PRESENTED TO

David TAYLOR

by the

TRAINING & EDUCATION COMMITTEE

of the

**NATIONAL ASSOCIATION OF
MASTER BAKERS
CONFECTIONERS AND
CATERERS**

E. L. Williams
Chairman

March 19 85

THE NEW INTERNATIONAL CONFECTIONER

The New International Confectioner

*Confectionery,
Cakes, Pastries, Desserts and Ices,
Savouries*

*Edited by Wilfred J. Fance F. Inst. B.B.
This metric edition revised by Michael Small, M.H.C.I.M.A., M.I.C.A.*

VIRTUE & COMPANY LIMITED
London, Dublin and Coulsdon

This edition revised by MICHAEL SMALL, M.H.C.I.M.A., M.I.C.A.

Michael Small is a widely experienced practical caterer, and is currently Catering Officer at Westfield College (University of London). He started his catering career in the kitchens of The Grosvenor House in London. Since then he has held many varied posts in the catering industry and regularly contributed to the trade press, in which capacity he was well known for his controversial views. He is a registered instructor for the HCITB. He is Editor of BUFFETS AND RECEPTIONS (Virtue) and has contributed to other Virtue books for the catering industry. He is author of CATERING FOR FUNCTIONS (Barrie and Jenkins).

British Library Cataloguing in Publication Data
The new international confectioner. — 5th ed.
  1. Confectionery
  I. Fance, Wilfred J.   II. Small, Mike
  III. International confectioner
664'.153   TX783

ISBN 0-900778-19-9

© Copyright International Editions René Kramer publisher, Lugano-Castagnola, Switzerland
© Copyright English Language Editions Virtue and Company Limited, London and Coulsdon
1st edition published 1968
5th edition 1981. Reprinted 1984.

Line drawing by Mrs. Sara Carolan, A.R.C.A., London, and Daniele Cleis, Lugano
Printed in Great Britain by Ebenezer Baylis and Son Ltd., The Trinity Press, Worcester, and London
Colour plates printed by IRL, Lausanne
Jacket design by Alex Hay of Balgrochan, Torrance of Campsie (Stirlingshire)

Acknowledgements

The publishers are indebted to the many people whose combined efforts have made this book possible. A work of this kind, with many international recipes received in different languages and styles, is not easy to put together into a co-ordinated whole. If we have succeeded, the credit rests largely with our Editor, W. J. Fance F. Inst. B.B. Without his first class knowledge of the whole field of baking and confectionery, this book could never have been completed.

We would like to thank the following authors and craftsmen who have contributed articles and recipes on their own particular subjects, helping to make this book truly international:

    GEORGES BÂTEAU, France
    WALTER BICKEL, Germany, Austria, France, Switzerland
    ARTHUR BOLLI, Switzerland
    JOSEF BÜRGI, Switzerland
    NEREO CAMBROSIO, Switzerland, Italy
    PAOLO CASCINO, Italy
    ALFRED CORLESS F. Inst. B.B., Great Britain
    CLAUDE DESARZENS, France, Switzerland
    WILFRED FANCE F. Inst. B.B., Great Britain, Turkey
    GERHARD GARTNER, Germany
    KARL GOETZ, Germany
    FRITZ HAHN, Germany, Austria
    PAUL HEINZ, Germany
    ARTHUR HOPE, Great Britain
    WISSE DE JONG, Holland
    HANS VAN DER KLINKENBERG, Switzerland
    ALEXANDER KOENE, Holland
    JAN LEIJEN, Holland
    SILVANO LULLINI, Italy
    MICHAEL SCHNÖKE, Germany
    PETER WHITELEY F. Inst. B.B., Great Britain

For the expert preparation of the products so well presented in the colour plates, we must thank especially the following:

THE RUSH GREEN COLLEGE, Romford, Essex
    W. J. FANCE F. Inst. B.B.

THE NATIONAL BAKERY SCHOOL, London
    J. SCADE F. Inst. B.B.

THE EALING TECHNICAL COLLEGE, London
    A. LITTLEWOOD F. Inst. B.B.

JOHN BENNETT, London

HOFKONDITOREI DEMEL, Vienna

HOTEL LA PALMA AU LAC, Locarno
>   A. BOLLI, propr.

CAFÉ KRANZLER, Frankfurt am Main
>   K. GOETZ and W. DISCHER

CONSERVENFABRIK EUGEN LACROIX, Frankfurt am Main

LUFTHANSA CATERING DEPT., Frankfurt am Main

MAISON MANUEL, Pâtissier et Confiseur, Lausanne
>   C. DESARZENS AND CH. VAUCHER

PARKHOTEL, Frankfurt am Main
>   F. EGGERT AND P. HEINZ

RESTAURANT RITZ, Berlin
>   M. SCHNÖKE

PASTICCERIA SALZA, Pisa
>   S. LULLINI

STATION VOOR MAALDERIJ EN BAKKERIJ, Wageningen
>   W. DE JONG AND J. LEIJEN

For outstanding photography:
>   BARRY BULOUGH, Carlton Artists, London
>   HANS FRÖHLICH, La Chaux-de-Fonds
>   GERHARD KÖLLING, Berlin
>   ERIC MÜLLER-GRUNITZ, Aschaffenburg
>   HANS STEGEMANN, Amsterdam

For special assistance, translation and advice:
>   MRS. ANNIE JACKSON, MRS. WITTINGHAM, London - MRS. A. CALANDRA, Lugano
>   MRS. B. RAMAKER, Amsterdam - MRS. COLETTE CHÂTELAIN, Lausanne
>   MR. MICHAEL VIRTUE, London
>   MR. KLAUS TINGELHOFF, Götzenhain
>   MESSRS. KRAFT FOODS LTD, London
>   MESSRS. LINSELL DEWELL LTD, Romford, Essex
>   MILK MARKETING BOARD, London
>   G. S. SELF M.R.S.H., Public Health Department, Barking, Essex
>   A. E. THEED, F. Inst. B. B., Hove, Sussex

Some of the drawings in Chapter V are reproduced by courtesy of MR. L. J. HANNEMAN from his book 'Cake Design and Decoration' published by APPLIED SCIENCE PUBLISHERS LTD.

There are many more who have done so much for the book - translators, advisers, typists and others too numerous to mention by name, but we thank them all.

London and Castagnola   THE PUBLISHERS

Contents

I   THE HISTORICAL DEVELOPMENT OF BAKING IN EUROPE   page 1

Ancient civilizations - the early confectioners - the wafer makers - honey-cake, pepper-cake, gingerbread - 'biskuit', sponge goods - puff pastry, Danish pastry - torten - marzipan and almond paste - Christmas fruit bread - panettone - brioche - twelfth cake - Baumkuchen - babas and madeleines - British traditional cakes and teabreads and their history

II   GENERAL INFORMATION   page 29

Food regulations - hygiene - apprenticeship and training - measuring heat and density - conversion tables - dough and cake mixing temperatures - yeast calculations

III   BAKERY TECHNOLOGY   page 37

The history and technology of aeration - formula balance - cake making methods - baking confectionery products - deep freezing and retardation - foodstuffs in the refrigerator - sugar boiling - plaiting

IV   RAW MATERIALS   page 57

Flour - eggs - cornflour - milk - fats and oils - sugars - honey - cocoa and chocolate - coffee - spices, aromatic seeds and fruits - salt - yeast - baking powders - alcohols

V   CAKE DECORATION   page 71

Colour - design - templates - textures - equipment - piping exercises - wedding cake proportions - casting moulds - lettering - monograms - stencils - modern cake decoration with royal icing

TECHNIQUES   page 107

VI   BASIC PREPARATIONS   page 173

Fermented doughs - batters - baking powder and prepared flour - pastries - cake bases - sponge mixtures - genoese - Baumkuchen - pound cakes - slab cakes - meringues - japonaise - almond and hazelnut products - fillings - toppings - creams and custards - icing and glazes - chocolate - modelling pastes - croquant - jellies

VII   YEASTED GOODS   page 257

Specialities from Great Britain, France, Holland, Switzerland, Germany

VIII	FRITTERS AND BATTERS	page 299
	Frying batter - specialities from Germany, Holland, Switzerland, France, Austria - waffles and wafers	
IX	BAKING POWDER AERATED GOODS	page 309
	Bread - buns - scones	
X	PASTRIES	page 315
	Sweet pastry - Scottish shortbread - puff pastries - choux pastries	
XI	SPONGE GOODS	page 345
	Specialities from Great Britain, Switzerland, Germany, France	
XII	GINGER AND HONEY GOODS	page 361
	Spices - gingerbreads - cakes - slabs - slices - ovals - honey cakes - Lebkuchen from Germany	
XIII	LARGE CAKES AND SLABS	page 381
	Large cakes from Great Britain, Austria, France, Germany, Switzerland, Italy - slab cakes from Great Britain	
XIV	SMALL CAKES AND AFTERNOON TEA FANCIES	page 407
	A selection from Great Britain, Germany, Switzerland, Holland, Italy, France, Austria	
XV	MERINGUES AND JAPONAISE	page 453
	Meringue goods from Austria, Switzerland, Italy, Germany, Turkey - japonaise from Great Britain, Switzerland, France	
XVI	BISCUITS	page 463
	Specialities from Great Britain, France, Italy, Holland, Germany, Switzerland, Canada	
XVII	PETITS FOURS	page 505
	Petits fours secs - petits fours glacés	
XVIII	ALMOND GOODS	page 531
	A selection from Great Britain, Germany, France, Switzerland	

XIX	GATEAUX AND TORTEN	page 545

Great Britain: sponge gâteaux - Swiss rolls - Battenburg - layer cakes - special gâteaux - gâteaux in paper cases - specialities from Austria, France, Switzerland, Germany, Holland, Hungary, Italy, Turkey

XX	DISPLAY AND SHOW-PIECES	page 597

Principles of display - show-pieces: croquembouche, harvest bread, tiered cake, Baumkuchen, sponge fancies - marzipan modelling

XXI	CHOCOLATES AND SUGAR CONFECTIONERY	page 617

Chocolates - liqueur chocolates - fondant chocolates - toffees and boiled sweets - fudges - fondants - pastilles - caramel fruits - fruit jellies - pulled sugar - sugar basket - spun sugar - blown sugar

XXII	SWEETS	page 649

Hot sweets: charlottes - croquettes - croûtes - dumplings - fritters - fruit desserts - omelettes - pancakes - pannequets - fruit and other pies - puddings - soufflés - strudels - tarts. Cold sweets: Bavarian creams - blancmanges - charlottes - cocktails - various creams - creams in goblets - small cream pots - fruit desserts - gâteaux and savarins - jellies - meringues - mousses and mousselines - pies - rice desserts - snow eggs - tarts and flans - yoghourt desserts - surprises - exotic sweets

XXIII	ICES	page 753

Cream ices - fruit or water ices - ice bricks - ice bombes - iced charlottes - ice cream coupes - ice gâteaux - iced mousses - ice parfaits - ice puddings - Italian semi-frozen desserts - baked ice creams - cassatas - sherbets - sundaes - assorted ices and iced desserts - spooms - artificial ices

XXIV	SAVOURY GOODS	page 813

Basic preparations - toppings - fillings - sauces - buttercreams - savoury goods made with puff, short and choux pastry to be served hot and cold - pies and pâtés - canapés - sandwiches

XXV	GLOSSARY	page 849
	HISTORICAL AND TECHNOLOGICAL INDEX	page 867
	RECIPE INDEX	page 871

List of Colour Plates

VI: BASIC PREPARATIONS
Easter Eggs 610
Moulded Chocolate 636, 657

VII: YEASTED GOODS
Apricot Streusel Slices 353
Bara Brith – Wales 272
Barm Brack 272
Bath Buns.................. 273
Chelsea Buns 276
Cherry Cheese Cakes 353
Cornish Saffron Loaves 273
Crumpets 270
Danish Ring 320
Dresdener Stollen 354
Easter Bread 274
Eierschecke 353
Gloucester Lardy Cakes 317
Hot Cross Buns 276
Kric-Krac 828
Muffins 270
Oxford Lardy Cakes 271
Plaited Goods 275
Raisin Slices............... 319
Sally Lunns 269
Savarins 353
Scottish Black Bun 272
Selkirk Bannocks 272
Simits 828
Taillaules 274
Wiltshire Lardy Cake 317

VIII: FRITTERS AND BATTERS – WAFFLES
Berlin Doughnuts 318
Choux Rings – Fried 318
Currant Puffs 318
Dairy Cream Waffles 355
Fritters 318
Snow – Balls 318
Spritzkuchen 318

IX: BAKING POWDER AERATED GOODS
Farls (Indian, Treacle) 396
Irish Soda Farls............. 396
Scones 389
Soda Bread 396
Soda Bread – Wheaten 396

X: PASTRIES
Apple Turnovers 319
Banbury Cakes 320
Choux 354
Coventry Puffs 320
Cream Slices 480
Eccles Cakes 320
Eclairs.................... 354
Maids of Honour Tartlets ... 317

Mince Pies 319
Palmiers 319, 478, 509
Profiteroles with Chocolate ... 640
Puff Pastry Goods 478
Salambos 354
Shortbread 389
Yorkshire Curd Tarts 658

XI: SPONGE GOODS
Carnival Heads 356
Desdemonas 482
Iagos 482
Othellos 482
Rosalinds 482

XII: GINGER AND HONEY GOODS
Almond and Hazelnut Fingers 356
Ashbourne Gingerbread 391
Baked Marzipan Santa Claus . 355
Butterspekulatius 355
Gingerbread 391
Ginger Nuts 391
Grasmere Gingerbread 391
Lebkuchen – Germany 395
Parkin Slab 395
Parkins 395
Speculaas Dolls 394
Spicy Speculaas 394
St. Gallen Biberli 355

XIII: LARGE CAKES AND SLABS
Birthday Cake 426
Butterletters 423
Caracas Cake 544
Cherry Cake 424
Coconut Cake 425
Date and Honey Cake 425
Dundee Cake 421
Genoa Cake 424
Madeira Cake 424
Simnel Cake 426
Slab Cakes 424
Wedding Cake............. 609

XIV: SMALL CAKES AND TEA FANCIES
Aidas 509
Almond Butter Biscuits 509
Almond Pretzels 481
Apple Poppy Seed Cakes 353
Apple Streusel Slices......... 478
Apple Strudel 481
Apricot Streusel Slices 353
Bee Sting 478
Bobes 509
Brassel Cakes 481
Butter Streusel Slices 478

Butter Wafers 509
Carracks 481
Cherry Cheese Cakes 353
Cherry Michel 478
Cherry Strudel 481
Chocolate Parfaits 481
Dutch Biscuits 479
Florentines 482
Flour Cakes 479
Fruits Tartlets 480
Genoese Glacés 560
Iced Tartlets 484
Lemon Rolls 481
Linz Beans 509
Linz Tartlets 481
Mille-feuille Slices 480
Raspberry Beans 509
Sanani 480
Selection for Afternoon Tea 480, 481
Sultana Cheese Slices 353
Tutti – Frutti............... 509
Victoria Fancies 480
Walnut Duchesses 509

XV: MERINGUES AND JAPONAISE
Coconut Meringues 390
Japonaise Gâteau 557
Meringue Fancies 393
Meringue Rocks 390
Moulded Meringues 392
Raspberry Kisses 392
Viennese Custard Rings 390

XVI: BISCUITS
Chocolate Rosettes 634
Duchess Biscuits 509
Dutch Biscuits 479
English Rout Biscuits 477
Fruit Biscuits 509
Ginger Nuts 391
Raspberry Rosettes 509

XVII: PETITS FOURS
Acorns 511
Amarena Sports 510
Amaretto 511
Assabesi 510
Bocche di Leone 511
Brasiliani 511
Calissons d'Aix 484
Cappucci 510
Cherry 511
Cherry Bowls 511
Cherry Sports 511
Chocolate Chantilly 510
Chocolate Kirsch 510
Chocolate Violets 511
Choux 511
Cocktails.................. 510

Coffee Walnut	511
Delina	510
Duchesses	509
Fiamme	510
Geneva Assortment	510, 511
Kirsch Glacés	511
Maraschino	510
Medusa	510
Mignon Amarena	510
Mocha	511
Nests	511
Nougatines Sports	510
Olivettes	511
Olivettes with Orange and Cherry	511
Pasticceria Mignon	510, 511
Petits Fours glacés	483, 510-512
Petits Fours secs	509, 634
Porto Rico	510
Punch Balls	634
Rosettes	511
Roulot	510
Sacripantini	510
Scodellini Pineapple	510
Scodellini Violetta	510
Sicily	511
Soupirs Chantilly	510
Viennese Petits Fours glacés	512

XVIII: ALMOND GOODS

Almond Crescents	393
Almond Rings	393
Bananas	480
Bethmännchen	391
Brenten	391
Honey Almond Tartlets	421
Macaroon Biscuits	393
Macaroon Fancies	634

XIX: GATEAUX – TORTEN

Battenburg	427
Bilberry Gâteau	542
Bilberry Tartlets	542
Birthday Torte	557
Black and White Fan Torte	543
Budapest Pineapple Torte	555
Buttercream Sponge Gâteau	544
Caracas Cake	544
Chessboard Gâteau	542
Children's Birthday Torte	556
Christmas Wreath	423
Dairy Cream Gâteau	558
Florida Tourte	543
Fudge Gâteau	556
Layer Cakes	428
Lemania Gâteau	422
Margret Cake	427
Mimosa Gâteau	559
Mocha Buttercream Torte	554
Nougatine Torte (Golden Book)	544
Peach Wine Cream Torte	563
Peppermint Cake	767
Pineapple Baumtorte	561
Red Currant Meringue Torte	562
St. Honoré – Italy	553
St. Honoré – Tuscany	553
Strawberry Dairy Cream Torte	563
Swabian Apple Tart	691
Swiss Buttercream Sponge Gâteau	544
Tarts	542, 690, 691
Torta Arancia	560
Torta Chantilly	558
Torta Cubana	558
Torta Dama	559
Torta Sorrentina	554
Tourte niçoise	422
Truffle Tourte	561
Walnut Torte	555
Wine Cream Tourte	562

XX: DISPLAY AND SHOW-PIECES

Baked Marzipan Santa Claus	355
Baumkuchen Pheasant	607
Baumkuchen Santa Claus	638
Clown	636
Croquembouche	789
Fruit Stall	639
Harvest Loaf I	604
Harvest Loaf II	605
Königsberg Marzipan Confections	636
Marzipan Dogs	637
Marzipan Fishes	637
Marzipan Frogs	637
Marzipan Fruits	606, 607, 639
Marzipan Hedgehogs	637
Marzipan Piglets	637
Marzipan Santa Claus	638
Marzipan Vegetables	606
Strawberry Kranzler	603
Sugar Parrot	634
Wedding Cake	608, 609
Window Display	541
Witch's Cottage	638

XXI: CHOCOLATES, SUGAR CONFECTIONERY

Blown Sugar	603
Caramel Fruits	635
Chocolates (Pralines)	633, 692
Fondants (Romborstplaat)	692
Glazed Chestnuts	636
Nut Dainties	633
Pineapple Triangles	633
Pulled Sugar	483, 603, 607, 633, 634
Rigi Peaks	633
Sorrento	633
Strawberry Kranzler	603
Stuffed Dates	634
Stuffed Walnuts	634
Sugar Basket with Chocolates	633
Sugar Basket with Petits Fours	634
Sugar Basket with Stuffed Fruits	634
Sugar Parrot	634
Torrone	664
Truffles	633
White Truffles	633

XXII: SWEETS

Adua Kat	768
Apple Tart, Swabian	691
Banana Fritters I	658
Bettina Tartlets	689
Champagne Flip	772
Christmas Pie	564
Christmas Pudding	659
Coupe Capriccio	792
Diplomat Bavarian Cream	661
Ecuadorian Banana Toddy	771
Florida Tourte	543
Fruits in Wine or Kirsch Jelly	640
Gâteau St. Honoré – Italy	553
Gâteau St. Honoré – Tuscany	553
Golden Tart	564
Harlequin Cream	794
Haupia Aloha	766
Kirsch Jelly	640
La Palma Bilberry Gâteau	542
La Palma Bilberry Tartlets	542
Mango Kohu Pee	769
Meringue Tart (Bilberry)	691
Mince Pies	564
Oranges Syracuse Style	664
Orange Tart	690
Peach Belle Forestière	791
Pears Helene	664
Pears Maja	794
Pineapple Kenya	790
Pineapple Ninon	660
Pineapple Roswitha	793
Pomegranate Cream	770
Profiteroles with Chocolate	640
Raspberry Gratin Eden	640
Rhubarb Pie	689
Rice Liguria	790
Russian Charlotte II	789
Snow Eggs	661
Strawberry Tart	690
Surprise havaïenne	792
Surprise sicilienne	793
Surprise Waldmeister	791
Tangerine Cream	660
Tarts	542, 690, 691
Tel Kadayif	635
Vacherin	795
Vanilla Soufflé	659
Williams Charlotte	789
Wine Jelly	640
Wune Wharn	770
Yorkshire Curd Tarts	658

XXIII: ICES

Christmas Parfait	789
Coupe Capriccio	792
Frosted Lemons	663
Ice Bombe	795
Mocha Ice Gâteau	794
Pineapple	663
Rose Ice Cream II	765
Semi-frozen Dessert	663
Twist	662
Zuccotto	662

XXIV: SAVOURY GOODS

Bacon and Egg Flan	829
Bacon and Egg Pies	830
Barquettes	825
Beef and Potato Pies	830
Boats and Bouchées	825
Bouchées	825
Brioches filled with Goose Liver Pâté	826
Canapés	826
Cheese Cannoli	827
Cheese Cream Savouries	831
Cheese Horns	827
Cheese Puffs	828
Cheese Scones	825
Cheese Soufflés	825
Goose Liver Medallions in Aspic on Brioches	831
Harlequin Slices	827
Pizza	829
Pork Pies	832
Sausage Rolls	830
Short and Puff Pastry Assortment	796
Steak and Kidney Pies	830
Veal and Ham Pie	796
Veal and Ham Pie, French	832

How to use this Book

Many of the recipes in THE INTERNATIONAL CONFECTIONER have been contributed from Continental sources. Care has been taken in the conversion of metric weights and measures to our own system and in the translation of preparation and methods from the language of the country concerned. Because materials and conditions vary in different countries, the reader should be prepared to make adjustments to recipes and methods should it become necessary.

The recipes given in metric units are not intended as an exact conversion from those given in British units. Each is a balanced recipe in either system.

To conform to the best British baking practice, when all liquid ingredients in a recipe are expressed by weights, so in the metric recipes, liquids are expressed in grammes. There are exceptions in Chapters XXII and XXIII which have a particular interest to the Hotel and Catering industry where liquid measurements are still in general use. Care has been taken in the compilation of recipes but adjustments may be necessary.

Most of the recipes in this book are complete in themselves and they are followed by the method of preparation. To avoid unnecessary repetition, reference is made in some of them to other recipes and preparations. Too many cross-references in the text, however, can be confusing, therefore they have been used only when it is felt that they are necessary.

If you find no cross-reference, you should refer to the indexes at the end of the book. There are two of these. The first covers technical terms and information of historical interest, and the second is a complete guide to all the recipes in the text. The comprehensive glossary will also assist the reader.

Introduction to the First Edition

This book has been published for those who are interested in pâtisserie; the student, the amateur, the craftsman and the artist alike. It does not pretend to present the sum total of knowledge on the subject, firstly because the sum total is not known, there is still much to learn, and secondly to present what is known would be beyond the compass of one volume.

An examination of the content page will show that the book has been constructed logically and progressively, starting with a short history of the development of baking in Europe together with short histories of better known British cakes and tea-breads.

A short history of aeration gives a picture of the results of trial and error from the time that man began to think about, and experiment with food, until such time as he learned technology and science and began to apply them to this thoughts and experiments. A well trained pâtissier today will know why and for what purpose certain techniques are employed.

Formula balance can be considered the mathematics of the craft, for with an understanding of the subject, time consuming trial and error can be cut to a minimum.

The closely guarded secrets that the old time craftsman hoarded in his brain and was able to delegate to his hands when necessary, which were once called 'the tricks of the trade', are no longer sacrosanct. It is true, of course, that the craftsman of the present day has specialist skills and an acute awareness of technique, all forged in the fire of industrial experience, nevertheless, these can be learned much more quickly today by the rapid growth of technology and science.

The review of bakery raw materials is of great importance, for without an understanding of them, there can be no basic comprehension of the possibilities inherent in them, or the limits set by them in the mixing, manipulative and baking processes.

Man has, at all times, sought to embellish, whether it be himself, his habitat, his possessions and his surroundings. His food is no exception, for colour, display and presentation render it more pleasing to the eye and through the eye to the palate. Presentation, display and decoration have been given an important place in this volume.

Because colour is of such importance in modern life and no less when it is applied to food, all the photographs of the finished products are in colour. In this way the visual affect on the reader will be total.

A great deal of thought has gone into the selection of items. The encyclopaedic approach was considered and discarded in favour of one more selective. It was felt that national characteristics should be the key to selection, opening the door to gastronomic history and tradition.

It is a saddening thought that in these days, when the foot of the world is on the accelerator, more and more of our delightful traditional products are no longer being made and are thus in danger of being forgotten. Some do not fit into the speed of automatic production, or into the standard size of a package. Some have been so altered and even debased that they are no longer a delight or even recognizable. Many British traditional products are included in this volume and rightly so, for they are part of our national heritage.

We are moving into a more affluent age when the economic level of the people is high as never before. With this changing pattern of life the imagination of bakery craftsmen should be sharpened. There are in this volume numerous examples of the pâtisserie of many countries. There is also a comprehensive survey of tea-breads, ices, chocolates, savoury goods and desserts. With the housewife becoming more and more dependent on the professional baker, this range should provide food for thought for bakers everywhere.

A good craftsman will be proud of his work. When he has finished it he will present it in such a way that its intrinsic beauty is heightened. This requires good taste in large measure and an understanding of the principles of display. A chapter has been included on this very important subject. It will be noticed also that care in presentation is manifest in all the colour photographs in this volume.

This work will be published in many languages. It is my hope that this English language edition will appeal to confreres in Australia, New Zealand, South Africa, Canada and the U.S.A., in fact everywhere that the English language is spoken. It has been said that craftsmanship is a link that binds one generation to another. It binds together also all those in the world today, who use their hands, their brains and their hearts in creative effort.

The publisher, René Kramer, who conceived this work, hopes that this volume will add to the world's knowledge of food in general and pâtisserie in particular, and that it will be read with interest and happiness. I share his sentiments.

LONDON   W. J. FANCE, F. INST. B. B.
1968

Publisher's Preface

More than 15 years have passed since the first edition of the International Confectioner was published. It has had such an appeal, that it has been translated and published in Dutch, French, German, Italian, Japanese and Serbo-Croat. Other language editions are in course of preparation.

In the introduction to the first edition, it was stated that the volume did not pretend to present the sum total of knowledge on the subject, because there is still much to learn. Nothing is static in life, and techniques and processes are constantly changing. The second English language edition, published in 1973, reflected these changes by including many additional colour plates and black and white illustrations together with recipes and text to correlate with them. This latest edition brings the book fully into line with the newest trends in the industry.

Since its first publication this book has been widely praised and has been accepted as a standard tool of the trade in many technical colleges and bakery schools throughout the world. The diversity of the recipes collected from many places and the international appeal of the book will ensure that it continues to be in demand wherever high standards are set for bakery technology and food production.

The Publishers
London and Castagnola

I. The Historical Development of Baking in Europe

The large number of flour confectionery lines which are produced daily throughout the world at the present time to delight the eye and palate have become so much a matter of course that it rarely occurs to those who enjoy them to wonder when and where these delicacies were first produced.

By discovering how to make fire, man acquired warmth and light and the ability to cook and bake. This laid the foundations on which man's future existence could be built up and radically altered.

The discovery of species of grass with seeds that could be used as food resulted in a hitherto unknown way of life; men began to settle in civic communities. By using heat, corn could be made into a pulp which was then turned into bread. It was not until much later, very many generations later, that experience and discoveries yielded the knowledge needed for the preparation of finer forms of bread - that is, *cakes*.

At that time all the prerequisites already existed for the production of flour confectionery - finer meal, other materials, and the art of baking. Undoubtedly, fat, milk, honey as a sweetener, some kinds of aromatic substances and possibly fruits were already in use.

ANCIENT EGYPT

The Egyptians had certainly learned the art of baking from the Babylonians and they developed an organized baking industry. A painted panel depicting the court bakery of Rameses III at Thebes in about 1175 B.C., shows the preparation of several kinds of cakes in addition to various types of bread. Animal-shaped moulds for sacrificial bread can be distinguished, proving that moulds were already in use in addition to shaping by hand. There are also small cakes and scrolls, called 'uten-t', fried in hot oil or fat, probably representing a coiled snake, one of the many sacred animals of that time. Cakes of the appropriate animal shapes were used for sacrifices as the poorer section of the population was often not in a position to spare live animals; this expedient later came into general use. Thus the types of cake known at that time were already shaped by hand in moulds, and baked in an oven or fried in hot fat.

An incentive for the creation of new forms of flour confectionery was provided by the rich of those times, who made extensive endowments in their lifetime to ensure that they would be adequately provided for after death. Erman gives an account of 5 kinds of wine, 10 kinds of meat and 14 kinds of cake in 'The Religion of the Egyptians'. As many as 16 different bakery products taking bread and cakes together, are known to have existed in the Old Kingdom.

ANCIENT GREECE

Long before Egyptian culture had passed its peak, knowledge of the art of baking gained a foothold in Greece. The general view is that the Greeks were the first to make use of the 'sweet substances' available to them by mixing them and incorporating them in dishes for their enjoyment at feasts. Greater use was made of flour confectionery of all kinds at various times of the day and on festive occasions. This explains why writers and actors seized upon this rewarding material. Aristophanes (450-385 B.C.) repeatedly mentioned a wide variety of baker's ware in his works.

They made a kind of fritter called 'encris' out of buckwheat flour, oil and honey. Their 'dispyrus' was a flat girdle-cake which they soaked in wine and ate hot. 'Trion' was a type of tart filled with grapes and almonds and served wrapped in a fig leaf.

The well-known wafers made in France called 'oublies' are thought to have originated in the 'obolios' which the Greeks cooked between two irons.

THE ROMAN EMPIRE

Centuries before the new era, Greek culture penetrated Roman territory, where it was transformed and in part took on a completely new shape. In view of the sensuality of the Romans, it was inevitable that festivities ran riot and the extravagance of the population became a political danger. As early as 186 B.C. the Roman Senate, at its 'Senatus consultum de Bacchanalibus' enacted stringent measures against the extent and excesses of these festivities. But Bacchus could no more be overthrown in Rome than Dionysus in Greece long before. While all baking had hitherto been done exclusively by women as part of their domestic duties, the baker's trade began to be a respected occupation for men in Rome. They made flour confectionery—'dulciarius'—but of a less sumptuous type - flat cheese cakes, cream or custard tarts, etc. The favourite was 'artocreas', a tasty pie which Cato mentions several times.

In Rome we find traces of a pastry-makers' association or craft guild called a 'pastillarium' as early as the fourth century A.D., proving that there must already have been quite a large number of consumers in those days.

Of course, as in any age, human existence did not consist solely of cake-baking and celebrations. With the new era, Christianity was on the move northwards; on account of shortage of land and the worsening of climatic conditions, the peoples of the north were on the move southwards. Later, Roman mercenaries marched north, and not only set up a temporary cultural frontier, but also acquainted other peoples with their customs and habits. The resulting mixture of forms of civilization spread to the northernmost countries, even to the British Isles.

THE COMING OF SUGAR

There is no doubt that flour confectionery was also being made in other parts of the world. A very long time ago, for instance, the Chinese were making biscuits, dried compote containing rice flour, fritters such as 'Tcheng-t'-Sin Maotsamm', sugar confectionery such as 'Nicupitsang', rose preserve and soya flour cakes.

Centuries later cane sugar from Asia Minor began its triumphant advance; it first conquered the mediterranean countries and was also brought north by clever merchants.

In about 700 B.C. flour confectionery sweetened with sugar was on sale in Egyptian bazaars.

THE EARLY CONFECTIONERS

In Venice there were already several confectioners in 1150. Sugar consumption in the East had also risen to quite a high level; it was even used for beverages— a great luxury! Almonds and sugar were used to prepare a 'sweatmeat'— marzipan. Costly things are most likely to give rise to falsification and this has time and again brought sugar and marzipan into disrepute. Even in the late Middle Ages Fulvio Pellegrino called marzipan a symbol of falseness. The oriental origin of sugar and its uses was deeply rooted in the minds of the educated classes; we can see how deeply from the fact that in 1682 Thiemen clothed his confectioner in an oriental robe.

Medicaments were at first still made by the doctors themselves. On the other hand the dealers in raw materials, or 'materialists', only dealt in these exotic commodities, which were the raw materials for most medicines. Sugar, in particular, was not only good to eat and sweet in taste; it could also be used in conjunction with costly spices to make many expensive, mysterious physics—and to earn a great deal of money. Several of the alchemists, while not giving up the idea of searching for the philosophers' stone, became 'apothecaries'. In the 'Constitutiones—utriusque Siciliae', of Emperor Frederick II, dated 1231, the apothecaries in Vienna are still called 'Confectarii'. Soon, disputes arose about 'rights' and 'privileges'; the authorities were called upon to decide what the apothecaries were entitled to do and what the 'materialists' were not allowed to do. Thus the burgomaster of Freiberg in Saxony granted the apothecaries the exclusive right to sell confectionery as early as 1294. In 1300 the Statute of Florence listed nearly 100 'Speciarii' who had for a long time been selling sugar in addition to honey and wax, almonds, marzipan and spices. In the town of Augsburg, too, several confectioners were already plying their trade in 1386. In 1432 Duke Albrecht II stipulated that in Vienna 'the merchants shall not bring any confections from Venice, neither shall they nor the shopkeepers sell them; but the apothecaries who reside here shall make such confections and trade in them', witness in a case involving a decision on 'confections'. Apothecaries must even have done some baking, for we find, in the apothecaries' ordinance and tax of Frankfort on the Main (1461), 'baked ... of good, hard sugar'.

THE WAFER MAKERS

But even more kinds of appetizing flour confectionery were created in the domestic kitchens, such as the so-called 'Eysenkuchen' (iron cakes) and 'Hyppeleyn' (little wafers) and many others. The importance of these 'waffles' in the life of the people at that time can be seen from the fact that even painters like Pieter Brueghel the elder and Jan van Bylert depicted the baking of such waffles as well as the waffles themselves and thus passed them on to posterity.

If we consult that valuable book, the 'Livre des Métiers' (Book of Crafts) we find that the trade of pastry-cook is only mentioned for the first time in the thirteenth century, in connection with the registration of the wafer-makers' articles of incorporation.

The wafer-makers were then granted the privilege of making the Host, the altar bread. Subsequently they joined up with the pastry-cooks to form a single guild.

HONEY-CAKE – PEPPER-CAKE – GINGERBREAD

Bakery products sweetened with honey probably represent the oldest type of flour confectionery. A good deal of information is available regarding the fact that they were made in ancient times, including lists of ingredients, but there are no clues of any kind as to proportions or the combinations of spices. We do know, however, from pictorial documents and descriptions, that even in its earliest days honey-cake was made in a wide variety of shapes. To emphasize the fact that it was designed as a sacrificial offering, suitable signs or, at a later date, seals were imprinted on the top of the cake until eventually it came to be baked in special clay moulds. On the occasion of the Roman New Year's

Fair, the Saturnalia and the Sigillaria, figures made of honey-cake flavoured with anise were most popular.

Particular care was devoted to the making of honey-cake in the monastery kitchens. As sour dough was the only aerating agent available for a very long time, these cakes were not particularly light or mellow. The Arabs are reported to have known how to prepare potash, but there is no evidence to indicate when this substance was first used to mellow honey-cake dough. Honey-cakes of all kinds were always connected in some way with feasts and festivals. The Christmas honey-cakes which were once customary in Bavaria, with their three praying female figures, date back to very early times and were once connected with 'Mothers' Day'. In England special cakes were baked for this occasion from about 700 A.D. onwards.

The spices used for honey-cake were cut up or finely pounded in a mortar before being added to the dough. In addition, spices were often used to decorate the top of the cake. The most popular decorations were cloves, small pieces of cinnamon, lemon peel and almonds. Occasionally sprigs of rosemary were also used.

Honey-cake dough was sometimes very difficult to work. The implement used for this purpose was the 'dough brake'.

Many of these honey-cakes were not intended for immediate consumption. They were stored for subsequent use in cooking as an essential ingredient for preparing, flavouring or thickening various dishes. One example of this use of honey-cake is the brown sauce for carp which is popular in some regions. It has not been possible to discover why this has always been called 'Polish sauce'.

While Torn became famous through its 'Katharinchen' ('Catherine cakes') with their unique shape, which have been made since 1640 and possibly even since 1557, Nuremberg first owed its fame to its 'Lebkuchen'. It is impossible to engage here in a detailed philological discussion of the development of the various names. The term 'Lebkuchen' originated in Nuremberg; in the strict sense of the word it means a spiced almond or nut mixture which is spread on wafers and then baked. The almonds naturally had to be as finely ground as possible. For this purpose a utensil was taken over from the primitive kitchen—this was the grinding-stone, which continued to be used in conjunction with rollers until a few decades ago.

From ancient times the ingredients for the 'Lebkuchen' mixture had been almonds and sugar, that is to say the same as for marzipan. Originally, however, only apothecaries were allowed to prepare and sell marzipan, so the capable Nuremberg 'Lebkuchen' makers had modernized their trade in their own way.

In actual fact, production centres that became widely known developed wherever honey was harvested. Three centuries ago there was far more honey per head of population than there is today. This fact alone explains why honey-cake, and later gingerbread, enjoyed so much popularity among the ordinary people in almost all the countries of Europe. Furthermore, these products were always considerably cheaper and easier to buy than marzipan, sugar confectionery and fancy cakes. In the old encyclopaedias the following were listed as being especially highly prized, the honey-cakes made in Rheims, Verdun and Metz; in Deventer (Holland) and in Basle, Danzig and Brunswick.

Switzerland has a few honey-cake lines which are among the finest of their kind. The plainer 'Züri-Tirggel', which date back to very early times, still find special favour with children. If ever the word 'Leckerli' is used anywhere, it can only refer to the 'Baseler Leckerli' which were already known as early as 1600.

The oldest Swiss speciality, however, is without doubt the 'Biber'. The oldest recipes for 'Biber' cakes are to be found in the Vadiana Municipal Library in St. Gallen. The 'Biber', which contains a filling, is decorated on top with a bear standing upright; it symbolizes the legend of Saint Gall (died ca. 645) who was said to have provided a bear with bread as a reward for supplies of wood.

There have been no attempts as yet to compile an exhaustive list of all the highly popular honey-cakes and gingerbread to be found in different parts of Europe.

'BISKUIT' – SPONGE GOODS

The original 'Biskuit' and its modern versions provided the basis on which confectionery developed into a separate, independent trade. The reasons for, and circumstances of, this development, as well as the time when it took place, have already been stated in the general survey. The word 'Biskuit' originally had a different meaning from today. In 1260 Tannhäuser, on a Mediterranean sea voyage, complains, 'My water is cloudy, my "piscot" is hard'. The 'piscot' was ship's biscuit—simply wheaten bread sliced after baking and then dried. For a long time to come this dried bread is mentioned in history as part of the rations for sea voyages and garrison stores, until the transformation of these products into high quality foods by modern methods of baking. The terms 'Zwybacken-Brot', 'Biscocten', 'Busquitt' and 'Krengel' were used for a long time side by side with the term 'Biskuit', the important one for confectioners, designating a product containing eggs, sugar and flour.

It is only possible to tell what type of product is meant where information on the ingredients and method of making is given at the same time as the name of the product. For instance, when Tabernaemontanus, in his 'New Herbal' (1551), mentions 'biscoct' and 'sweet bread' among the apothecary's wares, this gives no indication of the ingredients used or the method of preparation.

It was presumably in France that the way to prepare real 'Biskuit' (i.e. sponge) batters were first discovered. We must recall once again that the methods used in confectionery work were extremely primitive for a long time.

Mistress Schellhammer, in her 'Occasional Confectionery' (1699), had given the first description of a sponge batter beaten warm, calling it 'French sweet bread'. In the literature of the time there were soon a great many variations in the form of large and small sponge type goods based on the original mixture. The ingredients often included almonds or nuts and various spices; in addition to sugar, aniseed was used for sprinkling on the top. In 1622 'sweet bread, coarse, rough and hard biscuits' were listed as flour confectionery products. Efforts were made to improve these goods with all kinds of additional ingredients, such as rose-water or even attar of roses and malaga.

After 1700 it became the practice to beat up the egg yolks and whites separately before mixing them together. This at last made it possible to produce lighter, finer articles.

PUFF PASTRY AND 'PLUNDER' – DANISH PASTRY DOUGH

Leaving aside the indispensable butter content, we find that the principle of placing several thin layers of dough one on top of the other and then baking them was already followed in the New Kingdom of Egypt.

A large variety of pies were known in Rome in early Christian times. These so-called 'dish pies' (baked in a pie-dish) laid the foundations for two exceedingly important pillars of the confectioner's art—puff pastry and tarts—and have survived from ancient times to the present day. On the other hand, 'raised' pies, baked without a mould, only date back 600 years at the most. In the Wurzburg Parchment of about 1350, the author gives five pie recipes and repeatedly stresses that the dough, made of flour, wine and eggs, must be firm and thinly rolled out.

The term 'puff pastry' goes back nearly as far. A decree promulgated by the Municipal Council of Venice in 1525 against extravagant wedding feasts specifically mentions 'puff pastry' among the various dishes and bakery goods.

The 'Spanish' puff paste described by Rontzier owed its characteristics to the southern climate and is still made today. The pastry for French pies was the basis for the present-day process of spreading butter on a basic dough worked dry and giving it several 'turns'. From the original method of adding the butter in small pieces to the one by which the butter is sealed into the dough in a solid block all that was needed was one small step—that of attentive observation of the procedure. Claude Lorraine was unlucky in not being born until 1600, for from 1635 onwards he presented puff pastry as his own invention wherever he went.

Among the many recipes he published in his specialized book on 'The French Baker' in 1665, the Dutchman P.V. Aengeln did not forget puff pastry.

In those days and up to the end of the nineteenth century, puff pastry was often called 'butter paste'.

Today we still find the Spanish puff paste method used in Turkey. The pastries known as 'Baklava' are made in exactly the same way, except that the sheets of dough are each spread with butter instead of fat or olive oil, just soft enough for spreading. In accordance with oriental practice, orange or lemon syrup is poured over the pastries while they are still hot.

In Hungarian cooking, the dough for 'Schusterstrudel' (cobbler's strudel) is pulled and stretched until it is paper-thin and then folded over in several layers spread with butter. We may also mention that a puff paste case is used for several types of 'Pirogi', a group which comprises a great many Russian dishes.

In puff pastry then the lift is brought about by the expansion of steam from the water in the insoluble protein in flour which, when hydrated forms an elastic substance known to the miller and the baker as gluten. The gluten offers a resistance to the expansion and so the pastry lifts; the butter insulates the many hundreds of layers of dough and when the butter melts and begins to boil it helps to cook the dough layers and is absorbed by them. The laminated structure is then seen as flaky layers. In the case of 'Plunder' (Danish pastry dough) this function is assisted by yeast. It must have been a thrifty confectioner who first laminated a yeasted dough with butter and thus brought this group of products into the world.

Danish pastries so made in Copenhagen are a well-known speciality. The dough is somewhere between puff paste and yeasted dough in quality, but the special feature of these pastries is the filling, consisting of equal parts of butter, sugar, raw marzipan and very finely chopped candied lemon peel.

TORTEN

Ideas of what a 'Torte' is differ very widely, as regards both the derivation of the word and its popular and technical meanings. Professionally speaking, a 'Torte' was always of firm consistency compared with the softer 'Pastello', and it was always baked in a pastry case. The present-day 'Rheinischer Königskuchen' (Rhineland King Cake) is a typical example of these ancient products. In the early days of flour confectionery, any pie baked in a dish, even if it contained a fish or vegetable filling, was simply called a 'Torte'. This applies to Nero's 'Warm Tarts', the dessert tarts mentioned in Naples in 1476, and the 'Spanish Tarts' described by Marx Rumpolt in 1581. As the art of baking progressed and, in particular, as more was known about mixings, the two different types of 'Torten' parted company. Those that were really pies went their own way, together with puff pastry, while the others began to be made from almond mixtures, a practice which started in Italy, and thus developed into unfilled almond 'Torten'. At an early date these were coated with sugar glaze and decorated with candied citron peel, sliced almonds and even springs of rosemary.

The formula which the Dominicans used in Leipzig in 1500 to bake what they called 'an exquisite Italian "Torte"' was still a very amateurish affair. Almond 'Torten' are included in the list of prohibited confectionery goods in the Venice Municipal Council's decree of 1525. These were the first that could be termed 'Torten' in the strict sense of the word.

Of the standard 'Torten' known throughout the civilized world today, the oldest is 'Linzer Torte' (Linz Tart). Hagger (1719) gives several recipes for this and, on closer study, we find that these special types of paste were used for a great many small goods and even for large showpieces. In the past the white Linz tarts were more popular, but now the brown ones are more commonly made.

None of the other old varieties of 'Torte' have survived to the present day. 'Schaumtorten' (meringue tarts) first emerged in 1800, when they were known as 'Spanish wind tarts' and only contained a filling of stewed fruit. The use of fresh whipped cream as a filling for these tarts was very slow in becoming established. But this was the time when the heyday of the 'Torte' began. Only a few decades later *101 different* 'Torten' are described in one book on confectionery; the majority are based on batters or on the 'Viennese Torte' type, consisting either of a sponge base or of several rich sweet paste bases with a jam filling and a coating of water icing.

According to records which are still in existence, Franz Sacher, owner of a delicatessen shop, first made 'Torten' out of creamed chocolate cake batter in 1832. The original ones did not contain any filling and were coated with a film of apricot jam under their mellow-eating chocolate icing. Franz Sachers' son Eduard, who was a trained chef, naturally continued to produce his father's speciality. Franz Sacher was the founder of the Hotel Sacher, which is still of world-wide fame. Subsequently, due to special circumstances, the right to make 'Sacher Torte', was assigned to the confectioner Ch. Demel. His 'Torten' bore a chocolate seal with the name 'Edward Sacher Torte', still a registered trade-mark today, while the seal used by the Hotel Sacher has the name 'Hotel Sacher Torte' on it.

Meanwhile, the lighter sponge batters were more popular for 'Torten' than the heavier butter mixtures. One batter that became widely known was 'Viennese batter', which was beaten up either warm or cold, melted butter being added in either case. This type formed a transition to a completely different type of 'Torte'. The bases prepared from it could be split into several layers. Various wine creams flavoured with orange or lemon were now used as alternatives to the customary jam fillings and, very slowly and hesitantly, cream fillings became known and began to find a market. Butter cream fillings were not introduced until shortly before the end of the nineteenth century.

From Paris there came the 'Sarah Bernhardt Gâteau', named after the famous tragic actress, while Munich produced 'Prince Regent Torte'. In 1884 the Budapest chef Josef Karl Dobos created the 'Torte' named after him, with paper-thin bases of 'Baumkuchen' mixture, a particularly light chocolate cream filling and a coating of caramel on top. In 1885 Dobos was awarded a Gold Medal and a prize for his 'Torte'. Which of the many present-day formulas comes nearest to the original is still a matter for doubt. Dobos also wrote books on confectionery and there were plans for housing his works in the first European confectionery museum. In about 1890 'Parisian cream', the German name for ganache unsurpassed in delicacy, became popular as a filling for 'Torten'. 'Italian cream' filling became known much later; it was prepared by stabilizing egg whites whipped to a stiff snow with sugar boiled to the thread degree.

At the turn of the century the various 'Waffle Torten' came on the scene; the first of these was made by the Viennese confectioner Oscar Pischinger and its fame spread far beyond the frontiers of Austria.

MARZIPAN AND ALMOND PASTE

If we ask who 'invented' marzipan, we must also wonder about the origin of the word, its meaning and development.

A detailed account of how the word marzipan originated was given in 1904 by the Dutch philologist Kluyver. At the time of the Crusades, small silver coins were in circulation in the Levant, stamped with an effigy and the Arabic name 'mauthaban'. The name of these coins was later transferred to the small boxes made of wood shavings which were used for trading in costly drugs. In the thirteenth century boxes such as these served as containers for the 'sweetmeat' prepared from almonds, sugar and rose-water when it was offered for sale. Finally the name of the box was transferred to its contents, a common process in the history of language.

Marzipan itself is considerably older than its present name. Pharmaceutically, preparations such as this were regarded as 'Electuaries'. Strabon (65 B.C.-24 A.D.) in his 'Geographica' gives an account of the Medes, who inhabited northern Mesopotamia and whose customs and habits coincided with those of the Persians. While the rest of Media appears to be very well endowed, the northernmost mountainous region is barren. The inhabitants have to live on fruit and nuts; they make their cakes out of dried, pounded fruit and their bread out of roasted almonds. Almond bread has in fact survived here and there in the Arab world up to the present time.

The records of the 'Honest Brothers', a secret society founded in Basra in about 950, state that confectioners made a 'sweetmeat' out of almonds, sugar and oil. A Florentine statute enacted in 1300 refers to the 'Speciarii', who traded in marzipan and powdered sugar among other things.

The oldest detailed recipe for marzipan is contained in the cookery book by Bap. Platinam of Cremona (1481), which did not appear in German translation until 1542, in Augsburg. Yet we find detailed information on the preparation of marzipan in the Book of Electuaries published in 1540 by the Strasbourg doctor M. Gualter Ryff, who specifically mentions that it is beneficial to health. All Ryff's later works contain full description of marzipan. The Apothecary Tabernaemontanus also attributed a stimulating effect to marzipan in his extensive work published in 1588.

Finer marzipan products did not come into vogue until confectionery entered its phase of rapid development after 1800. Some of the new products of that time are still much sought after today, such as the marzipan specialities made in Frankfort on the Main and known as 'Brenten' and 'Beethmännchen', or 'Königsberger Teekonfekt' (Koenigsberg Tea Confections) which are made nowadays by many good confectioners in other countries.

In Lubeck there is a reference to marzipan in 1407 and again in the guild registers of 1530 but, according to the historian Warnke, it was not of real economic importance there until after 1800. In contrast to the conventional process, Lubeck marzipan was not—and is not—baked. Koenigsberg marzipan squares, however, are flashed after modelling and then decorated with rose-water glaze and glacé fruits.

CHRISTMAS FRUIT BREAD

'Stollen', sometimes called 'Christstollen', 'Strietzel' or 'Strützel', should undoubtedly be classed with the top products of modern confectionery. As the variety of names shows, an accurate historical analysis of their origin and meaning is now impossible. Loaves of bread were originally round, similar in shape to the ancient flat loaves. Later, when it became the practice to bake oblong loaves, perhaps to make fuller use of oven space, they were given names that described their shape.

There is evidence that 'Stollen' were baked for Christmas as early as 1329. Bishop Henry of Naumburg granted the bakers' guild a new privilege in that year, on condition that they supplied him and his successors with two 'Stollen' each made out of half a bushel of wheat, every Christmas.

No recipes for baking 'Stollen' have been handed down from the earliest times, but it may safely be assumed that they were always in keeping with the state of the baker's art of the day. Christmas bread is mentioned in Dresden as early as 1438. In that town an agreement was reached with the bakers of bread in 1528 whereby the production of flour confectionery became the province of the pastry-cooks; they also took over the baking of 'Stollen'. In 1496 'Christbrote uff Weihnachten' (Christmas loaves) were among the items sold at fairs and this product later gave its name to the Christmas Fair, which originally lasted only one day. 'Stollen' are mentioned relatively frequently as tributes paid to princes and Church dignitaries and even the famous 'Königsstollen' (Royal Christmas Bread) in Dresden is said to have originated as a tribute of this kind in 1529. Detailed recipes for 'Stollen' are not found in the literature until after 1700; they are listed as 'Butter Stollen' in reference books published in Leipzig and Berlin. Until only a few decades ago the production of 'Stollen', more than almost any other item of flour confectionery, was a field in which the art of home baking competed on equal terms with that of the professional confectioner.

PANETTONE

In Italy, where it originated, 'Panettone' has long been included among standard consumer goods and there are surely very few families whose table is not decked with this speciality at least on festive occasions and holidays, specially at Christmas.

The true origin of 'Panettone' ('big loaf') is, however, shrouded in the mists of time. There are only legends of how its name and form arose; according to some, it was first made in the 3rd century A.D., when the dough was left to rest for several days before baking. Another version of the origin of 'Panettone' is that it was first baked by a certain 'Ughetto' in a bakery of the Della Grazia in Milan at the time of Lodovico Il Moro and called 'Pane di Toni' ('Toni's Bread') after the master baker who owned the bakery.

BRIOCHE

Yeasted specialities which have been of international importance for several generations include the French 'Brioches', sometimes known as 'Apostle' or 'Prophet' cakes. The origin has been attributed to a certain Jean Brioche, who sold canary-bread on the Pont-Neuf in Paris, and to the pastry-cooks of St. Brieuc, who were called the 'Briochins'. It seems more likely that the name was made up of two separate parts—'Bri', because at first Brie cheese was used, and 'Oche' on the analogy of 'occhi', which were large, very popular Hyrcanian figs similar in shape to the typical brioche 'head'.

TWELFTH CAKE

A host of different customs have developed around Twelfth Night, 6th January, in the course of its history. Apart from the Christian ways of commemorating the Three Holy Kings, a charming secular custom of choosing a 'king' has developed. Some very optimistic historians of confectionery have come to the conclusion that Twelfth Cake originated in the Roman Saturnalia. These ancient festivities included the election of a king and general feasting and carousing, which even extended to the poorest people.

In France this custom is said to have existed in the tenth century; there is documentary evidence of it in Holland and Belgium in 1281, while in England the festival of the Bean King was celebrated at court by 1316.

This custom, which had spread as far as Eastern Europe, became confined to

France again in the eighteenth century. Gradually the practice of baking Twelfth Cake, to which adults and children were equally attached, almost died out in the bustle of the industrialized world and was in fact only upheld by a few traditionally minded families.

The original Twelfth Cakes were probably gingerbread or round, flat cakes. In Holland, waffles, cakes of the puff pastry type and even 'Torten' were baked for the occasion in the seventeenth century, while in France both round cakes and hollow rings were customary. Nowadays Swiss Twelfth Cake consists of a round centrepiece of good yeast dough surrounded by five to seven smaller balls, one of which contains a tiny china or plastic figure. The lucky finder is king.

The top of the cake is sprinkled with nibbed sugar before baking and with roasted almonds and pulverized sugar after baking. Finally a gold paper crown is placed in the centre and the masterpiece is complete.

It is usual to insert a bean into the cake before baking; this is why the holiday was called the 'Festival of the Bean King'. The practice of inserting coins or lucky charms into cakes before baking is still spread throughout Europe.

BAUMKUCHEN

Many touchingly ingenuous fairy-tales have been written about 'Baumkuchen', but they give no indication that this product occupies an exceptional position in the history of civilization.

The process of preparing food for consumption by cooking it on a spit over an open fire goes back to the beginnings of human civilization. The original spits were made exclusively of wood; a large proportion of the names—over 80 of them exist altogether by which 'Baumkuchen' is known—relate to the implement used: 'obelus', 'Spiss', 'Spisshut', 'Prügel', 'Stange' and 'Baum' (all meaning 'spit' or a wooden stick shaft or stake).

The oldest, most original form of this bakery product is found in the 'obelias' known in ancient Greece. This was wheaten bread shaped into long cords, wrapped round wooden poles, baked over an open fire and then carried on the shoulders of the 'obeliaphors' in Dionysian processions. It is even specified in Greek literature that 'obelias' were made from one to three talents of flour (56 to 170 lb. [26 to 78 kg.]). The worship of Dionysus is presumed to have originated in Asia Minor; thus it is possible that this form of bread also originated there.

Although it is rarely possible to make a clear distinction between 'bread' and 'cake' in the history of bakery products, the second generation of 'Baumkuchen' can unquestionably be regarded as cake. The Heidelberg manuscript 'Pal. Germ. 351' dating from the middle of the fifteenth century contains two relevant recipes entitled 'Von essen eins kuchen an eine spiss' ('on eating a spit-cake'). Starting in the monastery kitchens, these 'spit-cakes' soon found their way into the kitchens of the highest in the land and into middle-class homes. After 1500 such recipes are found in greater number; they also call for more delicately flavoured mixtures. In the Italian cookery book 'Epulario' (Venice, 1526) the frontispiece shows the baking of such a cake.

Unlike the previous ones, the third generation of 'Baumkuchen' was not shaped into cords and wrapped round rollers for baking. The oldest known recipe for this latest type of 'Baumkuchen' is described as early as 1547 by Balthassar Staindl von Dillingen, who writes 'Ain höflich essen haisst der raiff' ('The hoopcake is a courtly dish'). According to his recipe, the dough is pinned out to a rectangular shape, 'wrapped round a special spit and fastened securely with thread at intervals'. It is brushed with egg yolk seasoned with salt and then 'roasted' over an open fire in the same way as the earlier types of 'Baumkuchen'. Meanwhile, according to the recipe, the 'hoop-cake' is 'anointed' repeatedly with melted fat. An identical procedure is described by Marx

Rumpolt in both editions of his excellent book (1581 and 1604).

The Brunswick Cookery Book of 1692 already contains some recipes for the fourth generation of 'Baumkuchen' in addition to one relating to the second and one to the third generation. The mixtures prepared domestically on the basis of a pancake batter were the first ones to be applied to the spit in layers for baking. Mixings of this kind are very difficult to bake, it is true, and it was not a simple matter to obtain the desired indentations. A variety of directions for making 'Baumkuchen' can be found in each of the cookery books that appeared in about the seventeenth century and subsequently. Hagger, chef to the Prince Bishop in Salzburg, quotes five different types of 'Prügel- und Spiesskrapfen' ('spit fritters') in his book alone, and even includes an illustration of one. To facilitate the formation of indentations, the cakes were studded with strip almonds or tiny sticks of candied lemon peel while baking. In several of the recipes the egg yolks and whites are already prepared separately.

All efforts to discover exactly when the transition from the fourth to the fifth and last generation of 'Baumkuchen' occurred have proved vain. Various factors probably played a decisive part. Improved trade routes had made cane sugar cheaper and larger amounts could be used in baking. The first fifth generation recipe did not appear until 1769, when it was contained in Marcus Looft's work in addition to two fourth generation recipes. Yet by 1774 similar recipes were published in two different works in Berlin.

'Baumkuchen' was already produced professionally both in Nuremberg and in Frankfurt on the Main towards the end of the fifteenth century. Although every good cook knew how to bake this type of 'Baumkuchen', particularly able professionals had soon begun to specialize in this field. In the twelfth volume of 'Handwerke und Künste' ('Arts and Crafts'), published in Berlin in 1774, the production of 'Baumkuchen' is stated to form part of the 'urban activity of confectioners'. After the wars of independence 'Baumkuchen' became more widely known.

For nearly 200 years, then, 'Baumkuchen' has formed part of the range of goods supplied by confectioners. Krackhart's book on confectionery, published in 1870, does not as yet indicate any special types of 'Baumkuchen', but Birnbaum's encyclopaedia on confectionery (1898) contains recipes for 'Berlin' and 'Magdeburg' varieties of 'Baumkuchen'. Under the heading 'Salzwedel Baumkuchen' the reader is referred to the recipe for 'Berlin I Baumkuchen'. Accordingly, the special types of 'Baumkuchen' do not appear to have been developed until about the turn of the last century.

BABAS AND MADELEINES

The delicate 'baba' was invented at the Court of King Stanislas of Poland by the chef Chevriot. When the King took possession of the Duchy of Lorraine, which was given to him by his son-in-law, Louis XV, Chevriot served the 'baba' (an abbreviation of Ali Baba) which he made with flour and Hungarian wine. He soaked the slices of baba in Madeira and then rolled them in frying batter. Another discovery that followed the creation of the baba was that of the delicate 'madeleine'. A female cook in the service of King Stanislas served this cake for the first time at the end of a meal at which the King entertained Voltaire. It had such a delightful fragrance of orange-blossom and bergamot that Stanislas was enraptured by it and there and then sent some to his daughter, Queen Marie Leszczynska, at Versailles. She decided that this new delicacy should be called 'madeleine' after her father's faithful cook.

Babas, were first put in the market in 1836 by Sthorer, a Polish confectioner in the Rue Montorgueil. His shop is still in the same place, under the same name. It was Sthorer who had the brilliant idea of soaking these cakes in rum instead of selling them dry. When the Julien brothers subsequently opened their shop in the

Place de la Bourse in Paris, they imitated this idea to improve the flavour of the 'savarin', which they had invented, and first put on the market as 'Brillat-Savarin' in memory of the famous gastronome.

Another version is that madeleines were first made in Commercy, where a cook called Madeleine Paulmier is supposed to have invented the recipe long before King Stanislas arrived in Lorraine and to have passed it on to the Debouzie-Bray family at the Cloche d'Or Hotel. This family then specialized in the sale of the delicious cake.

MASTER CRAFTSMEN

Gradually, over the years, flour confectionery developed and increased its scope and resources during the reigns of Louis XIV and Louis XV and the Regency of the Duke of Orleans. A host of excellent chefs and masterly pastry-cooks invented new desserts of high quality for their noble masters. They include, in particular, Avice and Laguipiere and, the most famous of them all, Antoine Carême, who stimulated the development of what might be called 'Artistic Flour Confectionery'.

The man who was to become the King's chef and the king of chefs started his career in a poor cook-shop. Carême was a hard worker and loved his trade; he soon learned the rudiments of cookery and, in 1798, successfully applied for a post with one of the leading confectioners of Paris, the firm of Bailly; two years later, he was in charge of the tart and pie making department there. With his employer's encouragement he frequented libraries, where he copied etchings and engravings; he subsequently used these to illustrate his great work, 'Le Pâtissier Pittoresque' (Pictorial Confectioner's Guide) and his 'Pâtissier Royal' (Royal Confectioner).

The rest of the story is well-known. With his fine reputation, Carême became chef in ordinary to the most eminent men of the First Empire and the Restoration. He died in 1833 in his fiftieth year, leaving a large number of theoretical and practical works on cookery and flour confectionery for the benefit of professional confectioners and chefs.

One of those who carried on Carême's work was Pierre Lacam who, in 1860, created a large number of new lines—piped almond petits fours, Italian meringue sweets, etc. He collected a wide variety of recipes. He published them in 1865 in his book 'Le Pâtissier Glacier' (Flour Confectionery and Ice Cream) and later in the 'Mémorial de la Pâtisserie' (Book of Flour Confectionery).

British Traditional Cakes and Teabreads

BAKEWELL PUDDING

It was about a century ago that a cook was given orders and the ingredients to make short pastry strawberry jam tarts. These were to have been the dessert for the day. It happened at the Rutland Arms Hotel, then a great coaching inn situated in the Derbyshire town of Bakewell.

History tells us that puff pastry was used instead of short pastry and the cook, worried about the butter, sugar and eggs that were not used, and braving the possible anger of the proprietor, melted the butter and stirred it into the eggs and sugar which she had whipped together, then she poured it over the jam in the tart and baked it.

The guests in the hotel were delighted and, from that day to this, the Bakewell pudding, as this gastronomic mistake became known, has been made in the Rutland Arms and has become one of the classic dishes of the country.

BANBURY CAKES

The market town of Banbury in Oxfordshire has two claims to fame—the famous cross immortalized in the nursery rhyme and known wherever the English language is spoken, and the Banbury cake, equally famous and with an international reputation.

The origin of the cake is in some doubt, although it was believed to have been introduced by the returning Crusaders in the 13th century.

It is said that the Crusaders had met with a cake which was a mixture of fruit and spice, enclosed in a pastry envelope, during their campaigns in the Holy Land. They found the delicacy to their liking and brought the idea home with them, where by some happy chance it was developed in the Oxford market town of Banbury and given its name.

Banbury has a market charter granted by Henry II and for centuries breeding stock and cattle from distant counties were driven along the roads leading to the town. It is known that on market days, Banbury cakes were made and sold in large quantities, to be carried back to distant parts of the country by those who had business to do in such a busy market. In this way the fame of the Banbury cake spread throughout the land.

The visitor to Banbury will still find in Parsons Street the old original cake shop which dates, in part, from the 16th century. It was here that Ben Jonson, the great poet and dramatist, lodged for a time before writing the famous comedy, 'Bartholomew Fair' which contains reference to the Banbury cake and its maker.

BARA BRITH

During their long history, the people of Wales have, as far as possible, made their bread with the cereal produce of their own soil. If wheat was not available, then oats, barley or rye, or a mixture of these were used.

At some time in history, a Welsh cook sprinkled some dried fruit and some spice into a coarse meal dough and the national fruit loaf of Wales originated. It became known as Bara Brith, the word 'Bara' in the Welsh language meaning 'bread' and 'Brith' meaning 'speckled'. Nowadays, Bara Brith is made from white wheaten flour, but essentially it remains a rich fruited bread with a subtle flavour of spice.

BARM BRACKS

This is the national fruit bread of Ireland and is in everyday production in almost all bakeries throughout the country.

There is little known of its origin, although it is almost certain that it began as enriched bread. Early recipes show that butter or lard, sugar, and egg were mixed into a piece of bread dough. The only other addition at the time seems to have been caraway seeds.

Soon recipes began to include dried fruits; the modern Barm Brack being heavily fruited. The round shape almost certainly derived from the Irish pot oven which was an iron pot with a lid. The pot was heated by burying it in burning peat.

The name Barm Brack is a corruption of the Irish name Bairnin Breach, which means speckled or spotted bread—Bairnin meaning a small home made loaf and Breach meaning spotted. The present name is probably derived from the fact that when Bracks commenced to be made commercially by the baker, they were leavened by the use of barm which was made by the baker before compressed yeast was available.

Barm Bracks were specially enriched at Christmas time and at Hallowe'en. At the festival of Hallowe'en, small charms were baked in the Bracks, and great was the joy of the young who were lucky enough to get a slice containing a ring or some other charm.

BATH BUNS (LONDON TYPE)

The City of Bath has three distinct claims to fame; firstly as the magnificent Roman City, Aqua Sulis, which is now mostly buried, twenty feet below the present level of the City; secondly, as a fashionable eighteenth century spa conceived and dominated by Beau Nash; and thirdly because of its gastronomic history, probably unequalled anywhere in the world, for who has not heard of Bath Buns, Bath Chaps, Bath Oliver Biscuits and Sally Lunns.

The Bath Bun dates almost certainly from the fashionable era of Beau Nash. It is suggested, with some truth, that the bun was evolved from a type of dough which was used for making brioche, a delicacy introduced from France. This seems wholly credible because of the nature of the bun and because it is known that the bon ton of eighteenth century Bath favoured the French cuisine.

The original Bath buns were moulded into a round shape, carefully washed with egg yolks and sprinkled with caraway comfits before baking. Later the comfits lost their popularity and some currants mixed with coarse sugar nibs were sprinkled on top instead. This type of bun is still made and sold in the City of Bath.

It was during the nineteenth century that the London type of Bath bun was developed and this type is commonly met with at the present time, all over the country, outside the City of Bath.

BREADS OF NORTHERN IRELAND

By far the most popular breads in Northern Ireland today, as in the past, are soda breads. For many generations these breads have been baked on metal plates known as griddles. The griddle was suspended over a peat fire. A three legged pot was placed over a fire also and some of the bread baked in it, with red-hot peat placed on the lid in order to ensure thorough baking of both the bottom and the top of the bread. Today the modern hotplate has taken the place of the griddle and the oven has taken the place of the housewives' pot, although the old method of baking is still in use in outlying places.

This type of bread is aerated by the use of bicarbonate of soda and to confer a mellowness on the bread, buttermilk is used. The lactic acid in the buttermilk assists in the aeration also. The thin breads baked on the griddle or hotplate are known as farls and whilst fresh and warm, they are split, buttered and served with tea. They are also used as a base for sandwiches which are taken by workpeople for lunch in the shipyards, linen mills and factories of Northern Ireland. Fried lightly in hot fat they are served with hearty breakfasts of eggs and bacon. The soda breads are more popular for afternoon tea and it is usual to serve it sliced and buttered with jam and served with plenty of tea.

Another popular bread is made from potatoes and known as potato bread, 'tatie bread' 'pratie bread' or 'fadge'. It may reasonably be assumed that it originated as an easy way of using up mashed potatoes left over from supper, to be served at breakfast the following day. It is usual to serve potato bread either straight from the hotplate, or fried with bacon, eggs, or sausages.

There are many variations of potato bread made in different districts. There is the Potato Oaten or Rozel in which oatmeal instead of wheaten flour is used. In coastal areas cooked herring fillets are sometimes rolled inside the potato bread. Sometimes half cooked apples are sealed into a crescent shape of potato bread before cooking it more slowly on the hotplate.

OLD ENGLISH CHEESECAKES

English literature abounds in references to the cheesecake and cookery books of the 17th and 18th centuries are full of information for those who would learn how to make them.

As the basic ingredients of the cheesecake filling is the curd of sour milk, it is obvious that the cheesecake originated at no great distance from the dairy and, as in the distant past, the dairy and the kitchen were invariably under the same roof, the left hand, figuratively speaking, took the curds for the right hand to fashion into the old English cheesecake.

Daniel Defoe, in his book 'The Complete English Tradesman', published in 1726, mentions cheesecakes amongst other commodities when writing about a pastrycook's shop.

Cheesecakes were always on sale on the stalls in front of medieval houses and in the shopping halls built by wealthy merchants in the 14th century. Later they were always on sale on the stalls in the numerous annual fairs held all over the country, in particular Greenwich Fair, where vast quantities of cheesecakes were consumed.

It falls to Yorkshire as a county where the making of cheesecakes has been maintained and the Yorkshire cheesecake is justly famous throughout the world.

Hereford and Towcester, too, maintain the tradition, for there is little difference between them all and the old English cheesecake.

CHELSEA BUNS

Along the Thames at Chelsea there is, cradled in the curve of the river, a little haven for small ships. On the embankment nearby is a public house, the 'King's Arms'. Over a fireplace in the restaurant is a very old business poster on which is printed the Royal Arms and the date 1718, under which, in old English spelling, is the following:

RICHARD HAND
THE OLDEST ORIGINAL CHELSEY BUNN MAKER
AT THE 'KING'S ARMS' AT CHELSEY
REMOVED FROM
THE OLD ORIGINAL
CHELSEY BUNN HOUSE.
N.B. WHO HAS THE HONOUR TO SERVE
THE ROYAL FAMILY.

Chelsea has been famed for its buns since the beginning of the eighteenth century and now they are known all over the world. They were made originally in the 'Old Original Chelsea Bunn House' in Jew's Row. It was customery at that time for members of the Royal Family, the nobility and the gentry to visit the Bun House in the morning, where they partook of coffee and a Chelsea bun.

CHRISTMAS PIE

A few miles from the City of Guildford in the county of Surrey in England is the little hamlet with the curious name of Christmas Pie. It is one of the smallest hamlets in Great Britain and it is reported to have acquired its name because of the shape of the spring standpost on the village green, which was pie shaped.

Whether the hamlet has any connection with the delectable pie illustrated is not known. Nevertheless the little hamlet with the unusual name would do well to claim it, for it is wholly delicious and well worth adoption.

The history of the origin of puff pastry is obscure, although the method of making is fairly well documented. A book entitled 'Delightes for Ladies', written by Sir Hugh Plat in 1609, gives a recipe and the method of making puff pastry that is very similar to that which is used today. It is reasonably certain that at one distant point in history a piece of fermented dough was taken, and into it was rolled some fat, probably lard, when it was discovered that this manipulation, coupled with the yeast in the dough, gave the pastry an engaging lightness. This type of pastry has been used in Europe for many years in the making of Danish pastries, but there seems no record of it being used in Great Britain, save in the solitary instance of the pastry for the Christmas pie.

CHRISTMAS PUDDING

No British Christmas dinner table would be complete without the traditional Christmas pudding.

The pudding evolved from a savoury dish, known as plum pottage, which was always served at the beginning of a meal. It was made of meat balls, chopped tongue, wine, fruit juices, and spices, thickened with bread crumbs. The pottage was thoroughly cooked and served hot. Another name for it was plum broth. There are many references to it, in early English cookery books and in English literature.

The traditional pudding dates from the seventeenth century when some flour and some more breadcrumbs were used to stiffen the pottage. This mixture was boiled in a cloth on the morning of Christmas Days and served at the end of the Christmas dinner. It was at this time that the custom of stirring the pudding mixture with a wooden spoon, at the same time making a wish, originated, a custom that is still practiced today.

Another custom still practiced is the lighting of brandy after it has been poured over the hot pudding just before serving. The custom is vividly described by Charles Dickens in his well loved book, 'The Christmas Carol'.

It was perhaps during the reign of Queen Victoria that the custom of putting small charms into the pudding became popular. A ring meant marriage within a year; a thimble a year of spinsterhood for a girl; a button meant bachelorhood for a man; a small coin meant riches.

There are very many recipes for Christmas pudding, most households having one that has been passed down from mother to daughter over many years.

CORNISH PASTIES

The Cornish pasty is part of the folk history of the County and is based on household economy. The whole history of Cornwall shows the dependence of its people on the sea and on the soil. This maritime county is bounded on the north and north-west by the Atlantic Ocean, and on the south and south-west by the English Channel. The harvest of the sea is a constant challenge to Cornishmen. The fertile soil is prolific only in direct ratio to the work put into it.

Cornwall has always been rich in mineral wealth. It was the Phoenicians who bartered their fabrics and saffron for Cornish tin and copper.

Fishing, mining, quarrying and farming demand hard manual work. Meals must be readily transportable and sustaining, so in their early history Cornish people evolved the pasty, and as fish first came to hand it was enclosed in a pastry crust and cooked, so the shape of the pasty was established for all time.

Two other principles were established; firstly that the pastry crust must be sufficiently strong to withstand transport without breaking; secondly that the envelope acts as a container in which the filling cooks in its own juices, preserving the whole of its goodness and savour. The true Cornish pasty is always made with fresh, uncooked materials.

Because it was intended that the pasty must be strong enough to travel without breaking, the pastry should be of such strength that it would be intact when required. There is a favourite saying in Cornwall that it should be unbroken if, accidently, it was dropped down a mineshaft.

COVENTRY PUFFS

The origin of Coventry Puffs would seem to be connected with religious observance in some way and dates probably from the sixteenth century. They are almost certainly adapted from the God cakes which emanated from the City of Coventry. It was an Easter custom in this city for Godparents to send these cakes as presents to their Godchildren at Eastertide.

God cakes were puff pastry triangles filled with mincemeat but not turned over as with the Coventry Puff. They were washed with egg, sugared and baked with the folds uppermost. They were made in various sizes according to the wealth of the Godparent. Generally, the more wealthy or kindly the Godparent, the bigger was the gift of a God cake to the Godchild. It has been suggested, perhaps with some truth, that the three-cornered shape symbolized the famous 'Three Spires' of the City of Coventry.

DUNDEE CAKE

It is reasonably certain that this delightful cake originated in the Scottish city of Dundee from which it took its name. It is also reasonably certain that its origin is closely linked with a firm that has made marmalade in that city for well over two hundred years. The name of the firm is now world famous. Both marmalade and Dundee cakes are exported all over the world.

It is thought that the Dundee cake was first made in the city in the first years of the 19th century and is connected with the availability of orange peels as a by-product from the manufacture of orange marmalade.

A Dundee cake should contain fine flavoured butter and brown sugar. The crumb should be a delicate light brown in colour and should contain sultanas and orange peel only. The top should be decorated with split almonds placed in concentric circles and dusted with castor sugar before baking.

EASTER CAKES

Easter is one of the great festivals of the Christian Church and commemorates the resurrection of Christ. It also corresponds to the Jewish Passover. The festival is of great antiquity and occurs about the time of the vernal equinox, when the sun crosses the equator and day and night are equal in time.

The name Easter is derived from Eostre or Eastre, the Anglo-Saxon dawn goddess, whose festival fell in the spring. In Rome, the sacred fire in the Temple of the Vesta was kindled on March 1st, which date was the beginning of the Roman year. The custom still survives in the lighting of bonfires on Easter eve in many European countries, especially Germany. The Celts has a similar custom, known as the Beltane fires which demanded similar rituals.

At these festivals, games, dances and dramatic scenes were enacted and there was much feasting and drinking. Special cakes were made and provided for the feast. The cakes were made with coarse meal, animal, fat, eggs and honey. In course of time, spices and dried fruits were added. Because they came from the East it is possible that they were given a religious significance.

It can be assumed that the round, flat Easter cake is a direct descendent of the primitive cake, and it is to the West of England centred on Somerset, that we owe this link with the distant past, for it is there that the Easter Cake has been fostered and given continuity throughout the centuries.

ECCLES CAKES

No one knows when Eccles cakes were first made, certainly they have a claim to at least three centuries of history. If it is not known when first made, it is reasonably certain that they originated in the Lancashire town of Eccles, now almost a suburb of Manchester.

The word 'Eccles' means 'Church' and is derived from the Greek 'Ecclesia' which means an assembly. It therefore seems safe to assume that the old church in Eccles, which was built in 1111 A.D. was the point around which the town grew, and from which it took its name.

For centuries an annual service took place in the church, it being a vigil in commemoration of its dedication. This became known as the 'Eccles Wakes'. After the service, there was a fair, where stalls, shops and inns were busy with the selling of food and drink. Amongst the food items on sale were the popular Eccles cakes.

In 1650 A.D., when the Puritans gained power, they banned the wakes and Eccles cakes, because it was asserted they both had a pagan significance and that the Eccles cakes were too rich.

The visitor to the town of Eccles will not fail to note the bakery, where it is claimed that Eccles cakes have been made for hundreds of years. Arnold Bennett, the great English novelist, called this shop 'The most romantic shop in the world'.

ENGLISH PLUM CAKE

The plum cake is as English as roast beef and just as substantial. Recipes in old cookery books show that it was made from a piece of fermented dough into which fat, sugar, eggs, spices and dried fruits were mixed.

There are many references to plum cake in English literature and history. The records of Guildford, the County town of Surrey, show that it is an ancient custom for the High Steward of the County to present, on behalf of the Mayor, Alderman and Burgesses of the Borough, a plum cake on a wooden platter to Royal persons and other celebrities who visit the Borough. In 1674, the Duke of York, later King James II, visited Guildford and two plum cakes were purchased out of municipal funds. Again in 1702, a plum cake was presented to the husband of Queen Anne. There is a further record of a cake being presented to the King of Spain in 1704 and in the same year another cake was provided when the Queen was crowned.

In 1957, a plum cake made from an old recipe by bakery apprentices, was presented to Queen Elizabeth and the Duke of Edinburgh when they visited the City on the occasion of the 700 years since the original charter was granted in 1257, by King Henry III.

It is from the old English plum cake that present day fruited cakes originated.

GINGERBREADS

A volume could be written on the subject of gingerbread for it is recorded in the social history of the British Isles over a period of eight centuries. Ginger itself, has an even older history for it has been known and used as a spice since the earliest times.

It seems certain that gingerbread originated by adding ginger, spice and honey to a dough made from coarse meal, enriched with some fat, a measure of lightness being given by the natural fermentation of an ageing dough, assisted no doubt by the honey present.

The early Christian church did much to foster the popularity of gingerbread, for it was decreed that booths should be constructed in the precincts of the churches on the anniversaries of dedication and on all saints days, so that people could buy refreshments. These booths together with dancing and other festivities were the origins of the old English fairs.

Gingerbread figures in the form of a particular saint or other religious figures were a feature of the fair. Often the figures were gilded after baking.

After a time gingerbread was made in other forms and different regions of the country evolved their own recipes and finish.

THE HARVEST LOAF

The harvest loaf is traditional in Great Britain at the time of the harvest festival, when thanks are given in the churches for the harvest that has been safely gathered in. The harvest is significant in the lives of the people and throughout the world and through all the centuries, a bountiful harvest is a cause for thanks and rejoicing, for food is life and it must be lived fully until the harvest comes round again.

In all Christian countries, it is customary to decorate the church with products of the earth, and indeed in coastal towns the products of the sea also, so with gladness and humility to give thanks to a wise and benificent Deity.

In Great Britain, the harvest loaf can take many forms, from examples of the bread that daily sustains the local people to large moulded or plaited shapes that are made especially, partly to show the inate skill of the craftsman baker, and partly because only the best and the most ornate is good enough for such an occasion.

HOT CROSS BUNS

The God's Friday or Good Friday bun has a historical as well as a traditional background for it is in direct line with the sacrificial breads which were a part of pagan worship.

One of the links with the past is with the practice of fire worship. The sun was recognized by the ancients as the giver of life and became the deity of fire. The emblem of the fire worshippers in ancient Babylon was a circle with a cross dividing it into four. Cakes were made bearing this device and became associated with the rites of fire worship.

In Egypt, cakes were marked with a 'horn' device to symbolize the sacred heifer; these were called 'bous' from which almost certainly the English word 'bun' is derived.

In Greece, the goddess Hecate was worshipped at the full moon and round cakes dedicated to the Moon Goddess were crossed which symbolized the full moon and its four quarters.

In England, the pagan Saxons made crossed bread-cakes in honour of Eostre, the goddess of Spring, at which season her feast was held. With the spread of Christianity these pagan practices were adopted by the early Christian Church and cakes bearing the cross were consecrated and used at the Eucharist, the circular shape signifying eternity and the cross the symbol of the Christian Church.

The religious significance of hot cross buns invested them with magical powers and many curious superstitions and stories are connected with them. At one time, they were traditionally held to keep twelve months without going mouldy and were, in consequence, used as a charm against evil and as an effective cure for many ailments, including whooping cough. In some parts of Great Britain it was persistently believed that buns baked on Good Friday would save fishermen from shipwreck and wives would see to it that their men always had a bun with them as an insurance against disaster.

There are many references to hot cross buns in British folklore and literature. 'Poor Robin's Almanack' (1733) gives this quotation:

'Good Friday comes this month, the old
[woman runs
With one a penny, two a penny, hot cross
[buns,
Whose virtue is, if you believe what's said
They'll not grow mouldy like poor com-
[mon bread.'

On Good Friday morning, street vendors with buns for sale, piping hot, cried:

'Hot cross buns, hot cross buns,
One-a-penny, two-a-penny, hot cross buns
If your daughter does'nt like them, then
[give them to your sons,
And if you have'nt any of these pretty
[little elves
Then you simply can't do better than eat
[them all yourselves.'

MAIDS OF HONOUR

It was in 1514 A.D. that Sir Thomas Boleyn introduced his daughter Anne into the court of Henry VIII. She was appointed maid of honour to the King's sister Mary, whom she accompanied to the court of France. On her return her charm, gaiety and wit fascinated the King to such an extent that she became his Queen and later, mother of the girl-child who was destined to be Queen Elizabeth I. Her subsequent trial and execution is one of the tragic dramas of history.

Tradition tells us that Henry VIII, enjoying a festive occasion at Richmond, was induced to try a local cheese cake. He was as charmed with it as he was with the company of a bevy of young ladies of the court who were also enjoying the confection. Among the court ladies was Anne Boleyn. When nobody could advance the name of the delectable pastry, he ordered, with regal gallantry, that they be called 'maids of honour'. The name is ours in perpetuity and the association with Richmond in Surrey is for all time.

Maids of Honour tarts were made in a bakery claimed to be the original for many centuries, but alas! the bakery has finally closed its doors and the maid of honour has faded from sight. As with most traditional products, there are many recipes, each claiming to be the original, all of them basically the same, differing only in degree.

MINCE PIES

That Christmas in the British Isles and mince pies are synonymous is without doubt, for throughout the centuries, in folklore, story, poem and literature, there has been constant reference to mince pies. Even today, in a world where the traditions of the past are slowly being discarded and forgotten, the mince pie still graces the Christmas table.

A writer in the Gentleman's Magazine in 1783 suggests, and he may well have been right, that mince pies originated in the presentation of gifts to the Infant Jesus; gifts of gold, frankincense and myrrh with fruits, nuts and oil. It can reasonably be assumed that this event was commemorated by cradle shaped cakes filled with fruits and meats, spiced and sweetened. Spices have, from early times, been used for the preservation of meats although during the last half century meat in one form or another has been excluded from mincemeat, suet being the only contribution at the present time from animal sources.

Up to the Reformation, mince pies were still being made in the shape of a cradle. It is recorded that a cut was made in the top crust into which a small figure of the Infant Jesus was placed. When the figure was removed, the pie was eaten; in this way the religious significance of the mince pie was emphasized. The Puritans in an excess of zeal, condemned the mince pie, charging that the reverence given to it amounted to idolatry. When the Churches resisted, the Puritans counter-attacked and banned them. For good measure they banned the feast of Christmas also.

It was during the Restoration that the mince pie was restored to official favour, but with a difference, for the cradle shape gave way to the round pie, a shape that has endured to this day.

Mince pies can be made either from puff or short pastry. Both have their adherents and both can be seen in bakers' shops at Chrismas all over the British Isles.

MUFFINS AND CRUMPETS

One of the most welcome sounds in Victorian England was the bell of the muffin man who came on his rounds during cold autumn and winter afternoons, when the coal fires in the houses glowed and the kettles of water were boiling ready for tea.

He carried his wares on his head in a tray covered with a green baize cloth. Under the green cloth was a thinner white one which covered the muffins and crumpets which he had made earlier in the day.

The muffin which is rarely seen in Great Britain today, is a rather plump, soft, round, bread roll, flat on top and bottom. Muffins are torn open, toasted and spread at once with plenty of butter. They are made from a very soft fermented dough and baked in deep rings.

Whilst the sale of muffins has diminished in the United Kingdom, they are extremely popular in the United States where they are produced on a large scale.

Crumpets are made from a fermented batter, which is poured into shallow rings. They are thin and when held to the light show a fascinating network of holes. They also are toasted and served hot, plentifully spread with butter.

Both are baked on the hotplate which is lightly greased for muffins, but scoured and polished free from grease for crumpets.

OTHELLOS

When on April 23rd in the year 1564 a male child was born in Stratford-on-Avon to John and Mary Shakespeare, nobody could possibly have known that here was a child born to immortality. William Shakespeare achieved immortality.

It is perhaps fitting that we in England should claim as our own these four confections, Othellos, Desdemonas, Rosalinds and Iagos. The play Othello was written about 1604 and it tells of Othello the Moor who strangles his wife Desdemona after being inflamed to a murderous jealousy by the swarthy Iago. Rosalind is one of the central characters in the play, 'As you like it'.

The characters dictate the colours of the fondant finish. Chocolate for Othello the Moor; white for the unsullied purity of Desdemona; coffee for the swarthy Iago and pink for the gay adventurous Rosalind.

The bases for all four are the same. The fillings are different. Three methods of making can be employed.

OXFORD LARDY CAKE

The 'Old English Fair' was an eagerly awaited event in the lives of the people. It was a time when town and countrymen could meet their friends and neighbours. It was a time when the larder and the wardrobe could be replenished; when one's produce could be sold and when one could haggle over the purchase of the produce of others.

Some of the fairs in Britain can show a record of continuity extending over many centuries, some even preceding the legal status given them later by Royal Charter. It is said that Helston Fair dates back to Roman times, as did many fairs held in the vicinity of the Roman wall in Northumberland.

There seems little doubt that ancient pagan festivals were the origins of the fair and that later, when the Christian church replaced paganism, people continued to meet to perform their religious duties, after which they gave themselves up to merriment.

As food is a necessary concomitant to life, both religious and secular, booths and stalls on which food were displayed became customary. This was followed later by the products of other traders who saw in the assembled crowds an opportunity for trade and profit.

The history of the fair is also the history of gingerbread and the plum cake. Of the two, the plum cake was more substantial, being made from bread dough into which lard, sugar, spice and mixed fruit were mixed. A variety of this was the Lardy Cake which was similar in content to plum cake except that the fat was rolled in instead of being more closely incorporated by rubbing in.

Since time immemorial Lardy Cakes have been, with gingerbread, an integral part of the fair, differing only in degree, according to the county or district in which they are made.

It is thought that the history of the Oxfordshire Lardy Cake runs parallel with the history of Witney Fair and readers of 'Amaryllis at the Fair' by Richard Jefferies will be interested in his comments on both Oxford Lardy Cakes and Witney Fair.

PANCAKES

It is an interesting fact that throughout the whole span of human history, there have been but two major changes in the evolution of the hotplate as we know it today.

It is known historically that this type of baking was carried out in primitive times on a flat, heated stone. At some time in history, probably during the iron age, the stone was superseded by a metal plate which was scoured with sand, greased and heated over a fire.

This type of metal plate is still known in Wales as the bakestone. In Scotland and Northern England, it is known as the girdle, while further South and in Ireland, generations have known it is the griddle, a word derived from the early Norman 'gredil' meaning a gridiron. It is from this metal plate that our modern heat-controlled hotplate has evolved.

Froissart records that a flat metal plate for baking oatcakes was part of the equipment of the 14th century Scottish soldier; the plate was placed on a tripod over peat embers.

It is easy to visualize the primitive cook who saw in the hot, flat stone an opportunity for quickly baking a soft mixture of meal and water. It can be imagined also, that at some time in history a mixture soft enough to pour was put on the stone, then, when in a half baked state and easier to handle, turned over quickly to finish baking. It was at this moment of time that pancakes, crumpets, pikelets and fritters found their genesis.

It will never be known whether a measure of lightness was first conferred by using a slackened fermented dough, or by the use of a proportion of beaten eggs. There is little doubt that whichever came first it was soon followed by an awareness that milk was more enriching than water and that sugar and fat made the product more appetizing.

It becomes clear after an analysis of old recipes, that the English pancake is the slackest of all the mixtures of this type, for it contains a greater proportion of eggs and milk to the weight of flour than any other. With this in mind it is easy to understand the reason for the trend away from the griddle and in favour of the pan, in which the batter could be better confined and more expeditiously dealt with, and which led to the tossing of the pancake as the quickest way of turning.

Shrove Tuesday is the day dedicated to the pancake in Great Britain, and it is recorded that its observance was perpetuated in mediaeval times by a desire to feast and so use up the contents of the larder before the Lenten fast commenced on the day following, which is Ash Wednesday.

Shrove Tuesday derives its name from the custom of being shriven during Shrovetide; this was the term used for the confessing of sins and the receiving of penance and subsequent absolution before Lent.

History records that in mediaeval days the church bell was rung very early in the morning, as a reminder to the people of their religious obligations. The bell was known as the 'pancake bell'. The ringing of the pancake bell can still be heard on Shrove Tuesday in the Buckingham town of Olney, when it becomes the signal for the housewives to commence making pancakes and then, when the bell rings again, to race to the church, tossing the pancakes as they go. The first to arrive receives a kiss from the sexton and is adjudged pancake champion of the year.

THE PORK PIE

It is easy to imagine at some distant point in history, a cook who lined a mould or basin into which meat was placed with an addition of seasoning and possibly vegetables. It was cooked either by boiling, steaming or baking.

Legend has it that pies originated in Ancient Greece; later the conquering Romans learned the art. It seems certain that the Romans brought the art of pie making to England.

It seems possible that the fat used in the pastry came from the type of meat used: the amount of fat used and the nature of it, producing characteristics that were noticed by the discerning cook.

It will never be known who it was that first made a pie without the use of a supporting mould. It is possible that the same person had already discovered that the tensile strength of pie pastry could be increased by changes in the balance of the materials and by the use of boiling water, so that it could be hand raised and baked without a mould.

The English market town of Melton Mowbray is famous for all time by its association with two gastronomic delights—Stilton cheese and Melton Mowbray pork pies. The manufacture of Stilton cheese which originated in the village of Stilton, brought with it a surplus of whey, a by-product of cheese making. Because whey is useful in pig feeding, pig breeding became intensive in the district. Every means was used to market pig meat and one of the most popular was the delectable pork pie. Pies both large and small were sold to railway travellers to and from Melton Mowbray and soon their fame spread throughout the land. As fame can only be maintained by quality, everything used was of the best and experience showed that leg and loin of pork only should be used.

ENGLISH ROUT BISCUITS

The finest rout biscuits are made from raw marzipan made pliable with a little egg white or whole egg. They can also be made from a mixture of ground almonds, sugar, egg and orange flower water.

The Oxford dictionary defines the word 'rout' to mean 'assemblage or company of revellers; large evening party or reception'. It is the latter definition that gave the name to these biscuits for they were served at table with the wine or alternatively they graced the buffet table.

The word 'marzipan' seems to be of German origin and appears to have replaced the English 'marchpane' towards the end of the last century. There are many varieties of the word met with in English literature and old cookery books, 'marchpayne', 'marchepane', 'marspaine', and 'marcepaine' are examples. The 16th century French 'massepain' is also used in old cookery books. It is known that the manufacture of marzipan was developed in Italy in the fourteenth century, lending colour to a story that it refers to 'San Marco pani', shortened subsequently to 'Marcopani'—St. Mark's bread. (See also page 7.)

Withall's dictionary, 1568, refers to 'Dainty dishes as marchpayne, tarts etc.' William Harrison in 1592 mentions 'Marchpaine wrought with no small curiosity.' Shakespeare, in Romeo and Juliet, has one of Capulet's servants say, 'Away with the joint-stools, remove the court cupboard, look to the plate; good thou, save me a piece of marchpane . . .'

Sir Hugh Plat in his book 'Delights for Ladies' published in 1609, gives two recipes for making marchpane. Gervaise Markham (1568-1673) also gives a recipe for marchpane in his book 'The English Husife'. There are many references in English literature to this product, but it is not until the early 19th century that there are references to confections made from marzipan, which were served with a sweet wine.

A plastic paste such as marzipan is an ideal media, in the hands of a craftsman, for it can be wrought, twisted, and moulded into many shapes. Good taste in the use of colours and flavours and also in the finish is necessary, for not only must the biscuits be attractive, they are also meant to be eaten.

CORNISH SAFFRON CAKE

An old cookery book gives a recipe for 'goldwater'. This drink seems to have been concocted, not for any nutritional value, but because four or five leaves of beaten gold and some saffron, mixed with two quarts of brandy, added to its intrinsic worth—thus, at once, a drink and ostentation were both served.

Saffron like gold was, at one time, accepted as a standard of something rare and expensive, and so important was this standard that, in mediaeval times, those that adulterated saffron were promptly hanged. The gold standard is still with us. Saffron is now of botanical interest only.

Saffron is the dried, orange yellow stigmata of the crocus (crocus sativum) a species unknown in the wild state. One grain of saffron contains the stigmas of nine flowers, which is the equivalent of 4,320 flowers to the ounce.

Saffron has been cherished for centuries for its aroma, flavour and bright colour. That it was of value to the ancient Hebrews is clear, by the reference to it in the Bible (Solomon's Song IV.14). The name is of Arabic origin, for it was the Arabs who introduced it into Europe.

It was probably the Phoenicians who introduced it to England when they traded it and other products for Cornish tin. Hakluyt, the

English geographer, records that pilgrims brought saffron in hollow staves from the Holy Land in the reign of Edward III. In this way it was brought to the town of Walden in Essex where it was grown. Walden became known as Saffron Walden, a name that has endured to this day.

Saffron in mediaeval times, was assumed to have magical properties and it was carried to ward off the plague. Saffron mixed with apple juice was used as a medicine for jaundice and up to the beginning of the present century was considered a sovereign remedy for measles.

It is strange that saffron has been so well documented, yet there is no apparent record of its first introduction to cake. It seems possible that because of its then reputed magical and medicinal properties, it was introduced into the homely yeast cake, which was almost certainly the forerunner of the saffron cake as we know it today. The fact that saffron was first introduced into Great Britain through the County of Cornwall probably accounts for its popularity in the County in particular and the West of England in general.

It is customary in Cornish homes to serve saffron cake with Cornish clotted cream.

SALLY LUNNS

There is little or no doubt, that Sally Lunns originated in the City of Bath sometime in the 18th century. It is known that a pastrycook by the name of Sally Lunn, either originated this luscious tea-cake or was responsible for its fame.

Miss Sally Lunn had a bakehouse under her shop in Lilliput Alley in the City of Bath. It was from this shop that she and her assistants were kept busy, delivering the hot buttered tea-cakes to the houses of her many clients in the fashionable parts of the city.

At that time, Bath was one of the centres of fashion and elegance largely as a result of the industry and foresight of Beau Nash, a gambler, who drew up and maintained a code of etiquette and manners, eventually to become a virtual autocrat of society in the city.

To be fair to the memory of Beau Nash, there is little doubt that without his skill and prescience, Bath would not have become famous again in his time, as it was when it was known as Aqua Sulis by the Romans who built the magnificent baths over the only natural hot springs in Britain. Without Beau Nash, Sally Lunn would not have had such a large and distinguished clientele, and her name possibly would not have come down to posterity.

The existence of Sally Lunn is well authenticated, for William Hone (1780-1842) says that 'The cakes were named from a young woman of that name who 'cried' them at Bath'. Charles Dickens when writing from Italy in 1844 says, 'It is a sort of night that is meant for muffins, likewise crumpets, and also Sally Lunns.' W. S. Gilbert and Sir Arthur Sullivan raised the Sally Lunn to the eminence of comic opera, for he mentions it in 'The Sorcerer'.

Old cookery books abound with recipes for this traditional teabread and the great Marie Antoine Carême, who was cook to Tallyrand and subsequently to the Prince Regent, afterwards George IV of Britain, gave a recipe for this English delicacy.

SCONES

The scone is in direct line with the ancient Scottish bannock, which was a soft cake of barley meal baked on an iron plate heated over a fire. The plate was known in Scotland as a girdle. The bannock was round in shape and in course of time, it was cut into four triangular pieces so that it was easier to turn over on the girdle. In this way baking could be better accomplished. It was at this moment of time, when the bannock was first cut, that the scone originated. The triangular shape is now traditional.

With the introduction of bicarbonate of soda and its use with butter milk which contains lactic acid, together with the use of finer wheatmeal and wheaten flour, the scone gradually evolved from a thin hard biscuit to a thicker, softer cake; the action of the lactic acid not only increasing aeration but conferred a softening action on the flour gluten with a consequent mellowness in the baked scone, making them not only more attractive but much more digestible. At the same time, with this change in the character of the scone, came the opportunity for the craftsman to show a greater versatility in shape and variety. Today we have fruited, treacle, honey and potato scones, drop scones, coconut and chocolate scones, all refinements of an ancient past; all worthy representatives (if properly made) of Scotland, a country known all over the world as The Land O' Cakes.

SCOTTISH SELKIRK BANNOCK

The bannock is well documented in Scottish literature. It developed from the primitive flat, unfermented bread baked on hot stones. Later it was baked on a hot metal girdle.

Early records show that the meal used was a mixture of pease and barley which was made into a dough with cold salted water. There is a very close link between the bannock, the farl, the scone and the oatcake, all developing from the early bannock.

The bannock itself changed and there have been many types made in Scotland during the centuries; some made to celebrate Saint's days, national days, and to mark events such as births, fecundity and death.

One regional bannock is still made in the Scottish town of Selkirk from which town it takes its name. It was developed by one Robbie Douglas, who first sold them in his little bakery shop in a corner of Selkirk market place in 1859. Robbie Douglas said that the bannock should be a flat, round loaf with half its weight composed of large fleshy sultanas and with a pronounced flavour of butter.

SCOTTISH BAPS

The origin of the word 'bap' is unknown. Despite this lack of knowledge, the Scottish bap has been with us throughout many centuries and now is known all over the world.

There were references to baps in Scottish 16th century history when it was recorded that they were sold at 'nine for twelve pence'. The 'Blythsome Bridal' which is attributed to Sir Robert Semphill of Baltrees in Renfrewshire (1595-1660) or his son Francis, gives a description of the food of ordinary Scottish folk of that time, amongst which are bannocks of barley meal and farls and baps.

During the centuries, the Scottish teatable reached as high a level of perfection as the breakfast table, and the two meals, with the rich variety of scones, baps and other tea-breads, brought Scotland well-deserved renown, for, at their best, they could not be surpassed anywhere in the world.

Dr. Samuel Johnson said that 'In the breakfast, the Scots, whether lowland or highland, must be confessed to excel us. The tea and coffee are accompanied not only with butter, but with honey, conserves and marmalade. If an epicure could remove by wish in quest of sensual gratification wherever he has supped, he would breakfast in Scotland'.

Henry Kingsley (1830-1876) said, 'Brother, let us breakfast in Scotland, lunch in Australia and dine in Paris'. Baps were, at one time, served exclusively at the breakfast table.

The bap has been associated with the name of a famous Prime Minister of Britain. The grandfather of W. E. Gladstone kept a small shop in Leith Walk, Edinburgh, where he sold baps amongst other things. He was known popularly as 'small baps' because his baps were reputed to be smaller than those of his fellow tradesmen.

SCOTCH BUN

There is little doubt that the Scotch Bun was born out of the traditional hospitality of the Scottish people. It is customary for them to offer either a small slice of bun or a piece of shortbread as an accompaniment to a drop of whisky. The bun is always in evidence at festive occasions particularly at New Year celebrations.

Because of the heavily fruited nature of the bun and the addition of spirits in its making, it keeps excellently for a long time, even up to a year if properly stored, and the flavour and aroma is improved in keeping. This is an important quality for it means that the bun can be available, ready to serve with wine or whisky when visitors arrive.

Because of the close alliance between Scotland and France, there is a similarity between the culinary terms used in Scotland and France. It is suggested that the Scottish 'bun' is derived from the French 'bugne'.

Mary Stuart, whose mother was Mary of Lorraine, had many of her attendants resident in the tiny hamlet of Little France which was situated almost beneath the walls of Craigmillar Castle. It has been suggested that the Scotch Bun was synonymous with the Twelfth Cake *(page 9)* into which was baked a lucky bean. The finder of the bean was elected King or Queen of the Bean, and presided over the feast which followed the cutting of the bun. It is said that Mary Stuart abdicated for a day when the lucky bean was found by one of her attendants.

SCOTTISH SHORTBREAD

Scottish shortbreads are known all over the world, and properly made they are deservedly famous.

Shortbread originated as a rich oaten cake and it played, and still plays in its present form, a distinctive part in many Scottish customs and festivities.

That the shortbread should be rich and easily broken is understandable because it was, at one time, broken over the head of the bride when she set foot over the threshold of her new home, although this custom is fast dying out in favour of the symbolic cutting of the rich, highly decorated wedding cake.

Great quantities of shortbread are eaten at the festival of Hogmanay, accompanied by a dram or two of whisky. Immense quantities are exported from Scotland every year to Scots in every part of the world.

Basically, shortbread is a mixture of flour, butter and sugar. Small quantities of other ingredients can be added such as egg, marzipan, rice flour, peel, chopped almonds and walnuts. Some parts of Scotland have particular recipes, but the essential construction of the recipe varies but little.

SHREWSBURY CAKES AND BISCUITS

Probably the first record of the Shrewsbury cake was in the year 1561, when it was mentioned in the bailiff account that 'Lord Stafford was given a dozen of fine cakes at a cost of two shillings'.

In 1572, the Earl of Essex was a recipient of a dozen at the same cost. Sir Philip Sidney and his father in 1573-4 had, amongst other gifts, wine and Shrewsbury cakes. In 1581 two dozen fine cakes were given to Henry Bromley, son of the Lord Chancellor, at a cost of four shillings. Three years later, the same gentlemen received three dozen cakes, but this time the cost to the bailiffs was eight shillings.

Entries such as these went on well into the seventeenth century. It is recorded that in 1607, Lord Herbert of Chirbury, writing to his guardian Sir George More, said 'Lest you should think that the country ruder than it is, I have sent you some bread which is a kind of cake ... made in no place in England but in Shrewsbury... Measure not my love by substance of it, which is brittle, but by the form of it which is circular, which is the symbol of eternity'.

The making of Shrewsbury cakes were banned by the bailiffs towards the end of the sixteenth century as a result of a serious corn famine in 1596.

Eighteenth century literature was rich in reference to Shrewsbury cakes, but perhaps the greatest measure of literary publicity was given by Richard Barham in the 'Ingoldsby Legends'. A footnote to the poem says 'Oh Pailin! Prince of cake compounders, the mouth liquifies at thy very name'. Pailin was the name of the Shrewsbury cake maker at the time. The business, after changing hands many times, is still in existence, and Shrewsbury cakes can still be bought in this famous town.

THE SIMNEL CAKE

When Henry VII of England united the Houses of Lancaster and York by his marriage in 1486 to Elizabeth of York, he ended the bloodshed known in English history as the Wars of the Roses. A period was put to these wars by the battle of Bosworth where Richard III was finally defeated.

The crown did not lie easily on Henry's head, for the Lords Lovell and Stafford instigated the Easter rising by which they hoped to reassert the ascendency of the House of York. The rising was abortive. It was not until the king had overthrown two other pretenders to the throne, Lambert Simnel and Perkin Warbeck, that he firmly established the Tudor line on the throne of England.

The young man Lambert Simnel, the son of an Oxford baker, presented himself in Dublin in 1487 as the young Edward, Earl of Warwick, stating that he had escaped from the Tower of London. He was quickly joined by Lord Lovell and the Earl of Lincoln.

The real power behind Simnel, however, was a clever, but wily Oxford priest, one Richard Symonds. In 1487 Simnel was crowned King Edward VII in Dublin Cathedral.

A military force landing in Lancashire was subsequently defeated. Symonds and Simnel were captured; Symonds was executed, while Simnel was pardoned and employed in the royal kitchens. History records that Lambert Simnel was eventually promoted to the post of Royal Baker and was the originator of the Simnel cake, which, to please his royal master, was fashioned to the shape of a crown. The cake was vastly different in substance to what is accepted today.

The usage of these cakes is evidently one of great antiquity. It appears from one of the epigrams of the poet Herrick that, at the beginning of the seventeenth century, it was the custom in Gloucester for young people to carry Simnel to their mothers on Mid-Lent or Mothering Sunday. Pedantic people insist that the word Simnel comes through Old French from the Latin 'Siminellus' fine bread and the Latin 'Simila' the finest wheat flour.

YORKSHIRE PARKIN

Parkin is a form of gingerbread, one of the earliest and well documented forms of enrichment that evolved from the early types of bread made from coarse meal. (See Gingerbreads *pages 3, 18, 362-374*.)

Parkin has been a tradition in the West Riding of Yorkshire for centuries, particularly in November on Guy Fawkes night when it is eaten round the bonfire. What the significance of this practice is, it is difficult to know.

There are two well defined forms of Parkin, the biscuit and the slab.

YORKSHIRE TEA CAKES

These delightful tea cakes are known the world over and one can assume that there is a direct link with the bread cakes of coarsely ground meal that were baked on hot stones centuries ago. In the County of Yorkshire they owed their popularity to the fact that, during the Industrial Revolution, when they were cut and sandwiched with meat or cheese, they were an ideal portable meal for the men, women and children who worked in the hot steel and cotton mills. They kept moist in the hot atmosphere, quite unlike the sandwiches made from coarse bread which dried rapidly.

Nowadays, tea cakes are still immensely popular, not only in Yorkshire, but all over the British Isles.

There are two types of Yorkshire tea cake—plain and fruited, the former containing less sugar because they are invariably eaten with savoury foods. Both the plain and fruited varieties can be made either with white or wheatmeal flour.

II. General Information

Food Regulations

A study of the regulations pertaining to food in all countries will reveal a multiplicity of laws, each of which must be observed in a particular country, each of which generally has the force of law.

The pattern of legislation in general has a basic structure in that it is designed to protect the health of the worker and the consumer. It differs only in degree.

In all countries, the regulations are revised from time to time, some being wholly changed, some amended in part, whilst new regulations are added as more and more is known about foodstuffs. It is imperative that those engaged in the food industry should study all the food regulations in the country where they are working.

British confectioners will note the absence of egg colour in the recipes. The omission does not in any way suggest that it should not be used, it is omitted only because it may cause confusion in countries where it may not be used.

Copies of all regulations concerning food in general and the baking industry in particular in the British Isles can be obtained from H.M. Stationary Office or from most bookshops.

Hygiene

One of the facets in the making and preparation of foods that is of over-riding importance is hygiene. It cannot be stressed too emphatically that those engaged in the food industry have a special responsibility to their fellow men.

Food poisoning is still far too frequent and there can be no complacency about it, particularly when statistics prove that the greater proportion of it is due to personal carelessness, particularly after the use of the toilet, when the hands are not washed. This points to a lack of education on this very important subject, a laxity of control, with a consequent fall from the high standards of cleanliness necessary. Personal cleanliness must be a habit.

Dirt is a dangerous criminal, whether it is obvious to the eye or seen under a microscope. Never become an accessory to such a dangerous menace.

The hygiene standards laid down by law in almost all countries are very high. They can remain high only if people understand them and the principles involved.

Copies of the regulations can be obtained from the offices concerned in each country. In the British Isles, they can be obtained from H.M. Stationery Office in London, or advice will be given by the local health authority.

Apprenticeship and Training

Where there is food there is life; when there is none there is famine. Without food life will cease.

It follows then that all who are engaged in the production of food are important people, because they help to sustain life and bring happiness and contentment to mankind. This importance makes demands and creates responsibilities for all those who make a career in the food industry. This includes the pastrycook and confectioner.

The apprentice must never at any time forget this responsibility to his fellow man and he should so conduct himself not only to show that he is proud to serve the community in his chosen vocation but also that those with whom he is in contact will respect him.

Respect comes from many qualities, first of which is command of one's craft. To be a good craftsman, one has to seek perfection and this demands special qualities of character. He must develop a love of learning; this will establish a sense of humility, for it will be quickly found that the sum total of knowledge is but a fraction of the amount yet to be established. The apprentice will then know that he may ultimately be able to make his own contribution to this sum total and he can be proud of his effort, and merit the praise of others, even those as yet unborn.

From this humility will stem habits of precision and observation whilst at work, when every task will have an understood reason within the gastronomic scheme of things. The habit of precision will make him punctual and reliable always. All these attributes will lead to tolerance and good humour.

He must understand always that uncleanliness is a crime, particularly where food is concerned, therefore he will be neat and clean in all his habits and in his dress and appearance. He should not smoke, for smoking dulls the sense of taste and of smell. He will understand that the enjoyment of alcoholic drink and of food is a part of the art of living and calls for discrimination. It is better to leave alcoholic drink for the relaxed period after work is done. The practice of all this develops a healthy mind and a healthy body. With both, a happy and contented life is assured.

Apprenticeship varies from country to country. In some it is served in the place of work only, when the employer and/or his servants seek to teach the new entrant the elements of the craft. The level of success, however, is to a certain extent dependent on the amount of knowledge and the goodwill of those in the establishment. In other countries, the apprentice has the opportunity of spending a part of each week in school, where he will learn not only bakery subjects, but such subjects as civics, his native and one other language, chemistry, physics, microbiology and hygiene, calculations and commerce.

In Great Britain, the apprentice is released one day each week from his place of work to attend bakery school; he is expected also to attend two evenings each week in his own time. His training extends over four years.

The first two years of his study leads to the Basic Bakery Certificate of the City and Guilds of London Institute. He is then streamed, according to his talents, to either an Advanced Craft Course or a Technicians' Course, both leading to the appropriate City and Guilds Certificate; this will take a further two years. The Advanced Craft Course has a bias towards craftsmanship and takes a further two years.

The Technicians Course has a technological and scientific background. Finally, by arrangement with their employers, apprentices in either stream may continue with further studies leading to the Full Technological Certificate of the City and Guilds. At this level the subjects include Business Administration, Financial Control, Organisation of Production and Human Relations. The apprentice thus has the advantage of comprehensive study at school and at the same time he acquires industrial experience at his place of work; in this way he gets a balanced education. The policy and direction of bakery education is vested in advisory committees composed of members representative of all phases of the industry and there is close co-operation between all committees.

Each country, generally speaking, has its form of bakery education fitted to national need. Each country has something to offer another, and it is one purpose of this volume to bring closer the teachers and craftsmen of each country for the international advancement of the baking industry.

Measuring Heat and Density

Three items of small equipment very necessary in the bakery are the thermometer, sugar boiling thermometer and the saccharometer.

The thermometer is an instrument that measures temperature. Essentially it is a thick walled glass tube with a fine bore. At the lower end is a bulb generally filled with mercury. The stem, which is sealed, is calibrated in degrees which form the scale of the thermometer.

Mercury is generally chosen because of its wide range of expansion and contraction in the liquid state. The hotter the substance being measured, the greater the expansion, which shows as a rise in the tube. The cooler the substance, the greater is the contraction and the lower the level shown on the scale. Alcohol is sometimes used because it can be coloured red, which makes the thermometer easier to read.

The scale is fixed by placing the bulb in melting ice and making a mark on the stem. It is then suspended in steam from boiling water and a second mark is made. The first mark is the freezing point of water and the second, the boiling point. There are three types of thermometer, each calibrated differently since research has been carried out by various scientists:

1. The Swedish scientist Anders Celsius (1701-1744) who invented the Centigrade thermometer.

2. The Prussian physicist Gabriel-Daniel Fahrenheit (1686-1736) who invented the calibration named after him.

3. The French physicist René-Antoine Réaumur (1683-1757) who invented the thermometer which bears his name.

1. Centigrade (or Celsius). The scale shows 0° as the melting point of ice and 100° as the boiling point of water.

2. Fahrenheit. This shows 32° as the melting point of ice and 212° as the boiling point of water.

3. Réaumur. The scale in this case shows 0° as melting point of ice and 80° as the boiling point of water.

All this is confusing and it may be necessary for a craftsman in a particular country to convert one scale to another. Here is a conversion table.

Degrees Centigrade divided by 1.25 = degrees Réaumur: or multiply by 4 and divide by 5.

Degrees Centigrade multiplied by 1.8+32 = degrees Fahrenheit: or multiply by 9, divide by 5 and add 32.

Degrees Réaumur multiplied by 1.25 = degrees Centigrade: or multiply by 5 and divide by 4.

Degrees Réaumur multiplied by 2.25 + 32 = degrees Fahrenheit: or multiply by 9, divide by 4 and add 32.

Degrees Fahrenheit minus 32 divided by 1.8 = degrees Centigrade: or subtract 32, multiply by 5 and divide by 9.

Degrees Fahrenheit minus 32 divided by 2.25 = degrees Réaumur: or subtract 32, multiply by 4 and divide by 9.

Examples I

80° R	=	100° C	=	212° F
40° R	=	50° C	=	122° F
29.6° R	=	37° C	=	98.6° F
12° R	=	15° C	=	59° F
0° R	=	0° C	=	32° F

Examples II

80° C ÷ 1.25 = 64° R
80° C × 1.8 + 32 = 176° F
64° R × 1.25 = 80° C
64° R × 2.25 + 32 = 176° F
176° F − 32 ÷ 1.8 = 80° C
176° F − 32 ÷ 2.25 = 64° R

The sugar boiling thermometer is a more robust instrument mounted on a metal plate, the degrees being engraved on the metal. A thermometer with the Fahrenheit scale generally commences at 50° and extends to 480°.

The French chemist Antoine Baumé (1728-1804) perfected a saccharometer which is an instrument to determine the density of liquids. It consists of a thin glass tube with a bulb at the bottom. It is hermetically sealed. The bulb is filled with small shot, which enables the instrument to remain in a perpendicular position in a solution. The stem contains a calibrated scale, graduated through a range of 0 to 40 degrees Baumé, and on which the degree of density can be read. Distilled water will correspond to the 'zero' mark on the scale. An increase in the density of a solution will cause the instrument to rise and the higher figure will be clearly seen. For measuring, use a high, narrow container and pour in enough syrup to make it possible to put the saccharometer in without it touching the bottom.

The saccharometer should be used to measure the density of the syrup as this gives an exact measurement. Each degree marked on the saccharometer corresponds to 1 oz. sugar per 2 lb. 8 oz. water.

Example: A syrup at 30° contains 30 × 1 oz. = 1 lb. 14 oz. sugar. The table below may be helpful as it shows several examples of syrups and the relative degree upon the Baumé scale. The readings are made at boiling point. A margin of 2 or 3 degrees Baumé above these readings must be allowed for syrups which have cooled down. Syrups below 30° B do not keep well (they are non-saturated solutions). Syrups at 32° B and over are saturated solutions and will form crystals.

Table of Various Degrees Baumé

6 lb. 10 oz. sugar with 11 lb. water gives a syrup at 15°
6 lb. 10 oz. sugar with 8 lb. 12 oz. water gives a syrup at 20°
6 lb. 10 oz. sugar with 6 lb. 10 oz. water gives a syrup at 25°
6 lb. 10 oz. sugar with 4 lb. 8 oz. water gives a syrup at 28°
6 lb. 10 oz. sugar with 3 lb. 4 oz. water gives a syrup at 35°
6 lb. 10 oz. sugar with 2 lb. 4 oz. water gives a syrup at 38°

According to the use to which the syrup is to be put, increase or reduce the quantity of water. Here is a table of comparison between degrees Baumé, Réaumur, Celsius and Fahrenheit in sugar boiling. The hand tests are those used by Continental craftsmen. *See page 51.*

Hand test	Saccharometer Baumé	Réaumur	Thermometer Celsius	Fahrenheit
Coating	20°	78	97.5	207.5
Slightly smooth	25°	80	100	212
Very smooth	30°	82	102.5	216.5
Pearl	33°	84	105	221
Thread	35°	86	107.5	225.5
Small blow	37°	89	111.5	232.7
Large blow	39°	90	112.5	234.5
Soft or small ball	40°	92	115	239
Medium ball	41°	94	117.5	243.5

DOUGH AND MIXING TEMPERATURES

The temperature of a dough is one of the factors regulating the speed of fermentation.

The optimum temperature range is between 78-82° F (25-28° C). Above these temperatures the speed of fermentation increases but the yeast becomes more quickly exhausted. At a temperature of 120° F (49° C) yeast is in danger and at 140° F (60° C) it is destroyed.

Below the optimum range the speed becomes progressively slower until at 40° F (4° C) it is almost inactive, but is not damaged.

In an emergency, when yeast is in short supply, the temperature of a dough may be increased and the yeast content decreased, but it will not improve the quality of the finished product, there being a tendency to rapid staling.

Doughs may be made at temperatures below 78° F (25° C) but the yeast content must be increased until at temperatures below 72° F (22° C) the amount may have to be doubled, unless the doughs are required to ferment for long periods.

The finished dough temperature will be the average of the temperatures of all the raw materials used and it is clear that if a finished dough temperature is to be established, then a method must be used.

This is done by basing the calculation on the temperatures of the two main ingredients, the flour and the moistening agent used, milk and/or water. As the temperature of the liquid is more easily adjustable, then it is the liquid temperature that is to be calculated to make sure of a dough at the desired temperature.

The simplest calculation is as follows:

1. Note the desired dough temperature and double it.

2. Take the flour temperature and subtract it from the doubled figure.

3. The result can be taken as the required water, or milk, temperature so to establish the desired dough temperature.

4. It may be necessary in abnormal circumstances of heat or cold, particularly when small doughs are to be made, to add or subtract 2-4° to or from the water temperature.

Here is an example:
1. Desired dough temperature   78° F   78 × 2 = 156
2. Flour temperature   60° F   60
3. Water temperature   ─────
                                              96° F

Here is another example:
1. Desired dough temperature   80° F   80 × 2 = 160
2. Flour temperature   58° F   58
3. Water temperature   ─────
                                             102° F

CAKE AND PASTRY MAKING TEMPERATURES

The temperature of a cake mixing has a great influence on the quality and appearance of the baked product.

Research and experimentation have established the optimum temperature range to be 65-70° F (18-21° C). Most cake mixings are completed in stages and as it is the initial mixing temperature that is critical, there is no means of adjustment during the actual mixing, therefore the pre-mix storage conditions are important, raw materials being removed from the main store in sufficient time for them to be adjusted to the required temperature, ideally in a constant temperature room. Systematic control will see to it that only sufficient materials for a planned production period will be removed from bulk storage temperatures.

The temperature of materials intended for immediate use in the making of pastry is important. Pastries have a high fat content which is quickly subject to changing temperatures. In the case of puff pastry, the butter or pastry fat must be used at such a temperature that the fat films, during rolling and folding. If it is too hard, it will break down the laminated structure. If too soft, then it will squeeze out and shorten the pastry.

With short and sweet pastes, the fat should be in such condition that it can be rubbed finely into the flour without it oiling, which would make it difficult to use.

Storage temperature after making is important and this is dealt with in Chapter III.

Conversion Tables

METRIC WEIGHTS

Approximate equivalents

28.35 grams = 1 ounce	50 grams = 1 3/4 ounces
10 grams = .353 ounces	100 grams = 3 1/2 ounces
25 grams = .882 ounces	150 grams = 5 1/4 ounces
50 grams = 1.764 ounces	200 grams = 7 ounces
75 grams = 2.645 ounces	250 grams = 8 3/4 ounces
100 grams = 3.523 ounces	500 grams = 17 2/3 ounces
250 grams = 8.818 ounces	1 kilogram = 2 lb. 3 ounces
500 grams = 1 lb. 1.637 ounces	1 1/2 kilograms = 3 lb. 5 ounces
	2 kilograms = 4 lb. 6 ounces
	2 1/2 kilograms = 5 lb. 8 ounces
	3 kilograms = 6 lb. 10 ounces
1 oz. 28.35 gr.	12 oz. 340.20 gr.
2 oz. 56.70 gr.	13 oz. 368.55 gr.
3 oz. 85.05 gr.	14 oz. 396.90 gr.
4 oz. 113.40 gr.	15 oz. 425.25 gr.
5 oz. 141.75 gr.	16 oz. 453.60 gr.
6 oz. 170.10 gr.	17 oz. 481.95 gr.
7 oz. 198.45 gr.	18 oz. 510.30 gr.
8 oz. 226.80 gr.	19 oz. 538.65 gr.
9 oz. 255.15 gr.	20 oz. 567.00 gr.
10 oz. 283.50 gr.	21 oz. 595.35 gr.
11 oz. 311.85 gr.	22 oz. 623.70 gr.

1 cc (Cubic centimetre) equals 1 gram which can then be converted as above.

METRIC LINEAR MEASURES

Approximate Conversion Figures

1 millimetre =	0.001 metre =	0.0394 inch =	1/20 inch
10 millimetres =	1 centimetre =	0.3937 inch =	1/2 inch
10 centimetres =	1 decimetre =	3.937 inches =	4 inches
10 decimetres =	1 metre =	39.37 inches =	39 1/4 inches
10 metres =	1 decametre =	393.7 inches =	393 3/4 inches
10 decametres =	1 hectometre =	328 ft. 1 inch =	109 yards
10 hectometres =	1 kilometre =	3280 ft. 10 inches =	1093 2/3 yards

METRIC MEASURES OF CAPACITY

Approximate Conversion Figures

$1/2$ decilitre	= $1/3$ gill	= $1/12$ pt.	= 1 $3/4$ oz. (approx.)
1 decilitre	= $2/3$ gill	= $1/6$ pt.	= 3 $1/3$ oz. (approx.)
1 $1/2$ decilitre	= 1 gill	= $1/4$ pt.	= 5 oz. (approx.)
3 decilitres	= 2 gills	= $1/2$ pt.	= 10 oz. (approx.)
5 $3/4$ decilitres	= 4 gills = 1	pt.	= 20 oz. (approx.)
7 decilitres	= 5 gills	= 1 $1/4$ pt.	= 25 oz. (approx.)
9 decilitres	= 6 gills	= 1 $1/2$ pt.	= 30 oz. (approx.)
10 decilitres = 1 litre	= 7 gills	= 1 $3/4$ pt.	= 35 oz. (approx.)
11 $1/2$ decilitres = 1 $1/7$ litre	= 8 gills	= 2 pt.	= 40 oz. (approx.)
2 litres		= 3 $1/2$ pt.	= 70 oz. (approx.)
3.785 litres = 1 American gallon			
4.546 litres = 10 lb. distilled water = 1 Imperial gallon			

CALCULATION OF YEAST QUANTITIES

The quantity of fresh yeast in a mixing will depend on the time that the dough will ferment in bulk (doughmaking to scaling), the temperature of the dough, the method employed and the amount of enriching agents contained in it.

A yeasted dough will ferment best between 78-82° F (25.6-27.8° C). At higher temperatures, the speed of fermentation increases but gradually the yeast weakens. At temperatures exceeding 140° F (60° C) yeast is killed. As the temperature gets progressively below 80° F (26.7° C) the speed of fermentation slows down until at 40° F (4.4° C) it practically ceases, but the yeast is not damaged.

A good guide for the calculation of fresh yeast quantities for small doughs at 80° F (26.7° C) is to take the factor 12 and multiply it by the weight of flour calculated as a fraction of the weight of a sack of flour in pounds (280 lb.); multiply by 16 to bring the result to ounces and divide by the bulk fermentation time. Here are three examples.

Using 2 lb. of flour (1/140th sack) a dough at 80° F (26.7° C) is required to ferment in bulk for 2 hours.

$$\frac{12 \times 1 \times 16}{140 \times 2} = \frac{24}{35 \text{ oz.}} = 3/4 \text{ oz. (approx.)}$$

Using 3 $1/2$ lb. of flour (1/80th sack) a dough at 80° F (26.7° C) is required to ferment in bulk for 1 $1/2$ hours.

$$\frac{12 \times 1 \times 16}{80 \times 1.5} = \frac{8}{5 \text{ oz.}} = 1 3/4 \text{ oz. (approx.)}$$

Using 5 lb. of flour, a dough at 80° F (26.7° C) is required to ferment in bulk for 3 hours.

$$\frac{12 \times 5 \times 16}{280 \times 3} = \frac{8}{7} = 1 \text{ } 1/4 \text{ oz. (approx.)}$$

For cooler doughs, the weight of yeast needs to be increased progressively until in doughs at 70° F (21° C) about double the quantity is necessary. This can be calculated as an addition of 20 % for each 2° F (1.1° C) decrease in temperature below 80° F (26.7° C). Thus 20 % extra will be needed over the calculated quantity for a dough at 78° F (25.6° C); 60 % extra for a dough at 74° F (22.2° C) and 100 % extra for a dough at 70° F (21° C).

All doughs made with a thin preliminary ferment will need a little less yeast than calculated, depending on the time that the ferment is allowed to stand before it is made into a dough. Given time, yeast will multiply in a thin ferment.

Enriching agents, such as fat, eggs and sugar will slow down the speed of fermentation and unless a thin preliminary ferment is used before doughmaking, the amount of yeast will need to be increased or fermentation time extended.

Dried yeast must be used according to the instructions given on the package by the manufacturer.

The information given above must be used as a guide only; experimentation under the conditions where fermented doughs are made and processed are necessary for any degree of accuracy to be attained.

III. Bakery Technology

The History and Technology of Aeration

Aeration renders bakery products more attractive, more appetizing and more digestible. In order to aerate, a pressure must be induced within the product and a resistance offered to it so that volume may be increased during baking, until such time as the proteins coagulate and the volume is maintained without any collapse.

There are five methods of aeration
1. Panary   — yeast
2. Chemical   — baking powders
3. Physical   — whisking and beating
4. Lamination   — rolling and folding
5. Combinations of the above.

Panary
Right back in the dawn of human history, primitive man discovered that certain grains were edible. It was but a short step to the discovery that they became more readily consumable if they were broken. It seems obvious that the breaking was effected by means readily to hand—two heavy stones between which the grain was pounded. In this way, the first cornmeal was produced and milling got its inception.

The discovery of fire and its application to human comfort was a major achievement; used in cooking it rendered food much more appetizing and digestible. Baking was simple; all that was needed was a flat stone which could be placed into a fire and heated and on to which the rough breadcakes, made from cornmeal and water, could be placed and baked. The history of baking began at this point.

It was soon discovered that if the hot stone was enclosed by more stones, with the crevices sealed with clay, then heat was conserved. In this way the first oven was evolved.

A mixture of cornmeal and water shaped into rough pieces and baked on a hot stone resulted in a coarse bread quite hard in consistency, the only flavour being that conferred by the grain used and from that given by certain changes during baking. This was unleavened bread. The introduction of fermentation or leavening to bread was almost certainly the result of an accident, it being wholly possible, at one distant point in history, that a piece of old dough was mixed into one freshly made with the result that the baked bread was found to be less dense. In this way the bread became leavened and the art of panary fermentation got its inception. The art and practice of fermentation became highly developed in ancient Egypt, and amongst the early Jews. Soon it became common practice to save a piece of dough to mix with the new, so as to ensure continuity of the fermentation process.

Soon it was discovered that the speed of fermentation was partly controlled by the consistency of the dough, a soft dough fermenting more quickly than a tight dough. Very soft mixtures of malt, hops and water, together with a little of the coarse meal then used by the baker, were made up and left uncovered, to be innoculated by airborne yeast organisms (although this was not known at the time). After a period of time, during which the yeast cells multiplied, the barm, as it was called, was made into a dough. A piece of this dough was saved to act as a starter for the next barm and so the process went on. In many parts of the world, the sour dough method of fermentation is still used, particularly in the manufacture of rye breads.

All through the centuries it was thought that leavening was a spontaneous phenomena, until, in 1859, the great French scientist Louis Pasteur discovered that it was the result of living yeast micro-organisms, converting sugar into carbon dioxide gas (CO_2) which leavened or aerated the dough.

In the early part of the present century, compressed yeast was made available to the baker. Made under scientifically controlled conditions, it arrives at the bakery fresh and pure, ready to aerate, not only our daily bread, but the wide range of fermented goods that is the pride of the true craftsman.

The principle of panary fermentation is the production of CO_2. This is brought about by the action of enzymes in yeast and flour. The initial gas production comes from the breakdown of glucose present in flour, or contained in added ingredients. Further glucose is made available by the conversion of other carbohydrates by specific enzymes. The gas is entangled and held in the gluten network which is gradually made more elastic during the fermentation process and so the dough rises. There are acid and alcohol by-products of fermentation which make a contribution to flavour.

When in the oven, gas production is accelerated until at last the yeast is killed and activity ceases. The expansion of air and gas and the pressure of water vapour causes an increase in volume which is maintained by the coagulation of all the proteins present as baking proceeds.

Chemical

The evolution of cake, as we know it today, dates from a day in the past when an unknown cook decided, either as a result of a conscious desire to experiment, or in an effort to use up surplus ingredients, to introduce sugar, (probably in the form of honey) and some oil or fat into a fermented dough and was delighted when the enrichment produced a much nicer and more exciting addition to the range of foods then available. In this way, with the addition of dried fruit, the Old English Plum Cake was evolved, the method continuing until the introduction of chemical aeration, when it was discovered that certain chemicals would give off gas when moistened and heated.

When such chemical substances were first introduced into foodstuffs in not known. 'Pearl Ash' a form of potash was one of the first used. It was made originally by calcining wood and vegetable matter. Potassium carbonate is also obtained from residues of beet sugar refining. Centuries ago, it was discovered that if potash was added to a gingerbread dough, it would, during storage before baking, become aerated. The use of carbonate of potash still continues in the manufacture of continental spice breads, leckerlis and honey cakes.

Carbonate of soda has certainly been used for over 200 years. This alkali was used in domestic cookery when sour milk or buttermilk was the main moistening agent, it being evident that reaction with the lactic acid of milk effected a greater liberation of gas, and in consequence a greater degree of aeration.

As home baking decreased and the professional baker began to flourish, there was experimentation with other chemicals in an effort to find reliable aerating agents that were both harmless and tasteless when used in food. Alums and the carbonates of magnesia and lime were amongst the chemicals used. Old recipe books refer to muriatic acid, now better known as hydrochloric acid, being used with bi-carbonate of soda. The reaction released CO_2 with a residue of sodium chloride (common salt). Carbonate of ammonia, on moistening and heating, decomposes completely into CO_2 and ammonia gas.

This chemical is known by the British baker as 'Vol' and is still used in the manufacture of biscuits and choux pastry; in both cases the ammonia gas is quickly dissipated on cooling, without leaving the objectionable odour and flavour of ammonia in the finished product.

Tartaric acid then came into favour as an acid component of baking powder to be superseded by the slower acting cream of tartar which is less soluble in cold water so delaying the generation of CO_2 until the cake is in the oven so giving greater volume.

Because cream of tartar is comparatively expensive, many substitutes known as cream powders are now available to the baker. These are sold under various trade names, most of them being based on acid sodium pyrophosphate.

An efficient baking powder should comply with the provisions of the food regulations of the country in which it is used. It should liberate the maximum amount of gas during baking. After reaction, the residue substances remaining within the product must be harmless and not unpleasant in taste and aroma.

As with panary fermentation, the CO_2 generated by the chemicals is entangled in the gluten network, which holds and gives to it during expansion, until at last the proteins coagulate and the aerated structure becomes comparatively rigid.

Physical (cont. page 40).

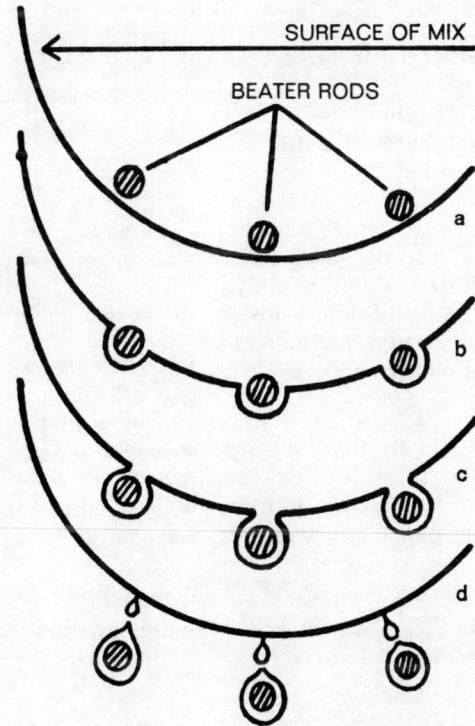

MECHANISM OF AIR INCORPORATION

Physical (cont.)

Long ago in our gastronomic history it was discovered that by beating a mixture, air was incorporated, and the baked product became lighter in texture, in fact it became aerated. It is probable that eggs were the media for the original discovery. Soon it was discovered that animal fats could be made much lighter by beating and the blending of other materials with it became much easier. In this way physical aeration got its inception.

There are two important bakery materials that are capable of holding air when beaten and they are fat and eggs. It soon became apparent that egg whites alone, when whipped, held more air than either whole eggs or egg yolks so that they became the ideal media for meringues and for royal icing.

An understanding of the mechanism by which air is drawn into a mixture during beating is of interest and importance to the craftsman.

It will be seen that the rapidly moving hand-whisk or beater breaks the surface on impact and moves into the mixture, temporarily extending the surface area.

The surface area will strive to remain at a minimum, thus offering a resistance, which drives the mixture behind the beating implement as it penetrates still further into the mix. It is during this fractional moment of time before the beater strikes again that air bubbles are drawn into the mixture behind the beating implement and become incorporated in, and held by, the fat or eggs, or both. In this way, countless bubbles are drawn into the mixing until at last it is thoroughly aerated.

To a lesser extent short pastry is also aerated by the introduction of air either during the rubbing in of fat into the flour or during the beating of fat and sugar prior to the mixing of them into the flour.

Lamination

Who it was that first rolled some fat into a dough will never be known. It may have happened by accident or by conscious design.

It is conceivable that a cook, wishing to enrich a piece of dough, decided to roll some fat into it, either because he or she did not relish the harder task of rubbing it in, or possibly because the fat was tough and hard. It is possible too that a cook, after adding everything else, discovered that the fat had been omitted and decided to roll it in. Perhaps some gastronomic genius reasoned it out, experimented and was amazed at the result. We shall never know.

The purpose of rolling and folding is to build up a laminated structure of alternating layers of dough and fat. If it was possible to count these layers when puff pastry is ready for baking, it would be found to consist of many hundreds. This build-up is known as aeration by lamination.

The reason for the lift in puff pastry has been the subject for conjecture over many years. Almost all of the reasons given are wide of the mark, some of them quite impossible.

If several pieces of gluten of equal weight are prepared and *each* put into an oven of different temperature, it will be seen that the rate of expansion differs, for it will be found that the higher the oven temperature the greater will be the expansion.

Gluten is insoluble wheat protein, hydrated in the ratio of one part protein and two parts water. It is the changing of water into steam and the consequent pressure within the gluten structure that is largely the reason for the lift.

Experiments with glutens of differing strengths, all placed together in one oven, will show that expansion is greater in the stronger glutens. It is thus seen that to produce good puff pastry fairly strong flour should be used and a correct baking temperature maintained.

Combination of Methods

A combination that comes readily to mind is that used for making Danish Pastries when butter is rolled into a fermented dough thus combining panary aeration with lamination.

The combination of physical and chemical aeration is quite common when mixtures of fat, sugar and eggs are beaten during the first stages of manufacture. Aeration is supplemented by the addition of baking powder during the later stages.

An example of a combination of panary and chemical aeration is the British fermented scone which is made by a preliminary yeast ferment before it is incorporated with other ingredients, to which baking powder has been added.

FORMULA BALANCE

A good formula is an accurate record of the weight of raw materials necessary to make a particular type of cake. If the formula is correctly balanced it will produce a good cake, always providing that the correct manufacturing procedure is adopted and that there is care in baking and packing.

A good cake is one showing no faults, either in appearance or in the eating. The quality of a cake may vary, but if the formula is correctly balanced, then it will produce a good cake.

An understanding of formula balance is of immense importance to the craftsman, for with this knowledge he can not only perfect his formulas, but can also recognize faults caused by the incorrect balance of raw materials, and be able to correct them.

When considering raw materials there are two points to be borne in mind; that there is one group that confers strength and structure to a cake and a second group that has to be carried by the first. The materials that confer strength and structure are flour and eggs, because both contain proteins that coagulate in the oven during baking to form the 'framework' of the cake. The group that has to be carried consists of fat, sugar, milk and fruit.

Two further considerations arise. Some materials open or lift the structure of the cake, whilst others tend to close it. Those that open the structure are sugar, baking powder and yeast, fat and eggs, the last two because they take in air when whipped or beaten. Those that close the structure are milk and water.

Consideration must also be given to other aspects of the basic raw materials used in cake-making. Fat enriches and when beaten holds air, thus assisting in aerating the cake. Sugar sweetens. Eggs moisten, and when beaten assist in aeration.

It is known that equal weights of flour, fat, sugar and eggs will produce a good cake, there being sufficient eggs to moisten the flour, sufficient sugar to sweeten and sufficient fat to enrich and also to hold the eggs when beaten, without 'curdling'. Fat and eggs combined hold sufficient air when beaten to aerate the cake. The flour and the eggs provide the strength and structure.

To lower the quality of the cake it is necessary, first of all, to increase the flour, with the weight of fat remaining constant. The weight of egg is equivalent to the weight of fat. The weight of sugar is increased. Because there is more flour to moisten, milk is introduced, and because there is a lower proportion of fat and eggs in relation to flour then baking powder is introduced to assist aeration.

Milk is added at the rate of 85 % of the weight of flour in excess of the weight of eggs.

Baking powder is added to complete aeration at the rate of 6 % of the weight of flour in excess of the weight of eggs for cakes of small size, 3 % for medium and 2 % for cakes of larger size. The weight of sugar should be approximately 25 % of the total weight of flour, fat, eggs and milk (if any).

Fat controls the quality of a cake, the better the quality of the fat the better the quality of the finished cake. The lower the proportion of fat in a cake, the lower the quality. The weight of fat should never exceed that of flour. A fat of good quality will take an

EFFECTS OF MILK

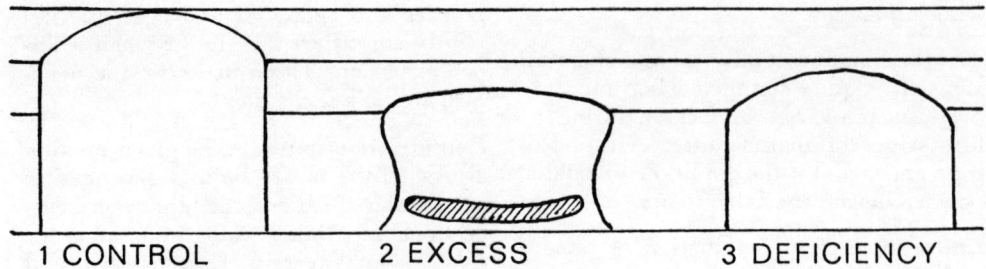

EFFECTS OF SUGAR

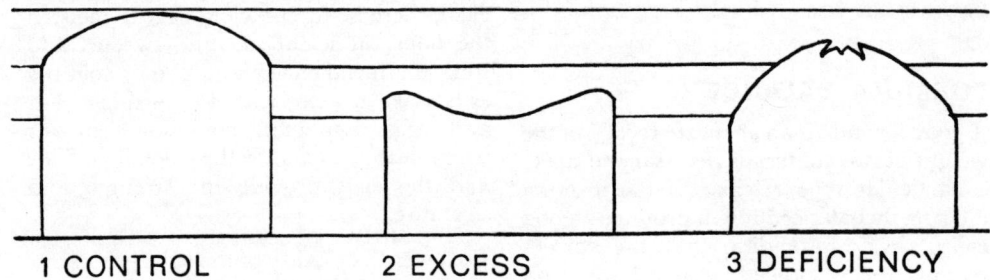

EFFECTS OF BAKING POWDER

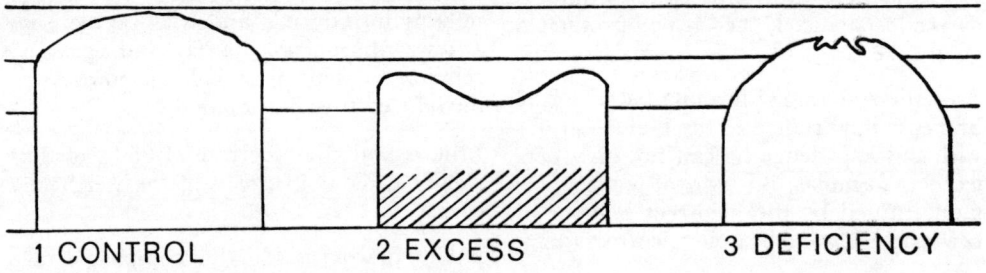

EFFECTS OF FAT

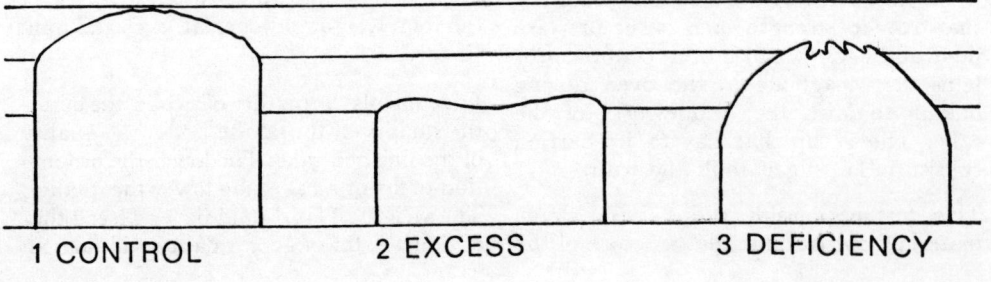

amount of eggs in the ratio of 1 : 1.25, and this ratio should not be exceeded.

Faults in cakes come under two main headings, collapse in the middle and collapse at the sides. The first can be described as the 'M' fault because the cut profile is similar to that of the letter 'M'. The second can be described as the 'X' fault because the collapse at the sides provides a profile similar to the letter 'X'.

The 'M' fault is almost always the result of an excess of baking powder or of sugar. It could be caused by an excess of both. An excess of baking powder will generate such a volume of CO_2 in the oven that the structural materials are ruptured, so causing collapse. This fault can be distinguished from that of excess of sugar by a darker crust colour and by a darkening of the crumb at the base of the cake.

The cake with an excess of sugar will show white sugar patches on the crust, the crumb will tend to be sticky and will be excessively sweet.

A cake with an excess of milk will not show any fault until it is removed from the oven and begins to cool when it will sink and collapse at the sides. While in the oven the volume is maintained by steam pressure, which diminishes as the cake cools. Apart from the collapse at the sides, there is a marked closeness at the base of the crumb which is visible when the cake is cut. Insufficient milk will cause a loss of volume, for part of the aeration of a cake is a result of steam expansion. The cake will be dry and it will stale quickly.

An excess of fat will show as a decrease in volume because the fat excess will weaken the structure. According to the amount in excess, the cake on inspection will have a greasy crust and crumb.

Cakes showing a high ragged top crust, known as a 'cauliflower' top, are a result of one or more errors. If the flour used is too strong for the formula used, then there will be too much resistance to expansion during baking. As this expansion cannot be denied, it causes a violent thrust upwards, the crust is ruptured and thrown back. Evidence of this thrust can be seen by the long tunnel shaped holes in the crumb leading to the point of eruption.

An oven too hot or with a lack of humidity will cause the same fault. In this case the crust forming before expansion is complete, offers a resistance and an eruption ensues because of the internal pressures.

Over-mixing after the inclusion of flour will cause the same fault. Over-mixing develops the potential strength of the gluten (flour protein) and the result is similar to that of using a flour that is too strong.

A formula deficient in fat and/or sugar will cause the same fault because both these materials have a softening effect on flour protein.

It must be understood that all faults differ in degree according to the extent of the inaccuracy in the balance of the formula. Slight faults can sometimes be corrected by an adjustment of flour strength or by a little less or a little more mixing time when the flour has been added. It is also interesting to note that it is impossible to have the 'M' and the 'X' faults together. Experiments will show that, within limits, the faults tend to cancel each other out and a new quality of cake becomes possible.

The illustrations on page 42 show the effects of the correct and incorrect balance of raw materials. The illustrations show the importance of an understanding of formula balance and will show that the simple rule is to so balance the formula that there is sufficient of the materials that provide structure to carry the rest of the materials, with due regard to a balance of those that open and those that close the structure.

Cake making Methods

There are several methods of making cakes, each dictated by the type of cake being produced, the balance and the type of materials used.

RUB-IN METHOD

This is perhaps the oldest method and the easiest to use. The method, however, is not successful unless the aeration is by means of baking powder.

The flour and baking powder are sieved together and the fat rubbed in finely. A bay is made in the mixture and the sugar, liquids and the flavour are added, after which the whole is well mixed. Any fruit should be placed round the outside of the bay.

Alternatively, the fats and an equal amount of flour are first creamed together, the liquids are added and finally the balance of the flour.

There is another method in which the fat and sugar are creamed, any eggs are added and the mixture rubbed into the flour; the addition of milk and flavouring and final mixing completes the operation.

Short pastes may be made by either of the first two methods. Sweet pastry by any of the three.

SUGAR BATTER METHOD

This method is used for better quality cakes containing higher proportions of fat, sugar and eggs in relation to the weight of flour. It is commercially popular because the materials can be assembled and the mixing completed in one operation.

The fat and sugar are first creamed during which air is beaten in and held by the fat. The eggs are beaten in a portion at a time and more air is incorporated. Finally the flour is carefully folded in and milk, if any, is added. Any fruit is added last. *Chapter VI.*

FLOUR BATTER METHOD

This method is used for cakes of any quality, since aeration is based mainly on the knowledge that a mixture of fat and flour will hold a great quantity of air when beaten. Any eggs used will assist in the holding of air. In the cheaper mixings, aeration will be supplemented by the addition of baking powder.

The fat and an equal amount of flour are well beaten together. Any eggs, with an equal amount of sugar, are whipped to a half sponge and carefully mixed with the fat/flour mix. Any balance of sugar is dissolved in the milk with the flavour added. Half is added to the mix, to be followed by the balance of flour and the rest of the sugar/milk solution. The baking powder (if any) is sieved with the flour. Any fruit is added last.

This method needs a careful lay-out of the formula before commencing and the use of more equipment. It is useful for large scale production of cheaper quality cakes and for high class exhibition work.

BLENDING METHOD

This is the method used for the production of cakes containing special cake flour and fat. It is carried out in three stages.

Firstly the flour is sieved with the rest of the dry materials and mixed with the fat to a crumbly consistency, care being taken not to turn it into a paste. The water is run in carefully until a smooth mixture is attained. After scraping down the bowl, the eggs are run in slowly. Further scraping and mixing completes the operation.

If a machine is used, the slowest speed only must be used, or the cake will shrink during baking.

Baking Confectionery Products

To have an understanding of raw materials; to be conversant with formula balance and types of aeration, is not enough. One other important factor follows, and that is baking. This must be done correctly and with understanding, otherwise at best the product will be sub-standard, and at worst it will be spoiled, so that time and materials are wasted.

There is always a correct temperature and baking time, but this will depend on many factors, such as:

1. Size
2. Thickness
3. Quality
4. Density
5. Oven loading
6. Oven humidity

A cake is cooked when the heat has penetrated to the centre, therefore it becomes obvious that the size of the cake is important. Generally speaking the larger the cake the longer it takes to bake, and the baking temperature must of necessity be lower. This, however, will depend to a certain extent on the thickness of the cake. A thicker cake is cooked when the heat has penetrated to the centre and then upwards to the centre of the crown. This is the last part of a thicker cake to bake because, at this point, the temperature is kept down because of the escaping steam; thus the thicker cake will need a lower baking temperature and longer baking time. An underbaked cake will have a damp patch just under the crown.

The quality of a cake has a bearing on baking temperature and baking time. If the cake contains a high proportion of sugar, then the baking temperature must be reduced and baking time increased because sugar will caramelize quickly at a high temperature, the crust will discolour, and there will be a bitter flavour.

A cake mixing that is dense, that is one containing a high proportion of sugar, fat, eggs and fruit, will need a lower baking temperature and the baking time will need to be extended, because heat penetration is delayed because of the increased density.

Oven loading must be taken into consideration, because the temperature of an oven full of cake will fall, depending on the type of cake being baked, and the size of the oven; therefore a higher initial temperature may be necessary. Humidity also is important because it will delay crust formation until full expansion has taken place. A correct baking temperature with insufficient oven humidity will not produce a good cake. An oven full of cake will generally provide sufficient humidity, otherwise supplementary steam becomes necessary, such as provided by water pots.

The same principles apply to baking on a hotplate, the larger the size and/or the greater the enrichment, then the lower the temperature of the hotplate.

The temperature of frying oil for doughnuts, fritters, beignets etc. is also critical. If the oil is too hot, then the desired expansion is not attained and distortion of shape becomes inevitable, together with possible under-cooking. If the temperature of the oil is too low, then expansion is excessive, the product will absorb oil and become greasy and oil laden.

If it is understood that a cake is not baked until the heat has penetrated for a sufficient time to finish baking, it will be understood also that care must be taken during the baking period. If the cake is knocked as a result of accident or carelessness, then the structure of the cake will surely be damaged, according to the extent of the knock and the degree of baking at the time.

If best quality materials are used, the formula is balanced, care is taken in the mixing and in the baking and then, after baking, the cakes are not treated with care, faults will be evident and this will be no credit to the person responsible, for it will be seen at once that he has forfeited his good name as a craftsman.

All baking temperatures and times given in this book are approximate and should be read with the information given above.

Deep Freezing and Retardation

There is historical evidence to the fact that in ancient China snow and ice were used for the preservation of food. All through the ages the principle of reducing the temperature of foodstuffs has been applied, so to delay deterioration and decay. Records of the social and gastronomic history of man show ample evidence of the use of ice caves, ice pits and, later, ice boxes. Not only was food preserved by this means, but in course of time, iced dishes were developed to bring greater variety to the menus of those who could afford them.

The principle is the same to-day as it was in the past; the lowering of temperature to such a degree that all living organisms and all physical and chemical changes responsible for spoilage are inhibited.

Science and engineering together, however, developed the modern controlled refrigeration process by which means vast quantities of foodstuffs are frozen, transported and stored all over the world.

One of the major advantages of deep freezing in the baking and catering industries is that products can be made in larger quantities, thus being produced more economically. In this way production peaks can be eliminated so that it is more even, thus preventing the strain of meeting abnormal production demands.

In the English speaking world a terminology has been established with regard to the refrigeration of foodstuffs and it may be subdivided under two headings.

1. Deep Freezing

This is a term used to describe the rapid reduction of temperature to below freezing point. The installation used is known as a 'deep freeze'.

This type of refrigeration unit can be built to any size from the large 'walk-in' freezing chamber to the small 'reach-in' cabinet. Competent refrigeration engineers are always ready to assist in this, and their advice that refrigeration space should be larger than required for normal production should be carefully noted. Units too small may lead to over-loading with a consequent lowering of efficiency. It is wise also to envisage a progressive increase in production as a result of up-to-date methods and the intelligent use of equipment.

Modern deep freeze installations are fully automatic irrespective of whether they are large or small; even so, there are considerations that must be observed if maximum efficiency is to be attained.

(a) The temperature of baked products must be reduced to that of the surrounding atmosphere before they are loaded into the deep freeze. This is important because the rate of freezing depends on the total weight and the temperature of the products loaded in per hour in comparison with the freezing capacity of the equipment.

(b) The size of the products to be frozen must also be considered. Small items will take 30/90 minutes, articles about 1 lb. in weight about four hours, and products about 2 lb. in weight up to six hours for the temperature to be reduced to 0° F (—17.8° C). The optimum storage temperature is approximately —10° F (—23° C).

(c) The length of storage time is also of importance. Some items can be made and stored overnight to be removed and baked in the morning, whilst others may be in deep freeze for longer periods. Consideration should be given to the possible loss of flavour and aroma from prolonged storage.

(d) Storage should be carried out systematically so that products can be removed in strict rotation. All trays and containers should therefore be clearly dated or code marked.

(e) All products to be frozen should be assembled first so that loading can be as rapid as possible, so to reduce the amount of warm air drawn in. The warm air not only increases the load, but the humidity present makes for a build-up of frost, even though the unit may have an automatic defrosting apparatus. Air locks or an air curtain system are an advantage in the larger units. Loading can be facilitated by the use of wheel-in racks.

Small cabinets generally have a heated door frame to prevent frost formation which would make door opening difficult.

Rapid freezing has two important aspects, for it is known that ice crystal size is in direct ratio to the speed of freezing; the quicker the freezing the smaller the crystal. This has two advantages. Firstly that the small crystal does not damage the structure of the food during formation as would larger crystal; secondly, small crystal will not leave large deposits of moisture in the food during defrosting.

The humidity of the refrigerator atmosphere has a marked effect on the frozen products. A relative humidity of about 80 % is necessary. Low humidity atmospheres will tend to bring about a partial dehydration before the freezing point is reached.

Some bakery products can be successfully deep frozen whilst others are less tolerant. Here is a list of items that can be successfully frozen:

Baked
1. Cakes, plain and fruited
2. Bread, buns and soft rolls
3. Small powder aerated goods
4. Almond goods
5. Short and sweet pastries
6. Puff pastries

Unbaked
1. Cake batters
2. Rich buns and rolls
3. Small powder aerated goods
4. Cake fillings
5. Short and sweet pastes
6. Puff pastes

Correct defrosting of baked products is necessary although the operation is relatively simple. All that is required is to bring the frozen goods into a warm part of the bakery. If the temperature is between 70°-85° F (21.1°-29.4° C) defrosting time is approximately the same as the time taken to freeze. Defrosting time can be shortened by the use of a forced warm air system, the air being at 100° F (37.8° C) with a relative humidity of 50 % and with air movement of 200 feet per minute.

Bread stales between temperatures of 75° F (23.9° C) and 0° F (—17.8° C). It stales rapidly between 40° F (4.4 C) and 30° F (—1.1° C), therefore rapid freezing takes the temperature quickly through, and below the staling range. The same applies to the temperature in reverse; bread, therefore, during defrosting, should be brought to a temperature figure of 70°-75° F (21.1°-23.9° C) as quickly as possible.

2. *Retardation*

This is the term used to describe the method of reducing the speed of yeast fermentation to a minimum. Temperatures between 32°-38° F (0°-3.3° C) will effect this. There are two methods of retarding yeast fermented doughs.

(a) In bulk. With this method the dough is made and given about one half or two-thirds of its bulk fermentation time. It is then flattened out in 8-10 lb. (3 ½ - 4 ½ kg.) pieces, wrapped in polythene and stored at 32°-38° F (0°-3.3° C).

When required for use, it is removed from the retarder and brought to room temperature, when it can be used in the normal way. Retarding for a period of over 72 hours is not recommended.

(b) In units. When a dough has reached a fermentation period as above, it is made up into the desired individual pieces and placed on the baking sheets. These are placed immediately into the retarder at the above temperature.

When required for baking, they are removed and brought to room temperature before baking in the normal way.

A combination of both methods will ensure that baked goods are quickly available and basic doughs are in reserve should they be required.

It is important that the made up individual pieces do not 'crust' whilst in the retarder. A relative humidity of 85 % will prevent this. If for some reason this cannot be maintained, then polythene sheets or greased paper should be used for covering.

Rich fermented doughs are retarded successfully up to 72 hours. Depending on the quality, less rich doughs have a limit between 24-48 hours.

The smaller domestic refrigerators maintain temperatures that will enable small quantities of yeast aerated goods to be retarded over a very limited period. The deep freeze compartment or ice box can also be used for small amounts that are already frozen, bearing in mind that overloading will always lead to a loss of efficiency.

There follows some detailed information concerning the use of the refrigerator for the smaller baker and caterer.

Foodstuffs in the Refrigerator

DAIRY PRODUCTS

Foodstuff	Container	Average period of storage	Remarks
Milk	Bottles or plastic containers	2-4 days	If in sterile containers. For longer storage boil the milk and then keep covered up.
Pasteurized or homogenized milk	Clean, sealed bottles	Several weeks	Only boil when ready to use.
Butter	Aluminium foil or greaseproof paper	Several weeks	As fats absorb smells and become rancid if exposed to the air, they must be thoroughly wrapped up.
Cream	Sealed containers	3-7 days	Cream keeps better in sealed glass jars.
Cream cheeses	Well sealed containers	Several days	Cream cheeses should be removed from their original wrappings which would not be sufficient to prevent dehydration.
Hard cheeses	Aluminium foil or greaseproof paper	15-20 days	Hard cheeses lose their flavour in the refrigerator although this is not so important if they are to be used in cooking.
Fermented cheeses	Special boxes or very careful wrapping	Variable	Camemberts, livarots are not put in the refrigerator unless they are ripe or overripe in order to arrest maturation. Careful wrapping is essential.
Eggs Whole eggs	Special egg boxes	1-3 weeks	
Egg whites Egg yolks	Sealed stainless containers	Several weeks	It is possible to store whites and yolks for longer periods in the deep freeze compartment.

Miscellaneous

Foodstuff	Container	Average period of storage	Remarks
Puff paste	Wrapped in plastic sheets	2-4 days	Give a final turn before cutting up.
Short paste	Sealed containers	1 week	Short paste made in advance and kept in the refrigerator gives very crisp pastry.
Sweetened or enriched paste	Earthenware or stainless metal containers	1 month approx.	Remove from the refrigerator some time before use.
Ice cream	Special containers	1 day to 1 week	Deep freeze compartment. Ices are smoother when eaten the day they are made as otherwise (water) crystals may form.
Confectioner's custard	Stainless containers	1-2 days	
Custards, soaked dried fruit, purée	Dishes, fruit bowls	Several days	
Left-overs	Sealed containers	1-4 days	Period of storage according to foodstuff.

Fruits

Foodstuff	Container	Average period of storage	Remarks
Redcurrants Cherries	Sealed bags or vegetable containers	Several days	Wash and drain before putting in the refrigerator.
Strawberries Raspberries	On covered dishes or in sealed containers		Two methods: 1. Sort out, place on a dish and cover over. 2. Sort out, wash, drain, sweeten with sugar and put in closed fruit bowls.
Melons Pineapples	Sealed bags		Fully ripe melons are not placed in the refrigerator except to be chilled. Wrap carefully to conserve flavour.

Foodstuff	Container	Average period of storage	Remarks
Peaches Pears Apricots Plums	Sealed containers	Variable according to ripeness	It is recommended to bring these fruits out of the refrigerator an hour before they are to be served so that their flavour can develop at a normal temperature.
Lemons			Should never be stored in the refrigerator.
Oranges			May be placed in the refrigerator for 30 minutes to be chilled before being eaten.
Bananas			Should never be put in the refrigerator as they would turn black.

Sugar Boiling

Sugar is soluble in water. Sugar is the solute and water the solvent. A given amount of water will dissolve a certain amount of sugar, any addition will precipitate. As the temperature of the water is raised, so more sugar will be dissolved. A solution holding the maximum of sugar without any precipitation at any given temperature is termed a saturated solution. If it is allowed to cool it will be found, provided that the boiling has been carried out correctly, that the excess sugar will not precipitate; the solution is then termed supersaturated. These solutions are very unstable and re-crystallization can be induced by agitation, or even by allowing them to stand for some time.

In the past, cube sugar was always advised for boiling because it was considered the best. Cube sugar was made from the first refined syrup crystallized and dried in the form of large thin slabs which were cut into cubes.

Cube sugar is now made by a new process. It is pressed into moulds which are lightly lubricated with edible oil. Oil traces are, therefore, present in the sugar solution. Preserving or mineral water sugar is now advised for sugar boiling.

It is standard practice to place six parts of sugar in a saucepan with two parts of water and take the solution to a temperature of 225° F. At this point care should be taken that all the sugar is dissolved and the sides of the pan are free from sugar crystals.

With the spatula removed, one part of warmed glucose is run in and allowed to mix by the action of the convection currents in the boiling solution. If no glucose is available a little weak acid is added instead; this will cause some of the sugar to change by hydrolysis to glucose. Glucose is necessary in most sugar solutions to prevent premature re-crystallization known to sugar boilers as graining. Premature graining can also be caused by failing to wash down the sides of the saucepan during boiling. Boiling should be done quickly and because copper is a good conductor of heat, a copper pan is ideal for the purpose.

Most experienced sugar boilers will use the hand tests to assess the degree of cooking; for the student the approximate temperatures are given. *(Illustration page 146)*.

Thread
If a drop of sugar is taken between the thumb and forefinger and a thin thread is formed when they are separated, then the sugar is boiled to the thread degree (225° F 107° C).

Pearl
If the test is repeated, it will be seen that the thread is stronger and when it breaks it will form a small pearl-like shape (230° F 110° C).

Blow
If a loop of wire is dipped into the solution it will, on removal, be glazed with a 'window' of sugar. If it is blown gently, the 'window' will be seen to bulge a little before bursting (235° F 113° C).

Feather
If the test is repeated and again it is blown, the sugar will fly off the wire like a string of feathers (240° F 116° C).

Soft or Small Ball
This is reached when a stick of wood dipped in cold water and then dipped into the sugar has a small, soft ball at the tip. If the ball is taken from the tip and allowed to drop on to a hard surface, it will be heard to drop with a dull thud (245° F 118° C).

Hard or Large Ball
When the test is repeated, the ball of sugar will be firmer and when dropped on to a hard surface a sharp crack will be heard (250° F 121° C).

Soft or Small Crack
This is reached when the stick of wood is dipped into cold water and then into the solution. After dipping into cold water again the sugar will break, but sticks to the teeth when bitten (270° F 132° C).

Hard or Large Crack
The degree is now reached where the sugar, dipped into cold water, breaks like glass and no longer sticks to the teeth. The sugar is at the correct degree for glazing cherries, orange segments, dates, etc. (280° F 138° C).

Sugar boiled over this degree will start to brown slowly, then more and more quickly until it caramelizes. *(Page 52)*.

THE VARIOUS DEGREES OF SUGAR BOILING - CONTINENTAL PRACTICE

Coating
Dip the skimmer in the boiling syrup and drain; the sugar will coat the utensil (20° B on the hydrometer).

Slightly Smooth
Take a drop of syrup between the thumb and forefinger; open them and a thin thread will form which breaks almost immediately (25° B on the hydrometer).

Very Smooth
If the same test is repeated, the thread is stronger and stretches further (30° B on the hydrometer).

Pearl
By this time the thread is stronger still and stretches further before falling back into a pearl-like drop (33° B on the hydrometer).

Small Blow
Dip the skimmer into the syrup and drain. Blow through the inside of the skimmer and little sugar bubbles will form on the other side of the holes (37° B on the hydrometer).

Large Blow
After boiling the sugar for a little longer, repeat the last test. The bubbles will be larger and some of them will float off (39° B on the hydrometer).

Soft or Small Ball
Dip a finger first in cold water, then in the boiling sugar and immediately in cold

water once more. The sugar remaining on the finger is very soft and can hardly be rolled into a ball (40°B on the hydrometer).

Medium Ball
After boiling a little longer, if the test is repeated, it is possible to roll the sugar into a soft ball (41° B on the hydrometer).

Hard or Large Ball
Shortly afterwards a ball of sugar forms easily between the fingers.

Soft or Small Crack
After further cooking, roll some sugar between the finger and thumb into a ball and elongate it into a strip which will break if bent.

Hard or Large Crack
The sugar crackles when dipped into cold water. It is hard and brittle and no longer sticks to the teeth.

Caramel
If boiled a little longer, the sugar turns yellowish and gives off a slight smell of burnt sugar. It is the final degree of sugar boiling and it is used to produce praline or brown nougat. After this the sugar becomes light brown, then dark brown and begins to smoke. When the sugar is sufficiently coloured, very carefully pour into the pan 10-14 oz. boiling water for every 2 lb. sugar and boil for a few moments to obtain the caramel. Caramel sugar syrup is used for colouring custards, ice-creams, etc. If the sugar is cooked any more, it turns into a dark, porous mass which is unusable.

CLARIFYING SUGAR SYRUPS

Nowadays the use of refined sugar obviates clarifying a syrup by the addition of whites of eggs. Only unrefined sugars and sugar by-products need clarifying, which is done in the following way:

3 lb. sugar
2 lb. 8 oz. water
½ egg white

Bring all the ingredients to the boil in a copper pan, stirring the while, and immediately remove from the heat in order to take off the scum; boil once more to bring the albumen (egg white) to the surface and skim again. Finally strain through a muslin cloth.

For a non-clarified syrup, take sugar and water in the same proportions but omit the egg white and boil twice in a copper pan. Stir frequently to help the sugar crystals to dissolve and wash the sides of the pan with a brush dipped in water to prevent the formation of crystals. Skim thoroughly and pour into a clean receptacle.

Plaiting

Plaiting is a pleasing and attractive form of decorative assembly. The shapes are built from strands of dough and in common with all forms of building, accuracy is essential. For this purpose there are rules that must be observed; they are as follows:

(a) The sub-division of the dough pieces must be accurate, each piece being the same size.

(b) Unless otherwise directed, each piece must be rolled to the same length.

(c) Each strand must be the same shape and thickness.

It can be seen from the above that successful plaiting is impossible if the strands are not properly prepared. *(Coloured illustrations page 275).*

One-strand Plait

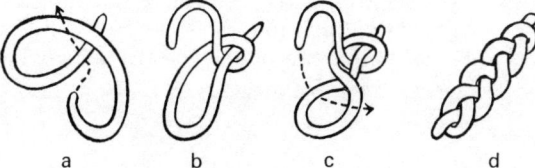

For this attractive and unusual plait, the dough piece is rolled to a fairly long rope. This is made into a loop with a long free end. The free end is drawn through the loop which is then twisted to the right. The end is then passed back and the loop twisted to the left, the sequence repeated until the plait is finished. *(Illustration page 275).*

Two-strand Plait

This simple shape is a twist rather than a plait. It is made by splitting the dough piece into two equal parts which are moulded round, after which they are given time to recover. They are then moulded into cigar shapes and twisted together as shown in the diagram. *(Illustration page 275).*

Three-strand Plait

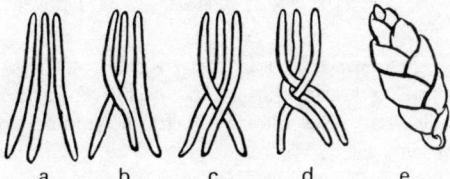

Probably the most popular of the plaited shapes. It is made by dividing the dough piece into three, which are first moulded round and then rolled to neat torpedo shapes and placed side by side. Commencing in the middle, the left hand piece is passed over its neighbour and the right hand piece brought over in a similar manner. This sequence continues until the end is reached. The whole arrangement is then turned over so that the free ends are brought to the bottom, when the plaiting is completed. Alternatively, the top ends can be fastened together and the plaiting done in one operation from top to bottom, but a better shape is given if it is done in two parts as described. *(Illustration page 275).*

Four-strand Plait

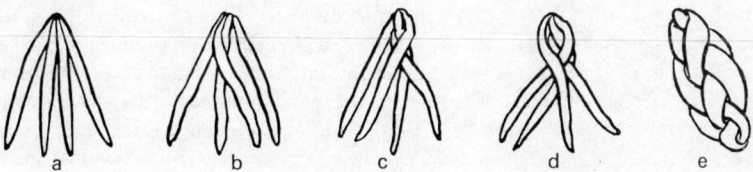

53

The strands are prepared as for the three-plait and the plaiting sequence is as follows, starting from the top where the strands are fastened together. The plaiting order is, two over three, four over two, and one over three, repeating this until the plait is finished. It is important to remember that after each move, the strands will bear the numbers one to four, reading from left to right: this can be seen clearly in the diagram. The finished shape can be seen in *illustration page 275*.

Five-strand Plait

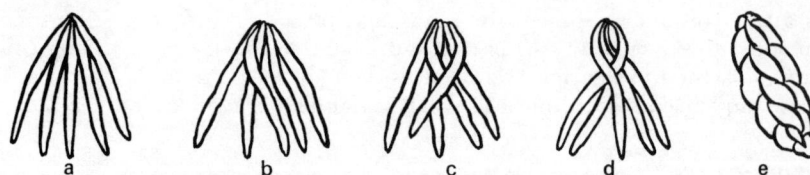

The five strands are fastened together at the top as for the four plait and the plaiting order is as follows. Two over three, five over two, and one over three, the sequence being repeated until the plait is finished. *(Illustration page 275)*.

Six-strand Plait

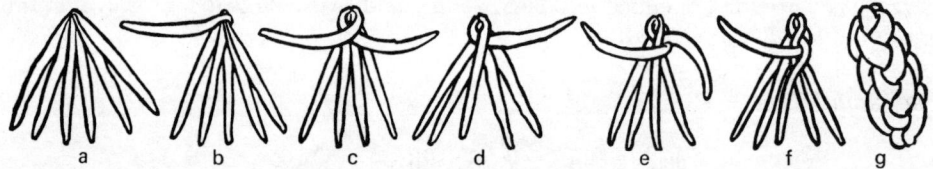

Mould the six strands as described and fasten together at the top. There follows an initial move that is not repeated and that is six over one. Then follows, two over six, one over three, five over one, and six over four, the sequence being repeated until the plait is complete. *(Illustration page 275)*.

Seven-strand Plait

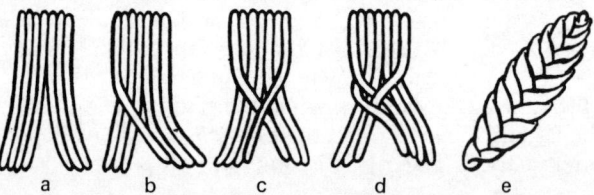

For this plait, the seven strands are rolled a little longer and placed side by side, opened at the bottom so that there are four strands at the left and three on the right. The outside left-hand strand is then brought to the middle and pushed to the right. The outside right-hand strand is next brought to the middle and pushed to the left. This sequence is repeated until the end is reached. The arrangement is then turned over and the other half completed in the same way. The moves are clearly shown in the diagram and the finished shape in the *illustration page 275*. Five, nine and eleven strands can be plaited in the same way.

Eight-strand Plait

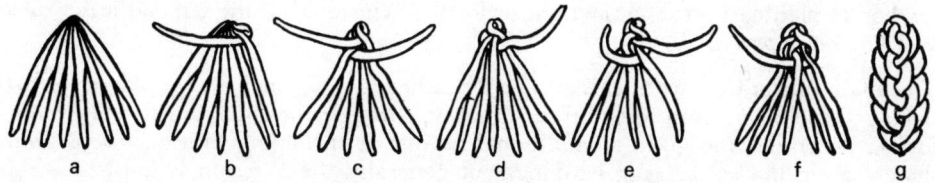

a   b   c   d   e   f   g

The eight pieces are moulded and arranged as for the four, five and six plaits. The first move, eight under seven and over one, is not repeated. There follow four moves which are repeated until the plait is completed. They are, two under three and over eight, one over four, seven under six and over one, and eight over five. The diagram shows the sequence and the *illustration* the finished shape. *(See page 275)*.

The Winston

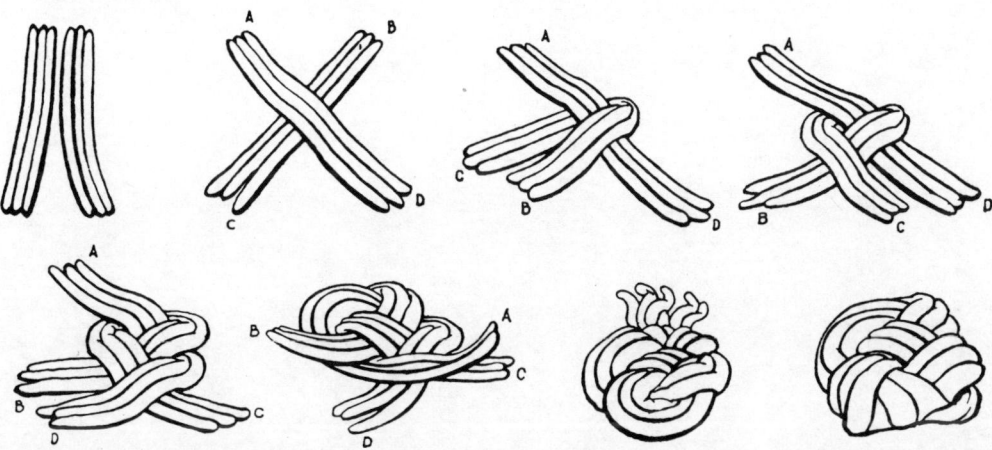

For this plait the dough piece is divided into six and each piece moulded round. After sufficient time for recovery, the pieces are moulded to fairly long ropes, three pieces being a little longer than the others. The three longer pieces are first placed together on the table with the shorter three pieces at right-angles as shown in the diagram. B is brought down over D, C is taken over B, and D over C. A is brought under B and over D, and C over A. The last two moves are repeated until the plait is finished. The tail end of the plait is then tucked underneath so that a round shape is formed. *(Illustration page 275)*.

Before baking, this plait is cut in the centre with a pair of scissors as illustrated. *(See page 275)*.

The Peardrop

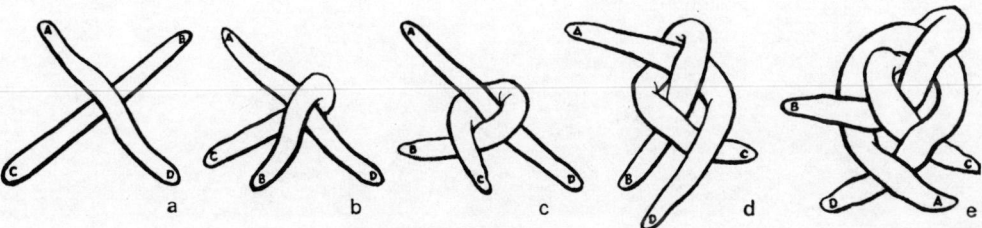

a   b   c   d   e

55

This plait is made with two strands, one piece being a little longer than the other. The method of plaiting is exactly the same as for the Winston, but the tail end is not tucked in. *(Illustration page 275)*.

The plaits illustrated were carefully egg washed twice; once when placed on to the baking sheets and again about three-quarters through the final proof. They may be further decorated and given an additional flavour by sprinkling with maw seeds immediately after the second egg washing, but generally the Winston is finished without seeds.

Very many more complicated forms of plaiting are possible both for commercial sale and for show pieces; the craftsman interested in this form of artistic work is recommended to acquire and study books on the subject.

Many of the simpler forms of plaiting can be used for small fancy dinner rolls.

IV. Raw Materials

The study of bakery raw materials is important. Firstly, because it will lead to more efficient buying, and secondly, an understanding of the interaction of them in manufacturing and baking processes will lead to better quality control. With this knowledge also, the craftsman will have the ability to adjust existing recipes according to a particular need.

This chapter deals with the sources and processing of the main ingredients found in the bakery. It should be read in conjunction with the sections in Chapter III (Baking Technology) which described the effects of raw materials in formula balance and the reaction of them in the mixing process and during baking.

They are given in the order as described in Formula Balance, i.e. the structural materials followed by those that have to be carried.

Flour

Flour is one of the two structural materials used in bakery products. By far the greater percentage of flour used today is milled from wheat, which, in varying quantities, is grown almost all over the world.

The wheat grain can be considered as having three main parts; the percentage figures being approximate:

1. The Bran   - 13 %
2. The Embryo or germ - 2 %
3. The Endosperm   - 85 %

The bran coatings protect the grain and provide a distinctive colour which ranges from a pale amber to a reddish light-brown. The bran comprises six principal layers. The bran coatings contain most of the vitamin B complex.

The germ contains the embryo plant and rootlet. It also includes the scutellum at the junction between the germ and the endosperm, the scutellum contains by far the greater percentage of the vitamin content of the wheat grain, particularly Vitamin E.

The endosperm consists of protein, starch, fat, water, sugar and mineral matter. It is from the endosperm that white flour is milled.

There are two methods of milling:

1. Stone Milling

This is the method of antiquity, although it is still practiced in many parts of the world.

The grain is broken and crushed between two heavy, grooved stones, the operation yielding a coarse meal.

The product of stone milling is wholemeal. The only possible adjustment comes from sieving out the coarse bran particles, resulting in a finer meal, the extraction rate of which depends on the fineness of the sieve.

2. Roller Milling

This originated in Switzerland to be developed commercially later in Hungary about 1870. Most of the world's wheat is now milled by this method.

After cleaning and conditioning, the wheats selected by the miller, known as the 'grist', are first broken between fluted rollers. Some flour is sieved off and the coarse particles remaining are sent to rollers set more closely together. The process is repeated until no endosperm is left on the bran coatings.

The coarse flour particles, free from bran, are passed to smooth reduction rollers, which grind them to a fine particle size. After sieving and other treatment, the flour is ready for dispatch to the baker. With roller milling, an extraction rate of flour can be produced by the miller from as low as 40 % to a wholemeal of 100 %. This is the essential difference between stone and roller milling. In its turn, these whiter flours, free from bran and germ, have a profound effect on bakery products so that a larger variety of fine bread and cakes becomes possible. Flours vary in strength and colour. This is due to effects of soil and climate on the growing wheat, the breed of wheat, the mixture of wheats used by the miller, by the length of time that the flour has been stored, and/or the chemical treatment to which the flour has been subjected.

Flour strength is defined by the quality of the gluten; elasticity and extensibility is the measure of that quality. Gluten is formed when the insoluble proteins are hydrated. Amongst other factors the degree of mixing and the presence of shortening agents have a bearing on gluten development.

The wheat flours available to the baker today may be divided into six types:

1. Wholemeals and Wheatmeals

These have an extraction rate of between 90 % and 100 %. Wholemeals contain all (100 %) of the wheat. Wheatmeals have the germ removed and, depending on the extraction rate, some of the bran. Because of the presence of germ and/or bran, the percentage of protein as compared with white flour, is less, so that doughs are less extensible, and the volume of the finished product is less. The use of these meals, however, confers a characteristic flavour.

2. Strong Flours

These are milled from wheats rich in good quality protein.

These wheats are grown in areas where the soil is rich in nitrogen, where the rainfall is adequate and where the hot sun is ideal for ripening and harvesting. The prairie provinces of Canada, parts of the U.S.A. and the U.S.S.R., together with parts of Europe referred to as Danubian, provide the strong wheats of the world.

The stronger flours are necessary in the making of bread, puff pastry, choux pastry and fancy tea breads.

3. Medium Strong Flours

These are milled from wheats grown in the Argentine, in areas watered by the River Plate. Australia produces some medium strong wheats, the flour of which is of excellent colour. Blends of strong and soft flours will also provide flours of medium strength.

4. Soft or Weak Flours

These are generally milled from European wheats, although some Pacific wheats from Canada and the U.S.A. and some Australian wheats can be included in this category.

Because of the low gluten content of these flours, they are admirably fitted for the production of rich cakes and biscuits which contain a high fat and/or egg content, or in products where a high tensile strength is not desirable, such as shortpastry, shortbreads and rich biscuits.

5. Special Cake Flour

This flour is also known as 'high-ratio' flour because, by its use, high ratios of sugar, eggs and milk are possible in a cake, producing a light mellowness in the crumb. This type of cake does not readily stale.

This flour is milled exceedingly fine from wheat of good quality, the fine granularity making it possible to hold more milk by adsorption, that is, held by surface tension, not to be confused with absorption, which means taking in. For the benefit of the student, adsorption can be illustrated by imagining the dipping of a ball of metal of a certain weight into water and then weighing it. The result will be the weight of the metal plus the weight of the water held on the surface. If the metal was made into pellets of the same total weight and these were dipped into water, it would be found that there was a greater amount of water held because of the greater aggregate surface area of the pellets. Flour of very fine granularity will thus hold more milk by absorption or surface tension than ordinary flour. In addition, all flours will absorb a quantity of liquid.

This type of flour is heavily chlorinated to break down the coherency of the gluten and, at the same time, it increases the acidity which renders the starch more soluble, increasing absorption of moisture.

6. Fractionated or High Protein Flour

This flour is produced by a new milling technique by which it is possible to control the protein quality and quantity in flour.

It is known that, during the normal roller milling process, the endosperm is broken into particles of different sizes. These can be measured in microns (the micron is one millionth of a metre). It is known also that particles less than 15 microns in size contain a high percentage of protein. It is thus clear that if the particles can be separated by particle size, then flours with different qualities can be produced simply by addition or substraction.

The separation is effected by a centrifugal air classifier, which fairly accurately divides the particles by size. With the development of this method, it becomes possible for the miller to produce flour according to specification.

The constituent composition of flour varies, here is what may be considered an average analysis of ordinary white flour:

Starch	70 %
Water	13 %
Insoluble proteins	11 %
Soluble proteins	2 %
Fat	1 %
Sugars	2.5 %
Mineral matter	0.5 %

The storage of flour needs careful planning. The store should be well ventilated and vermin proof with a temperature between 60° F and 70° F and with a relative humidity of about 60 %. The planning should provide for easy and systematic cleaning.

The walls should be treated with high-gloss mould resistant paint.

Eggs

Eggs are the second of the two structural materials used by the baker.

The word 'egg' in this context assumes that the eggs are hen eggs, for the vast percentage of eggs used are the product of the domestic chicken.

The egg has three main parts:

1. Shell   (12 %)
2. White   (58 %)
3. Yolk   (30 %).

The shell is of little use to the baker beyond use in the clarification of jellies.

The whites and yolks are of great importance.

Here is a table showing an average analysis of eggs.

	Whites %	Yolks %	Whole - egg %
Water	86-87	50-50.5	73-75
Protein	12-12.7	16-16.5	12-14
Fat	0.25	31-32	10-12
Mineral Matter	0.5-0.59	0.8-1.5	1-1.2

Shell eggs differ in weight, varying between 1 ½-2 ½ oz. (42-70 gr.) according to the grading. In the interest of accuracy, it is better to weigh eggs instead of using liquid measurement, and to record them in weight in a recipe, instead of as units or as a liquid measurement. Whites and yolks should also be weighed.

SHELL EGGS

The only possible objection to the use of shell eggs in bakeries, where large quantities are used, is the time taken in cracking and emptying the shells. Shell eggs arrive from the packing stations clean and well protected against breaking. Because of improved methods of transport and storage the bad egg is now comparatively rare.

FROZEN EGGS

Frozen eggs are always available to the baker and they are processed and refrigerated in vast quantities in many parts of the world. The low temperature completely inhibits bacterial activity, although under certain conditions putrefaction can commence from as short a time as 12 hours after defrosting. Provided that they have been correctly defrosted, they are an excellent alternative to fresh shell eggs.

Frozen egg whites and frozen yolks are also available. In the case of egg whites, there is little or no difference between them and freshly separated whites, again, provided that they have been correctly defrosted. Egg yolks are less successfully refrigerated and great care must be taken when defrosting.

The process of defrosting is of great importance. Eggs are frozen by the simple expedient of lowering the temperature below freezing point until they are a solid block. Correct defrosting means that this frost is gently taken out. This is done by immersing the can in cold running water, after which the eggs are removed from the can, thoroughly mixed, and brought up to bakery temperature. On no account must defrosting be attempted by the application of heat or the eggs will be damaged and lose their efficiency.

DRIED EGGS

Drieds eggs are egg solids after dehydration, that is the removal of water. As the average water content of an egg is 75 %, dried eggs are reconstituted by adding the water at the rate of three parts water to one part of dried egg powder.

To reconstitute correctly, a little of the water is added to make a smooth paste, the balance of water is added by degrees, stirring the whole time.

Dried whites, in the form of hard crystalline pieces, are reconstituted at the rate of one part dried whites to seven parts of water, the dried whites being sprinkled on the surface of the water.

Spray dried whites are reconstituted by combining one part of water and one part of powder by weight and allowing it to stand for 15 minutes. Nine more parts of water by weight are then added and the mixture well stirred.

Spray dried yolks are reconstituted by mixing one part by weight of water and one part by weight of powder. Leave for at least 15 minutes before use.

Eggs are an ideal media for the multiplication of harmful bacteria, therefore scrupulous cleanliness is essential at all times.

Cornflour

Commercial cornflour is chiefly produced from maize. It is white in colour with a particular crunchy feel when pressed in the hand.

Commercial production is commenced by soaking the maize in water containing sulphur dioxide. The soaking softens the maize and the SO_2 stops possible fermentation. It is then crushed and passed to water tanks where the germ floats off. The mass is then ground finely and, still in a semi-fluid state, passed through silk screens which removes the skin particles. After filtration the product, which is almost 100% starch, is dried.

Cornflour is gelatinized by mixing with water at a temperature in excess of 170° F. Cornflour is thus a thickening agent; it is used in custards, blancmanges and in confections such as Turkish delight. It will make an excellent glaze for fruit flans and on tea breads requiring a highly glazed appearance.

Cornflour, because it is almost 100% starch, can be used to dilute the strength of flour. It is the medium used for moulding chocolate centres.

Milk

Milk is a moistening agent containing about 87% water. It is an enriching agent depending on the amount used or whether it is full cream, half cream or skimmed.

Milk is available to the baker either as fresh liquid milk, in concentrated form, either sweetened or unsweetened, or in the form of dried milk powder.

One of the most important constituents of milk is milk fat because from it butter and cream are produced. Butter fat also contains the heat resistant fat soluble vitamins A, D and E. In nutrition, the protein and mineral contents of milk are also of great importance.

Most milk is pasteurized to destroy pathogenic bacteria. There are two methods of pasteurizing. The first method is to heat the milk to a temperature of 145° F and hold it at this temperature for 30 minutes. The procedure for the second method is to take the milk to a temperature of 162° F and hold it for only 15 seconds. Milk may be also sterilized at a temperature of 212° F after it has been homogenized.

Milk will vary in its composition. Here is a fairly average analysis.

	%	%
Fat		3.75
Solids not fat		
Milk protein	3.46	
Lactose	4.70	
Mineral matter	0.75	8.91
Water		87.34

Concentrated milks are available in two forms, condensed and evaporated. Both are produced by the evaporation of some of the water under vacuum. Here is a table showing analyses of condensed and evaporated milks.

	Condensed-Full Cream Sweetened %	Unsweetened %	Condensed-Separated Sweetened %	Unsweetened %
Water	25.3	69.24	30.3	49.3
Fat	10.8	9.6	1.8	2.9
Protein	8.03	9.66	11.1	18.0
Lactose	14.1	9.85	16.0	26.1
Added sugar	39.5	Nil	38.5	Nil
Mineral matter	2.27	1.65	2.3	3.7

It is usual to refer to the sweetened milks as 'condensed' and the unsweetened as 'evaporated'. Dried milk powder is very popular in the bakery because it occupies less space, it keeps well if correctly stored, it is easily reconstituted, it is 100 % soluble and, alternatively, it can be sieved with the flour and used in dry form.

Below is a table showing average analyses of milk powders.

	Full cream %	Half cream %	Separated (skimmed) %
Moisture	2.75	2.5	2.5
Fat	27.7	16.5	0.85
Protein	27.3	30.3	36.15
Lactose	36.5	43.8	51.8
Mineral matter	5.75	6.9	8.7

Full cream milk powder is reconstituted at the rate of one part milk powder to eight parts water. Half cream powder at the rate of one part powder to nine parts water, whilst the skimmed powder is reconstituted in the ratio of one part powder to ten parts of water.

The powder, which must be free from lumps, is mixed to a paste with some of the water, the balance being stirred in a little at a time.

Scrupulous cleanliness must always be observed; carelessness may result in inoculation with harmful bacteria.

Fats and Oils

There is no chemical difference between a fat and an oil. They are plastic or liquid according to temperature, each having different melting points.

All fats are enriching agents. They are shortening agents also, according to the amount and the method used.

BUTTER

Butter is manufactured by churning ripened milk fat. Churning causes the globules of fat to coalesce, during which buttermilk is separated and run off. Salt is added and the whole is worked to a homogenous mass. Colour also may be added to improve the appearance. The composition of butter varies according to source. Below is an average analysis.

Fat	82 -85 %
Water	10 -16 %
Curd (casein)	1.5- 2 %
Mineral matter (including salt)	1.4- 2 %

The fat content of butter contains in its composition a small amount of unstable volatile fats which are responsible for flavour. Under unsatisfactory storage conditions or because of age, they will break down causing rancidity. Ideally, butter should be stored at a temperature below 40° F.

The aroma of butter should be delicate and pleasing. There should be freedom from rancidity and oiliness. In texture it should be firm and plastic and for the baker it should have good creaming properties, retaining air after beating. Butter contains the vitamins A and D.

Provided that it is of good quality and flavour, butter is one of the finest fats for use in bakery products because of its characteristic flavour. It has a low melting point and because of this, it is ideal for puff pastry, although for this, it should be tough and stable, so that it will stand up to the rolling and folding necessary without squeezing out.

Butter is available to the baker both salted and unsalted, the latter being mainly used for buttercreams.

LARD

Lard is another fat that confers flavour. It is refined hog fat, the fat content being approximately 99 % and has probably the greatest shortening power of any plastic fat. As it does not cream satisfactorily, it is not used in any method of cake making where it has to be beaten. It is excellent for savoury pastries especially for pork and meat pies. It is essential in the making of lardy cakes and an excellent media for frying.

MARGARINE

Margarine originated as a butter substitute. It has now reached a peak of excellence as a result of research into the commercial application of hydrogenation. Margarine is a water in oil emulsion. It is composed of selected hardened (hydrogenated) oils, ripened milk, colouring matter and salt. It contains approximately 85 % fat and the grades made for the baker have excellent creaming properties and baking performance.

Toughened cake margarines are available for making puff pastry, but care is necessary because of the melting point which may be high, resulting in a fat film on the roof of the mouth after the pastry has been eaten.

Unsalted margarine may be purchased and this is mainly used for creams.

COMPOUND FAT

This type of fat was originally a lard substitute. It has now been developed into an excellent shortening in its own right. It is approximately 100 % fat, bland in flavour and usually white in colour. It is a compound of hardened oils given a fine texture by the modern Votator system of manufacture.

To replace 1 lb. (454 gr.) of butter or margarine in shortening value, 13 ½ oz. (372 gr.) of compound fat should be used together with a small amount of salt. It has excellent creaming properties and can be used for frying purposes. Pumpable shortenings are now available which can be delivered by tanker lorries and pumped into bulk supply tanks.

PASTRY FAT

This is a tough fat, white in colour, with a lower melting point than pastry margarine. In the absence of good butter it will make excellent puff pastry, although it will confer little or no flavour. Because it is white, it imparts no colour to pastry. It is almost 100 % fat, and because of this, 12 oz. (340 gr.) is recommended by the manufacturers to replace 1 lb. (454 gr.) of butter or pastry margarine.

SPECIAL CAKE FATS

These are high grade compound fats for use in conjunction with special cake flours in the manufacture of high-ratio cakes.

These fats owe their special qualities to the addition of emulsifying agents. Not only do they assist in holding an increased amount of liquid in the cake mix, they also increase the stability of the mix so that it does not collapse during baking. They are also known as super-glycerinated fats because of the higher glycerol content.

There are other compounds with a fat base that contain an emulsifying agent, together with other additions, depending on the specific purpose of its use, one such is for use with heavily fruited tea breads.

COOKING OILS

These are 100 % oils which, because of their low melting points, are liquid at normal temperatures. Because they are liquid, they have no creaming properties. They are useful for frying and tin greasing.

Oil is particularly useful in the making of enriched sponge cakes and light genoese which require the addition of a liquid fat to whisked egg and sugar.

Without doubt, olive oil is one of the finest of edible oils, the best is produced in Italy, while Spain produces the greater amount. It is, however, expensive so that other oils, of which there are many, are more extensively used.

Groundnut, palm, palm kernel, cottonseed, rape seed, sunflower seed, coconut and soya, amongst other fruits and seeds, are all oil bearing and are used in vast quantities by oil millers.

Sugars

Sugar in any form sweetens. It is refined commercially from either sugar cane or sugar beet. Chemically they are both the same and come under the general heading of carbohydrates.

There are many types of sugar available to the baker, each having special uses.

BROWN SUGARS

These are the unrefined raw sugars, some having names that refer to the country or area of origin, such as, Barbados, Trinidad, Demerara, etc. Some soft brown sugars are the residual crystals after the refining of white sugar.

All brown sugars confer colour and a measure of flavour, according to the type and the amount used. The darker sugars are ideal for rich cakes, such as wedding, birthday or Christmas cakes and for mincemeat and Christmas puddings.

WHITE SUGARS

Cube sugar is made in the refinery from first quality liquor and at one time was considered to be the best for sugar boiling. With the new method of manufacture, the cubes have traces of oil from the moulds and are less suitable for sugar boiling.

Granulated sugar is available as coarse or fine, differing only in crystal size. The coarse granulated is suitable for sugar boiling whilst the fine granulated is used for cakes and sponge goods.

Castor sugar is even finer and can be used in all kinds of cakes and for decorating the tops of pastries before or after baking. A proportion of castor sugar improves the eating qualities of almond paste.

Sugar nibs can be purchased as coarse, medium or fine. They are used in and on Bath buns, and as a dressing for fancy tea breads.

ICING SUGAR

This sugar can be bought in several grades depending on the fineness of silks used in the sieving. The finest is used in the making of royal icing, particularly if fine meticulous piping is necessary. Other grades can be used for water icing, glazes, for dusting cakes after baking and for almond paste.

GOLDEN SYRUP

This amber coloured syrup can be termed a by-product of sugar refining. When the syrup after many boilings ceases to yield crystals, it is filtered and concentrated. The best quality contains approximately 15-18 % water, the rest being sucrose, dextrose and levulose together with other substances that are partly responsible for flavour.

Some golden syrups are invert sugars coloured and concentrated.

Golden syrup is used by the baker for ginger cakes and biscuits.

TREACLE

This syrup is much darker and with a more pronounced flavour than golden syrup. It is made by diluting and filtering molasses and then concentrating. The lighter treacle can be used for ginger goods, the darker, also known as black treacle, is used to confer colour to bride and other dark heavily fruited cakes and Christmas puddings. The treacle replaces some of the sugar in the mix.

GLUCOSE

Commercial glucose, known also as corn syrup, is manufactured by boiling starch in water so that it is gelatinized. Weak acid is added to change the gel to sugar, after which, the acid is neutralized.

The viscosity of the syrup is reduced in vacuum pans until the water content is reduced to 15%. A new method of manufacture is by enzyme conversion. This glucose is approximately twice as sweet and three times as fluid as acid converted glucose.

Invert sugar, unlike corn syrup, is made from ordinary sugar boiled with water and sufficient dilute hydrochloric acid to invert the sugar to simple sugars. The acid is neutralized with sodium bicarbonate.

Like glucose, invert sugar is a thick colourless syrup. Both are used in cakes and biscuits and in sugar boiling.

HONEY

Honey was almost certainly the first form of sugar used by man.

It is a thick natural syrup obtained by bees from the nectar of flowers. Nectar contains about 80% water, 20% sugar together with essential oils and aromatic compounds that are responsible for the bouquet of honey. The bouquet will depend on the flora from which bees obtain the nectar.

The colour and consistency of honey vary with the source, ranging from a creamy white to a deep golden yellow.

The sugar content of nectar is inverted into levulose and dextrose in the approximate ratio of 38:35. Most of the water is evaporated by the heat in the hive during storage in the combs. Honey is the result of this concentration.

Honey is exported in large quantities from Canada, Australia, California, Hungary and Poland. English honey is considered to be one of the best and is sold mainly for table use.

Because of the percentage of invert sugars, care must be taken when baking cakes containing large amounts of honey. A lower baking temperature is necessary because the invert sugars caramelize at a lower temperature.

Honey is used in nougats, creams, in German Lebkuchen and French gingerbreads.

Honey is an excellent yeast food in fermented products.

Cocoa and Chocolate

Cocoa beans were first brought to Europe by Columbus in 1494. The cacao tree is cultivated in most tropical countries. It yields thick skinned pods containing seeds or beans surrounded by a soft pulp. The beans and pulp are allowed to ferment during which the pulp is changed to CO_2 and alcohol. The alcohol is oxidized to acetic acid which is allowed to flow away.

After a period of fermentation which destroys the embryo and effects internal changes at the same time, the beans are dried and packed for shipment.

At the chocolate factory the beans, after sorting and cleaning, are roasted. This renders the skins easy to remove and, at the same time, develops the flavour. The roasted beans are then broken into small pieces and blended with other broken beans in such a way that a desired flavour, colour and eating quality is eventually attained. The blended pieces are then milled to a fine particle size, during which the temperature rises causing the cocoa butter to melt so that the whole changes to a thick, viscous mass known as crude chocolate. After further milling it is run off into moulds and allowed to set. This is the unsweetened block chocolate that is ideal for flavouring and colouring creams, fondant and cakes.

COCOA

There are two methods of producing cocoa, the Dutch process and the natural process. With the Dutch process, the beans are treated with an alkali during roasting, resulting in the elimination of acetic acid giving the cocoa mass a better flavour and a richer colour. The mass is then pumped to hydraulic presses where some of the cocoa butter is removed. When cool, the press cake is reduced to powdered cocoa, sieved and packed.

The natural process differs only in that the beans are not treated with an alkali; grinding and pressing is the same as for the Dutch process.

CHOCOLATE

The blended and processed chocolate is mixed with cocoa butter, sugar, and, in the case of milk chocolate with milk solids, and then refined until the particle size is reduced to an extreme fineness. The viscosity is adjusted by the addition of more cocoa butter. The process is slow but necessary if fine chocolate is to be produced.

The chocolate now known as couverture is run into moulds and, when set, it is wrapped ready for distribution, or run into temperature controlled tanks from where it can be pumped into motor tankers for bulk liquid delivery.

BAKERS' CHOCOLATE

This is a chocolate specially made for coating cakes and fancies. It is similar to couverture except that most of the cocoa butter is removed and replaced by a hydrogenated fat together with a stabilizer such as lecithin.

Bakers chocolate cuts easily and, unlike couverture, it does not splinter. It may be bought as either plain or milk. Because of the removal of cocoa butter, which is a complex mixture of fats with different melting points, and replacement by other fats, this product does not have to be tempered.

The flavour is different from couverture. It is not suitable for chocolate dipping or for moulding unless specially made for these purposes.

Coffee

The word coffee is derived from Caffa, one of the provinces of Abyssinia, of which the original coffee-shrub is a native. It was introduced into Arabia in the fifteenth century and later into Turkey. It is now grown extensively in many parts of Central and South America and Central Africa. Brazil produces about four-fifths of the worlds' annual supply.

Commercial coffee beans are the seeds of the plant. They are sun dried and after all extraneous matter is removed they are put into bags for export. The quality and price of coffee will almost always depend on the care taken in the preparation before export. Coffee should be freshly roasted and ground immediately before use if the distinctive flavour of coffee is to be enjoyed, although the flavour can be retained by packing into hermetically sealed containers.

A strong infusion of roasted and ground coffee beans, or the use of coffee extract or soluble finely powdered coffee, will impart the desired flavour and colour to ices, creams, icings and cakes.

Coffee and vanilla flavours are excellent together. This combination is often erroneously referred to as Mocha. Mocha is in fact any strong coffee infusion.

Spices, Aromatic Seeds and Fruits

Spices, aromatic seeds and fruits have no food value, their chief function, if used correctly, is to stimulate the palate. Spices confer colour and flavour according to the amount and the spice, or mixture of spices, used.

Caraway

The dried aromatic fruit of a plant grown mainly in Europe. It has a pungent odour although this may depend on whether some of the essential oils has been removed with a suitable solvent. In Britain, caraway was used in what were known as 'seed' cakes, which, for some reason, have almost completely gone out of favour. They are, however, becoming increasingly popular in rye breads. Caraway is used in the manufacture of kümmel.

Cardamom

This spice is the fruit of a plant allied to the ginger family. They are the seeds of under-ripe fruit.

As the fruit ripens, a three cornered tripartite shell develops, divided by inner walls which are filled with many angular hard seeds. They have a very fine spicy, slightly hot flavour. Ground cardamom spice is used in Danish pastries.

Cassia

A spice very similar to cinnamon, but less pronounced in flavour and aroma. It is grown in China and India. Cassia is the spice flavour used in Easter cakes popular in the West of England. Cassia is also one of the components of ground mixed spice used in gingerbreads and Hot Cross Buns.

Cinnamon

The best quality cinnamon comes from Ceylon and is the dried inner bark of a species of laurel. It can be bought in the form of quills or in powder form.

Cinnamon is a flavour used in Chelsea buns, in Danish pastry fillings and in varieties of rich tea breads. It is used in German Lebkuchen and in French gingerbread.

Cloves

A clove is a dried bud of a species of myrtle grown in Zanzibar and the East Indies. Clove possesses a strong pungent flavour which has an affinity with apples. They are used in apple pies, tarts and dumplings. It is a delicious flavour for use in Banbury and Eccles cakes, and in German Lebkuchen and in French gingerbread.

Coriander

A spice which is the dried fruit of a plant grown in the Mediterranean region. It is the size of a peppercorn, hollow inside, which makes it easy to crush. This spice is used in jellies, ginger cakes and some varieties of Christmas confectionery.

Ginger

This is a popular spice in the bakery. It is produced from the roots of a herb cultivated in China, India, Australia and South Africa. The roots are carefully washed and dried and then ground to a powder. Ground ginger is used in all forms of gingerbread.

The preserved ginger used for decorative purposes is the boiled root preserved in a concentrated sugar solution. Finely chopped or crushed, it is used in ginger slab and in other types of ginger cakes. This type of ginger can also be crystallized.

Mace

Both mace and nutmeg are produced from the fruit of a tree grown in the East and West Indies. When the fruit, which is similar to a peach, is ripe, the skin is removed and dried, then ground to a powder. This is ground mace. It is used as a component of ground mixed spice and in some sauces.

Nutmeg

When the skin is removed from the peachlike fruit of the nutmeg tree, a hard shell is revealed. Within the shell is a hard nut which is the commercial nutmeg.

Ground nutmeg is the correct finish and flavour for a custard tart and the only added flavour that should be used in scones.

Mixed Spice
This is a mixture of ground spices that will vary according to the formula used by the manufacturer. Liquid mixed spice, known in Britain as bun-spice, is a mixture of essential oils sometimes in a suitable solvent. It is used in Hot Cross Buns. As it has a narcotic effect on yeast fermentation, it must be used with care, preferably added when the dough is half mixed.

Pepper
The dried fruit of a climbing shrub grown in the East and West Indies. Black pepper is the under-ripe berry after drying. Ripened berries, dried and with the outer shell removed is white pepper. Whole peppercorns keep their flavour longer than when they are ground. Pepper is used for seasoning meat pies and all savoury pastries.

Pimento
Sometimes known as 'allspice' because the flavour resembles a mixture of cinnamon, clove and nutmeg. It is the fruit of a species of myrtle grown in Jamaica and India. It is used as a flavour in savoury fillings.

The essential flavouring constituents of spices can be obtained in a much more concentrated form as essential oils, extracts and essences.

Salt

The chemical name for salt is sodium chloride. It is composed of 40% sodium and 60% chlorine. It is readily available in almost all parts of the world. It is indispensable to life.

Used by the baker, it confers flavour and if used carefully gently accentuates other flavours. It has a stabilizing effect on gluten and assists in controlling the speed of fermentation in yeast aerated goods. It also assists in retaining moisture in fermented goods.

Yeast

Yeast is one of the most important materials used by the baker. It is a living microorganism of the fungi family of plants. Because it is a living organism it must be treated with care.

Fresh yeast breaks with a sharp facture and has an aroma reminiscent of apples. It should be stored at a temperature of about 40° F and used in strict rotation.

The optimum temperature range for panary fermentation in a dough is 78-82° F. At lower temperatures the speed of fermentation gets progressively slower, but the yeast is not damaged. At 120° F yeast is in danger and at 140° F it is killed. Yeast should never be mixed in concentrations of salt or sugar.

As yeast gets stale, it becomes dry and crumbly and the temperature rises. After a time, by a process of autolysis, it becomes a sticky, evil smelling mass and is quite useless as an aerating agent.

Dried, or dehydrated yeast is available and this should be used as directed. Usually, one part of dried yeast is the equivalent of two parts of fresh compressed yeast.

Baking Powders

Baking powders are essentially aerating agents, generally made up of two parts of a baking acid and one part of sodium bicarbonate. The acid can be cream of tartar or one of the numerous proprietary cream powders sold under brand names. Cream powders are composed of one or more acids mixed with an inert substance such as starch so that the mixture can be used in the proportion of two parts to one part sodium bicarbonate. In this proportion the soda is completely neutralized and the maximum of carbon dioxide (CO_2) is evolved.

A good baking powder should not, provided that it is used in the correct proportion, leave an 'after-taste' in the mouth when the cake has been eaten.

It is the sodium bicarbonate which releases CO_2 when moistened and heated. If a suitable acid is used in the correct proportion, twice the amount of gas is released. Used alone or in excess, sodium bicarbonate will darken the crumb of the cake, producing at the same time a strong alkaline taste and aroma. In gingerbreads, where it is used alone, the extra depth of colour is an advantage, whilst the alkaline flavour is masked by the spices used.

Another chemical substance used for aeration is ammonium bicarbonate which, when moistened and heated, liberates CO_2, ammonium gas and water. It is useful in choux pastry and certain types of biscuits, because it gives the maximum amount of gas in the oven and in these products, the pungent ammonia gas is readily dispersed during and after baking.

A new substance, glucono-delta-lactone, used with sodium bicarbonate in the proportion of 2 to 1, is claimed to leave no 'after-taste' and because the reaction is comparatively slow, a greater volume of gas is liberated whilst the cake is in the oven, so giving an increased volume. An acid, used within limits, will strengthen protein. A small quantity in puff pastry will render the gluten of the stronger flour necessary for this type of pastry, more extensible so that the rolling and folding can be carried out more effectively. Lemon juice is excellent for this purpose or tartaric acid which is readily soluble in cold water.

A little baking acid will also strengthen egg whites in the making of meringues and royal icing.

Alcohols

Under the heading of alcohols, there may be included the numerous aperitifs, wines, dessert wines, liqueurs and spirits used by the pastrycook and confectioner. These alcohols are not only served to clients in restaurants, they are also used to flavour cakes and biscuits made in the bakery.

LIQUEURS

Liqueurs are spirituous liquors made from a mixture of spirits and sugar syrup in which fruits or aromatic plants have been macerated. There are three categories of liqueurs:

Ordinary - containing 20 % alcohol
High grade - containing 25 % alcohol
Very high
 grade - containing 40-45 % alcohol

Liqueurs may also be classified according to whether they are prepared from fruits or aromatic plants:

1. those prepared from fruits: apricots, mandarins, oranges, bananas, blackcurrants, cherries, cocoa, coffee, etc.

2. those prepared from aromatic plants: Anisette, Benedictine, Grande Chartreuse, Crème de Menthe, etc.

SPIRITS

Spirits are generally produced by distilling wine or other substances (e.g. fruit) and contain between 16 % and 70 % alcohol. The substance to be distilled is allowed to ferment, thus converting the natural sugar into alcohol. Water is then added and the mixture is heated. During distillation, the liquid containing alcohol evaporates and condenses at the beak of the alembic.

These spirits are used by the pastrycook and confectioner for flavouring either on their own or with the addition of sugar syrup.

V. Cake Decoration

The decoration of a cake, be it large or small, is creative work and as such is wholly satisfying because the craftsman has the opportunity of expressing himself by means of the various media used.

Craftsmanship is not only the ability to create, but also an understanding of why certain things are done and for what purpose. It calls also for proficiency gained by constant practice. Cake decoration demands manual skill, a sense of form and colour and an understanding of what is meant by good taste as applied to the decoration of food.

A cake is decorated so that it becomes more appealing to the eye and to the palate. If it fails in either of these, then the decoration is a failure, for it leads to a waste of time, effort and materials. Decoration can either be simple in form, or it can be extended so that it calls for a high degree of proficiency in manual skill and in art and design. Before practical work is commenced in earnest, an understanding of basic principles is necessary.

COLOUR

The great scientist Sir Isaac Newton discovered the source and natural order of colour. He found that when a beam of light is passed through a prism it is broken up into a band of colour, known as the spectrum. This is seen in the heavens when a rainbow is formed. The seven colours visible are violet, indigo, blue, green, yellow, orange and red.

Colours may be subdivided under the following headings.

Primary
These are red, blue and yellow from which all other colours can be made.

Secondary
These are formed by mixing two primary colours.

> Red and Yellow - Orange
> Yellow and Blue - Green
> Blue and Red - Mauve

Tertiary
The colours in this group are formed by mixing any two secondary colours. They are not edible in appearance and are generally not used in cake decoration except when they make coffee or chocolate colours.

Coffee colour is made by mixing green and orange in equal portions.

Chocolate colour is made by mixing green and mauve in equal portions.

To understand other terms used in describing colours a study of the colour circle is necessary.

COLOUR CIRCLE

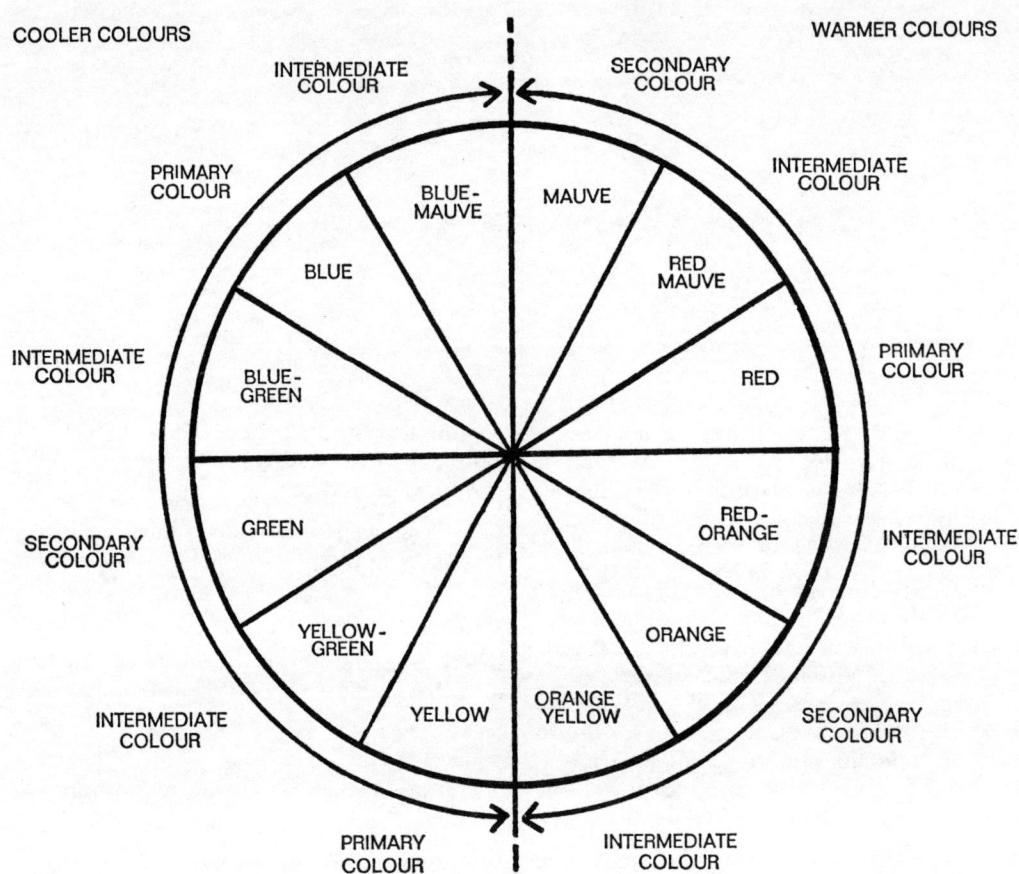

There are six complementary colours on the circle and they are immediately opposite each other. If they are placed side by side, each colour appears intensified, although much depends on the thickness, transparency and the amount of each colour. Complementary or secondary colours mixed together will produce a whole range of grey colours. These are the tertiaries.

Primary Colours

The primary colours are clearly seen and midway between them the secondary colours.

Intermediate Colours

These are seen between the primary and secondary colours.

Complementary Colours

There are six on the circle and they are seen immediately opposite each other. For example: Red and green.

Harmonious Colours

Any three colours together on the circle used in juxtaposition will produce a colour harmony. For example:

Orange, red-orange, yellow-orange.
Green, yellow-green, yellow.

Triad
Any three colours equi-distant on the circle constitute a triad. For example:

Orange, Green, Mauve.
Yellow, Blue, Red.

Tints
Any colour mixed with white, i.e. the luminosity is increased.

Shades
Any colour mixed with brown or black, i.e. the luminosity is decreased.

Monochromes
These are the tints and shades of one colour.

Neutral Colours
Black, white, and the greys constitute this group, to which may be added silver and gold.

Black and white are achromatic, that is, they have no colour.

Some colours have warmth and some are cool. The seven colours in the circle containing red have warmth differing in degree. The rest of the colours are cool.

With this understanding of colour, the application of it to cake decoration becomes easier.

The basic colour of a cake, excepting coffee and chocolate, should be white or a light pastel tint. Contrast can be given by the careful use of colours of deeper tone, or by the bright colour of decorative materials such as cherries, angelica, crystallized flowers etc., or by piped or modelled flowers, figures, and motifs, always bearing in mind that there must be a careful balance between cool and warm colours.

With chocolate and coffee as the base colour, lighter colours should be used to give contrast, using bright colour with the utmost care to provide interest.

Colours have an affinity with the seasons, for example:

Spring— Yellow, Pale Green, Lilac.
Summer—Pink, Darker Green, Gay colours.
Autumn—Brown, Yellow, Gold.
Winter— White, Blue, Red, Green.

Finally, the basic colour should bear some relation to the flavour. Lemon, orange, pistachio, coffee, pineapple, raspberry, strawberry, and chocolate are examples.

DESIGN

Cakes can be of any shape. Generally they are round, rectangular, oval or square. The shape is the frame which will contain the design.

Design as befits our streamlined age should be simple but interesting—the placing of it on the shape, however, is important. A simple division can be into two, created indirectly by the placing of decoration, or directly by a line which may be straight or curved.

Two or more lines which may be straight or curved will create more divisions. Here are examples:

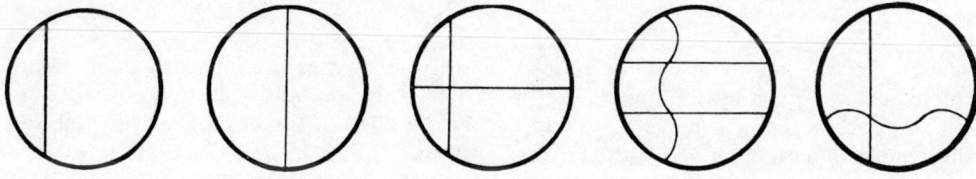

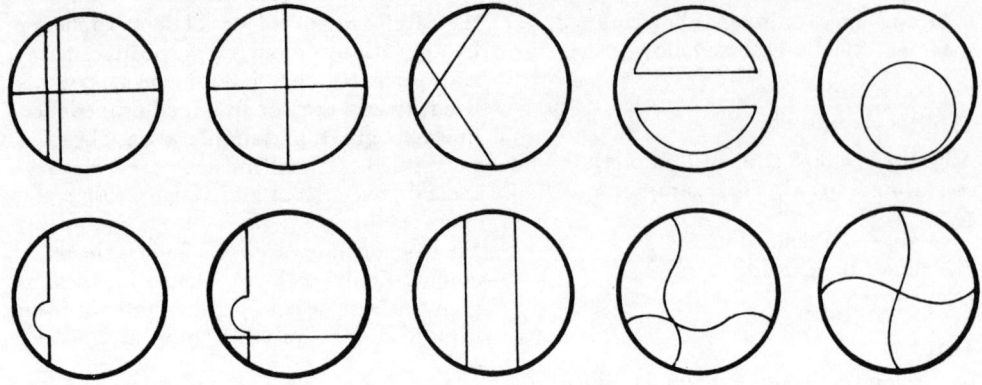

TEMPLATES

Templates are a ready means of establishing simple basic designs. They are simple to make and are generally cut as required from thin paper. For repetition work stronger material can be used, in which case more work will be required in the making.

An eight point star is made by taking a piece of paper and folding it into eight as illustrated. The design is marked with a pencil and cut with a pair of scissors. Several designs are shown in the following diagrams, the heavy lines indicating the scissor cuts.

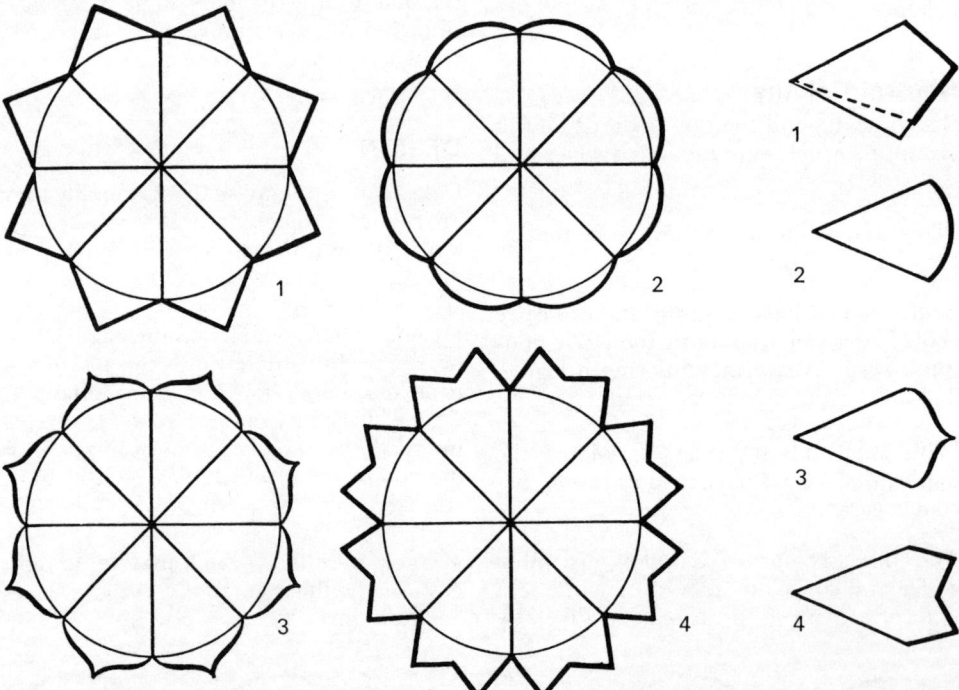

The size of the template can be quickly calculated by placing the point of the folded paper in the centre of the cake top, the outer dimensions of the template can easily be ascertained, bearing in mind always the possibility of a border design on the edge of the cake that will take up space.

For more permanent templates, the design must be drawn geometrically accurate before cutting. It is also a good idea to cut a little flap which can be folded up to facilitate the removal of the template without disturbing the piped outline which is the basis of the design and the reason for the template.

TEXTURES

The surface texture of decorative materials depend on the media used. Royal icing has a mat surface, whilst fondant and chocolate have a shiny texture. Jelly has a translucent texture. Various textures can be created by altering the reflective surface of the material. A comb scraper or a palette knife used on the surface will break up the reflection into patterns of light and shade according to how they are used. Sugars used for decoration provide different textures, according to the type of sugar used, and how it is applied.

EQUIPMENT

Certain tools and articles of equipment are necessary if cake decoration is to proceed smoothly and if the work is to be done with neatness and precision.

Turntable

This piece of equipment is designed to take the weight of a cake so that it can be rotated in any direction and at any speed. In its simplest form it is in two parts, the table which rotates and the base on which the table spins.

The turntable must, at all times, be kept clean and well oiled.

Palette Knife

Another indispensable piece of equipment. The blade should be about 7 in. (18 cm.) long and not too flexible. It must always be kept clean and bright.

Palette knives can be purchased in many sizes and are ideal for spreading icing and cake mixings. The smaller palette knife is excellent for mixing colour into small amounts of icing.

Icing pipes

For practice work, six pipes are all that are necessary. Later about ten more will be required. The six pipes suggested are Nos. 1, 2, 3 and 4, known as the writing pipes, and a small and large coarse star.

The types used are those made for use with paper or with nylon bags. Icing pipes should be treated with care. When work is finished the pipe should be taken from the bag and dropped into water and allowed to soak. If they are wanted again immediately, a camel hair brush will facilitate cleaning. Never allow the icing to harden in the pipes because time will be necessary for soaking before they can be cleaned. If a sharp instrument is used to clear the hard icing, the pipes may be seriously damaged.

Plastic Scrapers

Several plastic scrapers with straight edges are necessary. Some can be cut to provide decorative effects during the final coating of a cake. The diagram shows examples of cut edges:

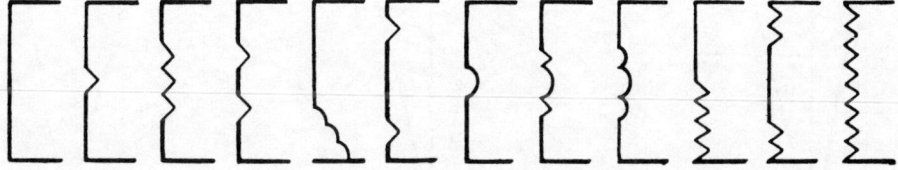

Other Equipment

Apart from basins, cloths, spatulas and a pair of scissors, a metal straight edge is useful to obtain a smooth unbroken surface on the top of a cake.

Piping Bags

There are three types of bag now generally in use.

1. The paper bag has been most popular for many years, particularly for fine delicate work. It can be cut from a standard sheet of parchment or strong greaseproof paper impervious to the effects of moisture.

The sheet can be folded into four, eight or sixteen rectangles, which, when cut diagonally, will provide bags in three sizes.

To make a bag, hold the paper with the right angle to the right (or vice versa if left-handed) (figure 1). Fold the top back to a point about halfway along the long edge (figure 2). Holding the point carefully, continue folding (figure 3). When the flap is tucked in, the bag is complete (figure 4). The bag should be folded quite tight or it will fall to pieces while in use.

The bag should never be over-filled or the icing will squeeze out when pressure is applied, quite apart from the fact that there must be enough paper to fold over to form a pressure lever (figure 5).

Paper bags can be used with or without pipes. To use without a pipe simply snip off the point of the bag with a pair of scissors after it has been filled. For special effects, however, pipes are necessary.

2. Light nylon bags are now available in several sizes. They are washable in hot water. This type of bag is used with a special metal device which holds the icing pipe securely. The pipe can be changed without emptying the bag.

3. Savoy bags made of close textured fabric are larger and used mainly for decorating with cream. Plain or star pipes with various aperture sizes are used with the savoy bag. The bags must be kept in a clean and sterile condition especially when used for dairy cream.

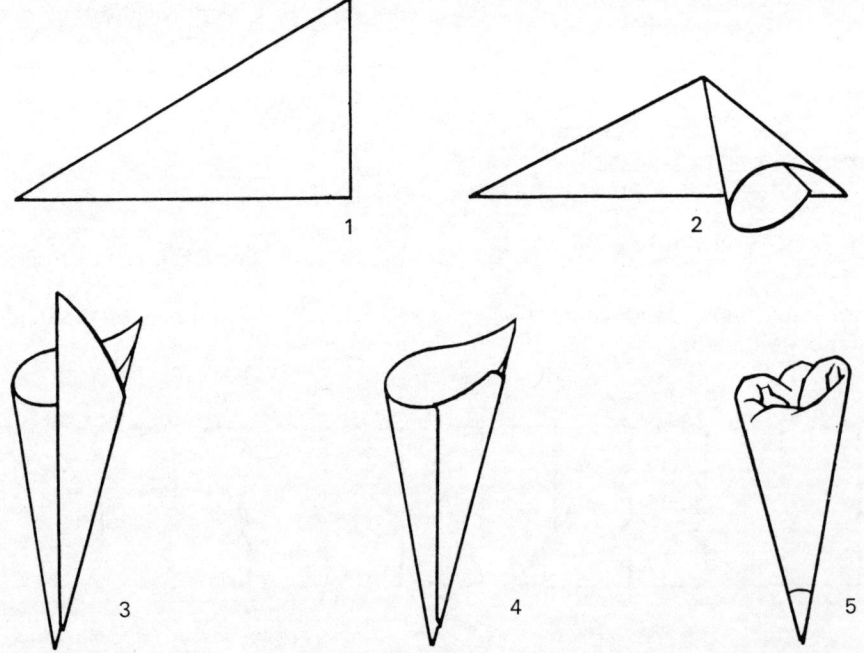

PIPING EXERCISES

Before commencing, there are two things of importance that must be learned.

Firstly, the necessity for hygiene which is imperative, for quite apart from the necessity for cleanliness and tidiness which is the hallmark of good craftsmanship, one habit must never be acquired and that is putting the icing pipe in the mouth to free the point from icing. Once the habit has been acquired it is extremely difficult to break. A damp cloth near at hand is much better for keeping the tip of the pipe clean.

Secondly, it is necessary to understand that accuracy in piping is impossible if a person is in a state of tension. One must therefore learn to be perfectly relaxed.

There is nothing highly technical about piping. It is simply a matter of wrist flexibility and pressure control, both of which can be learned only by constant practice.

The beginner can commence by taking a small bag of icing and snipping off the point and then just squeezing. There need be no formal design, just move the wrist about, applying and releasing pressure from time to time, until wrist movement and pressure control is attained.

When this has been achieved, pipe a series of straight lines, using pencil lines on a sheet of metal as a guide. Continue by piping parallel lines as close as possible to the original lines without touching. Follow this by piping lines at right angles. As pressure control is attained, pipe lines on top of the original lines in such a way that a pleasing design can be built up.

Lines, whether straight or curved, are piped by first placing the tip of the pipe at one end and applying gentle pressure, then by raising the bag a little, a thread of icing is suspended in the air so that it can be guided along the line. The value of the relaxed condition is apparent at this stage. Pressure is released just before the end is reached and the bag is carefully lowered so that the suspended thread of piping can be placed accurately to complete the line.

As proficiency is attained, more ambitious patterns can be attempted and different pipes can be used. Here are some patterns for practice:

Straight Line Exercises

Curved Line Exercises

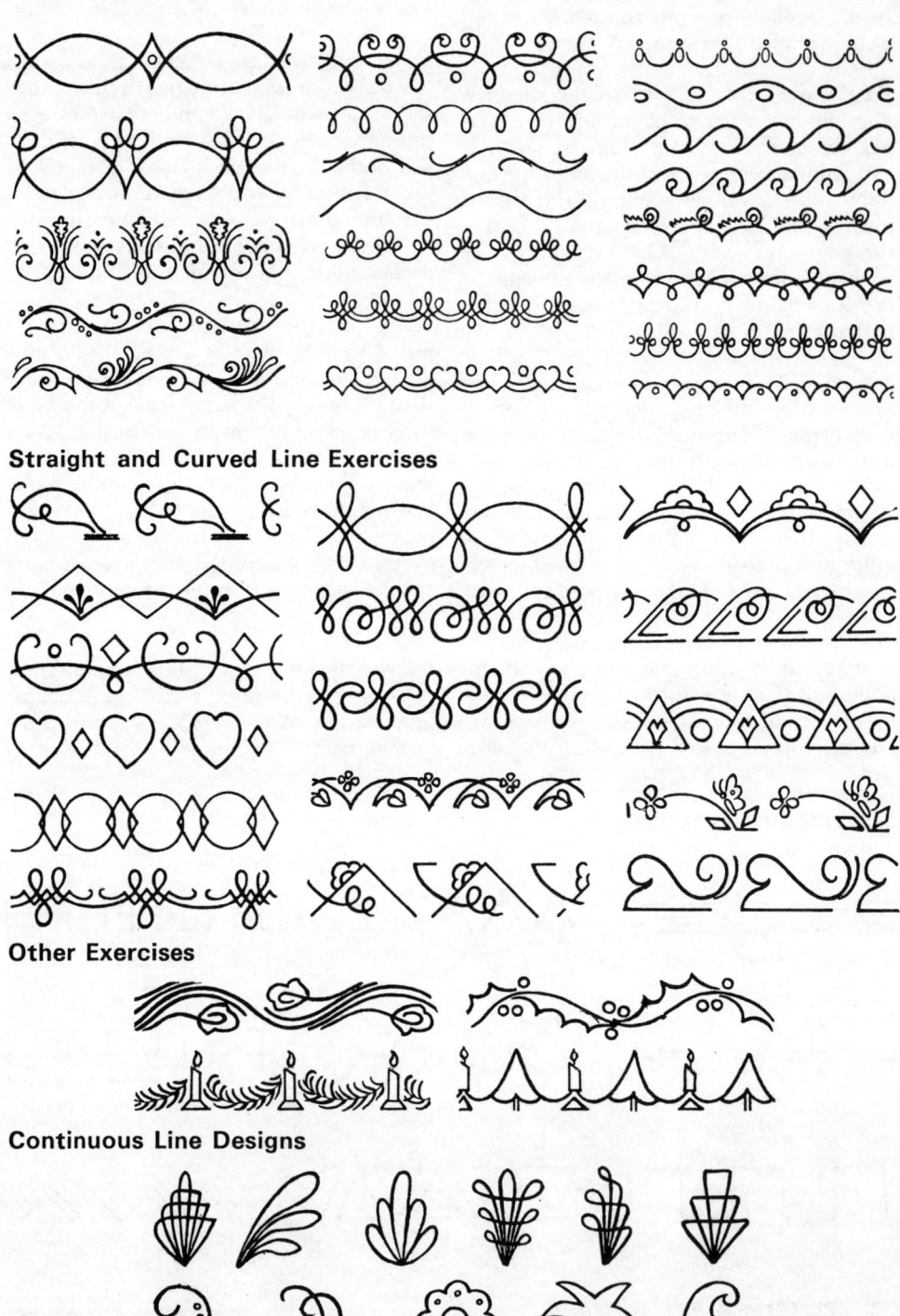

Straight and Curved Line Exercises

Other Exercises

Continuous Line Designs

Other Designs

Simple Natural Figures

Corner Designs

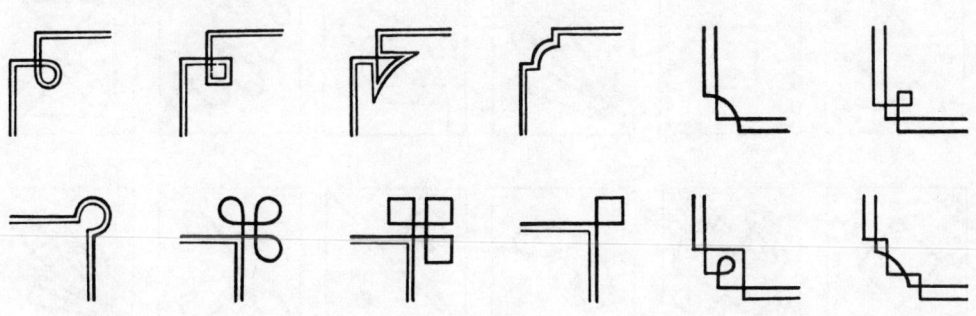

Decorative Breaks in Parallel Lines

Designs for Petits Fours glacés and Genoese Fancies

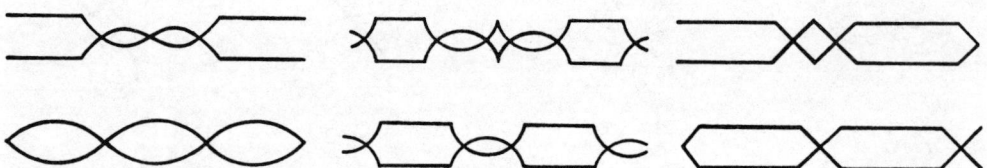

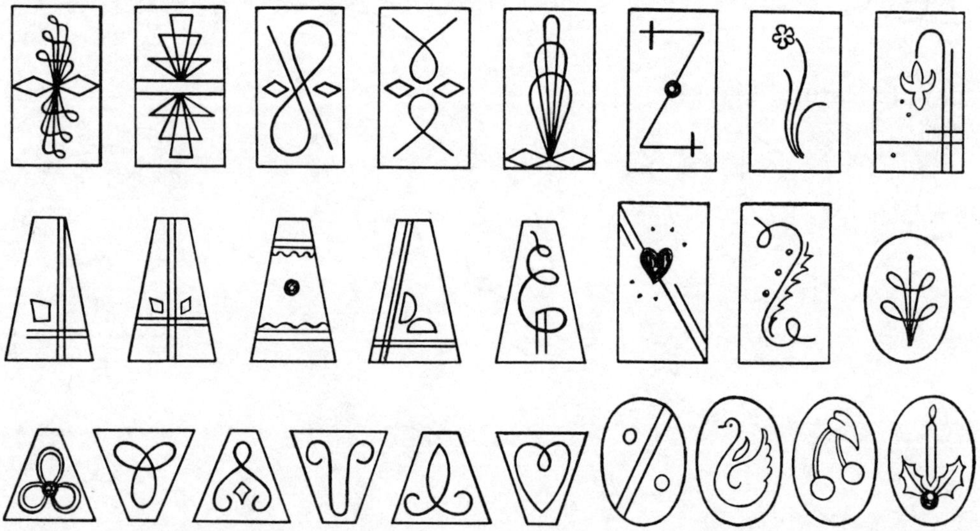

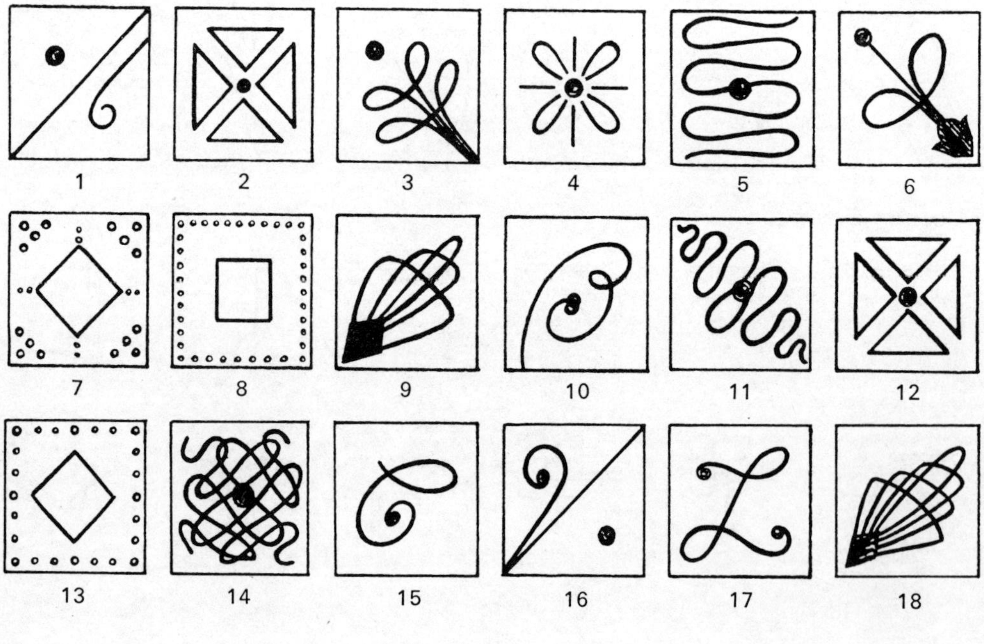

19
20
21
22
23
24
25
26
27
28
29
30
31
32
33
34
35
36
37

Piped Chocolate Motifs *(Text page 82)*

a
b
c
d
e
f
g
h
i
j
k
l
m
n
o
p
q
r

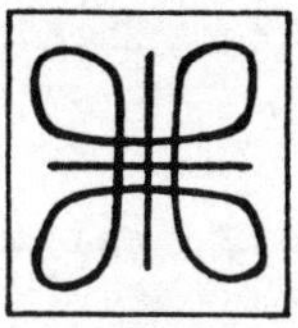

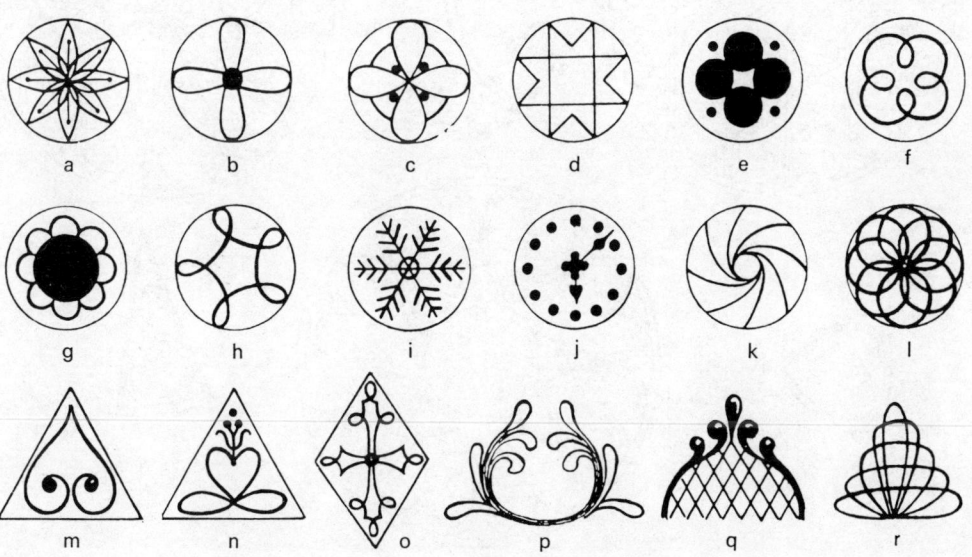

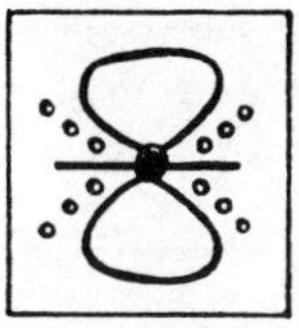

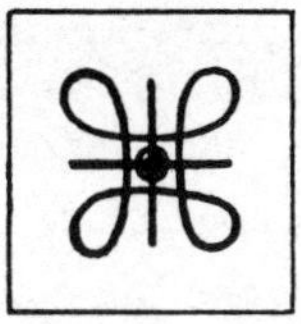

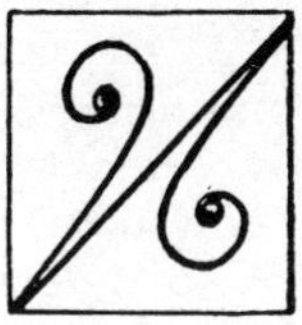

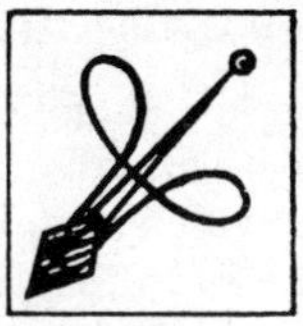

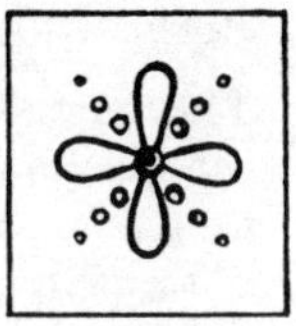

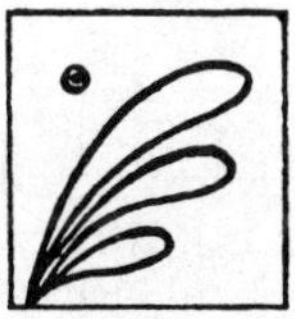

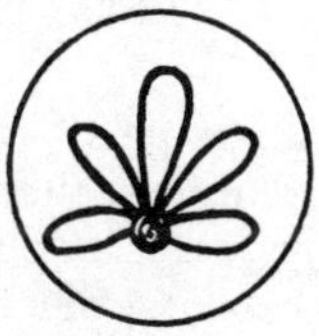

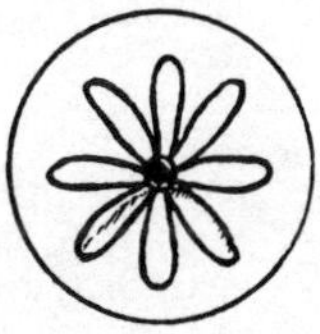

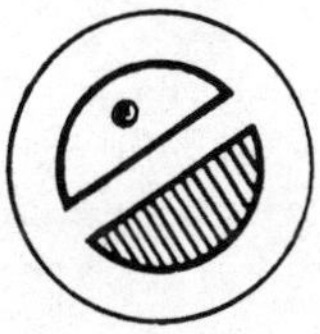

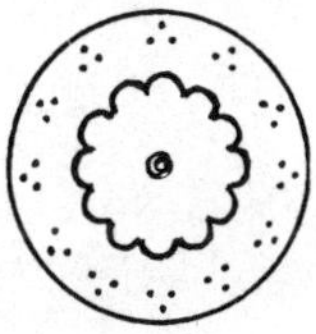

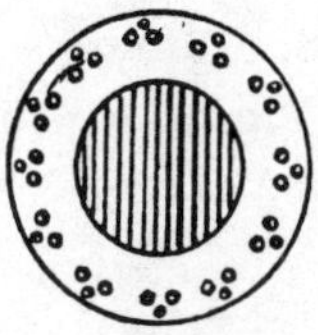

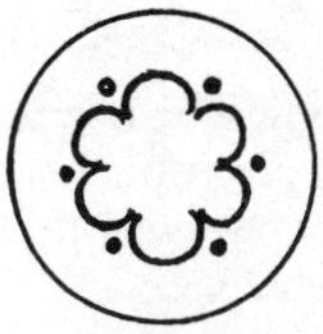

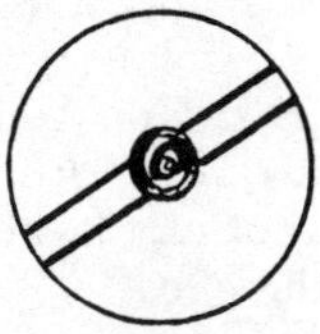

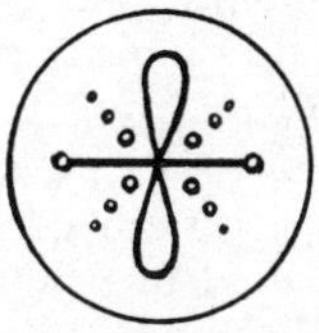

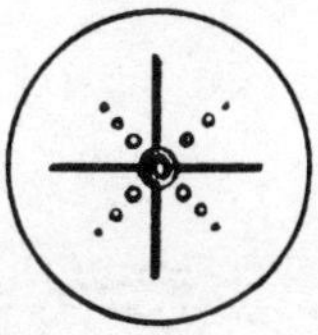

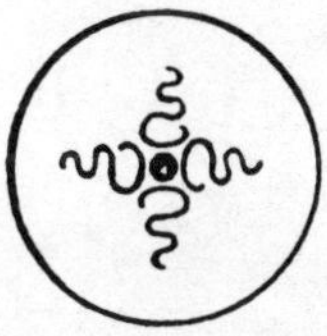

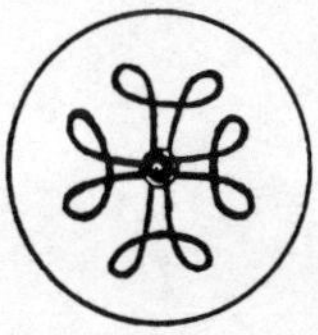

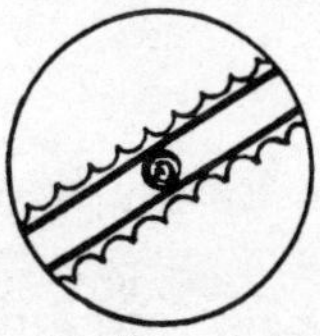

Piped Chocolate Motifs *(cont.)*

The outer circles, triangles and diamond shapes shown in the diagrams e, f, g, i, j, m, n and o are given to guide only and are not piped. The example j is piped on to a disc made of almond or sugar paste or chocolate.

The designs given are basic. The outlines can be carried out with fondant or chocolate. Royal icing can be used additionally but sparingly only.

The designs may be filled in with chocolate, fondant, jelly or with shaped pieces of almond or sugar paste, chocolate, crystallized fruits, angelica or croquant. Additional decoration, such as nuts, fruits, creams, crystallized and cut-out flowers can be used to brighten the effect.

The overall decoration, however, should be as simple and neat as possible and colour used with care.

These are piped with specially prepared chocolate on to wax paper. When set they can easily be removed with a small palette knife and deposited on torten, gâteaux, fancies and ices.

A *very small amount* of glycerine or stock syrup stirred into melted couverture will bring the mixture to piping consistency. Any piping chocolate left over should, on no account, be mixed with stock couverture.

Chocolate Run-out Pieces

These run-out pieces can be made during a slack period. They will keep well if properly wrapped and stored in a cool dry place.

Choux Pastry Designs *(Text page 83)*

First a shape such as a rabbit, parrot, angel, elephant, etc., is drawn on stout paper. Wax or greaseproof paper is laid over it and the outline of the drawing seen through the paper is piped with dark chocolate into which a very little stock syrup, glycerine or warm water is stirred. When the outline is set, the centres can then be filled in with milk or white chocolate or with fondant. When set, the shapes are removed from the paper, carefully wrapped and stored upside down in boxes. This type of run-out should be kept small.

They are used as a decoration for gâteaux, desserts, ice coupes, etc. (See drawings *pages 84-85.*)

Piped Choux Pastry

Delightful decorative patterns can be made with choux pastry for use on gâteaux, torten, fancies and ices.

The design can be piped freehand on to greased and floured baking sheets using a plain piping tube.

Alternatively the pattern can be drawn on thick paper which is covered with greased paper, through which the pattern can be clearly seen. It is a simple matter then to pipe over the outline.

The paper can be removed after baking.

Any of the recipes given on page 193 can be used, if the consistency is reduced with a little milk. Bake at 420-430° F (216-220° C).

After baking the patterns can be used plain, dusted with icing sugar or dipped into chocolate. (See drawings *page 82.*)

Cut-out Flowers

Flowers can be made quickly by cutting from almond or sugar paste. The paste is pinned out fairly thinly and cut out with a small fluted cutter. The pieces are placed in the palm of the hand and 'cupped' slightly by pressing the centres with a modelling tool.

Different textures can be given by marking the surface of the paste before cutting out, for example, with a ribbed roller using it one way, or twice at right angles. A further attractive texture can be given by sprinkling plain or coloured granulated sugar on the surface and rolling it in lightly before cutting out. A different texture again can be given by spraying with a contrasting colour, using an aerograph.

An attractive finish can be given by piping either fondant or jelly into the centres. Alternatively, fondant centres can be piped on to paper previously greased, then the centres can be dusted with coloured sugar. When set, the centres can be applied as soon as the flowers are cut out.

Piped Flowers

Flowers can be piped with royal icing. Flower nails are necessary which can be bought or made by simply pressing a long nail through a flat cork. With a small piece of wax paper attached to the cork head a flower can be piped on it whilst it is rotated by means of the stem. Special petal pipes are necessary and these can be bought in several sizes. When dry, the flowers can be easily removed from the paper.

Dainty flowers in glowing colour can be made without the petal pipes. Using a flower nail as described, pipe a small bulb first and then on it pipe sharp spikes by pulling the icing bag outwards until the bulb is covered.

Flowers of the daisy type can be piped by using a bag with the point neatly cut off or by using a fine plain icing pipe.

Buttercream flowers can be piped in the same way and placed in the refrigerator and then removed from the paper in the frozen state with a palette knife and placed on the cake.

Decoration - Outlines (See Chocolate Run-out Pieces *page 82*)

Decoration - Outlines (See Chocolate Run-out Pieces *page 82*)

Modelled Flowers

Beautiful flowers for decorating purpose can be modelled with almond and sugar pastes. Perhaps the most popular is the rose which can be made in a variety of colours to fit in with the colour pattern of a particular design.

To make a simple rose, first of all a sharp pointed cone must be fashioned. Two petals are then required which can be cutout discs with the edges made thin with the fingers, or simply small roughly rounded pieces of paste made very thin by pinching between the fingers into petal shape.

The petals are given a concave shape and then applied to the cone by dampening the base of each with a little water. The petals should be so placed that the centre is hidden. The edges of the petals are then folded back delicately to give a natural appearance to the rose bud.

Three more petals are made in the same way, but this time a little larger. They are fixed equidistant on the bud with the edges turned back a little more than with the rose bud petals. Larger roses can be made by adding more petals.

When set, the rose can be cut carefully from the base with a pair of scissors or a sharp knife and placed into position on the cake. (See Techniques *pages 141-145*.)

Other flowers can be made from these pastes and it is a pleasing exercise in craftsmanship to copy as near as possible the natural flower. For modelling pastes *pages 251-253*.

Flower shapes can be cut out of jelly or petals can be cut and assembled into flower shapes. Jelly shapes can be used in decorative patterns also as shown in the diagram.

Decorative Designs for Schnittorten

In Germany, round torten or rectangular shaped gâteaux are so decorated that they can be cut into individual units. After cutting, the pieces can be used as an assortment for afternoon tea or used for dessert.

The bases used can be either butter sponge or genoese (see Sponge Bars-Chapter XIX-Gâteaux and Torten). The decorative materials used can be either buttercream, fondant, chocolate, jelly or tasteful combinations of these with, as an addition, nuts, glacé or crystallized fruits. No very hard materials should be used.

Some of the designs given for Petits Fours glacés and Genoese Fancies on *pages 80-81* can be used. The designs on each torte can be uniform or they can be varied. *(Illustrations page 87.)*

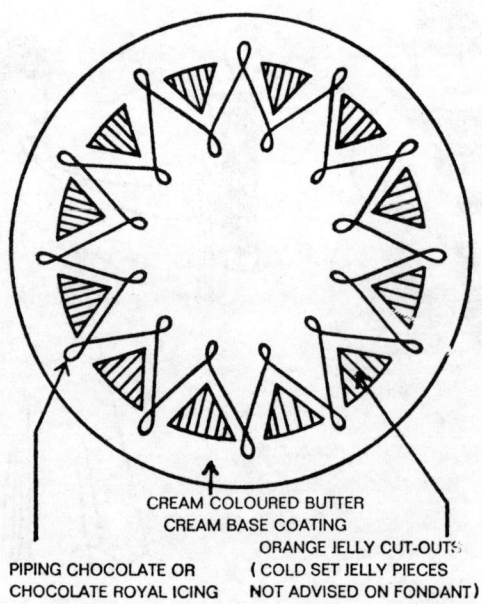

PIPING CHOCOLATE OR CHOCOLATE ROYAL ICING
CREAM COLOURED BUTTER CREAM BASE COATING
ORANGE JELLY CUT-OUTS (COLD SET JELLY PIECES NOT ADVISED ON FONDANT)

WEDDING CAKE PROPORTIONS

The most popular type of wedding cake is round in shape, the round ring shape being symbolical of eternity.

Running close in popularity is the square cake, its popularity probably being due to the greater ease in cutting slices.

Other shapes can be seen today, for example—heart, star, hexagonal and octagonal.

Generally speaking, wedding cakes are tiered—single tier, two, three or even more tiers, the most popular being the two and three tier cakes.

The tiers are separated by pillars made of gum paste by specialist manufacturers. Silver plated pillars were popular many years ago and these were hired, together with a stand and a knife, by the customer. At one time no pillars of any kind were used, each cake being placed directly on to the other, each cake becoming smaller according to the number of tiers.

Almost always, a wedding cake is finished with artificial flowers, silver leaves, sometimes silver dragees and an ornament for the top. This ornament is invariably made of gum paste. *(Cont. page 92.)*

Wedding Cake Proportions
Round cakes

Item	3 Tier - Total Weight 21 lb. (approx.) (9 1/2 kg.)			2 Tier ° Total Weight 15 3/4 lb. (approx.) (7 1/4 kg.)	
	Bottom Tier	Middle Tier	Top Tier	Bottom Tier	Top Tier
Size of frame	11" 28 cm.	7" 18 cm.	5" 12.5 cm.	10 1/2" 27 cm.	7" 18 cm.
Batter weight	7 lb. 8 oz. 3 kg. 400	2 lb. 12 oz. 1 kg. 250	1 lb. 6 oz. 625 gr.	6 lb. 0 oz. 2 kg. 720	2 lb. 12 oz. 1 kg. 250
Baking temperature	330° F 165° C	330° F 165° C	330° F 165° C	330° F 165° C	330° F 165° C
Baking times (approx.)	4 1/4 hr.	2 3/4 hr.	1 1/4 hr.	3 1/4 hr.	2 3/4 hr.
Baked weights (approx.)	7 lb. 0 oz. 3 kg. 175	2 lb. 8 oz. 1 kg. 135	1 lb. 4 oz. 565 gr.	5 lb. 8 oz. 2 kg. 500	2 lb. 8 oz. 1 kg. 135
Baked size (approx.)	10 3/4" × 2 3/4" 27 × 7 cm.	6 3/4" × 2 1/2" 17 × 6 cm.	4 3/4" × 2 1/2" 12 × 6 cm.	10 1/4" × 2 3/4" 26 × 7 cm.	6 3/4" × 2 1/2" 17 × 6 cm.
Almond paste for tops	3 lb. 0 oz. 1 kg. 360	1 lb. 0 oz. 450 gr.	8 oz. 225 gr.	2 lb. 0 oz. 900 gr.	1 lb. 0 oz. 450 gr.
Almond paste for sides	12 oz. 340 gr.	8 oz. 225 gr.	4 oz. 112 gr.	1 lb. 0 oz. 450 gr.	8 oz. 225 gr.

Size of boards	15" dia. 38 cm.	10" dia. 25 cm.	7½" dia. 19 cm.	15" dia. 38 cm.	10" dia. 25 cm.
Size when almond pasted (approx.)	11½" × 3¼" 29 × 8 cm.	7½" × 3" 19 × 7.5 cm.	5½" × 3" 14 × 7.5 cm.	10¾" × 3¼" 27 × 8 cm.	7½" × 3" 19 × 7.5 cm.
Apricot purée (approx.)	4 oz. 112 gr.	2 oz. 56 gr.	1 oz. 28 gr.	4 oz. 112 gr.	2 oz. 56 gr.
Weight of royal icing and decoration (approx.)	2 lb. 4 oz. 1 kg. 020	1 lb. 2 oz. 510 gr.	7 oz. 200 gr.	1 lb. 12 oz. 795 gr.	1 lb. 2 oz. 510 gr.

TOTAL WEIGHTS

Baked cake	7 lb. 0 oz. 3 kg. 175	2 lb. 8 oz. 1 kg. 135	1 lb. 4 oz. 565 gr.	5 lb. 8 oz. 2 kg. 500	2 lb. 8 oz. 1 kg. 135
Almond paste	3 lb. 12 oz. 1 kg. 700	1 lb. 8 oz. 675 gr.	12 oz. 337 gr.	3 lb. 0 oz. 1 kg. 350	1 lb. 8 oz. 675 gr.
Apricot purée	4 oz. 112 gr.	2 oz. 56 gr.	1 oz. 28 gr.	4 oz. 112 gr.	2 oz. 56 gr.
Royal icing and decoration (approx.)	2 lb. 4 oz. 1 kg. 020	1 lb. 2 oz. 510 gr.	7 oz. 200 gr.	1 lb. 12 oz. 800 gr.	1 lb. 2 oz. 510 gr.
	13 lb. 4 oz. 6 kg. 007	5 lb. 4 oz. 2 kg. 376	2 lb. 8 oz. 1 kg. 130	10 lb. 8 oz. 4 kg. 762	5 lb. 4 oz. 2 kg. 376

Wedding Cake Proportions
Square cakes

Item	3 Tier - Total Weight 25¼ lb. (approx.) (11½ kg.)			2 Tier - Total Weight 16¾ lb. (approx.) (7½ kg.)	
	Bottom Tier	Middle Tier	Top Tier	Bottom Tier	Top Tier
Size of frame	10" × 10" × 3" 25.5 × 25.5 × 7.5 cm.	7½" × 7½" × 3" 19 × 19 × 7.5 cm.	5½" × 5½" × 3" 14 × 14 × 7.5 cm.	9" × 9" × 3" 23 × 23 × 7.5 cm.	6" × 6" × 2½" 15 × 15 × 7 cm.
Batter weight	8 lb. 4 oz. 3 kg. 740	3 lb. 12 oz. 1 kg. 700	2 lb. 0 oz. 900 gr.	6 lb. 0 oz. 2 kg. 720	2 lb. 12 oz. 1 kg. 250
Baking temperature	330° F 165° C	330° F 165° C	330° F 165° C	330° F 165° C	330° F 165° C
Baking times (approx.)	4½ hr.	3 hr.	1 hr. 25 min.	3¼ hr.	2¾ hr.
Baked weights (approx.)	7 lb. 12 oz. 3 kg. 500	3 lb. 6 oz. 1 kg. 530	1 lb. 12 oz. 800 gr.	5 lb. 8 oz. 2 kg. 500	2 lb. 8 oz. 1 kg. 135
Baked size (approx.)	9¾" × 9¾" × 2¾" 25 × 25 × 7 cm.	7¼" × 7¼" × 2½" 18.5 × 18.5 × 6 cm.	5¼" × 5¼" × 2¼" 13.5 × 13.5 × 6 cm.	8¾" × 8¾" × 3" 22 × 22 × 8 cm.	5¾" × 5¾" × 2½" 14.5 × 14.5 × 7 cm.
Almond paste for tops	3 lb. 0 oz. 1 kg. 350	1 lb. 4 oz. 565 gr.	10 oz. 280 gr.	2 lb. 8 oz. 1 kg. 135	1 lb. 0 oz. 450 gr.
Almond paste for sides	1 lb. 8 oz. 675 gr.	12 oz. 340 gr.	6 oz. 170 gr.	1 lb. 4 oz. 566 gr.	8 oz. 225 gr.

Size of boards	15″ × 15″ 38 × 38 cm.	11″ × 11″ 28 × 28 cm.	8″ × 8″ 20 × 20 cm.	12″ × 12″ 30 × 30 cm.	8″ × 8″ 20 × 20 cm.
Size when almond pasted (approx.)	10¼″ × 10¼″ × 3¾″ 26 × 26 × 9.5 cm.	8⅛″ × 8⅛″ × 2¾″ 21 × 21 × 7 cm.	5⅞″ × 5⅞″ × 2¾″ 15 × 15 × 7 cm.	9¼″ × 9¼″ × 3½″ 23 × 23 × 9 cm.	6½″ × 6½″ × 3″ 16 × 16 × 8 cm.
Apricot purée (approx.)	5 oz. 140 gr.	2 oz. 56 gr.	2 oz. 56 gr.	4 oz. 112 gr.	2 oz. 56 gr.
Weight of royal icing and decoration (approx.)	2 lb. 7 oz. 1 kg. 105	1 lb. 4 oz. 566 gr.	10 oz. 280 gr.	2 lb. 0 oz. 900 gr.	1 lb. 2 oz. 510 gr.

TOTAL WEIGHTS

Baked cake	7 lb. 12 oz. 3 kg. 500	3 lb. 6 oz. 1 kg. 530	1 lb. 12 oz. 800 gr.	5 lb. 8 oz. 2 kg. 500	2 lb. 8 oz. 1 kg. 135
Almond paste	4 lb. 8 oz. 2 kg. 025	2 lb. 0 oz. 900 gr.	1 lb. 0 oz. 450 gr.	3 lb. 12 oz. 1 kg. 700	1 lb. 8 oz. 675 gr.
Apricot purée	5 oz. 140 gr.	2 oz. 56 gr.	2 oz. 56 gr.	4 oz. 112 gr.	2 oz. 56 gr.
Royal icing and decoration (approx.)	2 lb. 7 oz. 1 kg. 105	1 lb. 4 oz. 566 gr.	10 oz. 280 gr.	2 lb. 0 oz. 900 gr.	1 lb. 2 oz. 510 gr.
	15 lb. 0 oz. 6 kg. 770	6 lb. 12 oz. 3 kg. 052	3 lb. 8 oz. 1 kg. 586	11 lb. 8 oz. 5 kg. 212	5 lb. 4 oz. 2 kg. 376

It is important to remember that artificial decorations should be part of the design and not just put on because the customer expects them. They should be applied with care and with good taste.

If the gum paste ornament is white, then the 'whiteness' of the royal icing should match it as far as possible.

The cake is the 'pièce de résistance' of the wedding breakfast table and is probably the first article seen by the incoming guests. The first impression should be of beauty in colour and balance. These impressions are the first seen by the eye. *(Illustrations pages 608-609.)*

The wedding cake, including the top ornament, whether it be one or more tiers, should fit into an imaginary isosceles triangle. The height of the ornament then becomes critical and must be borne in mind.

Details of weights and sizes to assist the craftsman are given on *pages 88-91.*

Diagrams of Wedding Cake Construction

A rough guide for calculating the proportions of cake, almond paste and decorations (including icing) is to take the cake as 50 %, the almond paste as 25 %-30 %. The balance constitutes icing, board, decorations, etc., according to the amount used.

Thus a cake required to be 20 lb. (9 kg.) in finished weight, would require approximately 10 lb. (4 $\frac{1}{2}$ kg.) of cake, 5 lb. (2 $\frac{1}{4}$ kg.) of almond paste, and the remaining 5 lb. (2 $\frac{1}{4}$ kg.) would be made up of apricot purée, royal icing, board, decorations etc.

The weight of tiers before baking and the size of hoops required need careful attention. Balance is assisted if the tiers are graduated in depth, each one slightly less than the one underneath.

While trial and error is of importance in arriving at a system of cake weight proportion, there are two rough methods of proportioning for three tier cakes.

1. Put half the mixing in the largest hoop, two thirds of the balance in the middle size with the remaining third of the balance in the smaller size, i.e. 9 lb. (4 kg.), 6 lb. (2 $\frac{3}{4}$ kg.), 3 lb. (1 $\frac{1}{4}$ kg.) = 18 lb. (8 kg.)

2. $\frac{4}{7}$ bottom tier, $\frac{2}{7}$ middle tier, $\frac{1}{7}$ top tier, i.e. 8 lb., (3 $\frac{1}{2}$ kg.), 4 lb. (1 $\frac{3}{4}$ kg.), 2 lb. (1 kg.) = 14 lb. (6 $\frac{1}{4}$ kg.).

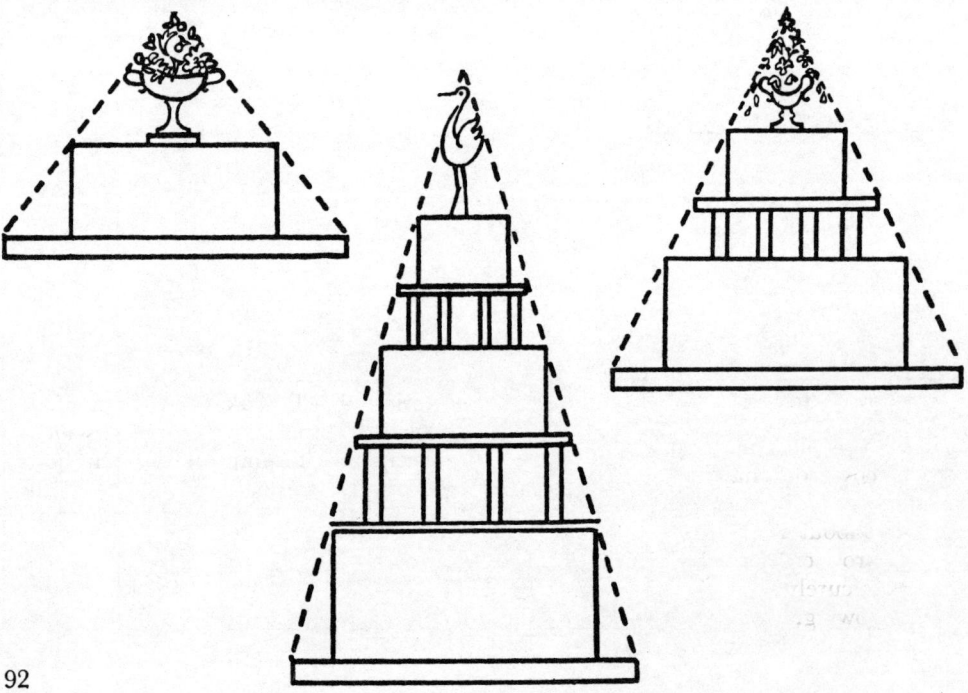

CASTING MOULDS

Moulds can be made from:

1. Plaster
2. Sulphur
3. Special commercial compounds.

They are used to make figure models and for decorative pressings.

Before moulding, a model should be selected. This should be as simple as possible and one that has no projections that would cause it to 'stick' in the mould and be impossible to remove.

The model should be flat and capable of being moulded in one piece, or it may be such that it has to be moulded in two pieces or more. In the latter case, the model should be carefully examined, because usually the joins in it can be seen and the number of pieces necessary easily assessed.

Plaster

For a flat model, a small piece of glass, plastic or metal is necessary on which the model is placed. This is surrounded by a wall of clay or plasticine leaving a space round the model.

The model, the base and the inside of the walls are then carefully covered with oil.

The plaster is made by placing an amount of water in a basin and adding the powdered dental plaster (never add water to plaster). When the mixture is the consistency of thick cream and it contains no lumps, it is carefully poured into the clay walls so that it covers the model. Take care not to pour quickly or air may be trapped, distorting the mould. After tapping the mould carefully to remove any bubbles, it is allowed to set.

If it is a two piece mould then it is necessary to cover one half of the model with plasticine or clay, extending the modelling material about half an inch around the model. Around this a band of stiff brown paper is securely fastened. The part of the model showing, the flange of clay and the inside of the brown paper is oiled before the wet plaster is poured in until the model is covered.

When set, the band is removed and the plaster cast carefully parted from the clay. This cast is then trimmed to remove all rough pieces and two wedge shaped incisions cut into the flange surface to act as keys.

Once again the brown paper band is secured around the cast, the model replaced and the whole oiled. Again plaster is run in and the same procedure followed. It will be seen that the new cast has the corresponding part of the key.

Sulphur

With this type of work, block sulphur and an old saucepan are required. The same procedure is adopted as for plaster casting except that for flat models glass or plastic cannot be used. Instead of plaster, melted sulphur is used.

Because sulphur is brittle when set, it is usual to strengthen the mould with plaster. This is done by placing the sulphur cast face downwards on to the base and surrounding it with a larger ring of oiled brown paper, deeper than the sulphur mould. Pad the bottom of the ring with clay on the outside to make it leak-proof. Cover with plaster completely and, when set, remove the clay and ring.

Commercial Compounds

These should be used according to the manufacturers instructions.

LETTERING

Lettering usually takes the form of the recipient's name or a specific message to the recipient. It is important that it should be carried out proportionally and skilfully, relative to the rest of the decoration of the cake.

The best proportional letters are the Roman and these are the most legible. One of the first essentials in good lettering is to keep all the vertical strokes vertical or, if the italic is used, to keep all the letters of the same height and slope. It is essential to know the relation of height to width of each letter, and to understand what is meant by 'lower case' lettering.

As a guide, letters can be grouped as follows:

1/2-3/4 Letters: — A. B. E. F. H. J. K. L. N. P. R. S. T. U. V. X. Y. Z.

The width is equivalent to from half to three quarters the height.

Full Letters: — C. D. G. O. Q.
The width and height are equal.
1 1/4 Letters: — W. M.
The width is one and a quarter times the height.
The letter 'I' needs the least space.
Here are the lower case letters: — a. b. c. d. e. etc.

When piping the Roman alphabet the strokes do not vary in thickness and usually lack ornamentation.

Piping should be executed with a fine writer tube and then highlighted with the use of a suitable colour scheme.

BASIC

ABCDEFGHIJKLMNO
PQRSTUVWXYZ

BASIC LETTERS WITH THICK AND THIN STROKES

ABCDEFGHIJ
KLMNOPQRS

BASIC LETTERS WITH THICK AND THIN STROKES AND SERIFS

KLMNOPQRS
TUVWXYZ

94

SPOT SERIF

ABCDEFGHIJKLMNO
PQRSTUVWXYZ

SERIF

ABCDEFGKLNRSTUV
WXYZ

Spacing

Spacing is one of the most important factors; there is no fixed rule to follow, merely the training of the eye. One has to create the effect of apparently equal intervals between the letters. Each letter shape varies because of its distinctiveness, therefore space between any two letters varies also.

Good spacing must allow the eye to flow smoothly over the words. C. T. L. V. A. by their shape create a certain amount of space and therefore need very little additional space. On the other hand, when two letters with vertical strokes come next to one another, more space is called for, e.g. M. I. N. D. J. Good spacing, although not immediately noticeable, plays its part in providing a feeling of well-being into lettering.

Layouts

A useful plan for successful arrangement is to make the lettering conform to a certain area, e.g. triangle, oblong, half circle, or a certain portion of the cake top. If it is necessary to centre a word, pipe the middle letter in the centre and build up the word.

In early stages of practice, it is useful to use paper templates to plan the layout and if so desired, pin-prick at specific points.

Legibility

Lettering must be easy to read. The simplest of styles should be chosen and embellished in various ways to add attraction. Care must be taken not to reduce legibility.

Always avoid a mixture of alphabets and capital and lower case letters.

It should be borne in mind that a child's knowledge of lettering is limited, therefore, when an inscription is required for a child's cake, lettering should be as simple as possible with no embellishments.

Ornamentation

Letters can be highlighted with smals amounts of ornamentation, e.g. the use of thick strokes, dots, etc. If using thick strokel the left stroke should be thickened. Serifs may be added which are a form of termination of the main letter strokes. A form of lettering without serifs is known as sans-serif.

Other Types of Lettering

1. Script Lettering

The slant of the upright strokes must be parallel and the height of the letters the same. The thick and thin strokes can be achieved by varying the pressure of the tube.

SCRIPT

ABCDEFGHI
JKLMNOPQR
STUVWXYZz
abcdefghijklmnopqrstuvwxy

A SCRIPT VARIATION

ABCDEFGHI
JKLMNOPQR
STUVWXYZ

2. Lombardic Lettering
A more ornamental type of lettering suitable for run-out letters and monograms.

LOMBARDIC

ABCDEFGHIJ
KLMNOPQRS

3. Old English

These letters are most beautifully formed. They may be simplified for piping directly on to cake.

OLD ENGLISH OR GOTHIC

4. Block Alphabet

This is constructed from thick strips, circles, half circles and triangles, most suitable for almond or sugar paste.

A BLOCK ALPHABET SUITABLE FOR CUTTING IN MARZIPAN

ABCDEFGH
IJKLMNOP
QRSTUVWX
▶▶▶ YZ ◀◀◀

'PLAYBILL' ALPHABET BASES AND CAPS LARGE ENOUGH TO DECORATE

ABCEGKMNQS
TVWXYZ123456

5. Stencilled Lettering
(See stencils *pages 101-102.*)

STENCILLED LETTERING

CHRISTMAS ★ GREETINGS
Birthday JOAN
SPRING *A Merry Xmas*

98

Birthday Greetings EASTER

STENCILLED ALPHABET

ABCDEFGH
IJKLMNOP
QRSTUVWX
WYZM

DECORATED LETTERS

S & C

Baby

6. Run-out Lettering

Run-out letters must be of such construction that they can be removed from wax paper and arranged on the cake. Firstly, the letters should be drawn acurately on paper and clear enough to be seen through the wax paper that is placed over it. The letters are then outlined with royal icing piped through a fine pipe. The outlines are then filled in with royal icing softened with a little egg white.

The colours of the outline and the soft sugar can be different or the soft sugar can be of two colours, the deeper colour being at the bottom to preserve a colour balance.

When dry, the letters can be removed from the wax paper and placed accurately on the cake. Run-out letters can be coloured with a brush or by the use of a spray after they are dry.

MONOGRAMS

These are letters that have been artistically intertwined to form a pleasing pattern. Any of the styles of lettering can be used.

Simple single line monograms can be piped directly on to the cake freehand. More ambitious monograms are done on wax paper, using the run-out technique already described.

Monograms are usually made up of the initial letters of the name of a person or persons or of an organization. Christening, birthday, coming-of-age, engagement, wedding and presentation cakes are examples when monograms may be needed.

At all times the monogram should fit into the design, balance and colour scheme of the cake. It should never obtrude at the expense of the rest of the cake.

MONOGRAMS

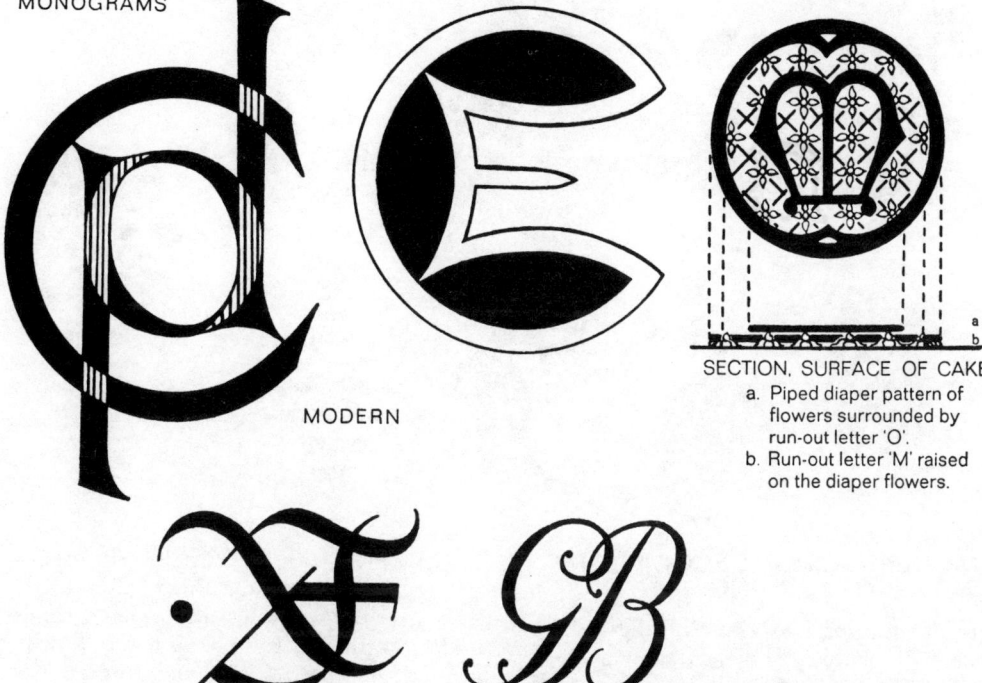

MODERN

SECTION, SURFACE OF CAKE
a. Piped diaper pattern of flowers surrounded by run-out letter 'O'.
b. Run-out letter 'M' raised on the diaper flowers.

BASED ON SCRIPT   TRADITIONAL

STENCILS

Stencils offer a ready means of decorating a cake, either with the help of a palette knife, a colour spray or even a sugar dredger. They have a further advantage in that they can, if made of durable material, be used over and over again.

The material used should be thin, water resistant and washable. Metal and plastic materials are ideal, the metal being more durable. A colourless plastic however has the advantage that it is transparent and thus can be placed over a drawing to facilitate cutting and, when completed, can be accurately placed on a cake.

A good stencil should allow the passage of icing, cream, edible powder or colour on to a cake. The design should be readily recognized when applied to the cake, but it should be so strengthened with ties that the pattern or letters remain in position.

With care the ties can become part of the pattern.

Stencils can be simple or more elaborate.

A stencilled inscription and border applied to a chocolate gâteau can be seen in the illustration, *page 119*. Here are some more examples.

STENCILS

MODERN CAKE DECORATION WITH ROYAL ICING

In life nothing is static; all things are in a state of change, some so slow as to be almost imperceptible, whilst others change more rapidly. Cake decoration is no exception.

In Great Britain, the changes that have taken place in cake decoration have been parallel with the contemporary scene and this is seen more clearly in decoration with royal icing.

In more spacious days, cakes were covered with fine work calling for painstaking effort which took a great deal of time. At present, as befits a streamlined age, fine tedious work is kept to a minimum giving place to prefabricated pieces that are added and built into an overall design. What little piping work is done, is carefully executed. Designs are not complicated and the modern craftsman will show that space can be made part of the design and not an area that has to be filled with decorative work as was the practice in the past.

Colour too, as part of the design, also reflects the contemporary scene, for the repetitive pink and white of the past has given way to delightful pastel tints. White, when used, is bright without any suspicion of greyness, so reflecting the maximum of light.

Because royal icing lends itself best to artistic precision work and is the medium used, it is necessary first of all to have some understanding of it; how it is made; how it is used; its possibilities and limitations.

Royal icing is an intimate mixture of icing sugar, egg whites and air in the proportion of about one part egg whites to six parts of icing sugar. *(Page 243)*. It is in fact the heaviest form of cold meringue.

Basins, spatulas and all materials used must be absolutely free from grease, otherwise the egg protein will be weakened and the air will escape as fast as it is beaten in and the icing will not reach the consistency necessary for either coating or piping.

To make royal icing, one third of the icing sugar is first stirred into the whites, another third is added and well beaten. The balance of the sugar is added a little at a time, each addition being well beaten in, until at last the correct consistency is reached.

The balance of air and sugar is critical; too much air results in a 'fluffy' icing with large air holes that will make fine precision piping impossible; too much sugar makes the icing 'heavy' and again it will be quite unfit for accurate piping. If the icing is made with the help of a machine, high speeds must be avoided because of the large air bubbles that will result. Correctly made royal icing should be capable of forming and maintaining a fine point when withdrawing the spatula slowly from the icing.

If the icing is to remain white, enough liquid blue colour should be mixed in during beating in order to impart a faint blue tinge, which will cause the icing to appear whiter when it is dry. If the icing is to be coloured, no blue should be used or the purity of any added colour will be distorted. The icing at all times should be covered with a damp cloth to prevent crusting. No metal objects, such as spoons or knives, should be left in the icing or discolouration will occur. Before the cake is coated with icing it must first be covered with almond paste. *(Page 112.)*

A piece of almond paste approximately half, or a little more, of the weight of the baked cake to be covered is weighed, and about one third of it is rolled out to a rope. This is then flattened with a rolling pin to a strip, which is trimmed with a knife to the depth and circumference of the cake. The strip is brushed lightly with well boiled apricot purée. If the cake is placed on its side at one end of the strip and then rolled along it, the cake will pick up the almond paste and be neatly coated. The rest of the almond paste is rolled up into a ball and flattened to the size of the cake top which has previously been brushed lightly with apricot purée. After the top has been placed into position it is pressed down and roughly shaped with the hands. It is then turned over on to the table top which has been dusted with castor sugar. With the careful pressure of one hand, the cake is slowly rotated and the top and the sides, particularly the top edge, can be given a geometrically accurate finish with the help of a metal tool known as an elbow scraper. The operation can be clearly seen in the *illustrations on page 112.*

Some craftsmen reverse this procedure by coating the top of the cake first with almond paste before completing the sides.

The cake is now ready for the first coating of icing. At this stage the cake is mounted on a cake board that is 3 to 4 inches (8-10 cm.) larger than the diameter of the almond pasted cake. The cake is fixed firmly by means of a little icing placed underneath. With the cake accurately mounted on the board, it is placed centrally on a turntable. A little royal icing is placed on the top of the cake with a palette knife and the turntable is slowly revolved while the icing is thoroughly spread to remove any large air bubbles that may be present. The side is then covered, using the same spreading motion, as the turntable is slowly revolved. With the edge of a plastic scraper held obliquely against the side of the cake, the turntable is rotated so that the cake turns against the scraper giving a smooth surface. *(Illustration page 113.)* Any surplus icing on the edge of the cake is drawn inwards on to the top with the palette knife. The top can then be finished by spinning the cake rapidly against the palette knife firmly held at a slight angle to the surface, the knife being withdrawn quickly as a smooth surface appears. *(Illustration page 113.)* Any surplus of icing on the edge of the cake can be removed by placing the blade of the palette knife, close to the handle, on to the edge and rotating the cake until a line of surplus icing is taken on the blade. This is repeated until the edge is cleared. *(Illustration page 113.)*

Some craftsmen prefer to coat the cake before placing on to a board. This is effected by placing the cake on a cake hoop smaller than the diameter of the cake and placing both on to the turntable. When the first coating is dry a second is given in the same way being careful on both occasions to trim the bottom edge of the cake so that no icing is below the edge. The cake, when dry, is transferred to a prepared cake board.

To prepare the board, it is first placed on to the turntable and kept in position by placing a weight in the centre. Softened royal icing is spread around the top edge of the board and smoothed with a palette knife, assisted by slowly rotating the turntable, until a perfectly smooth ring of icing is attained. The width of the ring should be just over the difference between the diameter of the cake and that of the board. *(Illustration page 114.)*

The second coating of the cake should be done with icing made a little softer by the addition of a small amount of egg white which should be carefully stirred in. To get a perfectly smooth second coating of the top, with no finishing mark visible, a straight edge can be carefully drawn across the surface. *(Illustration page 113.)*

In whichever way the first coating is applied the cake has to be prepared to receive the second coat. This is done by smoothing off any ridges and rough spots with a knife. For exhibition work sandpaper is used.

A knowledge of simple geometry is necessary for the preparation of the design which must be drawn accurately and clearly on thick drawing paper. Here are drawings of the top and bottom run-outs for the Christmas cake.

TWO RUN-OUTS FOR CHRISTMAS CAKE

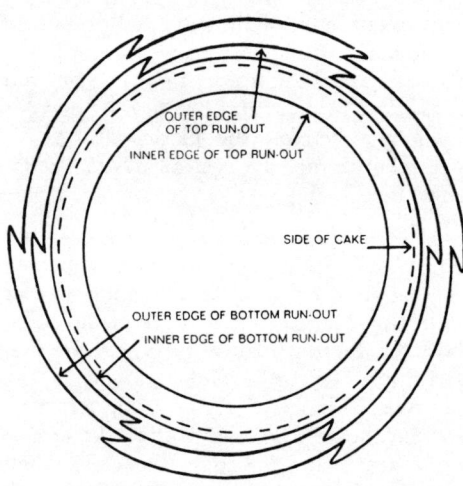

Detailed drawings of the lamp which is afterwards assembled on the cake top are also given.

LAMP FOR CHRISTMAS CAKE

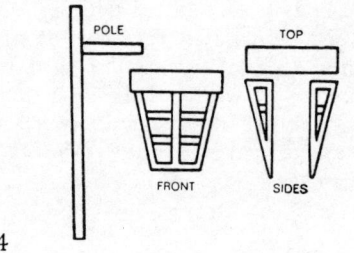

When the drawings are complete they are fastened on to a flat board and covered with strong wax paper which is also pinned down securely. The drawings should be clearly visible through the wax paper and it then becomes a simple operation to outline the designs with a thin thread of icing. For the Christmas cake, the outline can be piped with chocolate coloured icing.

The outline is then filled in with soft icing and it is most important that this icing is properly prepared so that it is of the correct consistency. Well prepared royal icing is softened by the addition of a little egg white or cold water, which is carefully stirred in without beating. The aim is a consistency that will not be so soft that it will quickly flow level when it is piped out. If prepared correctly it should run smooth and level only when gently agitated with the point of the icing bag or with the point of a small camel hair brush. Any air bubbles visible can be burst with the point of the brush or bag; then gentle rotatory agitation will soon effect smoothness.

Icing that is too soft will take longer to dry out and will lose its gloss. The run-out pieces will also tend to be brittle and will break when removing them from the wax paper. It is well to duplicate all pieces in case of accidental breakage. This is accomplished by removing the drawing pins and carefully sliding the drawing from underneath the completed run-out.

When filling in large ring shaped run-outs, it is well to pipe in at each end alternately because if the icing is piped in from one end continuously, a skin formation may be present where the first and last icing meets, making smoothness at the join impossible. The method of filling in is *illustrated on page 114.*

When perfectly dry and set, the pieces are freed from the wax paper in the manner as *illustrated on page 115.*

In the case of pierced designs, the insertions are piped in when the pieces are dry and before removal from the wax paper. If, however, the insertion is in the form of fine lines, the dry run-out is removed from the wax paper and turned over before the lines are piped. *(Illustration page 114.)*

Small pieces are made in the same way as the larger pieces, first being clearly drawn on to thick drawing paper. When multi-coloured pieces are to be made, different coloured icings can be run in, provided that each colour is allowed to form a crust before the neighbouring colour is run in, otherwise the two colours will run together. When dry, additional detailed colour may be added with a brush. Lettering and numerals are prepared in the same way and can be coloured also with a spray pencil.

With all the run-out pieces assembled and the cake twice coated and dry, the final stages can be commenced. If the inscription is to be piped freehand, this should be done first, taking care that it is placed correctly and will not be partially obscured when the top run-out is in position.

If the cake has been coated on the board, the run-out for the bottom is carefully placed over the cake and lowered on to the board. If the cake has been coated off of the board, the run-out is placed centrally on the board and the cake placed in the centre of it. The top run-out is fixed by piping two rings of icing just inside the top edge of the cake and lowering the run-out on to it making certain that it is placed accurately. To make it further secure, and to give a neater finish, icing is piped between the run-out and the cake top where it joins at the outer edge. This can be smoothed with a thin strip of plastic. The junction between the inner edge of the bottom run-out and the side of the cake can be similarly treated.

Finally, any smears of icing on the edge of the cake board must be wiped away with a damp cloth before the cake is put on display and before it reaches the customer's table.

This type of work is a challenge to those with an artistic bent. The most beautiful work can be accomplished if due attention is given to balance of form and colour and to clean accurate workmanship, always remembering that the finished cake is to be eaten. Anything that detracts from this is a waste of time and effort and brings no credit to those responsible.

Techniques

	Pages
Puff Pastry	109
Palmiers	110
Choux Pastry	111
Meringues	111
Cake Decoration for Wedding, Birthday and Christmas Cakes	112
Run-outs	114
Tempering Couverture	115
Chocolate Cut-out Pieces	118
Chocolate Rolls and Cigarettes	119
Piping Chocolate Ornaments	121
A Chocolate Centre Piece	124
Decorating a Birthday Gâteau	128
Fan Torte	130
Mocha Buttercream Torte	131
Parisian Strawberry Torte	132
Walnut Duchesses	133
Tubs made from Almond Wafer Mixture (Tuiles)	134
Almond Wafer Leaves	138
Chestnuts Monte Ceneri	138
Modelling a Marzipan Rose and Leaves	141
Sugar Boiling	146
Pulled Sugar	153
Blown Sugar	162
Assembling the Basket of Fruit	167
Pulled Sugar Ribbons	167
Pulled Sugar Bows	170

Puff Pastry

(*See also pages 181–182*)

The Scotch method of making puff pastry in which the whole of the butter in small pieces is mixed with the flour.

The pastry is pinned out to a rectangle.

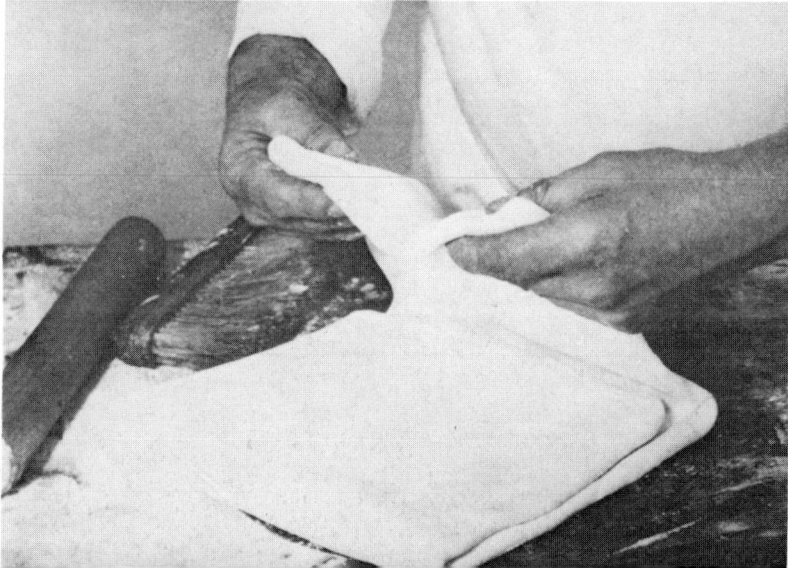

The pastry is folded into three. This is termed one half-turn.

With the French method of making puff pastry, only 2 oz. of butter are rubbed finely into the flour when the dough is made. The rest of the butter is placed in the centre in one piece and enclosed by the dough in the form of an envelope.
Rolling and folding proceeds as for the Scotch method.

For the English method, the dough is made in the same way as for the French method, but the butter is placed in small pieces so that it covers two thirds of the surface. Rolling and folding are then carried out exactly as for the Scotch method.

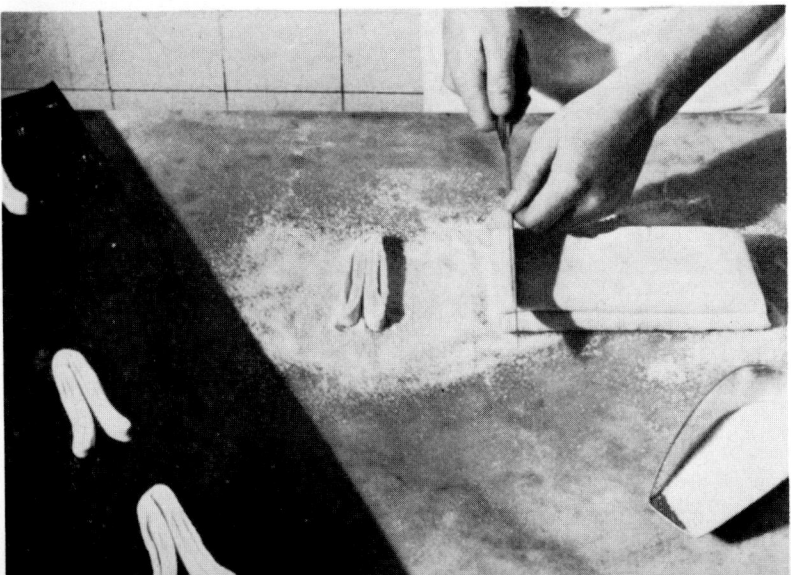

Palmiers

(*Recipe on page 330*)

The folded puff pastry is placed on fine granulated sugar and cut into strips, the ends of which are opened out as they are arranged on a greased baking sheet.

The baked pastries are removed immediately from the trays after baking to prevent sticking and possible breakage.

Choux Pastry
(*Recipes on pages 192–194, 338–343*)

Piping out choux rings.

Meringues
(*Recipes on pages 205–208, 457*)

Piping out meringues.

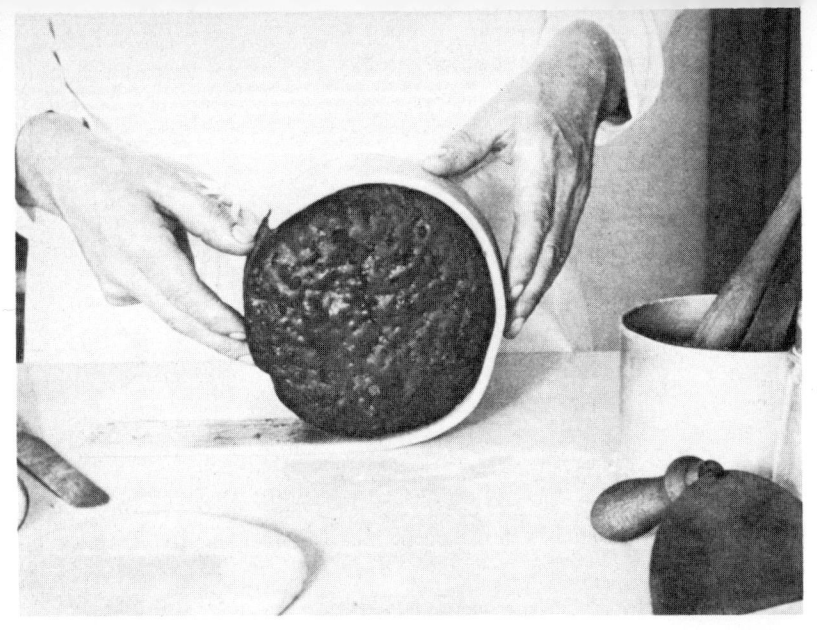

Cake Decoration for Wedding, Birthday and Christmas Cakes

(*See also pages 102–105*)

Almond pasting the side of a cake.

When the top has been fixed, the cake is turned over on to castor sugar and made level with the aid of a scraper.

Smoothing the royal icing on the side of the coated cake with a plastic scraper.

Smoothing the top with a palette knife.

Another method of smoothing the top by the use of a knife or a straight edge.

The method used to tidy the top edge.

Sometimes a cake is required to be placed on to a prepared board. Here is the method used.

Run-outs

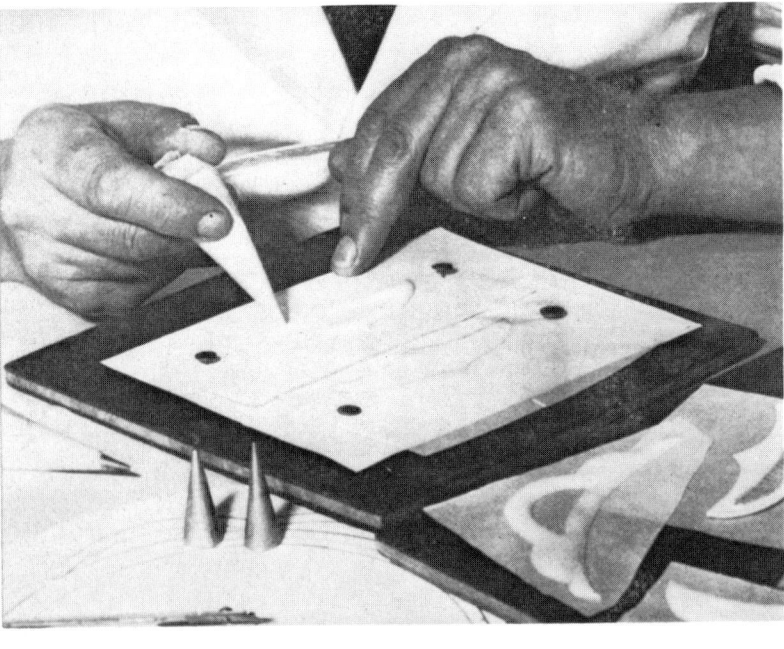

Making run-out pieces.

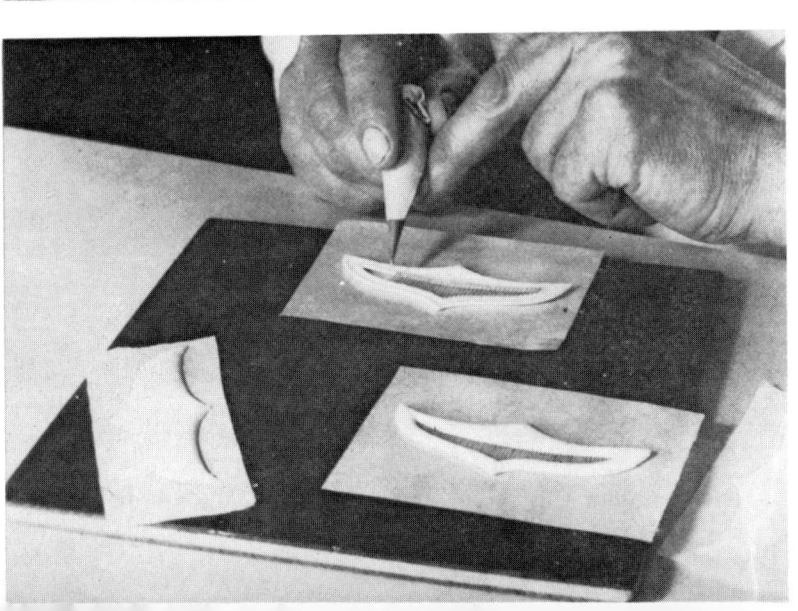

The method of piping pierced run-out pieces.

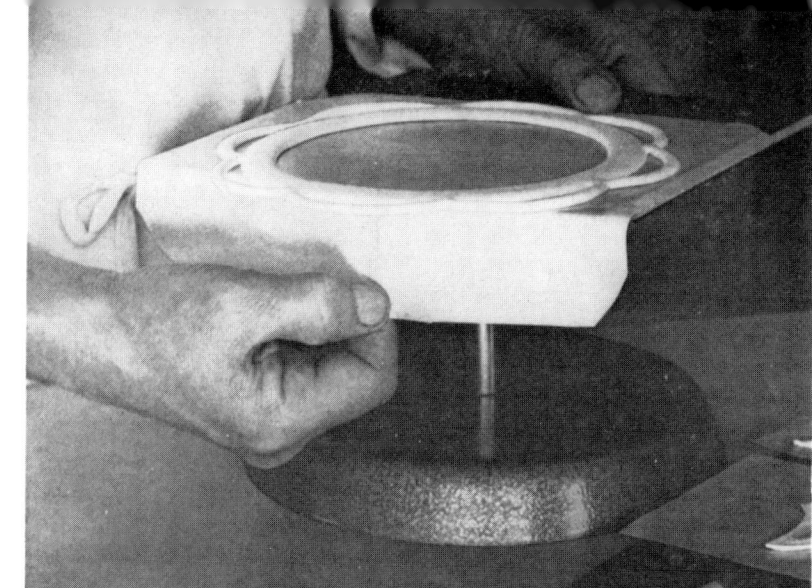

When run-outs are dry, they are released from the wax paper by the method shown in this photograph

Tempering Couverture
Please read carefully, Couverture – The importance of tempering, *pages 246, 247*.

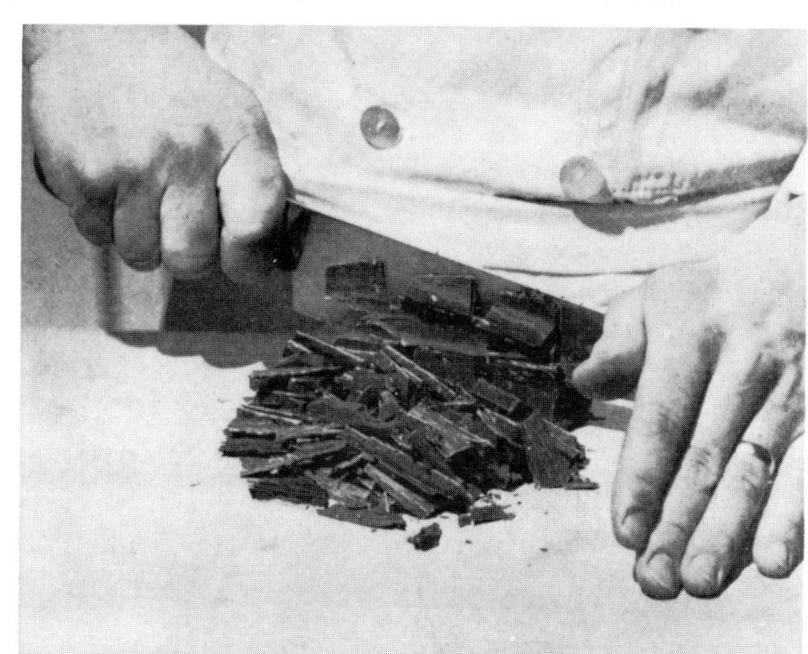

Cutting block of couverture into small pieces.

Melting some of the couverture over a bain-marie. The couverture should never come into contact with direct heat, water or condensed steam.

Adding a few pieces at a time to the melted couverture. The finished melted temperature should be as directed by the manufacturer.

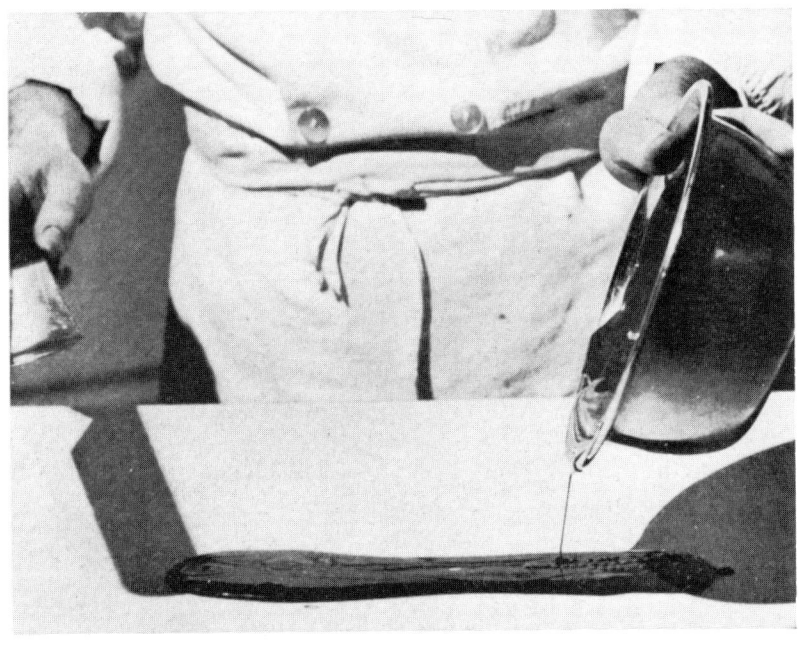

Pour two thirds on to a dry marble slab.

Leave one third in the bowl. Care must be taken that there is no water on the bottom of the bowl before pouring.

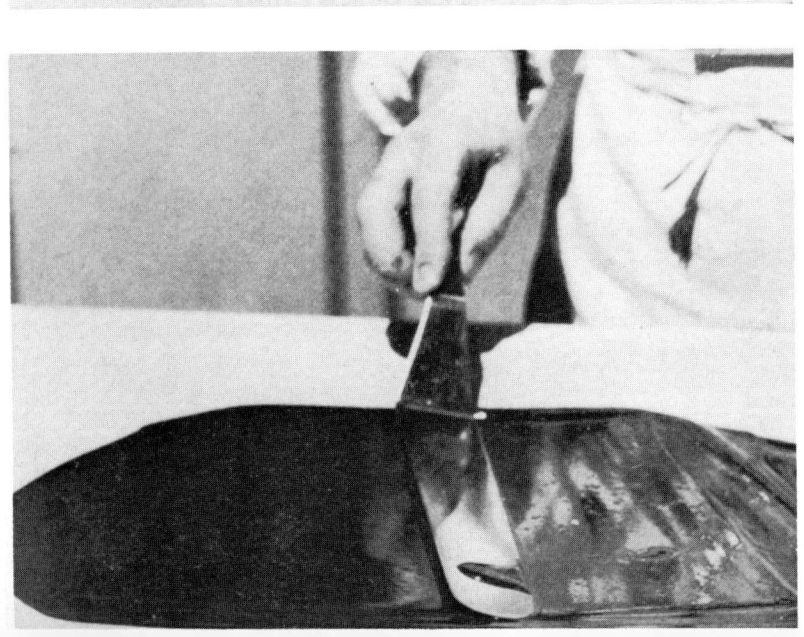

Spread the couverture with a trowel palette knife.

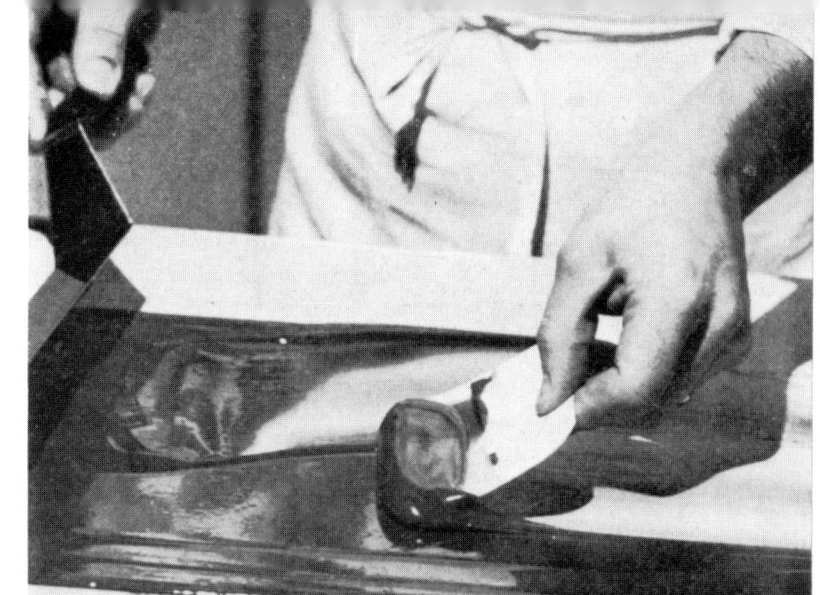

Scrape it towards the centre with a plastic scraper.

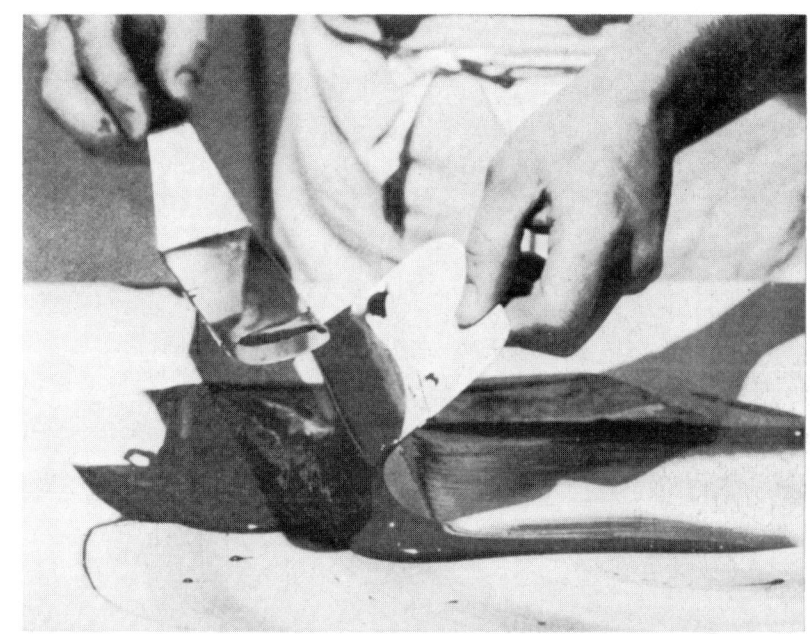

Clean off with a spatula and spread again.

As soon as the couverture begins to set, scrape it up, return it to the bowl and stir it a moment over the bain-marie. Care must be taken at this point, for the couverture will require very little time on the bain-marie before the required temperature is reached.

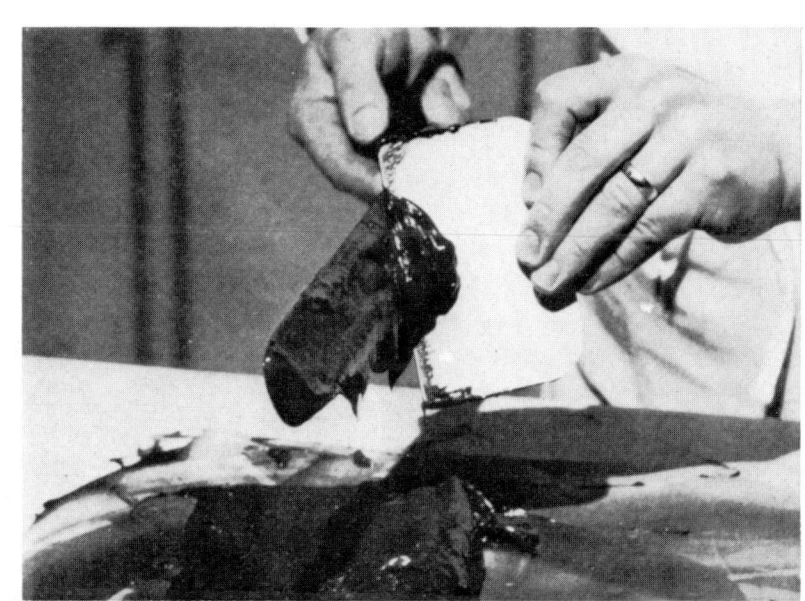

117

A simple method of tempering couverture is to add an unmelted piece to that which has been melted and stir. When the desired temperature is reached, remove the piece and stir again.

Chocolate Cut-out Pieces

(*See also page 248*)

The tempered couverture is spread thinly on greaseproof paper.

Examples of cut-out pieces.

Further examples.

An example of stencilling on chocolate.

Chocolate Rolls and Cigarettes

(*See also page 249*)

After spreading the couverture on the marble slab, warm it with the palm of the hand (see next illustration), then bring the blade of the knife down flat on the chocolate and pull it away making large rolls.

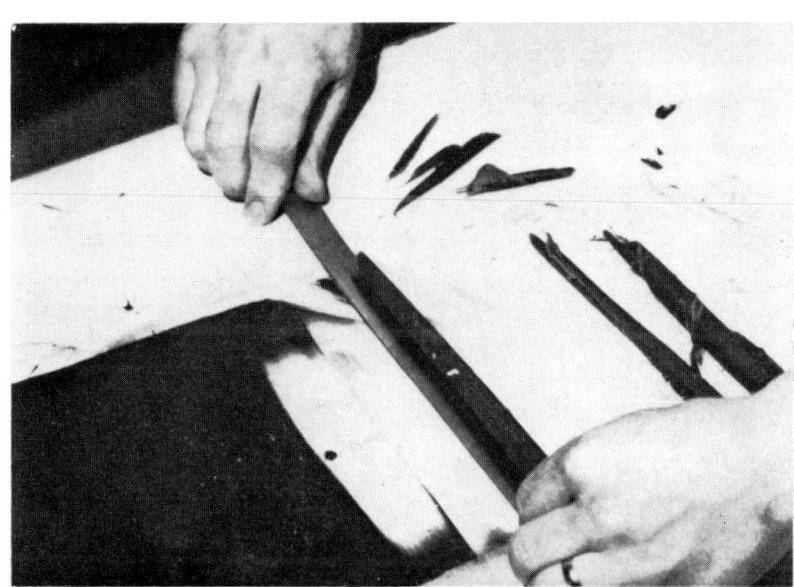

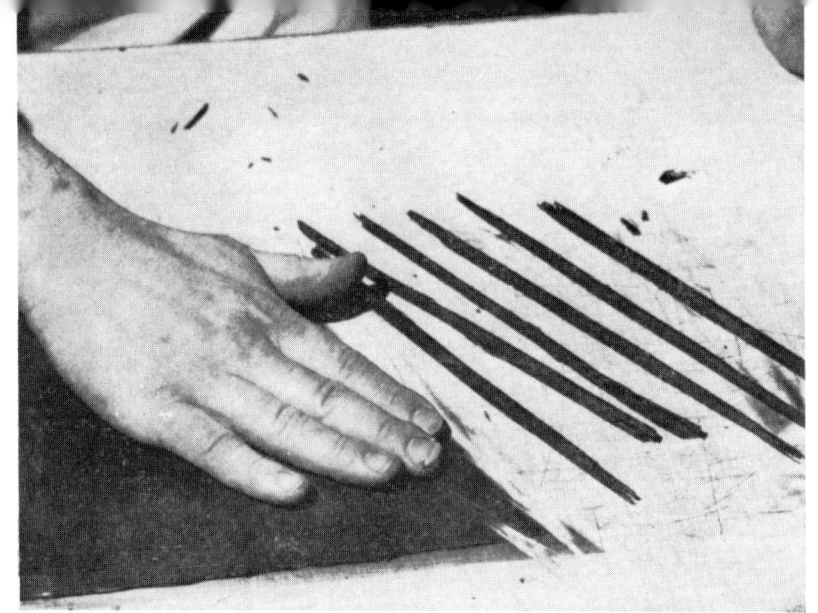

For the thinner cigarettes, warm the surface of the couverture with the palm of the hand.

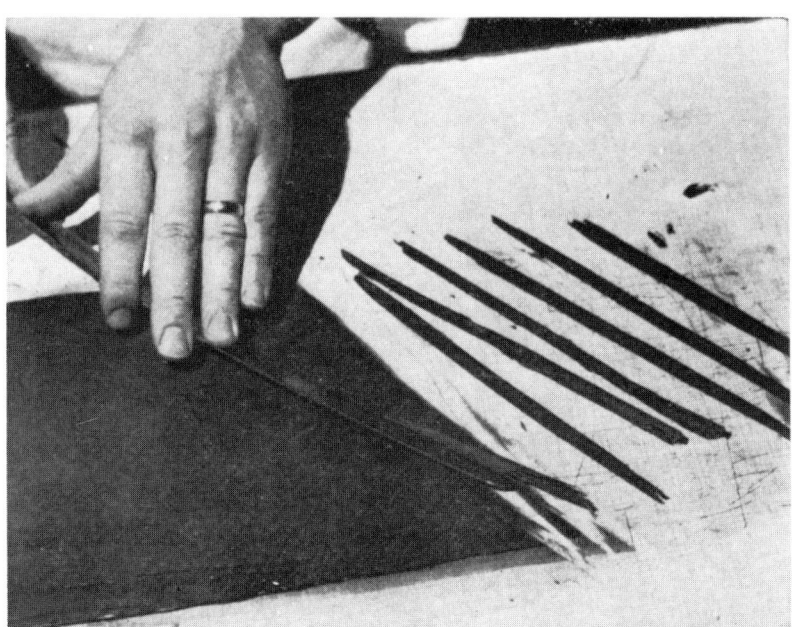

Hold the knife slightly on the slant and pull backwards a little.

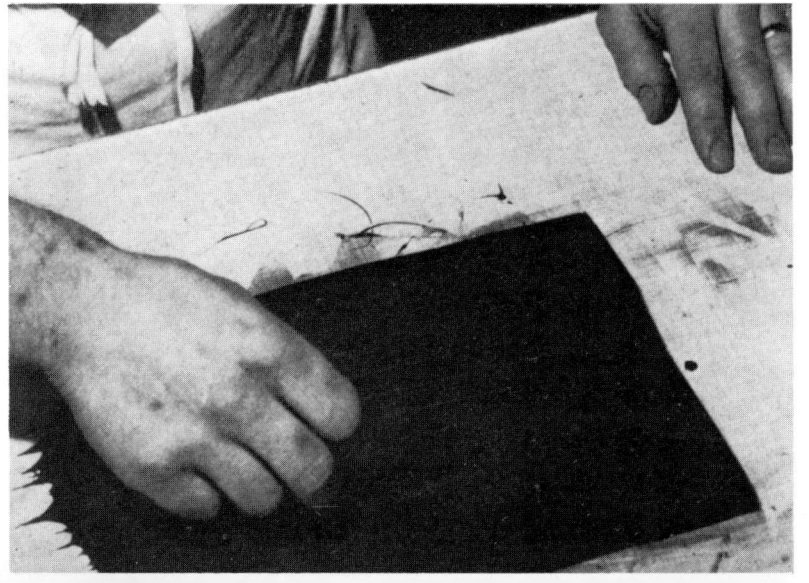

Small chocolate rolls for decorative purposes. Score into strips with the point of a sharp knife.

Divide into small rectangles by bringing the knife down on the transverse lines.

Carefully bring the knife forwards.

Piping Chocolate Ornaments
(*See also page 249*)

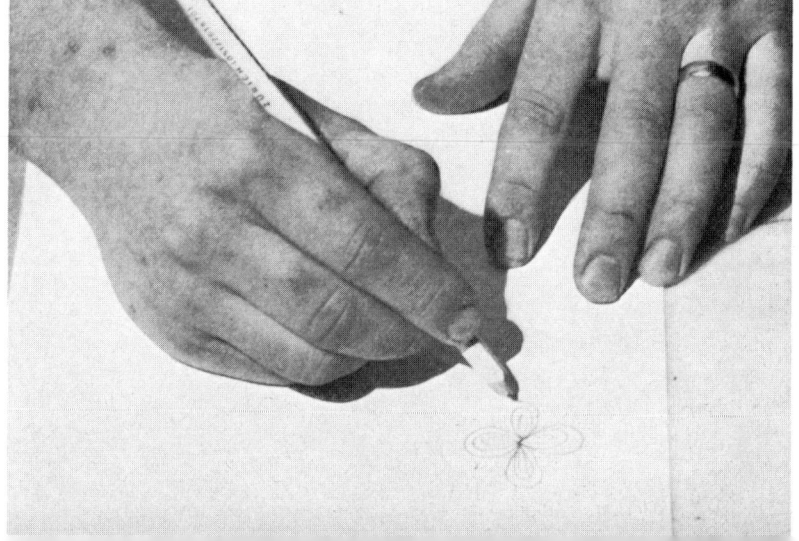

A pattern is first drawn on thick paper.

121

The melted couverture is thickened by adding a little stock syrup, glycerine or water. (Very little is required.)

The couverture is then brought to piping consistency.

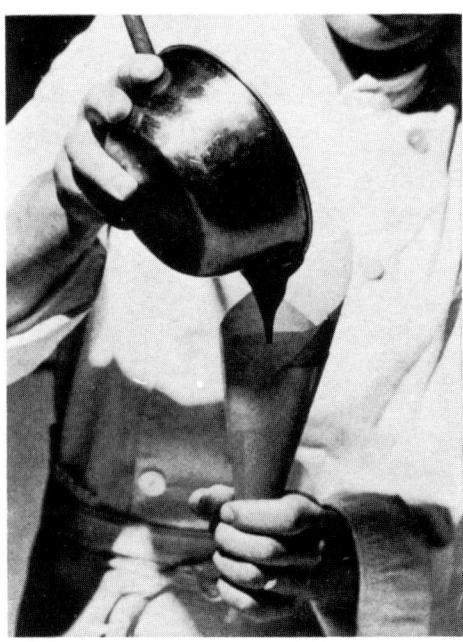

It is poured into a paper piping bag.

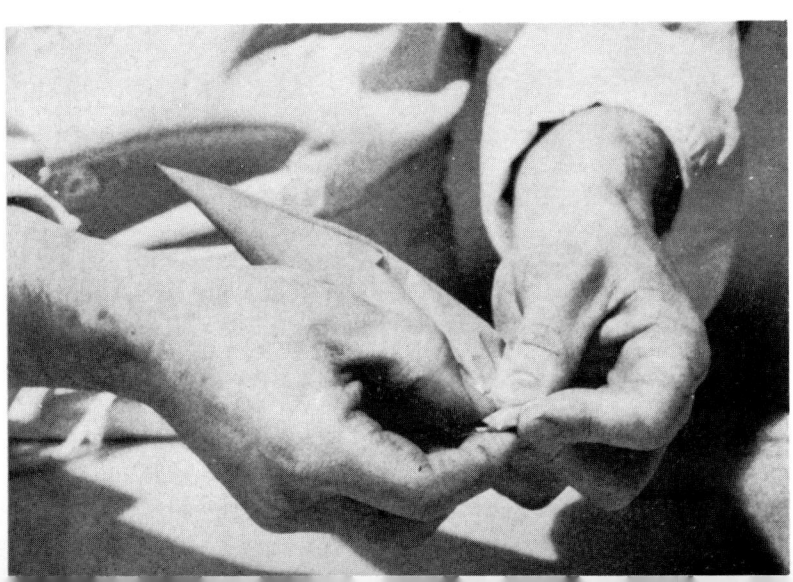

Closing the bag.

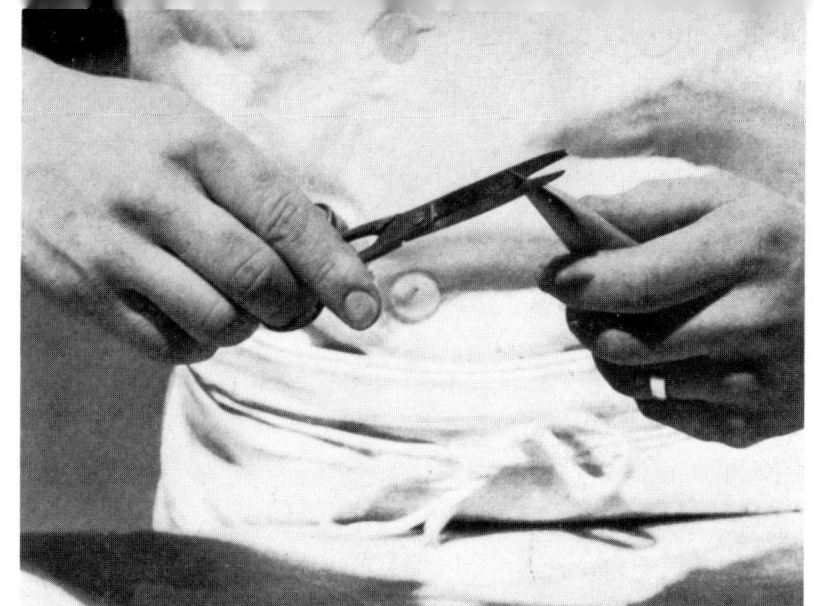

Snipping off the point.

Cover the drawing with a strip of greaseproof paper and pipe over the outline.

When piping, keep the bag raised a little so that the thread of chocolate is suspended.

A few finished ornaments.

Piping palm trees and swans.

A Chocolate Centre Piece

Used for gâteaux and festive cold sweets.

Cover the drawing with a strip of greaseproof paper.

Pipe the outline and the main section.

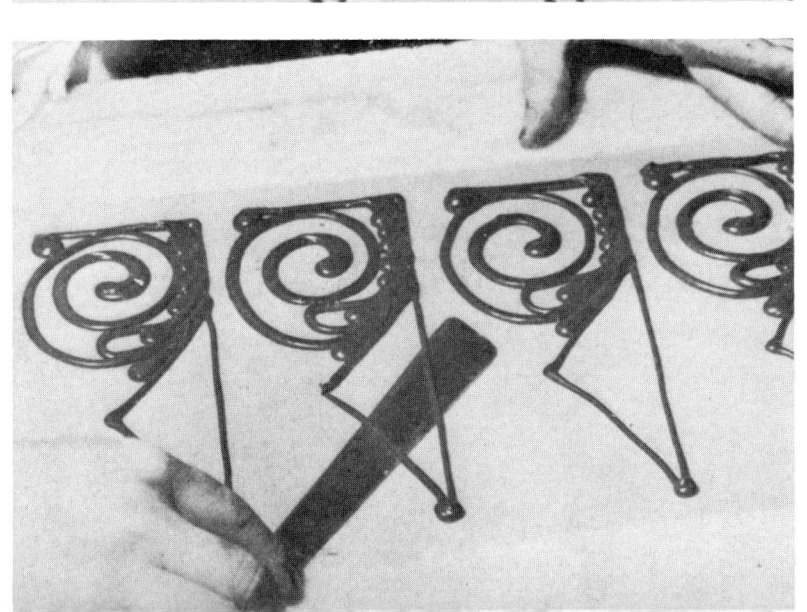

When set, detach the thin part with a palette knife.

124

Detach the other section.

Pipe the trellis work with a piping bag cut to a fine point.

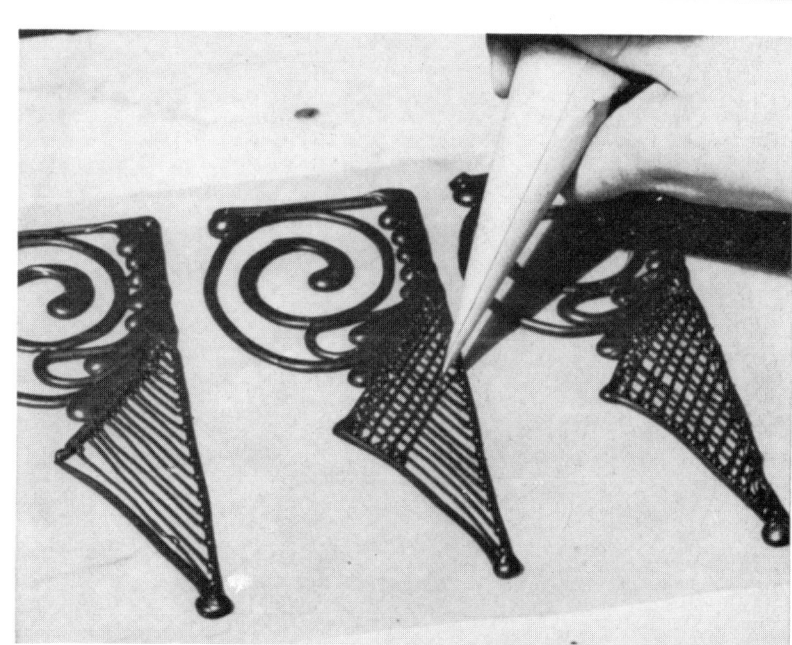

When set, detach the pieces.

Cutting out a chocolate base.

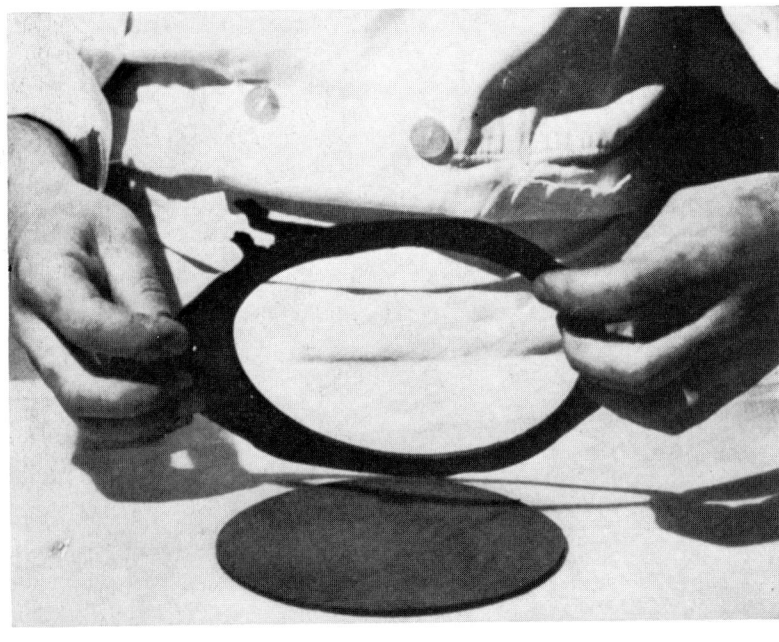

The surplus chocolate is removed when set.

Assembly commences. The sections are fitted together and fixed with melted chocolate.

The pieces are held until the chocolate used for fixing is set.

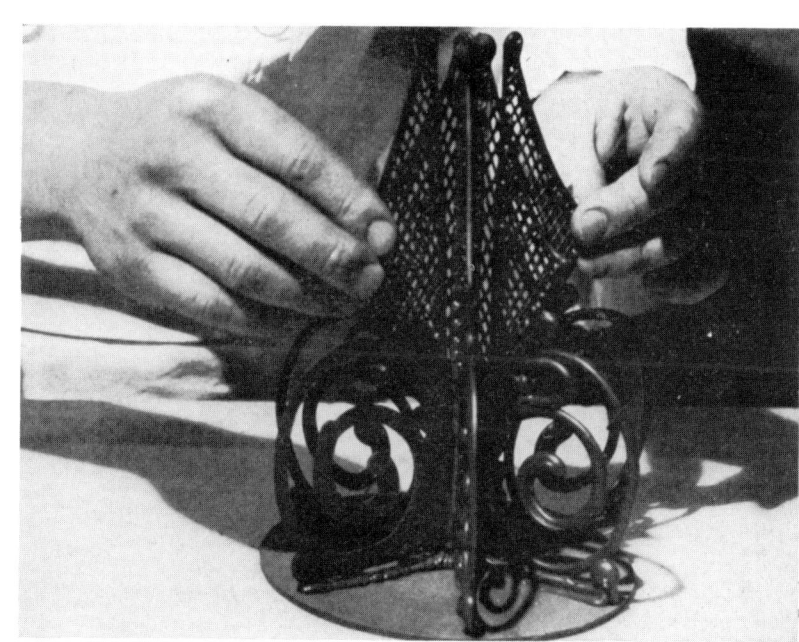

Work with the fingertips only to avoid leaving fingerprints.

As assembly continues make sure that every piece is firmly fixed.

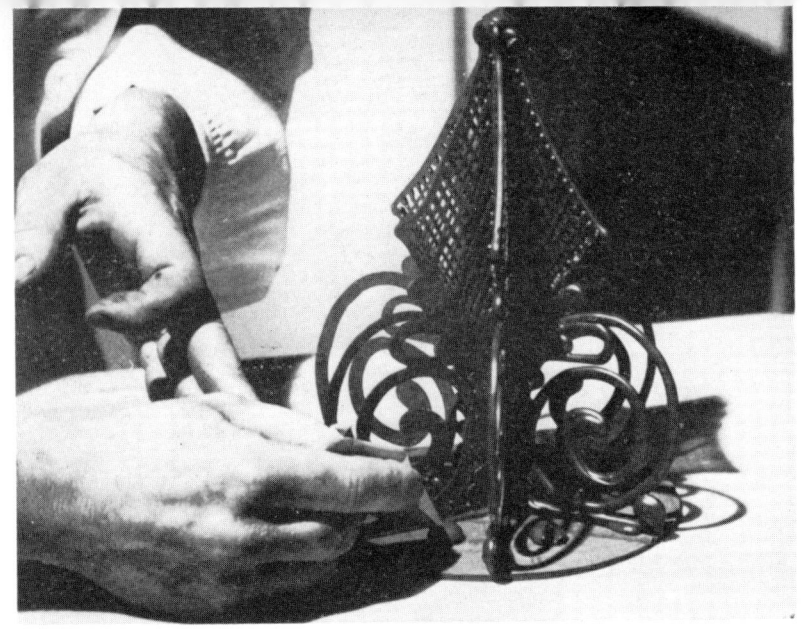

Pipe spots of chocolate in the spaces between the sections and place roses and leaves which have been prepared beforehand.

Finish with silver balls.

Decorating a Birthday Gâteau

Cut out circles of marzipan that have been impressed with a fluted roller. Cut the circles in half.

128

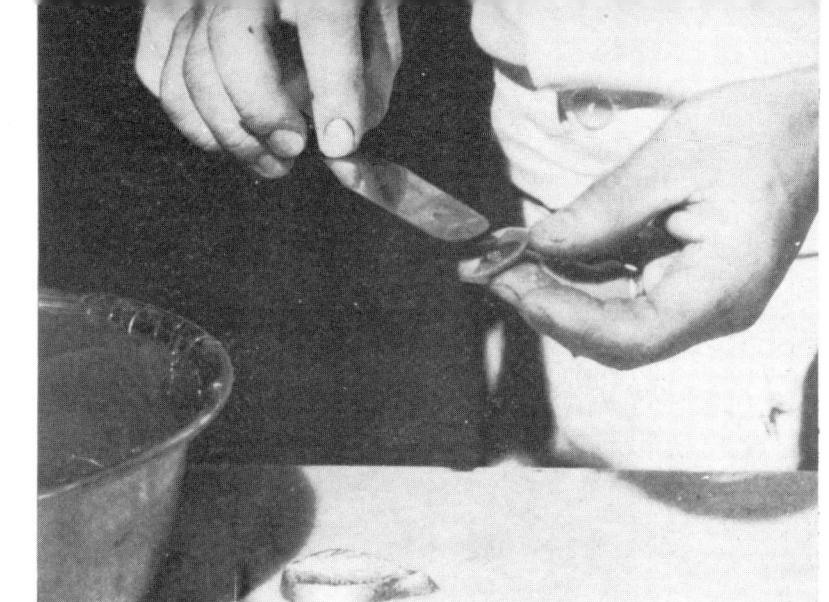

Spread the underside with a little chocolate.

Press them against the side all the way round.

Carefully lift the centrepiece with a spatula and place it on the top of the gâteau after piping on a spot of chocolate.

Finish with a fine piped border and silver balls.

This decoration is suitable if a cake of especially festive appearance is requested.

Fan Torte

(See recipe on page 579)

Building on the base to a height of about 1½ in. (4 cm.) with strips of almond sponge spread with nougat buttercream. The same cream is used to cover the base.

Assembling the segments in a fan design. The segments are made by spreading the top with chocolate and making a design with a comb scraper. When the chocolate is set, the top is cut into 18 pieces, half of which are dusted with icing sugar.

Mocha Buttercream Torte

(*See recipe on page 582*)

After covering a thin sweet paste base with nougat softened to a spreading consistency, lay a meringue base on top and spread with mocha buttercream. Sandwich the two almond sponge bases with mocha and place on top.

Coating the assembled torte with the coffee cream and combing the side.

Decorating with the same cream and with chocolate coffee beans.

Parisian Strawberry Torte

(*See recipe on page 582*)

Arrange the washed and dried strawberries on the base.

Glaze the strawberries with jelly.

Mask the side of the torte with roasted flaked almonds.

Walnut Duchesses

(*See recipe on page 452*)

Stencilling the mixture on to a lightly greased and floured baking sheet.

Piping the bases with nougat buttercream after baking and cooling.

After assembly, the tops are spread with chocolate and decorated with half walnuts.

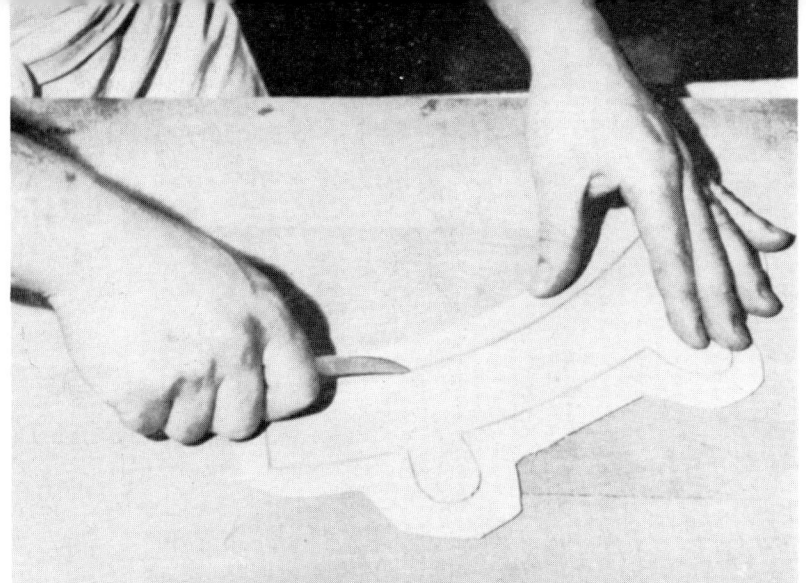

Tubs Made from Almond Wafer Mixture (Tuiles)

(See recipe on page 213)

First make a stencil from cardboard ⅛ in. (2–5 mm.) thick. For constant work a metal stencil is better.

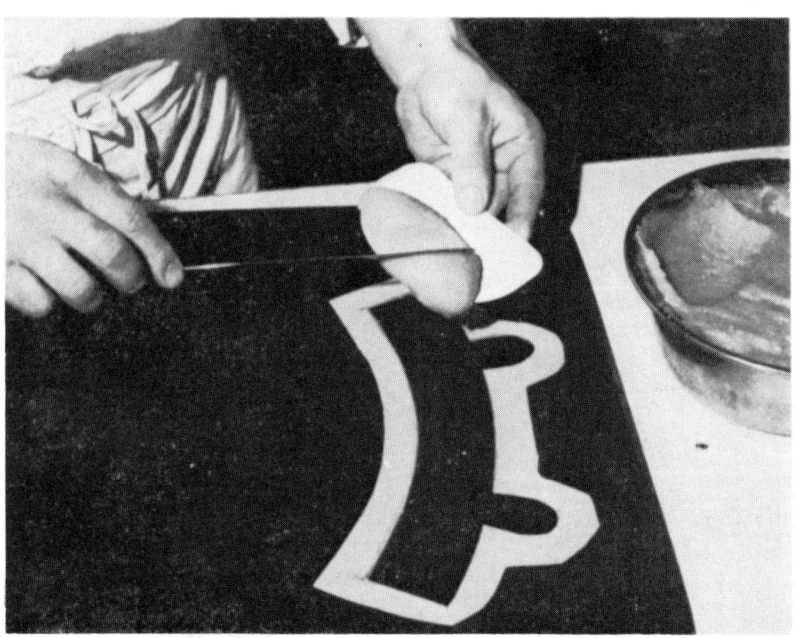

Lay the stencil on a lightly greased and floured baking sheet and spread the mixture in the centre.

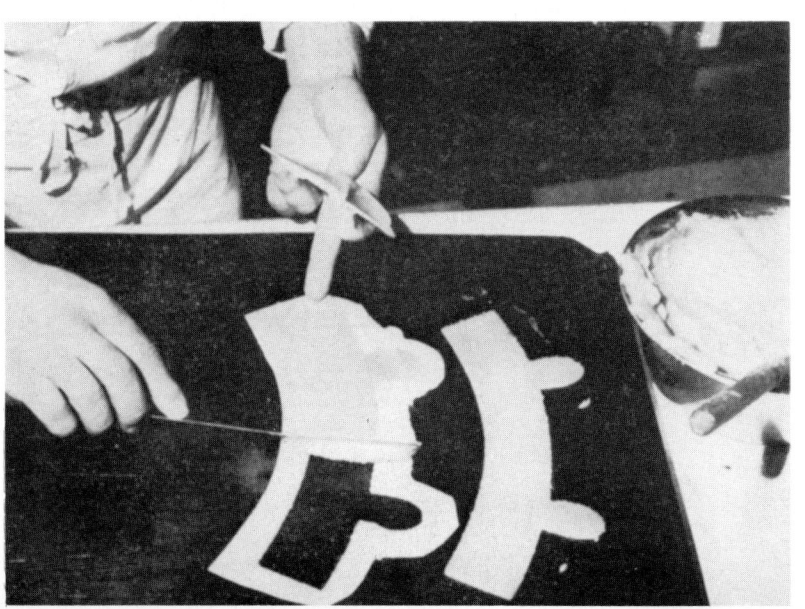

When spread, lift the stencil off carefully. Bake evenly in two stages.

134

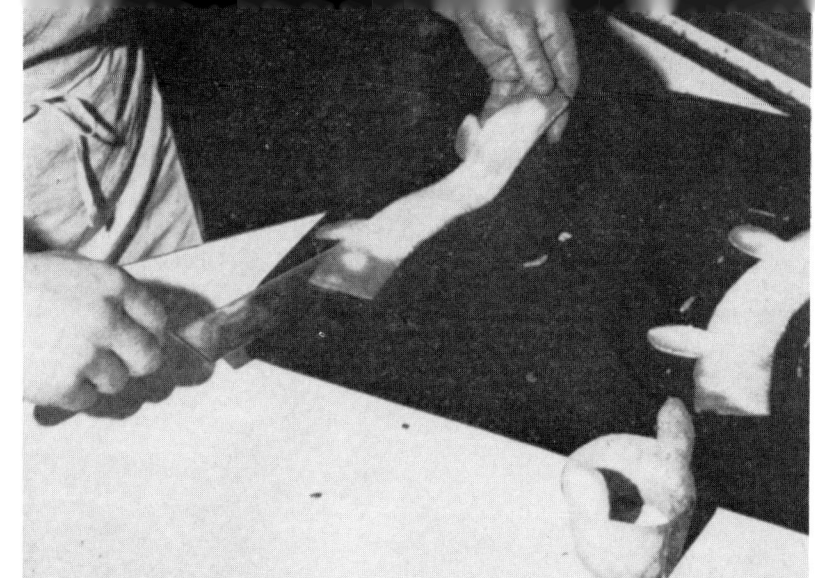

After baking, carefully remove the wafers from the baking sheet.

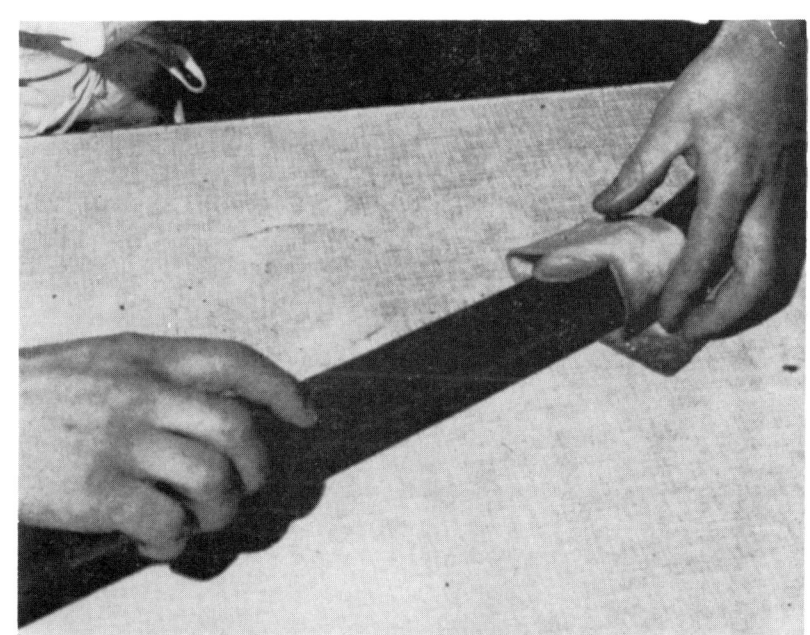

Curve them round a rolling pin pressing the ends together.

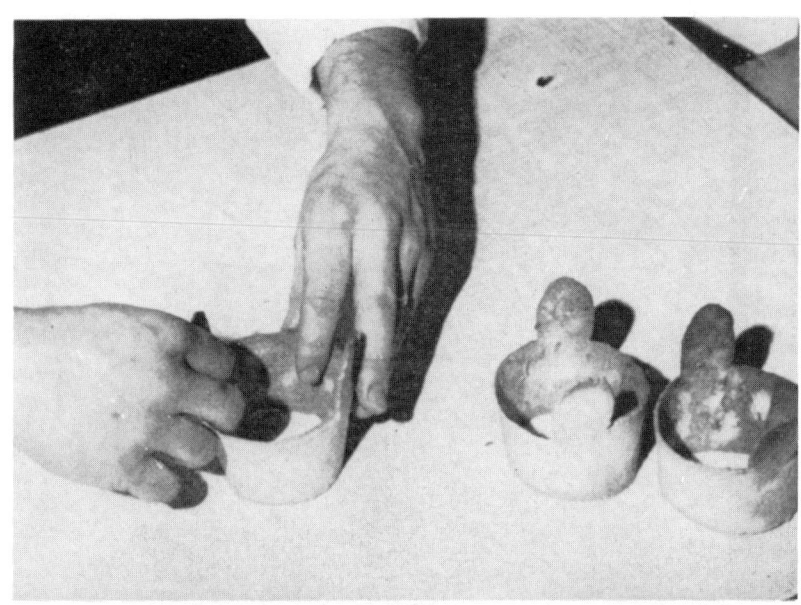

Finish rounding off by hand.

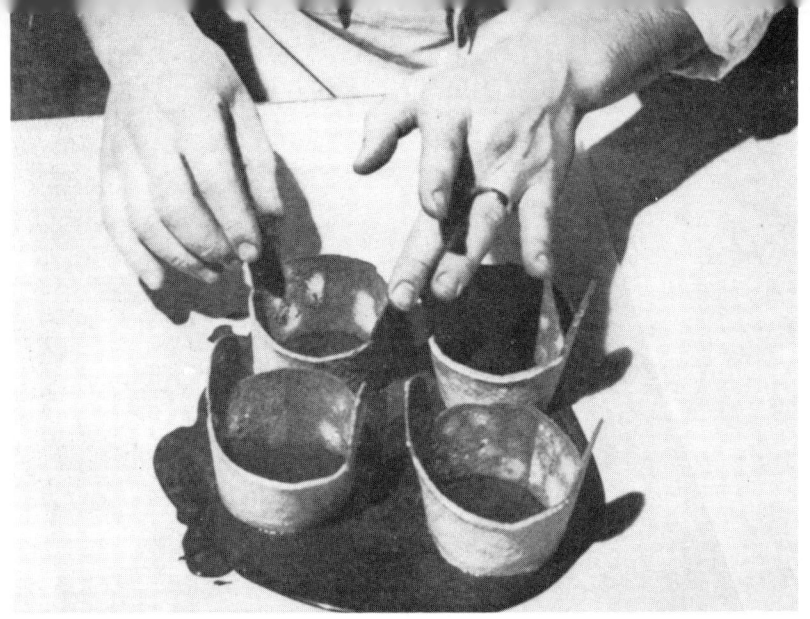

Spread an ⅛ in. (3 mm.) layer of chocolate on a sheet of paper and stand the tubs on it.

When set, carefully detach from the paper with a palette knife.

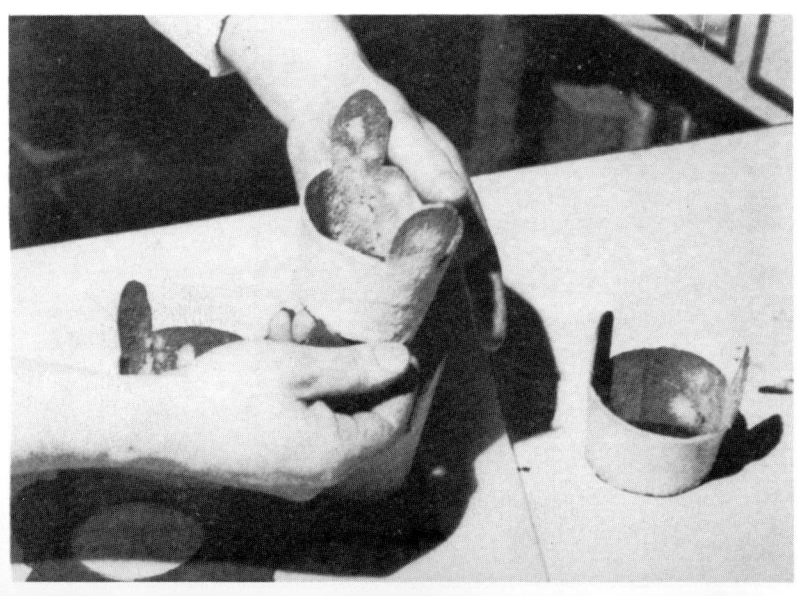

Break off the surplus chocolate.

Pipe a little chocolate round the inside lower edge to reinforce the tubs.

Brush the inside of the tubs with chocolate.

Leave to set.

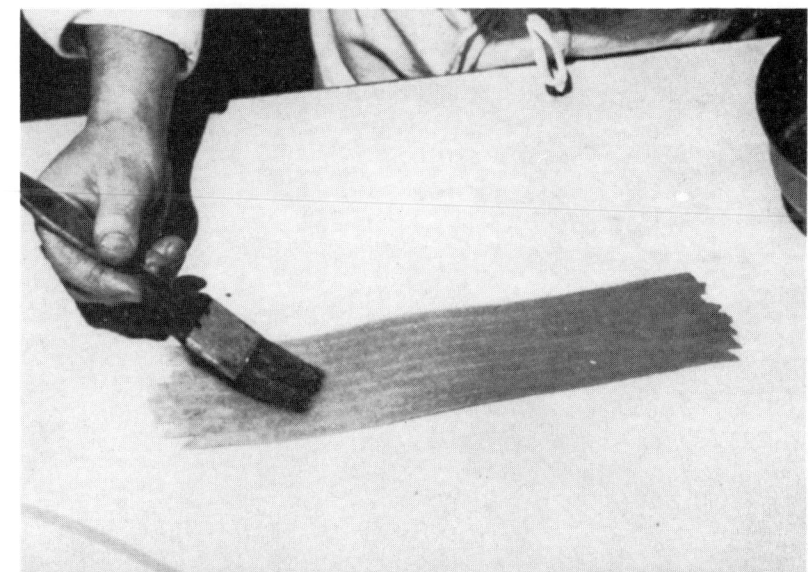

Cut a thin sheet of pale yellow marzipan into strips and brush with a little stock syrup.

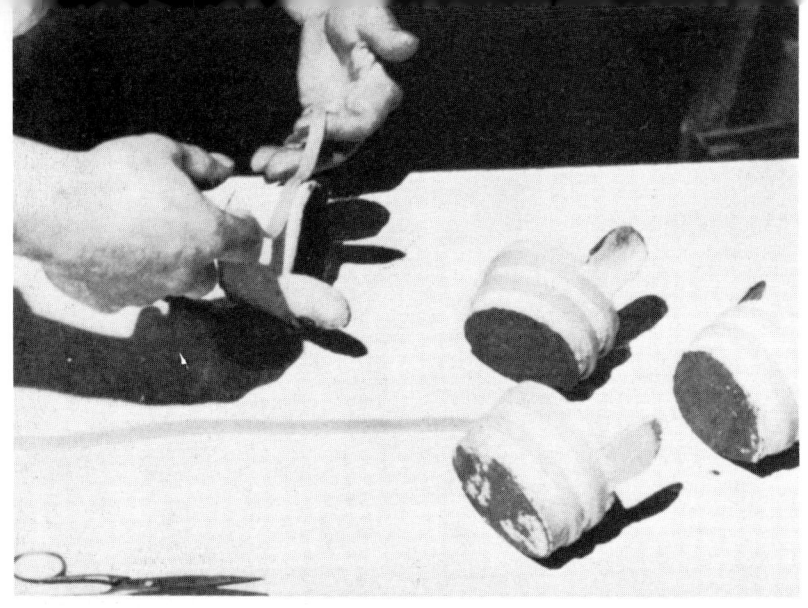

Fix two strips of marzipan right round the outside of each tub and press the ends together neatly. The tubs are now finished.

Almond Wafer Leaves
(See also pages 438, 515, 533)

The method of stencilling almond leaves and Christmas trees on to a lightly greased and floured baking sheet.

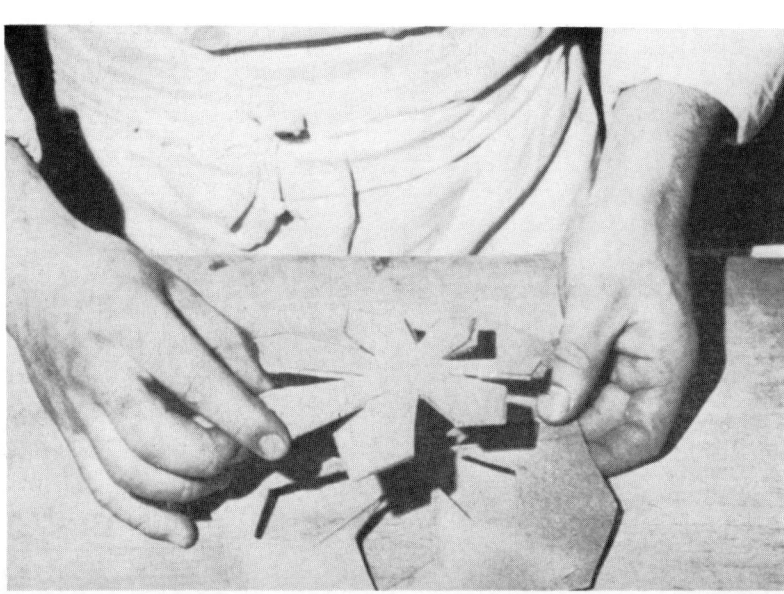

Chestnuts Monte Ceneri
A speciality of the Hotel La Palma, Locarno.

Make a stencil by cutting a chestnut leaf out of a piece of cardboard $\frac{1}{8}$ in. (2–3mm.) thick.

Place the stencil on a lightly greased and floured baking sheet. Spread almond wafer mixture in the centre. When the tray is full, bake off in two stages.

When baked to a pale golden colour, carefully remove the leaves from the baking sheet.

Gently press at once into small glass bowls.

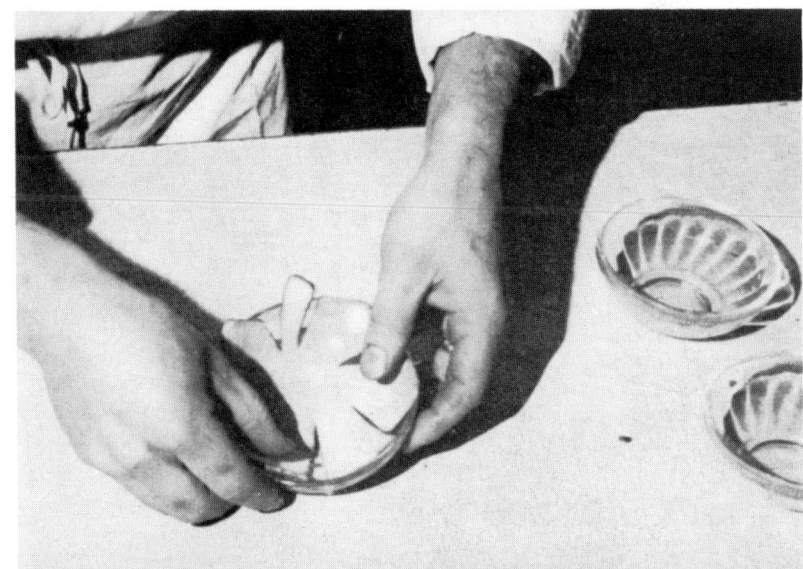

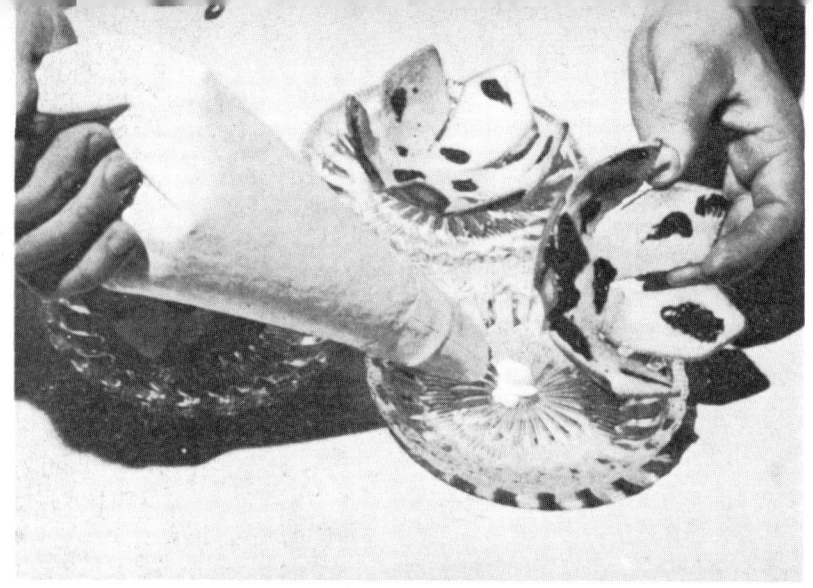

When cold, paint on small spots of chocolate.

Fix each leaf in position on a shallow cut-glass dish with a spot of whipped dairy cream.

Pipe a spot of whipped cream into each leaf and place half of meringue base on top.

Pipe on a little more whipped cream.

Using a fine noodle forcer, press out kirsch flavoured chestnut purée on top, then pipe on a whirl of whipped cream.

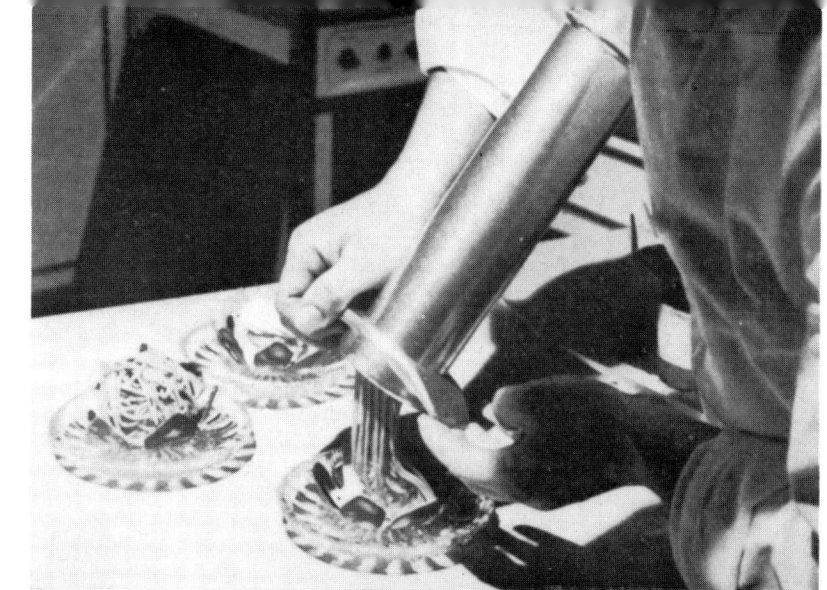

Place a marzipan chestnut in the centre for final decoration. (Wrap chocolate marzipan in green marzipan and decorate with prickles piped with green royal icing.)

Modelling a Marzipan Rose and Leaves

(*See also page 612*)

Roll a piece of prepared marzipan to a tapered shape. Lightly oil the marble slab.

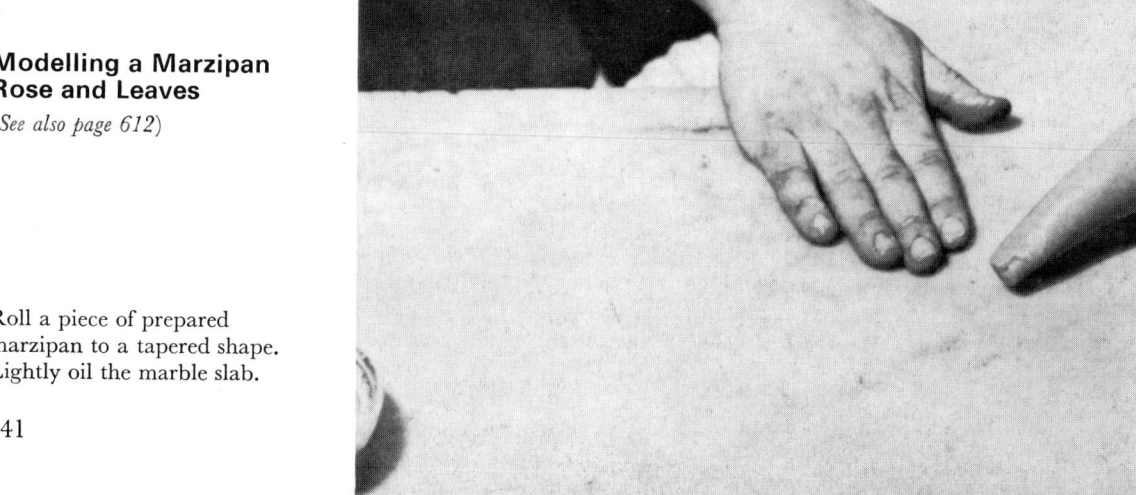

141

Mould a sharp pointed cone for the centre of the rose. From the tapered end of the marzipan press out a petal with a palette knife.

Make sure the edge of each petal is very thin.

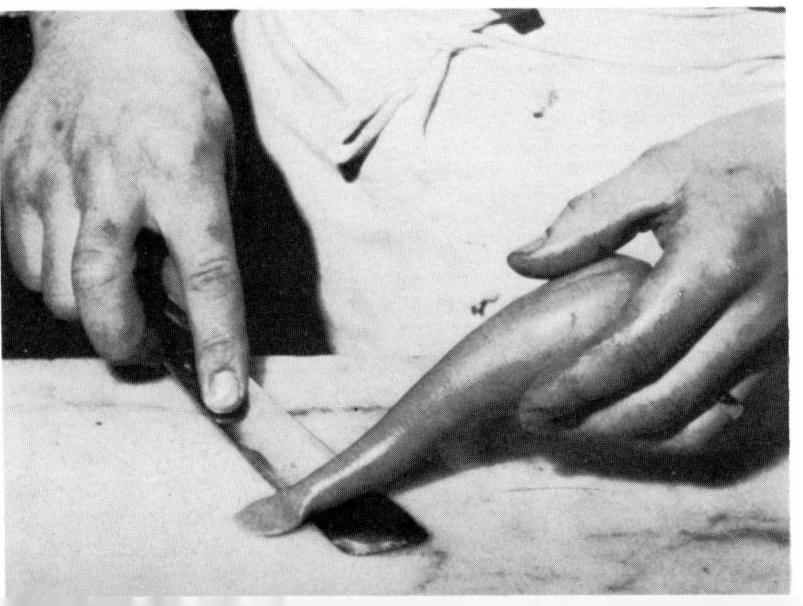

Detach with the palette knife.

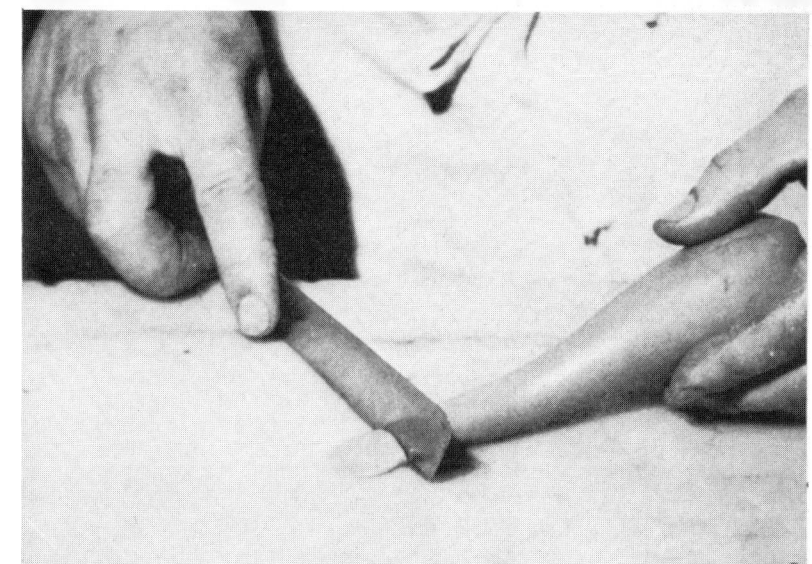

Cut off the end.

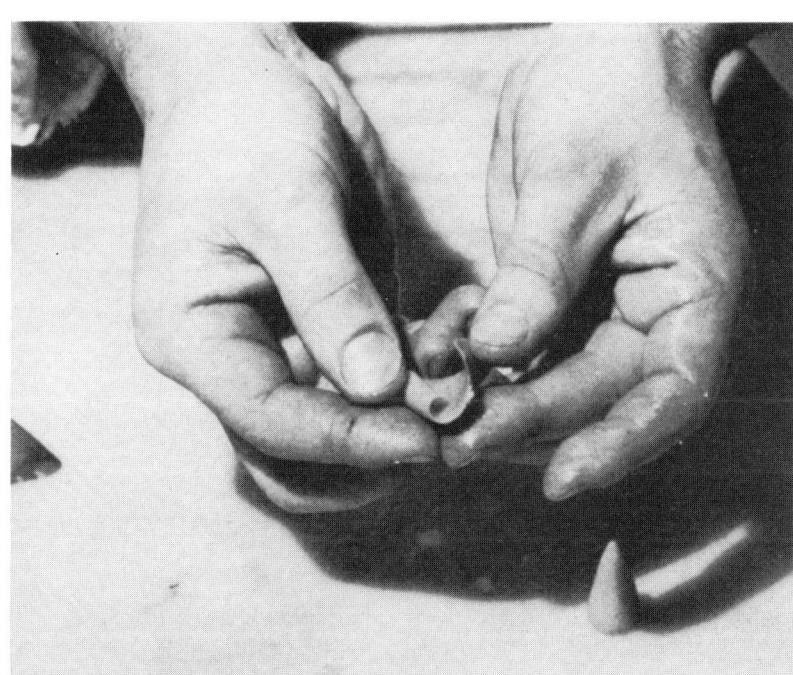

Roll the petal into a curl.

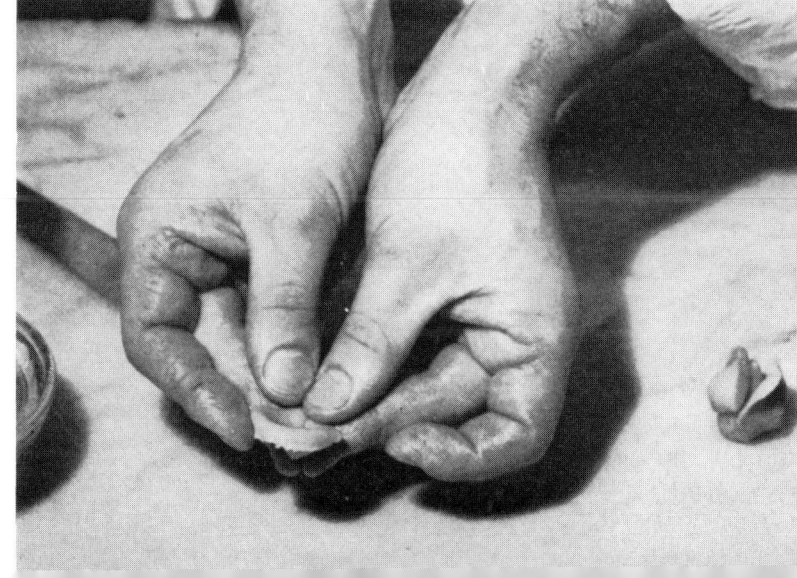

Make other petals in the same way, making a depression with the finger to form the concave centre.

Carefully attach the first petal to the cone leaving one side free.

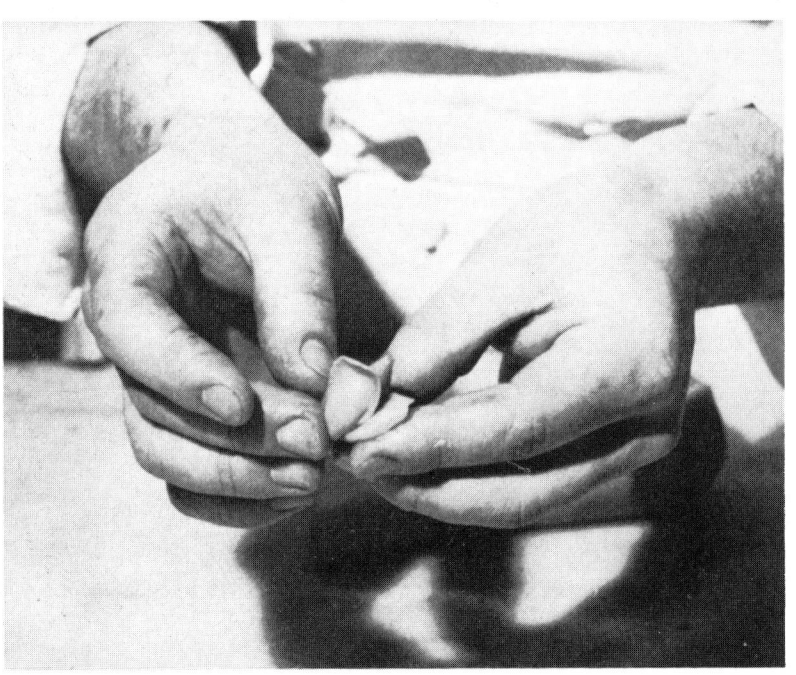

Attach the second petal by first inserting one side under the free side of the first. Bring both together and gently turn down the thin top edges with the fingers. The centre bud is now complete.

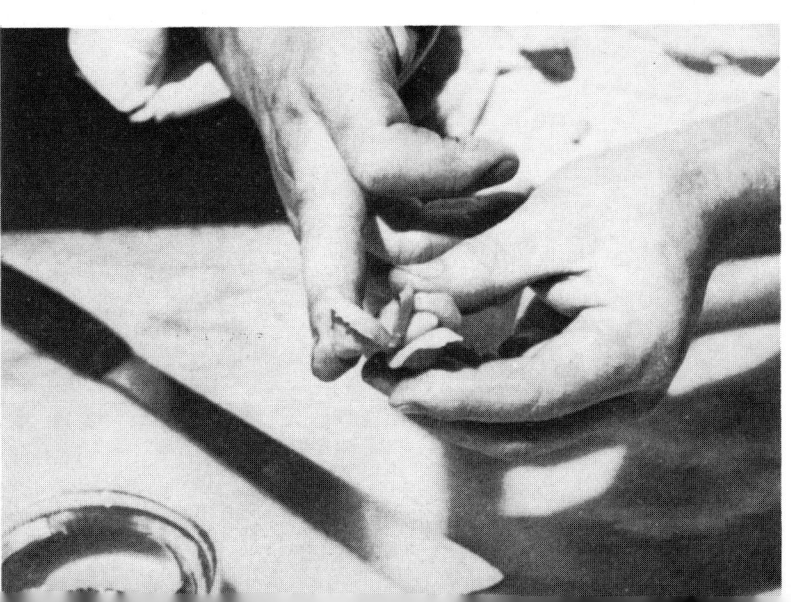

Make more petals but slightly larger. Always work with an uneven number of petals—three for the bud, followed by three a little larger for a medium size rose. Five more will make a large rose.

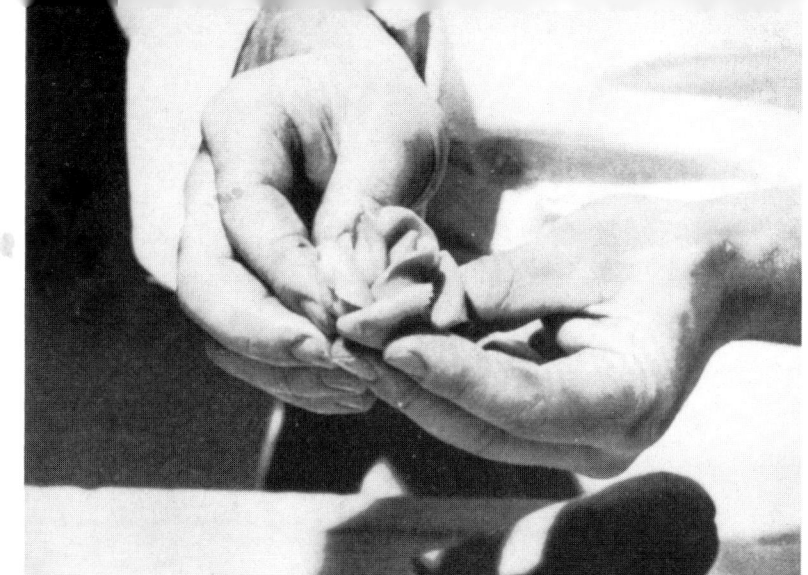

Attaching the individual petals.

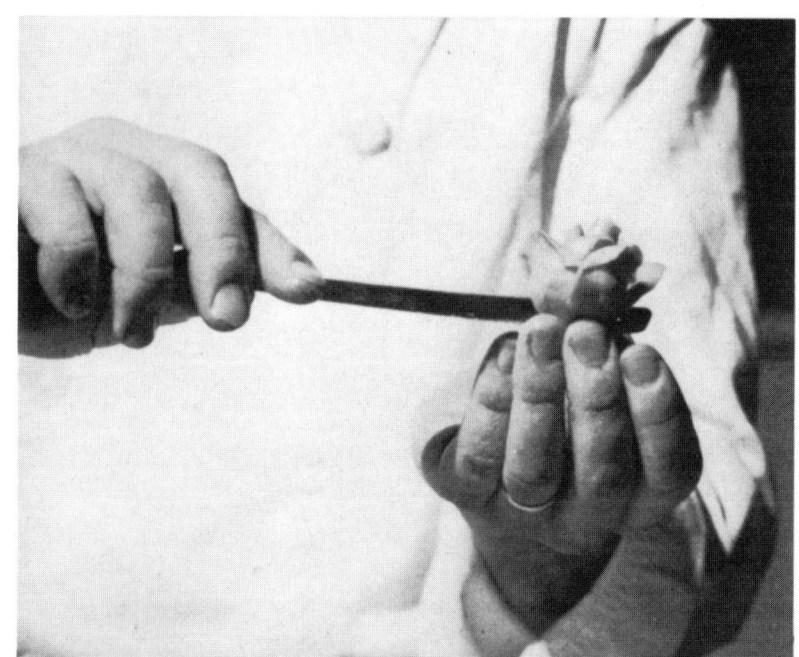

Cutting the finished rose off the base.

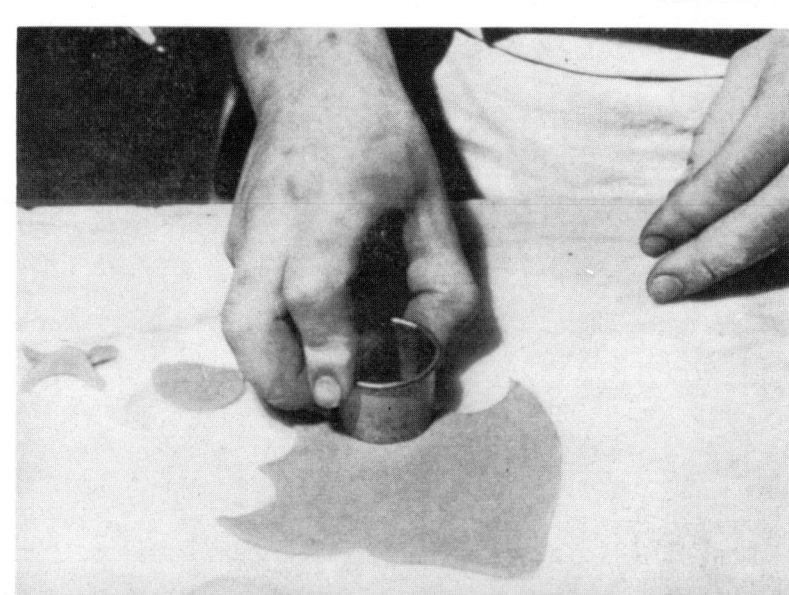

For the leaves, pin out marzipan thinly and cut out oval shapes.

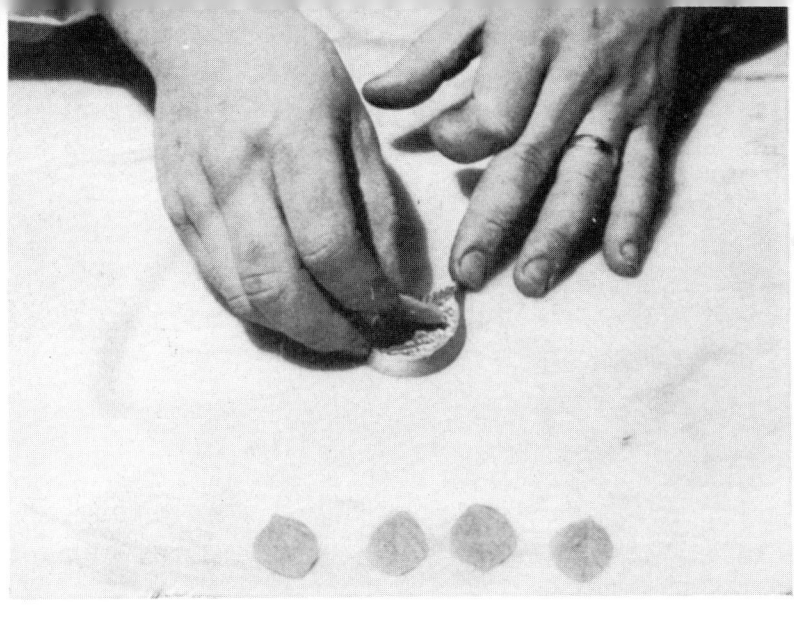

Press gently into a leaf mould.

Sugar Boiling
(*See also pages 50–52*)

Boil the sugar and water in a pan.

Remove the scum from the surface with a skimmer.

Wash down the side of the pan repeatedly with a brush dipped in water. This is to remove any sugar crystals.

Remove the last of the scum with a small strainer.

Strain the sugar through a cloth into a clean pan.

Add the glucose.

Place the Réaumur thermometer into the boiling sugar solution.

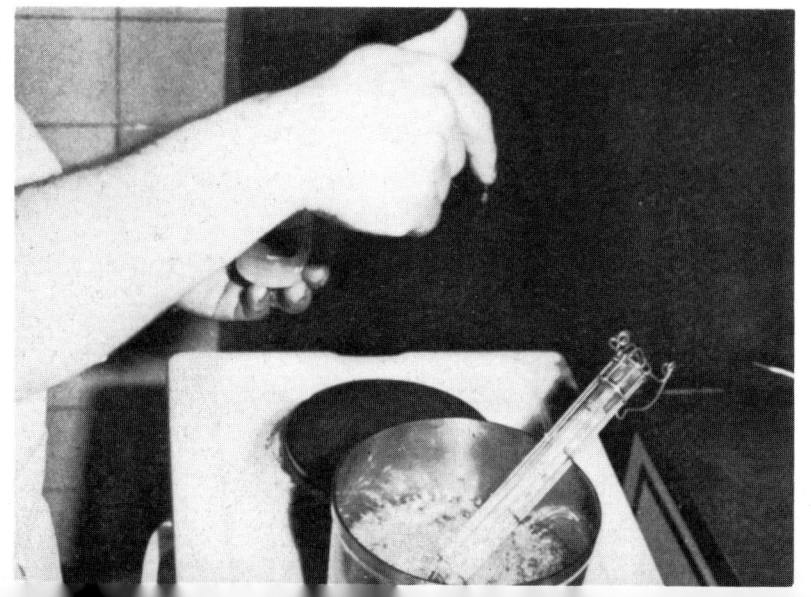

When it registers 110–112° R, add the cream of tartar.

At 122–124° R, stop further temperature rise by placing the pan in iced water for a moment.

Set aside for a short time until the sugar has reached the consistency of treacle.

Return to the heat and stir gently for a short time.

Pour on to a lightly oiled marble slab in long strips.

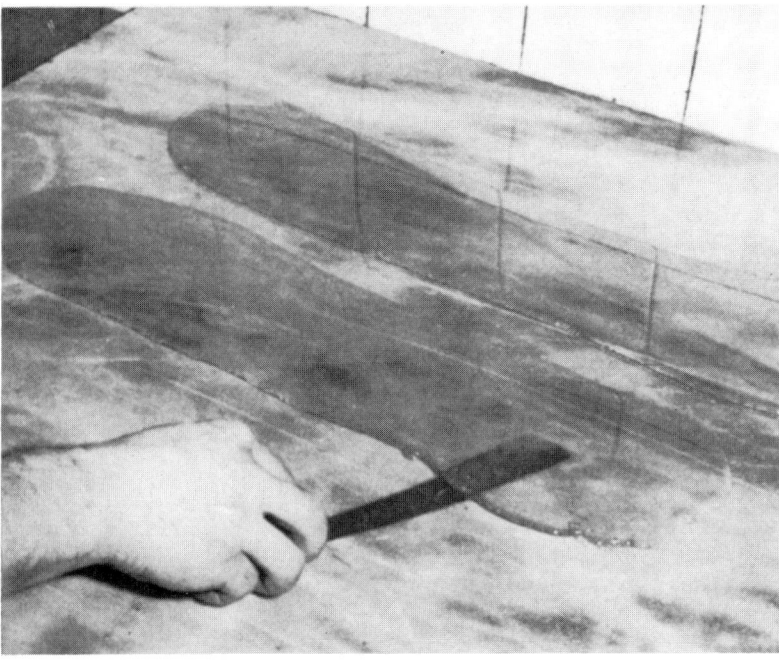

Detach the strips from the marble slab with a palette knife.

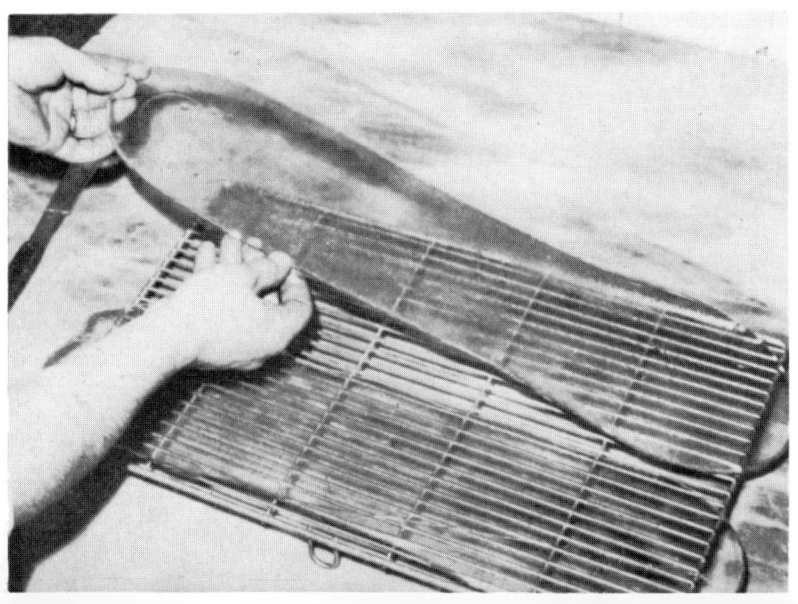

Leave them on a wire tray to cool thoroughly.

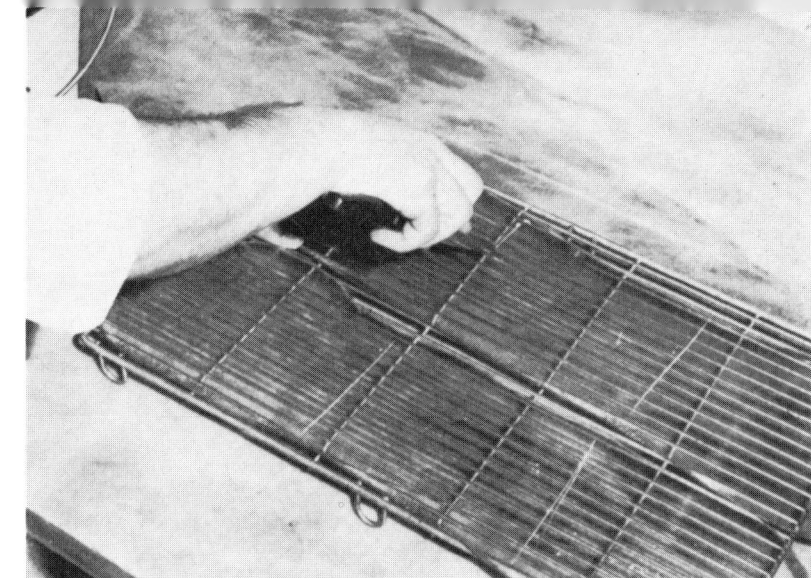

Score with a knife to the desired size to avoid splintering when breaking the sugar.

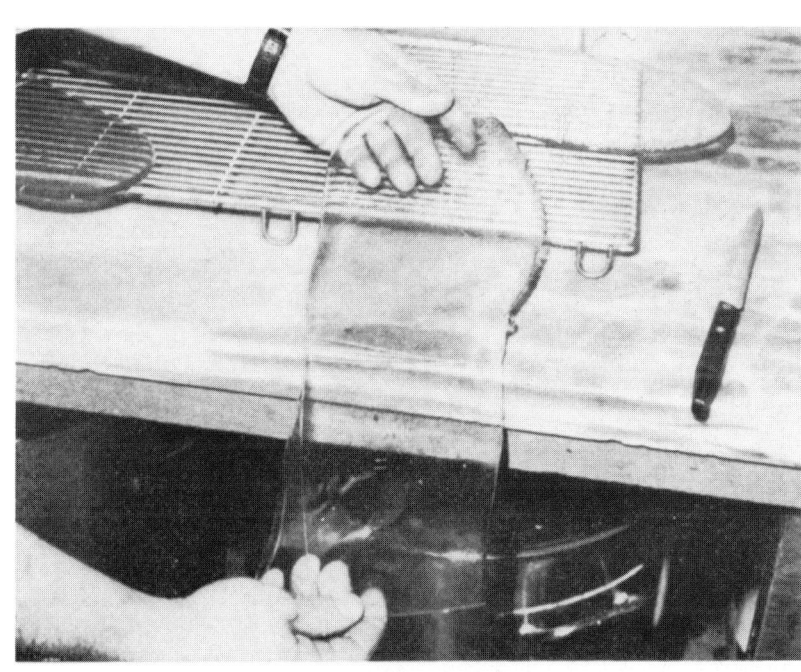

Breaking against the edge of the table along the score marks.

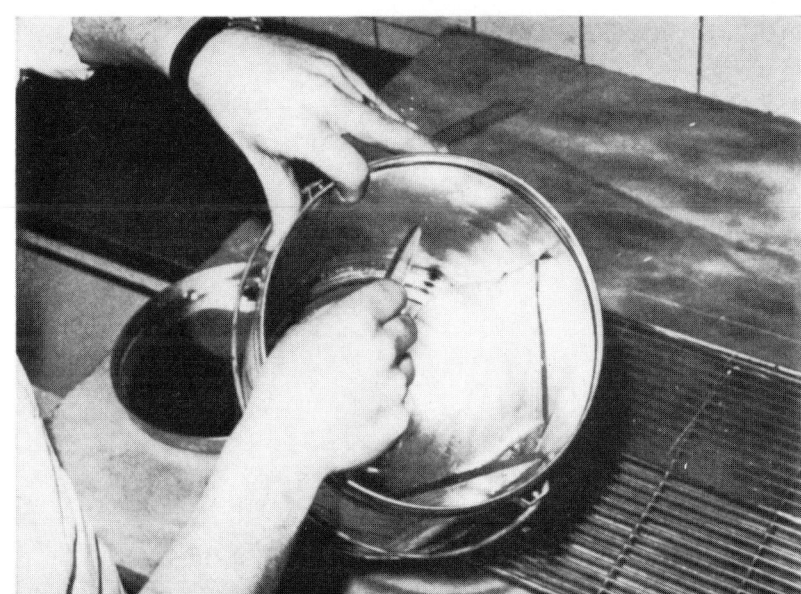

Store in a lightly oiled airtight container until required.

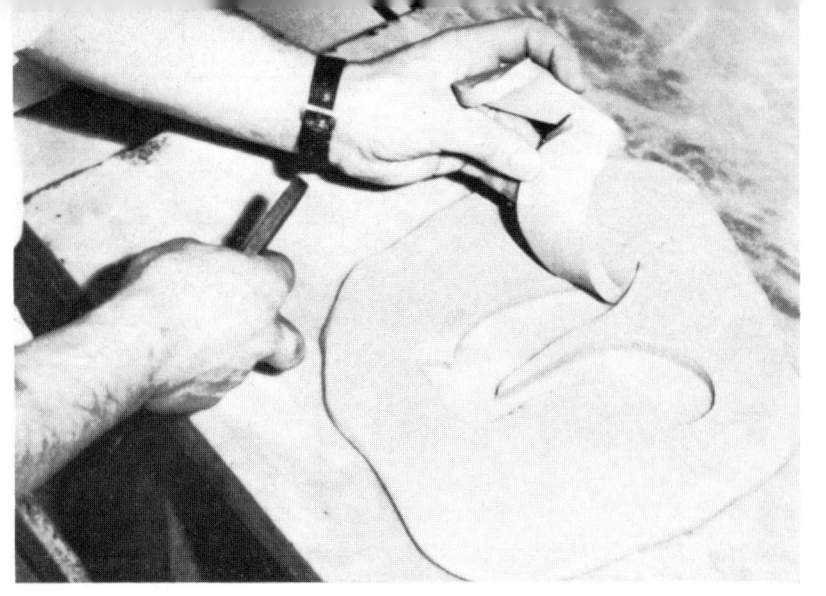

For casting small figures, pin out plasticine to about ½–¾ in. (1½–2 cm.) thick. Cut out the desired figure with the point of a knife and remove. Lightly oil the cut edges of the outline and the marble in the centre, so that the sugar does not stick when poured in and it has set.

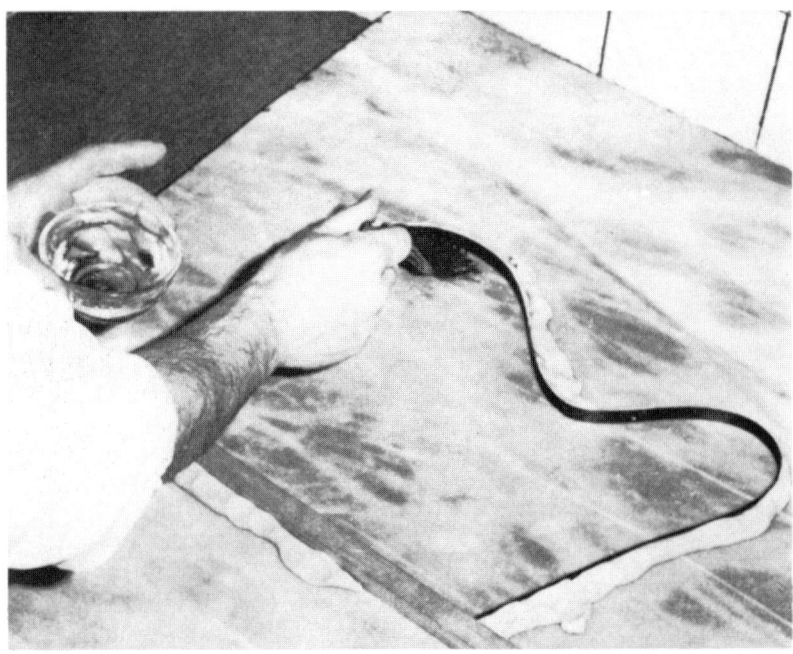

For larger pieces, use strip metal. Before pouring in the sugar, reinforce the outer edge with plasticine, and lightly oil the inside of the strip and the marble.

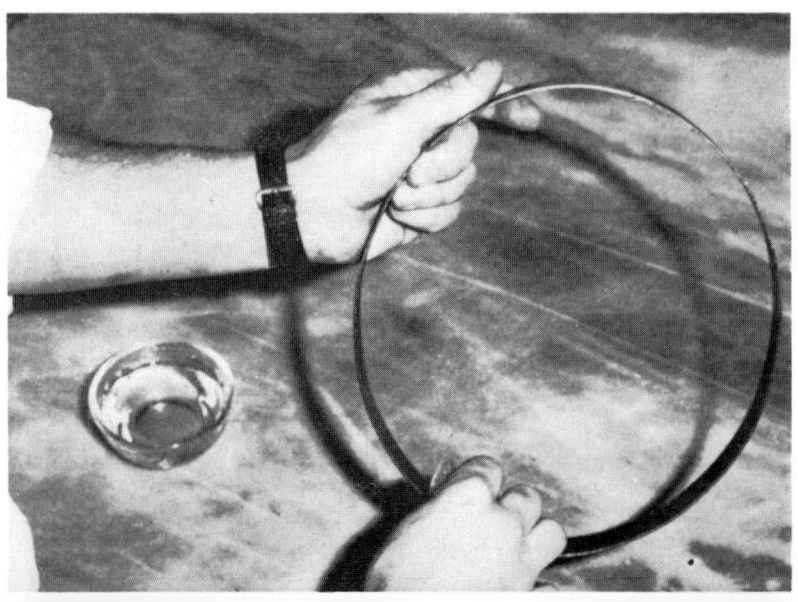

To make stands for baskets, figures, etc., use a lightly oiled flan ring. Proceed as above.

If only one colour is to be used, add it when straining the sugar. If several colours are required, divide the sugar into portions. Mix the colour with very little water.

Wait four or five minutes, depending on thickness, before removing the sugar from the mould or flan ring and detaching it from the slab with a palette knife. If this is done too soon, air bubbles will result.

Pulled Sugar

(*See also page 643*)
Decoration of a praline croquant basket.

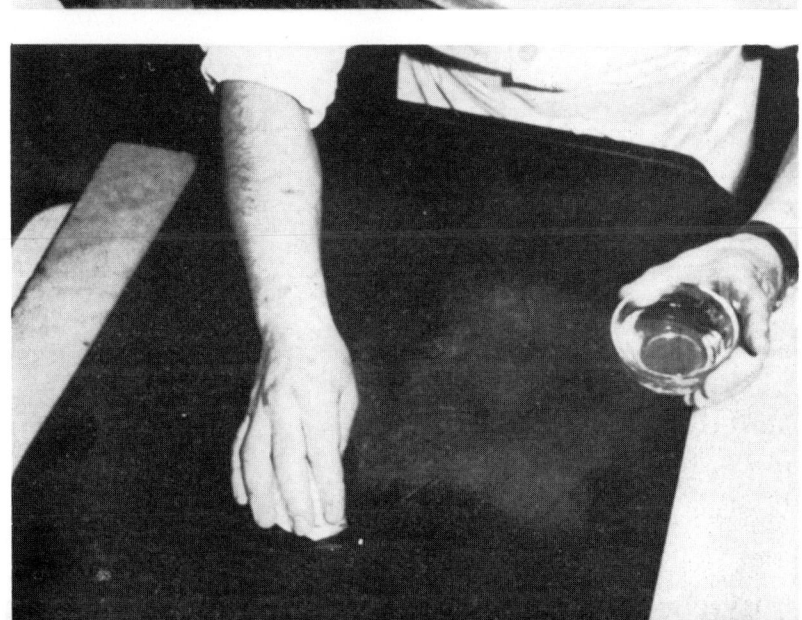

Oil a tray lightly.

153

Place on the tray as much boiled sugar as required and set into an oven that has been warmed a little.

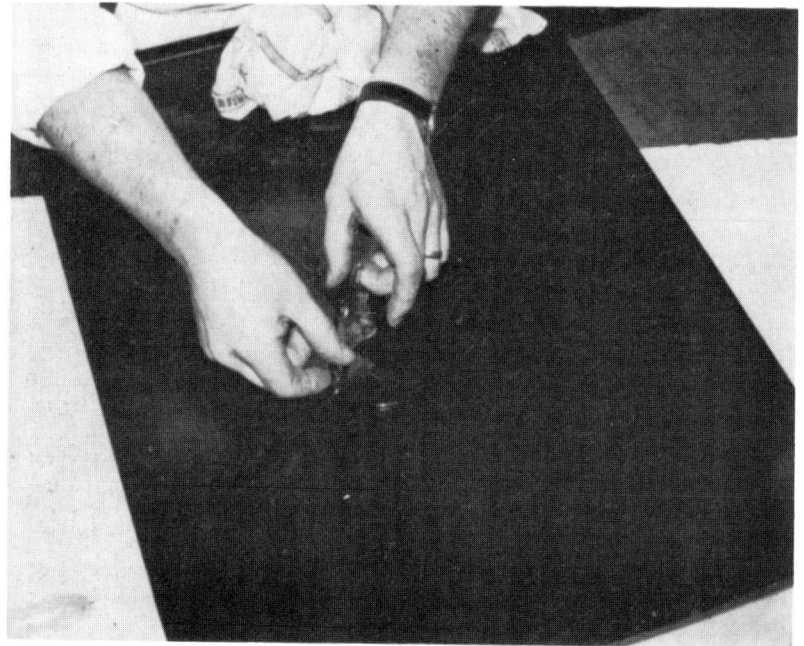

Remove from the oven and place the piece of sugar under a lamp.

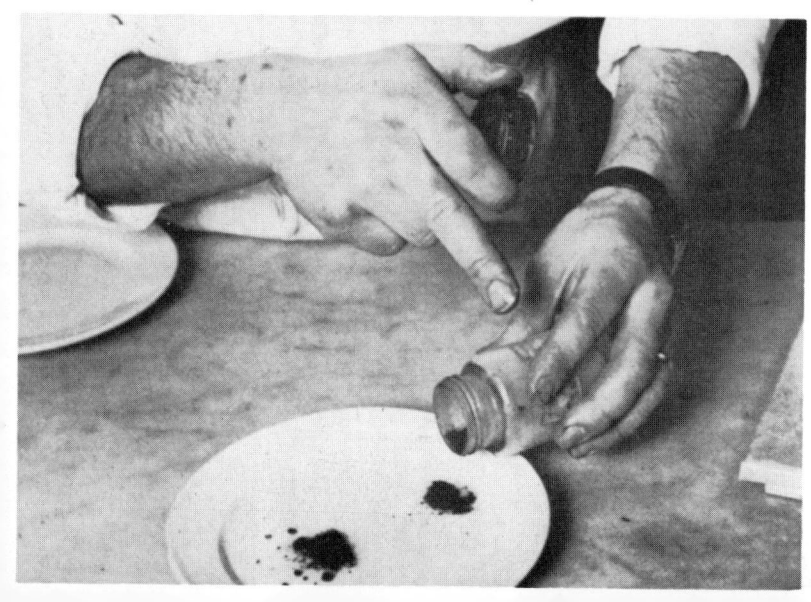

Blend the powdered colour with a little water or kirsch.

Spread the colour lightly on the sugar.

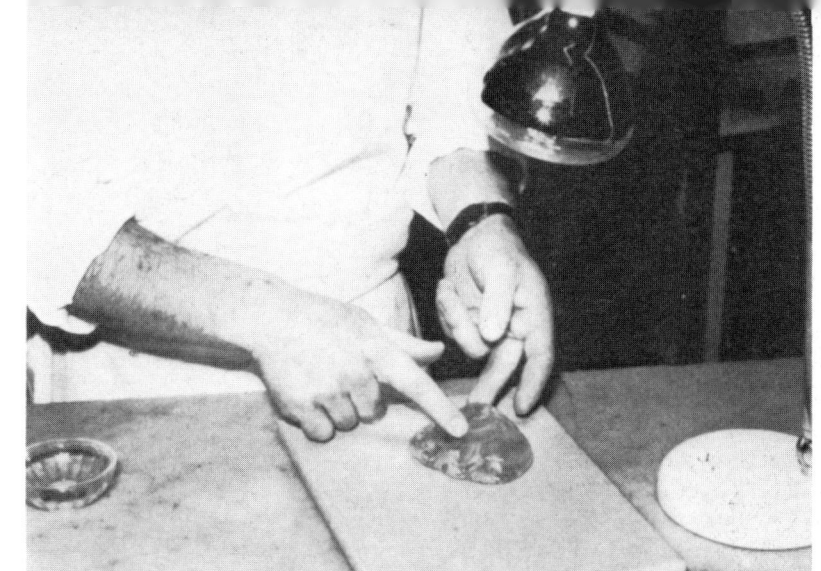

Fold the colour into the sugar.

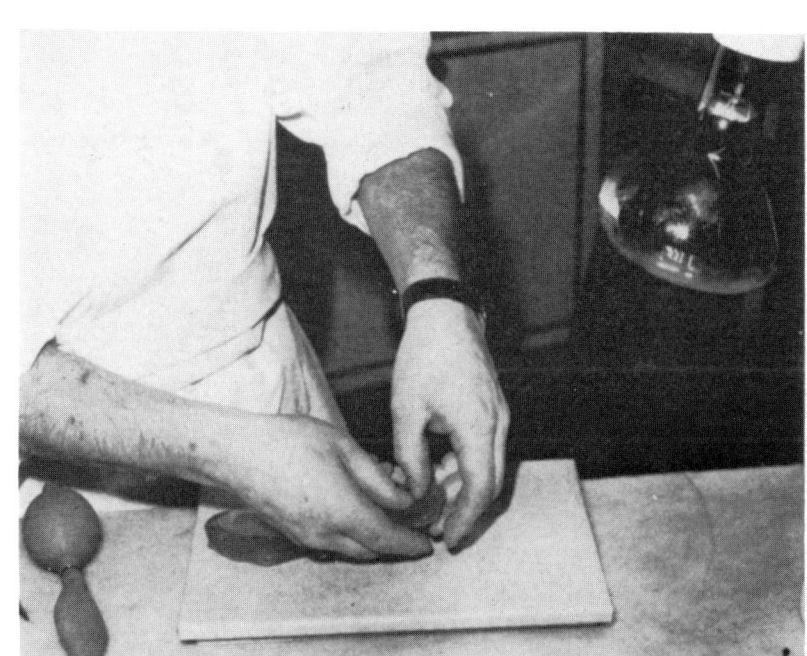

Distribute the colour evenly.

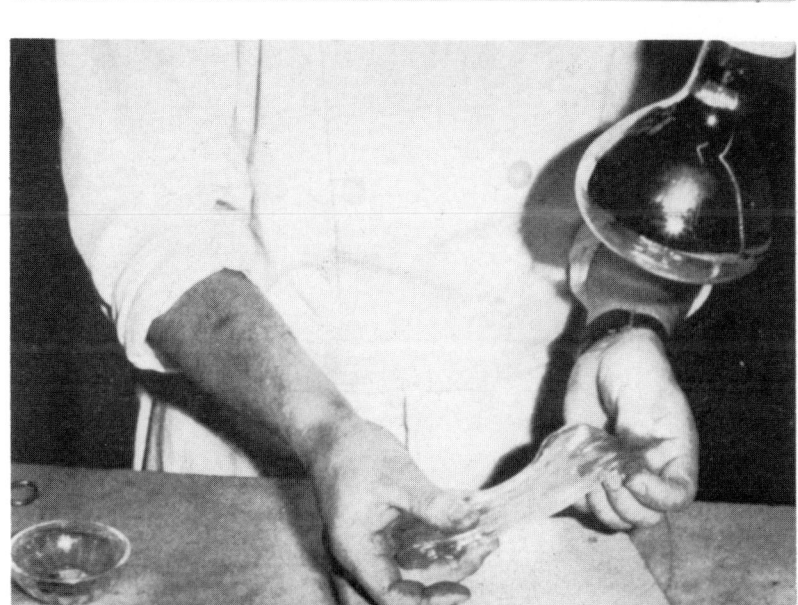

Mould the sugar into a ball.

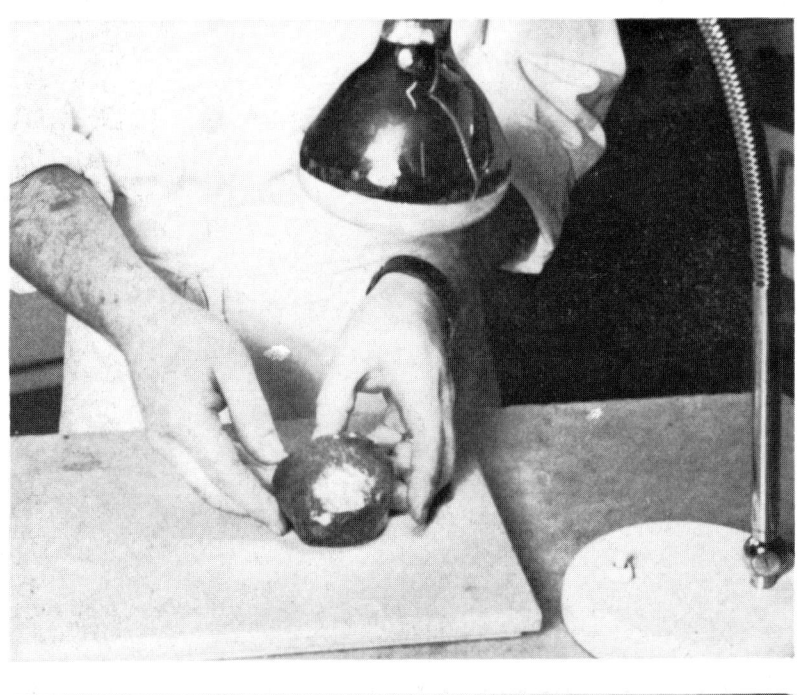

Place it under the lamp ready to fashion roses, leaves, etc.

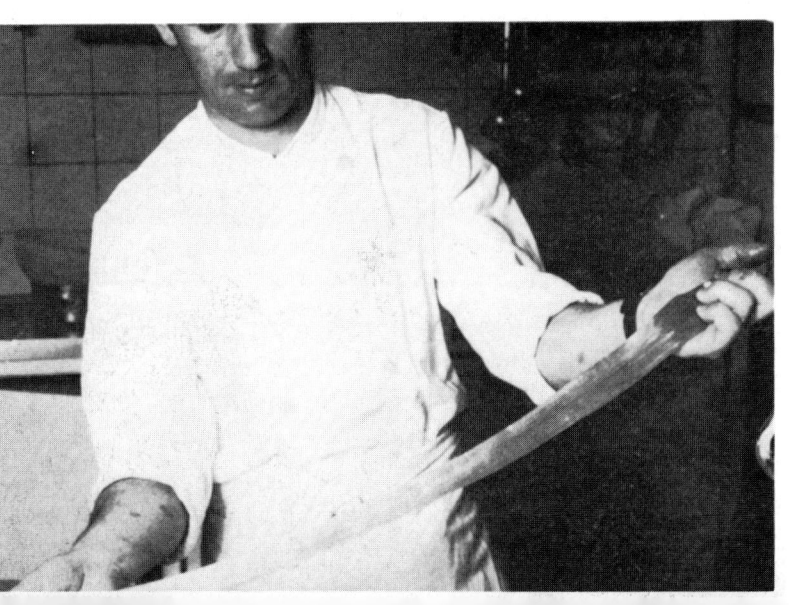

Pull a long uniform strip from the sugar.

156

Fold it in half.

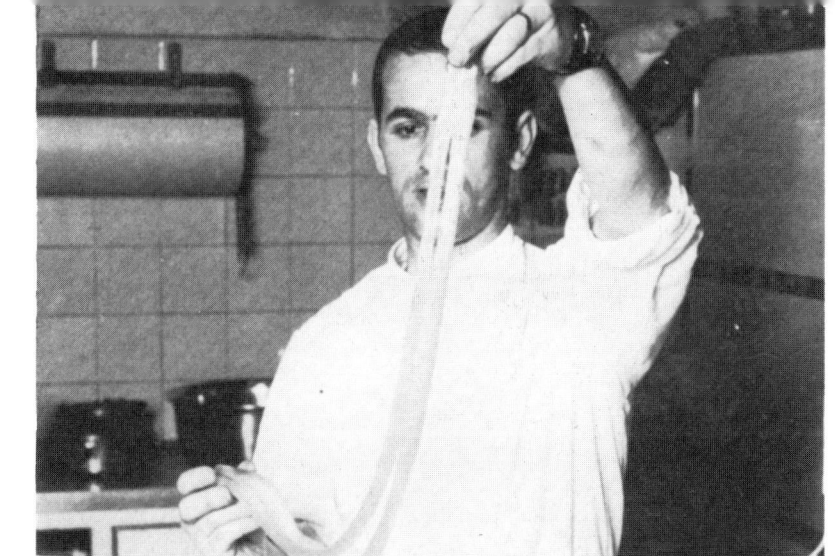

Twist it and then pull again.

Repeat this procedure.

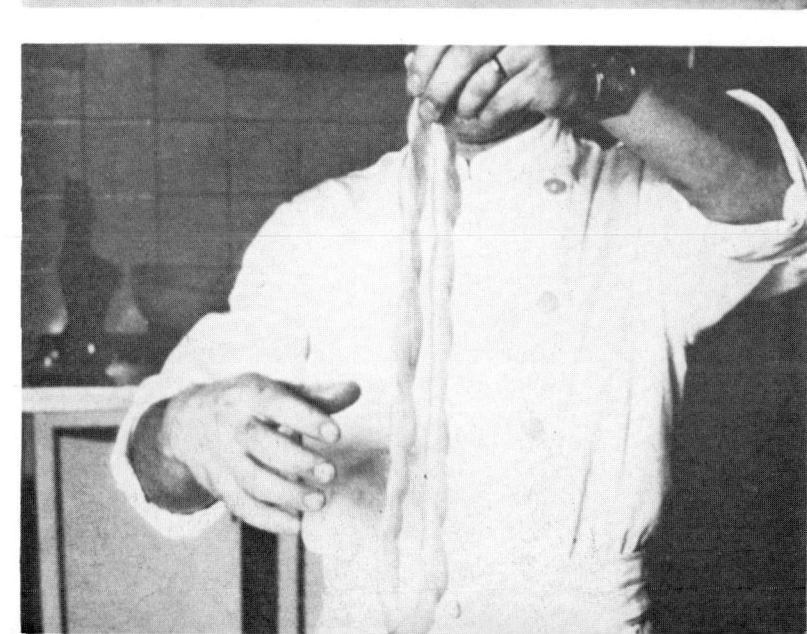

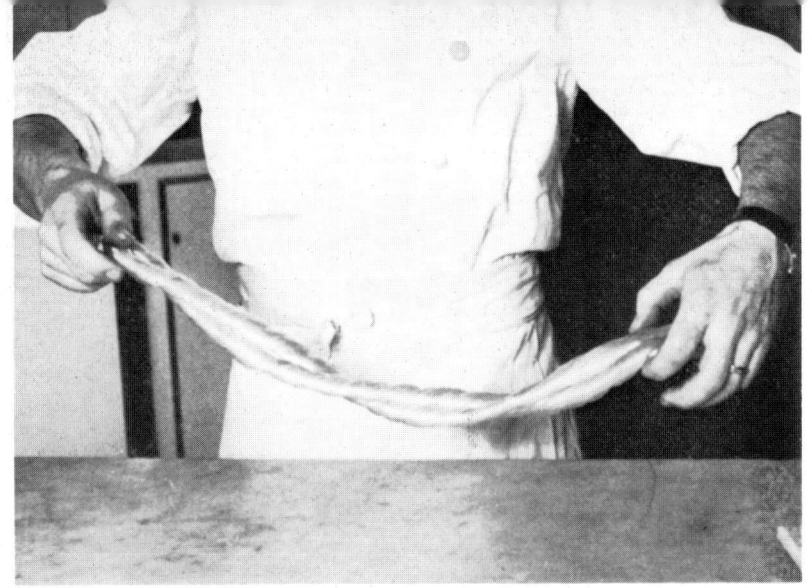

When the rope is of uniform thickness.

twist again.

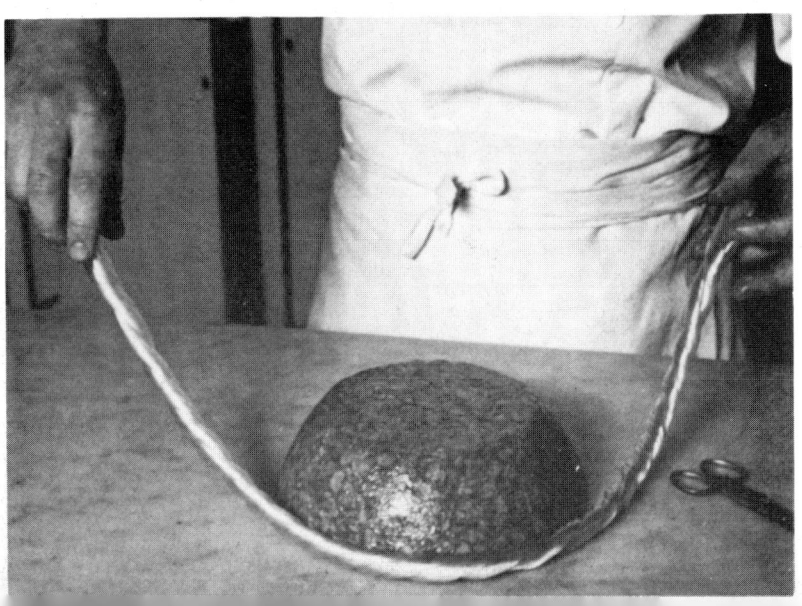

A stand is made by pressing praline croquant (*page 213*) into a lightly oiled basin. Lay the rope of pulled sugar round the prepared stand.

158

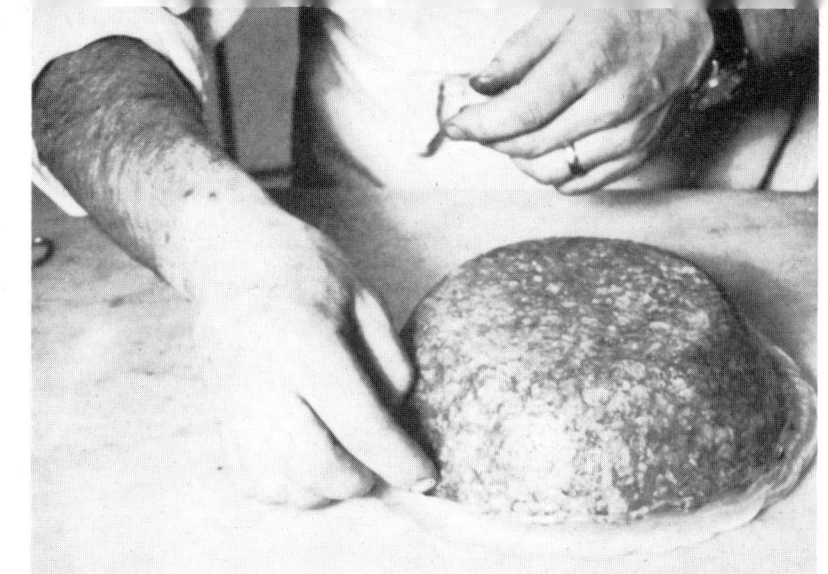

Fix it into position with a little warm sugar.

Cut off the surplus.

Fix a second praline croquant shell in position on top with a little warm sugar.

159

Edge with a twisted rope of pulled sugar.

Make and fix a handle of praline croquant.

Fill the empty basket with cellophane.

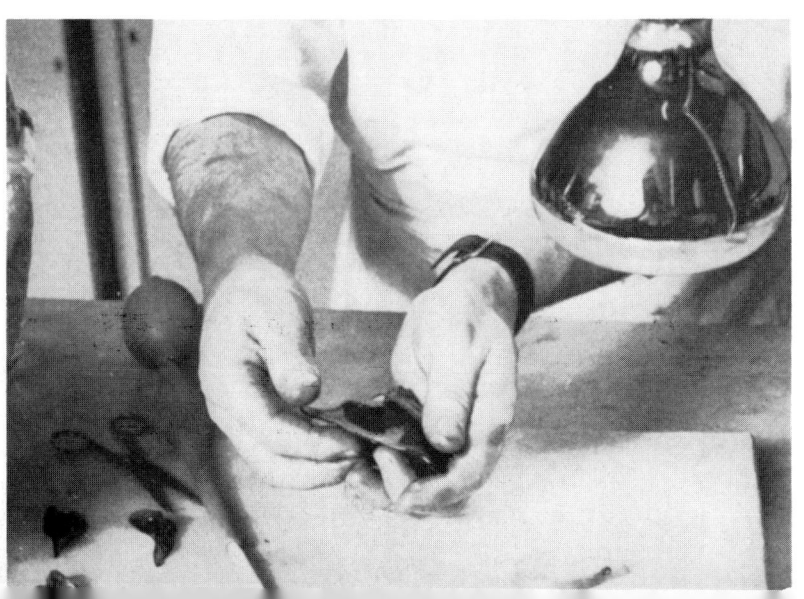

For pulled sugar leaves, pull out a piece of green coloured sugar to a fan shape between the thumb and forefinger.

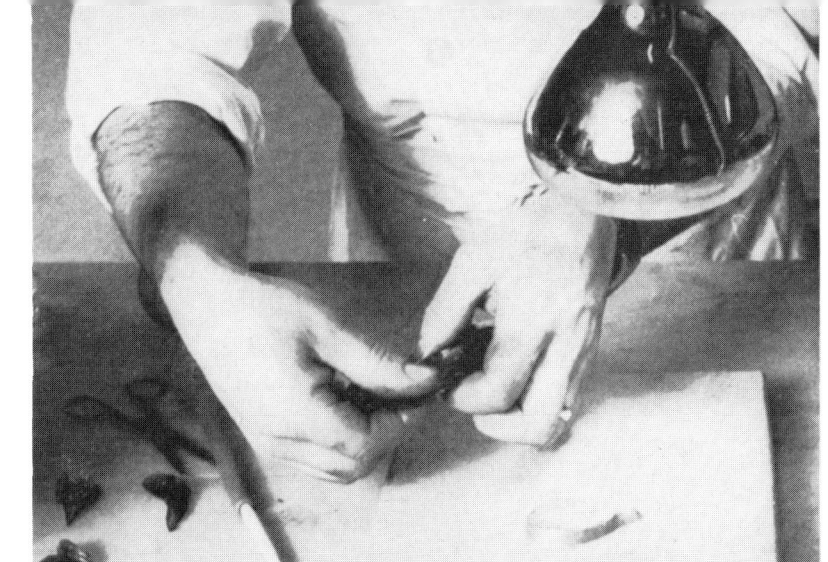

Pull off the leaves from the tapered ends.

Nip off with the forefinger and thumb.

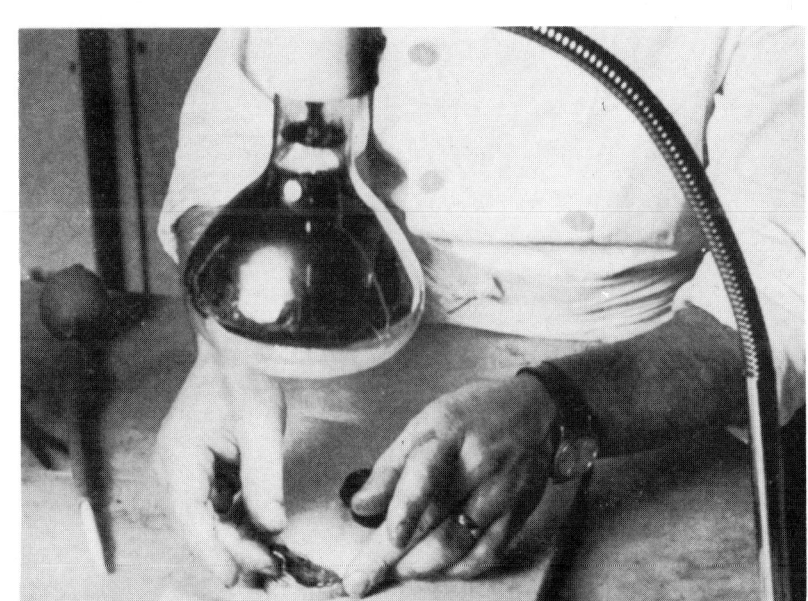

Press the pieces gently into a lightly oiled leaf mould.

161

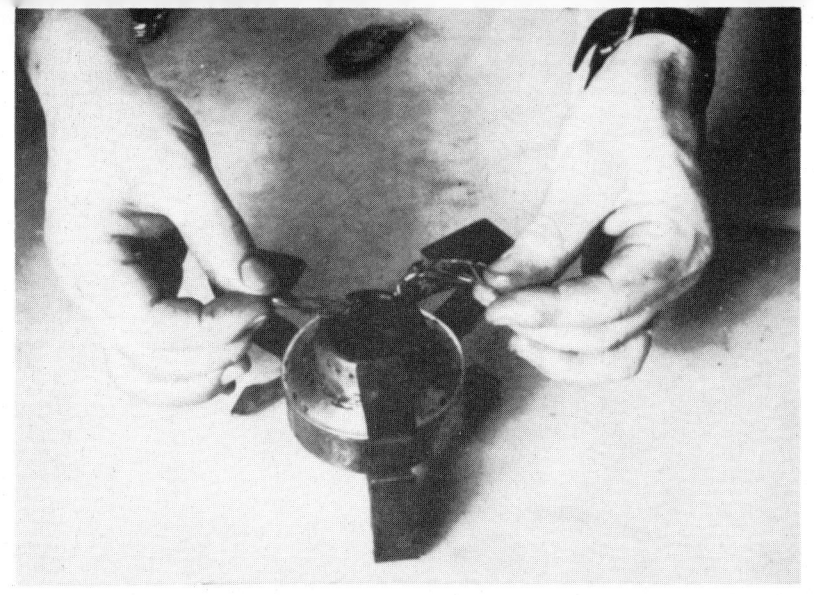

Warm the thick underside of the leaves a little over a spirit lamp and fix them to the basket, stems, etc.

Blown Sugar
(*See also page 645*)

Sugar blowing equipment.

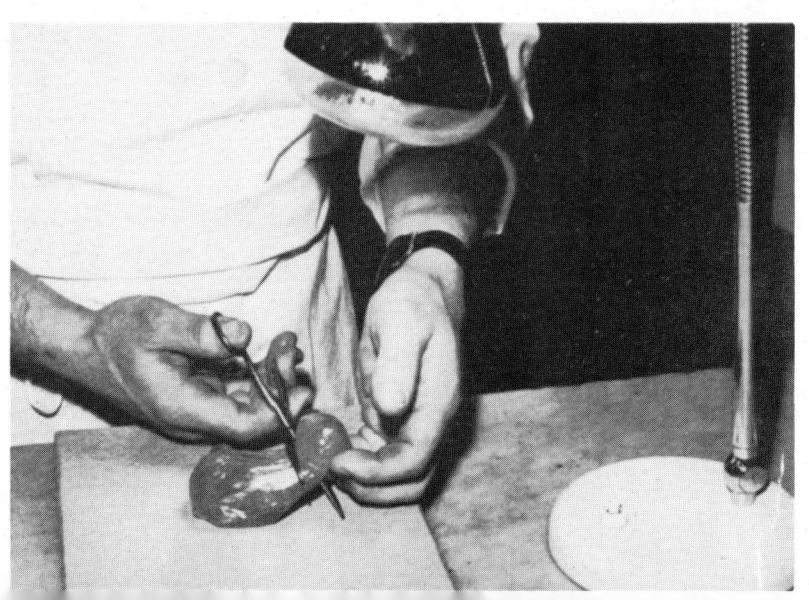

Blown sugar fruits.
I. BANANA
Cut off as much sugar as required.

162

Mould it into a ball and make a depression with the forefinger.

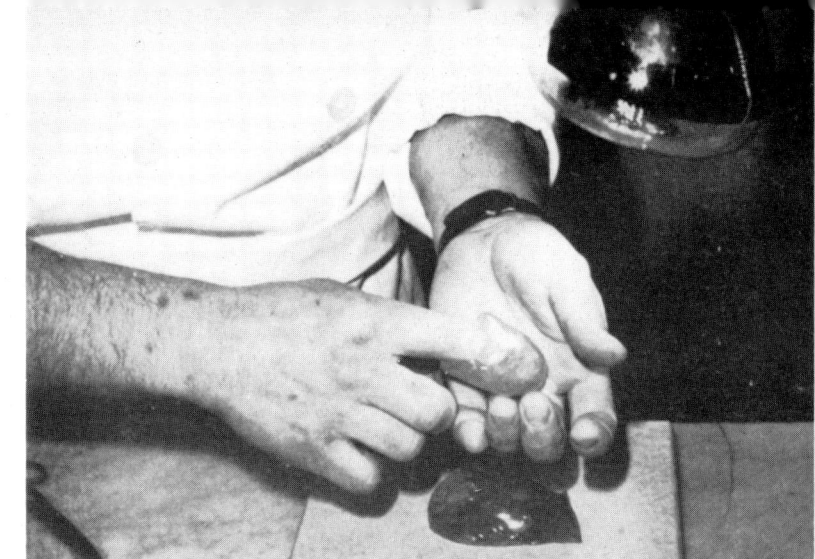

Insert the blowpipe into the depression and press the sugar round it well.

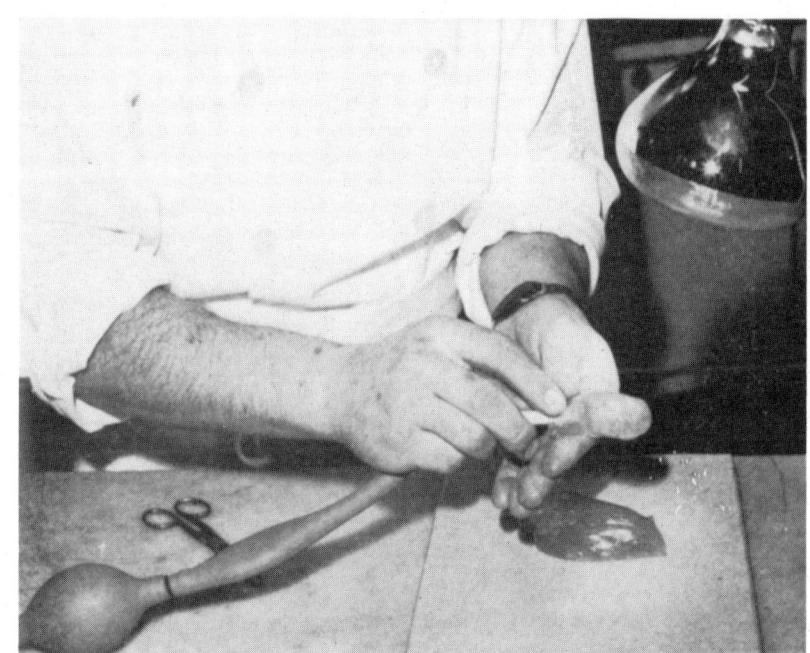

After blowing in a little air, stretch the sugar slightly.

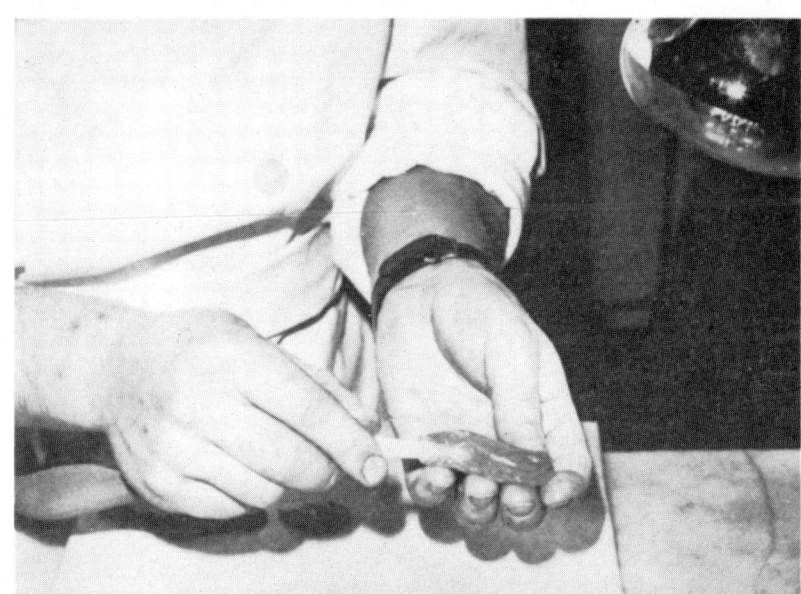

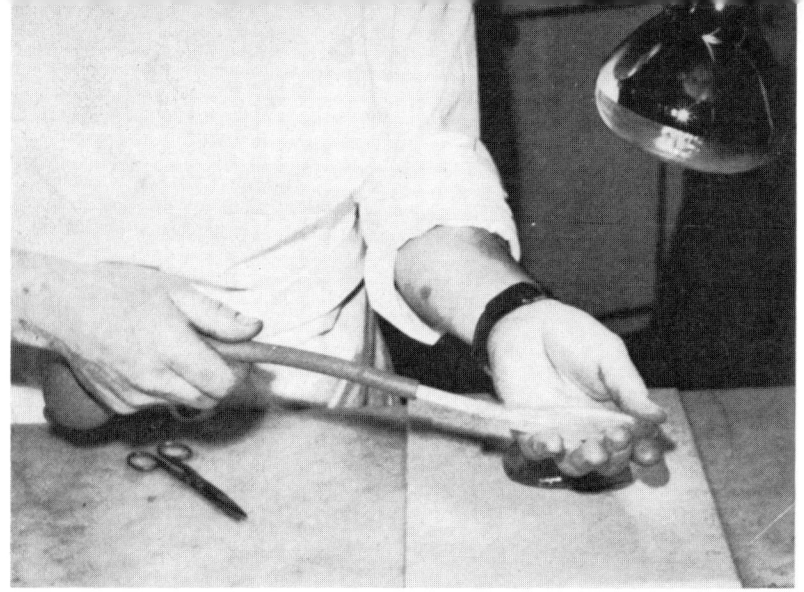

Keep on blowing in air with one hand while gently stretching the sugar with the other.

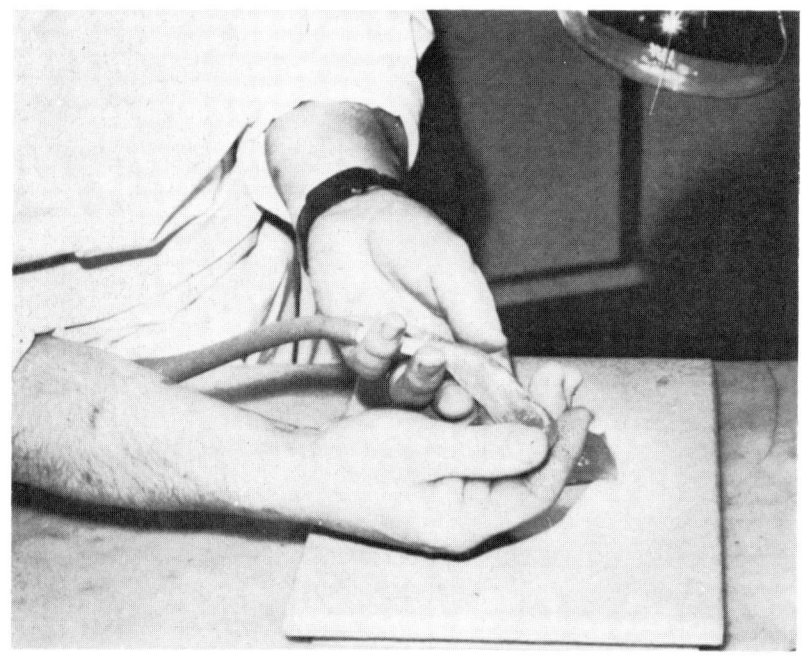

Then shape the banana, making it slightly curved.

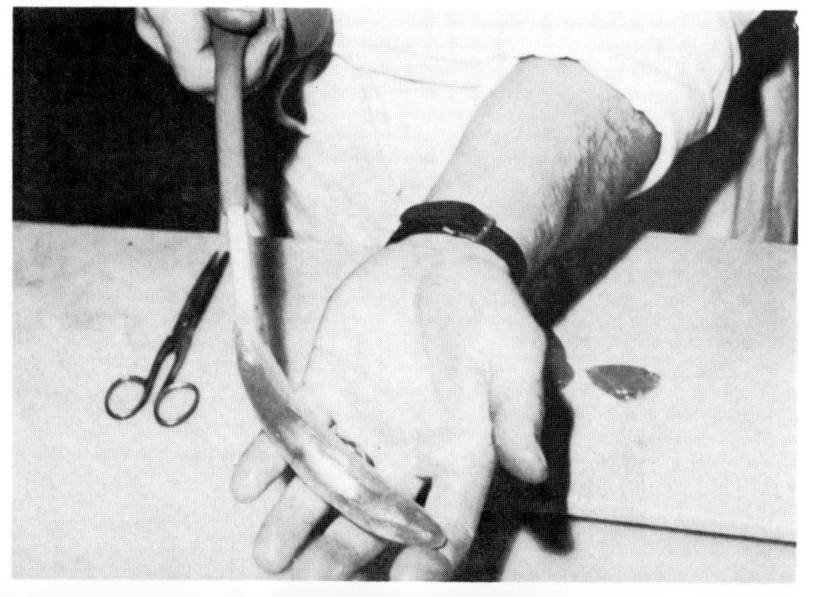

Carefully detach the sugar from the blowpipe at the point of insertion.

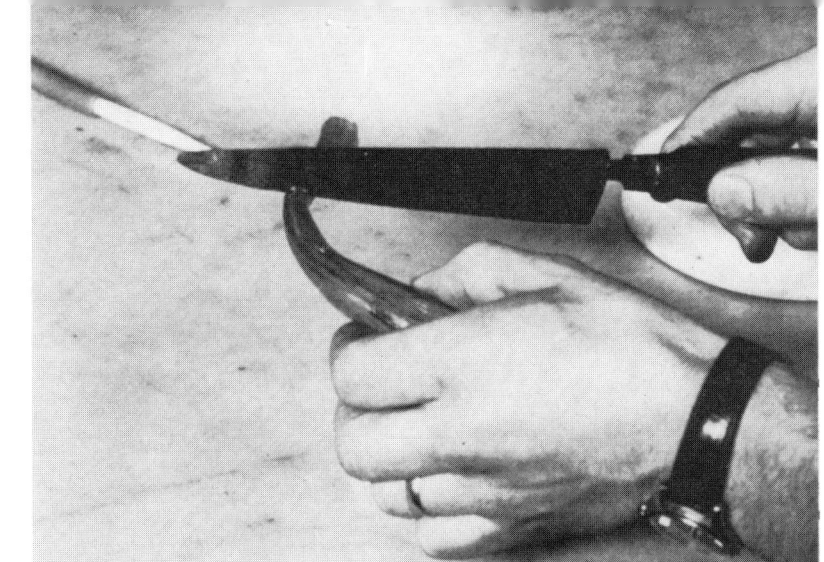

Alternatively, cut with a hot wire or knife.

Painting the banana.

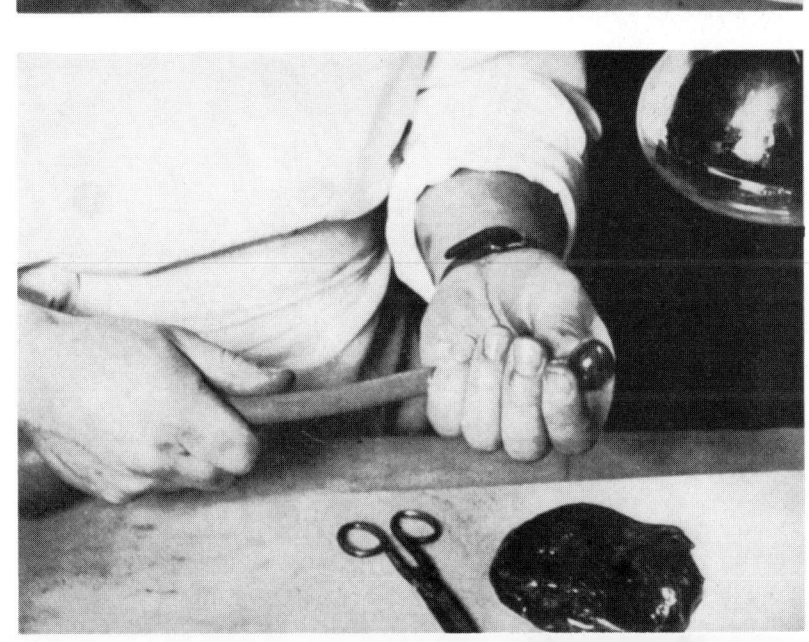

Blown sugar fruits.
II. BUNCH OF GRAPES
Blow each grape separately.

165

Place each grape on the neck of a bottle to cool.

Assemble to form a bunch.

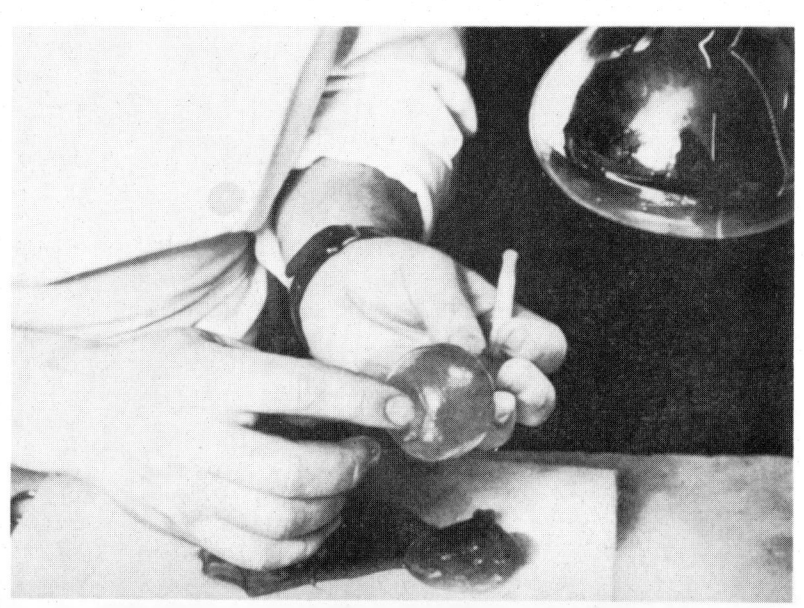

Blown sugar fruits.
III. PEAR
Blow and stretch the sugar to the shape of a pear. Make a depression for the calyx.

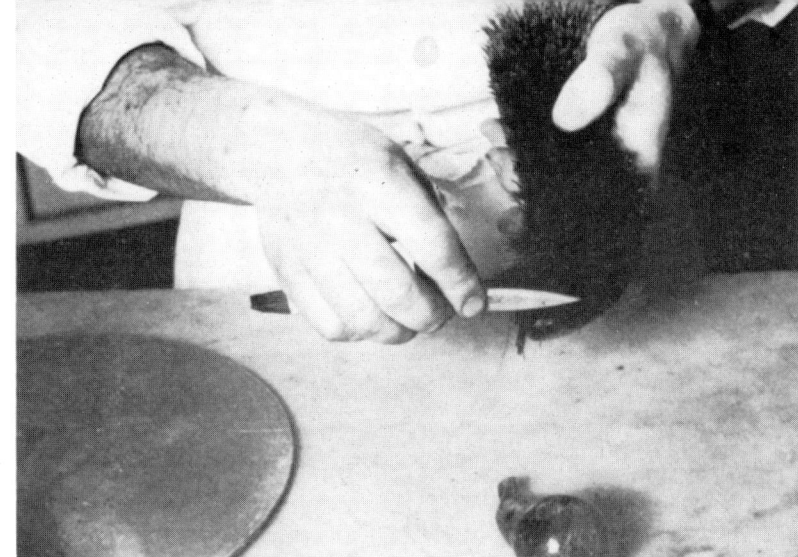

Paint the pear and speckle with colour. This is done by wetting the bristles of a brush with the desired colour and drawing a knife along the bristles towards the body. The specks of colour will fly forward. Insert the calyx in the depression.

Assembling the Basket of Fruit
Take particular care to achieve a harmonious combination of colours.

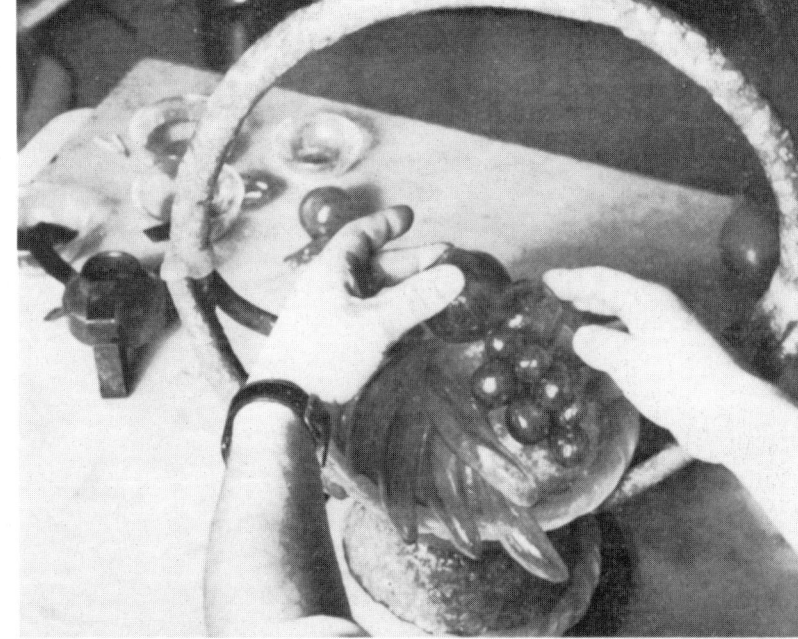

Fill the basket with blown bananas, grapes, pears, apples, plums, etc. and add a few leaves to fill the spaces.

Pulled Sugar Ribbons

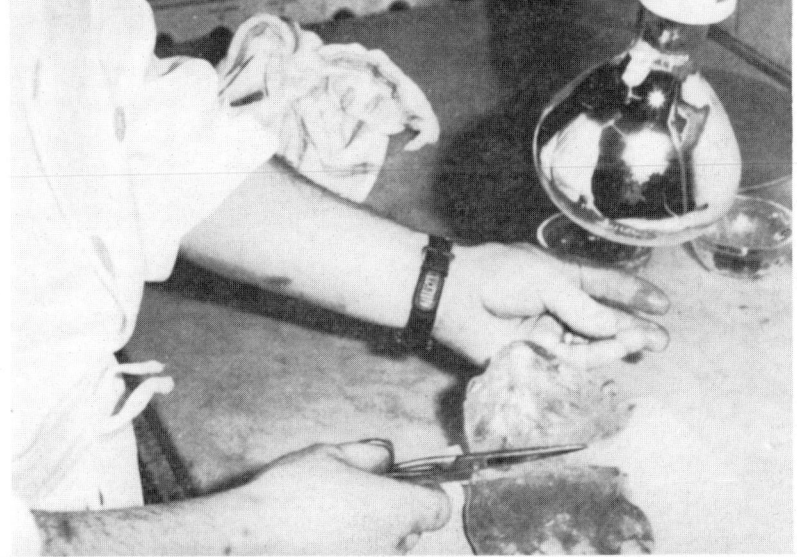

Colour three fifths and two fifths of the sugar respectively.

167

Shape into long strips and divide into two or three pieces.

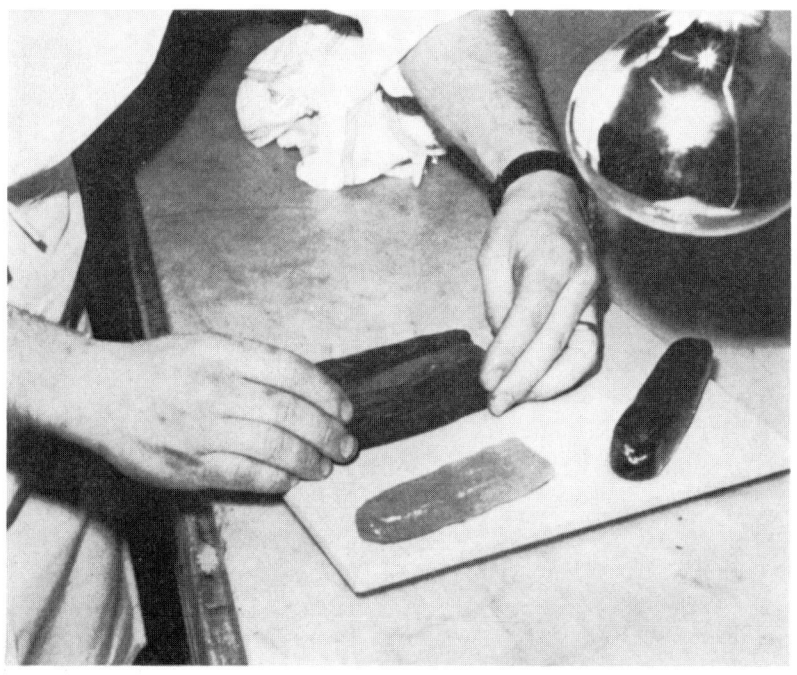

Start off with blue/yellow, blue and yellow/blue.

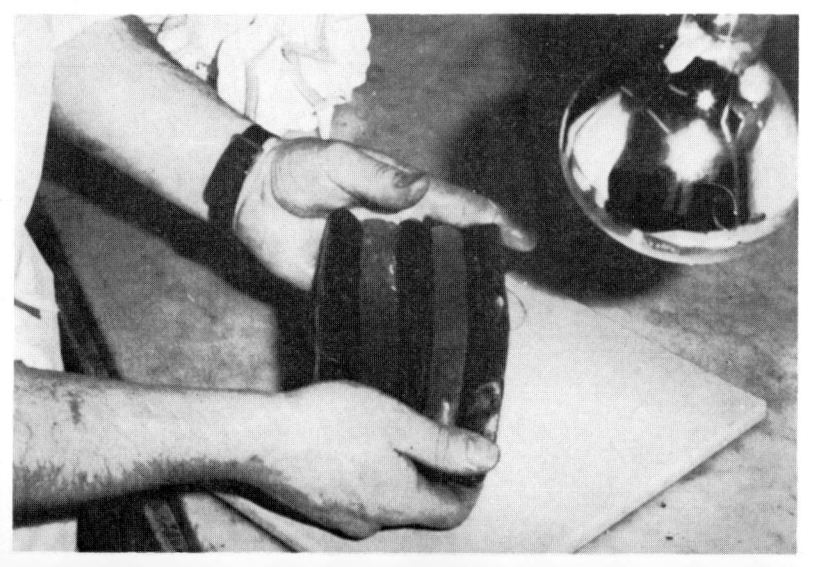

Make sure to warm the sugar right through.

Oil the underside of a baking sheet lightly, pre-heat in the oven, place the sugar on it and warm through in the oven.

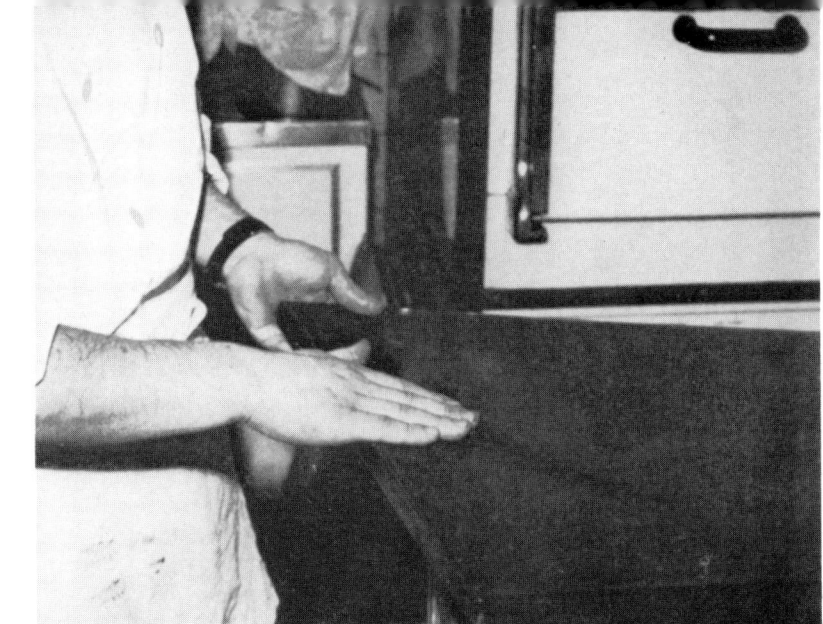

Commence pulling and continue until the strips of colour are of uniform width.

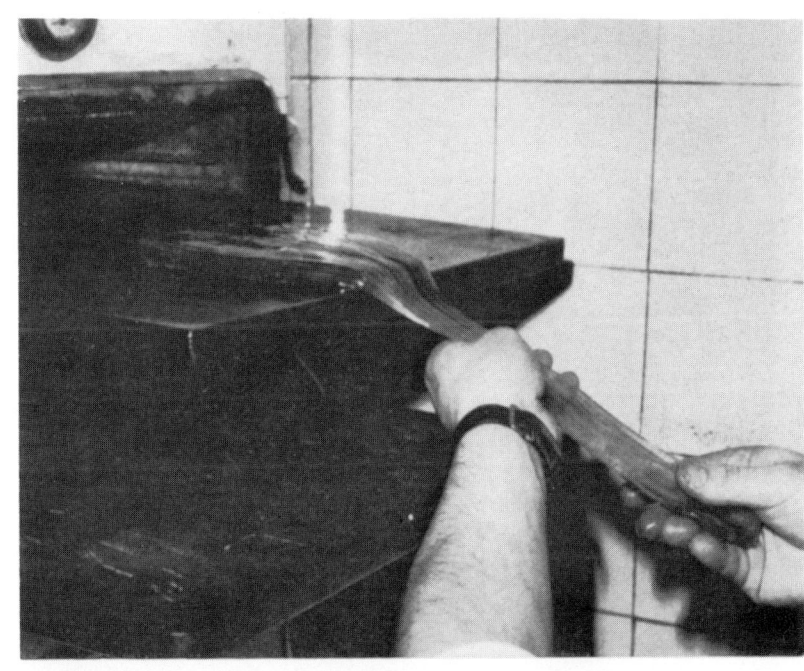

Pull carefully.

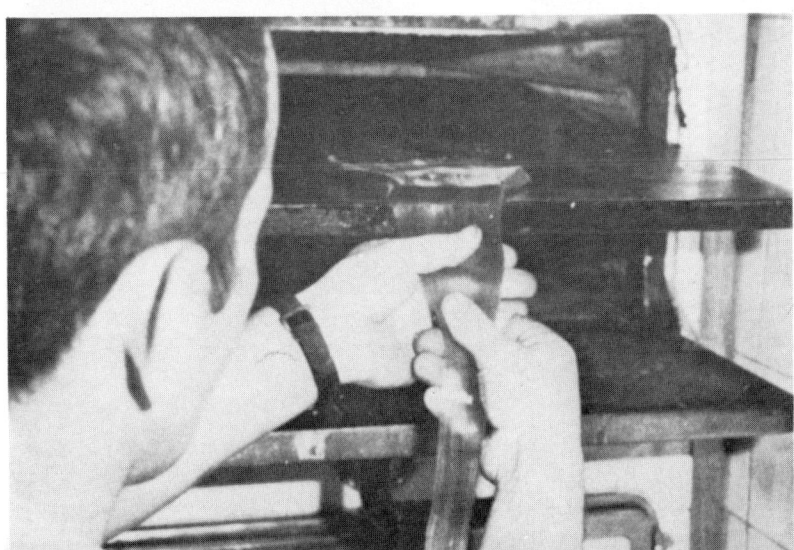

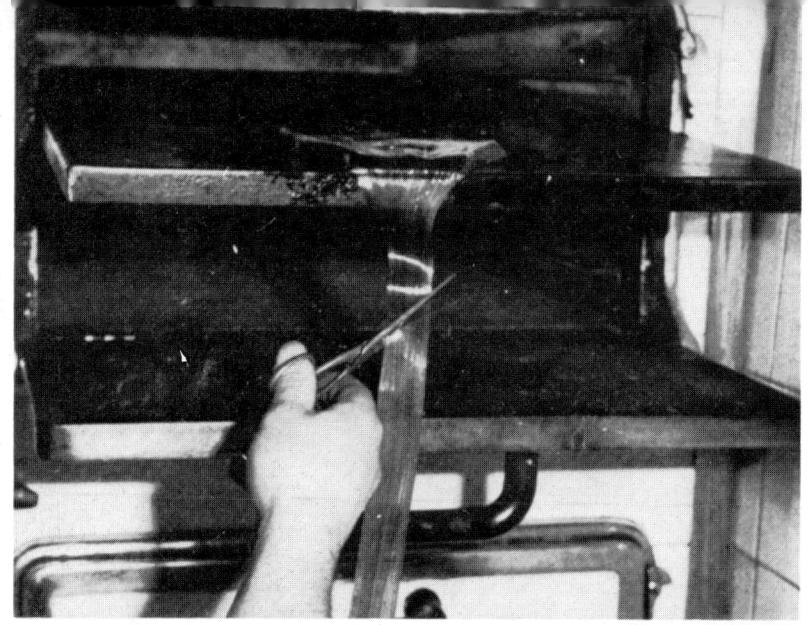

Cut off with scissors.

Drape the ribbon round the basket handle.

Pleat the ends neatly.

Pulled Sugar Bows

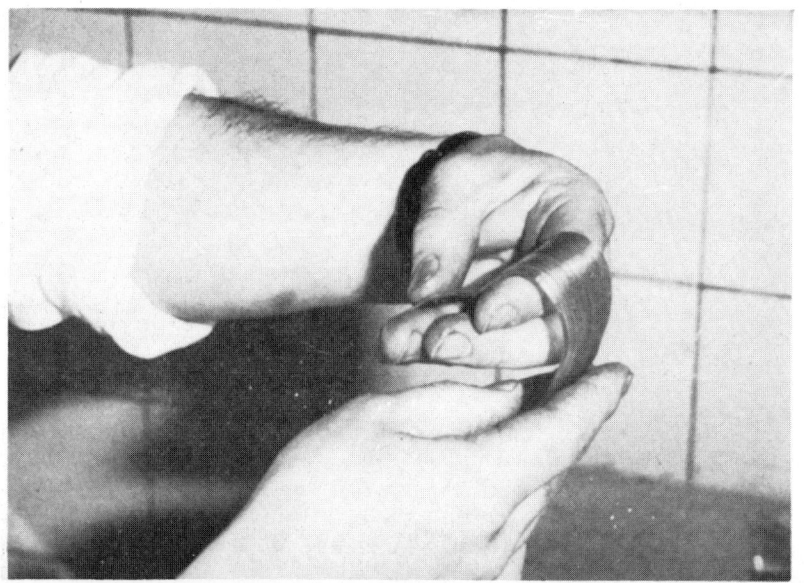

Pull the sugar into uniform ribbons and cut off at 4–6 in. (10–15 cm.) depending on the size of bow desired. Drape the ribbon over the fingers as illustrated.

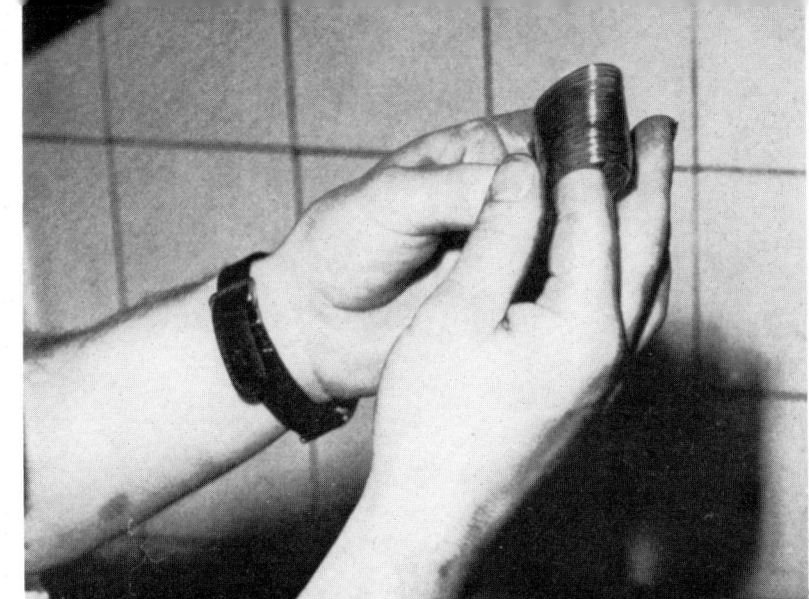

Shape neat loops with the forefinger.

Lay them on their edges to cool. Lightly oil ice cream coupes or moulds, warm the lower end of the loops over a spirit lamp.

Assemble in the lightly oiled coupes.

Assembling the bow.

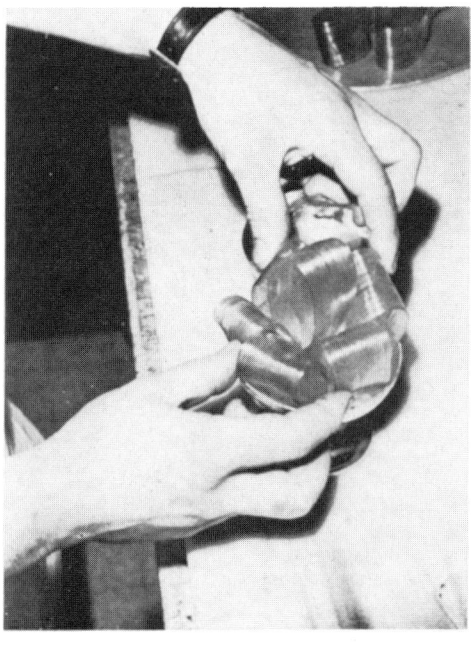

The completed bow.

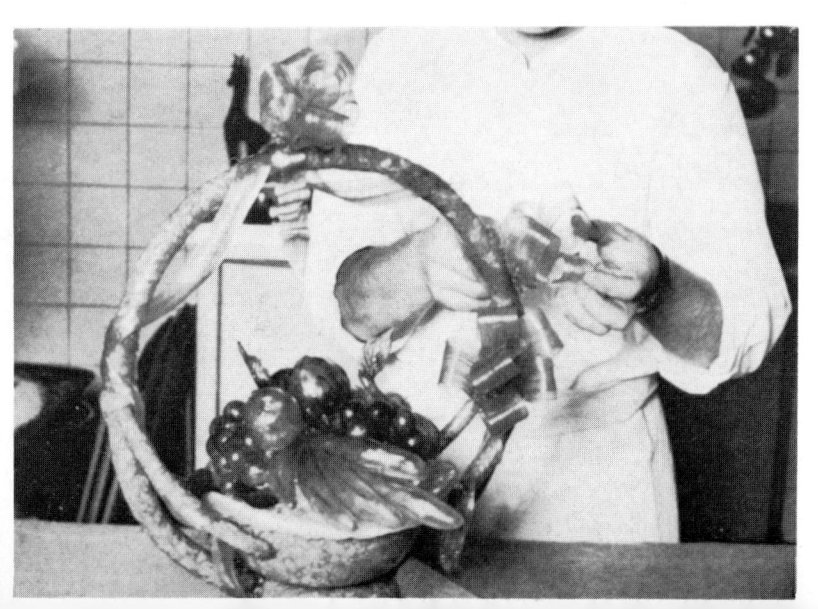

Fixing the bow on to the basket of fruit.

172

VI. Basic Preparations

Fermented Doughs

A basic fermented dough contains but four ingredients, flour, yeast, salt and water. If fat is added and the water (or part of it) is replaced by milk, then the dough becomes enriched.

As the fat content is increased and sugar and eggs are added the product ceases to be bread and becomes a bun. It can be said that when the product is no longer neutral in flavour and cannot be enjoyed with savoury foods, then it ceases to be bread.

There are three fundamental methods of preparing fermented doughs; sponge and dough, ferment and dough and straight dough.

The sponge is a modern form of the old sour dough or barm method. (Panary Fermentation, *page 37*). A sponge is thicker in consistency as compared with a ferment; it is generally cooler and is allowed to ferment for many hours, even overnight. A sponge generally contains approximately equal amounts of liquid and flour, together with the yeast. Sponges intended for long fermentation usually contain salt also.

In Great Britain it is usual to use ferments with a shorter fermentation time. The quickest is known as a 'flying ferment' which consists of all, or part of the milk, the yeast, a little sugar and about 4 oz. (125 gr.) of flour to each 20 oz. (625 gr.) of milk. This is allowed to ferment for the time necessary to prepare the balance of materials for the dough. It is, in fact, a fermentation 'boost' in which the yeast gets an excellent opportunity for vigorous activity. Longer time ferments are similar in composition, except that the yeast content is lower. With other ferments it is not common practice to extend fermentation time beyond about an hour.

A sponge or a ferment will gradually rise as it becomes full of gas. Depending on temperature, time and yeast content, it will eventually collapse as the gluten structure becomes softened by the water and enzymic activity, and over-extended by gas. During this time an increase in the acidity takes place which has the effect of hastening the ripening of the subsequent dough.

There is a school of thought that will suggest that a ferment must collapse before it is made into a dough, whilst others would say that if the ferment is collapsed by the simple expedient of whisking it, then it will ripen the subsequent dough just as quickly. It is all a matter of degree and the experienced craftsman will experiment and make his own decision.

A ferment is considered of particular benefit when a fermented dough is heavily enriched. Fat and sugar will inhibit the speed of fermentation so that if the yeast can work in a preliminary environment without fat and excess sugar, such as in a ferment, then initially, it will be more active than in a straight dough system where it is in immediate contact with such inhibitors. A straight dough can of course be employed if extra yeast is used or extra time given for fermentation.

Fermented doughs should be kept covered always to prevent 'skinning' which will show as streaks in the finished product. Unless the doughs are to be placed into a refrigerator, chilling should be prevented and all tins and baking sheets warmed before use.

The prover should not be too hot and must be slightly humid to prevent skinning which will produce a thick crust and prevent even expansion.

Basic Bread Dough
Straight Dough Method

lb	oz		kg	gr
1	14	Flour (strong)		935
	$1/2$	Salt		15
	$3/4$	Yeast		22
1	0	Water (approx.)		500
2	8	Flour (strong)	1	250
	$3/4$	Salt		22
	1	Yeast		30
1	8	Water (approx.)		750
3	8	Flour (strong)	1	750
	1	Salt		30
	$1\,1/4$	Yeast		35
2	0	Water (approx.)	1	
7	0	Flour (strong)	3	500
	2	Salt		60
	$2\,1/2$	Yeast		75
4	0	Water (approx.)	2	
14	0	Flour (strong)	7	
	4	Salt		125
	$4\,3/4$	Yeast		140
8	0	Water (approx.)	4	

Dough temperature 80° F (26.7° C). Knock back at 1 $1/2$ hours. Scale at 2 hours. Bake at 480° F (250° C). To enrich this dough $1/4$-$1/2$ oz. (10-15 gr.) of fat can be added to each 1 lb. 14 oz. (935 gr.) flour. The water (or part of it) can be replaced by milk. A proportion of the water or water/milk can be replaced with egg.

Sugar at the rate of $1/8$ oz. (4 gr.) for each 1 lb. 14 oz. (935 gr.) of flour can be added.

Enriched Bread
Sponge and Dough Method
Sponge

lb	oz		kg	gr
1	4	Water		625
	1	Sugar		30
	$1\,3/4$	Yeast		50
1	0	Flour (strong)		500

Dough

lb	oz		kg	gr
2	0	Flour	1	
	$2\,1/2$	Butter		75
	$3/4$	Salt		20
	5	Milk (approx.)		150

Sponge temperature 74° F (23.5° C). Allow to stand for 1 hour.

To make the dough rub the butter into the flour, dissolve the salt in the milk and stir both in the sponge. Add the flour and mix thoroughly. Scale after 30 minutes. Bake at 460° F (238° C).

Enriched Tea Bread
Straight Dough Method

lb	oz		kg	gr
1	4	Flour (strong)		625
	$1/4$	Salt		8
	2	Butter		60
	$3/4$	Sugar		20
	2	Egg		60
	1	Yeast		30
	9	Milk (approx.)		270

Finish the dough at 80° F (26° C). Knock back at 1 hour. Scale at 1 $1/2$ hours. This dough is suitable for plaited shapes. Bake at 450° F (232° C).

Straight Dough for Plaiting

lb	oz		kg	gr
5	0	Flour	2	500
	1 1/2	Salt		45
	3	Yeast		90
	1/2	Malt extract		15
	3 1/2	Egg		100
	9	Butter		270
2	4	Milk (approx.)	1	125

The dough should be 75° F (24° C) when made and it will be ready at 1 hour.

Basic Roll Dough

lb	oz		kg	gr
2	4	Flour	1	125
	3/4	Salt		20
	1 1/2	Lard		45
	2	Yeast		60
	1/2	Malt extract		15
1	7	Water (approx.)		710

Dough temperature 80° F (26° C). Dough ready for scaling at 30 minutes.

(Switzerland)

Basic Dough for Plaiting
Sponge

lb	oz		kg	gr
1	2	Flour		560
	1/2	Yeast		15
1	2	Water 55-60° F (12-15° C)		560

Dough

lb	oz		kg	gr
3	12	Flour	1	875
	1 1/2	Salt		45
	3/4	Malt extract		20
	3 1/2	Egg		100
	9	Butter		270
	2	Yeast		60
1	2	Milk (approx.) 70° F (21° C)		560

The sponge is allowed to stand overnight.

The dough is ready 15 minutes after making. *(Switzerland)*

Basic Dough for French Bread

lb	oz		kg	gr
3	8	Flour	1	750
	1 1/2	Salt		45
	1 1/2	Lard		45
	2	Yeast		60
2	4	Water (approx.) 40° F (4.5° C)	1	125

The dough is well mixed for 5 minutes, given a rest for 5 minutes and well mixed again so that it is well developed. It is ready for scaling after 1 1/2 hours.

(Switzerland)

Basic Bun Dough
Flying Ferment and Dough

Ferment

lb	oz		kg	gr
1	4	Milk 110° F (43° C)		625
	1/2	Sugar		15
	2	Yeast		60
	4	Flour		125

Dough

lb	oz		kg	gr
2	2	Flour (approx.)	1	60
	5	Butter		150
	6	Sugar		180
	4	Egg		125
	1/4	Salt		8

For fruited buns add 8 oz. (250 gr.) currants and 2 oz. (60 gr.) peel. Add flavour as desired.

The ferment after mixing is allowed to stand whilst the dough materials are assembled. The dough is made by rubbing the butter into the sieved flour. The sugar, salt, eggs and the desired flavour are added and mixed with the ferment and the whole is thoroughly mixed. Any fruit should be warmed and added at the knock back. The dough is knocked back at 45 minutes and it is ready at 1 1/4 hours.

Basic Bun Dough
Straight Dough Method

lb	oz		kg	gr
2	6	Flour	1	185
	1/4	Salt		8

lb	oz		kg	gr
	5	Butter		150
	6	Sugar		180
	2	Yeast		60
	4	Egg		125
1	4	Milk (approx.)		625
		Flavour as desired		

For fruited buns add 8 oz. (250 gr.) currants and 2 oz. (60 gr.) peel.

Dough temperature 82° F (28° C). Knock back at 60 minutes and the dough is ready at 90 minutes. The fruit should be warmed and added at the knock back.

Basic Bun Dough
Cold Sponge and Dough Method

Sponge

lb	oz		kg	gr
1	14	Water 60° F (15.5° C)		935
	1/2	Sugar		15
	1/8	Salt		5
	1	Yeast		30
2	0	Flour (strong)	1	

Dough

lb	oz		kg	gr
2	8	Flour (medium)	1	250
	12	Sugar		375
	12	Butter 100° F (38° C)		375
	10	Milk (approx.)		300
		Flavour as desired		

For fruited buns add double the fruit as above.

Mix the materials for the sponge until smooth and leave in a draught free place for 12-15 hours. The sponge will increase in temperature to 72° F (22° C).

Add the sugar, milk and flavour to the sponge and stir vigorously. Add the flour and when half mixed, the warm butter. The milk should be of such temperature that with the butter, the finished dough temperature will be 80° F (27° C). Knock back at 1 hour and scale at 1 1/2 hours. This time may be shortened by adding extra yeast at the doughmaking stage.

Kuchen Dough
Ingredients (for 4 lb. 4 oz. dough)

lb	oz		kg	gr
	2	Yeast		60
1	2	Milk (approx.)		560
2	2	Flour	1	60
	5	Sugar		150
	9	Butter		270

A little salt and lemon zest.

Disperse the yeast in the milk and mix in a little flour. Set aside to ferment, then work to a smooth dough with the rest of the flour, the sugar, butter, salt and lemon. Leave to recover for about 20 minutes. Then scale off the quantities required for the individual cakes. *(Germany)*

Focaccine

lb	oz		kg	gr
1	2	Flour		560
	3/4	Yeast (brewers)		20
	1 1/2	Olive oil		45
	3 1/2	Egg		100
	7	Milk		200
	3/8	Malt extract		12

(Italy)

Croissants I
Long Process

lb	oz		kg	gr
2	4	Flour	1	125
	3/4	Salt		20
	1/2	Malt extract		15
	3/4	Sugar		20
	1	Yeast		30
	3	Egg		90
1	2	Milk 55° F (12° C)		560
	12	Butter		375

The dough should not be overmixed. Place in the retarder for about 8 hours.

Knock the dough back and pin out to 1/2 in. (1 cm.) thick and cover one half with the butter and enclose it with the other half of the dough. Give three single turns at 5 minutes intervals. *(France)*

Croissants II
Medium Process

lb	oz		kg	gr
2	4	Flour	1	125
	3/4	Salt		20
	1 1/2	Sugar		45
	1	Malt extract		30
	1 1/2	Yeast		45
1	4	Milk 70° F (21° C)		625
	12	Butter		375

Make up as for the above and retard for 4-5 hours. Proceed as above. *(France)*

Croissants III
Quick Process

lb	oz		kg	gr
2	4	Flour	1	125
	3	Butter		90
	3/4	Sugar		20
	3/4	Salt		20
	2	Yeast		60
1	4	Milk (approx.)		625
	12	Butter		375

Make up a dough with all the ingredients and the first amount of butter. Allow it to ferment for 30 minutes. Pin out and enclose the remaining butter in the dough and give three half turns as for puff pastry. Allow to rest in the refrigerator for 15 minutes between each turn. *(France)*

Brioche

lb	oz		kg	gr
2	4	Flour	1	125
	1	Salt		30
	3/4	Malt extract		20
	3 1/2	Sugar		100
	14	Egg		435
	3 1/2	Yeast		100
	3 1/2	Milk (approx.)		100
	10	Butter		300

Mix the milk, salt, sugar and yeast together and, using as much flour as necessary, make a tight dough. Add the egg and the rest of the flour. The dough will still be tight and should be well mixed. Finally work in the creamed butter until the dough is smooth and silky. Keep in a cool place for one hour.

Sweet Dough
Recipe I

lb	oz		kg	gr
2	4	Milk 85° F (30° C)	1	125
	3 1/2	Yeast		100
	3/4	Malt		20
	5 1/4	Sugar		150
	3/4	Salt		20
3	8	Flour	1	750
	7	Butter		215
		Zest of 1 lemon		

Recipe II

lb	oz		kg	gr
2	4	Milk 77° F (25° C)	1	125
	10 1/2	Egg		300
	5 1/4	Yeast		150
	3/4	Malt		20
1	2	Sugar		560
	1 1/2	Salt		45
5		Flour	2	300
	14	Butter		435
		Zest of 3 lemons		

This sort of dough can be used for making fancy dinner rolls, filled plaited loaves, Russian crosses, escargots, currant loaves etc. *(France)*

Danish Pastry I

lb	oz		kg	gr
1	4	Flour (strong)		625
	2	Sugar		60
	1/8	Salt		4
	1	Yeast		30
	1 1/2	Egg		45
	10	Milk, cold (approx.)		300
	15	Butter		450
		Cardamom spice		

Rub one ounce of the butter into the flour. Place all except the rest of the butter into a bay and make into a dough which is just mixed together without in any way developing it. The rest of the butter is rolled in as for puff pastry giving three half turns. This pastry must be kept cool.

Danish Pastry II

lb	oz		kg	gr
2	0	Flour (strong)	1	
	5	Sugar		150

177

lb	oz		kg	gr
	1/8	Salt		5
	1 1/2	Yeast		45
	5	Egg		150
1	0	Milk, cold (approx.)		500
		Nutmeg or mace		
1	2	Butter		560

Make up as for Danish Pastry I.

Danish Pastry III

lb	oz		kg	gr
3	12	Flour	1	875
	5	Sugar		150
	3/4	Salt		20
	5	Yeast		150
	7	Egg		215
1	12	Milk 68° F (20° C)		875
2	10	Butter	1	300
		Zest of lemon		

Make up as for Danish Pastry I.
(France)

Danish Pastry IV

lb	oz		kg	gr
3	12	Flour (strong)	1	875
	5 1/2	Sugar		150
	1	Salt		30
	5	Yeast		150
	1	Malt		30
	7	Egg		215
1	12	Milk 68° F (20° C) (approx.)		875
1	2	Butter		560
		Zest of lemon		

Make up as for Danish Pastry I.
(France)

Danish Pastry V

lb	oz		kg	gr
1	2	Flour (strong)		560
	2	Sugar		60
	1/8	Salt		5
	1 3/4	Yeast		50
	2	Egg		60
	7	Milk, cold (approx.)		215
	10 1/2	Butter		300

Make up as for Danish Pastry I.
(Germany)

Danish Pastry VI

lb	oz		kg	gr
2	8	Flour	1	250
	1/2	Salt		15
	1/2	Malt extract		15
	3 1/2	Sugar		100
	1/4	Cardamom spice		8
	4 1/2	Egg		150
	2 1/2	Yeast		75
1	2	Milk, cold (approx.)		560
1	5	Butter		650
		Zest and juice of 1 lemon		

Make up the dough as for Danish Pastry I. Pin out to 1/2 in. (1 cm.) thick in rectangular shape and cover half of it with the butter. Enclose with the other half and give three single turns as for puff pastry.

Give 5-10 minutes rest between turns and 20-30 minutes after the last turn before cutting up. The pastry must always be kept cold and worked in a cool bakery.
(Switzerland)

Fermented Pastry

lb	oz		kg	gr
3	12	Flour	1	875
	1 1/4	Salt		35
	3/4	Malt extract		20
	1 3/4	Yeast		50
	7	Sugar		200
2	4	Milk (approx.)	1	125
	12	Butter		375
		Zest and juice of 1 lemon		

This pastry is made exactly as described for Danish Pastry I. The amount of yeast given will be sufficient if the pastry is stored in the retarder overnight. If required for use immediately, double the yeast quantity. *(Switzerland)*

Fermented Pastry

lb	oz		kg	gr
1	0	Basic bread dough		500
	4	Butter		125
	4	Lard		125

Suitable for Christmas Pie *(page 694)*.

Pin out the bread dough as for French puff pastry. Place the butter and lard that have been mixed together in the centre and enclose with the dough. Give four half turns, resting after each two turns.

(Great Britain)

Pizza Dough I

lb	oz		kg	gr
1	0	Flour		500
	3 ¹/₂	Lard		100
	¹/₂	Salt		15
	1 ¹/₂	Yeast		45
	10	Water, tepid (approx.)		300

Disperse the yeast in the water. Rub the lard into the flour. Mix all the ingredients to a smooth dough. After 30 minutes, knock back and scale at desired weights and mould round. After recovery, flatten to about ¹/₄ in. (5 mm.) thick.

Pizza Dough II

lb	oz		kg	gr
2	0	Flour	1	
	2	Margarine		60
	2	Olive oil		60
	³/₄	Salt		20
	2	Yeast		60
	3 ¹/₂	Egg		100
1	0	Water, tepid (approx.)		500

Proceed as for Pizza Dough I.

Strudel Dough I
Unfermented

lb	oz		kg	gr
2	0	Flour (strong)	1	
	3 ¹/₂	Lard		100
	3 ¹/₂	Egg		100
	³/₄	Salt		20
1	0	Water, tepid (approx.)		500

Rub the lard into the flour finely. Mix all the ingredients together. If the flour has a high water absorbing capacity, a little more water may be necessary. The dough should be elastic but not too soft. Mould into a ball, oil the surface, cover and allow to rest for at least 45 minutes.

Strudel Dough II
Unfermented

lb	oz		kg	gr
1	0	Flour		500
	2	Oil		60
	3 ¹/₂	Egg		100
	¹/₄	Salt		10
	8	Water, tepid (approx.)		250

Proceed as for Strudel Dough I.

Batters

These mixtures should be prepared with care, particularly when they are fried in deep fat. Fermented doughs especially should be soft and need developing until they become dry and smooth, as otherwise they could be flaccid and greasy. When making batters, it is important to use the exact quantity of butter required, since the addition of too much butter allows some of the cooking fat to be absorbed by the batter during frying. The normal proportions are one part of butter to five parts of flour. While frying, it is advisable to control the temperature of the cooking fat with a thermometer (approximately 347°-365° F [175°-185° C]). Either vegetable fat or ground-nut oil is generally used for frying. Individual recipes will be found in the recipes section.

Baking Powder and Prepared Flour

It sometimes happens that a very small amount of baking powder is required in a mixing, so small an amount that a chemical balance would be necessary to weigh it accurately. A chemical balance is not standard equipment in a bakery or in the home so that either guesswork or another method must be used to make certain of the correct amount. Guesswork is to be deplored.

A method to obtain reasonable accuracy is to prepare an amount of flour with a known quantity of baking powder thoroughly incorporated. This flour is variously known as self raising flour, scone flour, or, in Scotland, soda flour.

Here are three recipes. Whichever one is chosen it should remain constant in one bakery or kitchen, otherwise confusion and waste will result:

Scone Flour

1

lb	oz		kg	gr
2	0	Flour		900
	1 $1/2$	Baking powder		42

2

lb	oz		kg	gr
1	14	Flour		850
	2	Baking powder		56

3

lb	oz		kg	gr
1	0	Flour		450
	$3/4$	Baking powder		21
	$1/4$	Salt		7

Baking Powder

lb	oz		kg	gr
2	0	Cream of tartar (or substitute)	1	
1	0	Bicarbonate of soda		500

Each of these are thoroughly sieved and kept in a dry place. In each 2 $1/2$ oz. (70 gr.) of Nos. 1 and 3 there will be approximately $1/8$ oz. (3 $1/2$ gr.) of baking powder.

In each 2 oz. (56 gr.) of No. 2 there will be approximately the same amount ($1/8$ oz. [3 $1/2$ gr.]) of baking powder. In use, the appropriate amount of prepared flour replaces an equal amount of plain flour in the recipe.

Pastries

This part of the chapter describes the many types of pastry that have evolved during many centuries in which man has, by accident or by experiment, discovered that by adding enriching agents, by altering methods of making and shaping, and by ornamentation, many varieties can be produced from a basic paste.

It will never be known who the cooks were, in what century and in what country they were when they made their discoveries. We who are their heirs, know that it did happen and that our skills and our knowledge are the sum total of all that has gone before us.

PUFF PASTRY

How this delectable pastry originated is a matter for conjecture. Possibly the fat content of a dough had been accidently omitted and was rolled in after it was made, resulting in a delightful lightness. It may have been the result of experiment. We shall never know.

That the method of making puff pastry has been known for centuries is sure. Sir Hugh Plat in 1609 published a book entitled 'Delights for Ladies' and it contained a recipe and the method of making puff pastry. Except for the quaint Elizabethan English it is similar to the recipe and method used today.

There are several types of puff pastry such as 'Full', 'Three-quarter' and 'Half'. In Great Britain, the terms describe the amount of fat to the weight of flour. 'Full' denotes equal weights of fat and flour, 'Three-quarter' meaning three-quarter the weight of fat to the weight of flour, and so on.

The Continental term 'half pastry' refers to a full pastry given only three turns instead of six. Alternatively, puff pastry cuttings pressed together can be used. This is known as rough puff pastry.

In France and parts of Switzerland the butter content is calculated by taking half the weight of the finished dough. For example: if the finished dough weight is 2 lb. (1 kg.), then one pound (500 gr.) of butter is required.

There are many methods of manufacture. In Britain, there are three that are made commercially and they are 'English', 'French' and 'Scotch'. They differ only in the initial method of incorporating the fat.

The flour used for puff pastry should be strong, one having a stable gluten of good extensibility. Flours differ in the amount of water that they will carry; the water content in any recipe is therefore approximate. The consistency of the dough should be the same as that of the butter used.

The fat used should be butter, for no other fat will confer such flavour. It should be firm and stable so that it will film during rolling and folding but will not squeeze out. Butter also has a low melting point and will not leave a fat film on the roof of the mouth when the pastry is eaten. There are plastic fats on the market that will make excellent puff pastry, but they are without the exquisite flavour of good quality butter.

Although not absolutely necessary, a little weak acid can be used to confer a measure of extra extensibility on the gluten. Lemon juice is ideal for the purpose. Tartaric acid, because it is readily soluble in cold water, is a good alternative.

Puff Pastry
English Method

lb	oz		kg	gr
4	0	Flour (strong)	2	
	8	Butter		250
2	8	Water, cold (approx.)	1	250
		Lemon juice		
3	8	Butter	1	750

The 8 oz. (250 gr.) of butter is rubbed into the flour. A bay is made into which the water and the lemon juice are poured. The dough is mixed and well developed, and then allowed to rest while the butter is moulded into a plastic mass.

The dough is rolled to a long rectangle, taking care to keep the edges straight and the corners square.

The butter is then broken into small pieces to cover two thirds of the surface of the dough; the pieces should not be placed too near the edge.

The third of the dough without butter is brought up and the top third brought down, so that there are three layers of dough and two of butter. The pastry is then rolled out and again folded into three.

It is given six such turns with a rest of about 20 minutes between each two turns. In the rolling out, care must be taken to have the open ends parallel to the rolling pin. During rest periods, the pastry must be covered to prevent the formation of a skin on the surface.
(Illustrations page 110).

Puff Pastry
French Method

The formula is the same, but in this case the dough is rolled to a square shape with the corners thinner than the centre. The butter is formed into a square that will fit into the centre of the dough. The corners are then brought to the centre so that the butter is totally enclosed with the same thickness of dough around the butter.

It is given six turns in exactly the same way as for the English method, giving a rest between each two turns.
(Illustrations page 110).

Puff Pastry
Scotch Method

This is the quickest method of making puff pastry and is known at times as the 'blitz' method. The same formula is used. The butter is broken into pieces about the size of walnuts which are distributed throughout the flour. A bay is made into which the water and lemon juice are placed, the whole being made up into a dough, taking care that the lumps of butter are not rubbed into the dough.

The same manipulation follows as for the English and French methods.

It is imperative that in rolling and folding puff pastry, the edges should be kept straight and the corners square. The reason is because a laminated structure is being built up of alternate layers of butter and dough. Many hundreds of such layers are built up and if, because of carelessness, the layering is uneven, then the baked pastries will be uneven in size, some being small in volume whilst others will be distorted in shape.

All pastry pieces should be rested before they are baked, otherwise they will contract in the oven and the shapes will become distorted.

Provided that the materials used in puff pastry are of the correct quality and that care has been taken in the making, there will be a remarkable increase in volume during baking. This increase is due to the pressure of steam from the water in the gluten and the free water in the dough. Resistance to this pressure is offered by the dough structure, the gluten of which is extensible in a well made puff pastry. The pressure is greater than the resistance, so that the pastry rises in the oven until such time as the gluten coagulates under the influence of heat, and the structure becomes comparatively rigid and does not collapse. The flaking seen in the baked pastry is effected by the butter which insulates one layer from another. As it melts, it is absorbed by the dough layers which it helps to cook. *(Illustration page 109)*.

Puff Pastry I

lb	oz		kg	gr
1	0	Flour (strong)		500
1	0	Butter (approx.)		500
	¼	Salt		8
	9 ½	Water (approx.)		285

Make a bay in the flour and put therein the salt and cold water. Knead it briskly with the tips of the fingers without working the paste too much so as not to give it any elasticity. The mixing must be done so as to ensure a paste with exactly the same degree of consistency as the butter. It must always be rather firm and have a lot of body. This first step in making puff-paste called 'la détrempe' is the main agent of success. One has to take great care with it. It is well not to use all the water at once for fear of making the paste too soft, all flours have not the same faculty of absorption though giving an identical 'détrempe'. This is the reason why one cannot predetermine the exact quantity of butter to use. In order to know the required quantity of butter to use, one must weigh 'la détrempe' when it is finished; the amount will be equal to half the weight of 'la détrempe'. For example, for 1 pound (500 gr.) of 'détrempe', use 8 oz. (250 gr.) of butter. Working in this way, one has always a regular puff pastry.

Here is how one must incorporate the butter with the paste. Let 'la détrempe' rest first in a cool place for 15 minutes; then flatten it by beating it with a closed fist; then place the very firm butter in the middle and draw the four edges of the paste above it in order to cover it well.

With a rolling pin, roll out the paste evenly into a long and very regular oblong, rolling until one starts to see the butter through the dough. Roll very gently with a rolling pin dusted with as little flour as possible. When the paste has been rolled into a long straight oblong, fold it in three drawing one of the edges towards the middle of the paste and then draw the other one above it. This operation is called 'to give one turn'.

Then turn it lengthways, that is to say not on its other side but in the other direction and begin again rolling it with the rolling pin, then fold it again in three. This is the second turn and it is therefore in the opposite direction to the first turn.

Set the pastry to rest in a cool place for about 20 minutes before beginning again to give two more turns which, as before, will be in opposite directions. Set it to rest again in a cool place for 20 to 30 minutes and afterwards give it two further turns; these are the last, bringing the total number of required turns to six. It can be used for 'vol-au-vent', 'bouchées' and a multitude of other pastries.   *(France)*

Puff Pastry II

lb	oz		kg	gr
2	0	Flour (strong)	1	
1	8	Butter		750
	³/₄	Salt		20
1	0	Water (approx.)		500

Weigh the flour, sift it and place it on the table or in the mixing machine. Next rub in 2 oz. (60 gr.) of the butter and then add the salt and water. Thoroughly mix into a dough and shape it into a ball which is left standing for half an hour covered up with a damp cloth or a plastic sheet. Then take the dough, make two deep cuts in the shape of a cross with a knife and pull each quarter well apart so as to flatten and widen the cross.

To obtain good puff paste, the dough should be smooth but not overdeveloped as it will become too tight and elastic; this would be a great drawback when dealing with the next stage of the preparation (i.e. when the turns are given). When the dough has recovered, the butter (which should be of a plastic consistency) can be added. Place it in the centre of the cross and fold the four quarters of the dough over it. Next firmly seal the edges by nipping with a rolling pin without, however, squeezing the butter out. Then roll out into a long rectangle, either by hand, with a rolling pin, or by machine roller so as to give the necessary turns by folding the two ends of the rectangle towards its centre and then bringing both ends together in the form of a book.

For the preparation of puff paste, four book folds and one single turn are usually required. It is advisable to leave the paste in a cool place for 15-20 minutes between each turn. *(France)*

Dutch Puff Pastry

With this method the role of dough and butter is reversed.

lb	oz		kg	gr
2	8	Flour (strong)	1	250
1	14	Butter		900
	³/₄	Salt		8
1	2	Water (approx.)		560

Make a dough with 1 lb. 8 oz. (750 gr.) flour, the salt and the water and roll out into a rectangle. Then mix the butter with the rest of the flour (1 lb. [500 gr.]) into a paste, rolling it out into another slightly larger rectangle. Place the piece of dough on the piece of paste and then proceed to give the same number of turns as for the traditional puff paste. This method is favoured by many but it is left to the individual to decide which of the two is the most suitable. *(France)*

Lightning Puff Pastry

This third method of preparation is used in exceptional circumstances (last minute orders, etc.) when there is no time to follow either of the two recipes given above.

lb	oz		kg	gr
2	0	Flour (strong)	1	
1	8	Butter		750
	³/₄	Salt		20
1	0	Water (approx.)		500

Cut the butter while it is still firm into small cubes which are then lightly mixed with the flour. Next make a bay in the middle, pour in the water in which the salt has been dissolved and make into a dough; allow this to stand for a while and then give it four turns one after the other without interruption. This method enables one to obtain products made of puff paste within 40-45 minutes (including baking time). *(France)*

Half Puff Pastry

In 'grande cuisine' half puff-paste comes from the trimmings of full puff-paste, which are rolled into a ball and given one turn. When puff-paste is not used daily, one makes a half-paste as follows:

lb	oz		kg	gr
1	0	Flour (strong)		500
1	0	Butter		500
	¹/₄	Salt		8
	10	Water (approx.)		300

Make a bay in the flour, put therein the butter, salt, water and the juice of half a lemon. Knead it with the tips of the fingers but do not try to mix too well. As soon as the paste is made, give it 2 or 3 turns so as to finish the mixing and at the same time to make a flaky paste. Use it immediately. *(France)*

Half-and-Half Pastry

Pin out fresh puff pastry to a rectangular shape, cover two thirds of it with sablé pastry, fold over and give one single turn.

This pastry is particularly suitable for shutters ('jalousies'), apple dumplings, fruit slices, etc. *(Germany)*

Puff Pastry
Bases

lb	oz		kg	gr
1	0	Flour (strong)		500
1	0	Butter (tough)		500
	10	Water (approx.)		300
	1/8	Salt		3

Make a firm dough out of 14 oz. (435 gr.) flour, 3 oz. (90 gr.) butter, the water and salt. Then work the remaining butter and flour together and roll into the dough giving six turns, resting between each two.

To make a puff paste *base*, pin out approx. 7 oz. (200 gr.) prepared puff pastry and bake. *(Germany)*

Cheese Puff Pastry

lb	oz		kg	gr
2	0	Flour (strong)	1	
	4	Butter		125
1	3	Water (approx.)		590
1	12	Butter		875
	8	Bakers cheese		250
	4	Water		125

Rub together flour and butter. Dough up with the water. Allow to recover for 15 minutes.

Mix bakers cheese with water and blend the resultant paste with butter and refrigerate. Roll into the dough in the usual way giving five half turns.

SHORT PASTRY

As the word 'short' implies, this type of pastry, when baked, should be tender and fairly easily broken. When eaten it should 'melt in the mouth' suggesting a complete absence of toughness. This is brought about by the balance of materials used and the method of manufacture.

Toughness is caused by the hydration and development of the insoluble proteins in flour.

Water an insoluble protein together make gluten, an elastic substance which is more or less tough according to the type of flour used and the amount of working given it.

It becomes obvious that a soft flour, one with a low percentage of weak protein, is the best to use for short pastry. Even so, unless the method of making is correctly carried out, toughness will result.

All fats and oils are shortening agents because, when used correctly, they will insulate the particles of insoluble protein from water. That is why it is necessary to rub the fat finely into the flour before the water (contained in eggs and milk) is added.

To exert an influence on the paste, sugar, which has a softening effect on gluten, must, as far as possible, be in solution, therefore fine castor sugar is used because it is more readily soluble in the small amount of water contained in the eggs and milk. Even then toughening is possible if the pastry is roughly handled, because the water may be forced through the fat barrier to form gluten.

Short pastry can be subdivided under two headings, sweet and unsweetened. There are three methods of making sweet pastry:

A. Sweet Pastry
1. Rub-in Method

The flour is sieved and the butter is rubbed in finely without forming a paste. The liquids and sugar are added and the whole thoroughly dispersed without toughening.

2. Creamed Method

The butter and half the flour are creamed together. The sugar is dissolved in the liquids and partially mixed with the creamed flour/butter. The balance of the flour is added to make a smooth plastic paste.

3. Creamed Method

The butter and sugar are creamed together and the egg added. This emulsion is dispersed through the flour and a plastic paste formed.

B. Unsweetened Pastry

There are three methods of making unsweetened short pastry:

1. Short Pastry

As No. 1 or 2 above (omitting sugar).

2. Pie Pastry

The water is brought to the boil and added to the flour into which the fat has been finely dispersed. This is known as the semi-boiled method.

3. Pie Pastry

The fat and water are put in to a pan and heated until the fat is melted and the water boils. The mixture is then added to the flour and mixed in. This is known as the boiled method.

The use of boiling water causes some of the starch in the flour to gelatinize, which, when cool, gives a measure of rigidity to pie cases raised either by hand or by machine.

SHORT PASTRY-SWEET

Sweet Pastry I

lb	oz		kg	gr
1	0	Flour (soft)		500
	8	Butter		250
	4	Sugar (castor)		125
	2 1/2	Egg		75

Sweet Pastry II

lb	oz		kg	gr
1	0	Flour (soft)		500
	10	Butter		300
	5	Sugar (castor)		150
	2	Egg		60

Use any of the methods given (A).

The butter and sugar contents can be adjusted according to the use the pastry is to be put. An increase in either or both will mean a decrease in the egg/milk content and vice versa. *(Great Britain)*

Sweet Pastry I

lb	oz		kg	gr
1	4	Flour		625
	9	Butter		270
	1	Sugar (castor)		30
	1/8	Salt		3
	6	Water (approx.)		185

Method 1 (A).

Wrap and allow to rest overnight. For savoury tartlets etc., delete the sugar and double the salt. *(France)*

Sweet Pastry II

lb	oz		kg	gr
2	4	Flour	1	125
1	5	Butter		655
1	5	Sugar (icing)		655
1	2	Ground almonds		560
	12	Egg		375
	1/8	Salt		3

Use creamed method 2 or 3 (A).

(France)

Sweet Pastry III

lb	oz		kg	gr
2	4	Flour	1	125
1	2	Butter		560
	9	Sugar		270
	7	Egg		215
	1/8	Salt		3

Use creamed method 2 or 3 (A).

This pastry is useful for lining pans for fruit tarts, etc. *(France)*

Sweet Pastry IV

lb	oz		kg	gr
2	0	Flour (soft)	1	
	12	Butter		350
1	4	Sugar (castor)		625
	8	Egg		250
	1/8	Salt		4
		Zest of 1 lemon		

Use method 1 or 3 (A). *(France)*

Sweet Pastry V

lb	oz		kg	gr
1	0	Flour (soft)		500
	7	Butter		220
	8	Sugar (castor)		250
	2	Egg		60
	3	Egg yolks		90
	1/8	Salt		4
		Zest of 1 lemon		

A little baking powder may be added depending on the purpose for which the pastry is to be used.

Use any of the methods given (A).

This recipe and the one above are distinctive in that they both contain more sugar than butter, therefore the baking temperature should not be too high.

(France)

Sweet Pastry-Almond I

lb	oz		kg	gr
2	4	Flour (soft)	1	100
1	4	Butter		600
1	4	Sugar (icing)		600
1	0	Ground almonds		500
	10	Egg		300
	1/8	Salt		4

Use method 2 or 3 (A). *(France)*

Sweet Pastry-Almond II

lb	oz		kg	gr
1	4	Flour (soft)		600
	15	Butter		450
1	4	Raw marzipan		600
	5	Egg		150
	1/16	Cinnamon		2

Sieve the flour and the cinnamon. Reduce the marzipan with the egg. Mix all together. *(France)*

Sweet Pastry I

lb	oz		kg	gr
1	12	Flour		875
	4	Cornflour		125
1	2	Butter		560
	9	Sugar (castor)		270
	2	Egg yolks		60
		Lemon zest		
		Vanilla		

Method 1 (A). *(Germany)*

Sweet Pastry II

Ingredients for 12 bases:

lb	oz		kg	gr
1	2	Butter		560
	8 3/4	Sugar (castor)		280
	1 1/2	Egg yolks		45
1	10 1/2	Flour		800
	3 1/2	Cornflour		100
		Lemon		
		Vanilla		

Cream the butter and sugar and mix with the egg yolks. Then add lemon and vanilla and rub the mixture into the flour and cornflour. Work into a paste and leave until cold before pinning out. *(Germany)*

Sweet Pastry-Chocolate

lb	oz		kg	gr
1	8	Flour (soft)		750
	2	Cocoa powder		60
1	0	Butter		500
	8	Sugar (castor)		250
	3	Egg		90

Make up as for ordinary Sweet Pastry.

Sweet Pastry for Tea Biscuits I

lb	oz		kg	gr
1	0	Flour		500
	14	Butter		435
	5	Sugar (icing)		150
	1 1/2	Marzipan		45
	1	Egg yolks		30
	1/8	Salt		4
		Lemon zest		

Cream the butter and icing sugar. Work the marzipan and egg yolks until smooth and add to the butter/sugar mix. Rub into the flour adding the salt and lemon zest. Allow to cool. *(Germany)*

Sweet Pastry for Tea Biscuits II

lb	oz		kg	gr
3	5	Flour	1	650
	2	Cornflour		60
2	4	Butter	1	125
1	2	Sugar (icing)		560
	2	Egg yolks		60
	1/4	Salt		8

Make as for Sweet Pastry for Tea Biscuits I mixing the cornflour with the egg yolks. *(Germany)*

Sweet Pastry for Tea Biscuits III

lb	oz		kg	gr
1	0	Flour		500
	13	Butter		390
	5	Sugar (icing)		150
1	1/4	Egg whites		35
	1/8	Salt		3
		Vanilla		

Proceed as for Sweet Pastry for Tea Biscuits I. *(Germany)*

Sweet Pastry for Tea Biscuits IV

lb	oz		kg	gr
1	0	Flour		500
	1	Cocoa		30
	12	Butter		375
	5	Sugar (icing)		150
	1	Egg whites		30
	1/8	Salt		3

Proceed as for Sweet Pastry for Tea Biscuits I working the cocoa with egg whites. *(Germany)*

Sweet Pastry for Tea Fancies V

lb	oz		kg	gr
2	10	Butter	1	300
	14	Sugar (icing)		435
	3 1/2	Marzipan		100
	2	Egg yolks		60

lb	oz		kg	gr
3	6 1/2	Flour	1	685
	1/4	Salt		8
		Lemon juice		

Cream the butter and icing sugar, then work the marzipan and egg yolks until smooth and add to the butter/sugar mixture. Rub into the flour, add salt and lemon, work to a paste and leave until cold. *(Germany)*

Sweet Pastry for Piping

lb	oz		kg	gr
	12	Flour		350
	8	Butter		250
	8	Sugar (icing)		250
	3 1/2	Egg		100
	2	Egg yolks		60
		Zest of 1/2 lemon		

Cream the butter, sugar and lemon zest, adding the egg and yolks gradually. Lastly fold in the flour to make a mixture of piping consistency.

Vanilla sugar or other flavours may be used instead of lemon.

This type of mixture is mainly used for small fancies or biscuits.

Sweet Pastry
Mignon Bases — Mignon Böden

lb	oz		kg	gr
1	2	Flour		560
	13	Butter		390
	7	Sugar (icing)		200
1	1/2	Egg yolks		45
1	3/4	Marzipan		50
	1/8	Salt		3

Prepare a paste from the flour, butter, sugar, egg yolks, marzipan and salt.

Pin out 6 thin bases and bake until golden.

Milanese Pastry

lb	oz		kg	gr
2	4	Flour	1	125
1	2	Butter		560
1	2	Sugar (castor)		560

lb	oz		kg	gr
10	½	Egg		300
	⅛	Salt		3
		Zest of 2 lemons		

Use creamed method 2 or 3 (A) *(page 185)*.
(France)

Pasta Frolla

lb	oz		kg	gr
1	0	Flour		500
	10	Blanched almonds		300
	10	Butter		300
	10	Sugar (castor)		300
	3	Egg		90
	⅛	Salt		3
		Zest of lemon		

Grind the almonds and add the sugar gradually to prevent oiling. Add 1 ½ oz. (45 gr.) of egg and with the rest of the ingredients make all into a paste. *(Italy)*

Neapolitan Sweet Pastry

lb	oz		kg	gr
	12	Flour		375
	10	Almond paste (very firm)		300
	10	Butter		300
		Zest of ½ lemon		

Mix all the ingredients together and allow to rest.

Pasta brisée I

lb	oz		kg	gr
2	4	Flour	1	125
1	4	Butter		625
	3	Egg yolks		90
	1	Sugar (castor)		30
	1	Salt		30
	1	Milk (as required)		30

Make up as for ordinary Sweet Pastry.
(Italy)

Pasta brisée II

lb	oz		kg	gr
1	2	Flour (soft)		560
	11	Butter		330
	⅛	Salt		3
	5	Water (approx.)		150

Rub the butter into the flour and add the rest of the materials. Make into a smooth pastry. *(Italy)*

Sablé Pastry I

lb	oz		kg	gr
1	10	Flour		800
1	2	Butter		560
	9	Sugar (icing)		270
	2	Egg yolks		60
	½	Sugar (vanilla)		15
	⅛	Salt		3

Use creamed method 2 or 3 (A) *(page 185)*.
(France)

Sablé Pastry II

lb	oz		kg	gr
3	5	Flour	1	650
2	3	Butter	1	90
1	2	Sugar (icing)		560
	¾	Sugar (vanilla)		20
	6	Egg		180
	⅛	Salt		3

Use creamed method 2 or 3 (A) *(page 185)*.

Do not overmix. If not required for immediate use keep in refrigerator.
(France)

Sablé Pastry III

lb	oz		kg	gr
2	0	Flour	1	
1	7	Butter		700
	7	Sugar (icing)		200
	1	Egg whites		30
		Zest of ½ lemon		

Use creamed method 1 or 2 (A) *(pages 184-185)*.
(France)

Linz Pastry I

lb	oz		kg	gr
2	4	Flour	1	125
1	2	Butter		560
1	2	Sugar (castor)		560
	14	Ground hazelnuts		435
	5	Egg		150
	4	Egg whites		125
	3 ½	Milk		100
	⅛	Salt		3
	¼	Cinnamon		8

Grind the hazelnuts and sugar together, add the butter, then the egg, egg whites and milk and finally the flour, salt and cinnamon sieved together.
Do not overmix. *(France)*

Linz Pastry II

lb	oz		kg	gr
2	4	Flour	1	125
	14	Butter		435
1	2	Sugar		560
	9	Ground hazelnuts		270
	14	Egg		435
	1/8	Salt		3
	1/4	Cinnamon		8

Proceed as for Linz Pastry I. *(France)*

Linz Pastry III

lb	oz		kg	gr
2	4	Butter	1	125
	14	Sugar (castor)		435
2	8	Flour	1	250
	1/2	Baking powder		15
		Lemon zest		

Cream the butter and sugar before adding the flour and baking powder. This pastry is soft enough for piping. *(France)*

Linz Pastry I

lb	oz		kg	gr
1	0	Flour		500
1	0	Butter		500
	12	Sugar (castor)		375
1	0	Ground almonds		500
	5	Egg		150
	3	Egg yolks		90
	1/16	Cinnamon		2
		Zest of 1/2 lemon		

Mix the sugar, egg and egg yolks together. Blend with the softened butter. Add the flour, cinnamon, almonds and zest. Allow to rest before use. *(Austria)*

Linz Pastry II

lb	oz		kg	gr
	13	Flour		400
1	0	Butter		500
1	0	Sugar (castor)		500

lb	oz		kg	gr
	10	Ground hazelnuts		300
1	4	Egg		600
	13	Cake crumbs		400
	1/16	Cinnamon		2
		Ground cloves (pinch)		
		Vanilla		

Work all the ingredients together. Allow to rest before use. *(Austria)*

Linz Pastry III

lb	oz		kg	gr
1	4	Flour		625
1	4	Butter		625
	8	Sugar (castor)		250
	8	Ground almonds		250
		Zest of 1 lemon		
		Vanilla		

Proceed as above. *(Austria)*

Linz Pastry IV

lb	oz		kg	gr
1	4	Flour		625
1	4	Butter		625
	8	Sugar (icing)		250
1	0	Sponge crumbs		500
	1/8	Cinnamon		4
		Oil of bitter almonds (a few drops)		
		Zest of 1/2 lemon		

Proceed as above. Allow to rest for at least 2 hours before using. *(Austria)*

Linz Pastry V

lb	oz		kg	gr
1	2	Flour		560
	14	Butter		425
	7	Sugar (icing)		210
	10	Egg yolks		300
		Zest of 1/2 lemon		

Cook the egg yolks until hard and rub through a sieve. Work into a pliable paste with the other ingredients. Rest before use. *(Austria)*

Linz Pastry VI/Chocolate

lb	oz		kg	gr
1	7	Flour		700
1	7	Butter		700

lb	oz		kg	gr
	10	Sugar (icing)		300
	11	Ground almonds		330
	4 1/2	Block cocoa		140
	1/8	Cinnamon		4
		Vanilla		

Melt the cocoa in a bain-marie, mix with half the sugar and leave until cool, then work it with the rest of the ingredients to a pliable paste. Rest before use. *(Austria)*

Linz Pastry VII

lb	oz		kg	gr
	10	Flour		300
1	4	Butter		625
1	4	Sugar (icing)		625
	12	Ground almonds		360
	9 1/2	Cake crumbs		285
	10	Egg		300
	5	Orange peel (finely chopped)		150
	1/4	Cinnamon		8
	1/8	Ground cloves		4

Work all the ingredients to a pliable paste and allow to rest before use. This pastry is especially suitable for tartlets.

(Austria)

Crumb Pastry I

lb	oz		kg	gr
1	0	Crushed digestive biscuits		500
	8	Butter or margarine		250
	8	Sugar (castor)		250

Mix together.

Crumb Pastry II

lb	oz		kg	gr
1	0	Biscuit crumbs *		500
	3	Milk powder		90
	3	Sugar (castor)		90
	10	Butter or margarine		300

Melt the fat and mix with the other ingredients. These crumb pastes have to be pressed into the cases.

* Where possible the digestive type of biscuit should be used.

Apple Pie Pastry

lb	oz		kg	gr
2	0	Flour	1	
	1/2	Baking powder		15
	8	Butter		250
	8	Lard		250
	3 1/2	Sugar (castor)		100
	3/4	Salt		20
	8	Water, cold (approx.)		250

Sieve the flour with the baking powder and salt. Rub in the lard and butter. Dissolve the sugar in the water and add. Mix well and allow to rest for a few hours before use. *(U.S.A.)*

Basic Biscuit Pastry

lb	oz		kg	gr
2	4	Flour	1	
1	9	Butter		750
1	0	Sugar (castor)		500
	4	Egg yolks		125
	1/4	Salt		8
	1/8	Vanilla essence		3
	1/8	Lemon essence		3

Mix the butter, sugar and yolks together, adding the essences and salt. Mix into the flour. *(Italy)*

Basic Biscuit Pastry-Chocolate

lb	oz		kg	gr
2	4	Flour	1	
1	12	Butter		875
1	5	Sugar		625
	6	Egg yolks		180
	3 1/2	Cocoa powder		100
	1/8	Vanilla essence		3
	1/4	Salt		8

Proceed as above. *(Italy)*

Basic Cheese Pastry

lb	oz		kg	gr
2	4	Flour	1	
	10 1/2	Parmesan cheese (powdered)		300
1	8	Butter		750
	4	Egg yolks		125

lb	oz		kg	gr
	5	Milk (approx.)		150
	³/₄	Salt		22
		Pepper (pinch)		

Make up as for short pastry. *(Italy)*

SHORT PASTRY - UNSWEETENED
Basic Short Pastry

lb	oz		kg	gr
1	0	Flour (soft)		500
	6	Butter		180
	2	Lard		60
	3	Water (approx.)		90
	¹/₄	Salt		8

Method 1 (B) *(page 185)*. *(Great Britain)*

Short Pastry for Cornish Pasties

lb	oz		kg	gr
1	0	Flour (medium)		500
	6	Lard		180
	¹/₄	Salt		8
	7 ¹/₂	Milk (approx.)		225

Method 1 (B) *(page 185)*. *(Great Britain)*

Richer Short Pastry

lb	oz		kg	gr
1	0	Flour (soft)		500
	10	Butter		300
	1	Egg		30
	2	Milk (approx.)		60
	¹/₄	Salt		8

Method 1 (B) *(page 185)*. *(Great Britain)*

Short Pastry for Sausage Rolls

lb	oz		kg	gr
1	0	Flour (soft)		500
	8	Butter or lard		250
	¹/₈	Salt		3
	4	Water		125

Method 1 (B) *(page 185)*. *(Great Britain)*

Short Pastry for Lining Tarts

lb	oz		kg	gr
2	4	Flour (soft)	1	125
1	2	Butter		560
	³/₄	Salt		22
	9	Water (approx.)		270

Method 1 (B) *(page 185)*. *(France)*

Short Pastry - Pâte brisée fine

lb	oz		kg	gr
2	4	Flour	1	125
1	2	Butter		560
	³/₄	Salt		22
	8 ¹/₂	Water (approx.)		265

The method of preparation is the same as for the other type of short paste. Note, however, that this paste is more difficult to handle, especially in the summer, because of its high fat content.

(Switzerland)

Short Pastry for Lining Tarts etc. - Pâte brisée pour le fonçage des gâteaux

lb	oz		kg	gr
2	4	Flour	1	125
	7	Butter		200
	7	Lard		200
	1	Salt		30
	12	Water (approx.)		375

Mix the flour, butter and lard either on the table or in the mixing machine. Add the water in which the salt has been dissolved. This paste should not be handled for too long as it would become crumbly and difficult to roll out (too short).

(France)

SHORT PASTRY FOR PIES
Pie Pastry

Cold (a)

lb	oz		kg	gr
1	0	Flour (medium)		500
	7	Lard		200
	¹/₄	Salt		8
	5	Water (approx.)		150

Method 1 (B) *(page 185)*.

Semi-boiled (b)

lb	oz		kg	gr
1	0	Flour (medium)		500
	7	Lard		200
	¹/₄	Salt		8
	6	Water (approx.)		180

Method 2 (B) *(page 185)*.

Boiled (c)

lb	oz		kg	gr
1	0	Flour (medium)		500
	6	Lard		180
	1/8	Salt		3
	7 1/2	Water (approx.)		225

Method 3 (B) *(page 185)*. *(Great Britain)*

Pie Pastry

lb	oz		kg	gr
2	4	Flour	1	
	8 1/2	Butter		250
	3 1/2	Egg		100
	14	Water (approx.)		420
	1	Salt		30

Method 1 (B) *(page 185)*. *(France)*

Pastry for Pâtés, Croustades and Timbales

lb	oz		kg	gr
1	0	Flour (medium)		500
	5	Butter		150
	2	Lard or olive oil		60
	1	Egg yolk		30
	1/2	Salt		15
	6	Water (approx.)		180

After mixing, this pastry is developed well so that it has plenty of body, which is required of a pastry that has to bear a heavy weight of meat and which is to remain crisp after baking, despite the presence of so much humidity. Leave to rest some hours in a cool place before using. *(France)*

Pie Pastry - Pâte à Pâtés à chaud

This type of paste is particularly suitable for pies which have to be coated with (aspic) jelly, since it has the advantage of keeping firm and crisp after the pies have been coated with the jelly.

lb	oz		kg	gr
2	4	Flour	1	125
	3 1/2	Lard		100
	8 1/2	Softened margarine		275
	12 1/4	Water		375

To make this paste, melt the margarine and the lard to a temperature of about 104° F (40° C). Then use the same method of preparation as for short paste. In the summer it is better to add the water to the melted fats and pour this mixture on the flour. *(Switzerland)*

Pie Pastry

lb	oz		kg	gr
6	0	Flour	3	
1	14	Lard		900
	2	Salt		60
	10	Egg		300
1	10	Water (approx.)		800

Use Method 1 (B) *(page 185)*.

Sufficient pastry for three pies 18 in. (45 cm.) long. *(Germany)*

CHOUX PASTRY

Basically, choux pastry is a cooked mixture of fat, flour and water with possibly a little sugar and salt, in fact a roux into which eggs are beaten.

A study of recipes will show that there is a multiplicity of formulae all capable of producing good choux pastries. Some of the recipes are more suitable for use with certain grades of flour and/or different types of fat. It is difficult or even impossible to find a basis on which a formula balance can be worked out.

There are some good rules to follow:

1. The greater the proportion of egg used in the mix, provided that the consistency is correct, the lighter the choux pastries.

2. The more egg used, the less fat is necessary.

3. The recipes richest in fat are more suitable for small choux pastries.

Here are some recipes:

	1			2			3			4			5		
	lb	oz	gr	lb	oz	gr	lb	oz	gr	lb	oz	gr	lb	oz	gr
Water	1	4	600	1	4	600	1	4	600	1	4	600	1	4	600
Butter		10	280	1	0	450		10	280		8	225		6	170
Sugar	—	—	—	—	—	—	—	—	—	$1/8$		3	$1/8$		3
Flour (strong)		10	280	1	0	450	1	0	450	1	0	450	1	0	450
Egg (approx.)	1	10	700	2	0	900	1	10	700	1	8	625	1	6	625

	6 France			7 France			8 France			9 Germany		
	lb	oz	gr	lb	oz	gr	lb	oz	gr	lb	oz	gr
Water	1	4	600	1	4	600	—	—	—		10	300
Milk	—	—	—	—	—	—	1	4	600	—	—	—
Sugar		$1/8$	5		$1/8$	5		$3/8$	10	—	—	—
Salt		$1/8$	3		$1/8$	3		$1/8$	3		$1/8$	3
Lemon juice	—	—	—	—	—	—	—	—	—		1	30
Butter		7	200		10	280		8	225		6	175
Flour (strong)		9	250		14	400		14	400		12	350
Egg (approx.)	1	0	500	1	4	600	1	4	600	1	2	500

An analysis of these recipes will show limits to which the materials can be used, the percentage basis being on the total mix.

Water 25%-40%. Butter 10%-20%. Flour 15%-25%. Egg 20%-40%.

Formula 1 is suitable for éclairs. Formula 2 for very small choux. Formula 3 for larger choux and Gâteaux St-Honoré.

Formulae 4, 5, 6, 7, 8 and 9 are suitable for larger choux and beignets.

The butter and water are placed into a pan and heated until the butter is melted and the water boils. The sieved flour is stirred in and the mixture is cooked until it leaves the side of the pan without sticking. When the fierce heat has subsided, the egg is beaten in a little at a time until the desired consistency is reached. The amount of egg required will vary according to the degree of cooking and the type of flour and fat used.

The flour should be medium strong. Any type of fat can be used although better results will be obtained by using a good stable fat like butter or lard. Butter will confer the best flavour. A copper pan is not advised for cooking the roux because of the possibility of discolouration.

Sometimes a little carbonate of ammonia is used in the mix to increase the volume of cream buns. This chemical is better known to the British baker as 'vol'. It releases ammonia gas in the oven during baking, the gas being quickly dispersed as the choux pastries cool. It is important that the chemical is properly dissolved before adding to the mix; a concentration of it in the baked pastry will give a bad aroma and flavour.

The baking of choux pastries should be carried out with care, for unless the protein structure or the framework of the pastries has coagulated and dried sufficiently, then they will collapse. This is more likely in the case of large cream buns that are baked in large covered tins holding a number of buns or single buns each under a small tin.

The object in providing a closed environment is to create conditions for maximum expansion. The conditions necessary are slower heat penetration together with sufficient humidity. The slower heat penetration delays the coagulation of the protein structure and because the bun bakes in the humidity provided by its own steam, crust formation is slowed down; both conditions allow for maximum expansion.

Whilst timing will give an indication when choux pastries are baked, it should be supplemented by manual examination. Covered choux pastries need special care during a baking check. One cover only should be tilted for examination; removal of the cover will cause complete collapse if the choux pastry is not baked. Large covered baking tins generally have an inspection slot for examination.
(Illustration page 111).

Cake Bases

There are many types of cake bases suitable for decoration. The following points, however, must be borne in mind.

1. The base must be worthy of the decoration, that is, it must be of good quality. There is no advantage in decorating poor quality bases in an attempt to make them look better than they are.

2. The base should be suitable for the recipient or the occasion. A base for a child's cake, for instance, should be made from a light sponge or genoese. A base to be finished for dessert or afternoon tea should be light and tender. For bride, birthday and Christmas cakes a heavily fruited base is necessary, one with good keeping qualities.

3. The base should be suitable for the decorative media used. A heavily fruited cake would not be decorated with butter cream, for instance, or a soft base with hard icing.

4. The best use should be made of the raw materials available. Tins, frames and hoops should be properly prepared; the recipes used should be balanced; the correct manufacturing process used; colours and flavours in the mix used correctly; baking carried out properly; storage after baking should be under ideal conditions and the bases properly prepared before decoration commences.

5. The correct amount of mixing should be placed in the tins or hoops so that the bases are neither too thick nor too thin for the purpose required.

6. Consideration should be given to colour and flavour combinations. It is advisable to have some link between the base, the filling and the decoration. There should be a reason for the linkage, i.e. a continuity of colour and flavour throughout or, for contrasts that effect, a harmony of colour and flavour.

7. There should be a balance between the weight and size of the base and the weight of decorative material.

Here in tabulated form is a summary:

BASE	FORM	SUITABLE DECORATIVE MEDIA
Sponge	Sandwiches	Dairy cream, buttercream, water icing, fondant, icing sugar, jam.
Light genoese	Gâteaux	Fondant, buttercream, dairy cream.
Heavy genoese	Layer cakes	Chocolate, dairy cream, fondant, buttercream, ganache.
High sugar	Battenburg, Torten, Fancies	Ganache, almond and sugar paste, jam, jelly, fudge, fondant, buttercream, dairy cream.
Heavily fruited	Bride, Christmas, Birthday, Simnel	Almond paste, fondant, royal icing.

BASE	FORM	SUITABLE DECORATIVE MEDIA

Built-up bases
  Genoese
  Japonaise
  Sponge
  Sweetpaste
	Torten	Dairy cream, buttercream, fondant, almond and sugar paste, ganache, jelly, jam, special spreads.

Sponge Mixtures

A sponge cake is one usually containing eggs, sugar, flour and sometimes butter; in the latter case it is usually referred to as a butter sponge. The character of a sponge can be altered by adjustments in the balance of materials used and/or by additions.

Who first made a sponge cake is not known. It may have been by accident or by conscious experiment. It can be certain that, however it happened, the engaging lightness conferred on the cake by beating air into the egg and its consequent expansion during baking, opened the way to all types of sponge goods that are with us to-day.

During the centuries two methods have evolved.

1. Warm Method

The eggs and sugar are mixed together and warmed until the sugar is dissolved. The mixture is whipped until it is light, after which the flour is carefully mixed in. Any butter is melted and added with the flour.

2. Cold Method

The eggs are first separated. The yolks are whipped with some of the sugar and the whites with the balance. The two are blended together before the flour and butter (if any) is folded in.

According to the structural quality that is desired and the purpose of the finished sponge, each formula can be constructed within two limits.

Here are these formulae:

	Light lb oz		gr	Medium lb oz		gr	Heavy lb oz		gr
Eggs	1 4	50 %	600	1 4	40 %	600	1 0	33 $1/3$ %	500
Sugar (castor)	10	25 %	300	1 0	30 % (approx.)	500	1 0	33 $1/3$ %	500
Flour	10	25 %	300	1 0	30 % (approx.)	500	1 0	33 $1/3$ %	500
	Suitable for Swiss rolls			Suitable for fancies and gâteaux					

Eggs

The weight of egg can be adjusted by altering the proportion of yolks to whites.

An increase of egg yolks will add to the strength and deepen the colour of the sponge and at the same time reduce the moisture content. It will reduce the volume.

An increase in the amount of whites will have the opposite effect. It is inadvisable to use more than 50 % of yolks in the total weight of egg.

Flour

Some of the flour can be deleted and replaced with cornflour up to a proportion of 50 % flour and 50 % cornflour.

Almonds

Almonds can be added to a sponge mixture in the following way. Firstly grind down an equal weight of almonds and sugar. The mixture can be added without adjusting the weight of the other materials provided that the weight of the mixture does not exceed the weight of the sugar in the mix.

The cold method is used. Firstly the yolks are mixed with the sugar and almond mixture and beaten. The egg whites are whipped to a stiff snow and the two are carefully blended together before the sieved flour is folded in.

If ground almonds are used, they are sieved with the flour to a maximum of half the weight of sugar, the weight of almonds replacing the same weight of flour. The warm method is used in production.

Chocolate

Cocoa powder is used for colour and flavour, being well sieved into the flour at the rate of 2 oz. (60 gr.) cocoa powder to 14 oz. (430 gr.) of flour. To the weight of cocoa powder an equal weight of warm water should be stirred into the whipped egg/sugar, together with a little chocolate colour, before the flour is added.

It is important that the weight of cocoa powder that is added is sufficient to satisfy the Regulations current in Great Britain.

Butter

The butter is first melted and is carefully added with, or after, the flour.

For the warm method, butter can be added up to $4/5/80\%$ of the weight of sugar. For the cold method 50% of the sugar weight is sufficient.

Basic Butter Sponge

lb	oz		kg	gr
1	4	Egg		625
1	0	Sugar (castor)		500
1	0	Flour (soft)		500
	8	Butter (melted)		250
		Colour/flavour as desired		

Whisk the egg and sugar to a stiff sponge and add the colour and flavour. Fold in the flour and when half cleared pour in the melted butter and clear carefully.

Basic Chocolate Butter Sponge

lb	oz		kg	gr
1	4	Egg		625
1	0	Sugar		500
	14	Flour (soft)		440
	2	Cocoa powder		60
	2	Warm water		60
		Chocolate colour		

Sieve the flour and cocoa powder several times. Whisk the egg and sugar to a stiff sponge. Stir in the colour with the warm water. Fold in the flour and the melted butter.

Almond Sponge

lb	oz		kg	gr
1	4	Egg		625
	14	Sugar (castor)		435
	12	Flour (soft)		375
	6	Ground almonds		180

For a hazelnut sponge use ground hazelnuts.

Swiss Rolls

lb	oz		kg	gr
2	0	Egg	1	
	7	Egg yolks		200
1	0	Sugar (castor)		500
1	0	Flour		500

Whisk the egg, yolks and sugar to a stiff sponge. Fold in the sieved flour. Spread on to 3 paper lined baking sheets each about 24 in. × 18 in. (60 × 45 cm.).

(Germany)

Swiss Roll-Chocolate

lb	oz		kg	gr
1	4	Egg		600
	5 1/2	Egg yolks		160
	14	Sugar (castor)		400
	7	Couverture (dark)		200
	10	Flour		300
	3 1/2	Water		100

Whisk the egg, egg yolks and sugar to a stiff sponge. Stir the water into the melted couverture and carefully add to the sponge. Lastly fold in the sieved flour. Spread on to 2 baking sheets as above.
(Germany)

Swiss Roll-Hazelnut

lb	oz		kg	gr
	5	Egg yolks		150
	8	Egg whites		250
	5	Sugar (castor)		150
	3 1/2	Ground hazelnuts (roasted)		100
	3 1/2	Flour		100
	1/8	Cinnamon		4
	1 3/4	Butter		50

Whisk the hazelnuts and eggs yolks with one third of the sugar. Whisk the egg whites with the rest of the sugar to a stiff snow. Blend the two mixtures together, fold in the flour and cinnamon sieved together and lastly the melted butter. Sufficient for one baking sheet as above.
(Germany)

Swiss Roll-Lemon

lb	oz		kg	gr
1	2	Egg yolks		560
	14	Egg whites		420
	13	Sugar (castor)		400
	8	Flour		250
		Zest of 2 lemons		

Whisk the egg yolks with a quarter of the sugar, adding the lemon zest. Whisk the whites with the rest of the sugar to a stiff snow. Blend the two mixtures and fold in the sieved flour. Sufficient for two baking sheets as above. *(Germany)*

Almond Sponge Bases - Mandel-Biscuit-Böden

Ingredients for 4 bases 10 in. (25 cm.) in diameter.

lb	oz		kg	gr
	5 1/4	Egg yolks		150
	7 1/2	Egg whites		210
	5 1/4	Sugar		150
	7	Marzipan		200
	5 1/4	Flour		150

Beat the egg yolks and sugar until frothy, work into the marzipan until smooth. Whip the egg whites to a snow, fold in to the egg yolk/marzipan paste together with the flour. Divide into round hoops 10 in. (25 cm.) in diameter on baking sheets and bake. *(Germany)*

Walnut Sponge Bases

Ingredients for 5 thin bases 10 in. (25 cm.) in diameter.

lb	oz		kg	gr
	5	Egg		150
	3	Egg yolks		90
	6	Egg whites		180
	5 1/2	Sugar		165
	3 1/2	Ground walnuts		100
	3	Flour		90
	4	Fine sponge crumbs		125
		Cinnamon		
		Lemon zest		

Beat up the egg, egg yolks and 3 1/2 oz. (100 gr.) of sugar warming the mixture. Remove from the heat and continue beating until cool. Whip the egg whites and the rest of sugar (2 oz. [60 gr.]) to a stiff snow and fold into the egg/sugar sponge. Fold in the ground walnuts, flour, sponge crumbs, cinnamon and zest of lemon.

Deposit on to 5 circles of paper and bake quickly. *(Germany)*

Viennese Bases - Wiener Böden

Ingredients for 4 bases 10 in. (25 cm.) in diameter.

lb	oz		kg	gr
2	0	Egg	1	
1	4	Sugar		625
	4 1/2	Flour		140
	4 1/2	Cornflour		140
	9	Butter		270
		A little salt		

Beat the egg and sugar warm, remove from heat and continue beating. Blend in the flour and lastly add the hot butter. Fill into hoops and bake at 374-392° F (190-200° C). *(Germany)*

Mushroom Bases

Ingredients for 10 circular bases.

lb	oz		kg	gr
1	4	Egg		625
	12	Sugar		375
	12	Flour		375
	12	Butter		375
	2 1/4	Nougat		65

Whip the whites with half the sugar to a stiff meringue. Whip the yolks with the rest of the sugar and add the nougat paste. Blend the two mixtures and add the sieved flour and the melted butter.

Spread into circular shapes on to greaseproof paper and bake. *(Germany)*

Sponge Mixture for Othellos I
Very light

lb	oz		kg	gr
	7	Egg yolks		200
	10	Egg whites		300
	4	Sugar (castor)		120
	4	Flour		120
	4	Potato flour		120
	1 1/2	Water		45

Mix the yolks, water and flour to a paste. Whisk the egg whites, add the sugar, then carefully mix into the yolks/water/flour paste. Lastly fold in the potato flour. Bake at 320-340°F (160-170° C). *(Germany)*

Sponge Mixture for Othellos II
Heavy

lb	oz		kg	gr
	7	Egg yolks		200
	10	Egg whites		300
	8	Sugar (castor)		250
	7	Flour		200
	7	Cornflour		200

Whisk the egg yolks with half the sugar. Whisk the egg whites with the other half to a stiff snow. Blend the two mixtures and then fold in the sieved flour and cornflour. Alternatively the cornflour may be folded into the egg white/sugar snow, before blending with the yolk/sugar sponge.
(See also pages 345-346). *(Germany)*

Almond Sponge for Petits Fours

lb	oz		kg	gr
2	0	Raw marzipan *	1	
	7	Water		200
	8	Egg yolks		250
1	0	Egg		500
	7 1/2	Flour		220
	7 1/2	Butter		220

* Persipan may be used.

Mix the marzipan to a smooth paste with the water, add the yolks and egg and beat to a stiff sponge. Fold in the sieved flour and lastly the melted butter. Spread on to a greased and floured baking sheet about 14 in. × 22 in. (35 × 55 cm.). Bake at 424° F (220° C). *(Switzerland)*

Savoury Gâteaux Bases

lb	oz		kg	gr
1	0	1. Butter or margarine		500
1	2	Egg		560
	8	Liquid glucose		250
	8	Water		250
1	0	Special cake flour		500
1	0	Whey powder		500
	3/4	Cream of tartar		22
	1/4	Salt		8
	1	Bakers cheese		30
	2	2. Water		60
	3/8	Bicarbonate of soda		11

Place group 1 in machine bowl (liquid first) and whisk on top speed for 2 minutes.

Add group 2 and whisk 15 seconds on top speed.

Scale into greased and floured sandwich plates:

8 oz. into 8 in. plates (225 gr. into 20 cm.);
6 oz. into 6 in. plates (170 gr. into 15 cm.).
Bake at 360° F (182° C).

Genoese

In Great Britain it is common practice to use a basic formula for almost all fancies, gâteaux, layer cakes and battenburg, etc., varying it only to include pink colour or cocoa powder. Generally there are three types of genoese—light, heavy and high-sugar. It is the last, better known perhaps as high-ratio, which is mainly used at the present time.

Light Genoese - Butter Sponge

This is the true genoese and with variations, was used by British craftsmen in the past and by Continental craftsmen today. It is made by whisking the eggs—either whole or separated—with the sugar. When this is done the flour is carefully folded in whilst an assistant pours in the melted butter. This type of genoese is useful for fancies that do not have to be dipped into fondant or chocolate by hand. It is excellent for gâteaux bases and layer cakes also.

Here is a basic formula:

lb	oz		kg	gr
2	8	Egg	1	250
2	0	Sugar (castor)	1	
2	0	Flour (soft)	1	
1	0	Butter (melted)		500
		Colour/flavour as desired		

The genoese is made as described above. It is carefully spread on a paper lined baking sheet 18 in. × 36 in. (46 × 92 cm.) and baked at 370° F (187° C). For chocolate genoese, four ounces of the flour are replaced with four ounces of cocoa powder (sieved with the flour), some chocolate colour and four ounces of warm water. The colour and water are carefully stirred into the whisked egg and sugar.

Heavy Genoese

This is a genoese of extra tensile strength, so that pieces cut from it can be hand dipped into prepared fondant, without the pieces either breaking or crumbling.

It is made by beating the butter and sugar together until light, then beating the eggs in portion by portion; any colour and flavour is then added and lastly the flour is mixed in.

Here is a basic formula for this type of genoese:

lb	oz		kg	gr
2	0	Butter	1	
2	0	Sugar (castor)	1	
2	8	Egg	1	250
2	4	Flour (soft)	1	125
	4	Cornflour		125
		Colour/flavour as required		

The mixture is spread on a tray as described above and baked at 360° F (182° C). If chocolate genoese is required the adjustment is exactly as for light genoese.

(a) High-Sugar Genoese

This is the modern type of genoese made with special cake flour and super-glycerinated fat.

Here is a typical formula:

Stage I

lb	oz		kg	gr
2	0	Special cake flour		900
2	8	Sugar (castor)	1	125
	3	Dried milk powder		85
	1/4	Salt		7
	1 1/4	Baking powder		35
1	0	Special cake fat		450

Sieve the dry materials and place into the machine bowl with the fat. Mix to a crumbly consistency on low speed. Do not make into a paste.

Stage II

lb	oz		kg	gr
1	0	Cold water		450

Add gradually on slow speed, making certain that the mixture is free from lumps. Scrape the bowl down and mix for 4 minutes on low speed.

Stage III

lb	oz		kg	gr
1	8	Egg		680

Add slowly. Scrape the bowl down and the beater. Blend for a further 3 minutes on low speed.

Any flavour can be added at Stage II.

This type of mixture is always blended on low speed, never beaten at high speed, or the finished cake will be tough and it will shrink during baking. Here is a formula for a chocolate high-sugar genoese:

(b) Chocolate
Stage I

lb	oz		kg	gr
1	7	Special cake flour		655
	7 1/2	Cocoa powder		215
2	4	Sugar (castor)	1	20
	4	Dried milk powder		112
	1/4	Salt		7
	1 1/2	Baking powder		40
	15	Special cake fat		425

Stage II

lb	oz		kg	gr
1	3	Cold water		540

Stage III

lb	oz		kg	gr
1	6	Egg		625

The method of making and baking is exactly the same as for High-Sugar Genoese (a).

Here are formulae for delightful variations of Light Genoese-Butter Sponge.

Genoese

lb	oz		kg	gr
2	12	Egg whites	1	375
2	4	Egg yolks	1	125
2	8	Sugar (castor)	1	250
	5	Orange flower water		150
2	0	Flour (soft)	1	
	8	Ground almonds		250
2	0	Butter (melted)	1	

Whisk the yolks with the orange flower water and keep the mixture warm. Whisk the whites, adding the sugar gradually to a stiff meringue. Blend the yolks carefully with the meringue. Add the flour and ground almonds, previously sieved together, then blend in the melted butter. Spread on a prepared baking sheet and bake at 350° F (176° C).

Genoese-Almond

lb	oz		kg	gr
2	0	Butter	1	
2	0	Sugar (castor)	1	
2	8	Egg	1	250
1	8	Flour (soft)		750
1	0	Ground almonds		500
	2	Noyau		60

Firstly the butter and sugar are well beaten together, then the eggs are beaten in a portion at a time. Add the noyau then the flour and almonds that have been sieved together. Spread on to a prepared baking sheet and bake at 325° F (162° C).

This genoese is particularly suitable for gâteaux, slices and petits fours.

Genoese-Aveline

lb	oz		kg	gr
1	8	Egg yolks		750
1	12	Egg whites		875
1	2	Sugar (castor)		560
1	2	Flour (soft)		560
	8	Ground hazelnuts		250
	2	Ground bitter almonds		60
	12	Butter (melted)		375

The method of making is the same as for Genoese-Lemon sieving the flour and nuts together. It is baked at 400° F (204° C). This genoese is best spread thinly on prepared baking sheets, to be built up after baking, by sandwiching with jam, cream, etc.

Genoese-Chocolate I

lb	oz		kg	gr
1	12	Egg whites		875
1	4	Egg yolks		625
1	0	Sugar (castor)		500
	1	Vanilla sugar		30
	8	Ground almonds		250
	4	Flour (soft)		125
	8	Sponge crumbs		250
	4	Dark chocolate		125
1	0	Butter (melted)		500

Whip the whites to a stiff snow, then add the sugar until a stiff meringue is formed, then add the vanilla sugar. Stir in the yolks which have been whipped, then fold in the flour, ground almonds and sponge crumbs that have been well sieved together. Add the melted butter and, with the help of an assistant, stir in the melted chocolate. Care must be taken throughout, or the mixture will become tough. Bake at 350° F (176° C).

Genoese-Chocolate II

lb	oz		kg	gr
2	0	Butter		900
2	4	Sugar (castor)	1	20
2	8	Egg	1	135
1	12	Flour		795
	12	Ground almonds		340
	8	Cocoa powder		225
	1	Vanilla sugar		28
	4	Milk		112

The method of making is the same as for Genoese-Almond. The ground almonds and milk are added after the last of the eggs are beaten in. The flour and the cocoa powder, sieved together, are added last. Bake at 350° F (176° C).

Genoese-Coffee

lb	oz		kg	gr
1	12	Egg whites		875
1	4	Egg yolks		625
1	0	Sugar (castor)		500
	8	Flour (soft)		250
	2 1/2	Coffee infusion		75
	8	Ground almonds		250
	8	Sponge cake crumbs		250
1	0	Butter (melted)		500

Beat the yolks and coffee infusion together. Whip the whites, adding the sugar a little at a time until it is a stiff meringue. Stir in the yolks and coffee that have been previously whipped and kept warm. Carefully fold in the flour, ground almonds and sponge cake crumbs that have been sieved together and lastly the melted butter. Spread 3/4 in. (2 cm.) thick on to paper lined baking sheets and bake at 350° F (176° C).

This genoese is excellent for gâteaux bases, fancies and petits fours glacés.

Genoese-France

lb	oz		kg	gr
1	2	Sugar (castor)		560
1	10	Egg		800
1	2	Flour (soft)		560
	7	Butter		200

Break the eggs into a pan, add the sugar and beat up over a gentle heat until a temperature of about 104° F (40° C) is reached. Next whip up the mixture with the machine until it is completely cold. Remove from the machine and stir in the sieved flour and finally the cool melted butter. Bake the mixture in moulds or flan rings.

Genoese-Lemon

lb	oz		kg	gr
1	8	Egg yolks		750
2	8	Egg whites	1	250
2	0	Sugar (castor)	1	
1	8	Flour (soft)		750
1	0	Butter (melted)		500
		Zest of 2 lemons		

The whites are whisked to a still snow, adding the sugar gradually until a firm meringue is made. The yolks are whisked, and, with the zest of lemon, the two mixtures are carefully blended together. The flour is then added and finally the melted butter. The genoese is baked at 350° F (176° C).

Genoese-Margherita

lb	oz		kg	gr
2	4	Egg yolks	1	125
	14	Egg		400
2	10	Sugar (castor)	1	300
1	8	Flour (soft)		750
	10	Cornflour		300
1	0	Butter (melted)		500
		Maraschino		

Whip the yolks, egg, sugar and maraschino to a stiff sponge. Fold in the sieved flour and cornflour carefully, and then the melted butter. Bake at 350° F (176° C). This genoese is ideal for gâteaux bases.

Genoese-Marzipan

lb	oz		kg	gr
1	11	Egg yolks		840
	14	Egg		435
	10	Egg whites		300
1	0	Sugar (castor)		500
	8	Flour (soft)		250
	12	Ground almonds		375
	8	Butter (melted)		250
	2 1/2	Warm water		75
		Zest of 2 lemons		

Whip the yolks, egg and 12 oz. (375 gr.) of sugar to a stiff sponge. Whip the whites with 4 oz. (125 gr.) of sugar to a stiff meringue. Stir the flour and ground almonds, which have been sieved together, into the whipped yolks, egg and sugar, then blend in the meringue. Finally add the melted butter. This genoese is baked at 350° F (176° C).

Genoese-Rose

lb	oz		kg	gr
1	8	Egg whites		750
1	0	Egg yolks		500
1	4	Sugar (castor)		625
1	0	Flour (soft)		500
	8	Ground almonds		250
	8	Butter		250
	2 1/2	Rose water		75
		Carmine colour		

Whip the whites up stiffly adding the sugar in portions until a firm meringue is produced, then add the carmine colour. Stir in the yolks and rose water which have been lightly beaten, then the flour and almonds which have been well sieved together. Lastly stir in the melted butter which has been allowed to get nearly cold. Spread 3/4 in. (2 cm.) thick on to prepared baking sheets and bake at 350° F (176° C).

Genoese-Turin

lb	oz		kg	gr
1	12	Egg whites		875
1	12	Egg yolks		875
1	12	Sugar (castor)		875
1	4	Flour (soft)		625
1	0	Ground almonds		500
1	4	Butter (melted)		625
		Noyau		

Beat the yolks with 1 lb. (500 gr.) of the sugar and the noyau until the mixture is light. The whites with the balance of the sugar are whipped to a meringue, after which the flour is carefully folded in. The almonds and then the melted butter are blended into the beaten yolks. The two mixtures are then carefully blended together. It is baked at 350° F (176° C).

Care must be taken with this genoese because of its richness.

Genoese-Viennese

As for Viennese Bases *(page 197)*.

Genoese-Walnut

lb	oz		kg	gr
2	0	Butter	1	
2	0	Sugar (castor)	1	
2	8	Egg	1	250
2	4	Flour (soft)	1	125
	1/4	Baking powder		8
1		Vanilla sugar		30
	8	Finely chopped walnuts		250

The genoese is made exactly as for Genoese-Rose. The chopped walnuts are added last. Bake at 350° F (176° C).

Boiled Genoese

lb	oz		kg	gr
1	0	Butter		450
1	4	Flour		565
1	2	Sugar		510
1	4	Egg		565
	1/8	Baking powder		4
		Colour/flavour		

Bring the butter to the boil in a large bowl. Add 18 oz. (500 gr.) of flour. Whip the egg and sugar to a stiff sponge and add this a portion at a time into the hot butter/flour mixture. Add the balance of the flour which has been sieved with the baking powder, stirring carefully. Run the mixture onto a paper lined baking sheet, spread level and bake at 370° F (188° C).

Butter Sponge Bases and Sheet Genoese

Ingredients for 1 base 10 in. (25 cm.) in diameter.

lb	oz		kg	gr
	2 1/4	Egg yolks		60
	6 1/2	Egg whites		185
	7	Sugar (castor)		200
	3 1/2	Flour (soft)		100
	3 1/2	Cornflour		100
	1 3/4	Hot butter		50

For a sheet 36 in. × 18 in. (92 × 46 cm.).

lb	oz		kg	gr
	12	Egg yolks		340
2	0	Egg whites		900
2	4	Sugar (castor)	1	20
1	2	Flour (soft)		510
1	2	Cornflour		510
	9	Hot butter		255

Beat the egg yolks and half the sugar until foamy. Whip the egg whites and the rest of the sugar to a snow and fold into the egg yolk/sugar sponge with the flour and cornflour. Lastly add the hot butter, fill into a hoop and bake.

Sheets of butter sponge (genoese) are spread on to paper lined baking sheets.

(Germany)

Baumkuchen

Ingredients for approx: 10 lb. (4 1/2 kg.).

lb	oz		kg	gr
1	10	Butter		800
2	7	Sugar	1	200
	15	Egg yolks		450
2	2	Egg whites	1	50
1	7	Cornflour		700
	8	Ground almonds (roasted)		250
	1/8	Arrack		5
	1/4	Salt		10
		2 vanilla pods		
		2 lemons		

Method of making:

Cream the butter and 1 lb. 8 oz. (750 gr.) sugar. Whip the egg whites and the rest of the sugar to a stiff snow and gradually add the egg yolks.

Blend the cornflour and ground almonds with the butter/sugar mixture, then fold in the snow. Lastly add the lemons, vanilla, arrack and salt.

The Baumkuchen is baked on a special machine which in principle is a revolving spit. The spit is a tapered wooden roller which revolves in front of gas jets or electric elements. The speed of the spit is controlled by a variable speed electric motor and the spit can be raised and lowered according to the heat.

The spit is first covered with white paper which is fastened securely with thin string.

The mixture is poured or ladled evenly on to the papered spit as it slowly revolves. Up to 14-15 layers are put on successively, and at regular intervals some is removed with a brush in a similar manner that metal or wood is cut away on a lathe to make a design or pattern.

For the last layer, the mixture is thinned down a little with unwhipped dairy cream. When cool, the Baumkuchen is removed from the spit, brushed with well boiled apricot purée and coated with fondant or chocolate. It is usually decorated with paper sculpture on top or with flowers made from marzipan or pulled sugar. Sometimes the top decoration is a figure in blown sugar.

The Baumkuchen can be cut for use as gâteaux or fancies.

Pound Cakes

In Great Britain this name has been given to plain and lightly fruited cakes, usually baked in hoops, and which are about 1 lb. (500 gr.) in weight. The name probably derived from the fact that the basic formula for these cakes many years ago was 'a pound all round', that is:

BASIC CAKE MIX

	lb	oz	gr
Butter	1	0	500
Sugar	1	0	500
Egg	1	0	500
Flour	1	0	500

Sometimes this basic formula was extended to a pound all round and a pinch, the pinch being baking powder. If a fruited pound cake was desired, then 1 lb. (500 gr.) of fruit was added to the basic mix.

The method of making was either the flour or sugar batter, both of which are described on page 44.

At the present time, the range of such cakes has been extended. The shape now is usually an oblong, a shape which lends itself better to oven loading and to wrapping. In addition, the high sugar type of cake is becoming increasingly popular. This type of cake is made by using the blending method, see page 44. Special cake flour and super-glycerinated fat are both necessary for this type of cake.

The fruited cake originated from a piece of fermented dough, into which fat, sugar, fruit and some spice were mixed. It was known as a plum cake.

The discovery of the aerating properties of eggs and the introduction of baking powder eliminated the need for yeast as an aerating agent and opened the way for plain and lightly fruited cakes. The heavier substance of the old plum cake, however, was well liked and the only way to approach this heavier type of cake is by an increase in the fruit content.

Heavily fruited cakes are invariably dark in colour and apart from the amount and type of fruit used, this is effected by the use of dark sugar, black treacle and caramel. The flavour is augmented by the judicious use of spices and the zest and juice of citrus fruits. A table of fruit levels will be seen at the bottom of the page.

Slab Cakes

The mass manufacture of cakes of consistently high quality in Great Britain is a result of the introduction of machinery and technological control. It has happened only during the last half century. Before then, good quality cakes were the result of craftsmanship, good quality materials and careful baking.

With slab cakes the modern trend is for the wrapping of pieces of predetermined weight. Wrappers are transparent and this is ideal, for not only can the cut surface be seen, the wrapper itself retards staling; further, the cake can be easily and hygienically transported from the bakery to the shop and from the shop to the home.

Slabs can be of any size and of any type. They can be plain, or with additions such as coconut, caraway seeds, cherries, sultanas, currants, peel or a mixture of some

---

Lightly fruited	4 oz. (125 gr.)	of fruit to each 16 oz. (500 gr.) of batter
Medium fruited	8 oz. (250 gr.)	of fruit to each 16 oz. (500 gr.) of batter
Medium/heavy fruited	12-16 oz. (375-500 gr.)	of fruit to each 16 oz. (500 gr.) of batter
Heavy fruited	16-18 oz. (500-560 gr.)	of fruit to each 16 oz. (500 gr.) of batter

	Fruit	Batter
Birthday Cakes	45 %	55 %
Christmas Cakes	50 %	50 %
Wedding Cakes	55 %	45 %

At least 50 % of the fruit in a bride cake should be currants.

of these. Plain slabs can be sliced after baking and sandwiched with jam and/or cream. The tops of slab cakes can be decorated before baking with almonds or, after baking, with almond paste, fondant and preserved fruits.

Slab cakes can be baked either in metal tins or wooden frames. Metal tins will need more protection from the heat because metal is a more efficient conductor of heat than wood. The wooden frames necessary for the recipes given should be made of wood about $1/2$ in. (12 mm.) in thickness and approximately 12 in. × 8 in. (30 × 20 cm.) inside measurements. The same inside measurements are necessary for metal tins. For the high ratio type of madeira slab cake, wooden frames 12 in. × 6 in. (30 × 15 cm.) are suggested.

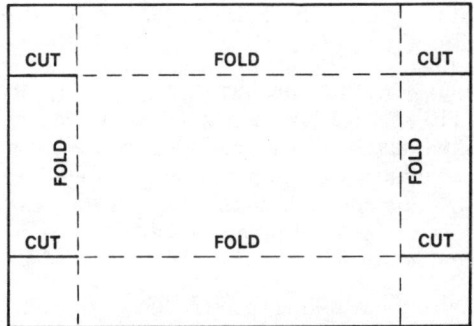

Paper slab cake lining-method of cutting

The frames are first lined with thick paper and then with greaseproof paper of special food quality. Metal tins will need several thicknesses of paper. The papers are cut as in the illustration, the dotted lines showing where the paper is to be folded.

When cut for display, slab cakes should be uniform in thickness. The crust should be thin and golden in colour; the crumb should be bright and attractive. The fruit should be well distributed and be bright and colourful in appearance. Cherries should be bold, clear red in colour, about $1/2$-$3/4$ in. (12-18 mm.) size. They should be washed in tepid water and well drained before use.

Meringues

The term meringue covers all forms of beaten egg whites and sugar, almost irrespective of the proportions used, the additions and any combinations.
(Illustration page 111.)

They can be subdivided under three headings. 1 Cold, 2 Hot, 3 Boiled (Italian). Each can be again subdivided into heavy or light meringue according to the proportion of sugar to egg whites used. Recipes based on 10 oz. (300 gr.) of egg whites ($1/2$ pint) are given at the bottom of the page.

The greatest care must be taken to keep all equipment and materials free from grease. No trace of egg yolk should be allowed in the whites. Grease will shorten the protein strands and prevent the inclusion of air.

	Cold Light lb oz	Cold Light gr	Cold Heavy lb oz	Cold Heavy gr	Hot Light lb oz	Hot Light gr	Hot Heavy lb oz	Hot Heavy gr
Egg whites		10		10		10		10
		300		300		300		300
Sugar (castor)	1 4	625	1 12	875	1 0	500	1 12	875
Sugar (preserving)	—		—		—		—	
Water	—		—		—		—	
Cream of tartar	*		*		*		*	
Glucose	—		—		—		—	
Couverture (Plain unsweetened)	—		—		—		—	

	Boiled (Italian)					
	Light		Heavy		Chocolate	
	lb oz	gr	lb oz	gr	lb oz	gr
Egg whites	10	300	10	300	10	300
Sugar (castor)	—		—		8	250
Sugar (preserving)	1 0	500	1 8	750	1 4	625
Water	5	150	7½	225	6	185
Cream of tartar	*		*		*	
Glucose	1½	45	2	60	1¾	50
Couverture (Plain unsweetened)	—		—		12	375

* Approximately $1/32$ oz. (1 gr.) of cream of tartar may be used to strengthen the meringue, but with firm egg whites it is not strictly necessary. The same amount of cream of tartar *or* the stated amount of glucose is used in the sugar boiling for the Italian meringue to prevent graining.

METHODS

Cold Meringue

The egg whites and the cream of tartar (if used) are placed into the machine and whisked until a stiff 'snow' is produced. With the whisking continuing on medium speed, half of the sugar is added a little at a time until a stiff meringue is formed. Any colour and flavour is now added and mixed in. The balance of the sugar is added either by folding in with a spatula or by the continued use of the machine.

Hot Meringue

Proceed as for cold meringue in the first stage. Make the sugar hot and run it into the whites while the machine is at medium speed. Continue whisking until a firm meringue is formed. Any colour and flavour is then added.

Boiled (Italian) Meringue

Place the sugar and water in a boiling pan and, after the sugar is dissolved, heat to 225° F (107° C). Remove any scum and wash the sides of the pan with a brush dipped into clean water. Remove the spatula and run in the cream of tartar, dispersed in a little water, *or* the warmed glucose. The addition will mix by the action of the currents set up by boiling. Stirring from this point on may cause the solution to grain.

Boil to the soft ball degree, 245° F (118° C), washing the sides of the pan at intervals. While the boiling is proceeding, the whites are whisked to a stiff 'snow' on medium speed, so that it reaches the peak as the sugar solution reaches the desired temperature.

With the whisking speed reduced, the boiling sugar solution is carefully poured in, then, with the speed increased to medium, whisking is continued until the meringue is firm. Do not attempt to scrape out the boiling pan or graining will result. Add colour and flavour last.

Chocolate Meringue

Whilst the greatest care must be taken to keep a meringue free from grease, chocolate, which contains fat, can be blended into a boiled meringue by making a slight alteration in the method.

The required amount of sugar and water is boiled to 250° F (121° C), proceeding as for boiled meringue and taking the same precautions. This solution is poured into a meringue made from the egg whites and a small proportion of castor sugar.

The couverture is melted to a temperature of approximately 100° F (38° C), and carefully blended in at the last.

The terms used to describe the types of meringue are those used in Great Britain. In France the 'cold' meringue is known as 'Swiss', the 'hot' as 'Spanish' whilst the 'boiled' is known as the 'Italian' as in Great Britain.

Swiss Method

lb	oz		kg	gr
1	4	Egg whites		625
2	4	Sugar	1	125

Whisk the egg whites with $^2/_3$ of the sugar until very stiff, then fold in the remainder of the sugar with a wooden spatula. This mixture is used for plain meringues.

(France)

Italian Method

lb	oz		kg	gr
	15	Egg whites		450
2	0	Sugar	1	
	7	Water		200

Cook 1 $^1/_2$ lb. (750 gr.) sugar with the water to a temperature of 245° F (118.3° C).

Whisk the egg whites with the rest of the sugar until stiff. Next pour in the cooked sugar slowly, whisking all the time. This mixture is used for petits fours and certain chocolate meringues (chocolate scrolls, kisses, soufflés, etc.). A slow oven 320° F (160° C) is used for this type of meringue mixture.

(France)

Spanish Method

lb	oz		kg	gr
1	0	Egg whites		500
2	10	Sugar	1	300

Whisk the ingredients in a pan over gentle heat until the mixture becomes frothy; then use the mixing machine to beat up until the mixture has cooled. *(France)*

Drying Meringues

Strictly speaking, meringues are dried and not baked. At temperatures suitable for baking, the sugar will caramelize and so spoil the colour internally and externally. It is usual to place in an oven at a temperature of approximately 270° F (132° C) until the meringues are set and then to place them in a warm cupboard or prover for some hours to completely dry out.

In Germany, it is usual to use an oven at a temperature of 320° F (160° C). The time in the oven is shorter, but they have much longer in the drier.

Meringue Bases

lb	oz		kg	gr
	10	Egg whites ($^1/_2$ pt)		300
1	2	Sugar		500

Whip up to a stiff snow. Pipe out the meringue into circles of the desired size on to paper lined baking sheets. The size of the circles may be pencilled on the paper. The circles are piped in whirl formation using a savoy bag fitted with a plain pipe.

Place in an oven at 320° F (160° C) and dry out in a warm cupboard. *(Germany)*

Chocolate Meringue

lb	oz		kg	gr
	12	Egg whites		375
2	0	Sugar (granulated)	1	
1	0	Water		500
	5	Block cocoa		150

Boil the sugar and water to 245° F (118° C). Melt the block cocoa and work to a smooth paste with a little stock syrup. Whip the whites to a stiff snow, then slowly pour the boiled syrup into the whites in a steady stream. Add the cocoa paste. *(Germany)*

Strawberry Meringue

lb	oz		kg	gr
	10	Egg whites		300
1	0	Sugar		500
1	0	Strawberry purée		500
	2 $^1/_2$	Glucose		75
	5	Water		150

Boil the water, sugar and glucose to 270° F (132° C). Stir in the strawberry purée which will reduce the temperature. Reheat to 245° F (118° C). Pour on to the stiffly whisked whites and add a few drops of cochineal.

This meringue can be made with all sorts of fruit purées. It is used as a filling for petits fours, cakes and iced soufflés.
(France)

Meringue for Decoration

lb	oz		kg	gr
	12	Egg whites		360
	15	Sugar (castor)		450
	1/2	Vanilla sugar		15

Whisk all the ingredients to a stiff meringue. The mixture may be coloured and flavoured as desired. *(Germany)*

Japonaise

Japonaise is a meringue with an addition of ground almonds or hazelnuts. Coconut also can be used. The nut addition can be to a maximum of two thirds (66 $\frac{2}{3}$ %) of the combined weight of sugar and egg whites.

For special mixtures, oil or melted butter can be added at the rate of one part to twenty parts egg whites. Flour or cornflour can be added also at the same rate.

Recipes can be constructed between two limits:

Light

    10 parts egg whites
    10 parts sugar
    10 parts ground almonds or hazelnuts *

Heavy

    10 parts egg whites
    20 parts sugar
    20 parts ground almonds or hazelnuts *

* The nuts may be used unroasted or lightly roasted. It is general practice, however, to lightly roast hazelnuts only.

Japonaise can be either piped or stencilled on to greased and floured baking sheets. The stencils are in the form of rubber mats with circles, ovals, or finger shapes cut at regular intervals.

Small japonaise shapes are used to make fancies. Larger circular shapes are used in the construction of torten; these are generally piped out into spiral shaped circles.

Here are some recipes that fall between the above limits:

	Almond		Hazelnut		Coconut		Torten bases		Stencils	
	lb oz	gr	lb oz	gr	lb oz	gr	lb oz	gr	lb oz	gr
Egg whites	10	300	10	300	10	300	10	300	10	300
Sugar (castor)	1 0	500	1 0	500	1 0	500	1 0	500	14	435
Ground almonds	8	250	—		—		10	300*	10	300*
Ground hazelnuts	—		8	250	—		—		—	
Coconut flour	—		—		4	125	—		—	
Coconut (fine desiccated)	—		—		4	125	—		—	
Cornflour	—		—		1/2	15	—		—	

* Ground hazelnuts can be used instead of ground almonds.

Japonaise made with Marzipan

lb	oz		kg	gr
	4	Egg whites		125
	15	Raw marzipan		500
	4	Sugar		125
	1 ³/₄	Cornflour		50
	6	Egg whites		175
	5	Sugar		150
	¹/₃₂	Cream of tartar		1

Mix the marzipan and a little of the egg white to make a smooth paste. Mix the sugar and cornflour together and add in portions alternatively with the whites.

Whisk the 6 oz. (175 gr.) of whites, the 5 oz. (150 gr.) of sugar and the cream of tartar to a firm meringue. Blend the meringue into the marzipan paste very carefully.

The japonaise made from ground almonds or hazelnuts have a more open texture than those made from marzipan; the latter, however, have a more pronounced flavour of almonds.

Japonaise Torten Bases

lb	oz		kg	gr
	13	Egg whites		400
1	0	Sugar (castor)		500
1	3	Ground hazelnuts		600
	2 ¹/₂	Flour		75
	1	Cocoa powder		30
	2 ¹/₂	Potato flour		75

Whisk the egg whites until firm gradually adding a little less than half the sugar and the potato flour. Mix the hazelnuts, flour, cocoa powder and the rest of the sugar and blend into the meringue. *(Germany)*

Japonaise for Piping

lb	oz		kg	gr
	10	Egg whites		300
	13	Sugar (castor)		400
	6 ¹/₂	Ground almonds or hazelnuts		200
	1 ¹/₂	Flour		50

Whisk the egg whites to a stiff snow gradually adding half the sugar. Lightly fold in the rest of the sugar mixed with the almonds and the flour. *(Germany)*

Japonaise for Roulades

lb	oz		kg	gr
	7 ¹/₂	Egg whites		240
	8	Sugar (castor)		250
	4	Ground almonds		125

Whisk the egg whites until firm gradually adding a little less than half the sugar. Mix the rest of the sugar with the almonds and fold in.

Using a savoy bag fitted with a plain pipe, this mixture is piped out in lines which are parallel and touching, on to greased baking sheets. After baking they are removed from the baking sheets and left in a place where the air is humid. Alternatively, they can be piped on to paper lined baking sheets. When baked they are turned over and the paper removed after damping. The roulades are spread with cream and suchlike fillings and rolled up as for Swiss rolls. *(Germany)*

Züngli Mixture

lb	oz		kg	gr
	10	Egg whites		300
	10	Sugar (castor)		300
	10	Ground almonds		300
	1	Flour		30
	3	Butter (melted)		90

Whisk the egg whites to a stiff snow, gradually adding a third of the sugar. Fold the almonds and the remaining sugar into the meringue and lastly blend in the butter carefully. *(Switzerland)*

Almond and Hazelnut Products

Basic mixes for almond goods can be subdivided under three headings: Marzipan and Almond pastes, Macaroon pastes and other Almond mixings.

MARZIPAN AND ALMOND PASTES

In Great Britain there has always been confusion in the use of these terms, often they are interchangeable being used to describe either one or the other.

Generally, the knowledgeable would assert that marzipan should contain two parts almonds and one part sugar, ground together and cooked. It is known as 'raw marzipan'. Almond paste or almond icing should contain one part almonds and two parts sugar, together with sufficient egg or glucose to make a pliable paste.

Alternatively, almond paste or almond icing can be made by mixing an equal quantity of marzipan and sugar. Orange flower water is the traditional flavour. In Great Britain a proposed Draft Code of Practice lays down that the terms shall be synonymous and that either should contain not less than 23.5 % dry almond matter and no other nut ingredient and not less than 75 % of the remainder shall be solid carbohydrate sweetening matter.

Very few craftsmen make raw marzipan in Great Britain, almost all of it being bought from large manufacturers. Reputable firms will guarantee a certain almond content.

Apart from orange flower water, marzipans and almond pastes can be flavoured according to taste with rosewater, rum, kirsch, and other spirits or liqueurs. For fruit flavoured marzipan, the zest of citrus fruits and sometimes some of the pulp can be ground together with the other ingredients.

Almond Paste I

lb	oz		kg	gr
1	0	Ground almonds		500
1	0	Sugar (castor)		500
1	0	Sugar (icing)		500
	6	Egg yolks (approx.)		185
	2	Orange flower water		60

Make into a pliable paste.

Almond Paste II - Warm

lb	oz		kg	gr
1	0	Ground almonds		500
1	0	Sugar (icing)		500
1	0	Sugar (castor)		500
	2	Egg		50
	4 $1/2$	Yolks		125
	2	Orange flower water		60

Warm the castor sugar, egg and yolks to 90° F (32° C). Add other ingredients and make into a plastic paste.

Almond Paste III - Boiled

lb	oz		kg	gr
1	0	Ground almonds		500
2	0	Sugar (granulated)	1	
	10	Water		300
	2	Glucose		60
	2	Orange flower water		60

Boil the water and sugar to 240° F (115° C) and stir in the glucose and the orange flower water. Finally add the ground almonds.

Almond Paste IV

lb	oz		kg	gr
2	0	Raw marzipan	1	
1	0	Sugar (castor)		500
1	0	Sugar (icing)		500

Blend together. The above quantities of sugar may include 3.5 % glucose.

Almond Paste V

lb	oz		kg	gr
2	0	Raw marzipan	1	
1	0	Fondant		500
1	0	Sugar (icing)		500

Blend together.

Almond Paste VI

lb	oz		kg	gr
2	3	Blanched almonds	1	100
	1	Bitter almonds		30
3	4	Sugar	1	625
1	0	Water		500
	2 $1/2$	Glucose		75

Shred the almonds after blanching and dry them a little. Boil the sugar, water and glucose to 245° F (117.5° C) and pour over the almonds. Mix and allow to cool. Grind to a fine paste. *(France)*

Almond Paste VII

lb	oz		kg	gr
1	0	Almonds		500
2	0	Sugar	1	
		Half a vanilla pod		

Blanch the almonds and pound very finely in a mortar with the scraped vanilla and a little water. Boil the sugar to the soft crack degree *(page 51)*. Add it to the almonds in a steady stream, pounding constantly meanwhile, and work to a soft paste. *(France)*

Almond Paste VIII

lb	oz		kg	gr
1	0	Ground almonds		500
1	0	Sugar		500
	8	Butter		250
		Water		
		Rosewater		
		Orange flower water		

Put the almonds, sugar and butter into a pan and add sufficient rosewater and orange flower water to flavour and sufficient water to make a rather soft paste. Heat and stir until the paste leaves the side of the pan. Allow to cool. *(France)*

Almond Paste IX

lb	oz		kg	gr
2	8	Almonds	1	250
4	8	Sugar	2	250
1	8	Water		750
	6 ½	Glucose		200

Grind the almonds until fairly oily; the right consistency has been reached when they can be pressed together with the hand. Bring the water and sugar to the boil and add the glucose. Boil to the small ball degree *(page 51)*. Remove from the heat and stir in the almonds thoroughly. Before the paste hardens, spread it thinly on a marble slab or work it a little longer. Break into several pieces and store in tins. Flavour as desired before use.

For chocolate centres the sugar should be boiled to the soft crack degree *(page 51)*. *(France)*

Almond Paste X

lb	oz		kg	gr
2	3	Blanched almonds	1	
	1	Bitter almonds		30
1	10	Sugar (icing)		800
1	14	Sugar (granulated)		935

Shred the freshly blanched almonds and grind coarsely with the granulated sugar. Dry the mixture out in a pan over heat. When cool, grind down, adding the icing sugar by hand. *(Germany)*

Hazelnut Marzipan

lb	oz		kg	gr
1	3	Blanched almonds		550
1	2	Lightly roasted skinned hazelnuts		500
3	5	Sugar	1	500
	2 ½	Glucose		75
1	0	Water		500

Proceed as for Almond Paste VI. *(France)*

Walnut Marzipan

lb	oz		kg	gr
1	8	Blanched almonds		750
	12	Green walnuts		375
3	5	Sugar	1	500
	2 ½	Glucose		75
1	0	Water		500

As for Almond Paste VI. *(France)*

Pistachio Marzipan

lb	oz		kg	gr
2	0	Blanched almonds	1	
	4	Blanched pistachio nuts		125
3	5	Sugar	1	500
	2 ½	Glucose		75
1	0	Water		500

As for Almond Paste VI. *(France)*

Chocolate Marzipan

lb	oz		kg	gr
2	3	Blanched almonds	1	
3	5	Sugar	1	500
	2 1/2	Glucose		75
1	0	Water		500
	3 1/2	Cocoa		100
	3 1/2	Stock syrup up to		100

As for Almond Paste VI. Add the cocoa during grinding. If the marzipan crumbles, add a little stock syrup. *(France)*

Coffee Marzipan

lb	oz		kg	gr
2	3	Blanched almonds	1	
3	5	Sugar	1	500
	2 1/2	Glucose		75
1	0	Water		500
	5	Coffee (strong infusion)		150

As for Almond Paste VI but boil the sugar to 288° F (142.5° C). *(France)*

Apricot Marzipan

lb	oz		kg	gr
1	0	Marzipan		500
1	0	Apricot jam		500

Mix thoroughly. *(Germany)*

MACAROON PASTES

These pastes are made as the filling for the great variety of almond goods made by the baker. They can be made in bulk. Small quantities are adjusted in consistency according to how the paste is to be used. Basically, it is a mixing of ground almonds, coarse sugar and egg whites. Sometimes the paste contains ground rice.

Macaroon Paste - Basic

lb	oz		kg	gr
1	0	Ground almonds		500
	8	Sugar (coarse granulated)		250
	1	Ground rice		30
	5	Egg whites (approx.)		150

Mix all ingredients together.

Macaroon Paste with Whole Egg

lb	oz		kg	gr
2	0	Basic macaroon paste	1	
	6	Whole egg (approx.)		185

Mix and allow to stand for at least 30 minutes before using. The zest of 1 lemon or 1 orange can be added to the above.

Macaroon Paste I

lb	oz		kg	gr
1	2	Blanched almonds		560
1	2	Sugar		560
	11	Egg whites (approx.)		330

Shred the almonds, mix with the sugar and whites and pass through the grinder twice. *(France)*

Macaroon Paste II

lb	oz		kg	gr
1	0	Blanched almonds		500
1	0	Sugar		500
	7	Egg whites (approx.)		200
	3 1/2	Double cream		100

Pound the almonds in a mortar, moistening with a few drops of water to prevent oiling. Mix with the sugar, then pound in the cream and sufficient egg whites to make a soft but not liquid paste. *(France)*

Macaroon Paste - Hot

lb	oz		kg	gr
1	2	Blanched almonds		550
1	9	Sugar		750
	10	Egg whites (approx.)		300

Grind the almonds with half the sugar, moistening with a little water to prevent the mixture from becoming oily. Put in a machine with the rest of the sugar and the egg whites and beat over heat until a temperature of 122° F (50° C) is reached. Leave to cool. *(France)*

Macaroon Paste-Hazelnut

lb	oz		kg	gr
1	2	Hazelnuts (blanched and coarsely ground)		560
1	10	Sugar		800
1	0	Egg whites (approx.)		500

Mix the hazelnuts and sugar with a third of the whites. Continue adding and mixing until the paste is of piping consistency.

Goods made from this paste may not be sold as macaroons in France. *(France)*

Macaroon Paste for Petits Fours

lb	oz		kg	gr
2	12	Marzipan	1	375
1	10	Sugar		800
	12	Egg whites (approx.)		375

Mix all the ingredients well together. For further details see recipe for 'Petits Fours' *(page 522)*. *(Germany)*

Egg Yolk Macaroon Paste

lb	oz		kg	gr
	9	Marzipan		280
1	0	Egg yolks		500
		Zest of lemon		

Mix the ingredients to a smooth paste. *(Germany)*

OTHER ALMOND AND HAZELNUT MIXINGS

There are variations possible when making gianduja.

1. Replace almonds with hazelnuts.
2. Replace 50 % almonds with hazelnuts.
3. Replace almonds with pistachio nuts.
4. Gianduja can be made white by using milk couverture instead of plain; by replacing half or all the couverture with cocoa butter; by lightly roasted the almonds or hazelnuts.

Gianduja I (dark)

lb	oz		kg	gr
1	0	Roasted almonds		500
1	0	Sugar (icing)		500
	7	Couverture (plain)		200

Grind the almonds and icing sugar together and add the melted couverture. When cool, grind once or twice again.

Gianduja II (lighter)

lb	oz		kg	gr
1	0	Almonds (lightly roasted)		500
1	4	Sugar (icing)		625
	8	Cocoa butter		250
	4	Couverture (milk)		125

Grind the almonds and sugar together until oily. Transfer to a bowl and mix in the melted couverture and cocoa butter. Pour the mixture on to a baking sheet lined with greaseproof paper. When completely cold, cut into strips and grind again, setting the rollers close together.

Gianduja Cream

lb	oz		kg	gr
1	0	Ground and roasted almonds		500
1	0	Sugar (icing)		500
	4 $1/2$	Groundnut fat		140
	8	Couverture		250

Suitable for filling tuiles, etc. *(page 518)*. Proceed as above.

Almond Wafer Mixture

lb	oz		kg	gr
	14	Blanched almonds		435
1	5	Sugar (icing)		650
	7	Flour		200
	7	Egg whites		200
	7	Milk (approx.)		200

Grind the almonds and sugar without moistening. Mix in the flour, followed by the egg whites and milk. *(France)*
(Illustrations pages 134-138).

PRALINE - CROQUANT - NOUGAT

There is much confusion over what is meant by the terms praline, croquant and nougat.

When sugar, with the addition of lemon juice, is heated carefully (caramelized), it becomes an amber coloured syrup. If warmed chopped or flaked almonds or hazelnuts are added, and the mixture is poured on to an oiled marble slab, it can be pinned out with an oiled rolling pin and cut into shapes for the decoration of petits fours, genoese fancies, gâteaux and torten. It can also be moulded (see illustrations *page 159*). For the purpose of clarity, this will be termed 'praline croquant'. (Croquant is a French word meaning crunchy). It is known in France as 'Nougat-de-Paris', not to be confused with the well known and entirely different product, Nougat Monté-limar.

If praline croquant is crushed, the pieces will be termed 'crushed praline croquant'. If the crushed praline nougat is sieved, the product is termed 'sieved praline croquant'. Both are used for inclusion in creams and ices, and for the decoration and masking of genoese fancies, gâteaux and torten.

When praline croquant is ground, a paste is formed by the release of almond or hazelnut oil. The delicately flavoured paste is termed 'praline paste'. It is used for flavour creams and ices. In Germany praline paste is known as 'nougat'. If chocolate is added to the paste it is termed 'chocolate nougat'.

'Krokant' consists of roasted almonds, hazelnuts or walnuts together with melted sugar and vanilla. It is used warm, e.g. for ornamental figures, Easter eggs, etc. Crushed, sieved 'Krokant' is used for desserts, buttercream, ice cream and cake and for decorating the top and sides of torten.

If the praline is made with peanuts or coconut, this must be clearly specified.

Nougat-de-Paris

lb	oz		kg	gr
1	10	Sugar		800
1	2	Flaked almonds		560
		Lemon juice		

Melt half the sugar in a long handled pan, adding the lemon juice and stirring briskly. Add the rest of the sugar a little at a time making certain that it remains a pale amber in colour. Mix in the almonds, which have been warmed and pour the mix on to an oiled marble slab. Fold in the edges toward the middle several times with a palette knife, before rolling out with an oiled rolling pin. *(France)*

Praline Paste

lb	oz		kg	gr
4	0	Sugar	2	
3	0	Hazelnuts	1	500
1	0	Almonds		500

Proceed as for 'Nougat-de-Paris' and when cool grind down finely to a paste. *(France)*

Chocolate Nougat I

lb	oz		kg	gr
1	0	Almonds		500
1	0	Sugar		500
	3 $1/2$	Couverture (plain)		100

Make praline croquant (Nougat-de-Paris) with the sugar and the almonds. Crush and grind between rollers to a smooth, semi-liquid praline paste. Add 3 $1/2$ oz. (100 gr.) couverture for a soft nougat and 11 $1/2$ oz. (350 gr.) for a nougat of cutting consistency. Lightly pass through the rollers once again. This nougat paste is dark in colour. *(Germany)*

Chocolate Nougat II

lb	oz		kg	gr
1	0	Almonds or hazelnuts		500
1	0	Sugar		500
	3 $1/2$	Couverture (milk) or cocoa butter		100
	5	Water		150

Lightly roast the almonds or hazelnuts. Boil the sugar and water to the crack degree *(page 51)* and add the almonds or hazelnuts. When cool, proceed as for Nougat I increasing the couverture or cocoa butter, or a mixture of both, if a nougat paste of thicker consistency is required. This is a nougat paste much lighter in colour. *(Germany)*

Praline Paste

lb	oz		kg	gr
4	0	Sugar	2	
3	0	Hazelnuts	1	500
1	0	Almonds		500
		Vanilla		

Proceed as for 'Nougat-de-Paris' and when cool grind down finely to a paste. *(France)*

Fillings

Fillings may be considered under two headings:

1. Those that are partially or totally enclosed in a pastry case, and then baked.
2. Those that are added after baking, such as creams, custards, jams, fruits, mixtures, etc.

Those that are baked, range from the lightest of genoese mixings to heavy mixtures such as mincemeat.

An English classic filling is that for the Eccles cake of which there are many, some of them claiming to be authentic. An analysis of the composition of these recipes shows that the fillings commonly contain currants, mixed peel, brown sugar, spices and butter. The filling should not contain cake crumbs.

The filling for Banbury cakes are also many, ranging from those that are delicious and tasty, down to nondescript mixtures of stale cake, jam, spice and currants. Those given will not degrade the good name of the Banbury cake, No. 1 being particularly excellent.

Mincemeat deserves a special mention for although good quality mincemeat can be purchased from suppliers, the craftsman may wish to prepare his own. If so there are precautions that must be taken.

Mincemeat derived its name from the fact that meats at one time could only be preserved by spicing and/or by the use of sugar. It was found that fruit, provided that is was not over ripe, contained acid in addition to sugar and it had a preserving effect on meats. In order that the fruit juices could permeate the meat more thoroughly, it was finely chopped or minced.

Earlier recipes show that calves tongues were used, to be followed later by tripe which is soft and mellow. Nowadays, the only constant ingredient of animal origin is suet.

All ingredients should be of the finest quality, the fruit clean and free from extraneous matter. The apples should be hard, undamaged, sour, cooking apples. Over-ripe apples will almost certainly cause the mincemeat to ferment during storage.

Raisins should be the larger, well flavoured stoned variety. Lemon juice will increase the acidity of the mincemeat, which will help in avoiding fermentation.

During storage, a syrup will be formed from the sugar and the liquids and it will be more juicy than when first made. This is an improvement and the mincemeat should not be used until this natural maturing has taken place.

Mincemeat should always be stored in a cool place. Over heated conditions may induce fermentation, particularly if the mincemeat is deficient in natural acidity.

If the mincemeat does ferment, the only remedy is to cook it in large lidded containers until such time as the yeasts that cause the trouble are killed.

Banbury Filling I

lb	oz		kg	gr
3	0	Cooking apples (peeled and cored)	1	500
3	0	Raisins (stoned)	1	500
2	8	Mixed peel	1	250
2	0	Barbados sugar	1	
3	0	Currants	1	500
	1/2	Ground cloves		15
	1/2	Ground cinnamon		15
		Zest and juice of 3 lemons		

Chop the apples and raisins very finely. Add the rest of the materials. Make fresh supply as required.
(Cont. page 217)

Mincemeat

	lb	oz	kg	gr	lb	oz	kg	gr	lb	oz	kg	gr
	1				2				3			
Sour apples	10	0	4	535	12	8	5	670	5	0	2	270
Suet	5	0	2	270	5	0	2	270	5	0	2	270
Raisins (seeded)	5	0	2	270	5	0	2	270	2	8	1	135
Sultanas	3	0	1	360	5	0	2	270	5	0	2	270
Orange peel	1	12		795	2	4	1	20	1	12		795
Lemon peel	1	12		795	2	4	1	20	1	12		795
Citron peel		4		112		8		225		8		225
Tripe	2	0		900	2	0		900	—			
Currants	7	8	3	400	12	8	5	670	7	8	3	400
Sugar (light Barbados)	3	0	1	360	3	12	1	700	4	0	1	815
Salt		1		28		1 1/2		40		1/2		14
Ground cloves		3/4		20		1		28		3/4		20
Ground nutmeg		1/2		14		3/4		20		1/2		14
Ground cinnamon		1/4		7		1/8		3		1/4		7
Ground mixed spice	—				—				—			
Rum	1	4		565	1	12		800		10		285
Brandy		10		285	—					10		285
Zest and juice of	5 lemons				6 lemons				4 lemons			
	4				5				6			
Sour apples	5	0	2	270	8	0	3	630	4	0	1	815
Suet	4	0	1	815	4	0	1	815	4	0	1	815
Raisins (seeded)	4	0	1	815	3	0	1	360	2	0		900
Sultanas	3	0	1	360	5	0	2	270	4	0	1	815
Orange peel	2	8	1	135	2	0		900	2	0		900
Lemon peel	1	0		450	2	0		900	1	0		450
Citron peel		8		225	1	0		450		8		225
Tripe	—				—				—			
Currants	5	0	2	270	6	0	2	725	6	0	2	725
Sugar (light Barbados)	4	0	1	815	6	8	2	950	3	8	1	590
Salt		1		28		1 1/4		35		1		28
Ground cloves	—				—				—			
Ground nutmeg		1 1/4		35		1		28		1/2		14
Ground cinnamon	—				—				—			
Ground mixed spice		4		112		4		112		1		28
Rum	1	4		565	1	4		565		10		285
Brandy	—				—					10		285
Zest and juice of	5 lemons				5 lemons				4 lemons			

The apples are peeled, cored and finely chopped together with the suet. The seeded raisins and peels are chopped and added. The tripe is cut up and minced, mixed with the sultanas, currants, sugar and spices, and added, together with the rest of the materials and then well mixed together. The spirits should be poured over the top of the mincemeat after it has been packed.

Banbury Filling II

lb	oz		kg	gr
2	0	Cake crumbs	1	
3	0	Currants	1	500
1	0	Mixed peel		500
	³/₄	Mixed spice		20
1	8	Brown sugar		750
		Zest of 8 lemons		

Apple pulp to moisten.

Banbury Filling III

lb	oz		kg	gr
1	8	Mincemeat		750
1	0	Sponge cake crumbs		500

Mix well together and keep in a cool place.

Banbury Filling IV

lb	oz		kg	gr
1	0	Sponge cake crumbs		500
1	4	Currants		625
	2	Mixed peel		60
	12	Sultanas		375
	¹/₂	Mixed spice		15
	4	Treacle		125

Eccles Filling I

lb	oz		kg	gr
1	0	Butter		500
1	8	Barbados sugar		750
	10	Egg		300
2	0	Cooking apples (peeled and cored)	1	
3	0	Currants	1	500
1	8	Mixed peel		750
	³/₄	Ground nutmeg		20
	¹/₂	Ground cloves		15
		Juice and zest of 2 lemons		
		Juice and zest of 2 oranges		

Chop the apples finely. Cream the butter and sugar and beat in the egg. Mix in all the dry ingredients. Add juice and zest of oranges and lemons last. Keep in a cool place.

Eccles Filling II

lb	oz		kg	gr
1	8	Cooking apples (peeled and cored)		750
1	0	Sultanas (small)		500
1	8	Barbados sugar		750
2	4	Currants	1	125
	8	Mixed peel		250
	¹/₄	Mixed spice		8
	¹/₈	Ground nutmeg		4
		Zest and juice of 3 lemons		

Chop the apples finely then mix all ingredients together.

Eccles Filling III

lb	oz		kg	gr
	8	Butter		250
	12	Apples (peeled and cored)		375
1	8	Currants		750
	¹/₄	Ground spice		8
	9	Sugar (brown)		270
	4	Egg		125
	7	Mixed peel		200
	1	Sherry		30
	1	Brandy		30

Chop the apples finely. Melt the butter and add the beaten egg, then mix all together.

Eccles Filling IV

lb	oz		kg	gr
2	0	Currants	1	
	8	Mixed peel (finely chopped)		250
	4	Butter (melted)		125
1	0	Sugar (brown)		500
	¹/₁₆	Ground nutmeg		2
	¹/₁₆	Ground spice		2

Frangipane Filling I

lb	oz		kg	gr
1	0	Butter		500
1	0	Sugar (castor)		500
1	0	Egg		500
	4	Flour		125
	12	Ground almonds		375
		Ratafia essence		

Cream butter and sugar lightly. Add egg in portions and finally add flour and ground almonds.

Frangipane Filling II

lb	oz		kg	gr
1	0	Butter		500
1	0	Sugar (castor)		500
1	0	Egg		500
	4	Ground almonds		125
	8	Sponge cake crumbs		250
	3	Flour		90

Proceed as for Frangipane Filling I.

Frangipane Filling III

lb	oz		kg	gr
1	0	Butter		500
1	0	Sugar		500
1	4	Egg		625
	4	Flour		125
	6	Sponge cake crumbs		180
	6	Ground almonds		180

Proceed as for Frangipane Filling I.

Frangipane Filling IV

lb	oz		kg	gr
1	0	Butter		500
1	0	Sugar (castor)		500
1	0	Egg		500
	12	Sponge cake crumbs		375
	8	Ground almonds		250
		Zest of 1 lemon		

Proceed as for Frangipane Filling I.

Frangipane Filling V

lb	oz		kg	gr
1	0	Butter		500
1	0	Sugar (castor)		500
1	0	Egg		500
1	0	Ground almonds		500
	1	Flour		30

Proceed as for Frangipane Filling I.

Frangipane Filling VI

lb	oz		kg	gr
1	5	Butter		650
	7	Sugar (castor)		215
1	9	Egg		770
1	12	Raw marzipan		875
	4	Flour		125

Rub the marzipan down with some of the egg. Cream butter and sugar, add the rest of the egg. Finally mix in rest of the materials.

Frangipane Filling VII

lb	oz		kg	gr
1	4	Butter		625
1	4	Sugar (castor)		625
1	4	Egg		625
	10	Ground almonds		300
	10	Flour		300

Proceed as for Frangipane Filling I.

Frangipane Filling VIII

lb	oz		kg	gr
1	0	Butter		500
1	0	Sugar (castor)		500
1	2	Egg		560
	8	Raw marzipan		250
	12	Sponge cake crumbs		375
	4	Cocoa powder		125

Proceed as for Frangipane Filling I.

Frangipane Filling IX

lb	oz		kg	gr
1	0	Butter		500
1	0	Sugar (castor)		500
1	4	Egg		625
	8	Ground hazelnuts		250
	8	Sponge cake crumbs		250

Proceed as for Frangipane Filling I.

Frangipane Filling X

lb	oz		kg	gr
1	0	Butter		500
1	0	Sugar (castor)		500
1	4	Egg		625
	8	Ground hazelnuts		250
	8	Flour		250

Proceed as for Frangipane Filling I.

Potato Curd

lb	oz		kg	gr
	8	Potatoes (boiled)		250
	8	Butter		250
	6	Ground almonds		180

lb	oz		kg	gr
	12	Sugar (castor)		375
	8	Egg		250
	1 1/2	Egg yolks		45
	1	Maraschino		30

Sieve the potatoes and beat to a light cream with the butter and maraschino. Beat in the egg and yolks and mix in the ground almonds. Add the sugar last of all just stirring it in. Store in a cold place. The firmer this curd becomes set, the less likely is it to curdle.

Old English Curd

lb	oz		kg	gr
3	12	Milk	1	875
	1	Rennet		30
1	8	Butter		750
1	8	Sugar (castor)		750
1	2	Egg		550
	1/8	Nutmeg		4
		Zest of 2 lemons		

Warm the milk to 100° F (38° C). Stir in the rennet and leave in a warm place for two hours. When firm, strain through a nylon mesh sieve. When the whey has run off and the curds are dry they are ready for use.

Cream the butter and sugar and add the egg a little at a time. Add the nutmeg and zest and finally the sieved curds. Keep in a cold place until ready for use.

Yorkshire Cheese Curd I

lb	oz		kg	gr
3	12	Milk	1	875
	1	Rennet		30
	12	Butter		375
	10	Sugar (castor)		300
	8	Egg		250
	4	Currants		125
	1/8	Nutmeg		4
		Zest and juice of 1 lemon		

Proceed as for Old English Curd.

Yorkshire Cheese Curd II

lb	oz		kg	gr
1	8	Curd		750
	9	Butter		270

lb	oz		kg	gr
	9	Sugar (castor)		270
	10	Egg		300
	8	Currants		250
	1/8	Nutmeg		4

Proceed as for the second part of Old English Curd.

Maid of Honour Curd

lb	oz		kg	gr
2	8	Milk	1	250
	3/4	Rennet		20
	5	Cream		150
1	0	Butter		500
1	4	Sugar (castor)		625
	12	Ground almonds (coarse)		375
	10	Egg yolks		300
	10	Egg		300
	1/8	Nutmeg		4
	2 1/2	Brandy		75
		Zest of 4 lemons and juice of 3		

The milk and rennet are mixed together and left in a warm place to set, after which it is drained and the curd allowed to dry a little.

The egg, egg yolks and sugar are whipped to a sponge and the melted butter is beaten in. If it shows signs of curdling, it is warmed and beaten smooth. Mix in the lemon zest and juice, the almonds and the strained curd. Last, add the lightly whipped cream and the brandy. Allow to stand in a cold place some hours before use.

Curd Filling

lb	oz		kg	gr
1	10	Cream cheese		800
	10	Curd cheese		300
	12 1/2	Sugar		375
	7	Egg		200
	3 1/2	Vanilla cream		100
	7	Flour		200
	6	Hot butter		180

Press the cheese through a sieve, mix with the sugar, egg, vanilla cream and flour. Lastly add the hot butter. *(Germany)*

Cheese Cream Filling

lb	oz		kg	gr
	15	Milk		450
	3	Egg yolks		90
	6	Sugar		180
1	2	Cream cheese		560
	12	Dairy cream		375
	3	Sultanas		90
		Half vanilla bean		
		10 sheets white gelatine		
		Salt		
		Lemon juice		

Cook the milk, egg yolks, sugar, vanilla, salt and lemon until fairly thick and smooth. Add the gelatine after soaking and squeezing out well, leave to cool, add the sieved cream cheese and lastly fold in the sultanas and whipped cream

(Germany)

Rice Tart Filling

lb	oz		kg	gr
1	0	Butter		500
1	0	Sugar (castor)		500
1	4	Egg		625
	12	Ground rice		375
	4	Flour		125
		Vanilla		

Cream the butter and sugar, add the egg a portion at a time, finally adding the sieved flour and ground rice, together with the vanilla.

Orange Rice Filling

lb	oz		kg	gr
1	0	Butter		500
	13	Sugar (castor)		400
	4	Orange marmalade		125
1	0	Egg		500
	12	Ground rice		375
	5	Flour		150
		Orange colour		

Cream the butter, sugar and marmalade together, and then add the egg a portion at a time. Add the colour and blend in the sieved rice and flour.

Orange and Date Filling

lb	oz		kg	gr
1	8	Dates		750
1	4	Apples		625
1	4	Sugar		625
1	8	Cake crumbs		750
	8	Orange juice		250
	2 $1/2$	Egg		70

Mince the dates and the apples and add the sugar and crumbs. Add the orange juice and blend in. Finally add the egg and mix until smooth.

Coconut Tart Filling

lb	oz		kg	gr
1	0	Sugar (castor)		500
	8	Butter		250
	8	Golden syrup		250
	10	Egg		300
	3	Flour		90
	$1/8$	Baking powder		4
	10	Milk (approx.)		300
	6	Coconut (fine)		180

Cream the sugar and butter and add the egg a little at a time. Add the warmed syrup and stir in the flour. Lastly add the milk and the coconut.

Coconut Orange Filling

lb	oz		kg	gr
1	12	Sugar (castor)		875
1	8	Coconut		750
	8	Egg		250
	3	Orange marmalade		90
	2	Honey		60

Mix all together.

Viennese Tart Filling

lb	oz		kg	gr
1	0	Marzipan		500
	14	Egg		435
	12	Butter		375
	4	Sugar (icing)		125
	2 $1/4$	Flour		60
		Lemon juice		

Work the marzipan and egg until smooth, add the butter and icing sugar and finally stir in the flour and lemon juice.

(Germany)

Swiss Tart Filling

lb	oz		kg	gr
1	0	Butter		500
1	0	Sugar (castor)		500
1	4	Egg		625
	8	Flour		250
1	8	Cake crumbs		750
	8	Ground almonds		250
	12	Currants		375
	12	Milk		375
		Zest and juice of 1 lemon		

Cream the butter and sugar. Add the egg in portions. Blend in the flour, crumbs, almonds and currants. Finally, mix in the milk.

Almond Tart Filling I

lb	oz		kg	gr
	12	Butter		375
1	0	Sugar (castor)		500
1	8	Macaroon paste		750
	13	Egg		400
	12	Flour		375
	4	Milk		125

Cream the butter and sugar. Add the macaroon paste and mix in well. Add the egg a portion at a time. Mix in the flour and finally the milk.

Almond Tart Filling II

lb	oz		kg	gr
1	0	Egg yolks		500
1	0	Sugar (castor)		500
	6	Scone Flour (No. 1)		180
	14	Ground almonds		435
	12	Egg whites		375
	4	Sugar		125
	$1/8$	Cream of tartar		4
	6	Butter		180

Beat the egg yolks and sugar until light. Blend in the sieved scone flour and almonds. Make a stiff meringue by whipping the egg whites with the cream of tartar, adding the sugar a little at a time.

Blend this carefully to the mixing, finally adding the melted butter carefully.

Cinnamon Tart Filling

lb	oz		kg	gr
	7	Almonds		210
	$10\,1/2$	Sugar		300
1	0	Egg		500
	$2\,1/2$	Flour		70
	5	Butter		150
	$1/4$	Ground cinnamon		8

Grind the almonds and half the sugar, moistening with a little water.

Whip up the egg and the rest of the sugar and blend in. Finally, stir in the melted butter and the flour and cinnamon which have been sieved together. *(France)*

Bakewell Tart Filling

lb	oz		kg	gr
1	4	Egg		625
1	4	Sugar (castor)		625
1	0	Butter (melted)		500
	12	Ground almonds		375
	4	Sponge cake crumbs		125

Whisk the egg and sugar. Add the melted butter. Blend in the almonds and crumbs.

Lemon Tart Filling

lb	oz		kg	gr
1	2	Butter		560
1	2	Sugar (castor)		560
1	4	Egg		625
	9	Flour (soft)		270
	6	Scone flour (No. 1)		180
	9	Cornflour		270
	2	Milk		60
	4	Lemon peel (finely chopped)		125
		Zest and juice of 2 lemons		

Proceed as for Rice Tart Filling.

Dutch Apple Tart Filling

lb	oz		kg	gr
2	0	Apples (peeled, cored and chopped)	1	
	4	Sultanas or raisins		125
	$1/8$	Ground cinnamon		4

Oxford Apple Tart Filling

lb	oz		kg	gr
1	2	Cooking apples (peeled, cored and finely chopped)		560
	6	Sponge cake crumbs		180
	6	Apricot jam		180
	1/16	Ground cinnamon		2

Victoria Cheesecake Filling

lb	oz		kg	gr
1	0	Butter		500
1	0	Sugar		500
1	0	Egg		500
1	0	Flour (soft)		500
	6	Ground almonds		180
		Zest of 2 lemons		

Cream the butter and sugar and add the egg in portions. Fold in the flour and ground almonds sieved together.

Royal Victoria Tart Filling

lb	oz		kg	gr
1	0	Butter		500
1	0	Sugar (castor)		500
1	0	Ground almonds		500
1	0	Egg		500

Put the ground almonds, sugar and egg together and beat until light. Add the butter, which has been melted, a little at a time, beating vigorously until it is soft and light. Keep in a cool place and use as required.

Iced Tart Filling

lb	oz		kg	gr
1	0	Sugar		500
1	0	Almonds		500
	14	Egg whites		435
	2	Flour		60

Grind the almonds and half the sugar with a little cold water. Whip up to a stiff meringue the egg whites and the rest of the sugar. Blend both mixtures and fold in the flour. *(France)*

Fruit and Nut Filling I

lb	oz		kg	gr
	12	Dates		375
	4	Walnuts		125
	12	Sultanas		375
2	4	Apricot jam	1	125
		Zest and juice of 1 lemon		

Damp the dates and pass through the mincer with the walnuts. Add the rest of the materials and mix well.

Fruit and Nut Filling II

lb	oz		kg	gr
	8	Flaked almonds		250
1	0	Apples		500
	12	Sultanas		375
	8	Apricot jam		250

Stir together.

Almond Nut Filling

lb	oz		kg	gr
	14	Butter		435
	2	Sugar		60
	5 1/2	Honey		150
	8	Dairy cream		250
1	0	Almonds		500
	12	Roasted hazelnuts		375

Bring the butter, sugar, honey and cream to the boil. Add the almonds and nuts and continue cooking for 5 minutes *(Germany)*

Honey Nut Filling

lb	oz		kg	gr
1	0	Butter		500
	10	Honey		300
	2	Glucose		60
1	4	Sugar		625
1	9	Cream		770
2	8	Flaked hazelnuts	1	250
		Lemon juice		

Bring all the ingredients to the boil except the nuts which are added last.

Coconut Slice Filling I

lb	oz		kg	gr
1	4	Egg whites		625
	1/8	Cream of tartar		4

lb	oz		kg	gr
1	8	Coconut		750
	6	Rice flour		180
3	0	Sugar (castor)	1	500
		Vanilla		

Whip the egg whites and vanilla flavour to a firm snow. Blend in the other materials that have been sieved together. Heat the mixture in a bain-marie to 110° F (43° C).

Coconut Slice Filling II

lb	oz		kg	gr
1	0	Sugar (castor)		500
	8	Coconut		250
	7 1/2	Egg whites		230
	1/2	Ground rice		15

Mix all ingredients together.

Chocolate Slice Filling

lb	oz		kg	gr
1	0	Butter		500
	12	Sugar (castor)		375
	2	Ground almonds		60
1	0	Egg		500
	4	Unsweetened chocolate		125
	10	Flour (soft)		300
1	12	Sponge cake crumbs		875
		Vanilla		

Cream the butter, sugar and almonds together and add the egg a portion at a time. Add the warmed chocolate and blend it in well. Finally, add the vanilla and the flour and crumbs.

Cherry Slice Filling

lb	oz		kg	gr
1	0	Butter		500
1	0	Sugar (castor)		500
	2	Ground almonds		60
1	4	Egg		625
1	4	Flour (soft)		625
	4	Scone flour (No. 1)		125
		Vanilla		

Cream the butter and sugar adding the egg in portions. Blend in the sieved flours.

Almond Slice Filling

lb	oz		kg	gr
1	2	Almonds		560
1	2	Sugar (granulated)		560
	12	Egg yolks		375
	14	Butter		435
	9	Flour		270
	15	Egg whites		450

Grind the almonds and sugar together moistening them with a little cold water. Stir in the egg yolks, the melted butter and the flour. Finally, fold in the stiffly whipped egg whites. *(France)*

Jap Slice Filling

lb	oz		kg	gr
1	8	Butter		750
1	8	Sugar		750
1	4	Egg		625
1	8	Coconut (fine)		750
1	0	Rice flour		500
		Vanilla		

Cream the butter and sugar and add the egg a portion at a time. Fold in the rest of the materials.

Hollandaise I

lb	oz		kg	gr
	14	Ground sweet almonds		440
	2	Ground bitter almonds		60
1	0	Sugar (castor)		500
1	0	Egg		500
1	0	Butter		500

Place the almonds and sugar into a bowl and mix in the egg, beating slightly. Make the butter quite hot and add, stirring well. *(France)*

Hollandaise II

lb	oz		kg	gr
1	0	Butter		500
1	0	Sugar (castor)		500
1	0	Blanched almonds		500
1	0	Egg		500
	8	Flour		250
		Zest of 1 lemon		

Cream the butter with half the sugar. Finely grind the almonds with the rest of the sugar. Amalgamate both mixtures and add the egg and the zest of lemon. Finally, mix in the flour.   *(France)*

Madeira Filling

lb	oz		kg	gr
1	0	Butter		500
1	0	Sugar (castor)		500
	5	Ground almonds		150
1	4	Egg		625
1	0	Flour (soft)		500
	4	Scone flour (No. 1)		125
		Zest and juice of 1 lemon		

Proceed as for Cherry Slice Filling.

Almond Cheesecake Filling

lb	oz		kg	gr
1	0	Ground almonds		500
1	12	Sugar (castor)		875
	2	Water		60
		Egg whites		

Add sufficient whites to make a soft paste. Beat thoroughly, adding the water last of all. The mixture should run flat.

Chorley Cake Filling

lb	oz		kg	gr
1	0	Currants		500
	4	Butter		125
	4	Sugar (brown)		125

Melt the butter and mix with the currants and sugar. Leave to cool.

Crumb Filling

lb	oz		kg	gr
1	0	Butter		500
1	0	Sugar (castor)		500
1	0	Egg		500
1	8	Cake crumbs		750
$1/8$		Nutmeg		4

Cream the butter and sugar. Beat in the egg in portions. Stir in the cake crumbs and nutmeg. This mixing should stand for a short while before use.

Andorra Filling

lb	oz		kg	gr
1	2	Confectioner's custard		560
	$3\,1/2$	Egg		100
	4	Chopped preserved fruits		125

Beat the egg and stir into the custard. Fold in the fruits which have been soaked in kirsch or maraschino.

Appenzell Honey Cake Filling

lb	oz		kg	gr
1	2	Ground roasted hazelnuts		560
	14	Sugar		435
	7	Brown pear syrup		218
	$7\,1/2$	Water		225
		Zest of 1 lemon		

Mix all together.

St. Gallen Biberteig Filling

lb	oz		kg	gr
1	2	Ground almonds		560
	14	Sugar		435
	$3\,1/2$	Syrup		100
	4	Water		125
	$1\,1/2$	Kirsch		45
		Zest of half a lemon		
		Orange flower water		

Mix all together.

Engadine Nut Filling

lb	oz		kg	gr
1	0	Sugar		500
	10	Dairy cream (single)		300
	1	Honey		30
	12	Walnuts (coarsely chopped)		375

Boil the sugar until it caramelizes. Pour in the cream and leave over the heat until the caramel has dissolved. Add the honey and lastly the walnuts. Leave to cool a little before filling into pans or rings lined with sweet pastry.

Cannoli Siciliani Filling

lb	oz		kg	gr
1	2	Cream cheese (sieved)		560
	9	Sugar (castor)		270
	2 1/2	Orange peel (cut finely)		75
	2 1/2	Chocolate (chopped into cubes)		75
	2 1/2	Pistachio nuts (halved)		75
	1/2	Rum		15
		Vanilla		

Mix all together. *(Italy)*

SPREADS SUITABLE FOR DANISH PASTRIES ETC.

Brown Plunder Filling

lb	oz		kg	gr
2	4	Ground hazelnuts (lightly roasted)	1	125
1	12	Sugar		875
	7	Glucose		200
	3/8	Cinnamon		10
1	2	Water		560

Mix thoroughly to spreading consistency. *(Switzerland)*

White Plunder Filling

lb	oz		kg	gr
1	2	Ground almonds		550
1	2	Sugar		550
	7	Egg whites		200

Mix as above. *(Switzerland)*

Butter Filling

lb	oz		kg	gr
1	0	Sugar (brown)		500
1	0	Butter		500

Cream together lightly. *(Switzerland)*

Almond Filling

lb	oz		kg	gr
1	0	Marzipan		500
2	0	Sugar	1	
2	0	Butter	1	

Beat all together.

Marzipan Filling

lb	oz		kg	gr
1	2	Marzipan		560
	7	Egg whites		210
		Zest of lemon		

Bring to a spreading consistency.

(Germany)

Cinnamon Filling

lb	oz		kg	gr
1	0	Butter		500
1	0	Sugar		500
	1/4	Cinnamon		8

Mix well together.

Hazelnut Filling

lb	oz		kg	gr
2	4	Roasted hazelnuts	1	125
2	4	Sugar (icing)	1	125
1	2	Water		560
	1/2	Cinnamon		15
		Zest of lemon		

Grind all the ingredients finely. *(France)*

Milk Chocolate Filling

lb	oz		kg	gr
2	0	Sugar (icing)	1	
	6 1/2	Butter		200
	10	Evaporated milk		300
	5	Unsweetened chocolate		150

Beat the sugar and butter with half of the milk. Add the melted chocolate and the rest of the milk.

Chestnut Paste

lb	oz		kg	gr
2	4	Chestnuts	1	125
	12	Sugar (icing)		375

Make a slit at one end of each chestnut and blanch them. Continue cooking after the skins have been removed. Grind the nuts with icing sugar. Broken marrons glacés can be used ground down with some syrup.

Suitable for spreading and piping.

(France)

Toppings

Butter Streusel I

lb	oz		kg	gr
1	2	Butter (unsalted)		500
1	2	Flour		500
	13	Sugar (icing)		375
		Ground cinnamon		

Mix all together. *(Germany)*

Butter Streusel II

lb	oz		kg	gr
1	0	Butter		500
	4	Ground almonds		125
	8	Sugar (icing)		250
1	4	Flour		625
		Zest of 1/2 lemon		

Melt the butter and add to the other materials. Mix well. Press the paste through a wide meshed sieve and allow to set.

Butter Streusel III

lb	oz		kg	gr
1	2	Butter		560
1	2	Sugar (icing)		560
2	0	Flour	1	
	1/4	Baking powder		8

Rub together until a crumbly mass is attained.

Butter Streusel IV

lb	oz		kg	gr
1	4	Flour		625
1	4	Butter		625
1	0	Sugar (icing)		500
		Zest of 1 lemon		

Mix all the ingredients together and pass through a coarse sieve. *(France)*

Baked Streusel

Reduce almond paste cuttings with a mixture of milk and egg whites. Pass through a grinder until smooth. Adjust to spreading consistency and spread thinly on to a greased and floured baking sheet. Bake carefully and when cold, break it up and pass through a coarse sieve.

Coconut Topping

lb	oz		kg	gr
1	0	Medium coconut		500
1	0	Sugar (icing)		500
	8	Butter		250

Mix evenly together.

Viennese Topping

lb	oz		kg	gr
1	2	Butter		560
	10	Sugar (castor)		300
1	4	Flour		625
	1/2	Baking powder		15
	5	Milk		150
		Vanilla		

Beat all together.

Danish Pastry Topping I

Mix together shredded unblanched almonds and sugar nibs.

Danish Pastry Topping II

Mix together nibbed almonds and sugar nibs.

Danish Pastry Topping III

Mix together ground almonds and sugar nibs.

Rum Apricot Topping

lb	oz		kg	gr
2	0	Marzipan	1	
1	0	Apricot jam (sieved)		500
		Rum		

Blend the marzipan with half the apricot jam making certain that it is free from lumps. Add the rest of the jam and the rum and mix thoroughly together.

Easter Bread Topping

lb	oz		kg	gr
	12	Ground hazelnuts		375
1	0	Sugar		500
1	4	Egg whites		625

Mix well together but without whipping.

Honey Topping

lb	oz		kg	gr
	6	Honey		180
	15	Sugar (castor)		450
	2 1/4	Fresh cream		75
1	5	Flaked almonds		655

Bring the honey, sugar and cream to the boil and add the flaked almonds.

Creams and Custards

CREAMS

There are many types of creams used by the baker for layering, filling or decorating. Perhaps the best of all is fresh dairy cream because of its unique flavour, its quality appeal and the ease with which it is prepared for use.

Other creams are mixtures of a fat and a sweetening agent either alone or with the addition of stabilizers which can be eggs, egg yolks, starch, agar-agar, gelatine, etc. Of the fats, good quality unsalted butter should be used because of the flavour that it confers.

Creams can be coloured and flavoured as desired and can contain additions such as chocolate, coffee, custard, lemon or orange curd, chopped fruit or nuts, etc. Marshmallow cream can be mixed with some creams to give extra stability.

Custards are mixtures of milk, eggs and sugar which are cooked together. Sometimes for extra stability, cornflour is added. Cooked custard is used on baked cakes and pastries with the exception of Danish pastries when it is usually applied before baking. For custard tarts, the custard is poured into the unbaked pastry cases, when both the pastry and custard are baked together.

Cooked custard can be added to buttercreams to make a custard cream. Custards generally are used in their natural colour, the exception being a chocolate custard, which is flavoured and coloured with plain chocolate. The cooked custard is known in France as 'crème pâtissière, in Italy as 'crema pasticcera'.

What are known as lemon or orange custards to Continental craftsmen are known in the British Isles as lemon and orange curds. They can be used alone as spreads or fillings, or blended with buttercream to confer the natural flavours of the fruits.

DAIRY CREAM

Probably the first cream used by the baker and still immensely popular to-day. Dairy cream consists largely of butter fat that has been separated, normally by mechanical means, from cow's milk. There are present also some other constituents of the original milk. The composition varies and can be expressed as follows:

Water	55-74 %
Protein	2.5 %
Butter fat	18-40 %
Lactose	4.5 %
Mineral salts	0.5 %

Whipping cream (35-40 % butter fat) is ideal for the baker and will be supplied on demand. If double cream is used, then it may be diluted with a little milk in the ratio of one part milk to four parts cream. The milk must be thoroughly mixed in before whipping.

Dairy cream should be about 24 hours old before use and at a temperature of 40° F (4° C). If the cream is whipped at a temperature too high, or in a room that is too warm, or it is whipped for too long a time, then it will turn into butter. The cream should be whipped until it is of a firm and stable consistency when whipping should cease immediately. The increase in volume as air is whipped in is known as 'over run'. It is recommended that for the highest quality confectionery, the over run should be $1\ 1/2$ to $1\ 3/4$ times the original volume, and for other use 2 to $2\ 1/2$ times.

It is of the utmost importance that meticulous cleanliness be maintained from the time of delivery until the point of sale. Here are four important points:

1. Cleanliness of all tools and utensils, including savoy bags and pipes.
2. Personal cleanliness.
3. Keep cream containers closed until ready for use and wipe the outside of the container before removing the lid.
4. Display the finished goods in a refrigerated counter.

Cream, by reason of its composition and the fact that it is not cooked, could be a suitable carrier of food poisoning bacteria, therefore all precautions must be taken against this possibility.

In Great Britain and Northern Ireland, Cream Regulations 1970 are now in operation. They specify requirements for the description and composition of dairy cream. There are eight categories listed. Whipping cream, used extensively in bakery products, is a new category and must contain a minimum of 35 % milk fat.

Permitted additives to prevent seepage and separation include certain stabilizers and emulsifiers. In addition, sugar may be added up to 13 %—21 oz. per gallon (130 gr. per 1 kg.).

Where the word 'cream' is used to describe confectionery products, only dairy cream may be used. The Regulations are subject to amendment from time to time.

Whipped dairy cream is known under various names in different countries and regions. In France and French speaking countries, it is known as 'Crème Chantilly'. Crème Chantilly in Italy is composed of 80 % dairy cream and 20 % crème pâtissière. In Austria 'Schlag-Obers', in Germany 'Schlagsahne' whilst in certain German speaking parts of Switzerland, whipped cream assumes the name of 'Nidel'.

Dairy cream is used in ice-cream, ganache, florentines, langues-de-chat biscuits, etc.

CLOTTED CREAM

This cream is special to the West of England, particularly Devon and Cornwall, where it is used as a filling for Cornish and Devonshire Splits and as an accompaniment to Saffron Bread. It is also used for desserts.

Milk is heated to a temperature between 110-120° F (43-49° C). The butter fat is separated off to produce a 50-60 % butter fat cream and held for 16-18 hours. It is then poured into shallow pans and scalded to a temperature of 190° F (87° C). The cream is then quickly cooled. Clotted cream is required to contain 55% butter fat.

BUTTERCREAM

There is, in Great Britain, a Code of Practice concerning Buttercream which says that the word 'Buttercream' may only be used to describe fillings containing mainly butter and sugar, and which contains at least 22 1/2 % butter fat, with no additions of other fat.

The approved word is 'Buttercream' not 'Butter Cream' or 'Butter-cream'.

All butters used should be of good quality and for buttercreams should be unsalted or lightly salted, or a blend of both.

Buttercreams must be carefully flavoured. Colours must never be brilliant; pastel tints are much nicer (chocolate excepted). Also *page 29*.

Basic Buttercream I

lb	oz		kg	gr
1	0	Butter		500
1	0	Sugar (icing)		500
		Colour/flavour		

Beat well together.

Basic Buttercream II

lb	oz		kg	gr
1	0	Butter		500
1	0	Fondant		500
		Colour/flavour		

Soften the fondant and beat well with the butter.

Buttercream with Eggs I

lb	oz		kg	gr
1	0	Egg		500
1	0	Sugar (castor)		500
1	0	Butter		500
		Colour/flavour		

Whisk the egg and sugar to a stiff sponge, add the butter which has been lightly creamed, a little at a time, beating well.

Buttercream with Eggs II

lb	oz		kg	gr
	15	Egg		450
	12	Sugar (castor)		375
2	0	Butter	1	
1	4	Sugar (icing)		625
		Colour/flavour		

Whisk the egg and sugar to a stiff sponge and add it a portion at a time to the beaten butter and icing sugar.

Buttercream with Egg Yolks III

lb	oz		kg	gr
1	0	Butter		500
1	4	Sugar (icing)		625
	4	Egg yolks		125
		Colour/flavour		

Beat the butter and sugar and add the egg yolks and continue beating.

Buttercream - Boiled

lb	oz		kg	gr
1	0	Butter		500
	6	Egg		180
1	0	Sugar		500
	5	Water		150
		Colour/flavour		

Boil the sugar and water to 240° F (115° C) and pour it into the well whisked egg. When cool, add the well creamed butter.

Buttercream I

lb	oz		kg	gr
4	0	Butter	2	
1	12	Fondant		875
1	6	Sugar		685

lb	oz		kg	gr
	7	Water		200
2	4	Egg	1	125

Boil the sugar and water to 240° F (115° C) taking the usual precautions. Pour this immediately over the well whisked egg and continue whisking. When cool mix with the butter and fondant that have been previously creamed. *(France)*

Buttercream II

lb	oz		kg	gr
3	0	Butter	1	500
2	0	Sugar (castor)	1	
	12	Egg whites		375

Whisk the egg whites with the sugar to a stiff meringue. Mix with the well creamed butter. This type of buttercream keeps well during the summer. *(France)*

Buttercream

lb	oz		kg	gr
2	4	Egg	1	125
1	6	Sugar		685
2	10	Butter (unsalted)	1	300
	8	Compound fat		250
		Vanilla		

Whisk up the egg and warmed sugar; cream the butter and compound fat. When the egg/sugar sponge is cold add it to the beaten fats. Sufficient for 6 torten.
(Germany)

Buttercream - Almond

lb	oz		kg	gr
1	8	Buttercream		760
	11	Raw marzipan		330
		Water (a little)		
		Kirsch (if desired)		

Work the marzipan down with a little water and beat with the buttercream.
(Austria)

Buttercream - Mousseline

lb	oz		kg	gr
	8	Stock syrup (28° B)		250
	4	Egg yolks		125
	8	Butter		250
		Flavour (as desired)		

Whisk the egg yolks and stock syrup in a bain-marie to a smooth, creamy consistency, then whisk until cold. Cream the butter well and lightly fold in the egg yolk/stock syrup mixture adding the desired flavour. The flavour can be vanilla, lemon or orange juice, a liqueur or a spirit. *(France)*

Buttercream - Vanilla

lb	oz		kg	gr
1	10	Milk		800
	4	Sugar		125
	2	Egg yolks		60
	2 1/2	Cornflour		75
1	2	Butter		560
	1	Sugar (icing)		30
		Vanilla		

Mix the sugar, yolks and cornflour with a little milk. Stir in the rest of the milk brought to the boil and cook to a smooth cream. Beat the butter and icing sugar together lightly and add the custard when cold. *(Germany)*

Buttercream - Chocolate Arrack

lb	oz		kg	gr
1	2	Buttercream		560
	2	Chocolate couverture		60
		Arrack		

Add the melted couverture and the arrack to the buttercream and beat well. *(Germany)*

Buttercream - Pineapple

lb	oz		kg	gr
1	2	Buttercream		560
	4	Pineapple jam		125
		Lemon juice		
		Egg yolk		

Stir the lemon juice, egg yolk and pineapple jam thoroughly into the buttercream. *(Germany)*

Buttercream - Mocha

lb	oz		kg	gr
	13	Milk		400
	2	Sugar (castor)		60
1		Egg yolk		30
1 1/2		Cornflour		45
8		Butter		250
	1/2	Sugar (icing)		15
	1/2	Coffee		15
		Brandy		

Mix the sugar, yolk and cornflour together with a little milk. Stir in the boiling milk and cook to a smooth cream.

Beat the butter and icing sugar together and add to the custard when cool. Lastly flavour with coffee and a dash of brandy. *(Germany)*

Buttercream - Nut or Hazelnut

To each 3 lb. (1 kg. 500) vanilla buttercream *(page 230)* add 4 oz. (125 gr.) of ground hazelnuts or walnuts. *(Germany)*

Buttercream - Chocolate Hazelnut

lb	oz		kg	gr
1	5	Egg		625
	10	Sugar (castor)		300
1	2	Butter		600
	10	Chocolate		300
	10	Ground hazelnuts		300
	1/2	Vanilla		15

Whip the egg and sugar with the vanilla over a little heat to a stiff sponge. When cold, beat in the butter, melted chocolate and the hazelnuts. *(Germany)*

Buttercream - Chocolate Hazelnut Praline

lb	oz		kg	gr
1	2	Butter		560
	6	Egg yolks		180
1	2	Sugar (icing)		560
	9	Chocolate		270
	3	Praline croquant (sieved)		90

Beat the butter and egg yolks and add the icing sugar. Beat well and add the melted chocolate. Add the croquant last.

(Germany)

Buttercream - Truffle

This cream is generally a beaten mixture of ganache and buttercream, flavoured with rum.

Buttercream - Lemon I

lb	oz		kg	gr
1	0	Butter	500	
1	0	Fondant	500	
	8	Sugar (icing)	250	
	8	Lemon curd	250	

Beat together until light. (Use a good quality lemon curd).

Buttercream - Lemon II

lb	oz		kg	gr
	1	Egg yolk		30
	1 3/4	Sugar (castor)		50
	1	White wine		30
1	2	Buttercream		560
		Zest and juice of 2 lemons		

Cook the egg yolk, sugar, lemon and white wine until thick, strain and leave until cool. When cold, mix well with the buttercream. To increase the flavour a little citric acid may be added. A little icing sugar may be added if necessary. The above quantity is sufficient for one Mignon Torte.

Buttercream - Madeira

Mix a well beaten buttercream with sufficient Madeira to flavour it. Malaga and marsala buttercreams are made in exactly the same way, using the appropriate wine.

Buttercream - Ginger

lb	oz		kg	gr
1	0	Buttercream	500	
	3	Ginger crush		90

Beat well together.

Buttercream - Nougat

lb	oz		kg	gr
1	4	Buttercream	625	
	4	Nougat paste		125

Beat well together.

Buttercream - Gianduja

lb	oz		kg	gr
1	0	Ground almonds or hazelnuts	500	
	8	Sugar (icing)	250	
		Milk (a little)		
	2	Cocoa powder		60
	4	Sieved sponge crumbs		125
	7	Couverture (milk)		200
	2	Couverture (unsweetened)		60
	3	Cocoa butter		90

Mix all together until smooth and leave twenty-four hours before use.

(Switzerland)

Buttercream with Marshmallow I

lb	oz		kg	gr
1	8	Butter	750	
1	0	Marshmallow	500	
1	0	Sugar (icing)	500	
		Colour/flavour		

Beat the whole of the ingredients until light.

Buttercream with Marshmallow II

lb	oz		kg	gr
1	4	Butter	625	
	6	Marshmallow		180
	6	Fondant		180
	6	Sugar (icing)		180
	4	Glucose (warmed)		125
	5	Evaporated milk		155
		Colour/flavour		

Beat the butter, marshmallow and sugar together. Add the softened fondant and the warmed glucose, beating all the while. Add the milk and the desired colour/flavour last.

Buttercream with Custard

lb	oz		kg	gr
1	8	Butter	750	
	12	Sugar (icing)		375
1	12	Custard (cold)	875	

Use custard I *(page 238)*. Beat the butter and sugar and blend in the custard.

Buttercream with Meringue

lb	oz		kg	gr
1	0	Butter		500
1	4	Sugar (granulated)		625
	6	Water		180
	4	Egg whites		125
	1/16	Cream of tartar		2
		Colour/flavour		

Make an Italian meringue. When cold add to the beaten butter a portion at a time.

Buttercream with Pectin I

lb	oz		kg	gr
	14	Egg whites		435
1	12	Sugar		875
	2	Pectin mixture		60
	3 1/2	Water		100
2	0	Butter	1	
	10	Compound fat		300
		Flavour (as desired)		

Pectin mixture

lb	oz		kg	gr
1	0	Sugar (castor)		500
	3 1/2	Sugar (icing)		100
	5 3/4	Pectin powder		160

Sieve well together. The egg white and sugar are beaten to a stiff meringue and the pectin which has been dispersed in the water is added. The butter and fat are creamed together lightly and added to the meringue. *(Switzerland)*

Buttercream with Pectin II

lb	oz		kg	gr
1	0	Butter		500
	2 1/2	Sugar (icing)		75

lb	oz		kg	gr
	10	Sugar (granulated)		300
	3/4	Pectin mixture		22
	6	Egg whites		180
		Colour/flavour		

Pectin mixture

lb	oz		kg	gr
	5	Pectin powder (40 %)		150
1	0	Sugar (granulated)		500

Sieved together. Place the sugar/pectin mixture, egg whites and water into a bain-marie and carefully heat to 96° F (36° C) stirring all the while. When cool, pour into the well beaten butter and icing sugar and beat until light and smooth.

OTHER CREAMS

Basic Fudge Mixture

lb	oz		kg	gr
	1/16	Salt		2
1	0	Fondant		500
1	0	Sugar (icing)		500
	2	Evaporated milk		60
	10	Special cake fat		300

Soften the fondant and blend with the icing sugar, milk and salt. Add the fat and mix. (Do not beat.)

Fudge Filling/Icing

lb	oz		kg	gr
1	0	Basic fudge mix		500
		Colour/flavour		
		Milk		

Add the desired colour and flavour together with sufficient milk to obtain the desired consistency, mixing on low speed.

Additions	
Orange/Lemon	to each 1 lb. (500 gr.) of fudge filling add 1/2 oz. (15 gr.) of minced whole orange or lemon minus seeds
Fruit jelly	to each 1 lb. (500 gr.) of fudge filling add 4 oz. (125 gr.) of jelly
Lemon/orange curd	to each 1 lb. (500 gr.) of fudge filling add 4 oz. (125 gr.) of curd
Chocolate	to each 1 lb. (500 gr.) of fudge filling add 4 oz. (125 gr.) of plain chocolate

Additions (cont.)	
Coffee	to each 1 lb. (500 gr.) of fudge filling add 1 oz. (30 gr.) (approx.) coffee infusion
Malt	to each 1 lb. (500 gr.) of fudge filling add 2 oz. (60 gr.) liquid malt
Chocolate malt	to each 1 lb. (500 gr.) of fudge filling add 2 oz. (60 gr.) of unsweetened plain chocolate to the above (malt)

Fudge of Lighter Consistency

Any of the fudges can be well beaten and used as for buttercream.

Fudge Covering

A fondant like covering can be made from fudge by warming in a bain-marie to 110-120° F (43-49° C) stirring all the while. Any air that may be present will be released while stirring. Should the fudge separate on warming, a little cold milk will soon bring about coherency. If properly prepared, the covering will set with a fine gloss.

Pistachio Marzipan Cream

Beat well a mixture of marzipan, pistachio colour and flavour and stock syrup.

Wine Cream

lb	oz		kg	gr
	8	White wine		250
	4	Egg yolks		125
	3	Sugar (castor)		90
	1 1/2	Cornflour		45
		Lemon juice		
		Gelatine (8 leaves)		
3	0	Whipped dairy cream	1	500

The wine, sugar, egg yolks, lemon juice and cornflour are made into a custard. The soaked gelatine is then stirred in thoroughly and before it sets, the whipped cream is folded in.

Wine Cream - Lemon

lb	oz		kg	gr
1	4	White wine		600
	14	Egg		400
	10	Sugar		300
		Juice of 6 lemons		
		Zest of 4 lemons		
	3 1/2	Custard powder		100
	7	Egg whites		200
	3 1/2	Sugar		100

Mix all the ingredients together except the last two. Bring them to the boil beating all the while. Strain and fold in the egg whites and the remaining sugar beaten to a stiff snow.

If intended for a basic cream, omit the egg white/sugar snow and leave in a cool place.

Mix with buttercream or whipped dairy cream as desired. Suitable for grape tartlets and desserts.

Wine Cream - Merlot

lb	oz		kg	gr
1	0	Merlot (red wine)		500
	10	Sugar		300
	1 1/2	Egg yolks		45
1	0	Whipped cream		500
		Salt (pinch)		
		Gelatine (4 leaves)		
		A piece of orange peel		

Boil up the Merlot, sugar, salt and orange peel for a few seconds. Stir the egg yolks and beat them into the hot mixture. Mix in the gelatine which should be previously soaked. Place the bowl containing the mixture into iced water to preserve the bouquet of the wine. As soon as the mixture begins to set, stir until it is smooth, then carefully fold in the whipped cream. Any other red wine may be used in which

case it may be called red wine cream. It can be transferred to individual glasses or goblets or used for pastries, in which case two extra leaves of gelatine should be used.
(Switzerland)

Stock Marshmallow

lb	oz		kg	gr
1	0	Sugar (granulated)		500
	8	Glucose		250
	6	Egg whites		180
	10	Water		300
	1/4	Agar-agar		8
		Cream of tartar		

The agar is soaked for some hours in the water and then brought to the boil. To make certain that the agar is properly dispersed, strain the solution. The sugar is then added and when properly dissolved it is taken to 225° F (107° C) when the warmed glucose is run in. The solution is then boiled to 245° F (118° C) taking the usual precautions.

Have ready the egg whites to which have been added a pinch of cream of tartar, beaten to a stiff snow. Whilst the machine is running pour in the boiling solution and continue beating until cool.

To use, add 10 oz. (300 gr.) of egg whites to each 2 lb. (1 kg.) of stock marshmallow. It can be coloured and flavoured.

Marshmallow Cream

lb	oz		kg	gr
	2	Gelatine		60
	10	Water		300
2	0	Sugar (granulated)	1	
	14	Glucose		435
	10	Water		300
	1/2	Tartaric Acid		15
		Flavour as desired		

Soak the gelatine in the 10 oz. (300 gr.) water. Boil the sugar, glucose, water and acid to 240° F (116° C) and cool to 200° F (93° C) and add the soaked gelatine and water.

Whisk until light.

Marshmallow - Strawberry

lb	oz		kg	gr
	2	Gelatine		60
1	0	Sugar (granulated)		500
	8	Glucose		250
1	0	Strawberry jam (sieved)		500
	10	Water		300
		Colour/flavour		

Take sugar, glucose, water and gelatine to the boil and cool. Whisk the mixture adding the warmed jam. Continue whisking until light.

Bavarian Cream

lb	oz		kg	gr
2	0	Milk	1	
	8	Sugar		250
	4	Egg yolks		125
3	0	Whipped cream	1	500
		Gelatine (12 leaves)		
		Vanilla pod		
		Liqueur (as desired)		

Add the vanilla pod to the milk and bring to the boil. Stir a little of the hot milk into the egg yolks and sugar. Add this to the rest of the milk and stir over gentle heat until the custard will coat a spoon. Stir in the gelatine previously soaked and squeezed out and leave in a cold place. As soon as the custard begins to set, stir it until smooth, flavour with liqueur as desired and carefully fold in the whipped cream. Fruit may be added as desired with the exception of acid fresh fruit such as pineapple, oranges, etc. Fill into large or small moulds. Decorate as desired after turning out.

This cream is particularly suitable for charlottes and other sweets. *(Switzerland)*

Bavarian Cream

lb	oz		kg	gr
1	4	Milk		625
	8	Sugar (castor)		250
	5	Egg yolks		150
	1/2	Gelatine		15
1	2	Cream		560
		Flavour		

Make a custard with the milk, 4 oz. (125 gr.) of sugar, egg yolks, the gelatine and flavour. When cool add the cream whipped with the balance of the sugar.
(France)

Charlotte Cream

lb	oz		kg	gr
1	4	Milk		625
	14	Cream		435
	8	Egg yolks		250
	8	Sugar (castor)		250

Prepare as for Bavarian Cream.
(France)

Diplomat Cream I

Stir cold vanilla custard *(page 241)* until smooth, flavour with liqueur as desired and carefully fold in 10 oz. (300 gr.) of whipped dairy cream. If required for Surprises *(page 746)*, add a small amount of a jellying agent (not more than ³/₈ oz. (10 gr.).

Diplomat Cream II

Mix one part of confectioner's custard with two parts whipped dairy cream and flavour well with kirsch or other liqueur or spirit.

St-Honoré Cream

lb	oz		kg	gr
1	8	Crème pâtissière		750
	5	Egg whites		150

Whisk the egg whites until stiff. Add the crème pâtissière while still boiling and mix thoroughly. In warm weather, two sheets of soaked gelatine may be added to the custard while still hot.
(France)

ITALIAN CREAMS

It will be noted that a high proportion of liqueur or spirit is used in many of these recipes. This is common practice in Italy.

Crema Pasticcera

lb	oz		kg	gr
2	0	Milk	1	
1	0	Sugar (castor)		500
	14 ½	Egg yolks		435
1 ³/₄		Egg		50
1 ³/₄		Flour		50
		Vanilla (1 pod)		

Crema Pasticcera (firmer)

lb	oz		kg	gr
2	0	Milk	1	
1	0	Sugar (castor)		500
	12	Egg yolks		375
	3 ½	Egg		100
	3	Flour		90
		Vanilla (1 pod)		

Crema Pasticcera (economic)

lb	oz		kg	gr
2	0	Milk	1	
1	0	Sugar (castor)		500
	7	Egg yolks		200
1 ³/₄		Egg		50
	3	Flour		90
		Vanilla (1 pod)		

Crema Pasticcera - Coffee

lb	oz		kg	gr
2	0	Coffee infusion	1	
1	0	Sugar (castor)		500
	10 ½	Egg yolks		300
1 ³/₄		Flour		50

The procedure for all these creams is to whip up the eggs and sugar and add the flour. Stir in the boiling milk. Return to the heat and cook very carefully until it begins to boil. Add a small nut of butter. If there is a need for rapid cooling, spread on a marble slab. The vanilla pod is boiled with the milk.

Flavouring Crema - Pasticcera

To each 2 lb. (1 kg.) of cream add:

lb	oz		kg	gr
	3	Chocolate		90
	3 ½	Gianduya		100
1 ³/₄		Pistachio paste		50
		Zest of 3 lemons		
		Zest of 3 oranges		
1 ³/₄		Liqueurs		50
1 ³/₄		Hazelnut paste		50

Orange Cream

lb	oz		kg	gr
	10	Sugar		300
1	1/2	Egg yolks		45
	4	Egg		125
1	3/4	Sugar		50
8	3/4	Butter		250
		Juice of 2 oranges		

Whisk the eggs and sugar. Add the other ingredients and allow to cook on a low heat. When it is cold, fresh whipped dairy cream can be blended in.

This cream can be filled into half orange caps for dessert.

As an alternative to orange, mandarins or lemons can be used.

Zabaglione

lb	oz		kg	gr
4	6	White wine (dry)	2	185
5	8	Marsala (dry)	2	750
1	1	Moscato		530
4	8	Egg yolks	2	250
1	2	Egg		560
6	8	Sugar	3	250
	3 1/2	Flour		100

Proceed as for Crema Pasticcera.

Zabaglione (whipped)

lb	oz		kg	gr
	7	Egg yolks (10)		200
	7	Sugar		200
	7	Marsala		200

Boil the above and whip until cold.

Zabaglione-Coffee (whipped)

lb	oz		kg	gr
	7	Egg yolks		200
	7	Sugar		200
	7	Instant coffee powder		200

Proceed as above.

Zabaglione-Chocolate (whipped)

lb	oz		kg	gr
	7	Egg yolks		200
	7	Sugar		200

lb	oz		kg	gr
1	3/4	Cocoa powder		50
5	1/4	Milk		150

Mix the cocoa powder with hot milk. When cool proceed as above.

Stracchino Cream for Mille-feuille

This is a particularly soft cream with a fine flavour used in the Venice and Lombardy regions. The finished gâteau should be eaten within 2 hours.

lb	oz		kg	gr
	7	Butter		200
	7	Sugar (icing)		200
	5	Egg yolks		150
	10	Egg whites (approx.)		350
		Vanilla		

Cream the butter, sugar and egg yolks. Whip the egg whites stiffly and fold into the mix. Add the vanilla.

Buttercream

lb	oz		kg	gr
2	0	Butter	1	
1	2	Sugar (icing)		500
	3 1/2	Alcohol		100
	3 1/2	Rum		100

Beat all the ingredients well together.

Buttercream Imperial

lb	oz		kg	gr
2	0	Butter	1	
1	12	Crema pasticcera		875
		Alcohol		
	3 1/2	Crème de cacao		100

Beat all the ingredients together.

Buttercream - Zabaglione

lb	oz		kg	gr
2	0	Butter	1	
1	12	Zabaglione		875
	3 1/2	Brandy		100

Proceed as above.

Buttercream - Meringue

lb	oz		kg	gr
2	0	Butter	1	
2	0	Meringue	1	
	5	Vanilla powder		150

Cream the butter and vanilla and fold in the meringue.

Buttercream (Various Flavours)

To each 2 lb. (1 kg.) of buttercream 3 1/2 oz. (100 gr.) of the following pastes may be added:

Pistachio	Coffee
Hazelnut	Praline
Chocolate	Almond
Macaroon	Croquant

Buttercream with Fruit

To each 2 lb. (1 kg.) of buttercream add 3 1/2 oz. (100 gr.) of orange essence or 7 oz. (200 gr.) of orange paste and the zest of 4 oranges.

Lemons or mandarins can be used in place of oranges.

Nougatine Buttercream

lb	oz		kg	gr
1	12	Butter		875
	12	Sugar (icing)		375
	12	Hazelnut praline		375
	8 1/2	Crème pâtissière		250
	3	Couverture (milk)		100
	5 1/2	Rum 70°		160
	1 1/2	Alcohol		45

Cream the butter and sugar then add the rest of the ingredients.

Argentina Cream

lb	oz		kg	gr
1	0	Butter		500
1	0	Almond mixture		500
	3	Egg yolks		85
	1	Alcohol		30

Beat well together.

Almond mixture

lb	oz		kg	gr
1	0	Sugar (granulated)		500
1	0	Blanched almonds		500

Grind to a powder.

Argentina Cream-Chocolate

To 2 lb. (1 kg.) of Argentina cream add 7 oz. (200 gr.) melted plain chocolate.

Buttercream (firmer)

lb	oz		kg	gr
4	6	White chocolate	2	
	10	Orange peel (ground)		300
2	0	Orange liqueur 30°	1	
1	0	Butter		500

Melt the chocolate and beat all the ingredients together.

Maraschino

lb	oz		kg	gr
3	8	White chocolate	1	750
1	12	Maraschino liqueur 30°		875
1	0	Butter		500

Essence of maraschino (1 gr. to 100 gr. of cream).

Proceed as above.

Hazelnut

lb	oz		kg	gr
3	0	White chocolate	1	500
1	0	Gianduja		500
1	0	Hazelnut praline		500
1	12	Rum		875
1	0	Butter		500

Coffee

lb	oz		kg	gr
4	0	White chocolate	2	
2	0	Coffee liqueur 30°	1	
	3 1/2	Coffee paste		100
1	0	Butter		500

Gianduja

lb	oz		kg	gr
3	0	White chocolate	1	500
3	0	Gianduja	1	500
3	0	Vanilla liqueur 30°	1	500
1	8	Butter		750

Alchermes

lb	oz		kg	gr
3	0	White chocolate	1	500
1	4	Alchermes liqueur 30°		625
1	8	Butter		750

Chocolate

lb	oz		kg	gr
4	0	White chocolate	2	
1	0	Cherry Brandy 30°		500
1	0	Zabaglione No. 8		500
1	0	Butter		500

Cream for Cappuccini

lb	oz		kg	gr
3	0	White chocolate	1	500
1	0	Alchermes liqueur 30°		500
1	0	Butter		500
	3 1/2	Alcohol		100

Arlecchini I

lb	oz		kg	gr
1	0	White chocolate		500
1	0	Gianduja		500
2	0	Butter	1	

Crema Arlecchino II

lb	oz		kg	gr
2	0	Butter	1	
1	0	Couverture (milk)		500
1	0	Gianduja		500

Beat well together

Chocolate Cream

lb	oz		kg	gr
2	0	White chocolate	1	
1	0	Gianduja		500
	8	Milk (boiled)		250
1	0	Butter		500

Chestnut

lb	oz		kg	gr
2	3	Chestnut purée	1	
	9	Rum or strega		250
	9	Butter		250

Pistachio

lb	oz		kg	gr
4	0	White chocolate	2	
	10	Pistachio paste		300
2	0	Vanilla liqueur 30°	1	
1	0	Butter		500

The procedure for making these creams, (chestnut excepted) follows:

Place the melted white chocolate and the other liquid materials in the machine and mix, adding the liqueur or essences made warmer. When well mixed store in a cool place for 24 hours, then beat in the butter a little at a time.

For the chestnut cream, mix the chestnut purée with half the rum, then add the butter and cream the mixture well. Finally add the rest of the rum.

CUSTARDS

See also Italian Crema Pasticcera *(page 235)*.

Custard I

lb	oz		kg	gr
1	4	Milk		625
	3	Sugar (castor)		90
	1/2	Cornflour		15
	5	Egg		150
		Flavour		

Mix cornflour, egg and sugar with a little milk and stir well. Add the rest of the milk and flavour desired. *(Great Britain)*

Custard II

lb	oz		kg	gr
1	4	Milk		625
	3	Sugar (castor)		90
	8	Egg		250
		Bay leaf		

Heat the milk, sugar and bay leaf to 180° F (82° C). Strain into the whisked egg.
(Great Britain)

Custard III

lb	oz		kg	gr
1	4	Milk		625
	4	Sugar (castor)		125
1	1/2	Custard powder		45
	4	Egg yolks		125
		Flavour		

Mix the cornflour, egg yolks and sugar with a little milk. Bring the rest of the milk to the boil and stir it in.
(Great Britain)

Custard IV

lb	oz		kg	gr
1	4	Milk		625
	3	Sugar (castor)		90
	2	Cornflour		60
	2	Butter (melted)		60
		Flavour		

Proceed as above stirring in the melted butter last. *(Great Britain)*

Custard V

lb	oz		kg	gr
1	4	Milk		625
	8	Egg yolks		250
	3	Sugar (castor)		90
		Bay leaf		

Proceed as for Custard III.
(Great Britain)

Custard VI

lb	oz		kg	gr
1	4	Milk		625
1	1/2	Sugar (castor)		45
	3/4	Cornflour		22
	4	Egg		125
	1	Butter (melted)		30
	1	Kirsch		30

Put the butter, sugar and nearly all the milk into a saucepan and bring to the boil. Pour it into the cornflour which has been mixed with the rest of the milk. Cook for one minute and beat in the egg a little at a time. Lastly add the kirsch.
(Great Britain)

Custard VII

lb	oz		kg	gr
1	4	Milk		625
	3	Sugar (castor)		90
	2	Ground almonds		60
	2	Ground rice		60
	2	Butter		60
	8	Egg		250

Proceed as above, adding the almonds in the first stage. *(Great Britain)*

Custard VIII

lb	oz		kg	gr
1	4	Milk		625
	5	Cream		150
	2	Sugar (castor)		60
	1/2	Arrowroot		15
3	1/2	Egg yolks		100
	8	Croquant (powdered and sieved)		250

Make up as for Custard VI, adding the croquant last. *(Great Britain)*

Custard IX

lb	oz		kg	gr
1	4	Milk		625
	5	Cream		150
	3	Sugar (castor)		90
	5	Egg yolks		150
	1/2	Arrowroot		15
		Bay leaf		

Make up as for Custard-Chocolate mixing the cream with the milk.
(Great Britain)

Custard-Chocolate

lb	oz		kg	gr
1	4	Milk		625
	10	Cream		300
	7	Sugar (castor)		200
	1	Arrowroot		30
4	1/2	Egg yolks		140
	4	Unsweetened chocolate		125
		Vanilla		

Mix the arrowroot in a little milk. Put the rest of the milk, the cream and the sugar into a saucepan and bring to the boil. Pour it into the arrowroot, mix and cook for one minute. Pour it on to the beaten yolks and stir well. Pour this mixture into the melted chocolate a little at a time stirring well at each addition. Add the vanilla last.

(Great Britain)

Custard-Caramel

Make up as for Custard-Confectioner's adding sufficient caramel to colour and flavour. *(Great Britain)*

Custard Cream

lb	oz		kg	gr
1	0	Milk		500
1	0	Cream		500
	8	Sugar (castor)		250
	4	Egg yolks		125
		Vanilla		

Heat the milk, cream and sugar with the flavour and pour over the egg yolks stirring constantly. *(France)*

Custard-Frangipane I

lb	oz		kg	gr
1	4	Milk		625
	4	Sugar (castor)		125
	5	Cream		150
	1/2	Arrowroot		15
	3 1/2	Egg yolks		100
	4	Ground almonds		125
	1	Maraschino		30

Put the cream, sugar and nearly all the milk into a saucepan and bring to the boil. Pour it into the arrowroot which has been mixed with the rest of the milk. Cook for about one minute, then pour it into the egg yolks, ground almonds and maraschino that have been mixed together. *(France)*

Custard-Frangipane II

lb	oz		kg	gr
2	0	Milk	1	
	6	Egg		180
	4	Egg yolks		125
	3 1/2	Sugar (icing)		100
	7	Flour		200
	2	Macaroons (crushed)		60
	2	Butter		60
		Salt (a pinch)		
		1/2 a vanilla pod		

Mix the egg, yolks, sugar and flour to a smooth paste. Heat the milk with the salt and vanilla. Pour slowly on to the egg/sugar/flour paste. Return to the heat and cook stirring all the while. Add the butter and the crushed macaroons. *(France)*

Custard-Confectioner's

lb	oz		kg	gr
1	4	Milk		625
	2	Sugar (castor)		60
	5	Egg yolks		150
	2	Arrowroot		60
	1	Butter		30
		Bay leaf		
		Vanilla		

Mix the arrowroot with a little milk. Put the rest of the milk, the bay leaf, butter and sugar together and bring to the boil. Remove the bay leaf and pour the mixture on to the arrowroot paste. Return to the heat and cook carefully for one minute. Add the vanilla last. *(Great Britain)*

Confectioner's Custard - Crème Pâtissière

Recipe I

lb	oz		kg	gr
1	4	Milk		625
	2	Custard powder		60
	4	Sugar (castor)		125
		Flavour		

Recipe II

lb	oz		kg	gr
1	4	Milk		625
	3	Egg yolks		90
	4	Sugar (castor)		125
	3/4	Cornflour		22
		Flavour		

Recipe III

lb	oz		kg	gr
1	4	Milk		625
	5	Egg		150
	4	Sugar (castor)		125
	1	Flour		30
	4	Egg whites		125
		Flavour		

Bring three quarters of the milk to the boil. Mix half of the sugar, the flour (cornflour can be used), the egg and the balance of the milk on which the boiling milk is poured. Return to the heat and cook.

Vanilla, chocolate, praline, kirsch, mocha, etc. can be used. Whisk the egg whites until stiff with half the sugar and fold into the custard whilst still warm. *(France)*

Custard - Almond I

lb	oz		kg	gr
	7	Almond paste		200
	7	Sugar (granulated)		200
	2 3/4	Butter		75
	3	Egg yolks		90
	1	Rum		30

Grind the almonds finely with the sugar. Add the egg yolks, butter and the rum. *(France)*

Custard - Almond II

lb	oz		kg	gr
	7	Almond paste		200
	3 1/2	Vanilla sugar		100
	2 3/4	Butter		75
	3	Egg yolks		90
	1	Kirsch		30

Cream the almond paste with the sugar. Stir in the egg yolks, butter and finally the kirsch. If the mixture is too thick add a few drops of water. This custard is used as a filling for various gâteaux and especially the Pithivier gâteau. *(France)*

Custard - Orange

lb	oz		kg	gr
1	4	Milk		625
	2	Vanilla sugar		60
	14	Sugar		435
	7	Egg		200
1	12	Butter		875
		Juice of 8 oranges		
		Zest of 2 oranges		
		Zest of 1 lemon		

Cook all the ingredients except the butter. Strain, then add the butter which has been well creamed. *(France)*

Custard - Wine or Sabayon

lb	oz		kg	gr
1	2	Sugar (castor)		560
	10	Egg yolks		300
1	2	Dry white wine		560
		Zest of 2 oranges		

Mix the sugar and the egg yolks, then add the wine and orange zest. Place on a low heat and stir vigorously until the custard becomes frothy and smooth (do not boil). This custard can be served on its own or poured over certain dessert puddings. *(France)*

Custard - Walnut

lb	oz		kg	gr
1	4	Milk		625
	2 1/2	Cornflour		75
	3	Sugar		90
	4	Egg		125
	4	Ground walnuts		100
	1/16	Cinnamon		2

Bring the milk to the boil. Beat the cornflour, egg and sugar until frothy and add the boiling milk. Stir until smooth and add the walnuts and cinnamon. Return to the heat and cook until smooth and compact. *(Germany)*

Custard - Vanilla

lb	oz		kg	gr
1	4	Milk		625
1	4	Cream		625
	3	Cornflour		90
	9	Sugar (castor)		270
	4 1/2	Egg		140
		Vanilla		

Bring the milk and cream to the boil and while boiling add it to the egg, sugar, vanilla and cornflour that have been mixed together. Cook until it is a smooth cream. Set in a cool place. *(Germany)*

Custard for Danish Pastry

lb	oz		kg	gr
1	4	Milk		625
	4	Sugar (castor)		125
	2	Cornflour		60

lb	oz		kg	gr
	4	Egg		125
	1/2	Butter		15
		Vanilla		

Bring the milk to the boil and pour it into the egg, cornflour, sugar and vanilla which have been stirred together. Return the mixture to the heat and cook for about two minutes, taking care that it does not burn. Lastly stir in the butter.

Lemon Curd

lb	oz		kg	gr
1	0	Egg		500
	8	Butter		250
	4	Lemon juice		125
1	8	Sugar (castor)		750

Heat all together over a water bath until it thickens. *(Great Britain)*

Orange Curd

lb	oz		kg	gr
1	5	Egg		650
1	8	Sugar (castor)		750
	14	Butter		435
		Juice of 1 lemon		
		Juice of 6 oranges		
		Zest of 2 oranges		

Place all the materials in a copper pan and cook carefully. Strain and store in a cool place. *(Great Britain)*

Lemon Curd - Uncooked

lb	oz		kg	gr
1	0	Egg		500
	8	Butter		250
	6	Lemon juice		180
1	0	Sugar (castor)		500

Mix the egg, sugar and the lemon juice and beat it until it is like a sponge. Warm the butter and beat in. Keep in a cool place until required for use.
(Great Britain)

Lemon Curd

lb	oz		kg	gr
1	8	Sugar (castor)		750
	10	Butter		300

lb	oz		kg	gr
	12	Egg		375
		Juice of 8 lemons		
		Zest of 4 lemons		

Place all ingredients into a copper pan and stir continuously until cooked. Remove from the heat and strain. *(France)*

Custard - Cheese

lb	oz		kg	gr
1	0	Milk		500
	2	Egg yolks		60
	6	Sugar (castor)		180
1	0	Cream cheese		500
	12	Dairy cream		375
	2 1/2	Sultanas		75
		Salt (a pinch)		
		Gelatine (10 sheets)		
		Zest of 1/4 lemon		
		1/2 vanilla pod		

Steep the vanilla in the milk, warming it gently. Mix the egg yolks, sugar, salt and lemon zest, pour in the milk and cook gently until the custard coats the spatula. Remove the vanilla and add the gelatine that has been previously soaked and squeezed dry. Chill well then add the sieved cream cheese. Lastly fold in the whipped cream and the sultanas.
(Germany)

Russe Cream

Plain Base Mixing

lb	oz		kg	gr
	5 1/4	Egg yolks		150
1	9	Milk		780
	10	Sugar		300
	4	Sheet gelatine		125
	1	Cornflour		30

Soak the gelatine in milk until soft and remove. Take the milk to the boil. Mix yolks, sugar and cornflour together, whisk well and add the boiling milk. Return to the double saucepan and cook until thick. Stir in the gelatine. Store in the cool until required.

Fruit Base Mixing

lb	oz		kg	gr
	4	Egg yolks		125
	6	Sugar (castor)		180
1	1/2	Sheet gelatine		45
1		Cornflour		30
		Juice and zest of 2 large oranges and 1 lemon		

Soak gelatine in cold water. Mix the sugar, egg yolks and cornflour together. Add the boiling juices and cook. Finally stir in the gelatine that has been removed from the water.

Rate of Usage

To each 1 lb. (500 gr.) of whipped dairy cream stir in 8 oz. (250 gr.) of either of the above base mixings. The basic mixing is carefully melted. The temperature is critical; if too hot the cream will melt; if too cold the gelatine base will set before it is properly mixed in.

Icing and Glazes

ICINGS

Water Icing I

lb	oz		kg	gr
1	0	Sugar (icing)		500
	2 1/2	Water (approx.)		75
		Colour/flavour		

Mix the water, which should be hot, with the icing sugar. Any colour and/or flavour is added last.

Water Icing II

lb	oz		kg	gr
1	0	Sugar (icing)		500
	2 1/2	Stock syrup (approx.)		75
		Colour/flavour		

Place the sugar and stock syrup in a pan and warm, adjusting the consistency as required.

Fondant

lb	oz		kg	gr
4	0	Sugar (preserving)	2	
1	4	Water		625
	12	Glucose OR		375
	1/6	Cream of tartar		5

For the method *see page 244*.

To prepare for use, place a sufficient quantity of the fondant into a pan and heat in a bain-marie to a temperature between 95-110° F (35-43° C). The consistency is adjusted with stock syrup *(page 244)*. Colour and/or flavour is added as desired. For chocolate fondant add melted chocolate. Any fondant not in use should be kept covered.

Fondant Meringue

lb	oz		kg	gr
1	0	Prepared fondant		500
	4	Meringue (boiled)		125
		Colour/flavour		

Carefully mix the meringue with the prepared fondant adjusting the temperature and the consistency as required.

Royal Icing

a.

lb	oz		kg	gr
7	0	Sugar (icing)	3	500
1	4	Egg whites (approx.)		625

b.

lb	oz		kg	gr
1	0	Sugar (icing)		500
	2 1/2	Egg whites (approx.)		75

For method *pages 244-245*.

Chocolate Icing I

lb	oz		kg	gr
	1	Gelatine (leaf)		30
3	0	Sugar (granulated)	1	500
	4	Glucose		125
2	8	Water	1	250
		Couverture* 100° F (37° C)		

Soak the leaf gelatine in cold water until it is soft. Bring the sugar, glucose and water to the boil. Remove the gelatine from the water and stir into the boiled syrup. Heat the couverture to 100° F (37° C) add syrup until the desired consistency is reached.

* Each 1 lb. (500 gr.) of couverture will need approximately 8 oz. (250 gr.) of the above syrup.

Chocolate Icing II

lb	oz		kg	gr
2	0	Sugar	1	
	8	Chocolate		250
1	4	Water (approx.)		625
		Vanilla		

Melt the chocolate, add the sugar and water, stir well and boil to the pearl degree *(page 51)*. Allow the icing to cool a little stirring occasionally until it begins to thicken and a thin skin forms on top. It is then ready for coating.

This is a fine type of icing suitable for torten and petits fours.

Chocolate Icing III

lb	oz		kg	gr
2	0	Sugar	1	
	7	Block cocoa		200
1	4	Water (approx.)		625

Mix the cocoa and sugar well with some of the water. Add the rest and boil to the pearl degree *(page 51)*. Proceed as above.

Orange Icing

lb	oz		kg	gr
1	8	Sugar (icing) (approx.)		750
	3 1/2	Stock syrup (38° B)		100
		Juice of 2 oranges		
		Lemon juice (1 teaspoon)		
		Thinly pared rind of 2 oranges		

Steep the orange rind in the hot syrup for 15 minutes. Add the orange and lemon juice, strain and allow to get cold. Mix with icing sugar until it is of a thick flowing consistency.

Stock Syrup

Stock syrup is used to make water icing and to adjust the consistency of fondant icing when it is prepared for use. It is made by boiling six parts of sugar with five parts of water and one part of glucose. Boil for a few minutes, remove the scum, strain, and when cool place in a bottle.

Fondant Icing

Using the recipe *page 243*, dissolve the sugar in the water and take the solution to 225° F (107° C). Pour into the solution the warmed glucose *or* the cream of tartar dispersed in a little water. Do not stir but let the addition disperse in the convection currents set up by boiling. Stirring may cause the solution to grain. Wash the inside of the boiling pan from time to time with a brush dipped in water and take the solution to 240° F (115,5° C). Next pour the boiling sugar solution into a square of steel bars which have been placed on a very clean marble slab moistened with cold water. Splash straight away with cold water to prevent crystals forming. When the syrup is tepid (100° F) remove the bars and work it on the slab with a steel spatula, turning it over from the outside towards the centre several times. As it is mixed, the syrup becomes opaque and then turns steadily whiter until it suddenly solidifies. Now place the fondant in a container and cover with a damp cloth. The water in the cloth causes it to soften and it will reach the right consistency after a few hours.

When ready for use, fondant should be white and malleable. If it is yellow or granular, it has either been over-cooked or worked while too warm.

Rock Sugar

lb	oz		kg	gr
4	0	Sugar (granulated)	2	
1	4	Water		625
	3	Royal (icing)		90

Boil the sugar and water to 280° F (137° C) taking the usual precautions during boiling. When it has reached this figure, dip the pan into cold water to prevent any further rise in temperature. Stir in the royal icing thoroughly and pour into a greased sieve or greased metal bowl and let it set.

The royal icing must be made with shell whites and contain no acid and be well beaten. When added to the boiling sugar solution it will froth and rise, in consequence of the air beaten in expanding under the influence of the heat. The egg whites will coagulate and when cool the rock sugar will set, when it can be broken up for decorating Christmas cakes, etc.

If the rock sugar is to be white, the royal icing is coloured a distinct blue. Any other colour may be used, bearing in mind that the royal icing must be rather heavily coloured to produce the colour effect in the rock sugar.

GLAZES
Apricot Glaze

lb	oz		kg	gr
1	0	Apricot purée		500
1	0	Fondant		500

Mix and boil well.

Honey Glaze

lb	oz		kg	gr
1	0	Sugar (icing)		500
	1 1/2	Honey		50
	2 1/2	Hot water		75
		Vanilla		

Mix together.

Cornflour Gel

lb	oz		kg	gr
1	8	Sugar (granulated)		750
1	9	Water		780
	3	Cornflour		90
	12	Glucose		350

Mix cornflour with a little of the water. Add the sugar, glucose and the rest of the water which have been brought to the boil. Cook for 1-2 minutes.

Jelly Glaze

lb	oz		kg	gr
	12	Sugar		375
2	8	Hot water	1	125
	1 1/2	Gelatine (powdered)		45
	1/4	Citric acid		8
		Colour/flavour		

Disperse the gelatine in the hot water, then add the sugar, acid, colour and flavour. Use this glaze when near the point of setting.

Arrowrot Glaze

lb	oz		kg	gr
1	4	Fruit juice		625
		Sugar*		
	1	Arrowroot		30
		Colour/flavour		

Mix the arrowroot with a little of the fruit juice. Stirring all the while, pour in the rest of the juice which has been brought to the boil. Use while hot.

* The amount will depend on the sweetness of the juice.

Bun Glaze I

Two parts fresh egg and one part water well whisked together.

Bun Glaze II

Two parts egg, one part sugar and one part water, well whisked together.

Bun Glaze III

lb	oz		kg	gr
1	4	Sugar (castor)		625
1	4	Water		625
	1/2	Gelatine (powdered)		15

Bring the water and sugar to the boil, removing any scum. Remove from the heat and add the gelatine that has been dispersed in a little water.

Gum Arabic Solution

lb	oz		kg	gr
	2	Gum arabic (powdered)		60
	10	Water		300
	4	Sugar (castor)		125

Mix the gum arabic and the sugar together and place into a bain-marie with the water and bring to the boil. Use while hot. A little apricot purée may be added.

Water Icing Glaze

lb	oz		kg	gr
1	0	Sugar (icing)		500
		Hot water		
		Lemon juice		

Mix the lemon juice with the sugar, adding hot water until the desired consistency is reached.

Cornflour Glaze

lb	oz		kg	gr
	1	Cornflour		30
1	0	Fruit juice		500
	6	Sugar		180
	1/2	Gelatine		15

Mix the cornflour with about 3 oz. (90 gr.) of juice. Boil remainder of the juice with the sugar adding colour if required. Add the cornflour mixture and cook until the mixture thickens. Stir in gelatine that has been dispersed in a little hot water. Cool a little before use.

Basic Leckerli Glaze

lb	oz		kg	gr
1	0	Sugar (granulated)		500
	4	Water		125

Dissolve the sugar in the water and boil to 185° F (85° C).

Magenbrot Glaze

lb	oz		kg	gr
2	8	Sugar (granulated)	1	250
	2	Cocoa powder		60
	14	Water		400
		Caramel		

Boil the sugar and water to the pearl degree *(page 51)*. Add the cocoa powder and tint with a little caramel.

Chocolate

Chocolate is a mixture of cocoa solids in fine fractions, cocoa butter and flavours. It may contain sugar and milk solids. Whether it is plain or milk it is known in the British Isles as couverture, as distinct from bakers' chocolate, made specially for coating and decorating cakes and fancies. It remains comparatively soft and unlike couverture does not splinter when it is cut. Couverture needs correct tempering before it is used; bakers' chocolate does not.

COUVERTURE

The Importance of Tempering

Cocoa butter, which is an important constituent of couverture, is a complex mixture of fats, each having a different melting and setting point. It is the presence of these different fat fractions that makes it so important that couverture is correctly tempered.

To prepare couverture, it is first cut into small pieces and put into a dry bowl placed on a saucepan containing warm water. It is of the greatest importance that no water, or water in the form of condensed steam, comes into contact with any chocolate or it will thicken and be useless for dipping and moulding, therefore, the bowl must be perfectly dry. It is of equal importance that the chocolate does not come into contact with direct heat, or the fine flavour will be lost; in addition, chocolate will quickly burn and will have to be thrown away.

Approximate temperatures for tempering are given below, but there may be variations due to the type of couverture used. Reputable chocolate manufactures will provide detailed instructions and these should be observed.

When the couverture, which should be stirred from time to time, has reached a temperature of 115-118° F (46-47° C) (milk couverture 110° F [43° C]) it is removed from the heat, and after the bottom of the bowl has been dried with a cloth, it is poured on to a dry marble slab and spread with a palette knife until it begins to set. It is then quickly returned to the bowl and very carefully taken to a temperature of 88° F (31° C) (milk couverture 84° F [29° C]). Great care must be taken at this stage for it will be found that the retained heat in the metal bowl is almost sufficient to take the couverture up to these figures. If the temperatures are exceeded, then the tempering must be started all over again. Couverture must at all times be stirred gently; vigorous stirring will introduce air bubbles which will spoil the smooth surface of the finished goods.

The reason for tempering is not easy to explain in simple terms, nevertheless an understanding of it is necessary if it is to be done consistently well. When couverture is taken to a higher figure, all the fats in the cocoa butter are melted and well distributed. The spreading assists in rapid cooling during which some of the fat fractions set. When the couverture is re-heated to the lower figures these fractions remain crystallized to act as nuclei on which complete crystallization is effected when the couverture sets after dipping and moulding.

If tempering is not done correctly, it will be found that the couverture will not set quickly and moulded figures will not leave the moulds. When at last the couverture sets, it will be found to have a fat bloom on the surface. This is due to the fat fractions not being mixed so that they float to the surface, to be seen as a grey film completely spoiling the gloss that is the beauty of correctly prepared couverture. Another form of bloom is a result of dampness when the sugar on the surface dissolves and re-crystallizes in larger form on drying. This is known as sugar bloom.

MOULDING

To produce chocolate figures, cups and Easter eggs, moulds are necessary, which may be either metal or plastic. Metal moulds are more durable, but plastic moulds being semi-transparent give the chocolate craftsman the opportunity of seeing whether or not the figure has come away from the mould.

The moulds are prepared by polishing them with a soft cloth or cotton wool, so that the moulding surface is not only perfectly clean, but with a high polish. If any of the moulds contain pieces of chocolate, they should be warmed and the melted chocolate wiped out. On no account should the chocolate be removed with a sharp instrument or the moulds will be scratched, which will show on the finished goods. When the moulds are not in use they should be cleaned and wrapped in soft paper before being stored in a clean dry place. Moulds for chocolate work are in one or two parts. Those in two parts are either totally enclosed or with open ends into which the chocolate can be poured.

Single section moulds are filled with the prepared couverture, tapped well to bring any air bubbles away from the moulded surface, and then allowed to set. When ready for removal, they should leave the moulds easily after a slight tap.

Enclosed moulds are opened and sufficient prepared couverture is deposited on one surface. The other half of the mould is placed over it and both sections securely fastened with clips. The mould is then rotated to distribute the chocolate over both surfaces, tapping the mould from time to time to remove any air bubbles from the inner surface. When set, the clips are removed, the mould carefully opened, and the figure taken out.

With open ended moulds, the two sections are first clipped together. Prepared couverture is then poured in until they are almost full, after which they are well tapped to remove air bubbles. After a short time they are taken one at a time and up-ended and tapped with a stick so that the balance of melted chocolate is returned to the bowl, leaving a shell of couverture in the mould. The moulds are then stood up on to greaseproof paper, so that any molten chocolate will run down, sealing the open end to form a pedestal so that the chocolate figure can be stood up.

When completely set, the moulds are unclipped and if the couverture has been properly tempered, the figures should leave the moulds with a fine gloss. *(Illustrations pages 636, 657.)*

Easter Eggs

Easter eggs are made in two ways:

1. Prepared couverture is poured into the polished moulds which are then tapped to remove bubbles. When about six have been filled, the first is inverted over the bowl and shaken with a rotary motion of the hand to remove the surplus chocolate. This will leave a shell of even thickness in the mould. As each is dealt with, it is inverted on to paper so that some of the molten chocolate runs down to form a flange round the inner rim.

2. The couverture is brushed into the prepared moulds with a soft dry brush. When it is set, another coat is added. A third may be given if necessary. When the last coating has been applied the moulds are inverted on to paper as described above.

If the couverture has been correctly tempered it will leave the mould on setting; this is because the chocolate will contract more than the metal or plastic of the mould. Before removal from the mould, however, the edge should be trimmed with a stout piece of plastic (never use a sharp metal instrument for this purpose) care being taken not to remove the flange.

To assemble eggs, a little melted chocolate is piped on the flange, two sections can then be fixed together. Easter eggs can be decorated in many ways, with piping chocolate, cut-out or modelled flowers, crystallized violets or rose petals. Nylon ribbon will also give an excellent finish. Care should always be exercised with finished chocolate products; careless handling will leave fingerprints and smears and the fine gloss will be spoiled.

When the confectioner is working with chocolate, he needs a special room for the dipping and moulding if good results are to be obtained. Ideally, the room should be kept at a temperature of 68° F (20° C). Praline centres to be coated with couverture must be dry and be of the same temperature as the room where the work is to be done. If they are colder, the couverture will set too rapidly and will have a dull appearance; on the other hand, if the centres are too warm, the couverture will turn grey on account of the separation of the cocoa butter from the chocolate. Even when the chocolates have cooled down, they must not be subjected to variations in temperature as they could become discoloured and lose their gloss. They should be stored at a temperature of 55-60° F (12-15° C) away from sunlight and dampness.
(See illustration page 610.)

Storing

In concluding this section, mention should be made of the means of storing chocolate products. Here are the advantages of wrapping them individually in cellophane:

1. The chocolate retains its flavour.

2. The mouldings are kept free from dust.

3. Finger prints and other marks are eliminated.

4. Storage is simplified, since some mouldings can be placed inside each other (the shells of Easter eggs, for instance).

CHOCOLATE CUT-OUTS

To make chocolate cut-outs for decorating gâteaux, fancies and ices, prepared couverture is spread on to thick paper. The paper is picked up and allowed to drop several times so that the chocolate runs level. When it is set, it is cut with the point of a knife or with sharp cutters to the desired shapes. The pieces are easily removed by inverting the paper on to a clean sheet and peeling it off. The shapes can then be collected and the debris returned for further use.
(See illustrations page 118.)

BAKERS' CHOCOLATE

This chocolate can be purchased as either plain or milk. It is similar to couverture except that almost all the cocoa butter has been removed and replaced by a hydrogenated fat, together with a stabilizer such as lecithin, to prevent the fat from separating. Because of the type of fat used and its increased stability, this chocolate does not need tempering.

Bakers' chocolate is prepared initially in the same way as couverture and then taken to a temperature of 130° F (54° C) (110-125° F milk [43-51° C]). The temperature is then allowed to drop until the desired consistency is reached; the higher the temperature, the thinner the chocolate. The generally accepted rule is that it should be warmer for larger articles such as gâteaux and cooler, 105-110° F (40-43° C) (100-105° F milk [37-40° C]) for smaller fancies. These are optimum temperatures, although it is possible to use bakers' chocolate at a temperature range between 90-130° F (32-54° C) with satisfactory results. As with couverture, no water or steam must come in contact with the chocolate or it will thicken and be useless for either dipping or spreading.

PIPING CHOCOLATE

Piping chocolate can be purchased from the manufacturer and should be used according to instructions. It can be made by the craftsman, however, by very carefully adding a little glycerine or stock syrup to melted couverture which can be either plain or milk. A very small addition will thicken the couverture to a consistency, so that it can be piped.

Piping chocolate is an excellent medium for piping, lettering outlines and chocolate motifs for gâteaux, torten, fancies and ices, etc. It can be applied directly on to the product, or on to wax paper, when after it is set, it can be removed and placed on to the article to be decorated.
(See illustration page 121.)

Chocolate Cigarette or Rolls

The successful making of chocolate rolls requires a great deal of skill and this is acquired only from patience and practice.

Pour a little tempered couverture on to a marble slab and spread thinly with a palette knife and continue working it until the surface is semi-set and has a grey appearance. With the edge of a knife or with a scraper on the surface of the chocolate, move it from left to right in an upward direction which gives a cutting action. If the couverture is in the correct condition the couverture will curl into rolls.
(See illustration page 119.)

Chocolate Shavings

Proceed exactly as for chocolate rolls but the couverture need not be tempered. Alternatively, the block of chocolate can be shaved with a sharp knife.

Chocolate Streusel

Temper some plain couverture and let it cool. Before it sets, press it through a coarse wire sieve on to a clean sheet of paper. After it has set completely, break up the threads by rubbing them gently through the fingers.

Chocolate Leaves

A variety of chocolate leaves can be made by using the natural or a plastic leaf as a mould. The leaf is carefully cleaned and dried, then very thinly smeared with olive oil, after which the chocolate is carefully spread on the surface. When set, the leaf will easily peel off.

Chocolate holly leaves make an excellent form of decoration for Christmas gâteaux, torten and fancies.

Chocolate Petals

These are made by placing dabs of tempered couverture on to greaseproof paper with a palette knife, so that as the knife is withdrawn from the paper, petal shapes are formed that are thicker at the edges and thin in the centres.

GANACHE

Ganache is an easily made mixture of chocolate couverture and cream. A cheaper variety can be made by using a mixture of cream and milk, or by using milk alone.

The couverture used may be either plain or milk. Because plain couverture imparts a pronounced flavour of chocolate, additional flavour is not generally used. Ganache made from milk couverture may be flavoured with an addition such as rum, kirsch or coffee. Here are recipes for ganache of three qualities.

Butter Ganache

Is prepared by replacing all or part of the cream with butter. This type of ganache is very palatable but does not keep so well. *(France)*

Egg Ganache

lb	oz		kg	gr
	4	Egg yolks		125
	5	Sugar		150
2	4	Fresh cream	1	125
3	4	Vanilla couverture	1	625

Beat up the egg yolks and stir in the sugar and cream. Cook over heat and add the couverture. *(France)*

	1			2			3		
	lb	oz	kg gr	lb	oz	kg gr	lb	oz	kg gr
Couverture	8	0	4	8	0	4	8	0	4
Cream	5	0	2 500	2	8	1 250	—		
Milk	—			2	0	1	4	0	2

Ganache is made by first melting the couverture, then bringing the cream or milk to the boil. The two are mixed thoroughly together and left in a cool place for 24 hours before use.

The consistency of ganache may be adjusted by decreasing or increasing the proportion of chocolate; an increase is advised in hot weather. A further increase will cause the ganache to set quite firm when it can be cut out for chocolate centres.

Ganache is normally used for spreading and piping. It is prepared by beating until it is light and workable. If it should curdle or separate during beating, it should be warmed, or a little warm chocolate may be run in. Properly prepared, ganache should be soft when used; it will, however, set quickly making it suitable for dipping into fondant or chocolate.

Here are further recipes:

Firmer Ganache

lb	oz		kg	gr
1	12	Fresh cream		875
	7	Vegetable fat		200
3	4	Vanilla couverture	1	625

Proceed in the same way as for cream ganache. *(France)*

Ganache flavoured with mocha, tea, various liqueurs, fruits or aromatics is prepared by replacing some of the cream with an infusion of coffee or tea, with liqueur or fruit purée.

Ganache

lb	oz		kg	gr
2	3	Dairy cream	1	
3	5	Couverture	1	500

Bring the dairy cream to the boil and add the grated couverture. When cold, beat well to a spreading consistency.

(Germany)

Fresh Cream Ganache

lb	oz		kg	gr
2	4	Fresh cream	1	125
4	0	Vanilla couverture	2	

Boil the cream in a copper pan and then add the finely grated couverture. Mix well to obtain a thoroughly smooth consistency and leave to set in a cool place. Beat the ganache well before use. *(France)*

MODELLING PASTES

In the whole range of decorative work many pastes are required for covering, moulding and modelling. The type of paste required depends on the purpose to which it is put.

Amongst the many uses are:

1. Toppings for fancies
2. Covering for cakes and gâteaux
3. Flower, fruit and figure work
4. Cut-out flowers
5. Extended borders
6. Structural support on large cakes
7. Pastillage and exhibition work
8. Display.

All modelling pastes may be coloured. Sugar and gum paste if required to be white may have a little blue added.

All pastes must be kept covered (gum paste in a container with a damp cloth) or they will skin and the quality and the smoothness of the paste will be affected.

Almond Paste for Genoese, Fancies, Gâteaux, Layer Cake and Battenburg

Recipe I

lb	oz		kg	gr
1	0	Raw marzipan		500
1	0	Sugar (icing) Stock syrup		500

Mix together carefully.

Recipe II

lb	oz		kg	gr
1	0	Raw marzipan		500
	8	Sugar (icing)		250
	8	Fondant		250

Almond Paste for Flower Modelling

Recipe I

lb	oz		kg	gr
1	0	Raw marzipan		500
	12	Sugar (icing)		375
	1/8	Gum tragacanth		4

Soak the gum tragacanth in water to a gel. Squeeze out the excess water through muslin. Mix all together.

Recipe II

lb	oz		kg	gr
1	0	Raw marzipan		500
	12	Sugar (icing)		375
	4	Gum paste		125

Recipe III

lb	oz		kg	gr
1	0	Raw marzipan		500
	12	Sugar (icing)		375
	12	Gum paste		375

Recipes II and III: Mix all the ingredients together.

Almond Paste for Fruits

Recipe I

lb	oz		kg	gr
3	0	Raw marzipan	1	500
3	8	Sugar (icing)	1	750
	1	Water		30
	1/8	Gum tragacanth		4

Proceed as for Almond Paste for Flower Modelling recipe I.

Recipe II

lb	oz		kg	gr
1	0	Raw marzipan		500
1	0	Sugar (icing)		500

Proceed as for Almond Paste for Flower Modelling recipe II or III.

Almond Paste for Figures, Press Moulding and Cut-out Pieces

Recipe I

lb	oz		kg	gr
1	0	Raw marzipan		500
	12	Sugar (icing)		375

Recipe II

lb	oz		kg	gr
1	0	Raw marzipan		500
	12	Sugar (icing)		375
	4	Sugar paste		125

Sugar Pastes

Recipe I

lb	oz		kg	gr
1	0	Stock marshmallow		500
	2	Fat (hard)		60
1	8	Sugar (icing) (approx.)		750

The fat, which can be palm kernel, or cocoa butter, is melted and added to the other materials and well mixed.

Recipe II

lb	oz		kg	gr
1	3	Sugar (granulated)		590
	6	Water		180
	10	Glucose		300
	1/2	Gelatine		15
	1 1/4	Fat (hard)		35
	1 1/2	Sugar (icing)		45
	1/8	Glycerine		4

Boil the sugar, water and glucose to 238° F (114° C) and allow to cool. Add the gelatine, soaked in a little water, the melted fat and the rest of the materials and mix well.

Recipe III

lb	oz		kg	gr
1	2 1/2	Glucose		560
	3 1/2	Fat (hard)		100
	1/8	Gelatine		4
3	8	Sugar (icing)	1	750

Heat the glucose and fat to 200° F (93° C). Add the soaked gelatine and the icing sugar. Mix to a plastic paste.

Recipe IV (Firmer)

lb	oz		kg	gr
	7 1/2	Water		225
	3/8	Gum tragacanth		12
	1/2	Gelatine		15
	1 1/2	Water		45
	8	Sugar (castor)		250
	2	Cocoa butter		60
2	8	Sugar (icing) (approx.)	1	250
	2	Cornflour		60

Soak gum in 7 1/2 oz. (225 gr.) water and strain. Soak gelatine in 1 1/2 oz. (45 gr.) water. Mix together and heat to 200° F (93° C) after adding castor sugar and cocoa butter. Mix in the icing sugar and cornflour.

Recipe V (Hard drying)

lb	oz		kg	gr
1	0	Sugar (granulated)		500
	5	Water		150
1	0	Glucose		500
	1	Gelatine		30
1	0	Royal icing		500
5	0	Sugar (icing)	2	500

Heat sugar, water and glucose to 200° F (93° C). Add the gelatine that has been soaked, then mix in the royal icing and sugar.

Recipe VI

lb	oz		kg	gr
1	8	Gum paste		750
	4 1/2	Glucose		140
	7	Sugar (icing)		200
	5 1/2	Cocoa butter		165
	6	Royal icing (no acid)		180

Melt the glucose and cocoa butter and blend into the royal icing. Add to the gum paste and finally add the icing sugar.

Gum Paste

Recipe I

lb	oz		kg	gr
	1	Gum tragacanth		30
	7 1/2	Water		225
	5	Cornflour		150
3	0	Sugar (icing) (approx.)	1	500

Soak gum for 12 hours and then squeeze water out through a cloth. Mix in dry materials.

Recipe II

lb	oz		kg	gr
	1	Gum tragacanth (powdered)		30
1	0	Royal icing		500
	2 1/2	Water		75
2	0	Sugar (icing)	1	

Beat the powdered gum into the royal icing, adding the water and sufficient icing sugar to make a smooth pliable paste.

Recipe III

lb	oz		kg	gr
2	0	Royal icing	1	
	1/2	Gum tragacanth (powdered)		15
1	0	Sugar (icing) (approx.)		500

Proceed as for recipe II.

Modelling Chocolate

lb	oz		kg	gr
1	0	Couverture (plain or milk)		500
1	0	Glucose		500

Melt the couverture and the glucose to 95° F (35° C). Mix together thoroughly. Keep the mixture for 24 hours in an air-tight tin, then mix well to a plastic paste.
(Great Britain)

White Chocolate Paste

lb	oz		kg	gr
	14	Cocoa butter		400
2	4	Sugar (icing)	1	
1	5	Glucose		600
	1/2	Gum tragacanth		15

Melt the cocoa butter and mix it with the icing sugar, glucose and the gum tragacanth that has been soaked in water. Pass through the grinding machine until the paste is perfectly smooth. *(France)*

Chocolate Modelling Paste

lb	oz		kg	gr
1	8	Couverture		800
	9	Glucose		275

Mix the glucose with the melted couverture and allow to stand. When the mixture sets, pass it through the grinding machine until it is of the correct consistency. Flowers made with this paste can be embellished with traces of gold. *(France)*

Selva

lb	oz		kg	gr
1	2	Plain couverture		500
1	2	Milk couverture		500
	3 1/2	Glucose		100
	3 1/2	Water		100

Melt the chocolate. Bring the glucose and water to the boil and add to the chocolate. When well mixed, place in the refrigerator for 5-6 hours, then pass through the refiner. Mould into one piece and return to the refrigerator. Cut off pieces as required and make into a thin ribbon by passing through the refiner. *(Italy)*

Jellies

Jellies have a gastronomic appeal because of their translucent appearance and colour. If fresh fruit is used then the flavour of the fruit is an added attraction.

Jellies are used for dessert either on their own or with other materials and/or embellishments. They are used to sandwich torten and can be used for decorative work, for bon-bons and for chocolate centres.

Basic Jelly

lb	oz		kg	gr
1	2	Sugar (castor)		560
	3	Gelatine		90
	15	White wine		450
	3	Egg whites		90
	15	Water (hot)		450
		Zest of 1 1/2 lemons		
		Juice of 3 lemons		

Soak the gelatine in cold water and disperse it in the hot water. Add the sugar, lemon juice and zest and bring to the boil. Cover over, remove from the heat and leave to stand for 10 minutes. Beat the egg whites with the white wine and gradually whisk in the syrup. Continue to whisk over heat until the jelly forms a crust. Simmer for 10 minutes. Cover over again, remove from the heat and leave to stand for a few minutes. Strain through a cloth which has been wetted with cold water and if the jelly is not completely clear, strain a second time. *(France)*

Basic Jelly

lb	oz		kg	gr
1	4	Water (hot)		625
	1	Gelatine		30
	3	Sugar (castor)		90
	2	Sherry		60
		Colour as desired		

Disperse gelatine and sugar in the water. Add the rest of the water and sherry. Place a few crushed egg shells in and strain.
(Great Britain)

Apricot Jelly for Bon-Bons

lb	oz		kg	gr
1	12	Strained apricot pulp		875
7	8	Sugar (granulated)	3	750
	12	Glucose		375
	6	Agar-agar		180
	1/8	Citric acid		4

Soak the agar overnight in plenty of water, then after straining it add it to the pulp. Heat until the agar is dispersed, add the sugar and boil to 244° F (117° C). Remove from the gas and gently stir in the citric acid. Pour 1/4 in. (5 mm.) on waxpaper lined trays and spread level. Keep in a warm room overnight.
(Great Britain)

Jelly for Cut Fondants

lb	oz		kg	gr
	4	Agar-agar		125
1	0	Glucose		500
4	0	Sugar (granulated)	2	
	1/8	Citric acid		4

Soak the agar in plenty of water overnight. When fully expanded, lift out into a pan and dissolve over a slow heat. Add the glucose and heat to nearly boiling point. Strain, return to the pan and add the sugar. If it will not dissolve, add a little water. Boil to 236° F (113° C).

Remove from gas and sprinkle the citric acid on the surface and gently stir. Pour 3/16 in. (1/2 cm.) thick on to waxpaper lined trays and leave to set in a warm room. This jelly may be coloured and flavoured as desired. *(Great Britain)*

Piping Jelly I
a.

lb	oz		kg	gr
1	1 1/2	Water		545
	1/2	Agar-agar		15

Soak for 10 hours.

b.

lb	oz		kg	gr
2	8	Sugar (granulated)	1	250
	12 1/2	Water		375
	2 1/2	Glycerine		75

Boil to 240° F (115° C).

c.

lb	oz		kg	gr
1	8	Apricot purée*		750
	1/2	Tartaric acid		15

Add a. to b. and stir well. Replace on heat and boil to 228° F (109° C). Then add c.

* Apricot purée is made by boiling equal weights of apricot pulp and sugar for 8 minutes.

Piping Jelly II
a.

lb	oz		kg	gr
1	1 1/2	Water		545
	1/2	Agar-agar		15

Soak for 10 hours.

b.

lb	oz		kg	gr
2	8	Sugar (granulated)	1	250
2	0	Apple juice	1	
	1/4	Pectin		8

Boil to 240° F (115° C).

c.

lb	oz		kg	gr
	2 1/2	Glycerine		75
	1/2	Tartaric acid		15

Add a. to b. then add c.
Boil the mixture to 220° F (104° C).

Piping Jelly III

lb	oz		kg	gr
3	8	Sugar (granulated)	1	750
	1 1/2	Glycerine		45
3	11	Water	1	830
	1 1/4	Powdered agar-agar		38
		Bring to the boil and stir in		
	1 1/2	Glucose		45
	1/4	Citric acid		8

All piping jellies may be coloured and flavoured as desired during manufacture.

Cold Set Jelly

This jelly will set very quickly in the cold state. It consists of a pectin syrup to which is added a complement, usually citric acid. If colour and flavour is used it is stirred in before the acid. Excellent cold-set jelly can be purchased from reputable manufacturers. Here is a recipe:

lb	oz		kg	gr
1	12	Water		875
	3/4	Pectin (acid free)		22

lb	oz		kg	gr
2	4	Sugar	1	125
	10	Glucose (low acidity)		300

Complement

lb	oz		kg	gr
	1	Citric acid		30
	1	Hot water		30

Blend the pectin with some of the sugar and place into the water which should be between 160-170° F (71-76° C). When all is dissolved, heat to boiling point and add the warmed glucose then the rest of the sugar. When dissolved, boil to 218° F (103° C). When cooled it is ready for use. The complement is used at the rate of 3-4 c.c's to each 1 lb. (500 gr.) of syrup.

Wine Jelly

lb	oz		kg	gr
1	0	White wine		500
2	0	Water	1	
1	8	Sugar		750
		Gelatine (15 leaves)		

Boil the wine, sugar and water together and skim well. Add the gelatine that has been previously soaked and well squeezed out. Depending on the purpose for which the jelly is to be used, it may be lightly coloured. Strain and do not keep too long. Especially suitable for sweets.

VII. Yeasted Goods

Abraham, Bread Doll

In many parts of the Netherlands it is a tradition to give an Abraham to a person who has reached the age of 50. This is a very charming tradition, especially as this biblical person is the symbol of wisdom and dignity. An Abraham can be made as a bread-doll or as a doll of puff pastry filled with almond paste. In both cases the doll is decorated with marzipan or sugar icing.

Here is a recipe:

lb	oz		kg	gr
2	4	Flour	1	125
	2 1/2	Yeast		75
	3/4	Salt		22
	1 3/4	Milk powder		50
	1 3/4	Sugar (castor)		50
	3 1/2	Butter or margarine		100
1	0	Water (approx.)		500

Mix the ingredients into a firm dough. Temperature of the dough 76° F (24° C). After 15 minutes, weigh a piece of dough at 2 lb. (1 kg.). Roll this piece into a shape 12 in. (30 cm.) wide and 18 in. (45 cm.) long. Spread with almond-paste that has been softened with some raw eggs. Sprinkle 3 1/2 oz. (100 gr.) of chopped preserved ginger, 7 oz. (200 gr.) of currants, 7 oz. (200 gr.) of raisins on top.

Roll up the slice and shape it into the model of a doll. Then shape the following parts from the rest of the dough, which has been rolled out very thin; cape, shoe,s crown, beard, nose, eye-brows, moustache, hair, etc. Then brush the doll with egg and, as soon as it is well risen, it is baked at 410° F (210° C).

When the doll is cool, glaze it with water icing.
(Holland)

Almond Custard Buns

Proceed as for Florentine Buns, but sprinkle flaked almonds on top. After they are cold, slice and sandwich with crème pâtissière. Dust with icing sugar.

Almond Knots

Weigh basic bun dough into 1 1/2 oz. (45 gr.) pieces and mould round. After allowing time for recovery, roll each into a rope and tie into a simple knot, tucking the ends underneath. Wash with egg and after proving bake at 450° F (232° C) for about 15 minutes. When cool, glaze the tops with water icing and dip each into lightly roasted flaked almonds.

Almond Rings

Pin out plain bun dough and spread over two thirds of the surface with almond filling *(page 225)*. Give two half turns as for puff pastry. When recovered, pin out 1/4 in. (1/2 cm.) thick and about 24 in. (60 cm.) wide. Cut into strips about 1 in.

(2 $^1/_2$ cm.) wide and twist each end in opposite directions so that a twist is formed. Place on to lightly greased baking sheets in the form of loose spirals. Egg wash and, when proved, bake at 420° F (216° C). Brush with apricot purée, glaze with thin water icing and sprinkle a few lightly roasted flaked almonds on top.

Apricotines

Half fill some fluted boat shaped moulds with savarin paste.

Place a quarter of a candied apricot in the centre and leave to rise.

Bake at 450° F (232° C). When cool, splash with rum and glaze with apricot purée. *(France)*

Apricot Streusel Cake I

lb	oz		kg	gr
	15	Kuchen dough		450
	7	Curd filling *(page 219)*		200
2	0	Apricot pulp	1	
1	4	Butter streusel *(page 226)*		625
		Sugar (vanilla)		
		Sugar (icing)		
		Butter (hot)		

Pin out the kuchen dough to a rectangle about 8 in. by 20 in. (20 × 50 cm.) and place it on to a baking sheet. Spread it with the curd filling. Cover this with the apricot pulp and sprinkle the streusel evenly on top. After proving bake until golden. Before cutting into slices, brush with hot butter, sprinkle with vanilla sugar and dust with icing sugar.
(Illustration page 353.) *(Germany)*

Apricot Streusel Cake II

lb	oz		kg	gr
	9	Kuchen dough		270
	4 $^1/_2$	Curd filling		140
	13	Halved blanched apricots		400
	3 $^1/_2$	Butter streusel		100

Line an aluminium foil flan case 7 in. (18 cm.) in diameter with the kuchen dough. Spread with the curd filling, cover with the apricots and sprinkle with the butter streusel.

After baking, dust the cake with icing sugar. *(Germany)*

BABAS AND SAVARINS

For these confections, the formula is the same except that the dough for babas contains fruit, while the savarin dough does not. Both can be made in small or large sizes. Babas are baked in dariole moulds or fluted tins and savarins in ring moulds.

The butter content of the mixture is important; too much, particularly when larger sizes are made, may, after soaking in syrup, cause collapse.

Babas and savarins may be made in advance and stored in tins with tightly fitted lids, although it is advisable to use them within one or two days.

Babas

lb	oz		kg	gr
1	0	Flour		500
	12	Egg		375
	1	Yeast		30
	$^1/_2$	Sugar (castor)		15
	$^1/_4$	Salt		8
	3 $^1/_2$	Milk (approx.)		100
	8	Butter		250
	2	Currants		60
	2	Sultanas or small raisins		60

All the ingredients except the butter and fruit are well mixed with a beating action. The dough should have a finished temperature of about 80° F (26° C). After 30 minutes, the butter at the same temperature is vigorously beaten in. Lastly the fruit is added. The greased moulds are half filled with the aid of a savoy pipe and plain tube. When fully expanded, smaller units are baked at 440° F (226° C) and larger babas at 420° F (215° C).

After soaking in syrup, babas are split, filled and finished with whipped dairy cream and decorated with glacé fruit. Babas may be brushed with boiled apricot purée, but this is optional.

Savarins

The above recipe can be used without the fruit. The same procedure applies but for savarins the mixture is piped into greased ring moulds. After baking at 450° F (230° C) they are soaked in flavoured syrup and, if a better appearance is required, brushed with boiled apricot purée. Into the centre cavity, whipped dairy cream is piped and glacé fruit used as a final decoration. Alternatively the cavity can be filled with a macedoine of fruit before the whipped cream is piped in. *(Illustration page 353.)*

Basic Syrup

lb	oz		kg	gr
2	0	Sugar (granulated)	1	
1	4	Water		624
		Lemon peel		
		Orange peel		

Boil together to a density of 20° Baumé. Add the flavour which may be rum or kirsch. Other liqueurs such as orange curaçoa, maraschino, etc., may be used. Alternatively, the zest and juice of an orange may be used. The same flavour can be used to sprinkle the confection before the application of apricot purée. After soaking, drain on wires.

Bara Brith

Ferment

lb	oz		kg	gr
1	4	Milk 100° F (38° C)		625
	1/2	Sugar (castor)		15
1	1 1/2	Yeast		45
	4	Flour		125

Let this ferment stand for 30 minutes.

Dough

lb	oz		kg	gr
2	8	Flour (strong)	1	250
	12	Butter or lard		375
	12	Sugar		375
	1/4	Ground spice		7
	5	Egg		150
1	0	Currants		500
1	0	Sultanas		500
	4	Peel		125
	3/4	Salt		20

When the ferment is ready it is made into a fairly soft dough with the rest of the materials. After 1 hour it is knocked back and allowed to ferment for another hour. It is weighed into pieces, moulded and washed over the top with egg diluted with a little water. The moulded pieces are placed into greased bread tins and set to prove. They are baked at 420° F (216° C). *(Illustration page 272.)* *(Wales)*

Barches

Ingredients for 25 plaits each weighing 1 lb. 2 oz. (560 gr.).

lb	oz		kg	gr
16	8	Flour	7	500
	14	Yeast		400
	3	Salt		100
1	8	Sugar (castor)		700
3	4	Butter	1	500
4	8	Milk (approx.)	2	

Make a ferment with approx. 4 lb. 8 oz. (2 kg.) flour. When the ferment is ready, mix the rest of the flour, the salt, sugar, butter and milk to a tight dough. Make the lower part of each 'Barche' by dividing 14 oz. (375 gr.) dough into 3 strands and plaiting them together. Place a thin strand made out of 4 oz. (125 gr.) dough on top. Wash the 'Barches' with egg, sprinkle with almonds, poppy seed or sugar nibs, and bake. *(Plaiting page 53.)* *(Germany)*

Barm Brack

Ferment

lb	oz		kg	gr
1	4	Milk 110° F (43° C)		600
1	4	Water 110° F (43° C)		600
	2	Sugar (castor)		60
	4	Yeast		125
	8	Flour		250

Set this ferment aside in a warm place until it rises and falls.

Dough

lb	oz		kg	gr
4	0	Flour (strong)	2	
	³/₄	Salt		20
	8	Sugar (castor)		250
	12	Lard		375
	10	Egg		300
6	8	Sultanas	3	250
1	0	Peel		500
		Zest of 3 lemons		

Warm the egg and mix with the sugar and salt. Add this mixture to the ferment and stir in. Add to the flour and commence to make a dough; when nearly made, add the lard and mix thoroughly. After 30 minutes, mix in the warmed fruit and allow the dough to recover for 15 minutes. When ready, the dough is weighed into pieces and moulded up round and then slightly flattened and washed with egg. They are placed into warmed, greased cake hoops set on slightly greased baking sheets. They are proved for about 55 minutes and baked at 420° F (216° C).
(Illustration page 272.)   *(Ireland)*

Bath Buns

London variety

Ferment

lb	oz		kg	gr
	10	Milk		300
	1	Sugar (castor)		30
	1 ½	Yeast		45
	4	Flour		125

Ferment temperature 85° F (29° C). Let the ferment stand until it drops.

Dough

lb	oz		kg	gr
2	0	Flour (strong)	1	
1	0	Butter		500
	10	Egg		300
	1 ½	Egg yolks		50
		Zest of lemon		
		A little nutmeg		

Add all except the butter to the ferment and make into a well developed dough. Then beat in the butter thoroughly. Knock back after 1 hour and again after another half hour. When at full proof, chop in the sugar nibs and peel.

lb	oz		kg	gr
1	2	Coarse sugar nibs		500
	6	Finely cut citron peel		180
	4	Finely cut orange peel		120

Lay out in rocky pieces on to greased baking sheets. Wash each one over with egg and place in a prover without steam. Before baking, sprinkle the tops with fine sugar nibs and bake to a rich, golden colour at 440° F (227° C).
(Illustration page 273.)   *(Great Britain)*

Bayrischzeller Striezel

(Court Recipe)

lb	oz		kg	gr
1	5	Flour		850
	1 ³/₄	Yeast		50
	3 ½	Egg		100
	2 ½	Egg yolks		75
	4 ½	Butter		140
	3 ½	Sugar (icing)		100
	8	Dairy cream		250
	3	Sour cream		90
	¼	Salt		8
	5	Raisins		150

Make a ferment with the yeast, a little cream and as much flour as necessary. When it is well developed add the remaining flour and other ingredients and mix well. Leave to ferment again, then mould to a narrow baton shape. Place on a greased baking sheet and cover with a floured cloth. Prove, then brush with egg. Bake at 440° F (225° C).   *(Austria)*

Bilberry Cake

lb	oz		kg	gr
	8	Kuchen dough		250
1	0	Bilberries		500

Line an aluminium foil flan case 7 in. (18 cm.) in diameter with the kuchen dough. Cover with bilberries, prove and bake, then dust the edge liberally with icing sugar. *(Germany)*

Bratislava Beugeln

lb	oz		kg	gr
2	0	Flour	1	
	1	Yeast		30
	5	Egg		150
1	4	Butter		625
	2	Sugar (icing)		60
	1/4	Salt		8
	12	Milk (warm) (approx.)		375

Filling

lb	oz		kg	gr
1	8	Ground hazelnuts		750
1	8	Sugar (granulated)		750
	7	Water		200
		Vanilla		

Disperse the yeast in the milk and make all the ingredients into a smooth semi-tight dough that does not stick. Cover and allow to rest for 30 minutes.

Boil the water, sugar and vanilla. Stir in the nuts while still hot. After cooling, the filling should be of spreading consistency.

When the dough is ready, weigh pieces of the desired size and mould round. Pin out to oval shape about 1/8 in. (4 mm.) thick. Spread some filling on each and brush one end with egg. Roll up, shape into crescents and place on to baking sheets. Brush with egg and allow to prove for 3 hours. Brush with egg again and prove for a further 30 minutes in a slightly lower temperature. Bake at 400° F (204° C). *(Austria)*

Breakfast Rolls
Ingredients for 80

lb	oz		kg	gr
4	6	Flour	2	180
	5	Yeast		150
2	12	Milk (approx.)	1	375
	3/4	Sugar (castor)		20
3	1/2	Butter		100
	3/4	Salt		20

Make a small ferment out of flour, milk and the yeast. Make a dough out of the butter, sugar and salt, add all other ingredients and the ferment and work up into a dough and mould up into rolls. Notch the rolls lengthwise, wash with egg yolk and bake briskly. *(Germany)*

Bridge Rolls

lb	oz		kg	gr
1	1	Flour (strong)		530
	1/4	Salt		8
	1/4	Sugar (castor)		8
	1	Egg		30
1	1/2	Butter		45
	1	Yeast		30
	10	Milk (approx.)		300

Dough temperature 80° F (27° C). Knock back at 20 minutes. Scale at 30 minutes.

Yield at 1 oz. (30 gr.) - 30
Yield at 1 1/2 oz. (45 gr.) - 20

Mould round and after a time for recovery, they are moulded into boat shape without having the ends too pointed. After placing on to greased baking sheets they are egg washed. They are egg washed again carefully before baking at 450° F (232° C).
(Great Britain)

Brioche

From the basic brioche dough *(page 177)* weigh off pieces at 1-1 1/2 oz. (30-45 gr.) according to the size of the tins used. Mould round and when recovered divide into tops and bottoms, the tops being about one quarter the size of the bottom. Mould both round and place them into greased fluted patty pans, making certain that the tops fit into a depression made in the bottoms. Prove and before baking, carefully wash with egg. Snip the base three times with scissors. Bake at 480° F (250° C).

Buns

lb	oz		kg	gr
2	4	Milk 77° F (25° C)	1	125
	10	Sugar		300
	7	Yeast		200
	1 3/4	Butter		50

lb	oz		kg	gr
	10	Egg		300
	1	Salt		30
	14	Sultanas		435
	7	Chopped candied orange peel		200
5	4	Flour	2	625
		Zest of 2 lemons		

Buns are shaped like round bread rolls. When they have been baked, they are dipped, while still hot, in melted butter and tossed in vanilla sugar. When cold, they are dusted with icing sugar. *(France)*

Bun Loaves

Fold into a basic, lemon flavoured bun dough, 12 oz. (375 gr.) warmed currants and 2 oz. (60 gr.) of finely chopped peel. Weigh at 13 1/2 oz. (420 gr.) and mould round. After time for recovery, mould to the shape of 1 lb. (500 gr.) bread tins. Wash the loaves with egg diluted with a little milk and place into the tins. After proving, bake at 430° F (220° C), for 20-25 minutes.

Bun Rounds I

From plain basic bun dough weigh pieces at 8 oz. (250 gr.) and divide each into six. Mould round and arrange five in a ring in well greased 6 in. (15 cm.) cottage pans with one piece in the centre. Wash with egg and allow to prove. Bake at 440° F (227° C) for about 15 minutes. When cool, spread warm vanilla flavoured white fondant on the top of each and place half a glacé cherry on the middle one.

Bun Rounds II

Weigh lemon flavoured plain bun dough into 8 oz. (250 gr.) pieces and mould round. When recovered pin out to about 6 in. (15 cm.) in diameter and place on to lightly greased baking sheets. Egg wash and divide into 8 segments keeping the round intact. When proved, bake at 440° F (227° C) for about 15-20 minutes. Immediately on removal from the oven glaze with a sugar wash and dust with castor sugar.

Bun Rounds III

Take lemon flavoured plain basic bun dough and weigh into 10 oz. (300 gr.) pieces. Divide into 7 pieces and mould round. Pin them out into circles about 5 in. (12 cm.) in diameter and egg wash the edges. Place a portion of mincemeat in the centre of each and shape into triangles as for Coventry puffs. Arrange each seven, folds uppermost, in such a way that a compact seven sided circular shape is formed. Wash with egg and when ready for baking, place a small heap of castor sugar on each triangle at the intersection of the folds. Bake at 440° F (227° C).

Alternatively, 10 oz. (300 gr.) pieces can be divided into 9 pieces and moulded round.

Mould into pear shape eight of the pieces and arrange in a circle, points inwards, placing the round ninth piece in the centre. Wash with egg and when ready, bake at 440° F (227° C). When cool, spread vanilla flavoured white fondant on the top of each pear shape and on the centre piece.

Butter Almond Buns

Weigh plain bun dough at 1 3/4 oz. (50 gr.) and mould round. After allowing time for recovery, pin out to about 6 in. (15 cm.) in diameter. Spread with almond mixture *(page 225)*. Fold in half and spread again with the mixture. Fold again so that they are triangular in shape. Place on to lightly greased baking sheets, egg wash, prove and bake at 420° F (216° C) for about 15 minutes.

Butter Buns
Straight Dough Method

lb	oz		kg	gr
4	0	Flour (strong)	2	
	10	Vegetable fat		300
	10	Sugar (castor)		300
	1/2	Salt		15
1	14	Milk 100° F (38° C)		935
	12	Egg		375
	4	Yeast		125
		Zest of 1 lemon		

Rub the fat finely into the sieved flour. Dissolve the sugar and salt in the milk and in it disperse the yeast. Add this mixture and the egg to the fat/flour and make into a smooth dough adding the zest of lemon. Allow to ferment for 25 minutes, knock back and leave for a further 10 minutes.

Roll out to a sheet 24 in. × 12 in. (60 × 30 cm.) and spread with soft butter. Sprinkle with brown sugar and some currants. Fold as for puff pastry, giving three half turns with a rest of five minutes between each turn. Roll out to $1/4$ in. (6 mm.) thick and cut into small diamond shapes. Place on baking sheets, egg wash and prove. When ready dust with castor sugar and bake at 440° F (227° C).

Butter Streusel Cake

lb	oz		kg	gr
	12 $1/2$	Kuchen dough		390
	7	Butter streusel		200
	1 $3/4$	Hot butter		50

Line a round aluminium foil flan case 7 in. (18 cm.) in diameter with the kuchen dough. Cover with the butter streusel and leave to prove for a short time.

After baking, spread the cake with the hot butter and dust with icing sugar.

(Germany)

Cadets

lb	oz		kg	gr
2	4	Flour	1	125
	1 $3/4$	Yeast		50
	$3/4$	Salt		20
	1 $3/4$	Milk powder		50
	$3/4$	Sugar (castor)		20
	1 $3/4$	Margarine		50
1	4	Water		625

Mix these ingredients to a very smooth dough. Temperature of the dough 77° F (25° C). After 30 minutes, divide into 30 equal pieces. Mould up round and let them rest. After a 15 minutes rest, brush the tops of the rolls with a little oil. Now mark the rolls into two equal parts with the aid of a thin round stick; press until the bottom of the dough is reached. Then, turn the rolls upside-down, and let them rest. When the rolls are well risen, they are turned again and baked in an oven at 482° F (250° C) into which steam is injected. The baking takes place either on the sole of the oven or on a baking-sheet. The rolls should be soft after being baked.

(Holland)

Carinthian Reinling

lb	oz		kg	gr
1	1	Flour		530
	1 $1/4$	Yeast		35
	3	Sugar (castor)		90
	1 $3/4$	Egg		50
	1 $1/4$	Egg yolks		40
	2 $1/2$	Butter (melted)		75
	$1/4$	Salt		8
	8	Milk (warm) (approx.)		250
	4	Raisins		125
		Zest of 1 lemon		

Make a ferment with the yeast, 1 oz. (30 gr.) of the flour, $1/4$ oz. (8 gr.) of the sugar and a little milk.

Mix together the egg, egg yolks, sugar, salt, lemon zest and milk. When the ferment is ready make into a smooth dough with the rest of the ingredients except the butter and the raisins. Add the butter and mix until the dough no longer sticks to the sides of the bowl. Cover and leave in a warm place. When the dough has developed, pin it out into a square about 16 × 16 in. (40 × 40 cm.). Sprinkle the surface with coarse granulated sugar mixed with a little cinnamon, and the raisins. Roll up like a swiss roll and shape into a ring with the ends well joined together. Place into a well greased gugelhupf mould with an upper diameter about 10 in. (25 cm.). Prove, then bake, brushing with butter two or three times during baking.

(Austria)

Carlsbad Crescents

Ingredients for 30

lb	oz		kg	gr
1	2	Flour		560
	11 $1/2$	Butter		345

lb	oz		kg	gr
2	1/2	Sugar (castor)		75
1	3/4	Yeast		50
		Salt		
		A little milk		

Disperse the yeast in a little milk, make into a dough with the flour, 2 1/2 oz. (75 gr.) butter, sugar and salt. Fold the remaining 9 oz. (270 gr.) butter into the dough three times, give the paste 3 single turns and leave to rest.

Shape into crescents, brush with egg and bake briskly. *(Germany)*

Cheese Bread and Rolls

lb	oz		kg	gr
10	0	Flour (strong)	5	
	8	Yeast		250
	4	Milk powder		125
	4	Compound fat		125
	4	Salt		125
	2	Sugar		60
5	12	Water (approx.)	2	750
2	0	Bakers cheese	1	

Dough temperature 76° F (24.5° C).
Allow dough to stand 1 hour before knock-back, leave 15 minutes to recover.
Scale to weight required and mould.
Bake at 400° F (204° C). Rolls 420° F (216° C).

This dough is suitable for all types of cheese bread, i.e. Morning-Rolls, Oven Bottom Bread, Tin Bread.

Cheese Baps

Weigh the dough as given above into 1 1/2 oz. (45 gr.) pieces and mould round. After time for recovery, pin out and place on to baking sheets. Flour the tops and about halfway through final proof make an impression in the centre of each with the finger tip. Bake at 420° F (216° C).

Pieces weighed at 8 oz. (250 gr.) made in the same way can be placed into 6 in. (15 cm.) cottage-pans. Bake at 400° F (204° C).

Chelsea Buns

Ferment

lb	oz		kg	gr
1	4	Milk		625
	1	Sugar (castor)		30
	2	Yeast		60
	6	Flour		180

Ferment temperature 85° F (29° C). This ferment is left until it drops.

Dough

lb	oz		kg	gr
3	0	Flour	1	500
	10	Butter		300
	6	Egg		180
	6	Sugar (castor)		180
	1/16	Ground nutmeg		2
		Zest of 1 lemon		

The butter is rubbed into the flour which has been sieved with the nutmeg. The egg, sugar and the zest is whisked into the ferment and made into a well developed dough with the flour. After an hour, the dough is divided into two pieces, each being shaped into a square. After time for recovery, each piece is pinned out to a strip about 10-12 in. (25-30 cm.) in width. Care must be taken to keep the sides straight and the corners square. The bottom edge is brushed with water or egg and the rest of the surface brushed with melted butter. Brown sugar, mixed with a little ground cinnamon, and then currants are strewn over the buttered surface, after which it is rolled up like a Swiss roll. This in turn is brushed all over with melted butter and then cut into pieces about 2 in. (5 cm.) wide which are placed, cut side down, side by side on a greased baking sheet. Care must be taken to place them uniformly in rows so that each has the same space and each, when baked, is supported by its neighbours. To keep the last row in position, a greased stick is firmly placed in position. After proving, the buns are baked at 420° F (216° C). As soon as they are removed from the oven, they are brushed with sugar wash and dusted with castor sugar.

(Illustration page 276.) *(Great Britain)*

Cherry Cheese Cakes
Ingredients for 20 cakes 2 in. by 4 in. (5 × 10 cm.).

lb	oz		kg	gr
1	0	Kuchen dough		500
4	6	Curd filling	2	180
1	5	Preserved morello cherries		650

Pin out the kuchen dough to a rectangular shape 8 in. by 20 in. (20 × 50 cm.). Spread with approx. 2 lb. (1 kg.) curd filling *(page 219)*, place the cherries evenly on top, cover with the rest of the curd filling and smooth off.

Bake at 374° F (190° C) for about 45 minutes until golden and then brush with butter and sprinkle with sugar.
(Illustration page 353.) *(Germany)*

Coconut Buns
Proceed as for Swiss buns and after dipping into fondant, press into pasteurized medium coconut.

Continentals
Weigh plain basic bun dough into 1 $\frac{1}{2}$ oz. (45 gr.) pieces. Mould round and when recovered, form into ropes about 9 in. (23 cm.) long. At one end make a circle, then thread the long end through it three times, turning slightly each time so that a five piece ring is formed. Egg wash and dip into flaked almonds. Prove and bake at 400° F (204° C).

Cornetti

lb	oz		kg	gr
2	4	Water 77° F (25° C)	1	125
	1 $\frac{3}{4}$	Yeast		50
	$\frac{3}{4}$	Malt		20
	$\frac{3}{4}$	Salt		20
	5 $\frac{1}{4}$	Oil or fat		150
4	4	Flour (strong)	2	125

To make cornetti, a tight dough must be used. Take pieces of dough weighing about 2 oz. (60 gr.) each, mould them up round and after recovery, roll them out into 8 in. (20 cm.) long strips. Allow to stand, then roll them up from both ends towards the centre and fit two together in the form of a cross. Brush with starch glaze when they come out of the oven. *(France)*

Cornish Saffron Loaves
Ferment

lb	oz		kg	gr
1	4	Milk		625
1	4	Water		625
	1	Sugar (castor)		30
	2 $\frac{1}{2}$	Yeast		75
1	4	Flour		625

Ferment temperature 78° F (26° C). Let the ferment rise and drop.

Dough

lb	oz		kg	gr
3	4	Flour (strong)	1	625
	10	Butter		300
	10	Lard		300
	7	Sugar (castor)		200
	$\frac{3}{4}$	Salt		20
	$\frac{1}{4}$	Saffron*		7
2	8	Currants	1	250
1	0	Sultanas		500
	8	Peel		250

The fats are rubbed into the flour and, when the ferment is ready, the whole of the ingredients are mixed to a rather firm dough which is allowed to ferment for 1 $\frac{1}{2}$ hours. When the dough is ready it is weighed into 1 lb. (500 gr.) pieces, moulded up and placed into greased bread tins.

After proving they are baked at 430° F (220° C).

* The saffron is prepared by making an infusion with boiling water. The infusion and the dregs are used in the dough.
(Illustration page 273.) *(Great Britain)*

Cream Cookies
Take a lemon flavoured basic bun dough and weigh in pieces 1 $\frac{1}{2}$ oz. (45 gr.). Mould round and place on to greased baking sheets. Prove in a little steam and bake at 460° F (238° C). They are neither

egg nor sugar washed. When cool they are cut just off centre and into the cut pipe a little raspberry jam. This is followed with vanilla flavoured whipped dairy cream piped in with a savoy bag and large star pipe. The tops are dusted with icing sugar.

Croissants

Take the completed dough (recipes on *page 176*) and pin out to a rectangle about $1/8$ in. (3 mm.) thick and cut into strips 8 in. (20 cm.) wide. Each strip is cut into triangles about 4 in. (10 cm.) at the base. Starting at the base, roll up the triangle tightly, form into a crescent shape and place on to warm, greased baking sheets. It is necessary to have a tall triangle to obtain a many storied structure when rolled up. Brush with egg and again after proving. Bake at 470° F (243° C). The prover must not be too hot or the butter in the croissants will melt, spoiling the flaky structure. *(France)*

Crumpets

lb	oz		kg	gr
2	8	Flour (medium strong)	1	250
	$1/4$	Cream of tartar (or substitute)		8
	$1/4$	Sugar (castor)		8
	$1 1/2$	Yeast		45
2	8	Water 100° F (38° C)	1	250
	$1/8$	Bicarbonate of soda		4
	$3/4$	Salt		20
	5	Water (cold) (approx.)		150

Beat these ingredients well together and let the batter stand for 45 minutes, then beat in the rest of the water, the salt and the soda.

The batter is poured into the crumpet hoops on a hotplate by means of a ladle. The hoops are slightly greased. When the crumpets have fully 'holed' they are turned over so that they may brown very slightly on top. This takes away the raw appearance and makes them more attractive. If the hoops are too heavily greased the butter will run on to the hotplate and the resultant crumpets will be 'blind', that is they will not show the characteristic network of holes. The hotplate must be burnished and absolutely free from grease.
(Illustration page 270.)

Currant Bread

lb	oz		kg	gr
2	2	Flour (strong)	1	60
	$1/2$	Salt		15
	5	Butter		150
	$1 1/2$	Sugar (castor)		45
	$1 1/2$	Yeast		45
1	4	Milk (approx.)		625
	10	Currants		300

Dough temperature 80° F (27° C). Fold in the warmed currants at $1/2$ hour. Scale at 1 hour. Wash each loaf with diluted egg before placing into greased tins. For sultana bread, replace the currants with sultanas. Bake at 450° F (232° C).

Currant Buns

Take a basic bun dough, add fruit and lemon flavour. Scale pieces at $1 1/2$-2 oz. (45-60 gr.) each and mould round. Mould again and place on to warmed, greased baking sheets. Prove and then bake at 460° F (238° C). Immediately on removal from the oven, wash with sugar wash. Alternatively they may be egg washed before proving.

DANISH PASTRIES

The varieties of Danish pastry described here are based on the recipes given in Chapter VI. It will be seen quite clearly that there can be many more added to those given, limited only by the ingenuity and inventiveness of the craftsman concerned, and by the standard of quality required. If these delicious pastries are to be fully enjoyed, they must be made of the finest materials, be light in structure so that they will literally 'melt in the mouth' and, above all, be oven fresh.

1. Pin out a piece of the pastry to a rectangle about 14 in. by 8 in. (35 × 20 cm.). Spread thinly with almond mixture *(page 225)*, sprinkle with currants, then roll up as for a swiss roll and cut into pieces about 1 1/4 in. (3 cm.) wide. Six shapes can be made.

(a) With the piece on its side, make one cut in the middle, leaving sufficient to form a hinge. Open the piece out so that it forms two overlapping circles.

(b) Proceed as for (a) but cut twice. On opening out, the piece will appear as three overlapping circles.

(c) Proceed as for (a) but cut three times. Open out to form four circles.

(d) Take the cut piece as for (a), but instead of cutting, press through the centre with a wooden skewer almost pressing in half. When baked, this pastry will have the shape of a butterfly.

(e) Place the piece, cut side down in a paper baking case. After egg washing, sprinkle a mixture of nibbed almonds and sugar nibs on the top.

(f) Flatten the piece and place directly on to a baking sheet cut side down.

2. Pin out a piece of pastry to a rectangle about 20 in. by 12 in. (50 × 30 cm.).

Spread thinly with the almond mixture *(page 225)* and fold into two so that a piece about 10 in. by 12 in. (25 × 30 cm.) is formed. Cut into strips about 3/8 in. (1 cm.) wide. Six varieties can be made.

(a) Twist each strip by placing the palm of the hands at each end. If one hand is pushed forward whilst the other is still, a spiral twist is formed. Arrange on a baking sheet in the form of a losely formed spiral.

(b) Proceed as for (a) but form into an 'S' scroll.

(c) Proceed as for (a) but form into a 'C' scroll. Egg wash (a), (b) and (c) and sprinkle with topping I, II or III *(page 226)*.

(d) Proceed as for (a) but form into a pretzel shape. Finish by egg washing and piping custard into holes.

(e) Proceed as for (a) but arrange by folding into three to form a round ended rectangle with three strands. Pipe custard between the three strands and egg wash.

(f) Proceed as for (a) but arrange so that four circles are formed. Egg wash and pipe custard into the circles.

3. Pin out a piece of pastry and cut into squares about 3 1/2 in. (9 cm.). Egg wash and bring each corner into the centre and press firmly. Egg wash again and pipe a spot of custard into the centre.

4. Pin out a piece of pastry and cut into strips about 6 in. (15 cm.) wide and then into triangles with a base about 4 1/2 in. (12 cm.). Egg wash and place on each a piece of marzipan into which a little egg is mixed. If each is held in the hands by the top corners and given a sharp twist, a crescent shape can be formed. These are egg washed and placed on a baking sheet.

5. Take a piece of pastry and proceed as for No. 1. Cut the roll to the width of a baking tray on which it is placed. With a sharp blade cut along the centre to the middle. During proving and baking the piece will open out. When baked, glaze and cut in to slices.

6. Pin out a piece of pastry and cut into strips about 3 in. (8 cm.) wide. Egg wash and place clove flavoured apple along the centre. Fold the top over and press firmly to secure the join. Egg wash and nick the joined edge with a series of small cuts. Cut the strip into pieces about 3 in. (8 cm.) long and arrange on a baking sheet, bending them into arcs with the nicked side outwards.

7. Pin out a piece of pastry and cut into a strip about 5 in. (13 cm.) wide. Egg wash. Place a roll of marzipan just under the top edge and a row of apple along the bottom edge. Cover the marzipan by

bringing over the top edge and cover the apple by bringing up the bottom edge. Pipe custard along the space between. When baked, glaze and cut into slices.

8. Pin out the pastry to about $1/8$ in. (3 mm.) in thickness and cut out with a $3 1/2$ in. (9 cm.) round fluted cutter. Wash with egg and in the centre of each place some of the fruit and nut filling *(page 222)*. Fold the pastry over to form a turnover. Egg wash. When baked glaze at once.

9. Pin out the pastry to about $1/4$ in. (5 mm.) thickness and into a strip about 12 in. (30 cm.) wide. Spread with marzipan mixed with egg to a spreading consistency and sprinkle with sultanas. Fold into three to give a strip about 4 in. (10 cm.) wide. Place on to a baking sheet and divide into fingers by pressing right through with a sharp scraper. Egg wash and sprinkle with flaked almonds before cutting. Glaze after baking.

10. Pin out the pastry and cut into a strip about 12 in. (30 cm.) wide. Spread with orange date filling *(page 220)* and fold into three as for puff pastry. Cut into slices and place them on to a baking sheet twisting each one beforehand. Egg wash. Glaze after baking.

11. Pin out the pastry to about $1/8$ in. (3 mm.) thick and cut into squares about 3 in. (8 cm.). Place a round piece of wood about $3/4$ in. (2 cm.) in diameter and 4 in. (10 cm.) long on each and bring two corners of the pastry to the top and press firmly. Tie across the centre with a piece of string. Egg wash. When baked remove the string and the wood. Fill in both ends with custard and decorate with cherry and angelica.

12. Pin out the pastry to about $1/4$ in. (5 mm.) thick and cut into squares about 3 in. (8 cm.). Fold each piece in half from corner to corner. With the long edge of the triangular piece in front make two neat cuts parallel with the short sides and about $1/4$ in. (5 mm.) from the edge. Make certain that the cuts do not meet at the top point. Open out the pieces and egg wash. Take one of the corners that has been completely cut through and fold it so that its point rests at the inside edge opposite. Do the same with the other cut corner. Pipe a small amount of mincemeat in the centre of each. When baked, glaze with apricot purée and fill centre in with white lemon flavoured water icing.

13. Pin out a strip of pastry to about $1/8$ in. (3 mm.) thick and 8 in. (20 cm.) wide. Brush with egg and spread a mixture of white plunder filling and confectioner's custard, in equal parts along the centre. The long ends are turned over to enclose the filling with the join underneath. After giving time for proof, the strip is egg washed and a line of custard is piped along the top. After baking, the strip is glazed with apricot purée and water icing and cut diagonally into fingers.

14. The dough is prepared exactly as for No. 13. A mixture of 3 parts white plunder filling and one part butterfilling is spread down the middle and enclosed as described above. After proof, the strip is egg washed, strewn with flaked almonds and baked. After baking, the strips are dusted with icing sugar and cut into diagonal slices.

15. Proceed exactly as for No. 13 but fill with 3 parts brown plunder filling and one part butter filling and sprinkle with flaked hazelnuts.

16. Prepare exactly as for No. 13 but use a filling composed of 2 parts apricot jam and 2 parts butter filling. Cut into fingers about $1 1/2$ in. (4 cm.) wide. Each piece is then cut lengthways in the centre and one end taken through the cut and pulled through. After egg washing, a bulb of confectioner's custard is piped in the centre. After baking, glaze with apricot purée and very thin water icing.

17. Prepare as for No. 13, using the filling given in either 15 or 16. Cut into fingers about $1 1/2$ in. (4 cm.) wide. Make a series of cuts along one side and place on to baking sheets. Bend into an arc with the cuts outside. Finish with egg wash and when baked glaze as above.

Sally Lunns, p. 291

Muffins, p. 285 — Crumpets, p. 266

Oxford Lardy Cake, p. 283

▲ Barm Brack, Ireland, p. 259 — Selkirk Bannock, Scotland, p. 292 — Bara Brith, Wales, p. 259
Scottish Black Bun, p. 292 ▼

▲ Cornish Saffron Loaves, p. 265   Bath Buns (London type), p. 260 ▼

274 ▲ Easter Bread, p. 278   Taillaules, p. 294 ▼

▲ Five Plait, Six Plait, Two Plait, Seven Plait, Eight Plait, p. 52-56

Winston, Three Plait, One Plait, Four Plait, Peardrop, p. 52-56 ▼

275

276 ▲ Chelsea Buns, p. 264

Hot Cross Buns, p. 282 ▼

LARGER DANISH PASTRIES

1. Cut out circles about 8 in. (20 cm.) in diameter from the pastry that has been pinned to a thickness of about $1/8$ in. (3 mm.). Egg wash and dock well. Take a spiral strip fashioned as described for 2 (a) about 8 in. (20 cm.) long and form a petal shape on the top with the ends firmly fixed in the middle. Repeat this seven or eight times until the petal formation is complete. Egg wash again and after proving fill the petal shapes in with custard and pipe a spot into the centre. Decorate the custard with glacé cherries and angelica and bake. Glaze after baking.

2. Proceed as for the above but cut into 10 in. (2.5 cm.) circles. Egg wash and dock well. Cut out an equal number of 8 in. (20 cm.) circles and fold each in half and cut eight times from the centre to within 1 in. (2.5 cm.) of the outer edge. After unfolding place on to the larger circles and fold back the points of the triangles to the outer edge. Egg wash again and bake. Fill in the centres with either canned fruits or fresh fruits in season. Glaze with purée and water icing.

3. Proceed as for No. 1 (page 277) and place the swiss rolled piece on a baking sheet in the form of a ring. Egg wash and then nick with a pair of scissors bringing one leaf to the right and one to the left alternatively. Sprinkle the tops with flaked almonds. Glaze after baking.

4. Make up as for No. 2 (page 277) using a cinnamon spread *(page 221)*. Cut out strips about $3/4$ in. (2 cm.) wide and plait them in threes and then form them into circles on a baking sheet. Egg wash and sprinkle with flaked almonds. Glaze after baking.

Finishes

All toppings including custard are added before baking, except where stated otherwise.

After baking and while still hot glaze immediately with apricot purée and then with a thin water icing glaze to which has been added fresh lemon juice.

The baking temperature is 400-420° F (204-216° C), according to the size of the pastry.

Danish Ring - Plunderkranz

Ingredients

lb	oz		kg	gr
	1 3/4	Yeast		50
1	2	Flour		560
	7	Milk (approx.)		200
	1 3/4	Sugar		50
	10	Butter		300
	1 3/4	Egg		50
	2	Sultanas		60
	2	Currants		60
	1/2	Chopped almonds		20
		Lemon		
		A little salt		

Filling

lb	oz		kg	gr
	9	Marzipan		270
	3 1/2	Egg whites		100

Bring the marzipan to a spreading consistency with the whites and flavour with a little lemon.

Make a ferment with the yeast, 7 oz. (200 gr.) flour and the milk. Add the remaining 11 oz. (360 gr.) flour, the sugar, 1 1/2 oz. (50 gr.) butter, the egg, lemon and a little salt to make a slack dough. Leave to ferment for a short time. Then roll the remaining butter into the dough, giving it 3 single turns. Take off 8 oz. (250 gr.) paste, pin out until 16 in. by 12 in. (40 × 30 cm.), spread with the prepared filling and sprinkle with the sultanas, currants and chopped almonds.

Then make a roll out of the whole, and cut it open lengthwise. Twist both parts together and shape into a ring. Leave to prove a little and bake off at 392° F (200° C). Brush with apricot purée, glaze with water icing and sprinkle lightly with roasted flaked almonds. *(Germany)* *(Illustration page 320.)*

Devonshire Splits

Weigh vanilla flavoured plain basic bun dough into 1 1/2 oz. (45 gr.) pieces, mould round and place in rows on a lightly

277

greased baking sheet. Prove and bake at 440-450° F (227-232° C) for about 15 minutes. When cool, split, just off top centre, with a sharp knife. Pipe in some raspberry jam and then clotted cream. Dust with icing sugar. *(Great Britain)*

Diamond Buns

Pin out plain lemon flavoured basic bun dough to $1/2$ in. (1 cm.) in thickness. Spread some softened butter over half the surface and sprinkle with currants, sultanas and chopped peel together with castor sugar. Bring the plain portion of the dough down and pin out carefully and give two half turns as for puff pastry. After time for recovery, give another half turn and pin out to $1/2$ in. (1 cm.) in thickness. Egg wash and dust with castor sugar. Cut into strips 2 in. (5 cm.) wide and then into diamond shapes. After proving, bake at 420° F (216° C).

Dough Cakes - Old English

Make up 2 lb. (1 kg.) of plain bread dough and, when ready, mix in the following materials:

lb	oz		kg	gr
	8	Lard		250
	4	Sugar (castor)		125
	8	Currants		250
	8	Sultanas		250
	2	Chopped peel		60
	$1/8$	Ground spice		4

Mix the lard, sugar and spice into the dough thoroughly, then carefully mix in the fruit. Let the dough recover for $1/2$ hour. Weigh at 18 oz. (560 gr.) mould and place into well greased 1 lb. (500 gr.) bread tins. Because of the amount of enriching materials in this mix, final proof will be prolonged, possibly nearly two hours. Bake at 400° F (204° C). They are brushed with melted lard as soon as they are removed from the oven.

Easter Bread

lb	oz		kg	gr
2	3	Milk 85° F (30° C)	1	
	5	Sugar (castor)		150
	1	Salt		30
4	0	Flour	2	
	9	Sultanas		275
	5	Almonds		150
	4	Yeast		125
	9	Butter		275
		Zest of 2 lemons		

Prepare in the same way as for sweet dough *(page 177)*, finally adding the lightly roasted, unskinned almonds. Leave the dough to rise and mould it into long pieces. Allow to rise again slightly. Place on baking sheets, brush with egg, make notches in the loaves and sprinkle the tops with flaked blanched almonds. Bake in a medium oven, avoiding steam, and, just before they are baked, dust them with icing sugar and replace them in the oven to glaze. *(France)*

Easter Bread

Ingredients for 7 loaves weighing 1 lb. 4 oz. (625 gr.) before baking.

lb	oz		kg	gr
1	8	Milk (approx.)		750
	$3 1/2$	Yeast		100
2	12	Flour	1	375
1	2	Butter		500
	$5 1/4$	Sugar (castor)		150
	$1/2$	Salt		15
2	4	Sultanas	1	125
	$4 1/2$	Nibbed almonds		125
	1	Bitter almonds		30
	7	Candied lemon peel		200
		Lemon fondant		
		Pistachio nuts		

First warm the milk, disperse the yeast in it and make into a ferment with part of the flour. Meanwhile cream the butter, sugar and salt until smooth. After leaving the sponge to ferment for the required time, mix thoroughly with the creamed ingredients and remaining flour and leave to ferment again. Then carefully pull in the sultanas, nibbed and bitter almonds and candied lemon peel. Scale off the number of pieces desired and mould into round loaves. Deposit on baking sheets, leave to prove, make a cross on the top of each loaf with a sharp knife and bake at 428° F (220° C). After baking, glaze with apricot purée while still hot, then ice with lemon fondant and sprinkle with pistachio nuts. *(Illustration page 274.)* *(Germany)*

Easter Bread

Sponge

lb	oz		kg	gr
2	4	Milk	1	125
	3 1/2	Yeast		100
4	8	Flour	2	250

Allow to ferment for 2 hours.

Dough

lb	oz			
	1	Salt		30
	3/4	Malt extract		20
	3 1/2	Sugar		100
	3 1/2	Honey		100
	7	Egg		200
1	0	Sultanas		500
	4	Orange peel (chopped)		125
	7	Pine nuts		200
		Zest of 1 lemon		

All the ingredients, except the fruit and nuts, are well mixed together and worked into the sponge until it is smooth. The fruit and nuts are then dispersed through the dough and it is allowed to ferment for another 1-2 hours. Weigh at the desired size, which can be from 4 oz.-1 1/4 lb. (125-625 gr.) and mould round; after time for recovery, mould again and place on to a baking sheet. When proved, spread with topping mixture *(page 226)*, sprinkle with pine nuts, dust heavily with icing sugar and bake at 360-375° F (182-190° C).

(Italy)

Easter Doves - Colomba Pasquale

Take the same dough as for Panettone, but replace the raisins with the same weight of orange and citron peel. Divide the dough according to the sizes required. Each piece is then divided into two, one part being a little larger than the other. The smallest piece is formed into wings in the shape of a 'U'. The larger piece is then shaped into the body of the bird. With the wings in position, the whole surface is covered with macaroon paste, ground almonds and granulated sugar. After proving, bake at 360-375° F (182-190° C). *(Italy)*

Eierschecke

Ingredients for 20 pieces 2 in. by 4 in. (5 × 10 cm.).

lb	oz		kg	gr
1	0	Kuchen dough		500
	13	Curd filling (page 219)		390
	3 1/2	Flaked almonds		100
	1/2	Lightly roasted ground almonds		15
	2 3/4	Sultanas		80
	7	Streusel		200
1	0	Butter		500
	5	Vanilla cream		150
	3 1/4	Egg yolks		100
	1 1/2	Flour		45
		Hot butter		
		Vanilla sugar		

Pin out the kuchen dough to a rectangular shape 8 in. by 20 in. (20 × 50 cm.), spread with the curd filling and sprinkle with the flaked almonds, sultanas and streusel. Beat the butter, vanilla cream, egg yolks and flour until frothy and add the ground almonds. Spread this mixture on the curd filling, smooth off and bake at 356° F (180° C) for about 45 minutes. After baking, brush with hot butter and sprinkle with vanilla sugar. *(Germany)* *(Illustration page 353.)*

Fermented Scones

Ferment

lb	oz		kg	gr
	5	Water 110° F (43° C)		150
	2	Yeast		60
	4	Flour		125

Let this ferment stand for 30 minutes.

Dough

lb	oz		kg	gr
2	8	Flour (medium)	1	250
	2	Baking powder		60
	2	Egg		60
	7 1/2	Butter		200

lb	oz		kg	gr
	7 1/2	Sugar (castor)		200
1	2	Cold milk (approx.)		560
	4	Sultanas		125

The flour and baking powder are sieved together and the butter rubbed in. The egg, sugar and milk are stirred into the ferment. The flour/butter mixture is added and the whole is mixed to a dough. Scale at 8 oz. (250 gr.) each and mould round. Re-mould after 10 minutes and pin out to about 7 in. (18 cm.) in diameter and place on to baking sheets. Cut each round into four without disturbing the circular shape. Wash with egg and allow to prove. Bake at 450° F (232° C).

Florentine Buns

lb	oz		kg	gr
14	0	Basic bun dough	7	
1	0	Butter		500
1	0	Sugar (castor)		500
	10	Honey		300
	12	Cherries (glacé)		375
1	0	Peel		500
	8	Sultanas		250
	14	Flaked almonds		435
	10	Strip almonds		300
	12 1/2	Dairy cream		390
		Dairy cream for filling		

Melt the butter, sugar and honey and take to boiling point. Add the rest of the ingredients. Weigh basic bun dough into 6 oz. (180 gr.) pieces and mould round. Allow to recover then pin out and place into 6 1/2 in. (16 cm.) cottage pans. Spread 3 oz. (90 gr.) of Florentine mixture on top of each and prove.

Bake at 400° F (204° C).

When cold, slice and pipe vanilla flavoured whipped dairy cream liberally on the bases. Cut the tops into eight pieces and arrange on the base. Dust with icing sugar.

Fougasse

lb	oz		kg	gr
1	0	Flour		500
	5	Butter		150

lb	oz		kg	gr
	4	Sugar		125
	4	Egg		125
	1	Yeast		30
	5	Water (approx.)		150

Disperse the yeast in the water and make up a dough with all the ingredients except 1 oz. (30 gr.) of butter. Develop the dough thoroughly. Prove for two hours. Melt the remaining 1 oz. (30 gr.) of butter and mix it in thoroughly. After recovery, make into three ropes and plait them. Form the plait into a ring. Egg wash and then prove. When ready bake at 400° F (204° C).

(France)

Fruit Bread
Ferment and Dough

Ferment

lb	oz		kg	gr
1	4	Milk 110° F (43° C)		625
	1	Sugar (castor)		30
	1 1/2	Yeast		45
	4	Flour (strong)		125

Let the ferment stand for 25 minutes.

Dough

lb	oz		kg	gr
2	2	Flour (strong)	1	
	5	Butter		150
	3	Sugar (castor)		90
	3/4	Salt		22
	2 1/2	Egg		75
	1/4	Ground nutmeg		8
	1/4	Ground spice		8
1	2	Currants		560
	4	Sultanas		125
	2	Peel		60

Rub the butter into the sieved flour, salt and spices. Stir the sugar and egg into the ferment. Add the flour and mix thoroughly. Fold in the warmed fruit at 1 hour. Scale at 1 1/2 hours. If a richer dough is required, increase the butter to 8 oz. (250 gr.), the currants to 1 1/2 lb. (750 gr.) and the sultanas to 8 oz. (250 gr.).

Fruited Almond Rings

Weigh a fruited bun dough into 8 oz. (250 gr.) pieces and mould round. After time for recovery, roll out into ropes about 8 in. (20 cm.) long. Fashion them into rings on a lightly greased baking sheet, dampening the ends to make a good seal. Egg wash, sprinkle with flaked almonds, prove and then bake at 380° F (193° C). Glaze with thin water icing containing fresh lemon juice.

Fruit Turnovers

Weigh plain basic bun dough into 1 $3/4$ oz. (50 gr.) pieces and mould round. When recovered, pin out to about 3 $1/2$ in. (9 cm.) in diameter. Wash the edges with water and place some good mincemeat in the centre of each. Enclose by bringing the top portion on to the bottom, sealing the join. Wash with egg and place on to greased baking sheets. Prove and then bake at 440° F (227° C). When cool, dust with icing sugar.

Guernsey Gauche - Channel Islands

lb	oz		kg	gr
1	4	Flour (strong)		625
	$3/8$	Salt		10
	1	Yeast		30
	12	Milk (approx.)		375

Make these ingredients into a dough at 80° F (27° C), and let it ferment for two hours.

lb	oz		kg	gr
	8	Butter		250
	$1/8$	Ground nutmeg		3

Work butter and nutmeg into the dough.

lb	oz		kg	gr
	8	Flour		250
	4	Lard		125

Start to work these in and when half mixed add the fruit.

lb	oz		kg	gr
1	8	Currants		750
	4	Cut mixed peel		125

Continue mixing until the fruit is well distributed throughout the dough. Shape the dough and place it in a well greased sloping sided tin, similar to a domestic baking tin. Let it prove for about 1-1 $1/2$ hours, then fold the dough back in the tin to make a smooth skin on the top. After another 15-20 minutes bake at 380° F (193° C) for about 1 $1/2$ hours.

For a sultana gauche use 2 lb. (1 kg.) of sultanas. For a butter gauche use all butter, add 2 oz. (60 gr.) extra sugar and use only 2 oz. (60 gr.) of well chopped lemon peel.

Gugelhupf I
Court Recipe

lb	oz		kg	gr
1	2	Flour		560
	1	Yeast		30
	9	Butter		280
	5	Sugar (icing)		150
	3 $1/2$	Egg		100
	12	Egg yolks		375
	6	Egg whites		180
	$1/4$	Salt		8
	7	Milk (warm) (approx.)		200
		Zest of $1/2$ lemon		

Make a ferment with the milk, yeast and 2 oz. (60 gr.) of flour. Cream the butter adding the zest and salt then the egg and egg yolks a little at a time. To this add the ferment and a quarter of the remaining flour and mix thoroughly. Whisk the egg whites and sugar to a stiff snow and fold it lightly into the dough together with the rest of the flour. Half fill well greased and floured moulds with the mixture, prove and then bake for about an hour at approximately 390° F (200° C).

(Austria)

Gugelhupf II

lb	oz		kg	gr
1	2	White flour		560
	3 $1/2$	Sugar (castor)		105
	5 $1/4$	Butter		160
	1	Yeast		30
	4 $1/2$	Raisins		140
	4 $3/4$	Milk (approx.)		140
1	$3/4$	Egg		50

lb	oz		kg	gr
	2	Egg yolks		60
	1/4	Salt		8
		1 grated lemon zest		
		Vanilla		

Make a ferment from the yeast, a little warm milk and some flour. Cream the butter with the sugar and add the salt, lemon zest and vanilla. Stir in the eggs. Mix all the ingredients to a fairly slack dough, adding a little water if necessary and drawing the raisins in at the end. Fill into a buttered, floured mould, leave to rise in a warm place, then bake in a hot oven. *(Austria)*

Kougelhopf

lb	oz		kg	gr
2	4	Flour	1	125
1	0	Egg		500
	3 1/2	Yeast		100
	3/4	Malt		20
	3/4	Salt		20
	7	Sugar		200
	7	Currants		200
	14	Butter		435
	4	Milk		125

Shape the dough into a ball, then make a hole in the middle and spread the dough out in the form of a crown so that it will slip into a chimney mould which has been greased and sprinkled with flaked blanched almonds. Bake in a medium oven. Brush with apricot purée and glaze when it comes out of the oven. *(France)*

Gugelhupf

Ferment

lb	oz		kg	gr
1	2	Milk		560
	1 3/4	Yeast		50
1	8	Flour		750

Dough

lb	oz		kg	gr
2	8	Flour	1	250
	1	Salt		30
	1/2	Malt extract		15
	10	Sugar (castor)		300

lb	oz		kg	gr
	10	Egg		300
	10	Butter		300
1	2	Milk (approx.)		560
1	0	Sultanas		500
	3 1/2	Orange peel (chopped)		100
		Zest and juice of 2 lemons		

Allow the ferment to drop and with the other ingredients except the fruit, make into a smooth dough. Finally add the fruit. After a rest of about 20 minutes scale at the desired weights and mould round. With the end of a rolling pin or by the use of the hand, make a hole in the centre of each and place into well greased and floured chimney moulds. The moulds should be little more than half full. Prove carefully until the dough is nearly at the top of the moulds. Wash with water and bake at 400° F (204° C).

When baked, turn out on to a cooling wire and when cold dust with icing sugar. *(Switzerland)*

Hot Cross Buns

Ferment

lb	oz		kg	gr
1	4	Milk		625
	1	Sugar (castor)		30
	2	Yeast		60
	4	Flour		125

Temperature of ferment 80° F (27° C). Let it stand for 30 minutes.

Dough

lb	oz		kg	gr
2	4	Flour	1	125
	6	Butter		180
	6	Sugar		180
	4	Egg		125
		Bun spice*		
	1/4	Salt		8
	12	Currants		375
	4	Cut mixed peel		125

Rub the fat into the flour. Stir the sugar, egg and salt in the ferment and add the flour/fat mixture. When half mixed, add

the bun spice and the fruit. Knock back at 40 minutes and scale at 2 oz. (60 gr.) each at 60 minutes. Mould round and place in ordered rows on to greased baking sheets and place into a prover. When ready, the buns are piped with a cross using crossing paste and baked at 440° F (227° C). Immediately on removal from the oven, the buns are glazed with sugar wash.
(Illustration page 276.) (Great Britain)

* Care must be taken in the use of bun spice which is available in liquid form. Bun spice is a mixture of spice oils, some of which have a narcotic action on yeast, therefore, it is better to add it during the mixing of the dough rather than add it directly to the ferment.

The amount used depends on its concentration and can be determined by test.

Bun Crossing Paste

lb	oz		kg	gr
	8	Flour		250
	2 1/2	Oil		75
	10	Water		300

The oil is mixed with the flour. The water is added gradually so that a smooth paste, free from lumps, is made. The piping is done through a fine pipe in a savoy bag. It is easier to pipe the horizontal lines along one row of buns and then to pipe the vertical lines a row at a time rather than pipe each bun individually.

Kirsch Pomponnettes - Pomponnettes au Kirsch

Place a seedless muscatel raisin in the bottom of small madeleine tins which have been greased. Three parts fill with savarin paste and prove. Bake at 450° F (232° C). Soak in kirsch syrup and dip into thin fondant slightly flavoured with kirsch.

(France)

Kric-Krac

Use the same dough as for Simits, pin out thinly and cut into strips. Place side by side on to baking sheets. Egg wash and sprinkle with sesame seeds. Bake at 450° F (232° C).

Alternatively, they may be rolled into thin ropes instead of being cut.
(Illustration page 828.) (Turkey)

Lardy Cake - Oxford

lb	oz		kg	gr
1	14	Flour (strong)		935
	1/2	Salt		15
	1	Lard		30
	1	Yeast		30
1	1	Milk (approx.)		530

Dough temperature 80° F (27° C).

This dough will be ready in 1 hour.

lb	oz		kg	gr
	12	Lard		375
	6	Sugar (brown)		180
		A little ground spice		

Roll the dough into a rectangle and spread over two thirds of its surface half the lard, brown sugar and spice mixed together. Fold as for puff pastry and give half turn. Repeat this using the other half of the lard mixture and give another half turn. The whole is cut into three of a size to fit flat tins 12 in. by 6 in. (30 × 15 cm.). Brush the tops with a mixture of egg and milk and score a trellis design with the point of a sharp knife. After sufficient proof, bake at 420° F (216° C).
(Illustration page 271.) (Great Britain)

Lardy Cakes - Gloucester

The same dough is used as above but with the addition of 12 oz. (375 gr.) sultanas and 4 oz. (125 gr.) of currants. Into this dough, 12 oz. (375 gr.) of lard and an equal amount of brown sugar and 1/8 oz. (4 gr.) of ground spice are rolled in after they are mixed together and given two half turns. The dough is then pinned out to a large rectangle and rolled up like a swiss roll. This is cut into six pieces and placed, cut side down into round pans of suitable size. The pans should be heavily greased with lard. When proved, they are baked at

420° F (216° C). When baked, the lardy cakes should be turned upside down from the pans immediately, or they will stick. Care should be taken, however, or the boiling lard will cause a painful burn.

The brown sugar and lard will, on cooling, show as a delightful glaze.
(Illustration page 317.)   *(Great Britain)*

Lardy Cake - Wiltshire

Use the same dough as for Oxford Lardy cakes with the addition of 8 oz. (250 gr.) currants. The procedure is the same except that 1 1/2 lb. (750 gr.) of lard, 6 oz. (180 gr.) of castor sugar and 1/8 oz. (4 gr.) of mixed spice are mixed together and rolled in as for puff pastry. After three half turns, the whole is placed on a baking sheet approximately 16 in. by 24 in. (40 × 60 cm.) in size and rolled flat. It is washed with egg diluted with a little milk and scored on the surface with the point of a sharp knife in a trellis design.

After sufficient time for the Lardy cake to prove, it is baked at 420° F (216° C).

When cool it is cut into slices.
(Illustration page 317.)   *(Great Britain)*

Lemon Buns

Weigh lemon flavoured basic bun dough into 1 3/4 oz. (50 gr.) pieces and mould round.

Wash with egg and dip the top of each into fine granulated sugar and place on to baking sheets. Press a little lemon peel firmly into the centre of each.

Alternatively, when half proved, the finger can be used to make an indentation in the centre of each into which lemon curd is piped. When proved they are baked at 430° F (220° C).

Lincolnshire Plum Loaf

Dough

lb	oz		kg	gr
2	4	Flour (strong)	1	125
	2	Lard		60
	2	Sugar		60
	1/2	Salt		15
	2	Yeast		60
1	4	Milk		625

This dough is made up with a finished temperature of 78° F (26° C). It is allowed to ferment for 1 hour when the following materials are mixed in.

Added materials

lb	oz		kg	gr
	6	Sugar (castor)		180
	6	Lard		180
	1/8	Ground spice		4
1	4	Currants		625
	8	Sultanas		250
	3	Peel		90

The sugar, lard and spice are well mixed into the dough, after which the fruit is carefully mixed in. The dough is then divided into six pieces (about 17 oz. (530 gr.) each). The pieces are moulded to the shape of the tins, washed on top with egg diluted with a little water and placed into greased bread tins. They are proved for about 100 minutes and baked at 400° F (204° C).   *(Great Britain)*

Liverpool Bun Loaf

This ferment stands for 30 minutes.

Ferment

lb	oz		kg	gr
	12	Milk 100° F (38° C)		375
	8	Egg		250
	4	Sugar (castor)		125
	1	Yeast		30
	8	Flour		250

Dough

lb	oz		kg	gr
1	8	Flour		750
	3/4	Baking powder		22
	1/2	Salt		15
	12	Butter		375
	14	Sugar (brown)		435
	1/2	Ground spice		15
	1/4	Ground nutmeg		8
	4	Egg		125

lb	oz		kg	gr
	8	Dark treacle		250
1	8	Currants		750
1	0	Sultanas		500
	4	Cut mixed peel		125

Cream the butter and sugar, beat in the egg and treacle. Add part of the flour and part of the ferment until all are blended well together. Add the fruit last. Weigh into 2 lb. (1 kg.) pieces, mould to the shape of the tins. Wash the tops with diluted egg and place into well greased oblong 2 lb. (1 kg.) bread tins. When proved, bake at 400° F (204° C), for about 1 hour.

Marignan

Pipe savarin dough into small boat-shaped pans and prove. Bake at 450° F (232° C). Soak in madeira syrup. Make a slit with a sharp knife and pipe in either Italian meringue or whipped dairy cream.

(France)

Milk Rolls

lb	oz		kg	gr
1	5	Flour (strong)		650
	1/4	Salt		8
	1/4	Sugar (castor)		8
	1 1/4	Butter		40
	1	Yeast		30
	12	Milk		375

Dough temperature 80° F (27° C).

Knock back at 40 minutes. Scale at 55 minutes.

Yield at 1 1/2 oz. (45 gr.) - 24
Yield at 2 oz. (60 gr.) - 18

Round, pointed or plaited shapes can be made from this dough. Egg wash before baking at 450° F (232° C).

Mozart Plaited Bread

lb	oz		kg	gr
2	4	Milk 77° F (25° C)	1	125
	5	Yeast		150
	1/2	Malt		15
	1 1/4	Salt		35

lb	oz		kg	gr
	7	Sugar (castor)		200
	7	Egg		200
	5	Finely chopped candied orange peel		150
5	4	Flour	2	625
	10	Butter		300
		Zest of 2 lemons		

When preparing the dough, the fruit is added last. When they come out of the oven, the eight strand plaited loaves are brushed with apricot purée and glazed. *(Plaiting page 55.)* *(France)*

Muffins

lb	oz		kg	gr
3	8	Flour (medium)	1	750
	1	Salt		30
	1/2	Butter		15
	1/2	Sugar		15
	1 1/2	Yeast		45
2	8	Water	1	250

Dough temperature 80° F (27° C). Knock back at 1 hour. Scale at 2 1/2 oz. (70-75 gr.) each after a further 1/2 hour. The fat is rubbed into the dry ingredients which are sieved together. After the yeast has been dispersed in the water, the whole is made into a very soft dough. After weighing, the pieces are moulded round and placed on to trays heavily spread with rice flour. When fully risen, they are carefully transferred to muffin hoops that have been placed on the hotplate. When they are half baked they are turned over to finish baking.
(Illustration page 270.)

Muffins - Oven Baked

Use a plain basic dough and weigh into 2 oz. (60 gr.) pieces. Mould them up into round shapes and allow to recover for five minutes. Roll each out to a circular shape about 4 in. (10 cm.) in diameter. Place on to lightly greased warm baking sheets. Egg wash and allow to prove. When ready, bake at 450° F (232° C) turning them over carefully when half baked.

Muffins-Sweet

Ferment

lb	oz		kg	gr
1	4	Milk 95° F (35° C)		625
	2	Sugar (castor)		60
	1 1/2	Yeast		45
	8	Flour (strong)		250

Allow to stand for 45 minutes.

Dough

lb	oz		kg	gr
1	4	Flour (strong)		625
	2	Butter		60
	3/8	Salt		10

Make into a well developed dough. Knock back at 1 hour and scale after another 15 minutes.

Proceed as for ordinary muffins, using a cooler hotplate.

Nut Rings

Ingredients for 30

lb	oz		kg	gr
	10 1/2	Kuchen dough		300
1	5	Sweet paste		650

Filling

lb	oz		kg	gr
	7	Chopped hazelnuts		200
	10 1/2	Fine sponge crumbs		300
	7	Raw marzipan		200
	3 1/2	Chopped walnuts		100
	3 1/2	Rum		100
	3 1/2	Finely chopped candied orange peel		100
	5 1/4	Egg		150

Mix together to a paste.

Work the kuchen dough and sweet paste together thoroughly, divide into 30 pieces and mould round. Pin out each piece to an oval shape 6 in. by 3 in. (15 × 8 cm.) and place the filling in the centre. Pinch up the paste so that the filling is completely enclosed. Shape into rings, arrange on baking sheets and brush with egg. After drying, brush with egg again and bake in a moderate oven for approx. 20 minutes.

(Germany)

Orange Blossom Bread - Duivekater

A kind of bread that is baked North of Amsterdam. This speciality is mainly baked in the period from the 5th of December until the 6th of January (Twelfth-night). Some bakers, however, are specialists in this kind of bread and they bake it the whole year round.

lb	oz		kg	gr
4	8	Flour	2	250
	7	Yeast		200
	1	Salt		30
1	8	Water (approx.)		750
1	2	Sugar (castor)		560
	5	Butter		150
		Lemon-oil to taste		

First make a ferment with the water, yeast, half of the flour and 3 oz. (90 gr.) of the sugar. Temperature of the ferment should be 77° F (25° C).

After a first rise of 15 minutes, mix in the rest of the sugar, the butter, and then the flour. The dough should be very firm and thoroughly mixed. Intensive mixing is necessary in order to obtain a fine structure. The dough can immediately be weighed and rounded up. After a sufficient time, the dough pieces can be moulded into the desired shapes. Put the loaves on a baking sheet allowing sufficient distance from each other. Brush the loaves with egg and decorate with cuts on the top. Prove the loaves for about 2 hours and then bake them at 410° F (210° C). *(Holland)*

Panettone

lb	oz		kg	gr
1	5	Flour		650
	1/2	Salt		15
	1 3/4	Yeast		50
	7	Butter		200
	5	Sugar (castor)		150
	3 1/2	Egg yolks		100
	10	Water (warm) (approx.)		300
		Zest of 1 lemon		
	5	Raisins (seedless)		150
	3 1/2	Citron peel (finely cut)		100

Disperse the yeast in the water and mix with the flour, salt, sugar and egg yolks to a medium firm dough, then work in the butter. Add the lemon zest, raisins and the citron peel. Divide the dough into three, mould round, cover and allow to recover for about 15 minutes. Re-mould into balls and place into hoops lined with a wide, oiled paper band. Allow them to prove until the volume has doubled, brush with egg, make an incision in the form of a cross on top and bake for 35-40 minutes at 400° F (204° C). *(Switzerland)*

Panettone I

Stage I - Sponge

Known in Italy as a Mother Yeast Mixture

lb	oz		kg	gr
	8	Flour		250
	1/4	Yeast		8
	4	Water		125
	4	White wine		125
	3 1/2	Wine vinegar		100

The sponge is set at 78-82° F (26-28° C). Fermentation time is approximately 2 1/2-3 hours although experience is necessary to recognize readiness for the next stage.

Stage II - Basic Dough

Known in Italy as a Mother Yeast Dough

lb	oz		kg	gr
1	2	Sponge as above (approx.)		560
1	7	Flour		700
	8	Water		250

The temperature of the basic dough should be as above.

Stage III - 1st Dough

lb	oz		kg	gr
3	0	Basic dough as above (approx.)	1	500
9	0	Flour	4	500
2	3	Butter	1	100
2	0	Sugar (castor)	1	
1	10	Egg yolks		800
	2 1/2	Honey		75
2	12	Water	1	375

Place the ripened basic dough in the mixer, add the melted butter and mix well. Add the rest of the ingredients and mix until the dough no longer sticks to the side of the mixer. Place the dough in a wooden trough and allow to ferment for about 9-10 hours at a temperature of 82-86° F (28-30° C).

Stage IV - 2nd Dough

lb	oz		kg	gr
20	8	The 1st dough	10	250
4	8	Flour	2	250
2	3	Butter	1	100
1	15	Egg		950
	2	Salt		60
	12	Water		375
	1/2	Butter essence		15
	1/2	Lemon essence		15
	1/4	Panettone essence		7
	1/4	Vanilla essence		7
3	0	Citron peel (chopped)	1	500
3	0	Orange peel (chopped)	1	500
5	4	Sultanas	2	625

When the first dough has risen to its maximum volume, return it to the mixer and add the flour, salt, egg and essences, then the butter and water in small quantities. Mix until the dough no longer sticks to the sides of the mixer. Add the peel and sultanas carefully.

Divide the dough into pieces weighing 8 oz. (250 gr.), 1 lb. (500 gr.), 1 1/2 lb. (750 gr.) or any other size as required. Mould into round balls and allow to recover for 30 minutes. Re-mould each piece and place it in a hoop lined with a special panettone paper band. Leave in the prover for 6 to 7 hours in a temperature of 82-86° F (28-30° C) and with a humidity of 50°. Shortly before full expansion, make an incision in the form of a cross on the top with a sharp knife, place a nut of butter in the centre and allow to prove for another 20 minutes. Lastly, carefully draw the four angles of the cut apart and bake at 360-370° F (180-190° C). After baking, invert on to a wire rack and leave until cold. Wait 12 hours before wrapping.

To ensure a light, high-quality product, first use the smallest possible quantity of 'mother yeast' to obtain a kind of sour dough composed of a large number of big 'daughter' yeast cells, as the finished panettone should be open grained. There is no point in using more yeast, as this will not produce the proper structure, volume or flavour. Sufficient time therefore must be allowed for the yeast to develop; the temperature should be between 82-86° F (28-30° C). It requires experience to recognize the exact point of time when the sponges and doughs have reached their optimum. Wooden troughs are best for the storage of sponges and doughs.

The flavourings used vary from one firm to another; in any event they should be used sparingly. A good flavour can be obtained by using citron and orange peel only.

If large quantities are made at one time, another dough stage will be required to provide sufficient aeration. Its weight should be one sixth of that of the dough.

A 2 lb. (1 kg.) panettone will need a hoop 7 in. (18 cm.) in diameter and 5-6 in. (12-15 cm.) deep. *(Italy)*

Panettone II

Stage I

lb	oz		kg	gr
4	8	Sponge (see Panettone I)	2	250
13	8	Flour	6	750
3	6	Butter	1	680
3	2	Sugar (castor)	1	560
2	12	Egg yolks	1	375
4	0	Water	2	
	4	Honey		125

Stage II

lb	oz		kg	gr
31	8	Dough as above	15	750
4	8	Flour	2	250
2	4	Sugar	1	125
3	6	Butter	1	680
3	12	Egg	1	875
	2 1/2	Salt		75

lb	oz		kg	gr
4	8	Citron peel (chopped)	2	250
4	8	Orange peel (chopped)	2	250
7	4	Raisins	3	625
1	2	Water (approx.)		560
	3/4	Butter essence		20
	3/4	Citron or panettone essence		20
	3/8	Vanilla		10

Proceed as for Panettone I *(Italy)*

Parisette

Take French bread dough, *page 175*. When ready weigh pieces at 10 1/2 oz. (315 gr.) and mould round. When recovered make into long cigar shapes and prove on cloths. Before setting on the oven bottom, the loaves are given three deep diagonal cuts. Bake at 450° F (232° C) in plenty of steam. Draw off the steam before baking is finished so that the bread can finish baking in a dry atmosphere. *(Switzerland)*

Party Buns

Weigh 1 3/4 oz. (50 gr.) pieces from a lemon flavoured basic bun dough *(page 175)* and mould round. When fully recovered, roll into ropes about 12 in. (30 cm.) in length. Curl each rope into a loose spiral on to a greased baking sheet, pinching the end to fasten. Egg wash and prove. Bake at 440° F (227° C). When cool, spread each with thin vanilla flavoured fondant. Alternatively, the ropes can be shorter and then fashioned into 'C' and 'S' scrolls.

Peaches

Take plain basic bun dough and into each 1 lb. (500 gr.) work in 4 oz. (125 gr.) butter. When recovered, scale into 1/2 oz. (15 gr.) pieces. Mould them round, and place on to warmed greased baking sheets. When proved, baked and cool, a small piece is taken from the bottom of each. Dip each piece into stock syrup and turn out on to granulated sugar. Pipe a filling cream into each cavity and stick them together in pairs. Place into paper cases.

Pineapple Buns

Weigh basic bun dough at 2 oz. (60 gr.) and mould round. After allowing time for recovery, pin out to about 3½ in. (9 cm.). Place on a lightly greased baking sheet and make a circular indentation in each, into which pipe a little vanilla custard. Place a pineapple ring on top with a glacé cherry in the centre. After proving, bake at 440° F (227° C). When cool, glaze with apricot purée and thin water icing made with the pineapple juice.

These can also be made by weighing 6 oz. (180 gr.) pieces into 6½ in. (16 cm.) cottage pans. Finish in the same way as above. Bake at 420° F (216° C).

Pitta

Serbian national pie made with:

lb	oz		kg	gr
4	0	Plait dough	2	
1	5	Peel		650
1	0	Thinly sliced apples		500
	10	Raisins		300
	7	Finely grated walnuts or hazelnuts		200
	9	Honey		275
		A little ground cinnamon		

Pin out the plait dough thinly on a table covered with a cloth and leave to dry a little. Thoroughly butter a square tin with upturned sides about 1 to 2 in. (3-5 cm.) high. Divide the dough into two and put one square in the bottom. Brush with melted butter and spread with a mixture of the peel, the apples, the raisins, previously soaked, the grated nuts, honey and cinnamon. Cover with the other square of dough after brushing its underside with melted butter. Brush the top with egg yolk and bake in a moderate oven for one hour.   *(Serbia)*

Plaited Bread - Vlechtbrood

This bread is composed of three or more strands of dough which are plaited together into the desired shape.

lb	oz		kg	gr
11	4	Flour	5	625
	5	Yeast		150
	3½	Salt		100
	10	Milk powder		300
	1 ¾	Sugar (castor)		45
	5	Margarine		150
5	4	Water (approx.)	2	625

Mix these ingredients thoroughly into a smooth firm dough. Temperature of the dough 77° F (25° C). After a rest for 20 minutes, divide into the desired weight and round up the pieces.

Example of weights into which one can divide the dough:

3 plait, 3 strands of 5 oz. (150 gr.) each,
4 plait, 4 strands of 4 oz. (125 gr.) each,
5 plait, 5 strands of 3 oz. (90 gr.) each,
6 plait, 6 strands of 2½ oz. (75 gr.) each.

The six plait can be shaped into a Winston. After the rounding up one can immediately start the plaiting. Roll out the strands equally; during this rolling the strands must not crack. Do not roll out more strands at a time than one uses for one loaf. After the rolling, start the plaiting which needs a very skilled hand. When the plait is finished it is brushed with egg. Let the egg dry and brush again. When the plaits are well risen, they are baked at 446° F (230° C).
(Plaiting pages 53-54.)   *(Holland)*

Portland Buns

lb	oz		kg	gr
4	0	Milk bread dough	2	
1	8	Lard		750
	8	Sugar (brown)		250
1	8	Currants		750
	8	Cut mixed peel		250
	¼	Ground nutmeg		8

Mix the dough, lard, sugar and nutmeg thoroughly together, then distribute the warmed fruit through the dough carefully. Allow about 30 minutes for the dough to recover. Weigh into 1 ¾ oz. (50 gr.) pieces and mould round. Place on to lightly greased baking sheets and prove carefully avoiding excessive heat and steam. Bake at 420° F (216° C) for about 15-20 minutes.

Alternatively, the dough can be pinned out on to a baking sheet and cut into squares after baking.

Pretzels

lb	oz		kg	gr
	7	Milk		200
	3/4	Yeast		20
	2	Egg		60
	1/4	Salt		8
1	2	Flour		560

When the pretzels have been given their shapes and have risen and are therefore ready for baking, they are dipped in a pickling brine to give them a special flavour.

For the pickling brine use 2 lb. 4 oz. (1 kg. 125) cold water in which 1 oz. (30 gr.) caustic soda has been dissolved. The brine should be prepared the day before it is required so that the pretzels have a better appearance when baked. The brine may be used for several days. Pickling brines can also be bought ready-made. *(France)*

Raisin Slices

lb	oz		kg	gr
2	0	Kuchen dough	1	
	7	Raisins		200
	4	Butter		125
	5	Flaked almonds		150
	7	Sugar (castor)		200
	5	Egg		150
	1/16	Cinnamon		2
		Zest of 1 lemon		

Work the raisins into the dough and pin out to a rectangular shape 24 by 16 in. (60 × 40 cm.) and place on to a suitable baking sheet.

Thoroughly mix the rest of the ingredients and cook over a low heat then leave to cool. After allowing the dough to recover, spread it with the mixture and bake at 400° F (200° C). After baking, and when cool, cut into slices of the required size. *(Illustration page 319.)* *(Germany)*

Rolls - Semmel

Take basic roll dough and weigh into 1 3/4 oz. (50 gr.) pieces and mould them round. When recovered mould again and set to prove on cloths. When ready for the oven give a diagonal cut with a sharp knife. Set on the oven bottom and bake at 450° F (232° C) in plenty of steam.
(Switzerland)

Rolls - Glarner Brötli

Proceed as for Semmel but at the second moulding elongate the rolls. Prove on a cloth and give a diagonal cut with a sharp knife just before baking at 450° F (232° C) with steam. *(Switzerland)*

Rolls - Doppelsemmel

Proceed as for Semmel but place the rolls two together on the cloth to prove. Cut both rolls together with a sharp knife before setting. Bake as above. *(Switzerland)*

Rolls - Schlumbergerli

Proceed as for Semmel but mould on a slightly oiled board. Prove on cloths and, just before baking, turn them over so that the moulding seam is at the top. Set on the oven bottom and bake at 450° F (232° C) in plenty of steam. The moulding seam will open during baking.
(Switzerland)

Rusks

Under the general heading of rusks are included unsweetened rusks, dietetic rusks (without salt) and sweetened rusks (zwiebacks). The rusk loses about 40 % of its original weight while being toasted. The toasting process causes the starch to be converted into dextrose, which is very easily digested and assimilated. It is for this reason that rusks are so suitable for invalids.

Nowadays rusks are no longer made on a small scale by individual craftsmen, but are mostly mass produced in specialized factories which supply some very good products. Here are three recipes, notwithstanding:

Rusks - Biscottes

lb	oz		kg	gr
2	4	Milk 85° F (30° C)	1	125
	5	Yeast		150
	³/₄	Malt		20
	1	Salt		30
	3 ¹/₂	Butter		100
4	6	Flour	2	180

(France)

Rusks - Zwiebacks

lb	oz		kg	gr
2	4	Milk 85° F (30° C)	1	125
	5 ¹/₄	Yeast		150
	³/₄	Malt		20
	7	Sugar		200
	7	Egg		200
	1	Salt		30
	5 ¹/₄	Butter		150
4	10	Flour	2	300

(Germany)

Rusks - Beschuit

lb	oz		kg	gr
2	4	Flour	1	125
	3	Yeast		90
	³/₈	Salt		10
	5	Egg		150
	1 ³/₄	Sugar		50
	4	Rusk-jelly (only to be obtained in the factories)		125
	6	Glucose		180
	12	Water (approx.)		375

First make a sponge from half of the flour, half of the sugar, the yeast, the egg and the water. Temperature of the sponge should be about 68° F (20° C). Fermenting time for the sponge is 15 minutes.

After this, add the rest of the sugar, half of the glucose, quarter of the flour, the rest of the glucose, half of the rusk-jelly, the rest of the flour, the salt and the rest of the rusk-jelly. One should only add the next ingredient if the former has been well mixed through the dough. After mixing all the ingredients, the dough must be mixed well for 30 to 45 minutes. Temperature of the dough 77-78° F (25-26° C). After mixing the dough let it rest for 15 minutes.

Weigh into 1 ¹/₂ oz. (45 gr.) pieces (the weight depends on the size of the mould). Smooth the pieces of dough and round them up into balls. Let the balls rise for a while and then roll them flat with a rolling pin and put them on a baking sheet and cover with special rusk-moulds 4 in. (10 cm.) in diameter and about 1 in. (3 cm.) deep.

These moulds are round with 5 holes. After the rolling, the last rise takes place in a prover with a temperature of 84° F (29° C). As soon as the rusks are well risen (this one can see through the holes in the moulds), they are baked at 536° F (280° C) for 5-7 minutes.

Immediately after baking, lift the moulds and allow the rusks to cool. They are cut into halves after half a day of cooling. After cutting, the rusks are dried and toasted in an oven at 410° F (210° C).

Dutch rusks should be golden-yellow, have a fine structure and be deliciously crisp.

(Holland)

Sally Lunns

Ferment

lb	oz		kg	gr
1	4	Milk 100° F (38° C)		625
	¹/₂	Sugar		15
	1 ¹/₂	Yeast		45
	4	Flour		125

This ferment is allowed to stand until it rises and drops.

Dough

lb	oz		kg	gr
2	8	Flour (strong)	1	250
	5	Butter		150
	5	Egg		150
	5	Sugar		150
		Zest of 1 lemon		
		A little ground nutmeg		

The butter is rubbed into the flour. This is made into a dough with the rest of the materials, taking care that the dough is not too soft. It is knocked back at 40 minutes and is ready for scaling after another 30 minutes. The dough is weighed at 8 oz.

(250 gr.) and each is moulded round. After time for recovery, they are re-moulded and placed into well greased 5 in. (12 cm.) cake hoops. When half proved, they are carefully egg washed. When fully proved, they are baked at 440° F (227° C). The hoops are removed as soon as the Sally Lunns are baked. Sally Lunns are cut as illustrated. They may be eaten with butter and such additions as jam, marmalade or honey. The slices may be toasted.
(Illustration page 269.) *(Great Britain)*

Scotch Baps

lb	oz		kg	gr
2	0	Flour (strong)	1	
	2	Butter		60
	½	Sugar		15
	½	Salt		15
	1	Yeast		30
1	7	Water (approx.)		700

Dough temperature 80° F (27° C).

The dough must be soft and well developed. Knock back at 1 hour. Scale at 1½ hours. Weigh into 3 oz. (90 gr.) pieces and mould round. After a time for recovery, pin out to oval shape, not too thin. Dust with flour and place on to baking sheets. When sufficiently proved, bake at 480-500° F (250-260° C). Do not overbake. Baps may also be made in round shapes.

Scottish Black Bun

Basic dough

lb	oz		kg	gr
1	0	Flour (strong)		500
	¼	Salt		8
	¾	Yeast		22
	11	Water (approx.)		330

Make dough at 76° F (24.5° C). Ferment for 1 hour.

Cover paste

lb	oz		kg	gr
1	9	Basic dough		780
	4½	Butter		140

Mix the butter into the dough and add sufficient soda flour to make a workable plastic paste.

Filling

lb	oz		kg	gr
	6	Soda flour		180
	⅛	Salt		4
	¾	Ground mixed spice		22
	⅛	Ground cinnamon		4
	⅛	Ground ginger		4
	3	Basic dough		90
	1	Treacle		30
	1½	Sugar (brown)		45
	2	Egg		60
	1	Butter (melted)		30
	1	Ground almonds		30
	2½	Milk		75
	6	Unblanched almonds		180
1	8	Sultanas		750
2	0	Currants	1	
	2	Preserved ginger (chopped fine)		60
	2½	Rum		75
		Caramel colour		
		Vanilla flavour		

The rum is poured over the cleaned fruit and given time to soak in. The butter, sugar and spice are creamed together and thoroughly mixed with the basic dough after which the fruit, treacle, caramel, vanilla and almonds are mixed in. The filling is weighed as required and blocked out by pressing into a square, rectangular or round tin. It is then turned out on to a dampened piece of cover paste, so that it can be completely covered. It is then inverted back into the baking tin, egg washed, docked and well pricked with a skewer.

After proving for about an hour, the buns are baked at 360° F (182° C). The above recipe will make two, weighing about 2 lb. (1 kg.) each and they will take about 2½-3 hours to bake. They are washed immediately on removal from the oven with rum flavoured egg wash.
(Illustration page 272.)

Selkirk Bannocks

Ferment

lb	oz		kg	gr
1	4	Milk 100° F (38° C)		625
	½	Sugar (castor)		15

lb	oz		kg	gr
	1 1/2	Yeast		45
	4	Flour		125

Let this ferment stand for 30 minutes.

Dough

lb	oz		kg	gr
2	0	Flour	1	
	6	Butter		175
	6	Sugar		175
	1/2	Salt		15
1	12	Sultanas		875
	4	Peel (orange)		125

When the ferment is ready it is made into a dough with the rest of the ingredients. It is knocked back after 1 hour and scaled into 1 lb. (500 gr.) pieces after another 1/2 hour. The pieces are moulded round and left to recover for about 15 minutes and moulded again. They are flattened and washed with egg. After proving they are baked at 440° F (227° C).
(Illustration page 272.)   (Scotland)

Simits

Into about 3 lb. (1 kg. 500) of basic bread dough rub 7 oz. (200 gr.) of butter or 6 oz. (180 gr.) of compound fat and stiffen with about 7 oz. (200 gr.) of flour.

Weigh off pieces, roll into ropes and fashion into circles.

Egg wash and dip into sesame seeds and place on baking sheets. After a short proof, bake at 450° F (232° C).
(Illustration page 828.)   (Turkey)

Spice Fingers

Pin out 2 1/2 lb. (1 kg. 250) of plain basic bun dough to a piece about 18 in. by 12 in. (46 × 30 cm.) and brush with melted butter except the bottom edge which is egg washed. Two thirds of the surface is sprinkled with sultanas and lightly dusted with ground mixed spice. Fold the dough into three, puff pastry fashion and pin out so that fingers 4 in. long. and 1 1/2 in. (10 × 4 cm.) wide are cut. Egg wash before cutting. Place the fingers on to warmed greased baking sheets and after proving, bake at 420° F (216° C).

Stollen I

An Old Danubian Recipe

lb	oz		kg	gr
2	0	Flour	1	
	1 1/2	Yeast		45
	3 1/2	Sugar (icing)		100
	9	Butter		280
	2	Egg		60
	1/2	Salt		15
	1/4	Cinnamon		8
1	0	Milk (warm) (approx.)		500
	8	Grapes (small)		250
	8	Raisins		250
	1	Rum		30
		Zest of 1 lemon		

Make a ferment with the yeast, a little sugar and some of the flour and milk.

Sieve the flour and cinnamon and add the lemon zest. When the ferment is ready add all the rest of the ingredients except the fruit and make into a smooth dough.

Carefully add the fruit last. Cover and allow to ferment for a while in a warm place. Divide into three pieces and mould each into a baton shape with one side slightly indented. Place on to a baking sheet and prove. Bake at 400° F (204° C). While still hot, brush with butter and sprinkle with vanilla icing sugar.
(Austria)

Stollen II - Dresden

lb	oz		kg	gr
1	5	Flour		650
	1 3/4	Yeast		50
	5	Sugar (castor)		150
	7	Butter (creamed)		200
	3 1/2	Egg		100
	2	Egg yolks		60
	1/2	Salt		15
	1/8	Nutmeg / Mace / Clove		4
	5	Milk (warm) (approx.)		150
	2 1/2	Sultanas		75
	2 1/2	Currants		75
	1 3/4	Peel (orange)		50

lb	oz		kg	gr
1 $3/4$		Peel (lemon)		50
		Zest of 1 lemon		
		Butter for brushing		
		Icing sugar for dusting		

Make a ferment with the milk, yeast and 4 oz. (125 gr.) of flour. When ready add the rest of the ingredients except the fruit, and mix thoroughly then work in the fruit. Allow the dough to ferment for a while then weigh to the desired size. Mould to a baton shape with a crease down the centre. After proving, bake at 420° F (216° C) for about 45-60 minutes according to size. As soon as baked brush with plenty of butter and dust twice generously with icing sugar. Do not cut for 24 hours.

Wrapped in cellophane, these loaves will keep well for several weeks. *(Germany)*
(Illustration page 354.)

Stollen III - Almond

lb	oz		kg	gr
10	0	Flour	5	
	10	Yeast		300
5	0	Butter	2	500
1	4	Sugar (castor)		625
	1	Salt		30
2	0	Milk	1	
5	0	Almonds (strip)	2	500
3	0	Peel (lemon)	1	500
		Zest of 2 lemons		
		Vanilla pods (2)		
2	0	Butter for brushing	1	
1	4	Vanilla icing sugar for dusting		625

Make a stiff sponge with one third of the flour, the yeast and the milk. When it has risen, add the sugar, butter, salt and the remaining flour and mix to a smooth dough. Draw in the fruit and almonds and allow to recover. Weigh into 2 lb. (1 kg.) or 4 lb. (2 kg.) pieces and mould into stollen shape. Prove for 30 minutes and bake at 400° F (200° C), in steam if possible. After baking, brush generously with butter and dust heavily with vanilla sugar. *(Germany)*

Sugar-Loaf - Suikerbrood

lb	oz		kg	gr
11	0	Flour	5	
1	0	Yeast		500
	3 $1/2$	Salt		100
	12	Margarine		350
	5	Sugar (castor)		150
5	7	Water (approx.)	2	700
6	0	Sugar nibs (lumps or chips)	3	
	1	Cinnamon		35

Mix a nice smooth dough from: flour, yeast, margarine, sugar and water.

Temperature of the dough 76° F (24° C). After a first rise of 20 minutes mix the sugar nibs and the cinnamon through the dough. Mould up the pieces of dough and have them rise for about 10 minutes. Then shape the pieces and put them in greased tins, (the weight depends on the size of the tin). The tins are greased and dusted with sugar in advance. Next let the dough rise until the tins are completely filled. Then bake at 420° F (216° C).

The colour of the loaf should be golden-yellow and the sugar sprinkled in the tins should be slightly caramelized. This is a palatable kind of bread that is mainly eaten in the North of the Netherlands.
(Holland)

Swiss Buns

From the same dough as for cream cookies, weigh pieces at 1 $3/4$ oz. (50 gr.) and mould them round. After time for recovery, mould them into finger shapes and place them side by side on a baking sheet, not too close together. Prove in a little steam and bake at 440° F (227° C). When cool carefully dip the tops into white vanilla flavoured fondant.

Taillaules

lb	oz		kg	gr
2	3 $1/2$	Milk (approx.)	1	
1	0	Egg		500
1	2	Sugar		550
	3 $1/2$	Yeast		100
	3 $1/2$	Malt		100
	2 $1/2$	Salt		75

lb	oz		kg	gr
8	0	Flour	4	
1	2	Butter		550
2	3	Sultanas	1	100
		Zest of 5 lemons		

To make this dough, use the same method as for a bun dough. When it is ready, mould long pieces of the dough into bread tins and leave to rise again. Then brush with egg and use scissors to make notches in the taillaules.

Bake in a medium oven 446° F (230° C). *(Illustration page 274.)* *(Switzerland)*

Teacakes - London

Weigh lemon flavoured basic bun dough into 2 oz. (60 gr.) pieces. Mould round and then pin out into circles about 3 in. (8 cm.) in diameter. Place on to baking sheets and wash with egg. When proved, place into an oven at 440° F (227° C). Turn over carefully when half baked and then finish baking.

Tijger Broodjes

Dough

lb	oz		kg	gr
2	4	Flour	1	125
	2	Yeast		60
	3/4	Salt		22
	3/4	Sugar (castor)		22
	1 3/4	Milk powder		50
1	4	Water		625

Mix a smooth dough from these ingredients. Temperature of the dough should be about 77° F (25° C). Let the dough rise for 30 minutes. Meanwhile make a batter with the following:

Paste

lb	oz		kg	gr
	7	Rice flour		200
	3 1/2	Flour		100
	3/4	Yeast		22
	3/4	Sugar		22
	3/4	Oil		22
	14	Water (tepid) (approx.)		435

Mix these ingredients and leave in a warm place. After the dough has risen, weigh into pieces of 2 oz. (60 gr.), mould up round and put them on a baking sheet. After approximately 15 minutes the rolls are brushed with the riceflour paste.

When the rolls are well risen, bake at 446° F (230° C). During the baking the top cracks, this gives the appearance of tiger skin. *(Holland)*

Triestines

lb	oz		kg	gr
	13	Egg		400
	5	Sugar (castor)		150
		Zest of 1 lemon		
	3 1/2	Yeast		100
2	0	Milk (warm) (approx.)	1	
	1 1/2	Malt		45
	1 1/2	Salt		45
5	0	Flour	2	500
2	0	Sultanas	1	
1	0	Peel (orange)		500
	3 1/2	Rum		100
	13	Butter		400

Whisk the egg, sugar and zest to a stiff sponge. Mix the milk, yeast, malt and salt and add to the egg/sugar sponge. Add the flour and mix thoroughly. Work in the butter until the dough ceases to stick. Mix the sultanas, previously soaked in the rum, with the orange peel. Dust with flour and work them into the dough. Leave to ferment and knock back twice with an interval of 40 minutes. Divide the dough into pieces of not more than 13 oz. (400 gr.), mould them round and place them on to tin foil plates or a baking sheet and prove well. Egg wash and sprinkle the tops generously with sugar nibs and bake about 400° F (204° C).

Weggen

lb	oz		kg	gr
2	4	Flour	1	125
	3/4	Salt		20
	1/2	Malt extract		10
	2	Egg		60

lb	oz		kg	gr
	1	Yeast		30
	4 1/2	Butter		140
1	2	Milk (approx.)		560

Make all the materials into a dough at 75° F (24° C). Let it ferment for 1 1/2 hours, knocking it back twice. Weigh at 4 oz. (125 gr.) or 10 1/2 oz. (300 gr.) and mould round. When recovered, re-mould and place on baking sheets and wash with egg.

Allow to prove and cut a cross on top before baking at 380° F (193° C).

(Switzerland)

Wheatmeal Bread

lb	oz		kg	gr
1	12	Wheatmeal		875
	1/2	Butter		15
	1/2	Salt		15
	1	Yeast		30
1	2	Water (approx.)		560

Dough temperature 78° F (25.5° C). Knock back at 1 hour. Scale at 1 1/2 hours. Bake at 450° F (232° C).

Wheatmeal Rolls

lb	oz		kg	gr
1	0	Wheatmeal		500
	1/4	Salt		8
	3/4	Butter		20
	3/4	Yeast		20
	11	Water (approx.)		330

Dough temperature 80° F (27° C). Knock back at 45 minutes. Scale at 1 hour.

Yield at 1 1/2 oz. (45 gr.) - 18
Yield at 2 oz. (60 gr.) - 14

Wheatmeal rolls may be moulded round or in boat shape. They may be washed with slightly salted water and the tops dipped into coarse meal or pinhead oatmeal. Alternatively, they can be egg washed only. Bake at 460-470° F (238-243° C).

Wholemeal Bread

lb	oz		kg	gr
1	12	Wholemeal		875
	1/2	Salt		15

lb	oz		kg	gr
	1/2	Butter or lard		15
	1	Yeast		30
1	4	Water (approx.)		625

Dough temperature 76° F (24.5° C). Knock back at 1 hour. Scale at 1 1/2 hours. Bake at 450° F (232° C). Keep final proof at a minimum.

Wholemeal Cheese Bread

lb	oz		kg	gr
3	8	Wholemeal flour	1	750
	1/2	Salt		15
	2	Compound fat		60
2	4	Water (approx.)	1	125
	1	Yeast		30
	8	Bakers cheese		250

1 hour dough - Temp. 80° F (27° C). Scale 1 lb. (500 gr.) into oblong bread tins. Bake at 400° F (204° C).

Small rolls can be made from this dough. They are egg washed and baked at 420° F (216° C). Very small rolls weighed at 1/2 oz. (15 gr.) are useful for the buffet table. They can be of any shape, plain of fancy.

Yorkshire Teacakes - White

lb	oz		kg	gr
1	12	Flour (strong)		875
	1/2	Salt		15
	3/4	Sugar (castor)		20
	3	Butter		90
	1 1/2	Yeast		45
1	0	Milk (approx.)		500

Dough temperature 80° F (27° C). Knock back at 45 minutes. Scale at 1 hour. Yield at 4 oz. (125 gr.) - 12.

Mould round and after a time for recovery, pin out to about 4 in. (10 cm.) in diameter and place on to baking sheets. Do not wash. When ready bake at 460-480° F (238-250° C).

Yorkshire Teacakes - White, fruited

lb	oz		kg	gr
1	8	Flour (strong)		750
	1/2	Salt		15

lb	oz		kg	gr
	1 1/2	Sugar (castor)		50
	2	Butter		60
	1 1/4	Yeast		35
	13 1/2	Milk (approx.)		400
	6	Currants or sultanas		180

Proceed exactly as for white teacakes. Yield at 4 oz. (125 gr.) - 12.

Yorkshire Teacakes - Wheatmeal

lb	oz		kg	gr
1	12	Wheatmeal		875
	1/2	Salt		15
	3/4	Sugar (castor)		20
	3	Butter		90
	1 1/2	Yeast		45
1	1	Milk (approx.)		530

Proceed as for plain white teacakes. Yield at 4 oz. (125 gr.) - 12.

Yorkshire Teacakes - Wheatmeal, fruited

lb	oz		kg	gr
1	8	Wheatmeal		750
	1/2	Salt		15
	1 3/4	Sugar (castor)		50
	2	Butter		60
	1 1/4	Yeast		35
	14	Milk (approx.)		435
	6	Currants or sultanas		180

Procced as for white teacakes. Yield at 4 oz. (125 gr.) - 12.

VIII. Fritters and Batters

Fritters

Frying Batter

lb	oz		kg	gr
	14	Flour		435
	1/4	Salt		8
	4	Olive oil		125
1	4	Water (tepid) (approx.)		625
	4	Egg whites		125
	1/3	Yeast (optional)		10

Place the sieved flour into a warmed bowl. Pour in the oil, salt and the water in which the yeast (if used) is dispersed. Mix briskly so as to obtain a smooth batter just able to coat the fingers.

Let the batter stand for 3-4 hours in a warm place. Before using fold in gently the stiffly whipped whites.

Beer Frying Batter

lb	oz		kg	gr
1	8	Flour		750
	2 1/2	Egg yolks		75
	1/2	Salt		15
1	3 1/2	Light ale		600
	5 1/2	Sugar (icing)		170
	4	Egg whites		125

Mix all the ingredients except the egg whites. Do not over mix, otherwise the batter will become elastic. Make the batter 3 to 4 hours before it is required. Shortly before use fold in the egg whites beaten to a stiff snow. Depending on the purpose for which the batter is required, the sugar may be omitted; it may also be added directly to the egg whites before whisking.

(Germany)

American Fritters

These fritters are ring-shaped and, when they have been fried, they are coated with cinnamon flavoured sugar. The candied fruits and currants which are incorporated in the batter are first soaked in rum.

The fritters can be eaten as they are or filled with confectioner's custard or raspberry jam.

lb	oz		kg	gr
	10	Milk (approx.)		300
	7	Dairy cream		200
	2 3/4	Yeast		80
	4	Egg yolks		125
	3/4	Salt		10
	3 1/2	Sugar (castor)		100
	7	Chopped candied fruits		200
2	10	Flour	1	300
	3 1/2	Butter		100
	7	Currants		200
	1 3/4	Rum		50

(France)

Carnival Fritters I
Beignets de Carnaval

lb	oz		kg	gr
1	5	Flour		650
	10 1/2	Egg		315
	5 1/4	Butter (melted)		150
	1 3/4	Sugar (castor)		50
		Zest of 1 lemon		
	1/2	Salt		15

(Switzerland)

Carnival Fritters II
Beignets de Carnaval

lb	oz		kg	gr
2	7	Flour	1	200
	2 3/4	Sugar (castor)		80
	7	Egg		200
	3 1/2	Kirsch		100
	1	Salt		30
	3 1/2	Dairy cream		100

Make up the dough as for Viennese Fritters. Mould the dough into round shapes about 1 oz. (30 gr.) in weight and leave to recover. Next shape the pieces into 5 in. (12 cm.) circles. After frying in hot fat, dust the fritters with icing sugar flavoured with vanilla sugar.

(Switzerland)

Carnival Fritters - Graz Style

lb	oz		kg	gr
1	2	Flour		560
	1 1/4	Sugar (icing)		35
	1	Yeast		30
	5	Egg yolks		150
	3 1/2	Butter (melted)		100
	13	Milk (warm) (approx.)		400
	1/8	Salt		4
		Zest of 1 lemon		
		Apricot jam		

Prepare the dough as for Viennese Fritters, but do not add the butter until the knock back. Rest for a short time, before proceeding exactly as for Viennese Fritters.

(Austria)

Choux Rings-Fried - Spritzkuchen

Using recipe 3 *(page 193)*, pipe out rings on to strips of greased greaseproof paper. Turn them upside down into boiling fat and remove the paper. When cooked and cool, roll them in castor sugar flavoured with ground cinnamon.

Alternatively, they can be dipped, while still warm, into a honey glaze.
(Illustration page 318.)

Currant-Puffs - Oliebollen

lb	oz		kg	gr
2	4	Flour	1	125
	2 1/2	Yeast		75
	1/2	Salt		15
	1 1/2	Sugar (castor)		45
	2 1/2	Margarine		75
1	14	Milk (approx.)		935
	1	Zest of lemon		30
1	2	Currants/raisins		560

Mix these ingredients except the currants and raisins to a rather smooth batter that is not too firm. Temperature of the dough should be about 77° F (25° C). After this, mix in the raisins and currants.

Let the batter rise for about 30 minutes. Then fry at 358° F (180° C). The small portions of batter are put into the basket with the aid of two spoons. This job wants a rather skilled hand.

After frying, the golden-brown puffs are dusted with icing sugar.
(Illustration page 318.) *(Holland)*

Cuisses-Dame

lb	oz		kg	gr
1	9	Flour		780
	10 1/2	Sugar		300
	12	Egg		375
	2 1/2	Butter		75
	1/8	Salt		4
	3/8	Baking powder		10
		Zest of 1 lemon		

Cuisses-Dame aux Amandes

lb	oz		kg	gr
2	4	Flour	1	125
1	5	Sugar		650
	9	Butter		270
	7	Blanched almonds		200
	14	Egg		435
	1/8	Bicarbonate of soda		4

Whip the egg and sugar. Add the creamed butter and the zest of lemon and the salt. Finally add the flour sieved with the baking powder.

For the cuisses-dame aux amandes, the almonds are ground with 4 oz. (125 gr.) of egg adding the rest of the materials to make a paste. It is shaped into sticks 3-4 in. (8 cm.) long and $1/3$ in. (1 cm.) thick. Fry until golden brown and toss into fine granulated sugar.

Fritters - Spritzkuchen

lb	oz		kg	gr
1	0	Egg		500
	4	Milk		125
	4	Water		125
	2	Butter		60
	2	Lard		60
	12	Flour		375
	$1/8$	Salt		4
	$1/4$	Sugar (castor)		7

Bring the milk, water, butter, lard, salt and sugar to the boil, then add the flour and cook until the paste leaves the side of the pan. Transfer to a clean bowl and beat in the egg a portion at a time while the paste is warm. Add a little lemon juice and pipe out in rings on to greased strips of paper, then fry in hot fat until golden. To give the finished fritters an attractive shape, a smaller star pipe should be used and the rings should be piped in pairs, one on top of the other, instead of singly. The shape will be improved if the deep fat fryer is covered at first. After frying, drain well and while still slightly warm, dip the fritters into lemon flavoured and coloured fondant and allow the excess to drain away on wires. *(Germany)*
(Illustration page 318.)

Muzen

lb	oz		kg	gr
	8	Flour		250
	2	Sugar (icing)		60
	2	Egg yolks		60
	$1\,3/4$	Egg		50
		Salt		
		Vanilla		
		Rum		

Make all the ingredients into a firm dough. After time for recovery, pin out thinly and use a pastry wheel to cut out 60 diamond shapes 3 in. (8 cm.) long. Fry and dust one side with icing sugar. *(Germany)*

Muzen Almond Puffs - Muzenmandeln

For approx. 4 lb. 6 oz. (2 kg.) after baking:

lb	oz		kg	gr
2	4	Flour	1	125
	9	Sugar		270
1	6	Egg		680
	$1/2$	Baking powder		15
	$1\,3/4$	Marzipan		50
	$4\,1/2$	Butter		140
	$1\,3/4$	Finely chopped candied orange peel		50
	2	Rum		60
	$1/16$	Cinnamon		2
	$1/16$	Salt		2

Sift the flour on to the table and form a bay. Beat the sugar, egg, baking powder and rum until well mixed. Work the marzipan into a smooth paste with a little milk. Soften the butter without warming it. Lightly work the egg mixture, marzipan and flour into a paste and mix in the softened butter.

After half an hour, pin out the paste, cut out with a 'muzen almond' cutter and fry in hot fat until pale golden, constantly agitating with a skimmer. Lastly roll the puffs in cinnamon flavoured sugar.

(Germany)

Pretzel - Choux

With a star tube pipe pretzel shapes with choux paste, on to greaseproof paper. Immerse in hot fat, when the choux will leave the paper. When fried and cool, split them and fill with confectioner's custard. Dust with icing sugar.

(Switzerland)

Rose Fritters - Beignets à la Rose

lb	oz		kg	gr
1	5	Flour		650
	4	Sugar (castor)		125

301

lb	oz		kg	gr
	³/₈	Salt		10
12		Egg		375
14		Dairy cream		435

Lightly beat the sugar and egg together then mix in the cream and flour to make a batter. Leave to stand in a warm place for about an hour and stir before frying. To obtain good fritters, the consistency of the batter is of paramount importance. That is why it is advisable to test it every time so that the fluidity of the batter can be adjusted if necessary. (Differences may arise due to the variable water absorption quality of the flour). Before use, immerse the fritter iron in the fat which should be 356° F (180° C). The batter will adhere to the heated iron. When well fried, leave the fritters to drain. When completely cold, dust with icing sugar. *(France)*

Fried Scones

Using recipe 1 or 2 *(page 311)*, make a smooth dough and pin out carefully to no more than ¹/₂ in. (12 mm.) in thickness. Cut into strips and then into fingers ¹/₂ in. (12 mm.) wide. Drop into boiling fat to cook. Drain and roll into cinnamon flavoured castor sugar.

The fingers can be split and filled with vanilla flavoured whipped dairy cream. Round shapes can be produced and finished in a similar manner.

(Great Britain)

Schenkeli

lb	oz		kg	gr
	14	Flour		425
	2 ¹/₂	Ground almonds		75
	9	Sugar (icing)		280
	3 ¹/₂	Butter		100
	5	Egg		130
	1	Egg yolks		30
	¹/₁₂	Ammonium		2.5

Sieve the flour and make all the ingredients into a dough. Shape the dough into an oblong roll. Cut off pieces and shape them into small rolls about 3 in. (7 cm.) long. Fry to a golden colour in hot fat. After draining, roll in cinnamon flavoured sugar. *(Austria)*

Schenkeli

lb	oz		kg	gr
2	0	Flour	1	
	³/₄	Baking powder		20
1	0	Sugar (icing)		500
	13	Egg		400
	¹/₄	Salt		7
	5	Butter (melted)		150
		Lemon zest		

Whisk the egg, sugar and zest over a gentle heat, then whisk until cold. Sieve the flour, baking powder and salt, then with the melted butter and the sponge make into a dough. After time for recovery, divide into pieces and roll each into finger thick ropes. Cut them into pieces about 3 in. (7-8 cm.) long. Round off the ends and fry in good quality fat.

If desired, a small incision may be made lengthways before frying, to obtain a uniform break. *(Switzerland)*

Shrovetide Fritters for Carnival

lb	oz		kg	gr
1	14	Flour		900
	1 ³/₄	Sugar (icing)		50
	¹/₄	Salt		7
	5	Dairy cream		150
	2	Butter (melted)		60
	10	Egg		300
		Zest of 1 lemon		

Whisk the sugar and egg together and mix with all the other ingredients except the flour. Sieve the flour, add and make up into a fairly firm dough. Allow to rest for a while. Weigh into 1 oz. (30 gr.) pieces and mould up into round balls. Flatten with the hands, dust with flour and stack in batches of six. Pin out by stages until each measures about 7 in. (12-14 cm.) in diameter. Insert a rod in the centre of each fritter and make a three quarter turn. Place the fritter in deep fat at 360° F (183° C). Leave the rod in position until the rosette shape has set, then with another rod free the first and turn the fritter over. Drain and dust with icing sugar.

(Switzerland)

Snow-Balls - Sneeuwballen

lb	oz		kg	gr
	3 1/2	Butter or margarine		100
1	2	Water		500
	7	Flour		200
	14	Egg (approx.)		400
	3 1/2	Currants/raisins		100

Boil the butter or margarine with the water. Then add the flour and stir the mixture until it is quite dry. The latter is of great importance.

Remove from the heat and add the egg in portions, then add the raisins and currants and the batter is ready. Cook in a frying fat at 338° F (170° C), the batter being piped in with the aid of a savoy bag and a pair of scissors.

During the cooking the snowballs increase their volume and they crack. Fry until they are golden-brown.

As soon as they are cooled they are opened and filled with whipped cream. Finally, they are dusted with icing sugar. Snowballs are usually eaten on New Year's Eve. *(Illustration page 318.)*   *(Holland)*

Tobacco Rolls - Tabac enroulé

lb	oz		kg	gr
1	2	Flour		560
	7	Butter		200
	1 3/4	Sugar (icing)		50
	1/8	Salt		4
	5	Almonds		150
	1/8	Cinnamon		4
	3 1/2	Egg		100
		Zest of 1 lemon		

Grind the almonds and sugar. Make all into a stiff paste and let it stand. Pin it out and cut into strips 3 in. (8 cm.) wide. Wrap the strips round greased wooden rollers and fry in deep fat. Spread each coil with raspberry jam and roll into cinnamon flavoured sugar.

Viennese Fritters - Wiener Krapfen

lb	oz		kg	gr
	3 1/2	Butter (melted)		100
1	0	Flour		500
	4	Egg yolks		120
	1 3/4	Sugar (castor)		50
1		Yeast		30
	15	Milk (approx.)		450
		Salt		
		Zest of 1/2 lemon		
		Apricot jam		

Cooking time: 6 to 7 minutes.

Disperse the yeast in a little lukewarm milk, mix with 2 oz. (60 gr.) flour to a paste and leave to ferment. Beat the egg or egg yolks and the sugar to a foam and add gradually the melted butter, salt, lemon zest, flour, the rest of the milk and the ferment. Knead dough thoroughly until it is smooth and fine and leave to prove in a warm place until it has doubled its volume. Knock back and allow to prove again. Roll the dough out to a thickness of about 1/16 in. (3 mm.) and cut out round bases of about 2 1/4 in. (6-7 cm.) in diameter. Water wash the edges of half the bases, pipe a dab of apricot jam in the centres and cover with the rest.

Seal the edges firmly, cover fritters with a floured cloth and leave to prove, but avoid excessive fermentation. Fry the fritters in hot lard, only a few at a time, and when they are nicely browned on one side, turn them over. As soon as they are done, drain them on a sieve and dust with icing sugar.
(Austria)

YEASTED DOUGHS FOR FRYING

These mixtures should be prepared with care, particularly when they are fried in deep fat. Fermented doughs especially should be soft and need developing until they become dry and smooth, as otherwise they could be flaccid and greasy. When making batters, it is important to use the exact quantity of butter required, since the addition of too much butter allows some of the cooking fat to be absorbed by the batter during frying. The normal proportions are one part of butter to five parts of flour. While frying, it is advisable to control the temperature of the cooking fat with a thermometer 347-365° F (approx.) (175-185° C). Either vegetable fat or ground-nut oil is generally used for frying.

Doughnuts

Lemon flavoured plain bun dough is weighed into 1 3/4 oz. (50 gr.) pieces and moulded round, the pieces being placed on to thickly oiled trays. After sufficient proof, they are dropped into oil at 370° F (188° C) and fried. When cool they are rolled into cinnamon flavoured castor sugar. Doughnuts have raspberry jam in the centre. This is accomplished in one of two ways.

1. Moulded pieces are flattened and raspberry jam is piped into the centre. The jam is then carefully enclosed by the dough, the join being carefully sealed to prevent the jam from escaping during frying. The seal is placed downwards on to the oiled tray.

2. Jam is injected into the centre of the doughnut after cooking, by a machine specially designed for the purpose.

Doughnut Rings

Proceed as for doughnuts and when proved, cut the centres out with a plain cutter. When cooked and cool, they are rolled in cinnamon flavoured castor sugar and then dusted with icing sugar.

Doughnut Twists

Using the same dough, weigh pieces at 1 3/4 oz. (50 gr.) each and mould round. When recovered from the moulding, roll out into ropes about 8 in. (20 cm.) long. Fold each one in two, twisting one end to form a corkscrew spiral. Prove, cook and finish as for doughnut rings.

Cream Doughnuts

Weigh plain basic bun dough into 1 1/2 oz. (50 gr.) pieces and mould them round. Make them into boat shapes and place them on heavily oiled trays. Prove and fry as for other types of doughnut. When cool, cut lengthways, just off centre with a sharp knife or a pair of scissors. Pipe a line of raspberry jam inside and finish by piping vanilla flavoured whipped dairy cream with a savoy bag and a star pipe. Dust with icing sugar to finish.

Berlin Doughnuts

Ingredients for 36 (approximately 3 1/2 lb. [1 kg. 150] dough)

lb	oz		kg	gr
1	0	Milk (approx.)		500
	1	Yeast		30
1	10	Flour		800
	2 3/4	Egg yolks		80
	4 1/2	Sugar		140
	5	Butter		150
	1/8	Salt		4
	3/4	Rum		20
		Zest of 1/2 lemon		

Make a ferment with the milk, yeast and a third of the flour. Beat up the egg yolks and sugar warm, remove from heat and continue beating, then add to the ferment with the butter. Mix in the salt, rum and remaining flour and clear the dough.

Weigh at 1 1/2 oz. (45 gr.). Mould round, then flatten and pipe on a spot of apricot, pineapple, raspberry or plum jam. Fold each one up tightly and prove. Fry in deep hot fat. Dust with icing sugar.
(Illustration page 318.) *(Germany)*

Berlin Tongues with a Cream Filling -
Langues de Berlin fourrées

When preparing this sort of fried product, use the same dough as for Berlin doughnuts.

Mould pieces of the dough into elongated shapes, which are left to rise. Next fry and toss in cinnamon flavoured sugar. When they are completely cold, cut the tongues lengthwise and, using a star pipe, fill them with a stiff Russe cream.

Waffles and Wafers

A good quality waffle does not depend solely on a formula, neither is the possession of a costly electric machine an assurance of success.

Successful baking depends on the heat of the iron and the time allowed. Both are critical, for if the waffle takes too long to bake, the flavour is destroyed and it becomes dry. If on the other hand the waffle is under-baked in an iron too cool, then it becomes tough with an unattractive centre.

Waffles should be served at once after baking or their crispness will be lost.

Waffle Batter I

lb	oz		kg	gr
	10	Egg whites		300
	7	Egg yolks		200
	5	Sugar		150
	7 $1/2$	Butter (melted)		225
2	8	Flour	1	250
	$1/2$	Salt		15
2	8	Milk (approx.)	1	250
	3	Baking powder		90

Sieve the dry materials thoroughly. Whip up the yolks and add the milk, then mix carefully with the dry mixture so as to get a smooth batter, free from lumps. Beat in the melted butter and finally fold in the egg whites, that have been whipped to a stiff snow.

Waffle Batter II

lb	oz		kg	gr
2	4	Flour	1	125
	15	Egg whites		450
	13	Egg yolks		390
1	2	Sugar		560
1	7	Butter		700
		Vanilla		

Waffle Batter III

lb	oz		kg	gr
2	4	Flour	1	125
1	8	Egg yolks		750
2	2	Egg whites	1	
	5	Yeast		150
1	8	Sugar (icing)		750
2	10	Butter	1	300
4	0	Dairy cream (whipped)	2	

Cream the butter, sugar and eggs thoroughly. Add the vanilla, then the stiffly whipped whites and finally the flour.

For the yeast waffles prepare a ferment which will be introduced to the mix before the egg whites. Add the cream last.

Use a spoon to deposit the batter on the iron, which has been heated and greased. Close the iron and cook one side after the other. When cooked, they are dusted with icing sugar.

Brussels Waffles I - Gaufres bruxelloises

lb	oz		kg	gr
1	0	Flour		500
	4	Butter		125
	3	Sugar (icing)		100
	$1/2$	Baking powder		15
	7	Egg		200
	$1/8$	Salt		4
		Milk		

Sieve the flour, baking powder and salt. Add the egg and sugar with sufficient milk to make a smooth batter. Finally beat in the warmed butter. Allow to stand in a warm place for 2 hours before baking.

Brussels Waffles II - Gaufres bruxelloises

lb	oz		kg	gr
	10	Flour		300
	2	Butter		60
	1 $1/2$	Sugar (icing)		50
	$1/4$	Yeast		8
	3 $1/2$	Egg		100
	$1/8$	Salt		4
		Milk		

Baking time 4-5 minutes.

Disperse the yeast in a little lukewarm milk, put it in the middle of the flour, add egg, sugar, salt and more milk if necessary, finally add the melted butter, mix and leave to rise for 2 hours. When the dough has doubled in volume bake, using a well greased waffle iron and dust with icing sugar when served.

Cinnamon Waffles - Gaufres à la Cannelle

lb	oz		kg	gr
	10	Flour		300
	4	Sugar		125
	3	Butter		90
	3 1/2	Egg		100
	1/4	Cinnamon		8
	1/8	Salt		4
		A pinch of baking powder		
		Milk		

Baking time 4-5 minutes.

Cream the butter and sugar, add the eggs one at a time, the salt, cinnamon, flour and baking powder, and finally sufficient milk to make a smooth batter. Leave to stand for an hour before baking the waffles in a well greased iron. *(France)*

Cinnamon Waffles

lb	oz		kg	gr
1	0	Butter		500
1	0	Sugar (icing)		500
1	0	Flour		500
	10 1/2	Egg yolks		320
1	0	Egg whites		500
	1/4	Cinnamon		7

Cream the butter adding the egg yolks a little at a time. Add the sugar, flour and cinnamon and mix well. Lastly fold in the egg whites that have been whipped to a stiff snow. Deposit on the waffle iron at once and bake. *(Germany)*

Dairy Cream Waffles

lb	oz		kg	gr
	12	Butter		375
	5	Egg yolks		150
	11 1/2	Egg whites		350
	1 3/4	Sugar (icing)		50
	12	Flour		375
1	0	Dairy cream		500
		Salt		

Beat the egg yolks and butter together until light. Whisk the egg whites and sugar to a stiff snow and fold into the yolk/butter mixture together with the flour and a pinch of salt. Lastly fold in the lightly whipped vanilla flavoured dairy cream. Bake in a well greased waffle iron. While still hot, dust with vanilla sugar and then with icing sugar. *(Germany)*
(Illustration page 355.)

Lille Waffles - Gaufres lilloises

lb	oz		kg	gr
	9	Flour		300
	5 1/2	Butter		175
	4	Sugar (icing)		125
	3	Egg yolks		100
	1/8	Salt		4
		Rum		
		Zest of 1/2 lemon or orange		

Make in the same way as sweet paste, divide into egg-sized pieces, roll into balls, press into hot, greased waffle iron and flatten by hand. Close the iron and bake at good heat. Note: These waffles will stay fresh and crisp if kept in a closed tin.
(France)

Sultan Waffles - Gaufres sultanes

lb	oz		kg	gr
	12	Flour		400
	9	Sugar		280
	4	Egg yolks		125
	5 1/2	Butter		175
	6	Egg whites		185
1	1	Milk (approx.)		500

Baking time 2-3 minutes.

Mix all the ingredients thoroughly and fold in the stiffly beaten egg whites last. Bake very thin in a special iron and fill in pairs with basic butter cream. *(France)*

Vanilla Waffles

lb	oz		kg	gr
	7	Butter		200
	7	Sugar (icing)		200
	8	Egg yolks		250
	11 1/2	Egg whites		350
	13 1/2	Flour		400
		Vanilla		

Cream the butter with the icing sugar and the vanilla and add the yolks a little at a time. Whisk the egg whites to a stiff snow and fold in together with the flour. Bake quickly.

Waffle Dressings

1. Butter and maple syrup.
2. Butter and diluted golden syrup.
3. Buter and honey.
4. Butter, crushed pineapple and un-whipped dairy cream.
5. Butter, crushed strawberry and whipped dairy cream.
6. Butter and jam.
7. Ice cream. *(U.S.A.)*

Butter Wafers

Pin out fine sweet pastry to a thickness of $1/4$ in. (5 mm.). Impress with a wafer roller and cut into pieces $1 \times 1 \, 1/2$ in. (3 × 4 cm.). Bake at 360° F (180° C).

After removing from the oven, spread with hot butter and dust with vanilla sugar. These wafers are served at tea-time.

Marzipan Wafers I

lb	oz		kg	gr
1	0	Marzipan		500
	8	Sugar (icing)		250
	2	Cornflour		60
	6	Egg		180
	2	Milk (approx.)		60
		Vanilla		

Marzipan Wafers II

lb	oz		kg	gr
1	0	Marzipan		500
	8	Sugar (icing)		250
	2	Cornflour		60
	5	Egg whites		150
	2	Milk (approx.)		60
		Vanilla		

Reduce the marzipan with half the egg or egg whites; when smooth add the icing sugar and cornflour. Add the rest of the egg or whites and finally, the milk. Stand the mixing overnight to mature which will increase the pliability when baked.

Stencil in various shapes or spread on to well greased and floured baking sheets and place into an oven at 420° F (216° C).

Half bake, cool and then return to the oven to take on a pleasing colour.

Stencilled circles can be formed into cornet shapes immediately on removal from the oven and then allowed to set on cream horn tins.

The mixture spread on a baking sheet can, when half baked, be cut into rectangles. When baking is completed, the pieces are immediately rolled over wooden cylinders about $3/4$ in. (2 cm.) in diameter to set.

Either of the recipes given can be coloured chocolate.

Parisian Wafers

lb	oz		kg	gr
	8	Flour		250
	5	Sugar (icing)		150
	3 1/2	Egg		100
	2	Butter (melted)		60
	2 1/2	Milk		75
		Orange flower water		
		Lemon zest		

Mix the egg with the sugar and flour. Add the milk, butter, zest and orange flower water and mix to a smooth batter.

Heat a special wafer iron, pour in a spoonful of the mixture, bake at a good heat, then turn the iron to bake the other side. When baking is completed, either roll the wafers immediately over a rolling pin to shape them into cones or alternatively leave them flat. *(France)*

Parisian Cigarettes I

lb	oz		kg	gr
	6	Butter		180
	4	Sugar (icing)		125
	2	Sugar (castor)		60

lb	oz		kg	gr
	6	Egg whites		180
	4	Flour		125
	4	Dairy cream		125

Cream the butter and icing sugar. Lightly whisk the whites and the castor sugar for a very short time, then mix with the butter/icing sugar mixture, fold in the flour and add the cream to make a smooth batter. Using a savoy bag with a plain tube, pipe on to greased baking sheets fairly far apart, shake to make the batter spread a little, then bake at 420° F (216° C). While still hot roll over small, thin cylindrical rods to the shape of cigarettes.

Parisian Cigarettes II

lb	oz		kg	gr
	7	Vanilla sugar		200
	4	Egg whites		120
	3 1/2	Butter		100
	3	Flour		90

Whisk the egg whites to a stiff snow and lightly fold in the sugar, sieved flour and finally the warm, melted butter. Test the mixture by baking off one or two small biscuits on a greased and floured baking sheet. If the biscuit breaks too easily, add a little sieved flour. If too solid, add a little more melted butter. When baked, roll up cigarette fashion.

IX. Baking Powder Aerated Goods

These are goods wholly or mainly aerated by the use of baking powder (Chapter III, Chemical Aeration, *page 38*).

In Great Britain they are generally known as morning goods, a name derived from the past when they were made early enough to be ready for sale when the shop opened in the morning. Scotland is the country where there is the greatest variety of morning goods, fresh and of excellent quality on sale every morning ready for breakfast.

There are two main methods of making powder aerated goods by hand.

1. Sieve the flour and baking powder; rub in the butter finely and make a bay. Into the bay place the sugar and the liquid. Any fruit is placed on the outside of the bay. The sugar is then dissolved and the flour slowly drawn in and all the ingredients mixed to a smooth dough.

2. A large bay is made in the sieved flour and baking powder into which the butter and sugar are placed and creamed well together. The eggs (if any) are mixed in and finally the milk. The flour is then brought in and the whole mixed to a smooth dough.

Either method can be employed if a machine is used.

The flour for powder aerated goods should be of medium strength. A flour too strong will offer too great a resistance to the sudden generation of gas when the product is in the oven, so distorting the shape.

Almond or Hazelnut Buns

Use the recipe for Raspberry Buns but flavour with almond. Either of the methods given above may be used. Scale at 1 $^1/_2$ oz. (45 gr.) for each and mould round and place on to the table smooth side downwards. Flatten slightly and pipe in the centre of each some almond or hazelnut filling. Bring the edge of the dough up to the centre so that the filling is totally enclosed. Make certain that the join is secure before turning them over. Wash with egg and dip into either flaked almonds or hazelnuts according to the nature of the filling. Arrange on to greased baking sheets and bake at 430° F (220° C).

Filling

lb	oz		kg	gr
1	0	Sugar (granulated)		500
1	0	Ground almonds or hazelnuts		500
	5 $^1/_2$	Egg		165
	1	Ground rice		30

Coconut Buns

lb	oz		kg	gr
2	0	Flour	1	
	1 $^3/_4$	Baking powder		50

lb	oz		kg	gr
	8	Butter		250
	8	Sugar (castor)		250
	5	Fine coconut		150
	4	Egg		125
1	5	Milk (approx.)		650
		Almond flavour		

Use any of the methods given. Weigh pieces at 1 $^3/_4$ oz. (50 gr.) each and mould round. Wash with egg and dip into medium desiccated coconut and place on to greased baking sheets. A trellis design is made on the top of each bun by pressing with the back of a knife. Bake at 430° F (220° C).

Coffee Buns

lb	oz		kg	gr
1	4	Flour		625
	1	Baking powder		30
	8	Butter		250
	10	Sugar		300
	2	Coffee infusion		60
	5	Milk (approx.)		150
	4 $^1/_2$	Currants		140

Make into a smooth dough and scale at 1 $^3/_4$ oz. (50 gr.) each. Mould round and arrange on to a baking sheet. Wash with egg and place a split almond in the centre of each. Bake at 420° F (216° C).

Raspberry Buns

lb	oz		kg	gr
2	0	Flour	1	
	1 $^3/_4$	Baking powder		50
	8	Butter		250
	8	Sugar		250
	4	Egg		125
1	2	Milk (approx.)		560
		Raspberry flavour		

Make up as for coconut buns, but dip into fine granulated sugar before placing on to greased baking sheets. Using the finger, make an indentation in the centre of each into which pipe a little raspberry jam. Bake at 440° F (227° C). Alternatively, they may be finished by flattening them after moulding them round, then piping a little raspberry jam in the centre of each. The jam is carefully enclosed by drawing the edge of the circular piece over the top of it and carefully sealing it by pressing with the fingers. The completed bun shape is turned over so that the join is underneath. All are egg washed, dipped into fine granulated sugar and arranged on to a baking sheet. After a slight flattening, a cross is made on the top of each with the point of a knife so that the jam will flow out during baking.

Rice Buns

lb	oz		kg	gr
2	0	Flour	1	
	1 $^3/_4$	Baking powder		50
	4	Rice flour		125
	8	Butter		250
	8	Sugar		250
	4	Egg		125
1	2	Milk (approx.)		560
		Vanilla flavour		

Use either of the methods given. Weigh pieces at 1 $^3/_4$ oz. (50 gr.) each and mould round. Wash with egg and dip into fine sugar nibs. Place on to greased baking trays and flatten slightly. Bake at 430° F (220° C).

Rock Cakes

lb	oz		kg	gr
2	0	Flour	1	
	1 $^3/_4$	Baking powder		50
	10	Butter		300
	10	Sugar		300
	4	Egg		125
	14	Milk		435
	4	Currants		125
	4	Sultanas		125
	2	Cut mixed peel		60
		Zest of lemon		

Use either of the methods given and place out in rocky pieces about 2 oz. (60 gr.) each on to a greased baking sheet. Wash with egg, sprinkle the tops with castor sugar and bake at 440° F (227° C).

Scones

Basic recipes on *page 311*.

Coconut Scones

Use any of the recipes given adding 2 oz. (60 gr.) of fine desiccated coconut. Scale at 12 oz. (375 gr.) and mould round. Pin out to about 8 in. (20 cm.). Wash with egg and dip into medium coconut. Cut into eight pieces and place on to a baking sheet. Bake at 430° F (220° C).

Devon Scones

As for farmhouse scones. After baking, split and pipe in raspberry jam and vanilla flavoured whipped dairy cream.

Farmhouse Scones

Use any of the recipes given. Proceed as for jam scones but instead of washing with egg, dust heavily with flour. Bake at 450° F (232° C).

Finger Scones

Pin out a plain scone dough to a thickness of 1/2 in. (1 cm.) and cut into rectangular pieces. Place on to greased baking sheets and egg wash. After resting for 10 minutes, bake at 440° F (227° C).

These scones can be finished by splitting, spreading with raspberry jam and piping in whipped dairy cream flavoured with vanilla, using a savoy bag fitted with a star pipe.

Fruited Scones

To any of the basic mixes, 4-6 oz. (125-160 gr.) of sultanas or currants can be added.

Jam Scones

lb	oz		kg	gr
2	0	Flour	1	
	1 3/4	Baking powder		50
	4	Butter		125
	2	Sugar (castor)		60
	2	Apricot jam		60
1	3	Milk		590
		Vanilla flavour		

Make a smooth dough and pin out to about 1/2 in. (1 cm.) thick and cut out with a 2 1/2 in. (6 cm.) plain cutter. Place on to greased baking sheets, wash with egg and after about 10 minutes rest, bake at 460° F (238° C).

Orange Scones

Use any of the recipes given, adding 4 oz. (125 gr.) of finely chopped orange peel. Proceed as for jam scones. When baked, glaze with orange flavoured water icing.

Scone Rounds

Scone rounds can be made with white flour or with wholemeal and be either plain or fruited. Any of the following recipes are suitable with the necessary adjustments.

The dough is weighed into 10 oz. (300 gr.) pieces and moulded round. After about 5 minutes they are re-moulded and then pinned out to a diameter of about 7 in. (18 cm.). Place on to baking sheets and cut into four pieces still maintaining the circular shape. Wash with egg and after about 10 minutes, bake at 450° F (232° C). *(Illustration page 389.)*

Scone Recipes

1. Basic

lb	oz		kg	gr
2	0	Flour	1	
	1 3/4	Baking powder		50
	4	Butter		125
	4	Sugar (castor)		125
1	4	Milk (approx.)		625
		Nutmeg - a pinch		

2. Richer mix

lb	oz		kg	gr
2	0	Flour	1	
	1 3/4	Baking powder		50
	5	Butter		150
	5	Sugar (castor)		150
	6	Egg		180
	15	Milk (approx.)		450
		Numteg - a pinch		

3. Richer mix

lb	oz		kg	gr
2	0	Flour	1	
	1 ³/₄	Baking powder		50
	8	Butter		250
	7	Sugar (castor)		200
	2	Egg		60
1	3	Milk (approx.)		590
		Nutmeg - a pinch		

Treacle Scones

Use recipe 1 or 2. Delete the sugar and replace with black treacle. Add ¹/₄ oz. (8 gr.) of mixed spice. Proceed as for jam scones. Bake at 430° F (220° C).

Turnover Scones

Any of the above recipes are suitable. Weigh into 8 oz. (250 gr.) pieces and mould round. After a short time re-mould and pin out to about 8 in. (20 cm.) and cut into four.

Arrange the pieces on a baking sheet and after about 10 minutes place into an oven at 450° F (232° C). Turn them over as soon as they can be moved without damage to the shape and replace in the oven to finish baking.

Alternatively, turnover scones may be baked on the hotplate, turning them when they are half baked.
(Illustration page 389.)

Victoria Scones

Take any of the basic recipes given, using white flour, wholemeal or wheatmeal and proceed as for jam scones, using the same size of cutter.

Victoria scones may be made smaller and when baked and cool they can be split and sandwiched with raspberry jam and vanilla flavoured whipped dairy cream. A finish is given by dusting with icing sugar.
(Illustration page 389.)

Wholemeal or Wheatmeal Scones

Any of the recipes given may be used, replacing the flour with wholemeal or wheatmeal. In recipes 1 and 2, the butter can be increased by an additional 2 oz. (60 gr.). The milk may have to be increased in all three mixes.

Soda Bread - Irish

lb	oz		kg	gr
3	0	Flour (soft)	1	500
	³/₄	Bicarbonate of soda		20
	1 ¹/₄	Cream of tartar		38
	³/₄	Salt		20
	4	Butter or lard		125
	¹/₂	Sugar (castor)		15
2	12	Buttermilk (approx.)	1	375

Sieve the dry ingredients and rub in the fat. Add the rest of the materials and mix lightly without over-working the dough. Weigh into 1 lb. (500 gr.) pieces and mould round; flatten a little and place on to a greased baking sheet or in a greased and floured hoop. Wash with a brine made from 1 oz. (30 gr.) of salt to 1 ¹/₄ lb. (625 gr.) of water. Dust heavily with flour and cut into four without separating the pieces. Bake at 440° F (227° C).
(Illustration page 396.)

Soda Bread - Wheaten

Use the same recipe as for Irish soda bread but replace 1 ¹/₂ lb. (750 gr.) of the flour with wholemeal. The procedure is the same.
(Illustration page 396.)

Soda Bread - Sultana Wheaten

lb	oz		kg	gr
1	8	Flour (soft)		750
1	8	Wholemeal		750
	³/₄	Bicarbonate of soda		20
	1 ¹/₄	Cream of tartar		35
	³/₄	Salt		20
	4	Butter or lard		125
	2	Sugar (castor)		60
	2	Egg		60
2	12	Buttermilk (approx.)	1	375
1	0	Sultanas		500

Make and finish as for Irish soda bread but bake at 420° F (216° C).

Soda Bread - Currant

Use the recipe as above but use all white flour and replace the sultanas with currants. Bake at 420° F (216° C).

Powder Aerated Goods - Baked on the Hotplate

Scotland is the country where one can purchase the greatest variety of hotplate goods. It is usual for the Scottish baker to use a prepared flour for most hotplate goods. It is prepared as No. 3, *page 180*.

The hotplate should be very lightly greased for powder goods unless otherwise directed. The heat depends to a large extent on the sugar content of the product being baked. The greater the amount of sugar, the cooler the temperature.

Irish Soda Farls

lb	oz		kg	gr
3	0	Flour (soft)	1	500
	3/4	Bicarbonate of soda		20
	1 1/4	Cream of tartar		35
	3/4	Salt		20
2	12	Buttermilk (approx.)	1	375

Sieve the dry ingredients and add the buttermilk. Make into a dough with the minimum of mixing. Turn out on to a well floured board because these doughs are so soft, and weigh into pieces of 1 1/4 lb. (625 gr.). Mould round and then pin out to about 10 in. (25 cm.) in diameter and cut into four quarters. Transfer immediately to the hotplate, turning them over when half baked. On removal from the hotplate, stack two high, cover with a clean cloth and allow to 'sweat'.
(Illustration page 396.)

Indian Farls

lb	oz		kg	gr
2	0	Flour (soft)	1	
1	0	Yellow maize meal		500
	3/4	Bicarbonate of soda		20
	1 1/4	Cream of tartar		35
	3/4	Salt		20
2	12	Buttermilk (approx.)	1	375

Proceed as for Irish Soda Farls.
(Illustration page 396.)

Treacle Farls

lb	oz		kg	gr
3	0	Flour (soft)	1	500
	3/4	Bicarbonate of soda		20
	1 1/4	Cream of tartar		35
	3/4	Salt		20
	6	Treacle		180
2	4	Buttermilk (approx.)	1	125

Proceed as for Irish Soda Farls.
(Illustration page 396.)

Wheaten Farls

Use the same recipe as for Irish Soda Farls replacing 2 lb. (1 kg.) of the flour with wheatmeal and adding 4 oz. (125 gr.) of coarse bran. Increase the buttermilk by 2 oz. (60 gr.) and proceed as for Irish Soda Farls.

Scotch Oatcakes

lb	oz		kg	gr
1	12	Medium oatmeal		875
	4	Flour		125
	1/2	Salt		15
	1	Butter		30
	3/4	Bicarbonate of soda		20
1	4	Water (approx.)		625

Rub the butter into the flour and oatmeal. Dissolve the soda in sufficient cold water to make a plastic dough. Scale at 6 oz. (175-180 gr.), mould round and pin out to 1/8 in. (3 mm.) in thickness. Cut into four, bake on the hotplate until nearly cooked, then reverse. Bake until they curl. Place them in a warm spot, or run them into the oven to dry completely.

Scotch Pancakes

lb	oz		kg	gr
2	0	Scone flour 3	1	
	1/4	Salt		8
	2 1/2	Butter (melted)		75
	10	Sugar (castor)		300
	5	Egg		150
1	12	Milk (approx.)		875

Mix the sugar, salt, egg and milk together and add the sieved flour. Pour in the melted butter and beat well. Using a savoy bag and a plain tube, pipe out on to a moderately heated and greased hotplate. Turn over carefully when half baked.

Pikelets
(Known as Crumpets in Scotland)

lb	oz		kg	gr
1	8	Scone flour 3		750
	9	Sugar (castor)		270
	2	Egg		60
	2	Butter (melted) or oil		60
2	4	Milk (approx.)	1	125

Make up as for Scotch pancakes and drop on to a greased hotplate by means of a ladle. Turn over when half cooked.

Potato Scones

lb	oz		kg	gr
1	0	Flour (strong)		500
	1 1/2	Baking powder		45
	8	Butter		250
2	0	Mashed potatoes	1	
	1/4	Salt		8
	10	Cold water (strained from cooked potatoes)		300

Sieve the flour and baking powder and rub in the butter finely. Sieve the cold mashed potatoes and mix in together with the salt and water. Scale at 7 oz. (210 gr.). Mould round, pin out thinly and cut into four. Place on to the hotplate and turn over when half cooked.

Salt Scones

lb	oz		kg	gr
2	0	Scone flour 3	1	
	3/8	Salt		10

lb	oz		kg	gr
	5	Oil		150
	2 1/2	Egg		75
1	2	Milk (approx.)		560

Make a bay in the flour and add the salt, oil, egg and milk. Make into a dough. Proceed as for soda scones.

Soda Scones

lb	oz		kg	gr
2	0	Scone flour 3	1	
	8	Lard		250
	2	Sugar		60
1	5	Milk (approx.)		650

Make into a smooth dough and scale at 8 oz. (250 gr.). Mould round and pin out to about 8 in. (20 cm.) in diameter and cut into four. Place on the hotplate and when half baked turn over to finish.

Welsh Cakes

lb	oz		kg	gr
2	0	Scone flour 3	1	
	9	Butter		270
	5	Sugar (castor)		150
	4	Egg		125
1	0	Milk (approx.)		500
	4	Currants		125
	1	Finely chopped peel		30
		Zest of 1 lemon		

Rub the butter finely into the flour and make a bay. Add the milk, sugar, egg and zest of lemon and mix to a dough, adding the fruit at the last. Pin out not too thick and cut out with a 2 1/2 in. (6 cm.) plain or fluted cutter. Bake on a moderately heated hotplate. Turn over when half baked and finish cooking.

X. Pastries

Sweet Pastry

In Great Britain, the term sweet pastry is given to a short pastry containing sugar. Recipes for the many sweet pastries and fillings are given in the Chapter 'Basic Preparations'.

Africans

Pin out sweet pastry to about $1/8$ in. (3 mm.) thick. Cut out with a 3 in. (7 cm.) round fluted cutter. Using a savoy bag fitted with a star pipe, filled with a viennese mixing *(page 220)*, pipe a circle on each, not too close to the edge and then halving the circle with a piped line. Bake at 400° F (204° C). When cool, fill in each section with jam or jelly of contrasting colours.

Apple Boats

Line small boat-shaped tins with sweet pastry and half fill with the following:

3 parts finely chopped sour apples
1 part chopped stoned raisins
1 part sieved apricot jam
Zest of 1 orange

Moisten the edge of the pastry. Pin out some pastry very thin and cut strips using a fluted pastry wheel. Place these in trellis fashion on the boats. Bake at 400° F (204° C).

Victoria Cheesecakes

Line some deep patty pans about $2 1/2$ in. (6 cm.) in diameter with sweet pastry cut with a fluted cutter. Thumb them into shape so that the pastry just reaches the top edge of the pans. Pipe a little raspberry jam in the bottom of each and three parts fill with the Victoria Cheesecake mixture given on *page 222*. Bake at 400° F (204° C). When cold, spread the top with warm vanilla flavoured fondant in such a way that there is a ring of the filling between the edge of the fondant and the pastry lining. Sprinkle a little finely chopped pistachio nut in the centre.

Mince Pies

Line patty pans with sweet pastry and place some mincemeat in each. Place a pastry lid on top cut with the same size cutter. Bake at 440° F (227° C). Sprinkle with castor sugar immediately on removal from the oven. Alternatively they may be egg washed and sugared before baking, in which case the baking temperature should be a little lower. A recipe for mincemeat will be found on *page 216*. *(Illustration page 319.)*

Pretorias

Pin out sweet pastry to a thickness of about $1/8$ in. (3 mm.) and cut out circles with a 3 in. ($7 1/2$ cm.) plain cutter. Place half of them on a baking sheet. Cut three small holes in triangular formation in the rest of the pieces and place them on another baking sheet. Bake at 400° F (204° C).

When cool they are sandwiched together with apricot jam, placing a pierced circle on a plain one. Dust with icing sugar and pipe different coloured jams or jellies in the holes.

French Puddings
Line some fluted pans with sweet pastry. Fill, just level with the edge of the pans with the following mixture:

lb	oz		kg	gr
	4	Butter		125
	4	Sugar (Barbados)		125
	4	Egg		125
	2 1/2	Rum		75
1	0	Currants		500
1	0	Sultanas		500
	4	Lemon peel (chopped)		125
2	0	Sponge cake pieces (soaked)	1	

Moisten the sponge cake cuttings with sufficient hot milk to break them down. Let them soak for a time and then stir well.

Cream the butter and sugar and add the egg a portion at a time; add the rum and finally the soaked cake. Bake at 350° F (176° C). When cold, mask with vanilla flavoured white fondant and place a neat line of finely chopped roasted almonds across the centre, with a half glacé cherry on each side.

Apricot Tarts
Line deep custard cups with sweet pastry and pipe a little apple conserve in the bottom. Bake at 425° F (218° C). When cold, place half a well drained apricot in each, cut side down and mask with well boiled apricot purée. Place a split almond on the top of each apricot and mask the edge of the tarts with finely chopped pistachio nuts.

Chorley Cakes
These traditional cakes, originating in the Lancashire town of Chorley, are similar to Eccles cakes except that a short pastry made with lard is normally used.

Short pastry-Sausage Rolls *(page 191)* will be suitable and this is pinned out to about $1/_4$ in. (6 mm.) thick and cut out with a 3-4 in. (7-10 cm.) plain cutter. The surface is moistened and the filling is placed in the centre *(page 224)*. The edges of the pastry are drawn over the filling to form a ball which is then flattened. Place on to baking sheets, seam downwards and make three cuts in the centre so that the filling is seen. Bake at 440° F (227° C) for about 15 minutes. Sprinkle with castor sugar immediately on removal from the oven.

Visiting Cards
For this pastry, special tins 16 in. long, 4 in. wide (40 cm × 10 cm.) and turned up $3/_8$ in. (1 cm.) all round are required. They are lined, not too thickly, with sweet pastry and pricked with a fork. A little greengage jam is spread on the bottom after which Victoria Cheesecake mixing *(page 222)* is piped in and spread level. Flaked almonds are sprinkled on top.

When baked at 380° F (193° C) and cooled, they are dusted with icing sugar, the ends are trimmed off and the strip cut into ten pieces.

Bird's Nests
Bake Royal Victoria filling adding one-fifth of its weight in cornflour, in greased savarin moulds, with blocked centres; turn out as soon as baked. The baking temperature is 350° F (176° C). For each pastry, three eggs are required, made by enclosing a small cherry in almond paste, making eggs of three colours. The pastry is brushed with hot apricot purée and masked with carefully roasted thread coconut and three eggs of different colours are arranged in the centre. Set each pastry on a disc of baked sweet pastry cut with a fluted cutter.

▲ Wiltshire and Gloucester Lardy Cakes, p. 283-284   Maids of Honour Tartlets, p. 336 ▼   317

318 ▲ Snow-Balls, p. 303 — Currant Puffs, p. 300
Berlin Doughnuts, p. 304 — Fritters (Spritzkuchen) and Fried Choux Rings, p. 300-301 ▼

▲ Mince Pies, p. 329 (puff pastry), p. 315 (sweet pastry)
Apple Turnovers, p. 337 — Raisin Slices, p. 290 — Palmiers, p. 330 ▼

319

320 ▲ Banbury Cakes, p. 327 — Coventry Puffs, p. 332 — Eccles Cakes, p. 329   Danish Ring, p. 277 ▼

Fruit Tarts

Recipes for large fruit tarts, suitable for desserts, can be found in Chapter XXII 'SWEETS'.

Large Jam Tarts

Line flan tins with sweet paste taking special care that no air is trapped between paste and tin. Fill with the desired amount of jam or curd and bake at 400°F (204°C).

Yorkshire Curd Tarts

Line rather large patty pans with sweet pastry and pipe a little raspberry jam in the bottom of each. Three quarters fill with the mixing given on *page 219*. *(Illustration page 658.)*

Alexandra Cream Tartlets

Prepare and bake exactly as for Victoria Cream Tartlets but put in slightly more filling. When cold, cut a slice from the top, leaving a narrow edge of the filling all round. On top of each tartlet pipe a rosette of whipped dairy cream flavoured with curaçao or chartreuse. Trim the cut slices with a small round cutter and dip the tops into well boiled apricot purée coloured red. Mask the edges with very finely chopped pistachio nuts. Place a circle on each rosette.

Almond Tartlets

Line patty pans with sweet pastry cut with a fluted cutter. Pipe in a little apricot jam and then some French macaroon paste. Place on top a cross made with sweet pastry and bake at 380° F (193° C). Brush with apricot purée. *(Holland)*

Almond Tartlets

Line fluted oval patty pans thinly with rich sweet pastry and pipe a spot of raspberry jam in each. Pipe in frangipane mixture and bake at 370° F (187° C). When cool spread with well boiled apricot purée. Make a caramel by melting 1 lb. (500 gr.) of granulated sugar with a little lemon juice, to a pale amber colour and mixing in 4 oz. (125 gr.) of warmed flaked almonds. Remove from the heat, but keeping it warm, quickly spread over half the surface of each tartlet. Coat the other half with white fondant. Finish with half a glacé cherry. *(Switzerland)*

Almond Cream Tartlets

With a small plain cutter take out circles from frangipane tartlet bases. Brush the pieces with apricot purée and dip into coarse crushed praline croquant. Pipe a whirl of whipped dairy cream in the centre and dust with icing sugar. Replace the tops.

Apple Frangipane Tartlets

Line deep pans with sweet pastry and three quarters fill with apples poached with cloves. Drain the apples well. Cover with frangipane mix and bake at 400° F (204° C). When baked, dust with icing sugar.

Chocolate Cup Tartlets

Proceed as for Walnut Tartlets, but pipe raspberry jam in the bottom. Pipe in chocolate frangipane filling. Bake at 375°F (190° C). When cool spread with chocolate buttercream and insert some strip almonds in the cream and place into the refrigerator. When set, dip into chocolate.

Christmas Tartlets

Line deep fluted pans with sweet pastry and trim off level. Place some mincemeat in the bottom and cover with frangipane mixing. Bake at 380° F (193° C). When cool, dust with icing sugar.

Custard Tartlets

Deep custard cups are necessary. These are lined with sweet pastry cut with a round fluted cutter, taking care that there is no air trapped between the pastry and the cup and making certain that there are no holes in the pastry through which the custard can percolate.

Fill three parts full with custard No. I *(page 238)* and sprinkle the surface with a pinch of ground nutmeg. Place into the oven carefully so that the custard does not spill or the tartlet will be difficult to remove from the pan without breakage. Bake at 440° F (227° C). Do not overbake or the custard will show the fault known as 'wateriness'.

Dutch Apple Tartlets
The same procedure is adopted as for mince pies except that a different filling is used. It will be found on *page 221*.

Fondant Marshmallow Tartlets
Proceed as for Lemon Marshmallow Tartlets, the bulb being placed with a plain pipe. When the marshmallow has set, dip into fondant and pipe a spiral on top. Many colours and flavours can be used for variety, but cream and fondant should match.

Ginger Tartlets
Proceed as for Walnut Tartlets but put ginger crush in the bottom and use chopped preserved ginger instead of walnuts in the mix. Bake at 375° F (190° C). When cool, place a large bulb of marshmallow cream on top and mask with brown sugar. Finish with a piece of preserved ginger.

Golden Tartlets
Line small patty pans with sweet pastry and fill with a mixture of golden syrup and bread crumbs, flavoured with fresh lemon juice.

The mixture should be of just flowing consistency when slightly warm. Bake at 400° F (204° C).

Gooseberry Tartlets
Line some pans with sweet pastry and bake them blind. When cool, brush inside with melted chocolate. Inside place a little sponge cake disc which is masked with apricot purée. Fill with poached gooseberries and mask with a pectin jelly.
(Switzerland)

Grape Tartlets
Line shallow patty pans with sweet pastry cut with a fluted cutter. Pipe in a little frangipane mixture and bake at 380° F (193° C). Brush with white wine. Spread with a mixture of whipped dairy cream into which broken macaroon and melted russe base have been stirred *(page 242)*. The proportion is two parts cream to one part base. Place halves of black and green grapes, which have been brushed with pectin jelly, alternately on each tartlet; pipe a rosette of cream in the centre and top with half a black grape.

Greengage Marshmallow Tartlets
Proceed as for Lemon Marshmallow Tartlets. Pipe on a bulb of vanilla flavoured marshmallow cream using a plain pipe. Pipe a small circle of greengage jelly on top and dust with castor sugar.

Hollandaise Tartlets
Line patty pans with sweet pastry using a plain cutter. Pipe in hollandaise filling. Sprinkle flaked almonds on top and bake at 380° F (193° C). When cold, brush with well boiled apricot purée and when this is set glaze with thin water icing into which some fresh lemon juice is mixed. Return to the oven for a few seconds to set the glaze.

Jam Tartlets
Pin out sweet pastry and cut out with a fluted cutter. Place into patty pans and use the thumbs to press lightly so that there is no air trapped between the pastry and the pan. Pipe in jam of the desired flavour and bake at 430° F (220° C). Orange or lemon curd can be used.

Lemon Marshmallow Tartlets
Line deep sharp edged pans with sweet pastry and pipe a little lemon curd in each, on top of which pipe frangipane mix. Bake at 375° F (190° C). When cool, pipe a bulb of lemon flavoured and coloured marshmallow cream and top with a round disc of chocolate. This is made by spreading

couverture on to greaseproof paper and when set, spreading thinly on top again and marking with a comb scraper. Cut out with a small plain cutter.

Lemon Meringue Tartlets
Line patty pans with sweet pastry using a fluted cutter and bake them blind. Place lemon curd in the bottom and, using a star tube, pipe a rosette of Italian meringue large enough to cover the top. Flash at 450° F (232° C).

Maraschino Tartlets
Line shallow fluted patty pans, oval in shape, with sweet pastry. Pipe in a little cherry jam, on top of which pipe frangipane mixture. Bake at 370° F (187° C). Cut the top of the tartlets halfway, to form a lid, under which, with a star tube, pipe pink buttercream flavoured with maraschino. Dust with icing sugar and place half a maraschino cherry in the centre of the cream.

Nougatine Tartlets
Prepare pans as for Nut Tartlets. Pipe in a little apricot jam and cover with hollandaise mixing. Cover half of the top surface with flaked almonds and bake at 370° F (187° C). When cool, mask the plain half of the top with apricot purée and cover it with pink fondant. *(Switzerland)*

Nut Tartlets
Line sharp edged pans with sweet pastry and trim off the edges neatly. Pipe a little raspberry jam in the bottom of each and sprinkle with chopped nuts which may be walnuts, hazelnuts or almonds. Pipe in hollandaise mixture. Sprinkle the top with the same type of chopped nuts and bake at 380° F (193 C). After baking, glaze with apricot purée. *(Switzerland)*

Orange Marshmallow Tartlets
Proceed as for Lemon Marshmallow Tartlets but use oval pans. Pipe orange coloured marshmallow cream, flavoured with orange juice on top using a star pipe. Finish with a finger shape strip of orange almond paste on which a pattern has been impressed with a patterned rolling pin.

Oxford Apple Tartlets
Proceed as for Apple Boats but use small deep pans. Three parts fill with the following:

3 parts finely chopped sour apples
1 part sponge cake crumbs
1 part sieved apricot jam
Zest of lemon
A little ground cinnamon

Pin out some sweet pastry very thinly and cut strips with a fluted pastry wheel. After dampening the edges of the tartlets, place four strips across to form an Oxford square, so that each strip lies across the end of the one before. Cut out very small fluted circles and place one in the centre of each square. Bake at 400° F (204° C). Whilst still hot, brush the centre circle with apricot purée.

Peach Tartlets
Line some pans with sweet pastry and half bake them. Pipe in some sponge mixture *(page 196)* and finish baking. When cool, brush with apricot purée and place half a peach on each. With piping chocolate, pipe a trellis pattern on the peach around which pipe a ring of buttercream. Mask the edge of the cream with roasted nib almonds. *(Switzerland)*

Pineapple Cup Tartlets
Line some deep pans with sweet pastry and bake blind. Brush the insides with well boiled apricot purée and one third fill with pineapple crush. Pipe in fresh whipped dairy cream leaving enough room to cover with pineapple flavoured and coloured fondant.

Pineapple Tartlets
Proceed as for Grape Tartlets. When cool, brush with well boiled apricot purée and place a pineapple ring on top with a cherry in the centre. Cover with pectin jelly.

Praline Tartlets

Line some patty pans with sweet pastry and bake blind. Place inside some broken sponge cake sprinkled with vanilla liqueur. Pipe a bulb of praline buttercream on top and when set dip into chocolate. Finish with a whirl of buttercream on top and sprinkle with a few lightly roasted flaked almonds. *(Switzerland)*

Punch Tartlets

Line custard cups with sweet pastry and fill with a mixture of sponge crumbs, chopped peel, raisins and cherries, cocoa powder and milk. Bake at 380°F (193°C).

When cold spread with confectioner's custard and mask with chocolate vermicelli. Pipe a spiral of white cream on the top and place half a glacé cherry at the side. *(Germany)*

Quayaquil Tartlets

Take baked sweet pastry cases and pipe in some raspberry jam. Fill with chocolate cream and spread level. On top of each place four small chocolate rolls. Place two narrow strips of paper at right-angles to the rolls and dust with icing sugar. Remove the paper strips carefully. *(Switzerland)*

Rice Tartlets

Using patty pans, proceed as for jam tartlets. Pipe a spot of raspberry jam in the base of each and add sufficient filling *(page 220)*. Bake at 420°F (216°C). When cold, spread with vanilla flavoured white fondant.

Victoria Basket Tartlets

Use small rather deep oval tins and proceed exactly as for Victoria Cream Tartlets. When cool, slice off the tops, mask them with apricot purée and finely chopped roasted almonds. Cut them in half and set aside. Make the handles from a sweet paste, baking them on paper so that they do not take on too much colour. Alternatively, strips of angelica can be used. Mask the top of the tartlets with hot apricot purée and pipe a rosette of whipped dairy cream at each end. Cut the masked slices in half to make lids and set them in position, tilted against the cream. Place a handle in each, pressing the ends into the filling.

Victoria Crown Tartlets

Proceed exactly as for Victoria Cream Tartlets and when cold cut a piece off the entire top of each. Mask half of these with pale green fondant and the other half with chocolate fondant. When set, cut each into six segments. Mask the top of the tartlets with red coloured apricot purée and pipe a rosette of vanilla flavoured whipped dairy cream in the centre of each, placing a half glacé cherry on top. Arrange the segments alternately, chocolate and green, sloping against the cream, so that the base of each segment is just inside the outer edge of the tartlet, giving the effect of an opening flower with the cream and cherry showing in the centre. Mask the edge with finely chopped roasted almonds.

Walnut or Frangipane Tartlets

Line small, rather deep custard cups with sweet pastry and pipe into each a little apricot jam. Pipe in frangipane mixture and bake at 360°F (182°C). Next day, with a small plain cutter, take out the centres, cutting right down to the base. In the cavity sprinkle a little chopped walnut. Dust with icing sugar and pipe a whirl of coffee buttercream on top of the chopped walnut. Spread the top of the cut-out pieces with cream and sprinkle with chocolate shavings. Dust then very lightly with icing sugar and replace on top of the cream whirl.

Walnut Marshmallow Tartlets

Proceed as for the Lemon Marshmallow Tartlets. Pipe a bulb of vanilla flavoured marshmallow cream on top and when set dip into chocolate couverture leaving a ring of white cream showing at the base. Top with half a walnut.

Walnut and Raisin Tartlets
Line some shallow patty pans with sweet pastry using a fluted cutter. Sprinkle the bottoms with chopped raisins and walnuts. Pipe in frangipane mixing and bake at 375° F (190° C). When cool, brush with well boiled apricot purée and mask with pale yellow fondant flavoured with muscatel.

St. Galler Törtli
Line patty pans with Linz pastry. Pipe in a little macaroon paste flavoured with lemon juice and zest. Cover with a lid of Linz pastry and bake at 380° F (193° C).

When baked turn upside-down. When cool brush with apricot purée, mask with chocolate fondant and finish with a half walnut. *(Switzerland)*

Venetian Chocolate Tartlets
Line some shallow patty pans with sweet pastry. Pipe in a spot of apricot jam and then three quarters fill with frangipane mixture. Bake at 370° F (187° C). When cool, pipe a neat spiral on top with a light ganache cream flavoured with rum. Dust with cocoa powder. In the centre of each place a chocolate cut-out circle that has been dusted with icing sugar.
(Switzerland)

Victoria Cream Tartlets
Line small custard cups with sweet pastry, pipe a little apricot jam in the bottom of each and half fill with Victoria Cheesecake filling. Bake at 400° F (204° C). When cold, brush the edges with apricot purée and mask with broken macaroon from which the crumbs have been sieved. Take a small plain cutter 1 in. (2 ½ cm.) in diameter and cut out the centre of the filling. Fill the hole with whipped dairy cream flavoured with maraschino and replace the cut piece on top. Dust with icing sugar, leaving the yellow sides of the cut piece showing.

Scottish Shortbread

Shortbread
Basic mixing

lb	oz		kg	gr
4	0	Flour	2	
2	0	Butter	1	
1	0	Sugar (castor)		500
	2	Marzipan		60

The butter, sugar and marzipan are mixed together without creaming and then mixed with half the flour. The rest of the flour is mixed in gradually. The shortbread will become plastic by thorough mixing, but it should not be allowed to become heated. If necessary a little egg may be added if the flour is dry. Leave for a time before working off.
(Illustration page 389.)

Decorated Shortbreads
Shortbreads may be decorated for special occasions such as, New Year's Day, Christmas or for a presentation. Decoration is effected by running in a mixture of royal and water icing into the centre. When dry, a neat border is piped with royal icing. Modelled roses or cut out flowers, preserved fruits, run-out motifs can be used for further decoration and an inscription is piped. Here are examples of inscriptions that can be used:

'Frae Bonnie Scotland'
'Frae the Land O'Cakes'
'For Auld Lang Syne'
'A Guid New Year Tae Ane An' A''
'Should Auld Acquaintance Be Forgot'
'Lang May Your Lum Reek'
'Guess Wha Frae'

Pitcaithly Bannocks
To every 1 lb. (500 gr.) of basic shortbread, add 2 oz. (60 gr.) of finely chopped citron peel and 2 oz. (60 gr.) of nibbed almonds. Weigh into 10 oz. (300 gr.) pieces, mould round and pin out to about 9 in. (23 cm.) in diameter. Dock well. Traditionally the edges should be pinched with the fingers,

but they may be pressed into moulds. Bake at about 370° F (187° C). Sprinkle with castor sugar after baking.

Shortbread Biscuits
See Chapter XVI, *page 498*.

Duchess Fingers
To each 1 lb. (500 gr.) of basic shortbread add 1 oz. (30 gr.) of nibbed almonds and 1 oz. (30 gr.) of praline paste. Proceed as for Shortbread Fingers.

Loundon Fingers
To each 1 lb. (500 gr.) of basic shortbread add 1 oz. (30 gr.) of chopped preserved ginger. Proceed as for Shortbread Fingers.

Blocked Shortbread
Press the shortbread into a carved wooden block and turn out on to a paper lined baking sheet. Dock well and bake at 370° F (187° C) for the larger sizes and at 400° F (204° C) for the smaller sizes. Great care must be taken over baking.

Shortbread Fingers
Using the basic shortbread mixing, pin out on to a baking sheet to about ³/₄ in. (2 cm.) thick. Place a stick at one end to keep it in position. Dock well and bake at 370° F (187° C). Cut into fingers as soon as it leaves the oven and dust with castor sugar. Separate when cold.

Tree Shortbreads
Roll out basic shortbread to a rope about 1 ³/₄ in. (4 ¹/₂ cm.) in diameter. Brush with egg and roll into demerara sugar. Cut slices about ³/₄ in. (1 cm.) thick and place them, cut side down, on to baking sheets. Pipe a little macaroon paste in the centre and bake at 370° F (187° C).

Walnut Shortbreads
To each 1 lb. (500 gr.) of basic shortbread add 1 ¹/₂ oz. (50 gr.) of finely chopped walnuts. Proceed as for Shortbread Fingers.

Puff Pastries
Recipes for puff pastries and fillings can be found in Chapter VI, 'Basic Preparations'.

Puff pastry toughens during manipulation and it is necessary to allow puff pastry pieces to recover from the manipulation for about 30 minutes before they are baked. If this is not done the pastries will be distorted in shape during baking. *(Illustration page 478.)*

Accordions
Prepare the puff pastry as for Parisian pastries, trimming both ends. Cut off narrow strips about ¹/₄ in. (7 mm.) wide and place them, cut side down, on to well greased baking sheets not too close together. After a sufficient rest, bake at 420° F (216° C). When half baked, turn them over carefully and finish baking. Remove from the baking sheet immediately on baking, or the caramelized sugar may cause them to stick. When cold, pipe kirsch flavoured whipped dairy cream in the form of a square on half of them, and fill in the square with pineapple crush mixed with well boiled apricot purée. Cover with the remaining pieces. When the cream is quite firm dip the two ends in chocolate.

Almond Cheesecakes
Prepare patty pans and fill with almond cheese cake filling *(page 224)*. After allowing sufficient rest, bake at 400° F (204° C). During baking the mixture should lift like a disc on the top of the pastry.

Almond Rolls - Amandelbroodjes
Roll out puff-pastry into a slice ¹/₁₂ in. (2 mm.) thick. Divide this into strips of 4 in. (10 cm.) wide and moisten. Apply a roll of almond paste softened with egg with a savoy bag, lengthwise along the centre of each slice. Fold the dough over the filling in such a way that the sides touch. Cut the slices into rolls 4 in. (10 cm.) wide. Moisten and dust thickly

with sugar. Put the rolls on a baking-sheet with the ends of the rolls touching each other. After a rest, bake at an oven temperature of 392° F (200° C).

Towards the end of the baking process, brush the rolls with water icing and place in an oven at 482° F (250° C) for the icing to set.

The almond rolls should have a flaky crust with a soft filling. *(Holland)*

Almond Twists

Pin out full puff pastry to $1/8$ in. (3 mm.) in thickness and approximately 15 in. (37 cm.) wide. Over two thirds of the surface spread with almond mixture and fold into three to give a strip 5 in. (12 $1/2$ cm.) wide. Cut slices $3/4$ in. (2 cm.) in thickness and give two twists. Place them together on the table and wash with egg and sprinkle with streusel. Arrange on to baking sheets. Bake at 420° F (216° C). When cool dip the ends in chocolate.

Apple-Balls - Appelbollen

For the filling, use cooking apples of equal shape and size. Peel these apples and remove the cores (drill core out while apple remains round). Roll the puff-pastry to about $1/12$ in. (2 mm.) thick. For each apple use about 2 $1/4$ oz. (70 gr.) of pastry.

Divide the piece of pastry into 6 in. (15 cm.) squares. Moisten and, after having filled the apples with a mixture of sugar, cinnamon and lemon peel, fold the pastry around the apples by squeezing together the 4 points. Now turn the apple-ball upside-down with the fold on the baking sheet; brush with egg. After a rest, brush again and bake. Oven temperature 482° F (250° C).

If so desired the apples could be filled in advance, and the holes closed with a piece of almond paste on both sides.

During and after the baking, the apples should keep their shape and remain white. *(Holland)*

Apricot Twists

Pin out puff pastry to about $3/16$th in. (6 mm.) and cut into fingers about 4 by 1 $1/2$ in. (10 × 4 cm.). Give them one twist before placing them on to baking sheets. Press a small round cutter halfway through the pastry at each end. Wash with egg and bake at 440° F (227° C). When baked, gently press in the two circles at either end and fill with apricot or peach jam *(Turkey)*

Banbury Cakes

Pin out puff pastry to about $1/8$ in. (3 mm.) thick and cut plain circles. Pin these out a little thinner and oval in shape. Place some filling in the centre of each. Fold so that the filling is enclosed and the shape is oval. Turn them over with the fold underneath and run the rolling pin over then so that all are of equal thickness. Wash with a beaten mixture of egg whites and water and dust liberally with sugar. Make three diagonal cuts on top and place on to lightly greased baking sheets. After a rest bake 420° F (216° C).
(Illustration page 320.) *(Great Britain)*

Butterflies - Papillons

Prepare puff pastry as for Palmiers. When the strip has been formed indent the middle with the rolling pin. Cut off pieces $3/8$ in. (1 cm.) wide and place cut side down on to greased baking sheets. Open the ends of each strip outwards a little. Bake at 380-400° F (193-204° C), turning after 5-6 minutes to prevent over-caramelization on one side. *(France)*

Coffee Rings

Pin the puff pastry to $1/8$ in. (3 mm.) thick and cut out with a plain cutter. Take the centre out with a smaller cutter. After a rest, bake at 460° F (238° C) for about 10 minutes. When cool, split and sandwich with coffee flavoured whipped dairy cream. Dip the top in coffee flavoured fondant. The dipping can be done first and the fondant allowed to set before the creaming is done.

Coques or Langues de Bœuf

Pin out puff pastry to $1/8$ in. (4 mm.) in thickness and cut out circles 2 in. (5 cm.) in diameter with a fluted cutter. Sprinkle the table with granulated sugar, lay the pastry circles on top and pin them to an oval shape. Place on to a baking sheet with the sugar coated side uppermost. Bake at 400° F (204° C).

(France - Switzerland)

Coronets

Proceed as for Square Jam Tarts, but instead of egg washing spread the surface with royal icing mixed with a little water and cornflour. Cut into squares and place a cross made from two thin strips of puff pastry from corner to corner on each. Bake at 380° F (193° C). When cool, split and pipe inside a little raspberry jam and then some whipped dairy cream.

Coventry God Cakes

These pastries are made exactly as for Coventry Puffs but with two important differences:

1. Jam is not used. They are filled liberally with mincemeat.
2. When folded they are not turned over, but are washed and sugared and then baked with the folds uppermost.

They can be made in all sizes.

Cream Fans

Pin out virgin puff pastry to about $1/16$ in. (2 mm.) in thickness and cut strips 12 in. (30 cm.) wide. Wash with water and dust well with castor sugar. Roll up as for swiss roll. Cut pieces about $1/4$ in. (5 mm.) wide and place, not too close together, cut side down on a greased baking sheet. With a sharp knife make a clean cut from the centre to the edge where it has been sealed. Allow to rest for a time and bake at 420° F (216° C) turning over when half baked. When cold, sandwich in pairs with whipped dairy cream and dust lightly with icing sugar.

Alternatively they may be left undusted and decorated with a rosette of cream at the point and topped with a small strawberry or other fruit.

Cream Horns

Pin out puff pastry cuttings very thinly and cut into strips about 16 in. (40 cm.) long and 1 in. (2 $1/2$ cm.) wide. Wash lightly with water. Take one strip at a time and fasten one end to the tip of a cream horn tin. Rotate the tin in such a way that the pastry covers the tin, each turn overlapping the previous one. At the top end, the strip is given a twist making a neat finish with the end tucked underneath. Wash with egg whites and dust with castor sugar. Bake at 400° F (204° C) and remove from the tin whilst still warm. The horns are finished by piping in some raspberry jam and filling with whipped vanilla flavoured dairy cream using a savoy bag and a star pipe.

Cream Oysters

Pin out some full pastry to about $1/8$ in. (3 mm.) in thickness and cut out with a $1 1/4$ in. (3 cm.) plain cutter. Cover the table top with castor sugar and on it pin out the pieces to an oval shape about 3 in. (7 $1/2$ cm.) long and $1 1/4$ in. (3 cm.) wide. Turn them over during rolling so that both sides are covered with sugar. Arrange on to greased baking sheets. Bake at 420°F (216° C). When cool fill with lemon curd and whipped dairy cream.

Cream Rolls

Provide a number of metal tubes 10 in. (25 cm.) long and $3/4$ in. (2 cm.) in diameter. Pin out puff pastry cuttings thinly and cut strips 14 in. (35 cm.) long and 1 in. (2 $1/2$ cm.) wide. After dampening the edges of the strips, twist along the tubes overlapping the paste a little, moistening the end of the strip to ensure adhesion. Run a knife along the tubes to ensure that they are all the same length, then divide each roll into two. Wash the tops with white of egg and water and dust with castor sugar. After a rest bake at

400° F (204° C). Remove while still warm. When cool, pipe in vanilla flavoured whipped dairy cream. To make certain that they are full, pipe in at both ends.

Crescents

Pin out puff pastry to a thickness of about $1/16$ in. (2 mm.) and cut into strips about $3\frac{1}{2}$ in. (9 cm.) wide. Brush the edges with water and place a rope of filling along the middle. Enclose the filling with the pastry and egg wash. Dust with castor sugar. Cut into pieces about 4 in. (10 cm.) long and place them, crescent shape, on to baking sheets. Bake at 420° F (216° C).

The filling is composed of a mixture of sultanas, currants, nib almonds, apricot or peach jam, flavoured with cinnamon.

(Turkey)

Cushions

Proceed as for Windmills but do not cut to the centre, instead bring each corner to the centre and then pin out to the original size. Wash with egg whites mixed with a little water and dust with castor sugar. After a rest, bake at 420° F (216° C) for about 15 minutes. When cool, pipe a thin cross with red jelly, from corner to corner, and finish the centre with a rosette of whipped dairy cream.

Eccles Cakes

Proceed as for Banbury Cakes but keep the pastry pieces round. Place some filling in the centre *(page 217)* enclose so that the shape is round when finished. To obtain uniformity of size, place each one fold uppermost in a plain ring of the desired size and flatten gently with the end of the rolling pin. Finish as for Banbury Cakes. *(Illustration page 320.)* *(Great Britain)*

French Pastries

Spread castor sugar on the table and on it pin out full puff pastry to about $1/10$ in. (3 mm.) in thickness and into a 20 in. (50 cm.) square. Turn the pastry so that both sides are covered with sugar. Starting at the top, fold over a $2\frac{1}{2}$ in. (6 cm.) piece, and then fold again and then once more. This will bring the folding to the centre. Starting at the bottom repeat this so that the two folds meet in the middle. From this folded strip, cut $1/4$ in. (7 mm.) slices. Dredge all of them with castor sugar and place half of them on to greased baking sheets cut side down. Take each of those remaining and turn them inside out so that the outer edges run down the centre. Give each one a twist and arrange on well greased baking sheets. These are the tops. Bake all at 400° F (204° C). When cool, sandwich with raspberry jam and whipped vanilla dairy cream.

Goldfish

Small fish shaped vol-au-vent cases can be made, using the appropriate cutters. After baking and when cool, the shapes can be filled with confectioner's custard, an eye being made with a small circle of cherry. The goldfish is finished with a pectin glaze.

Larger goldfish can be made when the scales can be simulated with mandarin orange segments, placed on the custard.

Greengage Cannons

Pin out puff pastry to a thickness of $1/16$ of an in. (2 mm.) and cut into rectangles 5 in. by 4 in. ($12\frac{1}{2} \times 10$ cm.). In the centre of each, place a good teaspoonful of firm greengage jam. Damp the shorter edges of the pastry pieces and fold them over the jam so that there is an overlap of about an inch. Press down and turn them over, setting them close together in rows, and should the edges not be square, trim them with a knife. With a small piece of bent metal, cut a 'V' shaped piece out of each end. Wash with a beaten mixture of egg whites and water and dust liberally with castor sugar. Place on to lightly greased baking sheets and, after a rest, bake at 400° F (204° C)

Mince Pies

Pin out puff pastry to about $1/8$ in. (3 mm.) in thickness and cut out circles with a plain or fluted cutter. Pin out the cuttings to a similar thickness and cut an equal number of circles which are placed on a baking sheet.

Wash these with water and place mincemeat in the centre. Cover with the circles first cut out and press down well all round. Wash with egg, dredge with castor sugar and make a neat cut in the centre. Allow to rest for 30 minutes and bake at 420° F (216° C) for about 15 minutes.

Alternatively the pies may be sprinkled with castor sugar immediately on removal from the oven or with icing sugar when they are cool.
(Illustration page 319.)

Palmiers

Reduce full puff pastry to about $3/16$ in. (4 mm.) thick. Cut into lengths 12 in. (30 cm.) wide. Brush with water and dredge with castor sugar. Fold the two long edges to the centre and wash the dry surface with water and dredge with castor sugar. Fold the two long edges again to the centre leaving a gap to allow for the final fold over. From the strip thus formed, cut pieces about $1/4$ in. (7 mm.) in thickness. Place them, cut side down, on to well greased baking sheets. Bake at 380-400° F (193-204° C). Turn over when partly baked and remove from the baking sheets immediately on baking. They may be sandwiched in pairs with cream.
(Illustrations pages 110, 319, 478.)

Parisian Pastries

Pin out full puff pastry to a thickness of $1/4$ in. (7 mm.). Brush over well with water and fold into three so that there is a strip of pastry $3/4$ in. (2 cm.) thick and $3 1/2$- 4 in. (9-10 cm.) wide. Cut the strip in half and from one piece trim the long edge that is not a complete fold. Cut off slices $3/4$ in. (2 cm.) wide, twist them in the middle and place, cut side down, on to well greased baking sheets. These are the tops. Cut away both long edges of the other piece and then cut slices the same thickness as the tops, placing them cut side down on other well greased baking sheets. These are the bottoms. Because the pieces expand outwards instead of upwards, the pieces must not be too close on the trays. Bake at 420° F (216° C). When cool, a little raspberry jam is piped on the bases, followed by a rosette of vanilla flavoured dairy cream on to which the tops are placed. The pastries are finished by dusting with icing sugar.

Pastry Leaves

Pin out full puff pastry to about $1/8$ in. (3 mm.) thick and cut out with a leaf shaped cutter. Spread the tops of each with royal icing mixed with a little corn flour and water. Pipe the veins on the leaves with red piping jelly. Bake at 420° F (216° C). When cool, split and fill with raspberry jam and whipped dairy cream.

Puits d'Amour

Pin out puff pastry to $3/16$ in. (4 mm.) thick and cut out rounds with a $2 1/2$ in. (6 cm.) plain cutter. Leave half of them as they are; cut out the centre of the others with a 2 in. (5 cm.) plain cutter. Moisten the edges of the round bases with water and place the rings on the top. Brush with egg and bake at 420° F (216° C). When cold, dust with icing sugar and fill with red currant jelly. *(France)*

Red Currant Crescents

Pin out puff pastry to $3/16$ in. (4 mm.) thick, and cut into oblongs $6 \times 2 1/2$ in. (15 × 6 cm.). Spread down the middle with red currant jelly and brush one end with egg. Roll up, shape into crescents and place on to baking sheets. Wash with egg, sprinkle with coarsely chopped almonds and sugar nibs and bake at 400° F (204° C).
(Austria)

Venetian Shutters

Pin out puff pastry to about $3/16$ in. (4 mm.) thick and cut into rectangles. Place on each some thin slices of apple in a shutter formation. Dust with castor sugar and after sufficient rest, bake at 420° F (216° C). When cool, dust with icing sugar and glaze the apple with pectin jelly. *(Switzerland)*

Victorias

Roll out puff pastry to 1/8 in. (3 mm.) thick. Cut out with a 7 in. (18 cm.) plain round cutter. Put the circles side by side and moisten them with water, and spread them with Victoria batter. Recipe for the Victoria batter:

lb	oz		kg	gr
1	2	Ground almonds		500
1	2	Sugar (granulated)		500
	1	Lemon peel		30
		Egg white		

Mix the ingredients carefully with so much egg white that the consistency of the mixture is not too firm and so that the batter can easily be applied. Put the circles with the victoria batter added to them on a baking sheet. After a rest, bake at 366° F (186° C). Towards the end of baking, dust with icing sugar. When cool decorate with whipped cream and fruits. *(Holland)*

Windmills

Pin out virgin puff pastry to about 1/8 in. (3 mm.) thick and cut into squares. Make four cuts in each from the corners but not quite to the centre. Moisten the centre and fold four alternate points to the centre which is pressed to make a good seal. From the cuttings, cut very small thin circles with a fluted cutter and place one in the centre of each windmill. Wash with a mixture of egg whites and water and dust with castor sugar. After a rest, bake at 420° F (216° C), for about 15 minutes. When cool, pipe a rosette of dairy cream in the centre.

PUFFS

Almond Puffs

Pin out full puff pastry to about 1/4 in. (6 mm.) thick. Cut out with a fluted cutter. Wash lightly with egg and dip the tops into nibbed almonds. Arrange on a baking sheet and bake at 380° F (193° C). When cool they are split and filled with raspberry jam and whipped vanilla flavoured dairy cream.

Caramel Cream Puffs

Pin out puff pastry cuttings quite thin and cut strips with a fluted pastry wheel. Damp them with a little water and wind them round well greased metal cylinders. Place a small round fluted disc on the top and egg wash. After a sufficient resting time bake at 400° F (204° C). When cool, fill with caramel flavoured whipped dairy cream. *(Switzerland)*

Cherry Puffs

From virgin puff pastry 1/8 in. (3 mm.) thick, cut plain circles with a 3 1/2 in. (9 cm.) cutter. Wash with water and fold the edges of the pieces slightly to the centre so that squares are formed. Rest for at least 30 minutes, egg wash and bake at 440° F (227° C) for about 15 minutes.

When cool, brush the centres with well boiled apricot purée and fill with poached fresh cherries or, if out of season, canned cherries and cover with a quick-set pectin glaze. Whatever cherries are used, make certain that they are stoned.

Currant Puffs

Take full puff pastry and during the sixth half turn sprinkle with currants. Pin out to 1/4 in. (5 mm.) in thickness keeping the sides as square as possible. Wash with egg and sprinkle with castor sugar, then cut into squares or oblongs. Bake at 410° F (210° C).

Coffee Puffs

Pin out puff pastry to 1/16 in. (2 mm.) thick and cut out circles with a fluted cutter. Pin these circles out on castor sugar to an oval shape. Place on to greased baking sheets. From the centre of half of them cut three small holes. After a rest, bake at 450° F (232° C) for about 10-12 minutes.

When cool, sandwich in pairs with coffee flavoured whipped dairy cream. Where the cream shows through the holes, pipe small rosettes with the same cream and top with a little finely chopped pistachio nut.

Coventry Puffs

Pin virgin puff pastry or puff pastry cuttings to about $1/16$ in. (2 mm.) thick and cut circles out with a 5 in. (12 $1/2$ cm.) plain cutter. Wash the edges with water and pipe in some raspberry jam just off centre. Fold over one edge to form the side of an equilateral triangle; the opposite side is folded over and finally the base is brought up to complete the shape. They are turned over and the tops are washed with a beaten mixture of egg whites and a little water, after which they are liberally dusted with castor sugar. After placing on to baking sheets they are rested for 30 minutes before baking at 400° F (204° C).
(Illustration page 320.)

Custard Puffs

Pin out puff pastry $1/8$ in. (3 mm.) thick and cut into 3 $1/2$ in. (9 cm.) squares. Damp the corners and pipe in confectioner's custard, on top of a small blob of greengage jam. Bring the corners of the paste to the centre, pulling each one slightly so that they overlap. Cut out twice as many very thin 1 $1/4$ in. (4 cm.) circles; wash and dust them with sugar and fold them in half, setting them back to back on the top of each pastry, which has been washed with a beaten mixture of egg whites and water, and lightly dusted with castor sugar.

After a rest, bake at 400° F (204° C) for about 15 minutes. While still hot, dust with icing sugar and return to the oven for a few seconds.

Custard Pineapple Puffs

Pin out full puff pastry to approximately $1/8$ in. (3 mm.) thick. Cut out into 2 $1/2$ in. (6 cm.) squares. Arrange on to baking sheets and bake at 440° F (227° C). When cool, split and fill with pineapple buttercream. Glaze the tops with pineapple coloured fondant that has been reduced with pineapple juice.

Custard Fruit Puffs

Pin out full puff pastry to about $1/4$ in (7 mm.) thick. Cut out with a square fluted cutter. Wash with egg and dip the tops in castor sugar. Arrange on a baking sheet and cut each one halfway through with a smaller square cutter. Bake at 470° F (243° C).

When cool fill the cases with custard filling. Place some well drained fruit on top and glaze with an arrowroot glaze.

Diamond Puffs

Pin out puff pastry to about $1/4$ in. (6 mm.) in thickness and cut into 3 in. (7 $1/2$ cm.) squares. Take each in turn and fold in half from corner to corner. With a sharp knife make two cuts parallel with each short side about $1/4$ in. (7 mm.) from the edge. The cuts should not meet at the top. Open out the pastry piece and wash with water. Take one of the corners that has been cut through and rest it on the opposite inside edge. Do the same with the opposite corner and press down. Place on to a baking sheet and egg wash. After a rest for about 30 minutes, bake at about 460-480° F (238-249° C). When cool, fill with jam or lemon curd.

Dutch Apple Puffs

Pin out puff pastry to $1/4$ in. (7 mm.) thick and cut into pieces 2 × 3 in. (5 × 8 cm.). Peel and core small apples, cut them into four and slice thinly. Arrange the slices, one overlapping the other in the centre of the pastry pieces. With the point of a sharp knife cut into the pastry about $1/4$ in. (7 mm.) from the edge to make a frame. Brush the edges with egg and bake at 400° F (204° C). When cold glaze with apricot purée or pectin jelly.

Lemon Puffs

Proceed as for Square Jam Tarts but cut into oblong shape. After washing and sugaring, arrange on a baking sheet. Bake at 410° F (210° C). When cool, cut along one side with a sharp knife and pipe in a little lemon curd. Using a savoy bag and a star tube, pipe some cream, flavoured with lemon curd along one edge.

Milan Puffs

Cut from puff pastry pinned out to a thickness of $1/8$ in. (3 mm.) circles, using a round fluted cutter, 3 in. (7 $1/2$ cm.) in diameter. Pin the centres lightly to make them an oval shape. Moisten the edges and place into the centre some apple conserve, a few stoned raisins and a little genoese mixture *(page 200)*. Fold the top half of the pastry over the other and press to seal the edges. Wash with a mixture of egg whites and water and dust liberally with castor sugar. Place on to baking sheets and, after a rest, bake at about 400° F (204° C).

Orange Puffs

Make vol-au-vent cases, washing with egg and dipping in castor sugar before baking. When baked and cool, fill with the following mixture:

lb	oz		kg	gr
	10	Egg whites		300
	10	Sugar (castor)		300
1	0	Water		500
	8	Sugar (castor)		250
	$1/16$	Zest of orange		2
	$1/8$	Salt		4
	3 $1/2$	Cornflour		100
	4	Water		125
	2	Orange juice		60

Whip the egg whites and 5 oz. (150 gr.) of sugar to a stiff meringue and stir in carefully another 5 oz. (150 gr.) of castor.

Bring the 1 lb. (500 gr.) of water, the 8 oz. (250 gr.) of castor sugar, the salt and the orange zest to the boil.

Stir the cornflour into the 4 oz. (125 gr.) of water and the orange juice and pour in the boiling mixture, stirring all the time. Cook gently for about 3-4 minutes, then carefully fold in the meringue. When the pastry cases are filled, top each one with a canned orange segment.

Orange Cream Puffs

Make small puff pastry cases and, before baking, wash the tops with egg and dip in castor sugar. After baking allow to cool, then fill with St-Honoré Cream *(page 235)* well flavoured with orange juice. Top with a small orange segment and glaze with pectin jelly.

Puff Pastries - Small

Pin out puff pastry $1/8$ in. (4 mm.) thick. Cut strips 1 $1/2$ in. (4 cm.) wide and cut the strips into diamond shapes. Place them on to baking sheets sprinkled with water, brush with egg and score the tops with the point of a knife. Bake at about 440° F (227° C) for about 8 minutes; 2 minutes before, dust them with icing sugar and return them to the oven to caramelize the sugar.

Pineapple Puffs

Take baked vol-au-vent cases and pipe in a little confectioner's custard, on top of which place a pineapple ring with a glacé cherry in the centre. Glaze with a cold-set pectin jelly or apricot purée. Brush the edge of the case with purée and mask with finely chopped pistachio nuts.

SLICES

Condés

Pin out puff pastry $1/8$ in. (4 mm.) thick and cut into strips 3-4 in. (8-10 cm.) wide. Spread with royal icing containing a generous amount of very finely chopped almonds, and dust with icing sugar. Using a knife dipped into hot water, cut evenly into pieces 1-1 $1/2$ in. (3-4 cm.) wide. Arrange them on a baking sheet sprinkled with water and bake in an oven with good bottom heat and low top heat to brown the surface without caramelization.

(France)

Conversation Slices

Pin out virgin puff pastry to about $1/8$ in. (3 mm.) thick and spread with royal icing into which a little cornflour and sufficient water is mixed to bring it to a spreading consistency. Pipe fine lines with a red piping jelly in a trellis design. Cut into rectangles and place on to baking sheets.

After resting for about 30 minutes, bake at 420° F (216° C) for about 15 minutes. When cold, split and pipe in a little red jam and whipped vanilla flavoured dairy cream.

Cream Slices

Pin out some well rested puff pastry cuttings $1/8$ in. (3 mm.) thick and line a baking sheet 18 in. (45 cm.) wide. After resting cut into four even strips, docking them well. Bake at 400° F (204° C) until crisp. When cool, spread half the strips with raspberry jam and then with either custard cream or whipped vanilla flavoured dairy cream, placing a strip on the top of each, bottom upward. Cover with vanilla flavoured white fondant or chocolate fondant. When the fondant is set, cut into slices. For an additional effect the fondant may be marbled.
(Illustration page 480.)

Frangipane Slices

From full puff pastry make strips $3 \, 1/2$ in. (9 cm.) wide and place half of them on to baking sheets. Wash the edges with egg and pipe a thick line of raspberry jam along the centre of each. On the jam, pipe a thick line of frangipane mixture. Take each of the remaining strips in turn and fold them in half lengthways, with the folded edge close to you. Make cuts $1/2$ in. (1 cm.) apart along its length and half its width. Open up the length and there will be a strip $3 \, 1/2$ in. (9 cm.) wide with cuts along the centre. These are used as tops to the jam and frangipane filled bases. Seal and notch the edges. Wash thoroughly with egg. Bake at 400° F (204° C). As soon as baked brush over with well boiled apricot purée. When cool cut into fingers.

Honey Nut Slices

From puff pastry cuttings cut out thin strips and place on to baking sheets. Spread honey topping *(page 227)* on half of them when half-baked and return to the oven. When cool, spread the plain strips with russe cream. Immediately the honey topped strips are removed from the oven, cut into fingers and when cool arrange on the creamed bases and finish cutting into individual fingers.
(Switzerland)

Pineapple Slices

Pin out puff pastry $1/8$ in. (4 mm.) thick and cut into oblongs $2 \, 1/2 \times 3$ in. (6 × 8 cm.). Cut well drained pineapple slices in four and lay three of the quarter-slices on each piece of puff pastry, one overlapping the other, leaving the edge of the pastry uncovered. Bake at about 380° F (193° C), then dust with icing sugar and glaze the pineapple with apricot purée.
(Switzerland)

Shutters

Pin out puff pastry to a thickness of $1/8$ in. (4 mm.) and cut into strips 3 in. (8 cm.) wide. Cover with vanilla flavoured Almond Custard II *(page 241)* leaving $3/8$ in. (1 cm.) uncovered on both sides. Moisten the uncovered edges with water and cover with a narrow strip of puff pastry. Cover the custard with thin strips of puff pastry in a shutter formation, pressing them firmly on to the narrow strips that have been moistened with water. Pinch the edge along each of the long sides and bake at 400° F (204° C). On removing from the oven glaze at once with apricot purée and cut into even sized slices. *(France)*

Strawberry Cream Slices

From puff pastry cuttings make thin slices and bake them well. Spread half of them with strawberry coloured and flavoured fondant. Spread the others with whipped dairy cream on top of which place strawberries. When the fondant strips have set, cut into fingers and place on the creamed strips and finish cutting. *(Switzerland)*

Strudel

For traditional Strudel *see page 688* for basic dough recipes, also *page 179* for recipes and methods.

Strudel - Apple

Peel and core good quality, fairly sour cooking apples, cut each one in four and slice thinly. Pin out puff pastry $1/8$ in.

(4 mm.) in thickness and 8 in. (20 cm.) wide and place it on a baking sheet. Sprinkle cake crumbs down the centre lengthwise and cover closely with the apples. Sprinkle with sugar and cinnamon and add some clean raisins. Fold both sides of the pastry over the filling and brush with egg. Make as large a lattice as possible with thinly cut strips of puff pastry on top and brush again with egg. Bake at 420° F (215° C), making certain that the strudel is baked right through. After baking dust with icing sugar. If desired, the strudel may be lightly glazed with apricot purée and coated with vanilla flavoured fondant. Cut into pieces of suitable size. *(Austria)*

Strudel - Cherry

Proceed exactly as for Apple Strudel but use stoned fresh cherries or well drained stewed cherries. After baking, cut into slices of suitable size and dust with vanilla sugar. *(Austria)*

Gooseberry Strudel

Pin out puff pastry cuttings to about $1/8$ in. (4 mm.) thick and cut strips about 8 in. (20 cm.) wide. Brush the edges with water and place a strip of sponge cake along the middle on which arrange gooseberries. Cover with broken sponge cake and enclose the whole with the puff pastry. Wash with egg and make a trellis pattern with thin strips of puff pastry on top. Bake at 380°F (193°C). When cool dust with icing sugar and cut into slices. *(Switzerland)*

Whipped Cream Slices

Pin out puff pastry to about $1/8$ in. (4 mm.) thick and cut into oblong pieces. Wash with a mixture of egg whites and water and dust with castor sugar. After sufficient rest, bake at 420° F (216° C). When cold slice in halves and spread raspberry jam on the bottom. Using a star tube, pipe a rope of vanilla flavoured whipped dairy cream along one side. Replace the top in a tilting position so that the cream can be seen.

SQUARES
Almond Squares - Amandelcarrés

For this palatable, remarkably well keeping pastry, line a baking sheet with puff pastry. Add a thick layer of filling.

The filling consists of:

lb	oz		kg	gr
2	4	Almond-butter (paste)	1	125
	7	Butter		200
	1	Lemon peel		30
	6	Beaten egg		175
	2	Flour		60

On this filling weave an open lattice of strips of puff pastry. After a rest, bake at an oven temperature of 338° F (170° C).

After baking and cooling, brush with apricot purée, then with very thin fondant. Cut into squares. *(Holland)*

Apple Squares - Appelcarrés

For this delightful pastry, roll puff pastry to $1/8$ in. (3 mm.) thick. Then divide into an equal number of strips of 4 in. and 6 in. (10 × 15 cm.) wide. Put the 4 in. (10 cm.) strips on a baking sheet, brush them with water, add a thick layer of filling in such a way that at both sides $1/2$ in. (1 cm.) remains uncovered.

For the filling use:

lb	oz		kg	gr
1	2	Sour cooking apples		500
	2	Raisins		60
	2	Lemon peel		60
	3 1/2	Sugar (granulated)		100
		Piece of sponge cake		

Dice the apples coarsely and mix them with lemon peel and raisins. Dice the sponge cake and add this carefully. After adding the filling, sprinkle a little cinnamon over it.

Now fold the 6 in. (15 cm.) strips longitudinally into two. Cut with a series of parallel cuts, open and cover the apple filling.

335

Press the sides gently, brush with egg plus extra egg yolk and bake immediately.

Oven temperature 446° F (230° C). After baking, brush the squares with apricot purée and cut them into slices. *(Holland)*

Lemon Squares

Pin out virgin puff pastry to $1/8$ in. (3 mm.) thick and cut into squares. Wash with an egg white and water mixture and dust with castor sugar. Place on to a baking sheet and after the necessary rest bake at 420° F (216° C). When cool, split and pipe in buttercream into which lemon curd has been beaten.

Pineapple Squares

Cut squares from virgin puff pastry about $1/8$ in. (3 mm.) thick. After a rest, bake at 440° F (227° C) for about 15 minutes. When cool, sandwich with a confectioner's custard into which a little meringue has been mixed, together with some pineapple crush. Coat the tops with pineapple coloured fondant flavoured with pineapple juice.

Swiss Cookies - Zwitsers

Roll out puff-pastry cuttings very thinly, moisten and prick with a fork. Apply a layer of fine almond-paste then spread with royal icing from the following recipe:

lb	oz		kg	gr
1 $3/4$		Egg whites		50
	$1/2$	Cornflour		15
	10	Sugar (icing)		300
		Vanilla		

Cut immediately after icing into 2 $1/2$ in. (6 cm.) squares and place a large half almond on top. Let the icing dry and place the squares on a baking sheet. Oven temperature 338° F (170° C). The Swiss cookies should have a light brown colour on top. *(Holland)*

TARTS

Apricot Tartlets

Take baked vol-au-vent cases and brush the centres with well boiled apricot purée. Place in each a well drained apricot half. Glaze with quick-set pectin jelly and sprinkle a little chopped pistachio nut on the top of each apricot.

Conversation Tarts

Pin out some puff pastry cuttings thinly and cut out with a plain round cutter. Use these pieces to line patty pans. Pipe into each a spot of apricot jam and some frangipane filling.

Cut out pieces from thin virgin pastry, using the same size plain cutter and after damping place one on the top of each tart. Press level and spread with royal icing mixed with a little cornflour and water. Place four thin strips of puff pastry on the top of each to form a diamond pattern. Bake at 370° F (187° C).

Dutch Apple Tarts

Reduce full puff pastry to about $1/4$ in. (7 mm.) in thickness and cut into pieces 2 in. by 3 in. (5 × 7 $1/2$ cm.). Peel and core small cooking apples, quarter them and then cut into very thin slices. Arrange them, each overlapping the other, on to the centre of the bases. With the point of a sharp knife cut a frame halfway through the paste close to the apple about $1/2$ in. (1 cm.) from the edge. Wash this frame with egg. Bake at 400° F (204° C). When cold fill with well boiled apricot purée or quick-set jelly.

Maids of Honour Tartlets

Line 2 in. (5 cm.) rather deep patty pans with puff pastry that has been prepared by placing cuttings inside a piece of fresh pastry and giving one half turn. Use a plain cutter and press with the thumbs so as to leave the centres very thin and the edges about $1/8$ in. (3 mm.) thick. Stab the base with a fork and place a little Maid of Honour filling in and, after resting for a time, bake at 400° F (204° C). These tartlets are quite small and should be eaten as soon as they are baked. *(Illustration page 317.)*

Old English Curd Tarts

Cut from virgin puff pastry ovals or circles using either a plain oval or round cutter. Press into oval or round patty pans leaving the centres thin and the edges quite thick. Coarsely notch the edges with a knife, making more an impression rather than a cut. Pipe raspberry jam in the bottom and then pipe in the cheese curd *(page 219)*. Sprinkle some strip almonds on top. After a rest bake at 410° F (210° C).

Orange Tartlets

Line patty pans with puff pastry cuttings, cut with a fluted cutter. Pipe in each a little confectioner's custard. After a sufficient rest bake at 400° F (204° C). When cool, pipe in more confectioner's custard, place two segments of mandarin orange on top and finish with a whirl of whipped dairy cream. *(Switzerland)*

Square Jam and Cream Tarts

Pin out full puff pastry to about $3/16$ in. (6 mm.) in thickness. Keep the pastry as square as possible. Wash with diluted egg and dredge with castor sugar. Cut into squares. Cut each square halfway through with a small round plain cutter and arrange on a baking sheet. Bake at 410° F (210° C). When baked and cool press the centres in and fill with jam. Pipe a neat rosette of whipped dairy cream at the edge of the jam, using a savoy bag and a star pipe.

Tarts - One Piece

Pin out full puff pastry to a thickness of about $3/16$ in. (6 mm.) and cut out with a plain or fluted cutter. Wash with egg, dip into castor sugar and arrange on a baking sheet. With a small plain cutter, press halfway through the pastry. Bake at 410° F (210° C). When baked, carefully push in the centre with the finger and fill with jam or curd.

Tarts - Two Pieces

Pin out full puff pastry to about $1/8$ in. (3 mm.) in thickness and cut out with a plain or fluted cutter. Cut the centre out of half of them and place the other half on to baking sheets and brush them lightly with water. Carefully place the ring tops on to the bases and wash with egg. Bake at 420° F (216° C). When baked and cool fill with jam or lemon curd, or with savoury fillings.

TURNOVERS

Apple Turnovers

From virgin puff pastry, cut out circles with a $3\,1/2$ in. (9 cm.) cutter, either plain or fluted. With a rolling pin, press the centres lightly to make into ovals. Brush the edges with water and place some clove flavoured apple in the centre. Fold the top over on to the bottom and press the edge to seal. Wash with an egg white and water mixture, dust with castor sugar and rest for awhile. Before baking make two cuts in the top of each. Bake at 420° F (216° C) aiming to get a slightly caramelized surface. *(Illustration page 319.)*

Apricot Turnovers

Pin out puff pastry to about $1/8$ in. (3 mm.) thick and cut into 4 in. (10 cm.) squares. Wash the edges lightly with water and place a little apricot or peach conserve in the centre and bring over one corner to make a triangle. Wash with egg and dust with castor sugar. Bake at 420° F (216° C). *(Turkey)*

Cream and Apple Turnovers

Make Apple Turnovers as described above. When cold, cut a wedge out of the front of each and pipe in whipped dairy cream, using a star tube.

Jam or Fruit Turnovers

Pin out full puff pastry to a thickness of about $3/16$ in. (6 mm.). Cut out pieces with a fluted cutter and elongate slightly by rolling the centre of each with a rolling pin. Wash the edge of each piece with egg whites or water and place some jam or fruit in the centre. Fold by bringing the one half of the paste on to the other, pressing the edges to make a complete seal. Make a small incision in the top of each before baking at 410° F (210° C).

Choux Pastries

Recipes for Choux Pastry and Creams will be found in Chapter VI 'Basic Preparations'.
(Illustration page 111.)

Apple Choux
Proceed as for Choux Baskets. Glaze the inside of the bottoms with apricot purée and the tops with lemon coloured and flavoured fondant on which place a half glacé cherry. Place some poached pieces of apple in the bottom and cover with a rosette of whipped dairy cream. Replace the tops.

Apricot Choux
Cut out 2 1/2-3 in. (6-8 cm.) circles from puff pastry cuttings, dock well and allow to rest. Brush the edges with egg and pipe a ring of choux pastry, not too close to the edge. Bake at 430° F (220° C). When cool dip the ring of choux into chocolate. Fill the centre with confectioner's custard flavoured with fresh lemon juice. Place half a poached or canned apricot on top and mask with pectin jelly. Finish with a small piped rosette of buttercream.

Caramel Choux
Fill round choux with caramel cream and dip the tops in caramel sugar. *(Italy)*

Cherry Choux
Split some eclair cases in half and cover the outside with milk chocolate. Pipe into the hollow a little confectioner's custard on top of which, with a star tube, pipe kirsch flavoured whipped dairy cream. Place three drained cocktail cherries on top.

Cherry Choux
Take choux pastry a little stiffer than usual, and pipe into greased coarse fluted queen cake tins. Make a depression in them by using an egg dipped in water. Fill the depression with custard. Bake at 420° F (216° C). When cool, fill the choux with a mixture of whipped dairy cream and custard and place four poached, stoned cherries on the top. Glaze with apricot purée or pectin jelly. *(Holland)*

Chocolate Choux
Make petits choux using a star pipe. When cool split them and dip the tops into thin couverture. Fill the bases with vanilla flavoured whipped dairy cream and replace the tops. *(Switzerland)*

Choux Baskets
Pipe bulbs of choux pastry on to a baking sheet and bake at 430° F (220° C). When cool slice in halves. Pipe a little fruit buttercream in the bottom halves and add a little well drained chopped fruit. Pipe in more cream. Cut the tops in half and place to form lids. Dust with icing sugar and fix handles previously made by piping choux paste on to paper lined tins.

Choux Grapes
Cut out circles of thin puff cuttings using a 4 1/2 in. (11 cm.) round cutter. Take out the centre with a 2 in. (5 cm.) cutter and cut each ring in half and arrange on to a baking sheet. After sufficient rest, pipe choux pastry on the top in grape formation. Bake at 430° F (220° C). When cold, split and spread with raspberry jam and then fill with vanilla flavoured whipped dairy cream. Finish by dusting with icing sugar.

Choux Rings - Fried - Spritzkuchen
(See page 300.)

Choux Slices
From a savoy bag fitted with a plain tube, pipe strips composed of three lines close together, on to a baking sheet. Bake at 430° F (220° C).

Spread chocolate russe cream on half of them. Brush the other strips with apricot purée and spread with chocolate fondant leaving the edges uncovered. When the fondant has set, cover it with a strip of paper and dust the edges with icing sugar. Cut into fingers and arrange them on the base and complete the cutting.

(Switzerland)

Cinderella Choux

Use recipe 1 or 2 *page 193*. Pipe into oval shapes using a plain pipe. Dust with icing sugar and bake carefully at 400°F (204°C). Cut and fill with vanilla flavoured whipped dairy cream.

Coffee Choux

Fill round choux with coffee cream. Dip into pale yellow fondant and place a sugar coffee bean on the top of each. *(Italy)*

Copenhagens

Cut some very thin circles of puff pastry cuttings. Wash the edges with egg and after sufficient rest pipe choux pastry round the edge of each. Bake at 430°F (220°C). When cool, dip the circle of choux pastry into chocolate and pipe a whirl of vanilla flavoured whipped dairy cream in the centre of each. Finish with a sprinkle of chopped pistachio nuts.

Cream Buns

Use recipe 4/5 *page 193*. Pipe into whirls on a baking sheet using a savoy bag and star pipe. The consistency of the pastry should be such that the marks of the pipe are just visible. Each bun is then covered with a bread tin. Alternatively, special cream bun tins may be used. These are specially made metal boxes fitted with a lid; many cream buns can be piped into them according to the size.

Cream buns are baked at 440°F (227°C). When cool they are filled with vanilla flavoured whipped dairy cream and dusted with icing sugar.

Duchess Rolls

Pipe choux pastry on to greased and floured baking sheets in the shape of small, long, pointed rolls. Brush with egg and sprinkle with sugar nibs. Bake carefully at 400°F (204°C). When cool, slit along one side and fill with apricot flavoured whipped dairy cream. *(France)*

Eclairs

Pipe the choux paste on to a baking sheet. They should be about the thickness of a finger. Brush with egg and bake at 430°F (220°C). When cold, slit them lengthways and fill with chocolate or coffee flavoured confectioner's cream. Lightly brush with apricot purée and finish with either chocolate or coffee fondant according to the filling. *(France)*

(Illustration page 354.)

Eclairs

The same choux pastry as for petits choux is used except that it is not quite so soft. Pipe out in finger shape, about 4 1/2 in. (11 cm.) long using a savoy bag and plain pipe. Bake at 430°F (220°C). When cool fill with vanilla flavoured whipped dairy cream and finish the top with chocolate fondant which should contain a minimum of one third block chocolate. Place into special paper cases ready for sale.

(Great Britain)

Eclairs - Andalusian

With a star pipe make éclairs from choux paste. When cool, coat the tops with lemon coloured and flavoured fondant. When this has set, slit them carefully and fill in with whipped dairy cream flavoured with curaçao and place a row of grapes on the cream. *(Switzerland)*

Eclairs - Hazelnut

Pipe out éclairs with a plain tube. When cool, fill with hazelnut crème pâtissière. Glaze the tops with coffee fondant. *(Italy)*

Eclairs - Marron

Split éclairs and fill the bottom with chestnut cream. Replace the top half upside down and spread this level with the same cream. With a fine plain tube, pipe a continuous haphazard rope on top similar to vermicelli.

Eclairs - Zabaglione

Pipe out with a star tube. Bake at 430° F (220° C). When cool, fill with a mixture of zabaglione and whipped dairy cream. Dust the tops with icing sugar.   *(Italy)*

Fabiola

Cut out long strips of puff pastry cuttings about 3-3 $^1/_2$ in. (7-9 cm.) wide and allow to rest. Pipe on choux paste in a zigzag pattern and bake at 430° F (220° C). When cool, split and sandwich with whipped chocolate dairy cream. Cut the top into fingers before replacing them on the base. Using a strip of paper placed lengthways on the strip, dust with icing sugar. Remove the paper and complete the cutting into fingers.   *(Switzerland)*

Favoris

Pin out sweet pastry $^1/_8$ in. (4 mm.) thick and cut out oval bases 3 in. (7-8 cm.) long. Moisten and pipe a figure 8 on each with a fairly large plain pipe, using a savoy bag filled with choux pastry. Bake at 380° F (193° C) and leave until cold. Place a bulb of vanilla flavoured custard inside each end of the figure 8 and top with a quarter glacé cherry.   *(France)*

Gooseberry Choux

With a star tube pipe a rather flat base with choux paste and finish with a ring around the edge. When baked, cut off the ring. Place a few gooseberries that have been poached in vanilla syrup on the base and cover with confectioner's custard. Brush the ring with apricot purée and glaze with rum flavoured fondant. Replace the ring. Place gooseberries in the centre and glaze with pectin jelly.   *(Switzerland)*

Lemon Choux

Pipe éclair shapes with choux pastry using a small plain tube. Instead of piping a plain strip, however, the finished pattern shows two parallel lines of small interlocked bulbs. Bake at 430° F (220° C). When cool, split and fill the bases with whipped dairy cream after piping in a little lemon curd. Brush the tops with well boiled apricot purée and, when set, spread with lemon coloured fondant flavoured with fresh lemon juice. Before the fondant has set sprinkle with finely chopped orange peel.

Leopolds

Proceed as for éclairs but use a star pipe. Sprinkle with fine sugar nibs and bake carefully at 400° F (204° C). Fill with vanilla flavoured whipped dairy cream.

Lucca Eyes

Pipe bulbs of choux pastry on to a baking sheet and bake at 430° F (220° C). Pipe vanilla flavoured whipped dairy cream or confectioner's custard in from underneath. Fix a black grape on the top of each with caramelized sugar and when set dip the top of the choux in the sugar to form a glaze.   *(France)*

Madelons

Pipe choux pastry into 'S' shapes with a star tube, brush with egg and sprinkle with sugar nibs. Bake at 430° F (220° C). When cool, fill with red currant jelly or, preferably, a mixture of whipped dairy cream and sieved red currant jelly.

(France)

Mecca Rolls

Using a star tube, pipe choux pastry on to greased, floured baking sheets in the shape of small ridged rolls about 3 in. (7 cm.) long and 1 $^1/_2$ in. (4 cm.) wide. Sprinkle the tops with granulated sugar and set aside for 15 minutes. Now impress the rolls lengthways down the middle with the back of a knife dipped into hot water. Bake carefully at 380° F (193° C) until crisp and golden.

When cold, the rolls may be filled with apricot flavoured whipped dairy cream.
(France)

Moors Heads - Moorkoppen

Using recipe 2 *(page 193)* pipe small bulbs on to a baking sheet, which has been lightly greased and floured. This paste is sufficient for 72 pieces. Bake at a temperature of 428° F (220°). The moors heads are coated with chocolate fondant. After coating, cut a hole in the side and fill with whipped cream.

Finally, pipe a rose of whipped cream on top and decorate it with a piece of orange.
(Holland)

Orange Rings

Proceed as for Copenhagens but use a small star pipe. Bake at 430° F (220° C). When cool split and fill with orange cream. They are dusted with icing sugar and a whirl of the same cream is piped into the centre followed by a well drained segment of mandarin orange.

Paris - Brest

Using a coarse star tube, pipe out a ring of choux pastry about 7 in. (18 cm.) in external diameter and 1 1/2 in. (4 cm.) wide. Brush with egg and sprinkle with flaked almonds. Lightly dredge with icing sugar, bake in a hot oven at first and then finish at a lower temperature. When cold, fill with chocolate praline buttercream *(page 230)* and dust with icing sugar.
(France)

Petits Choux

Pipe out some balls of choux paste on to a floured and greased baking sheet, using a savoy bag fitted with a plain pipe. Brush each one over with egg and bake at 430° F (220° C). When cold, slit them and fill with whipped dairy cream. Finish the tops with fondant, matching the colour and flavour to the colour and flavour of the cream filling. A different finish may be given by dredging with icing sugar. Place in paper cases.   *(Great Britain)*

Petits Choux

In contrast to cream buns, which may be large and uneven in shape, petits choux should be smooth, even and well formed. The choux pastry is piped out with a plain tube in bulbs the size of a walnut or a small apricot, then brushed well with egg and baked until dry and crisp.   *(France)*

Petits Choux - Almond

Mix 8 oz. (250 g.) of coarsely ground almonds, 7 oz. (200 gr.) of icing sugar and a little vanilla with sufficient egg white to make a paste that is just firm enough not to run. Pipe choux pastry on to greased, floured baking sheets as described above. Top each one with a dot of the almond mixture and bake at 380° F (190° C) until golden and dry. When cold split and fill with vanilla custard.   *(Germany)*

Petits Choux - Caramel

Dip some unfilled petits choux in pale coloured caramel. Make a hole in the base of the choux and fill with whipped dairy cream flavoured with hazelnuts.   *(France)*
(Illustration page 354.)

Petits Choux - Cévennes Style

Pipe petits choux as described above, brush with egg and bake. When cold, fill with chestnut purée thinned down with whipped cream and flavoured with kirsch.
(France)

Petits Choux - Chantilly

Proceed as above but fill with vanilla flavoured whipped dairy cream. Dust with icing sugar.   *(France)*
(Illustration page 354.)

Petits Choux - Chocolate

Proceed as above but fill with chocolate custard. Finish with chocolate fondant.
(Illustration page 354.)   *(Switzerland)*

Petits Choux - Coffee

Proceed in exactly the same way as described above. Fill with custard well flavoured with coffee. Coffee flavoured dairy cream may be used as an alternative filling.   *(France)*

Petits Choux - Frangipane

Proceed exactly as described above but fill with frangipane custard *(page 240)*.
(France)

Petits Choux - Parisian

Pipe out choux pastry as described above, wash with egg and sprinkle with nib almonds. Bake off until very dry. When cool, fill from underneath with vanilla flavoured whipped dairy cream. Dust with icing sugar and place into paper cases.

(France)

Pineapple Choux

Cut oval pieces from puff pastry cuttings pinned to about $1/8$ in. (3 mm). Allow to rest and then brush with egg. Pipe an oval bulb of choux paste on top leaving a border of puff pastry showing. Brush the bulb over with egg and sprinkle with nib almonds. Bake at 420° F (216° C). When cool make a slit in the choux and fill with confectioners custard into which chopped pineapple has been mixed. Mask with pineapple coloured fondant made rather thin with pineapple juice. Place a small piece of crystallized pineapple on top.

Polkas

Cut out sweet pastry circles about $2 1/2$-3 in. (7 cm.) in diameter and pipe a border of choux pastry round the edge of each. Brush with egg and bake at 430° F (220° C). When cold, brush the centre of each with hot apricot purée, then use a savoy bag with a plain tube to fill the centres with confectioner's custard mixed with a little butter. Dredge the border and filling with icing sugar and caramelize the sugar on top of the filling in the shape of a cross with a hot wire.

Pretzel Choux

With a star tube, pipe pretzel shapes with choux paste on to greaseproof paper. Immerse in hot fat, when the choux will leave the paper. When fried and cool, split them and fill with confectioner's custard. Dust with icing sugar.

(Switzerland)

Religieuses

Make an equal number of large and small cream buns from choux pastry which have been baked at 430° F (220° C) for 15 and 10 minutes respectively. Fill them with confectioner's custard and coat the large ones with chocolate fondant and the small ones with coffee fondant. Take some previously prepared tartlet cases made with short paste and fill these, too, with confectioner's custard. When these are quite cold, place a large chou in the middle with a small one on top. Using a savoy bag fitted with a star pipe, deposit round each a ring of coffee buttercream and add a little on top also.

(France)

Rognons

Using the same pastry as for éclairs and using the same pipe, make kidney shapes on a baking sheet. Bake at 430° F (220° C). Fill with coffee flavoured whipped dairy cream. Dip the tops into coffee fondant and then into roasted flaked almonds to which some chopped pistachio nuts or chopped green almonds have been added.

Royal Palace Choux

Use recipe 3 *(page 193)* and pipe out oval shapes with a plain pipe. With a wet scraper make a depression down the centre. Bake at 400° F (204° C). When cold, fill with vanilla flavoured whipped dairy cream and dust with icing sugar.

Using a star pipe fill in the depression with the same cream.

Salambos

Pipe éclair shapes with choux pastry on to greased, floured baking sheets, brush with egg and bake at 430° F (220° C) until dry. When cold, fill with confectioner's custard well flavoured with kirsch and dip the tops in sugar boiled to the crack degree *(page 51)*. While the sugar is still warm, the salambos may be sprinkled with chopped pistachio nuts.

(France)

Salambos

Pipe bulbs of choux pastry and bake at 430° F (220° C). When cool pipe in from underneath, either vanilla flavoured whipped dairy cream or confectioner's cream. Mask the tops with caramelized sugar. *(Illustration page 354.)*

(Germany)

Strawbery Rings

Pipe rings of choux pastry on to baking sheets using a star pipe. Bake at 430° F (220° C). Dip the tops into arrack flavoured apricot coloured fondant. When set, carefully slice the choux and pipe in arrack flavoured whipped dairy cream. Place some strawberries on the cream and replace the top. Finish with a strawberry dipped into pectin jelly. *(Switzerland)*

Swans

Make some oval choux buns. Using a small plain pipe, make the necks of the swans in the form of an 'S', piping these on a separate baking sheet. When both are baked, cut off the top of the buns carefully and cut each top into two to form the wings. Fill with whipped dairy cream and place the wings in position. Finally, fasten on the necks. Dust with icing sugar.
(France)

Swans from Locarno

Pipe out oval choux buns for the body, using a star pipe. Pipe 'S' shapes for the neck using a small plain pipe. Bake at 450° F (232° C). When cold, cut through the bodies horizontally halfway up and then cut the tops in two through the middle. Place a few strawberries in each base and pipe diplomat cream *(page 235)* flavoured with kirsch on top. Place the two halves of the top in position to form the wings and insert the neck in front. Lastly dredge well with icing sugar.
(Switzerland)

Swedish Choux

Pipe out bulbs of choux pastry on to baking sheets. Wash with egg and place a thin disc of sweet pastry on the centre of each. Bake at 430° F (220° C). Fill with whipped dairy cream flavoured with vanilla.

XI. Sponge Goods

Fruit Sponges

Well grease some custard cups or fancy sponge pans and flour them. Place half a glacé cherry or a few currants in the bottom. Two thirds fill with basic medium sponge mixture, using a savoy bag and plain pipe. Bake at 380° F (193° C). When cool, release from the pans and display upside-down.

Nut Fancies

Grease and flour some small deep custard cups and three quarters fill with medium sponge mixing. Bake at 400° F (204° C).

When cool, split and sandwich with vanilla buttercream. Spread top and sides with the same cream and mask the sides with lightly roasted mixed nib nuts. Pipe a rosette of cream on the top of each and top with half a walnut.

Othellos

There are three methods of making these delicate sponges.

lb	oz	1.	kg	gr
	12	Egg whites		375
	8	Egg yolks		250
	6	Sugar (castor)		180
	7	Flour (soft)		200
	1	Cornflour		30
		Cream of tartar (pinch)		

Whip the whites, sugar and cream of tartar to a stiff meringue. Break down the egg yolks with a whisk in a separate bowl and stir into the meringue. Carefully fold in the flour and cornflour that have been sieved together. Equal amounts of flour and cornflour can be used.

lb	oz	2.	kg	gr
	8	Egg whites		250
	8	Egg yolks		250
	5 1/2	Sugar (castor)		165
	5 1/2	Flour (soft)		165
	5 1/2	Cornflour		165
		Cream of tartar (pinch)		

Make a firm meringue with the egg whites, 3 oz (90 gr.) of sugar and the cream of tartar. Whisk the egg yolks and 2 1/2 oz. (75 gr.) of sugar to a sponge and blend the two together. Carefully fold in the flour and cornflour that have been sieved together.

lb	oz	3.	kg	gr
	8	Egg yolks		250
	11	Egg whites		330
	4 1/2	Sugar (castor)		140
	5 1/2	Flour (soft)		165
		Cream of tartar (pinch)		

Whisk the yolks and sugar to a stiff sponge and the egg whites to a stiff snow with the pinch of cream of tartar added. Add the sieved flour to the sponge and then fold in the meringue. The mixture is piped out on to sheets of paper by means of a savoy bag fitted with a $^1/_2$ in. (1 cm.) plain pipe. They are dusted with flour; the surplus is easily removed by holding up the sheet by two corners and quickly and carefully placing the sheet on to a baking sheet that is upside-down. Baking in this fashion prevents the formation of too much bottom crust. Bake at 400° F (204° C), with the oven door left open. It is the practice on the continent to bake at a higher temperature, even to 460° F (238° C), with the oven door slightly open.

The bases should be dry and biscuit-like. They can easily be removed from the paper. It is usual to scoop out a little from the under-side of each base to provide a cavity for the filling. Half of the bases should be trimmed off at the top; these will be required for the bottom halves of the finished confections, the trimming making certain that they will stand up properly when finished. All the bases should be equal in diameter, any too large must be trimmed to size with a plain cutter.

These are sandwiched with chocolate custard cream *(page 239)*, after which they are brushed over with well boiled apricot purée flavoured with curaçao. They are then dipped into chocolate fondant and placed on draining wires. They may be left undecorated or with a whirl of fondant piped on top. They are then placed in fancy paper cases.

Othello bases can be used to build up dainty afternoon tea fancies with a wide variety of finishes. Examples of these follow.
(Illustration page 482).

Almond Balloons I
Soften some raw marzipan with egg whites and beat it into buttercream. Use this cream to sandwich Othello bases. Spread the cream on the top and dip into lightly roasted flaked almonds. Dust lightly with icing sugar.

Almond Balloons II
Sandwich Othello bases with Almond Custard *(page 241)* flavoured additionally with vanilla, then brush with apricot purée. Dip into lemon coloured and flavoured fondant, pipe a spiral of chocolate on top and place into paper cases.

Carnival Heads
Take Moors' Head bases, sandwich them with jam and any desired buttercream or fine vanilla custard, then brush with apricot purée. Dip into well flavoured fondant of various colours and decorate the heads with almond paste and pipe in the facial characteristics with royal icing. *(Illustration page 356.)* (Germany)

Chocolate Balloons
Sandwich Othello bases with nougat buttercream. Brush the tops with apricot purée and dip into chocolate. Dip again roughing the surface with a palette knife before it sets. Sprinkle a few chopped pistachio nuts on top.

Another method of finish is to dip into chocolate once and sprinkle immediately with chocolate shavings. When the chocolate is set, dust lightly with icing sugar.

Chocolate Beans
Take oval Othello bases and sandwich together with rum flavoured ganache. Cover the top with the same ganache and mask with chocolate vermicelli. Make a small depression down the centre and fill with orange coloured and flavoured fondant.

Chocolate Cream Drops I
Fill hollowed out Othello bases with stiff vanilla flavoured chocolate custard cream and allow to set. Mask with chocolate and pipe a rosette of chocolate buttercream on top. On the rosette, place two small chocolate rolls. Dust with a mixture of cocoa powder and icing sugar and sprinkle with some chopped pistachio nut.

Chocolate Cream Drops II
Take Othello bases and dip the tops of half of them into plain chocolate. Spread the other half with raspberry jam and pipe on a whirl of whipped dairy cream. Place the chocolate coated drops on top.

Coffee Beans I
Pipe out an Othello mixing into bean shapes and bake. Sandwich with coffee cream or mocha buttercream, brush with apricot purée, and dip into coffee coloured and flavoured fondant. Place into paper cases.

Coffee Beans II
Bake and sandwich the bases as above. Brush with apricot purée and coat with milk couverture flavoured with a little instant coffee powder. Decorate with piping chocolate and place into paper cases.

Coffee Beans III
Make Othello bases as above and sandwich coffee cream well flavoured with kirsch. Dip into chocolate fondant flavoured with a little instant coffee, decorate with piping chocolate and place half a pistachio nut in the centre. Place into paper cases.

Desdemonas
Othello bases are sandwiched with vanilla flavoured whipped dairy cream. The tops are brushed with apricot purée and then dipped into white fondant flavoured with kirsch. Display in paper cases.
(Illustration page 482.)

Iagos
Othello bases are filled with custard cream flavoured with coffee, brushed with apricot purée and dipped into coffee coloured and flavoured fondant.
(Illustration page 482.)

Lemon Cream Fancies
Brush Othello bases with apricot purée and dip into lemon flavoured and coloured fondant. When set, sandwich them together in pairs with lemon flavoured dairy cream piped with a star tube. Finish with a small circle of candied lemon peel.

Marshmallow Drops
Pipe a bulb of marshmallow cream flavoured with lemon juice on the domed top of Othello bases. When set, dip into lemon flavoured and coloured fondant. Sprinkle with chopped pistachio nuts or green nib almonds.

Moors' Heads

lb	oz		kg	gr
	5	Egg yolks		150
1	7	Egg whites		700
	3 1/2	Sugar (castor)		100
	3 1/2	Flour		100
	7	Cornflour		200

Yield: 60 bases

Whisk the egg yolks, flour and half the sugar. Whisk the egg whites and the rest of the sugar to a stiff snow, blend the two together and lastly add the cornflour. Pipe out on to special Othello baking sheets and bake at 400° F (204° C). When cold, sandwich the bases with vanilla flavoured whipped dairy cream or good vanilla custard. Coat with cooked chocolate icing *(page 244).* *(Germany)*

Nougat Creams
Sandwich Othello bases with nougat buttercream. Brush the tops with apricot purée and dip into pale coffee coloured fondant. Finish with a few pieces of praline croquant.

Nut Balls
Sandwich Othello bases with nut buttercream *(page 230)* and glaze with apricot purée. Roll at once into roasted, coarsely chopped hazelnuts. Dip into white fondant well flavoured with nut liqueur and place into paper cases.

Orange Cream Drops
Take Othello bases and pipe on half of them a little orange marmalade and then

a whirl of whipped dairy cream. Cover with the plain bases and dust with icing sugar.

Praline Croquant Fancies

Sandwich Othello bases with vanilla flavoured whipped dairy cream. Brush the tops with apricot purée and sprinkle with broken pieces of praline croquant. Dip into rather thin, pale lemon coloured fondant.

Other nuts and fruits can be used but colours and flavours should correspond.

Rosalinds

Sandwich Othello bases with pink dairy cream delicately flavoured with rose. The same coloured and flavoured fondant is used for the finish after brushing with apricot purée. Display in paper cases.
(Illustration page 482.)

Strawberry Creams

Sprinkle Othello bases well with rum syrup and sandwich with strawberry jam and strawberry coloured whipped dairy cream. Brush with well boiled apricot purée and place a small strawberry on top. With chocolate fondant, pipe a haphazard pattern on the top.

Other Sponge Fancies

Many Afternoon Tea Fancies can be produced from a sheet of sponge cake. According to the thickness, the sponge base can be split once or twice and sandwiched with jam and/or cream. Alternatively, thin sheets can be sandwiched together, one on top of the other until the desired thickness is reached.

The sponge base can be made from the mixings given, of any colour, flavour and with many additions such as nuts and fruit. Excellent flavour is conferred by splashing with liqueur flavoured syrup, during the finishing.

Finishes are endless, giving the craftsman the opportunity of using his own artistic ability to the full with creams, fondant, chocolate and the multiplicity of decorative materials both natural or fabricated. Sponge can be used with other bases such as japonaise, sweet pastry, etc.

Shapes and sizes will depend largely on the demand of the customer and the circumstance, but at all times it must be remembered that smallness and daintiness generally go together.

Examples of such fancies follow.

Almond Croquant Slices

Sandwich two thin sheets of almond sponge with whipped dairy cream into which has been mixed a little gelatine and some sieved praline croquant. Sandwich two thin chocolate sponge sheets with the same cream and place on top. Refrigerate and then spread with chocolate; decorate with a comb scraper. Cut into strips and mask the sides with roasted flaked almonds. Cut into slices and place a caramelized blanched almond on the centre of each. *(Switzerland)*

Apricot Slices

Sandwich three layers of sponge with boiled apricot jam. Spread the top thinly with apricot coloured cold-set jelly. Cut into neat slices.

An alternative finish may be given by piping a trellis design on top of the jelly with white fondant, which has been acidulated with fresh lemon juice.

Cherry Slices

On strips of sponge, pipe three thick lines of kirsch buttercream. Fill in the spaces with cherries the juice of which has been thickened with cornflour. Place another sheet of sponge on top and spread top and sides with the same cream. Mask the sides with chocolate vermicelli and the top with chocolate shavings. Cut into slices.
(Switzerland)

Chestnut Slices

Spread a sheet of sponge rather thickly with chestnut purée. Spread on top whipped dairy cream and top with another sheet of sponge. Refrigerate and spread the top with chocolate. Cut into neat slices.

Chocolate Cream Slices

Sandwich chocolate sponge with buttercream and spread the top with the same cream which is decorated with a comb scraper. Cut into strips about 2 in. (5 cm.) wide and finish the sides with cream and chocolate shavings. Cut into slices.

Chocolate Wine Cream Fancies

Sandwich three thin sheets of chocolate sponge with wine cream *(page 233)*. Spread the top with chocolate and cut into squares. Pipe a rosette of cream in the centre of each and top with half a yellow glacé cherry. *(Switzerland)*

Christmas Triangles

Sandwich five thin slices of almond sponge with praline buttercream. Refrigerate, then coat the top with white fondant. Cut into strips about 2 in. (5 cm.) wide and then into triangles. In the centre of each place a fir branch piped with couverture and on each corner place a little star made from meringue that has been flashed in an oven of a higher temperature than normal. *(Switzerland)*

Costa Rica Slices

Two sheets of chocolate sponge are splashed with kirsch syrup and sandwiched with coffee buttercream. On top of this two hazelnut sponge sheets sandwiched with coffee ganache are placed. After refrigeration, the sheet is cut into strips and the sides masked with coffee cream and marked with a comb scraper. With a plain tube pipe two parallel lines along the centre so that they both touch. Cut into slices and on each pipe two lines at right angles to the others. On the intersection, place a small biscuit ring in the centre of which pipe a rosette of cream, on which is placed a small chocolate disc. *(Switzerland)*

Dobos Slices

Sandwich five or six very thin sheets of sponge with chocolate buttercream. Refrigerate and then cut into strips. In a copper or stout aluminium saucepan, melt some granulated sugar with a little added lemon juice to a light golden brown and spread quickly on the top of a single strip of sponge. With a warm greased knife, cut immediately into fingers. Arrange them together on the prepared foundation and cut through into slices. The caramel sugar sets quickly so only one strip should be dealt with at a time.

Harlequin Jelly Slices

Sandwich five or six layers of thin plain sponge with chocolate buttercream. Spread the top with a jelly made as follows.

Chop up some left-over jellies of different colours and mix with a plain cold-set jelly. Cut into slices.

Kirsch Cubes

Splash three sheets of sponge with kirsch syrup and sandwich with kirsch buttercream. Refrigerate and then cut into squares. Dip into apricot purée and then into white fondant. Spread some buttercream on to greaseproof paper and place into deep freeze. With a very small fluted cutter cut out small circles and place one on each fancy. Top with half a glacé cherry. *(Switzerland)*

Lemon Coconut Slices

Sandwich three layers of sponge, to which medium desiccated coconut has been added, with buttercream well flavoured with fresh lemon juice. Spread with cold-set jelly to which coconut has been mixed. Cut into slices.

Malaga Slices

Splash two sheets of chocolate sponge with malaga syrup and sandwich with malaga flavoured cream mixed with chopped pistachio nuts. Spread with pistachio flavoured and coloured cream and decorate with a comb scraper. Cut into strips about 2 in. (5 cm.) wide and spread the sides with pistachio cream and mask with chocolate vermicelli. Cut into neat slices.

(Switzerland)

Maraschino Slices

Splash two sheets of almond sponge with maraschino syrup and sandwich together with maraschino flavoured buttercream. Refrigerate and spread the top with pale green fondant and cut into strips. When the fondant has set, cut into diamond shapes.

In the centre of each, pipe a rosette of buttercream and top with a chocolate disc cut out with a fluted cutter. Place one or two silver dragées on the top of each disc.
(Switzerland)

Mocha Squares

Sandwich a heavy sponge with mocha buttercream and refrigerate. Cut into squares and dip into well boiled apricot purée. Mask the sides with roasted nib almonds and finish with a rosette of coffee cream and a sugar coffee bean.

Pineapple Cream Slices

Sandwich two sheets of swiss roll with pineapple buttercream into which finely chopped pineapple has been mixed. Refrigerate and cut into strips about 2 in. (5 cm.) wide. Spread the sides with the same cream and mask with chocolate shavings. Pipe two lines of cream along the length with a plain tube so that they are about $1/2$ in. (1 cm.) from each edge. Cut into slices and in the centre of each place a piece of pineapple and half a glacé cherry.
(Switzerland)

Pistachio Slices

Splash three sheets of chocolate swiss roll with rum. Sandwich them together with pistachio flavoured and coloured buttercream and refrigerate. Cut into strips about 3 in. (7-8 cm.) wide and spread the sides with the same cream and mask with a mixture of japonaise crumbs and cocoa powder. Spread some chocolate buttercream on greaseproof paper and place in the deep freeze. From it cut out fluted discs. Cut the strips into slices and place a buttercream cut-out on each, topped with half a pistachio nut. *(Switzerland)*

Praline Squares

Sandwich a sheet of heavy sponge with praline buttercream, spreading the top with the same cream. Refrigerate, then cut into squares. Mask the sides with buttercream and chocolate vermicelli. Finish with a rosette of cream and a sprinkle of chocolate shavings.

Rum and Red Currant Fancies

Sandwich alternately very thin sheets of sponge with red currant jelly and rum buttercream. Cut into cubes and place into paper cases.

Russian Slices

Four thin sheets of swiss roll are sandwiched together with a mixture of confectioner's cream and whipped dairy cream into which rum soaked sultanas are added. The top is spread with dairy cream on top of which roasted chopped hazelnuts are sprinkled. When the cream has set, cut into slices and pipe a rosette of cream in the centre of each.

Sponge Slice

This is the simplest of all fancies of this type. Take a sheet of sponge of the heavier type *(page 195)* and slice in half. Sandwich with whipped dairy cream or other cream after spreading with jam. Refrigerate for a while, dust with icing sugar and cut into slices.

Truffle Slices

Take two thin plain and two thin chocolate sponge sheets and sandwich them alternately with truffle buttercream. Spread the top thinly with cold-set jelly into which chocolate vermicelli has been mixed.

Savoy Fingers - Baguettes flamandes

lb	oz		kg	gr
	8	Egg		250
	4	Egg yolks		125
1	0	Sugar		500
1	0	Flour		500
	$1/2$	Vanilla		15

Whip the egg, yolks and sugar to a stiff sponge and fold in the sieved flour. Pipe out on to greased and floured baking sheets in finger shape (the thickness of the little finger and twice as long) and sprinkle with chopped almonds. Bake at 420° F (215° C). *(Belgium)*

Savoy Fingers

lb	oz		kg	gr
	9	Egg yolks		270
	12	Egg whites		350
	8	Sugar (castor)		250
	10	Flour		300

Whisk the egg yolks and half the sugar to a stiff sponge. Whisk the egg whites and the rest of the sugar to a stiff snow and fold it into the yolk/sugar sponge, together with the sieved flour. Using a plain tube, pipe out finger shapes on strips of paper, dredge with sugar, tip off the surplus, place on to baking sheets and bake until lightly coloured and dry at 375°F (190°C). Alternatively, after piping the fingers, the strips of paper can be carefully turned over on to a tray containing castor sugar, left for a few seconds, then the strip turned over again allowing the surplus sugar to fall off. *(France)*

Savoy Fingers

Use the same mixing as for Sponge Drops and pipe out into slender finger shapes and proceed as for sponge drops. After baking, reverse the sheets and wash with water. Take the fingers off and sandwich together in pairs immediately. There should be enough moisture on the base of each finger to accomplish this. *(Great Britain)*

Savoy Sponges

Take fluted or plain moulds of differing shapes and, after carefully wiping them out, grease evenly and then sugar and flour them, taking care to remove all surplus. Carefully fill them with basic medium sponge to two thirds the capacity without trapping air in the bottom. Bake at 360° F (182° C). When baked display upside-down.

To make certain that the eventual top is not overcoloured during baking, the moulds are supported on cake hoops or in bread tins placed on baking sheets.

Ring moulds lend themselves well to decoration. When greased, sugared and floured, cherries and angelica can be placed in a pattern on the base, showing a pleasing decorative effect when the sponges are baked and turned over.
(Great Britain)

Sponge Bricks

These are the old-fashioned sponge cakes, baked in rectangular frames that have six divisions. The frames are thoroughly cleaned, well brushed with grease, dusted with sugar and then flour making certain that any surplus sugar and flour is removed. The basic mix, as for sponge sandwiches, is piped in, using a savoy bag with a plain pipe. After dredging well with castor sugar, they are baked at 400° F (204° C). Turn out of the frames immediately after baking. If the frames are properly prepared, the crust of the sponge should show an unblemished surface.
(Great Britain)

Sponge Drops

lb	oz		kg	gr
1	0	Egg		500
	8	Egg yolks		250
1	0	Sugar		500
1	0	Flour (soft)		500
		Colour and flavour as desired		

Sponge Drops - Chocolate

lb	oz		kg	gr
1	0	Egg		500
	8	Egg yolks		250
1	0	Sugar (castor)		500
	14	Flour		435
	2	Cocoa powder		60
	2	Warm water		60
		Chocolate colour		

Whip the egg, yolks and sugar to a stiff sponge. Add the colour and flavour, stir in water in the case of chocolate drops, and fold in the flour. Pipe out on to greaseproof paper, dust with castor sugar, and bake on reversed baking sheets at

440° F (227° C). After removal from the paper, sandwich with jam, cream or lemon curd. The drops may be further decorated by dipping into fondant or chocolate with added decoration such as glacé cherries, angelica, almonds, walnuts, etc. *(Great Britain)*

Sponge Sandwiches

lb	oz		kg	gr
1	4	Egg		625
1	0	Sugar (castor)		500
1	0	Flour (soft)		500
		Colour and flavour as desired		

Whisk the egg and sugar to a stiff sponge. Add the colour and flavour and then fold in the flour carefully. *(Great Britain)*

Sponge Sandwiches - Chocolate

lb	oz		kg	gr
1	4	Egg		625
1	0	Sugar (castor)		500
	14	Flour (soft)		435
	2	Cocoa powder		60
	2	Warm water		60
		Chocolate colour		

Proceed as for sponge sandwiches, stirring in the warm water before the flour is folded in.

Well grease and flour eight 7 in. (18 cm.) sandwich plates and into each carefully place 6 oz. (15 cm.) of the sponge mix. Bake at 400° F (204° C). When cool the sandwiches may be filled with jam or cream and the tops sprinkled with castor or icing sugar. The tops may also be spread with water icing or fondant and decorated with glacé fruits, etc. *(Great Britain)*

Stencilled Sponge Fancies

Thin round, or oval discs of sponge cake can be made by stencilling light sponge mixtures on to greased and floured baking sheets. The delicate discs lend themselves admirably to unusually attractive finishes. Here is a suitable formula:

lb	oz		kg	gr
	4	Egg yolks		125
	3 $1/2$	Sugar (castor)		100

lb	oz		kg	gr
	5	Egg whites		150
	5	Flour		150

Whisk the egg yolks and sugar to a stiff sponge. Whisk the whites to a stiff snow and fold into the egg yolk/sugar sponge together with the well sieved flour. After stencilling, bake quickly at 440° F (225° C). The discs should be about 4-4 $1/2$ in. (10-12 cm.) in diameter.

Apple and Cream Turnovers

Stencil a light sponge mixing into round shapes about 4 in. (10 cm.) in diameter. Bake at 440° F (227° C). Bake quickly so that they do not dry. Place slices of well drained poached apple fanwise along one edge and glaze with a pectin jelly. Pipe bulbs of whipped dairy cream on the near end of the apple slices and fold over the other part of the sponge. Dust with icing sugar.

Cherry Turnovers

Proceed as above. Spread with cherry jam and then with whipped dairy cream to which gelatine and chopped cherries have been added. When nearly set, bring two sides to the centre and dust with icing sugar. Place a cherry at each end.

Red Currant Omelettes

Proceed as above. Spread with apricot purée and then with wine cream into which red currants have been mixed. Fold over and dust with icing sugar. Decorate in front with a few red currants that have been moistened with egg white and rolled in castor sugar and allowed to dry.

Strawberry Turnovers

Proceed as above. Spread with whipped dairy cream stabilized with a little gelatine. Cover the cream with cut strawberries. When the cream begins to set, roll the discs up like omelettes with the fold underneath. Place a strip of paper across the centre of each and dust with icing sugar, taking the paper away carefully. On the top of each, place a small strawberry glazed with pectin jelly. *(Switzerland)*

▲ Savarins, p. 259
　Apple Poppy Seed Cakes, p. 409 — Eierschecke, p. 279 — Sultana Cheese Slices, p. 448 —   353
　Cherry Cheese Cakes, p. 265, 416 — Apricot Streusel Slices, p. 258, 411 ▼

354 ▲ Petits Choux, p. 341 — Salambos, p. 342   ▲ Eclairs, p. 339

Dresdener Stollen, p. 293 ▼

▲ Baked Marzipan Santa Claus, p. 376
St. Gallen Biberli, p. 373 ▼

▲ Butterspekulatius, p. 364
Dairy Cream Waffles, p. 306 ▼

355

▲ Carnival Heads for a Children's Party, p. 346

Almond and Hazelnut Fingers, p. 376 ▼

Swiss Roll

lb	oz		kg	gr
	8	Egg		250
	5	Sugar (castor)		150
	5	Flour (soft)		150
		Colour and flavour as desired		

Swiss Roll
(special cake flour)

lb	oz		kg	gr
	10	Egg		300
	6	Sugar (castor)		180
	5	Special cake flour		150
	$1/2$	Glycerine		15
		Colour and flavour as desired		

Swiss Roll-Chocolate

lb	oz		kg	gr
	8	Egg		250
	5	Sugar (castor)		150
	4	Flour (soft)		125
	1	Cocoa powder		30
	1	Warm water		30
		Chocolate colour		

Swiss Roll-Chocolate
(special cake flour)

lb	oz		kg	gr
	10	Egg		300
	6	Sugar (castor)		180
	4	Special cake flour		125
	1	Cocoa powder		30
	$1/2$	Glycerine		15
		Chocolate colour		

The mixings given are for spreading on a papered baking sheet about 16 in. (40 cm.) square. Double the mix will be required for the standard 18 in. × 30 in. (45 × 76 cm.) baking sheet. The Swiss rolls are baked at 420° F (216° C). The Swiss rolls are spread with jam, buttercream or lemon curd, the Chocolate rolls with white or chocolate buttercream. Chopped glacé fruits and chopped nuts may be mixed in the cream for Swiss rolls. Swiss rolls may be decorated by covering with almond paste, fondant or chocolate and given suitable decoration with fruits, nuts, jellies, cut-out pieces, etc. They may also be used as the base for Christmas logs and may be cut up and decorated for Afternoon Tea Fancies.

Swiss Rolls - Miniature

Take three quarters of any of the Swiss roll mixings given above and spread on a baking sheet of the same dimensions. Bake at 430° F (220° C). When cool, spread with jam, lemon curd or buttercream and cut into three lengthways. Roll each strip up and cut into the desired sized pieces. These miniature rolls may be decorated with chocolate either by dipping one or both ends or dipping completely.

Swiss Rolls

Recipe I

lb	oz		kg	gr
	10	Egg yolks		300
1	0	Egg whites		500
1	2	Sugar (castor)		560
1	2	Flour		560
	6	Butter		180

Proceed as for sponge fingers, adding the melted butter last.

Recipe II

lb	oz		kg	gr
1	4	Egg		625
	10 $1/2$	Sugar (castor)		315
	10 $1/2$	Flour		315

Whisk the egg and sugar and then carefully fold in the flour. *(France)*

Swiss Rolls

The following three recipes are sufficient for two baking sheets about 18 in. by 36 in. (45 × 90 cm.).

1. Continental

lb	oz		kg	gr
	12	Egg yolks		375
1	1	Egg whites		525
1	2	Sugar (castor)		550
	9	Flour		300
	9	Cornflour		300
		Flavour		

2. Nut sponge

lb	oz		kg	gr
	9 1/2	Egg yolks		280
	15	Egg whites		470
	8	Sugar (castor)		250
	10	Flour		295
	8	Ground almonds or hazelnuts		250

3. Chocolate sponge

lb	oz		kg	gr
	10	Egg yolks		300
	15	Egg whites		450
	14	Sugar (castor)		400
	7	Flour		200
	7	Cornflour		200
	3 1/2	Cocoa powder		100

Whisk the whites until stiff gradually adding half the sugar. Beat the egg yolks with the rest of the sugar. Blend the two together and fold in the flours which have been sieved together. Spread on paper lined baking sheets. *(Germany)*

Almond Vanilla Rolls

Spread a light almond Swiss roll with apricot jam, then with vanilla flavoured buttercream. Roll up and refrigerate. Cut into neat slices and dip into vanilla flavoured white fondant, rolling the round sides only into lightly roasted nib almonds. Stand in paper cases. *(Switzerland)*

Apple Rolls

Spread a plain Swiss roll with wine cream *(page 233)* and place pieces of well drained lightly poached apple along the edge. Roll up so that the apple is in the middle. Refrigerate, dust with icing sugar and cut into dainty slices. *(Switzerland)*

Black Forest Rolls

On to a sheet of Chocolate roll, pipe kirsch flavoured buttercream in lines that do not touch. Fill in the spaces with well drained cooked black cherries and roll up. Refrigerate and then spread with cream. Cut into slices and decorate each piece with a small chocolate roll. *(Germany)*

Brandy Rolls

Proceed as for Roman Bridges but include some nib hazelnuts in the sponge before baking. Spread with brandy flavoured buttercream and roll up. Spread with brandy flavoured jelly and roll into lightly roasted flaked hazelnuts. Refrigerate and then cut into slices which are placed on thin discs of baked sweet pastry. Three grapes which have been dipped into pectin jelly are placed in the centre of each.

(Switzerland)

Budapest Rolls

lb	oz		kg	gr
	9	Egg whites		270
	1 1/2	Egg yolks		45
	6 1/2	Sugar (castor)		195
	1 1/2	Water		45
	4 1/2	Flour		140
	1 1/2	Cocoa powder		45

Whip the whites and the sugar to a meringue. Stir in the yolks that have been mixed with the water. Finally fold in the flour and cocoa that have been sieved together.

Spread on to a paper lined baking sheet about 16 in. by 30 in. (40 × 76 cm.) and bake at 420° F (216° C). Turn out and remove the paper and when cool sprinkle with kirsch syrup and spread with buttercream flavoured with the same liqueur.

Along the far edge place a line of preserved cherries and roll up as for Swiss roll. Spread with buttercream, dust with cocoa powder and again with icing sugar. Allow the cream to set and cut into neat slices.

(Switzerland)

Chocolate Cream Rolls

Spread a chocolate Swiss roll with raspberry jam and then with chocolate buttercream. Roll up and refrigerate. Spread the outside with chocolate cream and make a fluted design with the end of a palette knife. Cut into neat slices and decorate the tops with a chocolate disc.

(Switzerland)

Chocolate Roulade Rolls

lb	oz		kg	gr
1	6	Egg whites		680
	10	Sugar (castor)		300
	10	Sugar (granulated)		300
	3 1/2	Water		100
	11 1/4	Couverture (plain)		340
	3 1/2	Cornflour		100

Whisk the whites and the castor sugar to a stiff meringue. Bring the granulated sugar and the water to the boil and mix with the melted couverture. Add to the meringue and then fold in the cornflour. With a savoy bag fitted with a plain tube, pipe parallel lines on to paper lined baking sheets so that the lines just touch. Bake at 380° F (193° C). When baked, remove the paper and spread with kirsch buttercream. Make a rope of pink coloured marzipan and place along the top edge. Roll up and refrigerate. Cut into neat slices. *(Switzerland)*

Christmas Stars

Spread 1 1/2 lb. (750 gr.) of chocolate Swiss roll mix on a paper lined baking sheet. Bake at 420° F (216° C). When cool, remove the paper and spread with pineapple jam and then with cherry buttercream. Roll up, cover with buttercream and roll into lightly roasted flaked almonds. Refrigerate and then cut into dainty slices and place, cut side down, into paper cases. Pipe a rosette of cream in the centre of each and top with a choux paste star *(page 193)*. *(Switzerland)*

Coffee Cream Rolls

Spread a sheet of sponge with coffee buttercream on which sprinkle chocolate shavings. Roll up and spread with the same cream. Decorate by spinning chocolate on the top. When set, cut into slices and top each one with a sugar coffee bean. *(Switzerland)*

Easter Fancies

Spread a sheet of Swiss roll with raspberry jam. Roll up and refrigerate. Cut in half lengthways and place each half, cut side down, on to strips of baked sweet pastry, fixing with apricot purée. Cover with chocolate and cut into slices. Decorate each slice with an Easter motif such as a chick's head, a hare etc., which can be modelled with marzipan. Alternatively, the roll can be brushed with apricot purée and covered with lightly roasted nib hazelnuts or almonds and then lightly dusted with icing sugar before the motifs are put into place.

Harlequin Rolls

Make a plain sponge as for Roman Bridges, and spread with Russe cream *(page 242)* to which has been added a little gelatine. Sprinkle with small pieces of coloured quick-set jelly and roll up. Cover with buttercream and roll into lightly roasted nib almonds. Refrigerate and then cut into slices. Place into paper cases, cut side down. *(Switzerland)*

Lemon Cream Rolls

Proceed as for Pineapple Rolls and spread with lemon buttercream. Roll up as for Swiss roll. When set, dust with icing sugar and cut into neat slices.

Nougat Slices

Proceed as for Pineapple Rolls and spread with vanilla buttercream. Place a rope of chocolate nougat along the top edge and roll up as for Swiss roll. Cover with a thin strip of chocolate roll which has been spread with raspberry jam. Cover again with a thin strip of almond paste and coat with chocolate. Cut into slices. *(Germany)*

Pineapple Cream Rolls

Make an almond flavoured Swiss roll and spread with a pineapple flavoured buttercream into which a little gelatine and some finely chopped pineapple has been mixed. Roll up and refrigerate. Cover with plain chocolate and cut into triangular shaped slices. Stand them up in paper cases. *(Switzerland)*

Puckler Rolls

Spread a sheet of chocolate Swiss roll with buttercream into which chopped cherries have been mixed. Roll up and enclose

with a thin sheet of white sponge spread with apricot purée. Cover with chocolate and place two strips of marzipan along the roll. When set, cut into pieces.
(Switzerland)

Red Currant Rolls
Spread a plain Swiss roll thinly with red currant jelly, then with whipped dairy cream that has been stabilized with a little gelatine. Sprinkle with red currants and roll up. Refrigerate and then spread lightly with red currant jelly and roll into roasted flaked almonds. Cut into slices and place, cut side downwards, on to thin baked sweet pastry biscuits. *(Switzerland)*

Roman Bridges
Using 1 1/2 lb. (750 gr.) of white Swiss roll mixing, proceed as for Christmas Star Fancies. Spread with red currant jelly and then with almond flavoured buttercream. Refrigerate and then cut lengthways. Spread the halves with buttercream and cover with roasted flaked almonds. Place each half on to baked strips of rich sweet pastry, spread with red currant jelly. Cut into slices.

Truffle Rolls
Cut a sheet of white Swiss roll into three strips and spread with rum flavoured buttercream. Along one edge pipe a line of truffle buttercream. Roll up so that the darker truffle cream is in the centre. Dust with icing sugar and cut obliquely into little rolls. *(Switzerland)*

Victoria Sponge

lb	oz		kg	gr
1	0	Butter		500
1	0	Sugar (castor)		500
1	0	Egg		500
1	0	Flour (soft)		500
	1/2	Baking powder		15
		Zest of lemon		

Cream the butter and sugar and when light add the egg a little at a time. Add the zest of lemon and finally fold in the flour and baking powder that have been sieved together. Place into greased and floured sandwich plates and bake at 360° F (182° C). When cool, sandwich two together with lemon curd and dust with icing sugar. *(Great Britain)*

Windsor Rolls
Spread a sheet of chocolate Swiss roll with pistachio buttercream and sprinkle with some coarse sieved praline croquant. Roll up and refrigerate. Cover with the same cream and finish with spun chocolate. Cut into slices. *(Switzerland)*

XII. Ginger and Honey Goods

SPICES

Gingerbread and honeycakes depend to a large extent on spices for flavouring purposes. Excellent spices can be purchased ready for use from reputable firms who specialize in the production and compounding of ground spices and spice oils. Nevertheless, craftsmen may need to extend the range of flavours by compounding their own, so as to add a special piquancy and individuality to their goods.

Many craftsmen on the Continent possess spice mills which are used to grind spices to a fine powder immediately before use, so as to impart the full flavours of the spices used. When not in use, spices should be kept in containers with close fitting lids.

Here are some recipes for spice blends suitable for honeycakes and heavy gingerbreads. Further information on spices will be found on *page 66*.

Recipe I

lb	oz		kg	gr
	15	Cinnamon		450
	6	Clove		180
	2	Vanilla		60
	3	Bay leaf		90
	1	Coriander		30
	1	Fennel		30
	1	Pimento		30

Recipe II

lb	oz		kg	gr
	12	Cinnamon		375
	4	Clove		125
	1	Vanilla		30
	4	Ginger		125
	4	Bay leaf		125
	2	Nutmeg		60

Recipe III

lb	oz		kg	gr
	12	Cinnamon		375
	3	Clove		90
	3	Aniseed		90
	2	Nutmeg		60
	2	Cardamom		60
	1	Bay leaf		30
	1	Coriander		30

Recipe IV

lb	oz		kg	gr
	12	Cinnamon		375
	8	Aniseed		250
	8	Pimento		250
	3	Coriander		90
	2	Clove		60
	1	Ginger		30
	1	Vanilla		30

Recipe V

lb	oz		kg	gr
	8	Cinnamon		250
	8	Aniseed		250
	1	Pimento		30

lb	oz		kg	gr
	4	Coriander		125
	4	Clove		125
	2	Ginger		60
	1/2	Vanilla		15
	2	Nutmeg		60
	1	Fennel		30

Recipe VI

lb	oz		kg	gr
	9	Cinnamon		270
	3 1/2	Coriander		100
	3 1/2	Aniseed		100
	1	Clove		30
	1	Pepper		30
	1	Ginger		30

Lebkuchen Spice

Recipe VII

lb	oz		kg	gr
	4	Cinnamon		125
	3	Clove		90
	2	Nutmeg		60
	5	Aniseed		150
	3	Ginger		90
	5	Fennel		150
	5	Coriander		150

Biberteig Spice

Recipe VIII

lb	oz		kg	gr
	10	Cinnamon		300
	10	Coriander		300
	2 1/2	Nutmeg		75
	5	Sternanis		150
	3	Clove		90
	1	Ginger		30

St. Gall Honey Cake Spice

Recipe IX

lb	oz		kg	gr
	14	Cinnamon		435
	14	Coriander		435
	3 1/2	Nutmeg		100
	7	Aniseed		200
	4 1/2	Clove		140
	1/2	Ginger		15

Speculaas Spice

Recipe X

lb	oz		kg	gr
	9	Cinnamon		270
	2 1/2	Nutmeg		75
	2 1/2	Clove		75
	2	Ginger		60
	1	Cardamom		30
	3/4	Pepper		20

Aberdeen Gingerbread

lb	oz		kg	gr
1	2	Flour		560
	6	Oatmeal (medium)		180
	3/8	Ground ginger		10
	12	Butter		375
	6	Sugar (soft brown)		180
1	2	Golden syrup		560
	1/4	Bicarbonate of soda		8
	3	Milk (approx.)		90

Sieve flour and ginger and with it mix the oatmeal. Melt the butter and add the syrup and sugar and heat gently. Mix in the flour and lastly the milk into which the soda is dissolved. Turn the mix into three paperlined tins about 7 in. (18 cm.) square. Bake at 330° F (165° C) for about 50 minutes. Cut into squares when cool.

(Scotland)

Aberdeen Honey Cakes

lb	oz		kg	gr
1	8	Butter		750
1	8	Sugar (castor)		750
	3	Egg yolks		90
	4	Honey		125
2	8	Flour	1	250
	8	Scone flour*		250
	1/2	Ground spice		15
	1	Ground cinnamon		30
	1/8	Ground nutmeg		4
	10	Milk (approx.)		300

* *(Page 180).*

Cream the butter and sugar and add the egg yolks. Beat in the honey and then fold in the flour. Lastly mix in the milk. Fill into greased queen cake tins and bake at 380° F (193° C). *(Scotland)*

Almond Gingerbread

lb	oz		kg	gr
1	0	Flour		500
	1/8	Mixed spice		4
	1/4	Ground ginger		8
	1/8	Bicarbonate of soda		4
	4	Ground almonds		125
	4	Egg		125
	4	Milk (approx.)		125
1	0	Golden syrup		500
	8	Butter		250
	4	Sugar (soft brown)		125

Melt the syrup, butter and sugar and when cool add the egg and milk beaten together. Add the ground almonds and the flour, spices and soda which have been sieved together. Mix well and turn into two paperlined tins about 8 in. (20 cm.) square. Place split almonds on top and bake for about 50 minutes at 330° F (165° C). When cool, cut into fingers or squares.

Appenzell Honey Cakes

lb	oz		kg	gr
1	0	Wholemeal		500
	1/4	Carbonate of ammonia ('vol')		8
	1/2	Ground spice*		15
	7	Honey		200
	5	Sugar		150
	1 1/2	Egg		45
	2	Milk (approx.)		60

* (*Page 362, Recipe VIII*).

Warm the honey and sugar and stir in the milk. When cool, add the spice and the ammonia (vol) and when it begins to aerate and rise, work in the egg and the wholemeal. Leave overnight in a cool place. Weigh at 10 oz. (300 gr.) and mould round. Pin out to about 9 in. (23 cm.) and place on to a greased baking sheet. Wash with milk and decorate by marking with a fork. Place a split almond in the centre. Bake at 350° F (176° C).

The same dough can be used to make a filled variety. In this case the dough is weighed at 4 oz. (125 gr.) and moulded round. The pieces are pinned out to about 8 in. (20 cm.). Half of them have the edges washed with milk and about 3 1/2 oz. (100 gr.) of filling (*page 224*) placed in the centre and then covered with the plain pieces. Proceed as for Aberdeen Honey Cakes. *(Switzerland)*

Ashbourne Gingerbread

lb	oz		kg	gr
1	4	Flour		625
1	0	Butter		500
	10	Sugar		300
	1/4	Ground ginger		8
	3	Finely cut mixed peel		90

Sieve the flour and ginger. Rub in the butter and make up into a dough with the rest of the materials. Roll out into ropes which are flattened into strips. Divide into pieces about 1 in. (2 1/2 cm.) wide, cutting obliquely. Place on to lightly greased baking sheets and bake at 400° F (204° C). *(Great Britain)*
(*Illustration page 391.*)

Basle Leckerli

lb	oz		kg	gr
1	2	Honey		560
	13	Sugar		400
2	14	Flour	1	435
	1/8	Cinnamon		4
	1/2	Baking powder		15
	3/8	Potash		10
	1 1/4	Honey cake spice*		35
	4 1/2	Crumbs		140
	10 1/2	Mixed chopped peel		300
	5 1/2	Nib almonds		150
	12 1/2	Milk (approx.)		375
		Zest of 1 lemon		

* (*Page 361, Recipes II-V.*)

Warm the honey and sugar, then add all the other ingredients and make into a well mixed dough which is allowed to stand overnight. It is weighed into suitable pieces and then pinned out and placed on baking sheets about 1/4 in. (7 mm.) thick. It is well docked and baked at 420° F (216° C). While still hot, brush over with glaze. The glaze is put on with a rather stiff brush and worked backwards and forwards until it begins to grain. Cut into rectangles. *(Switzerland)*

Brandy Snaps or Jumbles

lb	oz		kg	gr
1	2	Butter		560
2	0	Sugar (castor)	1	
1	0	Golden syrup		500
1	0	Flour (soft)		500
	1/2	Ground ginger		15
	1/2	Ground spice		15

Sieve flour and spices and rub in the butter. Make a dough with the rest of the materials. Roll out into long ropes and chop into equal size small pieces and place them out 5 in. (12 cm.) apart on to well greased baking sheets. Flatten a little with the hand and bake at 320-340° F (160-171° C). As soon as they are baked and slightly cooled, roll each of them round a greased rolling pin about 1 in. (2 1/2 cm.) in diameter. They will set quickly and can be withdrawn at once from the rolling pin; do not bake too many at a time or they will set on the trays before they can be rolled.

Brandy snaps can be filled with whipped dairy cream.

Brandy Snaps

lb	oz		kg	gr
1	5	Golden syrup		650
1	5	Butter		650
1	2	Flour		560
1	0	Sugar (castor)		500
	2 1/4	Brandy		70
	3/4	Ground ginger		20
	4 1/2	Chopped walnuts		140

Add the melted butter to the syrup, then add the rest of the ingredients to make a fairly firm paste. Using a stencil with a round hole about 4 in. (10 cm.) in diameter, spread circles on to a greased baking sheet, keeping them well apart. Bake at 320-340° F (160-171° C). While still hot, roll them round a cylindrically shaped piece of wood to make tubes about 1 in. (2 1/2 cm.) diameter. Fill with whipped dairy cream flavoured with sweet sherry.

(Canada)

Butterspekulatius

lb	oz		kg	gr
3	0	Flour	1	500
2	0	Sugar (icing)	1	
	8	Sugar (vanilla)		250
2	0	Butter	1	
	3 1/2	Egg		100
1	0	Marzipan		500
	3/4	Ground cinnamon		25
	1/2	Ground tonka bean *		15
		Zest of 1 lemon		

* (See Glossary)

Cream the butter with the icing sugar and vanilla sugar. Reduce the marzipan to a smooth paste with the egg, then mix with the creamed butter and sugar. Add the spices and lemon zest and work up to a dough with the flour. Leave in a cold place, then press into wooden moulds or use a special machine to impress the figures in the dough. Place on baking sheets, brush with milk and bake for about 10 minutes at 400° F (204° C).

(Illustration page 355.) *(Germany)*

Cinnamon Stars

lb	oz		kg	gr
1	0	Ground almonds (roasted)		500
	7 1/2	Egg whites		240
1	8	Marzipan		750
1	4	Sugar (granulated)		625
1	0	Sugar (icing)		500
	1 1/4	Cinnamon		40
	2	Flour		60

Icing

lb	oz		kg	gr
1	0	Sugar (icing)		500
	5	Egg whites		150

Work all the ingredients together to make a firm dough and pin out to about 1/4 in. (6 mm.) thick. Beat the egg whites and sugar to a foam and spread on the surface of the dough. Cut out into star shapes and place on to baking sheets coated with beeswax. Bake for about 20 minutes at 360° F (180° C).

(Germany)

Dijon Honey Cakes

lb	oz		kg	gr
1	9	Flour		770
	1/4	Bicarbonate of soda		8
	1/16	Carbonate of ammonia		2
	1/8	Aniseed		4
	1/4	Lemon oil		8
	2	Egg yolks		60
1	4	Honey		625
	3	Milk (approx.)		90

Warm the honey and milk and when cool stir in the carbonate of ammonia (vol).

Add all the other ingredients and make into a smooth dough. Let it stand overnight and then pin out and place in a greased wooden frame on a greased baking sheet. Wash with milk and mark with a fork. Divide into rectangles with a wet scotch scraper. Place a split almond in the centre of each and bake carefully at 350° F (176° C). When cool, cut along the divisions with a sharp knife. Chopped orange and lemon peel may be added if desired.

(France)

Dumfries Gingerbread

lb	oz		kg	gr
	12	Butter		375
1	0	Sugar (brown)		500
	10	Egg		300
	4	Syrup		125
1	12	Flour (strong)		875
	1/2	Baking powder		15
	1/4	Bicarbonate of soda		8
	1/4	Ground spice		8
	3/4	Ground ginger		20
	10	Milk (approx.)		300
	6	Sultanas		180
	1/4	Caraway seeds		8

Cream the butter and sugar and add the egg a little at a time. Stir in the syrup and half the milk. Fold in the flour, baking powder, soda and spices that have been sieved together. Mix in the rest of the milk and finally the fruit and caraway seeds.

Weigh at 14 oz. (435 gr.) into well greased 1 lb. (500 gr.) bread tins. Bake at 360-370° F (182-187° C). *(Scotland)*

Ginger Boats

Line some small boat shaped tins with sweet pastry and place some ginger crush in the bottom of each on top of which pipe some frangipane mix *(pages 217-218)*. Bake at 380° F (193° C). When cool, spread the top with well boiled apricot purée into which chopped preserved ginger has been mixed. Dip the extreme ends in green nib almonds.

Gingerbread - Pain d'Epice

Recipe I

lb	oz		kg	gr
1	2	Flour		560
	1/2	Ground ginger		15
	1/8	Ground spice		4
1	2	Honey		560
	4 1/2	Sugar (icing)		140
	2	Orange peel (chopped)		60
	2	Lemon peel (chopped)		60
	2	Water (approx.)		60
	1/16	Potash		2

Warm the honey and dissolve the potash in the water. Make all the ingredients into a smooth dough and leave for 3-4 days.

Pin out to about 1 in. (2 1/2 cm.) thick on to a greased baking sheet and dock well. Bake at 340° F (171° C). Wash with milk as soon as it is baked. When cool cut into squares or fingers.

Recipe II

lb	oz		kg	gr
1	2	Rye meal		560
	6	Flour		180
	1/2	Ground ginger		15
	1/8	Ground spice		4
	12	Honey		375
	5	Sugar		150
	1/4	Salt		8
	1/16	Potash		2
	8	Milk (approx.)		250

Proceed as above. *(France)*

Gingerbread

lb	oz		kg	gr
1	0	Honey		500
1	0	Water		500
2	0	Flour	1	
	1/6	Baking powder		5
	6	Milk (approx.)		180
	4	Rum		125
	1/8	Salt		4
	1/8	Aniseed		4
	1/8	Cinnamon		4

Heat the honey, water, salt and the spices. Add the rum and flour into which the baking powder has been well sieved. Finally add the milk and fill into a tin lined with greased paper.

Bake at 350° F (176° C) for approximately one hour. This gingerbread can be enriched by adding:

lb	oz		kg	gr
	4	Angelica (diced)		125
	4	Glacé cherries		125
	4	Lemon peel		125

The top can be decorated with crystallized lemon peel and split almonds. *(Flanders)*

Gingerbread

lb	oz		kg	gr
2	0	Flour	1	
	3/4	Bicarbonate of soda		20
	1/4	Ground spice		8
	1/4	Ground ginger		8
	6	Butter		180
1	2	Golden syrup		560
1	2	Sugar (brown)		560
	6	Milk (approx.)		180
	12	Strip almonds		375
	8	Sultanas		250
	8	Finely chopped mixed peel		250

The flour, soda and spices are sieved together and with all the rest of the materials, mixed to a dough. After leaving for some hours, the dough is pinned out about 3/4 in. (2 cm.) in thickness on to a well greased baking sheet making certain that it is level.

Wash with egg diluted with water or milk and bake at 340° F (171° C).

When cold cut into squares.
(Illustration page 391.)   *(Great Britain)*

Gingerbread Slices

lb	oz		kg	gr
	5	Golden syrup		150
	5	Treacle		150
	7 1/2	Sugar (brown)		225
	6	Butter		180
	12	Milk		375
1	2	Flour (strong)		560
	3/4	Ground ginger		20
	1/4	Ground spice		8
	1/16	Ground mace		2
	3/8	Bicarbonate of soda		10
	1/8	Cream of tartar		4

Line a baking sheet 16 in. × 16 in. (40 × 40 cm.) with sweet pastry about 1/8 in. (3 mm.) in thickness. Mix the syrup, treacle and brown sugar together and stir in the butter which has been melted. Add the milk and then the flour, spices and chemicals that have been sieved together. Spread on to the prepared baking sheet and bake at 390° F (199° C). When cold, spread the top with thin white water icing into which finely chopped preserved ginger has been added. When set, cut into slices.

Gingerbread Squares I

lb	oz		kg	gr
1	0	Lard		500
1	0	Sugar		500
3	0	Syrup	1	500
5	0	Milk (approx.)	2	500
5	0	Flour (strong)	2	500
	2 1/2	Ginger		75
	2 1/2	Bicarbonate of soda		75
	2 1/2	Cinnamon		75
	2 1/2	Mixed spice		75

Proceed as for Ginger Spice Loaf.

This mixing will fill three trays about 16 in. × 16 in. (40 × 40 cm.) about 1 in. (2 1/2 cm.) deep. They should be well greased. Bake at 380° F (193° C). When cold, ice on top with ginger flavoured water icing. When set, cut into squares.

Gingerbread Squares II

lb	oz		kg	gr
1	0	Flour		500
	³/₄	Bicarbonate of soda		20
	¹/₂	Ground spice		15
	¹/₂	Ground ginger		15
	8	Butter		250
	10	Sugar (brown)		300
1	4	Golden syrup		625
1	0	Cake crumbs		500
1	0	Milk (approx.)		500
	8	Sultanas		250
	4	Peel		125
	4	Chopped preserved ginger		125

Sieve the flour, soda and spices. Rub in the butter and then mix in the crumbs. Mix the rest of the materials in thoroughly and spread on to a well greased baking sheet about 16 in. × 16 in. (40 × 40 cm.). Bake at 400° F (204° C). Brush over with stock syrup immediately on removal from the oven. When cool, cut into squares.

Ginger Cakes

lb	oz		kg	gr
1	4	Butter		625
1	8	Flour (soft)		750
1	7	Egg		720
1	2	Sugar		560
	3	Flour (soft)		90
	1	Cornflour		30
	12	Chopped preserved ginger		375

Using the flour batter method, proceed by first beating the flour (1 lb. 8 oz.) (750 gr.) and butter until light.

Whip the egg and sugar to a stiff sponge and blend carefully into the butter/flour mix. Sieve the rest of the flour and the cornflour and fold in. Weigh at 1 lb. (500 gr.) into well greased bread tins. Bake at 360° F (182° C). When cool, spread the tops with water icing and place thin slices of preserved ginger over the surface.

(Scotland)

Ginger Cakes I

lb	oz		kg	gr
	7	Butter		200
	7	Lard		200
1	0	Sugar (soft brown)		500
1	0	Egg		500
2	0	Syrup	1	
2	10	Flour (strong)	1	300
	1	Cornflour		30
	³/₄	Bicarbonate of soda		20
	¹/₄	Nutmeg		8
	1	Cassia		30
	¹/₂	Mixed spice		15
	¹/₄	Pimento		8
1	2	Milk		560

Cream the fats and sugar lightly and add the egg by degrees beating well after each addition. Add the warmed syrup and half the milk. Add the flours, the soda and the spices that have all been sieved together. Finally, add the rest of the milk. Scale at 1 lb. (500 gr.) into well greased oblong tins. Bake at 355° F (179° C).

Ginger Cakes II

lb	oz		kg	gr
1	4	Flour (medium)		625
	¹/₂	Baking powder		15
	¹/₂	Ground ginger		15
	12	Butter		375
	4	Sugar (dark brown)		125
1	8	Golden syrup		750
	6	Milk		180

Blend all the ingredients together and weigh the mixture into 1 lb. (500 gr.) bread tins at 14 oz. (435 gr.). The tins may be well greased or paper lined. Bake at 360-370° F (182-187° C).

Sultanas or chopped preserved ginger may be added.

Ginger Cakes - Small

lb	oz		kg	gr
	4	Butter		125
	4	Cooking fat		125
	6	Sugar		180
	8	Golden syrup		250
	9	Egg		270
1	0	Flour		500
	¹/₂	Ground ginger		15
	¹/₈	Ground spice		4

lb	oz		kg	gr
	1/8	Cream of tartar		4
	1/8	Bicarbonate of soda		4
	2	Milk (approx.)		60

Cream the fats and sugar and add the egg a portion at a time. Mix in the golden syrup. Add the sieved flour, spices and chemicals and lastly the milk. Pipe out into well greased fluted or plain pans into the bottom of which a few flaked almonds are sprinkled. Bake at 350-360° F (176-182° C).

Display upside down.

Ginger Ovals

lb	oz		kg	gr
1	0	Flour		500
	3/4	Baking powder		20
	4	Butter		125
	3	Sugar (castor)		90
	8	Golden syrup		250
	1/4	Ground ginger		8
	2 1/2	Egg		75
	1 1/2	Chopped preserved ginger		45

After sieving the flour, ginger and the baking powder, rub in the butter. With the rest of the materials make into a firm dough and weigh into 1 oz. (30 gr.) pieces. Mould round and then into pointed oval shapes. Place on to lightly greased baking sheets and bake at 345° F (174° C). When cool, spread the tops with finely chopped preserved ginger bound with well boiled apricot purée. Glaze with thin water icing and return to the oven for a minute or so to set.

Ginger Sandwiches

lb	oz		kg	gr
1	4	Butter		625
1	4	Sugar (castor)		625
	1	Glycerine		30
1	4	Egg		625
1	8	Flour (soft)		750
	1/2	Baking powder		15
	1/2	Ground ginger		15
	1/8	Ground spice		4

Cream the butter and sugar adding the egg in portions. Add the glycerine and then the flour sieved with the spices and baking powder. Scale into shallow hoops that have been well greased. Bake at 360° F (182° C).

When cold they are split and sandwiched with ginger marmalade. To complete, dust with icing sugar.

Ginger Spice Loaf

lb	oz		kg	gr
	8	Flour (strong)		250
2	0	Flour (soft)	1	
	1	Bicarbonate of soda		30
	1	Mixed spice		30
	4	Cake crumbs		125
	5	Lard		150
	6	Sugar (soft brown)		180
	6	Treacle		180
	6	Syrup		180
1	14	Milk (approx.)		875
	6	Currants		180
	6	Sultanas		180
	1 1/2	Ginger crush		45

Cream the lard and sugar and add the syrups. Stir in the milk. Fold in all the dry materials that have been sieved together, adding the fruit last.

Scale at 1 lb. 6 oz. (680 gr.) into well greased oval tins. Bake at 355° F (179° C).

Ginger Sponges

Into 7 in. (18 cm.) greased and floured sandwich plates, place 7 oz. (300 gr.) of basic heavy sponge *(page 195)*. Bake at 400° F (204° C). When cool, split and sandwich with buttercream into which chopped preserved ginger has been mixed.

Place thin slices of preserved ginger on top and mask with thin white fondant flavoured with ginger syrup. Alternatively the sponge can be coated with fondant and the thin slices of ginger placed on top after which they are dusted with castor sugar.

Mask the sides with buttercream and roasted nib almonds.

Grantham Gingerbread
(A white gingerbread)

lb	oz		kg	gr
1	0	Flour		500
1	0	Sugar (castor)		500
	4 1/2	Butter		140
	4 1/2	Egg		140
	1/4	Ground ginger		8
	1 1/2	Milk (approx.)		45
	1/4	Carbonate of ammonia		8

Sieve the flour and the ground ginger. Rub in the butter. Dissolve the ammonia in the milk and make all the ingredients into a fairly tight dough. Roll the dough into ropes about 2 in. (5 cm.) in diameter and cut pieces off about 3/8 in. (1 cm.) thick.

Place, cut side down, on to lightly greased baking sheets and bake at 400° F (204° C). Do not allow them to colour too much during baking.

Alternatively the dough can be pinned out to a thickness of 1/4 in. (7 mm.) and cut out with a 2 1/2 in. (6 cm.) plain cutter.

(Great Britain)

Grasmere Gingerbread

lb	oz		kg	gr
2	4	Flour	1	125
	1/2	Ground ginger		15
	1/8	Ground mace		4
	1/8	Ground cinnamon		4
	15	Sugar (soft brown)		450
1	12	Butter		875

The flour and spices are sieved together and the sugar added. The butter is rubbed in carefully until the mixture looks like breadcrumbs. Do not make into a paste.

Place about 1/4 in. (8 mm.) thick on to a well greased baking sheet and lightly press level. Bake at 400° F (204° C). After about 15 minutes, remove from the oven and cut into oblong shapes with the point of a sharp knife.

Return to the oven to finish baking. Remove from the baking sheet when cold.
(Illustration page 391.)   *(Great Britain)*

Honey Ginger Cake

lb	oz		kg	gr
	8	Butter		250
	8	Sugar (brown)		250
1	0	Honey		500
1	8	Flour		750
	3/8	Baking powder		10
	1/8	Ground cinnamon		4
	1/8	Ground ginger		4
	10	Milk (approx.)		300
	8	Egg		250

Cream the butter and sugar and add the egg in portions. Mix in the honey. Add the flour sieved with the baking powder and spices. Lastly add the milk. Weigh into well greased fluted tins. Bake at 345° F (174° C). Display them upside down.

Honey Squares

lb	oz		kg	gr
3	0	Flour	1	500
	1 1/4	Ground ginger		35
	1/2	Ground cinnamon		15
	1/4	Ground mace		8
	1/4	Ground nutmeg		8
	1	Bicarbonate of soda		30
	8	Butter		250
1	12	Sugar		875
1	0	Honey		500
1	0	Syrup		500
	12	Lemon peel (chopped)		375

Sieve the flour/soda and spices and rub in the butter. Make a smooth dough with all the ingredients. Lay out on to well greased baking sheets and roll level. Dock well and bake at 350° F (176° C). Whilst still warm brush over with gum arabic solution. Cut into squares.

Kirriemuir Gingerbread

lb	oz		kg	gr
2	12	Flour (strong)	1	375
	1	Bicarbonate of soda		30
	4	Glycerine		125
	3/4	Ground ginger		20
	3/4	Ground spice		20
	3/4	Ground cinnamon		20
1	8	Golden syrup		750

lb	oz		kg	gr
	8	Sugar (soft brown)		250
	9	Butter		270
	8	Water 110° F (43° C)		250
		If required to be fruited add:		
	12	Sultanas		375
	12	Whole almonds		375
	8	Orange peel (chopped)		250

Sieve the flour, spices and soda thoroughly then, with the rest of the materials, make into a smooth dough. Let it rest overnight. The gingerbread can be made in slab form or in 8 oz. (250 gr.) or 1 lb. (500 gr.) round cakes. If the latter, mould them round, pin out to the size of the greased hoops, docking well on top. Brush with egg and bake at 360° F (182° C). As a guide, a 1 lb. (500 gr.) plain gingerbread will take about 1 1/2 hours to bake, the fruited variety will take a little longer.

(Scotland)

Marmalade Gingerbread

lb	oz		kg	gr
1	0	Flour		500
	1/2	Baking powder		15
	1/4	Ginger		8
	1/8	Cinnamon		4
1	0	Orange marmalade		500
	12	Golden syrup		375
	4	Egg		125
	2	Water (hot)		60
	6	Butter		180

Proceed as for Almond Gingerbread stirring in the hot water last. There is no almond decoration.

Nottingham Gingerbread

lb	oz		kg	gr
1	0	Flour		500
	1/2	Bicarbonate of soda		15
	1 1/2	Ground ginger		45
	8	Butter		250
	8	Sugar (brown)		250
1	0	Golden syrup		500
	3 1/2	Egg		100
	10	Milk		300

Sieve the flour and ginger. Warm the butter, sugar, syrup and milk and stir in the bicarbonate of soda and add it, with the egg, to the flour mixture. Mix well and pour into a 7 in. (18 cm.) hoop which has been lined with greaseproof paper. Bake at 340° F (171° C), for 1 1/4-1 1/2 hours. Cool and wrap in greaseproof paper so that the gingerbread becomes sticky.

(Great Britain)

Old English Gingerbread

Gingerbread *(page 366)* (less the fruit and almonds) can be rolled into lengths about 1 1/2 in. (4 cm.) thick and cut into pieces. These are placed, cut side down, on to well greased baking sheets. Alternatively, they can be weighed, moulded round and placed on to baking sheets, allowing room for them to spread during baking. Bake at 340° F (171° C).

Old Fashioned Ginger Snaps

lb	oz		kg	gr
3	0	Flour	1	500
1	0	Butter		500
1	6	Golden syrup		680
2	0	Sugar (brown)	1	
	1	Ground ginger		30
		Zest of lemon		

Warm the syrup and mix with the melted butter. Make into a dough with the sieved flour and ginger. Let the dough lay for a day or two to mature. When ready, roll the dough into ropes and pinch pieces off the size of walnuts and place on to greased baking sheets in rows. Bake at 380° F (193° C).

Oval Ginger Cakes

lb	oz		kg	gr
	5	Butter		150
	4	Cooking fat		125
	8	Sugar (castor)		250
	6	Egg		180
	10	Golden syrup		300
1	4	Flour		625
	3/8	Baking powder		10
	1/4	Bicarbonate of soda		8
	3/8	Ground ginger		10
	10	Milk (approx.)		300

Proceed as for Small Ginger Cakes. Weigh into well greased oval bread tins at 15 oz.

(450 gr.). Bake at 355° F (179° C). There are three methods of decoration.

1. Sprinkle flaked almonds in the tins after greasing. Display upside down.

2. Turn upside down after baking and spread the top neatly with white water icing made with the syrup from preserved ginger.

3. Turn upside down after baking and spread the top with finely chopped preserved ginger mixed with well boiled apricot purée. Glaze with thin water icing and return to the oven for a short time to allow the glaze to set.

Panforte di Siena

lb	oz		kg	gr
1	6	Sugar (granulated)		680
2	0	Honey	1	
2	12	Candied melon	1	375
2	12	Orange peel	1	375
2	12	Citron peel	1	375
2	12	Candied apricots	1	375
2	12	Roasted ground hazelnuts	1	375
	10	Flour (soft)		300
5	8	Roasted almonds	2	750
1	10	Roasted hazelnuts		800
	3/4	Ground nutmeg		20
	3/4	Ground cinnamon		20
	3/8	Vanilla powder		10
	1/16	Ground cloves		2
	1/16	Ground coriander		2

Cook the sugar with a little water and add the honey. When boiling take to 310° F (154° C). Take away from the heat and mix in the other ingredients (the peels and the apricots are chopped). Line rings with very smooth paper and place an unconsecrated host in the bottom. Put the mixture in the rings and leave them for 5-6 hours then bake at 460° F (240° C). When baked and cool, dust with castor sugar. Wrap in metal foil. *(Italy)*

Parkins

lb	oz		kg	gr
1	8	Flour		750
1	8	Oatmeal (medium)		750
	1	Ground ginger		30
	1	Ground spice		30
	1 1/2	Bicarbonate of soda		45
	5	Butter		150
	2	Cooking fat		60
1	8	Golden syrup		750
	10	Sugar		300
	2	Milk		60

The flour and spices are sieved together and mixed with the oatmeal. The fats are then rubbed in finely. The soda is dissolved in the milk. All the materials are then mixed to a smooth fairly firm dough which is weighed into 1 1/2 oz. (45 gr.) pieces. The pieces are moulded round and placed on to lightly greased baking sheets. They are slightly flattened and washed with egg. Each parkin has a split almond placed in the centre. They are baked at 340° F (171° C). Parkins should not be placed too close together on the baking sheets because they will spread during baking.
(Illustration 395.)   *(Great Britain)*

Parkin Slab

lb	oz		kg	gr
1	0	Flour		500
	1/2	Ground ginger		15
	1/4	Baking powder		8
2	0	Oatmeal (medium)	1	
	12	Butter		375
2	0	Sugar (brown)	1	
2	0	Golden syrup	1	
1	4	Milk (approx.)		625

Sieve the flour, baking powder and ginger. Mix in the oatmeal. The sugar, butter and syrup are heated and poured over the dry materials together with sufficient milk to make a fairly soft mixture. It is then poured into well greased flat pans, or into tins lined with paper. They are baked at 325° F (162° C). *(Great Britain)*
(Illustration page 395.)

Parliament Cakes

lb	oz		kg	gr
2	0	Flour	1	
	1/2	Ground caraway		15
	2	Lard		60

lb	oz		kg	gr
	½	Bicarbonate of soda		15
1	4	Syrup		625
	2	Milk (approx.)		60
		Salt		

Sieve the flour and caraway and rub in the lard. Dissolve the soda in the milk and with the syrup make a smooth dough. Pin out to about ⅙ in. (4 mm.) thick and cut into rectangular shapes. Bake at 360° F (182° C).

Speculaas Dolls - Speculaas-Poppen

lb	oz		kg	gr
2	4	Flour (soft)	1	125
	1	Speculaas spice (page 362)		28
	¾	Baking powder		20
1	0	Butter		500
1	4	Sugar (castor)		625
	1	Zest of lemon		30
	1 ¾	Egg		50
	¼	Salt		6

Make a dough from these ingredients and let it rest in a cool place for a few hours. Roll the dough into ropes, and mould with the use of a special speculaas-board. Cut away the superfluous dough and loosen the doll from the mould and place on a baking sheet.

Brush with egg, cover the doll with almonds and brush again. Baking temperature 338° F (170° C). *(Holland)*
(Illustration page 394.)

Spiced Gingerbread - Ontbijtkoek

lb	oz		kg	gr
5	10	Grape sugar	2	800
4	8	Honey	2	250
3	12	Water	1	875
11	4	Rye flour	5	625
	3	Bicarbonate of soda		90
	1 ¾	Spice		50

Boil together the water, 2 lb. (1 kg.) honey and grape sugar.

Mix the boiling mass with the sieved flour. Let the dough rest for a few days and after this rest, mix with the rest of the honey, the soda and the spice *(page 362)*.

Weigh the dough into the desired weights and roll on to a greased baking sheet fitted with a greased wooden frame which will contain the gingerbread as it rises in the oven. Brush with water and bake at 356° F (180° C). Baking time 45-50 minutes.

After baking, turn the cake on to a board and let it cool. After cooling, cut into strips of the desired weight and shape (i.e. 1 lb.) (500 gr.). One can also add ginger, candied peel or sugar nibs to the dough. Depending on the addition or combination of additions the cakes are known as ginger cake, fruit cake, candied peel cake, etc.
(Holland)

Spicy Speculaas - Gevulde Speculaas

This pastry keeps well and is made of a combination of speculaas-dough, and almond paste.

Recipe for the dough:

lb	oz		kg	gr
2	4	Flour (soft)	1	125
	1	Spices		28
	⅜	Speculaas spice		10
	⅜	Baking powder		10
1	4	Butter		625
1	0	Sugar (castor)		500
		Zest of lemon		
	3	Egg		90
	¼	Salt		6

After mixing, let the dough rest in a cool place for a few hours. Next roll the dough ⅛ in. (4 mm.) thick which will cover a baking sheet. On this dough put a layer of almond paste, which has been rolled to a thickness of 1/16 in. (2 mm.). The almond paste is again covered with a layer of dough.

Brush with egg, cover well with almonds and brush again with egg. Bake at a temperature of 338° F (170° C). Cut after cooling.

Alternatively, they may be made in the same way as for Butterletters in which case they are baked at 437° F (225° C). Both types are illustrated. *(Holland)*
(Illustration page 394.)

St. Gallen Biber I

lb	oz		kg	gr
2	0	Honey	1	
	14	Sugar (castor)		435
	⁷/₈	Potash		25
	8	Milk (approx.)		250
	2 ¹/₂	Spice*		75
3	4	Flour	1	625
		Zest of 1 lemon		

* Page 362.

Warm the honey and sugar. Dissolve the potash in the warmed milk. When the honey/sugar mixture is at blood heat, make all the ingredients into a dough which is left to mature for from one to two weeks. When ready, it is put through the rollers three or four times and then rolled to ¹/₄ in. (7 mm.) thick. It is pressed into special wooden moulds and, after the filling (page 224) has been added, the pieces are lightly water washed and then covered with paste of the same thickness. Turn out on to baking sheets and bake at 380° F (193° C) to a golden brown and, whilst still hot brush with gum arabic solution.

(Switzerland)

St. Gallen Biber II

lb	oz		kg	gr
2	0	Honey	1	
1	0	Sugar		500
	4	Water		125
	1 ³/₄	Caramel colour		50
3	0	Flour	1	500
	¹/₄	Ammonium		7
	¹/₄	Bicarbonate of soda		7
	³/₄	Biber dough spice (page 362)		25
	2	Kirsch		60
		Zest of 1 lemon		

Filling: 8 oz. (250 gr.) marzipan brought to a spreading consistency with 8 oz. (250 gr.) sugar, kirsch and a little water. Alternatively the mixing on *page 224* can be used. Warm the honey with the water, sugar and caramel. Allow to cool, then add the other ingredients and mix to a smooth dough. Weigh into 3 ¹/₂ oz. (100 gr.) pieces, pin out into circles, sandwich in pairs with the filling, and edge with a rim one finger thick. Brush with egg, dock lightly, place almonds in the centre and bake at about 420° F (215° C).

(Switzerland)

St. Gallen Biberli

Take the same dough as for St. Gallen Biber and pin out about ³/₁₆ in. (4 mm.) thick and cut into strips 2 ¹/₂ in. (6 cm.) wide. Using a large plain tube, pipe the filling along the centre. The same filling as for St. Gallen Biber is used but of firmer consistency. Damp the bottom edge of the strip and fold over to enclose the filling. Shape into a roll with the seam underneath. Brush with milk and cut into blunt tipped triangles. Bake at 420° F. (215° C), then glaze with a gum arabic solution. During baking, the filling remains soft and spreads out a little. *(Switzerland)*
(Illustration page 355.)

Wholemeal Ginger Slices

lb	oz		kg	gr
1	8	Wholemeal		750
	8	Flour (soft)		250
	³/₈	Baking powder		10
	¹/₄	Ground spice		7
	7	Butter		200
	3	Ginger crush		90
	10	Sugar (brown)		300
1	8	Syrup		750

Sieve the wholemeal flour, baking powder and spice and rub in the butter. With the rest of the materials make a smooth dough. Pin out to about ³/₈ in. (1 cm.) thick and place on a baking sheet. Dock well and bake at 380° F (193° C). As soon as it is baked, brush over with well boiled apricot purée and, when set, mask with thin water icing. Return to the oven for a few seconds to form a dry glaze and when cold cut into fingers.

Wrexham Gingerbread

lb	oz		kg	gr
2	0	Molasses	1	
1	0	Sugar (brown)		500
2	8	Butter	1	250
	2	Ground ginger		60
	¹/₂	Ground clove		15
3	0	Flour	1	500

Boil the molasses, sugar and butter until they are nearly candied. Cool and add the sieved flour and spices. Pin out and place on a baking sheet. Dock well and bake at 360° F (182° C). When cold, cut into squares or rectangles. *(Wales)*

Lebkuchen - Germany

BASIC DOUGHS

Honey Dough - Honigteig

lb	oz		kg	gr
30	0	Honey	15	
30	0	Flour	15	
6-10		Rye meal	3-5	

Bring the honey to the boil over moderate heat and remove when it begins to rise. Strain and leave until fairly cool. Now add the flour and mix well by hand or machine. Store until required.

Sugar Dough - Zuckerteig

lb	oz		kg	gr
10	0	Sugar	5	
5	0	Water	2	500
16	0	Flour	8	

Heat the sugar and water until the sugar has dissolved and leave until cold. Add the flour and work well together. Use as required (without storing).

Treacle Dough - Syrupteig

lb	oz		kg	gr
30	0	Treacle	15	
30	0	Flour	15	
10	0	Rye meal	5	
3	0	Water	1	500

Bring the treacle almost to the boil over moderate heat and leave until cold. Add the flour and mix well by hand or machine. Store until required.

Water Dough - Wasserteig

Water dough is used to improve the consistency of Lebkuchen doughs which contain too much aerating agent or have been stored for too long and lost their firmness. It is simply prepared by kneading flour and water to a dough of the same consistency as the dough to be treated and is then worked into the latter by means of the brake or machine.

INFORMATION

Storage of Lebkuchen Doughs

After the basic Lebkuchen doughs have been well worked, they must be left to mature. For this purpose they should be stored in a cool, dry place in covered tubs or barrels. The age of a dough is important; doughs should preferably be stored for 3-4 months before use as this improves their baking properties and the appearance of the finished goods. New doughs require large amounts of aerating agent and tend to shrink during baking. There are exceptions, however, and every dough should be tested before use; some require long storage, while others are ready for use after 4-6 weeks.

RAW MATERIALS FOR BROWN LEBKUCHEN

In addition to the basic doughs, the following ingredients are used: candied orange and lemon peel, almonds, lemons, spices (cinnamon, cloves, cardamom and mace), ammonium or carbonate of ammonia, and potash.

Candied Orange and Lemon Peel

To prepare candied peel for use in Lebkuchen, the amounts required for external decoration should first be cut out of whole caps and the trimmings should be used for chopping.

Remove the crystallized sugar before cutting out. Orange peel is usually cut into diamond shapes for the decoration of Lebkuchen.

Lemon Zest

The zest may be grated or very finely chopped. If it is to be stored, it should be mixed with sugar.

Spices

The cinnamon, cloves, cardamom and spices used for Lebkuchen should be of excellent quality. The more finely ground they are, the better the flavour of the Lebkuchen.

Almonds

Almonds which are to be added to the dough should first be soaked in water; the excess water is then removed and the almonds are ready for use. The object of moistening the almonds is to make them sink to the bottom during baking; the dough then rises all round them, giving the finished goods a dimpled appearance. Choice almonds of uniform size should be used for decoration; they should be soaked in water overnight and dried before use.

Aerating Agents

Potash and ammonia should be used carefully. Potash is soaked in water and either pounded in a mortar or ground in a small mill before use. If the potash is not finely ground it may cause blistering. When potash is mixed with water it gradually gets warm, resulting in caking through evaporation of the water. It is therefore necessary to add water from time to time. Ammonium or carbonate of ammonia should be finely ground and sieved before use.

The most reliable procedure is to moisten the required amounts of potash and ammonium with water, grind them together in a mortar and add them to the dough through a hair sieve.

Dusting Flour

To give the underside of brown Lebkuchen a smooth finish and an attractive appearance, the baking sheets should be dusted with special dusting flour, prepared from flour, yeast, water and a little annatto colour mixed to a dough with water. The dough is divided into pieces of a convenient size, left to ferment, then baked, broken into small pieces, dried and ground ready for use.

ICINGS AND GLAZES

Brown Lebkuchen Glaze

Use 3 lb. (1 kg. 500) water to 1 lb. (500 gr.) potato flour or cornflour. Brown the flour, blend with the water over the fire and bring to the boil. Remove the scum which rises to the surface, then use as required, adding a little hot water if the glaze is too stiff. Brush on the Lebkuchen and dry in the oven.

Chocolate Icing

Use 8 oz. (250 gr.) cocoa paste and 2 lb. (1 kg.) sugar to approximately 1 lb. (500 gr.) water. Heat the cocoa gently in the water until the cocoa has completely dissolved, adding more water if necessary and stirring continuously. Add the sugar and a little vanilla flavouring and boil to the thread degree *(page 51)*. Remove from the heat, rub the icing against the side of the pan until a skin has formed and use as desired. Goods decorated with chocolate icing should be dried in a fairly warm place to give them a glossy finish.

Egg Glaze

Dilute the egg with milk.

Gum Arabic Glaze

See page 246. If not glossy enough, boil for a short time and glaze the cake again.

Lemon Icing

Mix the required quantity of icing sugar with sufficient water or stock syrup to produce a paste of the desired stiffness. Flavour either with citric acid or with very finely cut lemon zest rubbed off on loaf sugar and lemon juice squeezed through a cloth.

Meringue Icing

Use 1 lb. 2 oz. (500 gr.) sugar to 10 egg whites. Boil the sugar to the thread degree. Meanwhile whip the egg whites to a snow; remove the sugar from the fire and slowly pour it into the egg whites. Beat for a short time, then use as required. Goods decorated with meringue icing should be left to dry in a warm place.

Raspberry Icing

Raspberry icing may be made with stock syrup or water as described above. Alternatively, egg whites may be used; in this case, they are beaten with sufficient icing sugar to give a fairly stiff spreading consistency. Raspberry juice or essence is used for flavouring, and a little red colour may be added if desired.

Transparent Icing

Boil stock syrup to the thread degree. Remove from the fire, work against the side of the pan for a short time and spread thinly on the Lebkuchen, using a brush.

Vanilla Icing

Vanilla icing is usually prepared from egg whites and icing sugar flavoured with vanilla or vanilla sugar.

Stock Syrup

Use approximately 1 lb. (500 gr.) water per pound of sugar. Heat the sugar and water together over a fairly gentle fire until the sugar has completely dissolved. If a cheap grade of sugar is used, add one or two whipped egg whites, depending on the quantity of sugar, to make the scum rise to the surface. When the solution comes to the boil, chill the pan several times with cold water, wash down the sides of the pan and remove the scum from the surface. When cold, the stock syrup may be used for a variety of icings.

LEBKUCHEN-RECIPES

Almond and Hazelnut Fingers

lb	oz		kg	gr
20	0	Treacle dough	10	
10	0	Honey dough	5	
10	0	Sugar dough	5	
2	0	Water dough	1	
	2 ½	Cinnamon		75
	1	Ground cloves		30
	7	Potash		200
	5	Ammonium		150

Work the various doughs and the rest of the ingredients well together. Pin out thinly and cut into fingers 3 × 1 ¼ in. (8 × 3 cm.) or 4 × 1 ½ in. (10 × 3 ½ cm.). Sprinkle with chopped almonds or hazelnuts and bake at 360° F (180° C) for about 15 minutes. When cold, coat with bitter chocolate couverture. *(Germany)*
(Illustration page 356.)

Almond Lebkuchen - Mandellebkuchen

lb	oz		kg	gr
13	4	Blanched almonds	6	
19	12	Sugar	9	
6	9	Egg whites	3	
4	8	Flour	2	
2	4	Chopped candied lemon peel	1	
2	4	Chopped candied orange peel	1	
	5	Ground cinnamon		150
	2 ½	Ground cloves		75
	1 ¾	Ground mace		50
	1 ¾	Ground cardamom		50
	2 ¾	Ammonium		80
	¾	Potash		20
		Grated zest of 2 lemons		

Grate the almonds after blanching and drying, mix with one third of the sugar and moisten with egg whites. Then grind between rollers, add the remaining ingredients and work thoroughly. Scale off the mixing (approximately 2 oz. (60 gr.) to a wafer 4 in. (10 cm.) in diameter) and spread on the wafers.

Place on baking sheets covered with cardboard and decorate with halved, blanched almonds. After drying, bake off carefully. After baking, leave until cold before icing.
(Germany)

Baked Marzipan Santa Claus

lb	oz		kg	gr
4	0	Raw marzipan	2	
	1 ¾	Honey		50

Mix these two ingredients together and pin out to about 3/8 in. (1 cm.) thick. Cut out Santa Claus figures with a cutter or a knife and bake about 360° F (180° C). When cold, decorate with marzipan, royal icing, couverture, sugar nibs and golf leaf. *(Illustration page 355.)* *(Germany)*

Brown Lebkuchen Nuts
(Nuremberg Style)

lb	oz		kg	gr
6	0	Sugar (pulverized)	3	
1	8	Egg		750
	1 1/2	Potash		45
	3/4	Ammonium		20
	6	Ground cinnamon		180
	1	Ground cloves		30
	1/4	Ground cardamom		5
	1/4	Mace		5
1	0	Candied lemon peel		500
1	0	Candied orange peel		500
3	0	Honey dough	1	500
5	8	Flour	2	750
		Grated zest of 2 lemons		

Mix the egg and sugar together; then add potash and ammonium as aerating agents, the spices (cinnamon, cloves, cardamom and mace), the orange and lemon peel, grated lemon zest and honey dough. Lightly work to a firm dough with the flour, adding a little water if required. Then use the pastry brake or machine to work thoroughly. Pin out, cut into small rounds about 1 1/4-1 1/2 in. (3-4 cm.) across and place on lightly greased baking sheets. Lightly spray with water and bake in a hot oven. *(Germany)*
(Illustration page 395.)

Chocolate Hearts
Take the same dough as for Dominoes. Pin out fairly thinly, make heart shapes with a cutter or a mould, bake, leave until cold and coat with tempered couverture. *(Germany)*

Chocolate Lebkuchen

lb	oz		kg	gr
5	0	Almonds	2	500
11	0	Sugar	5	
2	4	Egg whites	1	125
2	0	Flour	1	
1	0	Finely cut candied lemon peel		500
1	0	Finely cut candied orange peel		500
	1/6	Ammonium		5
		Grated zest of 2 lemons		

First grate the almonds finely and grind them between rollers with part of the sugar and egg whites. Then mix to a paste with the remaining ingredients and work well. Spread on wafers 4 in. (10 cm.) in diameter at the rate of 2 oz. (60 gr.) per wafer. Place on baking sheets covered with cardboard and leave to dry. When a skin has formed, after about 1 1/2 to 2 hours, bake in a moderately hot oven.

When cold, coat the Lebkuchen with plain chocolate couverture. *(Germany)*
(Illustration page 395.)

Dominoes - Dominosteine

lb	oz		kg	gr
11	0	Honey dough	5	
22	0	Treacle dough	10	
11	0	Sugar dough	5	
2	4	Water dough	1	
	2 1/2	Ground cinnamon		70
	1	Ground cloves		30
	7	Potash		200
	5 1/4	Ammonium		150

Pin out the dough into even rectangular sheets approximately 35 in. by 18 in. (90 × 45 cm.) bake for about 30 minutes at 374° F (190° C) and leave until cold, if possible in a damp place. Then make the quince paste filling *(page 641)* and sandwich the sheets in pairs with a layer of filling about 1/2 in. (1 cm.) thick. When cold, cover the top with a thin sheet of lightly worked marzipan. Cut the sheets into 1 in. (2 1/2 cm.) cubes and lastly coat them with bitter chocolate couverture.
(Germany)

Elisen Lebkuchen

lb	oz		kg	gr
21	0	Sugar	10	500
15	0	Brown almonds	7	500

lb	oz		kg	gr
3	0	Candied orange peel	1	500
3	0	Candied lemon peel	1	500
10	0	Egg whites	5	
	7	Ammonium		200
6	0	Flour	3	
	8	Lebkuchen spices		250

Finely grind the sugar, almonds and candied peel moistened with a little egg white. Then mix in the remaining egg whites, together with the flour, ammonium and spices and spread the mixing on wafers. Leave to dry for a whole day and then bake for about 20 minutes in a moderate oven.

If desired, decorate some of the Lebkuchen with halved almonds and candied lemon peel before baking. In the illustration, the 1st and 3rd varieties are coated with water icing (boiled to the thread degree, 225° F [107° C]); the 2nd variety has been coated with plain chocolate couverture when cold and the 4th variety has been left undecorated. *(Germany)*
(Illustration page 395.)

Filled Honey Slices

Take the same dough as for Dominoes and pin out into thin rectangular sheets 36 × 18 in. (90 × 45 cm.). Bake, then sandwich the sheets in pairs with various fillings, as used for Dominoes and filled Lebkuchen, and cut into pieces 3 1/2 × 2 in. (9 × 4 1/2 cm.). Coat partly with almond couverture and partly with couverture containing sieved praline croquant. *(Germany)*

Filled Lebkuchen
(Liegnitz Style)

Dough as for Dominoes.
Filling

lb	oz		kg	gr
16	0	Apricot jam	7	500
5	0	Sultanas	2	500
3	0	Finely cut candied orange peel	1	500
3	0	Finely cut candied lemon peel	1	500
3	0	Chopped roasted almonds	1	500
1	0	Rum		500

First pin out the dough and cut into pieces 6 in. by 3 in. (15 × 7 1/2 cm.). Bake for about 30 minutes at 374° F (190° C). Meanwhile prepare the filling by bringing the apricot jam to the boil, stirring in the sultanas, peel and almonds and lastly adding the rum.

When the Lebkuchen are cold, sandwich in pairs with this filling, sprinkle the top with almond nibs and lastly coat with thin chocolate couverture. *(Germany)*

Lebkuchen Hearts

Use the same dough as for Dominoes. Either pin out the dough and use a cutter to make the hearts or fill into special moulds to make the impressions. After baking and cooling, coat with brown Lebkuchen glaze or couverture. Before it dries, place a picture on top if desired and decorate with royal icing and/or almonds.

Lebkuchen Triangles I - Spitzkuchen

lb	oz		kg	gr
13	0	Honey dough ready for use	6	
2	0	Sultanas	1	
2	0	Pounded brown hazelnuts	1	
2	0	Pounded brown almonds	1	

Mix the sultanas, hazelnuts and almonds with the honey dough. Divide into pieces each weighing 9 oz. (270 gr.) and pin each out to 28 in. (72 cm.) in length. Place on baking sheets, brush with water and bake for about 20 minutes at 356° F (180° C).

When cold, cut the strips into triangles and coat with bitter chocolate couverture. *(Germany)*

Lebkuchen Triangles II

lb	oz		kg	gr
10	0	Honey dough	5	
5	0	Sugar dough	2	500
	7	Egg yolks		200
1	0	Chopped almonds		500

lb	oz		kg	gr
	8	Flaked almonds		250
	2	Potash		60
1 1/4		Ammonium		40

Make all the ingredients into a dough, pin out to about 3/8 in. (1 cm.) thick and place on to a baking sheet. Bake at about 360° F (180° C). When cold, store in a cool humid place overnight. Cut into strips 1 in. (3 cm.) wide and each strip into blunt tipped triangles. Coat with tempered couverture. *(Germany)*

Lucerne Lebkuchen

lb	oz		kg	gr
2	0	Milk	1	
	10	Sugar		300
3	10	Flour (approx.)	1	800
	5	Lebkuchen spice		150
	5	Butter		150
1	8	Pear molasses		750
	1 3/4	Bicarbonate of soda		50

Dissolve the soda in the milk and mix with the sugar and molasses. Sieve the flour and the spice together and mix all the ingredients together, adding a little more flour if required. Weigh off pieces of the desired weight, but not exceeding 1 lb. (500 gr.), each. Mould round and place on lightly greased and floured baking sheets, not too close together. Bake at about 360° F (180° C). These Lebkuchen are intended to be eaten fresh. *(Switzerland)*

Nut Lebkuchen - Nuss-Lebkuchen

lb	oz		kg	gr
1	14	Grated brown hazelnuts		900
3	5	Sugar	1	500
	7	Chopped candied lemon peel		200
	7	Chopped candied orange peel		200
	14	Egg whites		900
	8	Flour		250
	2	Lebkuchen spices		60
	1/6	Ammonium		5

Heat the hazelnuts, sugar, lemon and orange peel and egg whites together to a paste. Then blend in the flour, Lebkuchen spices and ammonium and spread on wafers 4 in. (10 cm.) in diameter while still warm. At the rate of 2 oz. (60 gr.) per wafer, the yield is about 64 Lebkuchen. After leaving the spread wafers to dry for three to four hours, bake in a moderate oven for about 20 minutes. *(Germany)*

White Lebkuchen
(Finest Quality)

lb	oz		kg	gr
12	0	Sugar	6	
15	0	Flour	7	500
11	4	Egg	5	625
	15	Almond nibs (roasted)		450
1	0	Peel (lemon)		500
1	0	Peel (orange)		500
	7	Cinnamon		200
	1 1/2	Cloves (ground)		45
	1/4	Cardamom		8
	1/4	Mace		8
1	0	Treacle		500
	2 1/2	Ammonium		75
	3/4	Potash		20
		Zest of 2 lemons		

Make the dough in exactly the same way as for White Lebkuchen Nuremberg Style and bake. If the dough is too stiff, add a little more egg. Chop the almonds and peel a little more finely than for Nuremberg Lebkuchen to give a better spreading consistency. Wrap in exactly the same way as for Nuremberg Lebkuchen. *(Germany)*

White Lebkuchen -
(Nuremberg Style)

lb	oz		kg	gr
10	0	Sugar	5	
9	0	Egg	4	500
	1 3/4	Ammonium		50
	1/2	Potash		15
	7	Treacle		300
	5	Cinnamon		150
	2 3/4	Cloves		80
	1 3/4	Cardamom		50
	1	Mace		30
3	8	Roasted almonds	1	750

lb	oz		kg	gr
2	4	Candied lemon peel	1	125
2	4	Candied orange peel	1	125
9	0	Flour	4	500
		Grated zest of 5 lemons		

Stir the sugar well with 3 lb. 4 oz. (1 kg. 600) egg until the batter begins to froth. Add the remaining eggs and stir again thoroughly. Now add the ammonium, potash and treacle and mix well. (Be sure not to forget the treacle, which gives the Lebkuchen an attractive, freshlooking colour.)

Add the spices (cinnamon, cloves, cardamom and mace), the almonds, candied orange and lemon peel and grated lemon zest. Mix well once more and finally add the flour.

If the mixing is too soft, add a little sugar and flour in equal proportions to prevent it from running off the wafers. Spread the mixing on wafers and place on baking sheets covered either with three layers of paper or with cardboard. Decorate as desired with candied lemon peel or almonds and set away to dry. Make sure the place where they are drying is not too hot, otherwise their appearance may be spoilt by blistering. After drying, which will take two to three hours, leave in a cool place, then bake in a moderately hot oven. After baking, invert the Lebkuchen quickly and leave until cold. This will ensure a smooth surface and improve their appearance.

When cold, wrap them in transparent blue paper half a dozen at a time. *(Germany)*
(Illustration page 377.)

XIII. Large Cakes and Slabs

The term 'cake' in Great Britain embraces almost all of the products, large and small, usually produced in a confectionery bakery. The British cakes described in this chapter were at one time known as 'pound cakes'. A definition of this term and information concerning them will be found on *page 203*. A descriptive term now being used in Great Britain is 'oven finished', that is to say cakes that need no decoration after leaving the oven. The exceptions to be found in this chapter are Christmas, Simnel, Bride and Birthday Cakes which are included for convenience. Further information on these heavily fruited cakes will be found on *page 382*. Continental cakes included in this chapter are both oven finished and those that are decorated after baking, the latter not fitting the British understanding of gâteaux and torten, which can be found together in Chapter XIX.

Almond Cakes

lb	oz		kg	gr
1	8	Butter		750
	12	Compound fat		375
2	0	Sugar (castor)	1	
1	4	Raw marzipan*		625
2	4	Egg	1	125
2	4	Flour (soft)	1	125
		Zest of 2 lemons		

* The marzipan used must be two parts almonds and one part sugar.

Soften the marzipan with a little of the butter until smooth. Cream the butter, marzipan mix, sugar and lemon zest and add the egg a portion at a time. Fold in the flour and scale at 1 lb. (500 gr.) each into paper lined 5 ½ in. (14 cm.) cake hoops. Dust with castor sugar and bake at 370° F (187° C). *(Great Britain)*

Almond Dessert Cakes

lb	oz		kg	gr
1	4	Egg		625
	12	Butter		375
	4	Compound fat		125
	4	Raw marzipan		125
	1 ½	Glycerine		40
1	8	Flour (soft)		750
	1/16	Baking powder		2
1	4	Currants		625
1	8	Sultanas		750
	4	Citron peel (diced)		125
	4	Mixed peel (chopped)		125
	4	Cherries		125
	2 ½	Rum		75
	1 ½	Caramel colour		45
1	0	Sugar (brown)		500

Pour the rum over the prepared fruit and distribute it by rubbing lightly with the hands. Allow to stand overnight. Reduce the marzipan with a little butter. Cream the fats, sugar and glycerine lightly adding the egg a little at a time. Add the caramel colour. Fold in the flour that has been sieved with the baking powder and finally mix in the fruit. Scale 10 oz. (300 gr.) into paper lined tins about 8 in. by 3 ½ in. by 3 in. (20 × 9 × 7 cm.) deep. On top of this, lay a piece of raw marzipan about 3 ½ oz. (100 gr.) shaped to the size of the tin. Place another 10 oz. (300 gr.) of batter on top and spread level. Sprinkle the top with strip almonds and bake at 360° F (182° C).

Birthday Cakes

lb	oz		kg	gr
	12	Butter		375
	4	Compound fat		125
1	0	Sugar (dark brown)		500
	1	Caramel		30
	1	Glycerine		30
1	4	Egg		625
1	5	Flour (soft)		650
	⅛	Baking powder		4
	2	Ground almonds		60
	⅛	Ground nutmeg		4
	⅛	Ground spice		4
1	12	Currants		875
1	4	Sultanas		625
	12	Cherries		375
	8	Cut mixed peel		250

Zest and juice of one lemon and one orange. Sugar batter method, *page 44*.
(Illustration page 426.)   *(Great Britain)*

Budapest Sand Cakes

lb	oz		kg	gr
	5	Sugar (castor)		150
	5 ½	Egg yolks		160
	5	Egg		150
	5	Flour		150
	5	Butter (melted)		150
	1	Rum		30
		Zest of ½ lemon		

Whisk up the egg, egg yolks, sugar, zest and rum over gentle heat and then continue until cold. Fold in the sieved flour and lastly, carefully blend in the melted butter. Fill into a greased and floured, oblong, fluted convex based mould (as used for Roe's Back Cake) and bake at 380° F (190° C). When cool, dust with icing sugar or coat with chocolate icing.
(Austria)

Butterletters

Butterletters are made in Holland mainly around the 5th of December, Saint Nicholas' birthday. The majority of these letters weigh around 1 lb. (500 gr.) after being baked. For these letters weigh:

lb	oz		kg	gr
1	8	Almond paste		750
	14	Puff pastry		400

Make the almond paste in the following proportions:

lb	oz		kg	gr
2	4	Ground almonds	1	125
2	4	Sugar (granulated)	1	125
	1 ½	Lemon peel		45
	7	Raw beaten egg		200

Mix and keep this filling cool for a few days, then bring the dough to the desired consistency with raw egg. Roll the almond paste into a rope and cut this rope into equal pieces of about 22 in. (55 cm.).

Roll the puff pastry very thin into pieces 24 in. (60 cm.) wide and ¹/₁₂ in. (3 mm.) thick. Brush with water and use this to cover the ropes of almond paste. Take care that the flat bottom consists of a double layer of paste.

Form into letter shapes. Brush with egg to which an additional egg yolk has been added; after 30 minutes rest, brush again with egg and bake. Oven temperature: 437° F (225° C).

The butterletters should have a flaky crust with a soft yellow filling.   *(Holland)*
(Illustration page 423.)

Cake Financière

lb	oz		kg	gr
1	14	Egg whites		900
2	3	Sugar (castor)	1	100
	14	Blanched almonds		425
1	5	Melted butter		650
1	5	Flour		650

Adding half the sugar, whisk the egg whites until they are stiff. Grind the almonds dry with the rest of the sugar and fold in the meringue mixture with a spatula. Next blend in the flour and melted butter. Deposit this mixture into financière moulds, the inside of which have been greased and sprinkled with flaked almonds. Bake in a slow oven 356° F (180° C).

(France)

Caracas Cakes I

lb	oz		kg	gr
1	5	Almond paste		650
1	0	Egg yolks		500
1	8	Egg whites		750
	5 1/4	Sugar		150
	10 1/2	Melted unsweetened chocolate		300
	7	Flour		200
	7	Butter (melted)		200

Caracas Cakes II

lb	oz		kg	gr
1	3	Almond paste		600
1	0	Egg yolks		500
1	4	Egg whites		625
	5	Sugar		150
	10	Dissolved cocoa		300
	7	Flour		200
	7	Butter		200
		Cream Ganache flavoured with vanilla		
		Vanilla couverture		

With the mixing machine blend thoroughly the egg yolks and almond paste. Meanwhile whisk the egg whites with the sugar until stiff. Amalgamate both mixtures and finally stir in the chocolate (or nougat), flour and melted butter. Deposit in oval shaped hoops and bake in a medium oven 410° F (210° C). When the cakes have cooled, cut from the top of each a triangular piece. Fill the holes with vanilla ganache and replace the triangular pieces in a vertical position. Cover the whole of the tops of the cakes with ganache, cover with vanilla couverture and decorate the crest with golden balls or pistachio nuts. *(Illustration page 544.)* *(France)*

Cherry Cakes

lb	oz		kg	gr
	12	Butter		375
	5	Compound fat		150
1	1	Sugar (castor)		530
1	4	Eggs		625
1	8	Flour		750
	1/8	Baking powder		4
2	0	Cherries	1	
	4	Chopped citron peel		125
		Vanilla essence		

Use either the flour or sugar batter method. The citron peel should be in even size pieces. The cherries should be washed in tepid water, drained and dried. Scale at 1 3/4 lb. (875 gr.) into paper lined 6 1/2 in. (16 cm.) hoops. Bake at 360° F (182° C). *(Great Britain)*
(Illustration page 424.)

Christmas Cakes

Recipe I

lb	oz		kg	gr
	12	Butter		375
	4	Compound		125
1	0	Sugar (dark brown)		500
1	4	Egg		625
	1	Glycerine		30
	1	Caramel		30
1	5	Flour (soft)		650
	4	Ground almonds		125
	1/8	Baking powder		3
1	8	Currants		750
1	0	Sultanas		500
	12	Raisins		375
	12	Mixed cut peel		375
	1/8	Cinnamon		3
	1/8	Spice		3
		Zest and juice of 1 lemon		
		Zest and juice of 1 orange		

Sugar batter method *(page 44.)*

Recipe II

lb	oz		kg	gr
	12	Butter		375
	4	Compound		125
1	0	Sugar (dark brown)		500
	6	Honey		180
1	3	Egg		590
	1	Glycerine		30
	1	Caramel		30
1	3	Flour (soft)		590

lb	oz		kg	gr
	3	Ground almonds		90
	1/8	Baking powder		4
1	14	Currants		935
1	12	Sultanas		875
	12	Cherries		375
	8	Mixed cut peel		250
	1	Spice		30
		Zest and juice of 1 lemon		
		Zest and juice of 1 orange		

Sugar batter method *(page 44)*.

Coconut Cakes
Group 1

lb	oz		kg	gr
1	9	Flour (medium)		775
	8	Sugar (castor)		250
	1	Baking powder		30
1	0	Butter		500

Sieve flour, sugar and baking powder and rub in the butter.

Group 2

lb	oz		kg	gr
	9	Desiccated coconut		275
	5	Milk powder		150
	7	Sugar (castor)		200
	15	Water		450

Mix together one hour before needed.

Group 3

lb	oz		kg	gr
	5	Egg		150
	1	Glycerine		28

Add Group 2 to Group 3 and then beat with the crumbly flour/butter mix (Group 1) until smooth. Weigh at 12 oz. (375 gr.) into 5 in. (13 cm.) cake hoops or 1 lb. (500 gr.) bread tins. Sprinkle tops with coconut topping *(page 226)*. Bake at 340° F (171° C).
(Illustration page 425.)

Date and Honey Cakes

lb	oz		kg	gr
1	8	Flour (medium)		750
	14	Sugar (castor)		400
	1	Milk powder		30
	3/4	Baking powder		20
	4	Honey		125
	10	Butter		300

Sieve the dry ingredients and mix with the honey and butter until a crumbly consistency is reached.

lb	oz		kg	gr
	7 1/2	Egg		215
	9	Water		280
	3/4	Glycerine		20

Mix together and add to the above. Beat until smooth.

lb	oz		kg	gr
	12	Chopped dates		375
	4	Sultanas		125

Add to the above and mix. Scale at 1 lb. (500 gr.) into 6 in. (15 cm.) hoops or greased 1 lb. (500 gr.) bread tins. Sprinkle with sugar nibs. Bake at 360° F (182° C). *(Illustration page 425.)*

Diabetic Cakes

lb	oz		kg	gr
1	2	Butter		560
	8	Egg		250
	8	Ground almonds		250
	4	Gluten flour		125

Cream the butter and add the egg a little at a time. Fold in the ground almonds and the gluten flour. Spread about 1/2 in. (1 cm.) thick on a paper lined baking sheet. Bake at 400° F (204° C). Cut into fingers.

Dundee Cakes

lb	oz		kg	gr
	12	Butter		375
	4	Compound fat		125
1	0	Sugar (Trinidad)		500
1	4	Egg		625
	2	Ground almonds		60
1	5	Flour (soft)		650
	1/8	Baking powder		4
2	0	Sultanas	1	

lb	oz		kg	gr
	4	Orange peel		125
1		Rum		30
		Caramel colour		

Use the sugar batter method *(page 44)*. When scaled into hoops, the tops of the cakes are decorated in concentric rings with split almonds which are placed cut side down. There are two methods of completing the finishing.

1. Dusting with castor sugar.

2. Brushing with stock syrup immediately on removal from the oven.

Bake at 350° F (176° C). *(Scotland)* *(Illustration page 421.)*

Farmhouse Cakes I

lb	oz		kg	gr
1	0	Flour		500
1	12	Sugar (castor)		875
	2	Milk powder		60
1	0	Butter		500

Sieve the flour, sugar and milk powder and rub in the butter.

lb	oz		kg	gr
1	4	Egg		625
	2	Glycerine		60

Add to the above and cream for 5 minutes on medium speed.

lb	oz		kg	gr
1	4	Water		625

Add half the water on low speed.

lb	oz		kg	gr
	12	Flour		375
	1	Baking powder		30
1	12	Cake crumbs		875
1	0	Sultanas		500
1	0	Currants		500
	8	Cut mixed peel		250

Add the sieved flour and baking powder, the cake crumbs and the fruit and mix in. Add the rest of the water. Scale at 1 lb. (500 gr.) into 1 lb. (500 gr.) well greased bread tins. Bake at 370° F (187° C).

Farmhouse Cakes II

lb	oz		kg	gr
1	0	Flour		500
	1 $1/4$	Baking powder		35
1	0	Cake crumbs		500
	7	Butter		200
	10	Sugar (castor)		300
	$1/8$	Salt		4
	8	Egg		250
1	0	Milk		500
	10	Currants		300
	8	Sultanas		250
	2	Mixed peel		60

Sieve the flour, salt and baking powder and rub in the butter. Mix in the cake crumbs and make a bay (or put into the machine). Add the rest of the materials and mix thoroughly. The mixture will be soft at first but will become tighter as the crumbs absorb the milk.

Weigh at 15 oz. (450 gr.) into 1 lb. (500 gr.) bread tins which have been well greased. Bake at 400° F (204° C).

Farmhouse Cakes III

lb	oz		kg	gr
1	8	Flour		750
	1	Baking powder		30
	$1/8$	Salt		4
	8	Butter		250
	6	Golden syrup		180
	7	Egg		200
	10	Milk		300
	8	Currants		250
	8	Sultanas		250
	8	Chopped mixed peel		250

Sieve the flour, baking powder and salt and rub in the butter. Warm the syrup slightly and mix with egg and milk. Mix well and add the fruit. This mixture is enough for two well greased 2 lb. (1 kg.) bread tins or two 7 in. (18 cm.) paper lined hoops. Bake at 350° F (176° C) for about 1 $3/4$ hours. *(West of England)*

Fig Cakes

lb	oz		kg	gr
	10	Hazelnuts		300
1	4	Sugar (castor)		625

lb	oz		kg	gr
	12	Butter		375
1	0	Egg yolks		500
	12	Egg whites		375
	5	Flour		150
	1	Ground cinnamon		30
	1/8	Ground nutmeg		4
	12	Dates (chopped)		375
	10	Walnuts (chopped)		300
	10	Soaked figs (chopped)		300
		Zest of 1 lemon		

Grind the hazelnuts with half the sugar and beat up this mixture with the egg yolks and the butter. Meanwhile whisk the egg whites with the rest of the sugar until stiff.

Amalgamate both these mixtures and then fold in carefully the rest of the ingredients. Fill some moulds which have been lined with Linz paste and cover with figs. Bake in a medium oven. *(France)*

Fruit and Almond Cakes

lb	oz		kg	gr
1	12	Butter		875
	8	Compound fat		250
2	8	Sugar (castor)	1	250
2	8	Egg	1	250
	8	Ground almonds		250
3	8	Flour (soft)	1	750
	3/4	Baking powder		20
2	0	Sultanas	1	
1	12	Cherries		875
1	0	Dates (chopped)		500

Cream the fats and the sugar. Add the egg a little at a time. Fold in the flour, baking powder and ground almonds, thoroughly mixed together and lastly add the fruit. Do not overbeat at the creaming stage.

Weigh at 15 oz. (450 gr.) into paper cases placed in 6 1/2 in. (16 cm.) cottage pans. Sprinkle the tops with split almonds and bake at 375° F (190° C).

Genoa Cakes

lb	oz		kg	gr
	12	Butter		375
	4	Compound fat		125
1	0	Sugar		500
1	4	Egg		625
1	7	Flour		700
	1/8	Baking powder		4
	1	Ground almonds		30
1	0	Currants		500
1	0	Cherries		500
	12	Sultanas		375
	3	Cut peel		90
	3	Cut citron peel		90
		Essence of almond and vanilla		
		Zest of lemon		

Use the sugar batter method *(page 44)*. Sprinkle with split almonds.
(Illustration page 424.)   *(Great Britain)*

Honey Almond Cakes

lb	oz		kg	gr
1	8	Butter		750
	4	Compound fat		125
2	0	Sugar (castor)	1	
	14	Raw marzipan		400
	10	Honey		300
1	12	Egg		875
3	0	Flour (soft)	1	500
	1	Baking powder		30
1	0	Milk		500

Soften the marzipan with a little butter. Cream it with the rest of the butter, the fat and sugar, adding the egg a little at a time. Mix in the honey then the flour that has been sieved with the baking powder. Lastly add the milk. Weigh at 1 lb. (500 gr.) into 5 1/2 in. (14 cm.) diameter paper lined hoops or into paper lined 1 lb. (500 gr.) bread tins. Sprinkle with flaked almonds and bake at 370° F (185° C). After baking, glaze with honey mixture *(page 245)*.

Honey Walnut Cakes

lb	oz		kg	gr
1	12	Butter		875
	4	Compound fat		125
1	12	Sugar (castor)		875
1	0	Honey		500
2	8	Egg	1	250
3	0	Flour (soft)	1	500

lb	oz		kg	gr
	5	Milk		150
	12	Chopped walnuts		375
	$1/4$	Baking powder		8

Cream the fats and sugar and add the egg a portion at a time. Add the honey. Fold in the flour and baking powder that have been sieved together and add the milk and chopped walnuts. Scale at 1 lb. (500 gr.) into 7 in. (18 cm.) cottage pans lined with greaseproof paper baking cups. Sprinkle the tops with chopped walnuts. Bake at 380° F (193° C). Glaze as above.

King Cakes

lb	oz		kg	gr
1	0	Butter		500
1	2	Sugar (icing)		560
	6	Peel (citron)		180
	6	Peel (orange)		180
2	0	Raisins	1	
	11	Egg yolks		330
2	7	Flour	1	200
	14	Egg whites		425
	$3 1/2$	Rum		100
		Zest of 2 lemons		

Pour the rum over the peel and raisins and macerate for some hours. Cream the butter with 12 oz. (375 gr.) sugar and add the egg yolks a little at a time. Blend in the flour and zest then the peel and raisins.

(The citron peel must be finely cut.) Lastly fold in the egg whites whisked to a stiff snow with the rest of the sugar.

Fill paper lined King Cake moulds with the mixture and bake at 360° F (180° C).
(Austria)

King Cakes

lb	oz		kg	gr
1	4	Sugar		625
1	4	Butter		625
1	0	Egg		500
2	8	Flour	1	250
	7	Currants		200
	5	Sultanas		150
	$3 1/2$	Peel (citron)		100
	$3 1/2$	Peel (orange)		100

Cream the butter and sugar, adding the egg and 2 lb. (1 kg.) of the flour a little at a time. Lastly add the rest of the flour and the fruit. Fill paper lined King Cake moulds with the mixture and bake at about 360° F (180° C). *(Germany)*

Lemon Almond Cakes

lb	oz		kg	gr
1	8	Butter		750
3	0	Sugar (castor)	1	500
1	4	Egg		625
1	0	Lemon curd		500
	$1/2$	Salt		15
2	0	Milk	1	
3	12	Flour (special cake)	1	875
	2	Baking powder		60

Cream the fat and sugar with the lemon curd and salt. Add the egg in portions. Mix in half the milk then the flour and powder sieved together. Finally add the rest of the milk and mix to a smooth batter.

Prepare 6 in. (15 cm.) cottage pans by greasing well and flouring. Place three narrow strips of sweet paste parallel to each other on the bottom and sprinkle some flaked almonds inside. Weigh into each pan 12 oz. (375 gr.) of the batter and bake at 360° F (182° C). When cool, turn them over and glaze with thin water icing.

Lemon Cakes

Group 1

lb	oz		kg	gr
2	8	Flour (special cake)	1	250
3	0	Sugar (castor)	1	500
	$3/4$	Salt		20
2	8	Butter	1	250

Group 2

lb	oz		kg	gr
3	0	Egg	1	500
	7	Water		200

Group 3

lb	oz		kg	gr
1	4	Lemon curd		625
	2	Lemon juice		60
1	12	Water		875
	3	Glycerine		90

Group 4

lb	oz		kg	gr
2	8	Flour (special cake)	1	250
	3	Baking powder		90

Mix group 1 to a crumbly mass. Do not let it form a paste. Add group 2 and mix for 5-7 minutes on second speed. Scrape the mixing bowl down then add half of group 3 which has been well stirred together. Blend for a few minutes then add the sieved flour and baking powder. Finally mix in the rest of the liquid group 3.

Weigh at 9 oz. (270 gr.) into 5 in. (12 $\frac{1}{2}$ cm.) cottage pans lined with paper cases. Flatten the mix and pipe a trellis pattern on top with lemon curd. Bake at 370° F (187° C).

Lightly Fruited Cakes

lb	oz		kg	gr
1	0	Butter		500
1	0	Sugar (castor)		500
1	6	Egg		680
1	8	Flour (soft)		750
	$\frac{1}{4}$	Baking powder		8
	10	Sultanas		300
	4	Cherries		125
	4	Peel		125
		Almond flavour		

Cream the butter and sugar and add egg in portions. Fold in the sieved flour and baking powder and finally the fruit. Deposit in paper lined hoops or bread tins. Bake at 360° F (182° C).

Linz Cakes

lb	oz		kg	gr
1	14	Flour (soft)		935
	7 $\frac{1}{2}$	Scone flour		215
1	12	Sugar (castor)		875
1	14	Butter		935
	12	Roasted ground hazelnuts		375
	12	Egg		375
	10	Milk		300
	$\frac{1}{8}$	Vanilla essence		4
	$\frac{3}{4}$	Ground cinnamon		20
		Zest of 1 lemon		

Cream butter, sugar and flavours and add the egg in portions. Mix in the flours and the hazelnuts. Line 6 in. (15 cm.) flan rings with greaseproof paper and pipe in the mixture spiral fashion, using a plain tube. Spread 2-3 oz. (60-90 gr.) of apricot jam on to 5 in. (12 cm.) wafer paper circles and place on top of the spirals. Pipe another spiral on top, sprinkle with flaked almonds and bake at 350° F (176° C).

(Austria)

Lunch Cakes

lb	oz		kg	gr
1	0	Butter		500
1	4	Sugar (castor)		625
1	0	Egg		500
2	8	Flour (soft)	1	250
	$\frac{3}{4}$	Baking powder		20
1	0	Milk		500
		Lemon flavour		

Proceed as for Lightly Fruited Cakes.

Luncheon Cakes

lb	oz		kg	gr
1	0	Butter		500
1	0	Sugar (castor)		500
1	2	Egg		560
1	12	Flour		875
	$\frac{1}{4}$	Baking powder		8
	5	Milk		150
	6	Sultanas		180
	6	Currants		180
	4	Cherries		125
	3	Peel		90

Proceed as for Lightly Fruited Cakes.

Luxury Fruit Cakes

Group 1

lb	oz		kg	gr
1	12	Sugar (brown)		875
	15	Milk		450
	1 $\frac{1}{2}$	Milk powder		45
	$\frac{3}{4}$	Salt		20
	2 $\frac{1}{2}$	Rice flour		75
	4	Praline paste		125
	6	Ground almonds		180
	$\frac{1}{2}$	Mixed ground spice		15
1		Caramel colour		30

▲ Scone Rounds, Victoria Scones, Turnover Scones, p. 311-312   A Variety of Shortbreads, p. 325 ▼

390 ▲ Viennese Custard Rings, p. 458

Meringue Rocks, p. 457 — Coconut Meringues, p. 454 ▼

▲ Gingerbread Squares, p. 366 — Ashbourne Gingerbread, p. 363 — Ginger Nuts, p. 488 — Grasmere Gingerbread, p. 369

Bethmännchen, p. 533 — Brenten, p. 533 ▼

392 ▲ Raspberry Meringue Kisses, Germany, p. 457

Moulded Meringues, p. 457 ▼

▲ Macaroon Biscuits, p. 536 — Almond Rings, p. 532 — Almond Crescents, p. 531
Meringue Fancies, p. 456 ▼

▲ Speculaas Dolls, Holland, p. 372

Spicy Speculaas, Holland, p. 372 ▼

▲ Parkin Slab and Parkins, p. 371   A Selection of German Lebkuchen, p. 377-379 ▼

▲ Wheaten and Irish Soda Bread, p. 312

Farls, Ireland, p. 313 ▼

Group 2

lb	oz		kg	gr
1	9	Flour (high protein)		780
1	2	Fat (special cake)		560

Group 3

lb	oz		kg	gr
1	6	Egg		680

Group 4

lb	oz		kg	gr
4	0	Sultanas	2	
2	0	Currants	1	
	8	Cherries		250
	8	Chopped orange peel		250
	4	Chopped walnuts		125
	4	Strip almonds		125
1	1/2	Glycerine		45

The first group is mixed together and added to the second group, the whole being mixed for five minutes on slow speed, scraping the machine bowl down at least once. The egg is then slowly added and given four minutes on the same speed. Stir in carefully the rest of the materials in group four, which have previously been mixed together and left overnight. Weigh at 2 lb. (1 kg.) into paper lined 6 in. (15 cm.) hoops. Sprinkle the tops with halved cherries and chopped walnuts. Bake very carefully at 330° F (165° C). Glaze with gum arabic solution *(page 246)* immediately on drawing from the oven. It will be necessary to protect the cakes both underneath and on top during baking because of the richness of the mix.

(Great Britain)

Madeira Cakes

lb	oz		kg	gr
	12	Butter		375
	4	Compound fat		125
1	0	Sugar (castor)		500
	1	Glycerine		30
1	4	Egg		625
	1/4	Zest of lemon		8
1	7	Flour (soft)		700
	1/8	Baking powder		4

Use either the flour or sugar batter method. Scale into papered hoops or papered bread tins. Dust with castor sugar and place two thin strips of citron peel on top of each. Bake at 360° F (182° C). *(Illustration page 424.)* *(Great Britain)*

Mousseline Cakes

lb	oz		kg	gr
	14	Egg yolks		400
	14	Egg whites		400
1	12	Sugar (castor)		875
	14	Flour		400
	14	Cornflour		400
	10	Butter (melted)		300
		Zest of 1 lemon		

Whisk the egg yolks with the lemon zest and 14 oz. (400 gr.) of the sugar. Whisk the egg whites to a stiff snow, gradually adding the rest of the sugar. Blend the two mixtures together carefully. Fold in the flour and cornflour sieved together and lastly the melted butter. Fill into well greased and floured oblong moulds and bake at about 360° F (180° C). When cold, dust with icing sugar. *(France)*

Orange Cakes

lb	oz		kg	gr
	12	Butter		375
	12	Sugar		375
	15	Egg		450
1	2	Flour		560
	3/8	Baking powder		10
1	5	Candied orange peel		650
	7	Curaçao		200

Cream the butter and sugar. Beat in the egg and then blend the flour and baking powder which have been sieved together. Finally, add the orange peel and the liqueur in which it has been soaked. Fill some greased, oblong bread tins and bake in a medium oven. When the cakes are cool, brush them with hot apricot purée and glaze them with liquid fondant. Decorate the tops with triangular pieces of candied orange peel.

Pineapple Cakes

lb	oz		kg	gr
	9	Butter		280
	9	Sugar (icing)		280

lb	oz		kg	gr
	10	Egg		300
	4 1/2	Flour		140
	4 1/2	Rice flour		140
	9	Pineapple (finely diced)		280
	3/4	Rum		20
		Zest of 1/2 lemon		

Cream the butter and sugar. Sieve the flour and rice flour together and add to the creamed mixture a little at a time alternatively with the egg in small portions. Add the zest, the well drained cooked pineapple and the rum. Fill into a paper lined hoop and bake at 360° F (180° C). *(Austria)*

Pineapple Cakes

lb	oz		kg	gr
1	0	Butter		500
1	0	Sugar (castor)		500
1	8	Egg		750
1	8	Flour		750
	1/4	Baking powder		8
1	4	Finely diced pineapple		625
		Kirsch		

Cream the butter and sugar together, then add the egg a portion at a time. Blend in the flour and baking powder, which have been sieved together. Finally, mix in the diced pineapple that has been soaked in kirsch. Line oblong bread tins with parchment paper and fill them three quarters full with the mixture. Bake in a medium oven. When baked, brush the cakes with apricot purée and glaze with very liquid fondant. Decorate with triangular pieces of glacé pineapple. *(France)*

Raisin Cakes

lb	oz		kg	gr
1	0	Butter		500
1	8	Sugar (castor)		750
1	0	Egg		500
2	8	Flour	1	250
	3/4	Baking powder		20
1	2	Milk		560
2	0	Seeded raisins	1	
		Vanilla flavour		

Use the sugar batter method *(page 44)*. Scale at 15 oz. (450 gr.) into paper lined 1 lb. (500 gr.) bread tins. Bake at 380° F (193° C). *(Great Britain)*

Reginella Cakes

Grease a sandwich plate and line it with pasta frolla *page 188*. One third fill with a firm crème pâtissière. Add maddalena mixing so that it is two thirds full. Sprinkle the surface with curaçao and complete the filling with another layer of crème pâtissière. Decorate the top with a trellis design made from strips of pasta frolla which are washed with egg.

Place a morello cherry in each of the spaces in the trellis. Bake at 390° F (200° C).

(Italy)

Rhineland King Cakes

lb	oz		kg	gr
	4	Sugar (castor)		125
	5 1/2	Egg yolks		160
	7	Egg whites		200
	3 1/2	Butter		100
	4	Flour		125
	3 1/2	Sultanas		100
1	3/4	Candied orange peel		50
1	3/4	Candied lemon peel		50
		A little lemon and salt		
		Puff paste trimmings		

Beat the sugar and egg yolks until frothy. Add a little lemon and salt to the flour, rub in the butter, mix in the sultanas. Whip the egg whites to a snow, fold into the egg yolk/sugar sponge and blend with the other ingredients.

Line a flan mould 10 in. (25 cm.) in diameter with puff paste trimmings, spread the base with raspberry jam and fill with the mixing. Cover with a trellis of puff paste trimmings washed with egg. Bake at 356-374° F (180-190° C). *(Germany)*

Richelieu Ring - Richelieu-Kranz

Ingredients for 2 rings

lb	oz		kg	gr
1	0	Butter		500
1	0	Cornflour		500
	1/4	Baking powder		8

lb	oz		kg	gr
1	0	Sugar (castor)		500
1	0	Egg		500

Add the baking powder to the cornflour and cream with the butter. Beat the egg and sugar until frothy. Gradually blend the two mixtures together, mix thoroughly, divide evenly between two cake tins 8 in. (20 cm.) in diameter and bake at 392° F (200° C).

After baking, turn the rings out and leave to cool.

Lastly brush with hot apricot purée and sprinkle with roasted flaked almonds.

(Germany)

Roe's Back Cakes

Mixture 1

lb	oz		kg	gr
	5	Egg whites		150
	2 1/2	Sugar (castor)		75
	5	Ground almonds		150
	1	Cocoa powder		30
	3 1/2	Sugar (castor)		100

Mixture 2

lb	oz		kg	gr
1	0	Marzipan		500
	7	Butter		200
	10	Egg		300
	5 3/4	Flour		170
	1/8	Baking powder		5
		Zest of 1 lemon		
		Almond essence		

Thoroughly grease 'Rehrucken' moulds (oblong, fluted, convex based moulds) and sprinkle with blanched flaked almonds. For mixture 1, mix the almonds, cocoa powder and the 3 1/2 oz. (100 gr.) of sugar together well. Whisk the egg whites and the 2 1/2 oz. (75 gr.) of sugar to a stiff snow and carefully blend with the almond/cocoa/sugar mixture. Using a scraper, deposit in the middle of the mould and carefully draw up the sides until the mould is evenly coated. Now make mixture 2 by beating the butter, egg and marzipan until foamy. Add the essence and lemon zest, and blend in the flour that has been sieved with the baking powder. Fill the mould three quarters full with the mixture and bake at about 410° F (210° C). Turn out of the moulds and allow to cool. If desired, a wedge shaped slice lengthways may be cut out of the cake at the base, spread with kirsch buttercream and replaced. The almond covered side is turned uppermost and lightly dusted with icing sugar. *(Switzerland)*

Royal Cakes

lb	oz		kg	gr
1	0	Butter		500
1	0	Sugar (castor)		500
	9	Egg yolks		280
	11	Egg whites		350
1	0	Flour		500
	8	Peel (citron)		250
	3/4	Kirsch		20
		Half a vanilla pod		

Dice the citron peel finely, blanch well, pour the kirsch over and allow to macerate. Cream the butter and sugar, add the scraped vanilla then beat in the yolks and 8 oz. (250 gr.) of flour in portions. Fold in the egg whites whisked to a stiff snow, the rest of the flour and the peel. Fill into paper lined brick shaped tins and bake at about 360° F (180° C). *(Great Britain)*

Seed Cakes

Add to the formula as for madeira cakes, 1 oz. (30 gr.) of caraway seeds. Weigh into paper lined hoops or bread tins and sprinkle the tops with caraway seeds. Bake at 360° F (182° C). *(Great Britain)*

Simnel Cakes

lb	oz		kg	gr
1	0	Butter		500
1	0	Sugar (dark)		500
1	4	Egg		625
	1	Caramel colour		30
	1	Rum		30
	4	Ground almonds		125
1	4	Flour (soft)		625
1	8	Currants		750
1	0	Sultanas		500
	12	Peel		375
	1	Ground spice		30

Use the sugar batter method. 6 in. (15 cm.) cake hoops are prepared and into each 8 oz. (250 gr.) of the mix is placed and spread level. On to each, a 5 $\frac{1}{2}$ in. (14 cm.) diameter disc of almond paste is placed, each weighing 8 oz. (250 gr.). A further 8 oz. (250 gr.) of mix is added to each and smoothed down. Bake at 360° F (182° C), with plenty of protection underneath the cakes.

When cool, the bands are removed and the tops of the cakes are brushed with well boiled apricot purée. Almond paste weighed at 7 oz. (200 gr.) is used decoratively round the top edge of the cakes and washed with egg yolk. Greaseproof paper bands, high enough to stand about $\frac{1}{2}$ in. (1 cm.) above the level of the almond paste are fixed, and the cakes 'flashed' off in an oven at 450° F (232° C), care being taken to protect the bottom of the cakes.

On removal from the oven, the almond paste decoration is washed at once with gum arabic solution, *page 246*. The Simnels are finished by pouring a little white or pastel tinted fondant into the centres and decorating with preserved fruits or Easter motifs such as cut-out flowers, chicks, rabbits, etc., and adding an inscription such as 'Easter Greetings' or 'Happy Easter'. A deep gold or silver band adds considerably to the appearance, or a wide ribbon can be used.

Almond paste for middle

lb	oz		kg	gr
2	8	Raw marzipan	1	250
1	14	Sugar (icing)		900
	1	Egg yolk		30
		Rum		

Almond paste for top

lb	oz		kg	gr
2	6	Raw marzipan	1	180
1	0	Sugar (castor)		500
	2	Egg		60
		Yellow colour		

(Illustration page 426.)   *(Great Britain)*

Simnel Cakes
This cake is always referred to as the Bury Simnel and should not be confused with the Simnel cake above.

lb	oz		kg	gr
1	0	Butter		500
1	0	Sugar (demerara)		500
	10	Egg		300
2	8	Flour	1	250
	1	Baking powder		30
	$\frac{1}{4}$	Ground nutmeg		8
	12	Sultanas		375
	12	Currants		375
	4	Chopped peel		125
	5	Milk (approx.)		150

Rub the butter into the flour that has been sieved with the baking powder. With the rest of the ingredients, make into a clear dough. Weigh at 9 oz. (270 gr.) and mould to a round shape. Flatten with a rolling pin and place on to greased baking sheets. Wash with egg and decorate with split almonds to form a cross. Bake at 380-400° F (193-204° C), for about 25 minutes.   *(Bury, Lancashire)*

Streusel Cakes

lb	oz		kg	gr
1	10	Butter		800
1	10	Sugar		800
	14	Egg yolks		400
	10	Ground almonds		300
1	2	Egg whites		560
1	2	Flour		560

To make these cakes, first grease some oblong bread tins and line the bottoms with milanese paste covered with some glacé cherries. Then fill up with the mixture made in the following way:

Cream the butter and half the sugar, then add the egg yolks and almonds.

Whisk the egg whites until stiff, fold in the rest of the sugar and fold in the flour. Next amalgamate the two mixtures. Place into the prepared tins and sprinkle with streusel. Bake them in a medium oven. When they are cold, dust with icing sugar.
(France)

Sultana Cakes

lb	oz		kg	gr
	12	Butter		375
	4	Compound fat		125
1	0	Sugar (castor)		500
	1	Glycerine		30
1	4	Egg		625
	1	Ground almonds		30
		Vanilla essence		
1	7	Flour (soft)		700
	1/8	Baking powder		4
1	4	Sultanas		625
	6	Cut mixed peel		180

Use either the flour or the sugar batter method. When weighed into papered hoops or tins, sprinkle with strip almonds. Bake at 360° F (182° C). *(Great Britain)*

Sylvana Cakes

lb	oz		kg	gr
	14	Blanched almonds		400
	3 1/2	Dairy cream		100
	14	Butter		400
	7	Sugar		200
1	0	Egg		500
	3 1/2	Cocoa powder		100
	14	Flour		400

Grind the almonds with the cream and add the butter and sugar which have been creamed together. Beat in the egg a little at a time, then blend in the flour and the cocoa which have been sieved together.

Grease some hoops and after dusting them with flour, fill them with the mixture. Bake in a slow oven. When the cakes are cold, cut into three layers. Spread one layer with vanilla ganache and one with chocolate buttercream and sandwich together. Coat the cake with chocolate buttercream, covering the sides with chocolate granules and decorating the top with chocolate rolls.

(France)

Torta d'Arancio

lb	oz		kg	gr
2	3	Butter	1	
1	10	Sugar (granulated)		800
	7	Invert sugar		200
	14	Ground almonds		400
	14	Potato flour		400
	14	Flour		400
	13	Egg yolks		375
	14	Egg		400
	10	Orange peel (finely cut)		300
		Juice of 8 oranges		
		Juice of 4 lemons		
		Zest of 4 lemons		

Whip the egg, egg yolks, sugars and juices. Add the other ingredients carefully and finally mix in the butter which has been creamed. Fill into greased and floured sandwich plates.

Place, artistically, candied orange segments round the edge of the torta and when baked at 355° F (180° C) glaze while still hot with well boiled orange jelly.

(Italy)

Torta Maddalena

lb	oz		kg	gr
2	0	Sugar (granulated)	1	
2	0	Egg yolks	1	
6	0	Egg	3	
3	12	Cornflour	1	875
	7	Honey		200
2	8	Flour	1	250

Whisk the egg, egg yolks and sugar to a stiff sponge. Stir in the honey. Fold in the sieved cornflour and the flour and put into greased and floured sandwich plates. Bake at 355° F (180° C). They are finished by dusting with icing sugar. *(Italy)*

Torta Mandorlata

lb	oz		kg	gr
2	10	Butter	1	200
2	10	Sugar (granulated)	1	200
1	3 1/2	Cornflour		550
1	3 1/2	Flour		550
1	4	Egg yolks		575
1	5	Egg		600
1	5	Sieved praline nougat		600
		Vanilla		
		Zest of 1 lemon		

Proceed as for 'Torta Yolanda'. Sprinkle strip almonds on top and bake at 355° F (180° C).

The nougat is made from caramelized sugar and almonds (not roasted). It is poured on to a marble slab and when set it is crushed and sieved. *(Italy)*

Torta Margherita

lb	oz		kg	gr
2	0	Sugar (granulated)	1	
1	4	Egg yolks		625
1	10	Egg		750
1	10	Flour		750
	8	Potato starch		250
	10	Butter (melted)		300
		Vanilla		
		Zest of 1 lemon		

Whisk the egg, egg yolks and sugar to a stiff sponge. Fold in the sieved flour and potato starch carefully. Add the vanilla, zest and the butter which should not be too warm. Place into greased and floured sandwich plates and bake at 375° F (190° C). When cool dust with icing sugar. This base may be coated with fondant and an inscription piped on suitable for a birthday cake. *(Italy)*

Torta Yolanda

lb	oz		kg	gr
2	14	Butter	1	400
1	8	Sugar (icing)		750
	14	Sugar (granulated)		400
1	4	Egg yolks		625
1	2	Flour		550
1	12	Cornflour		875
1	5	Egg whites		650
	1 ¹/₂	Liqueur*		45

The butter and sugars are creamed lightly and the yolks are slowly added.

The flour and cornflour sieved together are next mixed in and finally the egg whites, whipped to a stiff snow, are carefully folded in. The mixture is baked in greased and floured sandwich plates at 374° F (190° C). When baked, the torta is dusted with icing sugar and a ready made flower or animal is placed on top.

* In Italy the liqueur used is considered to develop the flavour. It is also used in creams. *(Italy)*

Turban Cakes - Moscovische Tulband

lb	oz		kg	gr
	4	Egg yolks		125
	8	Sugar (granulated)		245
	4	Egg whites		125
	3 ¹/₂	Flour		100
	3	Butter or margarine		90
1 ³/₄		Raisins		50
1 ³/₄		Currants		50
1 ³/₄		Candied peel		50
		Zest of ¹/₂ lemon		

Whip together to a light fluffy mixture the egg yolks, zest of lemon and 3 oz. (90 gr.) sugar. Then whip the egg whites with 5 oz. (150 gr.) of sugar to a stiff meringue. Carefully stir together the egg yolk mixture with the meringue. Next stir in the melted butter or margarine, the flour, followed by the fruit. Pour this mixture into a greased turban mould. Bake in an oven at 356° F (180° C). Baking time about 40 minutes.

With this recipe one can also make small turban pastries.

This quantity of batter is sufficient for 24 small turbans. Oven temperature 428° F (220° C). Bake 12 to 15 minutes. *(Holland)*

Walnut Cakes

lb	oz		kg	gr
1	0	Egg		500
	14	Sugar		400
	14	Flour		400
	³/₄	Instant coffee		20
8	³/₄	Butter (melted)		270

Use the same method of preparation as for genoese sponge, but sift the flour with the coffee twice before mixing, so that they are well blended. Deposit in greased bread tins and bake in a medium oven. When the cakes are cold, cut them in half horizontally and sandwich together with a mocha flavoured buttercream containing chopped walnuts. Coat the cakes with the mocha cream, let this set and then cover all over with mocha fondant. Decorate with caramelized walnuts. *(France)*

Wedding Cakes

lb	oz		kg	gr
1	0	Butter		500
1	0	Sugar (dark)		500
1	4	Egg		625
	2	Roasted ground almonds		60
	2	Roasted nib almonds		60
1	0	Flour		500
	1/4	Cinnamon		7
	1/8	Ground nutmeg		4
2	0	Currants	1	
1	8	Sultanas		750
	8	Cut mixed peel		250
	8	Cherries		250
	1 1/2	Rum		45
	2	Caramel		60
		Zest and juice of 1 orange		
		Zest and juice of 1 lemon		

Use the sugar batter method. Scale into prepared hoops or frames. Bake at 330-340° F (165-171° C). Spirits, rum and/or brandy can be used in one of three ways.

1. In the mixing.

2. Poured over and rubbed gently into the fruit.

3. Sprinkled over the cakes after baking.

This type of heavily fruited cake should be wrapped and carefully stored for at least one month before decoration.
(Illustration page 609.) *(Great Britain)*

Wheatmeal Farmhouse Cakes

Group 1

lb	oz		kg	gr
1	9	Wheatmeal		770
1	4	Sugar (castor)		625
	3/4	Baking powder		20
	14	Butter		400

Group 2

lb	oz		kg	gr
	14	Milk		400
	7	Egg		200
	1	Glycerine		30
		Almond flavour		

Group 3

lb	oz		kg	gr
1	0	Sultanas		500
	6	Chopped cherries		180
	4	Chopped mixed peel		125

Place the first group in the machine and mix until they are like ground almonds. Do *not* mix into a paste. Mix the second group together and add half, mixing for one minute on second speed. Add the balance and give a further minute on the same speed. Carefully blend in the fruit and scale at 1 1/4 lb. (625 gr.) into paper lined 6 in. (15 cm.) hoops. Sprinkle with sugar and bake at 380° F (193° C).

Windsor Cakes

lb	oz		kg	gr
1	10	Butter		800
2	0	Sugar	1	
	15	Egg		450
1	7	Flour		700
	8	Cornflour		250
	10	Chopped almonds		300
1	0	Sultanas		500
1	0	Raisins soaked in rum		500
	14	Diced candied orange peel		400

Cream the butter and sugar and add the egg. Then stir in the rest of the ingredients (but not for too long so as to avoid making the mixture tough). Deposit the mixture on a baking sheet (approximately 15 in. × 20 in.) (38 × 50 cm.) lined with greaseproof paper. Bake at 356° F (180° C).

Covering mixing

lb	oz		kg	gr
	15	Egg whites		450
	8	Egg yolks		250
	8	Almond paste		250
	8	Sugar (castor)		250
	12	Flour		350
	2 1/2	Butter (melted)		75

Beat up the egg yolks with the almond paste. Whip up the egg whites and sugar to a meringue. Stir in the yolks/almond paste mix. Stir in the flour and melted butter. Spread on to two paper lined baking sheets, 15 in. by 20 in. (38 × 50 cm.). Sprinkle one of the sheets with flaked blanched almonds and bake them both in a hot oven. When they are cool, they are used to sandwich the cake; the almond strewn sheet on top, after brushing the cake with apricot purée. Trim the sides of the cake, cut up into squares (about 5 in. × 5 in.) (12 × 12 cm.) and dust the tops with icing sugar. It is advisable to wrap the cakes up straightaway in cellophane paper so as to prevent them from becoming dry.

(France)

Slab Cakes
RECIPES

	Madeira lb oz gr	Sultana lb oz gr	Currant lb oz gr	Cherry lb oz gr	Genoa lb oz gr
Butter	12 375	12 375	12 375	12 375	12 375
Compound fat	4 125	4 125	4 125	4 125	4 125
Sugar	1 0 500	1 0 500	1 0 500	1 0 500	1 0 500
Egg	1 4 625	1 4 625	1 4 625	1 4 625	1 4 625
Flavour	Lemon	Vanilla and lemon	Vanilla and almond	Vanilla	Vanilla, lemon, almond
Glycerine	1 30	1 30	1 30	1 30	1 30
Flour (soft)	1 8 750	1 4 625	1 4 625	1 6 700	1 4 625
Baking powder	¼ 8	¼ 8	¼ 8	¼ 8	⅛ 4
Cherries	—	—	—	2 4 1125	8 250
Currants	—	—	1 12 875	—	1 0 500
Sultanas	—	2 0 1000	—	—	1 0 500
Peel	—	—	4 125	—	4 125
Citron peel	—	—	—	4 125	—
Top decoration	—	Flaked almonds	Nib almonds	—	Split almonds
Baking temperature	370° F 187° C	360° F 182° C	360° F 182° C	360° F 182° C	350° F 176° C

The madeira slab can be sliced twice and spread with jam and cream.
The cherry slab can be finished on top with almond paste, white fondant and decorated with glacé cherries.

	Coconut lb oz gr	Almond lb oz gr	Seed lb oz gr	Ginger lb oz gr
Butter	12 375	12 375	12 375	12 375
Cooking fat	4 125	4 125	4 125	4 125
Sugar	1 0 500	1 0 500	1 0 500	1 0 500
Egg	1 4 625	1 4 625	1 4 625	1 4 625
Glycerine	1 30	1 30	1 30	1 30
Flour (soft)	1 4 625	1 2 560	1 8 750	1 8 750
Baking powder	¼ 8	¼ 8	¼ 8	¼ 8
Ground (sweet) almonds (bitter)	— —	2 60 2 60	— —	— —

	Coconut lb oz gr	Almond lb oz gr	Seed lb oz gr	Ginger lb oz gr
Caraway seeds	—	—	1 30	—
Coconut (fine)	4 125	—	—	—
Chopped ginger	—	—	—	*1 8 750
Flavour	Lemon	—	Lemon	Vanilla
Top decoration	Coconut	Flaked almonds	Caraway seeds	**
Baking temperature	360° F 182° C	360° F 182° C	360° F 182° C	360° F 182° C

* The preserved ginger is cut into small pieces and washed in tepid water and then dried.
** When cold the top of the ginger slab is spread with white fondant and then covered with thin slices of preserved ginger after which the top is dredged with castor sugar. The sugar batter or flour batter method can be used for making slab cake.
(Illustration page 424.)

Slabs using Special Cake Flour
Madeira

lb	oz		kg	gr
1	0	Special cake flour		500
1	0	Special cake fat		500
	1	Milk powder		30
	1	Soya flour		30
	1	Rice flour		30

Place into a machine and cream for five minutes at medium speed.

lb	oz		kg	gr
1	0	Egg		500
1	4	Sugar (castor)		625
	¼	Salt		8

Mix together and add over one minute on slow speed. Scrape the bowl down and cream for one minute on medium speed.

lb	oz		kg	gr
	10	Milk		300
		Flavour as desired		

Add carefully to the above.

lb	oz		kg	gr
	4	Special cake flour		125
	¼	Baking powder		8

Sieve together and add to the above and mix on medium speed for one minute scraping the bowl down once during this time.

Divide into two lined frames (6 in. × 12 in.) (15 × 30 cm.). Bake at 350-360° F (176-182° C). Baking time, 80 minutes (approximately).

Fruit slab

lb	oz		kg	gr
1	4	High-protein flour		625
1	0	Special cake fat		500
	1½	Milk powder		45
	2	Rice flour		60
	³⁄₈	Baking powder		10

On slow speed blend these materials to a smooth paste.

lb	oz		kg	gr
1	6	Sugar (castor)		680
	½	Salt		15
	10	Milk		300

Add over one minute on slow speed. Scrape the bowl and give six minutes on medium speed.

lb	oz		kg	gr
1	4	Egg		625
1	4	Currants		625
1	0	Sultanas		500

Add the egg on slow speed. Scrape down and add the fruit. Mix for another minute on slow speed. Sufficient for two slabs 12 in. × 6 in. (30 × 15 cm.). Bake at 350° F (176° C).

XIV. Small Cakes and Afternoon Tea Fancies

The subject matter of this chapter covers an almost unlimited range of confections; so many that they are almost impossible to classify under separate headings.

In Great Britain, afternoon tea fancies can include almost anything from a small piece of slab cake to a petit four, with perhaps genoese fancies or dipped genoese predominating. In France they are known as 'Les Petits Gâteaux' a selection of which is included in this chapter.

Tea in the afternoon is generally not taken in Germany, coffee being served instead and with it a variety of fancies ranging from a slice of torte to a petit four would be served. The same range would be served in Switzerland but tea instead of coffee is taken in the afternoon. In Italy pasticceria mignon are invariably served with afternoon tea.

It must be emphasized that many of the items described in other chapters can be served with afternoon tea.

A very large range of afternoon tea fancies can be made with genoese. These may be divided roughly under two headings:

1. Genoese Fancies

These are made by sandwiching the genoese base once or twice with jam and/or cream. The layers of genoese can be of one or more colours if desired. The top can be covered with a thin sheet of almond paste before spreading with chocolate or fondant. The genoese is then cut into shapes and additionally decorated with cream, fruit, nuts, chocolate, jelly etc. Alternatively, cream can be used for spreading.

Other varieties can be made by cutting the genoese base into strips after sandwiching, then coating the top and sides with cream, fondant, almond paste or chocolate. The strip can then be cut into small shapes and given additional decoration.

2. Genoese Glacés

These are perhaps better known as dipped fancies.

The preparation is as above, after which the base is cut into shapes with either a sharp knife or with cutters. If the base has not been given a topping with almond paste, then the pieces may be dipped into well boiled apricot purée. At this point a variety can be made by masking the sides of the dipped fancies with roasted nibbed or flaked almonds and the tops finished with cream. If not so finished, the pieces are dipped into prepared chocolate or fondant and decorated by piping with the same materials and finishing with candied fruit, crystallized or cut-out flowers, cream, nuts, or cut-out chocolate pieces.

Alternatively, a topping of cream, marshmallow, almond paste, meringue, ganache etc., can be applied before dipping, finishing with a spiral of chocolate or fondant and any of the decorative materials mentioned above. If cream is used for topping, the pieces must be refrigerated before dipping.

For genoese fancies a light genoese is generally used. For hand dipped fancies a heavy genoese is best. If however an enrober is used then a lighter genoese or one made with special cake flour can be used instead.

At all times care should be taken with colours and flavours. Generally the colour and flavour of the base should be matched by the fondant or cream. Alternatively, they may be in contrast but at all times they should be tasteful in appearance and flavour.

Detailed examples of some genoese fancies and genoese glacés are given in this chapter. *(Illustration page 560.)*

RECIPES
Aidas

lb	oz		kg	gr
2	4	Butter	1	125
	9	Sugar (icing)		270
	9	Marzipan		270
	9	Chocolate couverture		270
	15	Egg whites		450
3	4	Flour	1	625
		Salt		
		Nougat paste		

Beat the butter, icing sugar and marzipan until frothy. Melt the couverture and work with the egg whites until smooth. Add to the butter/sugar mixture alternately with the flour, pipe out bulbs using a plain tube and bake at 392° F (200° C).

After baking, fill the Aidas with nougat paste and half coat with couverture.
(Illustration page 509.) *(Germany)*

Almond Bread Slices - Mandelbrot

lb	oz		kg	gr
	5	Water		150
	6	Whole brown almonds		180
	4 1/2	Butter		140
	6 1/4	Sugar (pulverized)		180
1	6	Flour		680
		2 knife-points clove		
		1 knife-point cinnamon		
		1 knife-point ammonium carbonate		

First bring the water to the boil and scald the almonds, then pour them into a sieve and leave until cold. Meanwhile work the butter and pulverized sugar until smooth, add the clove, cinnamon, ammonium carbonate and lastly the flour, and work to a paste.

Add the scalded almonds to the paste, pin out to approx. $3/4$ in. (2 cm.) in thickness and 3 in. (8 cm.) in width, and leave overnight, preferably in a refrigerator. Next morning, cut the paste into very thin slices and finally bake on greased baking sheets at 392° F (200° C). *(Germany)*

Almond Butter Biscuits - Gemandeltes Buttergebäck

Pin out sweet paste to $1/4$ in. (7 mm.) in thickness and brush with egg. Sprinkle with chopped almonds, making sure to press them well down and brushing off any excess. Cut into pieces 1 1/4 in. by 1 1/2 in. (3 × 4 cm.) and bake at 356° F (180° C).
(Illustration page 509.) *(Germany)*

Almond Linz Crescents

lb	oz		kg	gr
1	4	Butter		625
	10	Sugar (castor)		300
	9	Egg		275
	14	Ground almonds (roasted)		425
1	8	Flour		750
	1/8	Ground cinnamon		3

Cream the butter and sugar, adding the egg a little at a time. Mix in the almonds and lastly the flour. Pipe out into crescent shapes using a star tube. Bake at 360° F (182° C). When cool, sandwich in pairs with hot apricot purée. Dip the ends into chocolate and the extreme tips into roasted nib almonds.

Almond Nut Slices - Nuss-Mandel-Schnitten

lb	oz		kg	gr
4	8	Sweet paste (approx.)	2	
	14	Butter		400
	2	Sugar		60
	5	Honey		150
	8	Dairy cream		250
	14	Almonds		400
	14	Roasted nuts		400

Pin out the sweet paste to a rectangular shape 18 in. by 28 in. (46 × 72 cm.) and bake lightly. Meanwhile, bring the butter, sugar, honey and dairy cream to the boil, add the almonds and nuts and continue cooking for 5 minutes. Spread this mixture on the sweet paste base and bake off until golden. After baking, cut into pieces 1 1/2 in. by 4 3/4 in. (4 × 12 cm.) while still warm. *(Germany)*

Almond Tartlets

lb	oz		kg	gr
	5 1/2	Ground almonds		160
	7	Sugar (castor)		200
	1 1/2	Flour		45
	2 1/2	Butter (melted)		75
	3 1/2	Egg		100
	1 1/2	Egg yolks		45
	2	Dairy cream		60
	1 1/2	Kirsch		45
		Sweet pastry		

Beat the almonds, egg and egg yolks until foamy, then gradually add the cream and kirsch. Fold in the flour and blend in the melted butter carefully. Line tartlet pans with sweet pastry, fill with the mixture and sprinkle with chopped almonds. Bake at 400° F (204° C). On removal from the oven, brush the tops with apricot purée. *(France)*

Apple Poppy Seed Cakes - Apfelmohn

For 20 cakes 2 in. by 4 in. (5 × 10 cm.)

lb	oz		kg	gr
2	10	Sweet paste	1	300
	8	Ground poppy seed		250

Bring 16 oz. (500 gr.) milk to the boil, let the ground poppy seed boil up in it, place in a strainer and drain.

lb	oz		kg	gr
	7	Vanilla cream		200
	7	Sugar		200
	5	Sponge crumbs		150
2	0	Apple slices (approx.)	1	
		Cinnamon		
		Vanilla fondant		
		Flaked almonds		

Pin out 1 lb. 10 oz. (800 gr.) sweet paste to a rectangular shape 8 in. by 20 in. (20 × 50 cm.) and bake lightly. Mix together the scalded poppy seed, vanilla cream, sugar, sponge crumbs, cinnamon and lemon and spread on the sweet paste base. Cover with the apple slices and then with a trellis made from 1 lb. (500 gr.) sweet paste. Bake at 356° F (180° C) for about 45 minutes.

After baking, brush with apricot purée. Glaze thinly with vanilla fondant and sprinkle lightly with roasted flaked almonds. *(Germany)*
(Illustration page 353.)

Apple Streusel Slices - Apfelstreusel

For 20 slices 2 in. by 4 in. (5 × 10 cm.)

lb	oz		kg	gr
1	2	Sweet paste		500
		Thin butter sponge genoese		
4	8	Stewed apples	2	
1	4	Butter streusel		625

Pin out the sweet paste to a rectangular shape 8 in. by 20 in. (20 × 50 cm.). Bake lightly, then spread with apricot jam and cover with a thin butter sponge genoese.

Add sultanas, currants and chopped almonds to the apples and flavour with lemon and rum. Arrange this mixture on the genoese and sprinkle evenly with the butter streusel. Bake at 374° F (190° C) for about 50 minutes, brush with hot butter and sprinkle with cinnamon flavoured sugar. *(Germany)*
(Illustration page 478.)

Apple Strudel

lb	oz		kg	gr
1	0	Puff pastry		500
		Butter sponge genoese		
1	0	Stewed apples flavoured with rum		500

Pin out a thin puff pastry base 4 in. by 16 in. (10 × 40 cm.). Place on a baking sheet so that the paste has upturned edges. Place a thin genoese in the centre, cover with the apples and spread with crème pâtissière. Lay a cover of puff pastry with evenly scored sides on top.

Bake the strudel at 356-374° F (180-190° C), then brush with apricot purée and glaze with water icing and cut into the desired number of portions. *(Germany)*
(Illustration page 481.)

Apple Tartlets

Line tartlet pans with puff pastry. After sufficient rest, pipe in crème pâtissière and place on each 3-4 apple segments. Bake at 375-390° F (190-200° C). When baked, glaze with apricot purée or other fruit glaze. *(Italy)*

Apple Tartlets - Barquettes aux Pommes

Peel and core some russet apples and dip them in lemon juice. Cut each apple into 6 to 8 segments shaped like half moons and poach them in a vanilla syrup. Also prepare a reduced apple purée. Line some boat-shaped tartlet moulds with sweet paste and bake blind. When they are cold, deposit in each some of the apple purée thickened with a little apricot jam. Place on top 5 or 6 pieces of apple with the round sides uppermost and coat with kirsch flavoured apricot purée. *(Switzerland)*

Apricot Slices

lb	oz		kg	gr
1	4	Sweet pastry		625

Filling

lb	oz		kg	gr
	1	Cake crumbs		30
	9	Sugar (castor)		270
	4	Ground almonds		125
	6	Ground rice		180
	7	Butter		200
	7	Egg		200
	8	Apricot jam		250

Line a baking sheet 16 in. by 16 in. (40 × 40 cm.) with sweet pastry and spread with apricot jam. Cover with well drained sliced apricots. Cover with the filling which is made by sieving the dry ingredients and rubbing in the butter until the mixture is a crumbly mass. Add the egg to make a smooth mixing. Bake at 390° F (199° C). Dust with icing sugar and cut into slices.

Apricot Slices

Pin out Linz pastry No. III *(page 189)* $^1/_4$ in. (5 mm.) thick, cut a rectangle about 12 × 4 in. (30 × 10 cm.) and place on a baking sheet. Egg wash and cover with a lattice of the same pastry about $^1/_4$ in. (5 mm.) thick and press it down. Egg wash the lattice and bake at 360° F (180° C) until light brown. While still hot, pipe apricot jam evenly into the spaces and cut into pieces of the required size. *(Austria)*

Apricot Slices

Line a baking sheet with rich sweet pastry about $^1/_4$ in. (7 mm.) thick and bake. Leave for a day to soften and then cut into strips about 3 in. (7.5 mm.) wide. Spread with well boiled apricot purée. Layer with half apricots and blanched gooseberries. Glaze with a cold-set jelly and pipe borders with whipped dairy cream. Cut into slices.

(Switzerland)

Apricot Streusel Slices - Aprikosenstreusel

For 20 slices 2 in. by 4 in. (5 × 10 cm.)

lb	oz		kg	gr
1	0	Kuchen dough		500
	7	Curd filling		200
2	4	Apricots (halved blanched)	1	125
1	5	Butter streusel		650

Pin out the kuchen dough to a rectangular shape 8 in. by 20 in. (20 × 50 cm.). Spread with the curd filling and cover this with the apricot pulp. Sprinkle the butter streusel evenly on top. Bake for about 45 minutes until golden. Before cutting, brush with a little hot butter and sprinkle with vanilla sugar and icing sugar.
(Illustration page 353.) *(Germany)*

Bakewell Tartlets

Cut out sweet pastry with a fluted cutter and line patty pans. Pipe a spot of raspberry jam in the bottom of each. Pipe in the following mixture:

lb	oz		kg	gr
	14	Butter		400
	10	Sugar (castor)		300
	10	Egg		300
	10	Flour (soft)		300
	4	Ground almonds		125
	4	Fine coconut		125
		Vanilla		

Cream the butter and sugar adding the egg in portions. Mix in the rest of the ingredients. Bake at 375° F (190° C). When cold, run in vanilla flavoured water icing.

Banana Marshmallow Slices

lb	oz		kg	gr
2	0	Stock marshmallow cream	1	
	12	Bananas		375
	8	Water (hot)		250
	1 1/2	Gelatine (powdered)		45
	1/4	Tartaric acid solution (8 oz. [250 gr.] tartaric acid and 8 oz. [250 gr.] water)		8
		Roasted coconut		

Whisk the marshmallow cream and the bananas on low speed until they are thoroughly mixed. Disperse the gelatine in the hot water and mix in. Whisk on an increased speed until stiff, then mix in the acid. Spread quickly into a frame lined with waxed paper. Cover the surface with lightly roasted coconut. When set, remove from the frame and remove the paper. Turn the slab over and cover with roasted coconut. Cut into slices.

Barcelona Ovals

lb	oz		kg	gr
1	0	Butter		500
	6	Sugar (icing)		180
	7	Ground hazelnuts (roasted)		200
1	0	Flour (soft)		500
		Vanilla		
		Zest of lemon		

Make a pastry with the above materials and pin out to about $3/16$ in. (5 mm.) thick. Cut out with a plain oval cutter. Bake at 370° F (187° C). When cool, sandwich together in pairs with red currant jelly and dip into pale yellow fondant flavoured with fresh lemon juice. Place a blanched roasted hazelnut on the top of each. *(Switzerland)*

Batavia Fancies

Sandwich three thin sheets of light genoese with a mixture of apricot jam, sponge crumbs, and arrack flavoured buttercream. Refrigerate.

Using a Parisian rout biscuit mixing pipe rings about 1 1/4 in. (3 cm.) in diameter, on to greased and floured baking sheets, using a fine star pipe. Let them stand for a time, then flash in a hot oven. Whilst still hot, brush with gum arabic solution.

Cut circles out of the genoese with a sharp round cutter 1 1/4 in. (3 cm.) in diameter and mask the sides with buttercream and roasted flaked almonds. Place an almond ring on each and fill in with pale yellow fondant. *(Switzerland)*

Battenburg Slices

These are built up with genoese of different colours. The simplest is to place a layer of one colour upon another with jam or cream in between. The combined layers should not exceed about 1 1/2 in. (4 cm.) in depth. The piece is cut into strips about 1 1/2 in. (4 cm.) wide and completely enclosed in a sheet of almond paste. The almond paste can be of any colour and flavour and can be marked on the surface with a patterned rolling pin. When completed, the strips are cut into slices.

Alternatives are as follows:

1. A strip composed of four squares fixed together with apricot purée. Two contrasting colours may be used such as pink and white or chocolate and white. Finish as above.

2. Right angled triangles of contrasting colours can be fixed, back to back, to form a triangle. Finish as above.

3. A rectangular strip composed of two triangular pieces of contrasting coloured genoese. Finish as above.

4. A triangular shape composed of alternating strips of contrasting colours. This is achieved by layering thin strips of plain and chocolate genoese with nougat cream so that a strip measuring about 2 in. (5 cm.) wide and 1 1/2 in. (4 cm.) deep is built up. The strip is placed flush on to the straight edge of a baking sheet and cut diagonally with a sharp knife, using the edge of the metal and the far top edge of the strip as guides. Sandwich the two pieces to form a triangle. It is important that the strip contains an even number of layers or the colours will not alternate. Finish as above.

Bee Sting - Bienenstich

20 pieces 2 in. by 4 in. (5 × 10 cm.)

lb	oz		kg	gr
1	7	Kuchen dough		700

Bee sting paste:

lb	oz		kg	gr
	5	Butter		150
	5	Sugar		150
	3 1/2	Flaked almonds		100
	1 3/4	Chopped almonds		50
	4	Unwhipped sweetened dairy cream		125
	1 1/2	Honey		45
		Half a vanilla pod		

Light vanilla cream:

lb	oz		kg	gr
1	0	Milk		500
	1 3/4	Cornflour		50
	1	Egg yolk		30
	2 3/4	Sugar (castor)		70
	5	Whipped egg whites		150
	4 1/4	Sugar (castor)		130
		Vanilla		

Pin out the kuchen dough to a rectangular shape 8 in. by 20 in. (20 × 50 cm.) and place on a baking sheet. Prepare the bee sting paste, cook it until it begins to leave the sides of the pan and spread it on the unproved kuchen dough. Now leave to prove for a short time.

Bake at 356-374° F (180-190° C) for about 30 minutes until golden. When cold, split ready for sandwiching.

Meanwhile cook the light vanilla cream. Whip the egg whites and the 4 1/4 oz. (120 gr.) sugar to a snow, fold into the cream and use it to spread on the base.

Cut the top-piece separately into fingers and arrange on the base. In this way the final cutting can be effected without the cream squeezing out. *(Germany)*
(Illustration page 478.)

Blidahs

lb	oz		kg	gr
	5	Egg whites		150
	7	Ground almonds		200
	7	Sugar (castor)		200
	1	Flour		30
		Zest of 1 orange		

Whisk the egg whites and half the sugar to a stiff snow, then fold in the rest of the ingredients. Stencil in small ovals on to greased and floured baking sheets, dust with icing sugar and bake at 355° F (180° C). *(France)*

Bobes

For approx. 36

lb	oz		kg	gr
	12	Butter		375
	7	Sugar (icing)		200
	3/4	Cornflour		20
	1 1/2	Egg yolks		50
1	0	Flour		500
	3 1/2	Finely chopped candied lemon peel		100
	3 1/2	Finely chopped candied orange peel		100
	3 1/2	Butter streusel		100

Filling

lb	oz		kg	gr
	11	Marzipan		325
	3 1/2	Arrack (approx.)		100

Bring the marzipan to a spreading consistency with the arrack.

Cream the butter and sugar, add the cornflour and egg yolks and mix to a smooth paste. Lastly work in the flour. Pin out the paste to the desired size, spread with the marzipan filling and cover with the candied orange and lemon peel and butter streusel. Roll up, brush with egg yolk and sprinkle with butter streusel. Cut the roll into slices 1 1/4 in. (3 cm.) thick and bake at 392° F (200° C). After baking, dust the individual slices with icing sugar.
(Illustration page 509.) *(Germany)*

Bordeaux Croquets - Croquets de Bordeaux

lb	oz		kg	gr
1	0	Flour		500
	6	Butter		180
	6	Sugar (castor)		180
	10	Unblanched almonds		300
	6	Egg		180
	1/4	Salt		8
	1/2	Baking powder		15

Make all the ingredients into a paste and then chop it to cut the almonds up a little. Make a rope about 3 in. (8 cm.) diameter and place on a baking sheet. Flatten slightly, but leave the centre rounded. Egg wash and mark with a fork in both directions. Bake at 380° F (193° C). The cake will rise during baking. When baked, cut into slices about 1 in. (2.5 cm.).
(France)

Brassel Cakes - Brasselkuchen

lb	oz		kg	gr
	14	Puff pastry		400
	9	Butter streusel		270

Pin out the puff pastry to a rectangular shape 8 in. by 12 in. (20 × 30 cm.). Cut into pieces 4 in. by 2 1/4 in. (10 × 6 cm.), sprinkle with the butter streusel, bake at 392° F (200° C) for about 20 minutes and then coat with white fondant.
(Illustration page 481.) *(Germany)*

Buddini

Line oval pans that have vertical sides with pasta frolla. Fill 2/3 with the following mixture:

lb	oz		kg	gr
1	0	Rice (cooked in milk)		500
	4	Egg yolks		120
	5 1/2	Crème pâtissière		175
	3 1/2	Orange peel (cut)		100
	2	Strega liqueur		60
		Zest of 2 oranges and 2 lemons		

Bake at 375° F (190° C). After baking, dust with icing sugar. *(Italy)*

Butter Streusel Slices - Butterstreusel

For 20 slices 2 in. by 4 in. (5 × 10 cm.)

lb	oz		kg	gr
1	8	Kuchen dough		750
1	4	Butter streusel		625
		A little milk		

Pin out the kuchen dough to a rectangular shape 8 in. by 20 in. (20 × 50 cm.). Brush with lukewarm milk and spread evenly with the butter streusel. Leave to

413

prove for a short time and bake at 374° F (190° C) for about 25 minutes until golden. After baking, brush with hot butter, sprinkle with vanilla sugar and dust with icing sugar. Cut into slices. *(Germany)* *(Illustration page 478.)*

Butter Wafers - Butterwaffeln

Pin out sweet paste to $1/4$ in. (6 mm.) in thickness, impress with a chequered wafer roller and cut into pieces $1 \, 1/2$ in. by $2 \, 1/4$ in. (4 × 6 cm.). After baking at 356° F (180° C) spread with hot butter and sprinkle with vanilla sugar. *(Germany)* *(Illustration page 509.)*

Butter Wedges - Butterwecken

lb	oz		kg	gr
	12 $1/4$	Butter		375
	7	Sugar (icing)		200
	3 $1/2$	Egg		100
1	2	Flour		500
		A little salt and vanilla		

Lightly cream the butter and icing sugar, add the egg, salt, vanilla and lastly the flour. Work into a sweet paste. Cut into rounds approx. 3 in. (8 cm.) in diameter using a fluted cutter. Cut each round into four quarters and bake at 392° F (200° C) until golden. After baking, dip the points of the butter wedges in chocolate couverture. *(Germany)*

Caen Sablés - Sablés de Caen

lb	oz		kg	gr
1	0	Flour		500
1	0	Butter		500
	$1/8$	Salt		4
	8	Sugar (icing)		250
	6	Egg yolks		180
		Zest and juice of 2 oranges		

Sieve the flour, sugar and salt and rub in the butter. Mix in the egg yolks which have been hard boiled and sieved. Add the zest and juice of the oranges and make into a smooth paste. Cut out with a 6 in. (15 cm.) round fluted cutter. Cut each into four and arrange on a baking sheet that has been sprinkled with water. Wash each with egg and bake at 400° F (204° C). *(France)*

Carracks

Line shallow patty pans with Linz paste. Bake the cases blind and, when cold, fill them with vanilla ganache. After refrigeration, coat with pistachio flavoured green fondant. When set, decorate the centre of each with a spot of chocolate fondant. *(Illustration page 481.)* *(France)*

Carracks - Small

Take a genoese about 1 in. (2.5 cm.) thick, split once and sandwich with chocolate buttercream. When set, cut evenly into squares about 2 × 2 in. (5 × 5 cm.) and coat the tops and sides with buttercream. Mask the sides with chocolate vermicelli, cover the tops with small chocolate cigarettes placed side by side and dust very lightly with icing sugar. *(France)*

Cats' Eyes - Katzenaugen

lb	oz		kg	gr
	13 $1/4$	Butter		375
	13 $1/4$	Sugar (icing)		375
	7	Unwhipped dairy cream		200
	9	Egg whites		270
1	2	Flour		500
		Vanilla		

Cream the butter and 8 oz. (250 gr.) icing sugar. Gradually add the cream. Whip the egg whites and the remaining icing sugar to a stiff snow and blend both mixtures with the flour. Pipe out on to greased, floured baking sheets in small half-spheres, using a plain tube. Flatten and bake at 392° F (200° C). After baking, sandwich the cats' eyes in pairs with nougat and decorate with chocolate couverture. *(Germany)*

Cats' Tongue Biscuits

lb	oz		kg	gr
	8	Sugar (icing)		250
	8	Flour		250
	8	Unwhipped dairy cream		250
	$1/2$	Sugar (vanilla)		15
	4	Egg whites		125

Mix the icing sugar with the cream, add the vanilla sugar and the flour and mix to a smooth paste. Fold in the stiffly whisked egg whites and pipe out finger shape on to greased and floured baking sheets, using a ¼ in. (5 mm.) plain pipe. Bake at 400° F (204° C) until the biscuits have a golden coloured edge. Make sure the fingers are not too close together, as they spread while baking. Remove from the baking sheets while hot. *(France)*

Cats' Tongue Biscuits - Fine

lb	oz		kg	gr
	8	Butter		250
	7	Sugar (icing)		200
	1 ½	Sugar (vanilla)		45
	2 ½	Egg		75
	8	Flour		250

Cream the butter with the two sugars and add the egg a little at a time. Fold in the flour and pipe out in fingers about 3 in. (8 cm.) long on to greased and floured baking sheets, using a plain ¼ in. (5 mm.) tube. Bake carefully at 400° F (204° C). *(France)*

Cat Tongues - Katzenzungen

lb	oz		kg	gr
	12	Butter		375
	12	Sugar (icing)		375
	7	Unwhipped dairy cream		200
	9 ¾	Egg whites		280
1	0	Flour		500
		Vanilla		

Cream the butter and 8 oz. (250 gr.) icing sugar. Gradually add the cream. Whip the egg whites and the remaining icing sugar to a stiff snow and blend both mixtures with the flour. Pipe out on to greased, floured baking sheets in small tongues, using a plain tube, and bake at 392° F (200° C). After baking, sandwich the cat tongues in pairs with nougat, placing the undersides inside, and cover diagonally with piped chocolate couverture.
(Germany)

Chatibeur

For 20 (40 halves)

lb	oz		kg	gr
1	0	Flour		500
	12	Butter		360
	4	Sugar (icing)		120
	2	Egg yolks		60
		(cooked in a bain-marie until thick, then strained)		
		Lemon juice		
		Salt		
		Vanilla		

Make a paste out of the above ingredients, pin out to approx. ¼ in. (5 mm.) in thickness and cut out rounds 4 in. (10 cm.) in diameter. Lightly pinch around the edges, cut in half and bake. After baking, fold over evenly (with the underside inside) and wrap in cellophane. *(Germany)*

Cheese Cakes

These cakes are well known in Great Britain, although they contain no cheese. Line patty pans with puff pastry cuttings and thumb up well. After a sufficient rest, pipe in the following mixture:

lb	oz		kg	gr
	8	Butter		250
	10	Sugar (castor)		300
	8	Egg		250
1	2	Flour (soft)		560
	⅜	Baking powder		10
	8	Milk		250
		Lemon flavour		

Bake at 400° F (204° C). When cold, spread with vanilla flavoured white water icing or fondant and dip into thread coconut. *(Great Britain)*

Cherry

Sprinkle a genoese base with maraschino and sandwich with maraschino cream. Spread the top with the same cream and decorate with a comb scraper. Cut into squares and decorate each with candied cherries and citron leaves. *(Italy)*

Cherry Barquettes

Line barquette pans with pasta frolla and fill ⅔ with apricot jam. Garnish each barquette with 3 candied cherries and bake at 375° F (190° C). *(Italy)*

Cherry Cheese Cakes - Käsekirsch-Kuchen

For 20 slices 2 in. by 4 in. (5 × 10 cm.)

lb	oz		kg	gr
	15	Kuchen dough		450
3	0	Curd filling	1	500
1	4	Preserved morello cherries		625

Pin out the kuchen dough to a rectangular shape 8 in. by 20 in. (20 × 50 cm.) Spread with 2 lb. (1 kg.) curd filling, *(page 219)*, place the cherries evenly on top, cover with the rest of the filling and smooth off. Bake at 374° F (190° C) for about 45 minutes until golden and then brush with butter and sprinkle with sugar.
(Illustration page 353.) *(Germany)*

Cherry Chocolate Slices

lb	oz		kg	gr
1	4	Sweet paste		625

Filling

lb	oz		kg	gr
	1	Cake crumbs		30
	1	Cocoa powder		30
	9	Sugar (castor)		270
	4	Ground almonds		125
	5	Ground rice		150
	7 1/2	Butter		215
	7 1/2	Egg		215
	8	Cherries		250

Line a tray about 16 in. by 16 in. (40 × 40 cm.) with sweet paste and spread with the filling. This is made by sieving all the dry materials and rubbing in the butter until the whole is a crumbly mass.

Add the egg slowly, and mix free from lumps. Place the cherries on top. Sprinkle all over with streusel. Bake at 390° F (199° C). When baked and cool, dust with icing sugar and cut into slices.

Cherry Michel - Kirschenmichel

For 20 slices 2 in. by 4 in. (5 × 10 cm.)

lb	oz		gr
1	0	Sweet paste *(pages 185-186)*	500
	8	Butter	250

lb	oz		kg	gr
	8	Sugar (castor)		250
	4	Egg yolks		125
	10	Egg whites		300
	12	Fine light sponge crumbs		375
3	0	Sweet black cherries	1	500

Pin out the sweet paste to a rectangular shape 8 in. by 20 in. (20 × 50 cm.) and bake lightly. Beat the butter, 4 oz. (120 gr.) sugar and egg yolks until frothy; whip the egg whites and the rest of the sugar to a snow, add to the butter mixture and draw in the sponge crumbs. Add the stoned cherries, fill the mixing on to the sweet paste base, smooth off until about 1 1/4 in. (3 cm.) deep and bake at 356° F (180° C) for about 1 hour. After baking, dust the individual slices with icing sugar.
(Illustration page 478.) *(Germany)*

Cherry Slices

Take six 1 lb. (500 gr.) pieces of sweet pastry and roll into ropes about 16 in. (40 cm.) long. Make a depression along the length of each with a rolling pin. With the thumb and forefinger, pinch a pattern along the sides. Place them side by side, so that they touch, on a baking sheet, placing a stick at one end to keep them in position. Place about 4 oz. (125 gr.) of cherries along each strip and cover with the following mix:

lb	oz		kg	gr
	8	Butter		250
	8	Sugar (castor)		250
	10	Egg		300
	9	Flour		270
	2	Scone flour		60
	1	Ground almonds		30

Bake at 400° F (204° C). When cold, dust with icing sugar and cut into slices.

Cherry Strudel - Kirschstrudel

lb	oz		kg	gr
1	0	Puff pastry		500
		Butter sponge genoese 1/2 in. (1 cm.) thick		
1	0	Thickened stewed cherries		500

(Strain the cherries and thicken the juice with 1 ³/₄ oz. [50 gr.] sugar and ¹/₄ oz. [8 gr.] cornstarch.)

Pin out the puff pastry thinly to a rectangular shape 4 ¹/₂ in. by 16 in. (12 × 40 cm.) with an upturned edge. Place a thin genoese in the centre, cover it with the stewed cherries and spread with vanilla cream or pastry cream.

Lay a cover of puff pastry with evenly scored sides on top. Bake at 356-374° F (180-190° C), then brush with apricot purée, glaze and cut into the desired number of portions.　　　　*(Germany)*
(Illustration page 481.)

Cherry Tartlets - Tartelettes aux Cerises

Stone the cherries and poach them in a syrup flavoured with lemon zest. When they have been cooked, reduce the liquor and thicken it slightly with cornflour. Line some pans with short paste and bake blind. When cold, fill with the cherries which have cooled down and sprinkle with finely chopped pistachio nuts. The fruit can also be covered with an almond meringue mixture which is dusted with icing sugar; in this case, the tartlets are returned to the oven for 5 minutes so that the tops become golden and crisp.　　　　*(France)*

Cherry Wedges

Sandwich a white genoese with kirsch buttercream into which chopped cherries have been mixed. Cut into strips about 2 ¹/₂ in. (6 cm.) wide and cover with pink almond paste marked with a ribbed rolling pin. Cut into blunt pointed triangles. With the same prepared almond paste, cut out very small fluted discs and cut them in half. Pipe a rosette of the same cream at the wide end of the triangles and place a half disc at the side so that they overlap the edge. Finish with a half glacé cherry on top of the rosette.

Chestnuts - Marrons

Take some oval biscuits made of sablé paste. Sandwich them with some maraschino flavoured chestnut paste *(page 225)* to which is added enough buttercream to bring the mixture to a consistency suitable for piping a bulb on the top of each from a savoy bag, fitted with a large star pipe.

When the cream has set, dip each into pale violet fondant flavoured with maraschino, placing each on to a wire tray to drain and set. Place half a glacé cherry on one side of each fancy. Place into paper cases.
(France)

Chestnuts - Kastanien

For 30

lb	oz		kg	gr
		60 Othello bases		
	9	Raw marzipan		250
1	0	Stock syrup (approx.)		500
		Nougat paste		
		Arrack marzipan filling		

Sandwich Othello bases in pairs with nougat and arrack marzipan. Thin down the raw marzipan with the stock syrup, warm (without bringing to the boil) and use to cover the filled Othellos.

When cold, coat with crushed croquant couverture and decorate with gold leaf.
(Germany)

Chinamen - Chinois

Line round shallow patty pans with Viennese paste. Fill with hollandaise filling and bake at 370° F (187° C). When cold, coat them level with praline buttercream and then mask with roasted ground almonds. On each, place a ball of praline paste and top this with a small disc of dark couverture. Pipe the features of a Chinaman with piping chocolate.　　　　*(France)*

Chocolate Coffee Slices

Sandwich a sheet of chocolate genoese with chocolate ganache buttercream. Cut into strips about 2 in. (5 cm.) wide and spread the top and sides with the same cream. Mask the sides with chocolate vermicelli. With a plain tube, pipe three lines of chocolate cream on the top with two lines of coffee cream between them. Refrigerate and cut into slices.

Chocolate Corn Flake Circles

Mix cornflakes with thin chocolate so that the flakes are covered. Using a ring about 2 in. (5 cm.) in diameter fashion circles on greaseproof paper about $1/2$ in. (1 cm.) thick. The ring can be removed immediately. When set, decorate the top with a rosette of buttercream topped with a chocolate disc.

Chocolate Fudge Slices

Line a baking sheet with chocolate sweet pastry. Bake at 380° F (193° C). Let the pastry stand for several days to soften, then sandwich two layers with well boiled apricot purée. Cut into strips and spread and decorate the tops with chocolate fudge. Cut into slices.

Chocolate Genoese Slices

Make a strip 2 in. (5 cm.) wide by placing strips of lemon and chocolate genoese side by side alternating the colours. Fix them together with apricot purée. Cover with chocolate almond paste marked with a ribbed roller. Cut into slices.

Chocolate Linz Fingers

lb	oz		kg	gr
1	4	Butter		625
	10	Sugar (castor)		300
	3	Egg		90
1	8	Flour		750
	3	Cocoa powder		90

Cream the butter, sugar and cocoa powder; add the egg and finally the flour. Using a star tube, pipe zigzag fingers on to baking sheets and bake at 360° F (182° C). When cold, sandwich in pairs with hot raspberry jam and dip one long side into chocolate.
(Same recipe for Linz Beans, *illustration page 509*.)

Chocolate Nougat Cup Cakes

To the Cup Cake recipe given add 9 oz. (270 gr.) of finely chopped plain couverture. Pipe chocolate coloured paper cases half full with this mixture and bake at 400° F (204° C). When cool, run in warm chocolate fudge.

Chocolate Nougat Rolls

Spread wafer mixing thinly on a greased and floured baking sheet. Half bake and cut into squares. Finish baking and quickly wrap each square round a wooden rod, applying a little pressure at the join. The wafers should be kept hot by keeping the baking sheet in the mouth of the oven. They may be stored in an air-tight tin until required for finishing.

They can be finished in a variety of ways.

For example:

1. Cover the outside with chocolate and pipe criss-cross lines on the top. Fill with whipped dairy cream.

2. Dip the ends in chocolate and fill with cream.

3. Spin with chocolate, add a little green nib almonds and fill with cream.

Chocolate Parfaits

Bake small round sablé biscuits, allow to cool, then sandwich in pairs with chocolate buttercream. Spread the tops with the same buttercream, leave until firm, then dip into fairly liquid couverture. Pipe a zigzag design on top with couverture and sprinkle a little chopped pistachio nut on top. *(France)*
(*Illustration page 481.*)

Chocolate Meringue Pies

Make tartlet cases of sweet pastry and bake them empty. When cold, brush them thinly with chocolate couverture. With a savoy bag fitted with a plain tube, fill them with chocolate custard in the form of a dome. With meringue, pipe a series of rings graduating to the centre, using a savoy bag with a plain tube. The centre ring should be about $1/2$-$3/4$ in. (1-2 cm.) in diameter. Mask the edge of the tartlets with lightly roasted flaked almonds. Flash in a hot oven to colour the meringue. Allow to cool. Fill the centres with red currant jelly and insert a chocolate cigarette in each.

(Germany)

Chocolate Sablé Slices

Line a baking sheet with rich sweet pastry and bake at 375° F (190° C). Store overnight to soften, then cut into strips about 2 1/2 in. (6 cm.) wide. Sandwich three or four strips with rum flavoured buttercream. Refrigerate, then coat with chocolate. Mark the top with diagonal lines with the back of a knife and then cut into slices. *(Germany)*

Chocolate Slices I

Line a baking sheet with fine almond sweet pastry pinned out to about 1/4 in. (5 mm.) thick and bake at 375°F (190°C).

Store overnight to soften, then cut into strips about 2 in. (5 cm.) wide. Sandwich three or four strips together with rum flavoured buttercream, leave until set, then coat with couverture. Mark the top with diagonal lines, using the back of a knife. When the couverture has set, cut into slices. *(Germany)*

Chocolate Slices II

lb	oz		kg	gr
2	0	Sweet pastry	1	

Filling

lb	oz		kg	gr
	12	Butter		375
	10	Sugar (castor)		300
	12	Egg		375
1	4	Cake crumbs		625
	8	Flour		250
	1	Ground almonds		30
	3	Unsweetened chocolate		90
		Vanilla		

Line a baking sheet with the sweet pastry and spread with apricot jam. Spread with the filling which is made up as for Osborne, the chocolate being melted and added before the flour, crumbs and almonds. Bake at 370° F (187° C). When cool, brush with apricot purée and cover with chocolate fondant. Cut into slices or squares.

Cinnamon Tartlets - Tartelettes à la Cannelle

lb	oz		kg	gr
	7	Almonds		200
	10	Sugar (castor)		300
1	0	Egg		500
	2 1/2	Flour		75
	5	Butter		150
	1/4	Ground cinnamon		8

Finely grind the almonds and half the sugar, moistening with a little water. Whip up the egg and the rest of the sugar. Mix in the almond/sugar mixture and then the flour and the butter which has been melted. Pour this mixture into patty pans lined with thin scrap puff pastry. Bake at 370° F (187° C). When baked, dust with icing sugar. *(France)*

Coconut Macaroons - Kokos Kransen

lb	oz		kg	gr
1	2	Dessicated coconut		560
1	5	Sugar (castor)		650
	9	Flour (soft)		270
	3 1/2	Egg		100
	10	Water (approx.)		300
		Yellow colouring		

Mix sugar and coconut with the rest of the ingredients into a mixture of piping consistency. Next, pipe rings with a star pipe on a baking sheet that has been lined with wafer paper. Bake at a temperature of 482° F (250° C). After baking, remove the superfluous pieces of wafer. *(Holland)*

Coconut Tartlets

Line deep patty pans or custard pans with sweet pastry and let them rest for 30 minutes. Make up the Coconut Tartlet Filling *(page 220)* and, while still warm, three parts fill the pastry lined shapes. Bake at 380-400° F (190-200° C). Larger units can be made in sandwich plates.
(Great Britain)

Coffee Balls

Sprinkle Othello bases with strong coffee and sandwich them together in pairs with coffee buttercream. Cover with the same

cream and roll into lightly flaked almonds. Pipe a small rosette of cream on the top of each and finish with a sugar coffee bean.
(Switzerland)

Coffee Barquettes
Line boat shaped tins with sweet pastry and bake blind. Fill with sponge cake cuttings mixed with rum, strong coffee and stock syrup. Spread the tops with coffee buttercream making a ridge along the middle.

Mask the edges with crushed meringue and place a sugar coffee bean in the centre. *(Switzerland)*

Coffee Cakes
Sprinkle a maddalena genoese *(page 40)* with a little cold, strong coffee, then split and sandwich with mocha buttercream. Mask the top with the same buttercream and decorate with a comb scraper. Cut into squares, pipe a whirl of coffee cream in the centre and top with a chocolate coffee bean. *(Italy)*

Coffee Fancies
Soak a maddalena genoese with a strong cold infusion of coffee. Sandwich and spread the top with coffee cream. Comb the surface and cut into squares. Pipe a rosette of the same cream in the centre of each and top with a sugar coffee bean.
(Italy)

Coffee Streusel Fancies
Sandwich a sheet of almond genoese with coffee buttercream. Refrigerate and cut out circles with a 1 1/2 in. (4 cm.) plain cutter. Cover top and sides with the same cream and roll into baked streusel *(page 226)*. Make little balls with a mixture of sponge cuttings and butter cream, roll them in streusel, dust with icing sugar and place in the centre of each fancy. *(Switzerland)*

Coffee Tongues
Sandwich in pairs 'S' shaped Othello bases with coffee buttercream. Dip into coffee flavoured chocolate and decorate the tops with an 'S' shaped scroll of white buttercream. *(Switzerland)*

Coffee Whirls
Take a sheet of coffee genoese and cut strips about 3 in. (8 cm.) wide. Cut the strips into fingers. On each, pipe a spiral whirl of coffee buttercream. Refrigerate and dip into milk chocolate. Place half a walnut at the end of each.

Commercy Madeleines

lb	oz		kg	gr
1	4	Sugar (icing)		625
1	4	Flour		625
	1/6	Bicarbonate of soda		5
1	3	Egg		600
	10	Butter (melted)		300
		Zest of 1 lemon		

Whisk the egg and sugar to a stiff sponge and fold in the zest and the flour and soda sieved together. Lastly carefully add the butter which should be barely lukewarm. Fill into greased and floured oval fluted madeleine pans and bake at about 400° F (204° C). *(France)*

Cream Baskets
Take frangipane tartlet bases *(page 324)* and slice off the tops fairly thinly. Using a fine star tube, pipe a rope of vanilla flavoured whipped dairy cream on either side. Cut the tops in half and arrange against the cream to form the lids of the basket. Dust with icing sugar.

Cream Cheese Tartlets
Line coarse fluted pans with sweet pastry and bake blind. Fill with the following mixture:

lb	oz		kg	gr
	7	Milk		200
	6	Egg yolks		180
	9	Sugar (castor)		270
1	12	Cream cheese		875
1	4	Whipped dairy cream		625
	4	Sultanas		125
		Gelatine (8 sheets)		
		Zest of lemon		

▲ Dundee Cake, p. 384

Honey Almond Tartlets, p. 536 ▼

421

422 ▲ Lemania Gâteau, p. 593   Tourte niçoise, France, p. 575 ▼

▲ Christmas Wreaths, p. 587

Butterletters, p. 382 ▼

423

▲ Cherry Cake, p. 383 — Madeira Cake, p. 397 — Genoa Cake, p. 386
Sultana Slab, Madeira Slab, Currant Slab, p. 404 ▼

▲ Date and Honey Cake, p. 384

Coconut Cake, p. 384 ▼

425

▲ Simnel Cake, p. 399

Birthday Cake, Great Britain, p. 382 ▼

▲ Battenburg, Great Britain, p. 547

Margret Cake, p. 581 ▼

427

428 ▲ Layer Cakes, Turkey, p. 548, 596 ▼

Take the milk and sugar to the boil and stir into the egg yolks. Return to the heat and cook carefully. Stir in the soaked gelatine, then the cream cheese and finally the whipped cream and sultanas. When the mixture has set in the tartlets, spin one way with chocolate and then at right angles. Finish each with a rosette of cream and half a glacé cherry. *(Switzerland)*

Cremasciutti
Line shell moulds with pasta frolla and fill ²/₃ with crème pâtissière. Top with pasta frolla and bake at 375° F (190° C). When cool, dust with icing sugar. *(Italy)*

Cup Cakes

lb	oz		kg	gr
	12	Butter		375
	14	Sugar (castor)		425
1	4	Egg		625
1	4	Flour		625
	¹/₄	Baking powder		8
		Colour and flavour as desired		

Cream the butter and sugar adding the egg by degrees. Add colour and flavour and fold in the flour. Pipe into small paper cases and bake at 400° F (204°C).

These cakes may be decorated before baking by sprinkling with currants, flaked almonds, coconut, etc., or with half a glacé cherry. They may be left plain and then decorated after baking, with fondant, buttercream, chocolate, jams and jellies etc.

Special metal sheets are available perforated with holes of a size to allow for the support of the paper cases during baking. In this way the shape is preserved, so reducing distorted shapes to a minimum.

Cup Cakes
(Using Special Cake Flour)

Group 1

lb	oz		kg	gr
1	2	Fat (special cake)		560
1	4	Sugar (castor)		625
	3	Milk powder		90

Group 2

lb	oz		kg	gr
1	2	Egg		560
	7	Milk (liquid)		200
	1	Glycerine		30

Group 3

lb	oz		kg	gr
1	11	Flour (special)		830
	1	Baking powder		30

Beat group 1 to a light cream. Add group 2 in six additions, beating well at each addition. Blend in group 3 that have been sieved together. Pipe into paper cases and bake at 420° F (216° C°.) The mixing will yield about 8 dozen small cup cakes. Colour and flavour can be used as desired.

For chocolate cup cakes, delete 3 oz. (90 gr.) of flour and replace with an equal amount of cocoa powder and add the same weight of milk, and at the same time a little chocolate colour.

Diamonds

lb	oz		kg	gr
	14	Sugar (icing)		425
1	10	Butter		800
1	0	Marzipan		500
	5	Egg whites		150
2	0	Flour	1	
		Salt		
		Vanilla		

Cream the butter, icing sugar, salt and vanilla. Work the marzipan and egg whites until smooth and add to the butter mixture. Force out in long bands through a biscuit forcer with a serrated plate and bake at 392° F (200° C). After baking, cut the strips into diamonds as desired and half dip in chocolate couverture.
(Germany)

Dipped Fondant Cubes
Split a sheet of butter sponge twice, sandwich with buttercream of the desired colour and flavour and refrigerate. Brush the sheet with hot apricot purée and cut into cubes, dipping the knife constantly in hot water. Dip into fondant of the same

colour and flavour as the cream. Use a fine plain pipe to decorate. Place into paper cases. *(Switzerland)*

Dobos

lb	oz		kg	gr
1	0	Butter		500
1	0	Sugar (icing)		500
1	0	Flour		500
1	0	Egg		500

Cream the butter and sugar together and add the egg a portion at a time. Finally fold in the flour. Spread the mixture out thinly on to greased and floured baking sheets. Bake at 420° F (215° C). Sandwich together five or six sheets with chocolate buttercream. Cut into strips about 2 in. (5 cm.) wide. Coat the tops with caramel and cut into slices. *(Hungary)*

Dome Slices

These are made in special gutter shaped moulds about 16-18 in. (40-45 cm.) long. They are lined with greaseproof paper into which a genoese mixing is spread. When baked and cool, the paper is removed and the genoese sandwiched with jam and/or cream and finished in many ways with almond paste, chocolate, jellies, fruit, nuts, fondant, etc. The strips are then cut into slices, or in half.

The same moulds can be used for shaping fancies. This is done by lining first with waxed or greaseproof paper and then with a strip of sponge. The concave space is then filled with cream and topped with another strip of sponge, which is brushed with apricot purée. Finally, a strip of baked sweet pastry is put on top. After refrigeration the strip is removed from the mould and decorated.

Dutch Tartlets - Hollandaise

Line some round patty pans with thinly rolled scrap puff pastry and pipe in the centre of each a spot of apricot jam. Fill the tartlets with some hollandaise mixture and place on top a cross made from two strips of puff pastry. Bake at 370° F (187° C). When baked, brush with apricot purée and glaze with kirsch flavoured water icing. Decorate with half a glacé cherry. *(France)*

Easter Cakes

lb	oz		kg	gr
	8	Butter		250
	5	Sugar (castor)		150
	3	Egg		90
1	0	Flour (soft)		500
	$3/16$	Baking powder		10
	8	Currants		250
	$1/8$	Ground cassia		4

Sieve the flour, baking powder and spice and rub in the butter. With the rest of the materials, make a pliable pastry. Pin out to about $1/4$ in. (5 mm.) thick and cut out with a 3 in. (8 cm.) fluted cutter. Place on baking sheets, wash with egg and dust with castor sugar. Bake at 400°F (204°C). *(Great Britain)*

Exquis

lb	oz		kg	gr
1	0	Almonds		500
1	0	Sugar		500
	7	Flour		200
	$4 \, 1/2$	Egg whites (approx.)		140
		Vanilla		

Grind the almonds and sugar. Add the vanilla and flour and make a stiff paste by adding the whites. Line some greased tartlet moulds with this paste and bake blind in an oven about 360° F (182° C). Fill each tartlet with butter ganache and refrigerate. Coat the tops with chocolate fondant and place half a pistachio nut in the centre of each. *(France)*

Fairy Cakes

lb	oz		kg	gr
	12	Butter		375
	14	Sugar (castor)		425
	12	Egg		375
	1	Glycerine		30
1	4	Flour (soft)		625
	$1/4$	Baking powder		8
	6	Milk		180

Proceed as for Queen Cakes. Pipe into well greased small fancy shaped pans. Place

two diamonds of angelica and half a glacé cherry on each. Bake at 425° F (218° C).
(Great Britain)

Fancy Crescents - Gipferl

lb	oz		kg	gr
1	2	Butter		560
	9	Sugar (icing)		270
	1	Egg yolks		30
1	10	Flour		800
		1 vanilla pod		
		A little salt		

Beat the butter, icing sugar, egg yolks, vanilla and salt until frothy, then mix with the flour. Pipe out this mixing in small crescents using a savoy bag and star tube and bake at 392° F (200° C). After baking, dip the ends in chocolate couverture.
(Germany)

Figs - Figues

Pipe out some sponge mixing in pear shapes on to greaseproof paper. Bake at 380° F (193° C). After baking, scoop out the middle of each and match up into pairs, filling with kirsch flavoured confectioner's custard.

Cover each one with thinly rolled green almond paste. Dip the base of each in cocoa and mark five lines on the sides with the back of a knife. *(France)*

Filled Pastries - Gevulde Koeken

A palatable cookie, made of two layers of paste between which almond-paste is applied.

lb	oz		kg	gr
	7	Butter or margarine		200
	7	Sugar (castor)		200
	1 1/2	Egg		45
	1/4	Zest of lemon		8
	1/16	Salt		2
	12	Flour (soft)		350
	3/8	Baking powder		10
		(2/3 bicarbonate of soda,		
		1/3 cream of tartar)		

Make a paste with the ingredients mentioned above. After resting in a cool place, roll out to a thickness about 1/8 in. (3 mm.).

Cut out with a 4 in. (10 cm.) fluted cutter and place half of them on a greased baking sheet.

Next, pipe about 3/4 oz. (20 gr.) of almond paste on each, and top with the other pieces. Brush with egg, put a half almond on top, brush again with egg and bake at 437° F (225° C). This recipe is sufficient for 24 pastries. *(Holland)*

Florettes

lb	oz		kg	gr
	10	Egg whites		300
1	0	Sugar (castor)		500
	12	Ground almonds		375
		Kirsch		

Whisk the whites stiffly and fold in the sugar, ground almonds and kirsch.

Line some fairly deep tartlet pans with sweet paste and pipe in a spot of apricot jam. Fill with the meringue mixture, sprinkle with strip almonds, dust with icing sugar and bake at 380° F (193° C).
(France)

Florentines

lb	oz		kg	gr
	5	Butter		150
	5	Sugar (castor)		150
	1 1/2	Honey		45
	1 3/4	Unwhipped dairy cream		50
	2 1/2	Flaked almonds		75
	1 3/4	Chopped almonds		50
	1 1/2	Nibbed almonds		45
	1 1/4	Candied orange peel		35
	1	Candied lemon peel		30
	3/4	Flour		20
		Half a vanilla pod		

Put the butter, sugar, honey and dairy cream into a pan, and cook over a fire to 248° F (120° C) stirring continuously. Add all the almonds, the orange and lemon peel, flour and vanilla and continue cooking until the mixture leaves the sides of the pan.

Deposit in 25 small heaps of equal size on a well greased, floured baking sheet, flatten

until 4 in. (10 cm.) in diameter and bake in 3 stages until golden. After baking, coat the underside with chocolate couverture and mark with a decorating comb.
(Illustration page 482.) *(Germany)*

Florentine Slices
Cut strips of florentine about 2 1/2 in. (6 cm.) wide and then into 1 in. (2.5 cm.) fingers. Place them side by side on a strip of genoese, fixing with nougat buttercream. The strip is built up of three layers of genoese sandwiched with the same cream. When set, cut into fingers.

Flour Cakes - Un Kurabiyesi

lb	oz		kg	gr
1	8	Flour (soft)		750
	1/4	Baking powder		10
	8	Cornflour		250
	8	Sugar (castor)		250
	4	Egg		125
1	0	Butter		500

The flour, cornflour and baking powder are first sieved together. The butter and sugar are mixed together and the eggs are added. The mixture is then mixed with the flour and a smooth paste is made.

Weigh into 2 oz. (60 gr.) pieces and mould into round shapes. Place on to lightly greased baking sheets and flatten slightly, then mark with a trellis design with the back of a knife. Bake at 350° F (176° C) so that they take on no crust colour.
(Illustration page 479.) *(Turkey)*

Frangipane Cream Slices
Line a baking sheet with sweet pastry about 1/4 in. (6 mm.) thick and half bake. Spread with raspberry jam and spread on top a frangipane mixing, 1/4 in. (6 mm.) thick. Bake at 375° F (190° C). When cold, cut into strips about 2 1/2 in. (6 cm.) wide. Pipe three lines of marshmallow cream on top. The cream should be lemon, chocolate and strawberry. When the marshmallow has set, cover with chocolate. Cut into slices.

Frangipane Fruit Slices
Line frames with sweet pastry as described under Fruit Almond Slices, and place a mixture of chopped cherries, ginger crush, sultanas with a little apricot jam. Fill in with frangipane filling. Bake at 360° F (182° C). When cold, brush with apricot purée and cover with roller marked almond paste. Cut into slices.

Frascati

lb	oz		kg	gr
1	0	Almonds		500
1	0	Sugar (granulated)		500
1	0	Chopped candied fruit		500
	8	Egg		250
	3	Egg yolks		90
	3 1/2	Kirsch		100
	13	Sweet paste		400

Line some tartlet pans with sweet paste. Grind the almonds with the sugar. Add the egg, egg yolks and the kirsch. Mix in the finely chopped fruit. Fill into the cases and bake at 400° F (204° C). Cover the tartlets with chocolate meringue and place into the oven to harden but not to change in colour (see as well *page 514*). *(France)*

Fromage de Brie
Sandwich a sheet of almond genoese twice with kirsch buttercream and refrigerate. Cut out circles with a 1 3/4 in. (4 cm.) plain cutter. Mask top and sides with the same buttercream and roll in castor sugar. Dust the tops with icing sugar and, with a knife, mark a trellis design on the top. Finish by sprinkling a little chopped pistachio nut or green nib almonds on top.
(Switzerland)

Fruit Slices

lb	oz		kg	gr
1	8	Flour		750
	3/4	Baking powder		20
	12	Butter		375
	15	Sugar		450
	14	Egg		400
	7 1/2	Milk		215
	8	Cherries		225
	6	Sultanas		180
		Vanilla		

Cream the butter and sugar, adding the egg in portions. Add the vanilla. Fold in the sieved flour and baking powder; add the milk and lastly the fruit. Spread this mixing on a paper lined tray about 16 in. by 16 in. (40 × 40 cm.). Bake at 400° F (204° C). When cold, remove the paper, dust with icing sugar and cut into slices.

Fruit Tartlets - Tartelettes aux Fruits divers

Line some boat shaped tartlet moulds with pasta frolla and bake blind. When cold, brush the inside with chocolate couverture and leave to harden. Deposit a layer of frangipane cream or confectioner's custard and place the fruit on top (grapes, mandarine segments, pineapple triangles, cherries, grapefruit). Lightly brush the fruit with apricot purée (optional) and surround with flaked roasted almonds.

(France)

Ginger Biscuits - Ingwer-Plätzchen

lb	oz		kg	gr
1	0	Butter		500
	7	Marzipan		200
	14	Sugar (castor)		400
1	0	Flour		500
		A little salt		
		A little finely ground ginger, cinnamon and cocoa powder		

Prepare a sweet paste from the above ingredients, adding the ginger, cinnamon and cocoa powder.

Pin out the paste to approx. $1/8$ in. (3 mm.) in thickness, cut out to small rounds, place 2 thin strips of ginger on each and bake at approx. 356° F (180° C) until golden.

(Germany)

Hazelnut Duchesses - Haselnussduchesse

lb	oz		kg	gr
1	0	Egg whites		500
1	0	Sugar (castor)		500
	7	Finely grated hazelnuts		200
	4	Flour		125
	7	Hot butter		200

Whip the egg whites and sugar to a stiff snow, blend in the finely grated hazelnuts and the flour and lastly draw in the hot butter. Mix well. Using a plain tube, pipe out in bulbs 1 $1/2$ in. (4 cm.) in diameter, sprinkle with flaked hazelnuts and bake off at 356° F (180° C). After baking, sandwich in pairs with nougat paste, placing the undersides inside, and dust lightly.

(Germany)

Hazelnut Fingers

Take rather short finger shaped Othello bases and sandwich with hazelnut buttercream. Cover the outside with the same cream and after refrigeration, dip into coffee coloured fondant. Decorate by spinning dark chocolate across the tops and finish with a blanched hazelnut.

(Switzerland)

Hazelnut Squares

lb	oz		kg	gr
2	8	Sweet pastry	1	250

Filling

lb	oz		kg	gr
	8	Sugar (granulated)		250
	5	Water		150
	12	Cake crumbs		375
	10	Roasted chopped hazelnuts		300
	10	Butter		300
	$1/8$	Cinnamon		4

Line a baking sheet with half of the sweet pastry. Take the sugar and water to the boil and stir in the crumbs and the hazelnuts and add the cinnamon. Spread on the lined tray and cover with the rest of the sweet pastry. Wash heavily with egg and mark a pattern of wavy lines with a comb scraper. Bake at 390° F (199° C). When cold, cut into squares.

Helvetia Slices

Make a light enriched sponge with the following:

lb	oz		kg	gr
1	8	Egg whites		750
1	8	Egg yolks		750
1	0	Sugar (castor)		500

lb	oz		kg	gr
	1/4	Cream of tartar		7
	8	Flour (soft)		250
	12	Arrowroot		375
	4	Dairy cream		125

The egg whites and half the sugar are whisked to a stiff meringue on medium speed. The yolks and the rest of the sugar are whipped stiffly using the same speed. The two mixtures are blended together carefully followed by the flour and arrowroot sieved together. Finally the cream is carefully mixed in.

This mixture is spread, about 1/4 in. (6 mm.) thick on paper lined baking sheets and baked at 380° F (193° C). When cool, five sheets are layered, one on top of the other, with kirsch buttercream. Cut into strips about 3 in. (7.5 cm.) wide and spread the same cream over the top and sides. Refrigerate and cover with white fondant. Run some chopped pistachio nuts or green nib almonds along the length and cut into triangles. Use the nuts sparingly. *(Switzerland)*

Honey Nut Boats
Line boat shaped tins with chocolate sweet pastry. Fill with honey nut mixture and bake at 360° F (182° C). When cool, spread the tops with truffle buttercream and mask the edges with chocolate vermicelli. Pipe three shells on the top of each using the same cream and a star pipe. *(Switzerland)*

Iced Tartlets - Tartelettes à l'Eau

lb	oz		kg	gr
1	0	Sugar (castor)		500
1	0	Almonds		500
	13 1/2	Egg whites		400
	2	Flour		60

Grind the almonds and half the sugar moistening with a little water. Into this mixture, fold in the egg whites which have been whipped to a stiff snow with the rest of the sugar. Finally fold in the flour. Fill into patty pans which have been lined with thinly rolled scrap puff pastry and bake at 380° F (193° C).

As soon as they are removed from the oven, coat with water icing and place a small quantity of roasted flaked almonds in the centre of each, or decorate. *(France)* *(Illustration page 484.)*

Ischl Linz Fancies
Pin out Linz Pastry I-Austria *(page 189)* to 1/4 in. (5 mm.) thick. Cut out with 1 1/2 in. (4 cm.) plain cutter and bake at 355° F (180° C). When cool, sandwich in pairs with apricot jam then coat with cooked chocolate icing. *(Austria)*

Jamaican Cakes
Sandwich together two sheets of genoese sponge with softened almond paste and then splash with rum to make the cake soft. Cut into diamond shapes and coat with rum flavoured buttercream. Refrigerate and then dip into pink fondant. Decorate with candied fruits. *(France)*

Jamettes

lb	oz		kg	gr
	12	Butter		375
1	0	Sugar (castor)		500
	12	Egg		375
1	8	Flour (soft)		750
	3/4	Baking powder		20
	9	Milk		270
		Lemon flavour		

Cream the butter and sugar adding the egg by degrees. Stir in half the milk, fold in the flour and baking powder and lastly the rest of the milk. Pipe out in small bulbs on to paper lined baking sheets, using a plain pipe. Bake at 400° F (204° C). When baked remove from the paper and sandwich them together in pairs with raspberry jam. Cover them all over with the same jam and roll in medium desiccated coconut.

Other finishes
1. Sandwich together in pairs with raspberry jam and buttercream. Dust with icing sugar.

2. Sandwich together in pairs with apricot jam and dip the tops in chocolate. Sprinkle a little green nib almond on top.

Jap Slices

lb	oz		kg	gr
2	0	Sweet pastry	1	

Filling

lb	oz		kg	gr
	12	Butter		375
	12	Sugar (castor)		375
	10	Egg		300
	12	Coconut		375
	8	Ground rice		250
		Vanilla		

Line a baking sheet with sweet pastry and spread with apricot jam. Make up the filling as for Osborne. Spread level and bake at 360° F (182° C). When cool, dust with icing sugar and cut into squares.

Jeannettes

Line a sandwich plate with milanese paste and spread a layer of hollandaise mixing over the bottom; next add some stoned white-heart cherries and cover with more hollandaise. Bake at 360° F (182° C) and brush immediately with apricot purée and glaze with water icing. Cut into pieces.
(France)

Lemons - Citrons

Line some round shallow patty pans with Linz paste and bake blind in a medium oven at about 370° F (187° C). As soon as cold, fill with lemon custard. Coat with lemon flavoured and coloured fondant, and write the word 'Citron' or 'Lemon' in chocolate on the top of each. *(Switzerland)*

Lemon Frangipane Slices

Sandwich two layers of frangipane with lemon curd. Cut into strips and spread lemon buttercream on the top, domed shape. Brush the sides with apricot purée and cover top and sides with a sheet of lemon coloured almond paste with the surface marked with a ribbed rolling pin.

Refrigerate and cut into slices.

Lemon Rolls - Zitronenrollen

For 24

lb	oz		kg	gr
	7 1/2	Egg whites		225
	3 1/4	Egg yolks		100
	3 1/2	Sugar (castor)		100
	3 1/2	Flour		100
	1	Water (approx.)		30

Beat up the egg whites, yolks, sugar and water warm for about 15 minutes; remove from heat, continue beating until cold and blend in the flour. Spread on paper to a rectangular shape 28 in. by 18 in. (70 × 45 cm.) and bake briskly at 392° F (200° C).

After baking, spread with the lemon cream, cut lengthwise into 3 equal parts and roll each of them up separately. When cold, cut each roll into 8 slices and dust with pulverized sugar.

Lemon cream

lb	oz		kg	gr
1	0	White wine		500
	4 3/4	Egg yolks		145
	5	Egg whites		150
	1 3/4	Cornstarch		50
	5	Sugar		150
		Juice and zest of 3 lemons		

Bring the white wine, egg yolks, cornstarch, 4 oz. (125 gr.) sugar, lemon juice and zest to the boil, whip the egg whites and 1 oz. (30 gr.) sugar to a stiff snow and add to the wine cream and allow to cool. *(Germany)*
(Illustration page 481.)

Lemon Tartlets - Tartelettes Citron

lb	oz		kg	gr
	14	Sugar (castor)		400
	7	Butter		200
	10	Egg		300
		Zest of 2 lemons		
		Juice of 6 lemons		

Put all the ingredients into a saucepan and cook. Line some patty pans with thin scrap puff pastry and half fill with the lemon mixture. Bake at 400° F (204° C). This type of tartlet differs from the usual lemon tart because the filling is cooked twice and they are not coated with fondant. *(France)*

Linz Beans
See recipe for Chocolate Linz Fingers, *page 418. (Illustration page 509.)*

Linz Chocolate Slices
Pin out Linz pastry ¼ in. (5 mm.) thick and cut into strips about 3 in. (8 cm.) wide. Bake at 340° F (170° C). When cold, sandwich in pairs with apricot jam and coat with cooked chocolate icing *(page 244)*. After the icing has set, carefully cut the strips into rectangles.
(Austria)

Linz Tartlets - Tartelettes de Linz
Line some tartlet pans with Linz paste, fill with raspberry jam and cover with a lattice of the same paste. Bake in a medium oven and glaze with raspberry jelly. *(France) (Illustration page 481.)*

Linz Fancies
Place small hoops on paper lined baking sheets. Pipe a white Linz mixing *(p. 189)* spiral fashion into the hoops, using a plain tube. Place on top a circle of wafer paper the same diameter as the hoops. Pipe a liberal amount of raspberry jam on each. Finish by piping a cross and an outer ring. Bake at 360° F (182° C). When cool, dust with icing sugar.
(Austria)

Linz Fruit Slices

lb	oz		kg	gr
1	4	Butter		625
	10	Sugar (castor)		300
	10	Ground almonds (roasted)		300
	2	Egg		60
1	8	Flour		750
	⅛	Ground cinnamon		4
		Lemon zest		

Pin this pastry out to about ¼ in. (5 mm.) thick and line a baking sheet. Bake at 380° F (193° C). Leave for a day, then sandwich three layers with hot raspberry jam. Cut into strips about 2 ½ in. (6 cm.) wide. Bring to the boil the following: sultanas, mixed chopped peel, currants, chopped cherries and preserved ginger, lemon zest, rum and sufficient apricot purée. Spread this mixture on the strips and glaze with thin lemon water icing. Stand in the oven to set the glaze, then cut into slices.

Lisettes

lb	oz		kg	gr
1	0	Almonds		500
1	0	Sugar (granulated)		500
	12	Candied orange peel		375
	12	Egg whites		375

Line some boat shaped pans with milanese pastry. Grind the almonds with the sugar. Fold in the stiffly whipped egg whites and the finely chopped orange peel. Pipe this mixture into the cases and decorate each with a diamond of orange peel. Bake at 380° F (193° C). Lightly dust with sugar.
(Switzerland)

Lucullus Slices
Split a strip of chocolate genoese about 2 in. (5 cm.) wide and sandwich two of them with arrack buttercream. Spread the top with kirsch flavoured buttercream and place small pieces of pineapple in two rows, each about ¾ in. (2 cm.) from the edge. With a savoy bag and plain tube, pipe three lines of the same cream along the strip, so that there are alternating lines of pineapple and cream. Place the third slice on top and refrigerate. When set, cover with chocolate. Cut into slices.
(Switzerland)

Madrid Dainties

lb	oz		kg	gr
1	0	Flour		500
	10	Butter		300
	4	Sugar (castor)		125
	7	Egg		200
	⅛	Ground bitter almonds		3

Mix all the ingredients to a plastic paste using a little cold water if necessary. Pin out ¼ in. (5 mm.) thick and cut out with a 2 in. (4 ½ cm.) plain cutter. Bake at

400° F (204° C). While still warm sandwich in pairs with well boiled apricot purée. Glaze the top and sides with purée and sprinkle lightly with sugar nibs.

(France)

Magali

Line some deep patty pans with milanese paste and bake blind. Fill with ganache and refrigerate. Coat the tops with chocolate fondant and decorate the edges with roasted ground almonds. *(France)*

Magdalena Slices - Magdalenen-Schnitten

lb	oz		kg	gr
1	0	Egg		500
1	0	Sugar (castor)		500
	8	Flour		250
	8	Cornflour		250
	8	Candied orange peel		250
	12	Butter (hot)		375
1	0	Fondant		500
	4	Candied orange peel		125

Whip the egg and sugar warm and continue whipping until cold. Add the flour, cornflour and finely chopped orange peel; lastly fold in the hot butter. Deposit in a greased tin, 8 in. by 11 in. by 2 in. (20 × 30 × 5 cm.) deep and bake at 360° F (182° C). When cold, coat the top with the fondant into which the finely chopped orange peel has been mixed. When set, cut into slices. *(Germany)*

Maltese Lemon Slices

Cut strips of sweet pastry about $3/4$ in. (2 cm.) thick and 3 in. (7.5 cm.) wide and spread them with redcurrant jelly. With a star tube pipe on the following mixture:

lb	oz		kg	gr
1	0	Butter		500
1	0	Sugar (castor)		500
1	0	Egg		500
2	0	Flour (soft)	1	
		Zest of lemon		

Bake each strip at 400° F (204° C), between metal bars. When cool, cut into slices. Cover the top and sides with arrack buttercream. Mask the sides with chocolate vermicelli and sprinkle chocolate shavings on the top. Dust lightly with icing sugar and cut into slices.

(Switzerland)

Marionnettes

lb	oz		kg	gr
	12	Finely ground roasted nuts		375
	8	Marzipan		250
1	8	Sugar		750
	3 $1/2$	Flour		100
		Cinnamon		
		Lemon juice		
		1 vanilla pod		

Prepare a paste from the above ingredients with sufficient egg white to bring it to a spreading consistency. Deposit on greased, floured baking sheets in rounds approx. 1 $1/2$ in. (4 cm.) in diameter, using a round stencil. Bake in 2 stages at 392° F (200° C). After baking, spread the undersides with chocolate couverture. *(Germany)*

Marshmallow Slices I

lb	oz		kg	gr
	10	Water		300
	3 $1/2$	Gelatine		100
2	0	Sugar (granulated)	1	
	10	Water		300
		Vanilla		
2	8	Desiccated coconut	1	250

Whisk the gelatine and 10 oz. (300 gr.) of water. (The gelatine is first dispersed in a little hot water.) Bring the sugar and the other 10 oz. (300 gr.) of water to the boil and pour it on to the whisking gelatine/water mix. When stiff, mix in the coconut and quickly spread on to a greased, paper lined tray. When set, cut into strips about 2 $1/2$ in. (6 cm.) wide and cover with chocolate, decorating the top with a comb scraper. Sprinkle a little green nib almonds along the length of the strip. Cut into fingers.

Marshmallow Slices II

Proceed exactly as above, but delete the coconut and replace with:

lb	oz		kg	gr
1	8	Cherries		750
1	0	Roasted nib almonds		500
1	0	Sultanas		500

Marzipan Sticks

Reduce raw marzipan to piping consistency with arrack, working in a little sieved praline croquant. Pipe out fingers with a star tube, about 2 1/2 in. (6 cm.) long. Bake carefully at 350° F (176° C). When cold dip into thin couverture. *(Switzerland)*

Marzipan Leaves

Using the wafer recipe *(page 533)*, stencil out leaf shapes. Bake at 420° F (216° C). Sandwich together in pairs with nougat buttercream. Dip halfway into chocolate. *(Illustration page 138.)*

Massillons

lb	oz		kg	gr
	7	Ground almonds		200
	10	Sugar (castor)		300
	3 1/2	Egg		100
	1 3/4	Egg whites		50
		Vanilla		
		Sweet pastry		

Beat the almonds, sugar, egg and vanilla until foamy and fold in the egg whites whipped to a stiff snow. Line tartlet pans with the sweet pastry, fill with the almond mixture and bake for about 10 minutes at 375° F (190° C). Spread the tops with a paste made up of 1 oz. (30 gr.) of egg whites mixed with 2 1/2 oz. (75 gr.) finely chopped almonds and about 5 oz. (150 gr.) of icing sugar. Return to the oven for 2 or 3 minutes to form a crust on top. *(France)*

Melide Slices

lb	oz		kg	gr
1	0	Sugar (castor)		500
	8	Honey		250
	6	Egg whites		170
	3	Cream		90
	3	Flour		90
1	0	Almonds (flaked)		500

Place the sugar, honey, cream and egg whites into a saucepan and heat carefully. When quite hot, mix in the flour and then the almonds. Spread this mixing when cool, 1/2 in. (1 cm.) thick on to a sweet pastry lined baking sheet that has been spread with raspberry jam. Bake at 360° F (182° C). When cold, cut into strips and then into fingers. Dip the ends in chocolate and place half a glacé cherry in the centre of each. *(Switzerland)*

Meringue and Citron Slices

Take a sheet of almond genoese and cut into strips about 2 1/2 in. (6 cm.) wide. Spread meringue on the top and sprinkle with chopped citron peel. Cut into fingers and flash in the oven.

Milan Slices - Mailänder Schnitten

For 48 pieces

lb	oz		kg	gr
	10	Butter		300
1	2	Sugar (castor)		560
	6	Ground almonds		180
1	10	Egg whites		800
	10	Flour		300

Macaroon paste:

lb	oz		kg	gr
1	0	Almond macaroons (crushed)		500
	8	Sugar (icing)		250
	3	Egg whites		90
		Juice of 3 lemons		

Cream the butter, 14 oz. (435 gr.) sugar and the almonds. Whip the egg whites and 4 oz. (125 gr.) sugar to a stiff snow and fold into the butter mixture together with the flour. Spread on a baking sheet in a rectangular shape 28 in. by 18 in. (70 × 45 cm.) and bake off. Cut into two and spread one with orange-flavoured apple jam. Brush the top half with apricot purée and divide into 48 sections. Prepare the macaroon paste and pipe out a whirl on each division. Flash and arrange on the base and cut into individual slices. Dip each one in hot apricot purée and glaze with lemon icing. For final decoration, place half a red glacé cherry and half a yellow glacé cherry on each slice, with a white almond stuck into the icing on the slant next to each half cherry. *(Germany)*

Mille-feuille Slices

Pin out very thinly some scrap puff pastry and line a baking sheet. Dock well before baking at 400° F (204° C). Cut the pastry into strips about 3 in. (7.5 cm.) wide and sandwich three together with a layer of apricot jam covered with a mixture of confectioner's cream and whipped dairy cream. Brush the tops with apricot purée and finish with marbled icing, using either fondant or water icing. When set carefully cut into slices.
(Illustration page 480.)

Mirlitons

lb	oz		kg	gr
	8	Egg		250
1	0	Sugar (castor)		500
		16-18 macaroon biscuits		
		Vanilla		

Line some fairly deep tartlet pans with thin scrap puff paste and allow to rest. Pipe a spot of apricot jam in the bottom of each. Whip up the egg and sugar stiffly and mix in the crushed and sieved macaroon. Fill into the cases and place three split almonds on the top in the form of a clover leaf. Dust generously with icing sugar and bake at 400° F (204° C). *(France)*

Mirlitons - Rouen

Line some patty pans with thin scrap puff pastry and allow to rest for some hours. Two thirds fill with the following mixture:

lb	oz		kg	gr
	3	Egg yolks		90
1	3/4	Sugar (castor)		50
	4	Butter		125
		Vanilla		
		Zest of 1 orange		

The yolks and sugar are well whipped, adding the zest and vanilla. Whilst still whipping, add the melted butter. After filling the cases, they are dusted with sugar and baked at 400° F (204° C). *(France)*

Nancéens

lb	oz		kg	gr
	8	Almonds		250
1	0	Sugar (castor)		500
	9	Egg whites		280
		Vanilla		

Finely grind the almonds, adding the sugar gradually and then moisten with 4 oz. (150 gr.) of egg whites. Warm this mixture until it is too hot to touch with the fingers. Remove from the heat and fold in the rest of the whites which have been stiffly whipped. Add the vanilla and fill into boat shaped tartlet pans lined with milanese paste. Place two split almonds on top; dust with icing sugar and bake at 380° F (193° C). *(France)*

Napoleon Slices - Napoleonschnitten

Bake a thin base of puff paste trimmings and cut in 3 in. (8 cm.) strips. Drain poached morello cherries, reduce the juice well, thicken with cornstarch and leave until cold. Sandwich three strips of puff paste together with vanilla-flavoured whipped cream and the cherries, glaze the surface with apricot purée and ice thinly with vanilla fondant. Cut into fingers and decorate with a rosette of whipped cream and a red cherry. *(Germany)*

Neapolitan Slices

Take a sheet of genoese and split. Sandwich with raspberry jam and cut into slices about 1 1/2 in. (4 cm.) wide. Spread the top with apricot purée and arrange three strips of different coloured almond paste, pyramid fashion, on top. Cover with white fondant. When set, cut into slices.

Neapolitan Peach Tartlets - Tartelettes aux Pêches à la napolitaine

Line some greased tartlet moulds with pasta frolla, prick with a fork and bake blind in a hot oven for 5 to 6 minutes. When they are baked, place in each half a choice peach which has been poached in syrup, coat with a little apricot purée and top with half an almond. *(France)*

Nichettes

Line small boat-shaped pans with sweet pastry, fill with Bourdaloue cream, sprinkle with strip almonds and dust with icing sugar. Bake in a hot oven so that the tops become slightly caramelized at the same time. *(France)*

Nougat Biscuits

Pin out chocolate sweet pastry *(page 186)* 1/4 in. (5 mm.) thick. Cut out discs with a 2 in. (5 cm.) plain cutter and bake at 375° F (190° C). When cold sandwich in pairs with nougat buttercream and coat with chocolate icing. Pipe on a cross of the same icing, slighty off centre and place half a glacé cherry in the middle of the cross. *(Great Britain)*

Nougat Fudge Biscuits

Pin out chocolate sweet pastry and cut out biscuits with a 2 in. (5 cm.) plain cutter. Bake at 380° F (193° C). Sandwich in pairs with nougat buttercream then cover the tops with warm chocolate fudge. Pipe a cross, just off centre, on the top of each and place half a glacé cherry on the intersection.

Nougatine

Sprinkle a maddalena genoese with rum and sandwich it with nougat cream. Spread the same cream on the top and cover with roasted nib hazelnuts. Cut into squares. Pipe a rosette in the centre of each with chocolate buttercream and place a liqueur cherry on top. *(Italy)*

Nougatines

Line some patty pans with Linz paste and fill with hollandaise mixing. Place some flaked almonds on half of the top of each tartlet. Bake at 400° F (204° C) and brush the tops immediately with apricot purée and coat the top of each pastry where there are no almonds with pink fondant. Decorate with half a glacé cherry rolled in granulated sugar.

Nougat Slices

Layer a thin sheet of chocolate genoese between two plain sheets, using nougat buttercream. Cut into strips about 2 in. (5 cm.) wide. Spread top and sides with the same cream and mask all over with lightly roasted flaked almonds. Cut into neat slices. Pipe a rosette of cream in one corner and top with half a glacé cherry.

Nut Balls

Glaze Othello biscuits with well boiled apricot purée. Place half a walnut on half of them and give a further glaze with thin rum flavoured fondant. Sandwich together in pairs with nougat buttercream, with the walnut decorated one on top. *(Switzerland)*

Nut Boats

lb	oz		kg	gr
	5	Ground almonds		150
	5	Sugar (icing)		150
		Linz pastry III		

Line small boat-shaped pans with the Linz pastry. Mix the almonds, sugar and a little milk to a fairly stiff paste. Fill into the lined pans, cover with the same pastry, press down well and trim the edges. Bake at 360° F (180° C). When cold, dust with icing sugar and place half a hazelnut in the centre, using a little apricot jam to fix in position. *(Austria)*

Nut Cubes - Nusswürfel

lb	oz		kg	gr
	8	Sugar (icing)		250
	14	Butter		425
	14	Ground roasted nuts		425
1	0	Flour		500
		A little cinnamon and salt		

Cream the butter, icing sugar and nuts until somewhat frothy, then add the flour together with the cinnamon and salt and work into a sweet paste. Shape into rectangular strips, put in refrigerator, cut into slices and bake at 392° F (200° C). After baking, spread the undersides with chocolate couverture. *(Germany)*

Orange Fancies

Sprinkle a maddalena genoese with orange liqueur and sandwich with orange buttercream. Spread the top with the same cream and comb the surface. Cut into squares and finish with a candied orange segment and leaves cut from citron peel.
(Italy)

Orange Tartlets - Barquettes aux Oranges

Line some boat shaped tartlet moulds with some sweet paste and bake blind. Deposit a layer of curaçao flavoured confectioner's custard in each tartlet case and fill with 5 to 6 segments of seedless Jaffa oranges, round sides uppermost. Coat with a curaçao flavoured wine jelly.
(Switzerland)

Osborne

lb	oz		kg	gr
2	0	Sweet pastry	1	

Filling

lb	oz		kg	gr
	12	Butter		375
	12	Sugar (castor)		375
	8	Egg		250
	4	Cake crumbs		125
	4	Ground almonds		125

Line a tray with the sweet pastry and spread with raspberry jam. Add and spread the filling which is made by creaming the butter and sugar and then adding the egg in portions. The crumbs and ground almonds are then mixed in. Bake at 400° F (204° C). When cool, skim off the top crust, brush with apricot purée and cover with chocolate fondant. Pipe a trellis design with the same fondant and sprinkle with chopped pistachio nuts or green almonds. When set, cut into slices.

Palisades

lb	oz		kg	gr
2	0	Butter	1	
1	0	Sugar (icing)		500
	4	Egg yolks		120
3	0	Flour	1	500
		Salt		
		Lemon		

Beat the butter, icing sugar, egg yolks, salt and lemon until frothy. Work into a paste with the flour, pipe out through a biscuit forcer and bake. After baking, cut into slices and dip one third in chocolate couverture.
(Germany)

Pashas

lb	oz		kg	gr
	7	Marzipan		200
	6	Sugar (castor)		175
	6	Egg whites		175
1	³/₄	Flour		50
		Half a vanilla pod		

Work the marzipan, 5 oz. (150 gr.) sugar and 2 oz. (60 gr.) egg whites to a semi-liquid paste. Then whip the flour, vanilla, remaining egg whites and sugar to a stiff snow. Blend the two mixtures together. Pipe out on greased, floured baking sheets in drops approx. ³/₄ in. (2 cm.) across (about 50 drops), bake lightly, leave until cold, then bake again at 356° F (180° C).
(Germany)

Peach Tartlets - Tartelettes aux Pêches

Line some moulds with pasta frolla and bake blind. As soon as they are cold, brush the insides with chocolate couverture and leave to set. Next deposit a small spoonful of frangipane cream at the bottom and place on top, half a choice peach which has been poached in a vanilla syrup, cooled down and been drained. Brush each peach with apricot purée, surround with chopped pistachio nuts and top with half a glacé cherry.
(France)

Pineapple Boats - Ananasschiffchen

Line about 20 small boat shaped moulds with sweet paste, fill with frangipane mixing and bake. After baking, cover with small pieces of pineapple and glaze with arrack fondant. Chopped almonds are recommended for final decoration.
(Germany)

Pineapple Pies

Line frangipane tins with puff pastry cuttings and pipe in some crème pâtissière mixed with chopped pineapple. Cover with frangipane mixing and bake at 375°F (190° C). When cool, mask with apricot purée and cover with a disc of pattern marked almond paste cut out with a fluted cutter. Place on top half a glacé cherry and a piece of candied pineapple.

Pineapple Truffle Balls

Cuttings of chocolate sponge cake are mixed with chopped pineapple and pineapple buttercream.

Fashion into balls, cover with buttercream and roll into chocolate vermicelli. Dust with icing sugar. *(Switzerland)*

Pommes-de-Terre

Sandwich small oval Othello bases together with chocolate rum flavoured ganache. Cover with almond paste and brush one end delicately with green colour. Roll into a mixture of cocoa powder and icing sugar. Mark the eyes with the point of a skewer. Place into paper cases. *(France)*

Pont-Neuf

Line some patty pans with thinly rolled scrap puff pastry and fill with a mixture made up of one part confectioner's custard and one part choux paste. Brush with egg and decorate with a trellis design made from strips of paste. Bake at 420° F (215° C) and dust with icing sugar.
(France)

Praline Cubes

Split a sheet of hazelnut sponge twice and sandwich with praline buttercream. Refrigerate and then cut into cubes. Coat with the same buttercream and mask with roasted ground hazelnuts. Starting at one corner, make an incision halfway across the top with a sharp knife, lift the flap up and pipe a small whirl of buttercream underneath. Dust with icing sugar.
(Switzerland)

Praline Duchesses

lb	oz		kg	gr
	5	Egg whites		150
	7	Sugar (icing)		200
	2	Ground almonds		60
	2	Almonds (roasted, crushed and sieved)		60
	2	Flour		60
	2	Butter (melted)		60
		Vanilla		

Whisk the egg whites to a stiff snow, then fold in all the dry ingredients and lastly blend in the melted butter carefully. Stencil in small ovals on to greased and floured baking sheets and bake at 400° F (204° C). When cold sandwich in pairs with praline nougat paste brought to spreading consistency. Dust with icing sugar. *(France)*

Pretzels - Almond

For 12

lb	oz		kg	gr
1	0	Puff pastry	500	

Pin out the puff pastry to a rectangular shape 8 in. by 14 in. (20 × 35 cm.). Divide into two pieces 4 in. by 14 in. (10 × 35 cm.) and cut into 12 strips.

Twist the strips and shape into pretzels, wash with egg and sprinkle with flaked almonds. Now bake the pretzels briskly. After baking, brush with apricot purée and then glaze with water icing. *(Germany)* *(Illustration page 481.)*

Pretzels - Almond, Chocolate and Vanilla

Use Sweet Pastry for Afternoon Tea Fancies *(page 186)* for the Almond and Vanilla Pretzels. Use No. IV for Chocolate Pretzels.

Force the pastry through a biscuit forcer with a No. 4 pipe and cut into 6 in. (15 cm.) lengths. Shape into pretzels and place on a baking sheet. Bake at 360° F (180° C). *(Germany)*

Almond Pretzels

Wash with egg and sprinkle with chopped almonds before baking.

Chocolate Pretzels

When cool, coat with thin, unsweetened couverture.

Vanilla Pretzels

When cool, coat with vanilla flavoured fondant.

Provence Crescents

lb	oz		kg	gr
	10	Ground almonds		300
	10	Sugar (icing)		300
	3 1/2	Egg whites		100
		Apricot jam		
		Vanilla		
		Almonds (chopped)		

Mix the ground almonds with the sugar, well boiled jam and the vanilla. Add the egg whites to make a paste that can easily be worked by hand. Divide into pieces about 1 oz. (30 gr.) and shape into small rolls about finger length using a little flour to prevent sticking. Brush with beaten egg and roll into chopped almonds. Arrange on a paper lined baking sheet in the shape of crescents, brush with egg and bake at 340° F (170° C). Immediately after removing them from the oven, brush with well sweetened milk to give a glossy finish.

(France)

Puits d'Amour I

Line some patty pans with puff pastry and half fill with confectioner's custard and bake. When completely cold, pipe a round of Russe cream *(see page 242)* on top and finish by flashing in a hot oven and then decorate with a hot iron. *(France)*

Puits d'Amour II

Pin out puff pastry 1/8 in. (3 mm.) thick and cut out 2 1/2 in. (6 cm.) circles with a plain cutter. Place half of them on a baking sheet and cut the centres out of the rest. Moisten the rings with water and place, wet side down on to the bases. Brush the rings with egg and after a rest bake at 420° F (216° C) for about 8 minutes.

Remove from the oven, dust with icing sugar, then return to the oven for a short time to caramelize the edges. When cool fill with confectioner's custard or, better still, red currant jelly. *(France)*

Queen Cakes

lb	oz		kg	gr
	8	Butter		250
	10	Sugar (castor)		300
	8	Egg		250
1	2	Flour (soft)		560
	1/2	Baking powder		15
	7 1/2	Milk		215
	4	Currants (optional)		125
		Lemon flavour		

Cream the butter and sugar and beat in the egg by degrees. Mix in the flour and baking powder, sieved together, then add the milk and, finally, the currants. Fill into carefully greased fluted queen cake tins. Bake at 400° F (204° C). Display upside down.

Alternatively, half a washed and dried glacé cherry may be placed in the bottom of the tin and a plain mixing used.

(Great Britain)

Raspberry Beans - Himbeerbohnen

lb	oz		kg	gr
1	2	Butter		560
	7	Sugar (icing)		200
	12	Marzipan		375
	3 1/2	Egg yolks		100
1	5	Flour		650
		Lemon juice		
		Salt		

First cream the butter, icing sugar and marzipan, then add the egg yolks and two thirds of the flour. Lastly fold in the rest of the flour. Pipe out in small bean shapes, using a No. 4 star tube, and bake at 392° F (200° C). After baking, sandwich the beans with raspberry jam and coat with chocolate couverture. *(Germany)*
(Illustration page 509.)

Raspberry Slices

Sandwich a sheet of genoese with raspberry jam. Cut into strips about 2 in. (5 cm.) wide and spread with pink cream on top, domed fashion. Brush the sides with apricot purée and cover the whole with a sheet of pistachio coloured almond paste marked with a ribbed rolling pin. Refrigerate and cut into fingers.

Raspberry Tartlets - Himbeertörtchen

lb	oz		kg	gr
6	0	Marzipan (approx.)	3	
		Chocolate couverture		
		Raspberry jam		
		Fondant		
		Raspberry essence		

Pin out the marzipan to $1/8$ in. (3 mm.) in thickness. Cut into rounds $1\,1/2$ in. (4 cm.) across, using a plain cutter. Place in small, plain petits fours moulds and bake lightly at 392° F (200° C). After baking, decorate the upper edge with couverture. Then half fill the tartlets with raspberry jam and outline them with pink fondant flavoured with raspberry spirit. Place a dot of white fondant in the centre.
(Germany)

Red Currant Slices

lb	oz		kg	gr
	5	Egg whites		150
	7 1/2	Sugar (icing)		215
	4 1/2	Almonds (nibbed)		140
		Vanilla		
		Red currant jam		
		Linz pastry III		

Pin out Linz pastry to $3/8$ in. (1 cm.) thick to make a rectangular base 20 × 4 in. (50 × 10 cm.). Place on a baking sheet in such a way that it is totally enclosed to prevent the pastry from spreading during baking. Half bake then spread with red currant jam. Whisk the egg whites until semi-stiff, stir in the icing sugar, vanilla and almonds and cook over gentle heat until the mixture is rather thick and not free-flowing. Spread this over the jam and bake at 375° F (190° C) using a double tray to prevent the pastry base from over baking. Cut into slices of the required size while still hot. *(Austria)*

Reginella

Line tartlet pans with pasta frolla. Pipe in a little crème pâtissière on top of which place maddalena that has been soaked with curaçao. Fill with crème pâtissière and place a cross of pasta frolla on each. Put a sour black cherry in the centre and bake at 375-390° F (190-200° C). *(Italy)*

Religieuses

Line patty pans with thinly rolled scrap puff pastry and bake blind. When cold, fill with a mixture composed of two parts almond paste and one part confectioner's custard. On top of each, drop a spoonful of uncooked meringue. Cover with flaked almonds and dust with icing sugar. Bake at 360° F (182° C) for about 15 minutes.
(France)

Roman Helmets

Line frangipane tins with almond sweet pastry and place some chopped pineapple in the bottom. Pipe in some frangipane mixture. Bake at 370° F (187° C). When cold, spread kirsch buttercream on the tops in dome shape. Mask the edges with grated milk chocolate and place a segment of pineapple in the top of each to simulate the plume of a helmet.
(Switzerland)

Rum Chocolate Cups

Into chocolate cups place a filling composed of sponge crumbs moistened with rum flavoured stock syrup. Fill with vanilla flavoured whipped dairy cream and level off.

Sprinkle with chocolate shavings, pipe on a rosette and top with a piece of pineapple.

Rum Fancies

Pin out a rich sweet pastry and cut out with a $1\,1/2$ in. (4 cm.) plain cutter. Bake at 375° F (190° C). Sandwich in pairs with rum flavoured buttercream. Dip into plain chocolate. Pipe a small rosette of the same buttercream on the tops and add a small chocolate disc that has been dusted with icing sugar. *(Germany)*

Sacher Slices

lb	oz		kg	gr
1	0	Butter		500
	12	Sugar (castor)		375
	8	Egg yolks		250
	8	Egg whites		250
1	0	Flour (soft)		500
	8	Plain couverture		250

Cream the butter and 8 oz. (250 gr.) of the sugar and add the yolks by degrees. Whisk the egg whites with the rest of the sugar and add. Blend the melted couverture and stir in, finally fold in the flour. Spread on to a paper lined baking sheet and bake at 360° F (182° C). When cold, cut into strips about 2 1/2 in. (6 cm.) wide and spread the tops with chocolate. When nearly set, make marks 1 in. (2.5 cm.) apart with the back of a knife. Refrigerate then split and sandwich fairly thickly with cream reinforced with gelatine. Cut the top section where marked, and pipe on each the word 'Sacher'. Place these pieces back on the base and return the strips to the refrigerator, to be cut up when required. *(Switzerland)*

Sacher Slices

lb	oz		kg	gr
	14	Butter		420
	9	Egg yolks		270
	12	Sugar (castor)		375
1	4	Egg whites		625
	7 1/2	Block cocoa		215
	7 1/2	Couverture		215
	9	Flour		270

Beat the butter with the egg yolks and half the sugar until light. Whisk the egg whites to a stiff snow with the rest of the sugar. Melt the block cocoa and the couverture and mix with the butter/egg yolks/sugar mixture. Fold in the stiff whites and the sieved flour and spread on a paperlined baking sheet of suitable size. When baked and cold, cut into strips about 2 1/2 in. (6 cm.) wide, split each strip four times and sandwich with ganache flavoured with rum. Coat with chocolate fondant, decorate with piping chocolate and pistachio nuts and cut into slices. *(Germany)*

Saint-André

Line some boat shaped pans with sweet paste and fill with cold reduced apple purée. Cover with royal icing and decorate with a St. Andrew's Cross made of strips of sweet pastry. Bake at 360° F (182° C).
(France)

Sanani

For approx. 20 pieces

lb	oz		kg	gr
	10	Marzipan		300
	10	Sugar (castor)		300
	4	Milk		125
	12	Egg whites		350
1	0	Mocha buttercream		500
		Flaked almonds		

Work the marzipan and milk into a smooth paste, add 5 oz. (150 gr.) sugar and beat until somewhat frothy. Whip the egg whites and the remaining sugar to a snow and fold into the marzipan mixture. Spread on a baking sheet to make a square 8 in. by 8 in. (20 × 20 cm.) sprinkle with flaked almonds and bake at 356° F (180° C) for about 20 minutes.

After baking, cut into 3, sandwich with the mocha buttercream well flavoured with cognac, cut up into 2 in. (5 cm.) squares and dust with pulverized sugar.

Lastly decorate each square with a bulb of fondant and lay a plaque inscribed 'Sanani' on top. *(Germany)*
(Illustration page 480)

Sand Biscuits, Filled - Sandgebäck, Gefüllt

lb	oz		kg	gr
1	0	Butter		500
1	0	Sugar (castor)		500
	8	Marzipan		250
	12	Egg		350
2	0	Flour	1	
		Lemon		
		Salt		

Punch marzipan filling:

lb	oz		kg	gr
1	0	Marzipan		500
1	0	Apricot jam		500
	5	Apricot brandy		150

Cream the butter and sugar; beat the marzipan, egg, lemon and salt until frothy. Blend the two mixtures together, lastly adding the flour. Pipe out on baking sheets using a variety of plain and star tubes (to make beans, sticks, etc.) and bake at 356-374° F (180-190° C).

After baking, sandwich half of them with punch marzipan *(see above)*, the other half with nougat. Individual biscuits may also be half dipped in couverture. *(Germany)*

Sand Rings

lb	oz		kg	gr
1	0	Butter		500
	10	Sugar (icing)		300
	5	Egg whites		150
	7	Milk		200
1	8	Flour (soft)		750
		Lemon zest		

The butter and sugar are well creamed together and the whites added by degrees followed by the flour and the milk. Using a star tube, rings are piped on to greased baking sheets. They are baked at 380° F (193° C). When cool, they are sandwiched together in pairs with red currant jelly. Plain chocolate is spun across the centre and a little crushed praline croquant is sprinkled on the chocolate before it sets.
(Switzerland)

Sand Stars - Sandsterne

lb	oz		kg	gr
	14	Butter		425
	14	Flour		425
	3 1/2	Sugar (icing)		100
	8	Egg whites (approx.)		250
		Vanilla		
		Salt		

Beat the butter and flour until frothy, add the icing sugar, egg whites, vanilla and salt. Work thoroughly until smooth and pipe out in star-shaped drops using a coarse star tube. Bake in a moderate oven (356-374° F, (180-190° C). *(Germany)*

Sapphos

Line some boat-shaped tins with viennese paste. Bake blind and allow to cool. Fill the boats with praline buttercream mixed with ground nougat. Refrigerate and coat with chocolate fondant. When set, pipe the word 'Sappho' in white fondant.
(Switzerland)

Scodellini Amarena

Line tartlet pans with pasta frolla and fill $^2/_3$ with sour black cherry jam. Place 3 sour black cherries in the centre and bake at 375° F (190° C). *(Italy)*

Scottish Slices

Cut a strip of almond genoese diagonally, using the method described for Battenburg Slices. Sprinkle with arrack syrup and spread with chocolate buttercream. Put the pieces together and refrigerate. Repeat this, cutting the other way so that a cross of St. Andrew is fashioned. Cut into fingers.

Short Cakes - Sprits Koeken

lb	oz		kg	gr
	10	Butter or margarine		300
	7	Sugar (castor)		200
	1 1/2	Egg		45
1	0	Flour		500
		Vanilla		
		Zest of lemon		
		Baking powder: a pinch		
		(See recipe for Filled Pastries)		

Cream the butter or margarine and add the sugar, salt, vanilla, lemon zest and egg and beat well. Add the flour in three equal portions (the baking powder is sieved with the flour). Pipe the mixture in zigzag strips with a bag fitted with a star pipe. Bake in an oven at 338° F (170° C). After baking, cut into pieces 4 in. (10 cm.) long. *(Holland)*

Shrewsbury Cakes

These are made exactly as given for Shrewsbury biscuits *(page 498)* except that a 4 in. (10 cm.) fluted cutter is used.

Sicilians

lb	oz		kg	gr
1	0	Macaroon paste		500
	1/2	Egg whites		15
	1/2	Honey		15
	1/4	Zest of orange		8
	1/2	Prepared flour		15
	4	Sultanas		125

Beat all the ingredients very well before mixing in the sultanas. Pipe out in long strips on greaseproof paper through a ³/₄ in. (2 cm.) plain savoy pipe. Bake on double trays at 350° F (176° C). The paper can be removed by turning the strips over and damping. Spin chocolate on the top and cut into slices.

Sighs

Line tartlet pans with sweet pastry, fill with confectioner's custard and bake. Pipe on a small dome of Italian meringue and return to the oven for a few minutes to dry the top, leaving the oven door open. When cold, coat with chocolate, coffee or kirsch flavoured fondant as required.

(France)

S-Shaped Sand Biscuits

lb	oz		kg	gr
	8	Butter		250
	8	Sugar (icing)		250
	5	Egg		150
1	0	Flour		500
		Salt		
		Lemon		

Beat the butter, icing sugar and egg with a little lemon and salt until frothy. Lastly blend in the flour. Using a savoy bag and star tube, pipe out in 'S' shapes and bake at 356° F (180° C). After baking, dip the ends of the 'S' shapes in chocolate couverture. *(Germany)*

Strassburgers

lb	oz		kg	gr
1	7	Butter		700
	7	Sugar (icing)		200
	7	Egg whites		200
1	10	Flour		800
		1 vanilla pod		

Cream the butter and icing sugar. Stir in the egg whites and vanilla and lastly add the flour.

Using a star tube, pipe out on small rectangular almond sweet paste bases approx. ³/₄ in. by 1 ¹/₂ in. (2 × 4 cm.) and bake in a moderate oven (356-374° F, (180-190° C).

Immediately after baking, glaze the Strassburgers with vanilla water icing. *(Germany)*

Strawberry Barquettes - Barquettes aux Fraises

Follow the same method as for peach tarts but use boat-shaped moulds. *(France)*

Strawberry Rolls

lb	oz		kg	gr
1	0	Raw marzipan		500
	8	Sugar (icing)		250
	2	Cornflour		60
	2	Milk		60
	5	Egg whites (approx.)*		150
		Vanilla		

* Alternatively, 6-7 oz. (180-200 gr.) of whole egg can be used instead of whites.

Stencil out mixing in round shapes on to a greased and floured baking sheet. Sprinkle with flaked almonds and bake at 420° F (216° C). Immediately on removal from the oven they are wrapped round a stick to form cylindrical shapes. They are filled with strawberries, with whipped dairy cream at both ends and sprinkled with roasted flaked almonds. A rosette of cream is piped on top of each, topped with a strawberry dipped into cold-set jelly. *(Switzerland)*

Strawberry Slices

Line a concave mould with a strip of sponge as for Dome slices, and fill with a strawberry cream. Cover with a sponge and then with a sweet pastry strip. Refrigerate and remove from the mould. Brush all over with well boiled apricot purée. Pin out pale green almond paste and mark the surface with a ribbed rolling pin. Cut two strips of such width that each will cover one third of the cake surface. With a small fluted cutter, cut small pieces out along one edge of each piece and place the strips on each side so that the cut-out designs run parallel on the top. On the apricot glazed surface between the strips, place small strawberries that have been glazed with cold-set jelly. In the centre of each cut-out, place a small diamond of angelica. The strip can be cut into lengths or into slices.

Many varieties of this type of fancy are possible by using sponge of different colours and flavours, different creams and decorations.

Strawberry Tartlets

Line frangipane tins with sweet pastry and bake blind. Brush the insides with chocolate. When set, fill with strawberries. Pipe a whirl of whipped dairy cream on top and sprinkle with roasted flaked almonds. Dust with icing sugar and place a strawberry, dipped into cold-set jelly on top of each.

Another finish is to line the baked sweet pastry cases with almond paste and fill with strawberry flavoured whipped dairy cream. This is covered with halved strawberries, which are glazed with strawberry jelly. *(Switzerland)*

Strawberry Tongues

Pin out chocolate sweet pastry to $1/8$ in. (3 mm.) thick and cut out ovals with a plain oval cutter. Bake at 380° F (193° C). Sandwich three together with maraschino flavoured buttercream, which has been mixed with strawberry purée. Refrigerate and dip into thin chocolate. Make thin circular ruffs of almond paste and place on top, in the centre of which place a strawberry dipped into cold-set jelly. *(Switzerland)*

Streusel Fancies

Take a sheet of almond genoese, cut out circles 1 $1/2$-2 in. (4-5 cm.) in diameter, split, sandwich with mocha buttercream and mask the top and sides with the same cream. Roll into baked butter streusel *(page 226)* and top each one with a little ball of sponge cuttings mixed with mocha buttercream, rolled in streusel and dusted with icing sugar. *(Switzerland)*

Sultana Cheese Slices - Käserosinen

For 20 slices 2 in. by 4 in. (5 × 10 cm.)

lb	oz		kg	gr
1	12	Sweet paste		800
1	0	Curd cheese		500
1	0	Cream cheese		500
	3 $1/2$	Flour		100
	3 $1/2$	Sultanas		100
	3	Egg yolks		90
	15	Egg whites		450
1	0	Milk		500
	14	Sugar (castor)		400
	3 $1/2$	Cornflour		100
	3 $1/2$	Hot butter		100
		1 vanilla pod		

Pin out the sweet paste to a rectangular shape 8 in. by 20 in. (20 × 50 cm.) and bake lightly. Meanwhile mix the cheeses, flour, sultanas, egg yolks, milk and vanilla to a firm paste, whip the egg whites and sugar to a stiff snow and fold into the paste with the cornflour. Lastly add the hot butter.

Fill the mixture on to the sweet paste base and bake at approx. 392° F (200° C). When well risen, score the sides all round at the level of the tin, remove from the oven and let the cake collapse. Now bake lightly once again, remove, and finally bake off until golden. Turn out, leave until cold and lightly glaze the top with lemon water icing. *(Germany)*
(Illustration page 353.)

Swedish Rings

lb	oz		kg	gr
1	5	Marzipan		650
	7	Sugar (icing)		200
	4	Egg yolks		125
		Lemon zest		

Cream all together thoroughly and, with a plain tube, pipe out ring shape on to greased and floured baking sheets. Using a star tube, pipe viennese mixing in the centre with a star pipe so that the centre is filled with a star formation. Pipe a little orange marmalade in the centre and bake

at 380° F (193° C). After baking, glaze the marmalade with some thin fondant.
(Switzerland)

Tommies

lb	oz		kg	gr
	10	Flour		300
	8	Butter		250
	4	Sugar (castor)		125
	5 1/2	Ground almonds (roasted)		165
		Salt		
		Milk		

Make all the ingredients into a plastic paste using a little milk. Pin out to 1/4 in. (5 mm.) thick, cut out with a 2 in. (5 cm.) fluted cutter and bake at 400° F (204° C°). When cold, sandwich in pairs with apricot jam and dust with icing sugar. *(France)*

Tottenham Cake

Take a sheet of heavy genoese, split and sandwich with raspberry jam. Spread the top with pink, raspberry flavoured fondant or water icing and cover with fine desiccated coconut. Cut into squares.
(Great Britain)

Tutti-Frutti

lb	oz		kg	gr
1	0	Sweet paste		500
		Raspberry jam		
		Glacé fruits		
		Almonds		

Cut the sweet paste base out into about 20 rounds 2 1/2 in. (6 cm.) in diameter and bake off quickly. After baking, sandwich in pairs with raspberry jam. Cover with chopped mixed glacé fruits flavoured with rum, brush these with apricot purée and sprinkle the edges of the rounds with chopped roasted almonds.

Decorate the centre of each pair of rounds with chopped pistachio nuts. *(Germany)*
(Illustration page 509.)

Tutti-Frutti Squares

Sandwich a sheet of genoese with apricot jam and cover the top with a thin sheet of almond paste. After cutting into squares, dip into well boiled apricot purée. On the top of each place a mixture of chopped glacé and candied fruits mixed with a little apricot purée. When set, dip into thin water icing flavoured with fresh orange juice. Stand in the oven for a little while for the glaze to set.

Utrechters

Pin out the sweet paste until 1/4 in. (5 mm.) in thickness and impress lengthwise with a fluted roller. Mark out into pieces 1 1/4 in. by 1 1/2 in. (3 × 4 cm.). Brush with egg, place 2 half almonds on each division and brush with egg again. Now cut through the pieces as marked. Bake at 356° F (180° C). *(Germany)*

Vanilla Almond Croquets

lb	oz		kg	gr
1	8	Raw marzipan		750
	8	Sugar (castor)		250
	2	Egg whites (approx.)		60
		Vanilla		

Make the above materials into a paste and pin out into strips about 3 in. (8 cm.) wide and 1/4 in. (6 mm.) thick. Spread with royal icing and cut into fingers about 1 in. (2.5 cm.) wide. Place the fingers on to greased and floured baking sheets and bake to a light golden colour.

Venetian Squares

Make a rich sweet pastry, coloured with caramel and flavoured with cinnamon and vanilla. Make it into a rope and then flatten four sides to a square about 1 1/2 in. (4 cm.). Wrap in waxed paper and refrigerate. Cut thin slices off and arrange on a baking sheet. Bake at 380° F (193° C). Sandwich in pairs with nougat buttercream and dip diagonally in chocolate. Place a split almond on top. *(Switzerland)*

Vienna Fruit Pastries - Harde Wener Vruchtengebakjes

lb	oz		kg	gr
	10	Butter or margarine		300
	5	Sugar (castor)		150
		Zest of lemon		

lb	oz		kg	gr
		A pinch of salt		
	1 ³/₄	Egg		50
1	0	Flour (soft)		500
		A pinch of baking powder		
		(²/₃ bicarbonate of soda		
		¹/₃ tartaric acid)		

Make a paste from these ingredients and line round and oval tartlet pans.

Pipe frangipane into each. The frangipane is made as follows:

lb	oz		kg	gr
	12	Almond paste		375
	3 ¹/₂	Butter or margarine		100
	3 ¹/₂	Egg		100

Bake at 356° F (180° C). After cooling, the pastries are brushed with apricot purée and decorated with fruits; pineapple, peaches, oranges, cherries, etc. After the decoration, finish the pastries with hot apricot purée or jelly. *(Holland)*

Viennese Desserts - Wiener Desserts

1 viennese butter sponge genoese
Apricot jam
Kirsch

Sandwich the genoese with apricot jam, sprinkle with kirsch, cut into shapes as desired approx. 1 ¹/₂ in. by 2 in. (4 × 5 cm.) and coat with arrack fondant.

Pieces of pineapple and a chocolate edging may be used as final decoration. *(Germany)*

Viennese Fancies - Wiener Mischung

lb	oz		kg	gr
1	7	Butter		700
1	2	Sugar		550
	7	Egg		200
2	10	Flour	1	300
		1 vanilla pod		
		A little cinnamon and salt		

Cream the butter and sugar, add the egg, vanilla, cinnamon and salt and lastly the flour. Divide this sweet paste into three:

Pin out the first portion to ¹/₈ in. (3 mm.) in thickness. Cut into rounds with a fluted or plain cutter 1 ¹/₂ in. (4 cm.) in diameter, brush with egg, sprinkle with fine hazelnuts and bake at 392° F (200° C).

Pin out the second portion to ¹/₈ in. (3 mm.) in thickness. Cut into ovals ³/₄ in. by 1 ¹/₂ in. (2 × 4 cm.) in size, brush with egg and sprinkle with streusel (made of 2 ³/₄ oz. (80 gr.) hot butter, 1 ³/₄ oz. (50 gr.) marzipan, 2 oz. (60 gr.) sugar, 4 ¹/₄ oz. (130 gr.) flour and a little salt). After baking at 392° F (200° C), sprinkle with vanilla icing sugar.

Pin out the third portion to ¹/₈ in. (3 mm.) in thickness. Cut into stars 1 ¹/₄ in. (4 cm.) in diameter with a serrated cutter, brush with egg and sprinkle with sugar nibs. Bake at 392° F (200° C). *(Germany)*

Viennese Fingers

Pipe Viennese Tart mixing in finger shapes on to baking sheets using the same pipe. Bake carefully at 400° F (204° C). When cool, sandwich together in pairs with pink, raspberry flavoured buttercream. Dip the ends in chocolate.

Viennese Macaroons

lb	oz		kg	gr
	14	Butter		425
	5	Sugar (castor)		150
1	4	Flour (soft)		625
	2 ¹/₂	Milk (approx.)		75

Make up as for Viennese Tarts adding the milk last. Using a savoy bag and star tube, pipe rings on to baking sheets. Into the centre of each, pipe some macaroon mixture *(page 212)*. Bake at 360° F (182° C). Place half a glacé cherry on the join of the ring before baking.

Viennese Rosettes

Pipe Viennese Tart mixing out in rosette shapes on to baking sheets with a star tube. Place half a glacé cherry on half of them. Bake at 400° F (204° C). When cool, sandwich them together in pairs with vanilla flavoured white buttercream, using the plain rosette as a base.

Viennese Sand Tartlets - Wiener Sandtörtchen

Line about 20 small fluted tins with sweet paste. Pipe a spot of raspberry or apricot jam in the bottom of each, fill with frangipane filling (No. VI) and bake for 20 minutes at 356° F (180° C). After baking, turn the tartlets out, then decorate with fruit and glaze. *(Germany)*

Viennese Shells

Using the same mixing and the same star pipe as for Viennese Tarts, make shell shapes on to baking sheets. Bake carefully at 400° F (204° C). When cool, sandwich together in pairs with vanilla flavoured buttercream. The tips may be dipped into chocolate and very little green nib almonds.

Viennese Squares

lb	oz		kg	gr
2	0	Sweet pastry	1	
	8	Butter		250
	2	Sugar (icing)		60
	2	Egg		60
	10	Flour		300
		Vanilla		

Line a baking sheet with the sweet pastry and cover thickly with raspberry jam. Pipe a trellis design on the top with the viennese mixing, using a savoy bag with a small star pipe. Bake at 390° F (198° C). When cold cut into squares. *(Austria)*

Viennese Tarts

lb	oz		kg	gr
1	0	Butter		500
	4	Sugar (icing)		125
1	0	Flour (soft)		500
		Vanilla flavour		

Beat the butter and sugar until light, adding the flour by degrees. Pipe whirls into paper baking cases with a savoy bag fitted with a star tube. Start the piping in the centre of the baking case and continue with a spiral movement round the sides until the shape is finished. Bake at 400° F (204° C). When cool, dust over with icing sugar and in the centre of each, pipe a spot of bright coloured jelly.

A variation can be made by piping the mixture directly into custard cups and piping apricot jam in the centre before baking.

Victoria Fancies

Cut out oval bases from a sheet of chocolate genoese *(page 200)*. Split and sandwich with chocolate buttercream mixed with chopped morello cherries. Coat the outside and roll into chocolate shavings and decorate the top with a fan-shaped piece of couverture.
(Illustration page 480.)

Victoria Slices - Viktoriaschnitten

lb	oz		kg	gr
	12	Butter		375
	8	Sugar (icing)		250
	8	Flaked almonds		250
	3 1/2	Egg		100
1	0	Flour		500
		Salt		
		Vanilla		

Work the butter and icing sugar until smooth, add the almonds and egg and work to a paste with the flour, vanilla and salt. Leave to cool off, then shape into square lengths approx. 1 1/4 in. by 1 1/4 in. (3 × 3 cm.) and cut into slices 1/8 in. (3 mm.) thick. Bake at 374-392° F (190-200° C). After baking, spread the undersides with plain chocolate couverture.
(Germany)

Visitants

lb	oz		kg	gr
	8	Ground almonds		250
	10	Sugar (icing)		300
	10	Egg whites		300
	3 1/2	Flour		100
	10	Butter (brown)		300
		Vanilla		

Beat the almonds, sugar and vanilla with 2/3 of the egg whites until very frothy, adding the egg whites a little at a time. Blend in the flour and the butter, previously heated until brown, then left until cold but still liquid and free from whey. Lastly fold in the rest of the egg whites whisked to a stiff snow. Fill greased and floured tartlet or boat shaped pans and bake for about 10 minutes at about 410° F (210° C). *(France)*

Vosge Slices

Sandwich a sheet of chocolate genoese twice with red currant jelly and buttercream, flavoured with raspberry liqueur. Cut into strips about 2 1/2 in. (6 cm.) wide and spread top and sides with the same cream. Mask the sides with chocolate vermicelli. On the top, pipe three lines of raspberry cream, using a plain pipe and in between, two lines of shells with milk chocolate whipped dairy cream, using a star pipe. Cut into slices. *(France)*

Walnut Desserts

Pin out a rich sweet pastry to about 3/16 in. (6 mm.) thick and cut out small ovals with a plain oval cutter. Bake at 380° F (193° C). When cool, sandwich in pairs with vanilla buttercream into which finely chopped walnuts have been mixed. Cover the tops and sides with the same cream and place two half walnuts on the top of each. Refrigerate and then dip into pale pink fondant. *(Germany)*

Walnut Domes

Hollow out Othello biscuits and fill with walnut buttercream. Place on to a circle of nut sweet pastry (*see* Nut Cubes). Dip into vanilla flavoured fondant. Pipe three parallel lines with chocolate across the centre and top with a half walnut. *(Switzerland)*

Walnut Duchesses

lb	oz		kg	gr
1	2	Egg whites		500
	14	Sugar		400
1	10	Finely grated walnuts		800
	1 3/4	Cornstarch		50
	5	Butter (hot)		150
		Vanilla		

Whip the egg whites and sugar to a stiff snow, add the walnuts and cornstarch. Lastly mix in the hot butter and the vanilla. Using a stencil, spread on greased baking sheets in halfcrown size rounds. Bake at 356° F (180° C). After baking, sandwich in pairs with nougat paste, placing the undersides inside, spread the top with couverture and decorate with walnuts. *(Germany)*
(Illustrations pages 133, 509.)

Walnut Ganache Slices

Cut strips of chocolate genoese about 3 in. (8 cm.) wide and spread on top a layer of milk chocolate ganache about 1/4 in. (5 mm.) thick. Place in a cool place for the ganache to set firm. Cut into slices and on top of each fix three walnut halves. Dip into milk chocolate.

Welsh Cakes

Line patty pans with puff pastry cuttings, thumbing the pieces up well. Pipe a little raspberry jam in the bottom and pipe in some of the following mixing:

lb	oz		kg	gr
1	0	Butter		500
1	0	Sugar (castor)		500
1	0	Egg		500
1	0	Sieved cake crumbs		500
	2	Flour		60
	4	Ground almonds		125

Cream the butter and sugar, adding the egg in portions. Mix in the dry ingredients. After a sufficient rest, bake at 420° F (216° C). When cool, dust with icing sugar.

Wine Biscuits - Weingebäck

lb	oz		kg	gr
	7	Butter		200
	2	Sugar (icing)		60
	3/4	Finely chopped fruit		20
	8 3/4	Flour		250
		A little salt and vanilla		

Prepare a sweet paste in the usual way from the above ingredients, including the fruit. Shape into rolls, put in refrigerator, then brush with egg yolks, sprinkle the sides with chopped almonds and cut into slices as desired. After baking at 392° F (200° C), coat with arrack fondant.
(Germany)

XV. Meringues and Japonaise

Meringues

Banana Meringues

Pipe on to greased and floured baking sheets an Italian meringue making them banana shape, using a plain pipe. The piping should be done zigzag fashion. Bake at 360° F (182° C). When cold, dip the bases of half of them in chocolate.

When set, pipe a little whipped dairy cream on top and then add half a banana cut lengthways. Top with the other half of the meringues. *(Switzerland)*

Banana Meringue Slices

Line a baking sheet thinly with sweet pastry and bake. Sandwich two pieces together with apricot jam. Make a meringue by whipping 1 lb. (500 gr.) of egg whites and gradually adding 2 lb. (1 kg.) of hot apricot jam. When very stiff add 1 lb. (500 gr.) of castor sugar. To each two parts meringue add one part chopped banana. Spread some of this on to the sweet pastry and pipe diagonal lines with the rest, using a savoy bag fitted with a star pipe. Dust with castor sugar and then cut into strips about 2 $1/2$ in. (6 cm.) wide and then into fingers. Place them slightly apart on to paper lined baking sheets and flash off in an oven about 450° F (232° C).

Chestnut Meringues

Proceed as for chocolate meringue nests. When cold, brush the inside with chocolate and when set, pipe in some whipped dairy cream on top of which pipe haphazardly in the form of vermicelli some marron cream which is made by beating equal parts of butter and chestnut purée.
(Switzerland)

Chocolate Cream Meringues

Stir into a cold meringue made from 1 pint of egg whites, 12 oz. (350 gr.) small pieces of plain couverture. Pipe shells on to greaseproof paper lined baking sheets, using a plain pipe in a rotating movement so that the shell is ridged. Bake at 250° F (121° C). Sandwich in pairs with a liberal amount of whipped dairy cream piped with a star tube. Place into paper cases.

Chocolate Meringue Nests

Take a heavy cold meringue mixing and pipe a series of bulbs on to a greased and floured baking sheet, using a savoy bag with a large plain pipe. With a smaller plain pipe, make a spiral edge on each bulb. Bake at 250° F (121° C). When thoroughly dried and cool, dip into chocolate. Spin the whole surface with chocolate and place three speckled eggs (*see* Meringue Nests) in the centre of each.

Chocolate Meringue Sticks

lb	oz		kg	gr
2	9	Sugar (granulated)	1	275
	3 1/2	Cocoa powder		100
	9	Couverture (chocolate coating)		275
	9	Egg whites		275
	5	Water		150

First boil 2 1/4 lb. (1 kg. 125) of sugar with 5 oz. (150 gr.) of water. Mix the cocoa with couverture (which has been melted in advance) adding a little warm water. Next mix in part of the boiling sugar syrup. Place the mixture in a warm place. Now beat the egg whites with the 5 oz. (150 gr.) of sugar until it is fluffy. Boil the rest of the sugar syrup to 212° F (100° C) and add this to the whipped egg whites. Fold a little of the egg-foam mixture with the chocolate batter, then add the rest of the egg-foam and stir with a spatula until a homogeneous chocolate meringue is made. Pipe quickly on to a baking sheet in fingers. The baking sheet should be greased and dusted with flour in advance.

After a rest of 5 minutes, bake in an oven at 338° F (170° C).

The meringues should be soft inside.
(Holland)

Chocolate Walnut Meringues

Mix chopped walnuts into Italian meringue and pipe out, finger shape, on to greased and floured baking sheets. Bake at 300° F (148° C). When cool, dip into chocolate and place half a walnut on the centre of each.

Coconut Cherry Meringues

To 4 lb. (2 kg.) of sugar made into an Italian meringue, carefully stir in 3 1/2 lb. (1 kg. 750) of fine desiccated coconut. With a star pipe fitted in a savoy bag, pipe whirls on to greased and floured baking sheets. Place half a glacé cherry on the top of each. Bake at 360° F (182° C). When cold, dip the bases into chocolate.

Coconut Meringues

Using a boiled meringue, add sufficient weight of desiccated coconut so that the mixture can be placed out in rough, rocky shapes on to greased and floured baking sheets. Bake at 330° F (165° C). The meringue can be coloured and flavoured as desired.

Coconut Meringues

With the same coconut meringue as used for meringue nests, pipe out whirls on to a greased and floured baking sheet. Bake at 250° F (121° C). *(Turkey)*
(Illustration page 390.)

Coconut Meringue Fancies

Proceed exactly as for Coconut Cherry Meringues but use a star tube and pipe fingers with a zigzag motion. Bake at 360° F (182° C) and, when cold, spin chocolate on the top using a paper bag with a very small aperture.

Alternatively they may be dipped at one end diagonally into chocolate and placed on greaseproof paper to set.

Coconut Pyramids

A different sort of meringue is made as follows:

lb	oz		kg	gr
	10	Egg whites		300
1	4	Sugar (castor)		625
	1/32	Cream of tartar		1
1	0	Sugar (granulated)		500
	10	Water		300
3	12	Desiccated coconut	1	875

Whisk the whites, castor sugar and the cream of tartar to a firm meringue. Bring the granulated sugar and the water to the boil, 225° F (107° C) and pour into the meringue on slow speed. Change up to medium speed and whisk until firm. Add any desired colour and flavour. Mix in the coconut and shape into pyramids on to greased and floured baking sheets. Allow to stand for one hour and bake at 360° F (182° C), just sufficiently to give the tops a deep tint. They may be finished by dipping the bases or the tops into chocolate.

Coconut Whirls - Hindistan Cevizli Koko

To each 2 lb. (1 kg.) of heavy meringue, fold in 8 oz. (250 gr.) of fine desiccated coconut. Using a savoy bag and star tube, pipe out in whirls on to greased and floured baking sheets. Bake, without allowing them to colour, at 250° F (121° C).
(Turkey)

Coffee Almond Balls

On to a greased and floured baking sheet, pipe bulbs of meringue. Dust them with ground almonds. Bake at 360° F (182° C). Sandwich together in pairs with coffee buttercream into which have been mixed some broken macaroon and some sponge cuttings, both of which have been sprinkled with rum. Finish with a small whirl of buttercream and a piece of fruit.
(Switzerland)

Coffee Balls

Proceed as for Coffee Almond Balls but after baking, return them to a very hot oven for a few seconds so that the surfaces caramelize to a light golden brown. Sandwich them together with coffee cream and pipe a small rosette at the join, on top of which sprinkle a little chocolate shavings.
(Switzerland)

Coffee Kisses

On a greased and floured baking sheet pipe out very small spirals, using a cold meringue. Bake at 360° F (182° C). Sandwich three or four together with coffee buttercream. Dip halfway into chocolate so that half of each spiral is covered. Place on end in a paper case. Finish the top with a rosette of cream and top with a small chocolate button. *(Germany)*

Copacabana Meringues

Using a light meringue and a large plain tube, pipe out strips $1/2$ in. (1 cm.) thick and $2 \, 1/2$ in. (6 cm.) long side by side to form squares $2 \, 1/2 \times 2 \, 1/2$ in. (6×6 cm.). Bake at 265° F (130° C). Dry thoroughly. Sandwich in pairs with chocolate buttercream flavoured with rum. Pipe stars of whipped dairy cream, vanilla flavoured, on top and sprinkle with chocolate shavings and finely chopped pistachio nuts.
(Germany)

Cream Points

On to a greased and floured baking sheet pipe small flat bulbs around the edges of which pipe circles of small stars. Bake at 360° F (182° C). When cold, brush the centres with chocolate and, when set, place in each a piece of well drained apricot. Pipe a rather tall spiral of whipped dairy cream on top and finish by placing at the sides some long chocolate shavings so that they meet at the top. *(Switzerland)*

Fraisalia Meringues

Scoop out meringue shells. Pipe in a little whipped cream and fill with small strawberries that have been macerated in sugar and a little kirsch. Sandwich together in pairs with vanilla flavoured whipped dairy cream. Place a strawberry at each end and place into paper cases. *(Switzerland)*

Fruited Meringues

Proceed as above but sandwich with vanilla flavoured whipped dairy cream that has been mixed with chopped fruit. Pipe a line of cream at the join and finish with a whirl of cream in the centre topped with half a glacé cherry. *(Switzerland)*

Goat's Paws

Pipe meringue into fingers about $2 1/2$-3 in. (6-8 cm.) long on to greased and floured baking sheets. Sprinkle with flaked almonds and bake at 250° F (121° C). When cold, sandwich in pairs with coffee buttercream and place in a cool place. Finally, dip the ends in chocolate.
(Holland)

Kaiserlaibl

Mix 2 lb. (1 kg.) light cold meringue with 8-10 oz. (250-300 gr.) sieved roasted crushed hazelnuts. Using a large plain tube, pipe out in the shape of half egg shells. Bake at 250° F (120° C) until set, then dry thoroughly. *(Austria)*

Meringue Boats

Prepare baking sheets by greasing and flouring. Use a heavy cold meringue of any colour and flavour. Have ready a piece of smooth wooden board about 12 in. (30 cm.) long and about 3 1/2 in. (9 cm.) wide. Place meringue on the board about 1 in. (2.5 cm.) thick in the centre and thinner at the sides. With a palette knife, take off some meringue the width of the board and drop it gently on to the baking sheet leaving a ridge down the centre. Repeat until the meringue is used up. Bake at 250° F (121° C).

Meringue Biscuits

Using a hot meringue, pipe out small shapes with a star pipe on to paper lined baking sheets. The meringue can be piped out in a variety of colours with the tops decorated with coloured sugar. Bake at 250° F (121° C). Dry thoroughly in a warm cupboard.

Meringue Fancies

Pipe a meringue mixture on to greaseproof paper lined baking sheets, in small bulbs. Dust lightly with cocoa powder and bake, without allowing them to colour, at 250° F (121° C). Sandwich together with ganache. *(Illustration page 393.)* *(Turkey)*

Meringue Figures

Delightful figures, particularly of animals and birds, can be made with meringue. It is first necessary to draw the figures in outline on stiff paper and to repeat the drawings in reverse. If the outlines are thick then they can be seen through greaseproof paper and act as a guide when piping the figures. Plain or star savoy tubes can be used according to the nature of the subject to be piped. When baked, the figures, after removal from the paper, can be sandwiched together with apricot purée after which the eyes, noses and other features can be piped on with chocolate or royal icing.

Meringue Fingers

Pipe out finger shapes on to greased and floured baking sheets using a cold meringue, which can be coloured and given the appropriate flavour. The pipe used can either be a plain or a star. Bake at 250° F (121° C). When thoroughly dried they can be sandwiched with creams of the same or contrasting colour and flavour. They are placed on their sides in long paper cases. Variety can be given in the following ways:

1. Sprinkling with coconut before baking.

2. Finishing with spun chocolate after creaming.

3. Dipping one or both ends into chocolate after creaming.

Meringue Nests

Mix 1 1/2 lb. (750 gr.) of desiccated coconut into a heavy boiled meringue, adding a little vanilla flavour. Pipe out bulbs on to greased and floured baking sheets. Make a cavity in each bulb using a wet cork or round piece of wood. Bake at 280° F (137° C). When cold, fill in the centres with various coloured fondants and place three small coloured eggs in the centre.

The eggs can be made from coloured almond paste or sugar paste. To speckle the eggs, apply some liquid colour to the bristles of a toothbrush and, holding the brush a little way from the eggs, run a skewer or thin stick along the top of the bristles, starting from the far end. As the bristles quickly return to shape the colour will be 'flicked' off on to the eggs.

Meringue Nuts - Mokkanootjes

lb	oz		kg	gr
	7	Egg whites		200
1	8	Sugar (granulated)		750
		Extract of mocca (coffee with caramel) to taste.		

Pipe the meringue out in small bulbs on a greased and floured baking sheet. The meringue should not be too light. Bake in an oven at 266° F (130° C).

Sandwich them with mocca buttercream.
(Holland)

Meringue Rocks

Make a vanilla flavoured, heavy boiled meringue and drop out into rocky heaps on to a greased and floured baking sheet. Make a slight cavity in the centre of each and drop in some lightly roasted flaked almonds. Bake at 250° F (121° C). The meringue should be perfectly white when baked. *(Turkey)*
(Illustration page 390.)

Meringue Shells

Using a light, cold meringue, pipe out bold oval shapes on to a greased and floured baking sheet, using a savoy bag fitted with a ⅝ in. (1.5 cm.) plain pipe. Dredge with castor sugar and bake at 250° F (121° C). When cool, press the base of each carefully to make a depression. Pack carefully on to papered trays and finish drying in a warm dry cupboard.

When required, pipe vanilla flavoured whipped dairy cream into the hollow base of the shell and place an uncreamed one on top. Place into paper cases on their sides so that the cream is visible.

A different finish can be given to shells before creaming by placing them for a very short time in a hot oven, so that the tops acquire a pleasing light caramel glaze.
(Illustration page 111.)

Meringue Shells - Chocolate

Proceed as above. Flavour the cream with melted, unsweetened chocolate or with couverture and sprinkle with flakes of couverture.

Moulded Meringues

Grease some small tinned moulds with cocoa butter. Pipe in some cold meringue and spread level with a palette knife. Turn the filled moulds over on to paper lined baking sheets. Place in the oven and as soon as the moulds are hot and the cocoa butter is melted, carefully remove the moulds. Dry the meringues thoroughly at 240° F (115° C). The meringues can be finished in a variety of ways with dairy cream, fresh fruit, chocolate, jam etc.
(Illustration page 392.)

Mushrooms

Using a cold meringue, pipe out plain bulbs. The size will depend on the purpose to which the mushrooms are to be put. Tiny ones for decorating a gâteau will only be about one inch in diameter.

Sprinkle carefully with a little cocoa powder to give a mottled effect. The stalks are piped out, as are the tops, on to greased and floured baking sheets. They are formed by piping first a small bulb then bringing the pipe up to form a peak. Both tops and stalks are baked at 250° F (121° C). When ready for finishing, a small hole is made in the centre of the base of each top, the base then being spread with chocolate. With the peaked end of the stalk inserted in the hole, the assembly of the mushroom is complete.

Peach Baskets

Make oval shapes from cold meringue as described for Strawberry Dairy Cream Meringues, but using a plain tube. When baked and cold, dip into chocolate halfway up the sides. Pipe a whirl of whipped dairy cream in the centre of each and sprinkle with chocolate shavings. Place a wedge of peach across the centres, thin edge downwards.

Raspberry Kisses

On a greased and floured baking sheet, pipe very tiny fingers each four touching, using a cold meringue. Bake as above and when cold, sandwich four pieces high with raspberry cream. When set, dip each end into chocolate. When finished each will look like a stack of sixteen small fingers.
(Illustration page 392.) *(Germany)*

457

Ring Bases

Using a cold meringue and a savoy bag fitted with a star pipe, proceed by piping bases on paper lined baking sheets and on them an outer ring so that there is a cavity in the centre for the filling. Bake at 240° F (115° C). When thoroughly dry, the bases can be finished in many ways with dairy cream, marron cream, fruits, etc.

Rochers

Take some Italian meringue mixture with the addition of flaked almonds and vanilla.

Use a tablespoon to deposit the meringue on a greased and floured baking sheet without, however, attempting to give any specific shape to the pieces. Dry them in a prover in such a way that the inside remains soft and creamy while the outside is crisp. Rochers can be flavoured with coffee, strawberry, chocolate, vanilla, etc.

(France)

Strawberry Cream Meringues

Using a star tube, pipe flattish bulbs with a cold meringue. Pipe two rings, one on top of the other round the bulbs to form a nest. Bake at 250° F (121° C). When cold, brush the inside with chocolate.

When set, pipe in a rosette of whipped dairy cream and sprinkle with chocolate shavings. Top with a strawberry.

Vacherin

Using a cold meringue and a plain tube, pipe out a spiral disc 6-7 in. (16-18 cm.) in diameter to form the base. Pipe a raised ridge round the edge. To make the top, pipe out a lattice work disc of the same size on paper. It is best to mark out patterns for the top and base on paper beforehand. When dried and cool, fill with vanilla flavoured whipped dairy cream, chestnut purée thinned down with whipped cream, a cream or custard, fruit or a combination of these fillings. Decorate as desired. *(Switzerland)*

Viennese Custard Rings

Proceed as for Ring Bases. Fill with custard and flash in a hot oven.
(Illustration page 390.)

Japonaise

When japonaise bases are sandwiched together, the slightly concave tops are placed together except where stated otherwise, so that, when assembled, the flat surfaces are the bottoms and tops respectively.

By altering the composition of the japonaise mixing, a range of drops and fingers can be made. A selection and details will be found under the heading, 'Almond Drops and Fingers' in Chapter XVIII - Almond Goods.

Almond

Sprinkle some bases with nib almonds before baking. Pipe some chocolate buttercream on to plain bases and place the almond bases on top (almonds upward). Spread the sides and when set, dip the bottom and sides into milk couverture. Dust carefully with icing sugar.

Burgdorfer

Sandwich two japonaise biscuits with rum flavoured ganache and smooth the sides. When set, brush with apricot purée and spread the top smoothly with ganache. Mask the sides with chocolate vermicelli. Dust the tops with cocoa and mark parallel lines with a knife. *(Switzerland)*

Buttercream Japonaise Fancies

A range of different finishes can be accomplished by using buttercreams of different colours and flavours. Here is an example. Sandwich round or oval japonaise biscuits together using the desired cream, sandwiching so that the rounded tops of the biscuits are inwards. Spread the tops and sides with the same cream and mask the sides with either sieved japonaise crumbs or roasted nib almonds. Dust the tops with icing sugar and mark a trellis design on top with the back of a knife. Sprinkle with chopped pistachio or green nib almond. Glacé cherries, angelica, crystallized violet or rose petals can also be used.

Capri Rolls

Using a square shaped stencil, lay out japonaise mixing on a greased baking sheet and sprinkle each with flaked almonds.

Bake at 360° F (182° C). Taking care to leave the almonds on the outside, roll round a wooden cylinder while the cakes are still hot. *(France)*

Cherry Japonaise Fancies

Pipe a whirl of kirsch flavoured ganache on to round japonaise biscuits, using a plain tube. Refrigerate and then dip into plain chocolate. Finish the tops with a half cherry.

Chocolate

Sandwich bases in pairs with chocolate buttercream and spread the sides evenly.

When the cream is firm, dip the fancies into milk couverture. Mark the tops with a dipping fork.

Chocolate Japonaise Slices

Spread greased and floured baking sheets thinly with japonaise mixture. Bake at 350° F (176° C). Next day, sandwich three sheets together with chocolate praline nougat. Cut into strips about 3 in. (8 cm.) wide and cover with chocolate thinly.

When set, cover again and decorate with a comb scraper. Sprinkle a little chopped pistachio nut or green nibbed almonds along the top. When set, cut into slices.

Chocolate Walnut Japonaise

Pipe a whirl of milk chocolate ganache, kirsch flavoured, on to a round japonaise biscuit, using a star tube. Refrigerate and when set, dip into milk chocolate and finish with half a walnut.

Coffee

Sandwich bases in pairs with coffee buttercream. Spread the same cream round the sides and on the top. Finish the sides with lightly roasted nib almonds and the top with a whirl of cream topped with half a walnut.

Coffee Dessert

Sandwich two japonaise biscuits together with coffee buttercream in such a way that the tops are inward; then spread the sides neatly. Pipe a spiral of coffee cream on the top and refrigerate. Dip into chocolate up to the base of the spiral. Place a sugar coffee bean at the edge.

(Switzerland)

Dragon Tongues

Take oval shape japonaise biscuits and sandwich three of them together so that they open at one side. Use coffee cream between the lower two with chocolate cream under the top one. Dust with icing sugar. *(Switzerland)*

Ginger Japonaise Fancies

Take oval japonaise biscuits and sandwich in pairs with chocolate buttercream, smoothing the sides neatly. Spread the tops with a mixture of well boiled apricot purée and ginger crush or finely chopped preserved ginger. When this has set, dip the fancies into milk chocolate so that only the bottom and sides are covered.

Ginger Japonaise Slices

Proceed as for chocolate japonaise slices but sandwich with a buttercream containing ginger crush. Sprinkle the tops with chopped crystallized ginger.

Hazelnut Japonaise Fancies

Sandwich round hazelnut japonaise biscuits together in pairs using praline buttercream. Spread the sides and tops with the same cream. Place roasted hazelnuts on the top and refrigerate. Dip into chocolate and sprinkle the tops with a little chopped pistachio or green nib almond.

Japonaise

Sandwich together some japonaise biscuits with praline buttercream. Refrigerate and cover the top and sides with the same cream. Mask top and sides with japonaise crumbs or finely chopped roasted almonds. Decorate the top with a spot of pink fondant.

The craftsman can use his skill and imagination in the finish of Japonaise biscuits thus envolving many varieties.

(Illustration page 557.) *(Switzerland)*

Japonaise Croquant Slices

Sandwich three strips of japonaise with nougat buttercream and spread the top and sides with the same cream. Mask the sides with sieved praline croquant. Pin out praline croquant and cut to the exact size of the required slices and place them in position, side by side on the top of the strip which can now be cut easily into slices.

Japonaise Fingers

A great variety of finishes are possible using japonaise finger biscuits. Here are two examples:

1. Pipe or stencil finger shaped japonaise biscuits and sprinkle with nib almonds before baking. When cool, sandwich together in pairs with buttercream of the desired colour and flavour, using a star pipe. Place together on their sides and decorate by spinning chocolate on top with a fine pipe.

2. Proceed as above but do not sprinkle with almonds before baking. Sandwich together in pairs with rum flavoured ganache and dip into plain chocolate, then decorate by spinning with white chocolate. Finish with a half pistachio nut or a few nib green almonds.

Japonaise Ganache Slices

Sandwich two slices of japonaise with ganache, then with a savoy bag fitted with a plain tube, pipe parallel lines along the top. Cover with milk chocolate. With a warmed, sharp knife cut very carefully into slices.

Japonaise Kirsch Slices

Spread japonaise mixing thinly on prepared baking sheets and sprinkle flaked almonds on half of them before baking. Spread a plain sheet with kirsch buttercream on top of which place a sheet of butter sponge. Sprinkle the sponge with kirsch syrup, spread with buttercream and place the flaked almond sheet on the top and press firmly. Cut into slices and dust with icing sugar, then cut into fingers.

Marbled Japonaise

Sandwich bases in pairs and spread sides with vanilla buttercream. Spread the tops with vanilla flavoured fondant and marble with chocolate fondant. Finish sides with sieved japonaise crumbs or roasted nib almonds.

Place a few pieces of chopped green almonds in the centre of each.

Alternatively, they may be spread with chocolate fondant and marbled with white.

Orange Japonaise Fancies

Pair up round japonaise biscuits and spread half of them with buttercream flavoured with curaçao. Cut circles of genoese the same diameter as the biscuits and with a sharp plain cutter take out the centre. Fill this with cream. Place the other biscuit on top with the flat side upwards. Tidy the sides with cream and refrigerate. Dip into milk chocolate and finish with a little candied orange peel.

Pineapple

Sandwich the bases together in pairs with rum flavoured buttercream and spread the sides neatly with a palette knife. Dip to the top edge in couverture and set on paper. Place on each a ring of almond paste that has been marked with a grooved rolling pin. In the centre of each, place a little chopped pineapple mixed with boiled apricot purée.

Pineapple Japonaise Slices

Prepare a filling by mixing sieved japonaise crumbs and chopped pineapple with ganache. Pin this out between wax paper to about $1/2$ in. (1 cm.) thick. Sandwich this between two sheets of japonaise which have been spread thinly with apricot purée. Cut into strips about 2 in. (5 cm.) wide and then into fingers. Dip into chocolate and decorate the top with a sprinkle of chopped crystallized pineapple.

Rochers

Pipe a mixture made up of meringue crumbs and chocolate buttercream into cone shapes on japonaise biscuits. Refrigerate and dip into chocolate fondant.

Royal Chantilly Japonaise

Sandwich three oval japonaise bases together with vanilla flavoured whipped dairy cream. Spread the top with two coats of vanilla couverture, using a comb scraper to decorate the second one. Sprinkle the centre with a few chopped pistachio nuts. *(France)*

Sarahs

Make japonaise biscuits using either an almond or hazelnut mixture. On to the biscuits pipe, in the form of a cone, some ganache or mocha flavoured buttercream.

Coat with chocolate or mocha fondant according to the filling. Decorate with a whirl of the same fondant and top with a silver dragee if chocolate, or a sugar coffee bean if mocha. *(Switzerland)*

Schaffhauser Slices

Sandwich four thin slices of japonaise with truffle buttercream. When set, cut into strips about $2 1/2$ in. (6 cm.) wide and cover with plain chocolate. Sprinkle roasted nib almonds along the length and when the chocolate is set, cut into slices.
(Switzerland)

Superlatives

Sandwich round japonaise bases with praline butter cream flavoured with kirsch. Spread the same cream on the top and round the sides. Place a ridged disc of almond paste on top and fill with chopped pineapple bound with well boiled kirsch flavoured apricot purée. Refrigerate, then coat with chocolate icing and decorate with a little gold leaf. Place half a walnut dusted with icing sugar in the centre.
(Germany)

Sylvana Fancies

A bulb of rum flavoured ganache is piped on to oval japonaise biscuits. After refrigeration the fancies are dipped into milk chocolate and, before the chocolate has set, three chocolate rolls are placed on top. Dust lightly with icing sugar.

Tongues - Schaffhauser Zungen

Using an oval shaped stencil, deposit hazelnut japonaise mixing on to a greased and floured baking sheet. Bake at 380° F (193° C) and when cool, sandwich together with praline buttercream. Dust with icing sugar. *(Switzerland)*

XVI. Biscuits

The term 'biscuit' has different meanings in different countries.

In Great Britain, the term generally refers to small, thin products of varying shapes, sweetened or unsweetened. They are usually sold by weight. The production of such biscuits is now almost completely in the hands of large scale manufacturers with automatic plants, where the biscuits are packaged and distributed within a short time of leaving the ovens.

The small baker, particularly in Scotland, still makes the much larger type of biscuit which sometimes are referred to as cakes. This type of biscuit is usually sold individually and not by weight.

Because, in this era of large scale production, there is need for streamlining and for the reduction of costs, many delightful biscuits are no longer made and have become memories. The recipes for many of these biscuits are given in this chapter. Freshly made from top quality materials, they will certainly please and delight the discriminating person.

Most of the recipes given are British and almost all of them fall under the heading of 'soft biscuits', that is, they are made from enriched doughs. These are distinct from 'hard biscuits' which are much less enriched and more heavily machined. Hard biscuits include those of the cracker type.

In continental countries the term 'biscuit' has many definitions. In France, Switzerland and in Italy, a great quantity of simple plain biscuits are made by large manufacturers, many varieties however are made by the baker. Biscuits which require more work and a degree of decoration are referred to as 'Petits Fours Secs' and are included in the chapter dealing with Petits Fours. There are, however, many items under the heading 'Tea Fancies' which, if made much smaller, would be referred to in France as 'Les Petits Gâteaux Secs' or, in Great Britain, as 'Fancy Biscuits'.

In Germany, the term 'biscuit' generally refers to a type of genoese. Items that would be known to the British craftsman as biscuits are referred to as 'Kekse' or 'Konfekt', but again, this would only be so, if they are small. If made in a larger size they would be defined as 'Tea Fancies' under which heading they will be found in this volume.

Because of the many varieties of biscuits possible and because the recipes cover such a wide field of bakery practice, in fact, almost anything made sufficiently small could be termed a biscuit; it is not thought advisable, because of duplication, to give a multiplicity of basic preparations.

Depending on the type of biscuit being made, however, the basic recipes given in Chapter VI will assist the enterprising craftsman, who will wish to experiment and evolve new types to please his customer, so to enrich and add to the sum total of gastronomic knowledge.

Abernethy Biscuits

lb	oz		kg	gr
1	0	Flour (soft)		500
	6 ½	Butter		195
	4	Sugar (castor)		125
	⅛	Salt		4
	¹/₁₂	Carbonate of ammonia		2
	4	Milk		125

Sieve the flour with the salt. Rub in the butter. Dissolve the ammonia in the milk. Make into a dough with the rest of the ingredients. Finish as for spice biscuits except that they are pinned out to the required size and docked. Bake at 420° F (217° C). *(Scotland)*

Alicante Biscuits

Grease very small boat shaped pans, dust them with potato flour and fill with Rheims biscuit mixture tinted pale pink. Place half an almond on each and bake at 355° F (180° C) after dusting well with icing sugar. *(France)*

Almond Biscuits

lb	oz		kg	gr
1	12	Flour (soft)		875
	4	Ground almonds		125
	½	Baking powder		15
1	4	Butter		625
	12	Sugar (castor)		375
	7	Egg		200

Sieve the flour and the baking powder and rub in the butter. Mix the ground almonds and add the sugar and egg. Make into a smooth paste. Pin out to about ³/₁₆ in. (4 mm.) and cut out with an oval fluted cutter, wash with egg and dip the tops into nib almonds. Bake at 380° F (193° C).

Almond Biscuits à la Charles X

lb	oz		kg	gr
1	0	Blanched almonds		500
	6	Sugar (granulated)		180
	2	Vanilla sugar		60

Grind the above to a paste and allow to stand for a while. Pin out and cut into strips about 1 ½ in. (4 cm.) wide, which are spread with apricot jam. The strips are then covered with the following paste:

lb	oz		kg	gr
1	0	Blanched almonds		500
	12	Sugar (castor)		375
	8	Sugar (icing)		250
		Egg		
		Rum		

The sugars and almonds are ground together with sufficient egg to make a paste. Dust with castor sugar and cut into small fingers. Place on to greased and floured trays and bake at 350° F (176° C).

(France)

Almond Biscuits - Jewish

lb	oz		kg	gr
2	0	Flour	1	
	10	Egg		300
1	8	Butter		750
1	8	Sugar (castor)		750
	⅛	Salt		4
	⅛	Cinnamon		4

Cream the butter and work it into the flour with the rest of the ingredients. Pin out the pastry and cut into the size and shape of the little finger. Brush with milk and dip into ground almonds. Bake at 380° F (193° C).

Almond Cookies - Pitmoppen

lb	oz		kg	gr
	10	Butter or margarine		300
	10	Sugar (castor)		300
	1 ¾	Egg		50
		Zest of lemon		
		Pinch of salt		
1	2	Flour (soft)		560
	¼	Bicarbonate of soda		8

Make a paste of these ingredients and, after cooling, roll into a rectangle about 1/8 in. (3 mm.) thick. Brush with egg. Cut squares 1 1/2 in. (4 cm.). Next, place two half almonds on each and brush again with beaten egg. Place the cookies on a baking sheet. Bake at an oven temperature of 356° F (180° C). *(Holland)*

Almond Crescents

lb	oz		kg	gr
1	0	Raw marzipan		500
	4 1/2	Sugar (icing)		140
		Lemon juice		

Mix all together and pin out to about 1/4 in. (5 mm.) thick and spread with thin royal icing. Cut out crescents with a small plain cutter and place on to greased paper on a baking sheet. Carefully bake until a pale golden colour. *(Germany)*

Almond Drops

lb	oz		kg	gr
	10	Ground almonds		300
	10	Sugar (castor)		300
	3	Cornflour		90
	2	Vanilla sugar		60
1	0	Egg whites		500

Whip the whites to a stiff snow and then fold in the dry ingredients mixed together. Pipe out into drops 1 in. (2.5 cm.) diameter on paper lined baking sheets. Sprinkle with nibbed almonds and dust with icing sugar. Bake at 360° F (182° C). When cold, sandwich with red currant jelly.

Almond Rocks

Pin out a rich sweet pastry to about 1/8 in. (3 mm.) thick and cut out with a plain cutter about 1 1/4 in. (3 cm.) diameter. Place on to baking sheets and wash with egg. Place strip almonds on the top of each. Bake at 400° F (204° C). *(Germany)*

Almond Rolls

lb	oz		kg	gr
1	0	Flour		500
	8	Finely ground almonds		250

lb	oz		kg	gr
1	0	Sugar (castor)		500
	4	Egg whites		125
	7	Egg		200
		Zest of lemon		

Mix to a smooth paste and stencil in circles on to a greased and floured baking sheet and bake at 420° F (216° C). While still hot, fold round a greased rolling pin.
(Germany)

Almond Rolls Richelieu

lb	oz		kg	gr
	10	Butter		300
	10	Sugar (icing)		300
	10	Almonds (nibbed)		300
	5	Flour		150
		Vanilla		

Cream the butter and sugar, add the vanilla, then mix in the almonds (finely nibbed) and the flour. Deposit in heaps the size of walnuts on greased and floured baking sheets, flatten a little and bake. While the biscuits are still warm, carefully remove them from the baking sheets and immediately press them round a rolling pin. *(France)*

Almond Scrolls

lb	oz		kg	gr
1	0	Ground almonds		500
1	10	Sugar (granulated)		800
	5	Egg whites		150
		Zest of lemon		

After beating well, the mixture, which should not be too soft, is piped out from a savoy bag fitted with a plain tube, on to nib almonds spread on paper. The mixture should be piped in parallel lines which should not touch. The lines are then cut with a wet knife into pieces about 2 1/2 in. (6 cm.) long. They are arranged on to either wafer paper or greased greaseproof paper. Bake at 350° F (176° C).

Almond Tea Biscuits

lb	oz		kg	gr
	12	Butter		375
	7	Sugar (castor)		200
	1 1/4	Egg whites		40

lb	oz		kg	gr
	1	Cornflour		30
	14	Flour (soft)		400
1 1/2		Marzipan		45

Sieve flour and cornflour and rub in the butter. Make a bay and place in the sugar and the marzipan that has been worked down with the egg whites. Mix to a pliable dough. Divide the dough into two and into one half work in 2 oz. (60 gr.) cocoa and 1 oz. (30 gr.) of egg whites and a little chocolate colour.

1. Build into Battenburg shape, (9 squares, alternate white and chocolate) wrap round with either white or chocolate.

2. Mould either white or chocolate into ropes and wrap in contrasting colour.

3. Layer alternate white and chocolate, wrap with either white or chocolate.

Wrap in waxed paper and refrigerate. When firm cut into slices 1/4 in. (5 mm.) thick. Bake at 380-400° F (193-204° C).

Anisette Biscuits

lb	oz		kg	gr
1	4	Flour (soft)		625
1	0	Sugar (castor)		500
	3/4	Aniseed		20
	7	Egg		200
	3 1/2	Water		100

Whisk the egg and sugar and add the water. Fold in the aniseed and flour. Pipe on to greased and floured baking sheets using a plain pipe. Dust with castor sugar and allow the biscuits to dry for about an hour. Bake at 375° F (190° C).

(Switzerland)

Amaretti di Cioccolato

lb	oz		kg	gr
2	0	Sugar (granulated)	1	
	6	Ground almonds (sweet)		180
	6	Ground almonds (bitter)		180
	4 1/2	Unsweetened chocolate		140
	1/8	Carbonate of ammonia		4
		Egg whites		

Proceed as for Amaretti di Saronno melting the chocolate before adding to the rest of the ingredients. *(Italy)*

Amaretti di Saronno

lb	oz		kg	gr
1	10	Sugar (granulated)		800
	9	Ground almonds		270
	2	Cornflour		60
		Egg whites		

Mix all together using sufficient egg whites to make a smooth macaroon paste. Pipe out small biscuits about 1 in. (2.5 cm.) diameter on to greased and floured baking sheets.

Bake at 390° F (200° C). Wrap them in special transparent paper inscribed 'Amaretti di Saronno'. *(Italy)*

Arnhem Cookies - Arnhemse Meisjes

(Named after the girls of the city of Arnhem.)

Roll out puff-pastry to 1/8 in. (3.5 mm.) thick. Cut out small ovals. After a short resting period, pin out these ovals in crystallized sugar. The top as well as the underside of the ovals should be very well covered with sugar.

Place on to well greased or silicone paper lined baking sheets. Rest before baking.

Oven temperature 392° F (200° C). When the pastries are nearly baked, brush over with water-icing and return to the oven for the icing to set as a glaze. *(Holland)*

Badener Chräbeli

lb	oz		kg	gr
	15	Sugar (icing)		450
	8	Egg		250
1 3/4		Water		50

lb	oz		kg	gr
1	2	Flour		560
	1	Aniseed		30
		Bicarbonate of soda (pinch)		1

Warm the egg, sugar and water a little then whisk until foamy. Add the aniseed and the flour and soda sieved together. Allow to rest for about half an hour, then pin out to about $1/2$ in. (1 cm.) thick and cut into strips about 3 in. (8 cm.) wide. Cut into fingers about $3/4$ in. (2 cm.).

Make three incisions on one side and bend with the incisions outside. Place on greased baking sheets; allow to dry a little and bake at 340° F (170° C).

(Switzerland)

Banbury Biscuits

lb	oz		kg	gr
1	0	Flour (soft)		500
	8	Butter		250
	8	Sugar (castor)		250
	2	Egg		60
	6	Currants		180
	$1/16$	Cinnamon		2

Mix the butter, sugar, cinnamon and egg together. Mix in the flour and make all into a plastic paste. Pin out to about $3/16$ in. (4 mm.) and cut with a 2 in. (5 cm.) fluted cutter. Dust the tops with castor sugar and bake at 390° F (198° C).

(Scotland)

Bannock Biscuits

lb	oz		kg	gr
1	8	Oatmeal (fine)		750
1	0	Flour		500
	$1/2$	Bicarbonate of soda		15
	$1/4$	Baking powder		8
	9	Butter		270
	8	Sugar (castor)		250
	8	Water (tepid)		250

Make all the ingredients into a smooth dough. Weigh at 7 oz. (200 gr.). Mould round and then pin out into circles. Dock well and cut into eight pieces. Bake at 420° F (216° C). *(Scotland)*

Barcelona Biscuits

lb	oz		kg	gr
1	0	Flour (soft)		500
	8	Butter		250
	8	Sugar (castor)		250
	2	Egg		60
	1	Egg yolks		30
		Zest of lemon		

Make into a smooth paste and cut out with a $1 \: 1/2$ in. (4 cm.) fluted cutter.

Pipe on the top of each a little of the mixture given in Vanilla Marzipan Biscuits. Bake at 328° F (162° C).

Basler Bruns I

lb	oz		kg	gr
	15	Almonds		450
	10	Sugar (granulated)		300
		Egg white		
	$7 \: 1/2$	Sugar (icing)		215
	10	Chocolate		300
	$1/8$	Cinnamon or vanilla		4

Pound the almonds and granulated sugar with sufficient egg white to make a fairly soft paste. Work in the icing sugar, chocolate, cinnamon, or vanilla if preferred, and leave to rest for a time. Pin out the dough to $1/4$ in. (5 mm.) thick, dusting the table and dough well with granulated sugar. Mark the surface with a fluted roller and cut out with a small plain cutter.

Place on to greased baking sheets and bake in a moderate oven after allowing them to dry a little. *(Switzerland)*

Basler Bruns II

lb	oz		kg	gr
1	0	Almonds		500
	12	Sugar (granulated)		375
	7	Egg whites		200
	10	Sugar (icing)		300
	2	Cocoa powder		60
	$1/8$	Cinnamon		4

Proceed exactly as for Basler Bruns I.

(Switzerland)

Bath Biscuits

lb	oz		kg	gr
1	2	Flour (soft)		560
	1/4	Baking powder		8
	12	Butter		375
	12	Sugar		375
	12	Egg		375

Cream the butter and sugar lightly and add the egg a portion at a time. Add the flavour and lastly the flour. Pipe out on to paper lined baking sheets, using a savoy bag and plain pipe.

For small plain drops, add zest of lemon. For fruited drops, add a little bun spice and 6 oz. (180 gr.) of currants.

For small plain fingers, add vanilla flavour. Bake at 380° F (193° C).

Bâtons parisiens épicés

lb	oz		kg	gr
1	8	Ground almonds		750
3	8	Sugar (icing)	1	750
	8	Egg whites		250
	1/2	Ground spice		15

Work all the materials up into a smooth paste. Pin out to about 3/16 in. (4 mm.) and spread with well beaten royal icing that has been softened with a little more egg white. Use no acid in the icing, but a small amount of cornflour may be added to prevent splitting during baking. Cut into strips about 2 1/2 in. (6 cm.) wide and then into fingers about 1 in. (2.5 cm.) wide. Place on to greased baking sheets about 1/2 in. (1 cm.) apart. Bake at once at 300° F (148° C). These biscuits will retain their shape as cut out, but will lift from the bottom, sometimes on both sides equally, but more frequently from one side only. *(France)*

Battenburg Drops

Use Almond Drop mixing and pipe out in the same way. Place half a cherry in the centre of each. Sprinkle with granulated sugar and bake at 370° F (187° C). Sandwich with warm pink fondant flavoured with noyau.

Biarritz Biscuits

lb	oz		kg	gr
1	0	Almonds		500
1	0	Sugar (granulated)		500
	11	Egg whites (approx.)		330

Grind the almonds with the sugar adding a little egg white. Reduce to a very soft paste with the rest of the whites. Stencil small circles on a greased and floured baking sheet. Bake at 350° F (176° C). When baked detach the biscuits from the baking sheet and keep them flat while cooling down. Coat the under surface, which is smooth, with chocolate couverture.
(France)

Biscuits Duc de Coburg

lb	oz		kg	gr
1	0	Ground almonds		500
1	0	Fine sponge crumbs		500
1	0	Flour (soft)		500
2	0	Sugar (icing)	1	
1	4	Egg (approx.)		625
		Zest of 2 oranges		

Mix all the ingredients to a smooth paste. The amount of egg required will depend on the dryness of the crumbs. Roll out the paste to a rope about 3/4 in. (2 cm.) thick and cut off small pieces. Roll these into balls and arrange on a greased and floured baking sheet. Flatten a little and put them aside until next day. With a sharp blade, cut a cross halfway through each biscuit. Bake at once at 375° F (190° C). *(France)*

Bitter Cookies - Bitterkoekjes

lb	oz		kg	gr
1	7	Blanched almonds		700
1	2	Blanched bitter almonds		600
4	0	Sugar (granulated)	2	
	10	Egg whites		300

Mix these ingredients together except the egg whites. Add the egg whites and mix to a consistency that can be piped. Line the baking sheet with rice paper and pipe the paste in little round balls. Moisten these rounds with water and bake immediately.

Oven temperature 356° F (180° C). The condition of the cracks is important. If the macaroons are not moistened sufficiently the cracks may be coarse; if too much moisture is used, the macaroons may be 'blind'. *(Holland)*

Bolero Biscuits

lb	oz		kg	gr
1	0	Flour		500
	3	Ground almonds		90
	10	Butter		300
	6	Sugar (castor)		180
		Vanilla		
	1 1/2	Egg		45

Make a pastry by rubbing the butter into the flour first and adding the rest of the materials. Pin out to about 3/16 in. (4 mm.) thick and cut out with a plain round cutter. Wash with egg and sprinkle with sugar nibs. Bake at 375° F (190° C).

(Switzerland)

Brauns

lb	oz		kg	gr
	9	Raw marzipan		270
	4	Sugar (icing)		125
	4 1/2	Couverture		140
	1/8	Ground cinnamon		4
	2	Egg whites		60

Mix into a paste. Pin out and cut with a small 1 in. (2.5 cm.) plain cutter. Bake at 400° F (204° C). There are three methods of treatment before baking.

1. Sprinkle baking sheets with granulated sugar so that after baking, partially caramelized sugar crystals are visible on the bottom of the biscuits.

2. Sprinkle the tops with sugar.

3. Combine both methods. *(France)*

Breton Biscuits

lb	oz		kg	gr
	12	Flour		375
	4	Butter		125
	6	Currants		180
	5	Sugar (castor)		150
	5	Egg		150
	1/16	Cinnamon		2
		Salt		

Prepare the dough as for Nantes Biscuits. Divide into pieces about the size of an egg, mould round and flatten with the hand. Place on to greased baking sheets, brush with egg, sprinkle a few currants in the centre (in addition to those used in the dough) and bake at 400° F (204° C). Vanilla or lemon can be used to flavour the biscuits instead of cinnamon. *(France)*

Brown Bread Drops

lb	oz		kg	gr
	12	Egg		375
	8	Sugar (castor)		250
	4	Flour (soft)		125
	8	Brown bread crumbs		250

Finely sieve the crumbs with the flour. Warm the egg and sugar to 100°F (37°C). Then whisk to a firm sponge. Carefully fold in the flour/crumb mixture. Pipe small oval shapes on to paper lined baking sheets. Sprinkle with crumbs. Bake at 400° F (204° C). When cool, remove from paper and sandwich with the following coffee cream:

lb	oz		kg	gr
	2	Unroasted coffee beans		60
	6	Sugar (granulated)		180
	2 1/2	Water		75
	1 1/2	Egg yolks		45
	8	Butter		250

Place 1 oz. (30 gr.) of butter in a pan and melt. Put the coffee beans in and stirring all the time, roast the beans a golden brown.

Crush the beans on a slab with a rolling pin, and return to the pan adding sugar and water, boil for two or three minutes and strain. Slightly beat the yolks and pour the syrup on them, beating well all the time. Add the butter in pieces and continue beating until firm.

Brussels Sticks

lb	oz		kg	gr
1	0	Butter		500
	7	Sugar (icing)		200
	12	Marzipan		350
	3 1/2	Egg yolks		105
1	4	Flour		600
		Lemon zest		
		Salt		

Cream butter and sugar. Reduce marzipan with egg yolks and beat in. Add the zest and salt and finally the flour. Using a small star tube, pipe out very small ribbed sticks on to a greased baking sheet.

Bake at 392° F (200° C). When cool, sandwich with apricot jam. Decorate the middle with 3 diagonal lines of chocolate and top with a little gold leaf. *(Germany)*

Butter Biscuits - Buttergebäck

lb	oz		kg	gr
3	0	Flour	1	500
2	0	Butter	1	
1	0	Sugar (icing)		500
	3 1/2	Cornstarch		100
	5	Egg		150
		Lemon zest		
		Vanilla		
		Salt		

Prepare a paste from all the ingredients, pin out to approx. 1/4 in. (6 mm.) in thickness, cut out shapes as desired, brush with egg and bake. After baking, sprinkle some of the biscuits immediately with cinnamon flavoured sugar. *(Germany)*

Butterscotch Biscuits

lb	oz		kg	gr
1	0	Butter		500
1	3	Sugar (brown)		590
	1/3	Salt		10
	1/4	Bicarbonate of soda		8
	6	Egg		180
1	12	Flour		875
		Zest of lemon		

Proceed as above.

Butterscotch Cookies

lb	oz		kg	gr
	12	Butter		375
1	4	Sugar (brown)		625
	1/3	Salt		10
	3	Egg		90
	10 1/2	Flour (strong)		315
1	0	Flour (soft)		500
	2/3	Bicarbonate of soda		20
	3	Milk		90
	5	Peel (finely chopped)		150
	6	Sultanas		180

Cream the butter, sugar and egg. Add the soda and salt, then add the flour and fruit.

Pin out to about $3/16$ in. (4 mm.) thick and cut out with a plain cutter. Alternatively the dough can be rolled into ropes about 1 1/4 in. (3 cm.) in diameter and pieces can be cut off and placed cut side down on to baking sheets. Bake at 400° F (204° C), after egg washing and sprinkling with sugar. *(Canada)*

Butter Pieces

lb	oz		kg	gr
1	0	Flour		500
	1/8	Salt		4
	1/8	Bicarbonate of soda		4
	10	Sugar (soft brown)		300
	8	Butter		250
	3	Egg		90

Mix all the ingredients together.

Scale in 1 lb. 2 oz. (560 gr.) pieces and put through a 36 piece divider. Place on greased baking trays and leave plain, or wash over with syrup and/or decorate with one of the following ingredients:

    Sugar nibs
    Coconut
    Broken wheat
    Nibbed nuts - various
    Flaked nuts
    Rolled oats

Bake at 380-400° F (193-204° C) for about 20 minutes on double trays.

Butter Rings

Pin out rich sweet pastry to about $1/8$ in. (3 mm.) thick and cut out with a 1 in. (2.5 cm.) fluted cutter. Take the centres out of half of them and wash these rings with egg. Bake at 360° F (182° C), being particularly careful in baking the rings. When cool, sandwich together in pairs with raspberry jam, placing a ring on each base. Half dip into chocolate. *(Germany)*

Carree Biscuits

lb	oz		kg	gr
1	4	Flour (soft)		625
1	2	Butter		560
	12	Sugar (castor)		375
		Salt		

Press into strips with a biscuit forcer on to baking sheets. Bake at 375° F (190° C). Brush with hot apricot purée and glaze with thin water icing. Cut into pieces.
(Holland)

Cherry Almond Biscuits

lb	oz		kg	gr
	7	Butter		200
	5	Sugar (castor)		150

Mix together without creaming.

	$1 1/4$	Egg		35

Add to above.

	11	Flour (soft)		330

Sieve and mix in.

	3	Whole almonds		90
	3	Cherries		90

Mix in.

Zest of $1/4$ lemon

Mould into rectangular bars, wrap in waxed paper and place into refrigerator. When quite firm cut into slices $1/4$ in. (5 mm.) thick and place on to greased baking sheets. Bake at 380-400° F (193-204° C). When cold, dip one corner into chocolate.

Cherry Rolls

lb	oz		kg	gr
	10	Flour		300
	10	Sugar (icing)		300
1	4	Dairy cream		625
	6	Cherries (finely chopped)		180
		Vanilla		

Proceed as for Almond Rolls. *(Germany)*

Chocolate Biscuits

lb	oz		kg	gr
1	0	Butter		500
	8	Sugar		250
	8	Ground almonds		250
1	0	Flour (soft)		500

Mix the butter and sugar without creaming. Add the flour and the ground almonds. Refrigerate the paste until it can be pinned out easily. Cut out with a plain 2 in. (5 cm.) cutter and arrange on baking sheets. Bake carefully at 380° F (193° C).

When cool, dip into plain couverture.

Chocolate Chip Cookies

lb	oz		kg	gr
	8	Butter		250
1	0	Sugar (castor)		500
	8	Egg		250
	$1/4$	Salt		8
1	8	Flour (soft)		750
	1	Baking powder		30
	12	Chocolate chips		375
	7	Milk		200
		Orange flavour		

Cream the butter and sugar and add the egg a portion at a time. Add the flavours. Fold in the flour and baking powder that have been sieved together and then the chocolate chips. Finally add the milk. Pipe out on to lightly greased baking sheets and bake at 400° F (204° C), until the edges are golden brown. *(Canada)*

Chocolate Kisses I - Bouchées au Chocolat

Pipe on to paper lined baking sheets small sponge drops, the size of very small macaroons. Without dusting them with sugar, bake at 380° F (193° C). Slightly hollow the under surface of the biscuits and sand-

wich in pairs with whipped dairy or St. Honoré cream. Dip into chocolate fondant and place a split almond on each.
(France)

Chocolate Kisses II

Using the same mixture as for Savoy Fingers *(page 351)* pipe out drops the size of small macaroons on to paper lined baking sheets. Bake off dry at 375° F (190° C). After cooling, hollow out the undersides a little and sandwich in pairs with whipped dairy cream or St. Honoré cream. Coat with chocolate fondant and place a roasted split almond in the centre.
(France)

Chocolate Macaroon Biscuits

lb	oz		kg	gr
	14	Raw marzipan		400
1	7	Sugar (granulated)		700
	2	Cocoa powder		60
	3 1/2	Ground hazelnuts (roasted)		100
	9	Egg whites (approx.)		275
		Vanilla		

The marzipan is first reduced with some of the egg whites. All the ingredients are then beaten over a lowered gas until the mixture is warm. With a savoy bag fitted with a plain tube, the mixture is piped on to wafer paper. Bake at 350° F (176° C), on double trays.
(Germany)

Chocolate Ovals

lb	oz		kg	gr
	12	Butter		375
	10	Sugar (icing)		300
	2	Egg yolks		60
	10	Ground almonds		300
1	0	Flour		500
		Zest of lemon		

Make a pastry of the above and pin out to about 1/8 in. (3 mm.) thick. Cut small ovals and arrange on a lightly greased baking sheet. Bake at 380° F (193° C). When cold, sandwich together in pairs with warmed chocolate praline nougat. When set, dip into chocolate. Finish with a sprinkle of chopped pistachio nuts.
(Germany)

Chocolate Pastille Macaroons

lb	oz		kg	gr
1	2	Sugar (icing)		560
1	2	Sugar (castor)		560
1	8	Ground sweet almonds		750
	4	Egg whites		125
		Maraschino		

Mix to a stiff paste and roll into long ropes using icing sugar for dusting. Cut into small pieces about the size of a large hazelnut. Roll each up round and leave to set.

Melt 8 oz. (250 gr.) of block chocolate and add to it soft royal icing a little at a time, stirring thoroughly at each addition. Add royal icing until the mix is a pale chocolate colour. The consistency should be suitable for dipping and this may be adjusted by adding a little egg white until the mixture will run a little and have a fine gloss.

Dip each sphere completely in the prepared icing and place on to the draining wires or on a very coarse sieve. When the surplus icing has drained off, lift the biscuits and place on to a clean lightly greased baking sheet and bake at 250° F (121° C).

Chocolate Raisin Biscuits

lb	oz		kg	gr
	10	Sugar (castor)		300
	4 1/2	Butter		140
	6	Raisins		180
	2	Plain chocolate		60
	9	Water		270
	1/16	Salt		2

Bring to boil and cool.

| | 2 | Egg | | 60 |

Add to above.

	12	Flour		375
	1/4	Baking powder		8
	1/16	Bicarbonate of soda		4

Sieve together and add it to the above mixture.

Pipe out with a savoy bag and plain tube on to greased and floured baking sheets. Bake at 380° F (193° C). Finish with beaten chocolate fudge icing.

Chocolate-Rosettes

lb	oz		kg	gr
	7	Sugar (icing)		200
1	0	Butter		500
	5	Egg		150
1	7	Flour		700
	1 1/2	Cocoa powder		45
		Orange essence		

Beat the sugar, butter, egg and essence until smooth. Fold in the flour and cocoa sieved together. Pipe out rosettes on to lightly greased baking sheets using a No. 7 star tube. Bake at 400° F (204° C). When cold, sandwich in pairs with orange flavoured nougat paste and dust lightly with icing sugar. *(Switzerland)*
(Illustration page 634.)

Chocolate Stars

lb	oz		kg	gr
	7	Persipan		200
	10	Butter		300
	8	Sugar (icing)		250
	5	Egg		150
1	8	Flour		750
	7	Ground hazelnuts		200
	3/4	Baking powder		20
	7	Chocolate		200
	3 1/2	Milk		100
	1/8	Salt		4

Mix the Persipan with the butter until it is free from lumps then add the melted chocolate, then the rest of the ingredients leaving the flour sieved with the baking powder till last. Leave to rest for a short time, then pin out to 1/4 in. (5 mm.) thick and cut out with a star shaped cutter. Bake at 400° F (204° C). When cool, pipe a small bulb of chocolate fondant on the centre of each. *(Switzerland)*

Christmas Stars

From rich sweet pastry cut small stars. Arrange on to baking sheets and bake at 360° F (182° C). When cold, dip into chocolate and place a small star cut from almond paste on top, in the middle of which place a silver dragée. *(Germany)*

Cinnamon Biscuits

lb	oz		kg	gr
1	4	Flour (soft)		625
	1/4	Baking powder		8
	1/2	Cinnamon		15
	7	Butter		200
	7	Sugar (castor)		200
	4	Milk (approx.)		125

Sieve the flour, baking powder and cinnamon and rub in the butter. Make a smooth dough with the rest of the materials. Pin out fairly thin and cut out with a small fluted cutter. Bake at 410° F (210° C). *(Scotland)*

Coconut Biscuits

lb	oz		kg	gr
1	0	Flour		500
	4	Coconut (fine)		125
	1/2	Milk powder		15
	1/8	Salt		4
	1/4	Baking powder		8
	6	Sugar (granulated)		180
	4	Sugar (soft brown)		125
	7	Butter		200
	3	Water		90
		Coconut essence		

Mix all the ingredients together. Pin out 3/16 in. (4 mm.) thick. There are two shapes:

1. Cut out with 2 in. (5 cm.) plain cutter.

2. Mark with ribbed marzipan roller. Cut into rectangles (using divider wheels) 2 1/2 in. by 1 1/4 in. (6 × 3 cm.).

Place on lightly greased baking trays, wash with light syrup. Bake at 380-400° F (193-204° C) on double trays for about 20 minutes.

Coconut Biscuits

lb	oz		kg	gr
1	2	Desiccated coconut		560
1	2	Raw marzipan		560
1	10	Sugar (castor)		800
	12	Egg whites		375

Soften the marzipan with a little egg white. Place it, together with 1 lb. (500 gr.) of sugar, the coconut and the egg whites into a bowl and, stirring all the while, bring the mixture to nearly boiling point. Stir in the rest of the sugar and pipe out in small heaps on to a greased and floured baking sheet. When cold, bake at 360° F (182° C). *(Germany)*

Coconut Cookies

lb	oz		kg	gr
1	0	Butter		500
2	4	Sugar (castor)	1	125
	12	Honey		375
	1/4	Salt		8
1	0	Egg		500
	1	Bicarbonate of soda		30
	15	Milk		450
4	2	Flour (soft)	2	60
2	0	Coconut (fine)	1	
	1	Baking powder		30
		Lemon		

Proceed as for Date Cookies. Cut into desired shapes. *(Canada)*

Coconut Crunchies

lb	oz		kg	gr
	6	Butter		180
1	2	Sugar (castor)		560
	1/4	Salt		8
	1/8	Ground ginger		4
	3/8	Bicarbonate of soda		10
	2 1/2	Egg		75

Cream 5 minutes on low speed.

	4	Treacle		125
	7 1/2	Milk		215

Mix and add to the above.

	10	Desiccated coconut		300
1	10	Flour (soft)		800
	1/2	Baking powder		15

Add and mix clear.

Pipe out, about 3/4 oz. (20 gr.) each, with a savoy bag and 1/2 in. (1 cm.) plain tube on to baking sheets. Allow to stand for 5 minutes. Egg wash carefully. Bake at 375° F (190° C).

Coconut Macaroon Biscuits

lb	oz		kg	gr
1	2	Coconut (fine)		560
1	9	Sugar (castor)		770
	10	Egg whites (approx.)		300
		Vanilla		
	3 1/2	Orange and lemon peel		100

All the ingredients are placed in a bowl and mixed over a low gas, heating to about 140° F (60° C). The finely chopped peel is then added. The mixture is then piped out with a star pipe on to wafer papered baking sheets and, after resting for a while, baked at 360° F (182° C). *(Germany)*

Coconut Rocks

lb	oz		kg	gr
	8	Coconut		250
	7	Sugar (castor)		200
	1 1/2	Egg yolks		45
	2 1/2	Egg whites		75

Whisk the sugar and egg yolks together with a little water. Whisk the egg whites to a stiff snow and fold into the sugar/yolks sponge together with the flour. Add the coconut and deposit in small heaps on to greased and floured baking sheets; dust with icing sugar and bake at 356° F (180° C). *(France)*

Coffee Biscuits

lb	oz		kg	gr
1	0	Flour		500
	3/4	Baking powder		20
	1/8	Salt		4
1	0	Sugar (brown)		500
	8	Butter		250
	4	Egg		125
	1	Coffee essence*		30
	4	Currants		125

Cream butter and sugar until light, add egg and coffee essence. Add the sieved flour, baking powder and salt, and when nearly mixed, add the fruit. Pipe on to lightly greased baking trays using 3/4 in. (2 cm.) plain tube. There are two methods of finish:

1. Flatten and bake plain.

2. Flatten and egg wash; sprinkle lightly with castor sugar.

Bake at 400° F (204° C) for about 15 minutes. (Do not double tray.)

* Coffee essence:
1 oz. (30 gr.) Instant coffee
2 oz. (60 gr.) Hot water

Coffee Biscuits

lb	oz		kg	gr
1	0	Flour (soft)		500
	3/4	Baking powder		20
	7	Butter		200
	8	Sugar		250
	3	Egg		90
	2 1/2	Milk (approx.)		75
	1	Coffee infusion		30
	4	Currants		125

Sieve the flour and baking powder and rub in the butter finely. Add the rest of the materials and partly mix. Add the currants and finish mixing. Pin out to the thickness of the currants. Cut out with a variety of small cutters. Bake at 410° F (210° C). *(Scotland)*

Corbet's Cookie

lb	oz		kg	gr
1	0	Flour		500
	4	Coconut (fine)		125
	1/2	Milk powder		15
	1/4	Salt		8
	3/8	Baking powder		20
	1/8	Sodium bicarbonate		4
	8	Sugar (granulated)		250
	8	Butter		250
	5	Water		150
		Vanilla essence		
	3	Currants		90
	2 1/2	Chocolate nibs		75

Mix all ingredients together.

Pipe out on to lightly greased baking trays using a 3/4 in. (2 cm.) plain tube. Flatten, using a light syrup wash. Bake at 380-400° F (193-204° C), on double trays for about 20 minutes.

Cornflake Toasties

lb	oz		kg	gr
1	0	Scone flour*		500
	3	Cornflakes		90
	8	Butter		250
	8	Sugar (castor)		250
	3	Egg		90
		Zest of lemon		

* *Page 180.*

Proceed as for Perkin Biscuits. Pin out to about 1/4 in. (5 mm.) thick and cut out with a small fluted cutter. Wash with egg and bake at 380° F (193° C). *(Scotland)*

Craquelins

lb	oz		kg	gr
1	0	Flour		500
	10	Butter		300
	1 1/2	Sugar (castor)		45
	1/8	Salt		4
	3	Egg yolks		90
		Milk (a little)		

Mix the ingredients to form a paste. Let stand for a while and then pin out to 1/8 in. (3 mm.). Cut out into small squares, brush with egg yolks. Trace lines on top with the point of a knife and bake at 440° F (226° C). Dust with icing sugar.
(France)

Cream Biscuits

lb	oz		kg	gr
2	0	Flour	1	
	3 1/2	Butter		100
	3 1/2	Malt		100
	3 1/2	Sugar		100
	3 1/2	Glucose		100
	7	Dairy cream		200
	3/8	Ammonium bicarbonate		10
	3/16	Salt		5

Mix the above ingredients together except the flour and butter. Leave the mixture in a cool place overnight and then add the flour and butter to make a paste. Roll out thinly and cut out with a plain round pastry cutter. Put the biscuits on greased baking sheets and bake in a medium oven.
(France)

Crescents

lb	oz		kg	gr
1	2	Butter		560
	9	Sugar (icing)		270
	1	Egg yolks		30
1	12	Flour		875
		Vanilla		
		Salt		

Cream butter and sugar and add yolks, vanilla and salt. Mix in the flour. Pipe out in small crescents with a savoy bag and small plain tube. Bake at 392° F (200° C).

When cool, dip ends in chocolate.

(Germany)

Croquant Biscuits

lb	oz		kg	gr
2	0	Flour (soft)	1	
1	4	Butter		625
1	0	Sugar (castor)		500
	6	Egg		180
		Zest of 2 lemons		

Make into a nice smooth paste and pin out to about $3/16$ in. (4 mm.) thick. Divide into strips 2 in. (5 cm.) wide. Cover the strips with a mixture composed of equal weights of strip almonds and icing sugar with sufficient egg whites to make a paste, and flavour with kirsch. The whites and kirsch are first mixed together and sprinkled over the almonds until they are damp. Cover with the icing sugar and mix. If all the sugar is not taken up, moisten again and so on, until all the sugar is used. If too much moisture is used, the mixture will run over the edges of the biscuits and be unsightly. Wash the strips with egg whites before spreading the mixture. Using a sharp knife, divide the strips into small fingers and place, $1/2$ in. (1 cm.) apart, on greased baking sheets and bake at 425° F (218° C).

(France)

Date Cookies

lb	oz		kg	gr
	12	Butter		375
1	4	Sugar (brown)		625
	7	Egg		200
	$1/2$	Salt		15
	$2/3$	Bicarbonate of soda		20
1	14	Flour (soft)		900
	10	Rolled oats		300
		Vanilla		

Cream the butter, sugar and egg, adding the soda, salt and vanilla. Add the flour and oats. Pin out to about $1/8$ in. (3 mm.) thick and cut with a $2 1/2$ in. (6 cm.) fluted cutter. Wash with water and place a generous portion of date jam in the centre of each. Fold over and place on to lightly greased baking sheets and bake at 400° F (204° C), after washing with egg.

(Canada)

Derby Biscuits

lb	oz		kg	gr
1	0	Flour		500
	10	Butter		300
	8	Sugar (castor)		250
	$2 1/2$	Egg		75
	6	Currants		180

Make up in the same way as for wine biscuits. Pin out to $1/8$ in. (3 mm.) thick. Cut out with a small fluted cutter. Egg wash and sprinkle with castor sugar. Bake at 390° F (199° C). *(Great Britain)*

Duchess Biscuits

lb	oz		kg	gr
	9	Egg whites		270
	$2 1/2$	Sugar (castor)		75

Whisk to a soft meringue.

	10	Sugar (icing)		300
	4	Flour		125
	6	Roasted ground almonds		180

Sieve flour and sugar, add roasted almonds, and blend into above.

	8	White compound fat		250

Melt and blend in.

Pipe out small bulbs on to greased baking sheets and flat them. Bake at 400° F (204°C).

Sandwich with a mixture of nougat and chocolate. Spin fine threads of chocolate at right angles on top.

(Illustration page 509.)

English Rout Biscuits, p. 485

478 ▲ Butter Streusel Slices, p. 413 — Cherry Michel, p. 416 — Bee Sting, p. 412 — Apple Streusel Slices, p. 409   Small Cakes made with Puff Pastry, p. 326 ▼

▲ Flour Cakes, p. 432   Dutch Biscuits, p. 485 ▼

480 ▲ Afternoon Tea Fancies, p. 407 — Mille-feuille Slices, p. 334, 439 — Fruit Tartlets, p. 433
Sanani, p. 445 — Bananas, p. 533 — Victoria Fancies, p. 451 ▼

▲ Almond Pretzels, p. 442 — Cherry Strudel, p. 416 — Apple Strudel, p. 410 — Brassel Cakes, p. 413
Lemon Rolls, p. 435 — Linz Tartlets, p. 436 — Carracks, p. 414 — Chocolate Parfaits, p. 418 ▼

482 ▲ Othellos, Desdemonas, Rosalinds, Iagos, p. 346-348

Florentines, p. 431, 513 ▼

Pulled Sugar Basket, p. 643, 644 — Petits Fours glacés, p. 520 — Parkhotel Frankfurt

▲ Calissons d'Aix, p. 507

Iced Tartlets, p. 434 ▼

Dutch Biscuits - Holländer

lb	oz		kg	gr
2	0	Butter	1	
1	0	Sugar (icing)		500
3	0	Flour	1	500
	1 ½	Cocoa powder		45
		A little salt and lemon		

Cream the butter and sugar, add the flour, a little salt and lemon and work into a paste. Take off three quarters of the paste, shape into long rolls and cool well.

Mix the cocoa powder into the remaining paste, cool and pin out thinly. Enclose the white rolls in the pinned out chocolate sweet paste, put in a cold place and finally cut into thin slices. Place cut side down on a baking sheet. Bake for about 15 minutes at 380°–400°F (190°–200°C). The finished biscuits are also called 'black and white' biscuits.
(Illustrations pages 479, 634.) *(Germany)*

English Rolls

lb	oz		kg	gr
	12	Flour		375
	12	Sugar (icing)		375
	10	Butter		300
	6	Ground almonds		180
	5	Egg		150
		Zest of 1 lemon		

Mix the almonds, egg and sugar to a soft paste. Add the rest of the ingredients and make into a plastic paste and allow to rest in a cool place for about 2 hours. Weigh into pieces about 1 ¾ oz. (50 gr.) and mould into roll shape. Place on to greased baking sheets, brush with egg, notch with the point of a knife and bake at 400°F (204°C). *(France)*

English Rout Biscuits

lb	oz		kg	gr
4	0	Ground almonds	2	
1	8	Sugar (icing)		750
	6	Egg whites or whole egg		180
		Flavour and colour		

The paste is divided into portions, flavoured and given the appropriate colour. For the biscuits illustrated, the paste was divided into three, coloured and flavoured as follows:

(a) Yellow colour and lemon flavour.

(b) Green colour and pistachio flavour.

(c) Red colour and raspberry flavour.

The biscuits illustrated were made according to the following directions:

1. Pieces of paste (a) are moulded between the hands into an oval shape. They are washed with egg and on to each a blanched almond is pressed; the finish after 'flashing' and glazing is with spun chocolate.

2. Small squares of paste (a) are cut with a cutter. Half of them have four small holes cut out. The plain squares are egg washed and on each a cut square is placed which is also egg washed. On removal from the oven, and after glazing, each small hole is filled with a coloured piping jelly.

3. Oval pieces of either (a) or (b) paste are moulded and egg washed. When removed from the oven and glazed, they are partially dipped into chocolate and chocolate vermicelli to simulate acorns.

4. Small circles of paste (a) are cut out with a fluted cutter and egg washed. Little balls of paste (b) are moulded and placed one on each of the circles. They are then egg washed and given the shape of apples by pressing on top with a point, so making a hole to receive a small stalk cut out from angelica.

5. Small balls of paste (c) are made, egg washed and pressed into nibbed almonds. A small cavity is made in the centre of each to receive white fondant after 'flashing' and glazing.

6. These filberts are made by rolling out a strip of paste (b) and trimming one edge with a serated cutter. The strip is cut into sections each one of which is wrapped round a whole blanched almond so that

about ¹/₃ of the almond is visible. Three of these are arranged into a triangle and one is placed upright in the centre. They are egg washed, 'flashed' and glazed.

7. Paste (a) is rolled out and cut into thin strips. A number of strips are made into a bundle which is tied in the middle with another strip. They are then egg washed, 'flashed' and glazed.

8. Two ropes of paste (b) are twisted together and cut into pieces and egg washed. After 'flashing' and glazing, the ends of each are dipped into chocolate.

9. Circles of paste (a) are cut out with a fluted cutter and egg washed. A half cherry is pressed on each. After 'flashing' and glazing, they are finished with spun chocolate.

The biscuits are placed on baking trays lined with silicone or greaseproof paper; if the latter, it is brushed with oil. They are 'flashed' at 450° F (232° C).

The glazing is done immediately on removal from the oven. The glaze is made with 2 oz. (60 gr.) of gum arabic which has soaked for some hours in 1 pint (625 gr.) of water. The suspension is heated over a water bath and used whilst hot.
(Illustration page 477.)

Farmhouse Treacle Biscuits

lb	oz		kg	gr
	10	Butter		300
1	4	Sugar (granulated)		625
	²/₃	Salt		20
	¹/₃	Bicarbonate of soda		10
	¹/₁₆	Ground cloves		2
	¹/₁₆	Ground ginger		2
	¹/₈	Ground cinnamon		4
	11	Black treacle		330
1	12	Flour		875
	5	Milk (approx.)		150

Mix all together to a smooth dough. Roll out into ropes and cut slices about ³/₄ oz. (20 gr.) each. Place on to lightly greased baking sheets, cut side down. Bake at 380° F (193° C).

Favourite Crunch

lb	oz		kg	gr
1	0	Flour		500
	2	Rolled oats		60
	1	Milk powder		30
	¹/₄	Salt		8
	¹/₂	Baking powder		15
	6	Sugar (granulated)		180
	4	Sugar (soft brown)		125
	8	Butter		250
	2	Golden syrup		60
	2	Water		60

Place all dry ingredients including sugar and butter in a bowl and rub in to a fine crumb. Dissolve the syrup in the water and add to form a clear dough.

1. Pin out ³/₁₆ in. (4 mm.) thick and cut out with 2 ¹/₂ in. (6 cm.) plain cutter. Place on lightly greased baking trays and wash with a light syrup (10 oz. [300 gr.] sugar in 1 lb. 4 oz. [625 gr.] water). Bake on double trays at 380-400° F (193-204° C) for about 20 minutes.

2. Hazelnut crunch

Use a 2 in. (5 cm.) cutter. Wash with syrup. Sprinkle with hazelnut flakes, proceed as before.

Fiches l'Orgeat

lb	oz		kg	gr
1	0	Sugar (icing)		500
	14	Ground sweet almonds		435
	2	Ground bitter almonds		60
1	0	Butter		500
	2	Orange flower water		60
1	4	Flour (soft)		625
	5	Milk (approx.)		150

Mix the ground almonds, milk and orange flower water together and stir until the mixture is white and milky. Let it stand awhile. Slightly cream the butter and sugar. Add the almond mixture, then add the flour and rub down into a smooth paste. Put in a cool place to mature. Using a savoy bag fitted with a flattened 16 point star, or a biscuit forcer with the appropriate plate, run the paste out in lengths

½ in. (1 cm.) apart on to lightly greased baking sheets. Bake at 440° F (227° C), to a rich golden colour. As soon as baked, brush the top surface with thin well boiled apricot purée and then with thin water icing flavoured with orange flower water. When cool, cut into small biscuits.

(France)

Fondant Pretzels

lb	oz		kg	gr
1	0	Flour		500
	10	Butter		300
	2 ½	Sugar		75
	7	Egg		200
		Salt		

Flavouring (aniseed or other flavouring)

Lightly mix the ingredients together to form a paste. Divide into pieces of equal size and roll into ropes. Fashion into pretzel shape and place on to a baking sheet. Brush with egg and sprinkle with nib sugar. Bake at 400° F (204° C). The nib sugar may be left off in which case the pretzels may be finished with vanilla, mocha or chocolate fondant. *(France)*

Fruit Biscuits, Filled - Früchtegebäck, Gefüllt

Sweet Pastry for Tea Biscuits I, *page 186.*

Filling

lb	oz		kg	gr
2	4	Marzipan	1	125
3	4	Mixed candied fruits	1	625
		Arrack		
		Fine granulated sugar		

Egg wash

lb	oz		kg	gr
	2 ½	Egg yolks		75
	¾	Honey		20

After preparing the sweet paste, chop the fruits very finely and bring the marzipan to a spreading consistency with arrack and granulated sugar. First pin out only half the sweet paste and cover with half the marzipan sprinkled with the chopped fruit. Cover the fruit with the remaining marzipan. Pin out the rest of the sweet paste and place on top, making quite sure that it is very well pressed down. Brush with the egg wash and mark with a decorating comb. Cut into pieces 1 ½ in. by ¾ in. (4 × 2 cm.) and bake at 392° F (200° C). *(Illustration page 509.)* *(Germany)*

Fruit and Nut Biscuits

lb	oz		kg	gr
	12	Sugar (castor)		375
	9	Butter		270
		Vanilla		
	¼	Ground cinnamon		8
	⅛	Ground mixed spice		4
	⅛	Ground nutmeg		4

Cream together on low speed.

| | 5 | Egg | | 150 |

Add on low speed.

	4	Broken almonds, walnuts, hazelnuts		125
	4	Currants		125
	2	Chopped citron peel		60
	¼	Zest of orange		8

Blend in.

| | 3 ½ | Milk (approx.) | | 100 |
| | ⅛ | Bicarbonate of soda | | 4 |

Mix and blend in. Lastly add:

| 1 | 0 | Flour (soft) | | 500 |
| | ⅛ | Baking powder | | 4 |

Pipe out with a savoy bag and plain tube on to greased baking sheets. Place half a glacé cherry on the top of each. Bake at 380° F (193° C).

Fruit Ovals

lb	oz		kg	gr
1	0	Flour		500
	10	Butter		300
	5 ½	Sugar (icing)		160
	2	Egg		60
	6	Cherries (halved)		170
	2	Nib almonds		60
	4	Raisins (small)		125

Make all into a smooth pastry, adding the fruit last. Roll out into ropes and flatten slightly to form an oval. Wrap in wax paper and refrigerate. When firm, cut into slices and place, cut side down, on to lightly greased baking sheets. Bake at 350° F (176° C). *(Germany)*

Ginger Biscuits

lb	oz		kg	gr
1	0	Butter		500
	12	Sugar (castor)		375

Mix but do not cream.

| | 4 | Egg | | 125 |

Add and mix.

1	12	Flour (soft)		875
	4	Cornflour		125
	1	Baking powder		30
	3/4	Ground ginger		20
	1/8	Bicarbonate of soda		4

Sieve well and blend into the above.

Mould into bars 4 in. by 1 1/4 in. (10 × 3 cm.). Wrap in waxed paper and refrigerate. When firm, cut into slices 1/4 in. (5 mm.) thick. Place on to greased baking sheets. Bake at 380-400° F (193-204° C).

Ginger Biscuits

lb	oz		kg	gr
1	2	Butter		625
	7	Raw marzipan		200
	14	Sugar (castor)		400
1	2	Flour		625
		Salt		
	3 1/2	Chopped ginger		100
	1/8	Cinnamon		4
	1/8	Cocoa powder		4

Make into a paste. Cut out with a 1 1/2 in. (4 cm.) plain cutter. Place 2 thin strips of preserved ginger on each. Bake at 356° F (180° C). *(Germany)*

Ginger Crisp

lb	oz		kg	gr
1	0	Flour		500
	1	Cake crumbs		30
	1/2	Salt		15

lb	oz		kg	gr
	1/4	Baking powder		8
	3/16	Bicarbonate of soda		5
	3/8	Ground ginger		10
	6	Sugar (granulated)		180
	4	Sugar (soft brown)		125
	6	Butter		180
	3	Water		90
		Lemon essence		

Mix all the ingredients together. Pin out 1/8 in. (3 mm.) thick, cut out with 2 in. (5 cm.) plain cutter. Place on lightly greased baking trays, wash with light syrup. Bake at 380-400° F (193-204° C) for about 20 minutes on double trays.

Ginger Nuts

lb	oz		kg	gr
1	0	Flour		500
	1/4	Baking powder		8
	1/4	Ground ginger		8
	1/4	Ground spice		8
	8	Sugar (castor)		250
	8	Golden syrup		250
	3 1/2	Butter		100
	1/2	Milk (approx.)		15

Sieve the flour, baking powder and the spices. Rub in the butter. With the rest of the ingredients make a plastic paste. It will be found that the mixture will need thorough working to get plasticity. Pin out to 1/8 in. (3 mm.) in thickness and cut out with a plain 2 in. (5 cm.) cutter. Place on to greased baking sheets. Bake at 340° F (171° C).
(Illustration page 391.)

Golden Bows

lb	oz		kg	gr
	10	Sugar (icing)		300
	1/2	Vanilla sugar		15
1	7	Butter		700
	3 1/2	Egg		100
2	0	Flour	1	
		Yellow colour		

Mix all the ingredients to a smooth piping mixture. Using a No. 5 plain tube, pipe out small crescents on to baking sheets.

488

Bake until golden in colour. When cold, sandwich with apricot purée and dip the ends in plain chocolate and finely chopped pistachio nuts. Some coconut coloured green may be used instead of pistachio nuts. *(Switzerland)*

Graham Biscuits

lb	oz		kg	gr
2	0	Graham flour	1	
2	0	Cornflour	1	
	14	Butter		400
	5	Honey		150
	2	Ammonium bicarbonate		60
1	4	Milk		625
	3/16	Salt		10

Make the ingredients into a paste in the same way as for milanese paste. Roll out and, using a plain, oval pastry cutter, cut out into biscuits. Put these on baking sheets and bake in a medium oven. *(France)*

Heckle Biscuits

lb	oz		kg	gr
1	0	Flour (soft)		500
	1/8	Bicarbonate of soda		4
	1/4	Cream of tartar		8
	5	Butter		150
	3	Sugar (castor)		90
	3 1/2	Milk (approx.)		100

Sieve the flour and chemicals together and rub in the butter. Add the sugar and milk and mix without toughening. Weigh into pieces of suitable size and mould round. Pin out and dock all over. Bake at 420° F (217° C) on wire mesh trays. *(Scotland)*

Honey Biscuits

Mix 2 lb. (1 kg.) of French sweet pastry with 7 oz. (200 gr.) of finely chopped candied fruits. Pin out 1/8 in. (3 mm.) thick and cut out with a 2 in. (5 cm.) plain cutter and bake at 400° F (204° C). While still hot, sandwich in pairs with honey and dust the tops with icing sugar. *(France)*

Jan Hagel Biscuits

lb	oz		kg	gr
	9	Butter or margarine		270
	7	Sugar (castor)		200
	1 1/2	Egg		45
	1/4	Cinnamon		8
	12	Flour (soft)		375
	1/8	Bicarbonate of soda		4
		Pinch of salt		

Make a paste of these ingredients. After cooling, roll into a rectangular shape about 1/8 in. (3 mm.) thick and put it on a lightly greased baking sheet. Brush with beaten egg and sprinkle with flaked almonds and nib sugar. Bake in an oven at 356° F (180° C). Cut cookies 1 1/4 in. by 1/2 in. (3 × 1 cm.) immediately after baking.

A delightful cookie, golden brown and crisp. *(Holland)*

Langues-de-Chat

lb	oz		kg	gr
1	0	Sugar (castor)		500
1	0	Flour (soft)		500
	1	Vanilla sugar		30
1	0	Single cream		500
	14	Egg whites		400

Whip the cream slightly until it just begins to thicken. Whip the whites to a stiff snow.

Add the sugar until it forms a stiff meringue adding the vanilla sugar. Fold in the flour and lastly the cream. Pipe out finger shape on to beeswaxed baking sheets *(see glossary)*, not too close together, using a 1/4 in. (5 mm.) tube. Bake very carefully at 420° F (216° C), so that the edges only are a light golden colour.

Here is another recipe:

lb	oz		kg	gr
1	0	Butter		500
1	0	Sugar (castor)		500
	10	Egg whites (approx.)		300
1	0	Flour (soft)		500

Cream the butter and sugar and add the whites a little at a time. Finally fold in the flour. *(France)*

Lemon Biscuits

lb	oz		kg	gr
	11	Butter		330
	3 1/2	Sugar (castor)		100
		Zest of 1/4 lemon		

Mix but do not cream.

| | 14 | Flour (soft) | | 400 |
| | 1/16 | Salt | | 2 |

Sieve and blend in.

Mould into bars 2 in. (5 cm.) square, wrap in waxed paper and refrigerate. When firm, cut into slices 1/4 in. (5 mm.) thick and place on to greased baking sheets. Pipe a bulb of macaroon paste on the centre of each biscuit. Bake at 380-400° F (193-204° C).

Lemon Scrolls

The same mixing as for almond scrolls is used. The mixture is piped out, using a savoy bag with a 3/8 in. (1 cm.) tube, on to greaseproof paper in fingers about 2 in. (5 cm.) long. After sprinkling with fine granulated sugar, a piece of angelica about 1 in. (2.5 cm.) long is placed on each. They are baked at 350° F (176° C).

Macarons à l'Orange

lb	oz		kg	gr
1	0	Blanched almonds		500
1	8	Sugar (granulated)		750
	7	Candied orange peel		200
	7	Egg whites (approx.)		200

Grind the almonds, sugar and egg whites, then add the finely chopped orange peel. Pipe out small round shapes on greaseproof paper and bake at 360° F (182° C). Peel off the paper when baked and when cool, dip the tops into orange coloured and flavoured fondant. *(France)*

Macarons de Nancy

lb	oz		kg	gr
1	2	Blanched almonds		560
2	4	Sugar (castor)	1	125
	12	Egg whites		375

Grind the almonds with 1 3/4 lb. (875 gr.) of sugar and 7 oz. (200 gr.) of egg whites. Let the mixture stand and then add the remaining 5 oz. (175 gr.) of egg whites which have been stiffly whipped with the rest of the sugar. Pipe out into small round shapes on to sheets of greaseproof paper. Sprinkle with sugar and bake at 360° F (182° C). *(France)*

Maraschino Dainties

lb	oz		kg	gr
1	0	Egg whites		500
	12	Egg yolks		375
1	0	Sugar (icing)		500
	10	Flour		300
		Pinch of salt		

Whip the whites to a stiff snow. Beat the yolks, sugar and salt until stiff. Fold in the whites and then the flour. With a savoy bag fitted with a small plain tube, pipe out on to a paper lined baking sheet in little bulbs so that each two are touching, giving an outline of a figure '8'. Sprinkle with nib almonds that have been moistened with maraschino flavoured egg whites and rolled in sugar. Bake at 350° F (176° C). When cold, spread the flat surface with pineapple jam and glaze with thin maraschino flavoured fondant. *(France)*

Marigolds

Pin out puff pastry to about 1/8 in. (3 mm.) thick and cut very small circles with a plain cutter. From the cuttings, cut out a similar number. Place them out on the table and cut out the centres. Wash the plain discs and place a ring on each. Sort out strip almonds of equal length and arrange them carefully around the inside of the rings in a slanting outwards direction. They should be pressed into the paste so that they stay in position during baking. Dust with icing sugar and bake at 400° F (204° C). When cool, insert some narrow strips of bright, firm red currant jelly between each piece of almond and a spot of apricot or greengage jam in the centre.

(France)

Melting Moments

lb	oz		kg	gr
	8	Butter		250
	4	Sugar (castor)		125
	2 1/2	Egg		75

Cream until light.

	2	Flour (soft)		60
	8	Ground almonds		250

Mix into the above.

Pipe out with a savoy bag and plain pipe three small bulbs together to form a shamrock pattern. Bake at 380°F (193°C).

Dip the three edges into chocolate.

Montagner Biscuits

lb	oz		kg	gr
1	0	Flour (soft)		500
	8	Butter		250
	8	Sugar (castor)		250
	5	Red wine		150
		Ground nutmeg (pinch)		

Cream the butter and sugar and beat in the wine. Fold in the flour. With a savoy bag fitted with a star tube, pipe on to greased and floured baking sheets in the form of stars. Bake at 400° F (204° C).
(Switzerland)

Montelman

lb	oz		kg	gr
	15	Sugar (icing)		450
1	2	Butter		560
	5	Egg yolks		150
	10	Mixed fruit		300
	8	Almonds (strip)		250
2	0	Flour	1	
		Zest of 1 lemon		
		Salt		

Make all the ingredients into a paste. Pin out as described for Nut Croquettes 3/4 in. (2 cm.) thick and refrigerate. Cut into strips 1 1/4 in. (3 cm.) wide. Cut each strip in slices 1/2 in. (1.5 cm.) wide, place them on greased baking sheets and bake at 350° F (180° C). *(Switzerland)*

Moque Biscuits

lb	oz		kg	gr
1	8	Flour (soft)		750
1	0	Butter		500
	8	Sugar (castor)		250
	1/2	Vanilla sugar		15
		Milk (a little)		

Sieve the flour and rub the butter and sugar into it, then making a firm, smooth, pliable dough with a little milk. Allow the dough to rest in a cool place for a while, then divide into pieces and roll them into ropes about 1 in. (2.5 cm.) diameter. Roll the ropes in fine granulated sugar so that they are well covered. Cut into little rounds about 1/4 in. (5 mm.) thick and arrange them on a baking sheet, cut side down. With a small round cutter, take out the centres and fill not quite full with frangipane mixture. Bake at 400° F (204° C).

Another variety, using the same basic mixing, is to proceed as above without removing the centres. As soon as they are baked they are dusted well with icing sugar and returned to the oven, care being taken that they do not take too much colour.

Another variety can be made from the same paste, but it must be handled differently. Divide the paste into half and one half into quarters. Add red colour and a little raspberry flavour to one quarter, and cocoa to the other. The half is left plain.

Take the red piece and mould up to a smooth ball; elongate it and square the ends. Mould up the plain piece and pin it out to the same length and size to enclose the red piece, keeping the sides perfectly square. Dampen the surface before enclosing. Do exactly the same with the chocolate piece, taking extra care as it will only be a thin coating. Roll out carefully to a rope about 1 in. (2.5 cm.) diameter, roll in sugar and cut into slices.

Bake carefully at 400° F (204° C), or the colours will suffer and the attractive appearance be lost.

Moss Biscuits

Raw marzipan is coloured a pale green. Pieces are then passed through a coarse sieve and taken off with a knife. The pieces are then placed on to paper lined baking sheets. They are flashed off at 425° F (218° C).

Nantes Biscuits - Galettes nantaises

lb	oz		kg	gr
1	0	Flour		500
	10	Butter		300
	7	Sugar (castor)		200
	5	Ground almonds		150
	3	Egg yolks		90
	1/4	Salt		8

Mix the ingredients into a smooth paste and let stand for one hour. Pin out to 1/8 in. (3 mm.) and cut out with a 2 in. (5 cm.) round fluted cutter. Brush the biscuits with egg and mark a criss-cross pattern with a fork. Drop a pinch of ground almond in the middle of each biscuit and sprinkle with sugar. Bake at 400° F (204° C). *(France)*

Neapolitan Biscuits

lb	oz		kg	gr
	10	Sugar (icing)		300
	5	Almonds (nibbed)		150
	2 1/2	Egg whites		75
	1/2	Flour		15

Mix the sugar, almonds, egg whites and flour to a compact paste. Pin out Neapolitan pastry *(page 188)* 1/8 in. (3 mm.) thick and cut out with a 2 in. (5 cm.) plain cutter and spread on each a little of the almond paste. Dust with icing sugar and bake in an oven with more bottom than top heat. *(France)*

Nice Biscuits - Biscuits de Nice

lb	oz		kg	gr
2	0	Flour	1	
	1	Cornflour		30
	7	Fine coconut		200
	3	Butter		90
	6	Compound fat		180
	14	Sugar (pulverized)		400

lb	oz		kg	gr
2		Golden syrup		60
	1/8	Bicarbonate of soda		4
	1/32	Carbonate of ammonia		1
3		Milk		90
		Pink colour (a little)		
		Vanilla		

Make into a smooth dough. Pin out thinly and cut into rectangles using a fluted cutter. Sprinkle surface with granulated sugar. *(France)*

Nougat Biscuits

lb	oz		kg	gr
1	4	Butter		625
	14	Sugar (castor)		400

Mix but do not cream.

	1 1/4	Egg		35

Add.

		Vanilla		
1	12	Flour (soft)		875
	1 1/2	Cocoa		45
	1/4	Salt		8

Sieve well and blend into above.

Mould into bars about 2 in. by 2 1/2 in. (5 × 6 cm.). Wrap in waxed paper and refrigerate. When firm, cut into slices 1/8 in. (3 mm.) thick and place on to greased baking sheets. Bake at 380-400° F (193-204°C). Sandwich with nougat cream and dip one corner into chocolate.

Nougatines

lb	oz		kg	gr
	5 1/2	Butter or margarine		175
	4 1/2	Sugar (castor)		140
	1	Water		30
	5	Flour (soft)		150
	1/8	Baking powder		4
	1 3/4	Nougat		50
		Vanilla		
		Salt		

Mix the butter or margarine with sugar, vanilla and salt. Next add the water and then the flour and baking powder. Lastly stir in the little pieces of nougat. The mixture should be a batter containing as little air as possible. Now pipe little rounds on a greased baking sheet and bake in an oven at 356° F (180° C). Loosen the cookies immediately after baking. The nougat is made by heating granulated sugar in a pan stirring all the time. The sugar will melt and then some flaked almonds are added and stirred in. The nougat is poured on a greased baking sheet. When it is cold, it is crushed, but do not add the powder to the paste, only use the small pieces. *(Holland)*

Nougat Ovals

lb	oz		kg	gr
	12	Butter		375
	12	Sugar (icing)		375
	7 1/2	Egg		225
1	4	Flour (soft)		625
		Vanilla		

Cream the butter and sugar and add the egg then the flour. With a small plain savoy tube, pipe out oval shaped biscuits. Allow room for spreading. Bake at 380° F (193° C). When cold, sandwich together in pairs with warmed chocolate praline nougat. When set, dip diagonally into chocolate and sprinkle with a little roasted nib almond. *(Germany)*

Nut Croquettes

lb	oz		kg	gr
1	0	Sugar (icing)		500
1	0	Butter		500
	3/4	Cinnamon		20
	7	Egg		200
1	0	Hazelnuts (chopped)		500
2	0	Flour	1	
		Zest of 1/2 lemon		
		Salt		

Mix all the ingredients together except the flour which is sieved with the cinnamon and then added. Shape the paste into a square, place it on a sheet of paper and pin out between two metal bars 3/4 in. (2 cm.) square, then refrigerate. Cut into strips 1 1/4 in. (3 cm.) wide and then cut into 1/4 in. (6 mm.) slices. Place them, cut side down, on to greased baking sheets and bake at 400° F (204° C). *(Switzerland)*

Nut Dessert Fingers

lb	oz		kg	gr
	10	Egg whites		300
	13	Sugar (castor)		400
	10	Ground hazelnuts		300
1		Flour		30

Whisk the egg whites and a quarter of the sugar to a stiff snow. Fold in the hazelnuts, the remaining sugar and the flour. Using a plain tube, pipe fingers 1 1/4 in. (3 cm.) long on to greased and floured baking sheets. Sprinkle with flaked hazelnuts, shaking off the surplus and bake in a medium oven. Remove from the baking sheets and sandwich in pairs with hot apricot purée flavoured with kirsch and with a little additional sugar. *(Switzerland)*

Orange Biscuits - Galettes à l'Orange

lb	oz		kg	gr
1	0	Nib almonds		500
1	0	Sugar (castor)		500
1	0	Orange peel		500
	12	Butter		375
	4	Flour		125
	4	Milk		125
		Cochineal		

Cream the butter and sugar, add the almonds, finely chopped peel, sieved flour, the milk and a little cochineal colour. Deposit in little heaps, the size of walnuts, on slightly greased baking sheets. Flatten slightly with a wet fork. Bake at 420° F (216° C). The biscuits should not be removed from the baking sheet until almost cold, since they are very fragile. *(France)*

Orange Macaroon Biscuits

lb	oz		kg	gr
1	0	Sugar (granulated)		500
1	8	Raw marzipan		750
	8	Egg whites (approx.)		250
		Zest of lemon		
	2	Orange peel		60

Reduce the marzipan with a little egg white and then beat all to a smooth paste of piping consistency. The orange peel is added last after being chopped very fine. Pipe bean shape on to paper lined baking sheets and bake at 350° F (176° C). When cool, remove from the paper and sandwich in pairs with orange marmalade and half dip into chocolate. *(Germany)*

Palace Biscuits - Paleis Banket

Pipe two strips of almond mixture of medium consistency (*see* English Rout Biscuits) on wafer paper with a savoy bag fitted with a star tube. Do not bake the strips at once but let them dry first. After drying, 'flash' in a hot oven at 500° F (260° C).

Brush with apricot purée, fill the open space between the two strips with warm raspberry jelly and pipe a strip of well flavoured fondant on top of the raspberry jelly. The open space between the two strips is pushed in before 'flashing' with a spatula to make a neat channel to receive the raspberry jelly and fondant. Cut the strips into small slices. The fondant is flavoured with maraschino liqueur and coloured pink. *(Holland)*

Palais de Dame

Recipe I

lb	oz		kg	gr
	3 1/2	Butter		100
1	0	Sugar (icing)		500
1	0	Flour		500
	1/2	Vanilla sugar		15
	10 1/2	Dairy cream		315
	7	Egg whites		200

Recipe II

lb	oz		kg	gr
	2	Butter		60
	9	Sugar (icing)		270
	10 1/2	Flour		315
	7	Dairy cream		200
	3 1/2	Milk		100
	12	Egg whites		375

Cream the butter and sugar and blend in the sieved flour. Add the cream and milk and finally the stiffly whisked egg whites. Pipe small round shapes on to a greased baking sheet and bake at 440° F (227° C) so that there is an even golden colour on the edge of each biscuit. The biscuit is very thin, like langues-de-chat. *(France)*

Parkin Biscuits

lb	oz		kg	gr
1	1	Oatmeal (medium)		530
1	0	Flour (soft)		500
	1	Bicarbonate of soda		30
	4	Sugar (castor)		125
	5	Butter		150
	14	Golden syrup		400
	4	Milk		125

Sieve the flour and rub in the butter. Mix with oatmeal. Dissolve the soda in the milk and with the rest of the materials make into a smooth dough. Finish as for spice biscuits. Bake at 320° F (160° C).

Pavilion Biscuits

lb	oz		kg	gr
1	0	Flour (soft)		500
	8	Butter		250
	8	Sugar (castor)		250
	4	Egg		125
		Zest of 1 orange		

Work the butter, sugar and orange zest together and add the egg. Make into a paste with the flour. Pin out to 1/8 in. (3 mm.) in thickness and cut out with a 1 3/4 in. (4.5 cm.) fluted cutter. Wash with beaten egg whites and sprinkle with a mixture of nibbed almonds and sugar nibs. Arrange on a baking sheet and bake at 400° F (204° C). After baking, dust lightly with icing sugar.

Pearl Biscuits

lb	oz		kg	gr
	7 1/2	Egg whites		215
	9	Sugar (castor)		270
	4 1/2	Flour (soft)		140
	1	Maraschino		30

Beat whites to a firm meringue, adding sugar gradually. Stir in the flour and the maraschino. Cut strips of paper and pipe on small fingers. Dredge with icing sugar, shake off surplus, and let stand for 15 minutes. Bake at 375° F (190° C) being careful that they do not colour. Dry out in a warm prover for 24 hours.

Perkin Biscuits

lb	oz		kg	gr
1	2	Flour		560
	14	Oatmeal (fine)		400
	3/4	Bicarbonate of soda		20
	1/8	Cream of tartar		4
	1/2	Ground ginger		15
	7	Butter		200
	6	Sugar (granulated)		180
	1 1/2	Egg		45
1	0	Golden syrup		500

Sieve the flour, chemicals and ginger and blend in the oatmeal. Rub in the butter finely. Mix the sugar, egg and syrup together and make all into a smooth dough. Cut out with a small plain cutter and glaze with egg. Place a split almond on each. Bake at 380° F (193° C). *(Scotland)*

Petits Beurres

lb	oz		kg	gr
1	10	Flour		800
	5	Cornflour		150
1	0	Sugar (castor)		500
	12 1/4	Butter		375
	2 1/2	Egg yolks		75
2	0	Milk (approx.)	1	
	1/8	Salt		4
	3/16	Carbonate of ammonia		5
	3/16	Sodium bicarbonate		5

Carefully mix the ammonium bicarbonate with the milk and pass the sodium bicarbonate, flour and starch through a sieve.

Make all the ingredients into a paste on the table. Leave to stand in a cool place, then roll out thinly and mark with a spiked roller. Cut up into oblongs, place on baking sheets and bake in a slow oven so that the biscuits become quite crisp.

Petits beurres should not be egg washed.

(France)

Pineapple Strips

lb	oz		kg	gr
	8	Sugar (icing)		250
	8	Butter		250
	7	Egg		200
1	4	Flour		625
		Lemon zest		
		Pineapple essence		

Mix the sugar with the butter, egg and essence until smooth, then add the zest and the flour. Force out in strips with a biscuit forcer on to lightly greased baking sheets and bake until golden. While still hot, brush with water icing flavoured with pineapple essence and cut into diamonds.

(Switzerland)

Pischinger

Pin out rich sweet pastry to about 1/8 in. (3 mm.) thick and cut out with a 1 1/4 in. (3 cm.) plain cutter. Place on lightly greased baking sheets and bake at 380° F (193° C). When cold, sandwich together in pairs with warmed chocolate praline nougat. Dip into chocolate and place a roasted hazelnut in the centre of each.

(Switzerland)

Plain Biscuits - Biscuits ordinaires

lb	oz		kg	gr
2	0	Flour	1	
2	0	Cornflour	1	
1	9	Sugar		750
1	9	Butter		750
	8	Egg		250
	7	Milk		200
	1	Salt		30
	1/4	Ammonium bicarbonate		8

Make the ingredients into a paste in the same way as for milanese paste. Leave to stand in a cool place for two days. Then machine the paste until it is smooth and roll it out thinly. Cut up into small oblongs, place on racks and bake in a medium oven. *(France)*

Puff Cracknels

lb	oz		kg	gr
1	12	Flour (soft)		875
	3	Sugar (castor)		90
	6	Egg		180
	2 1/2	Water		75
	1/16	Carbonate of ammonia		2

Dissolve the ammonia in the water and make all the materials into a stiff dough and allow to rest for 30 minutes covered with a damp cloth. Pass through rollers until a smooth skin is attained. Cover again with a damp cloth and rest for 1 hour. Pass through rollers once more and then pin out to a fairly thin sheet. Cut out with round or oval cutters and dock the centre of each. Throw the cut-out biscuits into boiling water. They will sink at first and then rise to the surface. Boil them for 3 minutes and then place into cold water. When cold, strain the water off and dry the biscuits in a cloth. Place on biscuit wires and bake at 450° F (232° C). Dry in a hot cupboard for some hours.

Raspberry Rosettes

lb	oz		kg	gr
1	0	Butter		500
	8	Sugar (icing)		250
	1/2	Egg yolks		15
	3/4	Egg whites		20
	1/2	Cornflour		15
1	8	Flour		750
	1/16	Salt		2
		Vanilla		
		Lemon juice		

Make into a paste. Cut one half of it out with a 1 1/2 in. (4 cm.) fluted cutter and cut out the centres with a plain cutter. Cut out a similar number without removing the centres. Place on a greased baking sheet and wash each with egg. Sprinkle sugar nibs on those with the centres removed. Bake at 356° F (180° C).

When baked and cool, pipe raspberry jam on the bases and sandwich each with a sugar ring top. Fill in the centres with kirsch fondant. *(Germany)*
(Illustration page 509.)

Raspberry Tartlets

Pin out raw marzipan, 1/8 in. (3 mm.) thick and line small petits fours moulds. Bake lightly at 392° F (200° C).

When baked decorate the upper edge with chocolate. Half fill with raspberry jam. Outline with raspberry fondant and place a spot of white fondant in the centre.
(Germany)

Ratafia Biscuits

lb	oz		kg	gr
1	0	Sugar (granulated)		500
	6	Ground sweet almonds		180
	2	Ground bitter almonds		60
	1	Ground rice		30
	7 1/2	Egg whites (approx.)		215

Place all together and beat for a few minutes. Pipe out in small bulbs on to greased and floured baking sheets or on greaseproof paper lined baking sheets. Bake at 360° F (182° C).

Rectangles

lb	oz		kg	gr
	8	Egg		250
	4	Egg yolks		125
	8	Sugar (castor)		250
	8	Butter		250
	8	Flour		250

Whisk the egg, yolks and sugar to a sponge. Carefully stir in the hot butter and the flour. Spread on paper as for swiss rolls. Sprinkle half with flaked almonds and bake for about 4 minutes at 480° F (250° C). Cut in half, spread the plain half with ganache or nougat paste and cover with the almond topped half. Dust with icing sugar and cut into rectangles.
(Switzerland)

Rheims (Champagne) Biscuits - Biscuits de Rheims

lb	oz		kg	gr
1	4	Sugar (castor)		625
1	5	Egg		650
1	4	Flour		625
	1/8	Bicarbonate of soda		4
	1/8	Cream of tartar		4
		Vanilla		

Whip up the egg and sugar, adding the soda and the cream of tartar. When stiff, fold in the flour, pipe into greased and floured special champagne biscuit moulds and dust with castor sugar. Bake at 380° F (193° C). These biscuits will keep well.

The cream of tartar and soda can be omitted. *(France)*

Rice Biscuits

lb	oz		kg	gr
1	0	Flour (soft)		500
	6	Butter		180
	8	Sugar (castor)		250
	1 1/2	Egg		45
	3 1/2	Milk		100
	1/2	Carbonate of ammonia		15

Rub the butter into the sieved flour. Dissolve the ammonia in the milk. Make a dough with the rest of the ingredients. Proceed as for spice biscuits. Bake at 340° F (171° C).

Rolled Oat Cookies

lb	oz		kg	gr
1	0	Butter		500
2	0	Sugar (brown)	1	
	8	Egg		250
	3/4	Salt		20
	1 1/2	Bicarbonate of soda		45
2	0	Flour (soft)	1	
2	0	Rolled oats	1	
	1/8	Mace		4
	7	Milk		200

Cream the butter and sugar and add the egg, salt and soda (dissolved in the milk). Add the flour and oats. Drop out on to greased baking sheets, flatten a little and wash with egg. Bake at 400° F (204° C).

(Canada)

Sablés

lb	oz		kg	gr
	5	Sugar (icing)		150
	3/4	Sugar (vanilla)		20
	7	Butter		200
	5	Margarine		150
1	0	Flour		500
	1 1/2	Egg whites		45
	1/8	Salt		4

Make the ingredients into a paste. Shape into ropes about 1 in. (2.5 cm.) in diameter and refrigerate. Brush with egg and roll into castor sugar, and cut into 1/4 in. (5 mm.) slices. Bake for about 5 minutes at 410° F (210° C). *(Switzerland)*

Sand Biscuits

lb	oz		kg	gr
	12	Butter		375
	8	Sugar (icing)		250
	4 1/2	Milk		140
1	8	Flour (soft)		750
		Lemon zest		
		Vanilla		

Cream the butter and sugar and, when light, add the milk a little at a time. Add the flavours and stir in the flour. Using a sixteen point savoy tube, pipe on to lightly greased baking sheets. Make a light impression in the centre and pipe in apricot jam. Bake at 400° F (204° C).

(Germany)

Sand Scrolls

lb	oz		kg	gr
1	0	Flour		500
	8	Cornflour		250
1	0	Butter		500
	10	Sugar (icing)		300
	2	Egg whites		60
	2	Milk (approx.)		60
		Lemon zest		
		Vanilla		

Cream the butter and sugar lightly, adding the egg whites and milk by degrees.

Fold in the flour. Pipe out 'S' shapes on to greased and floured baking sheets and let them rest for a while. Bake at 380° F (193° C). When cold, dip the ends into chocolate. *(Germany)*

Sand Stars

Proceed exactly as for Sand Biscuits but use an eight point star tube. Place half a glacé cherry on each before baking.

(Germany)

Sandmac Biscuits

lb	oz		kg	gr
1	0	Raw marzipan		500
	7	Sugar (icing)		200
	3 1/2	Egg yolks		100
		Lemon zest		

Make up the materials into a macaroon paste and pipe small biscuits about 1 in. (2.5 cm.) diameter on to greased and floured baking sheets. Pipe a small star of Sand Biscuit mixing on top of each and finish with a spot of raspberry jam. Bake at 350° F (176° C). *(Germany)*

Savoy Biscuits

lb	oz		kg	gr
	8	Eggs (separated)		250
	5	Sugar (castor)		150
	3	Flour (soft)		90
	2	Brown bread crumbs (dry)		60
	1	Kirsch		30

Pass the crumbs through a fine sieve. Whisk whites into a firm meringue, adding the sugar gradually. Stir in the beaten yolks and kirsch carefully. Fold in the flour and bread crumbs and pipe out into the bottom of sponge frames which have been greased and floured. Bake at 350° F (176° C).

Savoy Fingers - Biscuits à la Cuiller

Proceed as for Sponge Fingers but bake in an oven at 380° F (193° C), allowing the biscuits to dry out. These biscuits are not sandwiched together. *(France)*

Scottish Rolls

lb	oz		kg	gr
	8	Flour		250
	4	Butter		125
	5	Sugar (castor)		150
	3 1/2	Egg		100
	1/8	Bicarbonate of soda		4
		Zest of 1 lemon		

Make all the ingredients into a paste of medium firmness and allow to rest for two hours. Divide into pieces the size of a large walnut, shape into longish rolls, brush with egg and bake at 400° F (204° C). *(France)*

Shortbread Biscuits

lb	oz		kg	gr
1	12	Flour (soft)		875
	2	Cornflour		60
	2	Ground rice		60
1	0	Butter		500
	12	Sugar (castor)		375
	5	Egg		150

Mix the butter and sugar together without creaming. Add the egg, then the flours which have been sieved together. Mix to a smooth dough. With a variety of small cutters, many shapes can be made. Fruit and/or nuts can be used either inside the biscuits or on top as a decoration. Bake at 380° F (193° C). *(Scotland)*

Shortbread Drops and Biscuits

lb	oz		kg	gr
1	0	Sugar (fine castor)		500
1	8	Butter		750
	7	Egg		200
3	0	Flour (soft)	1	500
		Vanilla		

Cream the butter and sugar and add the egg. Add the flavour and fold in the flour. Pipe out with a plain tube on to lightly greased baking sheets. Alternatively a star pipe can be used and small fingers, shells and scrolls can be made. Decorate with cherries, angelica, etc. Bake at 380° F (193° C). *(Scotland)*

Shrewsbury Biscuits

lb	oz		kg	gr
1	0	Flour		500
	10	Butter		300
	10	Sugar (castor)		300
	3	Egg		90
	1/8	Cinnamon		4

Rub the butter into the flour and make a bay into which the sugar, egg and cinnamon are placed. The whole is made into a smooth paste which is pinned out to a thickness of $3/16$ in. (4 mm.). Cut out with a plain 2 in. (5 cm.) cutter and place on to paper lined baking sheets. Bake at 400° F (204° C).

Silver Drops

lb	oz		kg	gr
1	4	Egg whites		625
1	8	Sugar (castor)		750
	8	Cornflour		250
	1	Maraschino		30

Whip the whites to a stiff meringue adding the sugar a little at a time. Fold in the cornflour that has been thoroughly sieved. Add the maraschino.

Pipe out the size of a shilling on to papered trays and dust heavily with castor sugar, shaking off the surplus. Leave for a while until the surface sugar is partly melted and bake at 375° F (190° C), to a delicate but light tint. Sandwich in pairs with a fondant buttercream *(page 228)* flavoured with maraschino and lemon juice.

Souvaroff Biscuits - Souwaroffs

lb	oz		kg	gr
1	0	Flour		500
	12	Butter		375
	6	Sugar (icing)		180
	$1/8$	Salt		4

Mix the ingredients carefully with the finger tips since there is no egg or egg yolk in the mix. Leave to stand for an hour and then pin out to $1/8$ in. (3 mm.). Cut into small oval shapes and bake at 400° F (204° C). When the biscuits are almost baked, dust with icing sugar and replace in the oven to slightly caramelize. When cold, sandwich in pairs with redcurrant jelly. *(France)*

Speculaas

lb	oz		kg	gr
10	0	Flour (soft)	5	
	7	Speculaas spice		200
	$2 1/2$	Bicarbonate of soda		75
	$1 3/4$	Bicarbonate of ammonium		50
5	0	Butter	2	500
6	0	Sugar (castor)	3	
	5	Water		150
	2	Egg		60
	1	Salt		30
	$3/4$	Zest of lemon		20

Mix these ingredients to a dough, and let it rest in a cool place for a few hours.

Mould the special speculaas-shaped cookies from the dough with a cutting machine or a wooden speculaas-board and place them on a greased baking sheet.

Bake at a temperature of 375° F (190° C). The cookies should be rather firm and crisp. *(Holland)*

Spice Biscuits

lb	oz		kg	gr
1	0	Flour (soft)		500
	6	Butter		180
	6	Sugar (castor)		180
	4	Syrup		125
	$1/2$	Ground ginger		15
	$1/4$	Ground spice		8
	2	Milk		60
	$1/2$	Carbonate of ammonia		15

Sieve the flour, spice and ginger and rub in the butter. Dissolve the ammonia in the milk. With the rest of the ingredients make into a paste. Weigh according to the size required and mould each one round. Arrange on greased baking sheets and flatten slightly. Bake at 340° F (171° C).

Spiced Hazelnut Biscuits

lb	oz		kg	gr
	7	Butter		200
	7	Sugar (castor)		200

Mix on low speed. Do not cream.

	$1/8$	Ammonium carbonate ('Vol')		4
	1	Milk		30

Mix and add.

499

lb	oz		kg	gr
	3/4	Egg		20

Add and mix in.

lb	oz		kg	gr
	10 1/2	Flour (soft)		315
	3	Sponge-cake crumbs		90
	1/8	Ground cinnamon		4
	1/16	Ground mace		2
	1/8	Salt		4

Sieve well and blend in.

lb	oz		kg	gr
	3/4	Mixed peel		20
1	1/2	Roasted nib hazelnuts		45
1	1/2	Roasted ground hazelnuts		45

Add and mix in.

Mould into triangular bars and wrap in waxed paper and refrigerate. When firm, cut into slices 1/4 in. (5 mm.) thick and place on to greased baking sheets. Bake at 380-400° F (193-204° C). The edges may be dipped into milk chocolate.

Spicy Cookies - Taai-Taai

A delicacy that is made round the 5th of December, the birthday of Saint Nicholas.

lb	oz		kg	gr
5	0	Honey	2	500
5	0	Glucose	2	500
1	0	Water		500
5	10	Rye flour	2	800
5	0	Flour (soft)	2	500
	4	Bicarbonate of soda		125

Boil together the honey, glucose and the water. Mix this boiling mass with the sieved flours to a dough. Let the dough rest for a few days. After this rest, add 5 oz. (150 gr.) of Taai-taai spice (see end of this recipe) and the bicarbonate of soda. Shape the dough into dolls with Taai-taai moulds, brush with egg. To make these cookies extra tasty, add slices of ginger.

Taai-taai spice is composed of:
70 % of cinnamon, 30 % nutmeg and aniseed.

The exact composition is only known to the factories who produce it. *(Holland)*

Strassburg Sticks

lb	oz		kg	gr
	8	Butter		250
	4	Sugar (icing)		125
	2	Egg		60
	2 1/2	Marzipan		75
	12	Flour		350
		Salt		
		Lemon juice		

Cream butter and sugar. Work the egg and marzipan until smooth and add to the creamed butter/sugar. Add the salt and lemon juice and lastly the flour. Pipe out on to greased baking sheets in three parallel strips each touching, using a savoy bag and plain 1/4 in. (5 mm.) pipe. Wash with egg and bake at 380° F (193° C). Cut into pieces when cool. *(Germany)*

Sultana Biscuits

lb	oz		kg	gr
1	2	Butter		560
1	2	Sugar (icing)		560
	7	Egg		200
1	2	Flour		560
	5	Chopped sultanas		150

Cream the butter, icing sugar and egg together. Remove from the mixing machine and blend in the flour and the sultanas which have been previously soaked in rum. Pipe this mixture out in the form of little sticks on to greased baking sheets and bake in a medium oven. When the biscuits are baked, dip them diagonally in vanilla couverture. *(France)*

Swabian Rolls

lb	oz		kg	gr
1	4	Almond paste*		625
	10	Butter		300
	2 1/2	Egg yolks		75
1	0	Flour		500
	1/8	Cinnamon		4
		Lemon zest		

* One part unblanched almonds and one part sugar.

Mix the almond paste with the butter. Work in the yolks, zest and cinnamon and

500

lastly the flour. Roll into ropes about ¹/₄ in. (5 mm.) thick and then cut into small rolls. Place on to baking sheets, brush with egg, leave to dry a little and bake at 430° F (220° C). *(Switzerland)*

Swiss Biscuits - Galettes suisses

lb	oz		kg	gr
1	0	Flour		500
1	0	Almonds		500
	15	Sugar (granulated)		450
	5	Butter		150
	6	Egg yolks		180
		Vanilla		
		Salt		

Grind the almonds and the sugar, adding the egg yolks. Make into a stiff paste with the other ingredients. Let the paste stand for 1 hour. Pin out to ¹/₈ in. (3 mm.) and cut out with a small round plain cutter and wash with egg. Cover with flaked almonds, dust with sugar and bake at 400° F (204° C). Instead of flaked almonds, a split almond may be placed in the centre of each. *(Switzerland)*

Swiss Croquettes

lb	oz		kg	gr
1	0	Flour		500
	12	Butter		375
	12	Sugar (icing)		375
	1 ³/₄	Egg whites		50
	1 ³/₄	Egg yolks		50
	6	Almonds (nibbed)		180
	6	Cherries (chopped)		180

Cream the butter and sugar, then add the yolks and the whites. Blend in the flour, almonds and cherries then refrigerate. Shape into a long strip about 1 ¹/₂ in. (4 cm.) square and refrigerate again. Cut into slices ¹/₄ in. (6 mm.) thick and place them, cut side down, on greased baking sheets. Bake at 375° F (190° C). *(Switzerland)*

Tantallon

lb	oz		kg	gr
1	0	Flour (soft)		500
	¹/₈	Bicarbonate of soda		4
1	0	Rice flour		500
1	0	Butter		500
1	0	Sugar (castor)		500
	4	Egg		125
		Zest of lemon		

Sieve the flour, soda and rice flour. Mix the butter and sugar and add the egg. Make all into a smooth dough. Pin out fairly thin and cut out with a small fluted cutter. Bake at 390° F (198° C). Dust with castor sugar as soon as baked. *(Scotland)*

Tarragona Biscuits

lb	oz		kg	gr
2	4	Flour	1	125
1	2	Butter		560
	9	Sugar		270
	1 ³/₄	Cocoa powder		50
	3 ¹/₂	Chopped hazelnuts		100
	5	Egg yolks		150
	³/₈	Vanilla sugar		10
	³/₈	Ground cinnamon		10
	3 ¹/₂	Milk		100

Mix the ingredients in the same way as for milanese paste. Leave for half an hour in a cool place. Roll out thinly and cut out with a round pastry cutter. Bake in a medium oven. When they are cooked, sandwich the biscuits together with a little vanilla couverture. *(France)*

Thin Biscuits - Kletskoppen

lb	oz		kg	gr
	6	Butter or margarine		180
	14	Sugar (castor)		400
	1	Water		30
	3 ¹/₂	Flour (soft)		100
		Cinnamon		

Make a paste of piping consistency from these ingredients, then pipe small rounds on a baking sheet, not too close to each other. Place a half almond on each round.

Bake in an oven at 437° F (225° C). Loosen the cookies from the baking sheet before they are cold. *(Holland)*

Thin Wine Biscuits

lb	oz		kg	gr
1	0	Flour (medium)		500
	6 1/2	Butter		190
	1/4	Salt		8
	3/4	Sugar (castor)		20
	5	Water (approx.)		150

Chop the butter roughly into the flour and make into a rough dough. Give four half turns as for Scotch puff pastry. Wrap and allow to rest for 3-4 hours. Pin out very thin and dock the sheet well. After 10 minutes cut out with a round plain cutter. Bake at 400° F (204° C). *(Scotland)*

Trouville Biscuits - Sablés de Trouville

lb	oz		kg	gr
1	0	Flour		500
	12	Butter		375
	6	Ground almonds		180
	9	Sugar		270
	3	Egg yolks		90
		Salt		
		Zest of lemon		

Rub the butter into the flour and with the rest of the materials, make a smooth paste. Pin out to 3/16 in. (4 mm.) and cut out with a 3 in. (8 cm.) fluted cutter. Wash with egg, and cut each round into four. Trace lines on the tops with the point of a knife and bake at 400° F (204° C).

(France)

Tuiles

lb	oz		kg	gr
1	0	Sugar		500
1	0	Butter		500
1	4	Flour		625
	3 1/2	Egg yolks		100
	1/8	Salt		4

Make into a paste and pin out very thinly. Cut into small rounds with a plain cutter and bake at 450° F (232° C) for about five minutes on a greased baking sheet. Remove carefully at once from the baking sheet and allow to cool on a rolling pin to allow them to take a curved shape.

Brush with apricot purée and sprinkle either with fine sugar nibs or roasted nib almonds. *(France)*

Vanilla Biscuits

lb	oz		kg	gr
1	8	Flour (soft)		750
1	0	Butter		500
	5	Sugar (icing)		150
	1 1/2	Vanilla sugar		45

Make a smooth paste and leave in a cool place for a while. Pin out to 1/8 in. (3 mm.) thick and cut out with a small fluted cutter. Spread with heavy meringue into which a little sugar has been stirred until it becomes glossy. Bake at 300° F (148° C) until a light fawn in colour. The biscuits should have a beautiful glossy surface and the edges of the meringue should lift up slightly.

Vanilla Marzipan Biscuits

Make a paste as for Barcelona Biscuits. Pin out to 1/8 in. (3 mm.) thickness and then into strips 1 1/2 in. (4 cm.) wide. Spread over the surface:

lb	oz		kg	gr
	8	Ground almonds		250
	8	Sugar		250
	4	Egg whites		125
		Vanilla		

Beat lightly together. Sprinkle with nib almonds, cut into diamonds and bake at 325° F (162° C) on paper lined baking sheets.

Vanilla Patience Biscuits

lb	oz		kg	gr
1	4	Sugar (icing)		625
	10	Egg whites		300
	12	Flour		375
	2	Vanilla sugar		60

Whip the icing sugar and egg whites to a stiff meringue. Fold in the flour and vanilla sugar sieved together. Pipe out in small drops on to waxed trays. Let stand in a warm room for some hours and bake at 360° F (182° C).

Vanilla Sticks - Vanille Bâtons

lb	oz		kg	gr
	7	Butter or margarine		200
	9	Flour		270
	3	Sugar (icing)		90
		Vanilla		
		Pinch of salt		

Mix a paste of these ingredients. After cooling, it is rolled into a rectangle approximately 16 in. by 12 in. (40 × 30 cm.). Spread with royal icing which is made of 1 oz. (30 gr.) of egg white and about 5 oz. (150 gr.) of icing sugar, $^1/_2$ oz. (15 gr.) of cornflour, and a dash of vanilla. Let this icing dry, then cut into strips about 3 in. (8 cm.) wide. After this, cut into fingers $^3/_4$ in. (2 cm.) in width with the aid of a pastry wheel. Put the cookies on an ungreased baking sheet.

Bake in an oven at 338° F (170° C). The oven door should be slightly opened so that the steam can escape. *(Holland)*

Vanilla Sticks

lb	oz		kg	gr
2	0	Flour	1	
	8	Sugar (castor)		250
	12	Butter		375
	12	Egg		375
	$^3/_8$	Carbonate of ammonia		10
		Milk (sufficient)		
		Vanilla		

Make into a rather firm pastry and cut into little sticks. Bake at 360° F (182° C). *(Italy)*

Vendée Biscuits - Sablés vendéens

lb	oz		kg	gr
1	0	Flour		500
	11	Butter		330
	8	Sugar (castor)		250
	$^1/_4$	Salt		8
		Zest of 4 lemons		
		8 hard boiled egg yolks		

Make all the ingredients into a smooth paste, having previously forced the egg yolks through a sieve. Leave for two hours. Pin out to $^1/_4$ in. (5mm.), mark with a criss-cross patterned roller and cut out with a small triangular cutter. Bake at 420° F (216° C). *(France)*

Viennese Biscuits

lb	oz		kg	gr
1	0	Butter		500
	5	Sugar (icing)		150
	2	Egg		60
1	0	Flour (soft)		500
		Vanilla		

Cream the butter, sugar and egg together. Cream in half the flour and then the other half. With a savoy bag and a small star tube, pipe out small stars on to greaseproof papered baking sheets. Place half a glacé cherry on each and bake at 400° F (204° C). *(Austria)*

Viennese Horseshoe Biscuits

lb	oz		kg	gr
	7	Sugar (icing)		200
	15	Butter		450
	2 $^1/_2$	Egg whites		75
	2 $^1/_2$	Cocoa paste		75
1	0	Flour		500

Mix the sugar, butter and egg whites to a smooth paste, stir in the cocoa paste and lastly the flour. Using a No. 5 star tube, pipe out in small horseshoe shapes on to lightly greased baking sheets and bake at 400° F (204° C). Sandwich immediately with strawberry jam and dip both ends in milk chocolate and chocolate vermicelli. Alternatively dust lightly with icing sugar. *(Illustration page 634.)* *(Switzerland)*

Weesp Cookies - Weespermoppen
(from the City of Weesp)

lb	oz		kg	gr
2	4	Blanched almonds	1	125
2	11	Sugar (granulated)	1	300
	1 $^1/_2$	Lemon peel, finely chopped		50
	5 $^1/_2$	Egg		175
	1 $^1/_2$	Egg yolks		50

Mix these ingredients into a medium stiff macaroon paste. From this paste, roll ropes with a diameter of 1 in. (2.5 cm.) and roll these ropes in fine castor sugar, and cut them into slices of 1 oz. (30 gr.) and place them on a greased baking sheet. Let the tops dry for a while and then bake at a temperature of 437° F (225° C). The cookies should be somewhat tough once they are cooled. *(Holland)*

Wine Biscuits

lb	oz		kg	gr
1	0	Flour (soft)		500
	10	Butter		300
	8	Sugar		250
	2 $1/2$	Egg		75

Rub the butter into the flour finely. Make a bay and place in the sugar and the egg. Make into a smooth paste. Pin out to $1/8$ in. (3 mm.) in thickness and cut out with small fancy cutters. Finish the tops with nib almonds, sugar nibs, coconut etc. Bake at 400° F (204° C).

Zurich Nuts

lb	oz		kg	gr
	10	Sugar (icing)		300
	8	Butter		250
	7	Egg		200
	3 $1/2$	Ground almonds		100
1	0	Flour		500
	$1/8$	Vanilla sugar		5

Cream the butter and sugar, adding the egg a little at a time. Blend in the almonds, the vanilla sugar and lastly the flour. Using a star tube, pipe out in drops on to lightly greased baking sheets. Bake at 400° F (204° C). When cold, sandwich with nougat paste, dip the tops in couverture and place on paper.

(Switzerland)

XVII. Petits Fours

There is probably no confectionery so little understood in this country as petits fours.

The term is French. The word 'petit' means small and 'four' means oven or bakehouse. Colloquially, petits fours are simply small pieces that have been baked.

Petits fours may be broadly subdivided into petits fours secs and petits fours glacés. 'Sec' is a French word meaning dry; 'glacé' means iced. It is generally agreed that petits fours secs should contain no cream although chocolate is permissible. *(Illustrations pages 509, 634.)*

The word 'petit' is important because petits fours must be so small that they can be placed in the mouth in one piece.

In the quest for a greater understanding of this subject, it is conceded that the generic title covers all very small pastries and fancies, whether the bases be genoese or other pastes. The variety thus becomes endless and provides scope for further new varieties.

There is a further means of defining the difference between petits fours secs and glacés, for the former are those small unglazed confections that can be used as a decoration on, or served with desserts, such as ice creams, charlottes, fruit salads, coupes etc.

Petits fours glacés may be placed on the buffet table, or served with coffee at dinners, parties, particularly late parties, or at any such function where elegance, variety and small quantities are of importance.

Remembering always that they must be very small, petits fours secs can be made from the following:

(a) biscuits (d) puff pastry
(b) meringues (e) short pastry
(c) almond mixings

Petits fours glacés can be made from:

(a) any of the above that are additionally iced or creamed
(b) choux paste
(c) genoese
(d) small tartlets
(e) japonaise
(f) babas

There are three items that contain nothing baked:

(a) caramelized fruits (c) jellies
(b) fondants

All but petits fours secs should be placed in small paper cases.
(Illustrations pages 510-512.)

PETITS FOURS SECS

Almond Bread - Mandelbrot

lb	oz		kg	gr
1	4	Flour		625
1	0	Sugar (brown)		500
	8	Butter		250
	8	Almonds (strip)		250
	$1/8$	Ground cinnamon		4
	4	Egg yolks		125

Cream the butter and sugar and add the yolks. Add the rest of the materials and make into a paste. Mould into a long rectangle about $1\,^3/_4$ in. by $1\,^1/_4$ in. (4.5×3 cm.) across and refrigerate. Cut off slices about $1/4$ in. (5 mm.) thick and place, cut side down, on to baking sheets. Bake at 380° F (193° C). *(Switzerland)*

Almond Petits Fours - Fours aux Amandes

lb	oz		kg	gr
1	0	Blanched almonds		500
1	0	Sugar (granulated)		500
	15	Egg whites (approx.)		450
	$3\,^1/_2$	Apricot jam		100
		Zest of 1 lemon		

Grate the almonds, mix them with the sugar and 8 oz. (250 gr.) egg whites and then grind. Next, mix the rest of the egg whites, the jam and grated lemon zest, until a smooth consistency is obtained. From a savoy bag fitted with a small star pipe, make various shapes on parchment paper. Decorate with almonds or candied fruit. Flash the following day in a hot oven 482° F (250° C) and then brush with a solution of gum arabic. To remove the petits fours, pour some water between the paper and the baking sheet while the latter is still hot. These biscuits can be piped on to rice paper, which does not need to be removed. *(France)*

Almond Soufflés - Soufflés aux Amandes

lb	oz		kg	gr
	8	Egg whites		250
1	0	Almond paste		500
	$3\,^1/_2$	Apple jelly		100

Mix the almond paste and apple jelly together and then fold in the stiffly whisked egg whites. Deposit in small paper cases and bake in a slow oven. *(France)*

Amaretti

Use the same recipe as for those sold as individual cakes *(page 533)*. They should be made much smaller. *(Switzerland)*

Angelica Macaroons - Macarons à l'Angélique

lb	oz		kg	gr
1	0	Blanched almonds		500
1	5	Sugar (granulated)		650
	7	Egg whites		200
	5	Angelica		150

Grind the almonds and the sugar, add the egg whites and finely chopped angelica.

Deposit on greaseproof paper in the shape of crowns and sprinkle with granulated sugar. *(France)*

Anisette Biscuits - Anis

These are made in the same way as those sold as individual biscuits. Make much smaller. *(Switzerland)*
(Recipe page 466.)

Apricot Macaroons - Macarons Abricot

lb	oz		kg	gr
1	0	Almond paste		500
	8	Sugar		250
	$1\,^3/_4$	Apricot pulp		50

Mix all the ingredients into a stiff paste. Next make into little balls and roll these in granulated sugar. Place on baking sheets lined with parchment paper and make hollows with a piece of wood shaped like a pencil in the centre of each ball. After baking at 360° F (182° C), fill the hollows with hot apricot jam. *(France)*

Biarritz Biscuits

See recipe *page 468*.

Buttered 'S' Scrolls - 'S' au Beurre

lb	oz		kg	gr
	14	Butter		400
	7	Sugar (icing)		200
	3 1/2	Egg		100
	1 1/2	Egg yolks		45
1	5	Flour		650
		Zest of 1 lemon		
		Pinch of salt		

Cream the butter and icing sugar together, then mix in the egg and egg yolks. Remove from the mixing machine and blend in the flour and lemon with a spatula. Using a savoy bag fitted with a star pipe, deposit the mixture on to ungreased baking sheets and bake in a medium oven 400° F (204° C). *(France)*

Calissons d'Aix

lb	oz		kg	gr
1	0	Blanched almonds		500
	3 1/2	Sugar		100
1	0	Syrup		500
		Orange flower water		

Grind the almonds with sugar, moistening with water. Prepare the syrup until it reaches a density of 24 degrees Beaumé and mix it with the almond paste; flavour with the orange flower water and allow to evaporate over a low gas until a thick paste remains. Roll out the latter on top of rice paper between two strips of wood to ensure a uniform thickness of 1/5 in. (5 mm.). Ice the top with royal icing, cut out into oval shapes and bake for about 10 to 15 minutes in a slow oven. Dip one side in chocolate. *(France)*
(Illustration page 484.)

Chocolate Cornets

lb	oz		kg	gr
	7	Ground almonds		200
1	5	Sugar (icing)		650
	7	Flour		200
	7	Egg whites		200
	7	Milk		200

Beat the almonds, sugar and whites well, blend in the flour and milk to make a paste of spreading consistency. Pipe in small bulbs on greased baking sheets and bake at 400° F (204° C). Remove at once from the baking sheets and form into cones. Fill with a mixture of praline buttercream and ganache. Dip the ends into vanilla couverture. *(France)*

Chocolate Kisses - Baisers au Chocolat

lb	oz		kg	gr
	15	Egg whites		450
2	0	Sugar	1	
	10	Water		300
1	8	Couverture		750

Cook 1 lb. 12 oz. (875 gr.) of the sugar with the water to a temperature of 243.5° F (117.5° C). Beat up the egg whites with the rest of the sugar until stiff. Pour in the cooked sugar slowly, stirring all the time. Meanwhile melt the couverture and mix it with a little boiling water until a smooth mixture of medium consistency is obtained. Next add the melted couverture to the meringue mixture, stirring in the remainder gradually. From a savoy bag fitted with a plain pipe, small balls are piped on to a baking sheet. Bake in a slow oven 320-356° F (160-180° C).

When the biscuits are cold, sandwich them together with vanilla ganache. *(France)*

Chocolate Macaroons - Macarons au Chocolat

lb	oz		kg	gr
1	0	Almonds		500
2	0	Sugar (granulated)	1	
	15	Egg whites (approx.)		450
	3 1/2	Unsweetened chocolate		100

Grind the almonds, sugar and half the egg whites. Put this mixture in a basin and stir in the rest of the egg whites and the melted unsweetened chocolate. Deposit on greaseproof paper as for hazelnut macaroons and bake at 360° F (182° C). When baked, mark the centres of the macaroons and put a spot of chocolate fondant in the middle of each. *(France)*

Chocolate Soufflés - Soufflés au Chocolat

lb	oz		kg	gr
	8	Egg whites		250
1	0	Sugar (castor)		500
	5	Water		150
	8	Vanilla couverture		250

Prepare some Italian meringue mixture with the egg whites and cooked sugar. Stir in the couverture which has been diluted with a little boiling water, so that it has a very smooth, creamy consistency. Pipe little sticks on to greased baking sheets, using a savoy bag fitted with a plain pipe. Bake in a slow oven (about 356° F [180° C]) until the soufflés can easily be removed from the baking sheets. The inside of the soufflés should be soft and moist. *(France)*

Chocolate 'S' Scrolls - 'S' au Chocolat

Recipe I

lb	oz		kg	gr
	12	Egg whites		375
1	12	Sugar (castor)		875
	14	Vanilla couverture		400
	8	Water		250

Recipe II

lb	oz		kg	gr
	12	Egg whites		375
1	12	Sugar (castor)		875
	5	Unsweetened chocolate		150
	8	Water		250

The basic recipe is the same as for Italian meringue mixture *(page 207)*. When the mixture is quite stiff, fold in the melted unsweetened chocolate with a spatula. Pipe out into 'S' shapes through a star pipe on to greased baking sheets. If using the first recipe, bake immediately, but if using the second recipe, leave to dry slightly before baking in a slow oven (about 356° F [180° C]). The inside of the scrolls when cooked should be soft and moist. *(France)*

Cinnamon Leaves I - Zimtblätter

lb	oz		kg	gr
1	4	Flour		625
	12	Butter		375
	12	Sugar (castor)		375
	12	Ground hazelnuts		375
	4	Egg		125
	1/4	Cinnamon		7
		Zest of lemon		

Lightly mix the butter and sugar and add the egg. With the rest of the materials, make a smooth paste. Pin out to about 1/8 in. (3 mm.) thick and cut out with a leaf shaped cutter. Mark in the veins with a knife and arrange on a lightly greased baking tray. Bake at 380° F (193° C). When cold, dip halfway into chocolate. *(Switzerland)*

Cinnamon Leaves II

lb	oz		kg	gr
	8	Sugar (icing)		250
	8	Butter		250
	7	Ground hazelnuts		200
	3 1/2	Egg		100
	1 1/2	Egg yolks		45
	1/2	Cinnamon		15
1	0	Flour		500
		Lemon zest		
		Salt (a pinch)		

Make a paste with all the ingredients and pin out 1/4 in. (5 mm.) thick. Cut out with a leaf shaped cutter, mark in the veins with the back of a knife and leave to dry. Bake at 380° F (193° C) and, while still hot, brush with water icing. *(Switzerland)*

Cinnamon Stars - Etoiles à la Cannelle

lb	oz		kg	gr
1	12	Almonds		875
1	12	Sugar (granulated)		875
	10	Egg whites		300
	1/2	Cinnamon		15

Grind the almonds and sugar together, put on the table and make into a paste, stirring in the egg whites and cinnamon. Roll out the paste between two strips of wood so as to ensure uniform thickness. Coat with

▲ Selection of Biscuits and Petits Fours secs, p. 330, 407, 408, 414, 476, 513
Selection of Small Cakes and Biscuits, p. 413, 418, 443, 449, 487 ▼

509

510 ▲ Pasticceria Mignon, p. 524-529

Pasticceria Mignon, p. 524-529 ▼

▲ Pasticceria Mignon, p. 524-529

Pasticceria Mignon, p. 524-529 ▼

511

▲ Petits Fours glacés, p. 520

Viennese Petits Fours glacés, p. 520, 524 ▼

royal icing and cut out with a star-shaped pastry cutter. Place on a baking sheet lined with parchment paper and bake in a medium oven. This type of petit four can be listed among those made for Christmas. *(France)*

Coffee Soufflés - Soufflés au Café

lb	oz		kg	gr
	8	Egg whites		250
1	0	Sugar (castor)		500
	5	Water		150
	1/4	Instant coffee		8

Make an Italian meringue with the egg whites, sugar and water *(page 207)*. Pipe small bulbs on to a lightly greased baking sheet. Sprinkle with strip almonds. Bake at 250° F (121° C). *(France)*

Cressini

lb	oz		kg	gr
1	0	Flour		500
	5	Sugar (icing)		150
	10	Butter		300
	2	Egg yolks		60
		Salt (a pinch)		

Mix all the ingredients together to form a pliable pastry. Form it into ropes, flatten the sides to a square shape and refrigerate. Cut into slices about 1/4 in. (5 mm.) thick, place on to lightly greased baking sheets, cut side down and bake at 360°F (180°C). When cold, decorate with spots of fondant in different colours. *(Italy)*

Croquettes suisses

lb	oz		kg	gr
1	0	Flour		500
	12	Butter		375
	9	Sugar (icing)		275
	1 1/2	Egg whites		50
	1 1/2	Egg yolks		50
	6	Almonds (split)		180
	6	Cherries		180
		Zest of lemon		

Cream the butter and sugar together and add the egg yolks. Fold in the flour and add the cherries and almonds. Cool the paste and then fashion into a long square strip and refrigerate. Cut into 1/4 in. (5 mm.) slices and arrange, cut side down, on to baking sheets. Bake at 380° F (193° C). *(Switzerland)*

Duchesses

lb	oz		kg	gr
1	2	Egg whites		560
1	0	Sugar (castor)		500
	12	Hazelnuts		375
	3 1/2	Flour		100

Whisk the egg whites with half the sugar until stiff. Grind the hazelnuts and the rest of the sugar and add the flour.

Lightly mix all the ingredients with a spatula. Pipe out small sticks on to a greased baking sheet, sprinkle with finely grated hazelnuts and bake in a slow oven. Sandwich the biscuits together with praline flavoured ganache. *(France)*
(Illustration page 509.)

Equal Weight Cakes

lb	oz		kg	gr
	10	Sugar (castor)		300
	10	Egg		300
	10	Flour		300
	10	Butter		300
	1/16	Bicarbonate of soda		2
		Lemon zest		

Lightly whip the sugar, egg and soda, blend in the zest, flour and the melted, lukewarm butter. Fill into small greased fluted pans and bake at 400° F (204° C). *(Switzerland)*

Florentine Biscuits - Florentins

Recipe I

lb	oz		kg	gr
1	2	Evaporated milk		560
1	2	Dairy cream		560
	10	Butter		300
	14	Honey		400
	14	Sugar (castor)		400
1	5	Blanched almonds		650
1	5	Candied orange peel		650

513

Recipe II

lb	oz		kg	gr
1	2	Dairy cream		560
1	2	Sugar (castor)		560
	3 1/2	Butter		100
	3	Honey		90
1	2	Almonds		560
	15	Candied orange peel		450
	1 3/4	Flour		50

Cook the evaporated milk, cream, sugar, honey and butter in a copper pan at a temperature of 220° F (104° C), stirring the while. Remove from the heat and add the flaked almonds and the chopped candied orange peel. Pour on to a marble slab and leave to cool. Deposit on greased baking sheets in round balls and place in the oven. When the biscuits are half cooked, trim them with a round pastry cutter and return them to the oven. When they are cold, coat the under surfaces of the biscuits with vanilla or milk couverture and place, chocolate side down, on to a greaseproof paper. Leave to set, then peel off the paper, recoat with couverture and make a wavy surface with a comb scraper. *(Illustration page 482.)*

Frascati

See recipe *page 432.*

Half-Moons - Demi-Lunes

lb	oz		kg	gr
1	5	Walnuts		650
	14	Blanched almonds		400
1	10	Sugar (castor)		800
	12	Egg whites		375
	10 1/2	Flour		315
	2 3/4	Couverture (melted)		80
	1 3/4	Honey		50

Grind the walnuts, almonds, sugar and egg whites into a paste. Blend in the flour, couverture and honey. Allow to stand in the refrigerator, then roll out the paste between two strips of wood to ensure uniform thickness. Coat with pink royal icing and cut out half-moons with a plain pastry cutter. Put on a baking sheet lined with parchment paper and bake in a medium oven. This type of petit four is usually made for Christmas. *(France)*

Harlequins - Arlequins

Roll out some sablé paste thinly and cut out pieces with a plain pastry cutter 3/4 in. (2 cm.) in diameter. When they have been baked, sandwich them together with apricot jam. Finish off by covering the tops, half with yellow and half with red coloured apricot jam. Dip in water icing and leave to dry. *(France)*

Hittnauer Makronen

lb	oz		kg	gr
	10	Ground almonds		300
1	4	Sugar (castor)		625
	7	Egg whites		200
	6	Water		180
		Chocolate paste		

Whip up the almonds, egg whites and 4 oz. (125 gr.) of sugar. Boil the rest of the sugar and the water to 255° F (123° C). Pour this into the almond mixture and beat until cold. Pipe out small drops on to greased and floured baking sheets using a plain tube. Colour the rest of the mixing with the chocolate paste and pipe it directly over the white drops, completely covering them. Allow the drops to dry, then cut a cross on each with a sharp blade. Bake at 360° F (182° C). *(Switzerland)*

Italian Macaroons - Macarons italiens - Mandorlato all'italiana

lb	oz		kg	gr
	15	Egg whites		425
1	0	Sugar (castor)		500
1	3 1/2	Blanched almonds		600
		Zest of 2 lemons		
		Juice of 1 lemon		

Beat up the egg whites and sugar over a gentle heat, using a mixing machine.

When the mixture becomes stiff, add the flaked, blanched almonds and the zest and juice of the lemons. Deposit small spoonfuls of the mixture on greaseproof paper. Bake at 250° F (121° C) and when cooked, brush with a solution of gum arabic.

Macaroons - Macarons

There is a large variety of macaroon mixings but the most common are those mentioned under 'Macaroon Mixtures', and under 'Biscuits'.

Madeleines

lb	oz		kg	gr
	10	Sugar (icing)		300
	10	Egg		300
	4	Egg yolks		125
	7	Flour		200
	3 ½	Cornflour		100
	10	Butter (melted)		300
		Lemon zest		

Whip the sugar, egg, yolks and zest to a stiff sponge. Fold in the sieved flour and cornflour and lastly the butter. Fill into well greased shell patty pans and bake at 400° F (204° C). *(France)*

Madeleines

lb	oz		kg	gr
	10	Egg yolks		300
	7 ½	Sugar (castor)		220
	5	Blanched almonds		150
	5	Butter		150
	7 ½	Egg whites		220
	10	Flour		300
		Water (a little)		
		Lemon zest		

Grind the almonds finely with a little water and beat them with half the sugar, the egg yolks, zest and butter until light. Whisk the egg whites and the rest of the sugar to a stiff snow, fold into the almond mixture and lastly blend in the flour. Fill into greased shell patty pans and bake at 400° F (204° C). When cool, turn out and coat with chocolate.

Sultanas, orange peel and currants may be mixed with the madeleine mixture. In this case, a formula consisting of equal weights of sugar, egg, flour and butter should be used and the total weight of fruit should not exceed the weight of flour. For fruited madeleines, the best coating is rum icing (rum plus icing sugar). *(Switzerland)*

Mochas

Sandwich a thin sheet of genoese with mocha buttercream, refrigerate and cut out with a 1 in. (2.5 cm.) plain cutter. Spread the top and sides with the same buttercream and mask with roasted nibbed almonds. Dust the top lightly with icing sugar and place a tiny whirl of mocha buttercream in the centre. *(France)*

Nougatines

lb	oz		kg	gr
1	7	Sugar (granulated)		700
	10	Blanched almonds		300
	1 ¾	Glucose		50
	1	Butter		30
	3 ½	Dairy cream		100

Make light-coloured nougat out of all the ingredients, adding the butter and dairy cream last. Spread to a rectangular shape 10 × 14 in. (25 × 35 cm.) on an oiled marble slab, allow to cool, then coat with vanilla couverture. Decorate with wavy lines on the surface using a comb scraper and cut out in small rectangles. *(France)*

Oak Leaves - Feuilles de Chêne

lb	oz		kg	gr
1	0	Blanched almonds		500
1	10	Sugar (granulated)		800
	9	Flour		270
	10	Egg whites		300
	3 ½	Milk		100
		Zest of 2 lemons		

Grind the almonds and sugar into a paste, moistening with some of the egg whites. Then put it into a bowl and add the rest of the egg whites, the flour and milk. The same consistency is required as for cornet mixing. Using an oak-leaf shaped stencil, deposit on a greased baking sheet. Place on each oak-leaf a hazelnut and bake in a medium oven. *(France)*
(Illustration page 138.)

Orange Flower Soufflés - Soufflés à la Fleur d'Oranger

Use the same meringue mixture as for Coffee Soufflés, but flavour with orange flower water. Pipe out and bake in the same way, that is to say in a very slow oven 250° F (121° C), since these soufflés must remain white. *(France)*

Orange or Pistachio Balls - Boules à l'Orange ou Boules à la Pistache

Add some orange or pistachio flavouring to almond paste and colour it orange or green respectively. Shape into little balls and roll them in granulated sugar. Place them on a baking sheet lined with parchment paper and bake in a hot oven 482° F (250° C). It is recommended to use a double tray and not to bake for too long so that the centres remain moist. *(France)*

Orange Soufflés - Soufflés à l'Orange

Use the same mixture as for Coffee Soufflés, but flavour with some orange essence and add orange colouring. Pipe out on to greased baking sheets and bake in a slow oven 300° F (149° C). These soufflés have an oval shape. *(France)*

Parisian Kisses - Baisers parisiens

This sort of petit four is made with a meringue mixture beaten up over a source of heat. *(Spanish meringue mixture, page 207.)*

From a savoy bag fitted with a plain pipe, small balls of this mixture are piped out on to parchment paper. Sprinkle with granulated sugar before baking in a slow oven 320° F (160° C). The mixture can be given different colours and flavours, for instance:

Colour	Flavour
yellow	lemon
pink	raspberry
blue	kirsch
green	pistachio
white	almond

The kisses are sandwiched together with a stiff buttercream flavoured according to the colour of the kisses themselves. *(France)* (For buttercream, recipe II, *page 228.*)

Parisian Macaroons - Macarons parisiens

lb	oz		kg	gr
1	0	Almonds		500
	8	Sugar (granulated)		250
	3	Egg whites		90

Grind the almonds, sugar and egg whites. Make this mixture into little balls and, after dipping them in egg whites, place them on rice paper. Cut some almonds in half and press four pieces on each ball in the form of a square. Flash in a hot oven 450° F (232° C) and brush with a solution of gum arabic. *(France)*

Pearled Tuiles

lb	oz		kg	gr
	8	Butter		250
	8	Sugar (castor)		250
	10	Flour		300
	2 1/2	Egg yolks		75
		Salt (a pinch)		

Make all the ingredients into a pliable pastry and pin out 1/8 in. (3 mm.) thick. Cut out with a 1 in. (2.5 cm.) plain cutter, place on to greased baking sheets and bake at 450° F (230° C). Immediately after baking, bend them round a rolling pin to give them a curved shape, brush with apricot purée while still hot and sprinkle with roasted nibbed almonds or sugar nibs. *(France)*

Pertikus-Gipfel

lb	oz		kg	gr
1	0	Butter		500
	12	Sugar (castor)		375
	12	Ground hazelnuts		375
1	0	Flour		500
	2	Egg whites		60
	1/8	Cinnamon		3
	1/8	Nutmeg		3

Cream the butter, sugar and hazelnuts adding the egg whites by degrees. Blend in the flour and spices. Using a savoy bag fitted with a star tube, pipe the mixing in long strips on to the table. Cut into pieces about 2 in. (5 cm.) long and arrange in horseshoe shape on to baking trays. Bake at 380° F (193° C). *(Switzerland)*

Petits-Fours - Gevulde Progres Koekjes

Make a paste with the following ingredients:

lb	oz		kg	gr
	9	Nib almonds		270
	3 1/2	Sugar (granulated)		100
	1	Flour		30
	7	Egg whites		200
	5	Sugar (granulated)		150

Mix the almonds with 3 1/2 oz. (100 gr.) of sugar. Then add the flour. Beat the egg whites with 5 oz. (150 gr.) of sugar to a stiff meringue foam. Quickly fold the dry sugar/almond mixture into the meringue. Grease the baking sheet and dust it with flour. Pipe various shapes on the baking sheet. Sprinkle the products with nib almonds. Bake at a temperature of 356° F (180° C). Decorate in various ways using chocolate, fruits, nuts, cut-out flowers, etc. *(Holland)*

Pistachio Macaroons - Macarons à la Pistache

lb	oz		kg	gr
	10	Blanched almonds		300
	7	Pistachio nuts		200
1	12	Sugar (granulated)		875
	12	Egg whites		375
	1/2	Vanilla sugar		15

Finely grind the almonds, pistachio nuts, sugar, egg whites and vanilla sugar. To deepen the pale green colour, add a few drops of green colouring. Pipe the mixture on to greaseproof paper and bake in a slow oven. When baked, pistachio macaroons should show fine cracks to reveal the light green colour inside. *(France)*

Pistachio Rolls

lb	oz		kg	gr
	14	Almonds		400
1	3 1/2	Sugar (castor)		600
	7	Flour		200
	7	Egg whites		200
	7	Milk		200

Grind the almonds and sugar without moistening. Add the whites, flour and milk and mix well. Stencil out on to greased and floured baking sheets. Bake at 380° F (195° C) and while still hot fashion into tubes using an oiled rod. When cold, fill with pistachio marzipan *(page 211)* softened with kirsch and dip both ends of each roll in couverture.
(France)

Pretzels

Small almond, chocolate and vanilla pretzels can be made and included in a selection of petits fours, using the recipe on *page 442*. *(Germany)*

Punch Balls

These are made with high quality cuttings from genoese or sponge. They are placed in a bowl, sprinkled with rum and mixed well with buttercream, a little apricot jam and a few sultanas soaked in rum. This mixture is deposited in small heaps on paper and refrigerated. When firm, each heap is rolled into a ball and finished in the same way as truffles. Ordinary chocolate coating may be used instead of couverture. After dipping twice, roll into chocolate vermicelli, dust lightly with icing sugar and place into paper cases. These petits fours should be sold fresh.
(Illustration page 634.)   *(Switzerland)*

Raspberry Rosettes - Rosettes à la Framboise

lb	oz		kg	gr
	10	Butter		300
	4 1/2	Sugar (icing)		130
	10	Flour		300
	3 1/2	Cocoa powder		100
	1 1/2	Egg yolks		50

Cream the butter and icing sugar and then add the egg yolks. Remove from the mixing machine and blend in the flour which has been sifted with the cocoa. Pipe in the form of rosettes on ungreased baking sheets. Bake in a medium oven 400° F (204° C). Sandwich together with softened pink, raspberry flavoured almond paste. *(France)*

Richelieu

lb	oz		kg	gr
1	0	Egg whites		500
1	2	Sugar (castor)		560
	15	Blanched almonds		450
	2 3/4	Flour		75

Whisk the egg whites with the sugar until stiff and, with a spatula, mix in the flour and finely ground almonds. Using an oval shaped stencil, deposit the mixture on a greased baking sheet dusted with flour. Bake in a slow oven and remove the biscuits from the baking sheet as soon as they are baked. When they are cold, sandwich them together with praline flavoured ganache. To finish off, dip the biscuits in milk or vanilla couverture and mark the tops with a three pronged fork. *(France)*

Russian Cigarettes - Cigarettes russes

lb	oz		kg	gr
	10	Flour		300
1	0	Sugar (icing)		500
	12	Egg whites		375
	7	Dairy cream		200
	9	Butter (melted)		270
	1/2	Vanilla sugar		15

Put all the ingredients into a bowl in the same order as shown in the recipe and beat up, using a hand whisk, until the mixture becomes smooth. Then let it become firm in the refrigerator for two hours. Pipe out bulbs on to an ungreased baking sheet, not forgetting to leave enough space between each piece. Bake in a medium oven and then immediately roll round small wooden or metal cylinders. These biscuits are quite popular with ice cream. *(France)*

Schmelzbrötchen

lb	oz		kg	gr
	5	Egg		150
	7	Sugar (castor)		200
	7	Milk		200
	14	Flour		400
	3 1/2	Butter		100
	1/16	Bicarbonate of soda		2

Whip the egg and sugar together to a stiff sponge. Dissolve the soda in the milk and add to the sponge together with the flour and the melted butter. Fill into small greased fluted patty pans and bake at 400° F (204° F). These should be sold fresh. *(Switzerland)*

Small Fruits

These petits fours should be made very small and it is essential that they be absolutely fresh. To make them, pipe out an Othello sponge mixture on paper into small, round, oval, pear-shaped or oblong bases and bake. On removing from the oven, make a cavity on the underside of each by pressing the centre or carefully scooping a little away. Sandwich the bases with an appropriate filling, glaze lightly with well boiled apricot purée, wrap in pale coloured, thinly pinned out almond paste, then paint. When finished, place in paper cases.

The following fillings are suitable:

1. Half buttercream and half apricot jam, flavoured with liqueur.

2. Confectioner's custard strongly flavoured with liqueur or essence.

An assortment of fruits may consist of apples, pears, peaches, apricots, pineapple, oranges, bananas or chestnuts, or vegetables such as potatoes, tomatoes, etc.

For peaches, it is preferable to use a peach coloured almond paste which is pinned out thinly, and wrapped around the bases. A mark is made on one side with the back of a knife. A little carmine colour is carefully applied with a little cotton wool to simulate ripeness.

Potatoes should have a wrapping of almond paste tinted pale pink. They are rolled into cocoa powder and the surplus is brushed off. The 'eyes' are made with the point of a fine icing tube. *(Germany)*

Tuiles
Recipe I

lb	oz		kg	gr
	12	Egg whites		375
	14	Sugar (icing)		400

lb	oz		kg	gr
	5	Flour		150
	5	Candied orange peel		150
1	0	Blanched almonds		500
	5	Butter		150

Recipe II

lb	oz		kg	gr
	12	Egg whites		375
1	0	Blanched almonds		500
	12	Sugar (icing)		375
	3 1/2	Flour		100
		Zest of 2 lemons		

Lightly whisk the egg whites and blend in all the other ingredients, adding the melted butter last. Using a stencil, deposit the mixture on greased baking sheets and bake until the biscuits begin to change colour. Remove from the oven and allow to cool, then put back in the oven and, when the biscuits have a golden colour, take them off the baking sheets and place them immediately in trough-like moulds so as to give them a concave shape. The reason for baking the biscuits twice is to ensure that they are evenly baked.

(France)

Tuscanians - Toscani

Base

lb	oz		kg	gr
	4	Butter		125
1	0	Marzipan		500
	10	Egg		300
	2	Flour		60

The marzipan and butter are beaten together and the egg slowly added followed by the flour. The mixture is spread on to a paper lined tray and half baked.

Filling

lb	oz		kg	gr
1	4	Butter		625
1	4	Sugar (castor)		625
1	4	Glucose		625
1	12	Almonds (flaked)		875
	7	Water		200

All the materials are slowly brought to the boil continuing for about two minutes. The mixture is then spread on the base. Complete the baking and, while still hot, cut into small pieces. When cold, dip the base and sides in chocolate. *(Italy)*

Viennese Petits Fours - Viennois

Roll out a piece of viennese paste to a thickness of about $1/10$ in. (3 mm.) and cut out into biscuits with an oval pastry cutter. Bake them in a medium oven and, when they are cold, sandwich them together with a milk ganache to which praline has been added. To finish off, dip the biscuits half way in couverture.

Walnuts - Noix au Beurre

lb	oz		kg	gr
1	8	Butter		750
	10	Sugar (icing)		300
	4	Egg whites		125
1	12	Flour		875
	1/8	Powdered vanilla		4
		Pinch of salt		

Lightly cream the butter in the mixing machine, then add the icing sugar, egg whites, vanilla and salt. Remove the beater and work in the flour with a spatula. Using a savoy bag fitted with a star pipe, deposit this mixture on to greased baking sheets in the shape of half nuts. Bake in a medium oven, then sandwich the biscuits together with apricot jam. Finally, dip one end of each in some vanilla couverture.
(Illustration page 634.) *(France)*

Zurich Walnuts - Noix de Zurich

Thin out some marzipan with egg whites. Pipe on to parchment paper in the shape of half nuts. Leave to dry overnight, then flash in a hot oven and brush with gum arabic. Remove the paper and sandwich the pieces together immediately. It is advisable to use a double tray. There will then a minimum of bottom crust so that they stick together easily. This type of petit four is finished off in the same way as the walnuts in the preceding recipe.

(Switzerland)

NOTE

In concluding this section on petits fours secs, mention should be made of the fact that there are certain types of biscuits which are usually made in biscuit factories, but which can also be profitably produced by individual craftsmen, provided that they have adequate machinery and ovens available.

Petits Fours Glacés

These attractive delicacies with their different flavours and appearance must be made in a methodical manner. Providing that the work is organized systematically, petits fours glacés can be a profitable line. Moreover they allow the able and careful craftsman to present some charming table decorations, especially for running buffets at important functions.

Petits fours glacés are prepared on bases which have been made previously; they are covered as required with different sorts of creams or custards (buttercream, lemon custard, ganache, etc.). The bases are obtained by lining variously shaped little moulds with viennese or milanese paste or filling with genoese sponge mixture.

There may also be included in this category of petits fours those which are made from choux paste or assorted meringue mixtures.

It should be mentioned that in some cases petits fours glacés are called Parisian petits fours but, strictly speaking, these should be made in nougat cases; however both types are finished off in the same way.
(Illustrations pages 483, 512).

A SELECTION OF PETITS FOURS GLACÉS

Berolinas
Split a sheet of butter sponge *(page 196)* and sandwich with kirsch buttercream. Refrigerate until the buttercream is firm, then cut out into small ovals and spread with redcurrant jelly. Dip the tops in maraschino flavoured fondant and mask the sides with buttercream and chocolate vermicelli. Decorate with a small piece of pistachio nut and gold leaf. *(Germany)*

Caracks - Caraques
Make some tartlet cases with viennese paste and, after baking, fill with ganache. Leave in a cool place and then coat with green pistachio flavoured fondant. Finish with a spot of chocolate fondant. *(France)*

Cerisettes
Make some tartlet cases with milanese paste and, after baking, fill them with kirsch flavoured buttercream. In the centre of each tartlet, place half a glacé cherry which has been soaked in kirsch. Coat with white kirsch flavoured fondant. Decorate with two short lines of chocolate. *(France)*

Chestnut Turrets
Cut out thin, round bases of chocolate sponge about 1 in. (2.5 cm.) in diameter and pipe a dome of chestnut buttercream on top. Coat with cooked chocolate icing *(page 244)* and decorate with a mimosa ball. *(Austria)*

Chocolat
Pipe a little ball of ganache on to a base of milanese pastry and surround it with three discs of praline nougat. Leave in a cool place and then dip in chocolate fondant. *(France)*

Chocolate Drums - Tambours au Chocolat
Sandwich together pieces of chocolate sponge with chocolate buttercream. Leave in a cool place and then cut out with a round pastry cutter. Dip in chocolate flavoured fondant. Decorate with a silver ball. *(France)*

Chocolate Nougat I
Using a $^3/_4$ in. (2 cm.) round cutter, cut circles from genoese sandwiched with mocha

buttercream. Spread cream over top and sides, roll in nibbed sugar and pipe a star of mocha buttercream in the centre.
(France)

Chocolate Nougat II

Pipe a bulb of ganache on to small sweet pastry bases and cover with three tiny discs of praline nougat. Refrigerate, then dip into chocolate fondant and decorate with a mocha bean or a small piece of glacé cherry. *(France)*

Eaglets - Aiglons

Cut out thin round bases of genoese sponge about ³/₄ in. (2 cm.) in diameter. Decorate the top with a cone of coffee buttercream, using a piping bag and round tube.

As soon as the cream is set, dip into kirsch fondant. Spread couverture very thinly on a piece of stiff white paper and detach from the paper when cold. Cut the couverture into lozenges with a hot knife and stick three of them into each fancy.
(France)

Eclairs

Pipe out some small éclairs about 1 in. (2.5 cm.) long. Bake and fill with whipped dairy cream either coffee or chocolate flavoured. Coat the top with fondant.

Finish off with a sweet coffee bean or a little yellow mimosa ball. *(France)*

Gypsies - Gitanes

Cut out genoese as for Eaglets and pipe on an oval of strawberry butter cream with a plain pipe. Put in refrigerator to set, dip into fondant of a different colour, cut open with a knife dipped in hot water and slightly press the edges apart. *(France)*

Hazelnuts - Avelines

Fill some baked boat-shaped cases with buttercream containing chopped hazelnuts. Coat with pink fondant, mark with a chocolate line and finish off with half a blanched hazelnut. *(France)*

Hazelnut Petits Fours - Fours aux Noisettes

lb	oz		kg	gr
	7	Hazelnuts		200
	7	Blanched almonds		200
	14	Sugar (granulated)		400
	10	Egg whites (approx.)		300

Finely grind all the ingredients together and deposit on greaseproof paper. Bake in the same way as for almond petits fours. Glaze with water icing as soon as the petits fours come out of the oven. *(France)*

Hazelnut Soufflés - Soufflés aux Noisettes

lb	oz		kg	gr
	8	Egg whites		250
1	0	Sugar		500
	7	Hazelnuts		200

Whisk the egg whites and sugar until stiff. Then fold in carefully with a spatula the blanched and finely chopped roasted hazelnuts. Pipe on to greaseproof paper in the form of sticks and bake them until they are crisp, 300° F (149° C). Finish off by coating with vanilla fondant.
(France)

Japonais

The bases are made of japanese mixing and are about ³/₄ in. (2 cm.) in diameter. They are then finished in the same way as larger individual cakes. Chapter XV.
(France)

Jellies

lb	oz		kg	gr
4	4	Fondant	2	125
	15	Water		450
	4	Gelatine		125
		Colour		
		Flavour		

Bring the fondant and water to the boil and remove from the heat. Stir in the gelatine previously melted in a little warm water. Add the desired colour and flavour. Allow to cool a little and pour into a greaseproof paper lined tray. Place a sheet of greaseproof paper on top to remove any froth. When set, cut into cubes and roll into sugar. Present in small paper cases. Here are two examples of flavour and colour:

Lemon juice and rum - yellow.
Grand-Marnier - purple red.

Lemons - Citrons

Fill some small baked oval shaped cases with lemon curd. Leave to set in a cool place and coat with yellow, lemon flavoured fondant. Decorate, using a paper bag filled with chocolate and top with a quarter of a glacé cherry. *(France)*

Macaroon Petits Fours

lb	oz		kg	gr
4	0	Macaroon paste	2	
		To yield 100 petits fours		

Pipe out the macaroon paste to the small shapes required on to sheets of paper and bake at 350° F (176° C). When cool, spread the undersides with cherry or raspberry jam, pipe on buttercream flavoured with liqueurs or spirits, decorate with roasted chopped almonds and candied fruit, then refrigerate.

For chocolate petits fours, pipe on ganache and coat with plain or milk chocolate couverture.

For buttercream petits fours, coat with various well flavoured fondants when the buttercream is firm.

For decoration, the following are recommended: pistachio nuts, mocha beans, chocolate shavings, cherries or gold leaf. *(Germany)*

Marronnettes

Using oval shaped pieces of viennese pastry as bases, pipe on top whirls of maraschino flavoured chestnut cream. Dip in pale violet fondant. Decorate one end with a quarter of a glacé cherry. *(France)*

Martinique Moccatines

Cut genoese in small squares and garnish the top with coffee buttercream mixed with a little marzipan and rum. Let it set, dip into coffee fondant flavoured with rum and decorate with a chocolate coffee bean. *(France)*

Nut Boats

lb	oz		kg	gr
	3 ½	Ground hazelnuts		100
	3 ½	Ground almonds		100
	7	Sugar (icing)		200
	10	Egg yolks		300
1 ½		Egg		45
	4	Egg whites		125
1 ½		Flour		45
	4	Butter (melted)		125

Whip the egg, egg yolks, hazelnuts, almonds and half the sugar to a stiff sponge. Whip the egg whites and the rest of the sugar to a stiff snow and fold into the sponge together with the flour. Lastly blend in the butter which should be cool. Spread about ¾ in. (2 cm.) thick on to a greased and floured baking sheet. Bake at 375° F (190° C). After cooling, split three times and sandwich thinly with nut buttercream. Refrigerate and cut out with a small boat-shaped cutter, coat with coffee fondant and place a quarter of a caramelized hazelnut in the centre. *(Austria)*

Pavés

Sandwich together two pieces of genoese sponge with coffee or kirsch flavoured custard. Leave in a cool place and then cut up into small squares (sides about ½ in.) (1 cm.). Dip in the appropriate flavoured fondant. Decorate with a sweet coffee bean or a quarter of a glacé cherry. *(France)*

Petits Fours Expo

lb	oz		kg	gr
2	0	Persipan*	1	
1	2	Egg		560
	8	Egg yolks		250
	8	Flour		250
	8	Butter (melted)		250
	7	Water		200

* One part nut and one part sugar.

Work the persipan to a smooth paste with the water, then beat until foamy with the egg and egg yolks. Stir in the flour and the melted butter and spread on to a paper lined baking sheet 18 in. (45 cm.) square and bake for about 30 minutes at 375° F (190° C). Store in a refrigerator for a time. Divide into six pieces of equal size, then carefully split each piece twice. Make certain to use the undersides (from which the paper has been peeled) to make the tops or covers. Sandwich as follows: spread the bottom layer with well flavoured buttercream, place the second layer on it, spread this with buttercream, cover with the top layer and press it down firmly. Mask the top thinly with buttercream and refrigerate until firm. After 2 or 3 hours place a thin cover of almond paste (1 : 1) on top and coat thinly with apricot purée. Cut the squares into smaller squares, diamonds or triangles, or cut out with a small round or oval cutter. Thorough refrigeration is essential to ensure clean-cut edges. The diameter should not exceed $^3/_4$ in. (2 cm.).

The petits fours may be decorated in one or two ways:

1. They may be coated with fondant at 115° F (45° C), which should be of the same flavour as the buttercream used. After coating, they are placed in paper cases and decorated with a fine pipe *(see Designs for Petits Fours pages 80, 81).*

2. The petits fours may be topped with a quarter glacé cherry, almonds, pistachio nuts or small bulbs of buttercream, then dipped into fondant. The fondant over the cherry, nuts or buttercream is either dipped into coarse granulated sugar or have a design piped on top. If bulbs of buttercream are used, it is best to pipe them on paper, flatten them a little and then refrigerate. They can easily be removed from the paper with a small knife. When finished, the petits fours are placed in paper cases.

Particular attention should be paid to the need to make petits fours very small and to flavour the buttercream and fondant discreetly. The careful use of colour is also important. Liqueurs or spirits should be used with particular care. Any cuttings may be used to make small punch balls to avoid waste. *(Switzerland)*

Pineapple I - Ananas

Line some small oval, shell-shaped moulds with milanese paste and, after baking, fill with chopped glacé pineapple flavoured with kirsch. Coat with kirsch flavoured fondant and, using a chocolate filled paper bag, decorate with criss-cross lines. The fondant should be fairly liquid so as to allow the pineapple to show through.
(France)

Pineapple II - Ananas

Roll out some milanese paste and cut out pieces with a fluted pastry cutter (diameter 1 in. (2.5 cm.). Bake these and on them pile up cones of a mixture made of chopped, crystallized pineapple bound together with a little kirsch flavoured apricot jam. Dip in water icing and leave to dry on a wire rack. Decorate with a small piece of red, glacé cherry.

Pirandellos

Line small boat-shaped pans with milanese pastry and bake blind. Spread thinly with couverture and half fill with a mixture of chopped pineapple macerated in kirsch and with apricot purée added. Cover with a topping of maraschino buttercream finishing with sloping sides then refrigerate. When set, coat thinly with vanilla couverture and decorate with gold leaf. *(Germany)*

Pistachio Diamonds - Losanges Pistache

Sandwich two pieces of genoese sponge together with pale green, pistachio flavoured buttercream. Put in a cool place and then cut up into small diamonds. Dip in green, pistachio flavoured fondant. Decorate, using a paper bag filled with chocolate. *(France)*

Pistachio Soufflés - Soufflés à la Pistache

lb	oz		kg	gr
	7	Egg whites		200
	8	Sugar (castor)		250
	3 $^1/_2$	Pistachio nuts		100

523

Whisk the egg whites and sugar until stiff and fold in the finely ground pistachio nuts. Add a few drops of green colouring, deposit in paper cases and bake in a slow oven 300° F (149° C). Ice with pistachio flavoured fondant. *(France)*

Sarah
These petits fours are made in the same way as those sold as individual cakes *(page 461)*. *(France)*

Simone
Spread thin pieces of genoese with chestnut purée. Glaze with apricot purée and pipe an oval of Italian meringue on top with a large plain pipe. Sprinkle very finely stripped roasted almonds on top diagonally and put in a moderate oven for 3 minutes to dry the meringue mixture.

Viennese Petits Fours glacés
Ingredients for 140

lb	oz		kg	gr
4 ³/₄		Egg yolks		135
	12	Egg whites		350
	8	Marzipan		250
	8	Sugar (castor)		250
	8	Flour		250
	8	Hot butter		250

Beat the egg yolks, marzipan and 3 ¹/₂ oz. (100 gr.) sugar until frothy. Whip the egg whites and the rest of the sugar to a stiff snow and blend into the egg yolk mixture with the flour. Lastly, fold in the hot butter.

Spread on a baking sheet in a rectangular shape 28 in. by 20 in. (70 × 50 cm.) and bake at 392° F (200° C) for 20 minutes.

After baking, cut into 3 equal parts and sandwich with 2 lb. (1 kg.) raw marzipan brought to a spreading consistency with kirsch. Cut into 1 in. (2.5 cm.) squares, coat with flavoured fondant and decorate. *(Illustration page 512)*. *(Germany)*

Walnuts - Noix
Fill some small baked square tartlet cases with buttercream containing chopped walnuts. Coat with fondant and top with half a caramelized walnut. *(France)*

Walnut Cubes
Sandwich a sheet of butter sponge with maraschino buttercream mixed with ground walnuts. Refrigerate well, cut into cubes of not more than 1 in. (2.5 cm.) and dip into chocolate fondant. Place half a walnut dusted with icing sugar in the centre of each. *(Germany)*

Walnut Sablés - Sablés aux Noix

lb	oz		kg	gr
1	0	Flour		500
	8	Butter		250
	7	Sugar (icing)		200
	4 ¹/₂	Chopped walnuts		140
	1 ³/₄	Egg		50
		Pinch of salt		

First make as for ordinary sablé paste and with it form some ropes. Leave these to harden in a cool place and cut up into portions with a knife. Place on baking sheets and bake in a medium oven. As soon as they come out of the oven, glaze the sablés with kirsch flavoured water icing. *(France)*

PETITS FOURS - PASTICCERIA MIGNON - ITALY

In Italy, petits fours glacés are known as 'pasticceria mignon'. Petits fours secs are termed 'pasticceria secca', with the exceptions of small items of the biscuit type which have been piped out with a bag and pipe. These are known as 'petits fours'. Examples of pasticceria mignon follow. *(Illustrations pages 510-511.)*

Acorns - Ghiande
Split a sheet of maddalena genoese and soak with maraschino syrup. Spread with imperial cream containing chopped hazelnuts. Cut into ovals and glaze with apricot purée. Dip into coffee fondant and one end into milk chocolate vermicelli.

Amarena Sports - Amarene Sports
Sandwich pasta frolla biscuits in pairs with kirsch flavoured buttercream. Pipe a ring of the same cream on top and fill in with sour black cherries with thickened juice.

Amaretto - Tartellette all'Amaretto
Line small round frangipane tins with pasta frolla and bake blind. Pipe in some crème pâtissière and cover with half an apricot. Glaze with apricot purée and place half a pistachio nut on top.

Arancini - Oranges
Split maddalena and soak with orange liqueur. Spread with orange buttercream. Cut out in circles and glaze with apricot purée. Dip into orange flavoured white fondant and finish with a small circle of orange peel and a citron leaf.

Assabesi
Sandwich maddalena, after soaking with curaçao, with imperial chocolate cream. Cut into circles.

Cover with the same cream and roll into milk chocolate vermicelli. Dust with icing sugar.

Bocche di Leone
Sandwich two chocolate cut-outs with whipped cream.

Bombetta
Tiny bombe moulds are greased and three parts filled with margherita genoese mixing *(page 201)*. When baked and cool, a piece is hollowed out and filled with cream. The mignon is dipped into chocolate, and placed on a cut-out disc of almond paste so that the bottom is sealed. Before filling with cream, the hollow is brushed with liqueur.

Some examples follow.

Bombetta Coffee - Bombette Moka
Brush with strong coffee and fill with coffee buttercream. Dip into coffee fondant and finish with half a walnut.

Bombetta Hazelnut - Bombette Nocciola
Brush with rum and fill with hazelnut cream. Dip into milk chocolate. Place a caramelized hazelnut on top.

Bombetta Lemon - Bombette al Limone
Brush the hollow with vanilla liqueur and fill with lemon cream. Decorate the top with a citron leaf.

Bombetta Orange - Bombette all'Arancia
Brush with orange liqueur and fill with orange cream. Pipe a spot of orange fondant on top.

Bombetta Walnut - Bombette alle Noci
Brush with vanilla liqueur and fill with walnut cream. Place half walnut on top.

Brasiliani
Sprinkle pasta frolla baked circles with rum and pipe on each a bulb of gianduja, mixed with coarse sieved praline croquant. Dip into milk chocolate mixed with nib hazelnuts. Decorate with a pinch of chopped pistachio nuts.

Cannoli
Pin out puff pastry to about $1/8$ in. (3 mm.) thick and cut into strips about $3/4$ in. (2 cm.) wide. Damp them with water and roll them on to cream horn tins, starting from the bottom. Brush with water and cover with fine granulated sugar. Bake at 400° F (204° C) so that the surface is slightly caramelized. Fill with whipped vanilla flavoured dairy cream.

Cannoli Saratoga
Proceed as above but half fill with whipped dairy cream and complete the filling with gianduja whipped cream.

Cannoli Toscani

As above, but fill with a cream composed of equal parts whipped dairy cream and gianduja cream. Dust with icing sugar.

Cannoli Zabaglione - Cannoli allo Zabaglione

Proceed as described for Cannoli above, but wind the pastry strips round metal cylinders. When cool, fill with zabaglione and dust with icing sugar.

Cappucci

Pipe cone shaped spikes with chestnut paste on to pasta frolla biscuits soaked with vanilla liqueur. Fix in three pine nuts near the peak and refrigerate. Dip into chocolate.

Cherry Bowls - Tartellette alla Ciliegina

Into baked pasta frolla cases, pipe a little crème pâtissière and dust with icing sugar.

Place in the centre one cherry and glaze with apricot purée.

Cherry Sports - Sport con Ciliegia

Between two discs of pasta frolla, spread maraschino buttercream. Brush with apricot purée and dip into chocolate up to the top edge. Finish with half a cherry.

Chocolate Chantilly - Scodellini Chantilly

Into chocolate cups, place discs of maddalena; sprinkle curaçao liqueur and then pipe in a ring of chocolate cream. Pipe a tall cone of zabaglione cream. Refrigerate and finish with a spiral of chocolate.

Chocolate Kirsch - Scodellini Chantilly

Place discs of maddalena soaked with kirsch into chocolate cups. With a star tube, pipe a whirl of Italian Chantilly cream. Place a candied cherry on top.

Chocolate Pineapple - Hawaï

Into a little chocolate case, place some chopped pineapple. Pipe on top a whirl of whipped dairy cream. Finish with a piece of pineapple.

Chocolate Violets - Malaga

Take little round cut-out circles of rum soaked maddalena, sandwiched with chocolate buttercream. Dip into chocolate and pipe a circle of chocolate buttercream on top. Finish with a crystallized violet.

Choux

Very small cream buns and eclairs, filled with whipped dairy cream come under the heading of pasticceria mignon. Varieties of petits choux are given on *page 341*.

Small eclairs are made and finished in many ways. Here are three examples:

1. Pipe out small éclairs with a plain pipe. Fill with hazelnut crème pâtissière and glaze the top with coffee fondant.

2. As above but fill with chocolate crème pâtissière and glaze with chocolate fondant.

3. Pipe out with a star tube. Fill with a mixture of zabaglione and whipped dairy cream. Dust with icing sugar.

Choux à la Crème - Bigne alla Panna

1. Into small petits choux, pipe vanilla flavoured whipped dairy cream.

2. Fill with caramel flavoured cream and dip the tops in caramel sugar.

3. Fill with zabaglione cream. Cover the top with pink fondant and over pipe in trellis fashion with coffee fondant.

4. Fill with coffee cream. Coat the tops with yellow fondant and place a sugar coffee bean on top.

Cocktails - Tebaldi

Split maddalena and soak with orange liqueur syrup. Spread with chocolate buttercream. Cut into small rectangles and glaze with apricot purée. Dip into chocolate and, with white fondant, pipe a treble clef.

Coffee Walnut - Glassate alle Noci

Take small circles of vanilla liqueur sprinkled maddalena, sandwiched with walnut coffee cream, and dip them into coffee coloured and flavoured fondant. Place a piece of walnut on top.

Cri-Cri

Into baked pasta frolla cases, pipe a whirl of chocolate buttercream. On top, place balls made from a mixture of chopped hazelnuts and chocolate, rolled in chocolate vermicelli and dusted with icing sugar.

Delina - Scodellini allo Zabaglione

Into chocolate cups place discs of maddalena soaked with maraschino syrup. Pipe on top a bulb of zabaglione buttercream. Spin fine threads of chocolate at right angles on top and place a pistachio nut in the centre.

Diplomatici

Spread crème pâtissière on a sheet of baked puff pastry. Cover with maddalena genoese of the same size. Soak with vanilla liqueur. Spread again with the same cream and top with a sheet of puff pastry. Refrigerate and cut into squares. Dust with icing sugar and place into paper cases.

Fiamme

Proceed as for Capucci but soak the pasta frolla biscuits with vanilla syrup. Pipe a tall cone of chestnut paste with a star pipe. Refrigerate and then dip into chocolate.

Italians - Italiani

Proceed as for Diplomatici but use pasta frolla instead of puff pastry. Spread the top with imperial cream, sprinkled with caramelized nibbed hazelnuts. Cut into cubes and place into paper cases.

Kirsch Glacés - Glassate alla Ciliegina

Sandwich two layers of sponge with kirsch flavoured buttercream, cut into circles and glaze with apricot purée. Dip into maraschino flavoured white fondant. Add two cherries and pipe stalks and leaf outlines with chocolate. The leaves are filled in with green jelly.

Maraschino - Tranci di Maraschino

Split maddalena, sprinkle with maraschino and spread with maraschino flavoured buttercream. Cover the top with a thin sheet of pink coloured almond paste. Refrigerate and then cut into squares. Dip to the top edge in chocolate. Pipe on the top a small spot of yellow fondant and finish with a small piece of candied cherry.

Medusa - Meduse

Soak small pasta frolla biscuits with rum. Pipe a tall cone shape of crema arlecchini *(page 238)* against which place three pieces of praline croquant. Dip into chocolate and sprinkle with a little chopped pistachio nut.

Mignon Amarena - Visciole Mignon

Into baked pasta frolla cases place sour black cherries with thickened juice. Place a split almond on top.

Mocha - Glassate al Caffè

Slice maddalena and soak with strong coffee. Sandwich with coffee buttercream and cut out into small circles. Dip into coffee fondant and pipe a small rosette in the centre. Top with a sugar coffee bean.

Nests - Nidi

Split maddalena and soak with rum syrup. Spread with imperial chocolate cream.

Cut into circles, glaze with apricot purée and dip into coffee fondant. Finish with a circle of the same cream into the centre of which yellow fondant is piped.

Nougatines Sports - Sport Nougatine

Sandwich two discs of pasta frolla with nougat buttercream. Brush with apricot purée. Dip into roasted nib hazelnuts. Place a strip of paper across the top and dust with icing sugar. Remove the paper carefully.

Olivettes - Olivette

Proceed as for acorns but use crème de cacao for soaking. Glaze with apricot purée. Dip into chocolate fondant and finish with half a pistachio nut.

Olivettes with Orange and Cherry - Olivette all'Arancia e alla Ciliegia

Proceed as for Olivettes but use maraschino liqueur for soaking and maraschino buttercream for spreading. Dip half into pink fondant and finish with a small disc of orange peel and two angelica diamonds. Dip the other half into caramel fondant and finish with half a cherry and two citron leaves.

Persian Delights - Persiani

Pin out puff pastry thinly and cut into strips about 2 $1/2$ in. (6 cm.) wide and about 8 in. (20 cm.) long. In half of them cut incisions at right angles $1/2$ in. (1 cm.) apart. (These will be the tops.) Wash with egg yolks and after a sufficient rest, bake at 400° F (204° C). When cool, spread the bases with Chantilly cream and cover with the tops. Pipe the same cream into the incisions. Cut into slices.

Porto Rico - Tranci Moka

Sandwich two layers of sponge with coffee buttercream and place a thin sheet of coffee almond paste on top. Refrigerate and then cut into small rectangles. Dip to the top edge in chocolate and finish with piped chocolate design, a small rosette of white cream and a sugar coffee bean.

Rosettes - Rosette

Take baked pasta frolla cases and pipe in each a bulb of pink coloured, kirsch flavoured buttercream. Refrigerate and dip into chocolate. Make two incisions in the bulbs and sprinkle with a little chopped pistachio.

Roulot

Take a strip of swiss roll sponge soaked with vanilla liqueur and thickly spread with white vanilla buttercream. Place a row of strawberries along the length and roll up. Refrigerate and cut into small slices after covering the outside with cream and rolling into ground hazelnuts.

Sacripantini

Sandwich sponge bases with crème pâtissière after soaking with vanilla syrup. Cut into circles and cover with imperial vanilla cream. Roll into dry coarse maddalena crumbs and dust with icing sugar.

Scodellini Apricot - Scodellini Albicocca

Pipe crème pâtissière into baked pasta frolla cases and dust with icing sugar. Place half an apricot on top. Glaze with apricot purée and sprinkle chopped pistachio nuts on top.

Scodellini Pineapple - Scodellini Ananas

Pipe some crème pâtissière into baked pasta frolla cases and dust with icing sugar. Place a ring of pineapple on top into the centre of which place a cherry. Glaze with apricot purée.

Scodellini Violetta

Pipe a whirl of white cream on to pasta frolla biscuits. Top with chocolate cut-out discs with a crystallized violet on top.

Sicily - Tranci all'Arancia

Soak maddalena with orange liqueur and sandwich with orange buttercream. Cover with orange coloured and flavoured almond paste. Cut into strips and then into triangles. Glaze with apricot purée and dip to the top edge in chocolate. Finish with a rosette of cream, a small disc of orange peel and two diamond pieces of angelica.

Soupirs

Take baked pasta frolla cases and pipe in a tall cone of either hazelnut or pistachio buttercream. Refrigerate and dip the hazelnut cream mignons into pale yellow fondant and the pistachio mignons into pale green fondant. Starting at the top, pipe a neat spiral of the same fondant.

Soupirs Chantilly

Into baked pasta frolla cases soaked with vanilla syrup, spread apricot purée. Pipe a tall spike of whipped dairy cream mixed with crème pâtissière. Pipe two parallel lines with chocolate from one side to the other over the tip of the spike, and fill in with apricot purée.

GENEVA ASSORTMENT - ITALY

These are square or round cases generally made with couverture, filled with small cubes of liqueur flavoured genoese. Cream is piped in and other decorations added. Here follows a selection.
(Illustrations page 510.)

Bombetta Taormina

Bake maddalena mixture in small bombe moulds. When cold, cut the centre out and fill with ricotta cream. Brush with apricot purée and mask with caramelized nib pistachio nuts. Place half a candied cherry on top.

Cherry

As for Delizia but soak with maraschino. Fill in with coffee crème pâtissière topped with a candied cherry.

Coffee

Proceed as for Delizia but soak with a strong infusion of coffee. Pipe in a tall star of coffee cream which is topped with a sugar coffee bean.

Cremolini

As for Marsolini but soak with vanilla liqueur and fill with Italian crème pâtissière. Dust with icing sugar.

Delizia

Place pieces of maddalena soaked with maraschino into the chocolate bases and add crème pâtissière. Decorate with chocolate shavings and with a pistachio nut in the centre.

Marsolini

Proceed as for Bombetta Taormina. Soak with marsala and fill with zabaglione. Dust with icing sugar.

Nocciole

Proceed as for Delizia but soak the maddalena with rum. Pipe in a rosette of nougat whipped cream and finish with a caramelized hazelnut.

Orange

As for Delizia, soaking with orange liqueur. Fill level with orange cream. Finish with a rosette of whipped dairy cream sprinkled with chopped candied orange peel.

Super

Pipe tall stars of whipped dairy cream mixed with sieved praline croquant on to chocolate discs. Refrigerate and then dip into thin couverture. Dip the tips into granulated sugar.

XVIII. Almond Goods

Almond Bows

lb	oz		kg	gr
1	0	Sugar (granulated)		500
1	0	Almonds (nib)		500
	12	Egg whites (approx.)		375
	⅛	Ground cinnamon		3
1	1½	Flour		50
		Lemon zest		

Cook this mixture first and spread it on to wafer paper. With a sharp knife cut into strips and bake on a curved surface at 380° F (193° C).

Almond Crescents

Cut out crescent shapes from sweet pastry and proceed as for almond rings, except that the macaroon paste can be spread on with a palette knife. Dip into nibbed almonds. Bake at 350° F (176° C).

To provide variety, the crescents, after baking, can be decorated with spun chocolate or the tips may be dipped into chocolate. Alternatively, the crescents may be baked without the nibbed almond topping, instead, one single split almond is placed in the centre of each.
(Illustration page 393).

Almond Drops and Fingers

lb	oz		kg	gr
1	0	Marzipan		500
	12	Sugar (castor)		375
	6	Egg whites (approx.)		180

Reduce the marzipan to a smooth paste with some of the egg whites. Add the sugar and the remaining whites and mix thoroughly.

Care must be taken to avoid lumps in the mixture.

A wide variety of almond fancies can be made from this mixing by piping out drops and fingers on to greaseproof papered trays and sprinkling the tops with either nibbed or flaked almonds. Bake at 375° F (190° C) on reversed baking sheets. When cold they are sandwiched with either apricot jam, praline buttercream or pistachio marzipan cream.

Finish with either (a) chocolate (dipped or spun), (b) a spot of coloured fondant or, (c) dusting with icing sugar.

Almond Fingers

Take either of the mixtures given under the heading 'Macaroon Biscuits', and pipe out in finger form on to greased and floured baking trays. Sprinkle thoroughly with nib almonds, shaking off the surplus.

Bake at 360° F (182° C). When cool, remove from the trays and sandwich them together in pairs with ganache buttercream, flavoured with kirsch. Dip the ends in chocolate.

Almond Horseshoes

lb	oz		kg	gr
1	0	Raw marzipan		500
	8	Sugar (fine granulated)		250
		Zest of lemon		
		Egg white		
		Flaked almonds		

Mix the marzipan and sugar together with sufficient egg white to make a rather firm paste of piping consistency. Pipe small ropes on to flaked almonds. Roll the ropes in the almonds and arrange them in horseshoe shape on to greased and floured baking sheets. Bake at 350° F (176° C). When cold, pipe a line of chocolate along the top. *(Germany)*

Almond Meringue Puffs

Pin out puff pastry to about $1/8$ in. (3 mm.) thick and cut rectangles of 3 in. by 4 in. (8 × 10 cm.). Dampen the edges and pipe in some of the following mixture:

lb	oz		kg	gr
1	4	Sugar (castor)		625
	15	Egg whites		450
	12	Ground almonds		375
		Lemon zest		

Whip the whites to a stiff snow, gradually adding the sugar. Fold in the almonds and the zest. Fold over the pastry to enclose the filling, pressing the edges to seal and putting the fold underneath when arranging on to baking sheets. Wash with egg and sprinkle with flaked almonds. Bake at 420° F (217° C).

Almond Ovals

Cut out sweet pastry into oval shapes and proceed as for almond crescents, finishing with a single split almond in the centre. Bake at 350° F (176° C). When cold, dip the ends obliquely into chocolate.

Almond Puffs

Pin out puff pastry to about $1/4$ in. (6 mm.) thick and cut out with an oval fluted cutter. Reduce stock macaroon paste with egg to spreading consistency and cover the tops of the pastry. After a sufficient rest, bake at 380° F (193° C). Split when cold and pipe in raspberry jam and vanilla flavoured whipped dairy cream.

Almond Rings

Cut out rings of sweet pastry, using a fluted cutter and half bake them. Take the macaroon mix as for congress tarts and pipe on to the rings, using a savoy bag with a small plain pipe. Dip each into nibbed almonds and bake on double trays at 350° F (176° C). The rings may be decorated with spun chocolate or the bases may be dipped into chocolate.
(Illustration page 393).

Almond Slices I

Line a baking sheet with sweet pastry and half bake. Spread with raspberry jam and then with a layer of macaroon mix. Sprinkle with flaked almonds and bake at 350° F (176° C), on a double tray. When cold, cut into squares, diamonds or fingers. Decorate by partial dipping into chocolate. A tray about 16 in. by 16 in. (40 × 40 cm.) will need approximately 2 lb. (1 kg.) of sweet pastry and 3 lb. (1 $1/2$ kg.) of macaroon mix.

Almond Slices II

Take 1 lb. (500 gr.) pieces of sweet pastry and make into ropes about the width of a baking sheet. Make a depression along the centre with a rolling pin and place carefully along the width of the baking sheet after pinching the edges with the fingers. Proceed exactly the same with the rest of the pieces, placing them closely against each other on the sheet. Place a stick firmly against the last one to prevent spreading during baking.

Pipe a little raspberry jam along the centre of each and then pipe in about 8 oz. (250 gr.) of prepared macaroon mixture. Sprinkle with strip almonds and bake at 360° F (182° C). When cold, separate the strips and cut each into fingers.

Almond Triangles

Take rich sweet pastry and line a baking sheet to a thickness of about $1/4$ in. (6 mm.).

Wash with egg and sprinkle with flaked almonds. Bake at 350° F (176° C). Cut into slices about 3 in. (8 cm.) wide and then into triangles. Dip into chocolate so that it covers the base and comes just over the top edge.

Almond Wafers

lb	oz		kg	gr
1	4	Raw marzipan		625
	7	Egg whites (approx.)		200
	14	Sugar (icing)		400
	1/8	Cinnamon		3
	7	Flour		200

Mix all the ingredients together and stencil 2 in. (5 cm.) circles on to greased and floured baking sheets. Bake at 370° F (187° C), and when cool, sandwich together in threes with a beaten mixture composed of marzipan, fondant and chocolate praline nougat. Dip into chocolate and place a split almond in the centre of each. *(Germany)*

Amaretti

Warm a macaroon mix to 120° F (49° C), adding a little more egg white. Pipe out on to greased and floured baking sheets. The mixture should just flow. Leave for some hours until the surface has crusted and then with the finger tips, push the circles into squares carefully. Dust well with icing sugar as soon as they are piped out. Bake at 350° F (176° C). *(See also page 506).*

Apricot Almond Rings

Bake rings of rich sweet pastry cut out with a plain 2 1/2 in. (6 cm.) cutter, taking out the centres with a smaller plain cutter. When cool, pipe the following round the ring:

lb	oz		kg	gr
2	0	Raw marzipan	1	
1	0	Apricot jam (sieved)		500
	2	Rum		60

Blend half the apricot jam with the marzipan until it is free from lumps, then add the rest of the jam and the rum. Dip the rings into coarsely chopped roasted almonds and then into plain chocolate. Spin with either milk or white chocolate.

Bananas

lb	oz		kg	gr
	11	Raw marzipan		320
	3 1/2	Sugar (castor)		100
	2 3/4	Egg whites		80

Make a macaroon paste out of the above ingredients, shape into 20 'bananas' and bake. After baking, invert, decorate with piped lines of vanilla buttercream, place half a real banana on each macaroon banana and coat it with chocolate couverture. Sprinkle both ends with chopped pistachio nuts and the middle with a little gold leaf. *(Germany)*
(Illustration page 480.)

Bethmännchen

lb	oz		kg	gr
4	0	Marzipan	2	
	2	Honey		60
		Split almonds		

Mix the marzipan with the honey, pin out and cut into 1/2 oz. (15 gr.) pieces. Mould each piece into a ball, decorate with three split almonds and arrange on waxed baking sheets *(see glossary)*. Flash in a hot oven and glaze with hot gum arabic solution. *(Germany)*
(Illustration page 391.)

Brenten

lb	oz		kg	gr
4	0	Raw marzipan	2	
	2	Honey		60

Mix the marzipan with the honey and pin out 3/8 in. (1 cm.) thick. Use a modelling tool to impress various figures on it, then cut up and place on to waxed baking sheets. Bake for about 20 minutes at 360° F (180° C). *(Germany)*
(Illustration page 391.)

Chocolate Macaroons

lb	oz		kg	gr
1	0	Almonds (blanched)		500
1	8	Sugar (granulated)		750

533

lb	oz		kg	gr
	8	Egg whites		250
	6	Cocoa powder		180
		Vanilla		

Grind the almonds finely with the sugar and mix with the egg whites, cocoa powder and vanilla to a paste of piping consistency, adding a little more whites if necessary. Pipe out on to paper lined baking sheets and bake at 360° F (180° C) on double trays. When cold, the underside may be dipped in couverture. *(Germany)*

Christmas Macaroons

Take cooked macaroon paste and use a plain tube to pipe out triangles, rings, ovals and other shapes as desired on to greased and floured baking sheets. Decorate with small pieces of glacé cherry, angelica, almonds or pineapple and bake at 360° F (180° C). *(Germany)*

Cinnamon Macaroons - Zimtmakronen

Flavour macaroon paste with cinnamon and pipe out on to paper with a plain tube to make medium-sized macaroons. Pipe a whirl of the paste on top with a star tube and press a small piece of yellow glacé cherry into the centre. As soon as the macaroons are baked, glaze them with apricot purée. *(Germany)*

Coconut Macaroons

lb	oz		kg	gr
1	8	Sugar (castor)		750
1	0	Desiccated coconut (coarse)		500
	12	Egg whites (approx.)		375
		Vanilla		

The mixture is heated until quite warm and then placed in small heaps on to a greased and floured baking sheet and baked at 360° F (182° F) on double baking sheets. *(Germany)*

Congress Tarts

Line patty pans with sweet pastry cut out with a fluted cutter. Pipe a little raspberry jam in the centre of each and then either of the Macaroon Biscuit mixings made a little softer. Soften some sweet pastry with warm water to a piping consistency and pipe a cross on each. Bake at 350° F (176° C). An alternative method of making up the first mixing is to first whip the whites to a stiff snow and to add half of them to the dry ingredients, mixing thoroughly. The balance of the whipped whites is then added gently to the mix.
(Great Britain)

Cream Macaroon Slices

Pin out puff pastry about 1/4 in. (6 mm.) thick and cut into strips about 2 1/2-3 in. (6-8 cm.) wide. Spread with French macaroon mix, made a little stiff. Mark lengthways with a coarse cut scraper and allow to rest for at least an hour. Cut into fingers. Bake at 380° F (193° C). When cool, split and pipe in raspberry jam and vanilla flavoured whipped dairy cream.

Dutch Macaroons

lb	oz		kg	gr
1	0	Marzipan		500
1	0	Sugar (icing)		500
	4	Sugar (castor)		125
	7	Egg whites (approx.)		200

Soften the marzipan with some of the egg whites and then add the sugars and the rest of the whites. Warm the mixture in a bain-marie to 90° F (32° C). Pipe out in small oval shapes, using a savoy bag and plain pipe, on to greaseproof paper lined baking sheets. Allow to stand for some hours then make a cut lengthways on each with a sharp blade. Bake at 325° C (162° C). When cold, remove by damping the back of the paper. Sandwich together with apricot jam. These macaroons may be coloured pink and flavoured with raspberry essence or flavoured with chocolate.

Egg Yolk Macaroons

lb	oz		kg	gr
1	8	Marzipan		750
	7	Sugar (icing)		200
		Egg yolks		
		Vanilla		

Mix the marzipan with the sugar and vanilla and sufficient egg yolks to bring it to piping consistency. Pipe the desired shapes on to waxed baking sheets *(see glossary)*, using a star tube. Bake at 360° F (180° C). Immediately after baking, glaze with apricot purée or water icing.

(Germany)

Frangipane Macaroons

Proceed as for Viennese Macaroons, but fill the rings with frangipane mix. Bake at 360° F (182° C). When cool, mask the centres with apricot purée and then with thin water icing. Return to the oven to set the icing glaze.

French Macaroons

lb	oz		kg	gr
1	0	Marzipan		500
1	4	Sugar (castor)		625
	12	Egg		375

Work the marzipan down with a little of the egg. Add the sugar and the rest of the egg and mix thoroughly.

1. Pin out puff pastry to about $1/4$ in. (6 mm.) thick and cut out oval shapes with a fluted cutter. After a sufficient time for the pastry to recover, spread the tops with the above mixture and dust with castor sugar. Bake at 380° F (193° C). When cold, split and spread with raspberry jam and pipe in vanilla flavoured whipped dairy cream.

2. As for No. 1, except that flaked almonds are sprinkled on the top instead of castor sugar. Bake and finish as above, then dust with icing sugar.

3. Line patty pans with thin puff pastry, docking the bottoms well. Pipe a spot of lemon curd in the bottom of each, followed by the French macaroon mixture, into which a little zest of lemon is mixed. Dust with castor sugar and bake at 380° F (193° C).

4. Line deep patty pans, plain or fluted, with sweet pastry and proceed as follows:

a. Pipe in a spot of raspberry jam and then pipe the French macaroon mixture. Sprinkle with flaked almonds. Bake and sprinkle with icing sugar.

b. As for *a*. Dust with castor sugar and place a split almond on the top of each.

c. As for *b* but place a small cut-out ring of sweet pastry on the top of each.

d. Line oval patty pans with sweet pastry. Pipe in a spot of apricot jam and fill with the macaroon mixture. Sprinkle with flaked almonds and bake at 380° F (193° C). Immediately on removal from the oven, brush with hot apricot purée and then with thin water icing, flavoured with fresh lemon juice. Return to the oven for a short time for the glaze to set.

e. Line deep round or boat shaped pans with sweet pastry. Pipe in a spot of raspberry jam and then some macaroon mixing. Pipe diagonal lines with softened sweet pastry after dusting with castor sugar.

Fruit Almond Slices

For these, special metal frames are advised. They are about 28-30 in. (70-75 cm.) long, 3 in. (7.5 cm.) wide and with sides about $3/4$ in. (18 mm.) high. Line them with sweet pastry and place chopped apples or pineapples, black or red currants, sliced apricots or peaches, etc., and cover with a French macaroon filling. Dust with castor sugar and sprinkle with flaked almonds. Bake at 380° F (193° C). When cold cut into fingers.

Fruited Macaroon Tarts

A variety of fruited macaroon tarts can be made as follows:

First line patty pans with sweet pastry and into the bottom, place some fruit such as pineapple, apple, black currants, red currants, apricot, mincemeat, etc. Cover the fruit with French macaroon paste, dust with castor sugar and bake at 380° F (193° C).

Ganache Crescents

Cut out crescent shapes from sweet paste using a plain cutter. Bake carefully at 350° F (176° C). When cold, spread the tops with ganache cream and dip into chopped roasted almonds or hazelnuts. Dip the tops into milk chocolate and finish by spinning with dark plain chocolate.

Honey Almond Tartlets

lb	oz		kg	gr
1	0	Sugar (granulated)		500
1	0	Butter		500
	9	Honey		275
2	0	Almonds (strip)	1	

Boil the sugar, butter and honey and stir in the almonds. When a little cool, spread in to patty pans which have been lined with sweet pastry. Bake at 370° F (187° C). Decorate with glacé cherries.
(Illustration page 421).

Lemon Macaroons

As for macaroon biscuits. After piping on to rice paper a depression is made in the centre of each with a round piece of wood dipped into water. Pipe in lemon curd. After baking, more curd is piped in if necessary.

Macaroon Biscuits

1. with ground almonds

lb	oz		kg	gr
	8	Ground almonds		250
1	0	Sugar (castor)		500
	1 1/2	Ground rice		45
	5	Egg whites (approx.)		150

The dry ingredients are mixed together, the whites are added and the mixture well beaten.

2. with marzipan

lb	oz		kg	gr
1	0	Marzipan		500
1	0	Sugar (granulated)		500
	5	Egg whites (approx.)		150

Work down the marzipan with part of the whites then add the sugar and the rest of the whites.

Beat thoroughly.

Macaroon biscuits are piped out on to baking sheets lined with rice paper. A split almond, half a glacé cherry or half a walnut is placed in the centre of each. Bake at once at 350° F (176° C).
(Illustration page 393.)

Macaroon Bows

lb	oz		kg	gr
1	0	Raw marzipan		500
1	0	Sugar (granulated)		500
	5	Egg whites (approx.)		150

Mix the ingredients to a paste of spreading consistency and spread on to wafer paper. Sprinkle with flake almonds if desired. Cut into strips, place on to baking sheets and bake at 340° F (170° C). On removal from the oven, press the strips on a rolling pin and remove when cold. The wafer paper side may be coated with semi-sweet couverture. *(Germany)*

Macaroon Creams

Dip the rounded surfaces of small macaroon biscuits into milk chocolate and allow to set. Turn them over and spread with raw marzipan reduced with stock syrup. Pipe on a rosette of whipped dairy cream, topped with roasted flaked almonds.

Macaroon Fancies

Cut out shapes with a variety of cutters from sweet pastry. Pipe on the following with a small star pipe.

lb	oz		kg	gr
1	0	Marzipan		500
	12	Sugar (castor)		375
	4	Egg whites (approx.)		125

Rub down the marzipan with some of the whites. Add the sugar and the rest of the whites and make into a smooth paste which is heated over a pan of hot water to about 110° F (43° C). Pipe patterns on the sweet pastry bases and allow to

stand for some hours to set. Bake at 420° F (217° C). Brush immediately on removal from the oven, with hot gum arabic solution. The fancies may be decorated with cherry and angelica before baking, or with piping jelly after baking and cooling.
(*Illustration page 634.*)

Macaroon Fancies

Beat equal parts raw marzipan and castor sugar with sufficient egg white to bring to piping consistency. Pipe spirals on to paper lined baking sheets, using a small star pipe.

Make a depression in the centre of half of them into which pipe raspberry jam. Bake at 360° F (182° C). When cool, sandwich in pairs (with the jam one on top) with beaten milk ganache flavoured with kirsch. When the ganache has set, dip into chocolate up to the top edge. *(Switzerland)*

Macaroon Favours

These are used in the decoration of Christmas trees. Take a well beaten macaroon mixing and, with a plain tube, pipe out triangles, rings, stars, ovals and other fancy shapes, on to greased and floured baking sheets. Decorate with cherries and angelica. Bake at 360° F (182° C). *(Germany)*

Macaroon Frangipane Slices

On a paper lined baking sheet, pipe lines of macaroon paste, leaving about $1/2$ in. (1.5 cm.) space between each line. Fill in the spaces with frangipane mix and bake at 350° F (176° C). Take a sheet of butter sponge of equal size and spread it with apricot jam. Place the almond/frangipane piece on top and cut into fingers.

Macaroon Rings

Take the mixing as given for Macaroon Fancies and pipe rings with a star tube on to greased and floured trays. Place a split almond at the join. Allow some time for the rings to set. Bake at 420° F (217° C). Coat the tops of macaroon biscuits with chocolate and set a ring on each before the chocolate sets.

Macaroons on Sweet Pastry

Cut out a variety of shapes from sweet pastry and pipe the macaroon mixture on the tops. Decorate with almonds, cherries, walnuts or angelica. Bake at 350° F (176° C). Chocolate can be used as an additional decoration.

Macaroon Tea Fancies

1. Make small macaroon biscuits, piping them on wafer paper. When cold, dip them into plain chocolate without covering the wafer paper bottoms. When set, turn them over into paper cases and pipe a whirl or vanilla flavoured whipped cream on each. Finish by sprinkling with green chopped almonds.

2. Spread the bottoms of the macaroon biscuits with rum flavoured ganache cream which should be fashioned into a pyramid shape. When the cream has set, dip into chocolate and finish with a piped whirl of piping chocolate *(page 249)*, and some chopped pistachio nuts or chopped green almonds.

Nut Cakes

lb	oz		kg	gr
1	0	Sugar (castor)		500
1	3 $1/2$	Ground almonds*		600
	10	Egg		300

* Ground walnuts or hazelnuts can be used.

The ground nuts are lightly roasted and stirred into the sugar and eggs that have been whipped to a stiff sponge. The mixture is then piped out with a plain tube on to greased baking sheets. An almond, hazelnut or half walnut is placed on top. They are left until a crust forms, when they are baked at 350° F (176° C). When cool, they are glazed with a pectin jelly. These cakes should be baked on a double tin. *(Germany)*

Orange Crescents

Spread the table with flaked almonds and pipe on blobs of macaroon paste, flavoured with zest of orange. Roll the blobs into ropes about 6 in. (15 cm.) long so that they are covered with almonds. Arrange them on a greased and floured baking sheet in crescent shapes. Bake at 350° F (176° C). When baked, wash with hot gum arabic solution and place half a glacé cherry in the centre of each.

Orange Macaroons

Mix egg yolk macaroon paste with lemon zest and finely chopped orange peel. Pipe out in small bulbs with a plain tube on to paper. Indent slightly in the centre and fill the hollow with a spot of orange marmalade. Using a star tube, pipe out a whirl of the same paste on top, place a piece of glacé cherry in the centre and bake at 360° F (180° C). As soon as baking is completed, glaze with apricot purée or water icing. *(Germany)*

Ox Eyes

Pipe out macaroon mix into oval shaped rings on to greased and floured baking sheets. Sprinkle the tops with nib almonds. Fill the centres in with frangipane mixing and bake at 350° F (176° C). When cold, mask the centres with well boiled raspberry jam and glaze with thin water icing. Place in the oven for a short time for the glaze to set.

Parisian Macaroons

lb	oz		kg	gr
1	0	Almonds (blanched)		500
1	8	Sugar (icing)		750
	8	Egg whites		250
		Vanilla		

Grind the almonds finely, add 7 oz. (200 gr.) egg whites, the sugar and vanilla and mix thoroughly. Now add the rest of the whites and beat well. Pipe out small bulbs on to paper lined baking sheets. Dust with icing sugar and bake at 400° F (204° C). To remove from the paper easily, cover a hot baking sheet with a damp cloth and place the macaroons on top with the paper side underneath. The steam will release them from the paper quickly and easily. *(France)*

Pineapple Macaroons

Take small macaroon biscuits and brush with hot pineapple purée. Pipe on a bulb of marzipan reduced with maraschino syrup. Place a segment of pineapple on top and dip into chocolate so that the pineapple can still be seen. *(Germany)*

Raspberry Oval Macaroons

Proceed as for Almond Ovals, but pipe the macaroon paste round the edges only. Dip into nibbed almonds and bake at 350° F (176° C). Whilst hot, brush over with gum arabic solution and when cold, dust lightly with icing sugar. Fill the centres with raspberry jelly adding a little chopped green almond in the centres.

Scotch Macaroons

Cut out circles of thin puff pastry and dock well. Let them rest for at least two hours. On top of each, pipe macaroon mixture, using either of the mixtures given for macaroon biscuits. Bake at 350° F (176° C).

Sevastopol Slices

lb	oz		kg	gr
1	0	Unblanched strip almonds		500
1	8	Sugar (granulated)		750
	$1/8$	Ground cinnamon		3
	10	Egg whites (approx.)		300

Mix together and heat carefully without allowing the mixture to boil.

Line a baking sheet with sweet pastry and half bake. Spread with raspberry jam and pour the above mixing on and spread whilst hot. Allow to cool and finish baking. When cool, cut into fingers. *(Switzerland)*

Sicilians

Take stock macaroon mix, and to each 1 lb. (500 gr.) add 1 oz. (30 gr.) of egg white, 1 oz. (30 gr.) of honey and the zest of an orange. Beat the mixture on top speed for a few minutes, then add 1 oz. (30 gr.) of flour and 8 oz. (250 gr.) of sultanas.

Pipe out in long strips on to paper lined baking sheets, using a ³/₄ in. (18 mm.) piping tube. Bake at 350° F (176° C). When cool, remove from the paper and cut into pieces. They may be decorated with chocolate.

Soft Macaroons

lb	oz		kg	gr
1	0	Almonds (blanched)		500
1	0	Sugar (granulated)		500
	2 ¹/₂	Egg whites (approx.)		75
	2 ¹/₂	Dairy cream (approx.)		75
		Vanilla or lemon zest		

Grind the almonds with the sugar, add the flavour, then mix with sufficient egg whites and dairy cream in equal amounts to make a paste of firm piping consistency. Pipe out in bulbs the size of walnuts on to paper lined baking sheets and bake at 400° F (204° C). *(France)*

Truffle Macaroons

Take small macaroon biscuits and pipe a whirl of truffle buttercream on top. On top of the cream place a cut-out chocolate ring using a fluted cutter. In the centre of the rings, pipe a small rosette of the same cream and sprinkle with a little chopped pistachio nut or nib green almonds.

Vanilla Almond Crescents

lb	oz		kg	gr
1	2	Flour		560
	12	Butter		375
	9	Ground almonds		270
	3	Sugar (castor)		90
	1	Egg (approx.)		30

Make up as for sweet pastry. Roll out into long ropes and cut into equal size pieces. Fashion into crescent shapes and arrange on to baking sheets. Bake at 400° F (204°C), without allowing them to brown. While still hot, roll them in vanilla sugar.

Viennese Macaroons

Place viennese tart mixing *(page 451)* in a savoy bag fitted with a star tube and pipe rings on to paper lined baking trays. Fill the centres with macaroon mix. Place a glacé cherry at the join of the viennese ring. Bake at 360° F (182° C).

Walnut Tongues

lb	oz		kg	gr
1	0	Ground almonds		500
1	0	Ground walnuts		500
3	4	Sugar (granulated)	1	625
		Egg white		

The almonds, walnuts and 1 lb. (500 gr.) of the sugar are mixed together and placed in the oven for the nuts to lightly roast. When cool, the rest of the sugar is added and sufficient egg white is beaten in to bring the paste to piping consistency. Pipe out in finger shape on to paper lined baking sheets and bake at 360° F (182° C). When cool, remove from the paper and sandwich together with red currant jelly and dip diagonally into chocolate. Place a half walnut in the centre. *(Switzerland)*

Zurich Marzipan Leckerli - Zürcher Marzipanleckerli

The basic ingredient of the Leckerli is marzipan. To obtain a pleasing article, it is important to pay attention to the sugar content of the marzipan after it has been prepared for use (white paste plus nuts). The amount of sugar should not exceed 50%; in our recipe it is about 40%. The main varieties of Leckerli are: almond, hazelnut, walnut, pistachio, santal, chocolate, and orange. In this recipe be sure to use marzipan and almond paste in a ratio of 1 ¹/₄ : 1. 7 oz. (200 gr.) French marzipan, 5 ¹/₄ oz. (160 gr.) almond paste VI., plus ingredients to make varieties as listed below.

Almond Leckerli: 2 ³/₄ oz. (80 gr.) finely ground almonds.

Hazelnut Leckerli: 2 ³/₄ oz. (80 gr.) finely ground hazelnuts, cinnamon.

Walnut Leckerli: 2 ³/₄ oz. (80 gr.) finely ground walnuts.

Pistachio Leckerli: 2 ³/₄ oz. (80 gr.) finely ground pistachio nuts, bitter almond oil.

Santal Leckerli: 1 1/4 oz. (40 gr.) finely ground almonds, santal powder, raspberry pulp.

Chocolate Leckerli: 1 1/4 oz. (40 gr.) finely ground almonds, 1 1/4 oz. (40 gr.) liquid cocoa.

Orange Leckerli: 2 3/4 oz. (80 gr.) finely ground almonds, orange juice and paste.

Liquids such as liqueurs, juices, etc. should only be added to the marzipan in small quantities; first-class flavouring essences are preferable. To make up for any liquid used, it is advisable to add finely ground blanched almonds to the varieties concerned, but the total amount of ground nuts added may not exceed half the weight of marzipan indicated. When the marzipan has been prepared for use, leave it to rest for a time in a cool place.

Not only the marzipan, but also the fillings differ. Quince jelly is mostly used for white Leckerli; hazelnut, walnut and chocolate Leckerli are often filled either with almond paste flavoured with liqueur or with raspberry jam. The appropriate fillings for orange and lemon Leckerli are fruit pastes or flavoured apricot jam combined with almond paste. Santal Leckerli are filled mainly with raspberry jam thickened with santal powder.

After the marzipan has been allowed to rest, work it for a short time, then pin out 1/6 in. (4 mm.) thick. Cut to fit the mould to be used with a cutter or knife, depending on the type of mould. Lightly dust the mould, cover the inside with a piece of marzipan that has been cut to size and press down well so that the impression is clearly visible later on. Cover with the appropriate filling, then place the base on top and seal well. Invert on to a lightly dusted wooden board, cut out each Leckerli and arrange on a waxed baking sheet. Leave to dry for several hours and lightly bake in a fairly warm oven. While still hot, brush with vanilla icing, hot cocoa butter or gum arabic solution. To be on the safe side, start by making a test Leckerli of each variety, especially those involving the use of liquid cocoa, juices, etc.

(Switzerland)

Window Display, ▶
(See p. 597)

542 ▲ La Palma Bilberry Gâteau and Tartlets, p. 738, 739

Chessboard Gâteau, p. 593 ▼

▲ Black and White Fan Torte, p. 591   Florida Tourte, p. 738 ▼   543

544 ▲ Caracas Cake, p. 383, 592   ▲ Nougatine Torte (Golden Book), p. 594
Buttercream Sponge Gâteau, p. 567 ▼

XIX. Gâteaux and Torten

Gâteaux (Great Britain)

There are very few classic British gâteaux, almost all being the creation of individual craftsmen. They are generally sold as a 'week-end special'.

Most of the bases are made from plain or butter sponge, genoese mixings or from the basic mixings made with special fats and flours. Bases built up with sweet paste, sponge, and japonaise are becoming more and more into general use.

A selection of gâteaux follows, but the possibilities of variety are endless.

SPONGE GATEAUX

1. Cut the centre out of sponge sandwiches and sandwich with cream to one that is uncut. Dust with icing sugar and fill the centre with lemon or orange curd or with jam of any variety. The inner edge may be piped with whipped dairy cream.

2. Split a sponge sandwich and spread with jam or lemon curd. If the bases are not too thick, two can be sandwiched together instead of splitting one base. Using a savoy bag fitted with a star tube, pipe whipped dairy cream on the base making it thicker in the centre. Cut the top into eight segments, dust with icing sugar and carefully arrange on the base, tilting upwards towards the centre. Place a glacé cherry in the centre. The sides may be masked with cream and roasted nib or flaked almonds.

3. Proceed exactly as above but spread half the tops with chocolate fondant and half with white fondant. When set they are cut into eight. The segments are arranged on the bases alternating chocolate and white. Sprinkle a little green nib almond in the centre. Finish sides as described above.

4. Split and sandwich a sponge sandwich base with nougat buttercream containing chopped walnuts. Mask with apricot purée and cover with chocolate fondant. Pipe a freehand design on top with the same fondant and finish with halved walnuts.

5. Split and sandwich a sponge sandwich base with buttercream and spread the top thinly.

Pipe parallel lines of cream on top using a $1/4$ in. (5 mm.) plain pipe, the lines to be of two different colours, alternating, i.e. white and chocolate; white and pink; coffee and chocolate, etc. Whatever colours are chosen one of them should be used for sandwiching the base. Finish the top by a fine spinning of chocolate at right angles to the lines of cream. Sprinkle a few green nib almonds in the centre.

Mask the sides with cream and roasted nib or flaked almonds.

6. Split and sandwich a sponge sandwich base with raspberry jam and whipped dairy cream flavoured with vanilla. Glaze the top with apricot purée and cover with white fondant, meanwhile have chocolate fondant ready in a paper bag and quickly pipe lines right across before the white fondant has set. With a point, quickly draw it at right angles through the surface. Turn the cake round and repeat. 'Marbling' as this form of decoration is known is described in Mexican Gâteau *(page 572.)*

7. Proceed as for 1, but spread with pineapple jam before replacing the ring. Dust with icing sugar and fill in the centre with well drained small cubes of pineapple. Cover with cold-set jelly and then, with a star tube, cover with whipped dairy cream. Place the cut-out disc on the cream, but do not dust with sugar.

8. Slice a butter sponge sandwich base and spread with lemon curd. Brush the top with apricot purée and spread with a mixture of chopped cherries, angelica, flaked almonds and hazelnuts. Glaze with apricot purée. Mask side with buttercream flavoured with fresh lemon juice and then with roasted flaked almonds.

9. Slice and sandwich an almond butter sponge base *(page 198)* with nougat buttercream.

Coat top and sides with the same cream and mask with roasted flaked almonds. Place paper strips on the top about $1/2$ in. (1 cm.) apart and dust with icing sugar. Carefully remove paper strips.

10. Proceed as above. Mask the top and sides with the same cream. Finish the sides with roasted nib almonds. Arrange chocolate rolls on the top and lay strips of paper on at right angles. Dust with icing sugar. Remove paper strips very carefully.

SPONGES WITH FRUIT

Special tins, both large and small, can be purchased in which a sponge mixing can be baked. When turned over, the sponge base has a depression into which fresh or canned fruits can be placed and glazed with a cold-set jelly or other glazes. A variety of well drained fruits can be used and arranged in attractive patterns. Whipped cream can be piped on the inner edge to make them even more attractive.

SPONGE BARS

Sheets of sponge can be layered three, four or more high and sandwiched with jams and/or creams. After refrigeration the top can be either dusted with icing sugar, spread with cream, chocolate or fondant and then cut into rectangular units to be sold by the piece. Additional decoration can be given by the use of cream, nuts, fruit, etc. The decoration can be so placed that the unit can be divided into separate identical or different fancies.

Another method is to cut into squares or rectangles and cover completely with chocolate fondant or cream with additional decoration by piping and by the use of other decorative materials. Variety is endless.

SWISS ROLLS - BISCUIT ROULÉ

The basic swiss roll either white, chocolate, raspberry, orange, coffee, etc., can be given extra appeal by the use of a variety of fillings and/or by additional decoration. A selection follows.

1. Spread a sheet of coffee flavoured sponge with a cream into which has been mixed chopped cherries, pineapple, walnuts and angelica.

2. Spread a sheet of pink sponge with white cream, flavoured with maraschino into which chopped cherries have been mixed.

3. Spread a sheet of sponge with buttercream into which lemon, orange or tangerine curd has been mixed. The sponge can be coloured to correspond to the fruit curd.

4. Spread a sheet of sponge with a coffee cream.

5. Spread a sheet of white sponge with coffee cream into which chopped walnuts have been mixed.

6. Before baking, sprinkle the surface of a white sponge with nib or flaked almonds. When baked and cool, spread with an almond cream made by whipping in softened raw marzipan.

7. Any of the swiss rolls described can be refrigerated and then cut down the centre, each half being fixed, cut side down, to a strip of sweet pastry of equal width. The roll can then be covered with cream, fondant, chocolate, almond paste, etc., and given additional decoration.

Continental swiss rolls are invariably made by first separating the eggs. The yolks and part of the sugar are whisked and the whites whipped with the balance of the sugar. After both mixtures are blended, any mixture that may be composed of flour, cocoa powder, ground almonds or hazelnuts and cornflour is folded in. A great variety of fillings, usually flavoured with liqueur are used. Here is a selection. The basic recipes will be found on *page 357*.

8. Take a sheet of continental sponge and spread with lemon buttercream and roll up. Brush with apricot purée and cover with a thin sheet of almond paste marked with a ribbed rolling pin. Decorate by piping with the same cream and adding glacé cherries.

9. Spread a chocolate sponge with raspberry jam and then with buttercream flavoured with curaçao. When rolled up, brush with apricot purée and enclose with a thin sheet of almond paste. Coat with plain chocolate and spin with milk chocolate.

10. Before baking a continental sponge, sprinkle with crushed praline nougat. When baked, spread with a hazelnut buttercream and roll up. Glaze with thin warm fondant.

11. A nut sponge is spread with buttercream flavoured with cognac and rolled up. It is brushed with apricot purée and rolled in lightly roasted flaked hazelnuts and dusted lightly with icing sugar.

12. A continental sponge is spread with cream fortified with gelatine. Before rolling up, the surface of the cream is sprinkled with small cubes of different coloured jelly. Cover with buttercream and roll in lightly roasted nib almonds. Dust lightly with icing sugar.

13. Spread a nut sponge with a pineapple cream stabilized with gelatine and mixed with chopped pineapple. Roll up and cover with chocolate. Decorate with crystallized pineapple.

Many swiss roll fancies can be left uncut and sold by the piece. *(See chapter XI.)*

BATTENBURG

This type of decorated cake is popular in Great Britain and ranges from the simple to the more sophisticated.

The simplest of all is the chequer pattern which is built up from genoese of two colours. Generally pink and white is used with chocolate and white a close favourite. Many patterns of colour and form are possible, enclosed within a cover of almond paste, which can be left plain or marked with a patterned rolling pin. Extra decoration can be simple or more ambitious.

The bases for Battenburg are prepared from sheet type genoese. This type of cake requires good keeping and cutting qualities, an even texture, and brightness of colour to give contrast. It should be stored 24 hours before cutting.

Battenburg can be sold by weight, or cut into thin slices to produce a dainty fancy. For the former, the cross measurement should not exceed 3 in. (8 cm.); for the latter 2 in. (5 cm.).

The cake consists of coloured sections of genoese arranged in geometrical designs held together with apricot purée; the whole is then enclosed in a thin sheet of almond paste, either left plain, or grooved and finished on top in various ways.

A sheet of white genoese and one of pink or chocolate are trimmed to remove the crust, and cemented to each other with boiled apricot purée, which should be of good quality, and be applied quite liberally. It should contribute to the flavour of this type of cake as well as being the medium for holding the various portions of coloured genoese together.

The double sheet of genoese is now cut into strips about 1 in. (2.5 cm.) in width, and each strip laid over on its side. After the whole sheet has been cut and so treated, apricot purée is again liberally applied.

The strips are reversed and then fixed together, white to pink or chocolate to form a checkerboard pattern.

Almond paste is now pinned out to about $1/8$ in. (3 mm.) thick, trimmed to the same width as the genoese strip, and liberally covered with purée. The built up strip of genoese is now laid on to the almond paste at one end and turned over four times, picking up the almond paste and so becoming completely enveloped.

A knife is used to cut the strip free from the rest of the almond paste, and a second strip is covered in paste in the same way. Several pieces may be so wrapped before the almond paste is used up and another piece pinned out. Any paste remaining which is insufficient to cover at least one side of a strip may be worked into the next almond paste piece.

The strips of Battenburg may now receive an edge decoration by crimping either by hand or with the use of special metal nippers. Whilst the use of the latter can impart some very attractive designs, they are very much slower to apply, for they have to be done one side at a time. Hand crimping is more commercial, since the decoration is applied on the two edges simultaneously. Also with hand crimping the fingers are much kinder to the paste,

with the result that even a very thin paste coating may be crimped, which would be impossible with the nippers.

Two other treatments which may be given are as follows:

1. The paste may be textured with a special patterned roller prior to wrapping round the genoese strip.

2. The top of the Battenburg may be marked with a knife or specially shaped cutter before crimping the edges.

This is the maximum decoration that is usually applied to commercial Battenburg. However, for very little additional effort, attractive decoration may be added, which will certainly increase their popularity and sales. *(Illustration page 427.)*

LAYER CAKES

This type of decorated cake is made up of light genoese built up in layers and generally covered and finished with cream although chocolate and almond paste can be used for covering. Additional decoration is given by the use of other decorative materials. The dimensions are similar to those given for Battenburg.
(Illustrations page 428.)

Here are some examples:

1. Sandwich four layers of chocolate genoese with vanilla buttercream. Coat three sides with thin almond paste and cover with chocolate fondant. When set, pipe a continuous curly line diagonally on top and repeat it at right angles. Sprinkle in the centre, along the length, chopped pistachio nuts or green nib almonds.

2. Sandwich a layer of walnut genoese between two layers of chocolate genoese, using rum flavoured buttercream. Cover top and sides with thin chocolate almond paste and cover with chocolate, placing a line of halved walnuts on top. With a small star tube pipe little stars with pale green buttercream between each walnut.

3. Layer four sheets of almond sponge with pale green buttercream delicately

flavoured with pistachio. Enclose top and sides with thin pale green almond paste. Coat with pale green fondant flavoured with pistachio. Pipe a lattice pattern on top with chocolate and finish with a row of pistachio nuts.

4. Sandwich four layers of walnut sponge with vanilla buttercream into which finely chopped walnuts have been mixed. Cover top and sides with thin almond paste and coat with white vanilla flavoured fondant. Place halved walnuts along the length and finish by piping with chocolate.

5. Sandwich four layers of pink genoese with kirsch flavoured buttercream into which chopped cherries have been mixed. Cover top and sides with thin pink almond paste and coat with kirsch flavoured pink fondant. Place half cherries along the length with little stars in between piped with pale green buttercream.
(Other recipes see page 596.)

OTHER GATEAUX

Gâteaux in great variety can be produced by using bases made with either light or heavy genoese. The bases can be baked in cottage pans, round, oval and other shapes, or cut into shapes from the sheet. They may be coated with almond paste, fondant, meringue, creams, chocolate, etc., and finished with the same media and/or other decorative materials. Liqueur syrup may be sprinkled liberally on the base to confer additional flavour. Here are examples:

1. Split a light genoese base baked in a cottage pan and sandwich with vanilla buttercream. Coat the top and sides with the same cream and mask the sides with roasted flaked almonds. With the gâteau on the turn-table, place the top of a small palette knife in the centre, turn the table and make a neat spiral impression on the surface of the cream. Pipe eight cream whirls, equidistant about 1 in. (2.5 cm.) from the edge, using a star savoy pipe. Meanwhile cut some right angled triangles from chocolate spread on paper, the length of which should be a little less than the radius of the top of the gâteau. Place these on the top radiating from the centre with the tips inward and leaning back against the piped whirls. Dust very lightly indeed with icing sugar. Pipe a whirl of cream in the centre and sprinkle on a few green nib almonds.

2. Sandwich a light chocolate genoese baked in a sandwich plate with truffle buttercream. Cover the top and sides with the same cream and mask the sides with roasted nib almonds. Prepare a number of chocolate petals by placing dabs of chocolate on to greaseproof paper with a palette knife, so that as the palette knife is withdrawn from the paper, petal shapes are formed that are thick on the edges and thinner in the centres. Starting from the edge, place the petals on top of the gâteau in concentric circles overlapping each circle slightly. In this way a flower formation is effected. Dust very sparingly with icing sugar and finish with a whirl of cream in the centre; top with a little green nib almond.

3. Cut a square base from a pink genoese, split and spread with red currant jelly. Cover top and sides with white buttercream. With a knife, mark a cross on top from corner to corner. Using the lines as a guide, pipe lines of white buttercream stars on one triangle and repeat on the one opposite. Fill in, using the same star pipe, the other two triangles with pink or chocolate buttercream. Place cut langues-de-chat biscuits round the side and secure them with red ribbon tied with a neat bow. Sprinkle a little chopped pistachio or green nib almonds in the centre.

4. Layer a round almond light genoese base twice with nougat buttercream and coat top and sides. Cover the surface with piped chocolate by moving the point of the bag with a circular motion resulting in a pattern of interwoven irregular circles. Round the edge, place clusters made by mixing roasted strip almonds with chocolate and placing out on to greaseproof paper in neat heaps. They are lightly

dusted with icing sugar before placing on to the gâteau. Finish the bottom edge with green nib almonds.

5. Sandwich a light genoese base, baked in a cottage pan, with vanilla fudge cream. Coat top and sides and make a spiral pattern as described in No. 1. Pipe red jelly in the impression made and with a sharp point draw through the surface eight times to the centre. Finish with a pinch of chopped pistachio nut and mask the sides with roasted flaked almonds. *(Illustration page 556.)*

6. Split a light genoese base, baked in a cottage pan, and sandwich once with rum flavoured buttercream and once with raspberry jam. Brush over with well boiled apricot purée and coat with pale yellow fondant. Mask the bottom edge with chopped pistachio nuts. Decorate with various coloured fondants.

7. Sandwich a round almond gâteau base with apricot jam. Brush the top with apricot purée and pipe a trellis pattern with Parisian rout biscuit mixing *(page 485)* with a star pipe, finishing the border with a ring of stars. Flash the gâteau in a hot oven and then glaze with gum arabic solution. Brush side with apricot purée and mask with roasted flaked almonds. Fill in the intersections with contrasting coloured jam or jelly.

8. Sandwich a round, light genoese base with red currant jelly and cover with meringue *(page 205)*. Pipe a trellis design on top with a $1/4$ in. (5 mm.) plain savoy tube and finish the top edge with a ring of stars. (Do not pipe at the extreme edge.) Mask the sides with flaked almonds and flash the gâteau in a hot oven. Fill in the squares on top with contrasting coloured jellies.

SPECIAL GATEAUX

For special occasions, such as the following, special gâteaux are made.

New Year's Day	January 1st
St. Valentine's Day	February 14th
Mother's Day (Great Britain)	Mid-lent Sunday
St. Patrick's Day	March 17th
Easter	
Hallowe'en	October 31st
Guy Fawkes Day	November 5th
Christmas	December 25th

Colours and decorative motifs used should be symbolic of the event, always bearing in mind that the gâteaux are intended to be eaten, therefore good taste in colour and decoration are of primary importance. Special occasions such as birthdays, anniversaries, presentations, confirmations and engagements, all offer a challenge to the craftsman and special care should be taken to please the customer. It is well if something special and pleasing is known pertaining to the person or persons to whom the cake is to be presented. This knowledge can be used to give a special personal appeal to the gâteau. Names, professions, hobbies, etc., at once come to mind *(Illustrations pages 426, 556, 557, 608)*.

Elizabeth Gâteau

Take 1 lb. (500 gr.) of basic sponge mixing and pipe six spirals on to greased and floured baking sheets, using a savoy bag fitted with a plain tube. Bake at 375° F (190° C). When cold, sandwich five of them with chocolate hazelnut praline buttercream. Place into the refrigerator. Mask the top and side with buttercream. Spread the sixth sponge circle with caramel and cut into segments with a warm knife. Arrange them fanwise on the top of the gâteau. Dip the ends of savoy fingers into tempered chocolate and the tip into chopped pistachio nuts and arrange them, chocolate ends down, around the side of the gâteau. Make small cones from almond mixture and fill them with chilled kirsch flavoured whipped dairy cream. Place one on each of the segments. Place a deep red modelled marzipan rose in the centre.

This gâteau was designed in honour of the coronation of Her Majesty Queen Elizabeth II, in June 1953.

GATEAUX IN PAPER CASES

Genoese mixings of the orthodox kind and mixings using special flours and fats can be baked in paper cases; they lend themselves to easy finish, for decoration is only necessary on the top. Recipes can be found under the heading 'Genoese' in Chapter VI. A selection of finishes follows.

It will be seen that fudge icings can be warmed and used like fondant. Bases can be coated according to colour and flavour, the top being decorated by a neatly piped spiral with an appropriate decoration in the centre such as a cherry, walnut, almond, crystallized fruit, etc., or by a built up decoration such as an almond cluster or a truffle ganache ball.

1. The simplest form is to cover the top with a fudge icing or cream, making a pattern with sweeps of the palette knife. The colour and flavour of the icing should bear a relation to the colour and flavour of the cake base. For instance, a study of the fudge icings and creams on *pages 232-233* will suggest an orange or lemon fudge with a base similarly coloured and flavoured; a chocolate or coffee fudge on a chocolate or coffee base, or a malt fudge on a malt flavoured base.

2. Take an almond flavoured base and brush with apricot purée. Pipe stars or a ring of Parisian rout mixing *(page 485)* round the edge and flash in a hot oven. Brush with hot gum arabic solution *(page 246)*. When cool, fill in the centre with fondant and decorate. This type of finish is ideal for Easter gâteaux for which cut-out chicks, rabbits and other Easter motifs can be used.

3. Brush the top of a vanilla base with apricot purée and pipe a shell border with truffle buttercream. Fill in the centre with some of the following mixture:

Bring to the boil 6 oz. (180 gr.) of apricot purée to which 1 lb. (500 gr.) of castor sugar and a little fresh lemon juice have been added. Mix in chopped cherries, angelica, walnuts, pineapple and roasted flaked almonds or hazelnuts. Cool before use.

4. Make bases containing raisins flavoured with rum. When baked and cool, spread a thin coating of honey on top and sprinkle with seedless raisins that have been soaked in rum. Mask with thin water icing flavoured with fresh lemon juice.

5. Make bases containing chopped citron peel and when baked and cool, brush with apricot purée. Cover with lime coloured and flavoured fondant and spin with fine threads of milk chocolate. Place a ganache truffle ball in the centre.

6. Make bases which contain both white and chocolate mixing placed in such a way that a marbled effect is seen when the baked cake is cut. (Do not overdo this or the white cake will have a smudged appearance.) When baked and cool, brush with apricot purée and cover with dark chocolate vermicelli. Place a star shape template on the top, big enough so that the points reach the edge of the cake, and dust with icing sugar. Take the template away carefully, leaving the impression of a dark star against a white background.

7. Make lemon flavoured bases and when cool, brush with apricot purée. With a $1/4$ in. (5 mm.) plain savoy tube, pipe parallel lines, slightly apart, with meringue. Pipe a neat border and flash in a hot oven. When cool, fill in between the piped lines with lemon curd. Sprinkle a few green nib almonds in the centre.

OTHER GATEAUX

Almond Gâteau

Make a base from an almond butter sponge. Split twice and sandwich with nougat buttercream. Cover top and sides with the same cream and decorate the side with a comb scraper. Mark the top into twelve sections. Place a ring template on top which will leave a large circle of the centre exposed and spin chocolate across and then again at right angles. Remove the ring and pipe a three shell design on each segment with a star tube. Top each with a blanched almond, half dipped into chocolate. Mask the bottom edge with chocolate vermicelli.

Chessboard Gâteau

Bake white and chocolate genoese in separate 9 in. (22 cm.) sandwich plates. When cold, cut out the centre of each with a 1 in. (2.5 cm.) plain cutter, then into rings with a 3, 5 and 7 in. (8, 12.5 and 18 cm.) cutter respectively. This will result in a small disc and 4 rings each of a different diameter. Do this with all the bases. Now re-assemble them, using a white and chocolate piece alternatively, fixing with buttercream. When this is done, half the bases will have an outer ring and a centre of chocolate and the other half will have the opposite, i.e. an outer ring and a centre of white. Sandwich these opposites together in pairs with nougat buttercream. Spread the top and sides with the same cream.

Pin out white almond paste and cut strips about 1 in. (2.5 cm.) wide and then cut into squares. Do the same with chocolate almond paste. Arrange these squares on the top in a chequerboard design. Mask the sides with chocolate vermicelli. When cut, this gâteau will show a chequerboard formation inside.

Chocolate Choux Gâteau

Sandwich a 9 in. (22 cm.) genoese gâteau base with ganache buttercream. Cover top and sides with chocolate.

Before the chocolate sets, carefully place a patterned choux pastry ring, *(page 192)* that has been dusted with icing sugar on top. Place the gâteau on a board and finish the bottom edge with piped shells of pale green buttercream.

Choux Fruit Gâteau

Sandwich a 9 in. (22 cm.) genoese gâteau base with apricot jam. Coat the top and sides with lemon buttercream and pipe a ring of the same cream round the edge using a plain tube. Mask the side with roasted flaked almonds. Arrange well-drained fruits in the centre and cover with cold-set jelly. Place a patterned choux paste ring on top. *(Page 192)*.

Dutch Gâteau - Gâteau hollandais

8 persons:

lb	oz		kg	gr
	9	Puff pastry cuttings		270
	4	Sugar		125
	4	Butter		125
	4	Ground almonds		125
		2 eggs		
		Zest of 1 lemon		
1	3/4	Flour		50
		Apricot purée		
		Sugar (icing)		
		Kirsch		

Baking time: 25 minutes at 360° F (182° C). Line a flan ring with the puff pastry cuttings pinned out thinly, docking the bottom well to prevent the trapping of air. Prepare the filling by creaming the butter and sugar together with the zest of lemon; beat in the egg a little at a time and fold in the flour and ground almonds. Fill the mixture into the ring and smooth down. Roll out the remaining puff pastry very thinly and cut it into strips using a serrated pastry wheel. Arrange the strips into a trellis design on the top. Immediately on baking, brush with hot apricot purée and glaze with thin, kirsch flavoured water icing. Place a glacé cherry in the centre.

Japonaise Sponge Gâteau

Make japonaise spiral bases as described for Kirsch Torte. Spread one with ganache buttercream and top it with a circle of sponge. Spread the sponge liberally with apricot jam and a layer of cream. Top it with another japonaise disc. Spread with chocolate and decorate with a circular sweep of a comb scraper. Mask the side with buttercream and japonaise crumbs. Sprinkle a few green nib almonds on top before the chocolate sets.

Strawberry Meringue Gâteau

Sandwich a round 9 in. (22 cm.) genoese base with strawberry colouring buttercream mixed with cut strawberries. Spread top and sides with the same cream without strawberries. Mask the side with chocolate

▲ Gâteau Saint-Honoré Tuscany, p. 728

Gâteau Saint-Honoré, Italy, p. 728 ▼

553

554 ▲ Mocha Buttercream Torte, p. 581

Torta Sorrentina, p. 590 ▼

▲ Walnut Torte, p. 586

Budapest Pineapple Torte, p. 577 ▼

555

556 ▲ Children's Birthday or Party Torte, p. 578

Fudge Gâteau, p. 550 ▼

▲ Japonaise Gâteau, p. 460   Birthday Torte, p. 576 ▼

558 ▲ Torta Cubana, p. 589

Dairy Cream Gâteau or Torta Chantilly, p. 589 ▼

▲ Torta Dama, p. 589   Mimosa Gâteau, p. 589 ▼   559

560 ▲ Torta Arancia, p. 588

Genoese Glacés for Afternoon Tea, p. 407 ▼

▲ Pineapple Baumtorte, p. 583

Truffle Tourte, p. 594 ▼

561

▲ Red Currant Meringue Torte, p. 585

Wine Cream Tourte (other presentation), p. 595 ▼

▲ Strawberry Dairy Cream Torte, p. 586

Peach Wine Cream Torte, p. 583 ▼

564 ▲ Christmas Pie, p. 694

Golden Tart, p. 695 ▼

vermicelli and the top with broken meringue. Spin haphazard rings of chocolate over the top leaving about 5 in. (12.5 cm.) of the centre not piped. Place one large strawberry dipped in pectin jelly in the centre.

Gâteaux and Torten - Austria

Almond Torte

lb	oz		kg	gr
	4 1/2	Sugar (icing)		140
	4 1/2	Ground almonds		140
	5 1/2	Egg yolks		165
	5	Egg whites		150
	3 1/2	Flour		100
1	1/2	Water		45
		Zest of 1/2 lemon		

Whip the egg yolks with 3 1/2 oz. (100 gr.) of sugar and the almonds until foamy. Add the water and the zest and continue whipping for a short time. Whisk the egg whites and the rest of the sugar to a stiff snow and fold into the yolk/sugar/almond mixture, together with the flour. Fill into two shallow hoops and bake at 360° F (180° C). When cold, split both bases once, sandwich with almond custard *(page 241)* and coat neatly with lemon or maraschino flavoured fondant.

Chocolate Buttercream Torte

lb	oz		kg	gr
	3 3/4	Butter		105
	3 3/4	Sugar (icing)		105
	3 3/4	Ground almonds		105
	4	Egg yolks		125
	5	Whole egg		150
	5	Egg whites		150
	7	Chocolate		200
1	1/2	Flour		45

Melt the chocolate and keep it barely lukewarm. Cream the butter with 2 1/2 oz. (75 gr.) of sugar, beat in the yolks, egg and almonds and lastly the melted chocolate. Whisk the whites and the rest of the sugar to a stiff snow and fold into the egg / butter / sugar / chocolate mixture together with the flour. Bake in two hoops of suitable size at 360° F (180° C). When cold, split twice, sandwich with chocolate buttercream and coat with chocolate fondant or cooked chocolate icing.

Hazelnut Torte

lb	oz		kg	gr
	6	Sugar (icing)		175
	4 1/2	Ground hazelnuts (roasted)		140
	7	Egg yolks		200
	3 1/2	Egg		100
	6	Egg whites		175
	2 1/2	Cake crumbs		75
	2 1/2	Flour		75
	2	Water (approx.)		60
		Vanilla		

Whip up the egg yolks, egg, sugar and vanilla, add the water and the hazelnuts and continue whipping. Whisk the egg whites to a stiff snow and fold in together with the flour and the cake crumbs. Fill into a greased, floured circular tin and bake at 360° F (180° C). When cool, split twice, sandwich with hazelnut buttercream, coat with maraschino flavoured fondant and decorate with a ring of caramelized hazelnuts.

Linzer Torte I

lb	oz		kg	gr
	7	Ground almonds (unblanched)		200
	7	Sugar (castor)		200
	7	Butter		200
	5 1/4	Flour		160
	2	Egg yolks		60
		Cinnamon (pinch)		
		Juice and zest of half a lemon		

Proceed as for sweet pastry and allow to rest for a short time. Line an ungreased flan ring with half the pastry. Cut the remaining pastry into thin strips, using a pastry wheel and lay them on top lattice fashion. Lay a thicker strip of pastry round the rim and fill in the spaces between the criss-cross strips with red currant jam. Brush the top of the pastry with egg, sprinkle flaked almonds in the centre and bake at 350° F (176° C).

Linzer Torte II
Creamed Method

lb	oz		kg	gr
	4 1/2	Butter		140
	7	Sugar (icing)		200
	1 1/2	Egg yolks		45
	1 1/2	Egg		45
	3 1/2	Ground almonds		100
	4 1/2	Flour		140
		Zest of 1 lemon		

Cream the butter and sugar, add the egg and egg yolks a little at a time. Fold in the zest, the flour and the almonds. Place half the pastry on a greased and floured circle of paper and surround with a flan ring. Place the rest of the pastry on a floured table and shape part of it into a ring and the rest of it into strips. Spread the pastry base with red currant jam, edge it with the ring of pastry and place the strips on top lattice fashion. Brush with egg and bake at 360° F (180° C).

Linzer Torte III
Viennese Style

lb	oz		kg	gr
	6	Butter		175
	6	Sugar (icing)		175
	6	Ground almonds		175
	6	Sponge crumbs		175
	2 1/2	Flour		75
	3 1/2	Egg		100
	1/8	Baking powder		4
	1/16	Cinnamon		2
		Zest of 1 lemon		
		Ground cloves (pinch)		

Work all the ingredients to a pastry. Pin out half of it to form a round base, place on a lightly greased baking sheet, brush the edge with a little water and lay a rope of pastry round the edge. Spread with raspberry or red currant jam and cover with a lattice of strips of pastry. Brush with egg and bake at 360° F (180° C).

Panama Torte
Split a hazelnut torte base three times (making four layers in all) and sandwich with chocolate buttercream. Cover the top and sides with the same buttercream and mask with roasted flaked almonds. Dust the top with icing sugar.

Parisian Torte
Take three well dried, round bases made with cold meringue, measuring about 8 in. (20 cm.) in diameter. Sandwich them together with ganache. Coat the top and sides with ganache and mask the whole torte with chocolate vermicelli. Make some small balls of ganache, roll them in chocolate vermicelli, dust very lightly with icing sugar and arrange round the edge of the torte.

Pineapple Mousseline Gâteau
Split a deep sand cake twice and coat the top layer with fondant mixed with well boiled pineapple juice. Sandwich with stiffly whipped dairy cream mixed with cold well boiled pineapple juice and, if necessary, a little icing sugar, and place the fondant coated layer on top. Spread the sides with the same dairy cream mixture and decorate the gâteau with very thin, well drained slices of poached pineapple, glazing with a little jelly if desired. For one gâteau, 3/4 pint (3/8 l.) of dairy cream is required. The gâteau should be refrigerated well and used at once. Mousseline dairy cream gâteaux can be made in the same way, using other varieties of fruit.

Sacher Torte I
Original Recipe

lb	oz		kg	gr
	5	Butter		150
	5 1/2	Sugar (castor)		165
	6 1/4	Chocolate		185
	5	Flour		150
	5 1/2	Egg yolks		165
	8	Egg whites		250
		Vanilla		

Cream the butter with half the sugar. Add the melted chocolate and the vanilla and beat in the yolks a little at a time. Whip the whites to a stiff snow and fold in the rest of the sugar. Fold in the flour immediately and blend in the egg yolk/butter mixture. Fill into a flan ring and bake at 350° F (176° C). When cold, sandwich with apricot jam and cover with chocolate icing made as follows:

lb	oz		kg	gr
5	1/4	Chocolate (plain)		160
5	1/4	Sugar (castor)		160
4	1/2	Water (approx.)		140

Chop the chocolate into small pieces, add the sugar and water and heat gently until lukewarm and glossy. Mask the torte with apricot purée before coating with chocolate.

Sacher Torte II
Court Recipe

lb	oz		kg	gr
	3 1/2	Butter		100
	3 1/2	Sugar (icing)		100
	3 1/2	Ground almonds		100
	2 1/2	Egg yolks		75
	1 1/2	Egg		45
	3 1/2	Egg whites		100
	1 1/2	Flour		45
	4	Vanilla chocolate		125
		Vanilla powder		

Melt the chocolate and keep it lukewarm. Cream the butter with three quarters of the sugar, adding the yolks and eggs a little at a time. Whisk the egg whites to a stiff snow adding the rest of the sugar a little at a time. Quickly add the chocolate into the egg/sugar/butter mixture and fold in the egg whites together with the flour. Fill into a greased and floured paper lined hoop and bake at 360° F (180° C). When cold, brush with apricot purée and coat with cooked chocolate icing.

Sand Cake - Light

lb	oz		kg	gr
	3 3/4	Sugar (icing)		105
	3 3/4	Flour		105
	3 1/2	Egg yolks		100
	8	Egg		250
	2 1/2	Butter (melted)		75
		Zest of 1/2 lemon		

Whip up the yolks, egg, sugar and zest over a gentle heat, then continue beating until cold. Fold in the flour and lastly blend in the cooled melted butter. Fill into a hoop that has been greased and floured and bake at 360° F (180° C). When cold, sandwich with any desired jam and coat with fondant according to individual taste.

Thalhof Torte

lb	oz		kg	gr
	7 1/2	Butter		215
	6	Egg yolks		180
	10	Egg whites		300
	5	Chocolate		150
	5	Sugar (castor)		150
	7	Ground almonds		200

Cream the butter and chocolate lightly. Add the egg yolks a little at a time. Stir in the almonds and sugar and then fold in the egg whites beaten to a stiff snow.

Deposit 4 or 5 bases of the mixing, depending on the size required, on a greased and floured baking sheet. Bake at about 360° F (182° C), and set aside for 24 hours. Sandwich the bases together with chocolate hazelnut buttercream, and coat with chocolate fondant.

Gâteaux and Tourtes - France

In view of the fact that tourtes are very often bought by customers for some special occasion, particular regard should be paid to their presentation. In every case the tourte should enhance the appearance of the table—for this reason the craftsman will only be satisfied when he has applied all his artistic skill to the decoration of the tourte.

Tourtes fall into two categories: those which do not contain a filling and those which do, where the sponge is sliced horizontally one, two or three times and sandwiched together with buttercream, ganache or other mixture.
(Illustration page 544.)

Alcazar Gâteau

lb	oz		kg	gr
	4	Ground almonds		125
	4	Sugar (icing)		125
	2	Butter (melted)		60
	1 1/2	Egg yolks		45
	1 1/2	Egg		45
	2 1/2	Egg whites		75
	10	Sweet pastry		300

For decoration

lb	oz		kg	gr
	3 1/2	Ground almonds		100
	3 1/2	Sugar (icing)		100
		Egg white		
		Apricot jam		

Line a flan ring with the sweet pastry pinned out thinly and spread the bottom with apricot jam. Whip the almonds, sugar, yolks and egg together until foamy, add the egg whites whipped to a snow and lastly blend in the melted butter, which should be barely lukewarm. Fill into the flan ring and bake at 375° F (190° C).

For decoration, make a paste of piping consistency with the ground almonds, sugar and a little egg white. Using a star tube, pipe a trellis of this almond paste on top of the gâteau. Place in an oven for a short time to colour the almond paste decoration lightly, remove from the oven, glaze with apricot purée while still hot and place half a pistachio nut into each space in the trellis.

Amandine Tourte

lb	oz		kg	gr
1	2	Dairy cream		560
	14	Butter		400
	7	Honey		200
	8	Sugar (castor)		250
	12	Flaked blanched almonds		375

Place in a copper pan all the ingredients shown in the recipe, except for the almonds, and cook at a temperature of 220° F (104° C). Finally mix in the almonds. Make some round tartlet cases with sablé paste, (bake them and then fill them three quarters full with the mixture. Put back in a hot oven 485° F (250° C) for two or three minutes and decorate each tourte with a red glacé cherry.

Birthday Gâteau

Bake genoese mixture in a square frame. Split twice when cold, and sandwich with buttercream mixed with finely chopped candied fruits that have been macerated in Grand-Marnier. Coat the top with Grand-Marnier flavoured fondant. Coat the sides with buttercream with the same flavour but containing no fruit and mask with roasted chopped almonds. Arrange candied fruit on top in a floral design and pipe on an inscription in white fondant. Add final decorations, using piped fondant and praline croquant.

Brie Tourte

Take a round genoese sponge, slice it in two horizontally, splash well with kirsch and sandwich together with kirsch flavoured buttercream. Coat the sides and top of the tourte with buttercream; next cover the sides with roasted almonds and dust the top with icing sugar. Red glacé cherries are used for decoration.

Charlemagne Gâteau

Split a round genoese base twice and sandwich with hazelnut buttercream mixed with a little honey. Coat with coffee coloured and flavoured fondant, decorate with the same buttercream and finish off with a ring of caramelized hazelnuts round the edge.

Christmas Log - Bûche de Noël

lb	oz		kg	gr
	2 3/4	Sugar (icing)		80
	2 3/4	Flour		80
	1	Butter		30
	3	Egg whites		90
	3	Egg yolks		90

Baking time : 7-8 minutes.

Coffee buttercream

lb	oz		kg	gr
	4 1/2	Butter		140
	4 1/2	Coffee flavoured custard		140

Chocolate buttercream

lb	oz		kg	gr
	4 1/2	Butter		140
	4 1/2	Chocolate custard		140
		Sugar (icing)		
		Peeled chopped pistachios		

Stir the icing sugar with the yolks to a foam. Fold in stiffly beaten egg whites and the flour at the same time. Finally add the barely lukewarm butter. Do not handle too much. Spread the mixture on to a buttered sheet of paper, lining a baking sheet, and bake in a hot oven. When baked, turn out on a marble slab with the paper side on top. This will keep the cake pliable. Allow to cool. As soon as the cake is cold remove the paper and spread with coffee buttercream. Roll like a Swiss roll and place in the refrigerator to set the cream. Now, cut off both ends a little on a slant. Pipe lines of chocolate buttercream with a star tube close to one another on top and sides to imitate the bark of the log and coat both ends with buttercream. Scatter finely chopped pistachios here and there to imitate moss and dredge a little icing sugar on top to imitate snow.

Instead of coating with chocolate cream the cake may be iced with chocolate fondant and decorated with a Father Christmas and imitated fir-leaves, dredged lightly with icing sugar and a small shield of marzipan with the inscription 'Merry Christmas' placed on top.

Cussy Gâteau

lb	oz		kg	gr
	7	Egg		200
	1 1/2	Egg yolks		45
	4	Sugar (icing)		125
	4	Flour		125

lb	oz		kg	gr
	1 3/4	Ground almonds		50
	4	Butter (melted)		125
		Kirsch		

Beat the egg, yolks and sugar together over gentle heat, then whip until cold. Blend in the flour and the ground almonds and lastly the melted butter. Fill into a greased and floured square tin and bake at 360° F (180° C). On removal from the oven, moisten with a little pure kirsch, wrap in metal foil when cold. This gâteau will keep for several days.

Danicheff Gâteau

Bake genoese mixture in a square mould in a moderate oven for about 30-35 minutes. Allow to cool in the mould. Turn out, slice, and spread with a layer of red currant jelly. Spread with Italian meringue, and on top of this heap up Italian meringue fairly high. Shape it into a regular square, using a palette moistened with water. Heat an iron rod about as thick as a pencil until it is red hot and caramelize the meringue on top criss-cross, applying the rod lightly. Now cover the entire gâteau with strained apricot jam cooked almost to jelly. When the jam has drained, mask the sides with roasted chopped almonds without touching the meringue top.

Eaglet Gâteau

lb	oz		kg	gr
	8	Egg		250
	4	Sugar (icing)		125
	1 3/4	Cocoa powder		50
	2 3/4	Flour		80
	1 3/4	Egg whites		50
	3 1/2	Butter (melted)		100
		1 round sweet pastry base		

Filling

lb	oz		kg	gr
	1 3/4	Egg whites		50
	4	Sugar (icing)		125
	7	Butter		200
	5	Couverture		150

Whip up the egg and sugar over gentle heat, then continue whisking until cold. Sieve the flour and the cocoa powder.

569

Whisk the egg whites to a stiff snow, fold into the egg/sugar sponge, blend in the flour and cocoa and lastly the cooled melted butter. Fill a greased and floured fluted ring mould with the mixture and bake at 360° F (180° C). When cold, fix in position on the baked sweet pastry base with well boiled apricot purée. Make an Italian meringue with the egg whites and sugar for the filling, allow to cool, stir in the butter as for buttercream and lastly add the cooled couverture. Fill the centre of the gâteau with this mixture and refrigerate well.

Easter - Le Pascal

lb	oz		kg	gr
	3 １/２	Sugar (castor)		100
	3 １/２	Flour		100
	3 １/２	Butter		100
		4 eggs		

Filling and decoration

lb	oz		kg	gr
	5 １/２	Butter		165
	4 １/２	Custard		140
	2	Praliné		60
	14	Marzipan		400
	9	Pistachio fondant		270
	１/２	Egg white (approx.)		15
	3 １/２	Sugar (icing)		100
		Cocoa		
	7	Thick strained apricot jam		200

Baking time: 35-40 minutes.

This cake may be made in any shape. It may be baked in a square, round or oval mould, and decorated with Easter eggs, etc. Bake genoese mixture in an oval mould if possible, and allow to cool. Slice twice and spread with buttercream, mixed with praliné powder. Spread apricot jam very thinly all over the cake and cover with marzipan, rolled out to a thin sheet. Press on the sides and cut off the superfluous marzipan at the base. Coat the cake with pale green pistachio fondant flavoured with kirsch. Pipe 'Happy Easter' on top with royal icing mixed with cocoa and decorate top and base with royal icing.

Exotic Gâteau

Sponge mixture

lb	oz		kg	gr
	4 １/２	Sugar (icing)		140
	6	Egg		180
	2	Flour		60
	2	Ground coconut		60

Baking time: 35-40 minutes.

Buttercream

lb	oz		kg	gr
	4 １/２	Butter		140
	4 １/２	Thick custard		140
		１/２ liqueur glass rum		
	2	Ground coconut		60

Italian meringue

lb	oz		kg	gr
	2 １/２	Sugar (icing)		75
	1	Egg white		30

Decoration

    Candied orange peel
    30 small squares of coconut
    Ground coconut

Bake sponge mixture in a rectangular mould or in a deep baking sheet. If a baking sheet is used, cut the sponge cake in half so as to form a brick. Slice and spread with a layer of buttercream, mixed with ground coconut and flavoured with rum. Coat top and sides entirely with Italian meringue and cover the top with ground coconut. Decorate the sides with lozenge-shaped pieces of candied peel and small thin squares of coconut. Before serving, allow the meringue to get dry, but do not put the cake in the oven because of the buttercream.

Guayaquil Gâteau

lb	oz		kg	gr
	3 １/２	Ground almonds		100
	3 １/２	Sugar		100
	１/２	Flour		15
	5	Egg whites		150
	1 １/２	Butter		45

Buttercream

lb	oz		kg	gr
	4 1/2	Butter		140
	4 1/2	Thick custard		140
	2	Ground and sifted praline		60

Beat the egg whites stiffly, lightly fold in the flour and almond powder, and finally the melted, barely lukewarm butter. Spread this mixture in three round bases about 1/6 in. (4 mm.) thick and about 6 in. (15 cm.) diameter on a greased and floured baking sheet. Bake in a moderate to slow oven. Remove the rounds from the baking sheet, trim and place them on a flat surface to cool. Spread with praline buttercream, assemble and then coat top and sides with the same cream. Scatter granulated chocolate all around the sides and place chocolate cigarettes tightly packed against one another on top. Put two strips of paper on a slant on top, dredge with icing sugar, and lift off the strips of paper carefully.

Lemon Tourte

lb	oz		kg	gr
1	0	Butter		500
2	0	Sugar	1	
1	0	Eggs		500
		Juice of 6 lemons		
		Zest of 4 lemons		

Cook all the ingredients in a copper pan until the custard thickens and then pass it through a conical sieve. The tourte case is made with milanese paste and the edges are strengthened with a rope of paste. Bake in a medium oven. When it is cold, dust the edge of the tourte with icing sugar and fill it with the lemon custard.

Little Duke Gâteau - Gâteau Petit-Duc

Bake a round genoese sponge, to which 2 oz. (60 gr.) roasted ground hazelnuts have been added. When it is cold, slice and fill the gâteau with hazelnut buttercream, and coat top and sides with the same cream. Garnish tops and sides with very small rounds of the same mixture as for almond cornets, allowing them to cool flat instead of rolling them into cornets. Fill the spaces between the rounds with hazelnut buttercream, using a star tube.

Lutetia Chestnut Gâteau

lb	oz		kg	gr
		Round genoese sponge		
	7	Peeled and skinned chestnuts		200
	5	Butter		150
	3 1/2	Sugar (icing)		100
	1	Egg whites		30
		1/2 liqueur glass rum		
		Chocolate fondant		
		Marzipan		
		Royal icing		

Bake a genoese sponge in a buttered and floured round tin in a slow oven the evening before. Prepare Italian meringue with the egg whites and sugar, and allow to cool. Rub the cooked and well drained chestnuts through a wire sieve and mix the purée with the Italian meringue as soon as it is cold. Finally add softened butter and rum. Slice genoese into three layers and sandwich them with the chestnut cream. Place into the refrigerator to stiffen the cream. Coat entirely with chocolate fondant. Decorate with royal icing, using a very fine tube, and with chestnuts imitated with marzipan.

Marcelin Gâteau

lb	oz		kg	gr
	12	Sweet pastry		375
	4	Ground almonds		125
	5	Sugar (icing)		150
	2	Egg yolks		60
	2 1/2	Egg whites		75
	3/4	Kirsch		20
	3/4	Anisette		20

Line a flan ring with sweet pastry. Whip the egg yolks, sugar, almonds, kirsch and anisette together until very foamy, fold in the egg whites whisked to a stiff snow and fill into the flan ring. Dust with icing sugar and bake at 360° F (180° C).

Mascotte Gâteau

Bake genoese mixture in a round tin, allow to cool, split twice and sandwich with praline buttercream. Spread the top and sides with the same buttercream and mask with roasted nib almonds. Finish off by dusting the top with icing sugar.

Mexican Gâteau

lb	oz		kg	gr
	4 1/2	Sugar		140
	3 1/4	Flour		100
	2 3/4	Butter		80
	4	Egg whites		125
	3	Egg yolks		90
	1 1/4	Cocoa		40
		Apricot jam		
		Chocolate fondant		
		Royal icing		

Baking time: 35-40 minutes.

Whip sugar with yolks to a foam. Fold in the stiffly beaten whites and at the same time the cocoa and flour. Finally mix in the melted butter. Bake in a round greased and floured mould in a moderate oven. Allow to cool. Slice twice and layer with chocolate buttercream. Coat the cake with strained thick apricot purée and cover with lukewarm chocolate fondant. Spread it quickly over top and sides. Before the fondant has had time to cool, trace parallel lines across the top with white royal icing, using a strong paper bag or a very fine tube. Now pass the point of a knife lightly first in one and then in the opposite direction.

Mille-Feuille

lb	oz		kg	gr
1	2	Puff paste		560
	14	Jam		400
	10	Apricot jam		300
	10	Vanilla flowered whipped cream		300
	5	Wild strawberries		150

Baking time: 7-8 minutes.

Roll out paste 1/5 in. (5 mm.) thick and cut out 5-6 discs the size of a small gâteau ring. Cut out the middles of all except one which should be a little larger. Dock them all and bake in a hot oven. When cold stick the rings together with the jam, trim all the edges so that the cake is nice and round, brush the outside with apricot purée and place on to the larger base, also brushed with apricot purée. Decorate the outside with small puff paste decorations, baked separately, candied fruit or almonds, etc., and shortly before serving fill centre with whipped cream mixed with strawberries.

Mocha Gâteau

The Classic Method of Preparation

Bake a butter sponge or genoese mixture in a square or round tin. When cold, split twice and sandwich with a light mocha buttercream. Spread the top and sides with the same buttercream and mask the sides with roasted nib almonds. Using a star tube, decorate the top by piping small mocha buttercream stars close together in symmetrical lines.

Mocha Tourte

lb	oz		kg	gr
1	4	Egg		625
	14	Sugar (castor)		400
	14	Flour		400
	3/4	Instant coffee		20
	7	Butter		200

Follow the same method of preparation as for butter sponge. Before blending in the flour, sift it twice together with the coffee. When the sponge has been baked and is completely cold, slice it horizontally into two or three layers according to the size of the tourte and sandwich together with mocha flavoured buttercream. Spread buttercream thinly over the top of the tourte, leave in the refrigerator and then cover with mocha flavoured fondant. Decorate with piped fondant and some chocolate coffee beans.

Orange Mousseline Gâteau

lb	oz		kg	gr
	6 1/2	Sugar (castor)		190
	2 1/2	Flour		75
	2 1/2	Potato starch		75

lb	oz		kg	gr
	4	Egg yolks		125
	3 3/4	Egg whites		110
		Zest of 1 1/2 oranges		

Whip the egg yolks, sugar and zest until foamy. Fold in the egg whites whisked to a stiff snow together with the sieved flour and potato starch. Bake in a greased, floured round tin at 360° F (180° C). When cold, coat all over with orange flavoured and coloured fondant and decorate with thinly cut candied orange peel arranged in a design.

Orange Tourte

Cut a round genoese base into three slices and sandwich them together with some orange curd. An equal quantity of buttercream is mixed with some orange curd and this is used to coat the whole cake. Refrigerate and then cover all over with orange fondant. Decorate.

Pierrette Gâteau

Split a round butter sponge base twice and sandwich with almond buttercream. Coat the top and sides with the same buttercream and mask the sides with roasted chopped almonds. Cover the top with a thin disc of coffee marzipan which should be exactly the same size. Place a stencil with the silhouette of Pierrette and a crescent moon on top, dust very well with icing sugar and remove the stencil carefully so that the silhouette is clearly visible on the dark background.

Pineapple Tourte

Roll out some sablé paste, cut out round pieces (three for each tourte) and bake them in a medium oven. When they are cold, sandwich the pieces together with a kirsch flavoured buttercream containing some finely chopped glacé pineapple. Place in the refrigerator and then coat the tourtes with kirsch flavoured buttercream so as to obtain a smooth and even appearance. Cover completely with white or yellow fondant. Decorate with fondant using a paper bag and finish off with small oblong pieces of glacé pineapple.

Pistachio Tourte

lb	oz		kg	gr
1	0	Egg yolks		500
	10	Egg whites		300
1	5	Sugar (castor)		650
	7	Flour		200
	10	Ground pistachio nuts		300
	7	Ground almonds		200
	3 1/2	Butter (melted)		100

Whisk the egg whites with half the sugar and beat the yolks with the rest. Add the ground pistachio nuts and almonds. Amalgamate both mixtures, adding the flour and melted butter. Fill some 9 in. (22 cm.) flan rings and bake at 360° F (182° C). When they are cold, brush the tourtes with apricot purée and cover with pistachio fondant.

Polish Tourte

Soften some almond paste by mixing in some apricot purée and add the zest of a lemon. Roll out some scraps of puff paste. Cut out two rounds with pastry cutters, one of which is 3/4 in. (2 cm.) smaller than the other. Place the smaller round on a moistened baking sheet. Using a savoy bag fitted with a plain tube, pipe the filling into a spiral on to the smaller piece of puff paste. Brush the edges with egg and cover over with the larger piece of puff paste. Press down well to seal firmly and then trim the edges with the cutter. Brush all over with egg and mark with a knife. Bake at 380° F (193° C). Just before the Polish Tourte is completely baked, dust with icing sugar and glaze in a hot oven.

Praliné Gâteau

Bake genoese mixture in a round tin. When cold, split twice. Sandwich with praline buttercream, glaze the top and sides with well boiled apricot purée and mask with finely chopped roasted almonds. Lightly dust the top with icing sugar.

Praliné Tourte

lb	oz		kg	gr
	14	Egg yolks		400
1	2	Egg		560

lb	oz		kg	gr
1	5	Sugar (castor)		650
	10	Roasted ground hazelnuts		300
1	5	Flour		650
	14	Butter (melted)		400

Whip up the egg, egg yolks and sugar. Add the hazelnuts together with the flour and melted butter. Fill some 9 in. (22 cm.) flan rings and bake at 360° F (182° C). When the sponges have cooled down, cut them into layers and sandwich with praline buttercream which is also used to cover the whole tourte. Leave in a cool place, cover with pink fondant and decorate the sides with roasted almonds.

Queen Pomare Gâteau

Bake genoese mixture in a large dome-shaped mould which has been greased and floured. When cold, split four times and sandwich with praline buttercream. Coat with chocolate fondant, decorate with roasted split almonds and mask the bottom edge with finely chopped pistachio nuts.

Rosemary Gâteau

lb	oz		kg	gr
	4	Sugar (icing)		125
	2 ³/₄	Egg yolks		80
	1 ³/₄	Egg		50
	3 ¹/₂	Egg whites		100
	2	Ground almonds		60
	2 ³/₄	Flour		80
	3 ¹/₂	Butter (melted)		100

Filling

lb	oz		kg	gr
	3 ¹/₂	Ground almonds		100
	3 ¹/₂	Sugar (icing)		100
	2 ³/₄	Butter (melted)		80
	2 ³/₄	Chocolate		80

Whip the egg yolks and sugar to a stiff sponge, add the egg and almonds and continue whipping for a short time. Fold in the egg whites whisked to a stiff snow, together with the sieved flour. Lastly blend in the butter which should be barely lukewarm. Fill into a greased and floured round tin and bake at 360° F (180° C) and allow to cool. Split twice and sandwich with the filling made as follows: mix the almonds thoroughly with the sugar and butter, then add the melted chocolate. Allow to set after sandwiching the gâteau, then coat it with pink fondant, set aside for a few minutes and place a rose-shaped template on top. Dust with icing sugar and carefully remove the template.

Sans-Gêne Gâteau

Bake genoese sponge in a round buttered and floured tin, using only two thirds of the usual amount of sugar. The other third should be lightly caramelized, crushed and sieved when cold, and added to the genoese mixture. Bake in a very slow oven for about 30-35 minutes to prevent the gâteau from colouring too much because of the caramel sugar. Slice the gâteau, fill with praliné buttercream and spread buttercream thinly around the sides. Scatter on roasted chopped almonds all around the sides. Garnish with 8 small almond cornets filled with praliné buttercream with a star tube.

Success Gâteau

Sandwich four japonaise bases with hazelnut buttercream and coat with kirsch flavoured fondant on top. Spread the sides with the same buttercream and mask with roasted chopped almonds. Sprinkle a few of the almonds on top.

Sylvia Gâteau

lb	oz		kg	gr
	4	Egg whites		125
	7	Sugar (icing)		200
	5	Ground almonds		150

Whisk the egg whites to a stiff snow and carefully fold in the sugar and ground almonds. Using a savoy bag with a large plain tube, pipe out spiral bases, not too close together on to greased and floured baking sheets. Bake at 360° F (180° C). Remove from the baking sheets while still hot and cool on wire trays. Sandwich the bases with mocha buttercream, dust the top well with icing sugar, mark a lattice pattern using the back of a knife and place a pink marzipan bow in the centre, fixing it in position with a little fondant.

Tourte niçoise

Line a flan ring with scrap puff paste. Fill with some almond paste softened with curaçao and containing finely diced candied orange peel and the zest of one or two oranges to enhance the flavour. Cover the top of the tourte with a piece of puff paste made up of scraps and cut with a pastry wheel. Ice with royal icing, sprinkle with flaked blanched almonds, dust with icing sugar and decorate the centre with a crystallized orange slice. Leave to dry and bake in a slow oven 356° F (180° C). Before placing in the oven, prick the tourte several times with the tip of a pointed knife. *(Illustration page 422.)*

Tourte Religieuse

lb	oz		kg	gr
1	5	Marzipan		650
	7	Confectioner's custard		200
	3 1/2	Kirsch		100
	6	Egg whites		180
	7	Sugar (castor)		200
	5	Almonds (flaked)		150

Line some flan rings with puff paste. Leave in a cool place for 2-3 hours and then bake blind (that is to say with the bottom covered with cherry stones). When cold, fill with the marzipan which has been mixed with confectioner's custard and kirsch. Meanwhile whisk the egg whites with the sugar until stiff and use this mixture to cover over the tourte filling. Sprinkle with flaked almonds and dust with icing sugar. Bake at 380° F (193° C) for 10-15 minutes.

Turin Gâteau

lb	oz		kg	gr
1	2	Chestnuts		560
	3 1/2	Best butter		100
	3 1/2	Grated chocolate		100
	3 1/2	Vanilla sugar		100

Peel and boil the chestnuts, drain them well and rub through a sieve. While still hot, mix thoroughly with the butter, sugar and grated chocolate till very smooth. Fill this mixture into a cake tin, square if possible, covering the bottom with paper. Press down smoothly and put in a refrigerator for several hours to cool. When set, turn out and slice with a knife dipped in hot water. This excellent cake is not baked.

Valencia Gâteau

lb	oz		kg	gr
	4 1/2	Sugar (icing)		140
1	3/4	Flour		50
1	3/4	Potato flour		50
	3	Egg yolks		90
	3	Egg whites		90
	2 3/4	Candied orange peel (diced and soaked in curaçao)		80

Baking time: 40-50 minutes.

Filling and garnish

lb	oz		kg	gr
	5	Candied orange peel (diced, macerated in rum)		150
	3 1/2	Apricot jam (to bind the above)		100
	3 1/2	Rum flavoured fondant		100
	7	Orange flavoured fondant		200

Whip yolks and icing sugar to a foam. When it has doubled its volume fold in the stiffly beaten whites, flour and potato flour at the same time. Grease and flour a square mould and fill it with one half of the mixture. Scatter the drained, diced orange peel on top and cover with the remaining mixture. Bake in a moderate oven, and allow to cool. Slice and fill with the diced orange peel. Glaze with apricot purée. Carefully cover two opposite corners (tops and sides) with paper and coat the middle and the remaining two corners with yellow, rum flavoured fondant. When set, remove the paper and replace with orange coloured and flavoured fondant. Decorate with pieces of candied orange peel.

Viennese Tourte

lb	oz		kg	gr
	14	Sweet pastry		400
1	12	Raspberry jam		850
	7	Royal icing		200
	5	Egg whites		150
	7	Almonds (flaked)		200

After rolling the sweet pastry to a thickness of $1/10$ in. (3 mm.), cut out some round pieces, three of which are required for each tourte. Pipe out some royal icing in a criss-cross pattern on the third piece of paste. After baking, sandwich the pieces together with raspberry jam, placing the decorated piece on top. Coat the sides with meringue mixture and then with flaked almonds. Flash quickly in the oven.

Walnut Gâteau

lb	oz		kg	gr
1	0	Egg		500
	14	Sugar (castor)		400
	12 $1/2$	Flour		390
	$3/4$	Instant coffee		20
	8	Butter (melted)		250

Whip the egg and sugar over gentle heat, then remove from the heat and whip to a stiff sponge. Sieve the flour with the instant coffee, fold into the sponge and lastly add the butter. Fill into a greased and floured round mould and bake at 360° F (180° C). When cold, split and sandwich with mocha buttercream mixed with chopped walnuts. Cover the gâteau with mocha buttercream, allow to set, then coat with coffee coloured and flavoured fondant. Finish off with a ring of crystallized walnuts round the top.

Torten - Germany

Central European torten are becoming very popular in Great Britain and the British craftsman is applying his skill to this fine form of gâteau.

Essentially a torte is a built up round structure decorated with soft eating materials; particular care is taken with flavouring which should be a liqueur or a spirit. It can be said that a good torte is one with a pleasing decorative appearance inside and out.

The base can be built up with combinations of sweet paste, japonaise, sponge, stabilized cream, jelly, almond paste, etc. The torte, before final decoration, is marked into 8, 10, 14 or 16 parts according to the size of the base.

There are many classic torten well known to continental people and to visitors from all over the world. Many are given here.

Birthday or Anniversary Numeral

To make the numeral, either bake a butter sponge mixture in an appropriately shaped mould or cut the numeral out of a genoese. Sprinkle with kirsch and sandwich with one layer of raspberry jam.

Brush the whole numeral with apricot purée and cover with almond paste. Decorate the two outer edges with piped royal icing, then a thin border of chocolate next to it and pick out the centre in pink fondant. Finish off with glacé fruits, marzipan animals or candles, etc.

Birthday Torte

Any fondant coated torte base may be used. Decorate the edge all round with dots of coffee fondant. Pipe out fondant tulips and leaves freehand. Mimosa balls, crystallized violets and pistachio nuts may be used as additional decorations. Finish off with a suitably inscribed marzipan plaque or an inscription piped out freehand on the torte.
(Illustration page 557.)

Black Forest Cherry Torte

lb	oz		kg	gr
	7	Sugar (castor)		200
	5 $1/2$	Egg yolks		165
	1 $3/4$	Egg		50
	3 $1/2$	Sponge crumbs		100
	2	Ground almonds		60
	1 $3/4$	Cocoa powder		50

lb	oz		kg	gr
	7	Egg whites		200
	2	Flour		60
	14	Cherries		400
		(poached and stoned)		
1	4	Dairy cream		625
		Kirsch		
	½	Water		15

Whip the yolks, egg, sugar and water to a stiff sponge. Blend in the sponge crumbs, ground almonds, cocoa powder, egg whites whisked to a stiff snow and the flour. Fill into a greased and floured 10 in. (25 cm.) hoop and bake at 360° F (180° C). When cold, split twice. Cover the bottom layer with the cooked cherries and spread with a little vanilla flavoured whipped dairy cream. Place the second layer on top, spread it with whipped cream well flavoured with kirsch and cover with the top layer sponge. Spread kirsch flavoured whipped cream all over the top and sides, mask the sides with chocolate shavings, decorate the top with whirls of whipped cream round the edge and place half a red glacé cherry in the centre of each whirl. Finish the top decoration with chocolate shavings round the edge and a circle in the middle. Dust with icing sugar and refrigerate. This torte is intended for immediate consumption.

Bread Torte for a Housewarming

lb	oz		kg	gr
	12	Marzipan		375
	3 ½	Egg yolks		100
	6	Egg whites		180
	3 ½	Sugar		100
	3	Flour		85
	3 ½	Finely grated toasted pumpernickel		100
1	¾	Candied lemon peel		50
1	¾	Chocolate crumbs		50
		A little rum, cinnamon and salt		
		Red currant jam		

Beat the egg yolks and 7 oz. (200 gr.) marzipan until frothy; whip the egg whites and sugar to a snow and fold into the egg yolk/marzipan mixture together with the flour, pumpernickel, lemon peel, chocolate crumbs, rum, cinnamon and salt.

Fill into a round bread pan and bake off. After baking, slice through once, sandwich with red currant jam and cover with a disc made out of approx. 5 oz. (150 gr.) marzipan. Flash, then arrange glacé fruits in a ring on top.

Finish off with a salt cellar and pepper pot made of caramel and a marzipan plaque with the inscription 'Housewarming'.

Budapest Pineapple Torte

Ingredients for 5 thin bases approx. ½ in. (1 cm.) thick, 10 in. (25 cm.) in diameter.

Filling

lb	oz		kg	gr
1	4	Pineapple buttercream		600
		Buttercream for coating		
		Roasted almonds		
		Pineapple jam		

Sandwich the bases with pineapple buttercream and coat with buttercream. Mark the sides with a comb scraper and mark the top into 16 portions, sprinkle the centre with finely flaked roasted almonds and dust with icing sugar. Decorate each portion with a pineapple buttercream rosette and a quarter glacé cherry. An ornament made from piping chocolate may be used as an additional decoration. *(Illustration page 555.)*

Cheese Cream Torte

lb	oz		kg	gr
1	0	Cream cheese		500
	3	Egg yolks		90
	6	Sugar (icing)		180
	10	Milk		300
	2 ½	Sultanas		75
	10	Dairy cream		300
		Salt (a pinch)		
		Vanilla		
		Gelatine (8 sheets)		
	12	Scrap puff pastry		375

Pin out scrap puff pastry to make two bases 10 in. (25 cm.) in diameter. Allow to rest for at least 20 minutes before baking. Immediately after baking, cut one of the bases into sixteen segments. Line the bottom of a flan ring with paper, spread the uncut base with apricot jam and place it in the ring. Mix the egg yolks and sugar together, add the warm milk in which a little vanilla has been steeped, cook over gentle heat to a smooth custard that will coat a spatula, add a pinch of salt and the gelatine that has been soaked and squeezed dry, and allow to cool. Mix the sieved cream cheese with the custard, carefully fold in the whipped dairy cream, add the sultanas and quickly fill into the flan ring. Smooth over the surface, cover with the cut base, dust with icing sugar and refrigerate well.

Children's Birthday Torte

Any torte may be used, but a domed one is preferable as the design will stand out better. To decorate, prepare a paste of piping consistency from 1 oz. (30 gr.) egg, 1 oz. (30 gr.) sugar and 1 oz. (30 gr.) flour. Pipe out a small basket on a greased baking sheet and mould to shape as desired immediately after baking. Place on the torte, together with flowers made up of various glacé fruits. Finish off with a suitable birthday plaque and place a small marzipan rocking-horse in the basket.
(Illustration page 556.)

Chocolate Torte

lb	oz		kg	gr
	5	Butter		150
	5	Sugar (castor)		150
	2	Egg yolks		75
	6	Egg whites		175
	5	Grated chocolate		150
	2	Cornflour		75

Chocolate icing

lb	oz		kg	gr
	8	Sugar		250
	3 1/2	Water		100
	1	Block chocolate		30

(Boil to the thread stage and with a spatula agitate a little of the solution on the sides of the pan until it grains.)

Beat the butter, sugar and egg yolks until frothy, and mix with the grated chocolate. Whip the egg whites to a stiff snow, and fold into the butter mixture together with the cornflour.

Deposit in a hoop 10 in. (25 cm.) diameter and bake at 356° F (180° C). When cold, remove from the hoop, brush with apricot purée and coat with the chocolate icing.

Christmas Torte

Use a Baumkuchen (*see* Pineapple Baumtorte) for this torte.

Cover the top and sides with lightly moulded white marzipan (approx. 7 oz. [200 gr.]). Cut small round windows in the top edge with a savoy pipe, lay round pieces of pineapple in the windows and decorate the base of the torte with small bulbs of royal icing.

Use fondant angels and balls for additional decoration, make a fir branch out of pistachio nuts and chocolate, and finish off with a marzipan plaque bearing a Christmastide inscription.

Dairy Cream Cheese Torten

Into two 9 in. (22 cm.) flan rings place sponge bases about 1/2 in. (1 cm.) thick. Sprinkle with rum syrup. Spread on top the following filling which is enough for the two:

lb	oz		kg	gr
1	0	Cheese curd		500
	4	Sugar (castor)		125
	14	Lemon curd		400
	1 1/2	Gelatine		45
1	4	Whipped dairy cream		625
	6	Sultanas (soaked in rum)		180

The gelatine is soaked in water until pliable and then melted over heat. Mix the cheese, sugar and lemon curd. Add the gelatine and mix in. Fold in the whipped cream and the sultanas. Refrigerate.

Take two circles of sponge about $^1/_4$ in. (5 mm.) thick, cut into eight segments and dust with icing sugar. Carefully arrange them on the base and pipe a rosette of cream on each, sprinkling them with a little chopped pistachio nut or lightly roasted nib almonds.

Easter Torte

lb	oz		kg	gr
	7	Sugar (castor)		200
	7	Marzipan		200
	7	Flour		200
	6 $^1/_4$	Egg yolks		190
	10	Egg whites		300
		1 sweet paste base 10 in. (25 cm.) diameter		
		A little lemon		
	5	Pistachio (ground)		150
1	0	Pistachio buttercream		500

Mix the buttercream with pistachio nuts flavoured with a little kirsch.

Beat together the sugar, marzipan, flour, egg yolks and lemon, and fold in the egg whites whipped to a snow. After baking in a hoop, slice the base through three times and sprinkle with brandy. Brush the sweet paste base with any desired jam, cover with the sponge layers sandwiched with pistachio buttercream to make a dome shape and top with pistachio marzipan. Mask the side with roasted chopped almonds.

Decorate with a white marzipan hare coated with caramel, a little buttercream, marzipan Easter figures and a chocolate inscription 'Happy Easter'.

Estella Torte

Bake a light genoese in greased and floured 8 in. (20 cm.) cottage pans. Do the same with a Sacher torte mixing. When cold, cut each into four and re-assemble, using alternate layers of white and chocolate. The layering to be with nougat buttercream top and bottom and apricot jam in the centre. Cover with chocolate into which roasted nib almonds have been mixed. Mask the bottom edge with chocolate vermicelli. Mark the top into the required number of divisions. Into each, place an almond paste cut-out star in the centre of which a blanched roasted hazelnut is fixed.

Fan Torte

lb	oz		kg	gr
	2 $^1/_4$	Egg yolks		65
	6 $^1/_2$	Egg whites		190
	7 $^3/_4$	Marzipan		220
	4 $^1/_4$	Sugar (castor)		125
	4 $^1/_4$	Flour		125
	4 $^1/_4$	Butter (hot)		125
	4 $^1/_2$	Sweet paste		150
1	5	Buttercream		650
	3 $^1/_2$	Nougat paste		100
		Chocolate couverture		

Beat the egg yolks, 3 $^1/_2$ oz. (100 gr.) marzipan and half the sugar until frothy. Whip the egg whites and remaining sugar to a stiff snow, add to the egg yolk mixture, blend in the flour and lastly fold in the butter. Spread on to paper to make a genoese 14 in. by 10 in. (35 × 25 cm.) and approx. $^1/_2$ in. (1 cm.) thick, and bake at 392° F (200° C) for 20 minutes.

Pin out the sweet paste into a round 10 in. (25 cm.) in diameter and after baking and cooling, spread with part of the nougat buttercream (made by adding the nougat to the buttercream). Spread the rest of the buttercream on to the genoese, smooth off, cut into strips 1 $^1/_2$ in. (4 cm.) wide and arrange on the cream covered sweet paste base in a spiral. Coat the whole torte with cream and place roasted almonds round the sides. Mark the top into 16 portions and pipe a whirl of cream on each. Pin out the rest of marzipan into a disc 10 in. (25 cm.) in diameter and coat with couverture. After impressing with the fluted roller and cutting into 16 sections, dust 8 of them with icing sugar and place the dusted and undusted marzipan triangles alternately on top of the torte. *(Illustration page 130.)*

Florentine Torte

Spread warm Florentine mixing on 7 in. (18 cm.) wafer paper circles and bake at 380° F (193° C). When cool, trim to shape and cut into 12 sections. Sandwich a 7 in. (18 cm.) butter sponge with whipped dairy cream and spread the top and sides. Place the Florentine segments in place in top and mask the sides with roasted flaked almonds.

Frankfurter Kranz

lb	oz		kg	gr
	5	Sugar (castor)		150
	4	Butter		125
	7	Egg		200
	3 1/2	Flour		100
	3 1/2	Potato powder		100
	1/8	Baking powder		4
		Lemon zest		

For decoration

lb	oz		kg	gr
	12	Vanilla buttercream		350
	7	Praline croquant		200
	10	glacé cherries		
	20	pistachio nuts		

Baking temperature 360° F (182° C). Baking time 40 minutes. Cream the sugar and soft butter well. Beat in the egg portion at a time.

Add the sieved flour, potato powder and baking powder together with the lemon zest. Place this mixture into a tall circular savarin mould and bake. Leave to cool. Slice into four and sprinkle with rum, kirsch or Grand-Marnier. Sandwich all together with buttercream.

Cover with buttercream and sprinkle with crushed praline croquant. Decorate with buttercream whirls and place halved cherries and pistachio nuts on top.

Fruit Torte

lb	oz		kg	gr
	9	Sweet paste		270
		Viennese base 10 in. (25 cm.) in diameter		
1 3/4		Vanilla cream		50
		Raspberry jam		
		Various fruits		

Pin out the sweet paste into a flat disc 10 in. (25 cm.) diameter and bake off. After baking, brush with raspberry jam, lay a thin viennese base on top and cover it with vanilla cream. Place any fruit desired in a ring round the top of the torte and glaze.

Hazelnut Torte

Split an almond genoese base twice and spread with nougat buttercream. Coat top and sides with the same cream. Mask the bottom edge with chocolate vermicelli. Mark the top into the required number of divisions. Place a ring in the centre into which spread chocolate vermicelli. Remove the ring.

With a savoy bag fitted with a 1/4 in. (5 mm.) plain tube, pipe a line in the middle of each division starting from the edge of the vermicelli circle, terminating on the edge of the torte. At this end place a piped chocolate motif on which is placed a blanched roasted hazelnut.

Kirsch Torte

Pencil 9-10 in. (22-25 cm.) diameter rings on greaseproof paper and with a savoy bag fitted with a 3/8 in. (1 cm.) plain tube, pipe spirals with japonaise *(page 208)*. Bake at 350° F (176° C). When cool, remove from the paper and trim with a flan ring. Split a round, light genoese base the same diameter as the japonaise. Spread a japonaise base with pink, kirsch flavoured buttercream mixed with chopped cherries and place a sponge layer on top. Drench this with kirsch syrup, spread with cream and cover with the other sponge layer, repeat drenching and spreading, then top with another japonaise base, bottom uppermost. Spread top and sides with cream (without cherries), dust lightly with icing sugar and mark the desired number of divisions. Mask the side with sieved japonaise crumbs and sprinkle a few green nibbed almonds in the centre.

Macaroon Torte

1 butter sponge base 10 in. (25 cm.) diameter and 2 in. (5 cm.) deep.

lb	oz		kg	gr
	3 1/2	Egg		100
	3 1/2	Marzipan		100
		Apricot marzipan		
		(page 212)		
		Kirsch		
		Raspberry jam		
		Apricot jam		
		Egg yolk macaroon paste		
		Glacé cherries, angelica		
		Green almonds,		
		pistachio nuts, roasted		
		chopped almonds		

After baking, slice the butter sponge base through 3 times and sprinkle with kirsch. Spread the bottom layer with raspberry jam, the middle one with apricot marzipan and the top one with apricot jam. Coat the whole torte with 3 1/2 oz. (100 gr.) marzipan brought to a spreading consistency with 3 1/2 oz. (100 gr.) whole egg. Pipe out a design in egg yolk macaroon paste and flash. Glaze with hot apricot purée. Finally decorate with red glacé cherries, angelica, green almonds and pistachio nuts. Arrange roasted, chopped almonds in a small rosette in the centre and mask the sides with flaked almonds.

Margret Cake

lb	oz		kg	gr
2	7	Marzipan	1	200
	6	Butter		180
	10	Sugar (icing)		300
1	12	Egg		875
	8	Flour		250
	8	Cornflour		250
		Zest of 1 lemon		

Mix the butter and marzipan to a smooth paste. Separate the eggs. Whisk the egg whites to a stiff snow. Gradually adding the sugar. Work the egg yolks into the marzipan/butter paste. Fold the flour, cornflour and zest into the egg whites/sugar snow. Amalgamate both mixtures and fill into large fluted baking moulds that have been greased and floured. Bake at 400° F (204° C). When cold, brush over with apricot purée, coat with arrack flavoured fondant which should be thin enough to glaze only. Decorate with red glacé cherries and split roasted almonds round the top edge. Place yellow glacé cherries in the centre and finish off with pistachio nuts. Mask the bottom edge with finely chopped roasted almonds. *(Illustration page 427.)*

Mignon Torte

6 almond sweet paste mignon bases 10 in. (25 cm.) in diameter. *(Page 187)*.

lb	oz		kg	gr
1	5	Lemon buttercream		650
	3 1/2	Marzipan		100
	5	Lemon fondant		150
		Egg yolk macaroons		
		Roasted chopped almonds		
		Glacé cherries		
		Hot apricot jam		
		Pistachio nuts		

Sandwich and coat the mignon bases with the lemon buttercream. Pin out a very thin marzipan cover, place on top and coat with lemon fondant.

After flashing the egg yolk macaroons, dip them in hot apricot jam and decorate with a glacé cherry. Place a macaroon on each portion of torte and decorate with pistachio nuts.

Mark the sides of the torte with a comb scraper and mask the bottom edge with roasted chopped almonds.

Mocha Buttercream Torte

Sweet paste base 10 in. (25 cm.) diameter. Meringue base 10 in. (25 cm.) diameter. 2 almond sponge bases 10 in. (25 cm.) diameter.

lb	oz		kg	gr
1	5	Mocha buttercream		650
		Roasted chopped almonds		
		Mocha beans		
		Pistachio nuts		
		Flat chocolate shapes		
		Nougat paste		

Cover a thin sweet paste base with nougat softened to a spreading consistency, lay a meringue base on top and spread with a $1/2$ in. (1 cm.) thick layer of mocha buttercream. Sandwich the two almond sponge bases with mocha cream and place on top. Coat the top and sides of the torte with mocha buttercream, mark the sides with a comb scraper finish and the bottom edge with roasted chopped almonds.

Mark the top into 16 portions, sprinkle the centre with roasted almonds, using a ring to contain the almonds, pipe out three lines of different lengths on each portion using a No. 3 pipe and top each with a mocha bean and a quarter pistachio nut. Decorate the edge with small flat chocolate shapes previously piped on paper. *(Illustrations pages 131, 554.)*

Oracle Torte

Any torte may be used as desired (e.g. Sacher Torte, Budapest Pineapple Torte, Buttercream Torte).

Cover the torte with marzipan of the colour desired, mark into 18 portions, place a dot of fondant on each division and stand a comical figure as desired on each dot.

Top the centre (which was cut out and replaced when the torte was marked) with a caramel arrow that will turn easily, to represent the 'wheel of fortune'. Pipe small bulbs of royal icing round the top edge of the torte and tie a gold ribbon round the side.

Orange Torte

lb	oz		kg	gr
	9	Sweet paste		270
		1 butter sponge base		
	14	Thickened stewed morello cherries		400
1	4	Whipped sweetened dairy cream		625
	2 $3/4$	Sugar		80
	1	Egg yolk		30
		Red currant jelly		
		Juice and zest of 2 oranges		
		6 sheets white gelatine		

Line a hoop or a 10 in. (25 cm.) sandwich plate with sweet paste and bake until golden. After baking, spread with red currant jelly, lay the butter sponge base on top and cover with the cherries.

Make an orange cream out of the dairy cream flavoured with the oranges, the sugar and egg yolk, thicken with gelatine and fill the cream on to the cherries.

After it has set, mark the torte into 16 portions, decorate each one with a dairy cream rosette and a glazed orange segment. Mask the sides with roasted almonds, decorate the centre with chocolate shavings and finish with pistachio nuts and halved glacé cherries.

Painter's Palette

Cut a palette shape out of a butter sponge 6 × 12 in. (15 × 30 cm.), split and sandwich with buttercream. Cover with white marzipan and edge with coffee marzipan impressed with a fluted roller. The following are suitable for decoration: spots of fondant in various colours, caramel flowers such as tulips, narcissi, etc., and a paint brush.

Parisian Strawberry Torte

$1/2$ recipe cheese cream *(page 220)*.
Puff pastry base 10 in. (25 cm.) diameter.
Viennese base 10 in. (25 cm.) diameter.
Fresh strawberries
Strawberry jelly

Spread the cheese cream on the puff pastry base, cover with a thin viennese base, then the washed and dried strawberries. Lastly glaze with strawberry jelly and mask the sides with roasted chopped almonds. Any fresh, unblanched fruit, suitably prepared (e.g. bilberries, oranges, bananas, peaches) or apples may be substituted for the strawberries.

(Illustration page 132.)

Peppermint Cake

To make this cake successfully, the following preparations are necessary. Cut fresh peppermint before the beginning of the flowering season from the middle of

June to July to obtain a supply for the whole year. Pick off as many of the larger, more intensely coloured leaves as required, press them well and freeze in a suitable container. Dry the tender leaves in the shade, grind finely and store in a cool, dark place. When using the frozen peppermint, do not thaw it out, but break off small pieces and put through the well chilled mixer at once to obtain a very fine purée.

Make a genoese in the usual manner adding as much peppermint purée and ground peppermint as required to obtain the desired colour and flavour, spread on a paper lined rectangular baking sheet and bake. When cold, split into three layers and spread with fresh raspberry pulp, cover with ganache made with equal parts plain couverture and dairy cream and place all the layers together firmly. Cut the cake into strips and then into slices and serve with whipped dairy cream.
(Illustration page 767.)

Peach Wine Cream Torte

lb	oz		kg	gr
	9	Sweet paste		270
		Almond sponge base 10 in. (25 cm.) diameter		
		Raspberry jam		
		Peaches to decorate		
		Peach jelly		
		Marzipan to cover sides		

Wine cream

lb	oz		kg	gr
	9	White wine		270
	2 1/4	Sugar (castor)		70
	1	Egg yolk		30
		Juice of 1 lemon		
		4 sheets white gelatine		

Pin out the sweet paste into a flat base 10 in. (25 cm.) in diameter and bake off. After baking, spread with raspberry jam and cover with a thin almond base. Cook the wine cream ingredients until thick and spread the wine cream on top of the almond base. Decorate with peaches blanched in white wine and sprinkled with a few drops of arrack. Fill the space between them with stewed morello cherries and glaze the top of the torte with peach jelly.

Lastly encase the sides of the torte in white marzipan impressed with the fluted roller.
(Illustration page 563.)

Pineapple Baumtorte

lb	oz		kg	gr
	7	Butter		200
	7	Cornflour		200
	7	Sugar (castor)		200
	5 1/4	Egg yolks		150
	10	Egg whites		300
	3/4	Arrack		20
		Salt		
		Lemon		
		Apricot jam		
		Lemon fondant		
		Marzipan olives		
		Small pieces of pineapple		
		Pistachio nuts		

Cream the butter and cornflour, beat the egg yolks and 5 oz. (150 gr.) sugar until frothy, then blend together. Whip the egg whites and the rest of the sugar to a stiff snow and add to the batter with a little salt. Flavour with lemon, vanilla and lastly arrack.

For method of baking *page 602*.

After baking, take off the Baumkuchen, leave to cool, then trim the sides carefully so that the layers can be seen. Spread with apricot purée, coat the top with lemon fondant and mark into the required number of portions.

Decorate each portion with a marzipan olive and small piece of pineapple, coated with caramel.
(Illustration page 561.)

Pineapple Ice Parfait Torte

3 Butter sponge bases
7 in. (18 cm.) diameter, 1 in. (2.5 cm.) deep.

lb	oz		kg	gr
	5 1/4	Egg		150
	5	Sugar (castor)		150

lb	oz		kg	gr
2	12	Whipped dairy cream	1	375
	14	Pineapple cubes		400
	4	Cognac		125
	4	Curaçao		125
	4 1/2	Chopped almond macaroons		140

Make a sponge by beating up the egg and sugar warm, continuing until cool. Flavour the slightly sweetened dairy cream with the cognac and curaçao and add the pineapple cubes. Mix into the sponge and add the chopped macaroons. Deposit into three 7 in. (18 cm.) torte rings.

When the torten are frozen (after about 1 1/2 hours) turn out on to the butter sponge bases. Decorate with whipped dairy cream, mark into divisions and place a pineapple cube on each portion.

Pineapple Fruit Torte

lb	oz		kg	gr
	9	Sweet paste		270
		Butter sponge base 10 in. (25 cm.) in diameter.		
		Red currant jelly		

Cream

lb	oz		kg	gr
	10	Pineapple juice		300
	1	Cornstarch		30
	5	Sugar		150
	2 1/4	Egg yolks		65
	2 1/2	Egg whites		70
		Juice of 1 lemon		
		Pineapple slices		
		Glacé cherries		

Pin out the sweet paste into a flat disc 10 in. (25 cm.) in diameter and bake off. Brush with red currant jelly and place a thin butter sponge base on top.

Make the cream by cooking the pineapple juice, cornstarch, 3 1/2 oz. (100 gr.) sugar, egg yolks and juice of one lemon. Whip the egg whites and the rest of the sugar to a stiff snow and fold into the cream. Cover the butter sponge base with the cream shaped into a dome.

When cold, cover the top of the torte with pineapple slices, glaze with pineapple jelly and decorate each portion with a red glacé cherry.

Mask the side of the torte with roasted flaked almonds.

Prince Regent Torte - Munich

lb	oz		kg	gr
	3 1/2	Butter		100
	3 1/2	Sugar (castor)		100
	6	Flour		175
	1 3/4	Cornflour		50
	1/8	Baking powder		4
	5	Milk (approx.)		150
	3 1/2	Shell eggs (two)		100

Filling

lb	oz		kg	gr
	4 1/2	Butter		130
	4 1/2	Chocolate		130
	1	Sugar (icing)		30
	3 1/2	Egg		100

First separate the two eggs. Cream the butter, sugar and egg yolks together until light. Add the flour, cornflour and baking powder sieved together and then the milk. Finally fold in the stiffly whipped whites.

Pour out in 5 thin round bases on to greased and floured baking sheets, baking off one after the other to a pale golden colour. Alternatively, the mixture may be poured into torten rings that have been drummed with paper.

After the filling has been well beaten until very light, it is used to sandwich the five bases one on top of the other, leaving the top bare. Weight down overnight with a small board to prevent the layers curling.

Cover with 5 oz. (150 gr.) of melted chocolate into which a few drops of water have been mixed, working quickly so to ensure that the surface is smooth and even. The torte may be decorated with blanched almonds if desired, although the original recipe provides for a plain, dark surface with no additional decoration.

Red Currant Meringue Torte

Sweet paste base 10 in. (25 cm.) diameter

1 Viennese base

lb	oz		kg	gr
1	12	Red currants		875
		Red currant jam		

Meringue

lb	oz		kg	gr
	5	Egg whites		150
	4	Red currants		125
	7	Sugar (castor)		200

Line a 10 in. (25 cm.) torte ring with sweet paste and bake until golden. Spread with red currant jam, lay a thin viennese base on top and cover with red currants.

Top with the meringue (egg whites, red currants and sugar whipped up warm, removed from heat and whipped until cold). Mark the torte into 16 portions and pipe out a meringue rosette on each one. Then dust with icing sugar, flash quickly in a hot oven and place a red currant in the centre of each rosette. Finally dust the whole torte again with icing sugar.
(Illustration page 562.)

Regent Torte

lb	oz		kg	gr
	3	Egg yolks		90
	6	Egg whites		180
	4	Sugar		125
	2 1/2	Flour		75
	2 1/2	Cornflour		75
	1	Hot butter		30
1	5	Chocolate arrack buttercream		650
		A little lemon		
		Chocolate fondant		
		Chocolate shavings		

Beat the egg yolks and 3 oz. (95 gr.) sugar until frothy; whip the egg whites and 1 oz. (30 gr.) sugar to a stiff snow. Blend the flour and cornflour with the egg yolk/sugar sponge and the stiff snow. Lastly, add hot butter and a little lemon. Divide into 6 bases 10 in. (25 cm.) in diameter and approx. 1/4 in. (5 mm.) thick on a greased baking sheet and bake off briskly.

Sandwich these bases evenly with chocolate arrack buttercream. Brush the top with apricot purée and coat the whole torte with chocolate fondant. Mask the bottom edge with chocolate shavings.

Russian Charlotte Torte

Sweet pastry base 10 in. (25 cm.) diameter.

Apricot jam
Sponge fingers

lb	oz		kg	gr
1	4	Dairy cream		625
		Pineapple (1 slice)		
	2	Glacé cherries (mixed)		60
	1/2	Sherry		15
	1/2	Brandy		15
		Gelatine (8 sheets)		

1 Swiss roll made with:

lb	oz		kg	gr
	3	Egg yolks		90
	7 1/2	Egg whites		215
	3 1/2	Sugar (castor)		100
	3 1/2	Flour		100

Make up the Swiss roll and spread with apricot jam, roll up, cut into slices and line the bottom and sides of a 10 in. (25 cm.) flan ring with them. The ring should be placed on a sheet of strong greaseproof paper. Chop the pineapple and glacé cherries, macerate in the sherry and brandy, mix with the whipped dairy cream, stiffen with the gelatine, previously soaked and dissolved, and fill into the flan ring. Place the sweet pastry base on top, refrigerate, turn out, mark into portions, brush with well boiled apricot purée and glaze with fruit jelly. Place the sponge fingers round the side and decorate each marked portion with a whirl of dairy cream and a glacé cherry.

Sacher Torte

lb	oz		kg	gr
	3	Egg yolks		90
	6	Egg whites		180
	5	Sugar (icing)		150
	2 3/4	Flour		80

lb	oz		kg	gr
	2 3/4	Marzipan		80
	2 3/4	Butter (hot)		80
	1	Ground almonds		30
	1	Orange peel (finely chopped)		30
	1	Cocoa paste		30
	14	Ganache		400

Whisk the egg yolks and sugar to a stiff sponge and the egg whites to a stiff snow. Soften the marzipan with the cocoa paste and butter and add it to the sponge with almonds, peel and flour. Lastly fold in the egg whites. Fill into a paper lined hoop 10 in. (25 cm.) in diameter and bake for about 45 minutes at 360° F (180° C). When cold, split once and sandwich with ganache. Allow to set, then coat the torte with chocolate fondant. Decorate with a chocolate seal.

Spanish Vanilla Torte

lb	oz		kg	gr
	10 1/2	Marzipan		300
	5 1/4	Sugar (castor)		150
1	3/4	Whole egg		50
	3 3/4	Egg yolks		105
	7	Egg whites		200
	2 1/2	Flour		75
	2 1/2	Cornflour		75
	3	Butter (hot)		90
1	3/4	Plain chocolate shavings		50
		Chocolate couverture		
		Pistachio nuts		

Beat the marzipan, 3 1/2 oz. (100 gr.) sugar, whole egg and egg yolks until frothy. Whip the egg whites and the rest of the sugar to a snow. Blend both mixtures with the flour and cornflour and lastly add the hot butter.

Sprinkle the sides of a greased pan shaped mould with flaked almonds and deposit half the mixing in it. Sprinkle this with the chocolate shavings, cover with the rest of the mixing, smooth off and bake at 356° F (180° C) for about 45 minutes.

After baking, turn out the torte, let it cool, brush all over with apricot purée and spread the top with couverture.

Mark into 16 portions; pipe a ganache rosette on each and finish off with pistachio nuts.

Strawberry Dairy Cream Torte

lb	oz		kg	gr
	9	Sweet paste		270
		1 Viennese base		
1	12	Strawberries		875
	3 1/2	Strawberry pulp		100
1	4	Dairy cream		625
		Red currant jelly		
		Lemon juice		
		4 sheets white gelatine		

Pin out the sweet paste into a flat disc 10 in. (25 cm.) in diameter, bake off and spread with red currant jelly. Place the viennese base on top and cover with the washed and dried strawberries. Mix the whipped dairy cream with the freshly sieved strawberry pulp and a little lemon juice, thicken with the gelatine and shape into a dome on top of the whole strawberries.

After marking the torte into 16 portions, decorate each with a strawberry cream rosette and finish off with fresh sweetened strawberries. Sprinkle chocolate shavings on the centre of the torte and dust with icing sugar. A little chopped pistachio nut may be used for final decoration.
(Illustration page 563).

Walnut Torte

5 thin walnut bases
Walnut cream
Mocha buttercream
Marzipan to cover

Spread the walnut bases with walnut cream and put together while still warm.

When cold, mask the torte with mocha buttercream and flute the sides. Cover the top with a marzipan disc and coat it with mocha fondant.

Decorate the bottom edge of the torte with almonds and mark the top into 16. Top each portion with two half walnuts sandwiched with pistachio marzipan and coated with caramel.
(Illustration page 555).

Gâteaux - Holland

In Holland gâteaux are similar to those produced in France and Switzerland, but the emphasis is given to buttercream fillings and decoration.

Buttercream Gâteau

A sponge base containing chopped peel is sliced twice and sandwiched with buttercream or crème pâtissière. The top and sides are spread with buttercream and the side masked with lightly roasted flaked almonds. The top is piped with buttercream and finished with fruits.

Christmas Wreath - Kerstkrans

These wreaths are made before Christmas and resemble Butterletters. They can be baked in a similar way. The wreath, however, is decorated and the almond paste contains candied cherries. For a wreath, which after baking weighs 18 oz. (560 gr.), 9 oz. (270 gr.) of almond paste is used. Roll this filling into a rope 10 in. (25 cm.) long and make a deep longitudinal cut, put the cherries into this cut, close the cut and roll the rope to 24 in. (60 cm.). Enclose this rope with the paste, pinned out as for Butterletters, and shape it into a wreath. Brush with egg. After a rest, brush again and bake. Oven temperature: 446° F (230° C). After baking, brush with apricot purée and water icing and decorate with about 2 oz. (60 gr.) of candied fruits, almonds, marzipan, etc. Place a small candle on each.
(Illustration page 423.)

Hearts and Hams - Harten en Hammen

lb	oz		kg	gr
	4	Egg yolks		125
		Zest of ½ lemon		
	5	Almond paste		150
	5	Egg whites		150
	1 ½	Sugar (granulated)		50
	3 ½	Flour		100

This kind of pastry is often made for sale on 5th of December, the birthday of Saint Nicholas.

Mix together the egg yolks, zest of lemon and the almond paste, and whip to a fluffy but firm mixture.

Next, beat the egg whites to a stiff snow. Fold the egg yolk mixture into the egg white mixture and finally add the flour. Put this batter into greased moulds that have the shapes of hearts and hams.

Bake at a temperature of 338° F (170° C). As soon as they are cold enough they are split and spread with reduced apricot purée. Brush the top and sides with well-boiled apricot purée, and then glaze with a transparent water icing.

These pastries are decorated with candied fruits, such as cherries, angelica and candied peel.

Mathilde Gâteau - Mathilde Taart

Sandwich three discs of puff pastry using crème pâtissière for one layer and apricot jam for the other. Coat the top with rose coloured and flavoured fondant and finish the side with buttercream and lightly roasted flaked almonds. Round the top edge place small rings of baked puff pastry that have been dusted with icing sugar. Decorate the centre with fruit.

Nougatine Gâteau - Nogat Taart

Sandwich three circles of japonaise with coffee buttercream into which crushed praline croquant has been mixed. Spread top and sides with plain coffee buttercream and mask the side with crushed praline croquant.

Decorate by piping coffee buttercream on top, adding nuts and motifs made with piping chocolate.

Vanilla Gâteau - Ouderwetse Vanille Roomtaart

Into a baked puff pastry case spread crème pâtissière. Pipe a spiral of apricot purée on top and cover with meringue. Dust lightly with icing sugar, sprinkle with red cherries and flash in a hot oven.

Gâteaux - Hungary

Dobos Torte

Ingredients for 6 thin bases 10 in. (25 cm.) diameter.

lb	oz		kg	gr
	10	Egg		300
	6	Sugar (castor)		180
	³/₄	Honey		20
	5	Flour		150
		Lemon		
		Vanilla		
		Caramel (melted sugar)		
		Roasted chopped almonds		
1	5	Chocolate arrack buttercream		650

Beat the egg, sugar and honey for about 5 minutes until frothy, blend in the flour, flavour with lemon and vanilla and bake exactly the same as for Budapest Pineapple Torte. After baking, sandwich 5 bases with chocolate arrack buttercream, coat with the same cream and mark the top into 16 portions. Pipe out a long whirl on top of each portion. Coat the sixth base with caramel and cut into 16 portions with a firm, buttered knife before it is cold. Place a caramel coated triangle fanwise on each piped-out whirl using it to give each segment a tilt. Finish the bottom edge neatly with roasted chopped almonds.

Gâteaux - Italy

In Italy, gâteaux are served mainly as a dessert. There are two kinds.

1. Those that can be stored for a limited time.
For these, buttercreams are used for sandwiching and decoration because they do not deteriorate quickly.
They are ideal for shop sale and for transportation.

2. Those for immediate use.

These are sandwiched with cream containing eggs, such as crème pâtissière, and those containing whipped dairy cream. This type of gâteaux should be eaten the same day as prepared. They cannot be displayed unless in a refrigerated show case. If displayed without refrigeration, they will deteriorate rapidly.

The general procedure in Italy and in the Italian speaking part of Switzerland, is to slice the base into two or three, sprinkle with liqueur diluted in a sugar syrup and then spread with cream. Chopped fruit or crushed nougat may be sprinkled on the cream before sandwiching is complete. Liqueur is sprinkled on top before the base is coated and decorated. The liqueur syrup is composed of a genuine liqueur, such as Cointreau, Alkermes, Maraschino, Grand-Marnier, Strega etc., or liqueurs fabricated by the confectioner, mixed with stock syrup and water.

Arancia

lb	oz		kg	gr
2	0	Butter	1	
1	12	Sugar (castor)		875
	6	Glucose		180
	14	Ground almonds		400
	14	Cornflour		400
	14	Flour		400
	14	Egg yolks		400
	14	Egg		400
	12	Orange peel (chopped)		375
		Vanilla		
		Zest and juice of 8 oranges and 4 lemons		
		Orange liqueur		

Whip the eggs, yolks, sugars and juices stiffly. Add the zest and fold in the rest of the materials, adding the butter, which has been well creamed, last. Fill into round rings and bake at 360° F (182° C). When cold, slice and spread with orange buttercream. Cover the top with orange coloured and flavoured fondant. Mask the side with buttercream and sieved crushed praline croquant. Decorate.
(Illustration page 560).

Argentina

Make a rectangular box shape with meringue and bake. Fill with three alternate layers of chocolate and white argentine cream.

Refrigerate for 4 hours and cut into rectangles. Dust with icing sugar.

Autumn

Take a hazelnut maddalena base soaked with curaçao and sandwich it with imperial chocolate cream. Cover top and sides with the same cream. Decorate the top with candied fruit.

The side is masked with selva *(page 253)* almond paste or roasted nib hazelnuts.

Cubana

Prepare three round bases of maddalena genoese by soaking with curaçao 21°. Sandwich and coat with imperial chocolate cream and mask with chocolate shavings. Place in the centre a half sphere of built up maddalena coated with yellow fondant and piped with a trellis design with piping chocolate. Place a crystallized violet on top as illustrated.
(Illustration page 558.)

Dairy Cream Gâteau - Torta Chantilly

Prepare and bake a genoese in a round torten ring. (*See* recipe for Light Genoese on *page 199* or Genoese Margherita on *page 201.*) When cold and firm, split into two or three layers and sprinkle with vanilla syrup or a liqueur to taste. Prepare a cream by mixing 8 parts of whipped dairy cream with 2 parts of Crema Pasticcera *or* 2 parts of Zabaglione (whipped) *(pages 235-236)*. Spread the layers and cover the top and sides of the gâteau with the cream and mask the side with coarse genoese or sponge crumbs. Decorate the top with stars of the remaining cream. Finish the border with rosettes of whipped dairy cream alternatively topped with half a pistachio nut.
(Illustration page 558.)

Dama

Prepare three round bases of maddalena genoese by soaking with maraschino 21°. Sandwich and coat with imperial chocolate cream. Using a basket tube, pipe strips across the top with the same cream in a chequer pattern. Fill the squares alternately with pistachio and chocolate fondant as illustrated. Pipe a border with a fine star tube and mask the side with milk chocolate vermicelli.
(Illustration page 559.)

Fragola - Strawberry

Prepare bases as above by soaking with vanilla liqueur 21°. Sandwich with strawberry cream. Brush with apricot purée and coat the top with strawberry coloured and flavoured fondant. Mask the side with buttercream and sieved praline nougat.

Lucullus

Prepare five rectangular shaped thin layers of maddalena sponge by soaking with curaçao 21°. Sandwich alternately with white and chocolate imperial cream, mixing chopped candied cherries with the white cream. Brush with apricot purée and coat with chocolate fondant. Decorate with chocolate fondant and pipe inscription in white fondant.

Malaga

Soak a maddalena base with brandy and sandwich with imperial chocolate cream, mixed with sultanas and raisins. Spread top and side with the same cream and mask the side with chestnut granules and sugar. On the top, fashion a bunch of grapes with raisins that have been soaked in a bath of brandy.

Mimosa

Sandwich vanilla liqueur soaked almond maddalena genoese with imperial cream. Cover with the same cream and press a circle of almond paste in the centre. Mask with small cubes of maddalena and dust with icing sugar. Decorate with cherries and angelica in the centre.
(Illustration page 559.)

Moulin Rouge

Soak a round maddalena genoese base with maraschino liqueur 21°, and sandwich and coat with chocolate imperial cream and mask with chocolate vermicelli. Pipe eight rosettes of the same cream on the top, on each of which a cherry is placed.

Leaning against each, fanwise, eight chocolate half circles are placed, four of which have been dusted with icing sugar. Finish with a rosette in the centre topped with a cherry.

Novecento

Prepare a rectangular maddalena base by soaking with curaçao 21°. Slice into three and sandwich with white and chocolate imperial cream. Spread the top with white imperial cream and the sides with chocolate cream, and dust the top with icing sugar and, with the back of a knife mark a trellis design. Decorate with cherries.

Polenta e Osei

(This is a reproduction in gâteau form of a popular autumn dish.) Soak a round bombe shaped maddalena base with vanilla liqueur 21°, and sandwich with imperial zabaglione cream. Brush with apricot purée and cover with a thin sheet of yellow almond paste which has been rolled out on granulated sugar. Make a depression on top and pour in a little apricot purée or honey on which place skewered chocolate almond paste models of grilled birds. The birds are masked with apricot purée.

Portorico

Sandwich a maddalena base, soaked with strong coffee, with coffee imperial cream.

Cover with the same cream and mask the side with roasted chopped hazelnuts or crushed macaroon. Pipe alternate lines of white and coffee imperial cream on top.

Place a sugar coffee bean on each white line.

Rum

Take an oval maddalena base soaked with rum and sandwich with rum flavoured imperial cream. Cover tops and sides with the same cream. Write 'Rum' on top and mask the sides with chocolate vermicelli.

Selva

Soak a round maddalena genoese base with curaçao liqueur 21°. Sandwich with chocolate crème pâtissière. Coat with the same cream and dust with icing sugar. Decorate with a chocolate rose made with selva *(page 253)*.

Sorrentina

Bake a maddalena in a ring mould. When cold split twice and after soaking with vanilla liqueur, spread with chocolate buttercream. Brush with apricot purée and coat with chocolate fondant. Mask the bottom edge with a ring of half walnuts. Using the same cream, pipe twelve rosettes on the top, alternating with large and small rosettes. Place candied cherries on the large ones and half a pistachio nut on the smaller ones.
(Illustration page 554.)

St-Honoré

Various recipes, *see* chapter 'Desserts-gâteaux' *(pages 727-728)*.

Tirrenia

Soak a maddalena base with crème de cacao. Sandwich with imperial chocolate cream mixed with little cubes of chocolate. Decorate the top with alternate lines of piped white and chocolate imperial cream. Place a red sugar rose in the centre.

Torino

Soak a maddalena base with rum and sandwich with hazelnut imperial cream containing crushed praline croquant. Cover with hazelnut cream and decorate the top with the same cream. Mask the side with chopped roasted hazelnuts.

Gâteaux and Torten - Switzerland

Aargau Carrot Torte

lb	oz		kg	gr
	4	Egg yolks		125
	3 1/2	Sugar (icing)		100
		Salt (a pinch)		
	8	Carrots (grated)		250
	4	Ground almonds		125
	4	Ground hazelnuts		125
	1 3/4	Rusk crumbs		50
	1	Flour		30
	1/3	Baking powder		10
	5	Egg whites		150
	3 1/2	Sugar (castor)		100
		Zest of 1/2 lemon		
		Cinnamon		
		Ground cloves		

Whip the egg yolks, icing sugar, zest and salt until foamy. Stir in the carrots, hazelnuts, almonds, rusk crumbs, flour, baking powder and spices and lastly fold in the whites whisked to a stiff snow with the castor sugar. Fill into a greased and floured cake hoop or a deep flan ring and bake for about an hour at 360° F (180° C). The formula yields 1 gâteau 10 in. (25 cm.) in diameter. After baking, dust with icing sugar if desired. Marzipan carrots may be used for final decoration. If preferred, the gâteau may be enclosed in marzipan. With careful storage the gâteau will remain moist for a long time. It should not be sold before the second day.

Black and White Fan Torte

White base

lb	oz		kg	gr
	5	Egg		150
	3 3/4	Sugar (castor)		110
	3 3/4	Flour		110
	2	Butter		60

Chocolate base

lb	oz		kg	gr
	5	Egg		150
	3 3/4	Sugar (castor)		110
	3	Flour		90
	3/4	Cocoa		20
	2	Butter		60

From the recipes make two butter sponge bases 9 in. (23 cm.) in diameter. When cold and quite firm, split each one exactly in half. With the help of large cutters or cake rings, cut out into four absolutely uniform rings. Take a base made with a swiss roll mixing, spread it with arrack buttercream and cover with a concentric arrangement of two white and two chocolate rings, starting with a chocolate one and alternating the colours, so that the inside one will be a white disc. Spread again with the same buttercream and cover with chocolate and white rings in the reverse order, starting with a white one. Continue in the same way until all the sponge rings have been used, then cover the whole torte carefully with arrack buttercream and mask the sides with chocolate vermicelli. Run out some chocolate on paper and when nearly set cut out a circle the diameter of the torte and then cut into 12 segments. Place a circular template in the centre and dredge with icing sugar. Remove the template carefully. Mark the top of the torte into 12 divisions and pipe a whirl of buttercream on each one. Insert each chocolate segment obliquely on each whirl of buttercream.
(Illustration page 543.)

Black Forest Cherry Torte

Bake a thin round base of Linz pastry and spread with chocolate on one side. When set, place on a sheet of paper with the chocolate side underneath. Using a large plain tube, pipe three rings of chocolate buttercream or ganache on the base and fill the spaces with cooked morello cherries the juice of which has been thickened with cornflour. Cover with a thin chocolate sponge disc, sprinkled with kirsch flavoured stock syrup and press carefully round the edge. Cover this with a convex layer of kirsch flavoured whipped dairy cream stiffened with gelatine (3 sheets for each 1 lb. [500 gr.] of cream). Place a second disc of sprinkled chocolate sponge on top and cover this with the same cream. Mask completely with chocolate shavings and refrigerate. Cut into portions, pipe a whirl of whipped cream on to the rounded side of each one and insert a morello cherry. This torte is meant for immediate consumption or sale.

Caracas Cake

lb	oz		kg	gr
1	4	Almond paste I		625
		Egg yolks (24)		
		Egg whites (24)		
	5	Sugar (icing)		150
	10	Cocoa paste		300
	7	Flour		200
	7	Butter		200
		Ganache		
		Couverture		

Put the egg yolks and marzipan in the mixer and blend together. Whisk the egg whites to a stiff snow and stir in the sugar. Blend both mixtures and add the cocoa paste, flour and butter. Fill into paper lined oval hoops and bake at 410° F (210° C).

When cold, cut a V-shaped piece out of the top. Fill the space with fresh cream ganache and replace the wedge, point uppermost. Mask with ganache, coat with vanilla couverture and decorate with pistachio nuts.
(Illustration page 544.)

Caraque Tourte

Line a flan ring with viennese paste, taking care to strengthen the inside of the edges with a rope of paste. Bake in a medium oven. When it is cold, beat up the ganache and fill the pastry case with it.

Make the surface smooth, leave to set and then cover with pistachio flavoured and coloured fondant.

When this is dry, mark the centre of the tourte with a disc of chocolate fondant.

Caravelle

lb	oz		kg	gr
	8	Egg		250
	4	Sugar		125
	3	Flour		90
	1	Cocoa		30

lb	oz		kg	gr
	2	Butter (melted)		60
	12	Chocolate buttercream		375
	5	Vanilla couverture		150
	2	Chocolate vermicelli		60

Prepare a genoese base with the egg, sugar, flour, cocoa and butter. When cold, sandwich with two layers of buttercream, mask top and sides with the same cream and put the chocolate vermicelli round the side. Run the prepared couverture on to a sheet of rice paper; cut out in the shape of the flan. Heat a knife and divide the chocolate disc into 16 equal parts. Place these triangles on top, each one slightly tilted. Pipe a little cream under each to maintain the tilt. Pipe a whirl of cream in the centre.

Cherry Cheese Torten

lb	oz		kg	gr
2	6	Milk	1	175
	8	Sugar (castor)		250
	6 1/2	Cornflour		195
		Egg yolks (6)		
2	0	Curd cheese	1	
	4 1/2	Margarine		140
		Gelatine (7 sheets)		
		Egg whites (10)		
	1/2	Vanilla sugar		15
	2 1/2	Sugar (castor)		75
		Morello cherries		
		Zest of 1 lemon		
		Sweet pastry		

Lightly bake two sweet pastry bases 9 in. (23 cm.) in diameter and 1/4 in. (5 mm.) thick, cover them with morello cherries and surround them with rings 3 in. (7-8 cm.) deep, lined with greaseproof paper. Make a custard with the milk, sugar, cornflour and egg yolks, stirring vigorously while cooking, and add the previously soaked gelatine. Place the sieved curd, which should be warm, in a bowl with the margarine and zest and mix well, then blend into the custard. Lastly fold in the egg whites whisked to a stiff snow with the vanilla sugar and the 2 1/2 oz. (75 gr.) of castor sugar. Fill into the rings quickly, otherwise the torten will be spoilt. Set aside for 2 to 3 hours, egg wash and bake for 15 to 20 minutes at 500° F (260° C). Leave until cold before cutting.

Chessboard Gâteau

Cut chocolate sponge to the desired size, sandwich with chocolate rum buttercream and moisten with a little rum flavoured stock syrup. Envelop in marzipan and coat with couverture or ganache. Place the gâteau on a mirror or a tray with a reflecting surface, top evenly with the chequerboard design that has been prepared beforehand and add the final decoration. Even without the chessmen which are made with marzipan, this is an effective gâteau.
(Illustration page 542.)

Engadine Nut Torte

lb	oz		kg	gr
	15	Sugar (granulated)		450
	10	Single dairy cream		300
	1	Honey		30
	12	Walnuts (coarsely chopped)		375

Line two 9 in. (22 cm.) flan rings with sweet pastry. The depth of the rings should be 1 1/4 in. (3 cm.). Boil the sugar until caramelized and dissolve in the single dairy cream after which the honey and walnuts are stirred in. When cold, fill into the lined rings and cover each with a sweet pastry top. Brush with egg, make a design with a fork and lightly dock. Bake for about 25 minutes at 425° F (220° C). This torte remains moist for a long time.

Lemania Gâteau

lb	oz		kg	gr
	8	Viennese pastry		250
	6	Hollandaise filling		180
	3	Fresh cherries		90
		Glacé cherries		
		Sugar (icing)		

Line a flan ring with viennese pastry into which spread half the hollandaise filling. Add the stoned cherries and cover with the rest of the filling. Bake at 420° F (216° C) for about 30 minutes. When baked, turn the gâteau over so that the top flattens when cooling. To finish, place three strips of paper equidistant on top and dust with icing sugar. Carefully remove the strips of paper and in their place arrange lines of halved glacé cherries.
(Illustration page 422.)

Lemon Mousseline Torte

lb	oz		kg	gr
	2 3/4	Egg yolks		80
	8	Milk		250
	4	Sugar (icing)		125
	1/2	Custard powder		15
	4	Egg whites		125
		Gelatine (4 sheets)		
	3 1/2	Sugar (icing)		100
		Zest and juice of 3 lemons		
		1 japonaise base		
		1 almond sponge base		

Spread the underside of a japonaise base with chocolate. When set, place on a sheet of paper with the chocolate side underneath. Cover the base with a little lemon curd, place the almond sponge on top and brush with raspberry jam. Now surround with an adjustable torte ring. Cook the yolks, milk, the first amount of sugar, custard powder, juice and zest together to make a custard, add the previously soaked gelatine, mix until smooth and strain. Immediately fold in the egg whites whisked to a stiff snow with the second amount of sugar, fill into the prepared ring and smooth the top down with a scraper. Place in the refrigerator to set, then brush with slightly warmed apricot jelly. Carefully spread with lemon buttercream round the sides, either right to the top or only to the level of the filling. Mask the buttercream side with lightly roasted flaked almonds.

Recommended final decoration: a marzipan lemon with a green leaf on a thin disc of chocolate.

Mille-feuille Torte

Bake five puff pastry discs of equal size until quite crisp, turning them once while baking. When cool, sandwich together as follows: spread one disc with a little confectioner's custard flavoured with Grand-Marnier, cover with a second disc spread with cranberry jelly, cover with a third disc spread with praline nougat paste, then cover this with a fourth disc again spread with confectioner's custard flavoured with Grand-Marnier. Top with the last disc, smooth side upwards. With a sharp knife, trim the torte evenly all round, spread the sides with whipped dairy cream and mask with the puff pastry trimmings cut very small. Dust the top with icing sugar and sprinkle a few chopped pistachio nuts in the centre. Serve or sell at once.

Nougatine Torte (Golden Book)

Split a sheet of butter sponge three times and sandwich with nougat buttercream. Cut accurately to the desired size. Spread a little buttercream on one side and fix a grooved, slightly concave strip of marzipan in position. Use a slightly rounded strip of marzipan to make the spine of the book. Pin out chocolate marzipan to the required size and spread the right half with a little buttercream. Place the sandwiched butter sponge on it and spread the top lightly with the buttercream. Carefully bring the left half over and fix in position. Decorate with corner pieces and place the spine in position. The rest of the decoration depends on the occasion—an inscription, title, coat-of-arms, etc. This type of torte is very suitable for a cold buffet.
(Illustration page 544.)

Punch Tourte

lb	oz		kg	gr
1	0	Egg		500
	8	Sugar (castor)		250
	8	Flour		250
	3 1/2	Chopped orange peel		100
	5	Butter (melted)		150

Prepare in the same way as a butter sponge. When the cake has been baked and cooled down, cut it across into three slices and sandwich with rum flavoured, sweet orange marmalade. Coat with apricot purée and cover with rum flavoured white fondant. Decorate with candied fruit.

Rolla Gâteau

lb	oz		kg	gr
2 1/2		Egg whites		75
4		Sugar (granulated)		125
3 1/2		Chocolate		100
7		Butter		200
		Almonds (roasted)		
		4 Japonaise bases 8 in. (20 cm.)		

Make an Italian meringue with the egg whites and sugar, then add the melted chocolate. When cold, blend in the butter and use to sandwich the japonaise bases together and to coat the top and sides. Mask completely with roasted chopped almonds, lay strips of paper on top to form a wide trellis, dredge well with icing sugar and lift off the strips of paper carefully.

Truffle Tourte

lb	oz		kg	gr
1	10	Egg		800
1	2	Sugar (castor)		560
1	2	Flour		560
	1 3/4	Cocoa powder		50
	8	Butter (melted)		250

Whip up the egg and sugar over heat as for a genoese sponge.

Use a spatula to stir in the flour and cocoa powder, which have been sieved together, and finally add the melted butter. Fill some high brimmed tourte moulds and bake at 360° F (182° C). Turn out of the moulds and leave to cool. Cut the sponge across into three slices and sandwich with a good quality milk ganache which is also used to coat the whole tourte. Finish in the following way: Cover the sides with vanilla couverture and, using a bag fitted with a plain tube, pipe the word 'TRUFFLE' on top. Or pipe strips on top, dust with cocoa and garnish with mimosas. Finally sprinkle with dark coloured cocoa powder.
(Illustration page 561.)

Victoria Tourte

Prepare two thin almond sponge bases, and two puff pastry discs of equal size baked until crisp. Spread one of the sponge bases with vanilla buttercream and cover with the two discs of puff pastry sandwiched with strawberry jam. Spread with vanilla buttercream again and cover with the other sponge base. Brush lightly with apricot purée and coat with vanilla fondant.

Walnut Tourte

lb	oz		kg	gr
	4 1/2	Hazelnuts		125
	4 1/2	Walnuts		125
	8 3/4	Sugar (castor)		250
	10	Egg yolks		300
	8	Egg whites		250
	5	Flour		150

Grind the hazelnuts and walnuts with half the sugar and then work in the egg yolks.

Whisk the egg whites with the rest of the sugar until stiff. Amalgamate the two mixtures with a spatula and finally blend in the flour. Deposit into flan rings and bake in a slow oven, avoiding steam. When it is cold, cut the cake horizontally and sandwich together with buttercream containing chopped walnuts. Cover with a smooth layer of buttercream. Place in the refrigerator and cover all over with kirsch flavoured fondant. Decorate with piped fondant and finish off with caramelized half walnuts.

Wine Cream Tourte

Almond sponge base 10 in. (25 cm.) diameter

lb	oz		kg	gr
	9	Sweet paste		270
		Raspberry jam		
		Mixed compote fruits		

Wine cream

lb	oz		kg	gr
	9	White wine		270
	2	Sugar		60
	1	Egg yolk		25
	10	Whipped dairy cream		300
		1 lemon		
		4 sheets white gelatine		

Pin out the sweet paste into a flat disc 10 in. (25 cm.) diameter. Bake off, then brush with raspberry jam. Place a thin almond sponge base on top, decorate with mixed compote fruits as desired and place a hoop round the whole. Cook the white wine, sugar, egg yolk and lemon until thick, add the gelatine and, shortly before it sets, blend in the whipped dairy cream and fill into the hoop. When cold, remove the hoop and mark into the desired number of portions, decorate with compote fruits and glaze with a fruit jelly.

Mask the sides of the torte with roasted chopped almonds.
(Illustration page 562.)

Zigomar

lb	oz		kg	gr
	3 1/2	Egg yolks		100
	2 1/2	Egg whites		75
	2 3/4	Sugar (castor)		80
	1 3/4	Couverture		50
	1 1/4	Flour		40
	8	Pistachio buttercream		250
	3 1/2	Chocolate buttercream		100
	5	Vanilla couverture		150

Baking temperature 360° F (182° C). Baking time 30 minutes. Whip the egg yolks and sugar together. Add the couverture melted and mixed with a little warm water. Fold in the stiffly whipped whites and the flour.

Bake in a well greased and floured sandwich plate. When cold, slice into three and sandwich with pistachio buttercream. Cover thinly with chocolate buttercream. Cool and cover with vanilla couverture. Decorate with a border and a large 'Z'.

Zuger Kirschtorte

2 special japonaise bases are needed. Here is the recipe:

lb	oz		kg	gr
	8	Egg whites		250
	9	Sugar (icing)		270
	1	Potato starch		30

lb	oz		kg	gr
	10	Ground almonds (unblanched)		300
1		Flour		30
	1/2	Cocoa powder		15

Whisk the egg whites to a stiff snow and slowly add half the sugar. Lastly fold in the potato starch and carefully blend in the almonds, flour, cocoa powder and the rest of the sugar.

Mark two 8 in. (20 cm.) rings on a greased and floured baking sheet and spread or pipe the mixture to fill the rings. Bake at 360° F (180° C). While still hot, place an 8 in. (20 cm.) ring or cutter on top and carefully trim round. Save the trimmings for future use.

2 butter sponge bases are required from the following recipe:

lb	oz		kg	gr
	8	Egg		250
	1	Egg yolks		30
	6 1/2	Sugar (castor)		195
	6 1/2	Flour		195
	5	Butter (melted)		150

Whip the egg, egg yolks and sugar at around blood heat to a stiff sponge. Fold in the sieved flour, blend in the warm butter, fill into an 8 in. (20 cm.) drummed hoop and bake at 360° F (180° C).

When the sponge bases are cold and firm, skim off the top and bottom crusts and slice into two equal parts which should not exceed 1 in. (2.5 cm.) in depth. Sprinkle the top of each one with kirsch syrup. (One part stock syrup to one part kirsch.) Spread one of the japonaise bases with buttercream I *(page 228)* flavoured with kirsch and coloured a delicate pink, cover with a butter sponge disc so that the moistened side is undermost, then sprinkle the dry side with kirsch syrup. Repeat with the second sponge disc and the second japonaise base which should be placed on top, smooth side uppermost. Coat top and sides with buttercream and mask the side with sieved japonaise crumbs or with lightly roasted flaked almonds.

Refrigerate, then dredge well with icing sugar and mark in lozenge design with the back of a long knife. A decoration of glacé cherries and angelica makes the best finish.

Layer Cakes - Turkey

1. Sandwich four thicknesses of chocolate genoese with ganache buttercream. Coat with chocolate buttercream into which sufficient warm chocolate has been stirred until the mixture is of a consistency suitable for coating. When set, pipe a series of ovals on the top with the same mixture and place a piece of crystallized fruit between each. With white royal icing or buttercream, pipe a bird by each piece of fruit. Finish with a border along each edge.
(Illustration page 428.)

2. Proceed as for No. 1. Using a coarse star tube, pipe a line of chocolate buttercream along each edge between which arrange grapes.

Pipe a haphazard continuous line of white buttercream on top using a plain tube.

3. Proceed as for No. 2, but sprinkle a line of finely chopped pistachio nuts along the centre.

4. Sandwich four thicknesses of white genoese with vanilla flavoured white buttercream into which chopped peaches have been mixed. Coat with plain vanilla buttercream and, with a coarse star tube, pipe lines along each edge. Arrange peach slices along the top and overpipe with three parallel lines of buttercream, using a plain tube.
(Illustration page 428.)

5. Proceed as for No. 1. When set, pipe lines, using white royal icing or fondant as illustrated *(page 428)*. Finish with chopped pistachio nuts.

6. Proceed as for No. 4, but use grapes instead of peach slices.
(Illustration page 428.)

XX. Display and Show-Pieces

Principles of Display

Bakery products, with their shape, colour and fresh appeal are ideal for display. As articles of food they form part of the art of living.

The purpose of display is to attract and interest. In the past, attraction was created by the vendor ringing his bell and shouting his wares. Now, window display is designed to arrest the attention of the passerby, to interest and then to induce buying. *(Illustration page 541.)*

There are some who have an artistic flair for window dressing, a feeling for form and colour, an unerring sense of what is right. They confer dignity and good taste to the art of display and they have a profound respect for the products that they are displaying. Perhaps it would be difficult for them to explain why they do certain things, for an artist rarely bothers to explain his inner feelings or attempt an analysis of his motives. It is sufficient for him to know that he has expressed himself and that he has produced something to his satisfaction.

There are, however, fundamental principles involved in display, all followed, unconsciously perhaps, by the masters of the craft.

The creation of interest is of primary importance, for if the display is mediocre and fails in this respect, people will pass by and the whole purpose of display will be lost.

Having attracted attention, the display should maintain interest and so bring the prospective customer nearer the window for closer examination of the articles on display, which should induce a desire to buy.

It is at this point that the successful display artist will provide a subtle link between display and service, for the window should suggest the friendly, inviting character of the shop, suggesting also that the person is welcome to step inside. If the person does so and makes a purchase, then the display has been successful, for it must be remembered that a sale commences at the display point and ends at the cash desk.

To those who would wish to study window display, it is well to imagine the space available as a stage, and that one is the playwright, designer, dresser and stage manager all in one, with the objects of the display as the leading actors and the supporting cast.

A window has height, width and depth and it is within these limits that the display must be mounted. Here seven basic considerations are involved:

1. Design
2. Composition
3. Balance
4. Colour
5. Lighting
6. Background
7. Accessories

The design must be based on the space available, its dimensions and shape. The purpose will suggest the theme. It can be of seasonal, national, regional, local or historical interest, a special occasion, emphasis on one product alone or on a closely linked variety of products for a particular purpose. Within this the artist may discover a theme incorporating two or more of these.

1. The design should be such that the products to be shown will be clearly focussed in the eyes of the onlooker, all else being subordinate to this, but all exerting a subtle influence on the whole.

2. Everything within the display will have its rightful place, for care in composition is fundamental to harmony. Lack of harmony offends and irritates and the eyes of the viewer are turned away.

Eye levels are important, particularly when displays are designed to attract children. The direction of approach to the windows is also important.

3. A window should never be used as a store place, crowded with many items. Good balance demands restraint in the number of varieties displayed and in the number and type of props supporting them. There is a distinct aversion in almost all human beings to lack of balance, bringing an instinctive desire to put the matter right; a person then becomes more interested in the fault than in the products on display.

4. Correctly and skillfully used, colour is a joy. Colour gladdens, it gives life to any display with which it is associated. In the hands of a display artist it has infinite possibilities.

Black and white are achromatic, that is, they do not possess colour; together with most of the grey shades they are neutral. All other colours, according to their position on the chromatic scale, are either warm or cool, with the intermediates between. Black will give deliberate contrast and must be used sparingly, if at all, in the display of food, for food is a part of life, and aesthetically black has no association with the joy of living.

Generally, the neutral and cool colours are used for background; balance and harmony being given by the judicious use and placing of warmer colours.

Colour has association with and symbolizes the changing seasons. Spring suggests delicate light green, pale yellow and a warm lilac. In summer, warmer colours may be introduced. Autumn is the time of the harvest and rich brown, gold, together with red and deep yellow are symbolic of this season. During winter and particularly at Christmas, white and deep blue suggest themselves, with the careful use of deep green and red to provide contrast.

5. Lighting should always be used subtly to enhance the display, bearing in mind always that unless used with care and thought, it may distort both form and colour, destroying the essential harmony of the whole.

6. The background should never obtrude. Its purpose is to provide a pleasing screen against which the objects on display can be seen to the best advantage. The materials used and their colour are important, for both should suggest richness and quality without deviating from essential neutrality. A fabric of particular quality and colour can sometimes be used with added advantage, such as a rich deep blue velvet for a background to a white wedding cake.

The rich fabric suggests quality, and the colour, and the reflection from it will enhance the whiteness of the icing, as well as providing an excellent background against which the delicate work on the cake can be studied. A deep red, carefully placed and in correct amount, will bring complete colour harmony.

7. It must be remembered always that props must be subservient to that which is to be displayed. It is the products that are to be sold, not the props! The props may be divided under three headings:

(a) Those that support.

(b) Those that make a contribution to the harmony, balance and atmosphere of the display, both in form and in colour.

(c) Fittings specially designed for certain products or in common association with them.

Fittings that support are the bricks and girders that help build the display. They may vary in size, shape and form, and in the materials used. Depending on the type of display, they may be simple or more elaborate.

Other props may be termed accessories. These may be flowers to provide gaiety, colour or colour contrast or to provide balance. Toy balloons and coloured ribbons are examples of accessories that suggest a festive occasion. The display artist will never be at a loss in the use of the almost limitless variety of articles that are available. He will, however, use and place them carefully.

Examples of special accessories are the traditional wedding cake stand and the cutting knife. Tableware and napery come to mind when perhaps a meal or a party is the theme for a display. Informative showcards and price tickets are silent sales people and when used must be attractive. The lettering should also be attractive and easily read. The cards and tickets should be carefully placed and never be too obtrusive, above all, they should fit harmoniously in the display.

Remember that food is made to be eaten, and nothing should be allowed to detract from this fundamental concept. It should always be displayed with profound respect. *(Illustration page 541.)*

Show - Pieces

A show-piece is intended to be the focal point of attraction leading the eye to the articles displayed for sale. It follows that it should be of such form, colour and workmanship, and so placed that it will attract the passer by and bring him or her to the window or display stand. It should also be of such interest that it can become a topic of conversation in the locality, so as to bring others along to the display.

A display item can be typical of a sales product of the bakery; a show-piece fabricated from materials wholly or partly common to the establishment; fabricated from common and/or unusual objects or materials. It can be used to emphasize seasonal, regional, national or special products.

There are many possibilities, limited only by the capacity, artistry and imagination of the craftsman concerned and the display artist.

Here are a few examples.
(Illustrations pages 483, 541, 603-609, 633, 634, 636, 638, 639.)

LE CROQUEMBOUCHE

For this gâteau special moulds can be bought in different sizes. For a smallish cake a charlotte mould may be used. It must be inverted and oiled lightly on the outside. First of all bake very small buns of choux paste crisp and dry. Allow to cool and fill with pastry or other cream. Meanwhile boil 10 oz. (300 gr.) sugar, $1/2$ glass water and a tablespoonful glucose to pale caramel and keep it warm. Dip the buns in the caramel one by one with a confectioner's fork and stick them all around the mould close to one another row by row with the round side turned outwards. To give the pyramid the right form make the last rows smaller, finishing with two or three buns. The croquembouche may be placed on a base of Parisian nougat pressed into a lightly oiled cake hoop with the flat side up. Finally an aigrette of spun sugar or some ornament made of nougat is placed on top of the croquembouche.

Le croquembouche is one of the oldest French desserts. It may also be made with caramelized orange wedges although it is rather difficult to make evenly.
(Illustration page 789.)

HARVEST BREAD

The harvest loaf is traditional in Great Britain at the time of the harvest festival, a time when the churches are decorated with the produce of the land. Amongst the flowers, fruits and vegetables the harvest loaf takes pride of place. It is also used in window-display during the early autumn.

The moulding or modelling of dough into harvest bread or similar display pieces provides the baker with endless opportunities for developing traditional—and creating new—skills and standards of craftsmanship.

The dough, stiffer than that used for normal breadmaking, can be made from the following ingredients:

lb	oz		kg	gr
9	0	Bread flour	4	500
	2 1/4	Salt		70
	3/4	Sugar (castor)		20
	2 1/4	Milk powder		70
	1 1/4	Yeast		40
4	0	Water	2	

Temperature of dough:
74-76° F (23-24° C).

Allow dough to ferment 1 hour before commencing manufacture of a display piece, which should be carefully designed beforehand.

General Instructions

Cut the required amount of dough for each stage of the design from the bulk. Reduce this dough to the thickness required and rest sufficiently so that no distortion takes place during subsequent cutting or moulding. Keep the various moulded pieces under polythene sheets until required for assembly.

During the final formation of the piece egg-wash should be used, (a) to hold the pieces together and (b) to give an attractive glaze to the finished bread.

Bake carefully at 400° F (204° C).

Harvest Loaf 1

This loaf *(illustration page 605)* is built up in the following sequence. For the apples, scale off six 1 1/2 oz. (45 gr.) pieces of dough from the bulk. Mould each piece round, then flatten slightly before placing the pieces to prove under a plastic bowl. Now make a three strand plait, approximately 3 1/2 ft. (105 cm.) long. After shaping, place the plait under cover until required. To make the outer border a long thin strip of dough, 3 in. (8 cm.) wide and approximately 4 ft. (120 cm.) long, is laid on a flat bench. Cut the pattern with a sharp oval cutter and egg wash the surface. A thicker piece of dough, 2 in. (5 cm.) wide and 4 ft. (120 cm.) long, is then laid on top, level with the top edge. The surplus depth of the bottom oval pieces is now folded up on to the second piece and pressed to make secure. Turn this long strip over and then shape around a 15 in. (40 cm.) board. Cover with polythene sheeting until required.

By this time the apples will be proved and can now be coloured, using normal confectioners' colours. The next stage is the preparation of the ears of wheat, leaves, stalks, etc. The centre piece, 13 in. (33 cm.) in diameter, should then be cut from a thin piece of dough and allowed to recover under some protective sheeting. The base, consisting of a circle of dough, 24 in. (60 cm.) in diameter and about 1/2 in. (1 cm.) thick, is now formed and placed on a clean baking sheet. The build-up can now begin.

Dock the base and egg wash all over. Mould the centre piece and place neatly in position. Arrange the three-strand plait around the edge of the centre piece. Then follows the larger border, making a neat join. This join can often be hidden by the ears of wheat or some other part of the design. The surplus dough from the base is now cut away, leaving a rim of about 1 in. (2.5 cm.) all the way round. Cut this rim with scissors, spacing the cuts at regular intervals. Egg wash all over the surface.

Finally, arrange the fruit, wheat, leaves etc. Bake at 400° F (204° C) for 1 1/4 hours. It is necessary, in order to prevent deterioration of the colour, to protect the coloured areas during baking. A convenient method of doing this is to cover the apples with small paper cups. The cups can be removed just before baking is completed.

Harvest Loaf 2

This display piece is similar to the one described above. The outer border, however, is made up of oval pieces alternating with leaves cut with a leaf cutter.

The poppies are fashioned from thin dough, the centres being effected with maw seeds. The lettering is made from very thin ropes of dough. In this example the letters are carefully coloured.
(Illustration page 604.)

Harvest Loaf 3

For making a wheatsheaf, a piece of dough is first rolled out to about 3/4 in. (2 cm.) in thickness and cut into the shape of a wheatsheaf as illustrated. This base is well docked and kept damp by frequent washing with water.

The stalks are made from very thin strings of dough rolled out on the table by hand. They are then arranged on the bottom half of the base to look as natural as possible. Next, many pieces are formed in the shape of wheat ears, the cuts being made with a pair of scissors. The finished ears are placed into position over the top half of the base, taking care to cover the top of the stalks and to arrange them as naturally as possible. Several thin strands are next taken together, knotted in the centre and placed about halfway up the stalks, the ends being tucked under the base.

Finally, the wheatsheaf is carefully washed over with egg in such a way that each part is covered, making certain that there are no pockets of egg in the crevices. Bake at 400° F (204° C).

TIERED CAKE

(Wedding, Birthday, Confirmation or First Communion Cake) - France, Italy and Switzerland. (See also Chapter V - Cake Decoration.)

lb	oz		kg	gr
	10	Ground almonds		300
1	0	Sugar (castor)		500
	4	Egg		125
	7	Egg yolks		200

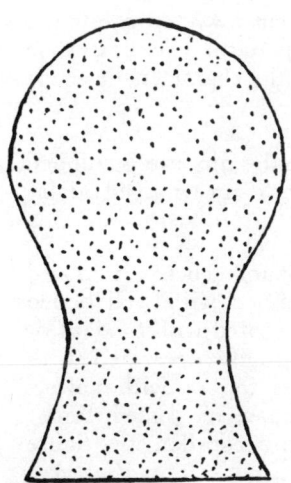 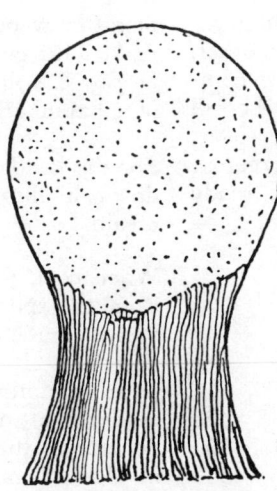 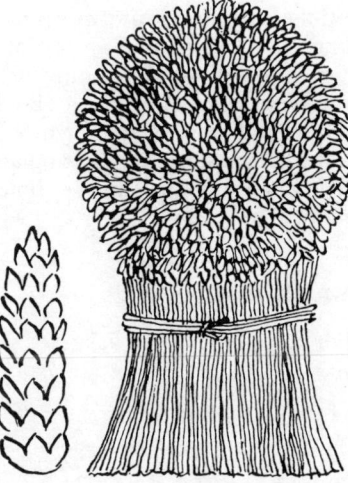

lb	oz		kg	gr
	10 ½	Flour		315
	14	Egg whites		400
		Zest of orange		

Baking time for the cakes 25-45 minutes according to size.

For this cake 8 or 10 plain round cake hoops of different sizes are required, but 4 or 5, graduated in size, are sufficient to make an attractive cake. There should be a difference of about 1 ½ in. (4 cm.) in diameter between each hoop, i.e. if the largest is 10 in. (25 cm.) in diameter the next one must be about 8 ½ in. (20-21 cm.) and so on. After the hoops have been greased and floured they are filled with the following mixture:

Beat the finely ground almonds to a foam with 4 ½ oz. (140 gr.) sugar and 4 oz. (125 gr.) egg. Add the remaining sugar, yolks and the zest of orange, and continue beating the mixture until quite white and very foamy. Fold in the stiffly beaten egg whites and the flour at the same time. Bake at 375° F (190° C). Remove the smallest cakes from the oven first and allow all cakes to cool. Place the cakes one on top of the other with red jam or jelly in between. Coat the whole cake very thinly with well boiled apricot purée and coat carefully with fondant, flavoured to taste. As soon as the fondant has set, decorate with candied fruit or with royal icing. Each layer may also be iced separately, one layer white, one pink and so on, and then placed one on top of the other. For a wedding, christening or first communion cake, the icing should be all white and some sort of symbol in sugar, a bridal couple, cradle, etc., placed on top. These ornaments can be bought ready made.

BAUMKUCHEN

For approx. 11 lb. (5 kg.)

lb	oz		kg	gr
1	12	Butter		875
2	3	Sugar (icing)	1	100
1	0	Egg yolks		500

lb	oz		kg	gr
2	5	Egg whites	1	150
1	9	Cornflour		770
	9	Finely ground roasted almonds		270
		2 lemons (juice)		
		2 vanilla pods		
		Arrack		
		Salt		

Cream the butter and 1 lb. 8 oz. (750 gr.) sugar. Whip the egg whites and the rest of the sugar to a stiff snow and gradually add the egg yolks.

Blend the cornflour and ground almonds with the butter/sugar mixture, then fold in the snow. Lastly add the lemon, vanilla, arrack and salt.

The Baumkuchen is baked on a special machine which in principle is a revolving spit. The spit is a tapered wooden roller which revolves in front of gas jets or electric elements. The speed of the spit is controlled by a variable speed electric motor and the spit can be raised or lowered according to the heat.

The spit is first covered with white paper which is fastened securely with thin string. The mixture is poured or ladled evenly on to the papered spit as it slowly revolves. Up to 14-15 layers are put on successively, and at regular intervals some is removed with a brush in a similar manner that metal or wood is cut away on a lathe to make a design or pattern. The illustration on *page 638* shows the characteristic shape of a Baumkuchen.

For the last layer, the mixture is thinned down a little with un-whipped dairy cream.

When cool, the Baumkuchen is removed from the spit, brushed with well boiled apricot purée and coated with fondant or chocolate. It is usually decorated with paper sculpture on top or with flowers made from marzipan or pulled sugar. Sometimes the top decoration is a figure in blown sugar. *(Germany)*

Strawberry Kranzler
An example of Blown and Pulled Sugar Work, p. 643

Harvest Loaf
Fine Example of Dough Modelling, Great Britain, p. 601

Harvest Loaf
Fine Example of Dough Modelling, Great Britain, p. 600

Marzipan Vegetables, Kranzler, p. 612

Baumkuchen Pheasant and Marzipan Fruits, Kranzler, p. 611-613

Wedding Cake
A fine Example of Pastillage Work from Italy

Three Tier Wedding Cake
Modern Style, Great Britain, p. 87-92, 403

Easter Eggs, Switzerland, p. 248

Baumkuchen Pheasant

See 'Baumkuchen'. The body weighs approx. 1 lb. 2 oz. (550 gr.) after icing, page 602.

Make the body out of a Baumkuchen baked to an oval shape. To decorate as a pheasant, use the following ingredients:
for the ruff and tail: caramel;
for the head and spiral: pulled sugar;
for the back: glazed pineapple slices;
for the wings: mix together 2 oz. (60 gr.) egg, 2 oz. (60 gr.) sugar and 2 oz. (60 gr.) flour; stencil out the wings on greased baking sheets and bake. *(Germany)*
(Illustration page 607.)

Baumkuchen Santa Claus

Make the body out of a Baumkuchen coated with plain couverture. Use marzipan moulded to the shape of an egg for the head and decorate with marzipan and royal icing. Fashion the hands from balls of marzipan and finish off with some small chocolates and a bow. *(Germany)*
(Illustration page 638.)

FRUIT STALL

Othello Sponge Mixture

lb	oz		kg	gr
	6	Egg yolks		180
1 1/2		Water		45
	3 1/2	Flour		100
	8	Egg whites		250
	3 1/2	Sugar (castor)		100
	3 1/2	Potato starch		100

Make up an Othello sponge mixture with the above ingredients. Pipe out on paper to the shapes of the various fruits and bake at 430° F (220° C) with the oven door slightly open. Make a depression on the underside of each base immediately after baking. Sandwich the bases, in pairs of equal size and shape, with a moist custard or cream, jam, etc., flavoured with a liqueur. Brush with apricot purée, wrap in marzipan, colour and lightly spray with a little marzipan varnish. Peaches should be rolled into very fine granulated sugar or icing sugar after they have been coloured.
(Illustration page 639.)

WITCH'S COTTAGE (HÄNSEL UND GRETEL)

First of all make a drawing of the cottage, then pin out Lebkuchen dough about 1/2 in. (1 cm.) thick for the various parts of the cottage, such as the base, outside walls (four) and roof. Take the piece for the front, cut out as necessary and decorate with almonds, orange and citron peel, etc. Bake all the parts. When cold, pour out liquid caramel to make the windows and mark lightly with a small round cutter to simulate the bull's eye panes. Now assemble the parts to make the cottage, fixing them together with melted couverture. Decorate the cottage with marzipan motifs, fancy Christmas biscuits, etc., fixed to the walls with melted couverture. It is advisable, however, to fix these in position before the cottage is assembled. The figures of Hänsel, Gretel and the Witch are modelled out of marzipan or cast in coloured caramel and assembled, and then finished off as appropriate. The small trees are made out of Baumkuchen and placed on a caramel base. Variation: the cottage minus the fairy tale characters may be used as a Christmas decoration; it is also suitable as a table decoration for a children's tea-party or a winter-time banquet.
(Illustration page 638.) *(Germany)*

BUTTER SPONGE CHICKS, HARES AND HENS - BISKUIT KÜCKEN, HASEN UND HENNEN

For about 10 butter sponge eggs:

lb	oz		kg	gr
	6	Egg yolks		180
1	0	Whole eggs		500
	2	Sugar (castor)		60
	9	Flour		270
	8 1/2	Cornflour		265
	13	Butter (hot)		400
		Lemon juice		
		Kirsch		

611

Beat up warm the whole eggs, egg yolks, sugar and a little lemon. Remove from heat and continue beating. Blend in the flour and cornflour, and lastly add the hot butter.

Fill into greased egg-shaped moulds 4 in. by 2 in. (10 × 5 cm.) and bake at 356° F (180° C) for about 30 minutes.

After baking, slice through the butter sponge eggs once, sprinkle with kirsch and sandwich with various kinds of jam. Put on heads made of Othellos and glaze with apricot purée.

Coat hens with kirsch fondant, chicks with yellow lemon fondant and hares with coffee fondant.

Using a paste made of 3 $^1/_2$ oz. (100 gr.) whole eggs, 3 $^1/_2$ oz. (100 gr.) sugar and 3 $^1/_2$ oz. (100 gr.) flour, pipe out wings and feathers, bake and finish off the chicks and hens with them.

Use croquant for the hares' ears.

Finally decorate with marzipan, piped royal icing and pistachio nuts.

These cakes are made in Germany at Easter.

SUGAR BASKETS

Sugar Basket with Chocolates

1st row:	Pineapple Triangles	*page 625*
2nd row:	Sorrento	*page 627*
3rd row:	Nut Dainties	*page 625*
4th row:	Rigi Peaks	*page 626*
5th row:	White Truffles	*page 627*

In the centre of the sugar basket:
    Truffles   *page 627*
(Illustration page 633.)

Sugar Basket with Petits Fours

1st row: Small tuiles with gianduja
2nd row: Punch Balls   *page 517*
(Illustration page 634.)

MARZIPAN MODELLING

The manufacture of marzipan animals, fruits and vegetables is an interesting occupation needing only good quality marzipan, suitable moulds, a few modelling tools and other small equipment that will be mentioned.

Small items of fruits and vegetables such as would be served with petits fours will not need the concentration to detail that larger articles will require, particularly if these are destined for display.

Natural fruits and vegetables should be used for reference. Shapes and colours can then be copied as faithfully as possible.

For display purposes marzipan fruits of natural size can be arranged in fruit bowls, either of metal or prefabricated with almond or sugar paste and suitably embellished with flowers made from the same media. Large animals, reinforced with wood and/or wire can also be made for display purposes.
(Illustrations pages 141-146, 606, 607, 636, 637-639.)

Marzipan for modelling is prepared as follows:

Marzipan Animals and Small Fruits

lb	oz		kg	gr
4	0	Raw marzipan	2	
4	0	Sugar (icing)	2	
	8	Glucose		250
		Colours and flavours		

Warm the marzipan and glucose and mix together. Work in the icing sugar and the colour and flavour desired.
(Illustrations pages 637, 639.)

Large Marzipan Fruits and Vegetables

lb	oz		kg	gr
3	0	Raw marzipan	1	500
3	8	Sugar (icing) (approx.)	1	750
	1	Water		30
	$^1/_8$	Gum tragacanth (powdered)		4
		Colours and flavours		

Soak the gum in the water and let it stand overnight. Strain it and mix with 8 oz. (250 gr.) of icing sugar. Work this into the marzipan and add icing sugar until the desired consistency is reached. Colour and flavour added as desired.
(Illustrations pages 606, 607, 639.)

Apple

Fashion an apple shape with pale green or pale yellow marzipan, keeping the skin perfectly smooth. Place on starch and make the impression on top with modelling tools. When set, colour with a brush or a spray, copying faithfully the colour formation of a real apple. Place a clove or suitably modelled marzipan piece in the centre of the impression on top. Varnish if desired.

Apricot

Proceed as for peaches, using apricot coloured marzipan. Do not dust with cornflour.

Banana

Make a banana shape with yellow marzipan, copying the natural fruit. Allow to set on a bed of starch, then carefully shade the ends with green and chocolate colour. Alternatively, the banana may be made from white marzipan and coloured after, when a further attraction may be given by carefully cutting and rolling back part of the skin, the fruit beneath being suitably marked with a blade.

Basket of Marzipan Fruits

The basket shown in the illustration is filled with various marzipan fruits modelled by hand and then painted.
(Illustration page 607.)

Bunch of Grapes

For display purposes, a bunch of grapes can be fashioned. First it is necessary to have pieces of stout wire 2, 2 $^1/_2$ and 3 in. (5, 6 and 8 cm.) long.

A pointed wedge shape is made with marzipan and mounted on a board. If the finished bunch is to be removed, cover the board first with waxed paper. Make a number of grape shaped pieces and impale them on a piece of wire which has been made red hot at one end. This will fix the grape on the wire. Dip all the grapes into couverture and allow to set. A perforated board is ideal or even a loaf of bread can be used to hold the wired grapes until the chocolate is set.

Commencing at the point of the wedge, insert the wired ends of the grapes continuing upwards until the wedge is covered. The grapes are lightly dusted with a mixture of cornflour and powdered blue. Finish the top with vine leaves made with green marzipan and a stem made with chocolate marzipan. Green royal icing can be used to pipe tendrils.

Cabbage

Proceed as for cauliflower but omitting the white flower and totally enclosing the centre piece.

Carrot

For this vegetable red-orange marzipan is used and a carrot shape made. After a depression has been made at the top it is carefully shaded green at that end. The cut-off foliage is represented by inserting short strips of angelica. Finally, lines are marked at right angles with a knife.

Cauliflower

For this vegetable two sulphur moulds are required, one for the flower which is modelled with white marzipan and one for the leaves for which green marzipan is used. A small ball of marzipan or a small cake is topped with the flower and the leaves arranged tastefully round the sides.

Chestnuts

First model the nuts themselves and dip the blunt end of each in milk chocolate couverture and the other half in plain couverture. Model the husks in two halves, tint them a greenish colour and press them

613

evenly round the nuts. Pipe the prickles on to the husks with milk chocolate couverture.

Lemon
Fashion lemon coloured marzipan to the shape of a lemon and make indentations as described for the orange. Brush one end lightly with green colour. The model can then be brushed or sprayed with lemon colour.

Orange
Make a smooth ball with orange coloured marzipan and roll it between two boards which have had pearl barley or sago glued on. This will give the indentations found on the skin of the orange. Put on to a bed of starch so that the shape is preserved and, with a modelling tool, mark the flower end and place in a small piece of greenish-chocolate marzipan. When set, brush off the starch and brush or spray with orange colour. If for display purposes, a marzipan varnish can then be applied. (See footnote at the end of this section.) The word 'Jaffa' can be painted on if desired.

Parsnip
The parsnip shape is made from a light caramel coloured marzipan. After a depression has been made at the top, lines are made on the root as for the carrot. Natural markings are made with chocolate colour.

Peach
Make an oval shape, keeping the skin smooth, using peach coloured marzipan. Make an impression at one end and a line along one side with modelling tools. Set on starch, and when firm, colour the sides with carmine powder, using cotton wool for this purpose. Dust very lightly with cornflour placed in a piece of fine muslin.

Pear
Use green, brown-green or brown-yellow marzipan and fashion a pear shape with a perfectly smooth skin. Lay sideways on a starch bed and make the necessary impression at one end. When set, colour with the brush or spray. Some pears are speckled with brown spots; this can be effected by dipping the surface of a tooth-brush in chocolate colour and placing it near the modelled fruit. If the bristles are brushed back with the edge of a knife they will flick forward and speckle the fruit with colour. Do not overload the brush. Finish with a chocolate marzipan stalk.

Peas in Pod
To fashion this vegetable it is necessary only to copy the natural vegetable carefully, using a marzipan coloured as near as possible to the original.

Plum
Model a plum shape with marzipan and when set, dip into thin couverture. From a muslin bag dust lightly a mixture of cornflour and powdered blue.

Strawberry
This fruit can be modelled by hand or a sulphur mould can be used. The marzipan should be red and when the model is set, it is dipped into hot raspberry jelly and sprinkled with yellow tinted sugar. An artificial hull is placed in the top.

Other fruits and vegetables can be modelled by copying the originals carefully.

Marzipan Dogs
Use appropriately shaped sulphur moulds to model the head, ears and body. Colour and assemble. Pipe out the eyes in royal icing and plain chocolate couverture, the tongue in red fondant and the nose in brownish coloured fondant. Lastly dip the underside in plain couverture.
(Illustration page 637.)

Marzipan Fishes
First press the marzipan into appropriate sulphur moulds and tint the fishes in suitable colours. Pipe on the eyes in royal icing and plain chocolate couverture.

Shape the remaining marzipan into small round pebbles, colour these and place them on transparent wrapping film. Impale each fish on a piece of wood, stick this into one of the pebbles and close the wrapping.
(Illustration page 637.)

Marzipan Frogs

First model the body and legs of each frog and colour them light green or dark yellow. Pipe on royal icing and plain chocolate couverture to make the eyes, red fondant to make the tongue and royal icing to mark the top of the head. Mount the frogs on wafer bases sandwiched with nougat and coated with plain couverture. Lastly mark out the feet in marzipan and add a marzipan plaque (e.g. with the inscription 'Good Luck').
(Illustration page 637.)

Marzipan Hedgehogs

First model the body, then tint the face a brownish colour. Make the eyes out of royal icing and plain chocolate couverture, and use a heartshaped piece of pink fondant for the tip of the nose. Stick a dozen or more almond slivers into the untinted part of the body, then dip this into plain couverture and mount at once on wafer bases sandwiched with nougat and coated with plain couverture. A marzipan plaque with the inscription 'Good Luck' (or a similar one) may be added for additional decoration.
(Illustration page 637.)

Marzipan Piglets

First model the bodies and colour them pink, touching up the backs in a reddish colour. Use split almonds to make the ears and feet, stick on a whole hazelnut to make the tail and dip the hindquarters and the base of the feet in plain chocolate couverture. Make the eyes out of royal icing and plain couverture and dip the snout in pink sugar. Mount the piglets on wafer bases sandwiched together with nougat and coated with plain couverture. Add a marzipan plaque with the inscription 'Good Luck' (or a similar one).
(Illustration page 637.)

Marzipan Poodles

Model the bodies. Coat all over with plain chocolate couverture and pipe on the eyes in royal icing and plain couverture, and the nose in red fondant.

Chicken Drumsticks - Hühnerkeulen

Line drumstick-shaped sulphur moulds with marzipan and fill the centre with chocolate nougat. Cover with marzipan. Colour a reddish brown and glaze with hot gum arabic solution. Sprinkle with sugar which has been tinted brown, allow to dry and glaze again. *(Germany)*

Christmas Tree

Take green coloured marzipan, flavoured with pistachio and make a tall cone shape. Make cuts, commencing at the top, with a pair of scissors, rotating the cone so that the cuts are even all round the cone. Fix on to a small cut-out plaque. Dust with icing sugar or brush with white royal icing. Coloured dragees may be placed on the branches as a further decoration.

Father Christmas Head

Make a ball of pink marzipan and then fashion into a pear shape with a sharp point. Pin out white marzipan or sugar paste and mark it with a ribbed roller. Cut out a small fluted disc and cut it in half at right angles to the ribbing. Fix this on the base as the beard. Above it, fix a nose made with very red marzipan. Pipe on eyes with white royal icing and the pupils with chocolate. Above the eyes, place a ring of white marzipan to make a brim for the hat. Tilt the point of the hat to one side.

Marzipan Santa Claus

First model the body round and the head to a slightly elongated shape. Dip the top part of the head in red caramel, the lower part in cocoa butter and pulverized sugar to make the beard. Then stick the head on to the body and use suitably coloured royal icing and plain chocolate couverture to make the eyes, nose, mouth, moustache and hands. Fix a flashed marzipan pretzel to the body on one side. Lastly mount each Santa Claus on a flashed marzipan star and pack in transparent wrapping.

Marzipan varnish can be bought from manufacturers of confectionery colours and flavours. It should be used only for display work.
(Illustration page 638.)

Königsberg Marzipan Confections

1. Cut marzipan into rounds and ovals, using various cutters. Place a neat rim on each of the shapes and decorate with nippers. Then flash, glaze with dextrin, fill with various kinds of jam and nougat and cover with fondant and chocolate couverture. Place a red or yellow glacé cherry on the fondant covering of the larger ones.
(Illustration page 636.)

2. Cut the marzipan into heart shapes, place a neat rim on each and decorate with the nippers. Flash in a salamander and fill with kirsch fondant. When it is firm, top the filling with a few brightly coloured crystallized fruits.

3. Model long and round marzipan loaves and flash in a salamander. Finally glaze with dextrin.

4. Model the desired marzipan shapes (e.g. pretzels, round rolls, crescents, sticks and plaits) and flash. Brush with dextrin and sprinkle with poppy seeds or sugar nibs as desired.

XXI. Chocolates and Sugar Confectionery

Chocolates

Chocolates have the advantage for the confectioner that they can be made all the year round since there is always a regular demand. Thus the confectioner is always able to offer them freshly made to his customers.

For first class chocolates, it is necessary to use only first quality materials, and to use great care in their preparation.

Chocolate centres are made from a variety of basic mixtures such as ganache, gianduja, marzipan, fondant, jelly and various nougats and praline. The centres are then coated with a layer of couverture thick enough to protect the centres of the chocolates while keeping them soft, and thin enough for them to be dainty and appealing. The chocolate coating should be bright and glossy and this can only be achieved if the couverture itself is correctly tempered, and the centres are at the same temperature as the room where they are being dipped.

According to the type of centre, the basic mixtures may be rolled or poured out between strips of wood and then cut out with cutters or a knife. For truffles, the mixture is forced out of a savoy bag fitted with a plain pipe into ropes which are then cut up with a special caramel cutter and the pieces rolled into balls by hand.

The confectioner is able to produce a wide range of chocolates by skilful blending of centres and flavours. The craftsman, proud of his products, will use parchment paper carrying the negative imprint of his name. On this he places the dipped chocolates, thus giving a personal touch to his products.

The variety of chocolates is unlimited. *(Illustration page 692.)*

Aidas

lb	oz		kg	gr
	7	Hazelnuts (roasted)		200
	7	Sugar (icing)		200
	14	Fondant		400
	4	Cognac		125

Grind the hazelnuts with the sugar until oily, then mix thoroughly with the fondant and cognac. Line small tinfoil cups with plain chocolate, fill up with the mixture, cover with the same chocolate and finish off with a small clef sign on top.

Algiers

lb	oz		kg	gr
1	0	Almonds		500
1	0	Sugar (icing)		500
	7	Dates		200
	2	Marsala		60
	10	Cocoa butter		300
	8	Couverture		240

Grind the blanched, roasted almonds with the icing sugar until oily, then mix with the cocoa butter and couverture. Chop the dates after stoning them and steeping them in the marsala, and mix well into the chocolate almond paste. When firm, work well again and pin out $1/4$ in. (8 mm.) thick. Cut out with a plain $1^1/_2$ in. (4 cm.) cutter and divide in half through the middle. Dip into plain couverture with a three pronged dipping fork and mark three lines.

Andalousians

lb	oz		kg	gr
2	4	Praline paste	1	125
1	2	Milk couverture		560
	3 $^1/_2$	Cocoa powder		100

Mix all the ingredients into a paste, roll out between strips of wood and cut out with a round cutter. Dip in milk couverture and mark with a fork.   *(France)*

Arabellas

lb	oz		kg	gr
	4	Orange peel		125
	4	Cherry jam		125
	5	Honey		150
	3 $^1/_2$	Gianduja		100
1	4	Milk chocolate		625
		Rum		
		Zest and juice of 1 orange		

Mix all the ingredients together well and pin out between metal bars $^1/_4$ in. (8 mm.) thick on greaseproof paper. When cold, cut into $^3/_4$ in. (2 cm.) cubes and dip in plain couverture. Finally place a tiny cube of orange peel in the centre of each.

Aromatic Centres

1. *Liquid centres.* Line small tinfoil cups or chocolate moulds with tempered couverture and pour in the required spirit (e.g. Fernet-Branca for aromatic centres) mixed with glucose. Cover over with couverture which has been brought to a piping consistency.

2. *Solid centres.* Mix one part raw marzipan with one part unsweetened pulped almonds or hazelnuts and work in $^3/_4$ oz. (20 gr.) finely ground tonka* beans per 2 lb. (1 kg.). Divide this basic paste into as many parts as required and add to each the desired variety of aromatic herb, spice or seed. Shape the centres, dry and coat with tempered couverture in the usual way.

* See Glossary, *page 866*.

Juniper, cardamom, thyme, pepper, nutmeg, cumin seeds

Each of these aromatic plants for these centres requires special preparation to provide the necessary flavouring, e.g.:

Cumin. Scald with thin stock syrup and boil until all the water has evaporated and the seeds look dry.

Ground nutmeg. Heat up in a little almond oil.

Thyme. Scald the air-dried leaves with heated brandy, cover and set aside until all the brandy has been absorbed.

Cardamom. Open the capsules, coarsely crush the seeds in a small mortar and brown lightly in a black pan.

Juniper berries. Take choice berries only, fry them lightly and quickly in oil, transfer to a strainer to drain, then leave them in a dry cloth to dry well. Chop into small granules resembling coarse semolina.

Peppercorns. Steep in red wine overnight and leave in a warm place, then dry and crush in a small mortar.   *(Germany)*

Brasilians - Brésiliens

lb	oz		kg	gr
	3 $^1/_2$	Ground almonds		100
	4 $^1/_2$	Sugar (icing)		140
	4 $^1/_2$	Chocolate		140
		A little milk		
		A dash of rum		
		A little coffee essence		

Mix the almonds, sugar, grated chocolate, rum, coffee essence and milk into a pliable paste. Shape into hazelnut-sized balls by hand. Roll the balls in grated chocolate or chocolate granules and cool well for several hours.   *(France)*

Caramel Sticks

lb	oz		kg	gr
1	0	Dairy cream		500
1	0	Milk		500
1	7	Sugar (granulated)		700
	7	Glucose		200
		1 vanilla pod		
		Couverture		

Mix together the above ingredients and boil to the ball degree. Then beat until firm. Pin out, leave until cold and cut into small sticks which are dipped into couverture. *(Germany)*

Chambery Truffles - Truffettes de Chambéry

lb	oz		kg	gr
	9	Praline nougat		275
	9	Couverture		275
	9	Fondant		275
	7	Butter		200

Sieve the crushed praline nougat and mix with the melted couverture, fondant and butter.

Divide this creamy mixture into very small pieces, put in a cold place for 1 hour, shape quickly into small balls, roll in cocoa powder mixed with castor sugar or in grated chocolate and put in a cool place until required. *(France)*

Chocolate Maraschino Centres

lb	oz		kg	gr
1	5	Butter		650
	3 1/2	Fondant		100
	3 1/2	Brandy		100
	7	Maraschino		200
3	12	Milk chocolate couverture	1	875
		Plain chocolate couverture		

Beat the butter and fondant to a light cream in the machine and add the brandy and maraschino. Stir in the tempered milk chocolate couverture. Prepare leaf-shaped cut-outs from the mixing; when they have hardened, coat with plain couverture and pipe on diagonal lines of milk couverture on top. *(Germany)*

Chocolate Nuts - Noix chocolatées

lb	oz		kg	gr
	5	Walnuts		150
	5	Sugar (icing)		150
	5	Chocolate		150

Blanch the walnuts and pound them to a firm paste with sugar and a little water and shape into walnut-sized balls. Boil up the chocolate with a little water, dip the balls in the mixture and when almost cold roll in cocoa. *(France)*

Chocolate Truffles - Slagroom Truffels

lb	oz		kg	gr
1	3 1/2	Whipped cream		600
2	0	Sugar	1	
2	0	Butter	1	
		Vanilla		

Bring to the boiling point the whipped cream, sugar and vanilla; next add the butter. Stir well and cool. Let this mixture rest for a few hours in a cool place. After this rest, whip the mixture until it is fluffy. Pipe into lines and cool again. Cut the cooled strips into small squares. Dip these squares into couverture and roll immediately in cocoa. *(Holland)*

Coffee Centres

lb	oz		kg	gr
5	0	Couverture	2	500
2	0	Fresh cream	1	
	3 1/2	Water		100
	3 1/2	Ground coffee		100

Infuse the coffee in the water, add the cream, warm without bringing to the boil and pass through a very fine meshed sieve. Now add the vanilla couverture to make a ganache and spread this mixture between strips of wood on parchment paper. Place another sheet of paper on top and level off with a rolling pin. Remove the paper and cut the mixture out with an oval cutter. Dip the pieces into vanilla couverture, mark with a fork and top with a sweet coffee bean. *(France)*

Coffee Cream Centres

lb	oz		kg	gr
1	2	Dairy cream		560
1	2	Milk		560
1	9	Sugar (granulated)		770
	7	Glucose		200
	1	Instant coffee		30

Boil the dairy cream, milk, sugar and glucose to the ball degree. Add the instant coffee and beat in the machine until firm. Pin out, cut out into small sticks when cold, and coat with plain chocolate couverture. *(Germany)*

Coffee Nougat

lb	oz		kg	gr
2	0	Nut nougat	1	
	5	Plain chocolate couverture		150
	³/₄	Instant coffee		20

Work the nut nougat and the liquid couverture until smooth and add the instant coffee. Spread this paste to the desired thickness, cut into pieces and decorate each with a coffee bean. *(Germany)*

Coccinelles

Lightly beat up ganache in the mixer and roll out between strips of wood ¹/₂ in. (1 cm.) thick on to marzipan that has been pinned out to a thickness of ¹/₈ in. (3 mm.). Cover with a sheet of pistachio marzipan of the same thickness and allow to set. Mark with a caramel roller, cut into small squares, dip into vanilla couverture and decorate with half a pistachio nut.
(Switzerland)

Countesses

Pipe out some good quality vanilla ganache into small ropes which are cut up into pieces ¹/₂ in. (1 cm.) long and then rolled by hand into balls. They are dipped first into kirsch fondant and, when this has set, into milk couverture. Using a paper bag, decorate with a thin line of couverture. *(France)*

Croquant Nougat

lb	oz		kg	gr
2	0	Almond nougat	1	
	5	Plain chocolate couverture		150
1	³/₄	Crushed croquant		50

Work the nougat and the liquid couverture until smooth and add the crushed croquant. Spread to the desired thickness, cut into pieces and pipe out an ornament in milk chocolate couverture on each.
(Germany)

Cuba

lb	oz		kg	gr
1	0	Sugar (granulated)		500
	1 ³/₄	Butter		50
	2 ¹/₂	Glucose		75
	2 ¹/₂	Dairy cream		75
	3 ¹/₂	Rum		100
	12	Almonds (flaked)		375

Melt the sugar as for praline croquant. Boil up the butter with the glucose and dairy cream and pour into the pan containing sugar to dissolve the caramel. Add the rum and the slightly warm, lightly roasted almonds. Roll out ¹/₂ in. (1 cm.) thick on a marble slab dusted with icing sugar, cut into squares, dip these in plain tempered couverture and place a sultana on top. *(Switzerland)*

Curaçao Truffles

lb	oz		kg	gr
	14	Butter		400
	7	Curaçao		200
	3 ¹/₂	Brandy		100
2	0	Milk chocolate couverture	1	

Beat the butter, curaçao and brandy to a light cream in the machine and add the milk chocolate couverture. Make into truffle shapes and coat with plain couverture. Using a plain tube, pipe out a turret shape on top of each one with the same cream and decorate with a small leaf-shaped couverture cut-out. *(Germany)*

Favourites

lb	oz		kg	gr
1	12	Butter		875
4	6	Milk couverture	2	180
2	10	Praline paste	1	300

Melt the butter with the milk couverture and when the mixture is cold, blend in the praline paste by hand. Roll out this mixture between iron bars 1/2 in. (1 cm.) thick. Leave to cool and then cut up into small oblongs which are dipped in milk couverture. Mark the tops of these chocolates with a fork. *(France)*

Florence

lb	oz		kg	gr
	10	Dairy cream		300
	9	Honey		280
1	0	Couverture		500
	7	Orange peel		200
	3 1/2	Praline croquant		100

Prepare ganache with the dairy cream, honey and couverture. As soon as it sets, add the orange peel that has been finely chopped and the finely crushed praline croquant. Line tinfoil cups with couverture; when set fill with the ganache and cover over with couverture. *(Switzerland)*

Ginger Triangles

lb	oz		kg	gr
2	0	Marzipan	1	
	3 1/2	Ginger		100

Chop the ginger and add to the marzipan. Pin out, cut into triangles and lastly coat with plain chocolate couverture.
(Germany)

Honey Nougat

lb	oz		kg	gr
	10	Honey		300
	10	Dairy cream		300
	3 1/2	Glucose		100
	5	Hazelnuts		150
	5	Almonds		150
	3 1/2	Orange peel		100

Boil the cream, honey and sugar to the medium ball degree *(page 51)*, then stir in the flaked roasted hazelnuts and almonds together with the very finely diced orange peel. Set aside for a short time, then roll out between metal bars 1/2 in. (1 cm.) thick on to an oiled marble slab. When cold, coat thinly with chocolate (on both sides), cut into strips and then cut these into lozenge shapes. Using a two pronged fork, dip into tempered couverture and mark the top with two lines.

Jamaica

lb	oz		kg	gr
1	4	Raw marzipan		625
	5	Sugar (icing)		150
	2 1/2	Rum		75
	5	Cherries		150
	3 1/2	Praline croquant		100

Mix the marzipan well with the rum and pass through close set rollers. Work in the sugar, then the chopped cherries and the coarsely crushed praline croquant. Chop again with a large knife, then roll out 1/2 in. (1 cm.) thick. Cut out into small ovals, allow to dry a little, dip into plain couverture and finish off by marking a line on top with a fork.

Kirsch Fondant Centres

lb	oz		kg	gr
	8	Butter		250
	8	Fondant		250
1	0	Couverture		500
	3/4	Kirsch		20

Beat the butter and fondant until light and fluffy, add the tempered couverture and lastly beat in the kirsch slowly. Place small discs of nougat on tiny dots of chocolate and press down firmly. Using a large star tube, pipe a whirl of the fondant mixture on top and when set, dip into plain couverture. *(Switzerland)*

Light Truffles

lb	oz		kg	gr
	8	Dairy cream		250
1	0	Couverture (milk)		500
	3 1/2	Cocoa butter		100
	1	Butter		30
		1 vanilla pod		

Boil up the cream with the vanilla pod, remove the pod, add the couverture, mix until smooth and pour on to a metal tray. Stir with a scraper from time to time and, as soon as the mixture is almost cold, blend in the butter and cocoa butter thoroughly. Make into truffles in the usual way.

Little Logs

lb	oz		kg	gr
2	0	Praline paste	1	
	7	Roasted chopped hazelnuts		200
1	0	Vanilla couverture (for the basic paste)		500

Mix all the ingredients into a paste and, using a savoy bag, pipe small ropes which are then cut into pieces $3/4$ in. (2 cm.) long. Dip the pieces into a vanilla couverture containing chopped roasted hazelnuts (7 oz. [200 gr.] per 2 lb. 4 oz. [1 kg. 125] couverture). *(France)*

Little Logs

lb	oz		kg	gr
	8	Butter		250
	8 1/2	Fondant		265
	5	Kirsch		150
1	0	Plain couverture		500
		Marzipan		

Beat the butter and fondant until light and fluffy, add the tempered couverture and lastly slowly blend in the kirsch. As soon as the mixture begins to set, pipe on to parchment paper in ropes, using a coarse plain pipe. Flavour some marzipan slightly with kirsch and tint it light green. Pin out $3/16$ in. (4 mm.) thick and brush with kirsch or cocoa butter. Place the ropes on the marzipan after leaving them to stand for a time and wrap it round them. Allow to dry a little, then cover with three coats of milk couverture and, using a hot knife, cut on a slant into $3/8$ in. (8 mm.) slices.

Ropes of gianduja may be wrapped in pistachio marzipan, brushed over with couverture and cut in slices in the same way. *(Switzerland)*

Malaga

lb	oz		kg	gr
	14	Dairy cream		400
1	12	Couverture (milk)		875
	7	Malaga muscatels		200
	2	Malaga wine		60

Boil up the cream and add the couverture. Finely chop the muscatels which have been macerated in malaga wine and stir them into cream/couverture ganache. Roll out $1/4$ in. (5 mm.) thick between parchment paper, allow to set, then cut out into circles. Using a three pronged fork, dip into milk couverture and place a muscatel in the centre.

Marie

lb	oz		kg	gr
	8	Almonds (roasted)		250
	10	Orange peel		300
	10	Sugar (icing)		300
	1/2	Rum		15
	10	Couverture		300

Grind the almonds finely with the orange peel and sugar, add the rum and then the tempered couverture. Fill into small tinfoil cups lined with couverture. Cover the tops with couverture.

Marzipan Centres

lb	oz		kg	gr
2	0	Marzipan	1	
		Plain chocolate couverture		

Pin out the marzipan, cut into rounds and coat with plain couverture. *(Germany)*

Marquisettes

lb	oz		kg	gr
	4 1/2	Ground almonds		140
	4 1/2	Sugar (icing)		140
	4 1/2	Grated chocolate		140
	1 1/2	Egg yolks (approx.)		45

Thoroughly mix the almonds with the sugar, chocolate and the egg yolks to make a firm paste. Make into hazelnut-sized balls, turn in grated chocolate and dry in the air for 2 hours or longer. *(France)*

Masked Hazelnuts - Noisettes masquées

Roast hazelnuts and rub off the skin by hand. When cold, dip in tempered couverture. *(France)*

Masked Pistachios - Pistaches masquées

Proceed as for masked hazelnuts but blanch and dry the pistachios without roasting them. *(France)*

May-Flies

Take a suitable quantity of good quality ganache, beat it up a little in the mixing machine and then spread it between strips of wood $1/2$ in. (1 cm.) high on a piece of pistachio marzipan $1/10$ in. (2 mm.) thick.

Cover over with another piece of pistachio marzipan and leave to set in a cold place before marking with a caramel roller and cutting into little squares. Dip the pieces in vanilla couverture and decorate with half pistachio nuts. *(France)*

Milano

lb	oz		kg	gr
2	4	Praline paste	1	125
	$1/4$	Coffee powder		8
1	12	Milk couverture		875
	$3\,1/2$	Milk		100

Dissolve the coffee powder in the warm milk and then stir in the praline paste and the liquid couverture. Leave to set, roll out between strips of wood $1/2$ in. (1 cm.) thick and cut out with a round cutter. Dip into milk couverture, mark three lines on each piece with a fork and top with a mimosa ball. *(France)*

Miniature Chessboards

Light gianduja

lb	oz		kg	gr
1	0	Almonds		500
1	5	Sugar (icing)		650
	12	Cocoa butter		375

Dark gianduja

lb	oz		kg	gr
1	0	Hazelnuts		500
1	0	Sugar (icing)		500
	15	Couverture (plain)		450
	2	Cocoa paste		60

To make the light gianduja, roast the almonds lightly, grind finely with the sugar and add the melted cocoa butter.

Mix thoroughly and, when firm, pin out several times between metal bars $1/4$ in. (5 mm.) thick, finally making it into a square of the same thickness on greaseproof paper and leave to set. For the dark gianduja, roast the hazelnuts lightly, grind finely with the sugar, add the couverture and the cocoa paste and proceed as for the light gianduja. Both squares should be the same size. Cut them once through the middle. Use one layer to form the base, brush it at once with hot cocoa butter, cover with a layer of the other colour and press down well, spread this with cocoa butter and place a further layer on top, continuing until a black-white-black-white formation is built up. Cut into $1/4$ in. (5 mm.) strips, lay these on their sides, sandwich in fours with hot cocoa butter to make a chequerboard pattern and spread tempered couverture round the sides with a small palette knife. Lastly cut into $1/2$ in. (1 cm.) slices.

(Switzerland)

Moccatines

lb	oz		kg	gr
	14	Sugar (granulated)		400
	8	Dairy cream		250
1	$1/2$	Instant coffee		45
	8	Hard fat		250
	$4\,1/2$	Sugar (icing)		140
1	$1/2$	Kirsch		45

Melt the sugar. Boil up the cream with the coffee, add to the caramel sugar and set aside. Cream the fat with the sugar, add the kirsch and lastly mix with the caramel coffee cream. Fill into small tinfoil cups lined with couverture. Cover the tops with couverture. *(Switzerland)*

Mont-Blanc

lb	oz		kg	gr
1	5	Butter		650
	14	Fondant		400
	7	Kirsch		200
3	5	Milk couverture	1	650
1	2	Vanilla couverture		560

Use the mixing machine to beat up the butter, fondant and milk couverture and then add the kirsch. Deposit the tempered vanilla couverture on some parchment paper and spread it out with a spatula. When it has set, cut out some rounds. Fill a savoy bag fitted with a plain pipe with the mixture already prepared and pipe it out on to the couverture bases making conical shapes. Leave to set and dip in some vanilla couverture. *(France)*

Moscovites

lb	oz		kg	gr
2	4	Fresh cream	1	125
1	2	Butter		560
2	4	Milk couverture	1	125
2	4	Vanilla couverture	1	125
2	4	Kirsch flavoured marzipan	1	125

Make a ganache with the cream, butter and all the couverture. Meanwhile roll out the marzipan to a thickness of $1/10$ in. (2 mm.) and cut out into rounds. When the ganache has cooled down, beat it up in the machine and then pipe it from a savoy bag fitted with a star pipe on to the marzipan rounds, raising the pipe so that a conical shape is achieved. Dip in either vanilla or milk couverture. *(France)*

Murano

lb	oz		kg	gr
2	4	Fresh cream	1	125
1	2	Honey		560
3	12	Milk couverture	1	875
1	8	Sultanas soaked in rum		750

Prepare a ganache with the cream, honey and couverture. When it has cooled down, mix in the sultanas. Make the mixture into ropes of uniform thickness and cut up with a knife. Roll by hand into egg shapes and dip them in milk couverture. Decorate with three lines piped with the aid of a paper bag.

N.B. As the mixture is soft, it should be well dusted with icing sugar before it is handled. *(France)*

Muscadin

Spread some green, pistachio flavoured marzipan between strips of wood $1/2$-$3/4$ in. (1-2 cm.) thick and cut out into rounds.

Make a hollow in each with the back of a dipping fork and fill with a little raspberry jelly which has been re-cooked with some sugar. Roll each piece into a ball and dip into vanilla couverture to which has been added some crushed roasted almonds (for 2 lb. 4 oz. [1 kg. 125] couverture use 10 oz. [300 gr.] almonds).

(France)

Noisettines

Roll out some hazelnut gianduja between strips of wood $1/4$ in. (5 mm.) thick and cut out into rounds. With a little couverture stick on each a coated roasted hazelnut. To coat the hazelnuts, put them in a copper pan with the sugar (use 7 oz. [200 gr.] sugar for 1 lb. 5 oz. [650 gr.] hazelnuts) and heat until it adheres to the nuts. Dip in either vanilla or milk couverture. *(France)*

Nougat Montélimar

lb	oz		kg	gr
1	9	Water		770
5	0	Sugar (granulated)	2	500
2	10	Glucose	1	300
	12	Egg whites		375
2	10	Honey	1	300
4	0	Chopped, roasted blanched almonds	2	
1	9	Chopped, roasted hazelnuts		770
1	2	Skinned pistachio nuts		560
		2 vanilla pods		

Prepare in the same way as that indicated for the basic recipe for Montélimar, but the sugar should be boiled to a temperature of 284° F (140° C). When the nougat is made, it should be rolled out between strips of wood $1/2$ in. (1 cm.) thick. The Montélimar should be thinly coated on both sides with couverture and then be cut up into little squares. These are dipped in vanilla couverture and marked with two lines with a fork.
(France)

Nougat Truffles

Fix a small disc of nougat on to paper with couverture. Pipe on ganache made with milk chocolate and place three more small discs of nougat at the top to look like wings. When set, dip in milk couverture and place a small silver ball on top. *(Switzerland)*

Nut Dainties

lb	oz		kg	gr
	7	Walnuts		200
	3 $1/2$	Almonds		100
	5	Honey		150
	10	Sugar (granulated)		300
	3 $1/2$	Water		100
		Curaçao (triple sec) *or* Maraschino		

Grind the walnuts and almonds until oily. Boil the sugar and water to 96° B and proceed as for marzipan, adding the liqueur. Roll out $1/2$ in. (1 cm.) thick and cut out into ovals. Dip into kirsch flavoured fondant, then place half a walnut on top immediately. When set, dip into couverture up to the top edge, without coating the top. *(Switzerland)*
(Illustration page 633.)

Olives

Roll out some pistachio flavoured almond paste between strips of wood $3/4$ in. (2 cm.) thick. Cut out into rounds which are then shaped by hand into olive shapes. Dip in vanilla or milk couverture to which coarsely ground roasted almonds have been added (10 oz. [300 gr.] almonds for 2 lb. 4 oz. [1 kg. 125] couverture).
(France)

Orange Marzipan

lb	oz		kg	gr
	3 $1/2$	Candied orange peel		100
2	0	Marzipan	1	

Chop the candied orange peel and work into the marzipan. Pin out, cut out into rounds, halve these and coat with plain chocolate couverture.

Decorate the top of each piece with a small triangle of candied orange peel and a leaf piped out in milk chocolate couverture. *(Germany)*

Orange Truffles

lb	oz		kg	gr
	8	Butter		250
	4	Fondant		125
	$1/2$	Grated zest of orange		15
	13 $1/2$	Plain chocolate couverture		400

First beat the butter, fondant and grated orange zest to a light cream in the machine. Then slowly add a little couverture. Spread the rest of the plain couverture on greaseproof paper and cut out into rounds. Lastly pipe out the mixture on the rounds, using a plain tube.

Pineapple Cups

Partly fill plain couverture into small tinfoil cups, top with pineapple jam brought to a liquid consistency with curaçao and cover over with plain couverture. The cups may be finished with a narrow paper band. *(Germany)*

Pineapple Triangles

Take some slices of glacé pineapple and cut them up into small triangles; dip them into warm kirsch fondant, coating three quarters of each piece; leave to dry and then dip the base in vanilla couverture.
(Illustration page 633.) *(France)*

Pistachio Marzipan

lb	oz		kg	gr
2	0	Pistachio marzipan	1	
		Plain chocolate couverture		
		Quartered pistachio nuts		

Pin out the pistachio marzipan to the desired thickness and cut out into half-moon shapes. Coat with plain couverture and decorate the centre of each with a quarter pistachio nut. *(Germany)*

Portugal

lb	oz		kg	gr
	14	Sugar (icing)		400
	5	Water		150
	8	Almonds		250
		Cinnamon (pinch)		
		Port (a little)		
		1 vanilla pod		

Make marzipan with the sugar, almonds, water and vanilla then grind finely with a little port wine, a pinch of cinnamon and, if required some glucose. Roll out $1/4$ in. (5 mm.) thick, cut into half-moon shapes and dip into couverture.

Pralines

lb	oz		kg	gr
2	0	Hazelnuts	1	
2	0	Almonds	1	
3	15	Sugar (icing)	1	950
6	0	Vanilla couverture	3	

Roast and skin the hazelnuts, roast the unblanched almonds and mix them all with the icing sugar. Now grind finely in the machine and finally add the melted couverture. Mix thoroughly into a smooth and firm paste. Roll out this paste between strips of wood $1/2$ in. (1 cm.) thick and cut out into rounds. Dip in vanilla or milk couverture and decorate by marking a circle on each chocolate with a fork. *(France)*

Princesses

lb	oz		kg	gr
2	4	Praline paste	1	125
	14	Cocoa butter		400
	10	Skinned pistachio nuts		300

Stir the melted cocoa butter into the praline mixture. Leave to set and then add the chopped pistachio nuts. Roll out this paste to a thickness of $1/2$ in. (1 cm.) and cut it up into strips $3/4$ in. (2 cm.) wide and 6 in. (15 cm.) long. Dip these pieces into milk couverture holding them with two forks and use a fork to decorate them with lines. The final step is to cut the strips up into pieces $1/4$ in. (5 mm.) wide. *(France)*

Rigi Peaks

lb	oz		kg	gr
	12	Butter		375
	12	Fondant		375
1	8	Couverture		750
	1	Kirsch		30

Beat up the butter and fondant until light and fluffy. Slowly beat in the tempered fondant and lastly add the kirsch. Pipe on to small discs of praline nougat, using a large star tube. *(Switzerland)* *(Illustration page 633)*.

Rochers

lb	oz		kg	gr
1	8	Flaked almonds		750
1	0	Milk or vanilla couverture		500

Take the flaked almonds and roast them. Once they have cooled down, mix them into the tempered couverture. Deposit from a spoon into small heaps.

N.B. Only the quantity needed should be prepared at any time, since if the mixture hardens, the couverture cannot be re-tempered owing to the presence of the almonds. *(France)*

Sicilians

lb	oz		kg	gr
2	4	Candied orange slices	1	125
	10	Marzipan		300
	1 $3/4$	Curaçao		50
		Vanilla couverture		

Thin the marzipan with the curaçao and spread this mixture on the slices of candied orange. Cut these into quarters and dip them in vanilla couverture. Mark the top of each with a fork. *(France)*

Sorrento

Fix small discs of praline croquant on to paper with a little couverture and pipe a small dome of ganache made with milk couverture on top. Fix three more small discs of praline croquant on to the top to resemble wings and, when firm, dip in milk couverture. *(Switzerland)*
(Illustration page 633.)

Surprise Truffles - Truffes en Surprise

Shape Parisian nougat into small balls by hand. Dip in couverture, allow to drain and roll in chocolate vermicelli. *(France)*

Truffles

The centres for truffles are made of different sorts of ganache (generally of the best quality). The mixture is beaten up and piped from a savoy bag fitted with a plain pipe into ropes. These are immediately cut up with the special caramel cutter. Leave to harden a little and shape into balls which are then rolled in the hand with a little couverture and placed on greaseproof paper. This thin coating of couverture gives the truffles a firmness necessary to enable them to be dipped in couverture and rolled on graters so as to roughen them. Different sorts of truffles can be produced by rolling kirsch truffles in chocolate granules, rum truffles (slightly elongated) in cocoa powder and coffee truffles in couverture chips. *(France)*
(Illustration page 633.)

Virginias

Cut Paris nougat in small lozenges and dip in couverture. *(France)*

Walnut Fondants

lb	oz		kg	gr
	3 1/2	Chopped walnuts		100
2	0	Marzipan	1	

First add the walnuts to the marzipan. Then pin out, cut out into the desired shapes, dip the top in fondant and edge with plain chocolate couverture.
Decorate with a glazed half-walnut.
(Germany)

White Truffles

lb	oz		kg	gr
	10	Dairy cream		300
1	8	Couverture (white)		750
	5	Nougat paste (light)		150
	5	Cocoa butter		150
	5	Butter		150

Boil up the dairy cream, add the couverture and mix until smooth. Pour on to a metal tray and leave until cold. Beat the nougat paste with the butter until light and fluffy, add the cold ganache and lastly blend in the melted cocoa butter, which should be cold. Stir until the mixture begins to set, then proceed as for other types of truffles.
(Illustration page 633.)

LIQUEUR CHOCOLATES

These chocolates are prepared by pouring a liqueur syrup into cavities made with moulds pressed into a bed of starch.

The starch should be very dry and sifted directly into shallow, wooden boxes about 1 in. (2.5 cm.) deep. The starch is then beaten up with a metal whisk so as to make it light and then is levelled off with a strip of wood and the excess starch removed. Plaster moulds attached to a strip of wood are then pressed into the starch to produce the cavities.

Boil the sugar (2 lb. 4 oz. [1 kg. 125] sugar to 14 oz. [400 gr.] water) to 221-223° F (105-106° C), carefully washing the sides of the pan and removing the scum. Take off the heat and when the sugar has cooled down, pour in 7 oz. (200 gr.) liqueur. Check with the hydrometer that the syrup is at 31-32° B. As liqueurs contain sugar, the sugar syrup is only boiled to 221-223° F (105-106° C), but for spirits the sugar syrup has to be boiled to 225.5-227° F (107.5-108.5° C), with the addition of 1 3/4 oz. (50 gr.) glucose for every 2 lb. 4 oz. (1 kg. 125) sugar. When the syrup is sufficiently cool, pour it gently into the cavities made in the starch; a conical fondant dropper with a rod inside is used for this purpose; next sieve some starch on top and leave to dry for 10-12 hours. Remove the centres from the starch and dust them with a fine brush before coating them with vanilla couverture. Liqueur chocolates are wrapped separately in silver paper bearing the name of the liqueur used.

LIQUEUR CHOCOLATES MADE WITHOUT STARCH

These are made by lining hinged metal moulds with couverture and then filling them three quarters full with the liqueur syrup at 28° B. Coat the lids of the moulds with couverture and close them. When they are cold, the chocolates are removed from their moulds and wrapped individually like other liqueur chocolates.

FONDANT CHOCOLATES

These are prepared in the same way as liqueur chocolates but flavoured and coloured fondant is poured while warm into the cavities in place of the liqueur syrup. When the fondant is quite set, remove the centres from the starch, brush them and dip in vanilla couverture. In the same way, novelties are obtained such as bells, mice, etc.

Sugar Confectionery

TOFFEES AND BOILED SWEETS

Boiled sweets are made from sugar which has been boiled to the large crack degree 290° F (144° C). To obtain a hard, smooth and transparent sweet, a quantity of glucose should be added to the water and sugar solution equal to about 15 to 20 % of the sugar. A simple boiled sweet is prepared by flavouring and colouring a sugar syrup containing 20 % glucose and which has been boiled to the large crack degree. The mixture is then poured on to the marble slab and cut up immediately into shapes. The more usual boiled sweets are no longer made by the craftsman, but are mass-produced and sold at competitive prices to the retailer.

Milk Caramels - Caramels au Lait

lb	oz		kg	gr
	9	Sugar (icing)		275
	2 ³/₄	Glucose or honey		75
	1 ³/₄	Butter or coconut oil		50

Put the sugar and honey in a sugar boiler that is not tinned inside, mix, bring to the boil and see to it that the syrup does not boil over. Stir from time to time to prevent it sticking and keep on brushing the sides of the pan with a brush dipped in cold water to prevent graining. Add the butter or coconut oil and boil to the ball degree. Pour on to an oiled marble slab surrounded by 4 oiled metal bars to prevent the mixture from running off. Do not cut into pieces until almost cold.

Vanilla Caramels - Caramels à la Vanille

Make in the same way as milk caramels, flavouring with vanilla.

Caramel Creams

lb	oz		kg	gr
3	4	Sugar	1	625
2	4	Cream	1	125
	9	Glucose		275
		Vanilla		

Cook all the above ingredients to 288° F (142.5° C). When the mixture is ready, pour it on to an oiled marble slab, level it off and mark with a fluted roller. Cut into pieces when almost cold.

Soft Caramels

lb	oz		kg	gr
1	8	Sugar (granulated)		750
3	0	Double cream	1	500
	7	Butter		200
	7	Glucose		200
		1 vanilla pod		

Place the sugar, cream, glucose and vanilla in a large copper pan that is not tinned on the inside. Bring to the boil, stirring constantly and carefully wash down the sides of the pan. As soon as the mixture has reached the thread degree, stir in the butter in small pieces and boil to the ball degree *(page 51)*. Remove from the heat, pour out to a thickness of about ³/₈ in. (6 mm.) on to an oiled marble slab surrounded by four metal bars and remove the vanilla. Leave until quite cold before cutting into pieces of the desired size with a caramel cutter or knife.

(France - Switzerland)

Cough Drops

lb	oz		kg	gr
4	0	Sugar (granulated)	2	
1	0	Glucose		500
	5	Honey		150
1	0	Herbal infusion		500
		Essence of menthol and eucalyptus		

Pour the infusion over the sugar, bring to the boil and skim; add the glucose and honey and cook to 288° F (142.5° C). Pour on to an oiled marble slab; splash with a few drops of the essences, fold over the mixture and finish off in the usual way.

Lemon or Orange Drops

lb	oz		kg	gr
2	0	Sugar (granulated)	1	
	10	Water		300
	7	Glucose		200
	¹/₄	Citric acid powder		8
		1 lemon or 1 orange		

Rub the lemon or orange peel on a lump of sugar and dissolve the latter in a little water. Meanwhile boil the sugar, water and glucose to 257° F (125° C) and then add the flavour solution. Cook the mixture to 290° F (144° C) and pour on to an oiled marble slab. Sprinkle with the citric acid and then fold over the sides towards the centre several times so that the acid is well mixed in. Spread the composition with the hands, flatten it out with a fluted roller and cut up into pieces.

Malt Drops

lb	oz		kg	gr
2	0	Sugar (granulated)	1	
	10	Crushed malt		300
1	8	Water		750
	7	Glucose		200

Cook the malt dissolved in the water until the quantity is reduced by half and strain. Add the sugar and glucose and boil to 288° F (142.5° C). Finish in the same way as above.

Peppermint Drops I

lb	oz		kg	gr
2	0	Sugar (granulated)	1	
	10	Water		300
	7	Glucose		200
		A few drops of peppermint essence		

Boil the sugar to 288° F (142.5° C) and add the peppermint essence a drop at a time. Stir well and then pour on an oiled marble slab. Finish as above.

Peppermint Drops II

lb	oz		kg	gr
1	12	Sugar (granulated)		875
	9	Water		270
	10	Sugar (icing)		300
		A few drops of peppermint essence		

Boil the sugar to 237° F (113.7° C) and stir in the icing sugar and peppermint essence. Pour into starch moulds, leave to dry and, after brushing off the starch, wrap in cellophane paper.

Poppy Drops

lb	oz		kg	gr
2	4	Sugar (granulated)	1	125
	7	Glucose		200
	14	Water		400
	¹/₄	Dried poppy flowers		8

Infuse the flowers in the water, strain and pour over the sugar; boil to 288° F (142.5° C). Finish as for lemon drops.

Strawberry or Raspberry Drops

lb	oz		kg	gr
3	4	Sugar (granulated)	1	625
1	0	Water		500
	10	Glucose		300
	1	Strawberry juice		30
		Red colouring		

629

Boil the sugar, water and glucose to 286° F (141° C). Pour in the fruit juice and bring back to the crack degree. Continue in the same way as for lemon drops.

Gum Drops

Gum arabic, first dissolved in water contained in a bain-marie and then filtered, is used for this kind of sweet. The gum is next blended with the sugar and stirred constantly while it is cooked in a pan. It must be simmered gently in order to obtain clear sweets. The mixture is adequately cooked when it begins to gel as it falls off the skimmer.

Gum Drops

lb	oz		kg	gr
6	0	Sugar (granulated)	3	
7	0	Ground gum arabic	3	500
2	0	Glucose	1	
2	0	Water (approx.)	1	

Dissolve and cook the sugar, glucose and water together in a pan. When the mixture is boiling vigorously, introduce the gum arabic and simmer gently, stirring with a spatula all the time. When the mixture begins to gel, skim and filter it. Flavour according to taste with different essences. Pour into starch impressions and leave to dry for a week to a week and a half in a slightly warm prover. When the sweets are dry, they are taken out and brushed clean and candied.

Marshmallows

lb	oz		kg	gr
	5	Marshmallow root		150
2	0	Sugar (granulated)	1	
2	0	Ground gum arabic	1	
	12	Egg whites		375
	5	Orange flower water		150
4	0	Water	2	

Soak the marshmallow root in the water, pass through a sieve and heat in a pan; add the gum arabic and sugar and, when these have dissolved, reduce the mixture until it reaches the consistency of a semi-liquid paste. Turn down the heat and add the whisked egg whites and orange flower water. Continue to evaporate over a gentle heat until the mixture no longer clings to the pan. Pour on to a marble slab, dust with starch and deposit with a savoy bag into starch impressions. Leave to dry and then remove and dust with a brush.

FUDGES
Cream Fudge

lb	oz		kg	gr
2	4	Cream	1	125
2	10	Sugar (granulated)	1	300
	9	Glucose		270
		1 vanilla pod		

Cook all the ingredients to 248°F (120°C), stirring all the while. Pour the mixture between metal bars about $1/2$ in. (1 cm.) thick on an oiled slab and level off. Wait until the mixture is completely cold before cutting it up into pieces.

N.B. Different flavoured fudges may be obtained by adding unsweetened chocolate, coffee essence or praline.

Cream Fondant Fudge I

lb	oz		kg	gr
1	0	Cream		500
1	0	Unsweetened evaporated milk		500
2	0	Sugar	1	
	1 $3/4$	Glucose		50
		1 vanilla bean		

Cream Fondant Fudge II

lb	oz		kg	gr
2	0	Cream	1	
2	0	Sugar	1	
	3 $1/2$	Glucose		100
		1 vanilla bean		

Cook all the ingredients to 248°F (120°C) in a copper pan and blend well by spreading the mixture against the sides of the pan with a spatula. Pour on to parchment paper between metal bars and level off before marking out the sweets. Only cut up when the fudge has become cold. This fudge can be flavoured with cocoa, coffee, hazelnuts or pistachio nuts. When the mixture is flavoured with an essence or a liquid, it must be cooked to 250° F (121° C).

FONDANTS

Fondants are made by heating fondant and pouring it into starch impressions. There are varieties of fondants which can be given different colours and can be flavoured with essences or liqueurs. By pouring two fondants at the same time, a marbled fondant can be obtained. Fondants may also be given centres of marzipan, hazelnut, paste, etc., which are dipped in fondant and then candied.

Fondants - Roomborstplaat

lb	oz		kg	gr
2	0	Sugar (icing)	1	
	7	Whipped cream		200
	³/₄	Water		20
		Vanilla		

Heat these ingredients to a temperature of 194° F (90° C) in a double boiler (a bain-marie). Pour into moulds with the aid of a funnel. In order to obtain an attractive assortment, various flavours can be used such as: cocoa, coffee, nutpaste, fruit pulp, etc. Directly after the pouring one can add nuts, candied fruits, etc. The fondant should be firm but soft eating. If one candies the outside of the fondants they will have a better appearance.

To candy the fondants dip them into a warm saturated sugar solution. After drying, the solution becomes unsaturated and crystallizes. *(Holland)*
(Illustration page 692.)

Little Fondants

lb	oz		kg	gr
2	0	Fondant	1	
	3 ¹/₂	Glucose		100
	¹/₁₆	Essence		2
	³/₈	Pectin		9
		Colour as required		

Heat the ingredients to about 120° F (49° C) in a bain-marie or on a low heat. Add essence (example: peppermint) and any colour. Pour into starch impressions. These fondants can be moulded in various forms and shapes.

PASTILLES

Pastilles are sweets obtained by giving various flavours to a mixture of sugar softened in water and icing sugar which have been heated together. They can be poured through a funnel into moulds, piped or be rolled out and cut up into pieces according to the consistency of the mixture.

N.B. Peppermint lozenges should always be dried in the open air and not in a prover in order not to lose their peppermint flavour.

Fruit Pastilles - Orange

lb	oz		kg	gr
1	0	Sugar (icing)		500
1	0	Sugar (granulated)		500
	1 ³/₄	Lump sugar		50
		Juice and zest of 4 oranges		

Rub the oranges against the sugar lumps and then squeeze the fruit to obtain the juice. Mix the latter with all the sugar and heat. Add colouring according to the type of fruit used. A savoy bag and pipe is utilised when making this type of pastille. Leave overnight to dry. These pastilles may be made with other fruit flavours.

Peppermint Pastilles

lb	oz		kg	gr
1	0	Sugar (granulated)		500
	9	Sugar (icing)		275
	9	Fondant		275
		A few drops of peppermint essence		

Thoroughly mix all the ingredients together, heat and pipe on to baking sheets. Dry in the air.

631

Orange Flower Water Pastilles

Use the recipe above (less peppermint). Moisten the sugar with concentrated orange flower water, add a little water until a semi-liquid mixture is obtained. Warm up the mixture until it liquifies but remove from heat before it starts to cook.

Pour through a funnel or out of a lipped pan. When the pastilles begin to set, remove from the baking sheet and finish drying them on a sieve in a prover.

CARAMEL FRUITS

Caramel fruits are made according to the following recipes. See *pages 211-212* for marzipan recipes.

Flavour 10 oz. (300 gr.) marzipan with arrack, shape 20 pieces round and place half a walnut on each side.

Flavour 10 oz. (300 gr.) marzipan with curaçao, shape 20 ovals and decorate each with 3 strips of candied orange peel.

Flavour 10 oz. (300 gr.) pale pink marzipan with cherry brandy, shape 20 pieces round and place 3 hazelnuts and 3 pistachio nuts on each.

Split open sugared green almonds and fill with pale yellow marzipan flavoured with rum.

Flavour 10 oz. (300 gr.) marzipan with arrack, shape about 15 pieces round and place a piece of crystallized pineapple on each.

Flavour 10 oz. (300 gr.) red marzipan with kirsch, shape 20 ovals, and place 2 red glacé cherries and 2 small pieces of pistachio nut on each.

Halve sugared black walnuts and cover each half with half a light-brown walnut.

Flavour 10 oz. (300 gr.) marzipan with kirsch, shape 20 ovals, and place one red and one yellow glacé cherry and two small pieces of pistachio nut on each.

Halve sugared 'chinois' (small green oranges preserved in brandy) and place a red glacé cherry on each half.

Stick the fruits on to needles, dip into caramel sugar (boil 4 lb. [2 kg.] sugar, 7 oz. [200 gr.] glucose and 1 lb. [500 gr.] of water to 286-293° F [141-145° C]) and then put on an oiled marble slab.
(Illustration page 635.)

Caramel Cherries - Cerises au Caramel

Drain brandy cherries well and dry them. With a fork, dip them into sugar taken to the crack degree 300-310° F (148-155° C) and place on marble slab to cool.
(Illustration page 635.)

STUFFED FRUITS AND NUTS
Stuffed Dates

Colour some marzipan lightly and flavour, preferably with spirits so that it does not taste too sweet (kirsch, raspberry brandy, slivowitz, cognac and similar spirits are suitable for this purpose). Roll out into bars, cut into ³/₄ in. (2 cm.) lengths and mould round. Stone and scoop out the dates, fill with the marzipan and roll the tops in coarse granulated sugar. Indent down the centre with a modelling tool and place the dates in paper cases.
(Illustration page 634.)

Stuffed Walnuts

Sandwich two half walnuts with the marzipan and proceed as above.
(Illustration page 634.)

Stuffed Prunes

Stone large prunes, fill with the marzipan and mark with a trellis pattern, using the back of a knife.

Instead of rolling the top in granulated sugar, spread with a little cocoa butter, dip into caramel sugar and flash under a salamander or glaze with hot gum arabic solution.

Sugar Basket with Chocolates ▶
(See p. 612, 643)

634 ▲ Sugar Basket, p. 643, with Petits Fours, p. 517, 612   ▲ Sugar Basket, p. 643, with Stuffed Fruits, p. 632

Sugar Parrot, p. 647, and Petits Fours, p. 473, 485, 503, 519, 536 ▼

▲ Tel Kadayif, p. 749   Caramel Fruits, p. 632 ▼   635

636 ▲ Clown, p. 599 　　　　▲ Moulded Chocolate, p. 247
　　　Königsberg Marzipan Confections, p. 616 ▼　　　Glazed Chestnuts, p. 642 ▼

▲ Marzipan Dogs, p. 614   ▲ Marzipan Fishes, p. 614

Marzipan Frogs, Marzipan Piglets, Marzipan Hedgehogs, p. 615 ▼

638 ▲ Marzipan Santa Claus, p. 615   ▲ Baumkuchen Santa Claus, p. 611
Witch's Cottage, p. 611 ▼   Fruit Stall, p. 611 ▶

640 ▲ Profiteroles with Chocolate, p. 745 ▲ Fruits in Wine or Kirsch Jelly, p. 729, 730
Raspberry Gratin Eden, p. 675 ▼

FRUIT JELLIES - GELATINE DI FRUTTA

Fruit jellies are served generally in the summer season instead of chocolates. They may also be served with petits fours.

Recipe I

lb	oz		kg	gr
1	0	Water		500
1	4	Sugar (granulated)		625
1	0	Glucose		500
	3/4	Pectin		20
	1/16	Fruit essence		2
	3/8	Citric acid		10
		Colour as required		

Heat the water to 140° F (60° C), then add pectin mixed with 3 1/2 oz. (100 gr.) sugar, allow to boil for 2 minutes, add the remaining ingredients, boil again, take from heat, add fruit essence and colour. Pour into starch impressions and leave to become set. Remove from the starch, wash them and roll into granulated sugar.

Recipe II

lb	oz		kg	gr
1	10	Sugar (granulated)		800
1	5	Glucose		650
1	12	Fruit pulp		875
	10	Fruit juice		300

Boil the ingredients to 212-221° F (100-105° C) and pour into starch impressions. Put in a drying cupboard and leave for 12 hours. Wash them and roll into granulated sugar. *(Italy)*

VARIOUS RECIPES

Loukoum or Turkish Delight

lb	oz		kg	gr
11	0	Sugar (granulated)	5	500
4	0	Glucose	2	
15	0	Water	7	500
1	5	Starch		650
		Juice of 8 lemons		

Pour 11 lb. (5 kg. 500) water over the sugar and add the starch, (which has been diluted in the remaining water), and the glucose and cook to 250° F (121° C). Immediately pour in the lemon juice, flavour according to taste and pour on a slab dusted with icing sugar between metal bars. Leave to dry for two days and cut into oblong strips which are then tossed in a mixture of icing sugar and starch. Loukoum or Turkish Delight can also be made with the addition of crystallized fruit, almonds, roasted hazelnuts or pistachio nuts.

Quince Paste - Quittenpaste

lb	oz		kg	gr
20	0	Quince pulp	10	
23	0	Water	11	500
27	0	Sugar (granulated)	13	500
13	0	Corn syrup	6	500
	2 3/4	Pomosin (retarder)		80
	5 3/4	Pomosin (pectin)		170
	6 1/4	Powdered tartaric acid		185

Boil up the quince pulp with 10 lb. (5 kg.) water, stir in the corn syrup, Pomosin retarder and 26 lb. 10 oz. (13 kg. 300) sugar and boil to 226° F (108° C). Then stir in the pectin and 6 oz. (180 gr.) sugar dissolved in 12 lb. 10 oz. (6 kg. 300) water and cool to 140° F (60° C). Now stir in the tartaric acid dissolved in 6 oz. (180 gr.) water and fill the mixing into 4 metal frames approximately 24 in. by 16 in. (60 × 40 cm.). *(Germany)*

Quince Slices

Make up quince paste as above. When cold, place on sheets of marzipan and also cover the top with marzipan. Flash and glaze, then cut into pieces about 3 in. by 1 in. (8 × 2.5 cm.). Dip into sugar if desired.

(One frame yields approx. 100 pieces.) *(Germany)*

Nougat Montélimar

Nougat Montélimar which is very well known originally came from the East. It is sold in bars or it is used for the centres of certain chocolates *(page 624.)*

641

Recipe I

lb	oz		kg	gr
2	0	Honey	1	
2	0	Sugar (granulated)	1	
	14	Egg whites		400
	3 1/2	Glucose		100
2	0	Lightly roasted blanched almonds	1	
	7	Skinned pistachio nuts		200
	10	Water		300

Melt the honey and with the egg whites, beat up in the mixing machine, adding after a while the sugar which has been boiled with the water and glucose to a temperature of 270° F (132° C). Continue to beat up the mixture over a moderate heat, until the ball or small crack degree 250-270° F (121-132° C) is reached according to the use to which the nougat is to be put. The small crack is reached when, after dipping the tip of a knife into the mixture, the droplet on the end breaks easily when cold. Add the warmed almonds, pistachio nuts or hazelnuts as the case may be, and mix them in with the aid of a spatula. When the mixture is ready, spread it on pieces of rice paper in a metal frame or between strips of wood (usually 1 in. [2.5 cm.] high). Level off the mixture, cover with some more rice paper and press down well. When the nougat is cold, cut into strips of the required width and pack in cellophane paper. When the nougat is intended for the centres of chocolates, the nuts should be chopped coarsely. For the best nougat, lightly roasted almonds should be used. It is possible to replace some of the almonds with red glacé cherries or roasted, skinned hazelnuts.

According to how the nougat is to be used, it may be flavoured with chocolate, vanilla or rose water.

Recipe II

lb	oz		kg	gr
3	8	Sugar (preserving)	1	750
1	0	Glucose		500
1	0	Honey		500
	15	Water		450
	6	Egg whites		180
	8	Chopped pistachio nuts		250
	8	Chopped cherries		250
	8	Nibbed almonds or hazelnuts		250

Bring the sugar and water to the boil and add the honey and glucose. Boil to 275° F (135° C). Whip the egg whites to a stiff snow. Remove the whisk and replace with the beater; continue beating while carefully running in the boiling syrup and continue until the mixture begins to become firm, then add the warmed cherries and nuts. Pour into a frame lined with wafer paper, spread level and cover with another sheet of wafer paper. Place a weighted board on top and leave to get cold. Cut with a hot wet knife. *(France)*

Glazed Chestnuts - Marrons glacés

Carefully peel 4 lb. (2 kg.) specially selected nice chestnuts. Put the peeled chestnuts in a colander with large holes and place this in a bowl of cold water mixed with a little flour. Put the bowl or pan on the fire, bring slowly to simmering point but do not let them boil. Simmer for 20 minutes. Remove chestnuts and place them immediately in fresh, boiling hot water without giving them time to cool. Simmer for another hour until they can easily be pierced by a needle. Remove the chestnuts from the water one by one, skin carefully so that they do not break and put them in a sugar boiler with boiling hot vanilla sugar syrup; the syrup must be kept constantly at simmering point but must never boil. Do not cover the pan so that the sugar is constantly becoming thicker as a result of evaporation; this may take up to 24 hours. As soon as a thin crust forms on the surface of the syrup the chestnuts are finished. At this stage the sugar should measure 34-36° B. Carefully remove the chestnuts and put on a wire tray to dry.

(Illustration page 636.)

Glazed Orange Slices - Oranges glacées en Tranches

Carefully peel the oranges—it is best to use the seedless ones—remove all white pith. Cut into slices and place upright on a sieve without allowing the slices to touch. Dry a little in gentle heat. Boil sugar to the crack 300-310° F (148-155° C). Dip in the slices and place on an oiled marble slab to set.

Glazed Tangerines - Mandarines glacées

Cut in slices and treat exactly the same as orange slices.

Salted Almonds - Amandes salées

Dry freshly blanched almonds well with a cloth, beat egg white lightly, moisten the almonds with it, place them on a thick, slightly hollow baking sheet, sprinkle with fine salt, shake up a little and place them in a cool oven. As soon as they start to colour shake up well. They should only be pale yellow. Treat hazelnuts and quartered walnuts in the same way. Roast the hazelnuts slightly first, so that the skin can be rubbed off.

Torrone

Same recipe as for Nougat Montélimar. Cut into rectangular pieces and dip into couverture.
(Illustration page 664.)

PULLED SUGAR

When sugar solutions are heated to very high temperatures most of the water in the solution is boiled off. At 312° F (156° C) a sucrose solution will consist of 98 % of sugar and only 2 % of water.

It follows that, when such a solution is cooled, a very high degree of super-saturation results and consequent agitation of such a solution will cause very rapid crystallization indeed. Since the speed of crystallization effects the crystal size, the crystals formed are very minute and the product, by the reflection of light from myriads of crystals, assumes a brilliant gloss or sheen. In practice, a solution cooled from 312° F (156° C) rapidly becomes plastic and then sets to a solid solution. The only method of working the mass (or agitating the solution), is to take it in the plastic state and pull it between the hands. Hence the term 'pulled sugar'.

A straight sugar solution, i.e. sucrose and water, tends to crystallize and to become very brittle soon after pulling commences, so that if fine and delicate work is to be produced from pulled sugar some method of control is required.

This control can be obtained by the careful addition of very small quantities of weak organic acid or by adding commercial glucose. The acid works by inverting some of the sucrose present in the boiling solution thus producing simple sugars, but since this is a continuing process too much inversion can take place and there is a tendency for the pieces produced to collapse. For this reason glucose is generally preferred.

The production of display pieces from pulled sugar is a craft that can be more easily demonstrated than explained. Since it is a craft, the worker must experience the 'feel' of the sugar, and this is not the same for all exponents. The amount of glucose added (the 'greasing' of the sugar) may well vary with different workers, but only within small limits.

Many delightful display pieces can be produced from pulled sugar, but probably the most popular are variations of the pulled sugar basket.
(Illustrations pages 153-162, 483, 603, 607, 633, 634.)

SUGAR BASKET

To produce the basket, a round or oval frame is required on which to weave the pulled sugar strands. The frame consists of a base into which are drilled an uneven number of holes, and short sticks to fit into the holes. The frames may be wood or metal and must be oiled before use.

Small batches of sugar are to be preferred, but if a great amount of pulled sugar work is to be done a stock of syrup can be prepared.

To 1 lb. (500 gr.) of sugar add 5 oz. (150 gr.) of water and the required amount of glucose or acid. (The writer prefers to add 2 oz. [60 gr.] of glucose and $1/16$ oz. [2 gr.] of cream of tartar for each 1 lb. [500 gr.] of sugar.)

Heat the batch until all the sugar is dissolved and then boil rapidly to 312° F (156° C) removing the scum repeatly and washing down the sides of the pan with water. As soon as this temperature is reached, pour the batch on to an oiled marble slab. As the solution cools it becomes more viscous and the edges must be turned in to keep the temperature even. As soon as possible, the batch must be taken up and pulled between the hands. As pulling proceeds, crystallization takes place, more resistance is felt to the pulling, and the sugar takes on a lustrous sheen; the batch 'turns'.

The sugar is now ready for use and half of it should be set aside to keep warm, while the other half is used. Any colour necessary is folded in while the solution is on the marble slab. A long continuous strip is pulled from the sugar and woven between the sticks of the frame as pulling proceeds. When the basket reaches the required height, the sticks of the frame are removed and replaced with sticks pulled from sugar. A strip of sugar is then pulled and twisted to a rope to place round the top edge of the basket; a similar rope is made for the base. The basket handle is then fashioned from wire, covered with sugar and set in place. (*Illustrations pages 483, 633, 634.*)

Roses, other Flowers, Stems and Leaves

Depending on the size of the basket, about 7-10 oz. (200-300 gr.) of pulled sugar is required for the flowers, ribbons and bows used in decoration. Colour is folded into the sugar at the commencement of the pulling process in exactly the same way as for the sugar used in weaving the basket. Roses may be coloured pale yellow, pale pink or a darker red. To produce them, each petal must be shaped separately; a natural rose should be used for reference so that it may be copied as faithfully as possible and this applies to all other varieties of flowers. Commencing with the inner petals, the sugar is pulled out thinly and the petals are shaped with the thumb and forefinger. The outer petals should be successively larger. The bud is modelled freehand from three small petals attached to each other. Finally all the larger petals are assembled and fixed over heat.

Other flowers, such as tulips, poppies, chrysanthemums, carnations, etc. are modelled in a similar fashion. In each case, it is necessary to study the natural flower closely so that the leaves and petals, blossoms and calyces, etc. may be assembled correctly.

The sugar for stems and leaves should be coloured a natural green. It can easily be pulled to the shape of a leaf, a blunt knife being used to simulate the veins and to produce a dentate leaf where required, though an easier, more effective method is to press the pulled leaves into a lightly oiled metal leaf mould to shape them and mark in the veins so that they resemble real leaves. After removal from the moulds, they can easily be attached to prepared stalks by warming the ends over a small flame.

Ribbons

Ribbons can be made in one or more colours and to be effective should be very thin. To produce a two colour ribbon, two pieces of sugar in suitable colours should be fashioned into blocks about 1 in. (2.5 cm.) long and $1/2$ in. (1 cm.) thick. It is important that the pieces be equally soft. These two pieces are stuck together, side by side, and pulled flat and wide. The piece is then folded to bring two sides together, thus giving three strips of colour. Pulled once more and folded again, five strips of colour are formed, and the piece is now pulled out long, flat and wide until very thin. It can now be fashioned to elaborate bows, or draped around the basket handle. Pulled sugar is very hygroscopic, that is, it will take up atmospheric moisture very quickly, leading to the early collapse of the sugar piece. For this reason pulled sugar pieces are stored in sealed display boxes containing calcium chloride, generally under a false bottom pierced with holes. The chemical takes up any moisture that may be present. *(See Techniques page 167.)*

(Illustrations pages 483, 634.)

SPUN SUGAR

The sugar is allowed to boil to the large crack 280° F (138° C). Whilst it is cooling slightly, a large wooden spoon is fixed on the table so that the handle projects beyond the edge. The handle is oiled and a clean oiled baking sheet is placed beneath it. A wire whisk with the end cut off is dipped into the sugar and taken out vertically, then, moving the whisk to and fro continuously with a flexible wrist, thin threads are thrown over the wooden handle of the spoon, dipping the whisk in the sugar again and again until the sugar is used. Remove the spun sugar from the handle and shape as desired, handling with care. The spun sugar, which can be previously coloured, is used to decorate gâteaux, show pieces, ice bombes, etc.

BLOWN SUGAR

Flower Vase

lb	oz		kg	gr
1	0	Sugar (preserving)	500	
	8	Water	250	
	5	Glucose	150	
		A little cream of tartar added at 230° F (110° C).		

Bring the sugar and water to the boil, remove all the scum from the surface, add the glucose and boil to 245° F (119° C). While boiling, repeatedly wash down the sides of the pan with a brush dipped in water to prevent the formation of crystals. Pour on to an oiled marble slab. Using a lightly oiled palette knife, repeatedly fold the sugar towards the centre until it can be handled. Any colour is added at this stage.

Mould the sugar into a ball. Leather gloves rubbed with glycerine are used to do this. Make a hole in the ball of sugar with a wooden implement. Remove the implement and insert the bellows in its place.

Apply light pressure to the rubber ball of the bellows to stretch the sugar. Bring it to the desired shape by turning it slowly and repeatedly blowing in a little air. Keep it moving in the hand until it is of the desired shape and completely cold.

Detach the blow-pipe from the sugar by holding the latter against the edge of the table at a point exactly corresponding to the end of the pipe inside the sugar and firmly tap it once with a knife.

If the vase is to have handles, the ends must first be warmed over a small flame and then carefully fixed into place. Large or small items made with blown sugar may be produced in a similar manner.

Sugar Cat

1. Parts a, b and c are made with blown sugar. Parts d, e and f are made with pulled sugar. The base is made of poured sugar.

2. Fix the body in position on the base. Fix on the head and tail and finish off with the ears, tie and whiskers.

3. Mix a little alcohol with some cornflour and powdered black and apply with a brush as illustrated. The whiskers may be made out of pulled sugar or painted on. The flower design is painted with a fine brush. The cat's body is white, the tie is blue, the flowers are ruby-red and the design surrounding them is dark green.

4. Three different views of the finished cat. *(Illustration page 646.)*

Sugar Cat

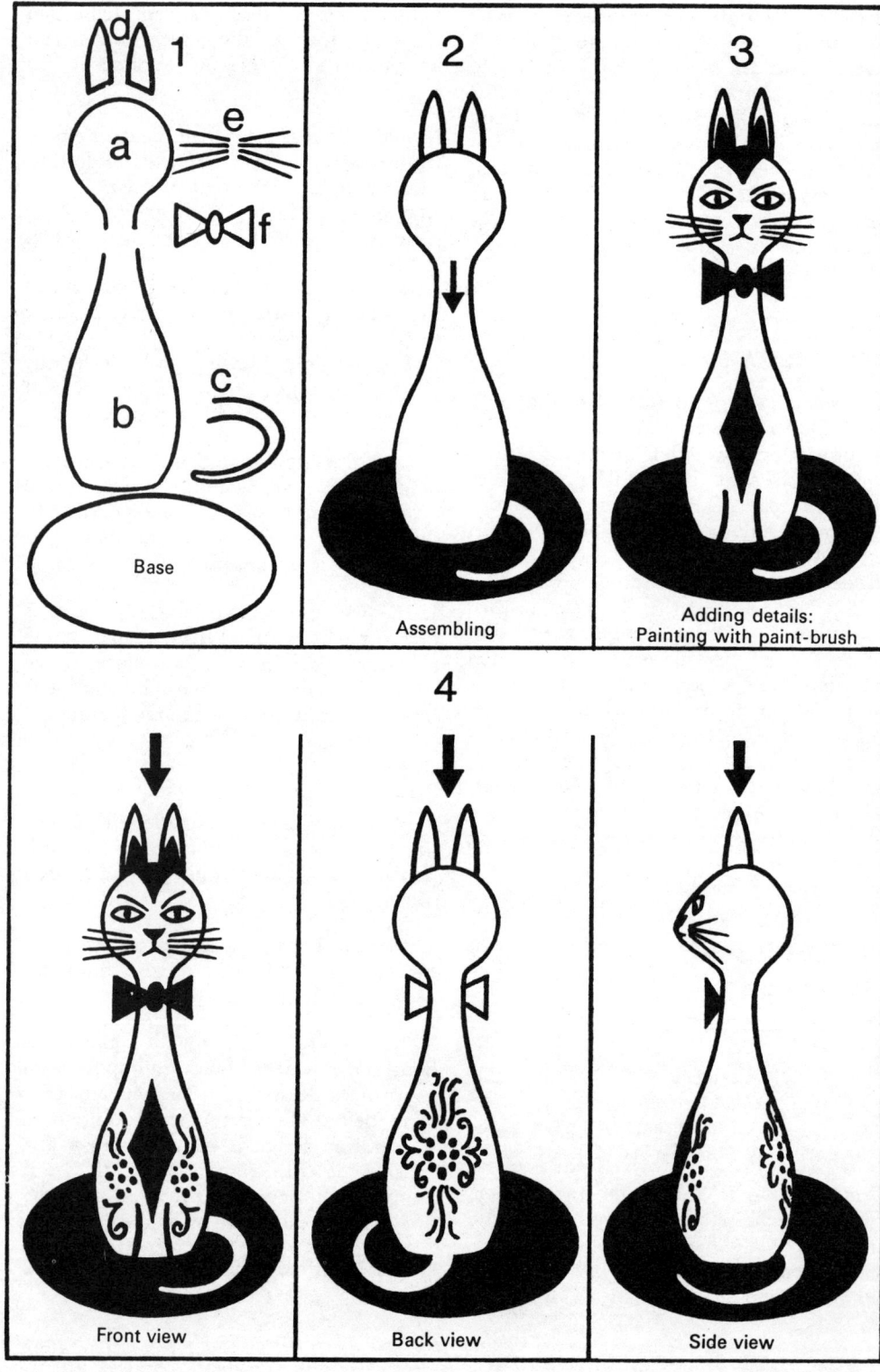

Parrot

1. Place a perch made of praline croquant and shaped like a sawn-off branch on a poured sugar base to support the body of the blown sugar parrot.

2. Using the thumb, pull 'feathers' of equal size from prepared sugar, then nip off with the middle fingers of the left hand and place on a lightly oiled marble slab.

3. Once sufficient feathers have been made, start fixing them in position, working from the bottom upwards, so that each slightly overlaps the other; hold the ends over a flame, then attach them by applying light pressure. Now fix the talons in place, slightly curved round the perch, then the beak which has been made in advance and allowed to cool before use.

4. Shape the wings out of a large piece of sugar, making them slightly curved. Allow to cool before use.

5. Lightly fix the wings on to the blown body, holding the rounded side over the flame for a moment, and add the feathers, starting at the tips.

6. Make a few pulled sugar scrolls and fix them on the base in twos or threes, or decorate with a few praline croquant branches with small flowers and leaves. Finish off with an upright slab of poured sugar fastened to the base behind the bird.

The parts made with poured sugar should be as dark as possible, while the blown sugar work should be executed in pale, delicate colours. To obtain different shades, place a little powdered colour on a plate, moisten it with alcohol or a few drops of water, dip a hard-bristled brush lightly into the colour and quickly run the fingers or the stick of a paintbrush over the bristles (towards you). Use this procedure to spray the parts for which a different or deeper shade is desired.

For smaller birds the feathers should be made with blown sugar, not attached afterwards. After blowing, the wings are set into place and painted with the different colours.

(Illustrations pages 634, 648.)

Various Fruits

(Illustrations pages 162-166.)

Sugar Parrot

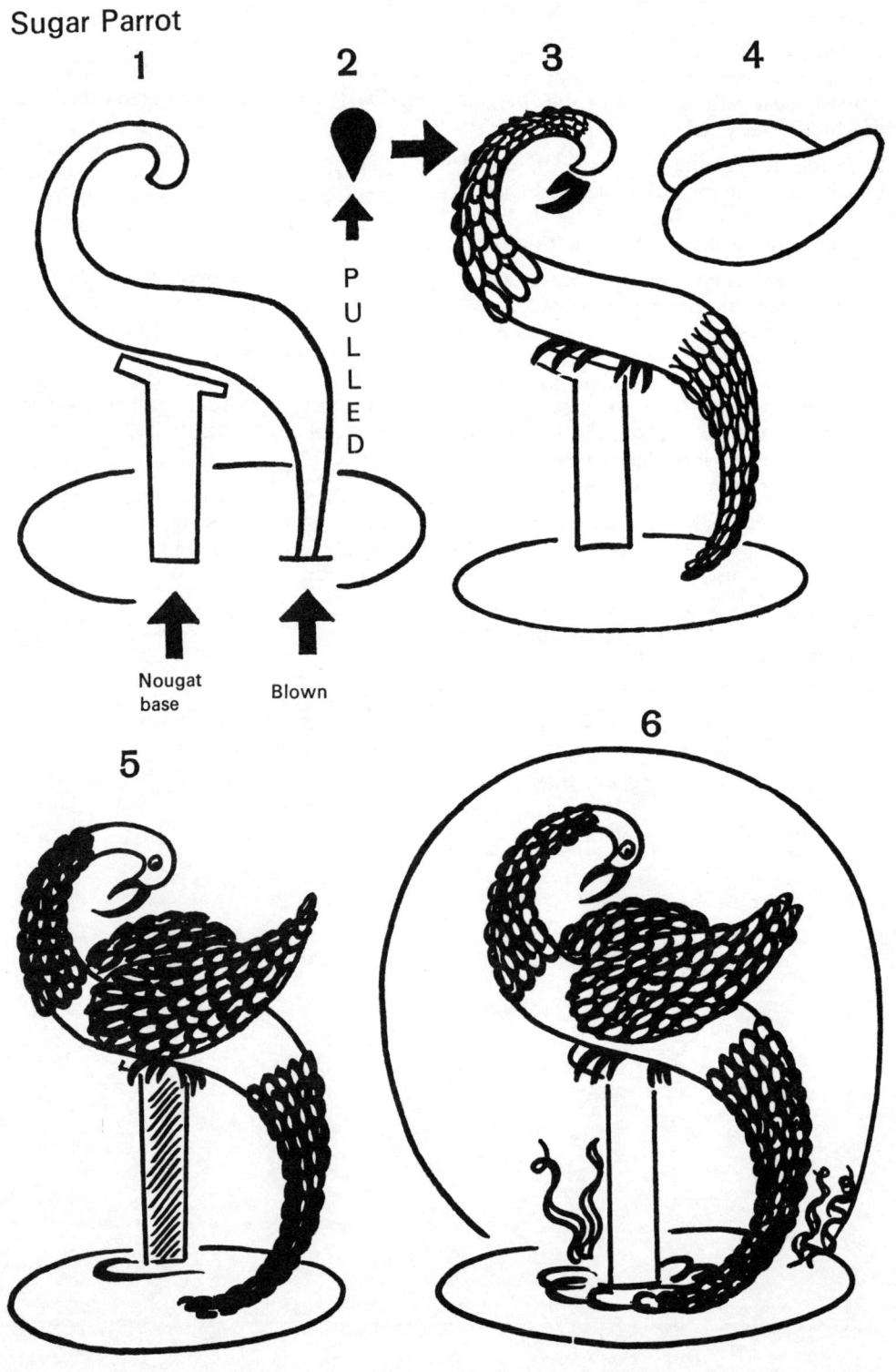

XXII. Sweets

In the introductory chapter to this book, it is stated that people are moving into a more affluent age, an age when the economic level of life is rising. It is within this context that this chapter is introduced.

The housewife, with a greater freedom from dull routine tasks that have been largely eliminated by better planning and labour saving devices, will turn more and more to the joys of creative effort and amongst the many, and probably by far the most important, is cooking.

Because food is essential to life, it is therefore necessary for it to be prepared several times a day and on each and every day.

Whilst the housewife, freed from a measure of unnecessary work, will find a certain amount of pleasure in cooking for herself and her family, she will not wish to be always tied to her kitchen; therefore, relief from the tyranny of compulsive necessity will be welcomed.

An awareness of this is seen in the huge market of prepared foods available for her today. These foods fall into three categories; those that have a very long shelf life, for example, canned and dehydrated foods; those that have a limited life such as refrigerated products; lastly, those that have to be consumed within hours. The greatest appeal of the last group is freshness.

It is here that the craftsman baker can become interested, for in this field are dessert dishes. There are, however, dessert dishes in bewildering variety, and a good deal of thought has been given to the task of presenting an interesting although limited selection, and giving a reason for that selection.

It was at last agreed that the choice should be, firstly, a selection of desserts that have bases, or a reasonable amount of materials useful for assembly or decoration, all of which can be made in, or bought from a bakery. Secondly, in view of the massive publicity given to the use of fresh dairy cream, it was thought advisable to include a selection of these. Finally, other attractive desserts that it is thought will stimulate the business acumen of the craftsman baker and restaurateur are included.

For those who would desire a greater knowledge of desserts, we would recommend the study of Modern French Culinary Art by Pellaprat, which is the companion to this volume.

Sauces - Syrups - Purées - Fruit Juices

VARIOUS SAUCES FOR SERVING WITH HOT AND COLD DESSERTS

Almond Sauce - Sauce aux Amandes
Prepare a custard cream but, while mixing it, add 1 3/4 oz. (50 gr.) finely ground almonds to 1 3/4 pt. (1 l.) of milk.

Apricot Sauce - Sauce à l'Abricot
Recipe 1
Use the same method as for cold sauce (page 651).

Recipe 2
Boil some apricot jam with a little water and sugar, pass through a fine-meshed sieve and flavour with kirsch, cognac or rum.

Bishop Sauce I
1 3/4 pt. (1 l.) fruit syrup
Finely pared zest of 2 oranges and half a lemon
1 3/4 oz. (50 gr.) strip almonds
3/4 gill (1 dl.) white wine
2 1/2 oz. (75 gr.) raisins
1 oz. (30 gr.) blanched finely cut pistachio nuts
1 oz. (30 gr.) cornflour

Cut the orange and lemon zest in julienne strips and cook until soft in a little stock syrup. Soak the raisins in warm water. Boil up the fruit syrup, thicken with cornflour that has been blended with the white wine, and strain. Add the julienne strips, the raisins, almonds and pistachio nuts before serving.

Bishop Sauce II
1 3/4 pt. (1 l.) red wine
10 oz. (300 gr.) sugar
Zest of 1 lemon
A small piece of cinnamon
1 clove
1 3/4 oz. (50 gr.) flaked almonds
Finely pared zest of 2 oranges
3/4 oz. (20 gr.) cornflour

Boil up the red wine, sugar, lemon zest, cinnamon and clove together. Thicken with the cornflour that has been blended with a little water, then strain. Add the orange zest that has been cut in julienne strips and cooked until soft, and also the flaked almonds before serving.

Brandy Sauce - Hard Sauce
Cream 9 oz. (250 gr.) butter with 5 oz. (150 gr.) icing sugar until the mixture is light and fluffy. Next gradually add about 2/3 to 3/4 gill (7 cl.) brandy and a few drops of lemon juice. This is a special sauce for Christmas pudding.

Caramel Sauce - Sauce au Caramel
Boil some sugar until it turns into a light caramel and blend it with a little boiling milk. Amalgamate a suitable quantity with some hot custard cream.

Cherry Sauce - Sauce aux Cerises
1 lb. (500 gr.) morello cherries
12 oz. (350 gr.) sugar
Lemon zest
3/4 pt. (4 dl.) red wine
1 small vanilla bean
Starch

Cooking time: 25 minutes

Stone the cherries and grind a few kernels. Cook the kernels with the cherries, sugar, vanilla or a little cinnamon, lemon zest and red wine. When the cherries are cooked, remove the lemon zest and vanilla and pass the cherries through a fine-meshed sieve. Reboil and thicken with a little starch.

Chocolate Sauce - Sauce au Chocolat
Recipe 1

Blend chocolate powder with a little water and mix into custard cream. Pass through a sieve.

Recipe 2

Melt some good quality chocolate in a double saucepan or in a bain-marie. Add fresh cream until a thick sauce is obtained.

Lemon Sauce - Sauce au Citron

Prepare some custard cream, add a generous amount of finely shredded blanched lemon zest and finally some fresh cream and lemon juice.

Maraschino Sauce - Sauce au Marasquin

Prepare a thick custard cream, add a little fresh cream and finally enough maraschino to give a pronounced flavour.

Orange Sauce - Sauce à l'Orange

Use the same method as for lemon sauce, replacing the lemons with oranges.

Pineapple Sauce - Sauce à l'Ananas

Recipe 1

Peel and core the pineapple. Mash it and cook it with sugar, vanilla and a little water. Rub through a sieve, reboil and thicken with a little starch. Add a little diced pineapple which has been cooked in its own juice.

Recipe 2

Slightly thicken some tinned pineapple juice with starch and flavour with kirsch. Add small strips of tinned pineapple.

Praline Sauce - Sauce au Pralin

Use the same method as for cold mousseline praline sauce *(page 654)*.

Thickened Syrups - Sirops liés

The juice of stewed fruit is very suitable for these syrups. Cook the juice and thicken it with a little starch. Flavour with spirit or liqueur according to taste.

VARIOUS SAUCES FOR SERVING WITH ICE CREAM PREPARATIONS AND COLD SWEETS

Almond Sauce - Sauce aux Amandes

1 lb. (500 gr.) almonds (blanched)
5 bitter almonds (blanched)
$^1/_2$ lb. (250 gr.) sugar
$^1/_2$ pt. ($^1/_4$ l.) water
1 tablespoonful kirsch
1 tablespoonful orange flower water
1 pt. ($^1/_2$ l.) cream

Pound the almonds to a paste, gradually adding the water, place in a stewpan and stir to the boil, cover and allow to cool. Force through a fine strainer to extract all the almond milk, add the sugar, stir until dissolved, then whip in the cream and flavouring.

Apricot Sauce - Sauce à l'Abricot

1 lb. (500 gr.) apricots (ripe)
1 lb. (500 gr.) sugar
2 oz. (60 gr.) glucose

Add a little water to the fruit, cover and simmer until mushed to a near pulp, remove some of the stones, crush them in a mortar, return to the pulp with the sugar and glucose and continue simmering to the correct consistency, strain, stir occasionally until cold.

All stoned fruits for sauces should be treated in this way. Edible food colours made especially for the purpose are used to finish the appearance of these sauces, such as yellow and carmine for apricot, carmine for cherry, green for greengage, etc. With peach and nectarine, the addition of zest of lemon and lemon juice enhances the flavour.

The addition of a liqueur or sherry gives general improvement.

Bar-le-Duc Sauce - Sauce Bar-le-Duc

12 oz. (375 gr.) red currants
4 oz. (125 gr.) raspberries
1 lb. (500 gr.) icing sugar
Juice of 1 lemon

Rub the uncooked red currants and raspberries through a hair sieve, mix with the icing sugar and flavour with the lemon juice.

Black Currant Sauce - Sauce aux Cassis

1 lb. (500 gr.) picked black currants
1 pt. ($^1/_2$ l.) syrup

Bring to the boil, simmer until tender and rub through a hair sieve. Stir until cold. Adjust with cream.

Black Currant Sauce (raw) - Sauce aux Cassis

1 lb. (500 gr.) ripe picked black currants
1 lb. (500 gr.) icing sugar
Cream to adjust

Crush the fruit in a mortar and run through a hair sieve, stir in the icing sugar, and an hour or so later adjust the consistency with cream.

Caramel Sauce - Sauce au Caramel

4 oz. (125 gr.) sugar
2 oz. (60 gr.) glucose
$1/2$ pt. ($1/4$ l.) water
1 pt. ($1/2$ l.) cream
1 piece of vanilla pod

Put sugar, glucose and water to boil, skim and simmer until the syrup becomes thick, remove the vanilla, continue cooking until a light brown colour, stand the stewpan in a basin of cold water to remove excessive heat, add the cream, bring slowly to scalding point, remove from heat and stir occasionally until cold.

Chantilly Sauce - Sauce Chantilly

1 pt. ($1/2$ l.) cream
2 oz. (60 gr.) sugar
1 oz. (30 gr.) vanilla sugar

Lightly whip to the right consistency.

Chocolate Sauce - Sauce au Chocolat

4 oz. (125 gr.) chocolate couverture
$3/4$ pt. (4 dl.) cream
2 oz. (60 gr.) glucose
Stock syrup

Melt the chocolate and glucose together at no more than 120° F (49° C), break down into a thick sauce with the syrup, flavour with a few drops of vanilla essence and stir in the cream.

Coffee Sauce - Sauce au Café

4 oz. (125 gr.) ground coffee
4 oz. (125 gr.) sugar
2 oz. (60 gr.) glucose
1 piece of vanilla pod
1 pt. ($1/2$ l.) cream
$1/2$ pt. ($1/4$ l.) water

Bring the water, glucose and vanilla to the boil, stir in the coffee, cover and allow to steep until cold. Force through a fine chinois to express all the liquid, add the sugar and stir until dissolved, then mix in the cream.

This sauce may also be made with soluble coffee powder.

Cold Custard Sauce or English Sauce - Crème ou Sauce à l'anglaise

6 egg yolks
4 oz. (125 gr.) castor sugar
$1/2$ pt. ($1/4$ l.) milk
1 piece of split vanilla pod
$1/2$ pt. ($1/4$ l.) cream
1 tablespoonful orange flower water

Put the milk to boil with the vanilla, cover and steep for 10 minutes. Whisk the yolks and sugar together, whisk on the strained milk and stir over gentle heat until the spatula is lightly coated. Place the cooking vessel in cold water to stop further cooking, stir until cold and fold in the part-whipped cream.

Dijon Sauce - Sauce dijonnaise

$1/2$ lb. (250 gr.) black currants
$1/2$ lb. (250 gr.) raspberries
1 lb. (500 gr.) icing sugar
Juice of 1 lemon

Rub the black currants and raspberries through a hair sieve, mix with the icing sugar and lastly add the lemon juice.

Lemon Sauce - Sauce au Citron

1 lb. (500 gr.) ripe white peaches
8 lemons
1 pt. ($1/2$ l.) syrup
2 oz. (60 gr.) glucose

Proceed as for orange sauce *(page 654)*.

Melba Sauce I - Sauce Melba

1 lb. (500 gr.) fresh raspberries
$1/2$ lb. (250 gr.) icing sugar
Juice of $1/2$ lemon

Crush and sieve the raspberries, add sugar and lemon juice and mix well.

Melba Sauce II

$1/2$ lb. (250 gr.) strawberry pulp
$1/2$ lb. (250 gr.) raspberry pulp
1 lb. (500 gr.) icing sugar
Juice of 1 lemon
Carmine to tint

Same procedure as above.

Melba Sauce III

$1/2$ lb. (250 gr.) raspberry pulp
$1/2$ lb. (250 gr.) strawberry pulp
$1/2$ lb. (250 gr.) red currant pulp
Stock syrup
Juice of 1 lemon

Pick, crush and sieve the red currants, then the raspberries and strawberries, add the lemon juice and break down to the required consistency with the syrup.

Mousseline Sauce - Sauce Mousseline

5 oz. (150 gr.) sugar
4 oz. (120 gr.) water
6 egg yolks
1 piece of vanilla pod
1 pt. ($1/2$ l.) cream

Bring water, vanilla and sugar to the boil, skim, strain and whisk on to the yolks, place in a bain-marie or over a pan of boiling water, scrape the sides down constantly until the mixture becomes like thick cream, remove from heat and whisk vigorously until cold. Part whip the cream and blend together.

This sauce will take the name of any added liqueur: sauce mousseline au maras-quin, au kirsch, etc.

Burgundy Mousseline Sauce - Sauce Mousseline à la bourguignonne

6 oz. (180 gr.) sugar
1 gill (1 $1/2$ dl.) Burgundy
6 egg yolks
1 pt. ($1/2$ l.) cream

Prepare as for mousseline sauce and adjust with Burgundy.

Other Fruit Mousseline Sauces - Sauce Mousseline aux Fruits divers

Prepare in the same way as for mousseline sauce, with the addition of the designated fruit pulp. It may be necessary to acidulate with a little lemon juice.

Lemon Mousseline Sauce - Sauce Mousseline au Citron

8 oz. (250 gr.) sugar
1 gill (1 $1/2$ dl.) lemon juice
6 egg yolks
1 pt. ($1/2$ l.) cream
Grated zest of 1 lemon

Usual procedure, adjust with white wine.

Orange Mousseline Sauce - Sauce Mousseline à l'Orange

5 oz. (150 gr.) sugar
1 gill (1 $1/2$ dl.) orange juice
6 egg yolks
Grated zest of 1 orange
1 pt. ($1/2$ l.) cream

Usual procedure, adjust with orange juice.

Port Wine Mousseline Sauce - Sauce Mousseline au Porto

5 oz. (150 gr.) sugar
1 gill (1 $1/2$ dl.) port wine
6 egg yolks
1 pt. ($1/2$ l.) cream

Prepare as for mousseline sauce and adjust with port wine.

Praline Mousseline Sauce - Sauce Mousseline pralinée

Same as for mousseline sauce with the addition of 4 oz. (125 gr.) almond or hazelnut praline.

Raspberry Mousseline Sauce - Sauce Mousseline aux Framboises

Add 1 gill (1 ½ dl.) of raspberry pulp to the mousseline sauce with a few drops of carmine to adjust the colour.

Tangerine Mousseline Sauce - Sauce Mousseline à la Mandarine

5 oz. (150 gr.) sugar
1 gill (1 ½ dl.) tangerine juice
Grated zest of 1 tangerine
6 egg yolks
1 pt. (½ l.) cream

Usual procedure, adjust with orange juice.

Orange Sauce - Sauce à l'Orange

1 lb. (500 gr.) ripe apricots
8 oranges
1 pt. (½ l.) syrup
2 oz. (60 gr.) glucose

Remove the zest from the oranges and cut into a fine julienne; cover with cold water, then bring to the boil. Refresh with cold water, strain and cover with the syrup, then bring to the boil and simmer for five minutes. Add the apricot pulp, the juice of the oranges and glucose and bring to the boil; simmer to the right consistency, remove from heat and stir occasionally until cold.

Praline Croquant Sauce - Sauce au Pralin

Stir 1 ¾ oz. (50 gr.) finely crushed, sieved praline croquant and a little vanilla sugar in to 1 pt. (½ l.) cold custard sauce.

Raspberry Sauce - Sauce aux Framboises

Prepare as for strawberry sauce.

Red Currant Sauce - Sauce Groseille

Prepare as for black currant sauce with the addition of the juice of 1 lemon. Carmine to tint.

Red Currant Sauce (raw) - Sauce Groseille

1 lb. (500 gr.) ripe red currants
1 lb. (500 gr.) icing sugar
Cream to adjust
Juice of 1 lemon

Same procedure as for black currant sauce.

These fruits contain so much pectin that either cream or stock syrup is necessary to adjust them to a consistency suitable for masking.

Sabayon Sauce - Sabayon

6 egg yolks
8 oz. (250 gr.) castor sugar
½ pt. (¼ l.) dry white wine
Juice of ½ lemon or orange or a little vanilla sugar

Put egg yolks, sugar and the fruit juice or vanilla sugar into a basin, stand in a bain-marie or over a pan of boiling water and whisk to a thick, creamy consistency. Remove from heat and whisk until cold. If not used at once, add two leaves of gelatine, previously soaked in cold water, to the mixture while whisking.

Lemon Sabayon Sauce - Sabayon au Citron

8 egg yolks
8 oz. (250 gr.) sugar
2 gills (3 dl.) white wine
1 gill (1 ½ dl.) lemon juice
Grated zest of 1 lemon

Proceed as for orange sabayon.

Liqueur Sabayon Sauce - Sabayon à la Liqueur

8 egg yolks
6 oz. (180 gr.) castor sugar
½ pt. (¼ l.) white wine
A few drops of lemon juice

¹/₂ gill (5 cl.) of the desired liqueur (cognac, rum, kummel, anisette, curaçao, Cointreau, Benedictine, etc.)

Place egg yolks, sugar, white wine and lemon juice into a basin and proceed as usual. Add the liqueur and whisk until cold.

Marsala Sabayon Sauce - Sabayon au Marsala I

8 egg yolks
6 oz. (180 gr.) castor sugar
¹/₂ pt. (¹/₄ l.) marsala
A few drops of lemon juice

Proceed as for plain sabayon. When cold, a few spoonfuls of whipped cream may be added to the sabayon.

Sabayon may also be prepared with all kinds of dessert wines such as malaga, madeira, port wine, sherry, etc.

Marsala Sabayon Sauce II

8 egg yolks
¹/₂ pt. (¹/₄ l.) cream
6 oz. (180 gr.) castor sugar
1 ¹/₂ gills (¹/₄ l.) marsala
A few drops of lemon juice

Proceed as above.

Orange Sabayon Sauce - Sabayon à l'Orange

8 egg yolks
6 oz. (180 gr.) sugar
2 gills (3 dl.) white wine
1 gill (1 ¹/₂ dl.) fresh orange juice
Juice of ¹/₂ lemon
Zest of 1 orange and ¹/₂ lemon

Proceed as usual and correct taste and consistency with orange juice.

Strawberry Sauce - Sauce aux Fraises

1 lb. (500 gr.) ripe strawberries
1 lb. (500 gr.) icing sugar
Juice of 1 lemon
Carmine to tint

Rub the strawberries through a hair sieve, stir in the sugar and lemon juice.

SYRUPS

Fruit and other Syrups

These are stock syrups flavoured with fruit or other vegetable substances.

Apple Syrup - Sirop de Pomme

Use the same methods as for rhubarb syrup, cooking russet apples which have been cut into quarters without, however, having their skins and pips removed. Not too much water should be used for cooking the apples and the resultant liquor is made into a syrup with an equal weight of sugar. Skim carefully and do not cook for too long or the liquid will turn to a jelly.

Blackberry Syrup - Sirop de Mûre

Crush 2 lb. 4 oz. (1 kg. 125) blackberries and leave overnight in an earthenware dish. Then extract the juice and filter it. Boil 3 lb. 4 oz. (1 kg. 625) sugar to 257° F (125° C), add the fruit juice and, just before the syrup begins to boil, skim and bottle.

Black Currant Syrup - Sirop de Cassis

Remove the stalks from the black currants, crush the fruit and squeeze out the juice. Cook in a pan with sugar using the following proportions: 1 lb. (500 gr.) sugar to 1 pt. (¹/₂ l.) of juice. Skim carefully and reduce to 31° B before bottling.

Cherry Syrup - Sirop de Cerise

1 quart (1 l.) cherry juice
2 lb. (1 kg.) sugar

Coarsely crush 3 lb. (1 kg. 500) cherries with the stones, cover and leave in a cool place for 24 hours, squeeze in a cloth to extract as much juice as possible, then strain. Boil up the juice with the sugar, remove all the scum from the surface, strain through a cloth again, leave until cold and bottle.

Coffee Syrup - Sirop au Café

Take 8 ¹/₂ oz. (250 gr.) coffee to make a very strong infusion. Filter well, add 3 lb. 4 oz. (1 kg. 625) sugar cooked to the ball degree and re-cook until the pearl degree is reached. Leave to cool and bottle.

May also be made with a strong infusion of instant coffee powder and syrup at 31° B, strained and bottled.

Gum Arabic Syrup - Sirop à la Gomme arabique

Grind 1 lb. (500 gr.) white gum arabic, soak it overnight in 10 oz. (300 gr.) cool water containing 7 oz. (200 gr.) orange flower water and the next day dissolve it in a bain-marie. Boil 6 lb. (3 kg.) sugar to 221° F (105° C), add the gum arabic mixture, boil and reboil, skim and pass through a muslin. Bottle when the syrup has cooled down.

Lemon Syrup - Sirop de Citron

Peel 6 or 7 lemons and squeeze out the juice. Put the rinds to infuse in a hot syrup at 22° B, using about 15 lb. (7 kg. 500) sugar to 8 quarts (9 l.) of water. Filter the lemon juice and add it to the syrup; it gives a sharp but pleasant flavour.

Lemon syrup may also be prepared like orange syrup.

Maidenhair Syrup - Sirop d'Adiante

Infuse 1 oz. (30 gr.) maidenhair leaves in 1 quart (1 l.) of boiling water. Cook this infusion with 4 lb. (2 kg.) sugar and 3 1/2 oz. (100 gr.) orange flower water. When the syrup is at 31° B, strain and bottle.

Orange Syrup - Sirop d'Orange

Squeeze out the juice of 15 very large oranges and 2 lemons and add the zest of 2 oranges and 1 lb. 10 oz. (800 gr.) sugar. Melt over heat until the liquid reaches about 140° F (60° C), and the sugar is dissolved; do not allow to boil. Strain through a muslin and cool before bottling.

Orgeat Syrup - Orgeat

Grind 1 lb. (500 gr.) sweet almonds and 1 3/4 oz. (50 gr.) bitter almonds, moistening them gradually with 3 pt. (1 1/2 l.) of cold water. Next squeeze the mixture through a cloth, adding 4 lb. (2 kg.) sugar. Melt over heat until the liquid reaches about 140° F (60° C), and then strain through a muslin. While the syrup is still tepid, add 1 3/4 oz. (50 gr.) orange flower water.

The syrup should not be boiled, as otherwise the almond juice will separate from the sugar and ferment.

Pomegranate Syrup or Grenadine - Grenadine, Sirop de Grenadine

Take about a dozen pomegranates and remove the pips, taking care to get rid of all the pith. Grind the pips and strain together with the juice through a cloth. Cook with 1 lb. 10 oz. (800 gr.) sugar for every quart (1 l.) of juice. Boil for 10 minutes, skim and bottle.

Quince Syrup - Sirop de Coing

Proceed in the same way as for cherry syrup, using 1 quart (1 l.) of quince juice and 3 lb. (1 kg. 500) sugar.

Raspberry Syrup - Sirop de Framboise

Proceed in the same way as for cherry syrup, using 1 quart (1 l.) of raspberry juice, 2 lb. 4 oz. (1 kg. 125) sugar and 10 1/2 oz. (300 gr.) glucose.

Red Currant Syrup - Sirop de Groseille

Prepare in the same way as cherry syrup, using 4 lb. 7 oz. (2 kg. 200) sugar with 2 quarts (2 l.) red currant juice. Do not boil longer than a minute or two to prevent the syrup turning into jelly.

Rhubarb Syrup - Sirop de Rhubarbe

Prepare about fifteen sticks of rhubarb and cut them up into pieces. Cook for 6 to 8 minutes in 2 pt. (1 l.) of water and then pour into a fine-meshed sieve in order to extract as much juice as possible. Simmer this for about 15 minutes with an equal weight of granulated sugar. Skim, bottle while still boiling hot and seal hermetically straight away.

658 ▲ Banana Fritters I, p. 669

Yorkshire Curd Tarts, p. 321, 695 ▼

▲ Vanilla Soufflé, p. 688   Christmas Pudding, p. 681 ▼   659

660 ▲ Pineapple Ninon, p. 720

Tangerine Cream, p. 708 ▼

▲ Diplomat Bavarian Cream, p. 699

Snow Eggs, p. 733 ▼

661

662 ▲ Zuccotto, p. 804

Twist, Italy, p. 804 ▼

▲ Pineapple Semi-frozen Dessert, p. 803

Frosted Lemons, p. 714 ▼

663

664 ▲ Oranges Syracuse Style, p. 715   ▲ Torrone, Italy, p. 643

Pears Helene, German presentation, p. 718 ▼

Syrup for soaking Savarins and Babas

1 lb. (500 gr.) sugar
1 pt. ($^1/_2$ l.) water
Zest of 1 orange and 1 lemon
$^1/_2$ cinnamon stick
$^1/_2$ gill (5 cl.) rum or other spirit or liqueur

Bring all the ingredients except the spirit to a boil. Simmer for 10 minutes and strain through a sieve. Stir in spirit or liqueur.

Rum is an essential ingredient when the syrup is to be used for rum baba or savarin. For other savarins the rum may be omitted and another spirit or liqueur used. Syrup for soaking savarins and babas is always used hot.

FRUIT PURÉES FOR ICES

In order to keep fruit purée for any length of time, it should be sterilized.

Apricot Purée - Purée d'Abricots

Stone the apricots, pass them through a sieve or the mincer, mixing them with 3 $^1/_2$ oz. (100 gr.) sugar for every 2 lb. (1 kg.) purée. Place in jars and sterilize.

Morello Cherry Purée - Purée de Guignes

Sieve the stoned cherries, adding 7 oz. (200 gr.) sugar to every 2 lb. (1 kg.) purée, place in jars and sterilize for 10 minutes.

Peach Purée - Purée de Pêches

Pass juicy peaches through a sieve, adding 1 lb. (500 gr.) sugar to every 2 lb. (1 kg.) fruit. Put in jars and sterilize for 10 minutes.

Raspberry Purée - Purée de Framboises

Proceed in the same way as for strawberry purée, but allow 7 oz. (200 gr.) sugar to every 2 lb. (1 kg.) raspberry purée.

Red Currant Purée - Purée de Groseilles

Heat the berries in water, using 3 $^1/_2$ oz. (1 dl.) water to 4 lb. (2 kg.) fruit.

When they burst, pass them through a sieve in order to remove the pips. Fill the jars and sterilize for 15 minutes.

N.B. This purée is made without the addition of sugar.

Strawberry Purée - Purée de Fraises

Pass clean strawberries through a sieve or the mincer. Mix 1 lb. (500 gr.) icing sugar with every 2 lb. (1 kg.) purée. Put in jars and sterilize for 10-15 minutes.

FRUIT JUICES

Fruit juice is an essential ingredient in the preparation of fruit syrups. If these fruit syrups are to be kept for any length of time, the fruit must be treated in a special way so as to eliminate its pectin content. This is done by allowing the fruit to ferment for a certain period of time during which the jellying substances become separated and can be removed by skimming and filtering.

The syrup itself must be perfectly clear and transparent. Dissolve over heat 3 lb. (1 kg. 500) sugar in every quart (1 l.) of fruit juice. Boil twice and carefully remove scum. When ready for bottling, the syrup should be at 33° B. It is poured while still warm into the bottles which are sealed and stored in a dry, cool place.

Fruit juice can be bottled with little or no sugar, provided it is sterilized.

Cherry Juice - Jus de Cerise

Stone the cherries and leave them in earthenware jars in the cellar for 5-6 days; stir once each day. When fermentation commences, the fruit is ready to be pressed. Leave overnight in the cellar or other cool place and the next morning skim and strain through a muslin. Fill the bottles and sterilize for 15 minutes.

Lemon Juice - Jus de Citron
Squeeze some lemons into an earthenware container, leave for a few days, skim, filter and put in bottles. Sterilize for 10 minutes.

Orange Juice - Jus d'Orange
Use the same method as for lemon juice.

Quince Juice - Jus de Coing
Grate the quinces and extract the juice from the purée so formed; leave it in an earthenware dish in the cellar. Two days later, decant, filter the liquid and fill the bottles. Sterilize for 20 minutes.

Raspberry Juice - Jus de Framboise
Crush the raspberries in an earthenware dish and leave for two days in a cool place. Next extract the juice from the fruit and, 24 hours later, skim and filter it. Bottle and sterilize for 15 minutes.

Strawberry Juice - Jus de Fraise
Use the same method as for raspberries.

Hot Desserts

CHARLOTTES

Apple Charlotte - Charlotte aux Pommes
6 persons:
1 tin loaf
4 oz. (100-125 gr.) butter
Apple purée
$1/3$ gill (4 cl.) rum
$1/3$ gill (4 cl.) apricot sauce
Cooking time: 45 minutes

Recipe 1: Cut from a tin loaf a dozen small, triangular pieces of bread which are dipped in melted butter and laid, overlapping each other, to cover completely the bottom of a charlotte mould. Next cut some strips of bread 2 fingers in width and the height of the mould, and dip these too in the butter. Arrange them closely round the side of the mould, overlapping each other.

Filling:
2 $1/2$ lb. (1 kg. 250) peeled, cored, sliced rennet apples
2 oz. (60 gr.) thick apricot jam
4 oz. (125 gr.) demarara sugar
4 oz. (125 gr.) butter
Grated zest of $1/2$ lemon
2 cloves

Melt the butter and sugar, add the apples, zest and cloves, cover and cook, stir in the jam and evaporate the moisture to a firm purée; allow to cool before filling the mould. Put the mould in a hot oven for 45 minutes. The slices of bread round the mould must be golden brown and fairly crisp so as to support the weight of the charlotte when it is turned out of the mould. A not too thick, hot, rum flavoured apricot sauce is served with this dessert.

Recipe 2: Although the true charlotte is that described above, it is rather difficult to cook unless a good oven is available. However, a simpler method is to use a fairly shallow, square mould and line it completely with little strips of bread dipped in butter and packed closely together without actually overlapping. Fill to the brim with a reduced apple purée and bake in a very hot oven. Serve with an apricot sauce or a rum flavoured custard sauce.

CROQUETTES

Chestnut Croquettes - Croquettes de Marrons
6 persons:
1 lb. (500 gr.) skinned chestnuts
3 $1/2$ oz. (100 gr.) sugar
Vanilla
1 pt. ($1/2$ l.) milk
1 $3/4$ oz. (50 gr.) butter
3 egg yolks
Fry for 3-4 minutes

Cook the chestnuts in the vanilla flavoured milk, rub them through a sieve and add the butter and egg yolks. Dry this mixture over heat and then leave to cool. Make into small balls the size of walnuts, dip these in egg and breadcrumbs and fry in extremely hot fat. Serve a kirsch flavoured apricot sauce separately. *(France)*

Rice Croquettes - Croquettes de Riz

6 persons:

4 １/₂ oz. (140 gr.) Carolina rice
3 oz. (100 gr.) sugar
1 pt. (¹/₂ l.) milk
1 oz. (30 gr.) butter
4 egg yolks
Vanilla

Fry for 3-4 minutes

Boil the rice in water for 3 minutes, drain it and finish cooking it in the milk, to which the vanilla and a pinch of salt have been added, until it is well cooked. Stir in the sugar, butter and egg yolks and continue stirring until the rice comes away from the sides of the saucepan. Spread this mixture in a dish and, when it is cold, divide it into small pieces the size of pigeons' eggs, which are then rolled on a floured marble slab to elongate them. Dip in egg and bread crumbs and fry in extremely hot fat. Serve together with a custard or a kirsch flavoured apricot sauce.

(France)

Fructidor Rice Croquettes - Croquettes de Riz Fructidor

Prepare in the same way as for rice croquettes, adding 4 ¹/₂ oz. (140 gr.) diced, candied fruit macerated in ¹/₄ gill (4 cl.) kirsch.

(France)

CROUTES

Apricot Croûtes - Croûtes aux Abricots

6 persons:

6 slices of savarin
12 stewed apricot halves
12 red cherries
2 ¹/₂ oz. (75 gr.) butter
¹/₂ pt. (¹/₄ l.) kirsch flavoured apricot sauce

Cooking time: 5-6 minutes

Bake the savarin at least one day in advance in a bread tin. Cut into slices ¹/₂ in. (1 cm.) thick and lightly fry on both sides in butter. Put two apricot halves on each slice with the hollow side uppermost to receive a cherry. Cover with a hot, kirsch flavoured apricot sauce.

(France)

Fruit Croûtes - Croûtes aux Fruits

8 persons:

1 savarin
1 lb. 4 oz. (625 gr.) stewed assorted fruit to which 3 ¹/₂ oz. (100 gr.) muscatels have been added
1 ¹/₂ gills (2 dl.) thick, apricot sauce flavoured with rum, kirsch or madeira, etc.
Icing sugar

Cooking time: 4-5 minutes

Cut a stale savarin into slices ¹/₂ in. (1 cm.) thick and place on a baking sheet. Dust with icing sugar and glaze in a hot oven. Arrange the slices on a round dish in the form of a crown with each slice overlapping the other. Add some apricot sauce to the stewed fruit and fill the centre of the dish.

(France)

Pineapple Croûtes - Croûtes à l'Ananas

6 persons:

6 slices of savarin as above
6 good slices of pineapple poached in kirsch flavoured syrup
6 red cherries
2 ¹/₂ oz. (75 gr.) butter
¹/₂ pt. (¹/₄ l.) kirsch flavoured apricot sauce

Cooking time: 5-6 minutes

Lightly fry the slices of savarin in butter. Place on each slice a cored slice of pineapple with a cherry in the centre. Cover with hot apricot sauce.

DUMPLINGS

Apple Dumplings - Mele in Gabbia

Pin out puff pastry to about ¹/₈ in. (3 mm.) thick. Cut into 6 in. (15 cm.) squares. Peel and core apples carefully so that they remain in one piece. Fill the centres with the following mixture:

4 oz. (125 gr.) cooked and crushed rice
4 oz. (125 gr.) crème pâtissière
2 oz. (50 gr.) raisins
2 oz. (50 gr.) cut candied orange peel
2 oz. (50 gr.) pine nuts
Zest of lemon

Other fillings can be used, such as: apricot jam, or a nut of butter to each apple flavoured with cinnamon, vanilla and zest of lemon.

Place each apple in the centre of a pastry square; fill the hole with the desired filling and then bring the four corners of the pastry to a point on the top of the apple. Brush at this point with egg and place on a small disc of pastry to make a seal. Brush all over with egg yolk and bake at 360° F (182° C).
(Italy)

Norman Apple Dumplings - Douillons à la normande

6 persons:

6 medium size apples
1 ³/₄ oz. (50 gr.) butter
2 oz. (60 gr.) sugar
10 ¹/₂ oz. (300 gr.) milanese paste
Baking time: 15 minutes

Peel and core the apples. Fill a little sugar and butter in the centre of each apple and wrap up in a piece of paste rolled out to the required size. Top with a piece of paste cut out with a round fluted pastry cutter, egg wash and bake in a hot oven (400° F, 204° C).
(France)

Bavarian Dumplings - Bayrische Dampfnudeln

Dough:

5 gills (³/₄ l.) lukewarm milk
1 ³/₄ oz. (50 gr.) yeast
2 lb. (1 kg.) flour
3 ¹/₂ oz. (100 gr.) sugar
3 ¹/₂ oz. (100 gr.) melted butter
5 eggs

Cooking liquid:

1 ³/₄ pt. (1 l.) milk
1 ³/₄ oz. (50 gr.) butter
1 ³/₄ oz. (50 gr.) sugar

Mix together the warm milk, yeast and flour and leave to ferment in a warm place for one hour. Then add the sugar, eggs and butter, work together and leave to rest.

Using a tablespoon, shape into small mounds the size of an egg and set in a warm place again to prove fully. Place the balls of dough in a shallow braising pan and cover them completely with the ingredients for the cooking liquid. Cover tightly and bake in a moderate oven until all the liquid has evaporated and the Dampfnudeln have turned a pale golden colour. Leave the top crust on the Dampfnudeln and serve with vanilla sauce.
(Germany)

Plum Dumplings - Zwetschgenknödel

1 lb. (500 gr.) white flour
³/₄ oz. (20 gr.) yeast
1 ¹/₄ gills (2 dl.) tepid milk
3 eggs
1 ³/₄ oz. (50 gr.) melted butter
Salt
1 pinch of sugar
Stoned plums

Break down the yeast in the tepid milk and prepare a yeasted dough with the flour, eggs, melted butter, salt, a pinch of sugar and a few tablespoons of extra milk if required. Work the dough vigorously until it leaves the sides of the basin. Leave to rise in a warm place for at least one hour. Shape the dough into balls the size of walnuts and press a stoned plum into the centre of each one. Leave in a warm place to rise again, then drop into boiling water and poach for 15 minutes, keeping the water just off the boil. Arrange on a serving dish, sprinkle with bread crumbs lightly fried in butter and serve at once.
(Austria)

FRITTERS

Apple Fritters - Beignets de Pommes

6 persons:

1 ¹/₂ lb. (750 gr.) russet apples
3 ¹/₂ oz. (100 gr.) sugar
¹/₃ gill (5 cl.) rum or kirsch
Coating batter
Vanilla sugar
Cooking time: 4-5 minutes

Peel and core the apples and cut them into not too thin slices. Sprinkle with sugar and splash with rum or kirsch. Macerate for an hour and dry on a cloth. Dip in coating batter and fry in very hot deep fat. Turn them over several times while they are being fried and then drain them on a cloth. Sprinkle with vanilla sugar and pile the fritters up on a dish.

Surprise Apple Fritters - Beignets aux Pommes en Surprise

6 persons:

3 good apples
1 1/2 gills (2 dl.) confectioner's custard
2 macaroons
Coating batter

Cooking time: 4-5 minutes

Cut medium sized russet apples in halves and scoop out the core. Poach them in a light syrup without letting them break. Fill the hollows with confectioner's custard to which are added the crumbled macaroons; dry well, dust with cornflour, dip in batter and fry in the ordinary way.

Apricot Fritters - Beignets d'Abricots

6 persons:

1 lb. (500 gr.) fully ripe apricots
Vanilla sugar
Coating batter

Cooking time: 4-5 minutes

Peel the apricots, halve them, sprinkle with vanilla sugar and let them stand. Drain and dry the fruit and lightly dust with cornflour before dipping into the batter. Fry in very hot fat.

Banana Fritters I

Same recipe as for Apple fritters.
(Illustration page 658.)

Banana Fritters II - Banane in Camiccia

1 lb. 4 oz. (625 gr.) flour
4 oz. (125 gr.) butter
4 oz. (125 gr.) sugar
5 eggs
1/3 gill (5 cl.) rum
Salt to taste

Prepare a paste. Pin out the paste thinly, cut out into rectangles and wrap a banana in each, brushing the edges of the paste with egg to make a good seal. Fry in oil. Glaze with thin water icing and turn them quickly into chopped pistachio nuts or almonds. *(Italy)*

Carlsbad Soufflé Fritters - Beignets soufflés Karlsbad

Prepare a choux paste with a large proportion of egg yolk and mix with finely chopped candied fruit and raisins. Dip a tablespoon in oil and use it to drop spoonsful of the paste into deep fat, which should be only moderately hot so that the fritters fry slowly. Drain well, roll in cinnamon flavoured sugar, dish and serve vanilla or lemon sauce separately as an accompaniment.

Fig Fritters - Beignets de Figues

6 persons:

6-8 ripe fresh figs
1/4 gill (2 cl.) kirsch
Castor sugar
Coating batter, vanilla flavoured icing sugar

Cooking time: 3-4 minutes

Peel figs carefully and cut them in quarters. Sprinkle with castor sugar and splash with kirsch. Macerate for one hour. Dip in coating batter and fry in deep, very hot fat. Drain on cloth and serve sprinkled with vanilla icing sugar. Sabayon sauce may be served separately.

Lyons Fritters - Bugnes

1 lb. (500 gr.) flour
2 1/2 oz. (75 gr.) butter
1 1/2 oz. (50 gr.) sugar
1 tablespoonful cognac
4 whole eggs

Cooking time: 4-5 minutes

Make the ingredients into a paste. Flavour according to taste and add a pinch of table salt. Knead the paste with the hand and shape into a ball which is left in a cool place for 2 hours. Then roll out and cut up into strips 1 to 1 $1/2$ in. (2 $1/2$-4 cm.) wide and 4 to 4 $1/2$ in. (10-11 cm.) long.

Make a loose knot with each strip, lower into deep, very hot fat and then drain and sprinkle liberally with icing sugar. These are a type of fritter made in the Lyons districts. *(France)*

Grand-Marnier Orange Fritters - Beignets d'Orange au Grand-Marnier

6 persons:
18 segments of large, pipless oranges
$1/4$ gill (3 cl.) Grand-Marnier
Castor sugar
Coating batter

Cooking time: 3-4 minutes

Soak the orange segments in Grand-Marnier and sugar for 2 hours. Dry them on a cloth, dust with cornflour, dip in batter and fry in very hot fat. Serve with a Grand-Marnier flavoured apricot sauce. *(France)*

Cheltonia Peach Fritters

Per portion:
1 large choice peach
1 tablespoon sponge cake crumbs
1 teaspoon grated almonds
1 dessertspoon maraschino
Coating batter
Apricot sauce
Sugar

Peaches are never served unpeeled; poach them in boiling water before peeling—the skins will then come away very easily. Carefully remove the stone and fill each peach with a mixture of the sponge cake crumbs, almonds and a little maraschino.

Dust the peaches with flour, coat with light batter and deep fry. Roll the fritters in castor sugar. Serve apricot sauce, flavoured with the rest of the maraschino, separately. *(Great Britain)*

Pineapple Fritters - Ananas-Krapfen

6 persons:
12 half slices of pineapple
$1/6$ gill (2 cl.) kirsch
Vanilla sugar
Coating batter

Cooking time: 4-5 minutes

Soak the pineapple slices in kirsch and sugar for 1 hour, drain, dry and dust with cornflour. Dip in the batter and fry in very hot fat. Drain on a cloth and sprinkle with vanilla sugar. *(Germany)*

Soufflé Fritters - Beignets soufflés

6 persons:
7 oz. (200 gr.) choux paste
Vanilla sugar
Custard cream or jam

Cooking time: 5-7 minutes

Prepare a choux paste with very little butter and make it into little, round balls which are then dropped into moderately hot frying fat, which is gradually further heated so that it is extremely hot when the fritters are completely cooked. These fritters are known to be cooked when they no longer turn over in the fat and are the same colour all over. Drain and pile them up on a napkin. Sprinkle with vanilla sugar. They can either be served with custard cream or with a jam filling. Usually, however, these fritters are served on their own. *(France)*

FRUIT DESSERTS

Bulgarian Apples - Pommes à la bulgare

6 persons:
6 apples
1 $1/2$ gills (2 dl.) confectioner's custard
1 oz. (25 gr.) almonds and hazelnuts, roasted and chopped
2 oz. (50 gr.) chopped muscatels
$1/2$ pt. ($1/4$ l.) red wine
2 $1/2$ oz. (75 gr.) sugar
$3/4$ gill (1 dl.) red currant jelly
6 tartlet cases made with milanese paste and baked blind

Cooking time: 10-12 minutes

Peel and core the apples and poach them in a syrup composed of red wine, sugar and a little water, taking care not to let them break up. Fill the centre of each apple with confectioner's custard mixed with the chopped nuts and muscatels. Dress the stuffed apples in the tartlet cases and mask them with the syrup, reduced, slightly thickened with cornflour and mixed with red currant jelly.

Apples Chateaubriand - Pommes Chateaubriand

6 persons:
6 apples
6 round croûtons fried in butter
7 oz. (200 gr.) red currant jelly
Cornflour

Cooking time: 10-12 minutes

Peel and core the apples and poach them in a vanilla flavoured syrup. Drain and place them on the croûtons and mask with red currant jelly, mixed with a little reduced syrup and thickened with cornflour.

Apples Condé - Pommes Condé

Proceed in the same way as for Apricots Condé.

Apples Manon - Pommes Manon

6 persons:
18 apple quarters poached in vanilla flavoured syrup
1 lb. 2 oz. (500 gr.) thick apple purée
18 little macaroons
$1/2$ pt. ($1/4$ l.) rum flavoured apricot sauce

Place the apple purée in a hot silver timbale and dress the apple quarters on top, which have been poached in a red coloured syrup. Place a macaroon between each piece of apple and mask with thick rum flavoured sauce.

Apples Marietta - Pommes Marietta

6 persons:
6 apples
7 oz. (200 gr.) chestnut purée sweetened and flavoured with rum
$1/2$ pt. (3 dl.) rum flavoured apricot sauce
$1\,3/4$ oz. (50 gr.) flaked, roasted almonds

Cooking time: 10-12 minutes

Peel and core the apples and poach them in a vanilla flavoured syrup without letting them break up. Drain them carefully and arrange them on a round dish. Fill the centre with chestnut purée, using a piping bag with a plain tube. Mask with apricot sauce and sprinkle with the almonds.

Apples Mary Stuart - Pommes Marie Stuart

6 persons:
6 apples
7 oz. (200 gr.) confectioner's custard
10 oz. (300 gr.) puff paste
1 egg
Icing sugar

Cooking time: 10-12 minutes

Peel, core and poach the apples in vanilla flavoured syrup without letting them get too soft. Drain and dry them on a cloth. Fill the centre of each apple with confectioner's custard and wrap in puff paste. Top with a piece of puff paste cut out with a round fluted pastry cutter, egg wash and bake in a hot oven.

Apricots Condé - Abricots Condé

6 persons:
12 choice apricot halves
$4\,1/2$ oz. (150 gr.) rice Condé
$1/2$ pt. (3 dl.) rum flavoured apricot sauce
Glacé cherries — Angelica

Dress a border of Condé rice on a round dish. Poach the apricots in vanilla flavoured syrup, drain them well and arrange them on top of the rice. Decorate with glacé cherries and diamond shaped pieces of angelica. Mask with apricot sauce. Serve the remaining sauce separately. (Rice Condé *page 697.*)

Flambéed Apricots - Abricots flambés

6 persons:
12 choice apricots
$1\,1/2$ gills ($1/4$ l.) apricot sauce
$1/4$ gill (3 cl.) kirsch

Cooking time: 5-6 minutes

Poach the apricots in vanilla flavoured syrup, peel and stone. Dress them in a fireproof dish and mask with hot apricot sauce. Pour the warmed kirsch around and ignite when serving.

Bananas Bourdaloue - Bananes Bourdaloue

6 persons:

1 flan case
6 bananas
1 1/4 pt. (3/4 l.) frangipane cream
3 macaroons
1 oz. (30 gr.) butter
Icing sugar
1 1/2 gills (1/4 l.) kirsch flavoured apricot syrup

Cooking time: 3-4 minutes

Bake the flan case blind. Cover the bottom with half the frangipane cream and arrange the bananas on top, which have been skinned, split lengthways, poached and drained. Mask with the remaining frangipane cream, sprinkle the crushed macaroons on top and dust with icing sugar. Sprinkle with melted butter and glaze in a hot oven. Serve the apricot syrup separately.

Flambéed Bananas Martinique - Bananes flambées Martinique

6 persons:

6 bananas, skinned and split lengthways
Juice of 1 orange
2 oz. (60 gr.) butter
3 oz. (90 gr.) sugar
1 1/2 gills (1/4 l.) apricot sauce
1 1/2 oz. (40 gr.) shredded, roasted almonds
1/2 gill (5 cl.) rum

Cooking time: 6-8 minutes

Service in front of the guests: melt the sugar and butter in a copper pan over a flambé réchaud with a high flame until it begins to caramelize. Add the orange juice to dissolve the sugar and then the apricot sauce.

Cook for a few seconds, add the bananas and simmer them in the sauce for 3-4 minutes. Pour over the rum and ignite. As soon as the flame goes out, serve the bananas on hot plates, masked with the sauce and sprinkled with the almonds.

Fried Bananas and Pineapple Javanese Style - Pisang and Ananas Goreng

3 1/2 gills (1/2 l.) water
2/3 gill (1 dl.) coconut milk
1 cup flour
3 eggs
Salt
Sugar
Sliced pineapple
Bananas

Peel the bananas and cut in half lengthwise; cut the slices of pineapple into two. Dust the fruit with sugar and flour. Prepare a thin batter with the remaining ingredients, coat the fruit with it and fry in deep oil.

Make a thick syrup with caramel sugar, water and ginger, and serve separately.

Soufflé Bananas - Bananes soufflées

6 persons:

8 choice bananas
3 oz. (100 gr.) vanilla sugar
1 1/2 oz. (50 gr.) butter
2 eggs
2 tablespoons rum

Cooking time: 6-8 minutes

Split the skin of 6 bananas carefully along three quarters of their length and remove the flesh without damaging the shells. Completely skin the other two bananas. Pass the flesh of all the bananas through a sieve and cook to a thick purée, adding the sugar and butter. Flavour the purée with rum, remove from the heat and mix in first the egg yolks and then the stiffly whisked egg whites.

Using a piping bag with a plain tube, fill the shells with the mixture, sprinkle with sugar and bake in a medium oven.

Cherries Eldorado - Cerises Eldorado

6 persons:
1 lb. 8 oz. (750 gr.) cherries
½ pt. (¼ l.) sabayon
  flavoured with cognac
Cooking time: 5-7 minutes

Stone and then poach the cherries in a vanilla flavoured syrup. Drain thoroughly, fill in a timbale or in individual cocottes and mask with the sabayon. Serve at once.

Flambéed Cherries - Cerises flambées

6 persons:
1 lb. 4 oz. (600 gr.) stoned cherries
¾ gill (1 dl.) red wine
3 ½ oz. (100 gr.) sugar
1 teaspoon cornflour
Cinnamon
¼ gill (3-4 cl.) kirsch
Red currant jelly
Cooking time: 5-7 minutes

Poach the cherries in the red wine with the sugar and a pinch of cinnamon. Drain them and reduce the red wine to a quarter of its volume. Thicken with the cornflour dispersed in a little water and add two tablespoons red currant jelly. Dress the cherries in a timbale or in individual cocottes (one per person) and mask with the sauce. Pour a tablespoon of warmed kirsch on each and ignite when serving.

Cherry Gratin - Gratin aux Cerises

18 oz. (600 gr.) stoned cherries
3 ½ oz. (100 gr.) sugar
2 eggs
A few macaroons
Cinnamon
1 ¾ gills (¼ l.) red wine
3 ½ gills (½ l.) milk
1 ¾ oz. (40 gr.) butter
Baking time:
25-30 minutes at 400° F (204° C)

Poach the cherries in the sweetened red wine with a little cinnamon. Make thin pancakes and place about a dozen cherries on each. Fold the ends over and place upside down on a buttered baking dish, scoring the tops of the pancakes slightly. Mix the milk, sugar, eggs and a little ground cinnamon and pour on to the pancakes; they should be completely covered. Sprinkle with broken macaroons and melted butter and bake until golden brown.

Peaches Andalusian Style - Pêches à l'andalouse

6 persons:
6 choice peaches
4 ½ oz. (150 gr.) Condé rice
8 oz. (250 gr.) Swiss meringue mixture
½ pt. (¼ l.) kirsch flavoured apricot sauce
Cooking time: 6-8 minutes

Poach the peaches in vanilla flavoured syrup, drain, peel and stone. Dress them on top of the rice and mask with meringue. Decorate with meringue mixture, using a piping bag and a star tube, dust with icing sugar and flash in a hot oven. Serve the apricot sauce separately.

Flambéed Peaches - Pêches flambées

Method 1. 6 persons:
6 choice peaches
¼ gill (4 cl.) kirsch
Castor sugar
Cooking time: 6-8 minutes

Poach the peaches in vanilla flavoured syrup. Dress them in a timbale with three to four spoons of the hot syrup. Pour over the warmed kirsch and ignite when serving.

Method 2. 6 persons:
6 choice peaches
1 ½ gills (2 dl.) strawberry purée
¼ gill (4 cl.) kirsch
Icing sugar
Cooking time: 6-8 minutes

Poach the peaches as above and skin. Arrange them on top of the strawberry purée warmed and slightly sweetened. Sprinkle with icing sugar, pour the warmed kirsch on top and ignite when serving.

Peaches Jan Gravendeel - Pêches Jan Gravendeel

1 portion:

1 choice peach (white if possible)
³/₄ gill (1 dl.) Grand-Marnier sabayon sauce (see Liqueur Sabayon Sauce)
4 crystallized violets

Cut the peach in half, remove the stone and skin. Carefully poach in syrup flavoured with Grand-Marnier. Dish the half peaches on a pre-heated plate and coat with sabayon sauce, then decorate with the crystallized violets and serve at once. (Speciality of the 'De Gravenmolen' Restaurant, Amsterdam.) *(Holland)*

The peaches can be replaced by preserved pears.

Stuffed Peaches Cancelliere - Pesche farcite alla Cancelliere

6 portions:

6 choice peaches
6 ¹/₂ oz. (200 gr.) amaretti or ratafia biscuits
2 ¹/₄ oz. (70 gr.) candied orange peel
2 ¹/₄ gills (3 dl.) custard cream
7 oz. (200 gr.) strip almonds

Cut the peaches in half, remove the stones and skin. Finely chop the candied orange peel and strip almonds, add the grated ratafias and mix with the custard cream. Fill the mixture into the centre of the peaches, using a savoy bag and plain tube.

Lightly butter a fireproof dish, place the peaches in it and cover with a mixture of 5 oz. (150 gr.) ground almonds, 3 eggs and 2 oz. (60 gr.) sugar. Bake at 320° F (160° C) and glaze with raspberry jam or jelly before serving. Can be served as well cold.

Pears à la Mode - Poires à la Mode

6 persons:

6 pears
¹/₄ pt. (¹/₈ l.) red wine
4 ¹/₂ oz. (150 gr.) Condé rice
2 oz. (60 gr.) glacé cherries
2 tablespoons cherry brandy
3 oz. (100 gr.) red currant jelly
Cornflour
Cinnamon
1 ¹/₂ oz. (40 gr.) nibbed pistachio nuts
Cooking time: 6-8 minutes

Peel and core the pears and poach them in red wine syrup flavoured with cinnamon. Drain the pears, reduce the syrup by half, add the red currant jelly, thickened slightly with cornflour and pass through a sieve. Mix the Condé rice with chopped glacé cherries macerated in cherry brandy. Dress the pears on top of the rice in a silver timbale, mask with the red wine sauce and sprinkle with nibbed pistachio nuts.

Flambéed Pears - Poires flambées

6 persons:

6 choice pears
2 oz. (60 gr.) apricot jam
¹/₂ gill (4 cl.) rum or kirsch
Icing sugar
Cooking time: 6-8 minutes

Peel and core the pears. Poach them in a vanilla flavoured syrup and dress them in a silver timbale. Cover with a few tablespoons of the reduced syrup thickened with the apricot jam. Dust the pears with icing sugar, pour over the warmed kirsch and ignite when serving.

Pears Schouwalow - Poires Schouvaloff

6 persons:

6 small pear halves
1 thin round genoese sponge
10 oz. (300 gr.) Swiss meringue mixture
³/₄ gill (1 dl.) reduced apricot jam
Red currant jelly
Halved pistachio nuts
Cooking time: about 10 minutes

Poach the pears in a vanilla flavoured syrup, drain and dry them on a cloth. Spread the apricot jam all over the sponge and arrange the pears on top with the stalk end pointing towards the centre. Mask with meringue mixture, smooth with a palette knife and pipe a criss-cross pattern with some of the meringue on top. Dust with icing sugar and put in the oven to colour the meringue. Drop a spot of red currant jelly in the spaces between the criss-cross lines and place half a pistachio nut on top. Serve a thickened kirsch flavoured syrup separately (optional).

Pineapple Condé - Ananas Condé
Dress thin half slices of pineapple on Condé rice, decorate and mask with rum flavoured apricot sauce.

Pineapple Marina - Ananas Marina
6 persons :
1 base of genoese sponge $^3/_4$ in. (2 cm.) thick
 and about 6 in. (15 cm.) in diameter
12 thin half slices pineapple
$^1/_2$ gill (5 cl.) kirsch flavoured syrup
12 oz. (360 gr.) stoned cherries
1 teaspoon cornflour
2 tablespoons brandy
1 oz. (30 gr.) shredded pistachio nuts
$^1/_2$ pt. (3 dl.) sabayon flavoured with
 Grand-Marnier

Poach the cherries in vanilla flavoured syrup, reduce the syrup and thicken with cornflour. Poach the pineapple slices with very little sugar and the brandy. Dress the genoese sponge on a hot round dish and soak very slightly with the kirsch flavoured syrup. Arrange the pineapple slices on top overlapping each other in the form of a crown and dispose the cherries in the centre. Sprinkle the cherries with flaked pistachio nuts and serve the sabayon separately.

Raspberry Gratin Eden - Gratin aux Framboises Eden
4 portions :
1 oval sheet of butter sponge $^1/_2$ in. (1 cm.) thick
14 oz. (400 gr.) raspberries
$^1/_2$ pt. ($^1/_4$ l.) confectioner's custard
$^1/_2$ pt. ($^1/_4$ l.) whipped dairy cream
Approx. $^1/_3$ gill (4 cl.) raspberry brandy
Lightly roasted flaked almonds
Praline croquant
Small knobs of butter

Line an oval fireproof dish with the butter sponge, moisten with raspberry brandy and cover with the raspberries that have been macerated in a little raspberry brandy and sugar. Blend the whipped cream and a drop of red colour into the confectioner's custard and flavour with raspberry brandy. Cover the raspberries completely with the custard cream, sprinkle with flaked almonds and a little praline croquant, dot the top with a few knobs of butter, dredge with icing sugar and brown quickly in a hot oven or under a salamander. *(Switzerland)*
(Illustration page 640.)

OMELETTES
Jam Omelette - Omelette à la Confiture
6 persons :
7 eggs
$^3/_4$ oz. (20 gr.) sugar
2 tablespoons jam (apricot, strawberry, raspberry, etc.)
1 $^1/_4$ oz. (40 gr.) castor sugar
Cooking time : 2-3 minutes

Season the eggs with sugar and a pinch of salt and prepare the omelette in the usual way. Just before rolling, fill the omelette with jam. Dress on an oval fireproof dish, dust with sugar and mark the surface in a criss-cross pattern with an electric rod or glaze quickly under the salamander.

Mousseline Omelette - Omelette Mousseline
4 persons :
3 egg yolks
5 egg whites
4 $^1/_2$ oz. (125 gr.) sugar
$^1/_6$ gill (2 cl.) kirsch
Vanilla or lemon zest
1 teaspoonful flour
1 tablespoonful fresh cream
1 $^3/_4$ oz. (50 gr.) butter
Cooking time : about 8 minutes

Beat up the egg yolks with the sugar, vanilla, kirsch and 1 oz. (30 gr.) melted butter until lighter in colour. Mix in the cream and lightly fold in the whisked flour and egg whites. Melt ³/₄ oz. (20 gr.) butter in a frying pan, pour in the mixture and warm for a moment over heat. Bake in a hot oven. Fold the omelette in half, serve on a long dish and dust with icing sugar.

Rum Omelette - Omelette au Rhum

4 persons:
7 eggs
³/₄ oz. (20 gr.) butter
²/₃ gill (3-4 cl.) rum
1 oz. (30 gr.) castor sugar
Cooking time: 2-3 minutes

Flavour the omelette with a pinch of salt and some sugar and prepare in the usual way. Place on a dish, sprinkle with sugar and splash with warm rum. Ignite when serving. In place of rum, kirsch, cognac or other spirits may be used.

Lemon or Orange Soufflé Omelette - Omelette soufflée au Citron ou à l'Orange

Proceed in the same way as for vanilla soufflé omelette, but replace the vanilla with finely grated lemon or orange zest.

Rum, Kirsch, Grand-Marnier, etc., Soufflé Omelette - Omelette soufflée au Rhum, Kirsch, Grand-Marnier etc.

Use the same method as for vanilla soufflé omelette, but add the liqueur or spirit to the egg yolks and sugar before folding in the whites.

Strawberry Soufflé Omelette

4 portions:
6 egg yolks
6 egg whites
5 oz. (150 gr.) sugar
1 small glass kirsch
14 oz. (400 gr.) strawberries

Remove the stalks from the strawberries, wash them well and add half the sugar and the kirsch. Beat the egg yolks with the rest of the sugar until very frothy, fold in the whites whipped to a very stiff snow, fill into a well-buttered fireproof dish and add the strawberries in layers. Bake in a slow oven for 10-12 minutes, transfer to a warm serving dish, sprinkle with sugar and serve at once. *(Great Britain)*

Vanilla Soufflé Omelette - Omelette soufflée à la Vanille

(Basic recipe)
4 persons:
5 oz. (150 gr.) castor sugar
3 egg yolks
5 egg whites
Vanilla
Cooking time: 8-10 minutes

Beat the egg yolks with the sugar and vanilla until lighter in colour. Fold in the stiffly whisked egg whites. Take a long, oven-proof dish which has been greased and sprinkled with sugar, and deposit the mixture in the form of an oval dome, the top of which should be slightly hollow. Smooth with a knife and decorate with some of the mixture which has been reserved for the purpose, using a savoy bag fitted with a star pipe. Sprinkle with sugar and bake in a slow oven (320° F [160° C]).

PANCAKES

Breton Pancakes - Crêpes bretonnes

6 persons:
4 ¹/₂ oz. (125 gr.) sifted flour
4 ¹/₂ oz. (125 gr.) sifted buck-wheat flour
A pinch ground cinnamon
¹/₃ gill (4 cl.) rum
About 1 pt. (¹/₂ l.) milk
2 ¹/₂ oz. (75 gr.) butter
Demarara sugar
Cooking time: 4-5 minutes

Mix both flours with a pinch of salt and a pinch of cinnamon. Next add the rum and enough milk to obtain a fairly liquid batter. Prepare the pancakes as usual but, before removing them from the pan, splash them with melted butter sweetened with demarara sugar. Fold into four and serve piping hot. *(France)*

Crêpes Suzette

Recipe 1. 6 persons:

12 small pancakes
2 oz. (60 gr.) butter
1 $^3/_4$ oz. (50 gr.) icing sugar
Zest of 2 oranges
$^1/_4$ gill (3 cl.) curaçao

Cooking time: 2-3 minutes

Cream the sugar with the best quality butter in a basin and add the grated orange zest and curaçao. Spread some of this mixture on each pancake and serve at once on a hot dish. Alternatively, it is possible to splash the pancakes with Fine Champagne (brandy) and to ignite when serving.

Recipe 2. 6 persons:

12 small pancakes
10 lumps of sugar rubbed against orange skin so as to be impregnated with the zest
Juice of 1 orange
$^1/_6$ gill (2 cl.) cognac
$^1/_6$ gill (2 cl.) Grand-Marnier
2 oz. (60 gr.) butter

Keep the pancakes hot, either between two plates or on a spirit lamp. Dissolve the sugar in the orange juice in a copper pan over the spirit lamp. Add the butter and allow to cook momentarily while shaking the pan to and fro. Pour in the Grand-Marnier and cognac and ignite. Dip the pancakes one after the other in the pan, so that they become thoroughly covered with the sauce, and roll them up using a spoon and fork. Serve on hot plates and pour the butter over them.

Ducal Pancakes - Crêpes ducales

Beat some butter with a little icing sugar, orange juice, grated orange zest and Grand-Marnier until foamy. Spread on to three small pancakes, fold over, brush with butter and flash in a hot oven. On removing from the oven, sprinkle the top with finely chopped orange peel and serve at once.

Georgette Pancakes - Crêpes Georgette

6 persons:

3 gills (4 dl.) pancake batter
5 $^1/_2$ oz. to 7 oz. (150-200 gr.) thin slices pineapple
$^1/_6$ gill (2 cl.) maraschino icing sugar

Cooking time: 3-4 minutes

Soak the pineapple in the maraschino icing sugar. Pour into the pan a film of batter; arrange the pieces of pineapple on top and cover with another thin layer of batter. When the pancakes are cooked they are served unfolded and dusted with icing sugar. *(France)*

Hawaii Pancakes - Crêpes Hawaii

Place a small pancake on a fireproof dish, cover the centre with confectioner's custard flavoured with Grand-Marnier and sprinkle generously with hazelnut praline croquant. Place a thin slice of pineapple poached in a mixture of stock syrup and orange juice on top and cover with a little more confectioner's custard. Lay a second pancake on top, dust with icing sugar, pour Grand-Marnier over and ignite.

(Switzerland)

Pancakes Greta Garbo - Crêpes Greta Garbo

10 small pancakes:

$^1/_2$ pt. ($^1/_4$ l.) lukewarm milk
3 $^1/_2$ oz. (100 gr.) melted butter
2 eggs
1 pinch of salt
$^1/_2$ oz. (15 gr.) sugar
3 oz. (90 gr.) flour
Compote of finely sliced peaches flavoured with Benedictine

Separate the egg whites from the yolks and whip the whites to a stiff snow. Make a batter with the yolks, milk, flour, butter, sugar and salt and fold in the whipped whites. Pour a little of the batter into a 5 in. (12 cm.) frying-pan and cook. The pancake is ready as soon as it has risen. Spread with the compote. Each portion usually consists of a pancake spread with compote of peaches, a second pancake, a second layer of compote and a third pancake on top. Serve with warm chocolate sauce decorated with crystallized violets and, if desired, hand round a little sour cream separately. *(Sweden)*

Jam Pancakes - Crêpes à la Confiture

Spread some red currant jelly or other jam on the pancakes and roll them up loosely. Sprinkle with castor sugar. *(France)*

Montenegrin Pancakes with Slivovitz

6 persons:

³/₄ gill (1 dl.) milk
³/₄ oz. (25 gr.) butter
³/₄ oz. (25 gr.) fine sifted maize meal
4 ¼ oz. (150 gr.) sloe jelly
30 prunes
3 cloves
Zest of 1 lemon
1 small piece of cinnamon
Ground cinnamon
5 ¼ oz. (150 gr.) sugar
³/₄ gill (1 dl.) sour cream
4-5 eggs
¹/₃ gill (4 cl.) cognac
¹/₂ gill (8 cl.) slivovitz

Cooking time: 10 minutes

Prepare a rather thin choux paste with the milk, butter, maize meal and 4-5 eggs. Bake 12 very thin pancakes with this mixture, spread them with sloe jelly, roll them up loosely and keep them warm in a chafing dish. Make a syrup with 3 gills (¹/₂ l.) water, 4 ¼ oz. (120 gr.) sugar, cloves, cinnamon and zest of lemon. Poach the prunes, soaked beforehand, for 10 minutes in the syrup, drain and stone them. Strain and reduce the syrup and flavour it with the cognac and half of the slivovitz. Final preparation in front of the guests: melt 1 ³/₄ oz. (50 gr.) butter in a copper frying pan placed on top of a spirit stove. Put the pancakes in the pan and add the prunes and a little syrup. Bring the syrup to the boil, pour the rest of the slivovitz over the pancakes and ignite. Place two pancakes and five prunes on each hot plate, cover with a tablespoon of syrup, mask with a teaspoon of sour cream and sprinkle with sugar mixed with ground cinnamon. *(Yugoslavia)*

Normandy Pancakes - Crêpes normandes

Cut some Caux calville or russet apples into quarters and fry lightly in a little hot butter to a light golden colour. Add sugar and a pinch of cinnamon. Make pancakes in the usual way, fill them with the apples, arrange on a dish, sprinkle with sugar and with very old Pays d'Auge calvados and set alight. *(France)*

Nougatine Pancakes - Crêpes Nougatine

Spread three thin pancakes with confectioner's custard flavoured with anisette, sprinkle generously with hazelnut praline croquant and fold over. Arrange on a fireproof dish, sprinkle with hazelnut praline croquant, dredge with icing sugar and flash in a hot oven. These pancakes may be splashed with liqueur and ignited if desired.

Palacinky

1 portion:

2 egg yolks
2 egg whites whipped to a snow
1 whole egg
1 teaspoon flour
1 tablespoon milk
1 pinch of salt
A little sugar
Thick vanilla cream
Raspberry purée
Whipped cream

Mix the egg yolks, whole egg, flour and milk thoroughly and fold in the whipped whites. Add a pinch of salt and a little sugar. Make pancakes from this mixture, cooking them on both sides to a pale golden colour. Without removing them from the pan, spread with 2 spoonfuls of thick vanilla cream, a spoonful of raspberry purée and a spoonful of whipped cream. Fold over like an omelette, dust the top with castor sugar and caramelize with a red-hot iron. *(Czechoslovakia)*

Pancakes Romantic Style - Crêpes à la romantique

For each person make a small, very thin pancake at the table over a spirit stove. Fill with a macedoine of bananas, pineapple, peaches, grapes and large cherries, together with a scoop of vanilla ice cream, and roll up. Pour a glassful each of maraschino and kirsch into the pan and set alight, continually basting the pancake. Transfer to a warmed plate, sprinkle with finely chopped nougat, add a pinch of freshly ground pepper and serve.

(Switzerland)

Prune Pancakes - Crêpes aux Pruneaux

Stone some prunes, chop them finely and macerate in armagnac or marc-brandy. Beat some confectioner's custard until smooth and mix in the soaked prunes. Fill small pancakes with the mixture, allowing three for each person, place them on a fireproof dish and spread with pancake butter flavoured with a little armagnac or marc-brandy. Flash under a salamander or in a hot oven.

Pancake butter:
7 oz. (200 gr.) butter
7 oz. (200 gr.) icing sugar
Juice of ½ lemon
Armagnac or marc-brandy to taste

Swedish Pancakes with Compote - Plätter med Sylt

Make a batter consisting of milk, white flour, eggs, salt, sugar and a little melted butter and whipped cream. Cook in butter in a frying pan a little at a time to make small thin pancakes similar to Russian blinis. Cover with thick strawberry or raspberry purée or bilberry jam. Serve 5-6 pancakes per portion, well sprinkled with sugar and cinnamon. *(Sweden)*

Soufflé Pancakes - Crêpes soufflées

6 persons:
12 small pancakes
About 8 oz. (250 gr.) vanilla, praline, chocolate or coffee flavoured soufflé mixture

Cooking time: 10-12 minutes

Put a tablespoonful of the soufflé mixture in the middle of each pancake and cover by folding the sides loosely towards the centre. Arrange on a greased dish and bake in a slow oven. *(France)*

Wafer Thin Pancakes - Crêpes fines

Grease a small, very hot frying pan and pour into it a thin film of batter. When the pancake is set on one side, turn it over and when it is completely cooked, fold it over in half and sprinkle with vanilla sugar. Serve on a hot dish. *(France)*

PANNEQUETS

Pannequets

These are larger pancakes filled with cream, custard, purée or jam. They are rolled up and after the ends have been trimmed diagonally, they are cut into two diamond-shaped pieces.

Jam Pannequets - Pannequets à la Confiture

Prepare some very thin pancakes and spread a tablespoon of jam on each. Roll them up to look like cigars and, after trimming the ends diagonally, arrange on a baking sheet. Dust with icing sugar and place in a very hot oven for about two minutes to caramelize the sugar.

Lyonnaise Pannequets - Pannequets à la lyonnaise

Spread the pancakes with some chestnut purée sweetened with syrup. Roll them up to look like large cigars, brush with apricot purée and sprinkle with chopped roasted almonds.

FRUIT AND OTHER PIES

This heading covers the many varieties which can be made at any time of the year in these days of fruit preservation. In smaller bakeries in the British Isles most small fruit pies are hand-made in deep custard cups, the fruit being totally enclosed with pastry. Small open fruit tartlets are made but are less common.

The coming of mass production by machine however has seen a further change for now they are made in square shallow pans and attractively packed. Metal foil cases are also used to eliminate breakage during transport. Essentially, the fruit pie is a mixture of fruit, sugar, a thickener of some sort and water, all enclosed in sweet pastry. The thickeners normally used are cornflour, rice flour, potato starch, wheat or other cereal starch, gelatine, agar-agar and pectin. There is now on the market an excellent soluble starch which should be used according to the manufacturer's instructions.

Fruit pies can be made both large and small and it is usual to use the fresh pastry for the tops, incorporating the cuttings with fresh paste for the linings.

The characteristics of a good pie are as follows:

(a) The pie should show plenty of fruit which should, as far as possible, be of good shape and colour. Fruit and juice should be compact showing no spaces.

(b) The juice should be clear and not too watery. It should be of a colour characteristic of the fruit used.

(c) Flavour is of the greatest importance and this is largely determined by the quality of the fruit, the amount of sugar used and the complementary flavour used (if any), i.e. clove used with apple.

Apple Pie

6 persons:

1 lb. (500 gr.) sweet short pastry
2 lb. (1 kg.) peeled, cored and thickly sliced apples
6 oz. (175 gr.) castor sugar
Grated zest of 1 lemon
$1/2$ gill (8 cl.) water
Juice of $1/2$ lemon
$1/2$ pt. ($1/4$ l.) cream
Cooking time: 40 minutes

Place the apples in a pie dish with the sugar, zest, juice and water. Cover with the pastry, pinch up and decorate the edges. Bake at 350° F (176° C) for half an hour, brush with water, bestrew with castor sugar and continue cooking until the fruit is tender. Serve with a sauce boat of cream. Alternatively cloves may be used for flavour instead of lemon. *(Great Britain)*

Blackberry and Apple Pie

6 persons:

1 lb. (500 gr.) sweet short pastry
$1 1/4$ lb. (625 gr.) peeled, cored and thickly sliced apples
$3/4$ lb. (375 gr.) blackberries
6 oz. (175 gr.) sugar
Juice of $1/2$ lemon
$1/2$ gill (8 cl.) water
Cooking time: 40 minutes

Proceed as for apple pie and serve with cream. *(Great Britain)*

Gooseberry Pie

6 persons:

1 lb. (500 gr.) sweet short pastry
2 lb. (1 kg.) gooseberries
8 oz. (250 gr.) sugar
Cooking time: 40 minutes

Proceed in the same way as for apple pie.
(Great Britain)

Maryland Pie

1 lb. 4 oz. (625 gr.) basic sweet pastry *(page 185)*
4 oz. (125 gr.) strawberry jam
4 oz. (125 gr.) currants
4 oz. (125 gr.) sultanas

Line a flan ring with part of the sweet pastry, prick the bottom, leave to rest. Cover with a layer of strawberry jam about $1/4$ in. (5 mm.) thick, then with a $1/2$ in. (1 cm.) layer of currants and sultanas, previously soaked. Cover with the rest of the pastry. Prick with a fork, brush with egg yolk, bake in a slow oven. Serve either hot or cold with custard or vanilla sauce. *(Great Britain)*

Mince Pies

(Page 329) (Illustration page 319).

Rhubarb Pie

6 persons:

1 lb. (500 gr.) sweet short pastry
2 lb. (1 kg.) peeled rhubarb cut into 2 in. (5 cm.) pieces
8 oz. (250 gr.) sugar
1/2 gill (8 cl.) water
A few drops of carmine

Cooking time: 30 minutes

Heat the sugar and water together and colour with the carmine. Arrange the rhubarb in a pie dish, pour over the syrup, cover with the pastry, pinch up the edges and bake at 380° F (194° C) for 25 minutes. Water wash, bestrew with castor sugar and continue cooking until the fruit is cooked but whole. *(Great Britain)*
(Illustration page 689.)

Rhubarb and Apple Pie

Line sandwich plates and place in alternate layers of finely cut floured rhubarb, sliced apple and diced beetroot. Add zest and juice of lemon, sugar and place on pastry lids. Bake at 400° F (204° C).

PUDDINGS

Cabinet Pudding also called Hot Diplomat - Pudding Cabinet ou Diplomate chaud

6 persons:

4 1/2 oz. (140 gr.) sponge fingers
3 oz. (90 gr.) castor sugar
3 eggs
3 1/2 oz. (100 gr.) raisins and diced candied fruit
3 gills (4 dl.) milk
3 gills (4 dl.) custard cream

Cooking time: about 25 minutes

Beat up the eggs and sugar in a basin and pour over them the milk which has been boiled with a vanilla bean, stirring all the time. Leave to stand and skim off the froth. Grease and sprinkle with sugar a pudding mould and fill it with pieces of sponge fingers; these may be replaced by genoese or other sponge. Fill the mould with alternate layers of sponge and diced fruit soaked in rum. Gradually pour in some custard so as to allow the sponge to soak it up and swell and continue until the mould is quite full. Put in a bain-marie in the oven for 25 minutes. To check that the pudding is cooked, test with a small knife which should come out without any trace of the custard. Five minutes after the pudding has come out of the oven, turn it out of the mould and pour over it a rum flavoured sabayon or custard cream. *(France)*

Christmas Pudding (Plum Pudding)

1 lb. (500 gr.) finely chopped beef kidney suet
1 lb. (500 gr.) raisins (stoned muscatels)
1 lb. (500 gr.) sultanas
1 1/2 lb. (750 gr.) currants
1 lb. (500 gr.) mixed candied peel (orange, lemon, citron) finely chopped
1 lb. (500 gr.) barbados sugar
1 lb. (500 gr.) fresh bread crumbs
5 oz. (150 gr.) strong flour
1 1/2 oz. (50 gr.) mixed spice
1/2 oz. (15 gr.) salt
1/2 pt. (1/4 l.) egg
Zest and juice of 3 lemons
Zest and juice of 3 oranges
Milk or beer or stout or sherry, brandy or whisky or an admixture of the above (optional)

Mix all ingredients together and allow to macerate for 48 hours. It is important that the basins are filled to the brim, the mixing forming a domed top, otherwise water in the form of condensed steam will form on the top of the pudding. Fill into buttered basins, cover with a buttered greaseproof paper and tie down with muslin or linen. Steam for about 4 to 6 hours according to size.

For service, unmould upon a round dish, dust heavily with icing sugar; place a sprig of berried holly in the centre, pour over a little warmed brandy or whisky and ignite upon sending to table. Serve with a sauceboat of cream, rum or whisky or brandy custard or hard sauce. Allow 4 oz. (125 gr.) of pudding per person.
(Illustration page 659.) *(Great Britain)*

Frankfurt Pudding I - Frankfurter Pudding

10 portions:

8 oz. (250 gr.) butter
6 oz. (180 gr.) sugar
4 oz. (125 gr.) brown bread crumbs
4 oz. (125 gr.) ground almonds
8 egg yolks
8 egg whites
2 oz. (50 gr.) finely diced candied fruit
$1/16$ oz. (2 gr.) cinnamon
1 pinch of salt
$1/3$ gill (5 cl.) red wine

Moisten the bread crumbs with the wine. Cream the butter with the sugar and add the egg yolks a little at a time. Stir in the bread crumbs, almonds, candied fruit, salt and cinnamon, then fold in the egg whites whisked to a stiff snow. Pour into buttered cup-shaped moulds that have been sprinkled with cake crumbs or bread crumbs made from rolls. Bake in a bain-marie in a moderate oven for about 45 minutes. Serve with bishop sauce or fruit sauce flavoured with kirsch. *(Germany)*

Frankfurt Pudding II - Frankfurter Pudding

15-16 portions:

$3 1/2$ oz. (100 gr.) butter
$3 1/2$ oz. (100 gr.) finely ground almonds
4 oz. (125 gr.) sponge cake crumbs
7 oz. (200 gr.) sugar
4 oz. (125 gr.) sultanas
10 egg yolks
10 egg whites
2 oz. (50 gr.) cornflour
Zest of 1 lemon
$1/8$ oz. (3 gr.) cinnamon
$1/8$ oz. (3 gr.) salt

Cream the butter with half the sugar and add the egg yolks a little at a time. Stir in the almonds, sponge crumbs, chopped sultanas, salt, cinnamon and grated lemon zest. Whisk the egg whites to a stiff snow with the rest of the sugar, fold into the above mixture and lastly blend in the cornflour. Three quarters fill into small buttered cup-shaped moulds which have been sprinkled with sugar. Bake in a bain-marie in a moderate oven for about 45 minutes, then remove from the oven and cook in a bain-marie on top of the stove for a further 15-30 minutes. Serve with bishop sauce. *(Germany)*

Jam Roly Poly Pudding

6 persons:

12 oz. (375 gr.) strong flour
$4 1/2$ oz. (150 gr.) finely chopped beef suet
Pinch of salt
$1/2$ oz. (15 gr.) baking powder
1 oz. (30 gr.) sugar
$1 1/2$ gills (2 dl.) water
1 lb. (500 gr.) jam (any kind)

Cooking time: $1 1/2$ hours

Sieve powder, sugar, salt and flour together, rub in the suet and make a well. Pour in the water and mix together with as little working as possible, cover and leave to rest. Roll out into an oblong shape, spread with jam to within $1/2$ in. (1 cm.) of the edge, water wash the edges, roll up like a Swiss roll and seal the edges well. Wrap in a buttered and floured cloth, tie up and steam or boil for $1 1/2$ hours. Remove from heat, let rest for five minutes, unwrap, cut into $1/2$ in. (1 cm.) thick slices and serve with a sauceboat of the appropriate hot jam. *(Great Britain)*

Mousseline Pudding - Pudding Mousseline

6 persons:

$2 1/4$ oz. (60 gr.) butter
3 oz. (80 gr.) sugar
5 egg yolks and 4 egg whites

Cooking time: 15-20 minutes

Cream the butter with the sugar and flavour according to taste (vanilla, lemon, etc.). Add the egg yolks one at a time and stir slowly on a gentle heat until the mixture reaches a consistency of a custard cream and coats the spoon. Remove from the heat and fold in straight away the stiffly whisked egg whites. Grease and sprinkle with sugar a mould which is large enough to contain the mixture without being more than half to three quarters full. Bake in a bain-marie in the oven (320° F, 160° C) and before turning the pudding out of the mould, wait for it to collapse a little for it will have risen considerably. Serve with a sabayon.

(France)

Queen's Pudding

1 lb. 4 oz. (625 gr.) milk
4 oz. (125 gr.) bread crumbs
2 oz. (60 gr.) butter
2 oz. (60 gr.) sugar
3 egg yolks
4 egg whites
Zest of 2 lemons
Juice of 1 lemon

Line a pie dish with sweet pastry. Boil the milk and pour it over the crumbs. Add the butter, and sugar and the zest and cool the mixture. Stir in the yolks and let the mixture stand for 30 minutes. Fill the pie dish and bake until the mixture sets. Spread with raspberry jam. Sprinkle with the juice of the lemon. Spread with a meringue made from the whites and a little sugar and flash at 450° F (232° C).

(France)

Tapioca Pudding

6 persons:

1 ³/₄ pt. (8 dl.) milk
3 oz. (90 gr.) tapioca
4 ¹/₂ oz. (120 gr.) sugar
4 eggs
2 oz. (60 gr.) butter
Lemon zest or vanilla

Cooking time: 30 minutes

Cook the tapioca for 15 minutes in the milk, flavoured with lemon zest or vanilla. Mix in the butter and leave to cool a little. Incorporate the eggs beaten up with the sugar; pour into a pie dish and bake in a moderate oven in a bain-marie.

(Great Britain)

Saxon Soufflé Pudding - Pudding soufflé Saxon

(Basic recipe)
6 persons:

3 oz. (80 gr.) sugar
3 oz. (80 gr.) butter
3 oz. (80 gr.) sieved flour
1 ¹/₂ gills (2 dl.) milk
4 eggs
Vanilla
Salt

Cooking time: 30-35 minutes

Cream the butter, blend in the flour and pour over this paste the hot milk in which the vanilla has been infused. Mix until smooth and dry out over heat as for choux paste. Remove from heat and add the sugar, a pinch of salt and the egg yolks.

When the consistency of a thick custard is reached, fold in the very stiffly whisked egg whites. Pour into a greased pudding mould sprinkled with sugar, filling it three quarters full. Bake in a bain-marie in a fairly hot oven, without allowing the water to boil. Cover the pudding with oiled greaseproof paper when the top has become sufficiently coloured. During cooking, the pudding should rise 1 to 1 ¹/₂ in. (2.5-3 cm.) above the top of the mould. Let the pudding stand for a few minutes before turning it out of the mould on to a round dish. Serve with either a vanilla flavoured custard cream, kirsch flavoured apricot sauce or white wine sabayon. This is the basic recipe for all soufflé puddings.

(France)

Chocolate Soufflé Pudding - Pudding soufflé au Chocolat

6 persons:

2 ¹/₄ oz. (70 gr.) sugar
3 oz. (90 gr.) sifted flour
3 oz. (90 gr.) butter
1 ¹/₂ gills (2 dl.) milk
4 eggs
4 ¹/₂ oz. (140 gr.) chocolate
3 gills (4 dl.) vanilla flavoured custard cream or chocolate sauce

Cooking time: 30-35 minutes

Prepare in the same way as Saxon soufflé pudding, using chocolate dispersed in milk in place of vanilla. Serve with a vanilla custard cream or a chocolate sauce.

Chocolate Almond Soufflé Pudding - Pudding soufflé au Chocolat et aux Amandes

6 persons:

2 ³/₄ oz. (80 gr.) sugar
2 ³/₄ oz. (80 gr.) sieved flour
2 ³/₄ oz. (80 gr.) butter
1 ³/₄ gills (¹/₄ l.) milk
2 ¹/₂ oz. (75 gr.) chocolate
1 ³/₄ oz. (50 gr.) ground almonds
4 eggs
3 gills (4 dl.) custard sauce flavoured with vanilla, chocolate or praline

Cooking time: 30-35 minutes

Use the same method as for chocolate (soufflé) pudding, but add the ground almonds to the mixture together with the egg whites. Serve with one of the suggested sauces. *(France)*

Fleur de Marie Soufflé Pudding - Pudding soufflé Fleur de Marie

6 persons:

3 oz. (80 gr.) sugar
3 oz. (80 gr.) semolina
3 oz. (80 gr.) butter
4 egg yolks
3 egg whites
2 gills (¹/₄ l.) milk
Vanilla
Salt

Cooking time: 15-20 minutes

Cook the semolina in boiling milk flavoured with vanilla; when it has thickened, add the sugar and butter and then, removing from the heat, the egg yolks and stiffly whisked egg whites. Pour the mixture into a plain pudding mould with a central funnel, which has been first coated with light coloured caramel. Bake in a bain-marie and serve with a custard cream to which some more caramel has been added. *(France)*

Grand-Marnier Soufflé Pudding - Pudding soufflé au Grand-Marnier

6 persons:

3 oz. (80 gr.) sugar
3 oz. (80 gr.) sieved flour
3 oz. (80 gr.) butter
1 ¹/₂ gills (2 dl.) milk
4 eggs
Grated zest of ¹/₂ orange
2 ¹/₂ oz. (75 gr.) macaroons
²/₃ gill (4 cl.) Grand-Marnier

Cooking time: 30-35 minutes

Cut up the macaroons into small pieces and soak them in Grand-Marnier. Prepare the pudding mixtures as for Saxon pudding, having infused the orange zest in the milk. Amalgamate both mixtures and bake. Serve with a Grand-Marnier flavoured custard cream. *(France)*

Killarney Soufflé Pudding

1 lb. 2 oz. (500 gr.) cream cheese
1 lb. 2 oz. (500 gr.) cream
9 oz. (275 gr.) castor sugar
Grated zest of 1 lemon
1 liqueur glass rum
15 egg whites
4 ¹/₂ oz. (135 gr.) white flour
4 ¹/₂ oz. (135 gr.) cornflour
7 oz. (200 gr.) raisins
A little saffron

Strain the cheese through muslin, then put through a sieve and mix with the cream, sugar, lemon zest and rum. Lightly colour the egg whites with saffron, whip to a stiff snow, add the sieved flour and cornflour and then the raisins, previously well soaked. Fill round moulds three quarters full and bake in a bain-marie.

Serve the pudding hot, sprinkling it with rum and setting it alight at the table.

Hand round a good sabayon sauce separately. *(Ireland)*

Lemon Soufflé Pudding - Pudding soufflé au Citron

6 persons:

Follow the same method as for Saxon soufflé pudding, using grated lemon zest instead of vanilla. Serve with a lemon flavoured custard cream. *(France)*

Queen's Soufflé Pudding - Pudding soufflé à la Reine

6 persons :

3 oz. (80 gr.) sugar
3 oz. (80 gr.) flour
3 oz. (80 gr.) butter
1 1/2 gills (2 dl.) milk
4 eggs
Vanilla
3 macaroons
1 3/4 oz. (50 gr.) pistachio nuts
3 gills (4 dl.) custard cream or sabayon

Cooking time : 35 minutes

Follow the same method as for Saxon pudding, but add the broken pieces of macaroons. Generously grease a pudding mould with softened butter and stick the chopped pistachio nuts round the sides. Pour the mixture into this mould. When the pudding is cooked, a custard cream or sabayon is poured round it or served separately. *(France)*

Royal Soufflé Pudding - Pudding soufflé royal

6 persons :

Line the bottom and sides of a charlotte mould or a shallow tin with some thin slices of apricot jam Swiss roll. Fill with Saxon pudding mixture and bake in a bain-marie in the oven. Turn out on a round dish and top with a decoration made with choux paste. Serve separately an apricot sauce flavoured with Madeira or Muscatel wine. *(Germany)*

Sans-Souci Soufflé Pudding - Pudding soufflé Sans-Souci

6 persons :

Follow the same method as for Saxon pudding, adding to the mixture together with the egg whites, 5 oz. (150 gr.) diced russet apples which have been cooked in butter. Serve with a vanilla flavoured custard cream.

Taiwan Soufflé Pudding - Pudding soufflé Taiwan

6 persons :

2 1/4 oz. (60 gr.) sugar
3 oz. (80 gr.) sieved flour
3 oz. (80 gr.) butter
1 1/2 gills (1/4 l.) milk
3 oz. (80 gr.) chocolate
2 oz. (60 gr.) finely diced stem ginger
3 gills (4 dl.) custard cream flavoured with syrup of stem ginger

Cooking time : 30-35 minutes

Prepare in the same way as Saxon soufflé pudding, using chocolate dispersed in milk and adding the diced stem ginger. Serve with custard cream flavoured with syrup of stem ginger.

SOUFFLÉS

There are two different types of soufflés—those based on a custard mixture and those made with a fruit purée.

To prepare a fruit soufflé mixture, the sugar is boiled to the crack degree and the fruit purée is added, causing the sugar to cool to the hard ball degree. If it cools below this degree, boiling must continue until the hard ball degree is reached before adding the stiffly whisked egg whites, otherwise the mixture would be too thin. Soufflé mixtures are filled into buttered soufflé cases or silver soufflé moulds that have been sprinkled with sugar and baked in a moderate oven so that the heat penetrates right through to the middle. Shortly before they are ready, soufflés are dusted with icing sugar to caramelize the surface lightly.

A soufflé must always be served immediately as it quickly collapses. To delay collapse, at least for a time, it is advisable to start baking the soufflé in a shallow bain-marie, removing it later on to finish baking.

Apple Soufflé - Soufflé aux Pommes

Prepare a fairly sweet, thick, reduced apple purée. To 9 oz. (275 gr.) of this purée, add 4 egg yolks and 3 stiffly whisked egg whites. Bake in the same way as other soufflés. To obtain a thicker mixture, a little frangipane or confectioner's custard may be mixed with the purée.

Cécilia Soufflé - Soufflé Cécilia

6 persons :

2 gills ($^1/_4$ l.) milk
1 $^1/_4$ oz. (40 gr.) flour
4 $^1/_2$ oz. (140 gr.) sugar
4 egg yolks
6 egg whites
3 $^1/_2$ oz. (100 gr.) hazelnuts
6 sponge fingers
Chartreuse
1 $^1/_2$ oz. (45 gr.) butter

Cooking time : 18-20 minutes

Proceed as for vanilla soufflé, but mix the milk first with the lightly roasted, ground and sifted hazelnuts. Fill the soufflé case with alternate layers of the soufflé mixture and sponge fingers splashed copiously with Chartreuse. *(France)*

Chocolate Soufflé - Soufflé au Chocolat

Follow the same method as for a vanilla soufflé, but add 2 $^3/_4$ oz. (80 gr.) chocolate to the milk and use $^3/_4$ oz. (20 gr.) less sugar, to allow for that in the chocolate; 1 more egg white should be used.

Cingalese Soufflé - Soufflé cingalais

6 persons :

3 gills (4 dl.) tea
2 $^1/_4$ oz. (70 gr.) flour
4 $^1/_2$ oz. (140 gr.) sugar
4 egg yolks
6 egg whites
7 sponge fingers
Rum

Cooking time : 18-20 minutes

Proceed in the same way as for a vanilla soufflé, replacing the milk by strong tea. Place in the centre of a soufflé case the sponge fingers which have been well soaked in rum.

Coffee Soufflé - Soufflé au Café

Follow the same method as for a vanilla soufflé, replacing half the milk by very strong coffee or adding a good tablespoonful of coffee powder or essence.

Colette Soufflé - Soufflé Colette

6 persons :

2 oz. (60 gr.) sugar
2 oz. (60 gr.) chocolate
2 $^1/_2$ oz. (75 gr.) ground almonds
1 $^1/_2$ oz. (40 gr.) flour
1 $^1/_2$ oz. (40 gr.) butter
1 $^1/_2$ gills (2 dl.) milk
4 egg yolks
6 egg whites
$^3/_4$ pt. (4 dl.) port flavoured sabayon

Follow the same method as for a vanilla soufflé. Serve together with a sabayon flavoured with white port. *(France)*

Estoril Soufflé - Soufflé Estoril

6-8 persons :

3 gills (4 dl.) milk
2 oz. (60 gr.) flour
2 oz. (60 gr.) butter
3 $^1/_2$ oz. (100 gr.) sugar
2 oz. (60 gr.) chocolate
2 oz. (60 gr.) hazelnut praline, ground and sieved
4 egg yolks
6 egg whites

Cooking time : 17-20 minutes

Melt the chocolate in the milk and proceed in the same way as for confectioner's custard and add the hazelnut praline. Let the mixture cool slowly before folding in the stiffly whisked egg whites. Pour into a soufflé dish which has been greased and sprinkled with sugar. Bake in a moderate oven and serve with a sabayon with port wine. *(Germany)*

Fruit Soufflé - Soufflé aux Fruits

(made with strawberries, raspberries, apricots, etc.)

6 persons :

9 oz. (275 gr.) thick fruit purée
7 oz. (200 gr.) sugar
Vanilla
5 egg whites

Cooking time : 18-20 minutes

Boil the sugar to the small crack degree and add the fruit purée. Pour on to the very stiffly whisked egg whites and mix together. Bake in the same way as other soufflés. If the addition of the fruit purée causes the sugar to cool below the hard ball degree, boil a little more until the small crack degree is reached again.

(France)

Grand-Marnier Soufflé - Soufflé au Grand-Marnier

6 persons:

3 oz. (80 gr.) sugar
1 ¹/₂ oz. (40 gr.) flour
1 ¹/₂ oz. (40 gr.) butter
1 ¹/₂ gills (2 dl.) milk
Grated zest of 1 small orange
¹/₂ gill (5 cl.) Grand-Marnier
4 broken large macaroons
4 egg yolks
5 large egg whites

Cooking time: 18-20 minutes

Soak the large pieces of macaroons in ¹/₄ gill (2.5 cl.) of the Grand-Marnier. Add to the mixture the orange zest and the other half of the Grand-Marnier together with the egg yolks. When filling the soufflé case, introduce layers of the macaroons. *(France)*

Jacqueline Soufflé - Soufflé Jacqueline

6 persons:

3 oz. (80 gr.) sugar
1 ¹/₂ oz. (40 gr.) flour
1 ¹/₂ oz. (40 gr.) butter
1 ¹/₂ gills (2 dl.) milk
6 egg yolks
5 egg whites
Vanilla
3 ¹/₂ oz. (100 gr.) strawberries (wild if possible)

Cooking time: 22-25 minutes

Use the same method as for vanilla soufflé, but add 2 more egg yolks and make the mixture thicker. Mix in the strawberry purée before folding in the egg whites. Bake in the same way as other soufflés. Serve together with strawberries macerated in sugar and kirsch. *(France)*

Lemon, Clementine or Orange Soufflé - Soufflé au Citron, aux Clémentines, à l'Orange

Proceed in the same way as for a vanilla soufflé, but flavour the milk with lemon, clementine or orange zest, which should not, however, be cooked as it would make the soufflé taste bitter. *(France)*

Palmyra Soufflé - Soufflé Palmyre

Proceed in the same way as for a vanilla soufflé. When pouring the mixture into the soufflé case, add alternate layers of sponge fingers cut into pieces and soaked in aniseed liqueur.

Semolina Soufflé - Soufflé de Semoule

1 pt. (¹/₂ l.) milk
3 ¹/₂ oz. (100 gr.) semolina
1 pinch of salt
¹/₂ vanilla pod
³/₄ oz. (25 gr.) butter
7 egg yolks
9 egg whites
2 ¹/₂ oz. (75 gr.) sugar

Boil up the milk with the vanilla, add the semolina, mix thoroughly and cook for 10 minutes over gentle heat. Remove the vanilla, stir in the butter and 1 oz. (25 gr.) sugar, remove from the heat and add the egg yolks. Whisk the egg whites to a stiff snow with 1 ¹/₂ oz. (50 gr.) sugar, fold in the cooked mixture, fill into buttered moulds and poach in a bain-marie in the oven. Serve with any desired sauce.

(Switzerland)

Strawberry Soufflé - Soufflé aux Fraises

4-6 portions:

12 oz. (275 gr.) strawberry purée
7 oz. (200 gr.) sugar
5 egg whites

Baking time: 18-20 minutes

Boil the sugar to the crack degree, mix with the strawberry purée and measure the temperature. If the ball degree has not been reached, continue boiling until it is. Allow to cool a little, then fold in the egg whites whisked to a stiff snow. Pour at once into a buttered soufflé case that has been sprinkled with sugar and bake in a moderate oven.

Proceed in the same way for raspberry, apricot and other fruit soufflés. *(France)*

Tyrolean Rice Soufflé - Tyroler Reisauflauf

3 1/2 gills (1/2 l.) milk
5 oz. (150 gr.) rice
2 oz. (60 gr.) butter
3 1/2 oz. (100 gr.) sugar
5 egg yolks
5 egg whites whipped to a snow
1 oz. (30 gr.) soft white bread crumbs
Salt
Vanilla
Lemon zest

Place the rice in the cold milk with the butter, salt, vanilla and a piece of lemon zest. Cook slowly for about 30 minutes. Remove the vanilla and lemon zest. Leave until fairly cool, then stir in the egg yolks and half the sugar. When quite cold, blend in the whipped egg whites, the remaining sugar and the bread crumbs. Fill a well-buttered, floured soufflé mould three quarters full and bake in a moderate oven. When the soufflé is cooked, brush the top with red bilberry jam, cover with Italian meringue and flash.
(Austria)

Vanilla Soufflé - Soufflé à la Vanille
(Basic recipe)

Recipe 1. 6 persons:
3 oz. (80 gr.) sugar
1 1/2 oz. (40 gr.) flour
1 1/2 oz. (40 gr.) butter
1 1/2 gills (2 dl.) milk
4 egg yolks
5 egg whites
Vanilla

Cooking time: 22-25 minutes

Melt a knob of butter, mix in the flour and then immediately pour in the milk which has been boiled with the vanilla. Add the sugar and stir briskly over heat until it comes to the boil. Remove from the heat, add the egg yolks, the rest of the butter and the very stiffly whisked egg whites. Stir the mixture vigorously to make it less light, as otherwise it would collapse before it was baked. Pour into a greased soufflé case which has been sprinkled with sugar, until it is three quarters full. Bake in a medium oven. This dessert must be served as soon as it comes out of the oven. As they say, a guest may wait for the soufflé, but the soufflé cannot wait. Cooking may be started in a bain-marie, but to finish a soufflé, it must be baked for 5-8 minutes out of water before it is served.

Recipe 2. 6-8 persons:
3 gills (1/2 l.) milk
2 3/4 oz. (85 gr.) flour
4 1/2 oz. (125 gr.) sugar
2 oz. (60 gr.) butter
1 egg
4 egg yolks
6 egg whites
Pinch powdered vanilla

Cooking time: 17-20 minutes

Proceed in the same way as for confectioner's custard. Let the mixture cool slowly before delicately folding in the very stiffly whisked egg whites. Pour into a soufflé dish which has been greased and sprinkled with sugar. Bake in a moderate oven.
(Illustration page 659.)

STRUDEL

Strudel

Dough 20-25 portions:
10 1/2 oz. (300 gr.) flour
1 3/4 oz. (50 gr.) either butter, margarine, lard or oil
1 egg
1 pinch of salt
1/4 pt. (1/8 l.) lukewarm water

Strudel dough is fairly simple to prepare, but requires somewhat sensitive fingers, as the finished article, especially its appearance, depends on the way the dough

▲ Bettina Tartlets, p. 743

Rhubarb Pie, p. 681 ▼

690 ▲ Orange Tart, p. 739

Strawberry Tart and Tartlets, p. 741 ▼

▲ Bilberry Meringue Tart, p. 739

Swabian Apple Tart, p. 736 ▼

691

692 ▲ Pralines « Lufthansa », p. 617

Fondants (Roomborstplaat), p. 631 ▼

is worked. The quality of the flour is important; strong flour is the best type to use.

Prepare a smooth dough from the above ingredients. The dough should not be too stiff; the amount of water will depend on the absorptive capacity of the flour. Mould the dough round, oil the surface and leave it to rest for a good half hour.

Pin out the dough as thinly as possible on a cloth dusted with flour and then stretch it carefully by hand to paper thinness.

Filling and baking the strudel

Cover two thirds of the dough with the filling; the remaining third is used to seal the strudel well after rolling. If the strudel is to be filled with fruit, first sprinkle the surface with toasted bread crumbs to absorb the fruit juice (if the fruit is very juicy, use untoasted bread crumbs sprinkled with a few drops of fat). Other types of filling are placed directly on the dough. Brush the uncovered part of the dough with melted butter to give the outside of the strudel a finer, crisper finish.

After spreading the filling over the surface, trim the edges and roll up with the help of the cloth, starting with the part covered with filling. Deposit on a greased tin or baking sheet. If the strudel is to be poached, leave it in the cloth until it is used. If it is baked in the oven, it should be brushed with lukewarm butter mixed with a well-beaten egg to make the crust more delicate and give it a more appetizing appearance. It is generally baked in a moderate oven.

Apple Strudel - Apfelstrudel

6 persons:

Strudel dough:

3 ½ oz. (100 gr.) butter or fat
3 ½ oz. (100 gr.) bread crumbs
2 lb. (1 kg.) apples
3 ½ oz. (100 gr.) sugar mixed with ground cinnamon (more or less sugar according to the acidity of the apples)
3 ½ oz. (100 gr.) raisins
A little rum to taste

Toast the bread crumbs in the butter or fat and sprinkle on the dough. Cover with the finely sliced apples, sprinkle with cinnamon and raisins and splash with a little rum. Roll up and finish off as above.

(Austria)

Old Vienna Apple Strudel - Altwiener Apfelstrudel

This special type of strudel is made in the same way as ordinary apple strudel, except that the apples are covered with sour cream, making the strudel softer, tastier and more nourishing. *(Austria)*

Cherry Strudel - Kirschenstrudel

Proceed as for apple strudel, using 2 lb. (1 kg.) cherries instead of apples. The flavour is better if the cherries are not stoned.

(Austria)

Curd Strudel - Topfenstrudel

8 portions:

5 oz. (150 gr.) butter
5 oz. (150 gr.) sugar
1 lb. 4 oz. (600 gr.) cheese curd
6 rolls without crust
3 ½ oz. (100 gr.) raisins
Sour cream
6 egg yolks
6 egg whites
Zest of ½ lemon
1 pinch of salt
Strudel dough

Baking time: 30-35 minutes

Beat the butter, half the sugar, the egg yolks, salt and grated lemon zest together until foamy. Mix with the sieved curd, the rolls which have been soaked in milk, squeezed dry and sieved, the sour cream and raisins. Lastly fold in the egg whites whisked to a stiff snow with the rest of the sugar. Spread this filling to the thickness of one finger on the strudel dough, which should not be sprinkled with bread crumbs; roll up and bake. Vanilla sauce may be served as an accompaniment.

(Austria)

Lower Austrian Strudel with Custard Sauce - Niederösterreichischer Strudel

Dough:

10 oz. (300 gr.) flour
1 oz. (30 gr.) oil
1 egg
1 pinch of salt
A few drops of vinegar
Approx. 1/4 pt. (1/8 l.) lukewarm water

Filling:

7 oz. (200 gr.) butter
7 oz. (200 gr.) sugar
6 egg yolks
6 egg whites whipped to a snow
2 oz. (60 gr.) currants
1 1/4 gill (2 dl.) sour cream
2 1/2 oz. (75 gr.) bread crumbs
Juice and grated zest of 1 lemon

Custard sauce:

Approx. 1 3/4 pt. (1 l.) milk
2 whole eggs
2 egg yolks
3 1/2 oz. (100 gr.) sugar
A vanilla bean
A little butter to grease the baking sheet and brush the strudel

Make the flour, oil, eggs mixed with the water, and the remaining ingredients into a soft dough on a pastry board and knead until smooth. Brush with oil and leave to rest for about half an hour on a corner of the board. Meanwhile, prepare the filling: beat the butter, sugar and egg yolks together until frothy, add the lemon juice and grated zest and then the sour cream and bread crumbs alternately. Lastly fold in the whipped egg whites very lightly.

Place a cloth on the table, sprinkle with flour, put the dough on it and punch down a little. Pin out very thinly to the edge of the table. Trim off the thick pieces round the edges and cover with the filling, leaving a narrow strip uncovered (about a quarter of the paste). Finally, add the currants and roll up, starting with the portion covered with filling. Place the strudel on a buttered baking sheet and brush with melted butter. Mix the ingredients for the custard sauce together thoroughly and pour a little over the strudel here and there when it is partly cooked so that it is steamed rather than baked for the remainder of the cooking process. Boil the rest of the custard sauce, beating until light and frothy, and pour over the strudel when about to serve.

(Austria)

Note: Strudels may be served hot or cold. Cold strudels are generally served with whipped dairy cream.

TARTS

These tarts can be served either hot or cold. (Tarts to be served cold, *see page 734*).

American Apple Tart - Tarte aux Pommes à l'américaine

1 lb. (500 gr.) sweet short pastry
2 lb. (1 kg.) apples
3 1/2 oz. (100 gr.) apricot jam

Shape the pastry into a square, moisten the edges, cover them with a rope of pastry the thickness of the little finger and crimp. Peel the apples, cut them in quarters, core them and cut into slices. Place these on the pastry, making sure that the slices forming the top layer are symmetrically arranged, each overlapping the other. Bake in a hot oven and glaze with apricot jam while still hot. *(France)*

Apple Curd Tarts

8 oz. (250 gr.) apple pulp
2 oz. (60 gr.) butter
3 oz. (90 gr.) sugar (approx.)
2 oz. (60 gr.) egg

Mix all together and fill into sweet paste lined sandwich plates as for Dilston Tarts *(page 695)*. Bake at 400° F (204° C). When baked, cover with meringue and flash.

Christmas Pie

Fermented puff pastry *(page 178)*
Mincemeat
Egg whites
Castor sugar

Pin out the pastry to about 1/8 in. (3 mm.) thick and cut circles to form the tops. Pin out the cuttings to about the same thickness and line flan rings. Fill with mincemeat, damp the edges of the pastry and fix the tops. Brush liberally with egg whites beaten with a little water and dust well with castor sugar. Make two holes in the top to allow the escape of steam and bake at 400° F (204° C), after proving for 15-20 minutes.

This pie can be served hot or cold with rum or brandy flavoured whipped dairy cream. *(Great Britain)*
(Illustration page 564.)

Dilston Tarts

1 lb. (500 gr.) butter
1 lb. 2 oz. (560 gr.) sugar
1 lb. (500 gr.) egg
14 oz. (400 gr.) mashed potatoes
4 oz. (125 gr.) flour
Salt

Line 7 in. sandwich plates or flan rings with sweet pastry. Spread a layer of lemon curd on the base of each and fill with the above mixture, which is made by creaming the butter and sugar lightly and adding the egg a little at a time. The potato, flour and salt are then blended in. Bake at 400° F (204° C).

Golden Tarts

Fill plates lined as above with a mixture of golden syrup and bread crumbs, flavoured with lemon juice. The mixture should be of just flowing consistency. Decorate with a trellis design made from strips of sweet pastry. Bake at 380° F (193° C).
(Illustration page 564.) *(Great Britain)*

Orleans Custard Tarts

Line plates as above and spread with raspberry jam. Three quarters fill with egg custard *(page 238)*, sprinkle with a little ground nutmeg and bake at 380° F (193° C).

Yorkshire Curd Tarts

6 oz. (180 gr.) sugar
6 oz. (180 gr.) butter
6 oz. (180 gr.) egg
1 lb. (500 gr.) milk curd
2 oz. (60 gr.) ground rice
4 oz. (125 gr.) currants
Zest and juice of 1 lemon
Nutmeg

Line large patty pans with sweet pastry. Cream the butter and sugar and add the egg gradually. Blend in the curd that has been well drained and sieved. Add the rice, currants, nutmeg, zest and juice. Fill into the shells and bake until the filling sets firmly at 390° F (200° C).
(Illustration page 658.) *(Great Britain)*

Various Hot Sweets

Buchteln (fine)

1 lb. 2 oz. (560 gr.) flour
9 oz. (280 gr.) butter
3 1/2 oz. (100 gr.) icing sugar
4 oz. (125 gr.) egg yolks
1 oz. (30 gr.) yeast
Zest of 1 lemon
Salt
Milk as required

Make a ferment with the yeast, a little flour and as much milk as required and leave to rise. Warm the rest of the flour, pour it into a bowl, make a bay, place the ferment in it, dust it lightly with flour, cover with a cloth and leave to rise again. Add the remaining ingredients to the flour, melting the butter first, and work all the materials to a semi-firm dough with some tepid milk. Cover with a cloth and leave to develop well, then transfer to a floured board or a table. Pin out about 3/4 in. (2 cm.) thick, cut into portions of suitable size and spread each piece with poppyseed, nut or curd filling as desired, or else with jam if preferred. Fold the ends up to enclose the filling, arrange close together on a greased baking sheet, prove well and bake in a medium oven.

Alternatively, the Buchteln may be made with Carinthian Reinling dough *(see page 263).* *(Austria)*

Cannoli - Ticino Style

Filling:

7 oz. (200 gr.) finely ground almonds
8 oz. (250 gr.) sponge cake cuttings
3 ½ oz. (100 gr.) finely crushed amaretti
3 ½ oz. (100 gr.) finely chopped orange peel
Milk

Dough:

1 lb. (500 gr.) flour
3 ½ oz. (100 gr.) fine semolina
¾ gill (1 dl.) oil
4 eggs
⅔ gill (7 cl.) milk

Pancake butter:

1 lb. (500 gr.) butter
1 lb. (500 gr.) icing sugar
Juice of 1 lemon

Pin out the noodle dough very thinly and cut into rectangles 2 ½ × 3 in. (6 × 8 cm.). Poach in lightly salted water for a few minutes, place in cold water at once, drain and dry well on a cloth.

Bring the filling to a spreading consistency with the milk, then pipe on to the noodle rectangles lengthwise, using a large plain tube. Roll up, pour the melted pancake butter over, flash in a hot oven, sprinkle with a few crushed amaretti and dust with icing sugar. *(Switzerland)*

Clafoutis limousin

6 persons:

1 lb. 4 oz. (600 gr.) black cherries
3 ½ oz. (100 gr.) sugar
1 ¾ oz. (50 gr.) flour
1 ¾ gills (¼ l.) milk
2 eggs
Vanilla
Salt

Mix the flour, sugar and the eggs, which are added one at a time, a pinch of salt, a little vanilla and the cold milk. When the ingredients have been thoroughly blended, pass the mixture through a conical sieve to eliminate any lumps. Meanwhile, stone the very ripe cherries, put them in an oven-proof, shallow pan and pour the mixture over. Sprinkle with sugar and place in a medium oven. This dessert may be served either warm or cold. Clafoutis may also be put in a dish lined with short paste, but this it not the authentic recipe. *(France)*

Emperor's Dessert - Kaiserschmarren

4 ½ oz. (140 gr.) butter
4 oz. (125 gr.) sugar
6 egg yolks
½ pt. (¼ l.) milk
1 pinch of salt
5 ½ oz. (165 gr.) flour
4 egg whites
Zest of ½ lemon
1 ¾ oz. (50 gr.) raisins

Beat the butter, sugar, salt and lemon zest together until foamy. Add the egg yolks in small portions and the milk and flour a spoonful at a time. Whisk the egg whites to a stiff snow and fold in together with the raisins. Pour into a well buttered shallow baking pan and bake in a moderate oven for about 40 minutes. After baking, cut or tear into cubes, sprinkle with sugar and serve with stewed fruit.

(Austria)

Fried Custard - Crème frite

6 persons:

3 ½ oz. (100 gr.) sugar
2 ¼ oz. (60 gr.) rice flour
2 whole eggs
2 gills (3 dl.) milk
Vanilla or other flavouring

Cooking time: 3-4 minutes

Whip the eggs and sugar, add the sifted rice flour and then the milk and flavouring. Boil for a moment to thicken the mixture to the consistency of a paste. Spread the mixture about ½ in. (1.5 cm.) thick on a greased and floured baking sheet and leave to cool. Divide into small diamond-shaped pieces, dip first into flour, then into beaten eggs and finally coat with white bread crumbs. Fry in very hot deep fat; just before serving, sprinkle with sugar.

(France)

Jam Puffs - Rissoles aux Fruits

6 persons:
14 oz. (400 gr.) puff paste
8 oz. (250 gr.) thick jam
Cooking time: 3-5 minutes

Roll out some scraps of puff paste to a thickness of $1/10$ in. (2.5 mm.) and cut out with a round, fluted pastry cutter; moisten all round and put in the middle of each piece some fruit purée or jam; fold the paste over in half as for turnovers and press down well to seal. Fry in extremely hot fat or bake in the oven; however, in the latter case, they are, strictly speaking, turnovers. Jam puffs may also be made with Krapfen dough filled with strawberry jam and they are known as dauphine jam puffs. Dust with icing sugar before serving.

Kesari Bhata - Sweet Rice Indian Style

5 oz. (150 gr.) rice
$3 \:^1/_2$ oz. (100 gr.) butter
1 oz. (30 gr.) raisins or sultanas
1 oz. (30 gr.) finely shredded blanched almonds
1 orange
1 tablespoon sugar
$^1/_2$ pt. ($^1/_4$ l.) water
1 pinch of salt
A little saffron

Cook the rice slowly for a few minutes in half the butter in a covered pan, add the water and boil for about 5 minutes. Add the orange flesh cut into cubes, together with the raisins or sultanas and cook for a further 10 minutes. Just before serving, carefully stir in the orange zest, finely chopped, the almonds, sugar, saffron and the rest of the butter. *(India)*

Prague Cakes - Livancen

6 persons:
10 oz. (300 gr.) flour
2 eggs
$1 \:^3/_4$ oz. (50 gr.) sugar
$1 \:^1/_2$ pt. ($^3/_4$ l.) lukewarm milk
$^3/_4$ oz. (20 gr.) yeast
Plum or other jam
Butter

Livancen are a well-known Czechoslovakian speciality similar to Russian blinis except for the fact that, unlike these, they are spread with sweet fruit purée before serving. Break down the yeast in the tepid milk and mix with the eggs, butter, lemon zest, sugar and salt. Beat well and work in the flour to make a fairly slack dough. Leave in a warm place to ferment for 1-2 hours. Cook gently in butter on both sides in small tartlet pans or special small frying pans.

Serve with jam, sweetened cream cheese or slightly sweetened sour cream flavoured with a little cinnamon.
(Czechoslovakia)

Rice Condé - Riz Condé

6 persons:
$6 \:^1/_2$ oz. (175-200 gr.) rice
4 oz. (120 gr.) vanilla sugar
$1 \:^3/_4$ pt. (1 l.) milk
$1 \:^3/_4$ oz. (50 gr.) butter
4 egg yolks
Cooking time: about 25 minutes

Blanch the rice in water for 3 minutes, drain, rinse and cook with the milk, sugar and a pinch of salt in a covered stew pan in the oven. As soon as the rice is cooked, add the butter and the egg yolks, stirring carefully so as not to break the grains of rice. This rice, which is usually served with fruit desserts, may also be served as a dessert on its own. *(France)*

Savarin rubané

6 persons:
1 savarin
1 lb. (500 gr.) macédoine of fruit
1 gill ($1 \:^1/_2$ dl.) thick apricot sauce
Syrup flavoured with brandy
$1 \:^1/_2$ tablespoons brandy
2 gills (3 dl.) sabayon flavoured with Grand-Marnier
$1 \:^1/_2$ oz. (40 gr.) chopped pistachio nuts

Soak the hot savarin in hot brandy flavoured syrup and place it on a round dish. Heat up the macédoine, drain and bind with thick apricot sauce flavoured with brandy. Glaze the savarin with apricot sauce, sprinkle with chopped pistachio nuts and fill the macédoine into the hollow. Serve the sabayon separately. *(France)*

Savarin Taiwan

6 persons:

1 savarin
1 lb. 4 oz. (600 gr.) pineapple
Syrup flavoured with curaçao
1/4 gill (4 cl.) curaçao
Cornflour
2 gills (3 dl.) hot orange sauce
1 1/2 oz. (40 gr.) blanched, shredded almonds

Dice the pineapple, poach in vanilla flavoured syrup, reduce the syrup, thicken slightly with cornflour and flavour with curaçao. Soak the hot savarin in hot syrup flavoured with curaçao and dress on a round dish. Fill the centre with the pineapple, mask the border of the savarin with orange sauce and scatter the shredded almonds on top. Serve remaining orange sauce separately.

Savarins may also be baked in individual moulds. *(Germany)*

Semolina Subrics - Soubrics de Semoule

6 persons:

1 pt. (1/2 l.) milk
3 1/2 oz. (100 gr.) sugar
4 oz. (125 gr.) semolina
2 oz. (50 gr.) butter
Vanilla
1 whole egg
3 egg yolks
Cooking time: 5-6 minutes

Sprinkle the semolina into the milk boiled up with the sugar and vanilla. Add the butter and finish cooking in a slow oven. Remove from the heat and thicken with the egg and egg yolks; spread on a greased baking sheet and leave to cool. Cut the mixture up into round, square or diamond shapes and fry in butter on both sides. Drain, dress on a dish and serve red currant, quince or apple jelly separately.
(France)

Timbale Bourdaloue

6 persons:

1 lb. 4 oz. (600 gr.) milanese paste
1 pt. (1/2 l.) frangipane cream
14 oz. (400 gr.) stewed and drained fruit
1/2 pt. (1/4 l.) kirsch flavoured apricot sauce
Cooking time: 40-45 minutes

Line a greased charlotte mould with milanese paste. Prick the bottom with a fork and fill three quarters full with alternate layers of frangipane cream and fruit, such as apricots, peaches, pineapple, etc., cut into rather large pieces. There should be three layers of cream and two of fruit.

Cover with a round piece of milanese paste, egg-wash and bake in a hot oven. Allow to stand for a moment before turning the timbale out on a round dish. Mask with a little apricot sauce and serve the remainder separately.

Tutti-Frutti Rissoles - Rissoles Tutti-Frutti

Pin out puff pastry 1/8 in. (3 mm.) thick and cut out with a round cutter. Mix confectioner's custard with a generous amount of finely chopped candied fruit and pipe on to the centre of the puff pastry circles, using a savoy bag. Brush the edges with egg, fold over to a half-moon shape, brush with egg again and, if desired, mark with a fork. Bake in a hot oven or deep-fry in hot fat and dredge lightly with vanilla icing sugar. Serve vanilla sauce separately as an accompaniment.

Cold Desserts

BAVARIAN CREAMS - LES BAVAROIS

These are very light creams which are filled into moulds, chilled and turned out. They may be made solely with cream or with the addition of fruit.

Plain Bavarian Cream I - Bavarois à la Crème

(Basic recipe)

6 persons:

3 egg yolks
4 oz. (125 gr.) sugar
½ pt. (3 dl.) milk
8 sheets gelatine
¾ pt. (4 dl.) whipped cream
½ vanilla bean

Beat up the egg yolks and the sugar until they are paler in colour. Add the milk, in which the vanilla bean has been infused, stir until the custard begins to coat the spatula, remove from heat and add the soaked gelatine. Leave to cool and, when the custard begins to set, fold in the whipped cream. Moisten a mould with cold water and pour in the mixture. Leave the cream in cold storage for a few hours before turning it out.

Bavarian cream may be flavoured with chocolate, coffee, praline, pistachios, almonds, etc., instead of vanilla.

Plain Bavarian Cream II - Bavarois à la Crème

1 ¾ pt. (1 l.) milk
4 oz. (250 gr.) sugar
6 egg yolks
12 sheets gelatine
Liqueur
2 ½ pt. (1 ½ l.) whipped dairy cream

Boil up the milk with the sugar, keeping back a little cold milk. Mix this with the egg yolks, pour in the hot milk and cook over gentle heat until the custard will coat the spatula. Stir in the soaked gelatine and leave to cool. When the custard begins to set, stir until smooth, flavour with liqueur or a spirit as desired, fold in the whipped cream and pour into moulds at once.

(Switzerland)

Apricot Bavarian Cream - Bavarois Apricota

6 portions:

8 oz. (250 gr.) apricot purée
4 oz. (125 gr.) icing sugar
Juice of ½ lemon
9 sheets gelatine
¾ pt. (4 dl.) whipped dairy cream
3 ½ oz. (100 gr.) sponge fingers or stale sponge cake
2 gills (3 dl.) curaçao
3 tablespoons apricot jam

For decoration:

Crystallized apricots
Whipped dairy cream

Mix the apricot purée, sugar and lemon juice together until the sugar has dissolved. Stir in the gelatine that has been soaked and dissolved in very little water. Cut up the sponge fingers coarsely and soak them in the curaçao. As soon as the purée has begun to set, blend in the whipped cream and fill into a mould alternately with layers of sponge fingers and apricot jam. Turn out when set and decorate with pieces of crystallized apricot and with whipped cream.

(Germany)

Cherry Bavarian Cream - Bavarois Cerisette

6 persons:

Bavarian cream
¼ gill (4 cl.) kirsch
3 ½ oz. (100 gr.) cherries in cognac

Flavour the Bavarian cream with kirsch and add the stoned cherries cut in halves.

Chocolate Bavarian Cream - Bavarois au Chocolat

Proceed in the same way as for Bavarian cream, but use ¾ oz. (20 gr.) less sugar and add ½ oz. (15 gr.) melted milk chocolate to the custard cream.

Coffee Flavoured Bavarian Cream - Bavarois au Café

Proceed in the same way as for Bavarian cream, but add a tablespoonful of coffee powder or essence.

Diplomat Bavarian Cream - Bavarois Diplomate

3 egg yolks
4 ½ oz. (125 gr.) sugar

¹/₂ pt. (3 dl.) milk
8 sheets gelatine
3 ¹/₂ oz. (100 gr.) finely diced candied fruit
2 ¹/₂ oz. (75 gr.) sponge fingers
¹/₄ gill (4 cl.) kirsch
Vanilla
³/₄ pt. (4 dl.) whipped cream

Prepare a vanilla Bavarian cream. Break the sponge fingers into pieces and soak them in kirsch. Fill a mould with alternate layers of Bavarian cream and pieces of sponge fingers and diced candied fruit. Decorate with Chantilly cream, sponge fingers and candied fruit. *(Germany)*
(Illustration page 66.)

Fruit Bavarian Cream - Bavarois aux Fruits

6 persons:

8 oz. (250 gr.) purée of fresh fruit
4 oz. (125 gr.) icing sugar
Juice of ¹/₂ lemon
8-10 sheets gelatine
³/₄ pt. (4 dl.) whipped cream

Rub the fruit through a hair sieve, mix it with the icing sugar, lemon juice and finally with the melted gelatine. Leave to cool down and when half set, fold in the whipped cream and pour into a mould.

Fruit Bavarois - Vruchten Bavarois

1 lb. 2 oz. (560 gr.) strawberry pulp 25 % sweetened
¹/₂ oz. (15 gr.) gelatine
1 lb. 2 oz. (560 gr.) whipped cream
2 oz. (60 gr.) sugar

This pudding can be made as well with raspberry pulp, pineapple juice, orange juice, etc.

First soak the gelatine in water. Whip the cream with sugar until not quite stiff. As soon as the gelatine is soft, dissolve it in a double-boiler and then mix it immediately with the strawberry pulp. At the same time add a few drops of lemon juice and colour more vividly with red food colouring. As soon as the mixture starts to set add the whipped cream carefully.

Pour the mixture into the moulds and allow it to chill. When the pudding is set, put the moulds in a pot with hot water for a little while, turn upside-down and turn out on to plates. Pipe the bavaroise with whipped cream and decorate with strawberries (fresh if possible). *(Holland)*

Layer Bavarian Cream - Bavarois rubané

Proceed in the same way as for Bavarian cream. Divide the mixture into four parts, flavouring them respectively with vanilla, chocolate, pistachio and coffee. Care should be taken to ensure that the layers do not mix. A similar effect may be obtained using other Bavarian cream mixtures.

Nesselrode Bavarian Cream - Bavarois Nesselrode

Proceed in the same way as for basic Bavarian cream, adding 2 extra sheets gelatine and ³/₄ oz. (20 gr.) sugar. Blend in chestnut purée. When the dessert is turned out of the mould, it can be decorated with marrons glacés and Chantilly cream. *(France)*

Orange Bavarian Cream - Bavarois à l'Orange

3 egg yolks
4 oz. (125 gr.) sugar
Grated zest of 1 choice orange
Juice of 1 orange
¹/₂ pt. (¹/₄ l.) milk
¹/₄ oz. (8 gr.) gelatine
³/₄ pt. (4 dl.) whipped cream

For decoration:

³/₄ gill (7 cl.) whipped cream
12 orange segments
A few poached red cherries

Proceed in the same way as for Bavarian cream, but infuse the orange zest in the milk. When the preparation is completely cold, flavour with the orange juice and then add the whipped cream. When it is turned out, the dessert is decorated with Chantilly cream, orange segments and cherries. *(Germany)*

Pistachio Bavarian Cream - Bavarois aux Pistaches

Proceed in the same way as for vanilla Bavarian cream, but add to the custard cream 2 oz. (60 gr.) blanched and finely ground pistachio nuts with a little kirsch.

Tea Bavarian Cream - Bavarois au Thé

Proceed in the same way as for Bavarian cream, but infuse $^1/_4$ oz. (8 gr.) tea in the milk.

BLANCMANGES

Blancmange - Blanc-Manger

6 persons :

9 oz. (250 gr.) blanched almonds
2 bitter almonds
3 $^3/_4$ oz. (100 gr.) sugar
10 sheets gelatine
$^3/_4$ pt. (4 $^1/_2$ dl.) whipped cream
Vanilla
Kirsch or orange flower water

Grind the almonds and moisten them gradually with $^3/_4$ pt. (4 $^1/_2$ dl.) of water. Next squeeze them through a cloth to obtain as much almond milk as possible, of which about 2 $^1/_2$ gills (4 dl.) are required. Dissolve the sugar in the cold almond milk and add the gelatine which has been melted in a water bath with very little water. When the mixture is almost set, flavour to taste and fold in the whipped cream. Pour into a mould with a central funnel and leave to set before turning out. *(France)*

Chocolate Blancmange - Blanc-Manger au Chocolat

Proceed in the same way as for ordinary blancmange, using $^3/_4$ oz. (20 gr.) less sugar and adding 1 $^3/_4$ oz. (50 gr.) chocolate melted in a bain-marie. *(France)*

Hazelnut Blancmange - Blanc-Manger aux Avelines

Proceed in the same way as above, but use fresh hazelnuts.

Liqueur Blancmange - Blanc-Manger aux Liqueurs

Prepare the blancmange in the usual way and flavour with $^1/_3$ gill (4-5 cl.) kirsch, maraschino, Cointreau, curaçao etc.
(France)

Raspberry Blancmange - Blanc-Manger aux Framboises

6 persons :

9 oz. (250 gr.) blanched sweet almonds
3 $^1/_2$ oz. (100 gr.) sugar
12 sheets gelatine
4 $^1/_2$ oz. (140 gr.) raspberry purée
$^3/_4$ pt. (4 $^1/_2$ dl.) whipped cream

Proceed in the same way as for ordinary blancmange, but mix in the raspberry purée before folding in the whipped cream.

Blancmange can also be made with strawberry, apricot, peach purée or orange juice, etc. *(France)*

CHARLOTTES

Chocolate Charlotte Princes' Style - Charlotte au Chocolat Princière

6 persons :

12 sponge fingers
Strawberry Bavarian cream
3 $^1/_2$ oz. (100 gr.) wild strawberries
3 $^1/_2$ oz. (100 gr.) chocolate granules
3 tablespoons sieved strawberry jam
$^1/_4$ pt. (1 $^1/_2$ dl.) Chantilly cream
A few small cultivated strawberries

Line the sides of the charlotte mould with the sponge fingers; fill with the strawberry Bavarian cream mixture containing the wild strawberries. Leave to set in a cold place. After turning the charlotte out of its mould, brush the top and sides with strawberry jam and sprinkle with chocolate granules. Serve on a round dish and, using a savoy bag fitted with a plain tube, decorate with Chantilly cream round the edge; on each dot of cream place a cultivated strawberry. *(France)*

Praliné Chocolate Charlotte - Charlotte au Chocolat pralinée

6 persons:

12 sponge fingers
3 egg yolks
3 １/₂ oz. (100 gr.) sugar
3 １/₂ oz. (100 gr.) not very sweet chocolate
１/₂ pt. (１/₄ l.) milk
8 sheets gelatine
2 oz. (50 gr.) praline ground and sieved
³/₄ pt. (4 dl.) whipped cream

Line the sides of a charlotte mould with sponge fingers. Fill with a chocolate Bavarian cream to which praline has been added. Leave to set and turn out on to a round dish. Decorate with Chantilly cream and candied fruits. A chilled vanilla custard cream may be served separately.

Malakoff Charlotte

6 persons:

12 sponge fingers
4 oz. (125 gr.) almonds
4 oz. (125 gr.) icing sugar
4 oz. (125 gr.) best butter
１/₂ pt. (3 dl.) whipped cream
Vanilla
１/₄ gill (3 cl.) kirsch

Line the mould as for charlotte russe apart from the bottom which is only covered with a round of greaseproof paper. Finely grind the almonds, gradually adding the sugar and powdered vanilla and mix in the slightly softened butter; all these ingredients are pounded in the mortar with the pestle until they become creamy and paler in colour. Add a liqueur glass of kirsch, put the mixture in a basin and fold in the whipped cream. Pour into the mould lined with sponge fingers and then surround it with crushed ice. When the charlotte is quite firm, trim the sponge fingers to the same height as the cream and turn out on to a dish covered with a d'oyley. Peel off the greaseproof paper and decorate the top with a vanilla flavoured, sweetened whipped cream, using a savoy bag fitted with a star tube. The cream should not have been fully whipped.

Royal Charlotte - Charlotte royale

6-8 persons:

Sponge mixture:
5 oz. (150 gr.) butter
4 oz. (125 gr.) sugar
10 egg yolks
10 egg whites
5 oz. (150 gr.) flour
4 oz. (125 gr.) strained and reduced apricot jam
3 oz. (100 gr.) red currant jelly
1 gill (1 １/₂ dl.) white wine jelly
7 oz. (200 gr.) coffee fondant

Custard:
³/₄ pt. (4 dl.) milk
2 egg yolks
3 １/₂ oz. (100 gr.) sugar
1 teaspoon cornflour
4 sheets gelatine
2 oz. (60 gr.) chopped candied fruit
１/₄ gill (3 cl.) maraschino
1 ³/₄ gills (１/₄ l.) whipped cream

Cooking time: 6-8 minutes

Cream the butter with 2 １/₂ oz. (75 gr.) sugar and incorporate the egg yolks one at a time. Whisk the egg whites with 1 １/₂ oz. (50 gr.) sugar until very stiff, mix in the flour and carefully amalgamate the two mixtures. Spread thinly on a greased floured baking sheet. Bake in a hot oven, ensuring that the sponge does not dry up. When it has cooled down, sandwich together five layers of the sponge alternately with apricot jam and red currant jelly. Cut up into strips 1 in. (2.5 cm.) wide and line a dome-shaped mould with them.

For the custard: Macerate the candied fruits in the maraschino. Mix the egg yolks, sugar, cornflour and milk together, finish cooking, and finally add the gelatine which has been soaked in water. When the custard begins to set, fold in the whipped cream and candied fruit. Fill the lined mould with this mixture and leave to set in a cool place. Turn out the charlotte on to a round jam sponge sandwich of the same diameter as the charlotte itself. The same sponge mixture is used to make heart-shaped petits fours which are brushed with apricot jam and iced with coffee fondant icing. Coat the charlotte with apricot jelly, glaze with white wine jelly and arrange petits fours all round.

(Germany)

Russian Charlotte I - Charlotte russe

6-8 persons:

12-15 sponge fingers
3 1/2 oz. (100 gr.) sugar
3 egg yolks
1/2 pt. (1/4 l.) milk
6-8 sheets gelatine
Vanilla
3/4 pt. (4 dl.) whipped cream

Take some very dry sponge fingers for lining the charlotte mould. First, for the bottom, cut some fingers into thin, triangular pieces and place these upside down with their tips meeting at the centre and packed closely together. Trim the sides and one end of the other sponge fingers so that they will fit more compactly round the sides of the mould; these, too, should be arranged with the upper surface against the side of the mould. It does not matter at all if all the fingers are not of the same height, because they will be trimmed to the height of the cream before the charlotte is turned out of the mould. The inside is filled with a vanilla or other flavoured Bavarian cream which contains rather less gelatine than usual. Leave to set in a cool place. Turn out just before serving on a napkin/doyley and decorate with Chantilly cream. *(France)*

Russian Charlotte II - Charlotte russe

8 portions:

Prepare a Bavarian cream, using a third of the quantities indicated in the basic recipe, flavour with kirsch and mix with 2 1/2 oz. (80 gr.) chopped candied fruit. Pour into a charlotte mould and leave to set in a cold place. Turn out on to a round dish and decorate with sponge fingers coated with couverture, whipped cream and a chocolate ornament. The sponge fingers may be glazed with water icing if desired. Serve with raspberry sauce.

(Illustration page 789.)

Valais Charlotte - Charlotte valaisanne

16 portions:

1 lb. 4 oz. (600 gr.) raspberries
3 1/2 oz. (200 gr.) sugar
5 sheets gelatine
1 1/4 pt. (7 dl.) whipped dairy cream
Juice of 1 lemon
12 oz. (400 gr.) raspberries
1/4 gill (3 cl.) raspberry brandy

Line a round, rather shallow mould with slices of filled Swiss roll. Cook 1 lb. 4 oz. (600 gr.) raspberries with the sugar, rub through a sieve, add the soaked gelatine and leave in a cold place. As soon as the mixture starts to set round the edge, stir, add the lemon juice and then the whipped cream, stir in the rest of the raspberries and the raspberry brandy and pour into the mould. Make small tubs out of almond wafer mixture and fill with whipped cream. When the charlotte has set, turn it out, brush the slices of Swiss roll with well boiled apricot purée and decorate with the cream tubs and a little whipped cream. On request, the coat of arms of the canton of Valais, made out of marzipan, may be placed in the centre. Serve raspberry syrup separately as an accompaniment.

(Switzerland)

Williams Charlotte - Charlotte Williams

8 portions:

Prepare a Bavarian cream, using a third of the quantities indicated in the basic recipe, flavour with pear brandy and mix with 6 half compote pears cut into dice. Fill a charlotte mould with the mixture, allow to set, then turn out on to a round dish. Arrange 8 half compote pears, coated with fairly thick chocolate sauce, evenly round the charlotte and decorate with whipped cream, chocolate triangles and a chocolate ornament. Serve with grenadine syrup.

(Illustration page 789.)

COCKTAILS

These desserts are usually served in 4 oz. (125 gr.) cocktail or port wine glasses, but champagne coupes may be used. The glass should never be filled up to the brim. All cocktails must be served well chilled.

Black Forest Cocktail - Cocktail de la Forêt-Noire

Place 6-8 stoned brandied cherries with a little of their juice at the bottom of the glass. Half fill with chocolate sauce mixed with chopped candied stem ginger.

Top with vanilla custard flavoured with Grand-Marnier and sprinkle with grated chocolate. *(Germany)*

Cherry Cocktail

Dress 6-8 stoned and quartered poached Morello cherries, macerated in Cherry Brandy, at the bottom of the glass. Fill three quarters full with kirsch sabayon, top with slightly sweetened whipped cream, smooth and sprinkle with chopped pistachio nuts. *(Germany)*

Cocktail Bonne-Femme - Hausfrauencocktail

Sieve some cream cheese, sweeten slightly with vanilla sugar and fold in a little whipped cream to bring it to a light, fluffy consistency. Fill the glass with alternate layers of the cream cheese and sweetened rapsberries or very small cherries, top with whipped cream and, just before serving, pour over a tablespoon of maraschino flavoured raspberry purée. *(Germany)*

Japanese Cocktail - Cocktail japonais

Cut 6 tangerine segments in pieces, macerate with curaçao and place them at the bottom of the glass. Half fill with orange sauce mixed with finely chopped candied orange peel and top with sherry sabayon. Sprinkle with flaked walnuts. *(Germany)*

Monk's Cocktail - Cocktail du Moine

Place 2 tablespoons salpicon of fresh fruit macerated with Benedictine at the bottom of a glass. Three quarters fill with vanilla custard mixed with chopped apricots, macerated in brandy, and top with Chantilly cream.

Sprinkle with roasted strip almonds. *(Germany)*

Oriental Cocktail - Cocktail à l'orientale

Dress 3 stoned dates, cut up into small pieces in brandy, with a little of their juice at the bottom of the glass. Half fill a glass with coffee custard sauce mixed with coarse crushed praline and top with slightly sweetened whipped cream flavoured with cinnamon. Place half a walnut dusted with icing sugar in the centre. *(Germany)*

Pierrette Cocktail - Cocktail Pierrette

Dress two tablespoons salpicon of fresh pineapple, macerated with kirsch, at the bottom of the glass. Three quarters fill a glass with chocolate sauce mixed with chopped brandied cherries. Top with whipped cream; pour a few drops of Cherry Rocher on the cream and sprinkle with crushed chocolate cigarettes. *(Germany)*

Shah Cocktail - Cocktail du Shah

Dice half a large fresh peach, macerated with peach brandy, and place at the bottom of a glass. Three quarters fill with white wine sabayon mixed with chopped maraschino cherries. Top with Chantilly cream and place a green maraschino cherry in the centre. *(Germany)*

Strawberry Cocktail - Cocktail aux Fraises

Cut 6 large strawberries in quarters, macerate with Cointreau and place them at the bottom of a glass. Half fill with Sabayon flavoured with Cointreau and top with slightly sweetened whipped cream mixed with strawberry purée.

Sprinkle with flaked pistachio nuts. *(Germany)*

VARIOUS CREAMS

Vanilla Custard Mould - Crème renversée à la Vanille

(Basic recipe)
5-6 persons:
2 eggs
4 egg yolks
1 pt. ($1/2$ l.) milk
$4\,1/2$ oz. (125 gr.) sugar
Vanilla
Cooking time: about 30 minutes

Beat up in a basin the egg yolks and sugar and stir in the boiling milk in which the vanilla has been infused. Leave to stand for a few minutes, remove the froth and strain. Pour into a slightly oiled or greased mould and poach in the oven in a bain-marie without letting it boil. Allow the custard to become completely cold before turning it out of the mould. *(France)*

Caramel Custard - Crème au Caramel

Proceed in the same way as for vanilla custard mould, but pour the mixture into a mould coated with caramelized sugar. *(France)*

Chocolate Custard Mould - Crème renversée au Chocolat

6 persons:
4 eggs
3 egg yolks
$3\,1/2$ oz. (100 gr.) sugar
$2\,1/2$ oz. (75 gr.) chocolate
1 pt. ($1/2$ l.) milk
Cooking time: about 30 minutes

Proceed in the same way as for vanilla custard mould, but first melt the chocolate in the milk. *(France)*

Coffee Custard - Crème renversée au Café

Prepare the same mixture as for vanilla custard mould without vanilla, but add instead a heaped teaspoonful of instant coffee powder to the warm milk. *(France)*

Royal Custard Mould - Crème royale

6 persons:
Mixture for a vanilla custard mould
$1\,3/4$ oz. (50 gr.) praline
$1\,3/4$ gills ($1/4$ l.) Chantilly cream
9 oz. (250 gr.) wild strawberries
Cooking time: 20-25 minutes

Stir the praline into the mixture. Poach in a border mould which has been greased and sprinkled with sugar. Leave to cool and turn out on to a round dish. Mix the Chantilly cream with the wild strawberries, retaining a few of the latter for decoration purposes. Fill the hollow with the strawberry cream and decorate with the rest of the strawberries. *(France)*

Amontillado Cream - Crème Amontillado

Moisten the rings of large cocktail glasses with egg white and dip them in finely chopped pistachios. Place coarsely crumbled sponge fingers soaked in sherry in the base of the glasses. Three quarters fill them with the following cream: mix 3 gills (4 dl.) custard cream with $1\,1/2$ tablespoons dry sherry and 5 leaves of gelatine (dissolved) and fold in $1/2$ pt. ($1/4$ l.) whipped cream. As soon as this cream has begun to set, decorate with a whipped cream rosette, an ornament of piped couverture and half a glacé cherry. *(Germany)*

Beau-Rivage Cream - Crème Beau-Rivage

6 persons:
2 eggs
4 egg yolks
1 pt. ($1/2$ l.) milk
$4\,1/2$ oz. (125 gr.) sugar
$1/2$ pt. ($1/4$ l.) Chantilly cream
Vanilla
6 cornets made with almond wafer paste
Chocolate fondant
Angelica
Glacé cherries
Cooking time: 20-25 minutes

Prepare a custard with the milk, eggs, egg yolks, 3 ½ oz. (100 gr.) sugar and 1 oz. (30 gr.) caramelized sugar. Poach in a savarin mould greased and sprinkled with sugar and leave to cool. Turn out on to a round dish, fill the hollow with Chantilly cream and decorate with glacé cherries. Fill the cornets with Chantilly cream, decorate with leaves of angelica and arrange them around the custard.

(France)

Harlequin Cream - Crème Arlequin

6 portions:

Cover the bottom of six small glass dishes with a layer of wine jelly about ¼ in. (4 mm.) thick. When set, fill up the dishes with a quarter of the amount of Bavarian cream given in the basic recipe, mixed with six half peaches cut into dice and flavoured with maraschino. Leave in a cold place until set. Dip the dishes in hot water for a moment, carefully loosen the cream round the edges, turn out and decorate each one with a marzipan head and chocolate wafers. Serve with grenadine syrup flavoured with maraschino.

(Illustration page 794.) *(Switzerland)*

Mogador Custard Cream - Crème Mogador

1 lb. (500 gr.) sugar
1 gill (1 ¼ dl.) water
2 ½ pt. (1 ½ l.) milk
3 ½ oz. (100 gr.) sugar
3 oz. (90 gr.) custard powder
4 egg yolks
Whipped dairy cream

Boil 1 lb. (500 gr.) sugar to the caramel degree and pour the water into the pan to obtain the caramel. Boil up the milk with the rest of the sugar and a pinch of salt. Blend the custard powder with the hot milk, add the egg yolks and cook to a custard.

Stir in the caramel and leave in a cold place. Before use, stir until smooth and fold in a little whipped cream.

(Switzerland)

Orange Harlequin Cream - Crème à l'Orange Arlequin

6 persons:

½ pt. (¼ l.) fresh orange juice
½ pt. (¼ l.) white wine
½ pt. (¼ l.) water
¼ oz. (10 gr.) cornflour
6 egg yolks
8 sheets gelatine
½ pt. (¼ l.) whipped cream
¾ gill (1 dl.) white wine jelly
Chocolate royal icing
Halved pistachio nuts

Beat up the egg yolks with the sugar until paler in colour and add the orange juice, white wine, cornflour and water. Thicken over heat as for a custard cream and, as soon as it coats the spoon, introduce the gelatine which has first been soaked in water. Leave to cool and, when the mixture begins to set, fold in the whipped cream. Pour into a cut glass dish and leave to set completely in a cool place. Decorate with chocolate royal icing and pistachio nuts and cover with partially set jelly.

Orange Cream Jeannette - Crème à l'Orange Jeannette

Prepare orange cream as for Harlequin cream. Cut 8 oz. (250 gr.) of genoese sponge into dice and steep in Cointreau liqueur. Fill the cream alternately with the diced sponge into a cut glass dish and leave to set. Pipe rings of couverture on top and when set fill with orange jelly. Cover with white wine jelly. *(France)*

Rob Roy Cream - Crème Rob Roy

6 persons:

4 egg yolks
5 oz. (150 gr.) sugar
½ oz. (15 gr.) cornflour
½ pt. (¼ l.) milk
6 sheets gelatine
3 egg whites
½ pt. (¼ l.) whipped cream
¾ gill (8 cl.) Scotch whisky
8 sponge fingers
1 gill (1 ½ dl.) Chantilly cream
3 glacé cherries

Break sponge fingers into small pieces and soak slightly in whisky. Soak gelatine. Mix egg yolks with sugar and cornflour, add the warm milk stirring constantly and whisk in bain-marie to a thick creamy consistency. Add the gelatine and allow to cool, stirring now and then. When the mixture is half set, mix in the whisky, fold in the whipped cream and finally the egg whites whisked to a stiff peak. Fill immediately into high glasses or goblets alternately with the sponge fingers. Pipe a rosette of Chantilly cream on top and place half a glacé cherry in the centre.
(Germany)

Sherry Cream - Crème au Xérès

6 persons:

3 egg yolks
2 １/₂ oz. (75 gr.) sugar
2 １/₂ oz. (75 gr.) cornflour
2 gills (3 dl.) milk
3 sheets gelatine
³/₄ gill (1 dl.) sherry
1 １/₂ gills (2 dl.) whipped cream
2 egg whites whisked stiff with
  ³/₄ oz. (25 gr.) sugar

Cooking time: 5 minutes

Beat up the egg yolks with the sugar and cornflour until paler in colour. Gradually add the hot milk and thicken over heat as for custard cream. Add the gelatine which has first been soaked in cold water. Leave to cool, stirring occasionally. When completely cold, stir in the sherry, fold in the whipped cream and then the egg whites. Pour into champagne glasses and decorate with a choux paste ornament.
(Germany)

Wine Cream Merlot

12 portions:

1 pt. (¹/₂ l.) Merlot or other good red wine
5 oz. (150 gr.) sugar
1 pinch of salt
2 egg yolks
4 sheets gelatine
1 pt. (¹/₂ l.) whipped dairy cream

Boil up half the wine with the sugar, beat in the egg yolks and add the soaked gelatine and the rest of the wine. Leave in a cold place until the mixture begins to set, then stir until smooth, fold in the whipped cream and pipe into claret glasses, goblets or cocktail glasses. When set, decorate with a mixture of slightly sweetened deep red wine and a little light buttercream or whipped cream (which should take on the colour of the wine). Place a marzipan or almond wafer vine-leaf on top for final decoration.

For a cold buffet, serve in cocktail glasses.
(Switzerland)

CREAMS IN GOBLETS

Creams in Goblets - Les Crèmes en Coupes

These are very delicate creams which are made so light that they do not require unmoulding. They can be filled into individual glass or cut-glass dishes, or into large champagne glasses or goblets, and suitably garnished and decorated. To improve the flavour, they may be mixed with cubes of sponge cake soaked in liqueur, fresh or crystallized fruit macerated in liqueur, etc.

Here are a few examples:

Banana Cream Caracas - Crème de Bananes Caracas

6-8 portions:

4 egg yolks
¹/₂ pt. (¹/₄ l.) milk
5 oz. (150 gr.) sugar
1 ¹/₂ oz. (50 gr.) chocolate
6 sheets gelatine
1 ¹/₂ tablespoons rum
5 ¹/₄ oz. (160 gr.) fresh banana purée
1 ¹/₄ pt. (6 dl.) whipped cream
1 teaspoon custard powder

Mix the egg yolks with the sugar and custard powder; warm the milk and disperse the chocolate in it. Beat the egg yolk mixture and the milk to a frothy cream over a bain-marie and stir in the soaked gelatine. Remove from the heat and beat until cold, then lightly fold in the banana purée, rum and, lastly, the whipped cream. Fill into individual dishes or goblets and, when set, decorate with whipped cream, triangles of crystallized pineapple and chocolate cigarettes. *(Germany)*

Peach Cream - Crème de Pêches

6-8 portions:

4 egg yolks
5 oz. (150 gr.) sugar
1/2 pt. (1/4 l.) white wine (not too dry)
6 sheets gelatine
1 1/4 pt. (6 dl.) whipped cream
2 1/2 oz. (75 gr.) candied apricots
2 1/2 oz. (75 gr.) sponge cake
1/8 gill (2 cl.) kirsch
1 teaspoon custard powder

Mix the egg yolks with the custard powder and sugar, add the wine and beat to a frothy cream over a bain-marie, mixing in the soaked gelatine at the same time. Remove from the heat and beat until cool; fold in the peach purée, then the whipped cream and the diced apricots and diced sponge cake, after soaking these in kirsch. Fill into individual dishes or goblets, leave until quite cold and decorate with a baked choux paste ornament and pistachio nuts. *(Germany)*

Tangerine Cream - Crème de Mandarines en Coupes

6 portions:

5 egg yolks
5 1/4 oz. (150 gr.) sugar
Juice of 10 tangerines
Grated zest of 2 tangerines
1/2 pt. (1/4 l.) white wine (not too dry)
1 teaspoon custard powder
6 sheets gelatine
1/8 gill (2 cl.) tangerine liqueur
6 savoy fingers
3 1/2 gills (1/2 l.) whipped cream

Mix the egg yolks well with the sugar and custard powder, add the tangerine juice and zest and the white wine and beat to a frothy cream over the heat. Add the soaked gelatine, remove from the heat and beat until cool. As soon as the mixture begins to set, lightly fold in the whipped cream and stir in the crumbled savoy fingers, previously moistened with tangerine liqueur. Fill into individual dishes, goblets or a fruit-bowl, leave until quite cold and decorate with whipped cream, chocolate shavings, canned mandarin orange segments, pistachios and red glacé cherries. *(Germany)*
(Illustration page 660.)

Vanilla Cream - Crème à la Vanille

6-8 portions:

5 egg yolks
5 1/2 oz. (150 gr.) sugar
3 gills (4 1/2 dl.) milk
1 teaspoon custard powder
1/2 vanilla pod (scraped)
1/4 oz. (8 gr.) gelatine
1 1/4 pt. (6 dl.) whipped cream

Prepare in exactly the same way as Wine Cream. *(Germany)*

Vanilla Cream Delmonico - Crème à la Vanille Delmonico

6-8 portions:

See Vanilla Cream. Prepare the cream as Wine Cream, but stir 3 1/2 oz. (100 gr.) diced candied fruit, previously macerated in Cointreau. Fill into individual dishes or goblets; when set, decorate with whipped cream, chocolate shavings and leaf shaped almond wafers. *(Germany)*

Wine Cream - Crème au Vin blanc

6-8 portions:

5 egg yolks
5 oz. (150 gr.) sugar
1 heaped teaspoon custard powder
3 gills (4 1/2 dl.) white wine
6 sheets gelatine
1 1/4 pt. (6 dl.) whipped cream

Mix the egg yolks with the sugar and custard powder, add the white wine and beat to a frothy cream over a bain-marie. Add the soaked gelatine, remove from the heat and beat until cold. Lightly draw in the whipped cream, fill into individual dishes or goblets and decorate with a chocolate couverture ornament and whipped cream. Small pieces of light jelly, small macaroons soaked in kirsch or cubes of butter sponge soaked in maraschino may be folded into the wine cream.
(Germany)

Wine Cream Benedictine Style - Crème au Vin à la Bénédictine

Prepare in the same way as Wine Cream but flavour with Benedictine and stir in savoy fingers soaked in Benedictine. Decorate with chopped pistachio nuts, whipped cream and leaf shaped almond or hazelnut wafers. *(Germany)*

SMALL CREAM POTS - PETITS POTS A LA CRÈME

Basic Recipe - Recette de Base

6 portions:

1 egg
3 egg yolks
4 oz. (125 gr.) sugar
1 pt. ($^1/_2$ l.) milk
Vanilla or lemon or orange zest

Cooking time: 15-20 minutes

Infuse the vanilla or zest in the milk, which should be warm, but not boiling. Beat up the egg, egg yolks and sugar, stir in the warm milk a little at a time and strain through a conical strainer. Fill individual fireproof cocottes up to the top with the custard and poach in a bain-marie in a moderate oven without letting the water boil. Allow to cool, then dust the top with icing sugar or pipe on a whirl of whipped dairy cream. *(France)*

Chocolate Cream Pots - Petits Pots à la Crème au Chocolat

Prepare the custard with 2 $^1/_2$ oz. (75 gr.) sugar and 3 oz. (80 gr.) of chocolate dissolved in the hot milk. Decorate with a rosette of Chantilly cream. *(France)*

Coffee Cream Pots - Petits Pots au Café

Proceed as in the basic recipe adding a tablespoon of soluble coffee powder or coffee extract. *(France)*

Geraldine Cream Pots - Kleine Cremennäpfchen Geraldine

6 portions:

1 egg
3 egg yolks
2 $^1/_2$ oz. (75 gr.) sugar
1 $^3/_4$ oz. (50 gr.) crushed and sieved croquant
1 pt. ($^1/_2$ l.) milk
$^1/_4$ pt. (2 dl.) whipped dairy cream
$^3/_4$ oz. (50 gr.) semi-bitter chocolate
$^1/_{10}$ gill (1 cl.) kirsch
3 red glacé cherries
Chopped pistachio nuts

Beat up the egg, egg yolks and sugar, add the warm milk, pass through a conical strainer and stir in the praline croquant. Pour into the cocottes and poach in the usual manner. Melt the chocolate over a bain-marie, mix with the kirsch, allow to cool, then blend with the whipped cream. When cold, decorate each pot with a whirl of whipped cream, place half a glacé cherry in the centre and sprinkle a few chopped pistachio nuts round it. *(Germany)*

Raspberry Cream Pots - Petits Pots de Crème Framboisine

Fill the cream pots not quite full with a vanilla flavoured custard cream and poach as usual. When they are cold, dress with a tablespoon of sugared raspberries on top, mask slightly with strawberry purée and decorate with whipped cream. *(France)*

Montmorency Cream Pots - Petits Pots de Crème Montmorency

Prepare the cream pots as usual with a vanilla flavoured custard, filling the pots not quite full. Dress a tablespoon of stoned cherries, poached in red wine and bound with a little red currant jelly on top and sprinkle with chopped pistachio nuts. *(France)*

Zabaglione Gritti - Zabaione Gritti

6 persons:

12 egg yolks
1 gill (1 $^1/_2$ dl.) marsala
5 oz. (150 gr.) sugar
6 sheets gelatine
$^1/_4$ pt. (1 $^1/_2$ dl.) whipped cream
3 glacé cherries
2 oz. (60 gr.) chocolate cigarettes

Beat egg yolks, sugar and marsala in a basin for a minute, add the gelatine, previously soaked, and place the basin in a bain-marie. Whisk to a thick creamy consistency and allow to cool stirring constantly. Beat the cream and add 2 oz. (60 gr.) sugar. Fill the zabaglione into individual goblets, decorate with whipped cream and half a glacé cherry and sprinkle the broken up chocolate cigarettes all around the cherry. *(Italy)*

FRUIT DESSERTS

Apples Brissac - Pommes Brissac

6 persons:

6 apples
1 round genoese base
$1/4$ gill (3 cl.) Grand-Marnier
5 oz. (150 gr.) red currant jelly
$1/2$ pt. (3 dl.) sabayon sauce flavoured with Grand-Marnier
Angelica

Poach the apples in a vanilla flavoured syrup and leave to cool. Steep the genoese base with a little syrup flavoured with Grand-Marnier and arrange the apples on top. Mask the apples with red currant jelly and stick two diamond shaped pieces of angelica into each apple. Serve the sabayon sauce separately. *(France)*

Apples Gabriella - Reinettes Gabrielle

Peel and core small apples. Fill with softened marzipan mixed with a little cinnamon, cook slowly and carefully in the oven and allow to cool. Arrange in a glass dish, coat with diluted Mogador custard cream (page *706*), decorate with whipped dairy cream and sprinkle with flaked almonds. *(Switzerland)*

Apples Maltese Style - Pommes à la maltaise

Peel and core russet apples and poach in white wine with a little sugar, a piece of quill cinnamon and lemon zest. Drain very well, fill the hollow in the centre with almond paste brought to a piping consistency with arrack and glaze each apple with wine jelly. Place a border of Maltese rice on individual glass plates, arrange an apple on top with a couverture ornament on it and pour round apricot sauce flavoured with orange juice.

Maltese rice:

$3 1/2$ gills ($1/2$ l.) milk
$3 1/2$ oz. (100 gr.) rice
Vanilla
Grated zest of 1 orange
5 leaves soaked gelatine
$1/2$ pt. ($1/4$ l.) whipped cream
12-15 orange slices
$3 1/2$ oz. (100 gr.) sugar
3 egg yolks

Blanch the rice, cook in the milk in the usual way with a piece of vanilla and the sugar, remove the vanilla, add the grated orange zest and, after squeezing out well, add the gelatine while the mixture is still hot and leave until cold. As soon as it begins to set, fold in the whipped cream and fill into small ring moulds. *(Germany)*

Apricots Countess Style

Cut large apricots in half, remove the stones and cook the fruit carefully in syrup. Leave until cold, fill the halves with vanilla ice cream, put them together in pairs and place in the refrigerator. When frozen dip the apricots in thick raspberry syrup and mask them with lightly roasted chopped almonds. Keep in the refrigerator until ready to serve and finally decorate with whipped cream.

Mascot Apricots - Abricots Mascotte

6 persons:

6 pastry cases made of shortpaste
1 pt. ($1/2$ l.) pastry cream
$1 3/4$ oz. (50 gr.) praline, pounded and sieved
2 oz. (60 gr.) apricot purée
6 apricots
Whipped cream
Almonds

Poach the small apricots carefully in vanilla flavoured syrup and allow to cool.

Mix the praline with the pastry cream and fill the pastry cases half full with this mixture. Place a well drained apricot, with the skin and kernel carefully removed, on top and brush lightly with apricot purée. Decorate with small stars of whipped cream round the edge and place half a roasted almond in the centre of each. *(France)*

Apricots Negrita - Abricots Negrita

6 persons:
9-12 apricots according to size
1 $^3/_4$ pt. (1 l.) vanilla ice
$^1/_2$ pt. ($^1/_4$ l.) sabayon sauce
$^1/_4$ gill (3 cl.) rum Negrita
Glacé cherries

Poach the apricots already halved, in syrup flavoured with rum, peel and leave to cool in the syrup. Garnish the bottom of a chilled timbale with the ice, drain and place the apricots on top. Cover with sabayon flavoured with rum and sprinkle with chopped glacé cherries.

Apricots West Indian Style - Abricots à la Mode des Indes occidentales

6 persons:
12 apricots
1 $^3/_4$ pt. (1 l.) banana ice
$^1/_2$ pt. ($^1/_4$ l.) apricot sauce flavoured with rum
Roasted shredded almonds

Poach the apricots in vanilla-flavoured syrup and leave to cool in the syrup. Garnish the bottom of a chilled timbale with the banana ice and place the drained and peeled apricots on top. Mask with the rum-flavoured apricot sauce and sprinkle with shredded almonds.
(Germany)

Avocados Louison - Avocats Louison

6 persons:
3 avocado pears
6 small scoops praline ice
$^1/_4$ gill (3 cl.) anisette
$^1/_2$ pt. ($^1/_4$ l.) Chantilly cream
$^1/_2$ pt. ($^1/_4$ l.) strawberry purée
Ground praline

Cut the avocado pears in two lengthwise and take out the stones. Scoop them out carefully, cut the flesh in small cubes and macerate with sugar and anisette. Cool. Fill it into the shells and place a scoop of praline ice on top. Pipe a border of Chantilly cream and sprinkle with ground, sieved praline. Serve the cold strawberry purée separately. *(U.S.A.)*

Bananas Copacabana - Bananes Copacabana

6 persons:
6 bananas
1 $^1/_2$ pt. ($^3/_4$ l.) vanilla ice
$^1/_2$ pt. ($^1/_4$ l.) cold chocolate sauce
$^1/_4$ gill (4 cl.) rum
1 oz. (30 gr.) shredded pistachio nuts

Peel the bananas, divide them in two and poach in syrup flavoured generously with rum. Leave to cool in the syrup. Place the vanilla ice at the bottom of a chilled timbale and arrange the drained bananas on top. Mask with chocolate sauce and sprinkle with chopped pistachio nuts.
(Germany)

Banana Lemon Custard Roll - Roulade de Citron aux Bananes

Spread a sheet of Swiss roll with lemon custard, roll up tightly and refrigerate. Cut into 1 $^1/_2$ in. (3 cm.) slices, lay these in a glass dish, pipe on a little thickened whipped dairy cream and arrange banana slices on top. Mask with thin rum sauce or strawberry pulp and decorate with whipped cream. *(Switzerland)*

Banana Meringues - Bananes meringuées

Using a coarse plain tube, pipe out an Italian meringue zigzag fashion to the shape of bananas on to greased and floured baking sheets. Bake, leave until cold, then dip the bases of half of them in couverture and allow to set. Pipe on a little whipped dairy cream, cover with half a banana cut lengthwise, pipe on a line of whipped cream and place the other half of the meringues on top. *(Switzerland)*

Bananas Theodor - Bananes Théodore

Slice bananas in half lengthwise and remove the flesh, keeping it and the skins intact. Fill the skins with banana cream, using a large plain pipe, and refrigerate for a short time. Place half a banana on each half-skin, mask with thin rum or apricot sauce and decorate with whipped dairy cream, tuiles and pistachio nuts.
(Switzerland)

Bananas Swedish Style - Bananes à la suédoise

6 persons:

4 large bananas
$1/2$ pt. ($1/4$ l.) Chantilly cream
$1/4$ gill (4 cl.) caloric punch (Swedish punch)

Peel and dice the bananas. Macerate in sugar and Swedish punch. Fill into individual goblets and decorate with Chantilly cream. *(Germany)*

Cherries Dijon Style - Cerises à la dijonnaise

6 persons:

$1 1/2$ lb. (750 gr.) stoned cherries
$1/4$ gill (4 cl.) black currant liqueur
$1/8$ gill (2 cl.) kirsch
Sponge fingers

Poach the cherries in syrup flavoured with black currant liqueur and leave to cool in the syrup. Dress the cherries in a chilled timbale and pour the kirsch on top. Serve with sponge fingers. *(France)*

Cherries Eltville - Cerises Eltville

Flavour Bavarian cream with cognac and mix with a little sieved praline croquant. Allow to set a little, then pipe out in bulbs forming a ring on to a glass dish. Place a few brandied cherries in the centre, decorate with a whirl of whipped dairy cream and sprinkle with sieved praline croquant. *(Switzerland)*

Cherries Montmorency

1 pt. ($1/2$ l.) milk
$1/2$ vanilla pod
1 pinch of salt
$3 1/2$ oz. (100 gr.) sugar
$1 1/4$ oz. (35 gr.) semolina
4 sheets gelatine
Orange zest
About $3/4$ pt. (3-4 dl.) whipped dairy cream
Stoned cherries poached in vanilla flavoured syrup

Boil up the milk with the vanilla and a little grated orange zest, pour in the semolina and cook over gentle heat for 3 to 4 minutes, stirring meanwhile. Add the salt, the sugar and the soaked gelatine, also a few sultanas if desired. Leave in a cold place until the mixture starts to set round the edge, then stir and blend in the whipped cream. Pour into ring moulds or glass dishes. If the latter are used, make a depression in the centre with the back of a spoon dipped in hot water and fill at once with the cherries. If ring moulds are used, refrigerate until set, then turn out on to glass dishes and fill the centre with cherries. Decorate with whipped cream before serving. Boil up the syrup again, thicken with a little cornflour and flavour with kirsch. When cold, coat the semolina lightly with the syrup or, preferably, serve the syrup separately in a sauce-boat.

Cherries Van Dyck - Cerises Van Dyck

6 persons:

$1 1/2$ lb. (750 gr.) stoned cherries
$1 1/2$ pt. ($3/4$ l.) vanilla ice
$1/2$ pt. ($1/4$ l.) thick custard sauce
$1/4$ gill (3 cl.) arrack

Poach the cherries in vanilla flavoured syrup and leave to cool in the syrup. Drain and dress on vanilla ice in a chilled timbale. Mask with the custard sauce flavoured with arrack.

Cherries Viennese Style - Cerises à la viennoise

6 persons:

$1 1/2$ lb. (750 gr.) stoned cherries
3 oz. (75 gr.) red currant jelly
1 egg

2 egg yolks
$1/2$ pt. ($1/4$ l.) milk
4 oz. (125 gr.) sugar
$1/2$ pt. ($1/4$ l.) Chantilly cream
$3/4$ oz. (20 gr.) shredded pistachio nuts

Cooking time : 25 minutes

Poach the cherries in vanilla flavoured syrup and drain. Reduce the syrup, bind with very little cornflour and the red currant jelly and cool. Bind the cherries with the syrup. Caramelize 1 $1/2$ oz. sugar and prepare custard with the egg, egg yolks, caramelized sugar and milk. Fill the mixture into a savarin mould and poach in a water bath in the oven. Allow to cool. Turn out on to a round dish, dress the cherries in the centre and sprinkle with shredded pistachio nuts. Decorate the custard with Chantilly cream.

(Austria)

Eaton Mess

6 persons :

1 $1/4$ lb. (600 gr.) strawberries
3 $1/2$ oz. (100 gr.) sugar
1 pt. ($1/2$ l.) whipped cream

Hull, wash and drain strawberries. Crush them slightly with a fork and incorporate sugar and whipped cream. Serve in a chilled timbale or glass bowl with sponge fingers. *(Great Britain)*

Figs Mistral - Figues Mistral

6 persons :

12 ripe fresh figs
$1/2$ pt. ($1/4$ l.) raspberry purée
$1/2$ pt. ($1/4$ l.) Chantilly cream
$1/8$ gill (2 cl.) cognac
Shredded almonds

Peel and cut the figs in halves and macerate them with icing sugar and cognac. Place them in the bottom of a chilled timbale and mask with raspberry purée. Decorate with Chantilly cream and sprinkle with shredded almonds. *(France)*

Figs Paradiso - Figues Paradiso

6 persons :

12 ripe fresh figs
1 $1/4$ pt. ($3/4$ l.) lemon ice
$1/2$ pt. ($1/4$ l.) cold apricot sauce
$1/8$ gill (2 cl.) Ricard
$1/8$ gill (2 cl.) kirsch
Lemon juice
Shredded pistachio nuts

Steep the figs for a moment in hot water, peel and cut them in halves. Macerate with sugar, kirsch and a few drops of lemon juice and chill. Garnish the bottom of a timbale with the lemon ice and place the figs on top. Mask with apricot sauce flavoured with Ricard and sprinkle with shredded pistachio nuts. *(Germany)*

Fried Eggs

Pipe blancmange into small flat dishes, using a plain tube. The blancmange should spread over the dishes a little. Refrigerate until set, then place a small half peach poached in orange syrup in the centre of each one and carefully mask with apricot sauce. Apricot halves may be used instead of peaches.

Gooseberry Fool

6 persons :

1 lb. (500 gr.) gooseberries
5 $1/2$ oz. (150 gr.) sugar
1 pt. ($1/2$ l.) whipped cream

Poach the gooseberries with 1 oz. (30 gr.) sugar and very little water and leave to cool. Rub through a sieve, add the remaining sugar and, if the purée is not sweet enough, add more. Incorporate the whipped cream and serve cold in individual goblets. *(Great Britain)*

Grapefruit Florida - Pamplemousse Florida

6 persons :

3 grapefruits
2 large oranges
5 oz. (150 gr.) stoned cherries
5 oz. (150 gr.) small strawberries
$1/2$ gill (7 cl.) sherry
4 oz. (125 gr.) sugar
2 oz. (60 gr.) shredded almonds

Cut grapefruits in two horizontally. Cut out the segments and remove the skin, then mix with the orange segments, cherries and strawberries. Macerate in sugar and sherry and leave to cool. Fill the shells with the fruit mixture, sprinkle with shredded almonds and serve very cold. *(U.S.A.)*

Frosted Lemons - Citrons givrés

6 persons:
6 lemons
1 ¼ pt. (¾ l.) lemon ice
Angelica

Cut the top of the lemons off lengthwise and remove the pulp carefully without damaging the skins. Prepare lemon ice with the pulp, fill into the shells and replace the top.

Place in deep freeze for 30 minutes, sprinkle lightly with water and allow water to frost. Remove from deep freeze, decorate with a flower made from almond or sugar paste, and serve immediately.

(Germany)

(Illustration page 663.)

Lychees Chinese Style - Lichis à la chinoise

6 persons:
2 lb. (1 kg.) tin lychees
1 ¼ pt. (¾ l.) vanilla ice
2 oz. (50 gr.) preserved stem ginger
½ gill (7 cl.) syrup of preserved stem ginger
½ gill (6 cl.) rice wine or dry sherry
1 teaspoon cornflour
1 tablespoon shredded pistachio nuts

Drain and stone the lychees, reduce the syrup by half and mix with the stem ginger syrup. Bind slightly with cornflour and flavour with rice wine. Leave to cool. Mix the vanilla ice with the diced stem ginger and place it at the bottom of a chilled timbale. Arrange the lychees on top, mask with the syrup and sprinkle with shredded pistachio nuts. *(Germany)*

Lychees Oriental Style - Lichis à l'orientale

6 persons:
2 lb. (1 kg.) tin lychees
1 pt. (½ l.) basic jelly
½ pt. (¼ l.) pomegranate juice
½ pt. (¼ l.) whipped cream
1 oz. (30 gr.) chopped roasted pine nuts
¼ gill (3 cl.) Benedictine

Drain the lychees and keep the juice. Reduce by half and filter together with the pomegranate juice. Mix with the liquid basic jelly (see jellies). Stone the lychees, drain again and fill them in a bowl or crystal dish. Cover with the half set jelly and mix carefully until the lychees sit in the jelly. Chill and decorate with slightly sweetened whipped cream flavoured with Benedictine, using a savoy bag and a star tube. Sprinkle with the chopped pine nuts. *(Germany)*

Lychees with Ricard - Lichis au Ricard

6 persons:
2 lb. (1 kg.) tin lychees
½ pt. (¼ l.) lychee syrup
½ pt. (¼ l.) dry white wine
3 ½ oz. (100 gr.) sugar
4 sheets gelatine
¼ gill (3 cl.) Ricard
½ pt. (¼ l.) Chantilly cream
1 tablespoon chopped, roasted pine nuts

Drain the lychees and stone them. Mix ½ pint of the syrup with the white wine and the sugar and bring to the boil. Add the gelatine, previously soaked in water and pressed, and leave to cool. Fill the mixture into a bowl set on ice, flavour with a tablespoon of Ricard and whisk to a foam. As soon as this mixture begins to set, fill into a timbale or glass dish and arrange the lychees on top. Decorate with Chantilly cream flavoured with the remaining Ricard and sprinkle with the pine nuts. *(Germany)*

Melon Majestic

6-8 persons:
1 ripe cantaloup melon
1 ¼ lb. (600 gr.) small strawberries
¼ pt. (2 dl.) Chantilly cream
¼ gill (3 cl.) kirsch
1 ½ oz. (50 gr.) chocolate cigarettes
2 ½ oz. (75 gr.) icing sugar

Cut out a circle around the stem of the melon. Take off the cap and remove water and seeds. Scoop out the flesh without damaging the shell and prepare melon water ice with the flesh. Macerate the strawberries in sugar and kirsch and cool. Place melon on crushed ice on a round dish, fill with melon ice and arrange the strawberries on top. Garnish with Chantilly cream, place the chocolate cigarettes on top and dust lightly with icing sugar.

Oranges Haifa

Cut off the top quarter of large, uniformly shaped oranges and carefully remove the pulp. Use it to prepare orange water ice, fill into the cleaned orange shells and deep freeze. Place small tartlet moulds in a pan, stand the oranges on them and fill up the spaces well with finely crushed ice. Top each orange with a spoonful of Grand-Marnier flavoured soufflé mixture (made in the same way as confectioner's custard) so that the orange ice is completely masked, then bake in the oven. Dust with icing sugar, then serve at once in a glass bowl on crushed ice. It is important to ensure that sufficient crushed ice is placed in the pan to prevent the orange ice from melting. *(Switzerland)*

Oranges Ilona

6 persons:

6 large oranges
$1/2$ pt. (3 dl.) chocolate ice
2 oz. (50 gr.) crystallized stem ginger
$1/8$ pt. (1 dl.) apricot sauce
$1/4$ pt. (2 dl.) Chantilly cream
$1 \, 1/2$ oz. (50 gr.) ground and sieved praline

Cut out a circle round the stem of each orange. Scoop out carefully without damaging the shell. Remove skin and pips and cut sections into dice, adding the sections of one or two more oranges if need be. Cut the stem ginger into dice, mix with the chocolate ice and fill the orange shells half full with the ice. Place a spoonful of diced oranges, bound with apricot sauce on top and decorate with a rosette of Chantilly cream. Sprinkle with praline and serve immediately. *(Germany)*

Oranges Riviera

12 persons:

1 very large orange in orange coloured blown sugar, top in marzipan, stem and leaves in green coloured pulled sugar
12 large oranges
1 large and 12 small lotus blossoms in almond modelling paste
About 2 pt. (1 l.) orange ice
Petits fours

Cut off top of the oranges, scoop out the pulp and prepare orange water ice with the juice. Clean the shells and tops and decorate with stems and leaves of green coloured modelling marzipan. Place the blown sugar orange on a large lotus blossom and fill with petits fours. Arrange the oranges filled with orange ice all around each on a small lotus blossom, and replace the tops. *(Germany)*

Oranges Surprise - Oranges en Surprise

6 persons:

6 large oranges
$3/4$ pt. (3-4 dl.) orange ice
8 oz. (250 gr.) Italian meringue mixture

Cut the top of the oranges off about three quarters of the way up and remove pulp without damaging the shells. Clean shells. Prepare orange ice with the pulp. Place the shells on crushed ice and fill with orange ice. Mask with Italian meringue mixture using a savoy bag with a plain round tube, dust with icing sugar and place in a very hot oven so that the meringue colours quickly. Dress on a napkin and serve at once. *(France)*

Oranges Syracuse Style - Arance Ripiene alla Siracusa

6 portions:

6 blood oranges
$4 \, 1/4$ oz. (125 gr.) almonds
$4 \, 1/4$ oz. (125 gr.) sugar
$1/2$ pt. (3 dl.) whipped cream
$1/4$ gill (3 cl.) Grand-Marnier

Cut off the top of each orange to make a lid, remove the pulp and squeeze out the juice. Blanch the almonds, roast lightly in the oven, pound in a mortar or grind, place in a basin, mix with the sugar, the juice of 3 oranges and the Grand-Marnier and lastly draw in the whipped cream lightly. Fill the mixture into the oranges, replace the lid on each, decorate with a leaf made of almond paste and chill at 40° F (5° C) for 2 hours. *(Italy)*
(Illustration page 664.)

Peach Belle Forestière - Pêche Belle Forestière

Line small carrack moulds with French sweet pastry, place a spot of apricot jam on the bottom of each one, pipe in Dutch mixing with a flat tube and bake in a medium oven. When cold, moisten with a little kirsch syrup and brush with praline cream. Place a small compote peach on top and coat lightly with kirsch sauce. Cover the bottom of a serving dish with bilberries, arrange the peaches on top and decorate with a little whipped dairy cream.

Dutch mixing: Beat 1 lb. (500 gr.) Persipan with 8 oz. (250 gr.) margarine and butter, add 5 eggs in small portions and lastly fold in 4 oz. (125 gr.) flour.

Kirsch sauce: Boil up ³/₄ pt. (4 dl.) milk with 2 ¹/₂ oz. (75 gr.) sugar. Thicken with 1 oz. (25 gr.) vanilla custard powder which has been blended with ¹/₄ pt. (1 dl.) cold milk. Allow to cool, then add ¹/₄ gill (3 cl.) kirsch. *(Switzerland)*
(Illustration page 791.)

Peaches Beau-Rivage - Pêches Beau-Rivage

6 persons:
6 peaches
1 ¹/₄ pt. (6 dl.) Plombière ice flavoured with kirsch
¹/₄ pt. (2 dl.) Chantilly cream
1 tablespoon crushed macaroons
1 tablespoon coarsely crushed crystallized violet

Poach the peaches in vanilla flavoured syrup, leave to cool and peel. Arrange the peaches on the ice filled in a chilled timbale and sprinkle with crushed macaroons and violets. Pipe a border of Chantilly cream around the peaches. *(France)*

Peaches Cléo de Merode - Pêches Cléo de Merode

6 persons:
1 ¹/₄ pt. (6 dl.) vanilla ice
¹/₂ pt. (¹/₄ l.) cold chocolate sauce
1 gill (1 ¹/₂ dl.) Chantilly cream
1 teaspoon chopped pistachio nuts

Poach the peaches in a vanilla flavoured syrup, leave to cool and peel. Place the ice at the bottom of a chilled timbale and arrange the peaches on top. Mask with chocolate sauce, pipe a border of Chantilly cream and sprinkle the sauce with chopped pistachio nuts.

Peaches Deslys - Pêches Deslys

6 persons:
6 small very choice peaches
3 gills (3-4 dl.) champagne jelly
Gold leaf

Poach the peaches in a kirsch flavoured syrup and leave to cool in the syrup. Drain, peel and stone each peach carefully and place each peach in a shallow champagne coupe. Mask entirely with very light champagne jelly mixed with gold leaf and leave to set in cold storage.
(Germany)

Flambéed peaches with Benedictine - Pêches flambées à la Bénédictine

6 persons, served at the table:
12 half peaches
6 slices pistachio parfait
1 ¹/₂ gills (2 dl.) hot apricot sauce
¹/₄ gill (3 cl.) Benedictine
¹/₈ gill (2 cl.) brandy
2 oz. (40 gr.) blanched and shredded almonds

Poach the peaches in vanilla flavoured syrup. In the dining room place a copper pan on a flambé réchaud, pour in the apricot sauce and 2 or 3 tablespoons of the vanilla flavoured syrup and allow to boil for a few moments. Heat the strained peaches in this sauce and ignite with the brandy and Benedictine. Place a slice of pistachio parfait on a cold plate, dress two half peaches on top, mask with a spoonful of apricot sauce, sprinkle with shredded almonds and serve immediately. *(Germany)*

Peaches Frascati - Pêches Frascati

6 persons :

6 peaches
1 1/4 pt. (6 dl.) almond ice
1/2 pt. (1/4 l.) strawberry purée flavoured with kirsch
1 tablespoon skinned, shredded walnuts
1/2 pt. (1/4 l.) double cream

Poach the peaches in vanilla flavoured syrup, leave to cool and peel. Arrange the peaches on the almond ice and mask with strawberry purée. Sprinkle with shredded walnuts and serve the double cream separately. *(Germany)*

Peaches Melba - Pêches Melba

6 persons :

6 choice peaches
1 1/4 pt. (6 dl.) vanilla ice
1/2 pt. (3 dl.) fresh raspberry purée

Poach the peaches in vanilla flavoured syrup and allow to cool. Garnish the bottom of a chilled timbale with the ice cream and arrange the drained and peeled peaches on top. Mask with the raspberry purée. *(France)*

Pears Almina - Poires Almina

6 persons :

6 pears
1 1/4 pt. (6 dl.) coffee ice cream
1 1/2 gills (1/4 l.) apricot sauce
1/8 gill (2 cl.) noyau liqueur
1/4 pt. (2 dl.) Chantilly cream
1 1/2 oz. (40 gr.) ground and sieved hazelnut praline

Peel, core and poach the pears in vanilla-flavoured syrup. Leave to cool. Fill the coffee ice at the bottom of a chilled timbale and dress pears on top. Mask with cold apricot sauce flavoured with noyau and decorate with Chantilly mixed with the ground and sieved praline. *(France)*

Pears Balmoral - Poires Balmoral

6 persons :

6 pears
1 1/4 pt. (6 dl.) hazelnut ice (the hazelnuts deeply roasted)
1/2 pt. (1/4 l.) cold chocolate sauce
1 1/2 gills (3 dl.) Chantilly cream

Peel, core and poach the pears in vanilla flavoured syrup and leave to cool in the syrup. Place the hazelnut ice at the bottom of a chilled timbale and arrange the drained pears on top. Mask with chocolate sauce and decorate generously with Chantilly cream. *(Great Britain)*

Pears Bristol - Poires Bristol

Pipe choux pastry on to baking sheets in oval rings and bake. When cold, coat the top with kirsch flavoured fondant. Split with a knife and sandwich with confectioner's custard flavoured with kirsch or pear brandy. Arrange on a glass dish, fill the hollow centre with a little whipped dairy cream and place half a glazed compote pear on top; it may be caramelized or simply coated with apricot jam. Add a marzipan stalk and leaf, mark in the calyx with the help of a paper piping bag and finally decorate with whipped cream. *(Switzerland)*

Pears Cardinal - Poires Cardinal

6 persons :

6 choice pears
10 oz. (300 gr.) raspberries
1 3/4 oz. (50 gr.) icing sugar
Juice of 1/2 lemon
2 tablespoons blanched and shredded almonds

Poach the pears in vanilla flavoured syrup and leave to cool. Rub the raspberries through a sieve and stir in the sugar and the lemon juice. Drain and peel the pears, arrange them in a chilled timbale and mask with the raspberry purée.

Sprinkle with shredded almonds. *(France)*

Pears in Château-Lafite - Poires au Château-Lafite

6 persons:

6 pears
½ bottle Château-Lafite
4 oz. (125 gr.) sugar
5 oz. (150 gr.) red currant and raspberry jelly

Peel, divide each pear in half, and core. Poach in the Château-Lafite and sugar and cool in the wine. Drain and reduce the wine to a fourth, bind with the red currant and raspberry jelly and chill. Arrange the pears in a timbale and mask with the wine sauce. *(France)*

Pears Châtelaine - Poires Châtelaine

6 large choice pears
Vanilla flavoured stock syrup
4 oz. (125 gr.) praline paste
1 lb. 4 oz. (600 gr.) vanilla ice cream

Sabayon sauce:

10 egg yolks
7 oz. (200 gr.) sugar
1 gill (1 dl.) Grand-Marnier
A little water
1 gill (1 dl.) custard cream flavoured with Grand-Marnier

Peel and core the pears, poach in vanilla-flavoured stock syrup and leave until cold. Drain and fill with praline paste.

Whisk the egg yolks, sugar, Grand-Marnier and a little water over a bain-marie until thick and smooth, remove from the heat and continue whisking until quite cold. Add the custard cream flavoured with Grand-Marnier. Place the pears in individual dishes on a scoop of vanilla ice-cream, coat with the sabayon sauce, sprinkle with roasted strip almonds and crystallized violets and decorate with whipped cream. *(Germany)*

Pears Dauphine - Poires Dauphine

8 persons:
Brioche dough
1 ¾ pt. (1 l.) pastry cream
1 liqueur glass of rum
8 small pears
¾ pt. (4 dl.) whipped cream

Line a lightly greased flan hoop with brioche dough and bake it without a filling. Peel and poach the pears in vanilla-flavoured syrup and allow to cool whilst in the syrup. When the shell is cold, fill with pastry cream flavoured with rum, and place the well drained pears on top. Decorate with whipped cream using a star pipe. Candied fruit may be mixed with the pastry cream. *(France)*

Pears Esmeralda - Birnen Esmeralda

Poach choice William pears in vanilla-flavoured syrup and leave in a cold place. Cover a long silver dish with a layer of sponge cake as for surprise omelette, top with vanilla ice cream and set in the refrigerator. Cut off a fifth of each pear at the stalk end and keep these caps. Core the remainder of each pear and cut into 4 or 5 slices. Spread the edges of the slices with a little butter to raise them and fill the centre with Bar-le-Duc red currant jelly. Stand them upright on the vanilla ice-cream, cover with a layer of soufflé omelette batter thin enough for the fruit to show through. Set in the oven for a short time until the batter takes on a slight colour and replace the stalk ends on top.

Decorate with long threads of red currant jelly, using a piping bag. Finish off by splashing with maraschino. *(Germany)*

Pears Helene - Poires Hélène

6 persons:

6 pears
1 ¼ pt. (6 dl.) vanilla ice
½ pt. (3 dl.) hot chocolate sauce

Peel and poach the pears in vanilla-flavoured syrup. Leave to cool in the syrup. Drain and arrange on the ice cream and serve the hot chocolate sauce separately. It is customary to sprinkle crystallized violets on top of the ice cream. *(France)*
(Illustration page 664.)

Pears Maja - Poires Maja

8 persons:

Peel and core William pears, poach in vanilla flavoured stock syrup and leave in the syrup until cold. Drain the pears very well and fill with almond paste (softened marzipan). Arrange a border of pistachio cream on individual glass plates, overpipe with couverture and leave until firm. Place a pear glazed with wine jelly in the centre and decorate with a stem made of couverture, a marzipan leaf and butterfly made of couverture.

Pistachio cream: Mix together 3 gills (4 dl.) custard cream, 1 ³/₄ oz. (40 gr.) ground pistachios, 1 ³/₄ oz. (40 gr.) ground almonds and 1 tablespoon maraschino. Soak and dissolve 5 leaves of gelatine, add to the mixture and fold in ¹/₂ pt. (¹/₄ l.) whipped cream. Fill into small ring moulds and leave to set. *(Germany)*
(Illustration page 794.)

Pears Tetrazzini - Poires Tetrazzini

6 persons:

6 pears
1 ¹/₄ pt. (6 dl.) raspberry ice
¹/₂ pt. (¹/₄ l.) apricot mousseline sauce
¹/₄ pt. (2 dl.) Chantilly cream
1 tablespoon crushed, sieved praline

Peel, core and poach the pears in vanilla flavoured syrup and leave to cool in the syrup. Place raspberry ice in the bottom of a chilled timbale and the drained pears on top. Mask with the sauce, decorate with a border of Chantilly cream and sprinkle the cream with the praline.

Persimmons Creole - Kakis à la créole

6 persons:

6 large ripe persimmons
¹/₂ pt. (3 dl.) pineapple ice
¹/₈ gill (2 cl.) curaçao
¹/₄ pt. (1 ¹/₂ dl.) whipped cream
3 glacé cherries

Cut a cap off the top of the persimmons, scoop out and mash the pulp. Mix the pulp with the pineapple water ice and flavour with curaçao. Fill the ice into the shells and place in deep freeze for half an hour. Decorate each persimmon with a rosette of whipped cream and place half a glacé cherry in the centre. *(Germany)*

Persimmons Cyrill - Kakis Cyrille

6 persons:

6 large ripe persimmons
1 banana
2-3 slices pineapple
¹/₈ gill (2 cl.) anisette
2 tablespoons thick apricot sauce
¹/₄ pt. (1 ¹/₂ dl.) whipped cream
6 small pieces glacé pineapple

Cut a cap off the top of the persimmon and scoop the flesh out carefully. Prepare a salpicon with the flesh, the peeled banana and the pineapple, macerate with anisette and chill. Bind this salpicon with thick apricot sauce and fill into the shells. Pipe a large rosette of whipped cream on top and place a piece of glacé pineapple in the centre. *(Germany)*

Pineapple Bourdaloue - Ananas à la Bourdaloue

Bake a sponge or genoese in a savarin mould and when cold soak lightly in kirsch flavoured syrup. Place it on a round dish and fill the middle with cold bourdaloue cream mixed with a little whipped dairy cream. Garnish all around with thin half slices of pineapple each overlapping. The slices should be macerated in sugar and kirsch beforehand. Decorate with whipped cream and candied cherries. Place the head of the pineapple on top as a final decoration.

Pineapple Haroun-al-Rashid - Ananas Haroun-al-Rashid

10-12 persons:

1 large pineapple
1 ¹/₂ pt. (1 l.) pistachio ice cream
1 pt. (¹/₂ l.) very thick raspberry purée
3 oz. (80 gr.) sugar
¹/₄ gill (4 cl.) kirsch
1 ¹/₂ oz. (40 gr.) blanched shredded almonds
1 ¹/₂ oz. (40 gr.) shredded pistachio nuts

Cut the pineapple in two lengthwise, including the green tuft and, using a sharp knife, scoop out the flesh without damaging the shells. Remove the stump, cut the pineapple into thin slices, macerate in sugar and kirsch and chill. Place the shells on crushed ice and fill cupola shape with pistachio ice. Arrange pineapple slices, overlapping each other on top and mask with raspberry purée. Sprinkle with shredded almond and pistachio nuts and serve the remaining raspberry purée separately. *(Germany)*

Pineapple Jamaican Style - Ananas à la Jamaïque

Cut off the top of a small pineapple, scoop out the flesh, cut out the core, then cut the pineapple into small pieces.

Macerate in sugar and rum and add a large peeled sliced banana. Drain well, mix with slightly sweetened whipped dairy cream and add a little more rum if necessary. Fill the pineapple shell with the mixture and add a few meringue cuttings.

Replace the pineapple top in its original position and dish the pineapple with crushed ice. *(Switzerland)*

Pineapple Kenya - Ananas Kenya

20 portions:

Line a rectangular silver dish with wine jelly (see Basic Preparations) and leave in a cold place to set. Cut two small pineapples in half lengthwise and remove the cores to leave a wedge-shaped hollow down the middle of each half. Place the head of a pineapple in the centre of the dish and lay the four evenly trimmed pineapple halves round it diagonally. Fill the wedge-shaped hollows with cherries, strawberries or other red fruits. Decorate with prunes, grapes and other fruits, taking particular care to achieve a harmonious combination of colours. Brush with wine jelly that is on the point of setting and refrigerate. This sweet is suitable chiefly for a banquet or a cold buffet.
(Illustration page 790.) *(Switzerland)*

Pineapple Ninon - Ananas à la Ninon

8 persons:

1 large pineapple
18 oz. (500 gr.) wild strawberries
4 bananas
8 pastry boats made from almond shortpaste
$1/2$ pt. ($1/4$ l.) whipped cream
$3/4$ pt. (3 dl.) raspberry sauce

Cut off the top of the pineapple without damaging the green leaves. Hollow it out neatly by placing in a sharp knife about $1/2$ in. (1 cm.) from the edge and cutting all round. Next place the knife in the base and pivot the pineapple round the blade so that the pineapple is removed in one piece without damaging the shell. Cut the part removed into thin slices then cut out the cores with a vegetable cutter. Macerate the slices in sugar and kirsch, and do the same with the strawberries and the bananas cut into slices. Chill well. Place the pineapple shell on a round dish and half fill with the strawberries and the banana slices. On top of these place the pineapple slices standing upright, each overlapping and coming a little over the edge of the shell. Fill up with whipped cream, using a savoy bag and star pipe, then replace the pineapple top in its original place. Fill the pastry boats with whipped cream, decorate them with small pieces of pineapple and a wild strawberry and arrange them around the shell. Serve with raspberry sauce. *(France)*
(Illustration page 660.)

Pineapple Roswitha

6 portions:

Line a 8 in. by 4 $1/2$ in. (21 × 11 cm.) tin with greaseproof paper. Lay a sheet of Swiss roll of the same size inside and brush with strawberry jam. Take a quarter of the amount of Bavarian cream given in the basic recipe, flavour it with Grand-Marnier and spread evenly on the Swiss roll. Leave until very cold, then cut out with a round cutter a little larger than a slice of pineapple. Cover with a well drained slice of pineapple and glaze with apricot jelly. Decorate with whipped dairy cream and place a chocolate ornament in the centre. *(Illustration page 793.)*

Raspberries Beatrice - Framboises Béatrice

6 persons:

1 lb. (500 gr.) large raspberries
$^1/_8$ gill (2 cl.) kirsch
1 $^1/_4$ pt. (6 dl.) hazelnut ice
$^1/_2$ pt. ($^1/_4$ l.) Melba sauce mixed with red currant jelly
1 tablespoon skinned, shredded walnuts

Macerate the raspberries with sugar and kirsch. Place the hazelnut ice at the bottom of a chilled timbale and arrange the raspberries on top. Mask with the Melba sauce and sprinkle with shredded walnuts.
(Holland)

Raspberries Côte d'Azur - Framboises Côte d'Azur

6 persons:

6 large oranges
$^1/_2$ lb. (250 gr.) raspberries
$^1/_2$ pt. (3 dl.) orange water ice
$^1/_8$ gill (2 cl.) curaçao

Cut a cap off the oranges, scoop out carefully and clean the shells. Macerate the raspberries in sugar and curaçao. Prepare water ice with the orange juice. Fill the orange shells half full of raspberries and place a dome of orange ice on top. *(France)*

Raspberries Erimar - Framboises Erimar

6 persons:

1 lb. (500 gr.) raspberries
$^1/_8$ gill (2 cl.) apricot brandy
2 oz. (50 gr.) sugar
6 oz. (200 gr.) red currant jelly
Blanc-mange
1 $^1/_2$ oz. (40 gr.) fresh shredded almonds
$^1/_2$ pt. ($^1/_4$ l.) double cream

Macerate the raspberries in the apricot brandy and sugar. Prepare blanc-mange in a border mould, and rub the red currant jelly through a sieve. Turn the blanc-mange out on a round dish and fill the raspberries in the centre. Mask with red currant jelly and sprinkle with shredded almonds. Serve with double cream.
(Germany)

Raspberries Kitty - Framboises Kitty

6 persons:

1 lb. (500 gr.) raspberries
1 $^3/_4$ pt. (1 l.) light Bavarian vanilla cream
$^1/_8$ gill (2 cl.) kirsch
4-5 oz. (150 gr.) red currant jelly
1 tablespoon chopped pistachio nuts

Macerate the raspberries with sugar and kirsch. Prepare a very light Bavarian vanilla cream. Fill a timbale or a cut glass bowl three quarters full with the cream and leave to set. Arrange the raspberries on top, and mask with red currant jelly and sprinkle with chopped pistachio nuts.
(Germany)

Strawberry Boats Congolese - Barquettes de Fraises à la congolaise

6 persons:

6 large barquettes of short pastry
1 banana
$^1/_4$ lb. (125 gr.) large strawberries
18 very small strawberries
2 tablespoons melted couverture
3 sheets gelatine
$^1/_2$ pt. ($^1/_4$ l.) whipped cream
2 oz. (50 gr.) icing sugar
$^1/_8$ gill (2 cl.) rum

Peel and dice the banana and macerate with the rum and $^1/_2$ oz. (15 gr.) of sugar. Prepare a cream as for 'Strawberries Princess Style' with a purée of the large strawberries, 1 $^1/_2$ oz. (50 gr.) icing sugar, the soaked and melted gelatine and three quarters of the whipped cream. Add the diced banana. Brush the inside of the pastry boats with couverture and leave to set. Fill them dome shape with the cream and decorate each barquette with whipped cream and three small strawberries.

Strawberries with Curaçao Mousseline Sauce - Fraises à la Sauce Mousseline au Curaçao

6 persons:

1 1/4 lb. (600 gr.) strawberries
Juice of 1 orange
1/2 pt. (3 dl.) cold mousseline sauce
1/4 gill (3 cl.) curaçao
1 oz. (30 gr.) shredded pistachio nuts

Steep the strawberries in orange juice and sugar, and cool. Dress them in a chilled timbale, mask with mousseline sauce flavoured with curaçao and sprinkle with shredded pistachio nuts. *(Germany)*

Eugenia of Strawberries - Eugénie aux Fraises

8 persons:

9 oz. (300 gr.) strawberries
1/2 pt. (1/4 l.) vanilla custard
3 gills (1/2 l.) whipped cream
8 leaves of gelatine
1/4 lb. (125 gr.) icing sugar
1 round genoese base

Rub the strawberries through a fine sieve and mix into the vanilla custard. Add the gelatine previously soaked and melted. When this mixture begins to set, add 1/2 pt. (1/4 l.) of whipped sweetened cream. Slice the genoese base and sandwich it with a thick layer of this strawberry cream. Cover with a layer of the remaining cream and allow to set. Decorate with small strawberries and whipped cream. Shortly before serving, cover with sweetened strawberry purée, to which the rest of the cream, whipped lightly, has been added. *(France)*

Strawberries Femina - Fraises Fémina

1 lb. (500 gr.) choice large strawberries
1/4 gill (4 cl.) Grand-Marnier
1 1/4 pt. (3/4 l.) orange water ice
1 3/4 oz. (50 gr.) sugar

Macerate the strawberries in Grand-Marnier and sugar and chill. Fill the orange ice, mixed with the Grand-Marnier used to macerate the strawberries, at the bottom of a chilled timbale and arrange the strawberries on top. *(France)*

Strawberries Lerina - Fraises Lérina

2 portions:

2 tablespoons vanilla ice cream
3 tablespoons whipped cream
2 crushed macaroons
2 teaspoons castor sugar
3 1/2 oz. (100 gr.) fresh strawberries
1 1/2 glasses Lerina liqueur
Genoese sponge approx. 1 1/2 in. (4 cm.) thick

Cut two pieces of genoese sponge about 3-4 in. (7.5-10 cm.) long and hollow them out slightly. Mix the vanilla ice cream with the whipped cream, the crushed macaroons and 1 teaspoon castor sugar and fill into the hollowed-out sponge. Mix the strawberries, either whole or halved, with 1 teaspoon castor sugar and the liqueur. Place on the ice cream filling and decorate with whipped cream and a touch of spun sugar. *(France)*

Strawberries Melba - Fraises Melba

6 persons:

1 1/4 lb. (500 gr.) choice strawberries
1 pt. (6 dl.) vanilla ice
1/2 pt. (3 dl.) slightly sweetened raspberry purée

Fill the vanilla ice at the bottom of a chilled timbale. Arrange the strawberries on top and mask with raspberry purée.

Strawberries Non Plus Ultra - Fraises Non Plus Ultra

6 persons:

1 lb. (500 gr.) strawberries
1 1/4 pt. (3/4 l.) almond ice mixed with 2 oz. (60 gr.) diced glacé pineapple
1/8 gill (1 cl.) curaçao
1/8 gill (1 cl.) cognac
1/2 pt. (3 dl.) cold orange sabayon
1 tablespoon shredded roasted almonds

Macerate the strawberries in sugar, cognac and curaçao. Fill the almond ice at the bottom of a chilled timbale and place the strawberries on top. Mask with the orange sabayon and sprinkle with the shredded almonds.

Strawberries Romanoff - Fraises Romanoff

6 persons:
Recipe 1
1 ¼ lb. (600 gr.) strawberries
Juice of 1 orange
¼ gill (4 cl.) curaçao
½ pt. (4 dl.) Chantilly cream

Macerate the strawberries in orange juice and curaçao. Arrange them in a chilled timbale and decorate with Chantilly cream, using a savoy bag and a star tube.

Recipe 2
1 ¼ lb. (600 gr.) strawberries
1 ½ gills (2 dl.) port wine
Sugar
½ pt. (3 dl.) Chantilly cream

Macerate the strawberries in port wine and very little sugar and chill. Fill the strawberries in high goblets or champagne coupes, cover with the port wine and top with Chantilly cream. *(France)*

Strawberries Verona - Fraises Vérone

Macerate strawberries of uniform size and shape in sugar and Grand-Marnier. Place a medium-size cream bun, filled with slightly sweetened whipped dairy cream mixed with strawberry pulp, in the centre of a glass dish and surround it with the strawberries. Mask the cream bun with cold strawberries sauce, decorate with whipped cream and sprinkle with chopped pistachio nuts. *(Switzerland)*

Paris Style Supreme of Fruit - Suprême de Fruits à la parisienne

On a previous day, cut the top off a mousseline brioche as a lid. Scoop the brioche out leaving ½ in. (1 cm.) thickness at the sides. Brush the outside and the lid with apricot purée and decorate with almonds and candied fruit. Fill the brioche with a warm fruit mixture bound with thick apricot jam and flavoured to taste. Put on the lid and serve at once. It is advisable not to get the filling too soft so that it does not soften the crust. Serve a little flavoured purée separately.

Tangerines Côte d'Azur - Mandarines Côte d'Azur

6 persons:
12 tangerines
4 oz. (100 gr.) pineapple
4 oz. (100 gr.) tangerine segments
4 oz. (100 gr.) peaches
2 oz. (50 gr.) stoned cherries
¼ gill (3 cl.) curaçao
2 ½ oz. (75 gr.) sugar

Cut all fruit into dice and macerate in curaçao and sugar. Trim the tangerines to form baskets, scoop out the pulp and prepare tangerine ice with the juice. Clean the shells and keep them cool. To serve, put a spoonful of the fruit mixture into each basket, cover with tangerine ice and serve immediately.

Frosted Tangerines - Mandarines givrées

6 persons:
6 large tangerines
¾ pt. (4 dl.) tangerine water ice

Cut off the top of the tangerines and scoop the pulp out carefully without damaging the shell. Clean shells and prepare tangerine water ice with the juice. Fill the shells with the tangerine ice, replace cap and place in deep freeze for 30 minutes. Sprinkle a few drops of water on top with a brush and leave to frost. Replace the tangerine leaves by those made of green blown sugar or green coloured marzipan. Dress tangerines on a napkin and serve immediately. *(France)*

Rote Grütze

6-8 persons:
1 ½ lb. (750 gr.) red currant
¾ lb. (350 gr.) raspberries
About 7 oz. (200 gr.) sugar
3 oz. (100 gr.) cornflour
½ pt. (3 dl.) custard sauce or fresh cream

Put the fruit in a saucepan with $^1/_2$ gill (8 cl.) of water and bring to a boil. Rub through a hair sieve, weigh the purée and add enough water to make 1 quart (1.2 l.) of purée. Boil up again and add the sugar. Mix the cornflour with a little water and pour it into the purée stirring constantly. Boil for a few seconds, take off the fire and allow to cool for a while before pouring the Grütze into individual glass bowls. Chill well and pour a little custard sauce or fresh cream on top or serve separately. For a lighter sweet only add 2 oz. (75 gr.) of cornflour. *(Germany)*

STEWED FRUIT COMPOTES

The fruits used in compotes should be of very good quality and not too ripe. They are cut in halves or quarters, according to their kind and size, and poached in syrup at about 18° B flavoured with vanilla, lemon or orange zest. Certain fruits, such as cherries, pears or prunes, may be poached in a syrup made of red wine and sugar and flavoured with cinnamon or lemon zest. When the fruit is cooked, the syrup should be reduced and, in certain cases, thickened with either red currant jelly, apricot jam or a little cornflour, but, in general, the reduced syrup is left as it is.

Compotes should be served cold but not chilled.

Mixed Stewed Fruit - Compotes composées

This is made up of several kinds of fruit. They are usually cooked separately in the same syrup, one after the other. Various fruits may, however, be cooked at the same time, and only those that give off their colour are cooked separately. All the fruits are then arranged together and covered with syrup lightly thickened with currant jelly or cornflour.

Stewed Apples - Compote de Pommes

If the apples are to be served whole, choose a small variety. Peel, core and rub them with lemon juice. Poach them in a vanilla flavoured syrup, covered with a sheet of white paper to avoid contact with the air, which may darken the fruit. They may also be cooked cut in quarters. Watch the cooking carefully, especially if the apples are soft.

Stewed Apricots - Compote d'Abricots

Cut the apricots in halves, remove the stones, plunge them for a few seconds into a hot syrup at 12° B and remove the skins. Poach them in the syrup flavoured with vanilla for 7 to 8 minutes. Drain and reduce the syrup to half. Arrange the apricots, cover with the syrup and decorate with the kernels extracted from the stones, split in half and macerated for a few minutes in kirsch flavoured syrup.

Stewed Bananas - Compote de Bananes

Leave very small bananas whole and cut the larger ones lengthwise. Poach them in a syrup at 16° B flavoured with rum. Reduce the syrup, thicken with a little apricot jam and strain over the bananas.

Stewed Cherries - Compote de Cerises

Stone the cherries carefully. For 2 lb. (1 kg.) fruit cook 10 oz. (300 gr.) sugar to the ball, pour it over the cherries and keep them covered at the side of the fire for 8 minutes, moving the stewpan from time to time until the sugar is dispersed. Flavour the syrup with a little kirsch before pouring it over the fruit.

Cherries may also be poached in a syrup made with claret, flavoured with cinnamon.

Stewed Figs - Compote de Figues

Fresh figs are poached in a syrup at 18° B, flavoured with vanilla or lemon zest. Dried figs are soaked in water overnight and cooked in a syrup at 12° B without any flavouring.

Stewed Greengages - Compote de Reines-Claudes

Stone the greengages, which should not be too ripe, and poach them in a vanilla flavoured syrup at 18° B for 10-12 minutes. Watch the cooking carefully and on no account allow the syrup to boil.

Stewed Mirabelle Plums - Compote de Mirabelles

Stone the mirabelles and poach them in the same way as greengages, without allowing them to boil.

Stewed Peaches - Compote de Pêches

Peaches may be cooked whole or cut in half. Poach them in a vanilla flavoured syrup at 18° B and do not remove the skins before they are cooked. They may be decorated with the kernels extracted from the stones and split in half.

Stewed Pears - Compote de Poires

Very small pears may be left whole, larger ones are cut in halves or quarters, according to size, peeled and cored. Soft pears are poached quickly in a vanilla flavoured syrup at 18° B. Cooking pears should be rubbed with lemon juice, blanched in water acidulated with lemon juice for a few minutes, to keep them white, and then poached in a vanilla flavoured syrup at 12° B.

Pears may also be poached in a syrup prepared with red wine and flavoured with cinnamon.

Stewed Plums - Compote de Prunes

All sorts of plums may be served stewed. Quetsches, for instance, are cut in half and poached carefully in syrup at 18° B. For fastidious guests they should be plunged into the syrup for a few seconds, to remove the skins, before being poached.

Stewed Prunes - Compote de Pruneaux

Soak large prunes overnight in water. Cook them in a syrup at 12° B, made of half water and half red wine, sugar and a little cinnamon. Before serving, the prunes may be stoned.

Stewed Raspberries - Compote de Framboises

Cook 7 oz. (200 gr.) sugar with a little vanilla to the ball and pour the syrup over 2 lb. (1 kg.) raspberries. Keep them covered for 10 minutes and put them in a fruit bowl. Reduce the syrup and thicken with a little red currant jelly. Allow to cool before pouring over the raspberries.

Stewed Rhubarb - Compote de Rhubarbe

Peel the sticks of rhubarb and cut them into pieces 2 in. (5 cm.) long. Put them in very little syrup at 28-30° B, cover with a sheet of white paper and poach in the oven, because rhubarb breaks up at the first boil and yields much water. Drain carefully and reduce the syrup before pouring it over the fruit.

Stewed Strawberries - Compote de Fraises

Proceed as for raspberries.

FRUIT SALADS-MACÉDOINES

Fresh Fruit Salad - Macédoine de Fruits

Apples and pears: peel, core, quarter and cut into thin slices.

Apricots: peel, stone and slice evenly.

Bananas: peel and cut into fairly thick slices.

Grapes: peel and remove seeds.

Peaches: peel, remove the stone, quarter and slice evenly.

Pineapple: peel, cut into thin rounds, remove the heart with a corer and cut the slices into eights.

Oranges: cut a cap off the top and bottom. Peel the skin from the sides with a sharp knife in a circular manner. Cut out the segments, which should not contain any skin.

Raspberries: remove hulls. Use only firm fruit.

Strawberries: remove hulls and, if very large, cut into quarters.

Thin slices of melon, tangerine and grapefruit segments, stoned cherries cut into halves and any other fruit in season may, of course, be used.

Add sugar and a few drops of lemon juice; optional flavour with liqueur and moisten with stock syrup. Mix carefully, chill well and serve in a silver timbale on crushed ice, or in a glass or crystal dish. For all fruit salads use fresh fruit in season as far as possible.

Optional: a large glass of dry champagne can be added.

Fresh Fruit Salad with Champagne - Macédoine de Fruits au Champagne

Prepare the fruit salad with fresh fruit as far as possible, sprinkle with a few drops of lemon juice and moisten with a little stock syrup. When serving, add a glass of dry champagne.

Fruit Salad Cardinal - Macédoine de Fruits à la Cardinal

Prepare fruit salad and flavour with kirsch. Chill, cover with strawberry sauce and sprinkle flaked almonds on top.

Fruit Salad in Jelly - Macédoine de Fruits en Gelée

6 persons:

20 oz. (625 gr.) fruit in season
3 gills (4 dl.) basic jelly
$1/2$ pt. ($1/4$ l.) white wine

Arrange fruit such as small strawberries, raspberries, stoned cherries; orange or tangerine sections, quartered ripe peaches or apricots, diced poached pineapple, small scooped out apple balls poached in vanilla syrup and drained etc. in a glass bowl or in champagne glasses. Mix the basic jelly with the wine and as soon as it begins to set, pour it over the fruit which must be entirely covered with jelly.

Fruit Salad Niçoise - Macédoine de Fruits à la niçoise

Place fruit salad flavoured with Grand-Marnier in the bottom and a scoop of orange ice on top.

Fruit Salad Ninette - Macédoine de Fruits Ninette

Flavour fruit salad with Grand-Marnier. Place a scoop of vanilla ice cream on top for each portion. Mask with strawberry purée and sprinkle with flaked walnuts.

Fruit Salad with Ice Cream - Macédoine de Fruits aux Glaces diverses

Flavour the fruit salad with kirsch or maraschino and serve with a scoop of vanilla, strawberry, raspberry or lemon ice for each portion.

Melon and Raspberry Salad - Salade de Melon aux Framboises

Peel a ripe Cantaloup or honeydew melon, remove seeds and scoop the flesh out with a dessertspoon. Mix with an equal amount of raspberries, macerate with very little sugar, a few drops of lemon juice and cognac. Chill and serve sprinkled with flaked walnuts.

Orange and Banana Salad - Salade de Bananes et Oranges

Peel and cut bananas in not too thin slices. Mix with the same amount of orange segments and macerate with sugar, rum and a few drops of lemon juice. Moisten with stock syrup, chill and serve with double cream.

Peach Salad with Melba Sauce - Salade de Pêches à la Sauce Melba

Cut peeled and stoned peaches in slices and macerate with sugar, a few drops of lemon juice and kirsch. Moisten with stock syrup, chill, fill in a silver timbale and mask with Melba sauce. Sprinkle with flaked pistachios.

GATEAUX

Italian and French gâteaux, tourtes and savarins are usually served as a dessert, as well as French and Swiss afternoon tea fancies. (All recipes *pages 408* and *565.*)

Meringue preparations in combination with fresh dairy cream are very popular on the continent.

A selection of classic gâteaux and famous meringue preparations follows:

Chocolate Rum Pie

8 persons:
1 flan crust
1 pt. milk ($^1/_2$ l.) milk
4 egg yolks
4 egg whites
1 tablespoon cornflour
$^1/_8$ gill (2 cl.) rum
3 $^1/_2$ oz. (100 gr.) chocolate
3 $^1/_2$ oz. (100 gr.) sugar
Vanilla
6 sheets gelatine
$^1/_2$ pt. ($^1/_4$ l.) cream
2 oz. (60 gr.) chocolate shavings

Prepare a custard with the milk, yolks, sugar, vanilla, chocolate and cornflour and add the gelatine, previously soaked in water. Leave to cool stirring constantly and before the custard begins to set, add the rum and fold in the egg whites whipped to a stiff peak. Pour the custard into the baked flan crust, cover with Chantilly cream and smooth the surface. Sprinkle with chocolate shavings and dust slightly with icing sugar. *(U.S.A.)*

Gâteau Forêt-Noire - Schwarzwälder Kirschtorte

12-14 persons:
8 egg yolks
1 egg
7 oz. (200 gr.) sugar
3 oz. (90 gr.) ground almonds
1 $^1/_2$ oz. (45 gr.) cocoa
2 oz. (60 gr.) flour
3 $^1/_2$ oz. (100 gr.) sponge crumbs
8 egg whites
14 oz. (400 gr.) Morello cherries stoned
1 pt. ($^1/_2$ l.) whipped dairy cream
$^1/_4$ gill (3 cl.) kirsch
A little chocolate
Cornflour or arrowroot
Baking temperature 360° F (182° C)
Baking time: about 25 minutes

Beat yolks of egg and egg with the sugar and a spoonful of water. Add the crumbs and ground almonds and then the whites beaten stiff, followed by the sieved flour and cocoa. Pour into a round sandwich plate, greased and floured, 10 in. (25 cm.) in diameter. When baked and cold, slice into three. Put the cold cherries cooked and bound together with cornflour on one of these layers, then another layer on top and cover with kirsch flavoured whipped dairy cream. Put on the third slice. Cover with the same cream. Decorate the edge and sides with chocolate shavings. Pipe rosettes of cream inside the top edge. Place chocolate shavings in the centre. Dust with icing sugar and set out the cherries. *(Germany)*

Gâteau Saint-Honoré

6-7 persons:
9 oz. (275 gr.) short pastry or pastry cuttings
Choux paste made from $^1/_2$ pt. ($^1/_4$ l.) water
3 $^1/_2$ oz. (100 gr.) butter
4 $^1/_2$ oz. (140 gr.) flour
$^1/_2$ oz. (15 gr.) sugar
4 eggs and a pinch of salt
1 pt. ($^1/_2$ l.) St Honoré cream
Whipped cream
6 oz. (180 gr.) sugar

Pin out a round base of short or puff pastry about $^1/_4$ in. (6 mm.) thick. Place this on a baking sheet and brush the outer edge with egg, then pipe choux paste round the edge with a plain pipe brushing with egg also. Bake in a moderate oven about 380° F (193° C).

Pipe out about 15 petits choux on to a baking sheet and bake about 420° F (216° C). Make certain that they are nice and brown and dry. They should be piped out about the size of a walnut and carefully egg washed before baking. Boil the 6 oz. (180 gr.) sugar with ¼ gill (4 cl.) water to the crack degree 280° F (138° C).

Impale the petits choux on a fork, dip them in the sugar and place at once around the edge of the base. The petits choux should be filled with cream before dipping. With a savoy bag and star pipe fill the centre with St Honoré cream and decorate with whipped cream and candied fruits.

(France)

Gâteau Saint-Honoré

Proceed as for St Honoré Tuscany, but fill the centre of the baked base with maddalena chopped into small cubes and soaked with vanilla liqueur. Spread Chantilly cream on top to make a level surface and place petits choux, prepared as above, round the top edge, piping a star of Chantilly cream between each. A pattern of alternate lines of white and chocolate Chantilly cream is arranged in the centre, put in with the help of a tablespoon.
(Illustration page 553.) *(Italy)*

Saint-Honoré Florentine

Proceed as for St Honoré Tuscany. Place Malaga raisins on the white piped Chantilly cream in the centre. *(Italy)*

Saint-Honoré Selva

Proceed as for St Honoré of Tuscany. The caramel on the choux however should be as dark as possible without being bitter in taste. The centre is filled with selva leaves instead of the piped pattern of Chantilly cream. *(Italy)*

Saint-Honoré Tuscany

Prepare a vol-au-vent base in the following way:

Cut out a large disc of puff pastry, prick the surface, place on to a baking sheet and brush lightly with water. Cut out the centres from two other discs of the same size, damp them with water and place one on top of the other, then put them neatly on the disc on the baking sheet. Brush the surface of the top ring with beaten egg, let stand for half-an-hour and bake.

Cut a disc of baked maddalena of a size that will drop into the baked base, split into two layers, soak with vanilla liqueur or Grand-Marnier and sandwich with Chantilly cream and drop it into the base. Spread evenly with Chantilly cream to make a level surface. Arrange petits choux round the edge of the base after they have been filled with zabaglione and dipped into caramel sugar. Between each chou a star of Chantilly cream is piped, topped with a piece of glacé cherry. A pattern of alternate white and chocolate Chantilly cream is piped into the centre using a savoy bag fitted with a star pipe. *(Italy)*
(Illustration page 553.)

MERINGUES

Fraisalia Meringues - Meringues Fraisalia

8 persons:

16 meringue shells
9 oz. (275 gr.) wild strawberries
½ liqueur glass kirsch
2 ½ oz. (75 gr.) castor sugar
1 pt. (½ l.) whipped cream
Vanilla

Macerate the strawberries in vanilla sugar and kirsch. Scoop out the meringue shells lightly and fill them, shortly before serving, with the strawberries. Join the shells and decorate them with whipped cream flavoured with vanilla sugar and place a small strawberry at each end. Do not use too much sugar in the cream because the meringue shells are so sweet.

Vacherin - Vacherin meringué

8 persons:

8 egg whites
14 oz. (400 gr.) sugar
1 pt. (½ l.) whipped dairy cream
   (barely sweetened)
Candied fruit

Mark 5 or 6 circles on a greased and floured baking sheet. Whip the whites to a stiff snow and fold in the sugar carefully. Starting in the centre of each circle, pipe 3 or 4 spiral discs. Pipe close lattice work in the remaining two circles. Bake in a cool oven about 250° F (121° C), without allowing the meringue to colour too much. Using meringue, sandwich the discs together starting with a lattice one and adding the spiral ones. Coat the top and sides with meringue adding a design on the side using a star tube. Return this base to the oven and bake until quite dry. When cool, fill the centre with cream and top with the remaining lattice disc. Pipe shells of cream round the top edge. Decorate with candied fruit.

According to season, coarsely crushed glazed chestnuts, chestnut purée, or wild strawberries may be mixed with the whipped cream.
(Illustration page 795.)

JELLIES

Basic Jelly - Gelée de Base

6 oz. (175 gr.) sugar
$1/2$ oz. (15 gr.) gelatine
$1/2$ gill (3 cl.) white wine
Juice of 1 lemon
Zest of $1/2$ lemon
1 egg white
1 pt. ($1/2$ l.) water
Cooking time: 20 minutes

Soak the gelatine, squeeze it out and melt it in the hot water. Add sugar, lemon juice and zest, cover and leave to infuse away from the heat for 10 minutes. Beat the egg white with the white wine to a light foam and mix little by little with the syrup. Bring to the boil stirring constantly and simmer for 10 minutes. Cover again and leave to stand for a few minutes away from the heat. Strain through a moistened cloth and, if the jelly is not quite clear, strain again.

Fruit Jelly - Gelée aux Fruits

6 persons:
1 pt. ($1/2$ l.) basic jelly
$1/2$-$3/4$ pt. (3-3 $1/2$ dl.) filtered fruit juice

For fruit jellies, berries such as strawberries, raspberries and blackberries or cherries are best; they must be fully ripe. Rub 1 lb. (500 gr.) of the desired fruit through a fine sieve adding about 1 gill (1 $1/2$ dl.) of water and filter the juice. Mix the cold basic jelly with the filtered juice, fill the jelly in a fancy mould with a central funnel and leave to set on ice or in cold storage. To unmould, dip the mould for a moment in hot water and turn out on a round dish. For a lighter jelly that can be served in champagne glasses or in a cut glass dish, mix 1 pt. ($1/2$ l.) of basic jelly with 3-3 $1/4$ gills (3-3 $1/2$ dl.) of filtered fruit juice.

Kirsch Jelly - Gelée au Kirsch

5 $1/4$ oz. (150 gr.) sugar
12 sheets gelatine
1 pt. ($1/2$ l.) water
$1/2$ vanilla bean
$1/4$ gill (4 cl.) kirsch
1 egg white
Cooking time: 2-3 minutes

Make a syrup with the sugar, vanilla and water, boil for 2 minutes, and add the soaked and squeezed out gelatine. Beat the egg white with very little water and clarify the jelly in the same way as for basic jelly. Strain through a cloth and when the jelly is cold but still liquid, add the kirsch. This jelly may also be flavoured with rum, curaçao, Grand-Marnier, Benedictine or other liqueurs. It is used mainly for coating moulds for cold sweets or as a garnish.
(Illustration page 640.)

Moscovite Strawberry Jelly - Moscovite de Fraises

6 persons:
3 gills (4 dl.) basic jelly
11 oz. (300 gr.) strawberries

Rub the strawberries through a sieve and mix the purée with the cold, still liquid jelly. Fill into a mixing bowl and beat on ice like egg white until it is foamy. As soon as it begins to set, fill into a fancy mould with a central funnel, moistened with cold water, and leave to cool until the jelly is set. Turn out on to a round dish and serve with custard sauce or strawberry purée.

This jelly can be made with raspberries, blackberries, cherries, peaches, apricots, etc. Peaches and apricots must be poached before they are rubbed through a sieve.
(Germany)

Orange Jelly - Gelée à l'Orange
6 persons:
1 pt. (5 dl.) basic jelly in which the grated zest of 2 oranges has been infused
$1/2$ pt. ($1/4$ l.) filtered orange juice (Juice of 8-10 oranges)

Mix the cold, but still liquid basic jelly with orange juice and flavour, if desired, with curaçao. Serve in champagne glasses, small china or silver containers or in half oranges scooped out and cleaned.

Wine Jelly - Gelée au Vin
6 persons:
1 pt. (5 dl.) basic jelly
$1/2$ pt. ($1/4$ l.) fine wine

Mix the basic jelly with a very fine wine such as Sherry, Madeira, Port wine, Marsala, Château Yquem, a very fine Rhenish wine, etc. To obtain a lighter jelly which can be served in champagne glasses, take 3-$3 1/4$ gills (about 4 dl.) wine. *(Illustration page 640.)*

MOUSSES AND MOUSSELINES

There are two methods of preparing mousses:

1. Using fresh cream.

2. Using stiffly whisked egg whites or whole eggs.

Chocolate Mousse - Mousse au Chocolat
6 persons:
Method 1
1 pt. ($1/2$ l.) fresh cream
7 oz. (200 gr.) vanilla couverture
1 pt. ($1/2$ l.) hot water
$3 1/2$ oz. (100 gr.) sugar

Melt the couverture in a bain-marie and pour in the hot water so as to obtain a smooth paste. Leave to cool. Fold in the whipped and sweetened cream and serve very cool in a fruit dish.

Method 2
4 egg whites
3 egg yolks
$1 3/4$ oz. (50 gr.) sugar
8 oz. (250 gr.) vanilla couverture
$1/2$ gill (4 cl.) milk

Whisk the whites until stiff. Melt the couverture in the milk in a bain-marie, add the sugar and leave to cool slightly. Stir in the egg yolks rapidly. Leave for 5 minutes and fold in the whisked egg whites. Pour into a fruit dish and serve very cool. *(France)*

Merlot Sabayon
6 persons:
$2/3$ gill (1 dl.) red wine (Merlot)
6 oz. (180 gr.) sugar
1 pinch of salt
3 egg yolks
3 egg whites
3 sheets gelatine

Boil up the wine with 4 oz. (120 gr.) sugar and a pinch of salt, thicken with the egg yolks and add the soaked gelatine. Leave in a cold place until the mixture begins to set, then stir, and fold in the egg whites whisked to a stiff snow with 2 oz. (60 gr.) sugar. Pour at once into individual dishes, decorate with whipped dairy cream and place a marzipan or almond wafer vine-leaf on top. *(Switzerland)*

Raspberry Mousseline - Mousseline aux Framboises
6 persons:
1 lb. 2 oz. (500 gr.) raspberries
$5 1/2$ oz. (150 gr.) icing sugar
Lemon juice
5 sheets gelatine
$3/4$ pt. (4 dl.) whipped cream

Pass the raspberries through a fine meshed sieve. Mix them with the icing sugar and when they are well blended, add the juice of half a lemon and the gelatine soaked and melted. Before the mixture begins to set, fold in the whipped cream. Pour into a glass dish or fruit bowl and leave to cool. Serve with a few choice raspberries on top and sponge fingers.

(France)

Strawberry Mousse - Mousse aux Fraises

6 persons:

1 lb. 2 oz. (500 gr.) strawberries
4 egg whites
5 1/4 oz. (150 gr.) castor sugar
3/4 pt. (4 dl.) whipped cream

Rub the strawberries through a hair sieve and mix them carefully with the stiffly whisked egg whites and the sugar. Fill into a glass dish and decorate with whipped cream and strawberries. Alternatively, sieve the strawberries, mix with sugar and whipped cream, pour into a glass dish and decorate. *(France)*

PIES

Introduction see page 679.

Banana and Apple Pie

Line sandwich plates with sweet pastry. Place in alternate layers of uncooked sliced apple and sliced banana. Sprinkle with sugar and a little cold water. Cover with pastry lids and bake at 400° F (204° C).

Banana Cream Pie

1 lb. 4 oz. (6 dl.) milk
5 oz. (150 gr.) sugar
1 oz. (30 gr.) flour
1 oz. (30 gr.) cornflour
3 eggs
1/2 oz. (15 gr.) butter
1 lb. (500 gr.) mashed banana
2 oz. (60 gr.) sugar
3 egg whites
3 oz. (90 gr.) sugar
Vanilla
Salt

Line plates as for dutch apple tart *(page 735)* and bake empty. Boil the milk and 5 oz. (150 gr.) sugar and add the flour, salt, cornflour and egg mixed together until it thickens. Add the vanilla and stir in. Allow the butter to spread over the surface. When cool stir in the mashed banana mixed with 2 oz. (60 gr.) sugar. Whisk the egg whites with 3 oz. (90 gr.) sugar to a stiff meringue and fold in. Pour in to baked shells and allow to cool. Decorate with whipped dairy cream.

(U.S.A.)

Canadian Cream Pie

Short paste:

2 lb. (1 kg.) flour
1 3/4 oz. (40 gr.) sugar
1 lb. (500 gr.) butter
1 egg
1 pinch of salt
Water as required

Filling:

1 lb. 8 oz. (750 gr.) icing sugar
1/2 pt. (1/4 l.) cream
2 oz. (60 gr.) flour

Make the short paste, leave to rest, pin out and use half the paste to line pie tins with a rim 1 in. (2.5 cm.) high. To make the filling, mix the flour with the cream, add the sugar, boil for a few minutes and leave until cold.

Spread the filling on the paste in the tins, cover with the remaining paste, brush with beaten egg, prick with a fork and decorate. Bake off and leave until completely cold before cutting up. Serve whipped cream separately. *(Canada)*

Lemon Meringue Pie

Paste:

6 oz. (175 gr.) flour
3 1/2 oz. (100 gr.) butter
1/2 oz. (15 gr.) sugar
1 pinch of salt
1/3 gill (5 cl.) water

Lemon cream:

6 oz. (180 gr.) sugar
1 oz. (30 gr.) butter

2 egg yolks
2 ⅓ gills (3 ½ dl.) hot water
1 ½ oz. (40 gr.) cornflour
Juice and grated zest of 3 lemons
A few drops of colour

Meringue:
3 egg whites
3 oz. (90 gr.) castor sugar

Mix the flour, sugar and salt with the butter, add the water and work together thoroughly. Pin out, line a flan ring with the paste, and bake blind in a slow oven.

Place the ingredients for the lemon cream in a pan and bring to the boil, stirring continuously. Fill into the pastry case while still warm. To make the meringue, whip the egg whites to a snow and fold in the sugar. Cover the lemon cream smoothly with the meringue and flash in a hot oven. *(U.S.A.)*

Honey Orange Raisin Pie
12 oz. (375 gr.) water
4 oz. (125 gr.) honey
4 oz. (125 gr.) raisins (seeded)
2 oz. (60 gr.) nib almonds
1 ½ oz. (45 gr.) cornflour
2 oz. (60 gr.) water

Bring to the boil the water, honey, raisins and almonds. Mix the cornflour with the 2 oz. (60 gr.) of water and add to thicken. When cool fill into sandwich plates prepared as for Dutch Apple Tart. Place lids on each with sweet pastry and bake at 425° F (217° C).

RICE DESSERTS

Palermo Style Rice - Riz à la palermitaine
Prepare Empress style rice as indicated and fill it into a border mould coated with blood orange jelly about ¼ in. (5 mm.) thick. Turn out on to a round dish, fill the centre with Chantilly cream and decorate with skinned orange segments macerated in curaçao. *(France)*

Rice Empress Style - Riz à l'Impératrice
5 persons:
3 ½ oz. (100 gr.) Carolina rice
3 ½ oz. (100 gr.) sugar
3 ½ oz. (100 gr.) candied fruit
3 egg yolks
1 pt. (6 dl.) milk
½ pt. (¼ l.) whipped cream
½ gill (5 cl.) red currant jelly (see jellies)
5 sheets gelatine
⅛ gill (2 cl.) kirsch
½ vanilla bean

Cooking time: 25 minutes

Blanch the rice for 2 minutes and finish cooking in ½ pt. (3 dl.) milk with the vanilla. Prepare a custard cream with the remaining milk, egg yolks and sugar, add the gelatine, previously soaked, pass through a chinois and leave to cool. When the rice is cooked, remove from the heat, incorporate the custard cream and leave the mixture until it starts to set. Then fold in the whipped cream and the diced candied fruit which has been macerated in kirsch. Cover the bottom of a mould with a central funnel, with the red currant jelly and when this has set, fill with the rice mixture. Place in cold storage before turning out on a round dish. *(France)*

Rice Liguria
1 pt. (6 dl.) milk
3 ½ oz. (100 gr.) rice
1 pinch of salt
1 vanilla pod
5 sheets gelatine
3 ½ oz. (100 gr.) sugar
1 pt. (½ l.) whipped dairy cream
10 half peaches cut into small dice and macerated in kirsch

Simmer the rice in the milk with the vanilla until it is well cooked. Add the soaked gelatine and the sugar, then leave in a cold place. Line the bottom of a timbale mould with wine jelly. As soon as the rice begins to set, fold in the cream, stir in the diced peaches and transfer to the mould. When cold, arrange on a dish with fresh peaches poached in stock syrup, allowing one peach per person, and serve with kirsch flavoured apricot sauce. *(Illustration page 790.)* *(Switzerland)*

Rice Trauttmansdorf - Riz Trauttmansdorf

6 persons:

3 1/2 oz. (100 gr.) Carolina rice
3 1/2 oz. (100 gr.) sugar
Vanilla
1 pt. (6 dl.) milk
1/2 pt. (1/4 l.) whipped cream
3 1/2 oz. (100 gr.) fresh fruit in season
5 sheets gelatine
1/4 gill (3 cl.) maraschino
1/2 pt. (1/4 l.) purée of fresh strawberries or raspberries

Dice the fruit and macerate in maraschino. Blanch the rice and finish cooking in the milk with the vanilla. When the rice is cooked, add the sugar and the gelatine which has first been soaked in water. Remove from the heat and allow to cool. Fold in the whipped cream, the diced fruit and the maraschino, pour into a jelly mould and leave to set. Turn out on to a round dish and serve with the fruit purée. *(Austria)*

Singapore Rice - Riz Singapour

6 persons:

3 1/2 oz. (100 gr.) Carolina rice
3 1/2 oz. (100 gr.) sugar
3 egg yolks
1 pt. (6 dl.) milk
1/2 pt. (1/4 l.) whipped cream
5 sheets gelatine
7 oz. (200 gr.) diced pineapple
1/4 gill (3 cl.) maraschino
1/2 pt. (1/4 l.) apricot sauce

Prepare the rice as indicated above and mix in the pineapple, poached and macerated in maraschino. Pour the mixture into a high mould with a central funnel and leave to cool. Turn out on to a round dish and serve with a cold apricot sauce, flavoured with the maraschino used to macerate the pineapple.

Tangerine Rice - Riz à la Mandarine

6 persons:

3 1/2 oz. (100 gr.) Carolina rice
3 1/2 oz. (100 gr.) sugar
3 egg yolks
1 pt. (6 dl.) milk
1/2 pt. (1/4 l.) whipped cream
5 sheets gelatine
5 tangerines
1/8 gill (2 cl.) curaçao

Prepare the rice in the same way as above, but flavour the custard with tangerine zest. Pour into a dome-shaped mould and leave to cool. Turn the rice out on to a round dish and decorate with tangerine segments macerated in curaçao. For this purpose tinned Japanese orange-tangerine segments may be used.

Turkish Creamed Rice - Mahallebi

6 persons:

2 1/4 oz. (60 gr.) rice
5 1/4 oz. (150 gr.) rice starch
1 pt. (6 dl.) fresh cream
9 oz. (250 gr.) castor sugar
Rose water

Cooking time: 1 hour

Simmer the rice in 2 1/4 gills (3-4 dl.) of water until it is well cooked and strain off the water through a cloth. As soon as this liquor is cold, mix it with the rice starch, add cream and sugar and cook slowly, stirring all the time. When the mixture begins to gel, remove from the heat and leave to cool while still stirring. Pour into small glass goblets, sprinkle with sugar and add a few drops of rose water.

(Turkey)

SNOW EGGS

Snow Eggs - Œufs à la Neige

6 persons:

5 egg whites
9 oz. (250 gr.) sugar
1 1/2 pt. (3/4 l.) milk
1/2 vanilla bean

Cooking time: 3-6 minutes

Beat the egg whites stiffly and fold in 7 oz. (200 gr.) sugar. Boil up the milk with the vanilla bean. Spoon the whites into the hot milk giving them egg shape and poach without allowing the milk to boil. After 2 minutes turn them over and when they are firm enough, take them out of the milk with a skimmer and drain on a cloth. Prepare custard sauce with the milk, egg yolks and the rest of the sugar, strain and leave to cool. Dress the snow eggs in a deep dish and coat with the custard sauce. Serve very cold. *(France)*
(Illustration page 661.)

Snow Eggs Carmen - Œufs Carmen

6 persons:

12 snow eggs
2 gills (3 dl.) whipped cream
Juice of $1/2$ orange
$1/8$ gill (2 cl.) curaçao
$1/2$ pt. ($1/4$ l.) fresh raspberry purée slightly sweetened
$1/2$ oz. (15 gr.) chopped pistachio nuts
2 sheets gelatine

Soak and squeeze out the gelatine, melt it in a bain-marie with a few drops of water and mix it with the orange juice. Bind the sweetened whipped cream with the gelatine, flavour with curaçao and dress in a glass bowl in dome shape. Leave to set. Arrange the snow eggs around, mask with raspberry purée and sprinkle with chopped pistachio nuts. *(Germany)*

Snow Eggs with Chocolate Sauce - Œufs à la Religieuse

6 persons:

12 snow eggs
2 gills (3 dl.) milk
2 egg yolks
$1 \ 3/4$ oz. (50 gr.) sugar
$3 \ 1/2$ oz. (100 gr.) chocolate
2 oz. (60 gr.) praline

Prepare the snow eggs as usual. Make a custard with the milk, egg yolks, sugar and chocolate. Strain and leave to cool. Coat the snow eggs with the cold chocolate sauce and sprinkle copiously with crushed praline. *(France)*

My Dream - Mon Rêve

6 persons:

5 oz. (125 gr.) not too sweet chocolate
$3/4$ gill (6 cl.) syrup
3 gills (4 dl.) whipped cream
$1 \ 3/4$ oz. (50 gr.) crushed, sifted praline
$1/8$ gill (2 cl.) kirsch
12 small snow eggs
$1/2$ pt. ($1/4$ l.) custard sauce

Disperse the chocolate in the syrup, stir well and leave to cool. Fold the chocolate and the praline in to the whipped cream and dress in a dome shape bowl. Arrange the snow eggs on top and mask them with custard sauce flavoured with kirsch.
(Germany)

TARTS

(Tarts to be served hot *see page 694*).

Fruit tarts are too often regarded by the craftsman as being of secondary importance. However it should not be forgotten that customers expect to buy tarts from the pastrycook which are different from what they make at home. The craftsman should in fact use great care and take pride in everything which he produces. The following points should therefore be observed:

1. Prepare a neat and trim pastry case.
2. Use top quality fruit.
3. Bake properly (the base especially).
4. Do not offer for sale any cakes or tarts which are not fresh.

Method of making: Line a tart mould or flan ring with short paste or puff paste (the best results are obtained if this is done the day before the tarts are required). Before filling with fruit (apricots, apples, pears, etc. according to the season), prick the paste with a fork so as to avoid it rising while it is being baked. Next arrange the fruit in the case, place knobs of butter here and there and sprinkle with sugar. When baked, glaze by brushing with boiling hot apricot purée. Alternatively it is possible to cover the

fruit before the tart is baked with a flan cream (guélon). When they come out of the oven, the tarts are finished ready for sale.
(Illustrations pages 690-691.)

Apple Streusel Tart

To make this tart a mould is lined with sweet, enriched dough *(page 176)* and a streusel mixture is sprinkled on top. Prepare this dough like a brioche dough *(page 177)*. When it has risen, use it to line some sandwich plates. Next put a layer of almond paste mixed with an equal quantity of confectioner's custard and cover up with chopped apples and sultanas. Finally sprinkle generously some streusel mixture on top *(page 226)*. Bake in a medium oven.

Amarena Tart - Crostata di Amarena

Line a deep flan ring with pasta frolla *(page 188)*. Cover the bottom with pastry cream. Bake at 375° F (190° C). When cool, cover the top with chopped amarenas and glaze with apricot purée. *(Italy)*

Alsatian Apple Tart - Tarte aux Pommes à l'alsacienne

7 oz. (200 gr.) flour
$1/2$ oz. (15 gr.) yeast
1 egg
$2/3$ gill (1 dl.) milk
$1/2$ oz. (15 gr.) icing sugar

Filling:

1 lb. (500 gr.) ripe apples
$2 1/2$ oz. (75 gr.) sugar
$1 3/4$ oz. (50 gr.) chopped almonds
$1/16$ oz. (2 gr.) cinnamon
Butter

Make a fermented dough with the flour, yeast, egg, milk and sugar. Leave to rise, then pin out and line a flan ring with the dough. Peel, quarter and core the apples, cut them into slices, mix with the sugar, almonds and cinnamon, fill into the lined flan ring, allow to prove, cover with small knobs of butter and bake in a hot oven.
(France)

Apple Tart Condé Style - Tarte aux Pommes Condé

1 lb. (500 gr.) sweet short pastry
1 lb. (500 gr.) thick apple purée
Royal icing

Line a flan ring with sweet short pastry, fill with the cold apple purée, moisten the rim of the pastry, cover with a circle of sweet short pastry, press down firmly round the edge and cut off any surplus pastry. Bake in a hot oven, remove, coat the top thinly with royal icing, allow to dry a little, then place in a moderately hot oven to dry out the icing without colouring it. *(France)*

Dutch Apple Tart

1 lb. 8 oz. (750 gr.) apples
$2 1/2$ oz. (75 gr.) water
5 oz. (150 gr.) sugar
8 oz. (250 gr.) raisins (seeded)
$1/4$ oz. (8 gr.) cinnamon

Line 7 in. (18 cm.) sandwich plates with sweet paste, allowing enough overlap to knit the lid. In each tart add 12 oz. (375 gr.) of the mixture. Cover with a lid of sweet pastry, trim the edge and bake at 400° F (204° C).

English Apple Tart - Tarte aux Pommes à l'anglaise

6-8 persons:

18 oz. (560 gr.) of short paste
18 oz. (560 gr.) thick apple purée
3 large cooking apples
$3 1/2$ oz. (100 gr.) apricot purée

Baking time:
25-30 minutes at 400° F (204° C)

Line a greased flan hoop with the short paste, keeping the rim a little thicker than the sides and base. Pinch the top edge into a neat design all round, so to form the ridge of the tart. Fill with cold apple purée and smooth down. Cover completely with thin slices of apple each overlapping. As soon as removed from the oven, spread a thin layer of apricot purée over the top. Alternatively, the top may be dusted with icing sugar.

Apple Meringue Tart - Tarte aux Pommes meringuée

8 persons:

18 oz. (560 gr.) short paste
18 oz. (560 gr.) thick apple purée

Meringue:

2 egg whites
3 ½ oz. (100 gr.) icing sugar
3 oz. (90 gr.) red currant jelly
3 oz. (90 gr.) apricot jam

Baking temperature 360° F (182° C). Baking time 25 minutes for the tart, 3-4 minutes to crust the meringue. Line a greased flan ring with short paste, prick the base, and press edges off with a rolling pin. Fill with apple purée and bake. Coat fairly thickly with meringue and smooth top and sides. Pipe a diamond pattern and a round edge on top. Dredge with icing sugar and place the tart in a slow oven to crisp the meringue and to brown it lightly. Finally fill the cavities alternately with red currant jelly and apricot jam.

Swabian Apple Tart - Schwäbische Apfeltorte

Scrap puff pastry
Red currant jelly
10 in. (25 cm.) butter sponge base

Custard:

½ pt. (3 dl.) milk
½ pt. (3 dl.) dairy cream
3 oz. (80 gr.) sugar
2 oz. (60 gr.) custard powder
5 oz. (150 gr.) egg
A little grated lemon zest and vanilla
2 lb. (1 kg.) peeled apples cut in half
Rum
Apricot jam
Apple jelly
3 ½ oz. (100 gr.) roasted strip almonds

Line a 10 in. (25 cm.) mould with tapered sides with the scrap puff pastry and brush with red currant jelly. Place the thin butter sponge base on top and cover with the custard. Arrange the apple halves on top after cutting them in slices part of the way through so that they still hold together. Bake for about 45 minutes at 375° F (190° C). When cold, moisten the apple halves with rum, brush with hot apricot jam, glaze with clear apple jelly and sprinkle round the edge with roasted strip almonds.
(Illustration page 691.) (Germany)

Trellised Apple Tart - Tarte aux Pommes grillagée

6 persons:

18 oz. (560 gr.) sweet paste
18 oz. (560 gr.) thick, cold apple purée
1 egg
3 ½ oz. (100 gr.) red currant jelly

Baking temperature 400° F (204° C).
Baking time 25 minutes.

Line a plain ring and trim off the paste at the edge. Fill up to the top with lightly sweetened apple purée. Cut the remaining sweet paste into strips and arrange them in a trellis on top. Press down well at the edges. Brush with egg on top and bake. After baking, brush the top with red currant jelly. Serve cold, decorated with whipped cream if desired.

Apricot Tart I - Tarte aux Abricots

6-8 portions:

1 lb. (500 gr.) sweet short pastry or puff pastry cuttings
2 lb. (1 kg.) apricots
Apricot jam
Icing sugar

Baking time: 25 minutes

Line a flan ring with the pastry, leaving it a little thicker round the edge to form the rim, then crimp the top. Dust the bottom well with icing sugar and arrange the halved, stoned, slightly flattened apricots on top each overlapping the other a little. Dust lightly with icing sugar and bake in a hot oven. After removing from the oven, glaze at once with hot apricot jam. (France)

Apricot Tart II - Tarte aux Abricots

14 oz. (400 gr.) French sweet pastry
1 ½ lb. (750 gr.) apricots
3 ½ oz. (100 gr.) icing sugar
7 oz. (200 gr.) apricot jam

Line a flan ring with the pastry and dust the bottom lightly with icing sugar. Cover evenly with halved, stoned, slightly flattened apricots each overlapping the other a little. Bake in a hot oven. On removing from the oven, glaze at once with hot apricot jam and, if desired, sprinkle with lightly roasted flaked almonds. *(France)*

Apricot Tart III - Tarte aux Abricots

8 oz. (250 gr.) butter
10 oz. (300 gr.) almond paste
7 egg yolks
5 egg whites
3 1/2 oz. (100 gr.) sugar
5 oz. (150 gr.) flour

Use the mixing machine to cream together the almond paste, butter and egg yolks. Whisk the egg whites with the sugar until stiff and fold in the flour. Next amalgamate both these mixtures carefully. Line a flan ring with milanese paste and brush the bottom with apricot purée. Then, after coating thinly with the prepared mixture, add a layer of halved apricots and cover over with the same mixture. Bake in a medium oven. Brush with apricot purée and glaze thinly with white fondant.

Apricot Streusel - Aprikosenstreusel

9 oz. (275 gr.) kuchen dough *(page 176)*
4 oz. (125 gr.) curd filling
12 oz. (100 gr.) halved blanched apricots (approx.)
3 1/2 oz. (100 gr.) butter streusel *(page 226)*

Line a round aluminium foil case 7 in. (18 cm.) in diameter with the kuchen dough. Spread with the curd filling, cover with the apricots and sprinkle with the butter streusel.

After baking, dust the cake with icing sugar. *(Germany)*

Bilberry Tart - Heidelbeerenkuchen

4 1/2 oz. (140 gr.) butter
5 1/4 oz. (150 gr.) sugar
4 1/4 oz. (125 gr.) nib almonds
3 1/2 oz. (100 gr.) bread crumbs soaked in milk
4 egg yolks
6 egg whites
1 3/4 oz. (50 gr.) flour
1 lb. 2 oz. (560 gr.) bilberries
1/8 oz. (3 gr.) cinnamon

Cream the butter with half the sugar and the cinnamon. Add the egg yolks one at a time, the nib almonds and the bread crumbs which have been passed through a sieve. Whisk the egg whites with the rest of the sugar until stiff. Blend in the flour and bilberries. Next amalgamate the two mixtures. Grease some flan rings and line with parchment paper. Fill with the mixture and bake in a medium oven. When cool, dust with icing sugar. The bilberries may be replaced by other fruit such as raspberries, black currants, etc.
(Germany)

Cherry Tart - Kirschenkuchen

8 3/4 oz. (250 gr.) butter
14 oz. (400 gr.) sugar
12 egg whites
8 egg yolks
5 1/4 oz. (150 gr.) strip almonds
7 oz. (200 gr.) flour

Cream the butter and half the sugar, gradually adding the egg yolks. Whisk the egg whites and remaining sugar until stiff and fold in the almonds and flour; blend both mixtures. Line flan rings with milanese paste, cover with some stoned cherries and fill up with the mixture. Bake in a medium oven. When cool, dust with icing sugar.

Covered Cherry Tart - Gedeckter Kirschenkuchen

9 oz. (275 gr.) sweet paste *(page 185)*
Thin butter sponge base *(page 196)*
10 1/2 oz. (300 gr.) stewed morello cherries
Raspberry jam
Vanilla custard *(page 241)*

Line a round aluminium foil case 7 in. (18 cm.) in diameter with the sweet paste and bake lightly. Spread with raspberry jam after baking and lay the thin butter sponge base on top. Cover with the cherries and top with the vanilla custard shaped into a dome. Sprinkle with flaked almonds, brown lightly in a hot oven and dust with icing sugar. *(Germany)*

Coconut Custard Tart

1 pt. ($^1/_2$ l.) milk
3 oz. (90 gr.) sugar
6 oz. (180 gr.) egg
$^1/_4$ oz. (8 gr.) cornflour
4 oz. (125 gr.) coconut
Vanilla

Blend all together. Proceed as for Dutch Apple Tart. Fill with the custard and bake at 390° F (200° C).

Coconut Meringue Tart

Proceed as for Coconut Custard Tart. When baked, cover with meringue and flash in an oven at 460° F (240° C).

Florida Tourte - Tourte Florida

10 portions:
Sponge:
3 whole eggs
1 egg yolk
3 $^3/_4$ oz. (110 gr.) sugar
3 $^3/_4$ oz. (110 gr.) sieved flour

Warm the eggs, egg yolk and sugar to blood heat and whip to a stiff sponge. Fold in the flour, fill into a 8 in. (21 cm.) mould and bake for 20 minutes at 400° F (204° C). When cold, split twice, sandwich with diplomat cream flavoured with kirsch and cover with the same cream. Sprinkle round the side with roasted almond nibs and cover the top with fruit of various kinds, paying particular attention to the combination of colours. Brush with pectin or wine jelly.
(Illustration page 543.) *(Switzerland)*

Fruit Tart - Crostata di Frutta

Fresh, preserved or canned fruit can be used.

Line a flan ring with pasta frolla and bake blind at 400° F (204° C). When cool remove from the ring and spread inside with a cream made from 3 $^1/_2$ oz. (100 gr.) of apricot jam and 3 $^1/_2$ oz. (100 gr.) of pastry cream. Place a disc of maddalena cake on top, impregnated with a liqueur which will correspond to the fruit which is to be used to decorate the top. Glaze with apricot purée. *(Italy)*

Gooseberry Tart

5 $^1/_4$ oz. (150 gr.) butter
12 oz. (375 gr.) sugar
7 oz. (200 gr.) ground almonds
3 $^1/_2$ oz. (100 gr.) Sauterne (white wine)
6 egg whites
4 egg yolks
1 $^3/_4$ oz. (50 gr.) flour
1 lb. 2 oz. (560 gr.) gooseberries

Line some tart moulds or flan rings with scrap puff paste and fill with the above mixture. Cream the butter and half the sugar. Add the egg yolks, almonds and white wine. Meanwhile whisk the egg whites with the rest of the sugar until stiff. Blend in the flour carefully. Next amalgamate the two mixtures, finally adding the gooseberries. Bake in a medium oven. As soon as the tarts come out of the oven, brush with apricot purée and glaze with white fondant.

Greengage Tart - Tarte aux Prunes Reines-Claudes

Make in the same way as plum tart, but mask with apricot jam to blend with their colour.

La Palma Bilberry Gâteau - Heidelbeertorte La Palma

Place a little kirsch flavoured diplomat cream on an evenly baked disc of French sweet pastry. Scoop the centre out of a butter sponge base, place it on the sweet pastry and moisten slightly with kirsch syrup. Fill the hollow with a little diplomat cream and with slightly sweetened bilberries. Cover the whole gâteau excepting the bilberries with meringue tinted pale pink and flash. *(Switzerland)*
(Illustration page 542.)

La Palma Bilberry Tartlets - Heidelbeertörtchen La Palma

Line tartlet moulds evenly with French sweet pastry and bake blind. When cold, spread the inside thinly with couverture, cover with a few sponge cuttings and moisten with kirsch syrup. Pipe a little diplomat cream on top, fill up with bilberries, decorate with meringue as above and flash. *(Switzerland)*
(Illustration page 542.)

Lemon Tart

6 oz. (180 gr.) butter
6 oz. (180 gr.) sugar
7 oz. (200 gr.) egg
4 oz. (125 gr.) bread crumbs
Zest and juice of 2 lemons

Proceed as for Dutch Apple Tart. Spread bottom of pastry with lemon curd and fill with the above filling. Bake at 400° F (204° C).

Lemon Chiffon Tart

1 $^3/_4$ pt. (1 l.) water
1 $^1/_2$ lb. (750 gr.) sugar
8 leaves gelatine
Grated zest of 3 lemons
Juice of 6 lemons
12 egg yolks
10 egg whites whipped to a stiff snow
Sweet short paste

Beat the water, egg yolks, sugar, gelatine, lemon zest and juice over gentle heat until thick, leave until almost cold and blend in the egg whites whipped to a stiff snow. Fill into tartlet shells made of sweet short paste, baked blind. Dust with castor sugar and lightly brown under a salamander.

Known in the U.S.A. as a pie. *(U.S.A.)*

Lemon Meringue Tart

10 oz. (3 dl.) milk
3 oz. (90 gr.) sugar
1 oz. (30 gr.) cornflour
3 oz. (90 gr.) egg
$^1/_8$ oz. (3 gr.) cinnamon
Zest and juice of 2 lemons
4 oz. (120 gr.) egg whites
3 oz. (90 gr.) sugar

Line plates as for Dutch Apple Tart. Boil the milk with the zest and thicken with the cornflour mixed with the egg. Add 3 oz. (90 gr.) sugar, the lemon juice and cinnamon. Fill into shells and bake at 400° F (204° C). Spread with meringue made with egg whites and 3 oz. (90 gr.) of sugar and flash in a hot oven.

Meringue Tart

This is a different sort of tart as it is composed half of meringue mixture (egg whites whisked with sugar until stiff) and half fruit. For the best meringue tarts, use small fruits such as strawberries, raspberries, blackberries, bilberries, etc.

Prepare the meringue tart in the following way:

Line a flan ring or a sandwich plate with milanese paste, puff paste or fine short paste and bake blind. Fill with a meringue mixture (14 oz. [400 gr.] sugar per pint [$^1/_2$ l.] egg whites) to which the washed fruit has been added. Keep aside a little of the meringue mixture not containing fruit to smooth over the tart and maybe to decorate the top, using a savoy bag fitted with either a plain or a star pipe.

Lightly dust with sugar and put in the oven at a temperature about 425-440° F (220-230° C). The tart must not stay too long in the oven as it would run. A good meringue mixture should have a nice golden colour. If the tart has to be cut into portions, it is advisable to use a wet knife.
(Illustration page 691.)

Mirabelle-Plum, Damson and Peach Tart, etc. - Tartes aux Mirabelles, Prunes de Damas, Pêches, etc.

Make in the same way as Apricot Tart and mask with apricot jam.

Orange Tart

8 persons:
1 lb. (500 gr.) sweet or puff pastry
 cuttings

2 lb. (1 kg.) shredded orange slices
Apricot jam
Orange and cherries crystallized

Baking temperature: 360° F (182° C)
Baking time: 25-30 minutes

Make a puff pastry case (see Apricot Tart) or line a flan ring with short pastry. When the pastry is cool, put in the orange slices. Glaze with a covering of hot apricot purée. Decorate with pieces of orange and crystallized cherries. Never decorate this tart in advance, the pastry will get soft.
(Illustration page 690.) *(France)*

Orange Chiffon Tart

Proceed as for Lemon Chiffon Tart but substitute zest of 2 oranges for zest of 1 lemon and 5 oz. (150 gr.) of orange juice instead of 3 oz. (90 gr.) of lemon juice.

Pear Tart - Tarte aux Poires

8 persons:

18 oz. (560 gr.) sweet paste
18 oz. (560 gr.) thick apple purée
4 pears
Red wine
Sugar
3 1/2 oz. (100 gr.) red currant jelly

Baking temperature: 360° F (182° C)
Baking time: 25-30 minutes

Line a ring with sweet paste and notch the edge. Prick the base with a fork and fill with apple purée and bake. Meanwhile, peel the pears, cut them in half and scoop out the core. Poach them in sweetened red wine. Drain well and arrange them on top of the apple purée, pressing them down a little. Coat generously with strained red currant jelly.

Pineapple Tart - Tarte à l'Ananas

10-12 persons:

10 oz. (300 gr.) butter
10 oz. (300 gr.) sugar
8 egg yolks
8 egg whites
8 oz. (250 gr.) flour
10 oz. (300 gr.) chopped pineapple

12 oz. (400 gr.) puff pastry cuttings
3 1/2 oz. (100 gr.) apricot jam
7 oz. (200 gr.) fondant
Crystallized pineapple

Baking temperature: 360° F (182° C)
Baking time: 30 minutes

Line flan rings with sweet paste as for apricot tart and fill with the above mixture. Beat the butter with half the sugar, add egg yolks one by one. Beat the whites stiffly with remainder of the sugar. Mix these two together with the flour and the pineapple and bake. Mask with apricot jam and spread with pale yellow fondant. Decorate with pieces of pineapple.

Plum Tart - Tarte aux Quetsches

8 persons:

1 lb. 2 oz. (560 gr.) short pastry
2 1/4 lb. (1 kg.) plums
3 1/2 oz. (100 gr.) icing sugar
7 1/2 oz. (215 gr.) red currant jelly

Baking temperature: 360° F (182° C)
Baking time: 20-25 minutes

Line a ring with short pastry, fill with halved, stoned and slightly flattened plums and overlap them slightly. Bake and mask with red currant jelly when done.

Prune Tart - Tarte aux Pruneaux

8 persons:

1 lb. 2 oz. (560 gr.) short pastry
10 oz. (300 gr.) nice large prunes
7 1/2 oz. (200 gr.) apricot jam or
  red currant jelly

Baking temperature: 360° F (182° C)
Baking time: 20-25 minutes

Soak the prunes, boil, cool and then stone them. Drain well, put into a lined ring and bake. Mask with red currant jelly or apricot jam. Do not sweeten the prunes when boiling.

Raisin Tart

Line sandwich plates as for Dutch Apple Tart and bake empty; when cool fill with this mixture:

2 lb. (1 kg.) raisins
1 lb. 4 oz. (625 gr.) water
1 $^1/_2$ oz. (45 gr.) arrowroot
3 oz. (90 gr.) water
8 oz. (250 gr.) sugar

Wash the raisins and boil in the 1 $^1/_4$ lb. (625 gr.) of water. Thicken with the arrowroot dispersed in 3 oz. (90 gr.) water and add the sugar. Fill into the shells and when cool decorate with whipped dairy cream.

Rhubarb Tart - Tarte à la Rhubarbe

8 persons:

1 lb. 2 oz. (560 gr.) short or sweet pastry
2 lb. (1 kg.) rhubarb
5 oz. (150 gr.) icing sugar
8 oz. (250 gr.) apricot jam

Baking temperature: 360° F (182° C)
Baking time: 30-35 minutes

Peel the rhubarb, cut in 1-inch (2.5 cm.) pieces and macerate with the sugar for 1 hour. Drain very thoroughly before filling the tart. Bake and mask with apricot jam.

Strawberry Tart - Tarte aux Fraises

8 persons:

1 lb. 2 oz. (560 gr.) sweet paste
2 lb. (1 kg.) strawberries
8 oz. (250 gr.) red currant jelly

Baking temperature: 360° F (182° C)
Baking time: 20-25 minutes

Line a ring with sweet pastry and make a nice roll round the edge. Bake unfilled, i.e. line with paper and fill with dried peas or broken rice, which can be used again and bake. Remove paper and peas and when cold fill with nice strawberries of the same size. Mask with red currant jelly. Do not fill too early, otherwise the fruit juice will soak the pastry. Most fruit tarts are baked with the filling; it is only in case of soft fruit such as strawberries, raspberries, blackberries, etc., that they are baked empty.

Note: To stop the bottom of the tart becoming soaked when soft fruit is used, sprinkle fine stale cake or rusk crumbs on the bottom before filling; they will absorb the moisture.
(Illustration page 690.)

Strawberry Tart Modern Style - Tarte aux Fraises à la moderne

14 oz. (400 gr.) sweet short pastry
1 $^1/_2$ lb. (750 gr.) medium-size even-shaped strawberries
About 7 oz. (200 gr.) red currant jelly
Couverture
Chopped pistachio nuts

Line a flan ring with the pastry and bake blind. Allow to cool, then spread the bottom thinly with couverture, allow it to set and fill symmetrically with the strawberries. Brush evenly with red currant jelly and decorate the edge with chopped pistachio nuts. *(France)*

FLANS

Andalusian Flan - Flan à l'andalouse

8 persons:

1 lb. 2 oz. (560 gr.) short pastry
1 $^1/_4$ lb. (600 gr.) orange-flavoured pastry cream
7 oz. (200 gr.) orange fondant
2 pieces of candied orange peel

Baking temperature: 375° F (190° C)
Baking time: 25 minutes

Line the ring with short pastry, prick it and fill with pastry cream heavily flavoured with orange. Bake and spread with orange fondant when cold. Decorate with pieces of candied orange peel.

Apricot Flan - Flan aux Abricots

8 persons:

1 lb. 2 oz. (560 gr.) sweet pastry or puff paste trimmings
2 lb. (1 kg.) apricots
3 $^1/_2$ oz. (100 gr.) icing sugar
Strained apricot jam

Baking temperature: 360° F (182° C)
Baking time: 25-30 minutes

Line a ring with the paste, prick, dust bottom lightly with icing sugar and fill with half stoned apricots, lightly flattened and overlapping slightly. Bake in a hot oven. When done glaze at once with thick, hot apricot jam.

Cherry Flan - Flan aux Cerises

8 persons:

1 lb. 2 oz. (560 gr.) sweet pastry
2 lb. (1 kg.) stoned cherries
3 1/2 oz. (100 gr.) icing sugar
4 oz. (125 gr.) red currant jelly
Baking temperature: 380° F (193° C)
Baking time: 25-30 minutes

Put a flan ring on a baking sheet, line it with the pastry, pinch the edge, prick the bottom several times and dust lightly with icing sugar. Place the cherries closely together with the hole left by stoning facing down and bake. After some time reduce the heat somewhat. When done dust heavily with vanilla flavoured icing sugar or, better still, glaze with strained red currant jelly. This flan can also be made from tinned cherries.

Alsatian Custard Flan - Flan au Lait à l'alsacienne

8 persons:

1 lb. 2 oz. (560 gr.) short pastry
4 eggs
3 1/2 oz. (100 gr.) sugar
Vanilla
1/2 pt. (1/4 l.) milk
10 oz. (300 gr.) apples
1 oz. (30 gr.) butter
Baking time: 30-35 minutes

Slice the peeled apples, simmer in butter and cool. Line the ring in the usual way, cover the bottom with apples, add vanilla-flavoured custard mixture and bake at 360° F (193° C).

Plain Custard Flan - Flan simple au Lait

8 persons:

1 lb. 2 oz. (560 gr.) short pastry
2 eggs
3 1/2 oz. (100 gr.) sugar
2 oz. (60 gr.) flour
1/2 pt. (1/4 l.) cold milk
Baking time: 25-30 minutes

Line ring in the usual way, fill with a mixture of the beaten eggs, flour, sugar and milk poured through a pointed strainer. Bake at 360° F (193° C).

Fisherman's Flan - Flan à la Batelière

8 persons:

14 oz. (400 gr.) short paste
9 oz. (275 gr.) thick apple purée
3 1/2 oz. (100 gr.) rice
5 oz. (150 gr.) vanilla sugar
1 pt. (1/2 l.) milk
2 egg yolks
1/4 gill (4 cl.) kirsch
2 egg whites
Apricot or gooseberry sauce

Line a flan hoop with the short paste. Fill with apple purée and bake in an oven about 400° F (204° C). Cook the rice in milk. When it is cooked add the sugar and egg yolks. Fold in the stiffly whipped whites and pile the mixture on the top of the flan. Smooth the top and sides of the rice and place in an oven about 356° F (180° C), to finish cooking. Take from the oven and dust heavily with icing sugar and caramelize the sugar in a criss-cross pattern with a red hot iron. Serve separately apricot or gooseberry sauce flavoured with kirsch. *(France)*

Frangipane Flan - Flan à la Frangipane

8 persons:

1 lb. 2 oz. (560 gr.) short pastry
12 1/2 oz. (375 gr.) frangipane custard
1 3/4 oz. (50 gr.) ground almonds
Baking time: 25 minutes

Fill the lined ring with frangipane custard with ground almonds. Do not fix a roll of pastry round the edge but cover with a lattice of crimp-edged strips of paste. Bake at 360° F (193° C).

VARIOUS COLD SWEETS

Bettina Tartlets - Bettina-Törtchen

6 persons:
Couverture
1/2 pt. (3 dl.) milk
2 egg yolks
2 oz. (60 gr.) sugar
2 oz. (60 gr.) cornflour
4 sheets gelatine
2 1/2 oz. (75 gr.) chopped candied fruit
1/4 gill (3 cl.) maraschino
1 1/2 gills (2 dl.) whipped cream
6 Florentine biscuits

Preparation: 30 minutes

Melt and temper couverture and line silver ice cream coupes or small vegetable dishes to a thickness of 1/5 in. (6 mm.). Allow the couverture to harden and, after trimming the edges, remove from the improvised moulds. Macerate the candied fruit in maraschino. Prepare the custard cream with the egg yolks, milk, sugar and cornflour and add the gelatine, which has first been soaked. When the custard begins to set, fold in the whipped cream and the candied fruit and fill the chocolate cases straight away. Cover with a Florentine biscuit of the same diameter as the chocolate case to serve as a lid.

Florentine biscuits:
7 oz. (200 gr.) butter
12 oz. (375 gr.) sugar
4 1/2 oz. (140 gr.) honey
1 lb. 2 oz. (560 gr.) nibbed almonds
4 1/2 oz. (140 gr.) chopped candied orange peel
4 1/2 oz. (140 gr.) glucose
1/4 pt. (1 1/2 dl.) fresh cream
Glacé cherries
Couverture

Baking time: 20 minutes

Place all the ingredients together in a saucepan and cook to the thread stirring constantly. Drop spoonfuls of the mixture on a waxed baking sheet and bake in a hot oven for about 10 minutes. Take out of the oven and cut each biscuit with a round pastry cutter. Place half a glacé cherry in the middle of each biscuit and replace in the oven to finish baking. Remove the biscuits from the baking sheet while they are still hot. As soon as they are cool, coat the base of each biscuit with couverture. Leave to harden and coat with a second layer of couverture which is then marked in wavy lines with a fork.
(Illustration page 689.) (Germany)

Cannoli Siciliani

1 lb. (500 gr.) flour
1 3/4 oz. (50 gr.) sugar
1 1/2 oz. (45 gr.) butter
1 3/4 oz. (50 gr.) egg
1 1/2 gills (2 dl.) marsala or red wine

Filling:
1 lb. (500 gr.) cream cheese (sieved)
8 oz. (250 gr.) castor sugar
2 1/2 oz. (5 gr.) orange peel (cut finely)
2 1/2 oz. (75 gr.) chocolate (chopped in cubes)
2 1/2 oz. (75 gr.) pistachio nuts (halved)
1/8 gill (2 cl.) rum
Vanilla

Mix all together. Make the ingredients into a dough, putting it through a roller two or three times. After a rest for about 20 minutes, pin the dough out very thinly and cut out with a plain cutter. Wash the pieces with egg and roll round a cannoli mould, which may be a metal cylinder or a round piece of wood. Fold over the join at the top neatly and firmly so that it does not unroll during the cooking. Drop into boiling oil and when cool and removed from the mould fill with the mixture given above. *(Italy)*

Champagne Flip - Champagner Flip

5 portions:
1/2 bottle champagne (goût américain)
1/3 gill (4 cl.) Cointreau
10 half maraschino cherries
1/4 oz. (6 gr.) agar-agar
3 egg yolks
2 1/2 oz. (75 gr.) icing sugar
2/3 gill (1 dl.) white wine
1 sheet gelatine

Blend the agar-agar with a glass of champagne and warm for 10 minutes to 122-140° F (50-60° C). Add the Cointreau, quickly pour in the rest of the champagne and immediately fill into semi-spherical moulds. While still lukewarm, place a well drained half maraschino cherry in each mould. When completely set, join together in pairs with a little gelatine to make balls and roll into sugar nibs.

Make a sabayon sauce with the egg yolks, sugar, white wine and a sheet of gelatine that has been previously soaked. Serve cold with the champagne balls. *(Germany)*
(Illustration page 772.)

Cherry Slices - Kirschenschnitten
Line a rectangular tin with puff pastry pinned out $1/8$ in. (2 mm.) thick. Sprinkle with lightly roasted ground hazelnuts, cover with stoned ripe cherries and bake in a hot oven with good bottom heat. Set aside for a short time and meanwhile whisk equal amounts of egg white and sugar to a stiff snow, adding a little vanilla sugar. Cover the cherries with this snow, pipe on a lattice work pattern and flash in a hot oven. Carefully remove from the tin; use a wet knife which is repeatedly wiped with a cloth to cut neatly into slices, and serve at once.

For red currant slices the proportion of sugar to egg white should be increased.
(Switzerland)

Chipolata Pudding
1 lb. 2 oz. (560 gr.) milk
7 oz. (200 gr.) sugar
4 oz. (125 gr.) egg yolks
$3/4$ oz. (20 gr.) gelatine
Bitter cookies (see recipe *page 468*)
1 lb. 2 oz. (560 gr.) whipped cream
2 oz. (60 gr.) glacé cherries
2 oz. (60 gr.) maraschino liqueur
Vanilla bean

Boil the milk with half the sugar and the vanilla bean. Beat the egg yolks with the rest of the sugar, and stir this egg mixture through the boiling milk. This mixture must not boil, or it will curdle. During the heating it should only thicken. When ready, add the gelatine, which has been dissolved in water, stir thoroughly. Allow to cool, stirring occasionally. Meanwhile, cut the cherries and the bitter cookies in little pieces and sprinkle them with some maraschino liqueur. Whip the cream. As soon as the mixture is cold, add the rest of the liqueur and as soon as the mass starts to set, stir in the whipped cream. Fill the pudding mould, adding layers of bitter cookies and cherries between the pudding layers. Put the filled mould in a cool place until the pudding is completely set. To loosen the puddings steep the moulds a little while in a pot with hot water and then turn them upside-down.

Pipe whipped cream on the pudding and decorate with fruits, chocolate, fondant and baked figures made as follows:

$3 1/2$ oz. (100 gr.) butter
11 oz. (320 gr.) water
7 oz. (200 gr.) fine white flour
4 oz. (130 gr.) egg yolks
$8 1/2$ oz. (240 gr.) egg whites

Make up as for choux pastry and pipe fine decorative designs on a baking sheet and bake carefully in a hot oven.
(Holland)

Curdled Milk Rolls - Rasgollah
6 persons:

For the syrup:

7 oz. (200 gr.) sugar
20 cardamom seeds
10 cloves
1 small piece of cinnamon
A strong pinch of saffron
2 tablespoons rose water

For the curdled milk:

2 quarts 3 gills (3 l.) milk
Juice of 3-4 lemons

Cooking time: 15 minutes

Cook the sugar and the spices in $2 3/4$ gills (3 dl.) of water for 10 minutes, and add the rose water. Do not strain. Bring the milk to the boil and curdle it with the lemon juice. Cover, leave to stand for

5 minutes and drain through a muslin cloth. While the curds are still warm, beat them up to make them smooth. Divide into 18 pieces and shape them like corks about 2 ³/₄ in. (7 cm.) long. Arrange the rasgollah in a deep dish and cover them with hot syrup. They may also be served with cold syrup. *(India)*

Délice Williamine

12 oz. (350 gr.) flour
5 oz. (150 gr.) castor sugar
5 oz. (150 gr.) butter
1 egg
2 egg yolks
Zest of ¹/₂ lemon
A pinch of salt
Compote pears
Confectioner's custard

Prepare sweet pastry with the flour, sugar, butter, eggs, lemon zest and salt, and set aside to rest. Pin out ¹/₈ in. (3 mm.) thick, cut into strips 4 ¹/₂ in. (11 cm.) wide, moisten the edges with water, make a rim all the way round with a thin strip of pastry and crimp. Bake until golden. Drain compote pears well, cut in thin slices and arrange in the centre of the pastry strips in a thin layer. Cover with a gable-shaped topping of confectioner's custard well flavoured with pear brandy or rum, leaving the edges uncovered. Sprinkle with coarsely granulated sugar, caramelize with a red-hot iron, cut into individual portions and serve at once.
(Switzerland)

Lemon Cream Madame Lacroix - Zitronencreme Madame Lacroix

6 persons:
6 ¹/₂ oz. (185 gr.) sugar
Juice of 2 lemons
Zest of a small lemon
7 sheets gelatine
1 ¹/₄ pt. (7 dl.) whipped cream, alternatively 7 stiffly whisked egg whites
Raspberry purée

Dissolve the sugar in the slightly warmed lemon juice and add the zest and the gelatine soaked and melted in a bain-marie. Leave to cool and fold in the whipped cream or, alternatively, the stiffly whisked egg whites. Fill into a glass dish, leave to cool and serve the raspberry purée separately. *(Germany)*

Montblanc of Chestnuts - Mont-Blanc aux Marrons

6 persons:
18 oz. (500 gr.) chestnuts
5 oz. (150 gr.) sugar
Milk
2 oz. (60 gr.) water
Vanilla
¹/₂ pt. (¹/₄ l.) whipped cream

Slit the chestnuts all round with a sharp knife. Put them on a baking sheet sprinkled with water and place them in a hot oven until they burst open. Remove peel and skin carefully and cook the chestnuts in hot sweetened milk flavoured with vanilla. Drain well and rub through a wire sieve. Boil the sugar and water to the ball with a small piece of vanilla. Remove the vanilla and mix the sugar with the chestnut purée. Add a piece of butter the size of a walnut and mix well. Butter and sugar a savarin mould. Fill the chestnut cream into a piping bag with a very small round tube. Pipe it into the savarin mould, imitating a bird's nest. Place a very cold round dish on top of the mould, and invert the dish in order to unmould the bird's nest. Fill the centre with whipped cream, using a fluted tube, and decorate with candied cherries, angelica or as desired.
(France)

Profiteroles with Chocolate - Profiteroles au Chocolat

9 oz. (275 gr.) choux paste
3 ¹/₂ gills (¹/₄ l.) vanilla flavoured whipped cream or pastry cream
3 ¹/₂ gills (¹/₄ l.) thick chocolate sauce

Make small cream buns with the choux paste, let them cool and fill with whipped or pastry cream, coat with hot chocolate sauce and serve at once. *Chocolate sauce:* Melt 5 oz. (150 gr.) of good chocolate with a little water, stir till smooth, add a small piece of fresh butter and pour over cakes.
(Illustration page 640.) *(France)*

Victoria Rings - Bordure Victoria

2 pt. (1 l.) milk
2 $^1/_2$ oz. (70 gr.) semolina
A piece of vanilla pod
5 oz. (150 gr.) sugar
7 sheets gelatine
1 $^1/_2$ pt. ($^3/_4$ l.) whipped dairy cream
3 $^1/_2$ oz. (100 gr.) sultanas
A pinch of salt

Boil up the milk with the vanilla and salt, pour in the semolina and simmer for 8 minutes. Remove from the heat, stir in the soaked gelatine and the sugar, and leave in a cold place. Before the mixture sets, stir for a moment, fold in the whipped cream and lastly add the sultanas which have been soaked and drained. Fill into small savarin moulds and refrigerate until set. Turn out on to small glass dishes and fill the centre with a salpicon of strawberries and peaches. Decorate with whipped cream and serve with grenadine syrup. Raspberry syrup may also be served as an accompaniment. *(Switzerland)*

YOGHOURT DESSERTS

Cassis Yoghourt Shake

Put one commercial yoghourt and one liqueurglassful of blackcurrant juice (full fruit) extract through the mixer and pour into a tall glass. Serve with a sponge finger.

Lemon Yoghourt Shake - Zitronen-Joghurt-Mixgetränk

Put one commercial yoghourt and the juice of one lemon through the mixer and serve at once in a tall glass, accompanied by a sponge finger.

SURPRISES

Specialities of the Hotel La Palma. Locarno

Meringue Topping for Surprises

10 egg whites
15 oz. (450 gr.) sugar
$^1/_3$ oz. (10 gr.) vanilla sugar

Make the meringue in the usual manner, whisking to a stiff snow.

Surprise hawaïenne

8 portions :

Cut a sheet of baked Swiss roll mixing to the shape of a pineapple. Cover with well-drained pineapple salad flavoured with curaçao triple sec. Cover this with a dome of diplomat cream also flavoured with curaçao triple sec and place another sheet of freshly baked Swiss roll mixing on top. Using a coarse star tube, pipe on meringue (lightly tinted red) to imitate the shell of a pineapple, flash, then decorate with half a pineapple top and eight half slices of pineapple (one per portion).

The diplomat cream may be replaced by pineapple ice or by any other variety of ice with the exception of chocolate and coffee ice cream.
(Illustration page 792.)

Surprise Belle-Alliance (or Surprise de Mariage)

10-12 portions :

Cut out a heart-shaped base from a sheet of baked Swiss roll mixing and cover with a $^1/_2$ in. (1 $^1/_2$ cm.) thick layer of fruit salad macerated in kirsch. Spread the top and sides evenly with kirsch flavoured diplomat cream, place strips of Swiss roll sponge round the sides and cover the top with a heart of the same size cut out of Swiss roll sponge. Cover and decorate with meringue, flash, then place a few sugar or marzipan roses in the centre. Refrigerate or else serve at once. With a filling of diplomat cream this sweet may be made a few hours in advance.

Surprise Marguerite Bolli

20 portions :

Arrange slightly sweetened strawberries on a Swiss roll sponge base of suitable size and splash with Grand-Marnier. Cover with diplomat cream flavoured with Grand-Marnier and place a thin layer of Swiss roll sponge on top. Coat with meringue, decorate and flash.

Surprise du Pâtissier

8 portions :

Cut out a round base of Swiss roll sponge 4 in. (10 cm.) in diameter and cover with 12 oz. (350 gr.) strawberries. Sprinkle with a little sugar and splash with cognac and orange juice. Turn out an ice bombe on top (half Grand-Marnier parfait, half cassata filling). Place thin slices of filled Swiss roll round the edge and pipe on a final decoration of meringue, using a plain tube. Flash under a salamander or in a very hot oven.

Surprise sicilienne

Bombe :

Lining : Warm 3 egg yolks with 2 1/2 oz. (80 gr.) icing sugar, whisk over gentle heat, continue to whisk until cold, add 1/4 gill (3 cl.) Grand-Marnier and a little grated orange zest, and lastly fold in 3/4 pt. (4 1/2 dl.) whipped dairy cream.

Filling : Warm 3 egg whites with 3 1/2 oz. (100 gr.) icing sugar, whisk until foamy, then blend in 1 3/4 oz. (50 gr.) roasted flaked hazelnuts, 1 3/4 oz. (50 gr.) finely chopped orange peel, 1/8 oz. (5 gr.) vanilla sugar, 5 drops orange flower water and 1/2 pt. (3 dl.) whipped dairy cream.

Cut a round base from a sheet of Swiss roll sponge or thin genoese, cover with 12 oz. (350 gr.) ripe strawberries macerated in Grand-Marnier and turn out the bombe on top. Decorate round the edge with thin slices of filled Swiss roll, mask and decorate with meringue, flash in a very hot oven and serve at once.
(Illustration page 793.)

Surprise Waldmeister

Line the bottom of an oval mould with Swiss roll sponge, arrange slightly sweetened raspberries on top and splash with anisette. Cover with anisette flavoured diplomat cream and place a thin oval of Swiss roll sponge on top. Coat with a cold (Swiss) meringue, decorate as desired and flash. It is preferable to use the same fruit for decoration as that selected for the filling.
(Illustration page 791.)

EXOTIC SWEETS

Specialities of the Restaurant Ritz, Berlin

In tropical and subtropical countries jellying agents of animal origin are less popular than the large selection of fruits, roots, leaves, flowers, etc. that is available there. For this reason, we are often compelled to use our own habitual jellying agents to prepare exotic sweets. To illustrate this, let us take the example of 'Kohu Pee'. This name does not stand for an actual sweet as we understand it, but rather describes a state. Literally translated, it means something like 'up and down fruit'. This does not mean, however, that the fruit is sometimes at the top and sometimes at the bottom of the tree; it simply refers to the springy consistency of fruit jelly. 'Kohu Pee' is found throughout the Polynesian islands, though it is sometimes called by a different name, and the meaning is always the same—a jelly of cutting consistency made from fruit pulp or merely from fruit juice in every possible colour, cut into different shapes and rolled in various kinds of sugar. Coconut punch is drunk as an accompaniment.

According to the original recipe, this famous dish is made with durians; the method of preparation is as simple as can be imagined. The ripe durian is split into five parts; the pale yellow, creamy fruit pulp surrounding the seeds, which are the size of walnuts, is beaten with switches and a certain amount of piri is added. Piri is a jellying agent of plant origin which, though it has the same properties as agar-agar, does not require warming. The prepared mixture is spread on to boards. It sets quickly and can then be cut and rolled into sugar. But, unfortunately, this famous 'Kohu Pee' cannot be produced in our part of the world for various reasons. The unique taste of the durian is only found in fruit that has ripened fully on the tree, but fully ripe durians will only keep for two days at the most. Another disadvantage is the pervasive, unpleasant smell of the untreated fruit, and yet another drawback lies in the fact that the pulp cannot be cooked or heated, but has to be prepared cold. The final difficulty is that piri, the only substance that will cause durian pulp to set, is not available. But since the term 'Kohu Pee'—as already mentioned—merely describes a state without reference to any particular fruit, it may be made out of almost any fruit purée or juicy fruit without deviating from its meaning.

Adua Kat (hot)

8 portions:

Sufficient annonae* for 8 persons
4-5 ripe bananas
20 cumquats (fresh or preserved in syrup)
3 ½ oz. (100 gr.) Rangoon beans**
3 ½ oz. (100 gr.) pulped peanuts
5 oz. (150 gr.) honey
1 ¾ oz. (50 gr.) butter
1 ½ gills (2 dl.) milk
1 chicken weighing 2 lb. (1 kg.)
1/16 oz. (2-3 gr.) pimento
Cornflour

* Only the following annonae are suitable for this sweet: custard apples, cherimoyas and sour-sops, possibly brick-red senegals too, although these barely grow to the size of a hen's egg.

** Before using Rangoon beans, always blanch them and pour away the water, as contact with water causes them to give off a toxic substance, prussic acid.

Blanch the chicken and cook until very tender together with the pulped peanuts, a pinch of salt and the juice obtained from the annonae when preparing and cutting them. While it is cooking, add the blanched Rangoon beans. As soon as the chicken is tender, plunge it in cold water and remove the skin. Boil the broth down to 1 pt. (½ l.), set it aside for a time to facilitate removal of the fat, then rub through a fine sieve with the beans. Warm the butter slightly, first add a little pimento and then, immediately afterwards, the honey and the warm milk, boil up and mix with the broth containing the beans. Place the resulting 1-1 ¼ pt. (6-7 dl.) creamy sauce on ice to cool.

Cut up the pulp of the annonae and bananas as for fruit salad and sprinkle with lemon juice if necessary. Cut the cumquats in halves or quarters only. Cut the chicken meat off the bones and shred it, then sprinkle with a little diluted honey and with pimento, mix with plenty of cornflour to separate the shreds, and deep-fry in hot oil until crisp and golden. Mix the fruit with the sauce and stir in part of the fried shredded chicken, or alternatively sprinkle all the shredded chicken on top to serve.
(Illustration page 768.)   *(Abyssinia)*

Baklava (warm)

15 portions:

1 lb. (500 gr.) flour
3 eggs
1 dessert-spoon oil
1 pinch of salt
3 ½ oz. (100 gr.) finely chopped almonds
3 ½ oz. (100 gr.) finely chopped pistachio nuts
3 ½ oz. (100 gr.) finely chopped hazelnuts or walnuts
5 oz. (150 gr.) butter
3 ½ oz. (100 gr.) honey
7 oz. (200 gr.) sugar mixed with ⅓ oz. (10 gr.) cinnamon

Baking time: 20-30 minutes

Make a noodle dough with the flour, eggs, oil and salt, cover and allow to rest for 1 hour. Divide into pieces and pin out each one until paper thin with plenty of potato flour. Butter a round or rectangular baking tray, cover the bottom with 5 or 6 sheets of pastry, laying one on top of the other, then sprinkle with a third of the sugar/cinnamon mixture, followed by the chopped almonds. Dot with a few knobs of butter and place 5 or 6 sheets of pastry on top. Repeat the process with a layer of pistachio nuts, then with a layer of hazelnuts or walnuts and finally cover with the remaining sheets of pastry. Before baking, cut the pastry in the baking tray into rectangles or diamond shapes with a sharp pointed knife, melt the rest of the butter and pour it over, then place in a moderate

oven. If less greasy baklava is desired, pour off some of the butter after baking. Heat the honey with a little water, flavour with grated lemon or orange zest and pour over the baklava while both the latter and the honey are still hot. The baklava tastes better when slightly warm than when quite cold. Allow to cool a little and place some Tel Kadayif on each portion.
(Turkey)

Tel Kadayif (cold)

1 lb. (500 gr.) flour
$^3/_4$ pt. ($^1/_2$ l.) water
$^1/_{16}$ oz. (2-3 gr.) yeast
1 pinch of salt

Work all the ingredients together to a very slack dough. Pass this through a special strainer made of metal finely pierced with small holes (and not of wire gauze) on to a large heated dish. Move the strainer backwards and forwards in long sweeps to produce thin threads. After 2 or 3 minutes, remove the threads from the heated dish and allow them to cool on a tray. They should remain quite white and resemble finely cut noodles, and they should dry rather than bake. To use, mix the threads with melted butter to separate them. Place half of them on a buttered baking sheet, sprinkle with a layer of chopped almonds, hazelnuts or pistachio nuts, cover with the rest of the threads and press down lightly. Brush lightly with melted butter, bake for 20-30 minutes in a slow oven and at once pour over some thin stock syrup flavoured with lemon or orange zest. Shape into rolls while still warm, or alternatively cut into pieces when cold or press gently into small moulds. When shaped into fairly large pieces, this sweet is a kind of baklava.
(Illustration page 635.)   *(Turkey)*

Ecudorian Banana Toddy (cold)

8-10 portions:

Custard cream:
3 egg yolks
1 $^3/_4$ oz. (50 gr.) sugar
$^1/_4$ gill (3 cl.) milk
$^1/_4$ gill (3 $^1/_2$ cl.) dairy cream
1 oz. (30 gr.) raw marzipan
1 ripe banana
 (5 oz. [150 gr.] with peel)
7 sheets gelatine
$^3/_4$ oz. (20 gr.) chopped pistachio nuts
$^1/_2$ pt. (2 dl.) whipped dairy cream
$^1/_4$ gill (4 cl.) rum
Juice of $^1/_2$ lemon

Jelly:
2 gills (3 dl.) white wine
1 $^3/_4$ oz. (50 gr.) sugar
2-3 unripe, green bananas
Juice of $^1/_2$ lemon
10-11 sheets gelatine
$^1/_8$ gill (2 cl.) rum

Peel the unripe bananas, cut them in thick, even slices and poach in the white wine mixed with the sugar and lemon juice. Allow to cool, then dry off the banana slices. Re-heat the banana syrup a little, dissolve the previously soaked gelatine in it and flavour with rum.

Warm the raw marzipan until dissolved in the milk and cream. Mix the egg yolks with the sugar and cook to a custard with the milk/cream/marzipan mixture. Put the ripe banana through the mixer with the lemon juice and at once stir the resulting purée into the warm custard together with the previously soaked gelatine. When sufficiently cool, add the chopped pistachio nuts and the rum, then fold in the whipped cream. Either mask suitable long curved moulds with the banana jelly and arrange the banana slices on it each overlapping the other, or else simply line the moulds with tinfoil and place the overlapping banana slices on top. Whichever alternative is adopted, fill the custard cream into the moulds and cover with jelly up to the top. If tinfoil has been used, coat the banana slices well with banana jelly immediately after unmoulding.
(Illustration page 771.)   *(Germany)*

Pomegranate Cream (cold) - Granatapfelcreme

6 portions:
7 egg yolks
2 $^1/_2$ oz. (75 gr.) sugar

1 gill (1 ½ dl.) fresh pomegranate juice
⅛ gill (2 cl.) lemon juice
⅓ gill (5 cl.) calvados
1 pt. (½ l.) dairy cream
15 sheets gelatine
7 oz. (200 gr.) finely chopped pistachio nuts

Mix the egg yolks with the sugar, add the pomegranate juice and lemon juice and cook to a custard over gentle heat. Stir in the gelatine, which has first been soaked, and the calvados while still lukewarm. When the mixture is about to set, fold in the whipped cream. Fill into semi-spherical moulds and leave until cold. After unmoulding, stick together in pairs with a little liquid gelatine to form spheres and refrigerate. When thoroughly chilled, roll each one into finely chopped pistachio nuts and decorate with a small, fresh, green leaf. Dish and serve grenadine syrup separately as an accompaniment.
(Illustration page 770.) *(Germany)*

Haupia Aloha (Chrysanthemum Cream) (cold)

8 portions:

1-2 medium-sized white or coloured chrysanthemums
1 pt. (6 dl.) milk
¾ gill (1 dl.) Mai Tai*
3 ½ oz. (100 gr.) jaggery**
¼ gill (4 cl.) arrack
¾ oz. (20 gr.) sugar
½ coffeespoon cinnamon
1 oz. (30 gr.) cornflour
¼ average-sized coconut

* Mai Tai is a syrupy drink with a low alcohol content. It is made out of pineapple, papaya, mango juice and palm wine and used in cocktails in the same way as grenadine.

** *See Glossary.*

Pull off the individual chrysanthemum petals and place them in a china bowl with the tender green leaves below the flowers. Sprinkle with cinnamon sugar, cover and set aside for an hour. Grate the white flesh of the coconut into the milk, heat to 194°F (90°C) and rub hard through a fine sieve. Dissolve the jaggery over a bain-marie and amalgamate with the milk. Blend the Mai Tai and arrack into the cornflour and use to thicken the coconut milk well. Mix the latter with the milk that is in the bain-marie and keep the temperature at the same level for 5 minutes, while stirring constantly. Now remove from the water-bath and boil up once over an open flame. Pour this creamy mixture at once over the sweetened chrysanthemum petals and leaves, stir quickly, fill into small individual dishes and refrigerate.
(Illustration page 766.) *(Hawaii)*

Mango Kohu Pee (cold)

2 lb. (1 kg.) tin mangos with juice
1 ¼ gills (18 cl.) palm wine
½ oz. (12 gr.) agar-agar
Juice of ½ lemon
A little grated tonka bean*
15-20 arbutus-berries**

Coconut punch:

1 ¾ pt. (1 l.) palm wine
4 oz. (125 gr.) jaggery* or brown cane sugar
3 ½ oz. (100 gr.) grated coconut
¾ gill (12 cl.) fresh cream
⅛ gill (2 cl.) white rum

* *See Glossary.*

** Arbutus-berries are the fruits of the strawberry tree. They are ½-¾ in. (1-2 cm.) in size, bright red and look a little like strawberries. They are pulpy, somewhat floury and sweet-tasting.

Drain off the mango juice—generally ½-¾ pt. (3-3 ½ dl.)—and make it up to 1 pt. (½ l.) with palm wine. Stir in the agar-agar, set aside for a short time to soak the agar-agar well, then slowly warm to 140°F (60°C) over a bain-marie. Now stir in the mangos which have been mashed in the mixer and flavour with lemon juice and tonka bean. Pour the mixture into a tin of suitable size to a thickness of about 1 in. (3 cm.), allow to set, then refrigerate. Cut into pieces of the desired shape. Just before serving, roll in sugar nibs and arrange the arbutus-berries on top.

To make coconut punch, heat the palm wine and sugar to 194° F (90° C), add the grated coconut flesh, cover and allow to stand for 10 minutes. Rub lightly through a fine sieve and mix with the cream and rum before serving. This punch is drunk with the Kohu Pee.
(Illustration page 769.) *(Polynesia)*

Wune Wharn (cold)

Banana leaves
Milk
Fresh coconut
Jaggery*
Arrowroot or tapioca
Agar-agar
Rice
Candied fruits
Nuts

* *See Glossary.*

1. Cut strips 9 in. (22 cm.) long and 1 ½ in. (4 cm.) wide from the banana leaves and make four even cuts halfway through each strip. Fold over and pinch the sides together like a small cardboard box, and also interweave the five flaps for the bottom similarly to a cardboard box. Fill these little boxes either with milk thickened with arrowroot, or else with fruit jelly made out of fruit juice and agar-agar. Here are some examples of suitable fillings: sweetened milk flavoured with almonds or vanilla; thick coconut milk with or without grated coconut; milk flavoured with flowers or leaves; the juice or pulp of any suitable fruit, or combinations of milk and layers of fruit.

2. Cook some ketan* in sweetened milk, as for rice pudding, flavour with grated tonka bean** and mix with a generous amount of finely cut candied fruit and chopped nuts. Shape into a thick slab, leave until cold, then cut into squares and wrap in banana leaves neatly trimmed to the right size. Skewer the four corners of each leaf in position with a small piece of bamboo-cane.

3. Cook some ketan with jaggery. When cold, spread on a banana leaf, place some small sticks of jaggery in the centre, roll up and cut into thick slices.
(Illustration of the three varieties, page 770.)

* Ketan is a very glutinous variety of rice with short, almost round-looking grains.
** *See Glossary.*

N.B. The above sweets cannot be made without banana leaves. *(Thailand)*

XXIII. Ices

Ice Creams and Frozen Confections

This large and varied field of production has produced many talented exponents, who never had the benefit of research and science as is available today. They depended on craftsmanship and a profound knowledge of raw materials and the reaction of them in the freezing processes.

From so many practitioners many recipes and methods have evolved, all of them excellent in their own right. The recipes and methods given in this chapter are therefore open to comment, perhaps even to vociferous questioning.

In extenuation, the writer has practiced the recipes and methods for over fifty years and found them popular, health giving because of their purity, beneficial because of their dietetic composition and pleasing because of subleties of flavour and presentation.

Ice cream production is basically a simple process, the practice, stretching back in one form or another, to Babylonian times. Once it called for an abundance of ice and salt and plenty of muscular effort. Today, because of the development of refrigeration, the original three basic requirements have been eliminated.

Cleanliness is essential in every phase of food manufacture and distribution; even greater care is imperative in the manufacture of ice cream because the principle materials used are so easily contaminated. Section 4 of the Food and Drugs Act must be carefully studied.

For the production of ice creams, a special room or compartment must be reserved and fitted, and kept solely for this purpose. A vitreous panelled ceiling, tiled or a similar type of wall finish and a tiled flood are necessary, together with an abundant supply of hot and cold water.

Equipment will vary according to the size of production and the variety of the products. Where high standards are the aim, the following will be necessary:

Sterilizer
Mechanically operated freezer
Conserving cabinet for finished ices
Deep freeze cabinet
Refrigerated cabinet for storage of cream and milk, etc.
A stainless steel topped table
Pestle and mortar
An electric or gas-fired stove
An earthenware or porcelain container with lid and tap for syrup
Hair sieves, whisks, screwtop jars, basins and covers
Wooden mushrooms
Piping bags and tubes

Hardwood spatulas
Turntable—to facilitate decoration
Tinned metal, muslin and medium gauge strainers
Plastic scrapers
Stainless steel knives, ladles and spoons
Storage container for finished ices
Storage containers for fruit ices in porcelain
Heavily tinned or pewter moulds
Covered storage containers for materials
Heavily tinned cooking vessels
A copper sugar boiling pan
Thermometers including sugar boiling thermometers
Saccharometers
Grinder
Mixer

The question of costs must arise in this competitive age, especially vis-à-vis the large manufacturer and the smaller unit.

The products of the large scale manufacturer are excellent and are of consistent quality; variety too, is good, but equating the variety and quality attainable by the small producer in relation to that of the large scale manufacturer, the small unit can so vary products and presentation that they can stand alone in unquestioned supremacy. This is the basic confrontation and in many products the cost should be less, for the production belt has not completely eliminated the human element, so much so that more sophisticated products need the employment of skilled and highly paid labour to supply a limited market, often out of all proportion to demand. The smaller unit can, therefore, create demand by its specialities, thus keeping overhead costs static.

ICES - GLACES

According to their composition, ices are divided into different sorts.

1. *Plain ices*, that require a freezer, are: Cream ice (custard ice), which is made of egg yolks, sugar, milk and/or cream and flavouring.

   Fruit or Water Ice, which is made of fresh fruit purée or fruit pulp and stock syrup, and liqueur ice.

   Fruit Cream Ice, which is made of fruit purée or fruit pulp, sugar, cream and/or milk.

2. *Light ices*, which are made with a special mixture and frozen in moulds; they are: iced bombes, iced parfaits, biscuit glacés, iced mousses, iced soufflés, iced gâteaux, iced puddings, iced charlottes, cassatas, etc.
   (Illustrations pages 765, 794, 795.)

3. *Various preparations* are: iced punch, spooms, ice cream coupes, iced sundaes, baked ice creams, etc.

CREAM ICES - GLACES CRÈME

The basic recipe for all cream ices (custard ices) is that of vanilla ice cream and numerous varieties may be obtained by changing the flavouring.

Vanilla Ice Cream - (Basic)
Glace à la Vanille

Basic recipe 1
1 pt. (½ l.) fresh cream
1 pt. (½ l.) milk
8 egg yolks
8-10 oz. (250-300 gr.) sugar
1 vanilla bean

Basic recipe 2 (without cream)
2 pt. (1 l.) milk
8 egg yolks
7-8 oz. (200-250 gr.) sugar
1 vanilla bean

Whisk up the egg yolks and sugar and then, stirring all the time, pour in the boiled milk and cream in which the vanilla bean has been infused. Place over heat again and continue to stir until the mixture thickens and coats the spatula. It is essential to avoid bringing the mixture to the boil as the egg yolks would curdle. It is cooked when, if one blows on to the spatula, the liquid forms itself into a rose. Pass through a very fine sieve and leave to cool before freezing.

Almond Ice Cream I - Glace aux Amandes

14 oz. (400 gr.) blanched sweet almonds
1 pt. ($^1/_2$ l.) cream
2 oz. (60 gr.) blanched bitter almonds
1 pt. ($^1/_2$ l.) milk
8 oz. (250 gr.) sugar
$^1/_3$ gill (6 cl.) sherry
5 drops essential oil of almonds

Pound the almonds to a paste, moistening with the sherry. Bring the milk to the boil, throw in the almonds and sugar, stir well together, cover and allow to become cold, then rub through a hair sieve. Add the essential oil and cream and freeze.

Almond Ice Cream II - Glace aux Amandes

Recipe 1

Pound 2 $^1/_2$ oz. (75 gr.) blanched almonds finely with a little water and infuse in the hot milk. Rub hard through a conical strainer and prepare the ice cream as directed in the basic recipe, but leave out the vanilla.

Recipe 2

Proceed according to the basic recipe, omitting the vanilla. When cold, mix thoroughly with 2 $^1/_2$ oz. (75 gr.) raw marzipan.

Almond Praline Ice Cream I - Glace aux Amandes pralinée

1 $^1/_2$ pt. ($^3/_4$ l.) cream
1 pt. ($^1/_2$ l.) milk
8 egg yolks
4 oz. (125 gr.) castor sugar
1 piece split vanilla pod
1 dessertspoonful noyau
1 dessertspoonful brandy

Praline:

4 oz. (125 gr.) castor sugar
4 oz. (125 gr.) blanched sweet almonds
Squeeze of lemon juice

Lightly roast the almonds. Melt the sugar in a sugar boiler, add the lemon juice and stir to a pale caramel or straw colour, blend in the almonds, and pour on to a slightly oiled marble slab. Bring one pint of cream and the milk and vanilla to the boil. Whip the yolks and the 4 oz. (125 gr.) sugar together, whisk on to the milk, return to the heat until the spatula is lightly coated, then stand in cold water to reduce the cooking heat.

Crush the praline with a rolling pin, sieve, crush the fragments left in the sieve and so on until all the praline is through. Add to the custard, stir together, strain when cold, add the noyau and brandy and the remaining of cream. Freeze.

Almond Praline Ice Cream II - Glace aux Amandes pralinée

For each quart (1 l.) of vanilla ice, stir in 2 oz. (60 gr.) praline when the ice is nearly frozen.

Caramel Ice Cream - Glace au Caramel

Same ingredients and method as for vanilla ice with this exception. Lightly caramelize the sugar, cool the sugar boiler in cold water to stop further cooking, then dissolve the sugar in the milk, and add this syrup to the cream.

Chestnut Ice Cream - Glace aux Marrons

1 $^1/_2$ pt. ($^3/_4$ l.) cream
1 pt. ($^1/_2$ l.) milk
10 oz. (300 gr.) sugar
1 tablespoonful rum
1 split vanilla pod
12 egg yolks
$^1/_2$ lb. (250 gr.) cooked chestnut purée

Bring 1 pint ($^1/_2$ l.) of cream, the milk and vanilla slowly to the boil. Whip the yolks and sugar together, whisk in the chestnut purée, strain on to the boiling liquid, put back and stir until the spatula coats a little more thickly than with plain vanilla ice. Place in a bowl of cold water to stop further cooking and allow to become cold, then add the rum and $^1/_2$ pint ($^1/_4$ l.) cream. Freeze.

Chocolate Ice Cream - Glace au Chocolat

2 pt. (1 l.) double cream
1 1/2 pt. (3/4 l.) milk
12 oz. (375 gr.) sugar
12 egg yolks
6 oz. (175 gr.) unsweetened chocolate
1 split vanilla pod
1 tablespoon rum

Take 1 pt. (1/2 l.) cream, 1 pt. (1/2 l.) milk and the vanilla pod and bring to the boil. Whip the yolks and sugar together, add the boiling milk and cream (1 pt. [1/2 l.] each) and whisk well together. Put back to cook until it lightly coats a wooden spatula, then stand in cold water to stop further cooking. Cover and let cool.

Break the chocolate into small pieces with a knife and gently melt with the remaining milk, mix into the custard. When cold, pass through a fine strainer. Part whip the rest of the cream and blend all together. Freeze. The addition of a little rum is generally much appreciated.

Coffee Ice Cream I - Glace au Café

Proceed as for vanilla ice cream and add coffee extract or instant coffee powder. Brandy is an improvement.

Coffee Ice Cream II - Glace au Café

1 1/2 pt. (3/4 l.) cream
1 pt. (1/2 l.) milk
10 oz. (300 gr.) sugar
4 oz. (125 gr.) coffee

Roast the coffee beans, not too highly, crack the beans in a cloth with a cutlet bat or rolling pin and cover with 1 pt. (1/2 l.) cream, 1 pt. (1/2 l.) milk and the sugar, together with a small piece of split vanilla pod. Heat to 200° F (94° C), cover and steep for 30 minutes, strain and allow to become cold, half whip the remaining half pint (1/4 l.) of cream, add the strained coffee preparation and blend well. Freeze. The addition of brandy will improve the flavour.

Coffee Praline Ice Cream - Glace au Café pralinée

1 1/2 pt. (3/4 l.) cream
1 pt. (1/2 l.) milk
9 oz. (275 gr.) sugar
4 oz. (125 gr.) coffee
A little brandy
1 piece of vanilla pod

Roast the coffee beans. Melt 4 oz. (125 gr.) sugar to caramel, mix in the beans, pour on to a lightly oiled marble slab, cool, crush and sieve. Put the milk, 1 pt. (1/2 l.) cream and vanilla pod on to boil with 5 oz. (150 gr.) sugar, add the coffee praline and allow to become cold, then strain, add the remaining cream and freeze.

White Coffee Ice Cream - Glace au Café blanche

1 1/2 pt. (3/4 l.) cream
1 pt. (1/2 l.) milk
10 oz. (300 gr.) sugar
6 oz. (180 gr.) coffee beans
A little brandy
1 piece of vanilla pod

Heat 1 pt. (1/2 l.) cream, the milk, the sugar and vanilla to 200° F (94° C). Roast the coffee beans and throw them into the milk unbroken. Cover and steep until cold and strain. Part whip the remaining cream, blend thoroughly and freeze.

Hazelnut Praline Ice Cream - Glace aux Avelines pralinée

1 1/2 pt. (3/4 l.) cream
1 pt. (1/2 l.) milk
4 oz. (125 gr.) sugar
8 egg yolks
1 piece of vanilla pod
1 small glass sherry

Praline:

4 oz. (125 gr.) sugar
4 oz. (125 gr.) hazelnuts
A few drops of lemon juice

Roast the hazelnuts, rub off the skin, melt the 4 oz. (125 gr.) sugar to a straw colour with the lemon juice, mix in the nuts and pour on to a marble slab to cool. Proceed as for Almond Praline I.

Pistachio Ice Cream I - Glace aux Pistaches

4 oz. (125 gr.) blanched pistachio nuts
4 oz. (125 gr.) blanched sweet almonds
1 $^1/_2$ pt. ($^3/_4$ l.) cream
9 oz. (275 gr.) sugar
1 pt. ($^1/_2$ l.) milk
8 egg yolks
1 tablespoonful maraschino
3 drops oil of almond

Pound the nuts to a fine paste in the mortar, adding a little milk during the process to prevent oiling. Whip the yolks and sugar together. Bring 1 pt. ($^1/_2$ l.) of cream and the milk to the boil, add the pounded nuts and whisk on to the yolks. Return to the heat and cook until it lightly covers the spatula. Remove and stand in a bowl of cold water immediately to stop further cooking, then cover and allow to become quite cold. Force through a fine strainer, add the oil of almond and maraschino, tint to a pale green colour, then stir in the remaining half pint ($^1/_4$ l.) of cream and freeze.

Pistachio Ice Cream II - Glace aux Pistaches

Prepare 1 quart (1 l.) of vanilla ice cream mixture and cool. Thin 3 $^1/_2$ oz. (100 gr.) German marzipan with a little of the mixture. Add $^1/_2$ oz. (15 gr.) ground pistachio nuts, the marzipan and $^1/_8$ gill (2 cl.) each brandy and curaçao to the mixture and freeze as usual.

Rose Ice Cream I - Glace à la Rose

5 oz. (150 gr.) fragrant rose petals
1 pt. ($^1/_2$ l.) syrup
2 oz. (60 gr.) crystallized rose petals
Juice of 2 lemons
3 drops attar of roses
Cream to dilute
Carmine to tint to rose pink colour

Scald the petals with the boiling syrup; infuse until cold; strain and add the lemon juice, dilute to 21° B with cream. Tint to a rose pink colour, add the attar of roses and freeze, then work in the crushed crystallized rose petals.

Rose Ice Cream II - Roseneis

1 $^1/_2$ pt. (9 dl.) dairy cream
$^3/_4$ gill (1 dl.) rose water
12 egg yolks
$^1/_2$ pt. ($^1/_4$ l.) stock syrup
Zest of 1 lemon
4 unsprayed wild roses
1 $^3/_4$ oz. (50 gr.) granulated sugar
8 drops rose oil

Beat the egg yolks, cream, syrup and lemon zest together, cook over gentle heat until the mixture will coat the spatula, strain, then cool on ice, stirring constantly. Add the rose water and rose oil and freeze. Pick the roses, wash them, then cut off the bottom third with scissors and discard. Finely chop the remaining upper part of the roses together with the sugar (which should absorb the moisture from the roses) and lightly work into the ice cream. For special occasions, decorate with fresh roses, enhancing their scent with rose oil.
(*Illustration page 765.*)   (*Germany*)

Rum Ice Cream - Glace au Rhum

Add 1 gill (1 dl.) of rum to 2$^1/_2$ pt. (1$^1/_4$ l.) vanilla or caramel ice.

Tea Ice Cream

Infuse about $^1/_8$ oz. (3-4 gr.) strongly flavoured tea in the milk, strain and prepare the ice cream according to the basic recipe, but leave out the vanilla. A little fine rum or cognac may be used for additional flavouring.

White Vanilla Ice Cream - Glace à la Vanille blanche

1 pt. ($^1/_2$ l.) milk
2 pt. (1 l.) cream
1 split vanilla pod
12 oz. (375 gr.) sugar

Scald the milk, 1 pt. ($^1/_2$ l.) of cream, the sugar and vanilla together; cover and allow to become cold; strain, add the other pint ($^1/_2$ l.) of cream and freeze.

Violet Ice Cream - Glace aux Violettes

5 oz. (150 gr.) Parma violet petals
1 pt. ($^1/_2$ l.) syrup
2 oz. (60 gr.) crystallized violets
Juice of 2 lemons
Cream to dilute

Pour the boiling syrup over the violets, cover and infuse until cold; strain and add the lemon juice. Dilute with cream to 21°B. Freeze and work in the crushed crystallized violets.

Walnut Ice Cream I - Glace aux Noix

1 $^1/_2$ pt. ($^3/_4$ l.) cream
1 pt. ($^1/_2$ l.) milk
9 oz. (250 gr.) sugar
4 oz. (125 gr.) walnuts
1 oz. (30 gr.) sweet almonds
1 piece of vanilla

Melt 4 oz. (125 gr.) sugar to a straw colour and add the lightly roasted walnuts and almonds. Pour on to a lightly oiled marble slab, cool, crush and sieve.

Bring 1 pt. ($^1/_2$ l.) of milk and 1 pt. ($^1/_2$ l.) of cream to the boil with 5 oz. (150 gr.) sugar and the vanilla, add the walnut praline, cover and allow to become cold. Strain and add the remaining cream. Freeze.

Walnut Ice Cream II - Glace aux Noix

Add 4 $^1/_2$ oz. (140 gr.) roasted and crushed walnuts to 3 $^1/_2$ pt. (2 l.) vanilla ice cream mixture and freeze as usual.

Ices Flavoured with:
Tea, Chartreuse, Maraschino, Kirsch, Absinthe, etc.

12 egg yolks
10 oz. (300 gr.) sugar
Zest of 1 lemon
1 piece of vanilla pod
2 pt. (1 l.) milk
1 pt. ($^1/_2$ l.) cream

Whip the yolks and sugar together. Bring to the boil the milk and half the cream, the zest of lemon and the vanilla pod. Whisk on to the yolks and stir over heat until the custard lightly coats the spatula. Remove, place the pan in cold water, stir occasionally, cover and allow to become cold, strain and add the remaining half pint of cream and freeze. Now gradually work in the desired liqueur or flavouring, such as: $^2/_3$ gill (1 dl.) maraschino, kirsch, absinthe, rum, brandy, Chartreuse.

FRUIT OR WATER ICES - GLACES AUX FRUITS

For fruit ices use equal quantities of fruit pulp and stock syrup at 30° B plus the juice of one or two lemons. The mixture must be reduced to 18-19° B by the addition of cold water and passed through a sieve before being frozen.

Stock Syrup for Water Ices (Approx. 28° B)

12 lb. (6 kg.) sugar
4 quarts (2 l.) water

Place the water in a copper sugar boiler, stir in the sugar and allow to dissolve as much as possible with an occasional stir. Bring slowly to the boil, with frequent skimming, if necessary clear the surface with a piece of absorbent paper. Strain through a muslin strainer. Cover with a piece of greaseproof paper with a small hole perforated in the centre. The best receptacle for these syrups is a glazed earthenware container with a lid and fitted chromium or silver tap.

Apricot Water Ice - Glace aux Abricots

1 pt. ($^1/_2$ l.) apricot pulp (preserved)
1 pt. ($^1/_2$ l.) syrup
Juice and zest of 1 orange
Juice of 1 lemon
$^3/_4$ gill (6 cl.) sherry or $^1/_4$ gill (3 cl.) rum
A few drops of yellow and carmine colour

Bring the pulp, syrup and orange zest to the boil, strain through a hair or silk sieve, allow to become cold, add the juice from the orange and lemon and the sherry or rum, adjust to 21° B and colour if necessary. Freeze.

Banana Water Ice - Glace aux Bananes

Proceed in the same way as for pineapple ice, using bananas instead, reducing the mixture to 20° B *(page 760)*.

Cherry Water Ice - Glace aux Cerises

1 1/2 lb. (750 gr.) picked Kentish reds
Juice and zest of 1 orange
Juice of 1 lemon
1 pt. (1/2 l.) syrup
A few drops of carmine
1/4 gill (4 cl.) kirsch

Remove the stones from the cherries and pound them in a mortar. Pass the fruit through a fine mincer. Cover the stones with 1 gill of water, bring to the boil, cover and allow to become cold. Cover the fruit with the syrup, bring to the boil, skim, cover and gently simmer until tender; add the zest, cover and allow to become cold, then rub through a hair sieve. Blend with the orange and lemon juice, strain in the liquor from the stones and kernels, adjust with water to 21° B, correct colour, add the kirsch and freeze.

Black Currant Water Ice - Glace aux Cassis

1 lb. (500 gr.) picked black currants
1 1/2 lb. (750 gr.) picked red currants
1 pt. (1/2 l.) syrup
Juice and zest of 1 orange

Cover the fruit with the syrup, bring to the boil, skim, add the zest of orange and cover and allow to cool. Strain through muslin, add the orange juice, adjust to 21° B. Freeze.

Red Currant Water Ice - Glace aux Groseilles rouges

1 1/2 lb. (750 gr.) picked red currants
Juice of 1 orange
1 pt. (1/2 l.) syrup
A few drops of carmine

Cover with the syrup, bring to the boil, cover, and allow to cool. Strain through a muslin bag and adjust with water to 21° B. Freeze.

White Currant Water Ice - Glace aux Groseilles blanches

1 1/2 lb. (750 gr.) picked white currants
Juice of 1 lemon
1 pt. (1/2 l.) syrup
1/3 gill (5 cl.) yellow Chartreuse

Cover the currants with the syrup, bring to the boil, cover and allow to cool. Strain through muslin, add the lemon juice and Chartreuse and adjust with water to 21° B. Freeze.

Greengage Water Ice - Glace aux Reines-Claudes

1 1/2 lb. (750 gr.) ripe greengages
  (do not use yellow plums)
1 pt. (1/2 l.) syrup
Juice of 1 lemon
1/4 gill (3 cl.) maraschino
A little green colouring

Cut the fruit in halves. Remove the stones and crush them in a mortar, cover with one gill of water, bring to the boil, cover and steep until cold, then strain. Cover the flesh with the syrup, bring to the boil, skim, and simmer until tender; rub through a hair sieve, add the lemon juice and infusion, colour to a very pale green, adjust to 21° B with water and mix in the maraschino. Freeze.

Lemon Water Ice - Glace au Citron

8 lemons
1 pt. (1/2 l.) syrup

Remove the zest from 4 lemons with a zesting knife, cut the lemons crosswise and squeeze out all the juice, remove seeds, place in a china bowl, add the syrup and sufficient water to bring the density to 21° B. Let macerate for half an hour and strain through a muslin chinois and freeze.

Loganberry Water Ice - Glace aux Ronces-Framboises

1 1/2 lb. (750 gr.) hulled ripe loganberries
Juice of 2 oranges
1/2 lb. (250 gr.) castor sugar
1/2 pt. (1/4 l.) syrup
Juice of 1 lemon
1 dessertspoonful kirsch

Place fruit in a shallow bowl, sprinkle with the sugar, cover with a sheet of grease-proof paper, place in a warm place (100° F [38° C]) and let heat gently through, remove and allow to macerate for at least two hours. Rub through a hair sieve, add the lemon and orange juice and the syrup, adjust to 21° B with water and add the kirsch. Freeze.

Melon Water Ice Cantaloup - Glace au Melon

1 1/2 lb. (750 gr.) Cantaloup melon flesh
Juice of 2 lemons
1 gill (1 1/2 dl.) ginger syrup from a jar of preserved ginger
3/4 pt. (4 dl.) syrup
1 dessertspoonful rum
3 drops essential oil of orange

Pound and rub the flesh through a hair sieve, add the other ingredients, adjust density with water to 21° B. Colour with a few drops of yellow colouring and freeze.

Melon Water Ice (Sugar or Musk) - Glace au Melon

1 1/2 lb. (750 gr.) melon flesh
Juice of 2 lemons
1 gill (1 1/2 dl.) ginger syrup
3/4 pt. (4 dl.) stock syrup
1 tablespoonful orange flower water
1 tablespoonful maraschino

Proceed as above.

Nectarine Water Ice - Glace aux Brugnons

The most distinctive of the peach ices.

1 1/2 lb. (750 gr.) ripe nectarines
Juice of 2 oranges
1 pt. (1/2 l.) syrup
A spot of carmine

Dip the fruit into boiling water for approximately 1 minute; refresh in cold water and peel, cut into halves with a stainless steel knife, remove the stones and crush them in a mortar, cover with 1 gill of water, bring to the boil, cover and steep until cold. Rub the nectarine flesh through a hair or silk sieve, blend in the orange juice and syrup, strain in the infusion, mix in the carmine and adjust with water to 21° B. Freeze.

Orange Water Ice - Glace à l'Orange

6 oranges
2 lemons
1 pt. (1/2 l.) syrup
Zest of 3 oranges

A few drops of yellow and carmine colouring to suggest the colour of the fruit. Same procedure as for lemon water ice.

Peach Water Ice - Glace aux Pêches

Proceed in the same way as for apricot ice, using peach pulp. Reduce to 18° B.

Pear Water Ice - Glace aux Poires

1 1/2 lb. (750 gr.) fresh, fully ripe Bartlet or Comice pears (peeled and cored)
1 pt. (1/2 l.) syrup
1/3 gill (5 cl.) brandy
Juice of 1 lemon

Rub the pulp through a hair or silk sieve, mix in the syrup, lemon juice and brandy and adjust to 21° B. Freeze.

Pineapple and Lemon Ice Cream

Flesh of 1 ripe pineapple pressed through a sieve; 1 3/4 pt. (1 l.) syrup at 18° B; 2 whipped egg whites; 1/3 pt. (2 dl.) good champagne; juice and zest of 6 lemons.

Pineapple Water Ice - Glace à l'Ananas

1 1/2 lb. (750 gr.) fresh pineapple flesh, free of rind and core (the best pineapples are the Hawaiian ones because of their fresh, distinctive taste)
1 pt. (1/2 l.) syrup
1 dessertspoonful rum

Mince the fruit through a fine plate, add the syrup, stir and let macerate for one hour and strain through a fine chinois strainer. Place the residual pulp in a tammy cloth and with you at one end and another person at the other, twist the cloth in opposite directions. This exerts enormous pressure and the pulp should give up every drop of juice. Mix all together with the rum, colour to the palest tone of yellow and adjust to 21° B with water.

Victoria Plum Water Ice - Glace aux Prunes

1 1/2 lb. (750 gr.) fully ripe Victoria plums
Juice of 1 lemon
Zest and juice of 1 orange
1 pt. (1/2 l.) syrup
A little carmine

Plunge plums into boiling water for approximately one minute, refresh in cold water and peel, cut into halves with a stainless steel knife and remove the stones. Crush the stones in a mortar, cover them with 1 gill (1 1/2 dl.) of water, bring to the boil, cover and allow to steep until cold and then strain.

Rub the flesh through a hair sieve, add the syrup infusion and juice of the orange and lemon. Rub one cube of sugar over the orange to collect the essential oil and dissolve in the syrup, adjust with water to 21° B and freeze.

Note. If one third of this plum ice is blended with two thirds peach ice, this produces a nectarine ice.

Raspberry Water Ice - Glace aux Framboises

1 1/2 lb. (750 gr.) hulled raspberries, Pine Royals if possible
1 pt. (1/2 l.) syrup
Juice of 1 orange
Juice of 1/2 lemon

Cover the raspberries with the syrup, bring to the boil and strain through muslin, allow to cool and add the orange and lemon juice with sufficient water to register 21° B. Freeze.

White Raspberry Water Ice - Glace aux Framboises blanches

1 1/2 lb. (750 gr.) hulled white raspberries
Juice of 1 lemon
1 pt. (1/2 l.) syrup

Cover raspberries with the syrup, bring to the boil, strain through muslin, cool, add the lemon juice, adjust with water to 21° B. Freeze.

Raspberry and Red Currant Water Ice - Glace aux Framboises et Groseilles

3/4 lb. (375 gr.) hulled raspberries
3/4 lb. (375 gr.) picked red currants
1 pt. (1/2 l.) syrup

Cover red currants with the syrup, bring to the boil, skim and simmer until tender, add the raspberries, cover and stand until only tepid and strain through muslin. Adjust syrup with water to 21° B and freeze.

Strawberry Water Ice - Glace aux Fraises

1 1/2 lb. (750 gr.) hulled alpine strawberries
Juice and zest of 1 orange
1 pt. (1/2 l.) syrup
Juice of half a lemon

Steep the orange zest in the syrup for half an hour. Pass the strawberries through a hair or silk sieve, mix with the orange and lemon juice, strain over the syrup, adjust to 21° B with water, add a few drops of carmine and freeze.

When using colour always remember that freezing will render it lighter.

Tangerine Water Ice - Glace aux Mandarines

1 1/2 pt. (3/4 l.) syrup at 30° B
Zest of 4 tangerines
Juice of 6 tangerines
Juice of 2 oranges
Juice of 1 lemon

Infuse the zest of the tangerines in the hot syrup. When this mixture is cold, add the juice of the tangerines, oranges, and lemon. Reduce to 20° B by the addition of cold water, strain and freeze.

Liqueur Ices - Glaces aux Liqueurs

Liqueur ices are made from syrup at 25° B flavoured with ³/₄ gill (7 cl.) of liqueur for every quart (1 l.) of syrup. The syrup is then reduced to 18-20° B with water or white wine. To enhance the flavour, a little lemon juice may be added during preparation; otherwise these ices are made in the same way as fruit or water ices. The most common flavours are anisette, armagnac, cognac, Cointreau, curaçao, Grand-Marnier, maraschino and rum, but, of course, other liqueurs may also be used.

FRUIT ICES WITH CREAM - GLACES AUX FRUITS À LA CRÈME

Apricot Cream Ice - Glace aux Abricots à la Crème

1 pt. (¹/₂ l.) preserved apricot pulp
1 pt. (¹/₂ l.) cream
1 pt. (¹/₂ l.) milk
12 oz. (375 gr.) sugar
1 tablespoonful noyau
Yellow and carmine to tint

Heat the pulp and sugar together to 200° F (93° C) stirring constantly. Then rub through a hair sieve and leave until cold. Mix in the cream and noyau, tint to the necessary colour, add the milk, mix well and freeze.

Cherry Cream Ice - Glace aux Cerises à la Crème

1 lb. (500 gr.) Kentish or morello cherries
12 oz. (375 gr.) sugar
1 ¹/₄ pt. (7 dl.) cream
³/₄ pt. (4 dl.) milk

Crush the picked cherries in a mortar, add the sugar, stir to the boil, cover and allow to simmer until the fruit is pulped, force through a coarse strainer to remove the stones, then rub through a fine sieve. Put away until cold, stir in the cream and start to freeze. Once the mixture attains a creamy consistency add the milk, making sure that everything is well blended. Finish freezing.

Black Cherry Cream Ice - Glace aux Cerises noires à la Crème

1 × 2 ¹/₂ lb. (1 kg. 250) tin of black cherries (Californian)
8 oz. (250 gr.) sugar
1 pt. (¹/₂ l.) cream
1 dessertspoonful noyau
1 pt. (¹/₂ l.) milk
Juice of ¹/₂ lemon
Carmine to tint

Stone the cherries, remove the syrup from the tin, add the sugar and lemon juice, bring to the boil, simmer until the fruit is easy to pulp, then rub through a hair sieve. Put away until cold. Thoroughly mix in the cream, then the milk. Freeze.

Black Currant Cream Ice - Glace aux Cassis à la Crème

1 lb. (500 gr.) picked black currants
³/₄ lb. (375 gr.) sugar
1 ¹/₄ pt. (7 dl.) cream
³/₄ pt. (4 dl.) milk

Crush the black currants in a mortar, remove to a stewpan, add the sugar, stir to 200° F (93° C), cover and cool; rub through a hair sieve, thoroughly mix in the cream, freeze to a creamy consistency and thoroughly mix in the milk, continue freezing.

Red Currant Cream Ice - Glace aux Groseilles rouges à la Crème

1 ¹/₂ lb. (750 gr.) ripe red currants (picked)
1 ¹/₄ pt. (7 dl.) cream
10 oz. (300 gr.) sugar
³/₄ pt. (4 dl.) milk

Crush the fruit in a mortar, remove to a saucepan, add the sugar and stir to 180° F (82° C), cover and allow to cool, rub through a hair sieve, then thoroughly stir in the cream, tint with carmine and mix in the milk. Freeze.

White Currant Cream Ice - Glace aux Groseilles blanches à la Crème

Same recipe and method as for red currants.

Greengage Cream Ice - Glace Reines-Claudes à la Crème

1 1/2 lb. (750 gr.) fully ripe greengages
1 1/4 pt. (7 dl.) cream
3/4 pt. (4 dl.) milk
10 oz. (300 gr.) sugar
Juice of 1 lemon
Green colouring to tint pale green

Remove the stones from the fruit with a stainless steel knife. Pound the stones in a mortar, cover with the milk and steep for half an hour. Stir the fruit and sugar together to 160° F (71° C), add the lemon juice, cover with a lid and allow to cool slowly. This undercooking is to retain the fresh fruit flavour, but is sufficient to soften the pulp to rub through a sieve. Mix in the cream and then strain in the infusion. Thoroughly mix and tint to a pale green. Freeze.

Lime Cream Ice - Glace au Limon à la Crème

16 West Indies limes
1 pt. (1/2 l.) syrup
3 egg whites
6 oz. (180 gr.) sugar
1 pt. (1/2 l.) cream
Green colour to tint

Remove zest from 8 limes, put in a bowl, add the juice from the limes and syrup, steep for half an hour, strain, adjust to 18° B and freeze. Moisten the sugar with a little water, boil, skim and cook to the feather 240° F (116° C), pour on to the stiffly whipped whites, continuously whisking, and continue until nearly cold. Put away until quite cold. Part whip the cream, blend with the meringue and mix thoroughly with the prepared ice.

Peach Cream Ice - Glace aux Pêches à la Crème

8 large ripe white peaches
Juice of 2 oranges
Juice of 1/2 lemon
Zest of 1 orange
10 oz. (300 gr.) sugar
1 pt. (1/2 l.) cream
1 pt. (1/2 l.) milk
Carmine to tint

Plunge the peaches into boiling water, then into cold water, remove the skins and cut into halves with a stainless steel knife. Remove the stones and crush them well in the mortar, place in a small basin, squeeze over the orange juice and steep for half an hour. Rub the peaches through a hair sieve, add the lemon juice, zest, sugar, and heat to 98° F (37° C), then allow to become cold. Squeeze the steeped kernels through a cloth to extract all the liquid, which is added to the peaches, strain again through a coarse strainer and blend with the cream, stir in the milk. Freeze.

Pineapple Cream Ice - Glace à l'Ananas à la Crème

1 pt. (1/2 l.) pulverized fruit and juice
1 pt. (1/2 l.) cream
1 pt. (1/2 l.) milk
Juice of 1 lemon
10 oz. (300 gr.) sugar

Choose a good firm pineapple, remove the rind and core and crush to a pulp in a mortar and strain through a hair sieve. Collect the fibrous part from the top of the sieve and squeeze out all remaining juice through a tammy cloth, stir into the purée the sugar and lemon juice and let stand, stirring occasionally until the sugar is completely dissolved. Blend in the cream, tint lightly with yellow and carmine, mix in the milk and freeze.

Pomegranate Cream Ice - Glace à la Grenadine à la Crème

6 to 8 large ripe pomegranates cut into quarters with a stainless steel knife, remove the seeds and pith with a spoon, place in a tammy cloth and with another person's help squeeze out the juice. The quantity needed is approximately 1 pt. (1/2 l.); zest and juice of 2 oranges; 1 gill (1 1/2 dl.) grenadine; juice of 1 lemon; 1 pt. (1/2 l.) syrup; 3 egg whites; 1 pt. (1/2 l.) cream; 6 oz. (175 gr.) sugar.

Add the orange and lemon juice to the pomegranate juice, zest, grenadine and syrup; steep for half an hour, then strain and adjust to 18° B and part freeze. Prepare a cooked meringue with the whites and sugar, part whip the cream, blend with the meringue and mix into the ice.

Raspberry Cream Ice - Glace aux Framboises à la Crème

1 pt. ($^1/_2$ l.) sieved ripe raspberry pulp
1 pt. ($^1/_2$ l.) cream
1 pt. ($^1/_2$ l.) milk
Juice of 1 lemon
12 oz. (375 gr.) sugar
Carmine to tint

Mix the sugar, lemon juice and pulp together and stir to blood heat. Allow to become cold, blend in the cream, mix in the milk, tint and freeze.

Strawberry Cream Ice - Glace aux Fraises à la Crème

1 pt. ($^1/_2$ l.) sieved strawberry pulp
1 pt. ($^1/_2$ l.) cream
1 pt. ($^1/_2$ l.) milk
Juice of 1 lemon
12 oz. (375 gr.) sugar

Mix the sugar, lemon juice and pulp together and stir to blood heat. Allow to become cold, blend in the cream, mix in the milk, tint and freeze.

Tangerine Cream Ice - Glace aux Mandarines à la Crème

1 pt. ($^1/_2$ l.) tangerine juice
1 pt. ($^1/_2$ l.) cream
Zest of 8 tangerines
1 pt. ($^1/_2$ l.) milk
Juice of 2 lemons
10 oz. (300 gr.) sugar
5 drops of essential oil of tangerine
1 tablespoonful apricot brandy
Carmine to tint

Steep the zests with the tangerine and lemon juice to which the sugar has been added. Leave for half an hour, then strain, add the liqueur, essential oil and cream and lastly the milk; tint to pale colour and freeze.

ICE BRICKS
Ice Bricks

Other recommended combinations:
torroncino - chocolate - vanilla
vanilla - coffee - zabaglione
vanilla - chocolate - almonds
croccantino rum - vanilla - pistachio
raspberry - banana - prunes
orange - lemon - melon
quince - sour black cherries - peaches
pineapple - strawberries - bananas
strawberries - pears - oranges

Mixture for Biscuits glacés

Old method for 8 persons:
6 egg yolks
7 $^1/_2$ oz. (200 gr.) castor sugar
3 $^1/_2$ oz. (100 gr.) Italian meringue
1 pt. ($^1/_2$ l.) whipped cream

Blend the yolks with the sugar, whisk over heat in a bain-marie to a thick creamy consistency and continue to whisk the mixture on ice until it is quite cold. Add the Italian meringue, the required flavouring and the whipped cream.

Modern method for 8 persons:
6 egg yolks
7 oz. (200 gr.) castor sugar
1 pt. ($^1/_2$ l.) whipped cream
Flavouring

Boil the sugar with a little water to the ball. Mix the yolks with the sugar, whisking continuously until the mixture is of a thick creamy consistency. Whisk on ice until cold, add the flavouring and fold in the whipped cream.

N.B. A bombe mixture may also be used for biscuits glacés.

How to mould and freeze Biscuits glacés

The moulds are round or brick-shaped, with removable lids, both at the top and bottom. The bottom lid is covered with a piece of greaseproof paper, at least an inch larger overall, then the lid is forced into position.

Haupia Aloha, p. 766
(Recipe p. 750)
Adua Kat, p. 768
(Recipe p. 748)

Rose Ice Cream, p. 765 ▶
(Recipe p. 757)
Peppermint Cake, p. 767 ▶
(Recipe p. 582)
Mango Kohu Pee, p. 769 ▶
(Recipe p. 750)

770 ▲ Wune Wharn, p. 751
Pomegranate Cream, p. 749 ▼

Ecuadorian Banana Toddy, p. 749 ▶

It is then filled, another piece of paper is used as a cover and the top lid is put into position. When frozen, the mould is dipped into cold water, both lids are removed, and a thin knife is passed round the inside of the mould to loosen the contents. The biscuit glacé is then cut into slices and arranged upon ice wafers (optional) and returned to deep freeze. Upon serving, biscuits glacés are usually decorated with whipped cream, glacé fruits, praline, chocolate ornaments or shavings, etc.

Biscuits glacés can be varied according to the composition of the ice cream.

Anisette -
Biscuit glacé à l'Anisette

Fill with aniseed mixture with the addition of 4 oz. (120 gr.) diced savoy fingers sprinkled with anisette. Decorate with a rosette of cream.

Apricot -
Biscuit glacé à l'Abricot

1 biscuit glacé mixture
$1/2$ pt. ($1/4$ l.) apricot pulp
1 tablespoonful apricot brandy

Blend pulp and apricot brandy into the mixture before adding the whipped cream. Garnish with a rosette of whipped cream and a small piece of glacé apricot.

Benedictine -
Biscuit glacé Bénédictine

$1/3$ strawberry
$1/3$ basic mixture flavoured with Benedictine
$1/3$ violet

Blanchette -
Biscuit glacé Blanchette

$1/3$ raspberry
$1/3$ vanilla
$1/3$ pistachio

Decorate with a rosette of cream and shredded pistachio nuts.

Cardinal -
Biscuit glacé à la Cardinal

Raspberry mixture.

Decorate with a rosette of cream and a sugared raspberry.

Carmen - Biscuit glacé Carmen

$1/3$ tangerine
$1/3$ sweetened whipped cream
$1/3$ praline

Decorate with a rosette of cream and a segment of tangerine.

Chocolate -
Biscuit glacé au Chocolat

1 biscuit glacé mixture
4 oz. (125 gr.) bitter chocolate

Melt chocolate with the syrup and proceed as usual.

Decorate with a rosette of whipped cream and a chocolate bean.

Coffee - Biscuit glacé au Café

1 biscuit glacé mixture
1 tablespoonful soluble coffee powder

Mix coffee powder with the syrup and proceed as usual.

Decorate with a rosette of whipped cream and a coffee bean prepared from marzipan and chocolate.

Coffee Praline -
Biscuit glacé au Café praliné

Prepare a coffee biscuit glacé mixture and add $2 \, 1/2$ oz. (75 gr.) ground and sieved praline. Decorate with a rosette of whipped cream and sprinkle with praline.

Creole - Biscuit glacé Créole

$1/3$ orange
$1/3$ rum
$1/3$ pineapple

Decorate with a rosette of cream and crystallized pineapple.

◀ Champagne Flip
(*Recipe p. 743*)

Duke of Orleans - Biscuit glacé Duc d'Orléans
$1/3$ coffee
$1/3$ sweetened whipped cream flavoured with maraschino and containing finely diced glacé pineapple
$1/3$ strawberry

Decorate with a rosette of cream and a sugar strawberry.

Excelsior - Biscuit glacé Excelsior
$1/3$ vanilla
$1/3$ raspberry containing diced savoy fingers soaked with maraschino
$1/3$ pistachio

Decorate with a rosette of cream, sprinkle with rose petals.

Fanchonnette - Biscuit glacé Fanchonnette
$1/3$ vanilla
$1/3$ pistachio
$1/3$ praline

Decorate with a rosette of cream and half a glacé cherry.

Impératrice - Biscuit glacé à l'Impératrice
$2/3$ kirsch
$1/3$ strawberry

Decorate with a rosette of cream and half a marron glacé.

Various Liqueur Biscuits
Blend in half a gill of liqueur to 1 biscuit glacé mixture.

Marie-Louise - Biscuit glacé Marie-Louise
Finely diced glacé fruits macerated in anisette and incorporated into the vanilla base. Decorate with a rosette of cream, half a glacé cherry and angelica.

Maxim's - Biscuit glacé Maxim's
$1/2$ champagne
$1/2$ raspberry

Decorate with a rosette of cream with a peeled and seeded grape in centre.

Mont-Blanc - Biscuit glacé Mont-Blanc
$1/3$ vanilla
$1/3$ rum
$1/3$ chestnut

Decorate with a rosette of cream and half a marron glacé.

Montmorency - Biscuit glacé Montmorency
Finely diced cherries macerated in a vanilla base. Decorate with a rosette of cream and sprinkle with diced or chopped glacé cherries.

Neapolitan I - Biscuit glacé à la napolitaine
$1/3$ vanilla
$1/3$ strawberry
$1/3$ pistachio

Rosette of cream.

Neapolitan II - Biscuit glacé à la napolitaine
$1/3$ vanilla
$1/3$ strawberry
$1/3$ chocolate

Rosette of cream.

Neapolitan III - Biscuit glacé à la napolitaine
$1/3$ vanilla
$1/3$ strawberry
$1/3$ praline

Rosette of cream.

Nesselrode - Biscuit glacé Nesselrode
Fill with chestnut mixture. Decorate with a rosette of cream and sprinkle with diced marrons glacés.

Odette - Biscuit glacé Odette
$1/2$ vanilla
$1/2$ praline

Rosette of cream, sprinkle with roasted shredded almonds.

Parisian - Biscuit glacé à la parisienne

$1/3$ red currants
$1/3$ vanilla
$1/3$ strawberry

Rosette of cream surmounted by a large sugared strawberry.

Pistachio - Biscuit glacé aux Pistaches

Add 3 oz. (90 gr.) blanched pistachio nuts ground to a paste with a few drops of kirsch in a mixer, and add to the basic biscuit glacé mixture.

Praline - Biscuit glacé praliné

Add 3 oz. (90 gr.) sieved praline to the basic mixture.

Raspberry - Biscuit glacé aux Framboises

1 biscuit glacé mixture
$1/2$ pt. ($1/4$ l.) raspberry pulp
Juice of $1/2$ lemon
2 egg whites
4 oz. (125 gr.) castor sugar
1 pt. ($1/2$ l.) whipped cream

Prepare Italian meringue with the sugar and the egg whites and allow to cool. Blend pulp and lemon juice into cream and meringue, then fold into basic mixture.

Rivoli - Biscuit glacé Rivoli

$1/2$ pistachio
$1/2$ chocolate

Decorate with a rosette of cream.

Strawberry - Biscuit glacé aux Fraises

1 biscuit glacé mixture
$1/2$ pt. ($1/4$ l.) strawberry pulp
Juice of $1/2$ lemon
Italian meringue prepared with 2 egg whites and 4 oz. (125 gr.) castor sugar
1 pt. ($1/2$ l.) whipped cream

Same procedure as for raspberry biscuit glacé.

Sylvia - Biscuit glacé Sylvia

4 oz. (125 gr.) roasted, crushed hazelnuts added to the vanilla base
2 oz. (60 gr.) diced savoy fingers soaked in apricot brandy and added to 1 pt. ($1/2$ l.) apricot mousse
$1/3$ hazelnut base
$1/3$ apricot
$1/3$ hazelnut base

Rosette of cream, surmounted by a piece of glacé apricot.

Tortoni I - Biscuit glacé Tortoni

$1/5$ red currant
$1/5$ vanilla
$1/5$ raspberry
$1/5$ vanilla
$1/5$ strawberry

Rosette of cream sprinkled with grated chocolate.

Tortoni II - Biscuit glacé Tortoni

Basic mixture with addition of 3 oz. (90 gr.) sieved praline croquant, and flavoured with kirsch. After turning out, pipe vanilla flavoured whipped dairy cream over the top spaghetti fashion, using a savoy bag and small pipe, then sprinkle with praline croquant and freeze again.

Vanilla - Biscuit glacé à la Vanille

1 biscuit glacé mixture
1 pt. ($1/2$ l.) cream
2 egg whites
4 oz. (125 gr.) sugar

Prepare an Italian meringue with the whites and sugar. Allow to cool. Make the syrup for the mixture with 1 split vanilla pod. Blend the Italian meringue into the part-whipped cream and finally into the biscuit glacé mixture.

Coffee and chocolate biscuits glacés can also be made with the basic mixture and Italian meringue. In this case the syrup is prepared with soluble coffee powder or melted chocolate.

ICE BOMBES

Ice bombes consist of a lining and a filling. The lining is generally made with plain ice cream prepared in the freezer, while the filling consists of 'bombe mixture'. There are countless possible variations in the production of ice bombes and only a small proportion of these can be listed here. It is advisable to turn ice bombes out on to a thin round slice of genoese or Viennese butter sponge to prevent them from sliding about the dish. It is then easier to decorate them and also to serve.

How to mould Bombes

Chill the moulds well before use, either placing them in the deep freeze cabinet or surrounding them with crushed ice. Line them quickly with a layer of ice prepared in the freezer to a thickness of at least 1/2 in. (1 cm.). Fill with bombe mixture, level off the top, cover with a sheet of paper, press on the lid and deep freeze. Work quickly to prevent the lining from sliding off. To unmould, hold the mould in warm water for a moment, wipe the outside, then slide on to a round dish.

There is no need for the lid if the bombe is placed in the deep freeze cabinet but, for hygienic reasons, it is advisable to cover it with a sheet of paper.
(Illustration page 795.)

Basic Ice Cream for Bombes

The following is the basic filling for ice bombes, which may be prepared in a bewildering number of combinations.

Bombe Mixture (basic recipe)

10 oz. (300 gr.) egg yolks
1 lb. 2 oz. (560 gr.) syrup at 32° B
1 lb. 2 oz. (560 gr.) whipped cream

Blend the egg yolks with the syrup, whisk over heat in a bain-marie as for a genoese sponge and continue to whisk until the mixture is completely cold. Then add the whipped cream and the required flavouring.

American Bombe - Bombe américaine

Line mould with strawberry ice and fill with tangerine bombe mixture. Garnish with pistachios.

Bombe Archiduc

Line mould with strawberry ice and fill with vanilla bombe mixture containing praline.

Bombe Aurélie

Line mould with vanilla ice and fill with strawberry parfait containing diced glacé fruits soaked in maraschino. Garnish with pineapple and orange sections dipped in caramel sugar.

Bombe Aurore

Line the mould with strawberry ice and fill with kirsch flavoured bombe mixture containing red glacé cherries soaked in kirsch.

Bombe Baroda

Line mould with coconut ice cream, and fill with chocolate mousse. Freeze, unmould and decorate with Chantilly cream and chocolate cigarettes.

Bombe Bourdaloue

Line the mould with vanilla ice cream and fill with anisette flavoured bombe mixture; decorate with crystallized violets.

Bombe Bragance

Line mould with lemon ice and fill with alternate layers of strawberry parfait and rum flavoured bombe mixture.

Brazilian Bombe - Bombe brésilienne

Line mould with pineapple ice and fill with vanilla bombe mixture flavoured with rum and containing diced pineapple soaked in rum.

Bombe Camargo

Line mould with coffee ice and fill centre with vanilla bombe mixture.

Bombe Chantilly
Line mould with chocolate ice and fill with bombe mixture flavoured with kirsch and maraschino. Freeze, unmould and decorate with Chantilly cream.

Bombe Chateaubriand
Line mould with apricot ice and fill with vanilla bombe mixture.

Bombe Créole
Line the mould with pineapple ice and fill centre with strawberry and pineapple bombe mixture.

Bombe Danicheff
Line mould with coffee ice and fill the centre with bombe mixture flavoured with kirsch.

Bombe dauphinoise
Line mould with pineapple ice and fill with bombe mixture flavoured with green Chartreuse and containing diced savoy fingers soaked in Chartreuse.

Bombe Dioclétian
Line mould with vanilla ice containing diced glacé cherries soaked in maraschino and fill with bombe mixture flavoured with Grand-Marnier and containing diced savoy fingers soaked in cognac. Unmould, place an ornament made of couverture on top and decorate with Chantilly cream and small leaf shaped wafers.

Bombe Diplomate
Line the mould with vanilla ice cream and fill with maraschino flavoured bombe mixture containing candied fruits which have been soaked in maraschino.

Bombe Esterhazy
Line mould with vanilla ice and fill with Chantilly cream containing diced glacé fruits soaked in kirsch.

Bombe Falstaff
Line mould with praline ice and fill with strawberry parfait mixture.

Bombe Fédora
Line mould with orange ice and fill with vanilla praline bombe mixture.

Bombe Hamlet
Line mould with tangerine ice and fill with vanilla bombe mixture containing diced preserved tangerines.

Bombe Hernani
Line mould with coffee ice and fill with walnut bombe mixture. Freeze, unmould and decorate with Chantilly cream and halved walnuts dipped in caramel sugar.

Japanese Bombe - Bombe japonaise
Line mould with peach ice and fill with tea flavoured bombe mixture.

Bombe Joinville
Line mould with chocolate ice mixed with chopped almonds and fill with maraschino flavoured bombe mixture containing chopped cherries.

Kranzler Bombe
Line mould to approximately 1 1/4 in. (3 cm.) thickness with pineapple ice mixed with diced pineapple and then with the same thickness of pistachio ice and chopped pistachios. Fill with praline parfait. Freeze, unmould and decorate with whipped cream, chocolate ornaments, glacé pineapple and red glacé cherries.

Bombe Madeleine
Line mould with almond ice and fill with vanilla bombe mixture containing diced glacé fruits soaked in kirsch.

Maltese Bombe - Bombe maltaise
Line mould with blood-orange ice and fill with mandarine flavoured Chantilly cream.

Bombe Marquise de Sévigné
Line mould with apricot ice and fill with Benedictine flavoured bombe mixture

containing diced savoy fingers soaked in cognac. Decorate with an ornament of piped baked choux paste, glacé pineapple and red glacé cherries.

Bombe Médicis
Line mould with cognac flavoured vanilla ice and fill with strawberry parfait mixture.

Bombe Ménélik
Line mould with tangerine ice and fill with rum flavoured bombe mixture.

Bombe Miss Hellyet
Line mould with raspberry ice and fill with vanilla bombe mixture.

Bombe Montmorency
Line the mould with kirsch flavoured ice cream and fill with a cherry brandy flavoured bombe mixture containing cherries which have been soaked in kirsch.

Bombe Nelusko
Line mould with praline ice and fill with chocolate bombe mixture.

Bombe Nesselrode
Line mould with vanilla ice cream and fill with Chantilly cream flavoured with kirsch and mixed with diced glacé chestnuts.

Oriental Bombe - Bombe orientale
Line mould with ginger ice and fill with pistachio bombe mixture.

Portuguese Bombe - Bombe portugaise
Line mould with tangerine ice and fill with curaçao flavoured bombe mixture.

Prince of Wales Bombe - Bombe Prince de Galles
Line mould with chocolate ice and fill with bombe mixture mixed with chestnut purée containing diced glacé chestnuts, unmould and decorate with whipped cream.

Bombe Princesse
Line mould with anisette ice and fill with vanilla bombe mixture.

Bombe Richelieu
Line mould with rum ice and fill with coffee bombe mixture containing chocolate coffee beans.

Bombe Riviera
Line mould with orange ice and fill with lemon sorbet flavoured with curaçao and roasted almond nibs. Unmould and decorate with palm leaf shaped wafers, chocolate ornaments, glacé fruits and a border of Chantilly cream bulbs.

Bombe Santiago
Line mould with cognac ice and fill with pistachio bombe mixture.

Bombe Sappho
Line mould with strawberry ice and fill with bombe mixture containing wild strawberries soaked in kirsch.

Scotch Bombe - Bombe écossaise
Line mould with orange ice mixed with chopped candied orange peel and fill with whisky flavoured bombe mixture. Decorate with whipped cream, orange segments and chocolate shavings.

Bombe Succès
Line mould with apricot ice and fill with Chantilly cream mixed with diced apricots soaked in kirsch.

Bombe Sultane
Line mould with chocolate ice and fill with vanilla bombe mixture containing praline.

Bombe Tosca
Line mould with apricot ice and fill with maraschino flavoured bombe mixture containing diced glacé fruits.

Bombe Trocadero

Line mould with orange ice mixed with chopped candied orange peel. Fill centre with Chantilly cream containing diced genoese sponge soaked in curaçao.

Tutti-Frutti Bombe - Bombe Tutti-Frutti

Line the mould with strawberry ice and fill with lemon bombe mixture containing mixed diced candied fruits which have been soaked in kirsch.

Bombe Victoria

Line mould with strawberry ice and fill with Plombières ice.

White Lady Bombe - Bombe Dame blanche

Line mould with vanilla ice and fill centre with bombe mixture containing almond milk.

Bombe Zamora

Line mould with coffee ice and fill with curaçao flavoured bombe mixture.

Bombe Zanzibar

Line mould with coffee ice and fill with bombe mixture mixed with almond powder and flavoured with curaçao.

ICED CHARLOTTES - CHARLOTTES GLACÉES

To prepare these ices, charlotte moulds are lined with savoy fingers as in the manner of Charlotte russe and then filled with various ice creams, bombe, biscuit glacé or mousse mixture and placed in the deep freeze until required. They are then unmoulded and decorated to taste. Sometimes a cold sauce is served with these preparations.

Iced Charlotte Aga Khan - Charlotte glacée Aga Khan

Line the mould with savoy fingers and fill with alternate layers of vanilla bombe mixture, to which small cubes of genoese sponge splashed with Cherry Rocher have been added, and chocolate parfait mixture containing diced glacé apricots macerated in kirsch. Unmould and decorate with dots of whipped cream tipped with leaf gold.

Iced Charlotte Berlioz - Charlotte glacée Berlioz

Line the mould with savoy fingers and fill with a bombe mixture containing small strawberries macerated in sugar and framboise. Unmould, decorate with Chantilly cream and strawberries.

Iced Charlotte Marie-Louise - Charlotte glacée Marie-Louise

Line the mould with savoy fingers which have been splashed with kirsch. Coat the interior with strawberry ice and fill with vanilla bombe mixture containing diced pineapple macerated in Cointreau. Freeze, unmould, decorate with Chantilly cream and chocolate shavings.

Iced Charlotte Procope - Charlotte glacée Procope

Line mould with savoy fingers and fill with two alternate layers of praline and coffee bombe mixture. Decorate with whipped cream and serve cold chocolate sauce separately.

ICE CREAM COUPES

These are ice cream and fruit confections served in individual containers of either glass or porcelain. It is wise to have these dishes sufficiently large, so that the contents do not slop over the sides. An attractively dressed coupe, too small in reality for its contents, giving no room for the diner to manipulate its contents, can only cause frustration.

Coupe Abricotine

Place a scoop of apricot ice in the bottom of the coupe, press down with a spoon, arrange three apricot halves on top, mask with apricot sauce. Pipe a border of whipped cream.

Coupe Adelina Patti

Fill coupe nearly full with vanilla ice cream. Place six brandied cherries on top and finish off with a rosette of whipped cream.

Coupe Alphonse

Place raspberries in the bottom, then pistachio ice, mask with mousseline sauce, pipe a border of cream, sprinkle with wild strawberries.

Coupe andalouse

Place orange segments macerated with sugar and curaçao in the bottom of the coupe, fill with lemon ice and decorate with orange segments and whipped cream.

Coupe Arlesian - Coupe arlésienne

Half fill a coupe with vanilla ice containing diced mixed glacé fruits macerated in kirsch. Place half a poached pear on top and mask with cold apricot sauce.

Coupe Belle Dijonnaise

Place black currants in the bottom of the coupe, cover with black currant ice, mask with black currant sauce and pipe a pyramid of Chantilly cream on top. Sprinkle with black currants moistened with egg white, rolled in castor sugar and dried.

Coupe berlinoise - Berliner Becher

Place a scoop each of vanilla and chocolate ice cream in the coupe and cover with diced mixed fruit macerated in sugar and rum. Pipe five rosettes of whipped cream on top, place a chocolate disc in the centre and add two glacé cherries and half a wafer.

Coupe Black Forest - Schwarzwaldbecher

Place three scoops of vanilla ice cream and a spoonful of morello cherries, macerated in cherry brandy and kirsch, in the coupe and add some chopped walnuts. Cover cone-shaped with whipped cream, flute with a knife, insert a few rolls of bitter chocolate vertically on top and place a rolled wafer with chocolate dots on one side of the coupe.

Coupe Black Forest II - Coupe Forêt-Noire

Place a piece of chocolate sponge in the coupe and soak in kirsch syrup. Cover with a large scoop of chocolate ice cream, make a depression with the back of the scoop and fill with slightly sweetened poached morello cherries. Pipe a few spots of whipped dairy cream all round and sprinkle chocolate shaving on them.

Coupe Brazilian - Coupe brésilienne

Place diced pineapple, macerated with sugar and maraschino, in the bottom of the coupe, cover with lemon ice and decorate with cherries and angelica.

Coupe Camargo

Place diced pineapple in the bottom, then an oval scoop each of coffee and vanilla ice.

Coupe Capriccio

Place 3 maraschino cherries in the coupe and pour a little grenadine over. Lay three thin slices of filled Swiss roll against the sides of the coupe and fill the cavity with diced peaches flavoured with maraschino. Pipe on kirsch ice cream with a large flat tube and mask with thin apricot jelly. Insert a heart made of piped chocolate in the centre of each coupe and serve at once. Alternatively, fruit ice or mousseline cream may be piped into the coupe, but the maraschino/kirsch combination is to be preferred. *(Switzerland)*
(Illustration page 792.)

Coupe Chateaubriand
Macerate strawberries with sugar and brandy and dress in coupes, then garnish with an oval scoop each of vanilla and apricot ice.

Coupe Cleopatra
Garnish bottom of coupe with maraschino ice containing coarsely crushed praline, then strawberries; mask with strawberry mousseline sauce; garnish with meringue mushrooms.

Coupe Coppelia
Place stoned cherries macerated in maraschino in the bottom of the coupe with an oval scoop each of coffee and praline ice. Sprinkle with roasted shredded almonds.

Coupe Diable rose
Macerate strawberries in kirsch and place in the bottom of the coupe, then cover with strawberry ice; pipe over a pyramid of raspberry cream; sprinkle with chopped glacé cherries.

Coupe Edna May
Place vanilla ice in the bottom of the coupe. Cover with cold cherry compote and pipe over a pyramid of whipped cream mixed with raspberry purée.

Coupe Elizabeth
Place stoned cherries macerated in brandy and sugar in the bottom, then a scoop of vanilla ice. Pipe on a pyramid of Chantilly cream and sprinkle with crushed crystallized rose petals.

Coupe Emma Calvé
Place praline ice in the bottom of the coupe, cover with cherry compote flavoured with kirsch and mask with raspberry purée.

Coupe Eugénie
Fill with vanilla ice cream mixed with crushed marrons glacés and flavoured with maraschino. Cover and decorate with Chantilly cream and sprinkle with crushed crystallized violets.

Coupe Fiammetta
Place stoned and skinned grapes macerated in sugar and brandy in the bottom, then apricot ice; pipe over a pyramid of brandy cream. Decorate with grapes.

Coupe Germaine
Place peach ice in the bottom of a coupe, then a peach. Mask with apricot sauce and pipe on a pyramid of Chantilly cream. Sprinkle with crushed macaroons and crystallized violets.

Coupe Gladstone
Place vanilla ice containing diced preserved stem ginger in the bottom of the coupe, then diced fresh pears macerated in gin. Pipe on a pyramid of Chantilly cream and decorate with glacé cherries and angelica.

Coupe Herriot
Put a scoop of vanilla ice cream mixed with chopped glacé fruits soaked in brandy in the coupe. Cover with a thin disc of sponge cake, place a very small ball of apricot ice on top and pour over a little liqueur Cherry-Heering. Pipe over a pyramid of whipped cream and place a candied walnut in the centre.

Coupe Jamaïque
Place diced pineapple macerated with rum and sugar in the bottom of a coupe, add coffee ice, then pipe a border of cream.

Coupe japonaise
Place raspberries in the bottom, then peach ice; mask with tea flavoured mousseline sauce; sprinkle with shredded almonds and crystallized orange blossom.

Coupe Java
Fill coupe with a scoop each of coffee and chocolate ice and a spoonful of morello cherries soaked in brandy. Decorate with rosettes of whipped cream, a red glacé cherry and flaked bitter chocolate.

Coupe Joséphine Baker

Put a tablespoonful of diced pineapple soaked in Cointreau in the coupe and cover with chocolate ice. Pipe over a pyramid of Chantilly cream and decorate with a chocolate ornament and half glacé cherries. Sprinkle chopped pistachios on the cream.

Coupe Jubilee

Not quite half fill a coupe with poached chopped cherries soaked in kirsch and place a scoop of vanilla ice cream on top. Decorate with whipped cream and sprinkle chopped pistachios on top.

Coupe Lucullus

Place a scoop of vanilla ice and two scoops of pistachio ice in a tall goblet, cover with a spoonful of chopped fresh fruit and crushed macaroons and pour over a little cherry brandy. Cover cone-shape with whipped cream and decorate with half a glacé cherry, shredded pistachio nuts and leaf-shaped wafers.

Coupe Madeleine

Fill coupe with vanilla ice cream mixed with diced preserved pineapple soaked in kirsch and maraschino. Cover with apricot sauce flavoured with kirsch and maraschino.

Coupe Marie-Brizard

Place stoned cherries in the bottom of a coupe, then an oval scoop each of coffee and anisette ice.

Coupe Marie-Louise

Place raspberries in the bottom of the coupe, cover with vanilla ice cream, mask with raspberry sauce and pipe a border of whipped cream.

Coupe Mercedes

Place vanilla ice in the bottom, then apricots, cover with a pyramid of Chartreuse flavoured whipped cream and sprinkle with shredded chocolate.

Coupe Metternich

Place a salpicon of pineapple soaked in kirsch in the coupe and cover with raspberry ice. Decorate with whipped cream flavoured with vanilla liqueur.

Coupe Miramar

Place diced pineapple and tangerine macerated in kirsch and sugar in the bottom of a coupe, then pineapple ice; mask with Chartreuse mousseline sauce; serve with savoy fingers.

Coupe Miss Helyett

Place raspberry ice in the bottom of a coupe, then apricots, mask with vanilla flavoured cream. Surround with a border of Chantilly cream.

Coupe Mistinguette

Place a scoop of almond ice in the coupe and cover with salpicon of fresh fruit macerated in Cointreau. Cover with strawberry ice, decorate with rosettes of whipped cream and a green maraschino cherry.

Coupe Monte-Cristo

Place diced banana, peach and orange, macerated in kirsch and sugar, in the bottom of a coupe; surmount with an oval scoop each of lemon and pistachio ice.

Coupe Montmorency I

Place stoned cherries macerated in kirsch and sugar in the bottom of a coupe, then a scoop of vanilla ice. Mask with red currant sauce. Pipe on a pyramid of Chantilly cream and sprinkle with chopped glacé cherries.

Coupe Montmorency II

Fill the coupe with vanilla ice flavoured with a little cherry brandy and smooth over the top. Pipe spots of whipped dairy cream all round the edge and cover the center with fresh compote cherries macerated in a little cherry brandy. Sprinkle with coarsely crushed praline croquant.

Coupe moscovite
Place stoned cherries, macerated in Kümmel and sugar in the bottom of a coupe, then a scoop of almond ice containing chopped glacé fruits. Pipe on a pyramid of Chantilly cream and sprinkle with roasted shredded almonds.

Coupe Mozart
Put alternate layers of vanilla and almond ice in the coupe, with sliced fresh peaches between the layers. Pour chilled raspberry syrup on top, decorate with whipped cream and sprinkle with chopped roasted almonds.

Coupe orientale
Place diced pineapple in the bottom of a coupe, then pineapple ice, mask with apricot sauce. Pipe a border of Chantilly cream and sprinkle with grilled shredded almonds.

Coupe Princesse
Place raspberries in the bottom of the coupe and then an oval scoop each of praline and orange ice. Pipe over a pyramid of whipped cream and garnish with strawberries.

Coupe Princesse Olga
Place apricot ice in the bottom of the coupe, then strawberries; mask with Kümmel mousseline sauce. Pipe a border of cream and sprinkle with crystallized violets.

Coupe Rêve de Bébé
Place a small scoop of pineapple ice in the coupe and surround with small strawberries soaked in orange juice. Cover with a scoop of strawberry ice, pipe a border of whipped cream and sprinkle with crystallized violets.

Coupe Rose-Chéri
Place strawberries in the bottom of the coupe, then pineapple ice; mask with white wine sabayon and sprinkle with crystallized rose petals.

Coupe Saint-Michel
Place Plombières ice flavoured with kirsch in the bottom of a coupe, then slices of pineapple. Decorate with cherries and greengages.

Coupe Savoy
Place raspberries in the bottom of the coupe, then coffee praline ice; mask with anisette mousseline sauce and sprinkle with crystallized violets.

Coupe Suzanne
Place diced pineapple, macerated in rum and sugar in the bottom of a coupe, then pineapple ice; mask with red currant sauce and pipe a border of whipped cream.

Coupe Thaïs
Place vanilla ice in the bottom of the coupe and place half a poached cold peach on top. Pipe over a border of Chantilly cream and sprinkle with chocolate chips.

Coupe tripolitaine
Place diced peach, orange and strawberry in the bottom of a coupe, and an oval scoop each of strawberry and lemon ice on top.

Coupe tunisienne
Place coffee ice in bottom of a coupe, then apricots and mask with chocolate sauce.

ICE GATEAUX
Ice gâteaux are among the finest, most delicate ice preparations, provided they are made with light ice and well flavoured. They generally consist of a base of genoese or Viennese butter sponge moistened with stock syrup which has been well flavoured with liqueur or spirits; this is covered with one or more layers of light ice and a second sheet of butter sponge is placed on top. After freezing, the gâteau is decorated with whipped cream, glacé fruits, etc. The sides are often masked with nuts. Japonaise bases may, of course, be used instead of butter sponge.

Ice Gâteau Green Goddess - Gâteau glacé Déesse verte

Place a layer of genoese sponge in the bottom of a round mould, fill with greengage ice and cap with a slice of genoese; both pieces of genoese to be sprinkled with maraschino. Freeze, unmould, mask with pistachio cream and decorate with the same cream, crystallized greengages and pistachio nuts.

Ice Gâteau Kranzler - Kranzler Eistorte

Prepare a bombe mixture containing pineapple chunks macerated in brandy and curaçao and freeze in a round mould. Turn out on a meringue base and divide the gâteau into the desired number of portions. Decorate each piece with whipped cream, a piece of pineapple and half a wafer. *(Germany)*

Neapolitan Ice Gâteau I - Gâteau glacé à la napolitaine

Place a layer of genoese sponge in the bottom of the mould, sprinkle with maraschino, $1/3$ fill with chocolate ice, another slice of genoese soaked with maraschino, $1/3$ more of pistachio ice, another layer of genoese soaked with maraschino, fill up the mould with orange ice, cover with another slice of genoese soaked in maraschino, put away in deep freeze to firm up, unmould, mask with strawberry cream. Decorate with Chantilly cream and strawberries.

Neapolitan Ice Gâteau II

Prepare three layers of genoese sponge (maddalena) by soaking with curaçao. Sandwich with one layer of vanilla ice cream and one of hazelnut. When frozen, unmould and coat with whipped dairy cream and decorate with pieces of pineapple and roasted chopped hazelnuts.
(Italy)

Ice Nut Gâteau with Cognac Cherries - Nusseistorte mit Cognackirschen

Prepare a parfait mixture and mix in some nut nougat worked to a smooth consistency with a little dairy cream. Arrange a layer of the mixture in a round mould, add a filling of cognac cherries, spread the rest of the parfait on top and put away in deep freeze to set. Divide into the desired number of portions, decorate with whipped cream, sprinkle with chopped roasted hazelnuts and serve with a wafer. *(Germany)*

Ice Gâteau Queen of Hearts - Gâteau glacé Reine de Cœur

Place a layer of sponge cake in the bottom of a round mould, fill with almond ice mixed with soft macaroons broken into pieces and splashed with kirsch, and cap with a slice of sponge cake; both pieces of sponge cake to be splashed with Cointreau. Freeze, turn out, brush sides and surface with apricot jam and scatter with chopped grilled almonds. Dust surface with a little icing sugar before serving.

Ice Gâteau Red Queen - Gâteau glacé Reine rouge

Place a layer of genoese sponge in the bottom of the mould, half fill with strawberry ice, another layer of genoese on top, complete filling with raspberry ice and cap with another slice of genoese. Freeze, unmould, mask with raspberry cream and decorate with raspberry cream and strawberries.

Siciliana

Prepare three layers of genoese sponge (maddalena) by soaking with orange liqueur. Sandwich with one layer of lemon and one layer of orange ice cream. Turn out when frozen, and coat with whipped dairy cream and orange segments. Place savoy fingers round the side. *(Italy)*

Ice Gâteau White Lady - Gâteau glacé Dame blanche

Place a slice of almond genoese in the bottom of the mould, sprinkle with kirsch, fill with white coffee ice, cover with another layer of almond genoese soaked with kirsch, put away in the deep freeze to set, unmould, mask with almond cream and decorate with Chantilly cream.

Mocha Ice Gâteau - Mokkaeistorte

Place a thin layer of Viennese butter sponge in the bottom of a round mould and moisten with kirsch syrup. Fill with mocha parfait mixture and freeze. Unmould, decorate all round the top with whirls of whipped dairy cream, insert a chocolate coffee bean in each one and sprinkle the centre of the gâteau with chocolate raspings. *(Germany)*
(Illustration page 794.)

Monte Bianco

Prepare three layers of genoese sponge (maddalena) soaked with rum. Sandwich with one layer of vanilla and one of gianduja ice cream. When frozen, unmould and finish as for Siciliana, but use pistachio nuts and cherries instead of orange segments. *(Italy)*

Monviso

Prepare three layers of genoese sponge (maddalena) by soaking with curaçao. Sandwich with one layer of coffee ice cream and one of zabaglione. When frozen, unmould and spread with whipped dairy cream and pieces of well drained canned fruits. *(Italy)*

Santa Lucia

Prepare three layers of genoese sponge (maddalena) by soaking with vanilla liqueur. Sandwich with one layer of banana ice cream and one of strawberry. When frozen, unmould and cover with whipped dairy cream and wild strawberries. *(Italy)*

Suzie

Prepare three layers of genoese sponge (maddalena) soaked with vanilla liqueur. Sandwich with one layer of almond and one layer of chocolate ice cream. When frozen, unmould and spread with whipped dairy cream and decorate the top with well drained canned peaches and cherries. *(Italy)*

Other recommended Ice Cream Combinations for Gâteaux

lemon - melon
sour black cherry - peach
prune - pear
apricot - pineapple
strawberry - apple reinette
strawberry - peach
strawberry - quince
raspberry - banana
vanilla - chocolate
vanilla - croccantino with rum

ICED MOUSSES

Ice mousses may be made in two different ways, using either a cream or a fruit mixture. They are served on their own or are used as centres for iced bombes, iced puddings or biscuits glacés.

Cream Iced Mousse - Mousse glacée à la Crème

8 persons:

Old method:

6 egg yolks
1 ½ gills (2 dl.) milk
6 ½ oz. (180 gr.) castor sugar
1 pt. (½ l.) whipped cream
Flavouring

Prepare custard cream with the egg yolks, milk and sugar and cool. Add flavouring to the cold custard cream and fold in the whipped cream.

Modern method:

5 egg yolks
3 egg whites
7 oz. (200 gr.) castor sugar
1 pt. (½ l.) whipped cream

Blend the egg yolks with the sugar and a few drops of water and whisk them over gentle heat in a bain-marie as for genoese sponge to a foamy consistency. Continue whisking on ice until the mixture is cold. Add the flavouring, then the egg whites whisked to a peak and fold in the whipped cream.

Cream iced mousses may be flavoured with vanilla, chocolate, soluble coffee powder, praline, ground pistachios, liqueurs, etc.

Fruit Iced Mousse - Mousse glacée aux Fruits

8 persons:
2 gills (¹/₄ l.) stock syrup at 35° B
2 gills (¹/₄ l.) fruit purée
A few drops of lemon juice
1 pt. (¹/₂ l.) whipped cream

Mix the cold syrup with the fruit purée and fold in the whipped cream. Fill into a mould and freeze.

This sort of mousse can be made with purées of various fruits such as apricots, bananas, peaches, raspberries, strawberries, etc. Watery fruits such as melons, pears, oranges, tangerines, etc. are unsuitable.

ICE PARFAITS

A parfait is a light ice frozen without lining and always made with a single flavour. Formerly parfait mixtures always had to be filled into special tall cylindrical moulds before freezing, but at present it is often produced in moulds of different shapes and decorated with whipped cream, etc. Since an ice parfait is very similar to a bombe mixture, the name should, in our view, be reserved for products frozen in a proper parfait mould and prepared in the standard manner.

Parfait Mixture

8 persons:
8 egg yolks
¹/₂ pt. (¹/₄ l.) syrup at 32° B
³/₄ pt. (4 dl.) whipped cream

Blend the egg yolks into the cold syrup and beat them over gentle heat in the same way as for genoese sponge until the mixture has doubled its volume. Continue whisking on ice until the mixture is completely cold. Add the required flavour and the whipped cream, fill in a mould and freeze.

Formerly parfait mixture was always filled into tall cylindrical moulds but at present it is often frozen in brick or other moulds and decorated to taste.

Parfaits may be varied by the addition of coffee, chocolate, praline, pistachios, liqueur, etc.

Chocolate Parfait - Parfait au Chocolat

Dissolve 3 oz. (90 gr.) of rather bitter chocolate in the syrup and proceed as usual.

Christmas Parfait - Weihnachtsparfait

6 portions:
1 ¹/₂ pt. (³/₄ l.) chocolate parfait
About 14 oz. (400 gr.) almond meringue
5 oz. (150 gr.) finely chopped almonds
6 Christmas trees and 6 bambis made out of almond wafer mixture
6 tiny stars made with French sweet pastry
6 glacé cherries
¹/₂ pt. (3 dl.) vanilla flavoured whipped dairy cream
A little couverture.

Stencil the almond meringue in 6 large triangles on to a waxed baking sheet and sprinkle with finely chopped almonds. Bake in a hot oven until brown, then remove at once and roll each one round a cream horn tin to make a cone. When cold, remove from the tin and fill each cone with whipped cream. Cut the parfait into 6 round slices and place each one on a chilled glass dish. Set a cream cone in the centre and fix a pastry star to the tip with a little couverture. Decorate with a Christmas tree, a bambi, whipped cream and a glacé cherry. *(Germany)*
(Illustration page 789.)

Coffee Parfait - Parfait au Café

Prepare parfait mixture as usual and add a heaped tablespoon of soluble coffee powder to the syrup.

Parfait Ice Princess - Parfait Eisprinzessin

Fill parfait mixture flavoured with Grand-Marnier in a brick mould and freeze. Unmould, cut into thick slices and decorate each portion with whipped cream, half glacé cherries, chocolate hearts and chocolate shavings. Stick a boot with skates attached, made of almond wafer mixture, on top of each portion.

Almond wafer mixture: work one part of flour and two parts of sugar into three parts of marzipan and thin with half milk and half egg white. Spread the mixture on a greased baking sheet with the aid of a stencil and bake in a hot oven. Allow to cool and decorate with spots of dark couverture. The mixture must not be thinned too much if the outlines of the shapes are to remain quite clear.

Parfait with Liqueurs - Parfait aux Liqueurs

Parfaits may be flavoured with spirits such as rum, cognac, whisky, armagnac, kirsch, etc., or with liqueurs, especially Benedictine, Grand-Marnier, Cointreau, Cherry-Heering and Prunella. For these parfaits add $1/4$ gill (4 cl.) of liqueur to the basic mixture before incorporating the whipped cream.

Parfait Marie-Brizard

Flavour parfait mixture with $1/4$ gill (4 cl.) of anisette and freeze in a rather tall brick mould. Unmould, cut into thick slices and decorate with anisette-flavoured whipped cream and angelica.

Pistachio Parfait - Parfait aux Pistaches

Grind 3 oz. (90 gr.) of very green pistachio nuts with 2 tablespoons of water and a few drops of kirsch to a very fine paste in a mixer. Mix this paste into the parfait mixture before adding the whipped cream and freeze as usual.

Praline Parfait - Parfait praliné

Prepare the parfait mixture as usual and add $2 1/2$ oz. (75 gr.) ground and sieved praline croquant together with the whipped cream.

Tea Parfait - Parfait au Thé

Infuse $1/8$ oz. (4 gr.) tea in the hot syrup, pass the syrup through a muslin cloth and allow to cool before preparing the mixture.

Vanilla Parfait - Parfait à la Vanille

Prepare the parfait with syrup flavoured with half a split vanilla pod.

ICE PUDDINGS

Ice Puddings - Puddings glacés

Formerly the designation 'iced pudding' was only used for chilled moulded creams served with a cold sauce. At present iced puddings are preparations similar to iced bombes, placed in deep freeze, unmoulded and served with cold sauce or syrup.

Japanese Ice Pudding - Pudding glacé japonaise

Line bombe mould with tangerine ice and fill with tea bombe mixture containing diced sponge cake and tangerine sections soaked in mandarine liqueur. Freeze, unmould and decorate with whipped cream and preserved tangerine sections. Serve a chilled syrup flavoured with mandarine liqueur separately.

Lyrical Ice Pudding - Pudding glacé lyrique

Fill bombe mould with vanilla bombe mixture containing diced glacé pineapple and savoy fingers soaked in kirsch. Freeze, unmould and decorate with an ornament of piped couverture, Chantilly cream, gold leaf and crystallized violets. Serve a purée of fresh raspberries separately.

Ice Pudding Majestic - Pudding glacé Majestic

Line a bombe mould with vanilla ice and fill with strawberry parfait containing wild strawberries and diced fresh pineapple macerated in kirsch. Freeze, unmould and decorate the top with an ornament made of piped choux paste and the base with dots of whipped cream and wild strawberries. Serve cold maraschino-flavoured custard sauce separately.

Ice Pudding Merville - Pudding glacé Merville

Line a round, not too shallow cake mould with slices of Swiss roll spread with apricot jam. Fill with a vanilla praline bombe mixture containing diced glacé fruits macerated in cognac. Serve with cold chocolate sauce.

Ice Pudding Miramar - Pudding glacé Miramar

Line charlotte mould alternately with savoy fingers, strips of pineapple and tangerine segments macerated in kirsch. Fill with pomegranate bombe mixture flavoured with kirsch and freeze. Unmould and serve with chilled vanilla syrup.

Ice Pudding Nancy - Pudding glacé Nancy

Line charlotte mould with savoy fingers splashed with Grand-Marnier and fill with chocolate parfait mixture containing crushed macaroons. Freeze, unmould and serve vanilla flavoured custard sauce separately.

BAKED ICE CREAMS

Omelettes soufflées en Surprise

As these ices have to be 'flashed' to a golden colour in a hot oven, they have first to be insulated against the heat with insulating material, which must be both pleasant and pleasing to eat. Firstly one must have a base of genoese or sponge upon a dish, which can be flavoured with any type of liqueur by lightly spinkling. Secondly there must be an easily manipulated material which can be spread quickly and evenly over the ice cream ensuring protection from the fierce heat of the oven. For this a meringue mixture is ideal.

Recipe for Meringue

Meringue I
4 egg whites
7 oz. (200 gr.) castor sugar
1 oz. (30 gr.) vanilla sugar
1 tiny pinch of salt

Whisk the egg whites to the peak, whisk in the warmed sugar a little at a time until the mixture is smooth and stiff.

Meringue II
8 egg whites
6 egg yolks
7 oz. (200 gr.) castor sugar

Whisk the yolks and the sugar over a pan of boiling water until the volume increases and the mixture becomes firm enough to hold its shape. Remove from heat, stand the bowl in a container with ice and water and continue whisking until cold. Whip the whites to the peak and with a large open whisk blend the two mixtures carefully together.

Omelette soufflée Belle-de-Nuit

Prepare as for Grand Succès with this difference—only use vanilla ice cream and heat sliced peaches in melba sauce.

Omelette soufflée Grand Succès

Place an oval piece of genoese upon an oval dish, sprinkle with kirsch. Arrange a thick piece of genoese about 3 in. (8 cm.) in diameter and 2 in. (5 cm.) thick in the centre of the bottom piece of genoese. Arrange strawberry and vanilla ice cream around this centre piece. Place a timbale mould upon the centre piece and cover to the rim of the timbale mould with meringue, shape and smooth with a palette knife, decorate, dust with icing sugar and 'flash' in an oven at 450° F (232° C). In the meantime, heat some stoned red cherries in red currant sauce. When the soufflé is a golden colour, remove from

▲ Williams Charlotte, p. 703
Croquembouche, p. 599 ▼

▲ Christmas Parfait, p. 786
Russian Charlotte II, p. 703 ▼

790 ▲ Pineapple Kenya, p. 720

Rice Liguria, p. 732 ▼

▲ Surprise Waldmeister, p. 747

Peach Belle Forestière, p. 716 ▼

792 ▲ Coupe Capriccio, p. 780   Surprise hawaïenne, p. 746 ▼

▲ Pineapple Roswitha, p. 720

Surprise sicilienne, p. 747 ▼

794 ▲ Harlequin Cream, p. 706   ▲ Pears Maja, p. 719
Mocha Ice Gâteau, p. 785 ▼

▲ Raspberry Bombe, p. 776

Vacherin, p. 728 ▼

796 ▲ Short and Puff Pastry Assortment, p. 820, 834

Veal and Ham Pie, p. 842 ▼

the oven, fill the timbale mould with the cherries, sprinkle with castor sugar, pour over some warmed kirsch and ignite when approaching the table.

Nero Soufflé Omelette - Omelette soufflée Néron

4 persons:

1 round base of genoese sponge
³/₄ pt. (¹/₂ l.) kirsch flavoured parfait
³/₄ gill (4 cl.) kirsch flavoured syrup
Italian meringue mixture made with
   4 egg whites and 7 oz. (200 gr.) sugar
1 very small round meringue with the
   centre scooped out
¹/₄ gill (2 cl.) kirsch
Castor sugar

Cooking time: 3-4 minutes

Place the genoese sponge at the bottom of a round dish and lightly splash with the kirsch flavoured syrup. Deposit the parfait on top of the sponge and cover over with the Italian meringue mixture. The surface should be dome-shaped, smoothed and decorated quickly with a paper bag containing the same mixture. Dust with sugar. Brown in a hot oven. Top with the small meringue with its hollow uppermost to receive the warmed kirsch which is then ignited. Serve at once.

Norwegian or Surprise Soufflé Omelette / Baked Alaska - Omelette soufflée norvégienne ou en Surprise

4 persons:

1 oval base of genoese sponge ³/₄ in.
   (2 cm.) thick
³/₄ pt. (4-5 dl.) ice cream or fruit ice
Meringue mixture made with 5 egg whites
   and 9 oz. (275 gr.) castor sugar

Cooking time: 3-4 minutes

Place at the bottom of an oval dish the genoese sponge which will keep the ice away from the heat. Pile the ice on top in the form of a pyramid and cover over with stiff meringue mixture. Smooth with a knife and decorate the top quickly with the same mixture, using a savoy bag fitted with a star pipe. Dust with sugar and put in a very hot oven to brown and harden the meringue without, however, warming the ice cream. The ice is better protected if it is completely covered with a second thin layer of genoese sponge.

Omelette soufflée Paquita

Prepare an oval base of genoese sponge upon an oval dish, arrange a layer of vanilla ice, leaving a depression in the centre, fill this cavity with a macedoine of fresh fruits flavoured with kirsch, cover over with another layer of strawberry ice and finish the omelette as usual. Serve with hot chocolate sauce in a sauceboat.

Soufflé riche Alexandra

Round base of genoese sponge sprinkled with maraschino, layer of strawberry ice with cavity. Fill the cavity with a macedoine of fresh fruit, cover with strawberry ice and finish as usual. When removed from oven garnish with strawberries.

Soufflé riche Délice

Round base of genoese sponge sprinkled with brandy, layer of pear ice with cavity. Fill cavity with strawberries, cover with pear ice and continue as usual.

Soufflé riche Edouard VII

Same as for George V substituting strawberry ice for vanilla.

Soufflé riche George V

Place a round base of genoese sponge upon a round dish, cover to within half an inch of the edge with vanilla ice, place a poached white peach upon the ice for each person, after stoning and drying on a serviette.

Colour the meringue a pale pink with carmine, heap it over the prepared base in a dome shape, smooth with a knife and decorate with a star tube, piping the lines from the base to the apex and finish with an overlapping rosette at the top. Dust with icing sugar and 'flash' as usual.

Soufflé riche Mon Rêve

Round base of genoese sponge sprinkled with maraschino, layer of pineapple ice with cavity, fill cavity with wild strawberries, complete covering with raspberry ice and finish as usual. Serve with Melba sauce.

Soufflé riche parisienne

Round base of genoese sponge sprinkled with kirsch, layer of coffee ice, poached stoned peach on top, cover with praline ice, and proceed as usual. Sprinkle with crushed praline when it leaves the oven.

ICE SOUFFLÉS - SOUFFLÉS GLACÉS

Iced soufflés can be divided into two groups. Cream soufflés are made with custard cream in the same way as iced mousse, while fruit soufflés are made of Italian meringue mixture, fruit purée and whipped cream.

How to mould and freeze Ice Soufflés

Take a soufflé mould or straight-sided silver timble. Wrap a strip of greaseproof paper or thin white cardboard round the edge 1-1 $1/2$ in. (3-4 cm.) higher than the mould and tie round securely. Fill the mould with the soufflé mixture until the latter reaches a point just $1/2$ in. (1 cm.) below the top of the paper, then deep freeze at once. To serve, dust the top lightly with cocoa powder and then a little icing sugar, carefully remove the string and paper and place the soufflé on a napkin in the centre of a round dish. For certain preparations, a cavity is made in the centre before dusting; this cavity is then filled as appropriate, the scooped-out mixture is spread over the top and the soufflé is finished off as above. Small individual soufflés are prepared in fairly large cocottes, which have strips of paper tied round them in the same way.

Iced Fruit Soufflé - Soufflé glacé aux Fruits

8 persons:

5 egg whites
9 oz. (375 gr.) castor sugar
$1/2$ pt. ($1/4$ l.) fruit purée or pulp
$3/4$ pt. (4 dl.) whipped cream

Boil the sugar to the soft ball and pour over the stiffly whisked egg whites. Continue whisking until completely cold, add the fruit purée and then fold in the whipped cream. Take straight sided silver or porcelain moulds, wrap a band of greaseproof paper round the edge at least 2 in. (5 cm.) higher than the moulds, tie round with a piece of string and fill up with the preparation at least 1 $1/2$ in. (4 cm.) higher than the mould. Put away to freeze. To serve, unwrap the paper surround and serve with savoy fingers.

Another method: Prepare the moulds as usual and place a tall mould of smaller diameter in the centre, then fill with the preparation as usual and freeze. To serve, remove the paper surround, pour some cold water in the centre mould to loosen it a little, then remove and garnish the cavity with various fruits or macedoine of fruits.

Benedictine Iced Soufflé - Soufflé glacé Bénédictine

Italian meringue made with 3 egg whites and 6 oz. (180 gr.) sugar
1 quart (1 l.) part-whipped cream
$3/4$ gill (1 dl.) Benedictine liqueur
4 oz. (125 gr.) diced savoy fingers

Splash the savoy fingers with Benedictine. Blend meringue with the whipped cream and the Benedictine and mix in the savoy fingers.

Iced Soufflé Cavalieri - Soufflé glacé Cavalieri

Fill the soufflé mould alternately with strawberry, chocolate and pineapple mixture, placing a thin round slice of genoese sponge splashed with kirsch, between the layers. Proceed as usual.

Iced Chocolate Soufflé - Soufflé glacé au Chocolat

2 oz. (60 gr.) unsweetened chocolate couverture
$1/2$ pt. ($1/4$ l.) syrup at 28° B
Italian meringue made with 3 egg whites and 6 oz. (180 gr.) sugar
1 quart (1 l.) whipped cream

Melt the chocolate in gentle heat, blend in the syrup, then mix in the meringue and lastly the cream.

Iced Coffee Soufflé - Soufflé glacé au Café

$1/2$ pt. ($1/4$ l.) syrup at 28° B.
1 heaped tablespoon soluble coffee powder
Italian meringue made with 3 egg whites and 6 oz. (180 gr.) sugar
1 quart (1 l.) whipped cream

Dissolve the coffee powder in the syrup and allow to cool. Mix in the meringue and lastly the whipped cream.

May also be made with a mousse mixture flavoured with soluble coffee powder.

Iced Liqueur Soufflés - Soufflés glacés aux Liqueurs

Italian meringue made with 3 egg whites and 8 oz. (250 gr.) sugar
1 quart (1 l.) part-whipped cream
$1/2$ gill (8 cl.) of the designated liqueur (Grand-Marnier, Cointreau, apricotine, etc.)
Usual procedure.

Iced Soufflé Miracle - Soufflé glacé Miracle

Prepare iced mousse mixture with tangerine. Macerate diced glacé pineapple and coarsely crushed macaroons with Grand-Marnier and mix with the mousse. Proceed as usual and serve with sugared wild strawberries.

Iced Soufflé Montmorency - Soufflé glacé Montmorency

Poach stoned morello cherries in vanilla-flavoured syrup, cool, drain and chop them coarsely. Macerate with sugar and kirsch.

Prepare iced mousse flavoured with kirsch, blend in the cherries and proceed as usual.

Iced Soufflé Paquita - Soufflé glacé Paquita

Place a round slice of sponge or butter sponge splashed with maraschino on the bottom of the soufflé mould. Cover alternately with a layer of strawberry ice and diced bananas, apricots, pineapple and very small strawberries macerated with sugar and maraschino. Dress Chantilly cream on top up to the edge of the strip of paper and freeze. Sprinkle grated chocolate and chopped pistachios on top and dust lightly with icing sugar.

Iced Pistachio Soufflé - Soufflé glacé aux Pistaches

4 oz. (125 gr.) blanched pistachio nuts
$1/2$ gill (8 cl.) syrup
$1/4$ gill (4 cl.) kirsch
Italian meringue made with 3 egg whites and 6 oz. (180 gr.) sugar
1 quart (1 l.) part-whipped cream

Pound the pistachio nuts with the syrup to a fine paste and rub through a sieve, or grind them in a mixer adding syrup and kirsch gradually. Blend the paste into the meringue, then fold in the whipped cream and proceed as usual.

Iced Praline Soufflé - Soufflé glacé praliné

Italian meringue made with 3 egg whites and 5 oz. (150 gr.) sugar
1 quart (1 l.) part-whipped cream
6 oz. (180 gr.) sieved praline

Blend meringue, praline and cream together and proceed as usual.

Iced Soufflé Tortoni - Soufflé glacé Tortoni

Not quite fill a soufflé mould with praline mixture. With a very small tube pipe Chantilly cream on top, letting it fall like spaghetti. Freeze. Sprinkle generously with roasted, crushed and sieved hazelnuts and dust lightly with icing sugar.

CASSATA

These ices are prepared in rather shallow round or oval basin-shaped moulds, but bombe moulds may also be used. The mould is first lined with three different sorts of ice; the final filling consists of an Italian meringue and cream mixture heavily garnished with glacé fruits.

Cassata Napoletana

Arrange a thick layer of vanilla ice in the mould, then a thick layer of chocolate ice, followed by a thick layer of strawberry ice leaving a central cavity.

Filling:

2 egg whites
5 oz. (150 gr.) sugar
1 gill (1 $^1/_2$ dl.) whipped cream
Essence, liqueur or essential oil to flavour
Finely diced glacé fruits

Boil the sugar to the soft ball. Whip the whites to a firm peak. Pour on the sugar, whisking constantly and continue whisking until nearly cold, allow to become quite cold and blend in the whipped cream. Mix in 8 oz. (250 gr.) glacé fruits and fill into the cavity. Put into the deep freeze until firm. *(Italy)*

Cassata Siciliana

Follow the same method as for Cassata Napoletana but with alternate layers of lemon, orange and chocolate ice. Fill cavity with the meringue mixture and cream containing finely diced angelica, halved pistachio nuts and crystallized water melon. *(Italy)*

Cassata Tortoni

Coat mould with praline, pineapple and chestnut ice. Fill centre with the meringue and cream mixture flavoured with noyau and containing diced glacé chestnuts. *(Italy)*

Cassata Tosca

Arrange thick layers of pineapple, apricot and praline ice in the mould and fill centre with the cassata mixture containing glacé cherries and pineapple. *(Italy)*

ITALIAN SEMI-FROZEN DESSERTS

These delightful desserts are produced only in Italy and the Italian part of Switzerland.

The basic creams are quite distinctive. The attention of the reader is called to the following information which emphasizes the importance of the egg yolk content of Zabaglione cream. In Italy the egg yolk content of the Zabaglione is critical and the success of these creams depends on this being rigidly observed. Zabaglione contains the equivalent of 10 egg yolks (counting 24 yolks to the pound) and therefore the egg yolks would need to be doubled in the basic mix for the above.

(For the basic Zabaglione cream Chapter VI - Basic Preparations *page 236*).

To make the creams for Bavarois, Damasco, Italian Zuppa, Java, Luisa, Poker, Sabrina, Soraya, first of all soak the gelatine in warm water until soft. Add the appropriate essence. Heat carefully until the gelatine is completely dispersed. Add the dispersion to the pastry cream or Zabaglione, then add the whipped cream and then the rest of the materials.

If chocolate is used, it is mixed with the pastry cream first. If fruits are used, they are added last.

Astrogel

Take a rectangular mould and place in whipped Zabaglione cream, followed by a layer of whipped dairy cream. Spread the surface with candied fruits. Refrigerate. Remove from the mould and cut into slices and dip into couverture so that the sides are coated only. Place on to paper and when the chocolate is set, the tops are dusted with icing sugar.

Bavarese St. Vincent

Cream:

White:

2 lb. (1 kg.) pastry cream
2 1/4 pt. (1.3 l.) dairy cream
Gelatine (8 sheets)

Dark:

1 lb. 9 oz. (700 gr.) pastry cream
1 lb. (500 gr.) couverture
2 1/4 pt. (1.3 l.) dairy cream
Gelatine (4 sheets)

In the bottom of a round or rectangular special hinged bavarois mould, place a piece of maddalena genoese and sprinkle with vanilla liqueur (30° B). Cover with white bavarois cream. Cover the surface with savoy biscuits sprinkled with the vanilla liqueur, then with the chocolate bavarois cream. Cover with genoese also sprinkled with vanilla. Refrigerate for 3-4 hours at freezing point.

Remove the bavarois by opening the mould.

Spread top and sides with chocolate dairy cream and mask with milk chocolate shavings. Dust with icing sugar.

Charlotte

1 lb. 5 oz. (650 gr.) soft cheese (mascarpone)
4 oz. (125 gr.) egg yolks
10 oz. (300 gr.) icing sugar
3 1/2 oz. (100 gr.) coffee infusion
1 3/4 oz. (50 gr.) rum
6 oz. (180 gr.) whipped egg whites

Whip the yolks and sugar, add the mascarpone cheese, the coffee and the rum.

The egg whites stiffly whipped are folded into the mix. Place savoy biscuits round the moulds, first dipping the insides into coffee. Fill the moulds with the cream. Refrigerate for 10-12 hours. Turn out and decorate the top edge of the charlotte with whipped dairy cream, piped with a star pipe. Place a coffee bean on each star and one in the centre.

Luisa Cream

14 oz. (400 gr.) dairy cream
14 oz. (400 gr.) zabaglione
3 sheets gelatine
3 1/2 oz. (100 gr.) chopped orange peel
2 oz. (60 gr.) crushed hazelnut croquant (coarse sieved)

In a square mould place maddalena genoese sprinkled with crème de cacao, then a layer of Luisa cream. Cover with another sheet of genoese. Refrigerate for 3-4 hours. Release from the mould and spread the surface thinly with dairy cream. With the same cream pipe six diagonal scrolls across the top using a star pipe. Between the four middle scrolls, glacé cherries are placed alternatively with leaves cut from citron peel.

The two opposing corner spaces have one piece of candied pineapple, on each side of which is placed a citron leaf.

Portuguese Cream

Cream caramel:

1 3/4 pt. (1 l.) milk
7 oz. (200 gr.) sugar
5 oz. (150 gr.) egg yolks
7 oz. (200 gr.) egg
Vanilla
Zest of orange
Zest of lemon
10 coffee beans

The milk is taken to the boil with the coffee beans, zests and the vanilla. The egg, egg yolks and sugar are stirred together and the boiling milk is added, beating well. The mixture is strained and put into cups into which a little caramel has been placed. They are cooked in a bain-marie for 1 1/2 hours at 356° F (180° C). Refrigerate for 2-2 1/2 hours and turn out.

Sabrina Cream

1 lb. 2 oz. (500 gr.) pastry cream
2 oz. (60 gr.) milk couverture (chopped)
5 oz. (150 gr.) mixed candied fruit
1 1/2 pt. (8 dl.) dairy cream
3 sheets gelatine

Candied fruits:

2 lb. (1 kg.) chopped orange peel
1 lb. (500 gr.) currants
1 lb. (500 gr.) cherries
1 lb. (500 gr.) pineapple
Zest of lemon

Mix all together and use as desired.

In a rectangular bavarois mould place savoy biscuits and sprinkle with mandarin liqueur 30°. Put in Sabrina cream and then another layer of savoy biscuits, sprinkled with the mandarin liqueur. Refrigerate for 3-4 hours. Release from the mould and spread with dairy cream on which maddalena genoese crumbs are sieved, using a very coarse sieve. Using a stencil, sieve icing sugar on the top so that there is a series of parallel white lines. In the centre of each line pipe a small whirl of whipped dairy cream and on the top of each a circle of orange peel is placed.

Italian Zuppa

1 lb. 5 oz. (600 gr.) pastry cream
5 oz. (150 gr.) orange peel
1 1/4 pt. (6 dl.) dairy cream
5 sheets gelatine (soak in orange liqueur 30° for 2 hours)

Take a mould about 10 in. (25 cm.) square. Place in a square of maddalena genoese sprinkled with vanilla liqueur 30°. Cover with Zuppa cream and top with another square of maddalena genoese sprinkled with vanilla. Refrigerate for 3-4 hours. Remove from the mould and spread thinly with dairy cream. Cover top and side with plain chocolate shavings. Pipe a border with dairy cream using a star pipe. Lightly dust with icing sugar.

Damasco

1 lb. 5 oz. (600 gr.) dairy cream
1 lb. 5 oz. (600 gr.) pastry cream
1 lb. 5 oz. (600 gr.) white chocolate
5 oz. (150 gr.) gianduja
6 sheets gelatine

Take a bombe mould and line in regular formation with small thin slices of chocolate roll and fill in with damasco cream. Cover with maddalena genoese and sprinkle with curaçao. Refrigerate for 3-4 hours. Release from the mould and turn over so that the rounded surface is uppermost. Cover the surface with whirls of whipped dairy cream placing each one in the centre of each slice of chocolate roll.

Decorate the top with a ball of gianduja rolled between two butter pats. Alternatively a cherry can be used.

Pipe whirls of cream round the base of the bombe at intervals with smaller whirls of gianduja in between.

Diplomatico

1 3/4 pt. (1 l.) dairy cream
1 1/4 pt. (6 dl.) zabaglione
   (10 yolk quality)

See footnote under the heading Italian semi-frozen desserts.

Take a square mould and place a sheet of sponge on the bottom. Cover with diplomatico cream. Cover with maddalena genoese sprinkled with vanilla liqueur. Cover the genoese with another layer of diplomatico cream and refrigerate.

Turn out of the mould, spread the top thinly with dairy cream and cover with chocolate shavings.

Java

3 1/4 pt. (2 l.) dairy cream
2 lb. 3 oz. (1 kg.) white chocolate
5 sheets gelatine

Proceed as for St. Vincent, but use Java cream instead. Refrigerate for 3-4 hours and remove from the mould. Spread the top with dairy cream and place cylinders made from selva chocolate *(page 253)* close together on the top. Place two strips of paper on the top and dredge with icing sugar. Remove the paper carefully to show a band of white sugar along the selva rolls. The rolls are moulded round a piece of wooden dowling.

Parfait Zabaglione

White:

1 ³/₄ pt. (1 l.) dairy cream
1 pt. (¹/₂ l.) zabaglione
   (9 yolk quality)
1 pt. (¹/₂ l.) Italian meringue

Dark:

1 ³/₄ pt. (1 l.) dairy cream
14 oz. (400 gr.) plain couverture
1 pt. (¹/₂ l.) Italian meringue

Instead of chocolate, hazelnut praline may be used.

Parfait Zabaglione Coffee

1 ³/₄ pt. (1 l.) dairy cream
1 ³/₄ pt. (1 l.) coffee zabaglione
   (20 yolk quality)

Line rectangular moulds with greaseproof paper and place in a layer of white parfait zabaglione or parfait zabaglione coffee and one of chocolate. Refrigerate and then take from the mould and remove the paper.

Pineapple

1 pt. (¹/₂ l.) dairy cream
7 oz. (200 gr.) pastry cream
10 ¹/₂ oz. (300 gr.) small pineapple cubes
Pineapple essence

Take a deep bombe mould and fill with the pineapple cream. Refrigerate for 10 hours. Remove from the mould and decorate all over with stars of dairy cream. Pipe a border of cream at the base and place segments of crystallized pineapple, between which are whirls of cream each topped with a split pistachio nut. Place four or five spikes of citron peel on the top to represent foliage.
(Illustration page 663.)

Poker Ace

4 lb. 6 oz. (2 kg.) pastry cream
1 lb. 9 oz. (700 gr.) white chocolate
1 lb. 9 oz. (700 gr.) gianduja
1 ¹/₄ pt. (7 dl.) dairy cream
12 sheets gelatine

Place the whipped cream in the bottom of the moulds. Place on top genoese sprinkled with curaçao. Place in refrigerator for 3-4 hours. Turn out and pipe a trellis design of Chantilly cream. Place an ace (heart, club, diamond, spade) on each division. The aces are made from white chocolate. Cover the sides of the genoese base with Chantilly cream and mask with chocolate shavings.

Soraya

1 lb. 9 oz. (700 gr.) pastry cream
5 oz. (150 gr.) white chocolate
8 oz. (250 gr.) plain couverture
1 lb. 9 oz. (700 gr.) dairy cream
6 sheets gelatine

Take a large savarin mould and place in Soraya cream and refrigerate for 3-4 hours. Turn out of mould and decorate with whirls of dairy cream piped with a star pipe, alternating with a glacé cherry.

Spumone Chocolate

The same procedure as below is adopted except that dark twist cream is used instead of the cream mixture and the beans are omitted.

Spumone Moka

The cream is a mixture of equal parts whipped dairy cream and whipped coffee zabaglione cream. Take a mould similar to a half-pint drinking glass but only about 3 ¹/₂-4 in. (9-10 cm.) high and drop into the bottom three coffee beans. Fill with the cream. Refrigerate for 10 hours. Turn out of the mould.

Spumone e Tartufi

3 ¹/₂ pt. (2 l.) dairy cream
1 lb. 2 oz. (500 gr.) gianduja

This base cream is used for both spumone and tartufi. They differ in form and appearance only.

For the spumone, take square moulds and fill them with the cream. Refrigerate and remove from the moulds. Spread the tops thinly with dairy cream and pipe five diagonal continuous whirls on the tops. Between the whirls pipe chocolate cream but in straight lines, not in continuous whirls.

For the tartufi, fill a shallower bombe mould with the same cream. Refrigerate and when turned out, cover with plain chocolate. The tartufi can be made much smaller for individual serving.

Twist

White:

3 ½ pt. (2 l.) dairy cream
2 lb. 7 oz. (1 kg. 200) zabaglione No. 8 (20 yolk quality)
7 oz. (200 gr.) sieved hazelnut croquant
7 oz. (200 gr.) chopped chocolate

Dark:

1 lb. 2 oz. (500 gr.) pastry cream
1 lb. 5 oz. (600 gr.) plain couverture
4 pt. (2 ½ l.) dairy cream

Take round moulds like a cottage pan, and place maddalena genoese on the bottom sprinkled with strega liqueur. Cover with white twist cream and place on a meringue disc. Cover this with the chocolate twist cream on which is placed another sheet of genoese also sprinkled with strega liqueur. Refrigerate for 3-4 hours. Turn out of moulds and spread tops and sides with dairy cream.

Place langue-de-chat biscuits round the sides. On the top place a pineapple ring and finish the decoration with dairy cream whirls, placing a pistachio nut on each. Pipe a whirl in the centre of the pineapple on which place a glacé cherry.
(Illustration page 662.)

Zuccotto

White:

1 ¾ pt. (1 l.) dairy cream
10 oz. (300 gr.) pastry cream
1 ¾ oz. (50 gr.) chopped orange peel
1 ¾ oz. (50 gr.) cherries
1 ¾ oz. (50 gr.) chopped chocolate
1 ¾ oz. (50 gr.) sieved hazelnut croquant

Dark:

2 lb. 10 oz. (1 kg. 200) dairy cream
10 oz. (300 gr.) pastry cream
10 oz. (300 gr.) plain couverture

Take a bombe mould and line it with maddalena genoese. Place in a layer of white zuccotto cream and then fill with chocolate. Cover with maddalena genoese sprinkle with crème de cacao and place in the refrigerator for 3-4 hours. Take from the mould, spread with dairy cream, and mask with very coarse maddalena crumbs, and then dust with icing sugar.
(Illustration page 662.)

SHERBETS - SORBETS

Sherbets are very light ices served in special glasses during banquets to refresh the palate, helping to better appreciate the flavour of the roast course. Nowadays, however, they are also served at lunchtime as a sweet or as a cool drink with light snacks. Sherbets are made with a syrup at 22° B containing wine, liqueur or fruit juice. Fruit sherbets are usually prepared with strained fruit juices. All sherbets are less sweet than ice creams and when they are set, Italian meringue mixture or whipped cream is added.

Fruit Sherbet - Sorbet aux Fruits

6 persons:

14 oz. (400 gr.) syrup at 20° B
About 14 oz. (400 gr.) fruit juice
Juice of 1 lemon
Italian meringue mixture made with
  1 egg white and 1 ¾ oz. (50 gr.) sugar

Mix the cold syrup with the fruit juice and lemon juice until the hydrometer registers 15° B. Freeze and amalgamate with the Italian meringue mixture. Fruit sherbets are generally made with the strained juice of strawberries, raspberries, red currants, cherries, pineapples, oranges, tangerines, lemons, etc.

Lemon Sherbet - Sorbet au Citron

6 persons:

1-1 1/4 pt. (5-6 dl.) syrup
  at 22° B
5-6 lemons
Italian meringue mixture made with
  1 egg white and 1 3/4 oz. (50 gr.) sugar

Infuse the zest of 2 lemons in the hot syrup and leave to cool down. Add the juice of the lemons and check with the hydrometer that the mixture is at 15° B. Strain and freeze. Finally add the Italian meringue.

Liqueur Sherbet - Sorbet aux Liqueurs

Prepare a syrup which should be at 18° B when the lemon juice has been added and it has cooled down. Freeze and, when it has set, mix in the Italian meringue made of 1 egg white and 1 3/4 oz. (50 gr.) sugar and 1 3/4 oz. (50 gr.) of the selected liqueur. Fill into chilled sherbet glasses and add a dash of the liqueur. Liqueur sherbets are made with kirsch, cognac, rum, curaçao, maraschino, Cointreau, Grand-Marnier, Chartreuse, Benedictine, etc.

Orange Sherbet - Sorbet à l'Orange

Prepare in the same way as lemon sherbet, adding to the juice of five oranges that of one lemon.

Wine Sherbet - Sorbet au Vin

6 persons:

14 oz. (400 gr.) syrup at 22° B
Approximately 7 oz. (200 gr.) wine
Juice of 1 lemon
Italian meringue mixture made of
  1 egg white and 1 3/4 oz. (50 gr.) sugar

Mix the cold syrup with the lemon juice and wine until the hydrometer registers 15° B. If the reading is higher, add some more water, if lower add some more castor sugar. Freeze and, when it has set, stir in the Italian meringue thoroughly. Serve in chilled glasses not more than three quarters full and pour into each glass a tablespoonful of the selected wine. Wine sherbets are made with good, matured quality wines such as sherry, port, madeira, sauternes, hock, marsala, malaga, etc.

Granites - Les Granités

These are sherbets made from fruit juices; their density should not exceed 14° B on the hydrometer. These ices are frozen in such a way that they become very granular. No Italian meringue mixture is added.

Marquises

Marquises are made mainly with strawberries or pineapple and with kirsch. Prepare syrup at 18° B and, when cold, add kirsch and lemon juice until the hydrometer registers 17° B. Freeze and add to every 1 lb. 2 oz. (500 gr.) of the frozen mixture 7 oz. (200 gr.) whipped cream mixed with strawberry or pineapple purée.

ICED PUNCH

Iced punch is made of stock syrup at 22° B diluted to 18° B with wine, mixed with lemon or orange juice and zest and left to infuse in a covered container. It is then strained and brought back to 18° B by the addition of syrup, frozen and mixed with Italian meringue in a proportion of one part meringue to four parts syrup/wine mixture. It is served in somewhat convex glasses and a teaspoon of the liqueur or spirit used for flavouring is sprinkled on top when serving.

Burgundy Punch - Punch glacé au Bourgogne

Juice of 5 lemons
Juice of 3 oranges
Zest of 3 lemons
Zest of 3 oranges
1 pt. (1/2 l.) syrup
Prepare as usual, adjust to 18° B. Freeze.
Cooked meringue made with 2 egg whites
  and 4 oz. (125 gr.) castor sugar
1/2 gill (8 cl.) brandy
1/2 gill (8 cl.) orange curaçao
1 pt. (1/2 l.) young Burgundy wine

Preparation: Roman Punch, *page 806.*

Claret Punch - Punch glacé au Bordeaux

Substitute claret for Burgundy, otherwise the same recipe.

Florentine Punch - Punch glacé à la florentine

Juice of 6 lemons
Zest of 3 lemons
$^2/_3$ pt. (4 dl.) syrup 18° B density
2 drops attar of roses (2 drops neroli oil of orange blossom)
8 drops violet essence
Cooked meringue made with 3 egg whites and 6 oz. (180 gr.) castor sugar
1 gill (1 $^1/_2$ dl.) green Chartreuse
1 bottle sauternes

Preparation: Roman Punch.

Lombard Punch - Punch glacé à la lombarde

Juice of 6 oranges and 2 lemons
Zest of 4 oranges
$^3/_4$ pt. (4 $^1/_2$ dl.) syrup

Prepare as usual, adjust to 18° B. Freeze.

Cooked meringue made with 3 egg whites and 6 oz. (180 gr.) sugar
1 gill (8 cl.) orange curaçao
1 bottle muscat wine

Preparation: Roman Punch.

Maraschino Punch - Punch glacé au Marasquin

Zest and juice of 6 lemons
$^2/_3$ pt. ($^1/_2$ l.) syrup

Prepare as usual, adjust to 18° B. Freeze.

Cooked meringue made with 2 egg whites and 4 oz. (125 gr.) castor sugar
1 gill (8 cl.) maraschino
1 pt. ($^1/_2$ l.) graves white wine

Preparation: Roman Punch.

Roman Punch - Punch à la romaine

Basic recipe for 6 persons:

Prepare $^2/_3$ pt. ($^1/_2$ l.) syrup at 22° B and leave to cool. Dilute with a good dry wine or dry Champagne until it reaches 18° B. Add the zest of half a lemon and half an orange and the juice of two lemons and oranges and leave to infuse in a covered container for one hour. Strain and add enough cold syrup to bring the mixture back to 18° B. Freeze and amalgamate with Italian meringue mixture made of two egg whites and 3 $^1/_2$ oz. (100 gr.) sugar. Before serving in chilled glasses, add $^3/_4$ gill (1 dl.) rum gradually to the mixture or pour a small tablespoonful in each glass on serving.

Rum Punch - Punch glacé au Rhum

Zest and juice of 5 lemons
Zest and juice of 5 oranges
$^2/_3$ pt. (4 $^1/_2$ dl.) syrup

Prepare as usual. Density 18° B.

Cooked meringue made with 2 egg whites and 4 oz. (125 gr.) castor sugar
1 gill (8 cl.) rum
1 gill (8 cl.) orange curaçao
1 pt. ($^1/_2$ l.) dry white wine

Same method and preparation as for Roman Punch.

Sherry Punch - Punch glacé au Xérès

Juice of 6 oranges
Zest of 6 oranges
Juice of 3 lemons
$^3/_4$ pt. (4 $^1/_2$ dl.) syrup
8 drops oil of tangerine

Prepare as usual, adjust to 18° B. Freeze.

Cooked meringue made with 2 egg whites and 4 oz. (125 gr.) castor sugar
$^1/_2$ gill (4 cl.) apricot brandy
1 pt. ($^1/_2$ l.) good dry sherry

Usual method and preparation.

SPOOMS - LES SPOOMS

These are sherbets which are made exclusively with good quality wines, preferably white wines or champagne. They are amalgamated with double the usual quantity of Italian meringue mixture to make them very light and frothy.

Apricot Spoom - Spoom à l'Abricot

1 $^1/_2$ lb. (750 gr.) ripe apricots
Juice of 2 oranges
Juice of 2 lemons
1 pt. ($^1/_2$ l.) syrup
Cooked meringue made with 2 egg whites and 4 oz. (125 gr.) castor sugar
1 tablespoon noyau
1 gill (8 cl.) apricot brandy
1 bottle sauternes

Cut the apricots in halves, remove and crush the stones, barely cover with water and bring to a boil. Cover and steep until cold and then strain. Rub the apricots through a sieve, then the juices, add the syrup and lastly the infusion and adjust to 18° B with the wine. Add the noyau and brandy and part freeze, then mix in the meringue and complete freezing.

Raspberry Spoom - Spoom aux Framboises

1 $^1/_2$ lb. (750 gr.) clean raspberries (Pine Royals if possible)
1 pt. ($^1/_2$ l.) syrup
1 gill (8 cl.) raspberry liqueur
Juice of 2 lemons
1 bottle muscat
Cooked meringue made with 3 egg whites and 6 oz. (180 gr.) castor sugar

Same method as for strawberry spoom.

Strawberry Spoom - Spoom aux Fraises

1 $^1/_2$ lb. (750 gr.) hulled alpine strawberries
Juice of 2 lemons
Juice of 2 oranges
1 pt. ($^1/_2$ l.) syrup
Cooked meringue made with 3 egg whites and 6 oz. (180 gr.) castor sugar
1 tablespoonful brandy
1 bottle graves

Rub the strawberries and the fruit juices through a hair sieve. Blend with the syrup, tint with carmine, adjust to 18° B with the wine, add the brandy and part freeze. Mix in the meringue and finish freezing.

SUNDAES

Iced sundaes are ice creams to which fruit, Chantilly cream and other ingredients (coffee, nougat, liqueur, nuts, syrup, etc.) have been added. They are served in oblong sundae dishes or in silver or glass cups. This dessert is preferably eaten at lunch-time. There are innumerable ways of making sundaes and some examples are given in the following recipes.

Creole Sundae

Half fill each dish with diced pineapple and banana soaked in rum; top with a scoop of lemon ice cream and decorate with Chantilly cream.

Imperial Palace Sundae

Place a small ladle of stoned and chopped lychees on a sundae dish and place a scoop of ginger ice in the centre and a small ball of pistachio ice cream on each side. Decorate with maraschino flavoured whipped cream and top off with a sprinkling of chopped walnuts.

Longchamp Sundae

Place three savoy fingers on a sundae dish and splash them with Benedictine. Place a small ball of vanilla and pistachio ice cream on top and coat with a purée of fresh strawberries. Garnish with whipped cream flavoured with Benedictine and sprinkle chopped pistachio nuts on the cream.

Morocco Sundae

Place at the bottom of each dish some pistachio ice cream to which whipped cream and ground nougat have been added. Top with a scoop of chocolate ice cream and decorate with Chantilly cream and a chocolate petal.

Ninon Sundae

Fill the bottom of each dish with some vanilla ice cream which has been softened with rum. Cover with morello cherries and decorate with Chantilly cream.

Osborne Sundae

Slice half a banana and arrange the slices on a sundae dish. Place a scoop of vanilla ice cream in the centre and cover with finely chopped figs mixed with maple syrup and a little honey. Decorate with whipped cream.

Pineapple Sundae

Place some diced pineapple which has been soaked in kirsch at the bottom of each dish, top with a scoop of vanilla ice cream and decorate with Chantilly cream.

Rainbow Sundae

Place a split banana on an oblong dish and on one side a small ball of pistachio ice cream and on the other a ball of strawberry ice cream. Garnish with orange segments and whipped cream and sprinkle chopped pistachio nuts on the cream.

Royal Banana Sundae

Place two small balls of vanilla ice cream on a split banana. Cover one of the balls with crushed pineapple and the other with whipped cream. Top each ball with a glacé cherry and sprinkle some chopped walnuts between the balls.

Royal Peach Sundae

Spread a little whipped cream on a sundae dish. Arrange 6 slices of fresh peach on the cream and place a dipper of vanilla ice cream on top. Cover with crushed pineapple and surround the base with whipped cream mixed with coarsely crushed praline. Top with a maraschino cherry.

Strawberry Whip Sundae

Mix crushed strawberries with the same amount of whipped cream. Spread a ladleful of the mixture on a sundae dish leaving the centre free. Place a scoop of strawberry ice in the centre, cover with raspberry syrup and decorate with whipped cream.

Temptation Sundae

Place a small ball of vanilla ice cream in the centre of a sundae dish and a ball of strawberry and chocolate ice cream on each side. Cover the vanilla ice cream with thick cold chocolate sauce flavoured with rum and sprinkle some chopped pistachio nuts on top. Garnish the strawberry and chocolate ice cream with Chantilly cream and a maraschino cherry.

Tutti-Frutti Sundae

Fill each dish with strawberry, lemon and pineapple ice cream and sprinkle with a mixture of diced candied fruit which has been soaked in kirsch.

Viennese Sundae

Soften some coffee ice cream with sweetened black coffee. Fill each dish three quarters full and top with whirls of Chantilly cream. These sundaes should be served in tall silver or glass goblets.

N.B. For chocolate ice cream or chocolate Viennese sundae, proceed in the same way as above, but replace the coffee ice cream with chocolate ice cream thinned with liquid ganache.

ASSORTED ICES AND ICED DESSERTS

Assorted Ice with Whipped Cream - Gemischtes Eis mit Schlagsahne

Fill three scoops of ice cream (e.g. vanilla, chocolate and strawberry) into a glass dish. Decorate with three large rosettes of whipped cream and place half a glacé cherry on each rosette. *(Germany)*

Baumkuchen ('Spit' cake) with Vanilla Ice Cream and Strawberries

Fill a small ring of Baumkuchen about $1/2$ in. (1 cm.) thick with vanilla ice, pile small fresh strawberries on top and dust with icing sugar. Pipe a fairly large rosette of whipped cream on top and sprinkle with chopped roasted almonds. *(Germany)*

Iced Chocolate - Eisschokolade

7 pt. (4 l.) milk
8 oz. (250 gr.) chocolate powder

Stir the chocolate powder into the milk and bring to the boil. Allow to cool, fill into tall goblets and add a small scoop of vanilla ice cream to each. Cap with a spiral of whipped cream, sprinkle with chocolate shavings and serve with a sponge finger. *(Austria)*

Christmas Candle - Weihnachtskerze

Take the top and bottom off an empty round tin (ex. of artichoke bottom) and line with a roll of paper. Alternatively, cut a roll of aluminium foil about 2 in. (5 cm.) in diameter, wrap it round a cylindrical piece of wood, stick it together and remove the wood. Fill the ring with strawberry parfait, freeze and cut to the desired length. Bake small Christmas trees made of wafer mixture, almost as tall as the candle but not quite as wide, and a large cinnamon star. The candle should fit the centre of the star. To serve, place the candle on the star and a Christmas tree by the side of the star. Top the candle with a sliver of roasted almond or a bright red marzipan leaf to represent the flame. *(Germany)*

Iced Coffee - Eiskaffee - Café liégeois

14 pt. (7 l.) milk
5 oz. (150 gr.) instant coffee powder

Stir coffee powder into the hot milk and chill. Fill goblets three quarters full of iced coffee, add a small scoop of vanilla ice cream to each and cap with a spiral of whipped cream. Decorate with a chocolate bean and serve with a sponge finger. *(Austria)*

Fior di Latte

8 oz. (250 gr.) sugar
5 egg whites
1 pt. ($1/2$ l.) cream
1 piece of split vanilla pod

Moisten the sugar with water, add the vanilla pod, bring to the boil and let infuse for 15 minutes, remove the pod and cook to the feather at 240° F (116° C [36° B]).

Whip the whites to a stiff snow, whisk on to the sugar and continue whipping until nearly cold, then leave until quite cold. Whip the cream and fold all together. Fill into a mould and deep freeze. A liqueur may be added to the meringue when cold. Only sufficient to give a subtle flavour is necessary. *(Italy)*

Fior di Latte Bellini

5 egg whites
8 oz. (250 gr.) sugar
1 split vanilla pod
2 oz. (60 gr.) shredded pistachio nuts
1 pt. ($1/2$ l.) whipped cream
2 oz. (60 gr.) each diced crystallized orange and lemon peel
Pineapple and cherries macerated in maraschino
Strawberry ice cream

Moisten the sugar with water, add the vanilla, bring to the boil, cover and allow to steep, then boil to the soft ball. Whip the whites to a firm peak and strain the boiling syrup in whilst whisking, continue whipping until nearly cold, allow to become quite cold, fold in the cream and fruits and pistachio nuts.

Coat the mould with a $1/4$ in. (5 mm.) coating of strawberry ice, fill with the prepared mixture, cover with greaseproof paper, force on the lid and freeze in the deep freezer. *(Italy)*

Fior di Latte Orlandini

5 egg whites
8 oz. (250 gr.) sugar
Grated zest of 1 orange
A piece of vanilla pod
8 oz. (250 gr.) finely diced crystallized citron peel
4 drops essential oil of orange
1 pt. ($1/2$ l.) whipped cream
Chocolate ice cream

Prepare an Italian meringue with the egg whites, vanilla, zest and sugar. When cold, fold in the cream, essential oil and citron peel. Coat the mould with the chocolate ice $1/4$ in. (6 mm.) thick, fill with the prepared mixture, cover with greaseproof paper and force on the lid. Freeze. *(Italy)*

Fior di Latte Violetta

2 oz. (60 gr.) violet petals
2 oz. (60 gr.) sugar
5 egg whites
6 oz. (180 gr.) sugar
1 pt. ($^1/_2$ l.) cream
4 drops essential oil of violet
2 oz. (60 gr.) crushed crystallized violets
Pistachio ice cream

Moisten the 2 oz. (60 gr.) sugar with a little water, bring to the boil, add the violet petals and cook to the crack, pour out upon a slightly oiled slab and when cold crush finely with a rolling pin and pass through a fine sieve, add to the cream and half whip.

Prepare an Italian meringue with the egg whites and sugar and when cold mix in the crystallized violets and essential oil, blend in the cream. Coat the mould with pistachio ice $^1/_4$ in. (6 mm.) thick, fill with the violet mixture and proceed as usual.
(Italy)

Iced Madeleine - Madeleine glacée

6 persons:
1 $^1/_8$ pt. (6 dl.) vanilla ice cream
1 $^1/_2$ gills (2 dl.) whipped cream
5 oz. (150 gr.) glacé fruits
$^1/_4$ gill (3 cl.) kirsch

Dice the glacé fruits and macerate in kirsch. Prepare vanilla ice cream and, before it sets too firm, mix in the whipped cream and glacé fruits. Fill mixture into a madeleine mould and freeze. *(France)*

Iced Meringues - Meringues glacées

6 persons:
1 pt. ($^1/_2$ l.) vanilla ice cream
12 meringue cases
1 $^1/_2$ gills (2 dl.) whipped cream

Sandwich the meringues together in pairs with the vanilla ice cream and, using a savoy bag with a star pipe, decorate with Chantilly cream. Serve on a napkin. Chocolate, coffee or other cream ice may be used instead of vanilla ice cream.

Iced Meringues Doris - Meringues glacées Doris

6 persons:
12 meringue cases
1 pt. ($^1/_2$ l.) vanilla ice cream
3 oz. (90 gr.) glacé fruits
$^1/_4$ gill (4 cl.) Grand-Marnier
1 $^1/_2$ gills (2 dl.) Chantilly cream
6 pieces glacé pineapple

Dice glacé fruits and macerate in Grand-Marnier. Mix this salpicon with the vanilla ice cream. Sandwich the meringues together in pairs with the ice cream, decorate with Chantilly cream and place a piece of glacé pineapple on top. Serve on a napkin. *(Germany)*

Iced Meringues Ravanola - Meringues glacées Ravanola

6 persons:
12 square meringue cases
1 pt. ($^1/_2$ l.) vanilla ice cream
3 oz. (90 gr.) marrons glacés
$^1/_4$ gill (3 cl.) kirsch
2-3 oz. (60-90 gr.) couverture
6 chocolate cigarettes
1 $^1/_2$ gills (2 dl.) Chantilly cream

Brush the inside of the meringue cases with melted couverture and allow to set. Crush the glacé marrons coarsely and soak in kirsch. Mix marrons with ice cream. Sandwich the meringues together in pairs, placing one on top of the other. Pipe a rosette of Chantilly cream on top and decorate with a chocolate cigarette.
(Germany)

Martinique Plate - Assiette martiniquaise

Cut bananas in rather thick slices and macerate them in rum and sugar. Arrange them on a plate around a large scoop of orange ice and decorate with Chantilly cream. *(France)*

Plombières Ice Cream - Glace Plombières

6 persons:
1 $^1/_4$ pt. (7 dl.) vanilla ice cream
1 oz. (30 gr.) glacé fruits
$^1/_4$ gill (3 cl.) kirsch
3 $^1/_2$ oz. (100 gr.) apricot jam

Dice the glacé fruits, macerate in kirsch, and mix with the ice cream. Fill a bombe mould with layers of the ice cream and the apricot jam. In place of the jam, sponge fingers soaked in kirsch may be used.
(France)

Profiteroles Mafalda - Profiteroles glacées au Chocolat

6 persons:
12 choux cases a little larger than usual
$^3/_4$ pt. (4 dl.) vanilla ice cream
1 $^1/_2$ gills (2 dl.) whipped cream
$^3/_4$ pt. (4 dl.) hot chocolate sauce
Chopped pistachio nuts

Fill the choux cases with the ice cream and pipe a rosette of whipped cream on top, using a savoy bag fitted with a star pipe. Sprinkle the whipped cream with chopped pistachio nuts and serve the hot chocolate sauce separately.

Snowball - Boule de Neige

6 persons:
1 $^1/_4$ pt. (6 dl.) vanilla ice cream
3 $^1/_2$ oz. (100 gr.) candied fruits
$^1/_2$ pt. (3 dl.) Chantilly cream
$^1/_4$ gill (3 cl.) kirsch
Crystallized violets

Dice the candied fruits and macerate them in kirsch. Incorporate them into the ice cream, which should be rather soft. Fill a ball-shaped mould with the mixture and place in the freezer for about 45 minutes. Turn out of the mould and pipe all over with dots of Chantilly cream, using a savoy bag fitted with a star pipe. Place crystallized violets here and there and leave the snowball in the freezer long enough for the Chantilly cream to set. Serve a kirsch-flavoured iced sabayon separately.
(France)

Temptation Plate - Assiette Tentation

Place half a peach on top of a portion of pistachio ice cream on a plate. Sprinkle with roasted, flaked almonds and surround with Chantilly cream.

ARTIFICIAL ICES

Artificial ices are used in window displays by way of advertisement. They should closely resemble real ices and to this end a special mixture is used which is prepared in the following way: make some royal icing with half castor sugar and half starch, but without adding any lemon juice. Continue to add both sugar and starch until the mixture reaches the consistency of a paste. Next, add a few drops of alum dissolved in water together with a small quantity of pure glycerine so as to make the mixture soft and malleable.

This mixture can be coloured with the various colourings used by the pastry-cook. Mould into the desired shapes, leave to dry thoroughly and then brush over with a transparent gum lacquer. These artificial ices can be shown cut across (for cassata, bombes, etc.) and it is only necessary to stick candied fruit, almonds, pistachio nuts, etc. into the slices and cover over with the gum lacquer.

If the ices are adequately covered with gum lacquer, they can easily be washed.

XXIV. Savoury Goods

Savoury goods may be divided under four general headings.

1. Small snacks for functions lasting about an hour such as a cocktail party.

2. More substantial items for functions such as a social evening, or for use as after dinner savouries.

3. Bigger and even more substantial items for such an occasion as a pre-theatre meal.

4. Items for a packed meal or as a course (with salad) in a meal.

One cannot be too rigid with this subdivision of savoury goods for occasions, because some items can be made small for one occasion or larger for another. There is scope for inventive craftsman.

As variety is the 'spice of life' so the variety, particularly for short functions, should be as comprehensive as possible. The first appeal should be to the eye, the second to the sense of smell and finally to the palate.

The range should vary too in the nature of the savouries; some should be short eating and others crisp and the variety should include nuts, potato crisps, olives, gherkins and even fruit which is becoming popular.

Consideration also should be given to mixtures that have a flavour and texture affinity one for the other, for instance cream cheese and chopped chives; salmon and cucumber; cheese and pineapple, etc.

Various Basic Preparations

BASES

These are many and varied and the more important are listed as follows.

Bread

This includes white, wholemeal, wheatmeal, rye, pumpernickel and savoury breads in small slices. The bread can be used as it is or it can be toasted or fried.

Rolls

These are small round or boat shaped rolls of the bridge roll type, made from an enriched dough unsweetened and quite soft. The shape is generally dictated by the type of filling. Very small salty unsweetened brioche rolls are also used.

Short Pastry

Short pastry is used for tartlets, barquettes, biscuits (which may be flavoured with cheese, spices, or other savoury flavours).

Puff Pastry

Puff pastry is ideal for bouchées, tartlets, barquettes and cannelons.

Choux Pastry

Petits choux that are baked and then filled and/or choux paste that is fried and filled all assist in variety.

Biscuits

Small unsweetened biscuits of the cracker type or small rye bread biscuits make ideal bases for savoury goods.

Scones

Small unsweetened scones or cheese scones made from white or wholemeal flour can be filled with savoury fillings.

SEASONINGS

The basic seasoning is a mixture of salt and pepper used to offset blandness and to give a zest to savoury goods. Salt also has the power of accentuating other flavours. Spices and herbs are added to the basic seasoning according to local taste and the savoury in which they are used. Zest of lemon is also a useful addition.

Pepper, salt, spices and herbs must be carefully stored in a dry place not only to preserve the aroma and the flavour, but also because salt is hygroscopic and attracts moisture which will upset the weight ratio of salt to other ingredients.

The spices used include ground nutmeg and ginger. The herbs used are sage, thyme, parsley, marjoram and basil amongst others.

1.
1 lb. (500 gr.) salt
5 oz. (150 gr.) pepper

2.
1 lb. (500 gr.) salt
3 oz. (100 gr.) pepper
$1/2$ oz. (15 gr.) nutmeg
$1/2$ oz. (15 gr.) dried crushed sage

3.
1 lb. (500 gr.) salt
3 oz. (100 gr.) white pepper
$3/4$ oz. (20 gr.) mace

4.
1 lb. (500 gr.) salt
4 oz. (125 gr.) white pepper
$1/2$ oz. (15 gr.) nutmeg

5.
1 lb. (500 gr.) salt
8 oz. (250 gr.) pepper
1 oz. (30 gr.) nutmeg
1 oz. (30 gr.) mace

6.
1 lb. (500 gr.) salt
4 oz. (125 gr.) pepper
$1/2$ oz. (15 gr.) ginger
$1/2$ oz. (15 gr.) pimento

7.
1 lb. (500 gr.) salt
3 oz. (100 gr.) pepper
$1/2$ oz. (15 gr.) nutmeg
$1/2$ oz. (15 gr.) sage

8.
1 lb. (500 gr.) salt
8 oz. (250 gr.) white pepper
$1/4$ oz. (8 gr.) Cayenne pepper
$1/2$ oz. (15 gr.) mace
$1/2$ oz. (15 gr.) nutmeg

SAUCES

Sauces are essential for some preparations. Recipes for sauces can be found in the new edition of Pellaprat's *Modern French Culinary Art* *(pages 141-162)*.

ASPIC

Aspic is made from veal bones, calve's feet, pork rinds, root vegetables and seasoning. It is clarified with minced beef and egg whites. A more up-to-date, economical method is the one using gelatine, i.e. heat up to a very concentrated stock, fat-free meat or chicken broth, fish or game stock and add 18-22 sheets of gelatine per 2 lb. (1 kg.) (20-24 sheets per quart [1 l.]), depending on the time of year. Before using the gelatine, soak it in water for a time and then squeeze it out. Stir it in well and then clarify the stock as follows—take 3 egg whites for each 2 lb. (1 kg.) (4 whites to 1 quart [1 l.]) of liquid, whisk them a little, gradually whisking them into the warm liquid, then boil up at once. Cover, set aside until the whites form a crust on top, then strain through a cloth or jelly bag. The liquid should now be absolutely clear.

The aspic will be stronger and tastier if the egg whites are well mixed with $2\,^1/_2$ oz. (75 gr.) lean, finely minced beef, $2\,^1/_2$ oz. (75 gr.) finely sliced leek and a little chervil before adding to the liquid. In this case 2 egg whites are sufficient for 2 lb. (1 kg.) of liquid (3 egg whites for 1 quart [1 l.]).

The aspic may be flavoured with madeira or sherry.

SAVOURY BUTTERS

These are many and their use apart from flavour, adds pleasing colour to savouries, provided that they are used with discrimination and good taste.
(See also 'Modern French Culinary Art', pages 162-164).

Almond

Mix 2 oz. (60 gr.) of finely ground blanched almonds with 4 oz. (125 gr.) of butter and pass through a fine nylon or hair sieve.

Anchovy

Crush or pass through a fine sieve 4 or 5 anchovy fillets in oil and mix the purée with 4 oz. (125 gr.) of soft butter. Do not add salt, as the anchovies are salt enough.

Cheese

Mix thoroughly 4 oz. (125 gr.) of crumbly cheese with 4 oz. (125 gr.) of butter.

Crayfish or Lobster

Pound crayfish or lobster shells and trimmings as fine as possible in a mortar; mix with an equal quantity of butter and pass through a fine nylon or hair sieve.

Maître d'Hôtel

Soften 2 oz. (60 gr.) butter without melting. Mix in salt, pepper, lemon juice and finely chopped parsley.

Mustard

Cream 4 oz. (125 gr.) butter with a pinch of salt and half a teaspoon of powdered mustard.

Sardine

The same as for anchovy butter using two sardines in oil instead of anchovies. Add a little salt and pepper.

Shrimp or Prawn

To 4 oz. (125 gr.) of butter use 2 oz. (60 gr.) of shrimps or prawns or the same weight in heads and shells. Proceed as for anchovy butter.

Tomato

To 4 oz. (125 gr.) of butter add 2 oz. (60 gr.) of tomato purée. Season with salt and pepper.

Watercress

Place some watercress leaves in boiling water and remove them when the water boils again. Cool, squeeze out thoroughly in a cloth and pass through a fine sieve. Mix with 4 oz. (125 gr.) butter and season with salt and pepper.

Yeast Extract

To 4 oz. (125 gr.) butter mix in sufficient commercial yeast extract.

TOPPINGS - COLD CUISINE

Many types of meat, poultry, fish, egg, cheese and vegetables can be used. There follows a selection:

Meats	Fish	Purées	Mousses	Other toppings
Roast beef Roast veal Roast chicken Corned beef Cooked ham Raw ham Ox tongue Tartar steak Salami Sausage	Anchovy Crab Herring Lobster Poached fish Prawns Sardines Shrimps Smoked salmon Tunny Caviar	Tomato Cheese Egg yolk Ham Liver sausage Fish	Ham Goose liver Chicken liver Fish	Cheese Egg Asparagus Tomatoes Salads

GARNISHES

Garnishes are used to decorate and to give a sense of completion to the savoury. There are many items that can be used. A selection follows:

Aspic Capers Caviar Champignons Cheese	Cucumber Egg Gherkins Olives Onions Paprika	Prawns Radish Roasted almonds Tomato Truffles

FILLINGS - HOT AND COLD CUISINE

The number of fillings are so numerous and so varied that space will not allow for them all to be dealt with. As many examples as possible however are given here:

Bacon and Egg Filling

2 oz. (60 gr.) lightly fried and chopped bacon
3 $1/2$ oz. (100 gr.) egg
2 $1/2$ oz. (75 gr.) milk

Mix well together. The mixing given will be sufficient for a 7 in. (18 cm.) flan.

Beef and Potato Filling

1 lb. 6 oz. (680 gr.) milk
$1/4$ oz. (8 gr.) salt
1 oz. (30 gr.) butter
1 $1/2$ oz. (45 gr.) dry oxtail (soup powder)
4 oz. (125 gr.) potato powder
3 oz. (90 gr.) minced cooked beef

Bring the first four items to the boil and add to the potato powder and finally add the minced beef.

Cheese and Onion Filling

2 lb. 8 oz. (1 kg. 250) minced Australian cheddar
15 oz. (450 gr.) milk
10 oz. (300 gr.) egg
1 oz. (30 gr.) seasoning No. 1
1 lb. (500 gr.) chopped semi-cooked onions

Cheese Filling I

1 lb. (500 gr.) bakers cheese

1 lb. (500 gr.) unsalted butter or margarine
1 lb. (500 gr.) water

Cream the cheese and fat lightly, adding the water gradually.

This filling can be piped through a savoy bag into bread rolls, spread on cocktail biscuits or slices of bread and toast.

Cheese Filling II

5 oz. (150 gr.) béchamel
3 oz. (100 gr.) egg yolks
4 oz. (125 gr.) butter
8 oz. (250 gr.) grated cheese
$2/3$ gill ($1/8$ l.) cream
Salt
Cayenne

Combine the thick hot bechamel with the egg yolks, cheese, butter and cream and season with salt and Cayenne.

Cornish Pasties

1 lb. 8 oz. (750 gr.) chopped lean beef
15 oz. (450 gr.) chopped potatoes
7 $1/2$ oz. (215 gr.) chopped turnip
3 $1/2$ oz. (100 gr.) chopped onions
Seasoning to taste

Cream Filling

1 lb. (500 gr.) butter
$1/4$ oz. (8 gr.) salt
15 oz. (450 gr.) cold béchamel
6 oz. (180 gr.) egg whites
5 oz. (150 gr.) mayonnaise

Beat the butter well, adding the salt. Beat in the béchamel. Fold in the whites of egg that have been whisked and finally fold in the mayonnaise.

Forfar Bridies

2 lb. (1 kg.) minced beef
4 oz. (125 gr.) rusk
1 oz. (30 gr.) seasoning No. 1
1 oz. (30 gr.) meat extract
3 lb. 4 oz. (1 kg. 625) water

Meat and Potato Filling

10 lb. (5 kg.) partly cooked potatoes
2 lb. (1 kg.) onion
4 lb. (2 kg.) lean beef
2 lb. 8 oz. (1 kg. 250) water
2 oz. (60 gr.) seasoning No. 6

The meat should be partly cooked with the water for these two fillings. The meat may be cut or minced before or after cooking. The seasoning is added prior to cooking. The gravy is thickened with flour.

Meat Stuffing

1 lb. (500 gr.) minced beef
7 oz. (200 gr.) egg
2 shallots finely chopped
1 leek finely chopped
Salt
Pepper

Lightly brown in a pan and when the mixture has cooled add the egg and seasoning.

Mutton or Lamb Pies

2 lb. (1 kg.) minced mutton or lamb
2 oz. (60 gr.) rusk
1 oz. (30 gr.) seasoning No. 3
6 oz. (180 gr.) onion
3 lb. 2 oz. (1 kg. 560) water

Pie Gravy

2 lb. 8 oz. (1 kg. 250) meat stock
$1/2$ oz. (15 gr.) meat extract
Seasoning
2 oz. (60 gr.) flour

Pie Jelly I

2 lb. 8 oz (1 kg. 250) water
2 oz. (60 gr.) gelatine
Seasoning

Pie Jelly II

Simmer pork rinds, feet, veal bones for some hours. Take off the scum, frequently strain, clarify and season to taste. If after testing the jelly is not firm enough, add a little gelatine. To clarify the jelly the stock is first strained and brought slowly to the boil, then with the heat lowered to simmering point, crushed egg shells and a little egg white are dropped in. After straining again it should be seasoned to taste.

Pork Pies

4 lb. (2 kg.) lean pork
1 lb. (500 gr.) fat pork
2 1/2 oz. (75 gr.) seasoning No. 2
10 oz. (300 gr.) water

To obtain a pink colour in the meat two methods may be adopted.

1. Dip the meat into mature brine before mincing and allow to drain.

2. Add to the recipe 10 % of cured pork or bacon trimmings. All bones, skin and gristle must be removed from the pork before mincing, using a 3/16 in. (4 mm.) plate.

Savoury Potato Fillings

Basic mixture 1
2 lb. 8 oz. (1 kg. 250) milk
1/2 oz. (15 gr.) salt
2 oz. (60 gr.) butter
9 oz. (270 gr.) potato powder

Heat the milk and reconstitute the potato powder and add salt and butter.

Basic mixture 2
3 lb. (1 kg. 500) mashed potato
1 oz. (30 gr.) butter
1 oz. (30 gr.) milk

Bacon and Onion
3 lb. (1 kg. 500) basic potato mixture
8 oz. (250 gr.) chopped bacon
8 oz. (250 gr.) chopped onion

Cheese and Celery
3 lb. (1 kg. 500) basic potato mixture
8 oz. (250 gr.) grated cheese
8 oz. (250 gr.) chopped celery

Cheese and Onion
3 lb. (1 kg. 500) basic potato mixture
8 oz. (250 gr.) grated cheese
8 oz. (250 gr.) chopped onion

Cheese and Tomato
3 lb. (1 kg. 500) basic potato mixture
8 oz. (250 gr.) grated cheese
8 oz. (250 gr.) tomato purée

Egg and Ham
3 lb. (1 kg. 500) basic potato mixture
8 oz. (250 gr.) minced ham
8 oz. (250 gr.) chopped, hard boiled egg

Steak Pies

2 lb. (1 kg.) lean beef
1 lb. 4 oz. (625 gr.) water
1 oz. (30 gr.) seasoning No. 6

Steak and Kidney Pies

2 lb. (1 kg.) lean beef
4 oz. (125 gr.) kidney
4 oz. (125 gr.) onion (if desired)
1 lb. 8 oz. (750 gr.) water
1 oz. (30 gr.) seasoning No. 6

Chop meat and stew gently until tender. Strain off the stock for making gravy and season.

Veal and Ham Pies

2 lb. 8 oz. (1 kg. 250) chopped veal
3 lb. 8 oz. (1 kg. 750 gr.) chopped pork
3 oz. (90 gr.) seasoning No. 8
10 oz. (300 gr.) water

Savouries made with Bread and Rolls

TO BE SERVED HOT

Finger Rolls

Soft finger rolls, large enough to be impaled on a heating device, which also provides the cavity into which a sausage is placed, is a quick and efficient method of providing a hot savoury.

TO BE SERVED COLD

Asparagus Rolls

Cut thin slices of white or wheatmeal bread, butter them and remove the crust. Place cooked asparagus on each and roll them up.

Bridge Rolls

These are cut, buttered and filled with meat, sausage, fish, cheese, egg, cucumber, lettuce, tomato, etc. or combinations of these. The crumb can be removed to give more room for the filling.

Hamburger Rolls

These are large, soft flat rolls which are sliced and buttered to receive a Hamburger seasoned with mustard.

Harlequin Slices

A long loaf from which the crust has been cut is required for these slices. It is then carefully cut into six slices. These are spread generously with the following savoury butter spreads:

Anchovy
Cheese
Tomato
Maître d'hôtel
Yeast extract

After assembling the slices one on top of the other, the whole is wrapped in aluminium foil and refrigerated, which makes it easier to cut into thin slices.
(Illustration page 827.)

Savoury Torte

Cut three slices of bread about $1/4$ in. (6 mm.) thick from a round coburg loaf and remove the crust. Butter one and on it place thin slices of tongue. Butter the second slice and turn it over on to the tongue. Spread the top with maître d'hôtel butter and put on the third slice. Mask the side with hazelnut butter and then with crushed roasted almonds or hazelnuts. Cover the top with slices of tongue and decorate with maître d'hôtel butter. Refrigerate and cut in a similar manner as for a torte.

Choux Pastry Savouries

Recipes can be found in 'Modern French Culinary Art', pages 196-242.

TO BE SERVED HOT
Cheese Fritters

Make a choux pastry from
$4\ {}^2/_3$ gills ($6\ {}^1/_2$ dl.) water
7 oz. (200 gr.) butter
11 oz. (325 gr.) flour
9 oz. (250 gr.) cheese (emmental or parmesan).
10 oz. (300 gr.) egg (approx.)
Salt
Pepper

Shape into fritters with a spoon and deep fry in hot fat. Drain well and serve at once.

Cheddar Pearls

Take some choux pastry and mix in half its weight with grated Cheddar cheese. Place it into a savoy bag fitted with $1/8$ in. (3 mm.) plain pipe. Hold it over a deep pan of hot fat and with a pair of oiled scissors cut off small pieces at it emerges from the pipe. Fry to a golden colour, drain well, season with paprika and serve at once.

Duchess Rolls

Pipe choux pastry into small oval shapes. Brush with egg and sprinkle with grated Parmesan cheese and bake well. When cool slit along one side and fill with cheese filling *(page 817)*. Serve hot.

TO BE SERVED COLD
Cheese Cream Buns

Pipe out walnut size pieces of choux pastry on to a baking sheet, brush with egg and sprinkle with grated Parmesan cheese and bake well. Make a small hole in the bottom of each and fill with cheese filling *(page 816)* using a bag and pipe. The filling should contain either Cheshire, Emmental or Parmesan cheese.

Cheese Soufflés

Pipe out choux pastry in very small bulbs or fingers on to a baking sheet and bake at 440° F (226° C). When cold fill with cheese filling.
(Illustration page 825.)

Cheese Swans

From unsweetened choux pastry pipe small oval shapes on a baking sheet. On another sheet pipe some thin 'S' shapes. Bake well. When cold cut the tops off the oval pieces and fill with cheese filling *(page 816)* but using either Cheshire, Emmental, Dutch or Compté cheese. Cut the tops in half and replace to represent wings and push in the 'S' pieces to represent the neck and head.

Choux Rings

Pin out short pastry to $1/8$ in. (3 mm.) thick and cut out with a 2 in. (5 cm.) plain cutter. Pipe rings of choux pastry neatly on each. Bake at 400° F (204° C). When cold, fill with one of the white sauce fillings and garnish as desired.

Foie gras Eclairs

Make very small éclairs and bake well. Slit along the side and fill with foie gras combined with butter and well seasoned.

The tops may be coated with blonde chaud froid sauce.

Puff Pastry Savouries

TO BE SERVED HOT

Boats - Barquettes

Barquettes and tartlets differ only in shape. At one time barquettes were used only for fillings of fish or shellfish, but this practice no longer survives. Barquettes are oval-shaped cases made with short pastry (or scraps of puff pastry) which are baked blind and then filled with the various salpicons or mixtures described below. They are then often reheated for a few minutes and served hot.
Recipes 'Modern French Culinary Art', pages 196-197.

Puff Pastry Cases - Bouchées

Roll out puff pastry $3/5$ in. (6 mm.) thick. Cut into circles with a fluted pastry cutter not more than 2 in. (5 cm.) in diameter. Care should be taken not to twist the cutter when cutting the circles. Place them on a baking sheet which has been sprinkled with cold water. Make a circular cut with a pastry cutter barely $1 1/2$ in. ($3 1/2$ cm.) in diameter to mark the cover of the *bouchée* case. Brush the top lightly with egg and bake in a hot oven 425° F (218° C) for 15-18 minutes. Watch these cases while baking. They should be quite dry when they are baked. Remove the lid with the point of a small knife; this cover should come off quite easily. Remove any dough in the centre of the cases that is not quite cooked. Fill with any of the mixtures.

An alternative method is to cut out circles of puff pastry cuttings $1/8$ in. (3 mm.) thick, dock them and moisten the edges. Top each circle with a hollow ring of $1/4$ in. (5 mm.) puff pastry, the diameter being the same as that of the base. Brush the rings twice with egg and after sufficient rest bake at 430° F (220° C). Cut out the lids separately, making them thin and a little larger as they will shrink a little during baking.

Special metal sleeves can be obtained from speciality shops. These are placed into the circular hole in the top which should be a little larger than the sleeve. This will prevent the pastry cases from skewing or falling over.
Recipes 'Modern French Culinary Art', pages 199-200.

Anchovy Sticks

Pin out some scrap puff pastry very thin. Place on to a baking sheet and arrange fillets of anchovy at regular intervals. Brush with egg and cover with a thicker piece of puff pastry. Brush with egg, cut into sticks and bake at 400° F (204° C).

Avondale Puff

Take some bouchée cases and fill with the following mixture:

Poach some haddock and mushrooms in butter, cut into dice and blend into oyster sauce and fill into the cases. Place an oyster on each and sprinkle with Cayenne. Serve hot.

Bacon and Egg Turnovers

Pin out virgin puff pastry to about $1/8$ in. (3 mm.) thick, and cut out with a fluted cutter. Wash with water and in the centre of each place a mixture of minced bacon and chopped hard-boiled egg. Fold over and seal the edges. Egg wash and make a cut in the top of each. After a rest bake at 440° F (226° C).

Bouchées à la Reine

1 lb. (500 gr.) chicken purée
or
7 oz. (200 gr.) chicken breast
5 oz. (150 gr.) poached mushrooms
1 oz. (30 gr.) truffle (optional)
4 oz. (125 gr.) sauce supreme
8 puff pastry cases

Cut the chicken, mushrooms and truffle in small dice, warm a little and bind together with the sauce supreme. Fill into the hot puff pastry cases. *(France)*

Cheddar Custards

$1/2$ pt. (3 dl.) milk
$1/4$ pt. (1 $1/2$ dl.) cream
7 oz. (200 gr.) egg
8 oz. (250 gr.) finely diced Cheddar
Salt, pepper
Mace

Line 24 small tartlet pans and allow to stand. Mix together the milk, cream, egg and seasoning. Divide the cheese out between the tartlets and fill up with the custard. Bake at 350° F (176° C). Serve hot.

Cheese Cushions

Pin out puff pastry to $1/8$ in. (3 mm.) and cut into small squares and egg wash. Cut some Gruyère or Emmental cheese into fingers and wrap each into a thin slice of salami or pork luncheon meat. Place diagonally on the squares. Fold two opposite corners to the middle, overlapping slightly and press to seal well. Wash with egg and place in the centre a small disc of pastry cut with a fluted cutter. After sufficient resting time, bake at 430-440° F (226° C).

Cheese Horns

Pin out scrap puff pastry to $1/8$ in. (3 mm.) and cut into strips and lightly brush with water. Carefully roll on to cream horn tins, overlapping the pastry as it is rolled. Make certain that the finish is under the tin. Egg wash and after a sufficient time bake at 400-420° F (204-216° C). Fill with cheese filling.
(Illustration page 827.)

Cheshire Cheese Rolls

3 $1/2$ gills ($1/2$ l.) thick béchamel
1 lb. (500 gr.) grated Cheshire cheese
4 oz. (125 gr.) egg yolks
1 lb. 12 oz. (875 gr.) scrap puff pastry
Salt
Paprika

Combine the hot béchamel with the cheese and egg yolks and add the seasoning and allow to cool, stirring occasionally.

Pin out the puff pastry to a thickness of about $1/6$ in. (4 mm.). Cut into strips 3 in. (7.5 cm.) wide and then cut each strip into 2 $1/2$ in. (6 cm.) pieces. Fill the pieces with the cheese cream and moisten the edge. Roll up, pressing the edges to enclose the cream. Brush with egg yolk and bake at 450° F (232° C).

Ham Croissants

Pin out some scrap puff pastry very thin and cut into rather long triangles. Brush with egg and at the base of each place some minced ham. Roll them up starting at the base and arrange them crescent shape on to a baking sheet. Egg wash and bake at 420° F (216° C).

Jura Tit-Bits

Pin out puff pastry $1/8$ in. (3 mm.) thick and cut out circles about 2 in. (5 cm.) in diameter. In one third of the circles cut out the centres. Place the complete circles on a baking sheet and wash with water. Place on each a cut out ring and place in the centre some cream as for cheese biscuits, using Parmesan cheese instead of Cheshire and increasing the seasoning. Wash the rings with water and cover with the remaining circles of pastry, pressing down firmly. Brush with egg yolk and prick the tops several times. Bake at 450° F (232° C) and serve at once.

Little Pies
Line tartlet or barquette moulds with thin puff pastry. Fill $^2/_3$ full with any of the fillings given. Cover with puff pastry, brush with egg yolk and place either an olive, almond or pistachio nut in the centre. Bake at 395° F (200° C). *(Italy)*

Fillings

a. Cooked minced spinach, cubes of mozzarella cheese and ham. Beat egg yolk with tomato sauce and mix with the other ingredients to a smooth paste. Fill round tartlet moulds.

b. Minced boiled or grilled chicken, mixed with béchamel to a smooth paste. Fill barquettes.

c. Tomato sauce and cubes of mozzarella. Fill barquettes.

d. Mushrooms and a cream sauce. Fill barquettes.

e. Anchovies minced with a little olive oil. Fill barquettes.

Picnic Puffs
Pin out virgin puff pastry to about $^1/_8$ in. (3 mm.) thick. Cut into strips about 2 in. (5 cm.) wide and wash with water. Pipe along the centre one of the savoury potato fillings *(page 818)*.

Place another strip of puff pastry on the top and seal the edges well. Egg wash and cut into small rectangles. Make deep diagonal cuts in the top and after resting bake at 420° F (216° C).

Richmond Cheese Cakes
$^1/_2$ pt. (3 dl.) milk
5 oz. (150 gr.) bread crumbs
3 oz. (90 gr.) egg yolks
3 oz. (90 gr.) egg whites
6 oz. (180 gr.) Cheddar cheese
Salt
Cayenne pepper

Line 24 small tartlet pans with thin scrap puff pastry and allow to stand. Boil the milk and add the bread crumbs and work to a thick consistency, cool, season and stir in the yolks. Whip the whites and fold in. Fill the tartlet cases and bake at 400° F (204° C). Serve hot.

Rissoles
Rissoles may be served as hors-d'œuvre or entrées. They may be of varying sizes and shapes, for instance, round or half-moon shaped, and are encased in an envelope of short pastry or puff pastry. If enclosed in unsweetened brioche dough, they are known as rissoles à la Dauphine. Rissoles are made of a salpicon of meat, poultry, game and mushrooms and are nearly always fried, although they can be baked.

For 8 rissoles: use $^1/_2$ lb. (250 gr.) paste, which is rolled out in a fairly thin strip and cut out with a fluted pastry cutter 3 in. (8 cm.) in diameter. Place 8 oz. (250 gr.) of the desired filling in the middle of each piece of paste, brush half-way round the edge with egg, fold over and press the edges together. Fry and serve very hot. *(France)*
(Recipes 'Modern French Culinary Art', *pages 222-223*.)

Rissoles
Roll out puff pastry to $^1/_4$ in. (5 mm.) thick and cut out round pieces with a 3 $^1/_2$ in. (9 cm.) fluted cutter. Extend them to an oval shape. Brush with egg and place into the centre of each one of many fillings, three examples of which follow this recipe. Fold over and press the edges to make a good seal. Wash with egg yolk and bake at 395° F (200° C).

Fillings
a. Spinach

2 lb. 4 oz. (1 kg. 125) spinach purée
10 oz. (300 gr.) béchamel sauce
5 oz. (150 gr.) grated Parmesan cheese
9 oz. (270 gr.) egg
Salt, pepper, nutmeg

Mix all together.

b. Artichoke

Prepare artichokes, boil and mince them.

Mix with the above ingredients.

c. Scampi

5 1/2 oz. (170 gr.) cooked shelled scampi
2 oz. (60 gr.) blanched champignons
2 oz. (60 gr.) blanched supreme of chicken
2/3 gill (1 dl.) béchamel sauce
3/4 gill (6 cl.) tomato sauce
1/4 oz. (10 gr.) butter
Salt, pepper

Mix the two sauces and the butter. Add the other ingredients. *(Italy)*

Sausage Rolls

There are two distinct types, those made with puff pastry and those made with short pastry. If puff pastry is used a three quarter paste is best, one that does not puff excessively. The pastry is rolled thinly and cut into strips on which are placed ropes of sausage meat. The edges of the strips are dampened with water, before the sausage meat is covered in one of two ways.

1. One edge brought over to meet the other.

2. The meat is so covered that there is an overlapping join underneath. The strips are brushed with egg or egg yolks and cut into pieces of a suitable size. Each roll is given 3 or 4 deep cuts on top making certain that the paste is cut through. After resting, bake at 420° F (216° C), making certain that the sausage meat is cooked. *(Great Britain)*
(Illustration page 830.)

Welsh Pastries

Pin out virgin puff pastry to about 1/4 in. (5 mm.) thick and cut out with a small round plain cutter. Lay out on a baking sheet and when about half baked, place on each a thin circle of cheese. Return to the oven to finish baking. Serve hot.

TO BE SERVED COLD

Bouchées Beauharnais

Filling: Diced chicken mixed with tarragon mayonnaise.

Decoration: Finely diced black truffle.
(Illustration page 825.)

Bouchées Joinville

Filling: Salpicon of shrimps mixed with tomato mayonnaise (Sauce Aurore).

Decoration: Dust with paprika. Shrimps on top.
(Illustration page 825.)

Bouchées Springtime

Filling: Vegetable salad mixed with mayonnaise.

Decoration: Disc of filled olive.
(Illustration page 825.)

Brie Pastries

1 lb. 2 oz. (560 gr.) puff pastry
11 oz. (330 gr.) ripe Brie
7 oz. (200 gr.) butter
5/6 gill (1/8 l.) whipped cream
3/4 gill (9 cl.) brandy
7 oz. (200 gr.) roasted ground hazelnuts
Paprika

Pin out puff pastry 1/6 in. (4 mm.) thick and cut out with a 2 in. (5 cm.) plain cutter. Dock each one and after resting bake until crisp.

Cream the butter and combine with the Brie which has been sieved; season with brandy and paprika and fold in the whipped cream. Sandwich in four with the cream and refrigerate. Finish the sides and tops with the cream and mask the sides with the roasted hazelnuts. Pipe a star of cream on the top of each.

Caraway Loops

Pin out puff pastry 1/8 in. (3 mm.) thick and cut into rectangles 2 by 3 in. (5 by 8 cm.). Using a knife or pastry wheel, make a cut lengthways down the centre about 2 in. (5 cm.) long. Draw one end of the pastry through the cut and arrange on baking sheets. Brush with egg, sprinkle with caraway seeds—mixed with a little pretzel salt if desired—and bake at 400° F (204° C). *(Switzerland)*

Cheese Butterflies - Kaas Vlinders

For these savoury pastries use the same recipe and method as for Salted Butterflies except that the slices of paste should be coated with melted butter and sprinkled with grated cheese. The cheese should be flavoured with salt and curry powder first. Just before the pastries are baked at 420° F (216° C), they should be moved against each other on the baking sheet, sprinkled with some grated cheese and put again in the oven for a little while until they are quite baked. *(Holland)*

Cheese Cannoli

Pin out puff pastry to $1/8$ in. (3 mm.) and cut into strips. Wash them lightly with water and roll them in spiral fashion round metal cylinders or pieces of dowling about $3/4$ in. (2 cm.) diameter. Egg wash and allow to rest before baking at 420-430° F (216-221° C). Finish by piping in cheese filling.
(Illustration page 827.)

Cheese Puffs

9 oz. (270 gr.) flour
5 oz. (150 gr.) butter
2 $1/4$ oz. (70 gr.) sieved cooked egg yolks
2 $1/4$ oz. (70 gr.) sieved Gruyère cheese
2 $1/4$ oz. (70 gr.) sieved Parmesan cheese
2 $1/4$ oz. (70 gr.) sieved Cheddar cheese
1 lb. 6 oz. (680 gr.) puff pastry
Paprika
Salt

Make a paste out of the flour, butter, egg yolks, cheeses, paprika and salt and roll it into the puff pastry. Give 5 half turns and let it rest for 2 hours. Pin out to $1/4$ in. (5 mm.) and cut into various small shapes. Egg wash and decorate with any of the following:

nib almonds, chopped walnuts, pistachio nuts, grated pumpernickel, caraway or poppy seeds, cheese or salt. Bake at 450° F (232° C). The cheese puffs illustrated have been split and filled with a cheese filling.
(Illustration page 828.)

Cumin Sticks

Pin out some scrap puff pastry quite thin (about $1/16$-$1/10$ in. (2-3 mm.)) and put out on a baking sheet. Brush with egg and sprinkle with cumin seeds mixed with a little salt, cut into sticks. Bake at 420° F (216° C).

Parmesan Sticks

Sprinkle some grated Parmesan cheese and a little paprika on to puff pastry during the last two turns. Roll to about $1/5$ in. (4 mm.) thick and cut into strips about 2 $3/4$ in. (7 cm.) width. Cut into sticks about $1/4$ in. (5 mm.) wide. Brush with egg yolk and sprinkle with grated parmesan. Dry gruyère may be used instead.

Poppyseed Ties

Pin out puff pastry to $1/8$ in. (3 mm.) thick, brush with egg and sprinkle evenly with poppyseed. Cut into rectangles 1 $1/2$ by 2 $1/2$ in. (4 by 6 cm.), twist the middle of each one right round and place on to baking sheets. Bake at 400° F (204° C).
(Switzerland)

Poppyseed Triangles

Pin out a piece of puff pastry and lay out on a baking sheet. Cut into small regular triangles. Wash with egg and sprinkle with poppy seed mixed with a little salt. Bake at 420° F (216° C).

Riviera Boats

Filling: Finely diced lobster and champignons or diced shrimps and champignons mixed with mayonnaise.

Decoration: shrimps, paprika and black olives.
(Illustration page 825.)

Sacristains

Pin out puff pastry to about $1/8$ in. (4 mm.). Cut into strips 4 in. (10 cm.) wide. Brush with egg and sprinkle with nib almonds

▲ Cheese Soufflés, p. 819 — Cheese Scones
Puff and Short Pastry Barquettes and Bouchées, p. 823, 824, 833 ▼

826 ▲ Assorted Canapés, Italy, p. 842

Brioches filled with Goose Liver Pâté, Maison Lacroix ▼

▲ Harlequin Slices, p. 819   Cheese Horns, p. 821 — Cheese Cannoli, p. 824 ▼   827

828 ▲ Simits, Turkey, p. 293 — Kric-Krac, p. 283   Cheese Puffs, p. 824 ▼

▲ Pizza, p. 835

Bacon and Egg Flan, p. 835 ▼

▲ Sausage Rolls, p. 823
Steak and Kidney Pies, p. 842 — Beef and Potato Pies, p. 840 — Bacon and Egg Pies, p. 840 ▼

▲ Goose Liver Medallions in Aspic, Maison Lacroix

Cheese Cream Savouries, p. 838 ▼

832 ▲ French Veal and Ham Pie, p. 842

Pork Pies, p. 841 ▼

mixed with a little salt. Cut into narrow strips, twist into spirals and place on a baking sheet. Alternatively, the strips can be curled round a stick. Bake at 400° F (204° C).

Salt Sticks

Pin out puff pastry to $1/8$ in. (3 mm.). Cut into strips 4-5 in. (10-12 cm.) wide, then cut into thin strips about $1/4$ in. (5 mm.) width. Twist each piece and arrange on a baking sheet. Dredge heavily with ordinary salt or celery salt. After a sufficient rest, bake at 450° F (232° C) for about 8-10 minutes.

Salted Butterflies - Zoute Vlinders

Take puff pastry that is ready except for the last turn and roll it to $1/8$ in. (3 mm.) thick. Cut slices about 24 in. (60 cm.) long, and sprinkle them with salt (1 oz. [30 gr.] salt to 2 $1/4$ lb. [1 kg. 125] paste).

Fold each slice of paste into 3 equal layers from both ends towards the middle; after this, fold these 2 triple layered slices together, so that one forms a strip of paste approx. 3 $1/2$ in. (9 cm.) wide, which is built up of 6 layers of paste.

Cut small slices of about $1/8$ in. (3 mm.) thick, put these slices cut side down on a greased baking sheet and bake immediately. Oven temperature: 420° F (216° C). The salted butterflies are ready as soon as they are set. *(Holland)*

Savoury Puff Slices

Pin out some scrap puff pastry very thin and cut into slices about 2 $1/2$-3 in. (6-8 cm.) wide. Dock well and after resting bake at 400° F (204° C). When cool, place prawns, diced cooked carrot and chopped tomato bound with mayonnaise on one strip and cover with another. Spread top with mayonnaise and with a knife mark into small rectangles. Garnish each rectangle with a slice of hard-boiled egg, a slice of gherkin and a slice of olive. Chill and glaze with aspic. Cut into slices where marked.

Strasbourg Boats

Filling: Buttered foie gras purée, which must have the consistency of cream.

Decoration: Disc of truffle.
(Illustration page 825.)

Sweet and Sour Fingers

Roll out puff pastry cuttings to about $1/8$ in. (3 mm.) thick. Cut into strips about 3 in. (8 cm.) wide and place half of them on a baking sheet. Dock them well and wash with water.

Fold the rest of the strips in half lengthways and make a series of cuts along the folded edge in a diagonal fashion so that when the strips are opened there is a chevron pattern of cuts.

Pipe filling along the base strips and place a patterned strip on the top of each. Egg wash and bake at 450° F (232° C) for about 15 minutes. When cool, cut into small fingers.

Filling

1 lb. (500 gr.) minced pork
8 oz. (250 gr.) chopped onion
1 $1/4$ gill (18 cl.) malt vinegar
6 oz. (175 gr.) castor sugar
2 oz. (60 gr.) cornflour
1 gill (15 cl.) water
Pepper, Cayenne pepper, salt, celery salt,
3 cloves of garlic

Sauté pork and onions until light brown. Add the seasoning and the vinegar in which the sugar has been dissolved. Cook until tender. Mix the cornflour and water, add to the above and cook until the mixture thickens.

Tunny Fish Boats

Filling: Cream of tunny fish.

Decoration: Strips of red peppers or tomatoes, finely chopped parsley.
(Illustration page 825.)

Turkish Specialities

1. Small triangles made from cheese puff pastry egg washed on top.

833

2. Small boat shapes made from cheese short pastry, egg washed and dipped into cumin seeds.

3. Three strips of puff pastry plaited together, egg washed and sprinkled with cumin seeds.

4. Savoury short pastry in which cheese curd is enclosed.

5. Puff pastry cut into rather tall triangles, the peaks of which are slit. Cheese curd is placed at the base and the pastry rolled up. They are egg washed.

6. Small squares of puff pastry, egg washed and dusted with salt.

Short Pastry Savouries

TO BE SERVED HOT

Berkely Tartlets

Line some small tartlet pans with short pastry and bake blind. Dice one chicken liver and 2 mushrooms and fry quickly in butter. Mix in 2 oz. (60 gr.) of devil sauce. Pipe a border of chicken purée mixed with a little béchamel round the tartlet cases and fill in the centres with the liver mixture. Garnish with half a stoned olive. Serve hot.

Cadogan Barquettes

Line small boat shape pans with short pastry and bake blind. Make a filling with the following materials in these proportions:

1 oz. (30 gr.) purée of ham
$1/4$ gill (3 cl.) cheese sauce
$1/2$ oz. (15 gr.) grated Lancashire cheese
A finely diced gherkin

Heat the ham and gherkin and fill into the pastry boats and mask with the sauce, sprinkle with cheese and reheat.

Calcutta Tartlets

Line some small tartlet pans with short pastry and bake blind.

Heat shrimps in curry sauce and fill into cases. Place some hot chutney in the centre of each and sprinkle with egg yolk. Serve hot.

Devilled Wensleydale Tartlets

Line 24 small short pastry tartlet cases and fill with the following:

8 oz. (250 gr.) Wensleydale cheese
$5/6$ gill ($1/8$ l.) béchamel
2 oz. (60 gr.) egg whites
$1/2$ gill (7 cl.) cream
Cayenne

Beat the cheese into the sauce. Whip the egg whites and cream separately, blend together and fold gently into the cheese mixture. Fill the cases and bake at 400° F (204° C). Serve hot.

Marion Delorme Tartlets - Tartelettes Marion Delorme

Take 9 oz. (270 gr.) puff pastry trimming and line tartlet moulds thinly with the paste. Pass 5 $1/2$ oz. (150 gr.) chicken and 4 $1/2$ oz. (130 gr.) raw mushrooms through the finest blade of the mincer or make into purée in a mixer. Boil this briefly with lemon juice and a piece of butter, stir into a thick cream with the $2/3$ gill (1 dl.) béchamel, season well, remove from heat, mix with 3 egg yolks and fill tartlets. Bake in a hot oven and serve at once. Enough for 12 tartlets.

Pastry Tartlets - Tartelettes

These are very similar to barquettes. They are round pastry cases made of short pastry (or scraps of puff pastry) which are baked blind and are then filled with the various fillings or mixtures described below.

Rajah Tartlets

Make some small short pastry tartlet cases and bake empty. Dice 8 oz. (240 gr.) prawns and heat in 8 oz. (240 gr.) curry sauce. Cook small mushrooms in butter. Fill the cases with the curry mixture and place a mushroom on the top of each. Sprinkle with paprika. Serve hot.

Reform Club Barquettes

Line some small boat shaped pans with short pastry. Cook two mushrooms and

2 oz. (60 gr.) of smoked haddock fillet in butter. Cut into small dice with a little ham and blend all the ingredients into 2 oz. (60 gr.) of cheese soufflé. Fill into the boats, sprinkle with cheese and bake at 420° F (215° C). Serve hot.

Rumanian Tartlets

Line small tartlet pans with short pastry and bake empty without letting them brown. Combine 9 oz. (270 gr.) choux pastry with 2 1/2 oz. (75 gr.) grated cheese and pipe three rings of the paste one above the other on to each tartlet. Fill the centres with a cream made from 9 oz. (270 gr.) béchamel, 1 1/2 oz. (45 gr.) egg yolks and 2 1/2 oz. (75 gr.) grated cheese, seasoned with ground nutmeg and paprika. Bake at 400° F (204° C) and serve hot.

Swiss Tartlets - Tartelettes suisses

12 tartlets :

1/2 lb. (250 gr.) puff pastry
2 eggs
5 oz. (160 gr.) Gruyère cheese
Mustard

Cooking time : 10 minutes

Heat 1/2 pt. (3 dl.) béchamel to the boil. Remove from the heat and add 2 eggs, 5 oz. (160 gr.) Gruyère cheese, stirring all the time. Season highly, add mustard and allow to cool. Line 12 small tartlet moulds thinly with the puff pastry. Fill to within 1/4 in. (6 mm.) from the rim of the moulds with the prepared mixture. Bake in a very hot oven, 450° F (232° C) and serve immediately, while the tartlets are still puffed up.

Flans

Bacon and Egg Flan

Line a 7 in. (18 cm.) flan ring or case with short pastry and dock the bottom. Fill with mixture *(page 816)*. Sprinkle the top with grated cheese and arrange sliced tomato round the edge. Bake at 400° F (204° C). *(Illustration page 829.)*

Cheese and Bacon Flan - Quiche à la lorraine

6 persons :

3/4 lb. (350 gr.) unsweetened short pastry
6 oz. (150 gr.) bacon
2 oz. (50 gr.) Gruyère cheese
3 eggs
3/4 pt. (4 dl.) milk

Cooking time : about 25 minutes

Place a lightly-buttered flan ring on a baking sheet and line with unsweetened short pastry; prick the bottom a few times with a fork and cover with very thin slices of grilled bacon. Cover the bacon with thin slices of cheese and on top of this pour the custard which has been made with the well-beaten eggs, the milk, salt, and pepper. Place in a hot oven, 400° F (204° C), bake and serve hot. It can be made with either cheese or bacon alone, but the eggs and milk are compulsory. It tastes better when the milk is replaced by thin cream or a mixture of half cream and half milk.

Onion Flan - Quiche aux Oignons

6 persons :

3/4 lb. (350 gr.) unsweetened short pastry
8 oz. (250 gr.) onions
2 oz. (50 gr.) butter
2 eggs
1/2 pt. (1/4 l.) milk

Cooking time : about 25 minutes

Slice onions thinly and simmer in the butter without allowing them to brown. Lightly butter a flan ring, place on a baking sheet and line with the short pastry. Fill with the onions when they are cool, pour on custard made with the well-beaten eggs mixed with the milk, salt and pepper and bake in a hot oven, 400° F (204° C).

Pizza

Roll out plain bread or pizza dough, and line flan rings about 3 1/2-4 in. (8-10 cm.) diameter. Allow to prove, then brush with olive oil. Sprinkle with origano. Spread with thick tomato pulp seasoned with salt and pepper. Arrange anchovy fillets on the surface and half bake at 375° F (190° C).

Place slices of mozzarella cheese and finish baking. Sprinkle with olive oil immediately on removal from oven. Puff pastry can be used instead of bread dough, especially when making small pizzas for a cocktail party. *(Italy)*
(Illustration page 829.)

Rarebits

Buck Rarebit
Make Welsh rarebit in the usual manner, then top with a small, neatly trimmed poached egg. *(Great Britain)*

English Rabbit (or Rarebit)
8 slices bread
1 lb. (500 gr.) Lancashire cheese
1/3 pt. (2 dl.) claret

Toast and cut away crusts, soak with claret, cover with the thinly sliced cheese, and bake until cheese is both melted and golden in colour.

Scotch Rarebit
8 bread slices
4 oz. (125 gr.) butter
1 lb. (500 gr.) Dunlop cheese

Toast, trim and butter bread. Cut cheese into 8 slices the same size as the bread, place upon the toast and cook in a fierce oven until golden.

Welsh Rarebit I
8 bread slices
1 lb. (500 gr.) Cheshire or Gloucester cheese
4 oz. (125 gr.) butter
1 tablespoonful of made mustard

Toast and trim and butter. Cut cheese into 8 slices and toast on one side. Place toasted side to the bread, spread other side with mustard, bake in fierce oven until golden.

Welsh Rarebit II
8 slices trimmed toast
4 oz. (125 gr.) butter
3/4 lb. (375 gr.) Cheddar cheese
1 gill (1 1/2 dl.) beer
1 teaspoonful mustard
1 gill (1 1/2 dl.) béchamel
2 egg yolks
1 teaspoonful Worcester sauce

Butter toast and lightly sprinkle with beer. Dice cheese, add rest of beer and sauce, melt, beat in yolks with mustard. Pour over toast and colour under the salamander.

Toasts

Anchovy Toast
Spread some toast with anchovy butter and garnish with rinsed anchovy fillets. Cut into squares, rectangles or diamonds, spread again with butter and serve warm.

Baron's Toast
For one portion take a large grilled mushroom cap and place on a round of buttered toast with the stalk side uppermost, then place a piece of grilled bacon on either side and a slice of poached beef bone marrow in the centre. Lightly sprinkle with chopped parsley.

Bloater on Toast
Carefully cut the bloater open, skin it, remove the backbone and the small bones, place it in a buttered tin, brush with butter, sprinkle with a little Cayenne pepper and place in a hot oven. Serve on a rectangular piece of toast. *(Great Britain)*

Captain's Toast
For one portion, grill a thin slice of gammon 1 1/2 in. (4 cm.) square and place it on a square of toast. Spread a slice of lobster lightly with mustard, warm with a few drops of Worcester sauce and place on top. Garnish the centre with a stoned olive wrapped in an anchovy fillet which have been warmed in a little butter.

Croque-Monsieur
For one portion, take a slice of bread about 2 1/2 by 3 1/2 in. (6 by 9 cm.) and cover

with a thin slice of Gruyère cheese then with a slice of ham of the same size. Top this with another slice of cheese and a slice of bread. Press down very carefully and fry in clarified butter until brown and crisp.
(France)

Derby Toast
Heat 1 oz. (30 gr.) of ham purée with one tablespoonful of béchamel sauce and season with a good pinch of Cayenne pepper. Heap on a round of toast in a dome shape and place a warmed half walnut in the centre. *(Great Britain)*

Diana Toast
For one portion, cut a large chicken liver into small dice, fry quickly in hot butter, leaving it a little underdone, then bind with a tablespoonful of hot Diable sauce. Spread on toast at once and place a small grilled mushroom cap in the centre.

Dutch Toast
For one portion, cook 1 oz. (30 gr.) of smoked haddock fillet in butter, mash and bind together with one tablespoonful of béchamel sauce. Heap on to a round of toast in a dome shape and top with three overlapping slices of hard boiled egg. Sprinkle lightly with Cayenne pepper.

Findon Toast
Spread a square piece of smoked haddock with mustard butter, wrap it in a rasher of streaky bacon, grill and place it on a piece of toast.

Guards Club Toast
For one portion, spread a thin square piece of gammon with mustard and grill with a little butter. Warm a tablespoonful of chopped mango chutney. Place the gammon on a square of toast, cover with the chutney and place a grilled mushroom cap in the centre. *(Great Britain)*

Ivanhoe Toast
For one portion, cook 1 oz. (30 gr.) of smoked haddock in butter, chop finely, bind together with one tablespoonful of béchamel sauce and season with a good pinch of Cayenne pepper. Heat half a pickled walnut in butter. Place the haddock on a round of toast with the walnut in the centre.

Marrow on Toast
Poach four, large thick slices of beef bone marrow in well salted water, drain thoroughly and place the slices side by side on a square of toast. Dust with Cayenne pepper and sprinkle with chopped parsley.

Montrose Snack
For one portion, mix one tablespoonful of purée of groundgame with a teaspoonful of chopped mango chutney, bringing to a spreading consistency with some mushroom ketchup and a splash of red wine, and season with a good pinch of Cayenne pepper. Spread on a round of toast to a dome shape, press half a pickled walnut in the centre, sprinkle with grated cheese and brown the top quickly in a hot oven or under a salamander.

Mushrooms on Toast
Grill a very large mushroom with bacon fat or butter, place it on a round of toast and season with salt and a good pinch of Cayenne pepper.

Sardines on Toast
For one portion, take one skinned and boned sardine, sprinkle with Cayenne pepper and heat in butter. Place on a piece of toast cut to the same shape and sprinkle with a few drops of lemon juice.

Scotch Woodcock
Cover a square of buttered toast with lightly cooked scrambled egg and arrange strips of anchovy fillet on top in a lattice pattern. Place a caper in each space and serve at once. *(Great Britain)*

Soft Roes on Toast
For one portion, roll up a large herring roe and cook under cover with a little butter. Place on a round of buttered toast and dust lightly with Cayenne pepper.

Yarmouth Toast

Place one large grilled mushroom cap on a round of toast with the stalk side uppermost. Place one rolled up herring roe, cooked under cover, in the centre, and sprinkle with paprika and chopped parsley.
(Great Britain)

Various Savouries

Angels on Horseback

Trim the 'beards' off three oysters and wrap each one in a small thin rasher of bacon. Thread all three on to one skewer, grill briskly and place on a square of toast.

Cheese Biscuits

1 lb. 6 oz. (650 gr.) flour
12 oz. (350 gr.) butter
14 oz. (400 gr.) Cheddar cheese
1/2 oz. (15 gr.) salt
1/2 oz. (15 gr.) paprika
1/8 oz. (3 gr.) white pepper

Blend the butter and the cheese (which has been grated) until smooth, but do not beat. Sieve the flour and the seasoning and add to the butter/cheese mixture. Make into a smooth paste. The biscuits are cut 1/8 in. (3 mm.) thick and baked at 400°F (204°C).

Cheese Fans

5 oz. (150 gr.) flour
4 oz. (125 gr.) butter
4 oz. (125 gr.) Parmesan cheese
3 1/2 oz. (100 gr.) dairy cream
2 egg yolks
Salt
Paprika

Grate the cheese and keep a little back. Make a dough with the rest of the ingredients, but only work it lightly. Allow to rest for 2-3 hours, pin out 1/4 in. (5 mm.) thick and cut out circles 4 1/2 in. (12 cm.) in diameter. Cut each circle into four fan shaped segments, brush with egg, sprinkle with the cheese and bake at 430° F (220° C). Serve cold. *(France)*

Cheese - Fried

Cut Camembert cheese that is not too ripe in triangles, dust with flour, coat twice with beaten egg and white breadcrumbs and deep fry until golden. Serve with toast.

Cheese Rolls

3 1/2 oz. (100 gr.) butter
4 oz. (125 gr.) egg yolks
3 1/2 oz. (100 gr.) Parmesan cheese
5 oz. (150 gr.) egg whites
5 1/2 oz. (165 gr.) flour
Salt
Paprika
Nutmeg

Filling

3 1/2 oz. (100 gr.) béchamel sauce
3 1/2 oz. (100 gr.) cheese (brie or camembert)
2 1/2 oz. (75 gr.) butter
Salt
Paprika

Cream the butter, add the egg yolks a little at a time and season with the salt, paprika and grated nutmeg. Fold in the egg whites whisked to a stiff snow, the grated cheese and the flour all at once, and spread thinly on greased, floured paper. Bake off briskly at 430° F (220° C) and leave until cold. Peel off the paper, spread with the filling, roll up, wrap in foil and refrigerate. To serve, cut into slices 3/4 in. (1.5 cm.) thick.

To make the filling, sieve the cheese, mix with the hot béchamel sauce, season with salt and paprika and blend in the butter. Stir occasionally until cold. *(Switzerland)*

Cheese Cream Savouries

Cream 8 oz. (250 gr.) of butter until very soft and light and mix with a similar amount of grated cheese (Gruyère, Cheshire or Gouda), season with Cayenne pepper and fold in 3 1/2 oz. (100 gr.) of whipped dairy cream. Cut unsweetened short pastry into small circles, squares, ovals or rectangles and use some to line small tartlet pans. Bake, leave until cold,

pipe on the cheese cream using a plain or a star tube and garnish with small pieces of tomato, roasted split almonds, pistachio nuts, cherries, etc. *(Germany)*
(Illustration page 831.)

Cheese and Potato Scones

3 lb. (1 kg. 500) reconstituted potato powder
12 oz. (375 gr.) butter or margarine
1 oz. (30 gr.) salt
12-16 oz. (375-500 gr.) (variable) flour
8 oz. (250 gr.) bakers cheese

Melt fat in warm potato and mix with remainder of ingredients using 12 oz. (375 gr.) of flour adding the balance if required. Scale at 4 oz. (125 gr.) and mould round. Pin out very thinly to 6 in. (15 cm.) diameter and cut into 4 quarters. Bake on a hot plate at moderate heat. Check heat by baking one or two first.

Cheshire Cheese Biscuits

Paste
1 lb. (500 gr.) flour
12 oz. (375 gr.) butter
13 oz. (400 gr.) grated Cheshire cheese
4 $1/2$ oz. (130 gr.) egg yolks
Salt
Cayenne pepper

Filling
$3/4$ pt. (4 dl.) béchamel
2 oz. (60 gr.) egg yolks
3 oz. (90 gr.) butter
6 oz. (180 gr.) grated Cheshire cheese
5 $1/2$ gills (8 dl.) cream
Salt
Cayenne pepper

Make the paste up in the usual way and after one hour pin to a thickness of $1/4$ in. (5 mm.). Cut out round biscuits 1 $1/2$ in. (4 cm.) diameter. Bake at 400° F (204° C). Sandwich the biscuits together with the filling cream. They may be served either hot or cold.

Devils on Horseback

Proceed as for angels on horseback, but season well with Cayenne pepper after grilling.

Eel Rolls - Paling Broodjes

A speciality made mainly by the bakers of the province of Zeeland.

4 lb. 8 oz. (2 kg. 250) flour
4 oz. (125 gr.) yeast
1 $1/2$ oz. (45 gr.) salt
3 $1/2$ oz. (100 gr.) milk powder
5 $1/2$ oz. (160 gr.) margarine
2 pt. (1 $1/8$ l.) water (approx.)
Eel

Mix these ingredients to a smooth dough in the usual way. Temperature of the dough 75° F (24° C).

After about 20 minutes the dough is divided into 2 oz. (60 gr.) pieces. Next mould up the pieces and let them rest for a while. Pin them out with rolling pin. Meanwhile take the skin from the raw eel and cut into slices, and salt them. On each piece of dough place a piece of eel, and then fold. The rolls are put on a baking sheet, brushed with egg, and, as soon as they are well risen, they are baked in an oven at 446° F (230° C).

Eel rolls are best when they are still warm. The consumer may be advised to warm them up at home before they are eaten.

Furthermore, one should advise the client to start eating the roll from the side so that the removing of the bone will be easier.
(Holland)

Oyster Fritters

For one portion, simmer four oysters in their own liquor until firm, trim off the 'beard' and season with lemon juice and a good pinch of Cayenne pepper. Coat in frying batter and deep fry in hot fat until golden. Drain well and serve garnished with fried parsley and edges of lemon.

Parmesan Fans

6 persons:
5 oz. (150 gr.) flour
4 oz. (125 gr.) butter
4 $1/4$ oz. (130 gr.) grated Parmesan cheese
2 egg yolks
$2/3$ gill (1 dl.) cream
Salt
Paprika

Keep back a little yolk and cheese. Make a paste with the rest of the materials and allow to rest for 2-3 hours. Pin out to about $1/5$ in. (5 mm.) thick and cut into rounds 5 in. (12 cm.) in diameter. Wash with egg yolk, sprinkle with grated cheese, cut into four, thus making fan shapes. Bake at 420° F (216° C).

Salmon Roll

8 oz. (250 gr.) egg yolks
$1/8$ oz. (3 gr.) salt
$1/4$ gill (3 cl.) hot water
Nutmeg
Pepper
12 oz. (375 gr.) egg whites
$1/8$ oz. (3 gr.) salt
8 oz. (250 gr.) flour

Whip the yolks and $1/8$ oz. (3 gr.) salt until light and creamy. Stir in a pinch of nutmeg, a little pepper and the hot water.

Fold in half the egg whites, that have been whipped stiffly with $1/8$ oz. (3 gr.) salt. Fold in the flour and then the remaining whites. Spread on to two baking sheets 16 in. × 16 in. (40 × 40 cm.) which have been lined with greased tissue paper. Bake at 420° F (216° C) in an oven with plenty of top heat to colour. Slip on to a cold tin immediately so that the paper 'sweats' making it easier to remove.

Spread with mashed salmon bound with fish velouté sauce. Roll up as for swiss roll. Wrap in foil and refrigerate. Cut into neat slices.

Stilton Corks

6 oz. (180 gr.) Stilton cheese
2 oz. (60 gr.) white breadcrumbs
$1/2$ oz. (15 gr.) chopped parsley
$1/2$ oz. (15 gr.) chopped chives
1 glass of port

Sieve the cheese, mix with the breadcrumbs and herbs and add just enough port to make a thick, smooth paste. Make into 8 cork shapes on a floured table, pass through beaten egg, coat with the breadcrumbs and deep fry in hot fat. Dish on a napkin with fried parsley.

British Pies and Pasties
Bacon and Egg Pie

Line $3\,1/2$ in. (9 cm.) diameter 1 in. (2.5 cm.) deep pans with short pastry. Place in 1 oz. (30 gr.) of lightly fried bacon and one shell egg. Cover with a pastry lid, cut with a fluted cutter, egg wash, make two holes in the top and bake at 400° F (204° C).

For 7 in. (18 cm.) pies, 12 oz. (375 gr.) of bacon and four eggs are required.
(Illustration page 830.)

Beef and Potato Pies

Line 3 in. (8 cm.) diameter deep pie tins. Place the meat filling *(page 817)* in the cases and cover with gravy. Bake at 430-440° F (221-226° C) and add more gravy if necessary. Cover the meat with potato filling, using a savoy bag with a coarse star pipe. Return to the oven to delicately brown the potato.
(Illustration page 830.)

Cheese and Onion Pasties

Filling

1 lb. (500 gr.) reconstituted potato powder
12 oz. (375 gr.) bakers cheese
4 oz. (125 gr.) reconstituted onion
8 oz. (250 gr.) egg
Mix well together.

Pin out short pastry $1/4$ in. (5 mm.) thick and cut with $4\,1/2$ in. (11 cm.) cutter; place 2 oz. (60 gr.) of the filling in the centre. Moisten edges and bring together to form a pointed oval shape. Pinch edges together firmly. Egg wash. Pierce twice. Bake at 440° F (227° C) for 30 minutes. This recipe produces 20 pasties.

Cheese and Onion Patties and Turnovers

$4\,1/3$ gills (6 dl.) milk
3 oz. (85 gr.) cornflour
8 oz. (250 gr.) bakers cheese
$5/6$ gill ($1/8$ l.) water
8 oz. (250 gr.) reconstituted onion

Cook cornflour and milk; mix bakers cheese and water and add to cooked cornflour. Mix in chopped onion. Line patty pans with wafer thin cheese puff paste. Add filling and place thin puff pastry on top. Egg wash and bake at 420° F (216° C).

Cheese and onion turnovers can be made on the same principle as a jam turnover, substituting the above filling instead of jam and using wafer thin pastry. Egg wash and bake at 420° F (216° C).

Cheese and Onion Pies

Line rings with short pastry and dock the inside well and place on a baking sheet. Fill with filling *(page 816)*. Bake at 400° F (204° C). They may be made in large or small sizes.

Chicken Pies

Line rings with short pastry and fill with the meat of a boiled chicken chopped small. Add white sauce, place a pastry lid on each and make a hole for a steam escape. Bake at 400° F (204° C).

Cornish Pasties

Pastry *(page 191)*
Filling *(page 817)*

The recipes given will make 15.
The meat must be lean and tender and cut into small pieces; the potatoes, turnips (or swedes) and onions are sliced thinly after peeling. The meat must be raw, and the whole is mixed together with seasoning to taste.

The pastry pieces are moulded round and pinned out to receive 3 oz. (100 gr.) of filling. The pastry edges, after damping, are joined on top, sealed neatly by giving what is known as the Cornish twist; make two small holes in the top.

The pasties are baked at 400° F (204° C) for about 35 minutes. Pasties of larger size can be made.

Forfar Bridies

Cut out circles of unsweetened short pastry, wash with water and place in the centre of each a little filling *(page 817)*. Fold over and seal the edges, egg wash and make a cut in the top of each. Bake at 420° F (216° C).

Mutton Pies

Line pie rings or pans with boiled short pastry and fill with filling *(page 817)*. Cut out lids and place on the top. Make a hole in the centre for a steam escape and bake at 460° F (237° C).

Pork Pies

Reference to *Chapter VI (pages 191-192)* will show that one of three pastries are used for making pork pies. For hand raising, probably the boiled paste is the best.

The pastry is weighed according to the size of the pie, moulded round and allowed to rest.

Take each ball of pastry, using flour to prevent sticking, and tap the edge with the side of the hand, turning the pastry continuously until it assumes the shape of a hat.

After a rest, the pieces are turned upside down and with the thumbs, each is hollowed out in turn until they are of such size that a wooden pie block of the appropriate size, readily fits inside.

The art of raising is to obtain a slightly thicker base than the sides, and to work the sides up on the block perfectly smooth with the hands, so that they are very slightly tapered. The block is then carefully removed and the pie cases left to set.

The pie cases are filled with meat *(page 818)* at the appropriate weight. It is essential that the meat, water and seasoning are thoroughly mixed. The filling is made into a ball and dropped into the case and then carefully pressed to exclude air spaces.

The lids are made from the same pastry which is rolled to a thickness of $1/8$ in. (3 mm.) and cut with a plain cutter a little larger than the diameter of the pie. To make a steam vent a hole is cut in the top of each lid. The lids are lightly washed with water and placed on top of each case in close contact with the meat, and then joined with the fingers and thumb along the inside top of the pie. The top edge is then trimmed level and decorated with marzipan nippers.

The pie is egg washed and a pattern of diamond shaped leaves is placed on the top taking care not to cover the steam escape hole. The leaves are also egg washed.

The pies are transferred to baking sheets ready for baking at a temperature depending on the size of the pie.

Here are essential details:

Veal and Ham Pie

Line rectangular pie tins with savoury pie pastry *(page 191)*. Fill halfway with filling *(page 818)* and place hard boiled eggs along the length. Complete the filling with the meat and press down gently. Place on the tops and fasten firmly by giving a decorative edge with marzipan nippers. Wash with egg and make holes for the release of steam.

Bake at 430° F (221° C). Using the holes in the top, fill with jelly and when cool add more jelly if necessary. *(Illustration page 796)*. The illustration on page *832* shows the French method: strips of ham and truffles instead of eggs.

	Weight of filling	Weight of pastry	Baking temperature	Baking time
½ lb. (250 gr.) pies	3 oz. (90 gr.)	4 oz. (125 gr.)	410° F (210° C)	50 min.
1 lb. (500 gr.) pies	7½ oz. (215 gr.)	7 oz. (200 gr.)	400° F (204° C)	60 min.
2 lb. (1 kg.) pies	16 oz. (500 gr.)	14 oz. (400 gr.)	400° F (204° C)	100 min.

The weight will be made up with jelly. It is of the utmost importance that baking temperatures and times be carefully adhered to because meat not thoroughly cooked may not be sterile and thus may be the cause of food poisoning.

About thirty minutes after baking, the pies are ready to be filled with jelly *(page 817)*. This is done carefully through the holes in the top. Some of the jelly will be absorbed by the meat, so that it will be necessary to add more jelly from time to time until the pies are full.
(Illustration page 832.)

Steak and Kidney Pies

Line either 3 in. (8 cm.) diameter 1 in. (2.5 cm.) deep round pans or 2 in. × 4 in. (5 × 10 cm.) rectangular pie dishes, with short pastry. Fill with filling *(page 818)* and add gravy *(page 817)*. Brush the edges with water and put on the lids and seal firmly. Make two holes in the top, egg wash and bake at 430-440° F (221-226° C) for about 40 minutes.
(Illustration page 830).

Canapés

Canapés are very small square, rectangular, oval or round shapes which may be bread or biscuit. The bread can be white, wholemeal or rye, and can be left plain, toasted or fried. The pieces are spread with butter or butter mixture before finishing. *(See also Modern French Culinary Art: recipes pages 168-177 and illustrations pages 174-175.)*

Elegant presentation *illustrated on page 826*.

Alsatian

Fry oval slices of white bread in butter or toast them. When cold spread with butter, cover with a thin oval slice of goose liver and place a round truffle slice in the centre. Glaze goose liver and truffle lightly by brushing with aspic.

Anchovy

Spread rectangular pieces of toast with anchovy butter. Mask the short ends with chopped parsley and the long ends with chopped hard boiled egg. Make a cross in the centre with two strips of anchovy fillet.

Bradford
Toast round slices of white bread and butter them. Crush hard boiled egg yolks with a spoonful of cream, season with salt, pepper, lemon juice and a little curry powder and spread the canapés with the mixture. Place a salted and peppered slice of tomato on top and sprinkle with tiny gherkin dice.

Celery
Take a round piece of buttered croûte biscuit, and cover it with a cooked celery heart. Cover with aspic jelly, and place a piece of tomato in the centre of the celery heart.

Egg
Spread cold pieces of rectangular toast with mayonnaise. Garnish with 3-4 overlapping slices of hardboiled egg, decorating the yolk with a slice of gherkin.

Ham
Take a round piece of croûte biscuit, and butter it very thinly. Spread with meat paste, and add a layer of ham slightly smaller than the biscuit itself. Cover with aspic jelly. Add four small square pieces of beetroot. In the centre of the beetroot pipe a spot of mashed potato and on top place a cooked pea.

Hungarian
Spread oval slices of white bread with butter to which a little paprika has been added. Cover with a mound of chopped chicken bound with mayonnaise and sprinkle with a very short fine julienne of red or green peppers.

Mushroom
Butter thickly a round piece of croûte biscuit. Take a mushroom which has been fried, preferably in a frying pan in an oven, so as to retain its shape, and from which the stalk has been removed, divide it into quarters and in the centre place a small piece of carrot, and then pipe a small amount of potato on the mushroom, sprinkling it with pistachio.

Parisian
Rub hardboiled egg yolk through a sieve, mix with highly seasoned mustard mayonnaise, and spread this cream on round canapés fried in butter. Garnish centre with a sprig of watercress.

Pâté de Foie gras
Smear a thin layer of butter on an oblong piece of croûte biscuit, piping duck's liver in butter on top. (Goose liver preferred, but more expensive.) Cover with aspic jelly. Add small pieces of carrot and lettuce.

Russian Salad
Cover a round piece of croûte biscuit with Russian salad, and add a small piece of parsley.

Salami
Lightly butter a round piece of toast. Wrap a small piece of gherkin in salami, place this on top of the toast and cover with aspic.

Salmon
Put small pieces of smoked salmon on top of small oblong pieces of brown bread (not toasted). Cover with aspic jelly, and pipe on a small star of mashed potato, adding a small piece of celery.

Sardine
Spread rectangular pieces of toast with lemon butter. Garnish edges, place a small skinned and boned sardine in the centre and dust lightly with paprika.

Shrimp
Fry round slices of bread in butter. Spread with shrimp butter and roll in chopped hardboiled egg yolks. Place 6 shrimp tails in a rose pattern on top, and decorate centre with butter using a piping bag, with a small fluted tube.

Tartare
Spread rounds of toast with dressed steak tartare. Place a small rolled anchovy fillet in the centre and fill with a few capers. Serve at once well chilled.

Tomato

Butter a round piece of croûte biscuit lightly, place a round piece of tomato on top and cover sparingly with finely grated cheese. Put a caper in the centre.

Tongue

A square piece of buttered toast. Cover it with a piece of tongue the exact size required. Cover with aspic jelly, and pipe a star of potato. Add a small piece of pickled walnut. Scatter sieved yolk of hard boiled egg round the walnut.

Sandwiches

Sandwiches are made with thin slices from a tin or sandwich loaf without crust, spread with butter and filled, and cut in half or in triangles. The bread can be white, wheatmeal or rye. They may be filled with ham, meat, poultry, cheese, pastes, purées, etc. Here is a selection.

When the sandwiches have to be made in advance they may be kept fresh for several hours by wrapping them in metal foil or in a napkin, placing a light weight on them and keeping them in the refrigerator. If this is omitted the corners will curl upwards and dry out. Sandwiches are seldom served as hors-d'oeuvre. They are served mainly for tea, small cold buffets, as snacks at cocktail parties, etc.

Brioche Sandwiches

Use $1^3/_4$ lb. to 2 lb. (875 gr.-1 kg.) brioche dough to make a large brioche (but without its top ball) and place it in a plain pan about 5 in. (13 cm.) high and 6 in. (15 cm.) in diameter. Leave to rise, brush with egg and bake in a moderate oven. When it is cold, place the brioche in the refrigerator until the next day. Cut off the top slice (about $1/_5$ in. [4 mm.]) and keep on one side. Slice the rest of the brioche thinly (about $1/_{10}$ in. [2 mm.]) and make up into sandwiches, buttering and filling each pair of slices with ham, salami, salmon or pâté de foie gras, cheese spread, etc. Place the sandwiches on top of each other and cut across with a serrated knife into eight equal portions. Replace the top slice of the brioche and serve on a round dish or, in some circumstances, wrap in cellophane paper. These brioche sandwiches are very popular at parties since people can help themselves easily, as each sandwich is quite separate. *(France)*

Sandwiches made with Bridge Rolls

Cut the bridge rolls horizontally, butter and fill as for ordinary sandwiches. For cocktail parties and other receptions, it is a good idea to make small bridge rolls (about $3/_4$ oz. [20 gr.] of dough for each roll).

Sandwiches made with French Sticks

Cut up the loaf into pieces about 4 in. (10 cm.) long, split in two, butter and fill as ordinary sandwiches.

Sandwiches made with toasted Bread

These are prepared in the same way as those made with a tin loaf except that the bread is lightly toasted. In Italy it is common to be served with toasted sandwiches. These are composed of ham and cheese between buttered slices of bread. They are then put into the toaster.

Anchovy Sandwiches - Sandwiches aux Anchois

Spread with anchovy butter, fill with well-drained anchovy fillets in oil and sprinkle chopped hardboiled egg on top. Cut in small triangles.

Sandwiches with Chester, Gruyère and other Cheese - Sandwiches au Chester, Gruyère, etc.

Spread with butter or mustard butter, spread with very thin cheese slices and cut in triangles. Soft cheeses such as camembert, brie, etc., are best passed through a sieve and mixed with $1/_3$ the weight of butter, seasoned with a pinch of Cayenne pepper and spread on the bread.

Club Sandwiches

On the same principle, it is possible to make multiple sandwiches which are composed of layers of bread and different fillings. For instance, the top of a ham sandwich may be spread with mayonnaise and sprinkled with chopped hard-boiled egg; another slice of bread is put on top and this in turn is buttered and covered with mustard, diced base of globe artichoke and thinly cut roast beef; finally a further slice of bread and butter with a little mustard is put on top. The whole is pressed together and, after the crusts have been trimmed off, the sandwich is cut up into triangles. These are served individually in paper serviettes. If free rein is given to the imagination, there are endless possibilities for the composition of multiple sandwiches.

Crayfish Sandwiches - Sandwiches aux Ecrevisses

Butter the bread, fill with chopped crayfish tails and cut in triangles.

Cucumber Sandwiches - Sandwiches aux Concombres

Spread with herb butter and cover with very thin slices of cucumber, without seeds and cut in rectangles.

Egg Sandwiches - Sandwiches aux Œufs durs

Spread with mustard and cress butter, fill with thin slices of hardboiled egg and cut in squares.

Ham Sandwiches - Sandwiches au Jambon

Spread with mustard butter, fill with very thin slices of ham and cut across the middle once to make a sandwich of 1¹/₂-3 in. (4-8 cm.).

Lettuce Sandwiches - Sandwiches à la Laitue

Spread bread with mustard butter, fill with finely shredded, slightly salted lettuce and cut once diagonally.

Pickled Tongue Sandwiches - Sandwiches de Langue écarlate

Spread with cress butter, fill with thin slices of very red tongue and cut in rectangles.

Poultry Sandwiches - Sandwiches de Volaille

Spread with mustard or horseradish butter, cover with thinly sliced or chopped poultry meat and cut in rectangles.

Radish Sandwiches - Sandwiches aux Radis

Spread with butter, fill with thinly sliced radishes and salt lightly. Cut in rectangles.

Sausage Sandwiches - Sandwiches de Salami ou Mortadelle

Spread with herb butter, fill with thin slices of any sausage and cut in triangles.

Smoked Salmon Sandwiches - Sandwiches au Saumon fumé

Spread with unsalted butter or with horseradish butter, fill with very thin slices of smoked salmon, and cut in triangles.

Tomato Sandwiches - Sandwiches à la Tomate

Spread with horseradish butter, fill with thin slices of skinned tomatoes from which seeds and liquid have been removed and cut in triangles.

Tunny Sandwiches - Sandwiches au Thon

Spread with butter, fill thinly with tunny preserved in oil crushed finely with a fork; cut in rectangles.

Veal Sandwiches - Sandwiches de Veau

Spread with horseradish or plain butter, fill with thin slices of cold roast veal and cut in rectangles.

Open Sandwiches

Open sandwiches are becoming increasingly popular. They are attractive and nutritious. The instructions for making are simple and need only care, together with good taste in the arrrangement of the toppings and in presentation.

Here is a selection of open sandwiches from Denmark where, in common with other Scandinavian countries, they are known as smorrebrod.

Bread is used as the base and it can be white, brown, or rye. It is cut into slices about $1/2$ in. (1 cm.) thick and about 2×4 in. (5×10 cm.) in size. The slices are spread with butter, on which the toppings and the garnish are arranged. A cake slice or one similar is used for serving. They are eaten with a knife and fork.

GARNISHES

They are chosen for colour and flavour. Gherkins, onions, lemon, egg radishes, cucumber, tomato, orange, beetroot and aspic jelly are examples.

Twists

Beetroot, cucumber, tomato and lemon and orange slices can be used for added decorative affect by twisting. This is done by slitting through the centre but leaving a hinge at the top and then twisting in opposite directions.

Roses

Choose small radishes and leave a small leaf on each. Trim off the root and cut in petal formation from the base to the stalk. They will open if left in cold water.

Fans

Cut a gherkin in slices for three quarters of its length, leaving a hinge at the top. The slices can be pressed apart in the form of a fan.

Anchovy

Arrange anchovy fillets on a new potato salad. Decorate with sliced tomato.

Bacon I

Use crisp-fried back rashers with sliced mushrooms. Decorate with tomato and cucumber twists.

Bacon II

Arrange grilled collar, potato salad and pickles on the base. Decorate with a tomato twist and chopped parsley.

Bacon III

Take middle gammon slices and arrange with scrambled egg, tomato and cucumber twists. Decorate with finely chopped chives.

Bacon IV

Arrange crisp-fried streaky bacon with slices of hard boiled egg, tomato and cucumber twists and a little mustard and cress.

Chicken I

On a bed of lettuce, arrange slices of cold roast chicken. Add tomato and cucumber slices and small bacon rolls.

Chicken II

On a bed of lettuce, place chopped chicken in mayonnaise. Add tomato slices and a gherkin fan.

Chicken III

Arrange slices of chicken and tongue on the base with Russian salad, cress, tomato and radish.

Danbo Cheese

Thin slices of Danbo cheese with caraway seeds on lettuce. Decorate with a gherkin fan.

Danish Blue Cheese

Thin slices of Danish Blue on a bed of lettuce. Place in the centre three halves of black grapes that have been de-seeded. They are placed cut side down.

Esrom Cheese

Thin slices of Esrom cheese with chopped celery and tomato.

Fynbo Cheese
Thin slices of Fynbo cheese on a bed of lettuce with cress and tomato twists.

Ham
Arrange slices of ham on a bed of lettuce. Add vegetable salad, mushrooms and a cucumber twist.

Liver Paté
On a slice of liver pâté, arrange butter-fried mushrooms, bacon, a tomato twist and a gherkin fan.

Luncheon Meat
On slices of luncheon meat, place some horseradish cream, a little lettuce, two prunes and an orange twist.

Maribo Cheese
On thin slices of Maribo cheese, arrange a radish rose.

Pork and Ham
On slices of chopped pork and ham, place Russian salad, lettuce and a tomato twist.

Pork and Tongue
On slices of chopped pork and tongue, arrange vegetable salad, watercress and a radish rose.

Salami
Arrange thin slices of salami on the base and decorate with onion rings and parsley.

Cocktail Sausage
Slice cocktail sausage and mix with potato salad. Place this on the base, add crisp-fried bacon and garnish with tomato.

Frankfurter Sausage
Split the sausages lengthways and arrange with lettuce, tomato and spring onion salad.

XXV. Glossary

Technical terms used in different countries can be confusing. The same word, in different languages, may have totally or partially different meanings. In each country too, there may be confusion due to the regional use of words, or even the use of different words to describe the same things. Sometimes the same word has a subtly different meaning according to the context in which it is used.

For these many reasons mainly British bakery terms are used in this volume.

Absorb
To suck in; to take in by chemical or molecular action.

Adsorb
To hold by surface tension.

Aeration
The rendering of bakery products more appetizing, palatable and digestible by the incorporation of air and/or gas, in one or more of the stages of production before baking. Air is introduced during mixing, beating or whisking. Gas is introduced by the production of carbon dioxide gas (CO_2) from yeast or baking powder. The internal expansion of air and gas and the pressure of steam during baking, all make a contribution to total aeration.

Albumen
One of the many proteins. When the term is used in the bakery, it is generally accepted to mean the whites of eggs.

All-in process
All the ingredients are mixed together without any preliminary stages.

Almond paste
Almond paste is a mixture composed of approximately two thirds sugar and one third ground almonds together with sufficient egg to make a plastic paste. It is flavoured with orange flower water.

Angelica
The young leaf-stalks of a plant of the family Umbelliferae found in Northern Germany, Austria, Switzerland and Scandinavia. The stalks are candied and used for decoration. The essential oil derived from the roots is used to flavour liqueurs such as Chartreuse and Benedictine.

Anisette
A fine liqueur made with aniseed and other complementary flavouring ingredients.

Annonae
The fruits of certain species of Annona, which are tropical trees. The fruits vary

in size; the smallest are the size of apples, while the largest may be as big as a coconut. One variety, the custard apple, in rather like a greenish, giant strawberry in appearance and has a rough, scaly surface. The pulp has a sweet, creamy flavour; it is very soft and can only be used fresh.

Apricot purée

Apricot pulp and an equal quantity of sugar that is boiled together to a degree that it will set as a glaze on cooling. Alternatively, well boiled sieved apricot jam can be used.

Arrack

A fine spirit made in India, Java, Ceylon, Thailand and neighbouring regions. It is produced from fermented rice, molasses or sweet-sapped plants.

Bag

(a) 140 lb. (63 $^1/_2$ kg.) of flour. Two bags make a sack (280 lb. [127 kg.]).

(b) A paper or nylon bag for icing and piping. A paper bag is fashioned from a triangular piece of paper.

Bain-marie

(a) An apparatus in the form of a water bath which can be kept at a controlled temperature so that fondant, chocolate, etc., can remain melted and at an even temperature.

(b) A double saucepan in which the lower part contains water. The upper part contains the material to be heated; in this way the material is kept from direct contact with the source of heat.

Bake blind

A term used to describe the making of unfilled flan and tartlet bases. The flan ring or tartlet pan is lined with pastry—usually sweet or short pastry. The centre is then filled with dried peas, rice, cherry stones, etc., which after baking are removed, leaving the flans or tartlets ready for filling.

Bake off

A term used by bakers to describe the operation of baking cakes after they have been prepared for the oven.

Baking

To render bakery products suitable for human consumption and digestion by cooking in an oven at correctly controlled temperatures.

Baking powder

Any chemical, or mixture of chemicals which, when moistened and heated, generates gas (usually CO_2) which will aerate bread and cakes. Ideally the residual salts of reaction should be tasteless and without odour. The baking powder must comply with the Food and Drugs Acts of the country in which it is used.

Baking sheet

A metal plate on which buns, cakes, pastries and biscuits are baked. Generally they have three up-turned sides and an open end. The open end will facilitate cleaning.

Basin

A round earthenware or plastic container used for making small quantities of icing etc.

Batch

The entire mixing of bread or cakes. The contents of the oven.

Batter

A soft, completed cake mixture. A very soft fermented mixture as for crumpets.

Baumé, Antoine

French chemist (1728-1804). Inventor of the hydrometer (saccharometer). The degrees on the scale are called '° B' after him.

Bay

A well, made in a heap of flour and other dry materials to receive the liquid ingredients preparatory to mixing.

Beat

The aeration of fat, sugar, eggs and other materials by beating together. This can be done by hand or by machine.

Beater

A hand shaped implement which, when fixed to a machine, beats ingredients such as fat, sugar and eggs.

Beeswax

The rendered product of combs built by bees for the storage of honey.

If clean baking sheets are warmed and rubbed with beeswax, they are suitable for baking certain confectionery products such as langues-de-chat biscuits.

Biscuits

Thin cakes that are dry, crisp and flat. They are soft or hard according to the amount of fat and other enriching agents contained therein. They are small and of varying shapes. Some may be unsweetened.

Black Jack

A common name given to a thick solution of dark caramelized sugar. It is used for colouring richly fruited cake mixtures.

Blanch

To treat food with boiling water:—to remove the skins of nuts and fruit by plunging them first into boiling water and then into cold; to scald fruit for preserving or freezing; to scald vegetables in order to remove excessive flavour or smell.

Bloom

The healthy sparkle on the crust of unglazed fermented goods, the result of the use of good quality materials, correct fermentation and baking. Good bloom on cakes is the result of using good quality materials, a balanced formula and correct baking conditions. Bloom should not be confused with the glaze imparted by egg washing.

Bloom on chocolate is the greying of the surface with a consequent loss of gloss. There are two causes.

(a) Fat bloom. This is the result of incorrect tempering, when some of the fat fractions, not being fixed, float to the surface of the chocolate and are seen as a grey film.

(b) Sugar bloom. This is caused by dampness or condensation which dissolves the surface sugar causing re-crystallization in larger form as it dries.

Blue

To add blue colouring to white icing so that it appears even whiter.

Bowl

A rounded metal container used in the bakery for mixing, beating or whipping by hand. A bowl specially made for a machine is known as a machine bowl.

Brake

A machine that consists of two metal rollers, either hand or mechanically operated, for rolling pastry or for biscuit doughs.

Brioche

A fancy sweet bread or yeast cake. Both large and small types are made, but they are always shaped with a "head". In France small brioches are used as breakfast rolls.

Buckwheat

A cereal grown in parts of the European and American Continents. It is ground to a flour which contains about 15 % protein, 6.4 % carbohydrates, 13 % water together with fat, mineral matter and fibre.

Bun

A small yeast fermented or chemically aerated, sweetened cake.

Bun wash

A sweetened liquid brushed on yeasted buns immediately on removal from the oven so as to give a shiny glazed appearance. The wash can be made from:

(a) Sugar solutions; (b) egg, sugar, milk mixtures; (c) either (a) or (b) with the addition of gelatine.

Cake

Refers generally to a baked mixture of fat, sugar, eggs and flour, with or without milk, baking powder, fruit, etc. A cake can be of any shape or size.

Cake hoop

A metal ring which supports a cake during baking.

Cake tins

Small or large metal shapes in which cakes are baked. They may be plain or fluted.

Candied

Preserved by immersion in a super-saturated sugar solution. The subsequent drying results in a covering of thick sugar crystals. Orange, lemon, angelica and citron caps are candied.

Caramel

(a) Sugar heated above its melting point so that it takes on a pale amber colour.

(b) A sugar solution boiled to over 312° F (155.5° C) when dehydration begins to occur causing the solution to take on a brown colour.

Caramel colour

See black-jack.

Caramel fruits

Orange segments, stuffed dates, grapes, etc., dipped into a sugar solution boiled to 280° F (138° C).

Caramelize

A term used to describe the change in sugar on a cake during baking.

It is the caramelization of sugar in the crust that is mainly responsible for crust colour. Sugar sprinkled on the top of a cake before baking is partially caramelized.

Caramels

Toffees composed of sugar, butter, cream, etc., and boiled to a degree, that, when cold and cut into pieces, they are of a semi-solid consistency.

Carbonate of ammonia

Better known to the baker as 'Vol'. The commercial product is a mixture of ammonium bicarbonate and ammonium carbamate. It completely volatilizes when moistened and heated, into ammonia gas, CO_2 and water. It is used in choux paste and biscuits.

Carbon dioxide (CO_2)

A heavy colourless gas produced as a result of the fermentation of sugar by yeast. This gas is also evolved from a carbonate or a bicarbonate alone or in the presence of an acid, when moistened and heated. It is used also for aerating commercial mineral waters. Solid CO_2 is used as a refrigerant known as dry-ice because it changes directly from the solid to the gaseous state.

Carbonize

To burn.

Centigrade

Divided into 100 degrees, as the centigrade thermometer (first constructed by Celsius, 1701-44), in which the freezing point is zero and boiling point is 100°.

Centrepiece

An ornament made with praline croquant, caramel sugar, chocolate, macaroon paste or similar substances, and used to decorate a festive table or gâteaux, sweets, etc. It may consist of several sections. A drawing must first be made and a cardboard stencil prepared so that the sections may be produced accurately. Particular care should be taken to ensure purity of style.

Centres

A term used to describe moulded fondants, jellies, cut-out almond paste, caramels, etc., ready for dipping into couverture or boiled sugar.

Chaffing
The careful final moulding of buns, scones, etc., to procure a perfectly smooth skin.

Charlotte
A word derived from the old English, charlyt, meaning a dish of custard.

1. A hot sweet made with stewed fruit and strips of white bread, and baked in a round mould or tin.

2. A delicate cold sweet consisting of a cream mixture in a casing of sponge fingers, decorated with whipped dairy cream.

Checking
The appearance of fine cracks on the surface of biscuits after baking.

Cheese curd
A curd produced by adding rennet to warm milk, or by souring. When set, the whey is drained from the curd. Curd is used in the making of maids of honour tartlets and Yorkshire curd tarts.

Cherry Brandy
A fine liqueur made with cherry juice, kirsch, alcohol, sugar and water.

Chinois
A fine meshed conical shaped sieve.

Chlorination
The chemical treatment of a substance with chlorine. If used in excess on flour it will denature the gluten and break down its coherency. The flour, if finely milled, will take a high ratio of sugar, milk and eggs to the weight of flour. Chlorination also increases the acidity which assists in the gelatinization of starch during baking. The flour is known as special cake flour.

Chocolate
A term used to describe both couverture and bakers' chocolate. Bakers' chocolate is made specially for use on cakes because it cuts without splintering and needs no tempering. It may be either plain or milk. *(See* Couverture.*)*

Chocolate vermicelli
Polished granules of chocolate used for the decoration of gâteaux, torten, fancies, ices, etc.

Clarify
The removal of all extraneous material from a liquid syrup or jelly so to attain a pure transparency or translucency.

Coagulate
The partial or complete solidification of a protein in suspension by heat. A weak acid will also cause coagulation.

Coat
To cover a cake with almond paste and/or icing, fondant, cream or chocolate.

Cocoa butter
Fat obtained by pressing cocoa nibs at a temperature of 160-195° F (70-90° C) and then filtering. No chemicals or fat solvents may be used

Cognac
Brandy based exclusively on the wines made in the Charente region.

Colourings
To colour creams, ice cream, fondant, sweets, marzipan or sugar products, only permitted food colours may be used. They are covered by the food regulations which have been laid down in almost every country and about which it is necessary to be informed.

Comb scraper
A plastic scraper with a serrated edge which makes a pattern on the surface of royal icing or chocolate.

Compound fat
A white fat, bland in flavour, made from hydrogenated oils. It is approximately 100 % fat.

Cones

Coarsely ground rice or maize, used to prevent a dough from sticking during manipulation and proving.

Constituent

A component part of the whole; one ingredient in a formula.

Coupe

An ice cream confection containing fruit and other ingredients, and served in individual goblet-shaped containers.

Couverture

A chocolate which can be either plain or milk, which has to be correctly tempered before use so to produce a fine gloss on finished chocolate goods.

Cream

(a) To beat fat and sugar or fat and flour together until light and fluffy.

(b) To add cream as a decoration or filling to a baked cake.

(c) A generic term once used to describe all kinds of creams such as dairy cream, buttercream, marshmallow cream, custard cream, etc. In Great Britain, the term must only be used to describe dairy cream.

Cream of tartar

(Potassium Hydrogen Tartrate).

One of the best acid components of baking powder. It is sparingly soluble in cold water, but readily soluble in hot water. It is used with bicarbonate of soda in the proportion of 22.4 parts of cream of tartar to 10 parts of bicarbonate of soda.

Cream powders

The name used by commercial firms to describe various acids or mixtures of acids suitable for use in baking powders. They are diluted with an inert substance such as starch, so that they can be used in the proportion of two parts cream powder and one part bicarbonate of soda.

Crimping

Giving a decorative edge to shortbreads, marzipan, almond and sugar pastes by pinching between the thumb and index finger. An alternative term is 'pinching'.

Croquant

Sugar with the addition of a little lemon juice melted to a light amber colour to which lightly roasted nibbed or flaked almonds or hazelnuts are added. Croquant can be rolled out, cut into shapes and built up into ornamental figures. If put through rollers, praline paste is formed. It is sometimes known as nougat.

Crystallization

The formation of crystals. Small fruits, pineapple, ginger and fondants are crystallized by immersion in supersaturated sugar solutions after which they are dried; fine crystals then form on the surface.

Cup cakes

Small cakes baked in crimped paper cups or cases.

Curaçao

A fruit flavoured liqueur which derives its flavour from the zest of the bitter orange used in its production. There are three varieties: sec — fairly sweet, — double sec — dry —, and triple sec — very dry.

Curd

A name given in Britain to a cooked mixture of orange or lemon juice, eggs, sugar and butter. The correct name should be orange or lemon custard.

Curdle

When fat, sugar and eggs are beaten together carefully, an emulsion is formed. If during the beating, the eggs are added too quickly, or are too cold, or the initial creaming of the fat and sugar is not complete, then the mixture will separate and lose its smooth consistency. Some aeration is lost when a mixture curdles.

Cut-out
To cut units from the mass with a knife or a cutter. Almond paste, sugar paste or chocolate cut into shapes for assembly into a pattern or design on cakes, torten or gâteaux.

Cutters
Implements, either plain or fluted, used to cut out biscuits and pastries in various shapes and sizes.

Decorate
(a) To add fruits, nuts, sugar, etc., to cakes before baking for the purpose of decorating. This is known as being 'oven decorated'.

(b) To add such decorating materials as the above; almond paste, chocolate, cream or icings after baking, generally to make a pattern or a design. The word is given special significance in describing artistic work in royal icing.

Deep freeze
A refrigerator designed to take the temperature of certain baked goods rapidly below freezing point, where staling is inhibited. Defrosting restores the goods to their original state.

Deposit
The act of putting cake batter into hoops, pans, tins, etc., either by hand or by machine. The machine used is known as a depositor.

Develop
To thoroughly mix a dough to increase its elasticity by the complete hydration and the development of the gluten.

Divider
A machine that will divide accurately a piece of dough or pastry into a number of smaller pieces. The number of pieces depends on the make of the machine. Generally it is 30 or 36.

Docker
An implement containing spikes which is used to mark certain bakery goods before baking. The spikes decorate and also provide small holes for the escape of steam.

Dough
A term used to describe a yeast fermented mixture. It describes also the basic mixture for puff pastry before rolling and folding is commenced.

D'Oyley
A fancy lace mat made either of fabric, plastic or paper, used in the presentation of foodstuffs.

Dragees
Small silver or gold coloured sweets used in the decoration of cakes.

Draw
To remove bread or cakes from the oven.

Dredger
A small container with a perforated lid used to sprinkle sugar, flour, etc.

Drummed hoop
A cake hoop across the bottom of which is stretched a sheet of strong greaseproof paper. The paper is kept in position by twisting the edges over the wired rim of the hoop. The hoop is drummed to prevent the bottom edge of a rich cake from becoming overbaked. It is also done to prevent soft semi-liquid batters from flowing beneath the hoops during baking.

Durian
The fruit of Durio zibethinus, an Indian tree. The fruit is almost as large as a melon and, when fresh, its pulp has a delicious sweet taste reminiscent of pineapple and peaches. After a few hours, however, it develops a repulsive smell; for this reason the fruit is picked before it is fully ripe.

Dust

(a) To sprinkle flour on the table top to prevent dough or pastry from sticking.

(b) To sprinkle sugar over a cake or pastry, an operation known as dusting.

Egg wash

To wash dough and pastry pieces with beaten egg (generally diluted with water) to produce a glazed surface when baked.

Elasticity

The effect of manipulation on a dough. The extent will depend on the quality and the complete hydration of the gluten.

Emulsion

An intimate mixture of two fluids that normally would not mix, such as oil and water. This is done by means of an emulsifier, a machine that will break down the oil and water to minute particles while under pressure. If an emulsifying agent is used then the emulsion may become permanent. Fat, sugar and eggs correctly beaten together form an emulsion, the lecithin in egg yolks being a good emulsifying agent.

Enrichment

The addition of enriching agents such as fat, sugar, eggs, etc., to doughs and pastries.

Enrobe

The mechanical coating of cakes, pastries, biscuits and ices.

Enrober

A machine that sprays chocolate or fondant of correct viscosity and temperature over goods passing through on a wire belt. Surplus chocolate or fondant is drained back to a holder tank so that the enrobing is continuous.

Essences

Aromatic compounds used for flavouring confectionery. They can be natural or synthetic or blends of both.

Fahrenheit scale

A thermometric scale showing freezing point at 32° and boiling point at 212°.

Fancies

Small decorated cakes of any kind.

Fancy

That which is enriched, shaped, baked and/or given extra decoration so that it is above the ordinary.

Ferment

A soft liquid mixture of water, yeast, yeast food and flour brought to a controlled temperature and allowed to ferment before being made into a dough. Ferments are used as the preliminary stage for rich fermented doughs.

Fermentation

Panary fermentation is brought about by the action of yeast on sugars in solution which produces CO_2, alcohol and other by-products. The CO_2 causes the dough to expand; the alcohol and by-products play a part in the resultant flavour.

Final proof

The last stage in the production of yeasted goods before they are baked. It is the time between final shaping and full expansion.

Fingers

Small finger shaped rolls, biscuits, meringues, sponge cakes, fancies etc.

Flaked

Cut very thinly into slices, i.e. flaked almonds.

Flambé réchaud

A chafing-dish. A small charcoal or spirit heated stove.

Flan

An open pastry case that is baked in a flan hoop, into which fruit is arranged. It is then glazed with a pectin or starch jelly.

Flash
To place a cake decorated with meringue or almond paste into a very hot oven, which confers a delicate golden additional colour. Petits fours, such as rout biscuits etc., are also flashed.

Fondant
A form of icing made by boiling sugar, water, glucose or a weak acid to 240° F (115° C), then agitating when it is cool until it forms a mass of minute crystals. It is the reflection of light on the tiny crystals that explains the gloss on correctly prepared fondant.

Full proof
The point of maximum expansion in a dough before collapse.

Ganache
A paste made by mixing boiling dairy cream with melted couverture, suitably flavoured.

Garnish
To embellish so as to add interest to a dish before presentation, i.e. decorate savoury goods with parsley.

Gâteau
A decorated cake that can be cut into individual portions. The term refers to a light, unfruited cake that has been sandwiched with jam and/or cream and coated with cream, fondant, water icing or chocolate.

Gelatine
A transparent, colourless, tasteless substance derived from lean calves' heads, calves' feet and beef bones. These are boiled, then the clarified broth is poured on to sheets of glass, cut into slabs and sheets, placed on nets and either air-dried or subjected to artificial heat. Gelatine is sold in powdered or sheet form. It is used in the production of creams and custards, jellies, moulds, etc.

Gelatinization
The heating of starch in water so that the cells burst. On cooling, a gel is formed.

Genoese
A generic term used for describing sheets of good quality plain cake that are cut into small shapes for making genoese, fancies and petits fours. Genoese can be cut into larger pieces for gâteaux or into strips for Battenburg, layer cakes, etc. Genoese can be made in various colours and flavours.

Glaze
(a) To give a glossy surface to tea-breads and pastries by washing with egg before baking.

(b) To give a dry, glossy finish to buns by washing with a sugar solution immediately on removal from the oven.

(c) To brush with highly boiled apricot purée.

(d) To finish fruit flans by adding a pectin or a starch-jelly.

(e) To brush rout biscuits with a hot gum arabic solution immediately on removal from the oven.

Gloss
(a) The shiny surfaces of correctly tempered chocolate, visible on chocolates and moulded chocolate figures.

(b) The fine reflective surface on correctly prepared fondant.

Glucose
A thick, viscous, colourless syrup used in boiling sugar, to prevent premature graining.

Gluten
Insoluble wheat protein after hydration. It is an elastic substance that assists in trapping CO_2 in a dough. On ripening, the gluten becomes extensible so that expansion can take place without a loss of gas. During baking the gluten coagulates and forms, with other proteins, the structure of the bread or cake.

Glycerine
A colourless, odourless syrup with a sweet taste. It is soluble in water and alcohol. Because it is highly hygroscopic it is used in cake mixings to delay staling.

Golden wedding cake
A cake of the same quality as a wedding cake made to celebrate the 50th anniversary of a wedding. It is usual to use gold leaves in the decoration.

Graining
The operation of re-crystallizing a supersaturated sugar solution by agitation.

Grease
To brush fat into cake tins or to smear fat over baking sheets.

Greasing boiled sugar
This is a term used by sugar boilers to describe the prevention of premature graining. Glucose or a little weak acid is used in the boiling syrup for this purpose.

Gum arabic
A dried gum derived from African, Indian and Australian species of acacia. It is sold in the form of round or oblong grains or lumps of various shades from colourless to a less transparent reddish-brown. It is water-soluble. In confectionery it is used to glaze marzipan, macaroons and some other goods, and also to glaze burnt almonds.

Gum paste
A paste made from icing sugar, starch and soaked gum tragacanth. It is used for modelling ornaments for wedding cakes. During use it must be kept covered with a damp cloth because it dries rapidly.

Hair sieve
A sieve made of horsehair, which is used for sieving red fruits as these would lose their bright colour if rubbed through a wire sieve.

Handing-up
The shaping into balls of yeasted dough pieces and scones after weighing, in preparation for final shaping.

High-ratio cakes
The name 'Hi-ratio' is registered in the U.S.A. The term is used to describe cakes containing high percentages of sugar and liquids based on the weight of flour. Special flour and superglycerinated fats are used for this type of cake.

Hotplate
A heated flat, metal plate on which muffins, crumpets, pikelets and pancakes are baked. The heating may be by electricity, gas or by steam tubes.

Hydrometer
An instrument for determining the approximate specific gravity of a liquid at a certain temperature. A similar instrument is the saccharometer used in sugar solutions. Baumé and Brix saccharometers are commonly used.

Hygroscopic
The power of attracting moisture, i.e. glycerine is hygroscopic.

Ice cream powder
A thickening agent for ice cream. It contains gelatine, gum tragacanth, pectin or similar substances with jellying properties.

Icing
The coating and decoration of a cake with royal icing. The term is sometimes used to describe the decoration of cakes with fondant and water icing.

Icing sugar
Finely powdered sugar that has been sieved through a fine mesh. The finest is used in the making of royal icing.

Jaggery
A brown sugar made from the sap of various palms in tropical regions. The

highest yield is obtained from Arenga sacchifera, a palm found in Africa, Indonesia and India. It produces about 22 gal. (100 l.) sap, yielding 2 1/4 gal. (10 l.) syrup.

Jelly

There are many types of jelly used in confectionery.

(a) Aspic. This is made from vegetable flavoured clarified stock usually fortified with gelatine.

(b) Cold-set. This is a clear solution of pectin and sugar in water which, when mixed with a small amount of citric or tartaric acid in solution, sets very quickly.

(c) Piping jelly. A sweetened, coloured and flavoured jelly of such consistency that it can be piped on to fancies and gâteaux.

(d) Starch jelly. This consists of gelatinized starch with added sugar. The starch can be gelatinized with boiling water or fruit juice.

(e) Sweet jelly. A clear translucent jelly made with gelatine, flavoured with fruit juice and suitably coloured and sweetened. It can be whipped to a foam while still liquid if taken before setting point.

Jellying agents

Substances, such as agar-agar, gelatine, gum tragacanth or pectin, of animal or plant origin, which cause a liquid to set.

Jigger

A tool containing a serrated brass wheel for cutting strips of pastry at the same time decorating the edges.

Kirsch

A fine liqueur distilled from fermented cherry mash. No other ingredients may be added. The minimum alcohol content is 38 vol. %, but a good kirsch may reach a level of over 50 vol. %. Kirsch is used in creams, gâteaux and torten, petits fours, fruit salad, ice cream and many other products.

Knock-back

A term now used instead of 'cut-back'. The operation of de-gassing a fermented dough either by hand or machine. If by hand, the dough is punched down, folded and stretched. Large doughs are returned to the mixing machine where in a very short time the operation is completed. Knocking-back takes place about two thirds or three quarters through the bulk fermentation time.

Krapfen

A very soft, well developed yeasted dough used for doughnuts. (Chapter VIII page 303. Viennese Fritters-Wiener Krapfen.)

Lamination

The formation of numerous alternate layers of dough and butter as in the making of puff pastry. This is done by rolling and folding.

Lecithin

A phosphorized fatty substance which has a great power as an emulsion stabilizer. Egg yolks and soya beans are both rich in lecithin.

Liqueurs

Spirits sweetened with sugar and flavoured with essences, fruit juice, distillates or essential oils. The alcohol content must be at least 30 vol. %. Very fine liqueurs used to flavour buttercream, sweets, ice cream, etc. include Cointreau, Benedictine, curaçao, Chartreuse, Grand-Marnier, Cherry Heering and Apricot brandy.

Macerate

To pickle briefly; to steep; to souse. The term is generally applied to fruit, usually diced, sprinkled with sugar and liqueur in order to improve the flavour.

Maidenhair fern

A dried and pressed fern used in the decoration of cakes, particularly in conjunction with marzipan roses or piped flowers.

Manipulation

A term used to describe the use of the hands or machine in moulding, folding, rolling, shaping and plaiting.

Maraschino

A delicate liqueur made from a type of sour black cherry grown in Dalmatia. It is colourless and usually sold in bottles surrounded with bast fibre. Maraschino is used to flavour buttercream, fruit salad and a large variety of sweets.

Marble icing

A decorative effect given when lines of icing are piped in various colours on to an iced surface. Before the surface icing has set a point is drawn quickly in various directions, so producing a marble effect.

Marmalade

A preserve made of oranges, lemons or grape fruit, containing the finely shredded rinds of the fruits. The term refers to no other type of preserve in Great Britain.

Marzipan

A paste consisting of approximately two thirds freshly blanched almonds and one third sugar, which has been ground finely through rollers and then cooked.

Masking

To cover a cake or suchlike base with apricot purée, buttercream, etc. To cover a prepared base or part of the base with chocolate vermicelli, chocolate shavings, roasted nuts, etc.

Maw seeds

Seeds from a species of poppy used to sprinkle on tea breads and rolls. They can be bought as either 'blue' or 'white'.

Mincemeat

Originally finely chopped meats preserved with sugar, spices and fruits. It is now a confection composed of about equal parts currants, peel, sultanas, raisins, suet, sugar, and apples to which are added spices, lemon juice and brandy or rum. It is used for making mince pies and tarts.

Mould

(a) The operation of shaping dough either by hand or by machine.

(b) A hollow form, which may be of metal, wood, plaster or plastic into which marzipan, almond paste, sugar paste and biscuit dough can be cast.

(c) To shape chocolate by the use of moulds.

(d) Minute micro-organisms of the fungi family of plants, that grow in suitable conditions.

Musty

A taint developing in flour and eggs when stored in unsuitable conditions. The taint can be strongly evident after bakery products in which they are used are baked.

Nibs

Small cube shaped fragments such as almond nibs. Sugar nibs are small accumulations of crystals which are of irregular shape.

Nougat

(a) A confection made from a boiled solution of sugar and honey which is poured over whipped egg whites. Nuts, angelica and fruits are added. The best known is nougat Montélimar.

(b) A name given to a mixture of melted sugar and flaked or nibbed almonds ground to a paste and mixed with chocolate (Great Britain and Germany),

(c) Nougat de Paris: a name given in France and in Switzerland to a mixture of sugar and almonds which in this country is known as praline-croquant.

Orange flower water

A distillate obtained from the flower of the orange tree, having a delicate aroma and flavour. It is used in almond paste.

Palette knife
A thin, flat, knife with a rounded end used for spreading icing and cake batter. A trowel palette knife has the blade at a lower level than the handle. It is used for spreading cake mixtures on to baking sheets.

Palm wine
The fermented sap of various tropical palms. The inflorescences are cut off to obtain the sap, which is fermented to make a wine with a low alcohol content.

Pan
A broad, shallow baking tin.

Panary
From the latin *panare* meaning bread. The fermentation of a yeasted dough is termed panary fermentation.

Pastillage
Paste made from icing sugar and gelatine mucilage. It is similar to gum paste but is less hard and brittle when set.

Pastries
Used generally to describe all products made by the pastrycook and confectioner. In particular the term refers to products made from puff pastry.

Pasty
A small savoury containing meat and vegetables.

Patty
A small pie baked in a shallow pan known as a patty pan.

Pectin
A gum like substance found in most fruits and vegetables. Some fruits and vegetables are rich in pectin, particularly the apple. Pectin can be bought in liquid or powder form. It is used in cold-set jelly, and in jams containing fruits deficient in natural pectin.

Peel
(a) A flat wooden blade fixed to a long pole, used for setting and drawing bread and cakes from the oven. A thin metal blade is sometimes used.

(b) The halved, candied rinds of oranges, lemons and citrons known as caps which are usually cut into small pieces for use in the bakery.

Persipan
A paste used as a substitute for marzipan or almond paste. It is made by warming moist ground apricot or peach kernels with sugar after removing their bitter taste. The moisture content may not exceed 20 %. To use Persipan, work one part raw Persipan with up to one and a half parts sugar. German legislation requires clear labelling of all Persipan products.

Petits fours
The term used to describe very small fancy cakes, so small that they can be placed in the mouth in one piece. They can be divided under two headings.

(a) Petits fours secs, which are small cakes dried, baked in the oven and then glazed, such as English and Parisian rout biscuits.

(b) Petits fours glacés. Very small cakes that are finished with icing.

Pie
Fruit or meat in a pie-dish covered with a pastry lid. Hand or machine raised pies are made from a pie paste which is shaped, allowed to set and become rigid, before they are filled with meat or fruit and then lidded.

Pincers
A tool with two prongs made from a springy metal. The prongs can be of different widths and shapes, with a fluted design on the edges. They are used for pinching a design on almond paste in the decoration of Battenburg, layer cake and gâteaux. The same tool is used to mark the edges of pork and other meat pies.

Pinched

The decoration on the edge of shortbreads. It is done by pinching the edge between the thumb and forefinger. It is a manual skill that is dying out and for this reason almost all shortbreads are now blocked out by machine. Wooden moulds are used in small bakeries.

Pinning

The operation of rolling dough or pastry into a flat sheet with a rolling pin.

Piping

(a) The fine, sometimes intricate decoration on a cake.

(b) The operation of forcing icing contained in a bag through the aperture at the point of an icing pipe. The pipe may be plain or designed at the point to give certain decorative effects.

Plaiting

The weaving of one or more ropes of dough into an ordered design.

Plaster moulds

Moulds made from plaster of Paris (calcium sulphate) which are used to cast models from gum paste, sugar paste and almond paste.

Poach

To simmer dishes in a mould in a water-bath until cooked. To cook food in water that is kept just on boiling point without letting it actually boil.

Pound cakes

A term used at one time to describe cakes made from 1 lb. (500 gr.) each of butter, sugar, eggs and flour. The term is now used for all cakes baked in a round hoop or oblong tin such as madeira, genoa and cherry.

Praline

Croquant that has been passed through rollers to produce a smooth paste. It is the natural oil in the almonds (or hazelnuts) that makes a paste possible. Praline paste has an excellent flavour and is used in creams, ices, etc.

Precipitate

To throw out of solution. To be deposited as a solid from a solution.

Prove

The filling of a yeasted dough with gas. Final proof is the time between final shaping of the dough piece and the time when it is placed into the oven.

Prover

A cupboard wherein yeasted goods are placed for final proof before baking. The atmosphere of the prover must be warm to assist fermentation and humid to prevent skinning.

Pudding

(a) A soft, sweetened mixture baked in a dish or steamed in a basin.

(b) A savoury dish that is boiled or steamed in a basin.

(c) A Yorkshire pudding which is baked in a dish may be sweet or savoury.

Puff pastry

Puff pastry is a laminated structure built up of alternate layers of dough and butter. The structure is built by rolling out and giving sufficient turns until there are hundreds of layers of dough and butter.

Pulled sugar

A solution of sugar in water with a little glucose or weak acid, boiled to 312° F (156° C). It is poured on to an oiled slab, coloured, and as soon as it can be handled it is pulled and folded until it attains a satin like sheen. It is used generally to fashion baskets of flowers for table decoration.

Quicklime

A hygroscopic substance which is placed in storage units for pulled or blown sugar products.

Recipe

An exact formula which will include the weights of the materials to be used for a particular type of bread or confectionery. All other details such as temperature, times, yields, etc., will also be recorded.

Recovery time

The time necessary for a dough to lose its toughness after manipulation.

Rennet

An infusion of the inner membrane of the fourth stomach of the calf which contains the enzyme rennin. It is used to coagulate milk for the manufacture of cheese and curd.

Retardation

The arresting of fermentation activity by holding dough in bulk or in small made up units at a temperature between 34-38° F (1-3° C). Retardation must not be confused with deep freezing.

Rice flour

Finely milled rice used in rice cakes, macaroons, shortbreads and for dusting purposes.

Ripening

The action of fermentation, manipulation, time, salt, water and temperature on gluten, all of which have an effect in changing it from its original toughness to a mellow extensibility.

Rock sugar

An aerated decorative material in various colours that is made by stirring a small quantity of royal icing into a sugar solution boiled to 280° F (138° C). The heat causes the air in the royal icing to expand and the albumen to set. The water vaporizes and the sugar crystallizes. When it is cold it is broken into pieces of suitable size.

Rolls

Small bread shapes used at breakfast, dinner and tea. They may be crisp or soft and of any shape, some of which may be plaited.

Rose oil

The essential oil obtained from rose petals. It is creamy in colour and is only rose-scented in high dilutions. 6000 to 10.000 lb. (3000 to 5000 kg.) rose petals only yield 2 lb. (1 kg.) rose oil.

Rose water

A by-product of rose oil distillation. It is occasionally used for Christmas goods, sweets and ices.

Royal icing

An intimate mixture of icing sugar and egg white, sometimes with the addition of lemon juice. It is beaten until it maintains a peak, when it is then ready for coating and piping.

Run-outs

Dried pre-fabricated pieces made with royal icing for fitting into a design on a cake. They can be made from coloured icing or they can be coloured after drying. The outline and essential details are first drawn on paper which is covered with wax paper so that the drawing is clearly visible. The outlines are then piped over with a fine piping tube. Royal icing, softened with water or egg white, is then piped in so that it runs level. Small pieces can be made in the same way with coloured fondant.

Sack

(of flour) 280 lb. (127 kg.). Flour is still invoiced by the sack but delivered in two bags of 140 lb. (63 $^1/_2$ kg.) each.

Saffron

The dried stigmas of the saffron crocus. The deep orange-yellow colouring matter is extracted by making an infusion in boiling water.

Salamander

A hot metal plate used for browning or 'flashing' food.

Salpicon
A mixture of several kinds of food diced small.

Sandwich plates
Round shallow metal tins in which sponge sandwiches are baked.

Saturated solution
Some substances are more soluble in hot water than they are in cold, sugar is an example. If the maximum amount of sugar is dissolved in a certain amount of water and more sugar is added it will be seen as a precipitate. If the solution is heated, the extra sugar will dissolve. This will go on until boiling point when $1\,{}^1/_2$ times the amount of sugar will be in solution as compared with the amount in cold water. A solution is termed saturated when none of the sugar precipitates.

Savoy bag
A triangular shaped bag made of cloth or a plastic material into which a pipe is inserted. It is used for piping meringue, sponge fingers and drops, soft biscuits, choux paste, etc., on to baking sheets. It is also used to pipe cream on, or in, cakes and pastries.

Savoy pipe
A metal nozzle, either plain or star shaped, through which mixtures or creams are forced after placing into a savoy bag.

Scaling
The technical term that is used for the operation of weighing dough or cake before baking.

Scoop
A small rounded short handled shovel for holding small amounts of dry materials. A scoop can be used to transfer small amounts from bulk supply.

Scraper
(a) A small oblong piece of plastic material, with two corners rounded for scraping down mixing bowls. The straight edge of the scraper can be used to smooth the side of a cake when coating with royal icing. The straight edge can also be cut in many ways so that a pattern can be made in the icing.

(b) A metal blade in a wooden handle that is used to scrape the surface of a bench.

Scuffle
A mop tied on the end of a pole with a length of rope, which, when wetted, is used to clean the sole of an oven.

Season
The operation of dulling the shiny surfaces of new pans and baking tins so that the heat will penetrate and not be reflected. It is done by putting the new tins in the oven for some hours at a temperature of less than 440° F (226° C).

Seasoning
The adding of salt, pepper, spices and herbs to meats and other savoury foods.

Setting
The operation of filling an oven with bread or cakes.

Short pastry
A friable, easily broken pastry made from flour, fat, sugar and egg. For savoury pastry the sugar is omitted.

Sieve
Utensil with a wire or nylon mesh through which dry materials are passed. Sieving removes coarse particles, extraneous materials and also it is a means of blending. Coarse sieves are used for the cleaning and draining of fruit. A sieve can also be used for fluids or semi-fluids.

Silver wedding cake
A cake made to celebrate the 25th anniversary of a wedding. The cake will have silver leaves as part of the decoration.

Skinning
If doughs or dough pieces are left uncovered the surface moisture is evaporated and a skin is formed. The skin will form streaks in the crumb of the baked product. After shaping, skinning will result in a loss of bloom and a hard crust.

Slab cake
Plain or fruited cake baked in rectangular tins or frames. The slabs generally weight about 5-7 lb. (2 $^1/_2$-3 $^1/_2$ kg.) each, according to whether they are plain or fruited.

Slack dough
A soft dough; one containing extra water.

Snow
A term used to describe well beaten egg whites. The direction is to 'whip to a stiff snow'.

Sodium bicarbonate
The constituent of baking powder that liberates CO_2. The maximum is liberated when the correct amount of acid is present.

Soft flour
A flour containing a weak gluten.

Spatula
A wooden tool with a flat blade for beating and mixing.

Splash
The act of spraying water with a brush on to baking sheets ready for baking puff pastry. The term is also used to describe the light spraying of liqueur on to torten and gâteaux bases.

Sponge
(a) A light plain cake produced by whisking eggs and sugar together until stiff and thoroughly aerated, then carefully blending in flour. To make a butter sponge, melted butter is carefully blended in with the flour.

(b) A rather thick fermented batter.

Spun sugar
A solution of sugar in water when boiled to 280° F (138° C) can be spun into fine threads by dipping wires into the solution and waving them to and fro over a rod. The solution may be coloured. The spun sugar can be gathered up and used for decorative purposes.

Stencil
A pattern cut in a waterproof material or in metal, through which a decorative design in sugar or icing can be applied to a cake. A similar implement can be used to deposit japonaise or similar mixings on to baking sheets.

Stock syrup
A solution of sugar in water boiled to 225° F (107° C). It is used to adjust the consistency of fondant. It is also used for making water icing. The normal recipe for stock syrup is 3 lb. (1 kg. 500) of sugar to 2 $^1/_2$ lb. (1 kg. 125) of water.

Strong flour
Flour containing a strong stable gluten.

Sugar paste
A paste made with icing sugar, egg whites, glucose, cocoa butter and soaked gum tragacanth.

Super saturated solution
A saturated solution that is allowed to cool without crystallization occurring.

Tart
A pastry case baked with a filling of fruit, jam, custard, frangipane, macaroon, etc.

Tea breads
Small yeasted goods made from an enriched dough, shaped in many ways. They may be finished with a fondant or water icing glaze and decorated with roasted nuts. Some may be sprinkled with maw seeds before baking or dusted with icing sugar afterwards.

Tight dough

The term used to describe a stiff dough. A dough containing insufficient water.

Tonka beans

The ripe seeds of a tree growing in Brazil, Venezuela and Guiana and sometimes reaching a height of 67 feet (20 m.). They contain 1 to 3 % coumarin, which is their most important constituent. They are used to flavour various products, such as Baumkuchen, and exotic sweets.

In Great Britain, in 1965, the Food Standards Committee published a Report recommending that a number of flavouring agents, including tonka bean and coumarin, should be prohibited by regulations for use in food. In 1966, the Committee was asked to reconsider the whole question. At the time of going to print, the Committee has not reported. In the meantime, it seems wise to regard the 1965 Report as a guide, as the use of tonka bean and coumarin in food could be criticized by enforcement authorities.

Turntable

A piece of equipment that is designed to take the weight of a cake. It can be rotated at any speed, so that a smooth coating of icing can be applied and piping carried out with precision.

Vanilla sugar

A mixture of white sugar and finely ground vanilla.

Wafer paper

Edible sheets of paper-like material on to which macaroon, ratafia and Parisian rout biscuits are piped. It is made from gelatinized starch and gum, sheeted and dried. It is sometimes erroneously referred to as rice-paper, although rice flour may be used in its preparation.

Wash

(a) To brush with egg, milk, water, before baking. (b) To brush with a glaze after baking.

Wash brush

A soft haired brush for washing cakes or pastries with egg or other liquids before baking, or for glazing after baking.

Wedding cake

Also known as bride cake. A richly fruited cake covered with almond paste, coated and piped with royal icing. It can be made in one or more tiers, each tier supported by gum paste, plastic or silver pillars. The top tier generally supports a gum paste ornament.

A similar cake can be made for anniversaries of the wedding day (see golden and silver wedding cakes).

Whip

To rapidly aerate a sponge, meringue or cream by means of a hand or machine whisk.

Whisk

An implement made of wire used to whip sponges, meringues and cream by hand. A similar implement is specially made to fix in a machine.

Yeast

A living micro-organism of the fungi family of plants. Under favourable conditions of temperature, moisture and food, the cells multiply by splitting off into daughter cells. Compressed yeast is generally used for fermented goods although excellent dried yeast is available particularly for use in hot climates and for emergencies. Aeration is effected by the production of CO_2 from sugars. The gas is held in the dough by the gluten network.

Yield

The calculated units from or the total baked weight of a particular formula.

Zest

The coloured outer rinds of oranges and lemons. The zest contains the essential oils of the fruit.

Historical and Technological Index

A

Absorb	849
Adsorb	849
Aeration	37, 849
Albumen	849
Alcohols–liqueurs	69, 859
– spirits	69
All-in process	849
Almond paste and marzipan	849, 860
– history	8
Angelica	849
Anisette	849
Annonae	849
Apprenticeship and training	30
Apricot purée	850
Aromatic seeds and fruits	66
Arrack	850

B

Babas and madeleines–history	11
Bag-flour weight	850
– icing	850
Bain-marie	850
Bake blind	850
Bake off	850
Bakewell pudding–history	12
Baking	850
Baking confectionery	44
– powder	38, 68, 179
– sheets	850
Banbury cakes–history	12
Bannocks-Selkirk–history	25
Baps-Scottish–history	25
Bara-brith–history	13
Barm brack–history	13
Basin	850
Batch	850
Bath buns–history	13
Batter	850
Baumkuchen	10
Baumé	32, 850
– saccharometer tables	32
Bay	850
Beat	851
Beater	851
Beeswax	851
Biscuit (sponge)–history	5
Biscuits	851

Black jack	851
Blanch	851
Blending method	44
Bloom–bread and cakes	851
– chocolate	851
Blue	851
Bowl	851
Brake	851
Bride cake–proportions	87-92
Brioche	851
– history	9
British traditional cakes and teabreads–history	12
Buckwheat	851
Bun	851
Bun wash	245, 851
Butter	62

C

Cake	852
Cake decoration	71
Cake hoop	852
Cakemaking methods	42
Cake mixing temperature	33
Cake tins	852
Calculations of yeast quantities	35
Candied	852
Caramel	852
Caramel colour	852
Caramel fruits	852
Caramelize	852
Caramels	852
Carbon dioxide	852
Carbonate of ammonia	852
Carbonize	852
Carême Antoine	12
Casting moulds	93
Centigrade–Celsius	31, 852
Centrepiece	852
Centres	852
Chaffing	853
Charlotte	853
Checking	853
Cheese cakes–Old English–history	14
Cheese curd	853
Chelsea buns–history	15
Cherry brandy	853
Chinois	853
Chlorination	853

Chocolate	66, 853
– bakers'	66
– couverture	66, 854
– piping	84
– vermicelli	853
Christmas pie–history	15
– pudding–history	15
Clarify	853
Clarifying sugar syrup	52
Coagulate	853
Coat	853
Cocoa and chocolate manufacture	65
Cocoa butter	853
Coffee–sources	66
– preparation	66
Cognac	853
Colour	71
Colourings	853
Comb scraper	853
Compound fat	63, 853
Cones	854
Confectioners–early	2
Constituent	854
Conversion tables	34, 35
Cornflour	61
Cornish pasties–history	16
– saffron cake–history	23
Coupe	854
Couverture	854
Coventry puffs–history	16
Cream	854
– of tartar	854
– powders	854
Crimping	854
Croquant	854
Crumpets–history	20
Crystallization	854
Cup cakes	854
Curaçao	854
Curd	854
Curdle	854
Cut-out	855
Cutters	855

D

Danish pastry–history	5
Decorate	855
Deep freeze	45, 855
Defrosting bread and cakes	47

Defrosting eggs	60
Density–measuring	31
– tables	32
Deposit	855
Design	73
Develop	855
Display	597
Divider	855
Docker	855
Dough	855
– temperatures	33
– temperature calculations	33
D'Oyley	855
Dragees	855
Draw	855
Dredger	855
Dried eggs	60
– reconstitution	60
Drummed hoop	855
Dundee cake–history	16
Durian	855
Dust	856

E

Easter cakes–history	17
Eccles cakes–history	17
Egg wash	856
Eggs	59
Egypt, Baking in ancient	1
Elasticity	856
Emulsion	856
English plum cake–history	17
Enrichment	856
Enrobe	856
Enrober	856
Essences	856

F

Fahrenheit	31
– degrees	856
Fancies	856
Fancy	856
Fats and oils	62
Ferment	856
Fermentation	856
Final proof	856
Fingers	856
Flaked	856
Flambé réchaud	856
Flan	856
Flash	857
Flour batter method	44
Flours	57
Flowers cut-out	85
– modelled	85
– piped	85
Fondant	857
Food regulations	29
Formula balance	41
– faults	42
Frozen eggs–defrosting	60
Frying fat–temperature	45
Full proof	857

G

Ganache	857
Garnish	857
Gâteau	857
Gelatine	857
Gelatinization	857
Genoese	857
Gingerbread–history	18
Glaze	857
Gloss	857
Glucose	65, 857

– manufacture	65
Gluten	857
Glycerine	858
Golden syrup	64
– manufacture	64
Golden wedding cake	858
Graining	858
Grease	858
Greasing boiled sugar	858
Greece, Baking in ancient	2
Gum arabic	858
Gum paste	858

H

Hair sieve	858
Handing-up	858
Harvest bread–history	18
Heat measuring	31
High-ratio cakes	858
Honey cakes–history	3
– composition	65
Hot cross-buns–history	18
Hotplate	858
Hydrometer	858
Hygiene	29
Hygroscopic	858

I

Ice cream powder	858
Icing	858
– sugar	858
– pipes	75
Irish breads–history	14

J

Jaggery	858
Jelly	859
– aspic	859
– cold-set	859
– piping	859
– starch	859
– sweet	859
Jellying agents	859
Jigger	859

K

Kirsch	859
Knock-back	859
Krapfen	859

L

Lamination	859
Lebkuchen–history	3
Lecithin	859
Lettering	93
Liqueurs	69, 859
Louis Pasteur	38

M

Macerate	859
Madeleines–history	11
Maidenhair fern	859
Maids of Honour–history	19
Manipulation	860
Maraschino	860
Marble icing	860
Margarine	63
Marmalade	860
Marzipan	860
– history	8
Masking	860
Master craftsmen	12
Maw seeds	860
Measuring density	31

– heat	31
Milk	61
Milk powder–reconstitution	62
Mince pies–history	20
Mincemeat	860
Mixing temperatures	33
Monograms	100
Mould shaping	860
– fungi	860
Muffins–history	20
Musty	860

N

Nibs	860
Nougat	860

O

Orange flower water	860
Othellos–history	20
Oxford lardy cakes–history	21

P

Palette knife	861
Palm wine	861
Pan	861
Panary fermentation	37, 861
Pancakes–history	21
Panettone–history	9
Parkin, Yorkshire–history	27
Pastillage	861
Pastries	861
Pastry making–temperatures	33
Pasty	861
Patty	861
Pectin	861
Peel-oven	861
– fruit	861
Pepper cakes–history	3
Persipan	861
Petits fours	861
Pie	861
Pincers	861
Pinched	862
Pinning	862
Piping	862
– bags–nylon	76, 850
– paper	76, 850
– savoy	76, 864
Piping chocolate	84
– exercises	77
– tubes	75
Plaiting	52, 862
Plaster moulds	93, 862
Plum cake–history	17
Plunder–history	5
Poach	862
Pork pie–history	22
Pound cakes	862
Praline	862
Precipitate	862
Prove	862
Prover	862
Pudding	862
Puff pastry	862
– history	5
Pulled sugar	862

Q

Quicklime	862

R

Raw materials	57
Réaumur René Antoine	31
– degrees	31, 32
Recipe	863

868

Recovery time 863	Selkirk bannocks–history 25	Temperatures 33
Refrigeration 45	Setting 864	Tempering chocolate 246
Rennet 863	Short pastry 864	Templates 74
Retardation 45, 863	Shortbread–history 26	Textures 75
Rice flour 863	Show–pieces 597	Thermometers 31
Ripening 863	Shrewsbury cakes–history 26	Tight dough 866
Rock sugar 863	Sieve 864	Tonka beans 866
Rolls 863	Silver wedding cake 864	Torten–history 6
Roman Empire, Baking in .. 2	Simnel cakes–history 27	Training 30
Rose water 863	Skinning 865	Treacle 64
Rout biscuits–history 23	Slab cake 865	Turntable 866
Royal icing 863	Slack dough 865	Twelfth cake–history 9
Rub-in method 44	Snow 865	
Run-outs 863	Soda breads, Ireland–history . 14	**V**
	Sodium bicarbonate 865	
S	Soft flour 865	Vanilla sugar 866
Saccharometer 32	Spatula 865	
Sack-of flour 863	Spices 66, 361	**W**
Saffron 863	Spirits 69	
– cake, Cornish–history 23	Splash 865	Wafer makers–history 3
Salamander 863	Sponge–cake 865	Wafer paper 866
Sally Lunns–history 24	– ferment 865	Waffles–early makers 3
Salpicon 864	Sponge cakes–history 5	Wash 866
Salt 68	Spun sugar 865	Wash brush 866
Sandwich plates 864	Stencils 865	Wedding cake 866
Saturated solution 864	Stock syrup 865	Whip 866
Savarins–history 12	Stollen–history 8	Whisk 866
Savoy bag 76, 864	Strong flour 865	
– pipe 76, 864	Sugar batter method 44	**Y**
Scaling 864	Sugar boiling 50	
Schnittorten–designs 86	– degrees 51	Yeast 68, 866
Scones–history 24	Sugar paste 865	– quantities–calculations 35
Scoop 864	Sugars 2, 64	Yield 866
Scotch baps–history 25	Super saturated solutions 865	Yorkshire parkin–history 27
Scotch bun–history 26		– teacakes–history 27
Scraper 864	**T**	
Scuffle 864	Tart 865	**Z**
Season 864	Teabreads 865	
Seasoning 864	Teacakes, Yorkshire–history .. 27	Zest 866

Recipe Index

A

Aargau Carrot Torte 591
Aberdeen Gingerbread 362
– Honey Cake 362
Abernethy Biscuits 464
Abraham Bread Doll 257
Accordians 326
Acorns 524
Africans 315
Afternoon Tea Fancies 407
Aidas 408
Alcazar Gâteau 568
Alchermes Cream 238
Alexander Cream Tartlets ... 321
Algiers 617
Alicante Biscuits 464
Almond and Hazelnut
  Products 209, 213, 531
– Apricot Rings 533
– Balloons 346
– Biscuits à la Charles X 464
– Jewish 464
– Bread 506
– – Slices 408
– Bows 531
– Buns 309
– Butter Biscuits 408
– Cakes 381
– Cheese Cakes 326
– – Filling 224
– Cookies 464
– Cream Tartlets 321
– Crescents 465, 531
– Croquant 213
– – Slices 348
– Custard 241
– – Buns 257
– Dessert Cakes 381
– Drops 465, 531
– Filling 225
– Fingers 531
– Frangipane Tartlets 321
– Fruit Slices 535
– Fruited Rings 280
– Gâteau 550
– Genoese 200
– Gianduja 213
– Gingerbread 363
– Goods 531

– Honey Tartlets 536
– Horseshoes 532
– Japonaise 460
– – Recipes 208, 458
– Knots 257
– Linz Crescents 408
– Macaroon Paste 212, 213
– Marzipan 211, 212
– Meringue Puffs 532
– Modelling Pastes 251
– Nougat 213
– Nougat-de-Paris 214
– Nut Filling 222
– – Slices \ 409
– Ovals 532
– Pastes 210, 211
– Petits Fours 506
– Praline 213
– Pretzels 442
– Puffs 331, 532
– Rings 257, 532
– Rocks 465
– Rolls 326, 465
– – Richelieu 465
– Scrolls 465
– Slice Filling 223
– Slices 532
– Soufflés 506
– Sponge Bases 197
– Squares 335
– Tart Filling 221
– Tartlets 321
– – Holland 321
– – Switzerland 835
– Tartlet Filling 221
– Tea Biscuits 465
– Torte 565
– Triangles 532
– Twists 327
– Vanilla Crescents 539
– Vanilla Rolls 358
– Wafers 533, 786
– Wafer Mixing 213
Almonds, salted 643
Amandine Tourte 568
Amarena Sports 525
Amaretti 506, 533
– di Cioccolato 466
– di Saronno 466
– Switzerland 506

Amaretto 525
American Fritters 299
Anchovy Sticks 820
Andorra Filling 224
Angelica Macaroons 506
Anisette Biscuits 506
Anniversary Torte 576
Appenzell Honey Cakes 363
– Filling 224
Apple and Cream Turnovers . 352
– Balls 327
– Boats 315
– Charlotte 666
– Choux 338
– Curd Tart 694
– Dumplings 667
– Dutch, Tartlets 322, 326
– Frangipane Tartlets 321
– Fritters 668
– – Surprise 669
– Oxford, Tartlets 323
– Pastry 190
– Poppy Seed Cakes 409
– Rolls 358
– Squares 335
– Streusel Slices 409
– Strudel 334, 410, 693
– Tart (U.S.A.) 694
– Tartlets, Italy 410
– – Switzerland 410
– Turnovers 337
– – and Cream 337
Apricot Almond Rings 533
– Choux 338
– Fritters 669
– Glaze 245
– Jelly 254
– Macaroons 506
– Slices 348, 410
– Streusel Cake 258
– – Slices 411
– Tartlets 336, 410
– Tarts 316
Apricotines 258
Arabellas 618
Arancia Gâteau 588
Arancini 525
Argentine Chocolate Cream . 237
– Cream 237
– Gâteau 589

Arlecchino Cream 238	– – Choux 192	– – Tea 465
Arnhem Cookies 466	– – Pie 191	– Amaretti Cioccolato 466
Aromatic Centres 618	– – Puff 180	– – di Saronno 466
Arrowroot Glaze 245	– – Short 190	– Anisette 466, 506
Ashbourne Gingerbread 363	– – Sweet 184	– Arnhem Cookies 466
Asparagus Rolls 818	– Pound Cakes 203	– Badener Chräbeli 465
Aspic 814	– Praline 213	– Banbury 467
Assabesi 525	– Prepared Flour 179	– Bannock 467
Autumn Gâteau 589	– Savoury Goods 813	– Barcelona 467
Aveline Genoese 200	– Slab Cakes 204	– Basler Bruns 467
Avelines 521	– Sponge Mixtures 195	– Bath 468
Avondale Puffs 820	– Spreads 225	– Bâtons parisiens épicés 468
	– Toppings 226	– Battenburg Drops 468
B	Basket, Sugar 643	– Biarritz 468, 506
Babas 258	Basle Leckerli 363	– Bitter Cookies 468
Babas and Savarins 258, 259	Basler Bruns 467	– Bolero 469
– Basic Syrup 259	Batavia Fancies 411	– Brauns 469
Bacon and Egg Filling 816	Bath Biscuits 468	– Breton 469
– Flan 835	– Buns 260	– Brown Bread Drops 469
– and Onion Filling 818	Bâtons parisiens épicés 468	– Brussels Sticks 470
– and Egg Turnovers 821	Battenburg 547	– Butter 470
Badener Chräbeli 466	– Drops 468	– – Pieces 470
Baked Streusel Topping 226	– Slices 412	– – Rings 471
Bakewell Filling 221	Batters 179	– Butterscotch 470
– Tartlets 411	– Beer 299	– – Cookies 470
Baking Powder 179	– Standard Waffle 305	– Carree 471
– Goods 309	Baumkuchen Recipe 203, 602	– Champagne 496
– and Recipes 179, 180, 309	– Pheasant 611	– Cherry Almond 471
Banana Fritters 669	– Santa Claus 611	– – Rolls 471
– Marshmallow Slices 411	Bavarian Creams 698	– Chocolate 471
– Meringues 453	– Apricot 699	– – Chip Cookies 471
– Meringue Slices 453	– Basic Recipe 699	– – Kisses 471, 472
Bananas 533	– Cherry 699	– – Macaroons 472
Banbury Biscuits 467	– Chocolate 699	– – Ovals 472
– Cakes 327	– Coffee 699	– – Pastille Macaroons 472
– Filling 215, 217	– Diplomat 699	– – Raisin 472
Bannock Biscuits 467	– Fruit 700	– – Rosettes 473
– Pitcaithly 325	– Layer 700	– – Stars 473
– Selkirk 292	– Nesselrode 700	– Christmas Stars 473
Bara Brith 259	– Orange 700	– Cinnamon 473
Barches 259	– Pistachio 701	– Coconut 473
Barcelona Biscuits 467	– Tea 701	– – Cookies 474
– Ovals 411	Bavarian Dumplings 668	– – Crunchies 474
Barm Brack 259	Bayrischzeller Striezel 260	– – Macaroons 474
Barquettes (Puff Pastry) 820	Bee-sting 412	– – Rocks 474
– (Short Pastry) 820	Beef and Potato Pies Filling .. 816	– Coffee 474, 475
Basic Preparations 173	Berkeley Tartlets 834	– Corbet's Cookies 475
– Almond Products 209	Berlin Doughnuts 304	– Cornflake Toasties 475
– – Pastes 210	– Tongues 304	– Craquelins 475
– Baking Powders 179	Berolinas 520	– Cream 475
– Batters 179	Bethmännchen 533	– Crescents 476
– Baumkuchen 203	Beugeln, Bratislava 261	– Croquant 476
– Cake Bases 194	Biarritz Biscuits 468, 506	– Date Cookies 476
– Chocolate 246	Bibeteig Filling 224, 373	– Derby 476
– Creams 227	– St. Gallen 373	– Duc de Coburg 468
– Croquant 213	– Spice 362	– Duchess 476
– Custards 227, 238	Bilberry Cake 260	– Dutch 485
– Danish Pastry 177	Bird's Nests 316	– English Rolls 485
– Fermented Doughs 173	Birthday Cakes 382	– Rout 485
– Fillings 215	– Children's Torte 578	– Farmhouse Treacle 486
– Ganache 250	– Gâteau 568	– Favourite Crunch 486
– Genoese 198	– Numeral Torte 576	– Fiches l'Orgeat 486
– Gianduja 213	– Torte 576	– Fondant Pretzels 487
– Glazes 245	Biscuits 463	– Fruit 487
– Hazelnut Products 209	– Abernethy 464	– Fruit and Nut 487
– Icings and Glazes 243	– Alicante 464	– – Ovals 487
– Japonaise 208	– Almond 464	– Ginger 488
– Jellies 253	– – à la Charles X 464	– – Crisps 488
– Macaroon Pastes 212	– – Cookies 464	– – Nuts 488
– Marzipan 211, 212	– – Crescents 465	– Golden Bows 488
– Meringues 205	– – Drops 465	– Graham 489
– Modelling Pastes 251	– – Jewish 464	– Heckle 489
– Nougat 213	– – Rocks 465	– Honey 489
– Other Pastes 213	– – Rolls 465	– Jan Hagel 489
– Pastries 180	– – Richelieu 465	– Kletskoppen 501
– – Biscuit 186, 187, 190	– – Scrolls 465	– Langues-de-Chat 489

872

– Lemon	490	
– – Scrolls	490	
– Macarons à l'Orange	490	
– – de Nancy	490	
– Maraschino Dainties	490	
– Marigolds	490	
– Melting Moments	491	
– Montagner	491	
– Montelman	491	
– Moque	491	
– Moss	492	
– Nantes	492	
– Neapolitan	492	
– Nice	492	
– Nougat	492	
– – Ovals	493	
– Nougatines	492	
– Nut Croquettes	493	
– – Dessert Fingers	493	
– Orange	493	
– – Macaroons	493	
– Palace	494	
– – Palais de Dame	494	
– Parkin	494	
– Pavilion	494	
– Pearl	494	
– Perkin	495	
– Petits Beurres	495	
– Pineapple Strips	495	
– Pischingers	495	
– Plain	495	
– Puff Cracknels	495	
– Raspberry Tartlets	496	
– – Rosettes	496	
– Ratafia	496	
– Rectangles	496	
– Rheims	496	
– Rice	497	
– Rolled Oat Cookies	497	
– Sablés	497	
– Sand	497	
– – Scrolls	497	
– – Stars	497	
– Sandmac	498	
– Savoy	498	
– – Fingers	498	
– Scottish Rolls	498	
– Shortbread	498	
– – Drops	498	
– Shrewsbury	498	
– Silver Drops	499	
– Souvaroff	499	
– Speculaas	499	
– Spice	499	
– Spiced Hazelnut	499	
– Spicy Cookies	500	
– Strassburg Sticks	500	
– Sultana	500	
– Swabian Rolls	500	
– Swiss	501	
– Croquettes	501	
– Tantallon	501	
– Tarragona	501	
– Thin	501	
– – Wine	502	
– Trouville	502	
– Tuiles	502	
– Vanilla	502	
– – Marzipan	502	
– – Patience	502	
– – Sticks	503	
– Vendée	503	
– Viennese	503	
– – Horseshoe	503	
– Weesp	503	
– Wine	504	

– Zurich Nuts	504	
Blancmange-Ordinary	701	
– Chocolate	701	
– Hazelnut	701	
– Liqueur	701	
– Raspberry	701	
Blancmanges	701	
Blidahs	412	
Bobes	413	
Bocche di Leone	525	
Bombetta	525	
– Coffee	525	
– Hazelnut	525	
– Lemon	525	
– Orange	525	
– Taormina	529	
– Walnut	525	
Bordeaux Croquets	413	
Bouchées 820,	823	
Brandy Rolls	358	
– Snaps	364	
Brasiliana	525	
Brassel Cakes	413	
Bratislava Beugeln	261	
Brauns	469	
Bread Doughs, Basic	174	
– Enriched	174	
– – Tea	174	
– French, Basic	175	
– Torte	577	
Breakfast Rolls	261	
Brenten	533	
Breton Biscuits	469	
Bridge Rolls	261	
Brie Pastries	823	
– Torte	568	
Brioche	261	
– Basic Dough	177	
– Sandwiches	844	
British Pies and Pasties	840	
– Bacon and Egg Pie	840	
– Beef and Potato Pie	840	
– Cheese and Onion		
– – Pasties	840	
– – Pies	841	
– – Turnovers	840	
– Chicken Pies	841	
– Cornish Pasties	841	
– Forfar Bridies	841	
– Mutton Pies	841	
– Pork Pies	841	
– Steak and Kidney Pies ...	842	
– Veal and Ham Pie	842	
Brown Bread Drops	469	
Bruns, Basler	467	
Brussels Sticks	470	
– Waffles	305	
Bûche de Noël	568	
Budapest Pineapple Torte ...	577	
– Rolls	358	
– Sand Cake	382	
Buddini	413	
Bun Crossing Paste	283	
– Doughs, Basic	175	
– – Ferment	175	
– – Sponge	176	
– – Straight	175	
– Glaze	245	
– Liverpool Loaf	224	
– Loaves	262	
– Rounds	262	
– Scotch Black	292	
Buns Almond	309	
– – Custard	257	
– Bath	260	

– Butter	262	
– – Almond	262	
– Chelsea	264	
– Coconut	265	
– Coffee	310	
– Currant	266	
– Diamond	278	
– Florentine	280	
– France	261	
– Hazelnut	309	
– Hot Cross	282	
– Lemon	284	
– Party	288	
– Pineapple	289	
– Portland	289	
– Raspberry	310	
– Rice	310	
– Swiss	294	
Burgdorfer	458	
Butter Almond Buns	262	
– Biscuits	470	
– Buns	262	
– Filling	225	
– Pieces	470	
– Rings	471	
– Sponge Animals	611	
– Sponges	196	
– Streusel Cake	263	
– – Slices	413	
– – Topping	226	
– Wafers	414	
– Wedges	414	
Buttercream, Basic	228	
– Almond	229	
– Boiled	229	
– Chocolate		
– – Arrack	230	
– – Hazelnut	230	
– – Praline	230	
– Coffee	237	
– Gianduja	231	
– Ginger	231	
– Imperial	236	
– Italian 235-238		
– Lemon	231	
– Madeira	231	
– Maraschino	237	
– Meringue	237	
– Mocha	230	
– Mousseline	229	
– Nougat	231	
– Nougatine	237	
– Nut or Hazelnut 230,	237	
– Pineapple	230	
– Truffle	231	
– Vanilla	230	
– Various	237	
– with Custard	231	
– – Egg	229	
– – – Yolks	229	
– – Fruit	237	
– – Marshmallow	231	
– – Meringue	232	
– – Pectin	232	
– Zabaglione	236	
Buttercream Gâteau	587	
– Japonaise Fancies	458	
Buttered "S" Scrolls	507	
Butterflies	327	
– Cheese	824	
Butterletters	382	
Butterscotch Biscuits	470	
– Cookies	470	
Butterspekulatius	364	
Butter Sponge Chicks, Hares,		
etc.	611	

873

C

Cadets	263
Cadogan Barquettes	834
Caën Sablés	414
Cake Bases	194
– Built-up	194
– Butter Sponge	196, 203
– Heavily fruited	204
– Heavy Genoese	199
– High Sugar	199
– Light Genoese	199
– Toppings	226
Calcutta Tartlets	834
Calissons d'Aix	507
Canapés	842
– Alsatian	842
– Anchovy	842
– Bradford	843
– Celery	843
– Egg	843
– Ham	843
– Hungarian	843
– Mushroom	843
– Parisian	843
– Pâté de Foie gras	843
– Russian Salad	843
– Salami	843
– Salmon	843
– Sardine	843
– Shrimp	843
– Tartare	843
– Tomato	844
– Tongue	844
Cannoli	525
– Cheese	824
– Saratoga	525
– Toscani	526
– Zabaglione	526
Cappucci	526
Cappuccini Cream	238
Capri Rolls	459
Caracas Cake	592
– Cakes	383
Caracks	520
Caramel Choux, France	341
– – Italy	338
– Cream Puffs	331
– Creams	628
– Custard	240
– Fruits	632
Caramels	628
– Milk	628
– Soft	628
Caraque Tourte	592
Caravelle Gâteau	592
Carinthian Reinling	263
Carlsbad Crescents	263
– Fritters	669
Carnival Fritters	300
– Heads	346
Carracks	414
– Small	414
Carree Biscuits	471
Cat's Eyes	414
Cat's Tongues	414, 415
Cerisettes	520
Champagne (Rheims) Biscuits	496
Chantilly Torta	589
Charlemagne Gâteau	568
Charlottes	701
– Apple	666
– Chocolate Prince's Style	701
– Custard Cream	235
– Malakoff	702
– Praline Chocolate	702
– Royal	702
– Russian (Charlotte russe)	703
– Valais	703
– Williams	703
Chatibeur	415
Cheddar Pearls	819
Cheese-almond Cakes	326
– Baps	264
– Biscuits	838, 839
– Bread	264
– – Wholemeal	296
– Butterflies	824
– Cakes	415
– Richmond	822
– Cannoli	824
– Cheddar Pearls	819
– Custards	821
– Cherry Cakes	265
– Cheshire Biscuits	839
– – Rolls	821
– Cream Buns	819
– Torte	577
– Fillings	816-818
– Cushions	821
– Custard	242
– Fritters	819
– Horns	821
– Pastry	190
– Puffs	824
– Rolls	264
– Soufflés	819
– Swans	820
– Victoria Cake	315
– and Bacon Flan (Quiche à la lorraine)	835
– and Onion Filling	816
– – Pasties	840
– – Patties	840
– – Turnovers	840
– and Potato Scones	839
– and Tomato Filling	818
Chelsea Buns	264
Cheltonia Fritters	670
Cherry	415, 529
– Almond Biscuits	471
– Barquettes	415
– Bowls	526
– Cakes	383
– Cheese Cakes	265, 416
– – Torte	592
– Chocolate Slices	416
– Choux	338
– Japonaise Fancies	459
– Michel	416
– Puffs	331
– Rolls	471
– Slice Filling	223
– Slices	348, 416
– Sports	526
– Strudel	335, 416
– Tartlets	417
– Turnovers	352
– Wedges	417
Cheshire Cheese Biscuits	839
– – Rolls	821
Chessboard Gâteau	552, 593
Chessboards-Miniature	623
Chestnut Cream	238
– Croquettes	666
– Meringues	453
– Paste	225
– Slices	348
– Turrets	520
Chestnuts	417
– glazed	642
Chicken Pies	841
Child's Birthday Torte	576
Chinamen	417
Chocolat, France	520
Chocolate, Bakers	249
– Balloons	346
– Beans	346
– Biscuits	471
– Buttercream	237, 238
– – Torte	578
– Chantilly	526
– Chip Cookies	471
– Choux	338
– – Gâteau	552
– Cigarettes	249
– Coffee Slices	417
– Cornets	507
– Cornflake Circles	418
– Couverture	246
– Cream Drops	346
– – Meringues	453
– – Rolls	358
– – Slices	349
– Cup Tartlets	321
– Custard	239
– Cut-outs	248
– Drops	351
– Drums	520
– Eclairs	339
– Fudge	232
– – Slices	418
– Genoese	200, 201
– – High Sugar	200
– – Slices	418
– Hearts	377
– Icing	244
– Japonaise	459
– – Slices	459
– – Walnut Slices	459
– Kirsch	526
– Kisses	471, 507
– Leaves	249
– Linz Fingers	418
– Macaroon Biscuits	472
– Macaroons	507, 533
– Meringue	453
– – Nests	453
– – Pies	418
– – Shells	457
– – Sticks	454
– – Walnut	454
– Modelling Paste	253
– – White	253
– Moulding	247
– Nougat	520, 521
– – Cup Cakes	418
– – Rolls	418
– Ovals	472
– Parfaits	418
– Pastille Macaroons	472
– Petals	249
– Pies	418
– Pineapple	526
– Piping	249
– Potatoes	442
– Pretzels	402
– Raisin Biscuits	472
– Rolls	249
– Rosettes	473
– Roulade Rolls	359
– "S" Scrolls	508
– Sablés Slices	419
– Shavings	249
– Slice Filling	223
– Slices	419
– Soufflés	508
– Sponge Sandwiches	352

– Stars 473	– Apple 338	– Biscuits 474, 475
– Streusel 249	– Apricot 338	– Buns 309
– Sweet Pastry 185	– Baskets 338	– Buttercream 237
– Tempering 246	– Caramel 338	– Cakes 420
– Torte 578	– Cherry 338	– Choux 339
– Walnut Meringue 454	– Chocolate 338	– Cream 237
– Wine Cream Fancies ... 349	– Cinderella 339	– Rolls 359
Chocolates and Sugar	– Coffee 339	– Crema Pasticcera 235
Confectionery 617	– Fruit Gâteau 552	– Dessert 459
Chocolates, Aidas 617	– Gooseberry 340	– Fancies 420
– Algiers 617	– Grapes 338	– Geneva 529
– Andalusians 618	– Lemon 340	– Genoese 201
– Arabellas 618	– Petits 341	– Japonaise 459
– Brazilians 618	– Pineapple 342	– Kisses 455
– Caramel Sticks 619	– Pretzel 342	– Puffs 331
– Centres 619, 621, 622, 628	– Rings-fried 338	– Rings 327
– – Aromatic 618	– Royal Palace 342	– Soufflés 513
– – Coffee 619	– Savouries 819	– Streusel Fancies 420
– – Cream 620	– Slices 338	– Tongues 420
– – Kirsch 621	– Swedish 343	– Walnut 527
– – Maraschino 619	Christmas Cakes 383	– Whirls 420
– – Marzipan 622	– Log 568	– Zabaglione Cream 236
– Coffee Nougat 620	– Macaroons 534	Cold Desserts 698
– Coccinelles 620	– Pie 694	– Bavarian Creams 698
– Countesses 620	– Stars 359, 473	– Blancmanges 701
– Croquant Nougat 620	– Tartlets 321	– Charlottes 701
– Cuba 620	– Torte 578	– Cocktails 704
– Favourites 621	– Triangles 349	– Creams, various 705
– Florence 621	– Wreath 587	– – in Goblets 707
– Ginger Triangles 621	Cigarettes Parisian 307, 308	– – Petits Pots 709
– Honey Nougat 621	Cinderella Choux 339	– Exotic 747
– Jamaica 621	Cinnamon Biscuits 473	– Flans 741
– Liqueurs 627, 628	– Filling (Spread) 225	– Fruit 710
– Little Logs 622	– Leaves 508	– – Compotes 724
– Malaga 622	– Macaroons 534	– – Salads 725
– Marie 622	– Stars 364, 508	– Gâteaux 727
– Marquisettes 622	– Tartlet Filling 221	– Italian Semi-frozen .. 800
– Masked Hazelnuts 623	– Tartlets 419	– Jellies 729
– – Pistachios 623	– Waffles 306	– Mousselines 730
– May Flies 623	Clotted Cream 228	– Mousses 730
– Milano 623	Club Sandwiches 845	– Pies 731
– Miniature Chessboards ... 623	Coccinelles 620	– Rice 732
– Moccatines 623	Cocktail Desserts 704	– Snow Eggs 733
– Mont-Blanc 624	– Black Forest 704	– Surprises 746
– Moscovites 624	– Bonne-Femme 704	– Tarts 734
– Murano 624	– Cherry 704	– Various 743
– Muscadin 624	– Japanese 704	– Yoghourt 746
– Noisettines 624	– Monk's 704	Cold Meringue 206
– Nougat Montélimar 624	– Oriental 704	– Set Jelly 255
– Nut Dainties 625	– Pierrette 704	Colomba di Pasqua 279
– Olives 625	– Shah 704	Commercy Madeleines 420
– Orange Marzipan 625	– Strawberry 704	Condés 333
– Pineapple Cups 625	Cocktails Tebaldi 526	Confectioner's Custard .. 240
– – Triangles 625	Coconut Buns 265, 309	– Crema Pasticcera 235
– Pistachio Marzipan ... 625	– Biscuits 473	– Crème Pâtissière 240
– Portugal 626	– Cakes 384	Congress Tarts 534
– Pralines 626	– Cherry Meringues 454	Continentals 265
– Princesses 626	– Cookies 474	Conversation Slices 333
– Rigi Peaks 626	– Crunchies 474	– Tarts 336
– Rochers 626	– Macaroon Biscuits 474	Copacabana Meringues 455
– Sicilians 626	– Macaroons 419, 534	Copenhagens 339
– Sorrento 627	– Meringue Fancies 454	Coques (Langues-de-Bœuf) .. 328
– Truffles 619, 627	– – Fingers 456	Corbet's Cookies 475
– – Chambéry 619	– Meringues 454	Cornetti 265
– – Curaçao 620	– Orange Filling 220	Cornflake Toasties 475
– – Light 621	– Pyramids 454	Cornflour Glaze 246
– – Nougat 625	– Rocks 474	Cornish Pasties 841
– – Orange 625	– Scones 311	– Filling 817
– – Surprise 627	– Slices Filling 222	– Saffron Loaves 265
– – White 627	– Tartlets 419	Coronets 328
– Virginias 627	– Topping 226	Costa Rica Slices 349
– Walnut Fondants 627	– Whirls 455	Couverture 246
Chorley Cakes 316	Coffee Almond Balls 445	– Tempering 246
– – Filling 224	– Balls 419, 445	Coventry God Cakes 328
Choux Pastries 192, 338	– Barquettes 420	– Puffs 332
– à la Crème 339	– Beans 347	Craquelins 475

875

Cream Baskets	420	
– Biscuits	475	
– Buns	339	
– Cheese Tartlets	420	
– Cookies	265	
– Dairy Gâteau	589	
– Fans	328	
– Horns	328	
– Macaroon Slices	534	
– Oysters	328	
– Points	455	
– Rolls	328	
– Slices	334	
Cream, Butter	227	
– Clotted	227	
– Dairy	227	
Cream in Goblets	707	
– Banana Caracas	707	
– Peach	708	
– Tangerine	708	
– Vanilla	708	
– – Delmonico	708	
– Wine	708	
– – Benedictine	709	
Cream, Petits Pots	709	
– Basic	709	
– Chocolate	709	
– Coffee	709	
– Geraldine	709	
– Montmorency	709	
– Raspberry	709	
– Zabaglione Gritti	709	
Creams, Italian	235	
Creams and Custards	227	
Creams, other	232	
– Additions to	232, 233	
– Bavarian	234, 698	
– Charlotte	235	
– Diplomat	235	
– Fudge, Basic	232	
– – Covering	233	
– – Filling	232	
– – Lighter	233	
– – Marshmallow	234	
– – Stock	234	
– – Strawberry	234	
– Merlot	233	
– Pistachio Marzipan	233	
– Russe	242	
– St-Honoré	235	
– Wine	233	
Creams, Various Dessert	705	
– Amontillado	705	
– Beau-Rivage	705	
– Caramel Custard	705	
– Chocolate Mould	705	
– Coffee Custard	706	
– Harlequin	706	
– Mogador Custard	706	
– Orange Harlequin	706	
– Orange Jeannette	706	
– Rob Roy	706	
– Royal Custard	705	
– Sherry	707	
– Vanilla Custard	705	
– Wine Merlot	707	
Crema Pasticcera	235	
Cremasciutti	429	
Crème Pâtissière	240	
Cremolini	529	
Crescents	329, 476	
– Almond	465, 531	
– – Vanilla	539	
– Turkey	329	
Cressini	513	
Cri-cri	527	

Croissants	176, 266	
Croquant	213	
– Biscuits	476	
– Japonaise Slices	460	
Croquembouche	599	
Croquettes	666	
– Chestnut	667	
– Fructidor	667	
– Rice	667	
– suisses	501	
Croûtes	667	
– Apricot	667	
– Fruit	667	
– Pineapple	667	
Crumb Pastry	190	
– Filling	224	
Crumpets	266	
Cuba	620	
Cubana Gâteau	589	
Cuisses-Dame	300	
– aux Amandes	300	
Cumin Sticks	824	
Cup Cakes	429	
– Chocolate Nougat	418	
– with Special Cake Flour	429	
Curd Filling	219	
– Lemon	242	
– – uncooked	242	
– Maids of Honour	219	
– Old English	219	
– Orange	241, 242	
– Potato	218	
– Yorkshire	219	
Curd Tarts		
– Maids of Honour	336	
– Old English	337	
– Yorkshire	321	
Currant Bread	266	
– Buns	266	
– Puffs	331	
– Slab	404	
Cushions	329	
Cussy Gâteau	569	
Custard	238	
– Almond	241	
– Bavarian	234, 698	
– Caramel	240	
– Charlotte	235	
– Cheese	242	
– Chocolate	239	
– Confectioner's	240	
– – France	240	
– – Great Britain	240	
– – Italy	235	
– – Cream	240	
– Danish Pastry	241	
– Frangipane Cream	240	
– – Fried	696	
– Fruit Puffs	332	
– Lemon (curd)	242	
– – uncooked	242	
– Orange (curd)	242	
– Pineapple Puffs	332	
– Puffs	332	
– Sabayon	241	
– St-Honoré	235	
– Tartlets	321	
– Vanilla	241	
– Walnut	241	
– Wine	241	
Custards and Creams	227	

D

Dairy Cream	227	
– Cheese Torte	578	
– Torte	589	

Dama Gâteau	589	
Danicheff Gâteau	569	
Danish Pastries	266	
– Pastry	177, 178	
– – Custard	241	
– – Ring	277	
– – Spreads	225	
– – Toppings	226	
Date and Honey Cakes	384	
– Cookies	476	
Decorated Shortbread	325	
Delina	527	
Delizia	529	
Derby Biscuits	476	
Desdemonas	347	
Desserts, cold	698	
– hot	666	
Devilled Wensleydale Tartlets	834	
Devon Scones	311	
Devonshire Splits	277	
Diabetic Cake	384	
Diamond Buns	278	
– Puffs	332	
Diamonds	429	
Dijon Honey Cakes	365	
Diplomat Cream	235, 699	
Diplomatici	527	
Display and Show-Pieces	597	
– Principles	597	
Dobos	430	
– Slices	349	
– Torte	588	
Dome Slices	430	
Doppelsemmel	290	
Dough Cake, Old English	278	
Doughnuts	304	
– Berlin	304	
– Cream	304	
– Rings	304	
– Tongues	304	
– Twists	304	
Dragon Tongues	459	
Dresdener Stollen	293	
Drums, Chocolate	520	
Duc de Coburg Biscuits	468	
Duchess Biscuits	476	
– Fingers	326	
– Rolls	339	
Duchesses	513	
Dumfries Gingerbread	365	
Dumplings	667	
– Apple	667	
– Bavarian	668	
– Norman	668	
– Plum	668	
Dundee Cake	384	
Dutch Apple Puffs	332	
– – Tartlets	322, 336	
– – Tart Filling	221	
Dutch Biscuits	485	
– Gâteau	552	
– Macaroons	534	
– Rusks	291	
– Tartlets	430	

E

Eaglet gâteau	569	
Eaglets	521	
Easter Bread		
– France	278	
– Germany	278	
– Italy	279	
– Topping	226	
Easter Cakes	430	
– Doves	279	
– Eggs	248	

– Fancies	359	
– Gâteau (le Pascal)	570	
– Torte	579	
Eccles Cakes	329	
– Fillings	217	
Eclairs	339, 521	
– Andalusian	339	
– Chocolate	339	
– Coffee	339	
– Foie gras	820	
– France	339	
– Great Britain	339	
– Hazelnut	339	
– Marron	339	
– Zabaglione	340	
Eel Rolls Stuffed	839	
Egg and Ham Filling	818	
Egg Glaze	375	
Egg Yolk Macaroons	534	
Eierschecke	279	
Elisen Lebkuchen	377	
Elizabeth Gâteau	550	
Engadine Nut Filling	224	
– Torte	593	
English Rarebit	836	
– Rolls	485	
– Rout Biscuits	485	
Enriched Bread	174	
– Teabread	174	
Equal Weight Cakes	513	
Estella Torte	579	
Exotic Desserts	747	
– Adua kat	748	
– Baklava	748	
– Ecudorian Banana Toddy	749	
– Haupia Aloha	750	
– Mango Kohu Pee	750	
– Pomegranate Cream	749	
– Tel Kadayif	749	
– Wune Wharn	751	
Exotic Gâteau	570	
Expo petits Fours	522	
Exquis	430	

F

Fabiola	340	
Fairy Cakes	430	
Fan Torte	579	
– Black and White	591	
Fancy Crescents	431	
Farls, Indian	313	
– Soda	313	
– Treacle	313	
– Wheaten	313	
Farmhouse Cakes	385	
– West of England	385	
– Scones	311	
– Treacle Biscuits	486	
Favoris	340	
Favourite Crunch	486	
Fermented Doughs	173	
– Pastry	178	
– Scones	279	
Fiamme	527	
Fiches l'Orgeat	486	
Fig Cakes	385	
– Fritters	669	
Figs	431	
Filled Honey Slices	378	
– Pastries	431	
Fillings-Cakes and Pastries	215	
– Almond	225	
– – Cheesecake	224	
– – Nut	222	
– – Slices	223	
– – Tart	221	

– Tartlet	221	
– Andorra	224	
– Appenzell	224	
– Bakewell Tartlets	221	
– Banbury	215, 217	
– Butter	225	
– Cannoli Siciliana	225	
– Cheese Cream	220	
– – Curd	223	
– Cherry Slice	223	
– Chocolate Slice	223	
– Chorley Cake	224	
– Cinnamon Tartlets	221	
– Coconut Orange	220	
– – Slice	222	
– – Tartlets	220	
– Crumb	224	
– Curd	219	
– Dutch Apple	221	
– Eccles	217	
– Engadine Nut	224	
– Frangipane	217, 218	
– Fruit and Nut	222	
– Fudge	232	
– Hazelnut	225	
– Hollandaise	223	
– Honey Nut	222	
– Iced Tartlet	222	
– Jap Slice	223	
– Lemon Curd	242	
– – Tart	221	
– Madeira	224	
– Maids of Honour	219	
– Marzipan	225	
– Milk Chocolate	225	
– Mincemeat	216	
– Old English Curd	219	
– Orange Curd	242	
– – and Date	220	
– – and Rice	220	
– Oxford Apple	222	
– Plunder, brown	225	
– – white	225	
– Potato Curd	218	
– Rice Tart	220	
– Royal Victoria	222	
– St. Gallen Biterteig	224	
– Swiss Tart	221	
– Victoria Cheesecake	222	
– Viennese Tartlet	220	
– Yorkshire Cheese Curd	219	
Fillings, Savoury	816	
– Bacon and Egg	816	
– Beef and Potato	816	
– Cheese	816, 817	
– – and Onion	816	
– Cornish Pastie	817	
– Cream	817	
– Forfar Bridies	817	
– Lamb	817	
– Meat Stuffing	817	
– – and Potato	817	
– Mutton	817	
– Pie Gravy	817	
– – Jelly	817	
– Pork Pie	818	
– Potato	818	
– Steak	818	
– – and Kidney	818	
– Veal and Ham	818	
Financière Cake	382	
Finger Rolls-Savoury	818	
Fingers Almond	531	
– Duchess	326	
– Hazelnut	433	
– Sweet and Sour	833	

Flans	741	
– Alsatian Custard	742	
– Andalusian	741	
– Apricot	741	
– Cherry	742	
– Fisherman's	742	
– Frangipane	742	
– Plain Custard	742	
Flans, Savoury	835	
Florence	621	
Florentine Biscuits	513	
– Buns	280	
– Slices	432	
– Torte	580	
Florentines	431	
Florettes	431	
Flour Cakes	432	
Flower Vase	645	
Focaccine	176	
Foie Gras Brioche	844	
– Eclairs	820	
Fondant Cubes	429	
– Marshmallow Tartlets	322	
– Meringue	243	
– Pretzels	487	
– Recipe and Method	243	
Fondants	631	
Forfar Bridies	841	
– Filling	817	
Fougasse	280	
Fragola Gâteau	589	
Fraisalia Meringues	455	
Frangipane Cream Custard	240	
– Slices	432	
– Fillings	217, 218	
– Fruit Slices	432	
– Macaroon Slices	537	
– Macaroons	535	
– Slices	334	
Frankfurter Kranz	580	
Frascati	432, 514	
French Bread (Parisette)	288	
– Basic Dough	175	
French Croissants	176, 177, 266	
– Gâteaux	567	
– Macaroons	535	
– Pastries	329	
– Puddings	316	
– Stick Sandwiches	844	
Fried Choux Rings	300	
– Scones	302	
Fritters and Batters	299, 668	
– American	299	
– Apple	668	
– – Surprise	669	
– Apricot	669	
– Banana	669	
– Carlsbad	669	
– Carnival	300	
– Cheese	819	
– Cheltonia Peach	670	
– Cuisses-Dame	300	
– – aux Amandes	300	
– Currant Puffs	300	
– Fig	669	
– Grand-Marnier Orange	670	
– Lyons	669	
– Muzen	301	
– Muzen Almond Puffs	301	
– Pineapple	670	
– Pretzel Choux	301	
– Rose	301	
– Scones, fried	302	
– Schenkeli	302	
– Shrovetide	302	
– Snowballs	303	

877

Fritters and Batters (cont.)
- Soufflé 670
- Spritzkuchen 301
- Tobacco Rolls 303
- Wiener Krapfen 303
Fromage de Brie 432
Fruit Bread 280
Fruit Compotes 724
- Apple 724
- Apricot 724
- Bananas 724
- Cherries 724
- Figs 724
- Greengages 725
- Mirabelle Plums 725
- Mixed 724
- Peaches 725
- Pears 725
- Plums 725
- Prunes 725
- Raspberries 725
- Rhubarb 725
- Strawberries 725
Fruit Desserts, cold 710
- Apples Brissac 710
- - Gabriella 710
- - Maltese Style 710
- Apricots Countess Style ... 710
- - Mascot 710
- - Negrita 711
- - W. Indian Style 711
- Avocados Louison 711
- Bananas Copacabana 711
- - Lemon custard 711
- - Meringue 711
- - Theodor 712
- - Swedish Style 712
- Cherries Dijon Style 712
- - Eltville 712
- - Montmorency 712
- - Van Dyke 712
- - Viennese Style 712
- Eaton mess 713
- Figs Mistral 713
- - Paradiso 713
- Fried eggs 713
- Gooseberry Fool 713
- Grapefruit Floride 713
- Lemons frosted 714
- Lychees Chinese Style 714
- - Oriental Style 714
- - with Ricard 714
- Melon Majestic 714
- Orange Haifa 715
- - Ilona 715
- - Riviera 715
- - Surprise 715
- - Syracuse 715
- Peaches Beau-Rivage 716
- - Belle Forestière 716
- - Cleo de Merode 716
- - Deslys 716
- - Flambéed with Bénédictine 716
- - Frascati 717
- - Melba 717
- Pears Almina 717
- - Balmoral 717
- - Bristol 717
- - Cardinal 717
- - Château-Lafite 718
- - Châtelaine 718
- - Dauphine 718
- - Esmeralda 718
- - Hélène 718
- - Maja 719
- - Tetrazzini 719

- Persimmons Creole 719
- - Cyrill 719
- - Pineapple Bourdaloue .. 719
- - Haroun-al-Rashid 719
- - Jamaica Style 720
- - Kenya 720
- - Ninon 720
- - Roswitha 720
- - Raspberries Beatrice 721
- - Côte d'Azur 721
- - Erimar 721
- - Kitty 721
- - Rote Grütze 723
- Strawberry Boats Congolese 721
- - Curaçao 722
- - Eugenia 722
- - Femina 722
- - Lerina 722
- - Melba 722
- - Non Plus Ultra 722
- - Romanoff 723
- - Verona 723
- Supreme of Fruit,
  Paris Style 723
- Tangerines Côte d'Azur... 723
- - frosted................. 723
Fruit Desserts, hot 670
- Apples Bulgarian 670
- - Chateaubriand 671
- - Condé 671
- - Manon 671
- - Marietta 671
- - Mary Stuart 671
- Apricots Condé 671
- - flambé 671
- Bananas Bourdaloue 672
- - Martinique 672
- - and Pineapple,
  Javanese Style 672
- - Soufflé 672
- Cherries Eldorado........ 673
- - flambéed 673
- - Gratin................. 673
- Peaches Andalusian 673
- - flambéed 673
- - Jan Gravendeel 674
- - Stuffed Cancelleria 674
- Pears à la Mode 674
- - flambéed 674
- - Schouwalow 674
- Pineapple Condé......... 675
- - Marina 675
- - Raspberries Gratin Eden .. 675
Fruit Jellies 729
Fruit Juices 665
- Cherry 665
- Lemon 666
- Orange 666
- Quince 666
- Raspberry 666
- Strawberry 666
Fruit Levels in Cakes 204
Fruit and other Pies 679
- Apple 680
- Blackberry and Apple 680
- Gooseberry............... 680
- Maryland 680
- Mince 680
- Rhubarb 681
- Rhubarb and Apple 681
Fruit Purées 665
- Apricot 665
- Cherry 665
- Peach 665
- Raspberry 665
- Red Currant 665

- Strawberry 665
Fruit Salads 725
- fresh 725
- Cardinal 726
- in Jelly 726
- Melon and Raspberry 726
- Niçoise 726
- Ninette 726
- Orange and Banana 726
- Peach 726
- with Ice Cream 726
Fruit Almond Cakes 386
- - Slices.................. 535
- and Nut Biscuits 487
- and Nut Filling 222
- Biscuits 487
- Bread 280
- Ovals 487
- Slices.................... 432
- Sponges 345
- Stall 611
- Tarts 321, 738
- Tartlets.................. 433
- Torte 580
- Turnovers 281, 337
Fruited Macaroon Tarts 535
- Meringues 455
- Scones 311
Fruits, small 518
Frying Butter 299
Fudge, Chocolate 232
- Covering 233
- Cream 232
- Filling 232
- - lighter 233
- Gâteau 550
Fudges 232, 630

G

Ganache Recipes 250
- Butter 250
- Egg 250
- Firm 250
- Fresh Cream 251
- Crescents 536
- Japonaise Slices 460
Garnishes
- Open Sandwiches 846
- Savouries 816
Gâteaux and Torten 545
- Austria 565
- - Almond Torte 565
- - Chocolate Buttercream
    Torte 565
- - Hazelnut Torte 565
- - Linzer Torte 565, 566
- - Panama Torte 566
- - Parisian Torte 566
- - Pineapple Mousseline
    Torte 566
- - Sacher Torte 566, 567
- - Sand Cake 567
- - Thalhof Torte 567
- France 567
- - Alcazar Gâteau 568
- - Amandine Tourte 568
- - Birthday Gâteau 568
- - Brie Tourte 568
- - Charlemagne Gâteau .. 568
- - Christmas Log 568
- - Croquembouche 599
- - Cussy Gâteau 569
- - Danicheff Gâteau 569
- - Eaglet Gâteau 569
- - Easter Gâteau 570
- - Exotic Gâteau 570

– – Guayaquil Gâteau 570	– – in Paper Cases 551	– Cherry 529
– – Lemon Tourte 571	– – Other Gâteaux 549, 551	– Coffee 529
– – Little Duke Gâteau 571	– – – Almond 551	– Cremolini 529
– – Lutetia Chestnut Gâteau . 571	– – – Chessboard 552	– Delizia 529
– – Marcelin Gâteau 571	– – – Chocolate Choux 552	– Hawai 529
– – Mascotte Gâteau 572	– – – Choux with Fruit 552	– Marsolini 529
– – Mexican Gâteau 572	– – – Dutch 552	– Nocciola 529
– – Mille-feuille 572	– – – Jap Sponge 552	– Orange 529
– – Mocha Gâteau 572	– – – Strawberry Meringue . 552	– Super 529
– – Orange Mousseline	– – Special Gâteau 550	Genoa Cakes 386
Gâteau 572	– – – Anniversaries 550	Genoese 198, 200
– – Orange Tourte 573	– – – Elizabeth 550	– Almond 200
– – Pierrette Gâteau 573	– Sponge	– Aveline 200
– – Pineapple Tourte 573	– – – Bars 546	– Boiled 202
– – Pistachio Tourte 573	– – – with Fruits 546	– Chocolate 200
– – Polish Tourte 573	– – – Swiss Rolls 195, 546	– Coffee 201
– – Praline Gâteau 573	– Holland 587	– Fancies 407
– – – Tourte 574	– – Buttercream 587	– Glacés 407
– – Queen Pomare Gâteau .. 574	– – Christmas Wreath 587	– Heavy 199
– – Rosemary Gâteau 574	– – Hearts and Hams 587	– High Sugar 199
– – Sans-Gêne Gâteau 574	– – Mathilde Gâteau 587	– – Chocolate 200
– – St-Honoré 727	– – Nougatine Gâteau 587	– Lemon 201
– – Success Gâteau 574	– – Vanilla Gâteau 587	– Light 199
– – Sylvia Gâteau 574	– Hungary 588	– Margherita 201
– – Tourte niçoise 575	– – Dobos Torte 588	– Marzipan 202
– – Tourte Religieuse 575	– Italy 588	– Rose 202
– – Turin Gâteau 575	– – Arancia 588	– Sheet 203
– – Valencia Gâteau 575	– – Argentina 589	– Turin 202
– – Viennese Tourte 576	– – Autumn 589	– Walnut 202
– – Walnut Gâteau 576	– – Cubana 589	Gevulde Koeken 431
– Germany 576	– – Dairy Cream 589	Gianduja 213
– – Anniversary Numeral ... 576	– – Dama 589	– Cream 213
– – Birthday Torte 576	– – Fragola 589	Ginger and Honey Goods 361
– – – Children's 578	– – Lucullus 589	Ginger Biscuits 433, 488
– – Black Forest Cherry Torte 576	– – Malaga 589	– Boats 365
– – Bread Torte 577	– – Mimosa 589	– Cake 367
– – Budapest Pineapple Torte 577	– – Moulin Rouge 590	– Cakes 367
– – Cheese Cream Torte ... 577	– – Novecento 590	– – oval 370
– – Chocolate Torte 578	– – Polenta e Osei 590	– Crisps 488
– – Christmas Torte 578	– – Portorico 590	– Honey Cakes 369
– – Dairy Cream Cheese Torte 578	– – Rum 590	– Japonaise Slices 459
– – Easter Torte 579	– – Selva 590	– Nuts 488
– – Estella Torte 579	– – Sorrentina 590	– Ovals 368
– – Fan Torte 579	– – St-Honoré 590, 728	– Sandwiches 368
– – Florentine Torte 580	– – – Florentine 728	– Snaps 364, 370
– – Forêt-Noire Torte 727	– – – Selva 728	– Spice Loaf 368
– – Frankfurter Kranz 580	– – – Tuscany 728	– Sponges 368
– – Fruit Torte 580	– – Tirrenia 590	– Tartlets 322
– – Hazelnut Torte 580	– – Torino 590	– Wholemeal Slices 373
– – Kirsch Torte 580	– Switzerland 591	Gingerbread 366
– – Macaroon Torte 581	– – Aargau Carrot Torte 591	– Aberdeen 362
– – Margret Cake 581	– – Black and White Fan	– Almond 363
– – Mignon Torte 581	Torte 591	– Ashbourne 363
– – Mocha Buttercream Torte 581	– – Black Forest Cherry Torte 591	– Dumfries 365
– – Oracle Torte 582	– – Caracas Cake 592	– Flanders 366
– – Orange Torte 582	– – Caraque Tourte 592	– France 365
– – Painter's Palette 582	– – Caravelle Gâteau 592	– Grantham 369
– – Parisian Strawberry Torte 582	– – Cherry Cheese Torte ... 592	– Grasmere 369
– – Peach Wine Cream Torte 583	– – Chessboard Gâteau 593	– Great Britain 366
– – Peppermint Cake 582	– – Engadine Nut Torte 593	– Kirriemuir 369
– – Pineapple Baumtorte ... 583	– – Lemania Gâteau 593	– Marmalade 370
– – – Fruit Torte 584	– – Lemon Mousseline Torte. 593	– Nottingham 370
– – – Ice Parfait Torte 583	– – Mille-feuille Torte 593	– Old English 370
– – Prince Regent Torte ... 584	– – Nougatine - Golden Book 594	– Slices 366
– – Red Currant Meringue	– – Punch Torte 594	– Spiced 372
Torte 585	– – Rolla Gâteau 594	– Spices 361
– – Regent Torte 585	– – Truffle Tourte 594	– Squares 366, 367
– – Russian Charlotte Torte . 585	– – Victoria Torte 594	– Wholemeal 373
– – Sacher Torte 585	– – Walnut Torte 595	– Wrexham 373
– – Spanish Vanilla Torte ... 586	– – Wine Cream Torte 595	Glarner Brötli 290
– – Strawberry Dairy Cream	– – Zigomar 595	Glazed Fruits 643
Torte 586	– – Zuger Kirschtorte 595	Glazes 245
– – Walnut Torte 586	– U.S.A.	– Apricot 245
– Great Britain 545	– – Chocolate Rum Pie 727	– Arrowroot 245
– – Battenburg 547	Geneva Assortment 529	– Bun 245
– – Layer Cakes 548	– Bombetta Taormina 529	– Cornflour 246

879

Glazes Cornflour Gel 245	– Walnut Cakes 386	– – Riche-Alexandra 797
– Egg 375	Honey Cakes 361	– – – Délice 797
– Gum Arabic 246	– Aberdeen 362	– – – Edouard VII 797
– Honey 245	– Appenzell 363	– – – George V 797
– Jelly 245	– Dijon 365	– – – Mon Rêve 798
– Leckerli 246	– Ginger 369	– – – Parisienne 798
– Magenbrot 246	– Squares 369	– Bombes 776
– Water Icing 246	Hot Cross Buns 282	– – Basic Mixture 776
Gloucester Lardy Cakes 283	– Crossing Paste 283	– – American 776
Goat's Paws 455	Hot Desserts 666	– – Archiduc 776
Golden Bows 488	– Charlottes 666	– – Aurélie 776
– Tart 695	– Croquettes 666	– – Aurore 776
– Tartlets 322	– Croûtes 667	– – Baroda 776
Goldfish 329	– Dumplings 667	– – Bourdaloue 776
Gooseberry Choux 340	– Fritters 668	– – Bragance 776
– Strudel 335	– Fruit 670	– – Brazilian 776
– Tartlets 322	– Omelettes 675	– – Camargo 776
Graham Biscuits 489	– Pancakes 676	– – Chantilly 777
Grand-Marnier Orange	– Pannequets 679	– – Chateaubriand 777
Fritters 670	– Pies 679	– – Créole 777
Grantham Ginger Bread 369	– Puddings 681	– – Danicheff 777
Grape Tartlets 322	– Soufflés 685	– – Dauphinoise 777
Greengage Cannons 329	– Strudel 688	– – Dioclétian 777
– Marshmallow Tartlets 322	– Tarts 694	– – Diplomate 777
Guayaquil Gâteau 570	– Various 695	– – Esterhazy 777
– Tartlets 324	Hot Meringue 206	– – Falstaff 777
Guernsey gauche 281	Hotplate Goods,	– – Fedora 777
Gugelhupf 281, 282	– Baking Powder 313	– – Hamlet 777
– Viennese 281	– – Farls, Indian 313	– – Hernani 777
Gum Arabic Glaze 246	– – – Soda 313	– – Japanese 777
– Pastes 252	– – – Treacle 313	– – Joinville 777
Gypsies 521	– – – Wheaten 313	– – Kranzler 777
	– – Oatcakes 313	– – Madeleine 777
H	– – Pikelets 314	– – Maltese 777
Half Moons 514	– – Potato Scones 314	– – Marquise de Sévigné ... 777
Ham Croissants 821	– – Salt Scones 314	– – Médicis 778
Hamburger Rolls 819	– – Scotch Pancakes 313	– – Ménélik 778
Harlequin Jelly Slices 349	– – Soda Scones 314	– – Miss Hellyet 778
– Rolls 359	– – Welsh Cakes 314	– – Montmorency 778
– Slices 819	Hotplate Goods–yeasted 313	– – Nelusko 778
Harlequins 514	– – Crumpets 266	– – Nesselrode 778
Harvest Bread 600, 601	– – Muffins 285	– – Oriental 778
Hawaï 526	– – – sweet 286	– – Portuguese 778
Hazelnut and Almond		– – Prince of Wales 778
Products 209, 213. 531	**I**	– – Princesse 778
– Avelines 521	Iagos 347	– – Richelieu 778
– Buns 309	Iced Tartlets 434	– – Riviera 778
– Cream 237	– Filling 222	– – Santiago 778
– Duchesses 433	Ices 753, 754	– – Sappho 778
– Filling 225	– artificial 811	– – Scotch 778
– Fingers 433	– assorted 808	– – Success 778
– Japonaise Fancies 521	– – Baumkuchen 808	– – Sultane 778
– Petits Fours 521	– – Christmas Candle 809	– – Tosca 778
– Soufflés 521	– – – Parfait 786	– – Trocadero 779
– Spiced Biscuits 499	– – Chocolate 808	– – Tutti-Frutti 779
– Squares 433	– – Coffee 809	– – Victoria 779
– Torte 565, 580	– – Fior di Latte 809	– – White Lady 779
Hazelnuts 521	– – – Bellini 809	– – Zamora 779
Hearts and Hams 587	– – – Orlandini 809	– – Zanzibar 779
Heavy Genoese 199	– – – Violetta 810	– Bricks 764
Heckle Biscuits 489	– – Madeleine 810	– – to mould and freeze ... 764
Helvetia Slices 433	– – Martinique 810	– – – Old Method 764
High Sugar Genoese 199	– – Meringue 810	– – – New Method 764
– – Chocolate 199	– – – Doris 810	– Anisette 773
Hittnauer Makronen 514	– – – Ravanola 810	– Apricot 773
Hollandaise Filling 223	– – Plombières 810	– Benedictine 773
– Tartlets 322	– – Profiteroles Mafalda ... 811	– Blanchette 773
Honey Almond Cakes 386	– – Snowball 811	– Cardinal 773
– – Tartlets 536	– – Temptation 811	– Carmen 773
– Biscuits 489	– – with Cream 762	– – Chocolate 773
– Glaze 245	– baked 788	– – Coffee 773
– Nut Boats 434	– – Belle-de-Nuit 788	– – Praline 773
– Nut Filling 222	– – Grand Succès 788	– Combinations 764
– Nut Slices 334	– – Nero 797	– Créole 773
– Squares 369	– – Norwegian 797	– Duke of Orléans 774
– Topping 227	– – Paquita 797	– – Excelsior 774

– – Fanchonnette 774	– – Saint Michel 783	– Mousses 785
– – Imperatrice 774	– – Savoy 783	– – Cream 785
– – Liqueurs-Various 774	– – Suzanne 783	– – Fruit 786
– – Marie-Louise 774	– – Thaïs 783	– Parfaits 786
– – Maxim's 774	– – Tripolitaine 783	– – Basic Mix 786
– – Mont-Blanc 774	– – Tunisienne 783	– – Chocolate 786
– – Montmorency 774	– Creams 754	– – Christmas 786
– – Neapolitan 774	– – Almond 755	– – Coffee 786
– – Nesselrode 774	– – – Praline 755	– – Marie-Brizard 787
– – Odette 774	– – Caramel 755	– – Pistachio 787
– – Parisian 775	– – Chestnut 755	– – Praline 787
– – Pistachio 775	– – Chocolate 756	– – Princess 787
– – Praline 775	– – Coffee 756	– – Tea 787
– – Raspberry 775	– – – Praline 756	– – Vanilla 787
– – Rivoli 775	– – – White 756	– – with Liqueurs 787
– – Strawberry 775	– – Hazelnut Praline 756	– Puddings 787
– – Sylvia 775	– – Liqueur Flavours 758	– – Japanese 787
– – Tortoni 775	– – Pistachio 757	– – Lyrical 787
– – Vanilla 775	– – Rose 757	– – Majestic 787
– Cassatas 800	– – Rum 757	– – Merville 788
– – Napolitana 800	– – Tea 757	– – Miramar 788
– – Siciliana 800	– – Vanilla (Basic) 754	– – Nancy 788
– – Tortoni 800	– – – white 757	– Punch 805
– – Tosca 800	– – Violet 758	– – Burgundy 805
– Charlottes 779	– – Walnut 758	– – Claret 806
– – Aga Khan 779	– Fruit with Cream 762	– – Florentine 806
– – Berlioz 779	– – Apricot 762	– – Lombard 806
– – Marie-Louise 779	– – Cherry 762	– – Maraschino 806
– – Procope 779	– – – black 762	– – Rum 806
– Coupes 779	– – Currant, black 762	– – Roman 806
– – Apricotine 780	– – – red 762	– – Sherry 806
– – Adelina Patti 780	– – – white 762	– Sorbets and Granites 804
– – Alphonse 780	– – Greengage 763	– – Fruit 804
– – Andalouse 780	– – Lime 763	– – Granites 805
– – Arlesian 780	– – Peach 763	– – Lemon 805
– – Belle Dijonnaise 780	– – Pineapple 763	– – Liqueur 805
– – Berlinoise 780	– – Pomegranate 763	– – Marquises 805
– – Black Forest 780	– – Raspberry 764	– – Orange 805
– – Brazilian 780	– – Strawberry 764	– – Wine 805
– – Camargo 780	– – Tangerine 764	– Soufflés 798
– – Capriccio 780	– Gâteaux 783	– – Bénédictine 798
– – Chateaubriand 781	– – Combinations 785	– – Cavaliera 798
– – Cleopatra 781	– – Green Goddess 784	– – Chocolate 799
– – Coppelia 781	– – Kranzler 784	– – Coffee 799
– – Diable rose 781	– – Mocha 785	– – Fruit 798
– – Edna May 781	– – Monte Bianco 785	– – Liqueur 799
– – Elizabeth 781	– – Monviso 785	– – Miracle 799
– – Emma Calvé 781	– – Neapolitan 784	– – Montmorency 799
– – Eugénie 781	– – Nut with Cognac Cherries 784	– – Paquita 799
– – Fiammetta 781	– – Queen of Hearts 784	– – Pistachio 799
– – Germaine 781	– – Red Queen 784	– – Praline 799
– – Gladstone 781	– – Santa Lucia 785	– – Tortoni 799
– – Herriot 781	– – Siciliana 784	– Spooms 806
– – Jamaïque 781	– – Suzie 785	– – Apricot 807
– – Japonaise 781	– – White Lady 784	– – Raspberry 807
– – Java 781	– Italian semi-frozen Desserts. 800	– – Strawberry 807
– – Joséphine Baker 782	– – Astrogel 800	– Sundaes 807
– – Jubilee 782	– – Bavarese St. Vincent ... 801	– – Creole 807
– – Lucullus 782	– – Charlotte 801	– – Imperial Palace 807
– – Madeleine 782	– – Damasco 802	– – Longchamp 807
– – Marie Brizard 782	– – Diplomatico 802	– – Morocco 807
– – Marie-Louise 782	– – Java 802	– – Ninon 807
– – Mercedes 782	– – Luisa Cream 801	– – Osborne 808
– – Metternich 782	– – Parfait Zabaglione 803	– – Pineapple 808
– – Miramar 782	– – – Coffee 803	– – Rainbow 808
– – Miss Hellyet 782	– – Pineapple 803	– – Royal Banana 808
– – Mistinguette 782	– – Poker Ace 803	– – Royal Peach 808
– – Monte-Cristo 782	– – Portuguese 801	– – Strawberry Whip 808
– – Montmorency 782	– – Sabrina 801	– – Temptation 808
– – Moscovite 783	– – Soraya 803	– – Tutti-frutti 808
– – Mozart 783	– – Spumone, Chocolate ... 803	– – Viennese 808
– – Orientale 783	– – – Moka 803	– Water or Fruit Ices 758
– – Princess Olga 783	– – – and Tartufi 803	– – Apricot 758
– – Princesse 783	– – Twist 804	– – Banana 759
– – Rêve de Bébé 783	– – Zuccotto 804	– – Cherry 759
– – Rose-Chéri 783	– – Zuppa 802	– – Currant, black 759

881

Ices Water Currant red 759	– Almond 458	– Oxford 283
– – – white 759	– Burgdorfer 458	– Wiltshire 284
– – Greengage 759	– Buttercream Fancies 458	Large Cakes 381
– – Lemon ......·......... 759	– Cherry 459	Layer Cakes 548
– – Liqueur 762	– Chocolate 459	– Turkey 596
– – Loganberry 759	– – Walnut 459	Lebkuchen 374
– – Melon 760	– Coffee 459	– Doughs, basic 374
– – – Cantaloup 760	– – Dessert 459	– – Storage 374
– – Nectarine 760	– Dragon's Tongues 459	– – Sugar 374
– – Orange 760	– Fingers 460	– – Treacle 374
– – Peach 760	– – for Piping 209	– – Water 374
– – Pear 760	– – for Roulades 209	– Raw Materials 374
– – Pineapple 760	– Ginger 459	– – Aerating Agents 375
– – – and Lemon 760	– Hazelnut 459	– – Almonds 375
– – Plum, Victoria 761	– Marbled 460	– – Candied Peel 374
– – Raspberry 761	– Orange 460	– – Dusting Flour 375
– – – white 761	– Pineapple 460	– – Lemon Zest 374
– – – and Red Currant 761	– Piping 209	– – Spices 375
– – Stock Syrup for 758	– Rochers 458, 461	– Icings 375
– – Strawberry 761	– Royal Chantilly 461	– – Brown Glaze 375
– – Tangerine 761	– Sarahs 461	– – Chocolate 375
Icings 243	– Schaffhauser Tongues 461	– – Egg 375
– Fondant 243	– Slices, Chocolate 459	– – Gum Arabic 375
– Fondant Meringue 243	– – Croquant 460	– – Lemon 375
– Orange 244	– – Ganache 460	– – Meringue 375
– Royal 243	– – Ginger 459	– – Raspberry 376
– Soft Chocolate 243, 244	– – Kirsch 460	– – Stock Syrup 376
– Water 243	– – Pineapple 460	– – Transparent 376
Ischl Linz Fancies 434	– – Schaffhauser 461	– – Vanilla 376
Italian Creams 235	– Sponge Gâteau 545	– Almond 376
– Alchermes 238	– Superlatives 461	– Brown-Nürnberg 377
– Argentina 237	– Switzerland 460	– Chocolate 377
– – Chocolate 238	– Torten Bases 209	– Elisen 377
– Arlecchini 238	– Zungli Mixture 209	– Filled Liegnitz 378
– Buttercream 236	Jeannettes 435	– Hearts 377, 378
– – Imperial 236	Jellies 253, 729	– Lucerne 379
– – Meringue 237	– Basic 253	– Nut 379
– – Nougatine 237	– Apricot 254	– Triangles 378
– – Various Flavours 237	– Cold Set 255	– White, Nürnberg 379
– – With Fruit 237	– – Complement 255	Leckerli, Basle 363
– – Zabaglione 236	– Fondants 254	– Glaze 246
– Cappuccini 238	– Petits Fours 521	– Zurich 539
– Chestnut 238	– Piping 254	Leipzig Danubian Stollen 293
– Chocolate 238	– Wine 255	Lémania Gâteau 593
– Coffee 237	Jellies, Dessert 729	Lemon Almond Cakes 387
– Crema Pasticcera 235	– Basic 729	– Biscuits 490
– – Coffee 235	– Fruit 729	– Buns 284
– – Flavourings for 235	– Kirsch 729	– Cakes 387
– Gianduja 238	– Moscovite 729	– Choux 340
– Hazelnut 237	– Orange 730	– Coconut Slices 349
– Maraschino 237	– Wine 730	– Cream Fancies 347
– Meringue 237	Jelly Glaze 245	– – Rolls 359
– Orange 237	Jewish Almond Biscuits 464	– Curd 242
– Pistachio 238	Jumbles 364	– Frangipane Slices 435
– Stracchino 236		– Genoese 201
– Zabaglione 236	**K**	– Macaroons 536
– – Chocolate 236	Kaiserlaibl 455	– Marshmallow Tartlets 322
– – Coffee 236	King Cakes 387	– Meringue Tartlets 323
Italian macaroons 514	Kirriemuir Ginger Bread 369	– Mousseline Torte 593
Italian meringue 206, 207	Kirsch Cubes 349	– Puffs 332
Italians 527	– Fondant Centres 621	– Rolls 435
	– Glacés 527	– Scrolls 490
J	– Japonaise Slices 460	– Squares 336
Jam and Cream Tarts 337	– Pomponnettes 283	– Tart Filling 221
– Scones 311	– Torte 580	– Tartlets 435
– Tartlets 322	– – Zuger 595	– Tourte 571
– Tarts, large 321	Koenigsberg Marzipan 616	Lemons 435
– Turnovers ......·........ 337	Kougelhopf 282	– Petits Fours 522
Jamaica 621	Krik-krak 283	Leopolds 340
Jamaican Cakes 434	Kuchen Dough 176	Liegnitz Lebkuchen 378
Jamettes 434		Light Genoese 199
Jan Hagel Biscuits 489	**L**	Lightly Fruited Cakes 388
Jap Slice 435	Langues-de-Bœuf 328	Lille Waffles 306
– Filling 223	Langues-de-Chat Biscuits 414, 489	Lincolnshire Plum Loaf 284
Japonais 521	Lardy Cakes 283	Linz Beans 436
Japonaise 208, 458	– Gloucester 283	– Chocolate Slices 436

882

– Pastry 188-190	Malaga 622	– – Ring 458
– Tartlets 436	– Gâteau 589	– Banana Slices 453
– Cakes 388	– Slices 349	– Basic Recipes 205, 206
– Fancies 436	Maltese Lemon Slices 437	– Biscuits 456
– Fruit Slices 436	Maids of Honour Filling 219	– Boats 456
– Torte 565, 566	– Tartlets 336	– Boiled (Italian) 206, 207
Liqueur Chocolates 627	Maraschino Cream 237	– Chocolate 206, 207
– without Starch 628	– Dainties 490	– – Pies 418
Lisettes 436	– Mignons 527	– – Sticks 454
Little Duke Gâteau 571	– Slices 350	– Citron Slices 438
– Logs 622	– Tartlets 323	– Coconut Fancies 454
– Pies 822	Marbled Japonaise 460	– – Pyramids 454
Livancen 697	Marcelin Gâteau 571	– – Whirls 455
Liverpool Bun Loaf 284	Margherita Genoese 201	– Coffee Almond Balls 455
London Bath Buns 260	Margret Cake 581	– – Balls 455
– Tea Cakes 295	Marie 622	– – Kisses 455
Loukoum 641	Marignan 285	– Cold 205, 206
Loundon Fingers 326	Marigolds 490	– Cream Points 455
Lucca Eyes 340	Marion Delorme Tartlets ... 834	– Custard Rings 458
Lucullus Gâteau 589	Marionnettes 437	– Fancies 456
– Slices 436	Marmalade Gingerbread 370	– Figures 456
Lunch Cake 388	Marronnettes 522	– Fingers 456
Luncheon Cakes 388	Marrons glacés 642	– for Decoration 208
Lutétia Chestnut Gâteau 571	Marshmallow 630	– Goat's Paws 455
Luxury Fruit Cake 388	– Cream 234	– Hot 205, 206
Lyons Fritters 669	– Drops 347	– Mushrooms 457
	– Slices 437	– Nests 456
M	– Strawberry 234	– Nuts 456
Magali 436	– Walnut Tartlets 324	– Peach Baskets 457
Macarons de Nancy 490	Marsolini 529	– Raspberry Kisses 457
– à l'Orange 490	Martinique Moccatines 522	– Rochers 458
Macaroon Biscuits 536	Marzipan and Almond Pastes. 210	– Rocks 457
– Bows 536	– Filling 225	– Shells 457
– Cream Slices 534	– Genoese 202	– – Chocolate 457
– Creams 536	– Leaves 438	– Spanish 207
– Fancies 536, 537	– Modelling 612	– Strawberry 207
– Favours 537	– Models, Apple 613	– Swiss 207
– Frangipane Slices 537	– – Apricot 613	– Vacherin 458
– Fruited Tarts 535	– – Banana 613	Meringues 205, 453
– Pastes 212	– – Basket of Fruit 613	– Banana 453
– Petits Fours 522	– – Bunch of Grapes 613	– Chestnut 453
– Rings 537	– – Cabbage 613	– Chocolate Cream 453
– Tea Fancies 531	– – Carrot 613	– – Walnut 454
– Torte 581	– – Cauliflower 613	– Coconut 454
Macaroons, Angelica 506	– – Chestnut 613	– – Cherry 454
– Apricot 506	– – Christmas Tree 615	– Copacabana 455
– Chocolate 533	– – Dogs 615	– Drying 207
– Christmas 534	– – Father Christmas Head . 615	– Fraisalia 455
– Cinnamon 534	– – Fishes 614	– Fruited 455
– Coconut 534	– – Frogs 615	– Kaiserlaibl 455
– Cream Slices 534	– – Hedgehogs 615	– Moulded 457
– Dutch 534	– – Königsberg 616	– Strawberry Cream 458
– Egg Yolk 534	– – Lemon 614	Mexican Gâteau 572
– Frangipane 535	– – Orange 614	Mignon Bases 187
– French 535	– – Parsnip 614	– Torte 581
– Hittnauer 514	– – Peach 614	Mignons Amarena 525
– Italian 514	– – Pear 614	Milan Puffs 333
– Lemon 536	– – Peas in Pod 614	– Slices 438
– Nancy 490	– – Piglets 615	Milanese Pastry 187
– on Sweet Pastry 537	– – Plum 614	Milk Chocolate Filling 225
– Orange 490, 538	– – Poodle 615	– Rolls 285
– Parisian 538	– – Santa Claus 615	Mille-feuille Gâteau 572
– Pineapple 538	– – Strawberry 614	– Slices 439
– Pistachio 517	– Pistachio Cream 238	– Torte 593
– Raspberry Oval 538	– Sticks 438	Mimosa Gâteau 589
– Scotch 538	Marzipans 211, 212	Mince Pies-Puff Pastry 329
– Soft 539	Mascotte Gâteau 572	– Sweet Pastry 315
– Truffle 539	Massillons 438	Mincemeat 216
– Viennese 539	Mathilde Gâteau 587	Miniature Chessboards 623
Maddalena Torte 401	Meat and Potato Filling 817	Mirlitons 439
Madeira Cakes 397	– Stuffing 817	– Rouen 439
– Filling 224	Mecca Rolls 340	Moccatines 522
Madeleines 515	Medusa Mignons 527	Mocha 527
Madelons 340	Melide Slices 438	– Buttercream Torte 581
Madrid Dainties 436	Melting Moments 491	– Gâteau 572
Magdalena Slices 437	Meringue Bases 207	– Mignons 524

883

Mocha Squares	350	
– Torte	581	
– Tourte	572	
Mochas	515	
Modelling Pastes	251	
– Almond	251	
– Chocolate	253	
– Gum	252	
– Selva	253	
– Sugar	252	
– White Chocolate	253	
Montagner Biscuits	491	
Montélimar Nougat	641	
Montelman	491	
Moors Heads	340, 347	
Moque Biscuits	491	
Moss Biscuits	492	
Moulded Meringues	457	
Moulin-Rouge Gâteau	590	
Mousseline Cake	397	
Mousses and Mousselines	730	
– Chocolate	730	
– Merlot Sabayon	730	
– Raspberry	730	
– Strawberry	731	
Mozart Plaited Bread	285	
Muffins	285	
– Oven Baked	285	
– Sweet	286	
Munich Prince Regent Torte	584	
Mushrooms	457	
Mutton Pies	841	
– Filling	817	
Muzen	301	
– Almond Puffs	301	

N

Nancéens	439
Nantes Biscuits	492
Napoléon Slices	439
Neapolitan Peach Tartlets	439
– Biscuits	492
– Slices	439
– Sweet Pastry	188
Nests Mignons	527
Nice Biscuits	492
Nichettes	440
Niçoise Tourte	575
Nocciole	529
Nottingham Gingerbread	370
Nougat	213
– Biscuits	440, 492
– Buttercream	231
– Chocolate	214
– Creams	347
– Fudge Biscuits	440
– Montélimar	641
– Ovals	493
– Paste	214
– de Paris	214
– Slices	359, 440
– Truffles	625
Nougatine	440
– Buttercream	237
– Gâteau	587
– Sports	528
– Tartlets	323
– Torte	594
Nougatines	440, 492, 515
Novecento Gâteau	590
Nürnberg Lebkuchen	379
Nut Balls	347, 440
– Boats	440, 522
– Cakes	537
– Croquettes	493
– Cubes	440

– Dainties	625
– Dessert Fingers	493
– Fancies	345
– Rings	286
– Tartlets	323

O

Oak Leaves	515
Old English Curd Tarts	337
– – Filling	219
– Dough Cakes	278
Oliebollen	300
Olivettes	528
– with Orange and Cherry	528
Omelettes	675
– Grand-Marnier	676
– Jam	675
– Kirsch	676
– Lemon	676
– Mousseline	675
– Orange	676
– Rum	676
– – Soufflé	676
– Strawberry	676
– Vanilla	676
One Piece Tarts	337
Onion Flan	835
Open Sandwiches	846
– Anchovy	846
– Bacon	846
– Cheese	846
– – Danbo	846
– – Danish blue	846
– – Esrom	846
– – Fynbo	846
– – Maribo	847
– Chicken	846
– Ham	847
– Liver Pâté	847
– Luncheon Meat	847
– Pork and Ham	847
– Pork and Tongue	847
– Salami	847
– Sausage, Cocktail	847
– – Frankfurter	847
Oracle Torte	582
Orange Balls	516
– Biscuits	493
– Blossom Bread	286
– Cakes	397
– Cream	232
– – Drops	347
– – Puffs	333
– Crescents	537
– Curd	241, 242
– Date Filling	220
– Fancies	441
– Flower Soufflés	515
– Geneva	529
– Japonaise Fancies	460
– Macaroon Biscuits	493
– Macaroons	538
– Marshmallow Tartlets	323
– Marzipan	614
– Mousseline Gâteau	572
– Puffs	333
– Rice filling	220
– Rings	341
– Scones	311
– Soufflés	516
– Tartlets	337, 441
– Torte	582
– Tourte	573
Orange (Marzipan)	614
– Mignons	525
Osborne	441

Othellos	345
Other Gâteaux	549, 551
Ox Eyes	538
Oxford Apple Tartlets	323
– – Filling	222
– Lardy Cakes	283

P

Painter's Palette	582
Palace Biscuits	494
Palais de Dame	494
Palisades	441
Palmiers	330
Panama Torte	566
Pancakes	676
– Breton	676
– Crêpes Suzette	677
– Ducal	677
– Georgette	677
– Greta Garbo	677
– Hawaii	677
– Jam	678
– Montenegrin	678
– Normandy	678
– Nougatine	678
– Palacinky	678
– Prune	679
– Romantic Style	679
– Scotch	313
– Soufflé	679
– Swedish	679
– Wafer Thin	679
Panettone	286
Panforte di Siena	371
Pannequets	679
– Jam	679
– Lyonnaise	679
Paris-Brest	341
Parisette	288
Parisian Cigarettes	307
– Kisses	516
– Macaroons	516, 538
– Pastries	330
– Strawberry Torte	582
– Torte	566
Parkin Biscuits	494
– Slab	371
Parkins	371
Parliament Cakes	371
Parmesan Fans	839
– Sticks	824
Party Buns	288
Pashas	441
Pasta Brisée	188
– Frolla	198
Pasticceria Mignon	524
– Acorns	524
– Amarena Sports	525
– Amaretto	525
– Arancini	525
– Assabesi	525
– Bocche di leone	525
– Bombetta	525
– – Coffee	525
– – Hazelnut	525
– – Lemon	525
– – Orange	525
– – Taormina	529
– – Walnut	525
– Brasiliana	525
– Cannoli	525
– Saratoga	525
– Toscani	526
– Zabaglione	526
– Cappucci	526
– Cherry Bowls	526

– – Sports 526	– Great Britain 341	– – or Pistachio Balls 516
– Chocolate Chantilly 526	– Parisian 342	– – Soufflés 516
– – Kirsch................... 526	Petits Fours 505	– Parisian Kisses............. 516
– – Pineapple-Hawaii 526	– – Geneva 529	– – Macaroons 516
– – Violets, Malaga.......... 526	– – Glacés 520	– Pearled Tuiles 516
– Choux..................... 526	– Berolinas 520	– Pertikus-Gipfel 516
– – à la crème 526	– Caracks 520	– Pistachio Macaroons 517
Cocktails-Tebaldi 526	– Cerisettes 520	– Pretzels, Almond.......... 517
– Coffee Walnut 526	– Chestnut Turrets........... 520	– – Chocolate 517
– Cri-cri 527	– Chocolat-France 520	– – Vanilla 517
– Delina..................... 527	– Chocolate Drums 520	– Punch Balls 517
– Diplomatici 527	– – Nougat 520	– Raspberry Rosettes 517
– Fiamme 527	– Eaglets 521	– Richelieu 518
– Italians 527	– Eclairs 521	– Russian Cigarettes 518
– Kirsch glacés 527	– Expo 522	– Schmelzbrötchen........... 518
– Maraschino 527	– Dutch 517	– Small Fruits 518
– Medusa 527	– Gypsies 521	– Tuiles 518
– Mocha 527	– Hazelnut 521	– Tuscanians 519
– Nests 527	– – Avelines 521	– Viennese.................. 519
– Nougatine Sports 528	– – Soufflés 521	– Walnuts 519
– Olivettes 528	– Japonaise 521	– – Zurich 519
– – Orange and Cherry 528	– Jellies 521	Picnic Puffs 822
– Oranges 525	– Lemon 522	Pie, Fillings (Meat) 816-818
– Persian Delights 528	– Macaroons 522	– Gravy 817
– Porto Rico 528	– Marronnettes 522	– Italian 822
– Rosettes 528	– Martinique 522	– Jelly 817
– Roulot 528	– Nut boats 522	– Pastry 191
– Sacrapantini 528	– Pasticceria Mignon........ 524	– – Methods 184
– Scodellini Ananas 528	– Pavés 522	Pierrette Gâteau 573
– – Apricot 528	– Pineapple 523	Pies and Pasties (British) 840
– – Violetta 528	– – Ananas 523	– Bacon and Egg Flan........ 835
– Sicily..................... 528	– Pirandellos 523	– Beef and Potato Pies....... 840
– Sports, Amarena 525	– Pistachio Diamonds 523	– Cheese and Onion Pasties.. 840
– – Cherry 525	– – Soufflés 523	– – Patties.................. 840
– – Nougatine 528	– Sarah 524	– – Pies 841
– Super 529	– Secs 506	– Chicken Pies 841
– – Chantilly 529	– Simone 524	– Cornish Pasties 841
– Tebaldi................... 526	– Walnut Cubes 524	– Forfar Bridies 841
Pasticceria Mignon,	– Walnuts 524	– Mutton Pies 841
Geneva assortment 529	– – Sablés 524	– Pork Pies 841
– Bombetta Taormina 529	Petits Fours secs 506	– Steak and Kidney 842
– Cherry 529	– Almond 506	– Veal and Ham 842
– Coffee 529	– – Bread 506	Pies, Dessert............. 679, 731
– Cremolini 529	– – Soufflés 506	– Apple 680
– Delizia 529	– Amaretti................. 506	– Banana Apple 731
– Marsolini 529	– Angelica Macaroons 506	– – Cream 731
– Nocciole 529	– Anisettes 506	– Blackberry Apple 680
– Orange 529	– Apricot Macaroons 506	– Canadian Cream 731
– Super 529	– Biarritz Biscuits 506	– Chocolate Rum 727
Pastry, Choux 192	– Buttered "S" Scrolls 507	– Christmas 694
– Pie....................... 191	– – Chocolate 508	– Fruit 679
– Puff 180	– Calissons d'Aix 507	– Gooseberry............... 680
– Short................ 184, 191	– Chocolate Cornets 507	– Honey Orange Raisin 732
– Sweet.................... 185	– – Kisses 507	– Lemon Meringue 731
Pastry Leaves 330	– – Macaroons 508	– Maryland 680
Pavés 522	– – Soufflés 508	– Mince 680
Pavillon Biscuits 494	– Cinnamon Leaves 508	– Rhubarb 681
Peach Baskets 457	– – Stars 508	– – and Apple 681
– Tartlets............... 323, 441	– Coffee Soufflés 513	Pikelets 314
– Wine Cream Torte 583	– Cressini 513	Pineapple Buns 289
Peaches..................... 288	– Croquettes suisses 513	– Baumtorte 583
Pearl Biscuits 494	– Duchesses 513	– Boats 441
Pearled Tuiles 516	– Dutch 517	– Cakes 397, 398
Peppermint Cake 582	– Equal Weight 513	– Choux 342
Perkin Biscuits 495	– Florentine Biscuits 513	– Cream Rolls.............. 359
Persian Delights 528	– Frascati 514	– – Slices................... 350
Pertikus-Gipfel 516	– Half-Moons 514	– Cup Tartlets 323
Petit Beurre Biscuits 495	– Harlequins 514	– Fritters 670
Petits Choux 341	– Hittnauer Makronen 514	– Fruit Torte 584
– Almond 341	– Italian Macaroons 514	– Ice Parfait Torte 583
– Cévennes 341	– Macaroons 515	– Japonaise 460
– Chantilly 341	– Madeleines............... 515	– – Slices................... 460
– Chocolate 341	– Mochas.................. 515	– Macaroons 538
– Coffee 341	– Nougatines 515	– Mousseline Torte 566
– Frangipane 341	– Oak Leaves 515	– Petits Fours 523
– Germany 341	– Orange Flower Soufflés 515	– Pies 441

Pineapple Puffs 333
– Slices..................... 334
– Squares 336
– Strips 495
– Tartlets................... 323
– Tourte 573
– Truffle Balls 442
Piping Jelly 254
Pirandellos 523
Pischinger 495
Pistachio Balls 516
– Cream 233, 237
– Diamonds.................. 523
– Macaroons 517
– Marzipan 625
– – Cream 233
– Rolls 517
– Slices..................... 350
– Soufflés 523
– Tourte 573
Pitcaithly Bannocks 325
Pitta 289
Pizza 835
– Dough 179
Plain Biscuits 495
Plaited Bread................ 289
– Dough 175
– Mozart 285
Plum Dumplings............. 668
Plunder Filling ....
– brown 225
– white.................... 225
Plunderkranz 277
Polenta e Osei 590
Polish Tourte 573
Polkas 342
Pommes-de-Terre 442
Pomponnettes 283
Pont-Neuf 442
Poppyseed Ties 824
– Triangles 824
Pork Pies 841
– Filling 818
Portland Buns 289
Porto Rico Gâteau 590
– Mignons 528
Portugal 626
Potato Curd Filling 218
– Filling 818
– Scones.................... 314
Pound Cakes 203
Powder Aerated Goods 309
Praline 213
– Croquant 213
– – Fancies 348
– Cubes 442
– Duchesses 442
– Gâteau 573
– Nougat 214
– Paste 214, 215
– Squares................... 350
– Tartlets................... 324
– Tourte 573
Prepared Flour 179
Pretorias 315
Pretzels 290, 517
– Almond 442
– Chocolate 442
– Choux................... 342
– Fondant 487
– France 290
– Germany 442
– Pickling Brine 290
– Vanilla 442
Prince Regent Torte......... 584
Progress Koekjes 517

Provence Crescents 443
Puckler Rolls 359
Puddings 681
– Cabinet 681
– Chocolate Soufflé 683
– – Almond 684
– Christmas 681
– Fleur de Marie Soufflé 684
– Frankfurt 682
– Grand-Marnier Soufflé 684
– Jam Roly-poly 682
– Killarney Soufflé 684
– Lemon Soufflé 684
– Mousseline 682
– Queen's 683
– – Soufflé 685
– Royal Soufflé 685
– Sans-souci Soufflé 685
– Saxon Soufflé............. 683
– Taiwan Soufflé 685
– Tapioca 683
Puff Cracknels 495
Puff Pastries................. 326
– small 333
Puff Pastry
– Recipe and Methods .. 180-184
– Savouries, Cases 820
– – Barquettes 820
– – Bouchées 820
Puits d'Amour 330, 443
Pulled Sugar 643
– Basket 643
– Flowers 644
– Leaves 644
– Ribbons 644
– Roses 644
Punch Balls 517
– Tartlets................... 324
– Tourte 594

Q

Quayaquil Tartlets 324
Queen Cakes 443
Queen Pomare Gâteau 574
Quiche à la lorraine 835
Quince Paste 641
– Slices 641

R

Raisin Cakes 398
– Slices 290
Rajah Tartlets 834
Rarebit, English 836
– Scotch 836
– Welsh 836
Raspberry Beans 443
– Buns 310
– Kisses 457
– Oval Macaroons 538
– Rosettes 496, 517
– Slices 443
– Tartlets 444, 496
Ratafia Biscuits 496
Rectangles 496
Red Currant Jelly Crescents . 330
– Meringue Torte 585
– Omelettes 352
– Rolls 360
– Slices 444
Reform Club Barquettes 834
Regent Torte 585
Reginella 444
– Cakes 398
Reinling, Carinthian 263

Religieuse Tourte 575
Religieuses 342, 444
Rheims (Champagne) Biscuits 496
Rhineland King Cakes 398
Rice Biscuits 497
– Buns 310
– Filling 220
– Tartlets 324
Rice Desserts 732
– Condé 697
– Croquettes Fructidor 667
– Empress Style 732
– Liguria 732
– Palermo Style 732
– Singapore 733
– Soufflé 688
– Tangerine 733
– Trauttmannsdorf 733
– Turkish creamed 733
Rich Fruit Bread 280
Richelieu 518
– Ring 398
Richmond Cheese Cakes 822
Rigi Peaks 626
Ring Bases 458
Rissoles à la dauphine 822
Riviera Boats 824
Rochers 458, 626
Rock Cakes 310
– Sugar 244
Roe's Back Cake 399
Rognons 342
Rolla Gâteau 594
Rolled Oat Cookies 497
Rolls Asparagus 818
– Basic Dough 175
– Bridge 261, 819
– Cheshire Cheese 821
– Duchess 819
– Finger 818
– Hamburger 819
– Milk 285
– Sausage 823
– Stuffed Eel 839
Roman Bridges 360
– Helmets 444
Rosalinds 348
Rose Fritters 301
– Genoese 202
Rosemary Gâteau 574
Roses 85, 644
Rosettes Mignons 528
Roulot Mignons 528
Roumanian Tartlets 835
Rout Biscuits, English 485
Royal Cakes 399
– Chantilly Japonaise 461
– Icing 243
– Palace Choux 342
– Victoria Cheese Cakes 315
– – Filling 222
Rum Apricot Topping 226
– Chocolate Cups 444
– Fancies 444
– Gâteau 590
– Red Currant Fancies 350
Rusks 290
– France 291
– Germany 291
– Holland 291
Russe, Charlotte 703
– Cream 242
Russian Cigarettes 518
– Charlotte Torte 585
– Slices 350

S

"S" Scrolls, Buttered	507
– Chocolate	508
Sabayon Custard	241
– Gritti	709
– Sauces	654, 655
Sablé Biscuits	497
– Pastry	188
Sacher Slices	444, 445
– Torte	566, 567, 585
Sacripantini Mignons	528
Sacristains	824
Saffron Loaves, Cornish	265
Saint André	445
Salambos	342
Sally Lunns	291
Salmon Roll	840
Salt Scones	314
– Sticks	833
Salted Almonds	643
– Butterflies	833
Sanani	445
Sand Biscuits	445, 497
– Cake	567
– Rings	446
– "S" shaped Biscuits	447
– Scrolls	497
– Stars	446, 497
Sandmac Biscuits	498
Sandwiches, Open	846
(see under Open Sandwiches)	
Sandwiches	844
– Bridge Roll	844
– Brioche	844
– French Stick	844
– Toasted Bread	844
– – Anchovy	844
– – Cheese	844
– – Club	845
– – Crayfish	845
– – Cucumber	845
– – Egg	845
– – Ham	845
– – Lettuce	845
– – Pickled Tongue	845
– – Poultry	845
– – Radish	845
– – Sausage	845
– – Smoked Salmon	845
– – Tomato	845
– – Tunny	845
– – Veal	845
Sans-Gêne Gâteau	574
Santa Claus-Baumkuchen	611
– Marzipan	615
Sapphos	446
Sarahs	461, 524
Sauces, Hot and Cold Desserts	650
– Almond	650
– Apricot	650
– Bishop	650
– Brandy	650
– Caramel	650
– Cherry	650
– Chocolate	650
– Lemon	651
– Maraschino	651
– Orange	651
– Pineapple	651
– Praline	651
– Thickened Syrups	651
Sauces, Ice Creams and Cold Desserts	651
– Almond	651

– Apricot	651
– Bar-le-Duc	651
– Black Currant	651, 652
– Caramel	652
– Chantilly	652
– Chocolate	652
– Coffee	652
– Custard	652
– Dijon	652
– Lemon	653
– Melba	653
– Mousseline	653
– – Burgundy	653
– – Lemon	653
– – Orange	653
– – Other Fruits	653
– – Port Wine	653
– – Praline	654
– – Raspberry	654
– – Tangerine	654
– Orange	654
– Praline Croquant	654
– Raspberry	654
– Red Currant	654
– Sabayon	654
– – Lemon	654
– – Liqueur	655
– – Marsala	655
– – Orange	655
– – Strawberry	655
Sausage Rolls	823
Savarins	259
– à la Crème	259
Savoury Goods	813
– Aspic	814
– Bases	813
– – Biscuits	814
– – Bread	813
– – Choux	814
– – Gâteaux Bases	198
– – Puff Pastry	814
– – Rolls	813
– – Scones	814
– – Short Pastry	813
– Butters	815
– – Almond	815
– – Anchovy	815
– – Cheese	815
– – Crayfish	815
– – Lobster	815
– – Maître d'Hôtel	815
– – Mustard	815
– – Prawn	815
– – Sardine	815
– – Shrimp	815
– – Tomato	815
– – Watercress	815
– – Yeast Extract	815
– Fillings	816
(see under Fillings, Savoury)	
– Garnishes	816, 846
– Seasonings	814
– Toppings	816
Savoury Goods with	
– Bread and Rolls	818
– – Asparagus	818
– – Bridge Rolls	819
– – Finger Rolls	818
– – Hamburgers	819
– – Harlequin Slices	819
– – Savoury Torte	819
– British Pies and Pasties	840
– Canapés	842
(see under Heading)	
– Choux Pastry	819
– – Cheddar Pearls	819

– – Cheese Cream Buns	819
– – – Fritters	819
– – – Soufflés	819
– – Swans	820
– – Choux Rings	820
– – Duchess Rolls	819
– – Foie gras Eclairs	820
– Flans	835
– – Bacon and Egg	835
– – Cheese and Bacon	835
– – Onion	835
– – Quiche à la lorraine	835
– – Pizza	835
– Puff Pastry, cold	823
– – Bouchées Beauharnais	823
– – – Joinville	823
– – – Springtime	823
– – Brie Pastries	823
– – Caraway Loops	823
– – Cheese Butterflies	824
– – – Cannoli	824
– – – Puffs	824
– – Cumin Sticks	824
– – Parmesan Sticks	824
– – Poppyseed Ties	824
– – – Triangles	824
– – Riviera Boats	824
– – Sacristains	824
– – Salt Sticks	833
– – Salted Butterflies	833
– – Savoury Puff Slices	833
– – Strasbourg Boats	833
– – Sweet and Sour Fingers	833
– – Tunny Fish Boats	833
– – Turkish Specialities	833
– Puff Pastry, hot	820
– – Boats, Barquettes	820
– – Cases, Bouchées	820
– – Anchovy Sticks	820
– – Avondale Puffs	820
– – Bacon and Egg Turnovers	821
– – Bouchées à la Reine	821
– – Cheddar Custards	821
– – Cheese Cushions	821
– – – Horns	821
– – Cheshire Cheese Rolls	821
– – Ham Croissants	821
– – Jura Tit-bits	821
– – Little Pies	822
– – Picnic Puffs	822
– – Richmond Cheese Cakes	822
– – Rissoles	822
– – – à la dauphine	822
– – – France	822
– – – Italy	823
– – Sausage Rolls	823
– – Welsh Pastries	823
– Rarebits	836
– – Buck	836
– – English	836
– – Scotch	836
– – Welsh	836
– Sandwiches	844, 846
(see under Heading)	
– Sauces	814
– Scones	314, 839
– Short Pastry, hot	834
– – Berkeley Tartlets	834
– – Cadogan Barquettes	834
– – Calcutta Tartlets	834
– – Devilled Wensleydale Tartlets	834
– – Marion Delorme Tartlets	834
– – Pastry Tartlets	834
– – Rajah Tartlets	834
– – Reform Club Barquettes	834

887

Savoury Short Pastry (cont.)
- - Rumanian Tartlets 835
- - Swiss Tartlets 835
- Toasts 836
- - Anchovy 836
- - Baron's 836
- - Bloater 836
- - Captain's 836
- - Croque-Monsieur 836
- - Derby 837
- - Diana 837
- - Dutch 837
- - Findon 837
- - Guards Club 837
- - Ivanhoe 837
- - Marrow 837
- - Montrose Snack 837
- - Mushrooms 837
- - Sardines 837
- - Scotch Woodcock 837
- - Soft Roes 837
- - Yarmouth 838
- Various Savouries 838
- - Angels on Horseback ... 838
- - Cheese Biscuits 838
- - Cheese Cream Savouries . 838
- - Cheese Fans 838
- - Cheese, fried 838
- - - Rolls 838
- - - and Potato Scones ... 839
- - Cheshire Cheese Biscuits . 839
- - Devils on Horseback 839
- - Eel Rolls 839
- - Oyster Fritters 839
- - Parmesan Fans 839
- - Salmon Roll 840
- - Stilton Corks 840
Savoy Biscuits 498
- Fingers 350, 351, 498
- Sponges 351
Schaffhauser Slices 461
- Tongues 461
Schlumbergerli 290
Schmelzbrötchen 518
Schnittorten 86
Schwarzwälder Torte 727
Scodellini Amarena 446
- Ananas 528
- Apricot 528
- Violetta 528
Scone Flour 180
Scones, basic 311
- Cheese and Potato 834
- Coconut 311
- Devon 311
- Farmhouse 311
- fermented 279
- Finger 311
- fried 302
- fruited 311
- Jam 311
- Orange 311
- Potato 314
- Rounds 311
- Salt 314
- Soda 314
- Treacle 312
- Turnover 312
- Victoria 312
- Wheatmeal 312
- Wholemeal 312
Scotch Baps 292
- Macaroons 538
- Pancakes 313
Scottish Black Bun 292
- Shortbread 325

- basic 325
- Biscuits 326, 498
- blocked 326
- decorated 325
- - Inscriptions 325
- Drops 498
- Duchess Fingers 326
- Loundon Fingers 326
- Pitcaithly Bannocks 325
- Rolls 498
- Shortbread Fingers 326
- Tree Shortbreads 326
- Slices 446
- Walnut Fingers 326
Seasonings, Savoury 814
Seed Cakes 399
Selkirk Bannocks 292
Selva 253
- Gâteau 590
Semmel Rolls 290
Sevastopol Slices 538
Shortcakes 446
Short Pastry 184, 191
- sweetened 185
- unsweetened 184, 191
Show-pieces 597
- Baumkuchen, pheasant ... 611
- Santa Claus 611
- Butter Sponge Animals ... 611
- Harvest Bread 600, 601
- Le Croquembouche 599
- Marzipan Models
- - Animals and Fruits . 613-615
- - Santa Claus 615
- Tiered Cake 601
Shrewsbury Biscuits 498
- Cakes 446
Shutters 334
Sicilians 446, 538
Sicily (Mignon) 528
Sighs 447
Silver Drops 499
Simits 293
Simnel Cake 399
- Bury 400
Simone 524
Slab Cakes 204, 404, 405
- Almond 404
- Cherry 404
- Coconut 404
- Currant 404
- Fruit 405
- Genoa 404
- Ginger 404
- Madeira 404
- Seed 404
- Sultana 404
Slices, Almond 532
- - Croquant 348
- - Fruit 535
- - Nut 409
- Apple Streusel 409
- Apricot 348, 410
- - Streusel 411
- Banana Marshmallow 411
- - Meringue 453
- Battenburg 412
- Bee-Sting 412
- Butter Streusel 413
- Cherry 348, 416
- - Michel 416
- Chestnut 348
- Chocolate 419
- - Coffee 417
- - Cream 349
- - Fudge 418

- - Genoese 418
- - Japonaise 459
- - Walnut 459
- Choux 338
- Condés 333
- Conversation 333
- Costa Rica 349
- Cream 334
- Croquant japonaise 460
- Dobos 349
- Dome 430
- Florentine 432
- Frangipane 334
- - Cream 432
- - Fruit 432
- Fruit 432
- Gingerbread 366
- Harlequin 349
- Helvetia 433
- Honey filled 378
- - Nut 334
- Japonaise 453
- - Chocolate 459
- - Croquant 460
- - Ganache 460
- - Ginger 459
- - Kirsch 460
- - Pineapple 460
- - Schaffhauser 461
- Lemon Coconut 349
- - Frangipane 435
- Linz Chocolate 436
- - Fruit 436
- Lucullus 436
- Macaroon Frangipane 537
- Magdalena 437
- Malaga 349
- Maltese Lemon 437
- Maraschino 350
- Marshmallow 437
- Melide 438
- Meringue and Citron 438
- Milan 438
- Mille-feuille 439
- Napoleon 439
- Neapolitan 439
- Nougat 359, 440
- Pineapple 334
- - Cream 350
- Pistachio 350
- Quince 641
- Raisin 290
- Raspberry 443
- Red Currant 444
- Russian 350
- Sacher 444, 445
- Savoury Harlequin 819
- Schaffhauser 461
- Scottish 446
- Sevastopol 538
- Sponge 334
- Strawberry 334, 447
- Sultana Cheese 448
- Truffle 350
- Victoria 451
- Vosge 452
- Walnut Ganache 452
- Whipped Cream 335
- Wholemeal Ginger 373
- Wine Cream 349
Small Cakes and Afternoon
- Tea Fancies 407
Snow Balls 303
- Eggs 733
- - Carmen 734
- - My Dream 734

888

– – with Chocolate Sauce ... 734	– Swiss Rolls 196, 357, 546	Sugar Confectionery 628
Soda Bread 312	Spreads..................... 225	– Caramel Creams 628
– Currant 313	– Almond 225	– Caramels, Milk 628
– Sultana 313	– Butter 225	– – Soft 628
– Wheaten 312	– Chestnut.................. 225	– – Vanilla 628
– White 312	– Cinnamon 225	– Drops, Cough 629
– Flour 179	– Hazelnut 225	– – Gum 630
– Scones 314	– Marzipan 225	– – Lemon 629
Soft Caramels 628	– Milk Chocolate 225	– – Malt 629
– Chocolate Icing 244	– Plunder, brown 225	– – Orange 629
– Macaroons 539	– – white................... 225	– – Peppermint 629
Sorrentina Gâteau 590	Spritzkoeken 446	– – Poppy 629
Sorrento 627	Spritzkuchen 300	– – Raspberry 629
Soufflés 685	Spun sugar.................. 645	– – Strawberry 629
– Almond 506	Square Jam and Cream Tarts 337	– Fondants, Holland 631
– Apple 685	St. Gall Honey Cake Spice ... 362	– – Little................... 631
– Basic 685	– Biber 373	– Fruit, Caramel 632
– Cecilia 686	St. Gallen Biberli 373	– – Jellies 641
– Cheese 819	– – Biberteig Filling 224	– Fudges 630
– Chocolate 686	St. Galler Törtli 325	– – Cream 630
– Cingalese 686	St-Honoré	– – Cream Fondant......... 630
– Coffee 686	– Cream 235	– Marshmallows 630
– Colette 686	– Gâteau (France) 727	– Pastilles 631
– Estoril 686	– Florentine 728	– – Fruit 631
– Fruit 686	– Selva 728	– – Orange Flower 632
– Grand-Marnier 687	– Tuscany 728	– – Peppermint 631
– Hazelnut 521	Steak and Kidney Pies 842	– Various................... 641
– Jacqueline 687	– Filling 818	– – Caramel Fruits 632
– Lemon 687	Steak Pies Filling 818	– – Fruit Jellies 641
– Orange 687	Stock Syrup 758	– – Glazed Chestnuts 642
– – Flower 515	Stollen, Almond 294	– – – Orange Slices 643
– Palmyra 687	– Austria 293	– – – Tangerines 643
– Semolina 687	– Dresdener................. 293	– – Nougat Montelimar 641
– Strawberry 687	Stracchino Cream 236	– – Quince Paste 641
– Tyrolean Rice 688	Strasbourg Boats 833	– – – Slices................. 641
– Vanilla 688	Strassburg Sticks 500	– – Salted Almonds 643
Souvaroff Biscuits 499	Strassburgers 447	– – Stuffed Fruits 632
Spanish Meringue 207	Strawberry Barquettes 447	– – – Dates 632
– Vanilla Torte 586	– Cream Slices 334	– – – Prunes 632
Special Gâteaux 550	– – Meringues 458	– – – Walnuts 632
Speculaas, Biscuits 499	– – Torte 586	– – Sugar, Basket........... 643
– Dolls 372	– Creams 348	– – – blown 645
– Spice 362	– Meringue 207	– – – Cat 645
– Spicy..................... 372	– – Gâteau 552	– – – Leaves 644
Spice Biscuits 499	– Parisian Torte 582	– – – Other Flowers 644
– Fingers 293	– Rings 343	– – – Parrot 647
Spiced Hazelnut Biscuits 499	– Rolls 447	– – – Ribbons 644
Spices 361	– Slices..................... 447	– – – Roses 644
– Biberteig.................. 362	– Tartlets................... 448	– – – Spun 645
– Lebkuchen 362	– Tongues 448	– – Torrone 643
– Speculaas 362	– Turnovers 352	– – Turkish Delight......... 641
– St. Gall Honey Cake 362	Streusel, Apricot Slices....... 411	Sultan Waffles 306
– Various Blends 361	– baked 226	Sultana Biscuits 500
Spicy Cookies 500	– Butter 226	– Cakes 401
Sponge Bases 197, 198	– Cake 400	– Cheese Slices 448
– Almond 196, 197	– – Apricot 258	– Slab 404
– Basic Recipes 196	– Chocolate 249	Super Chantilly.............. 529
– Butter 196	– Fancies 448	– Mignon 529
– Chocolate 196	– Toppings 226	Superlatives 461
– Mignon 198	Striezel, Bayrischzeller 260	Surprises
– Mushroom 198	Strudel 334, 688	– Belle-Alliance 746
– Savoury.................. 198	– Apple 334, 693	– du Pâtissier 747
– Viennese.................. 197	– Basic Dough............... 179	– hawaiienne 746
– Walnut 197	– Cherry 335	– Marguerite Bolli 746
Sponge, Bars 546	– Curd 693	– Meringue Topping 746
– Bricks 351	– Gooseberry 335	– sicilienne 747
– Chocolate 196	– Lower Austrian 694	– Waldmeister 747
– Drops 351	– Old Vienna 693	Swabian Rolls 500
– Fancies 348	Stuffed Eel Rolls............. 839	Swans 343
– Fruit 345	– Fruit and Nuts 632	– from Locarno 343
– Gâteaux 545	– Dates 632	Swedish Choux 343
– – with Fruit 546	– Prunes 632	– Rings 448
– Othellos 198	– Walnuts 632	Sweet Dough 177
– Sandwiches 352	Success Gâteau 574	Sweet Pastry 184, 315
– Slices..................... 350	Sugar Boiling 628, 643	– Almond 186
– Stencilled 352	Sugar Bread, Suikerbrood ... 294	– Chocolate 186

889

Sweet Crumb 190
- Linz 188-190
- Mignon Bases 187
- Milanese................. 187
- Neapolitan 188
- Pasta brisée 188
- - Frolla 188
- Piping 187
- Sablé 188
- Tea Biscuits 187
- - Fancies 187
Sweet and Sour Fingers 833
Sweets (Desserts)........... 649
Swiss Biscuits 501
- Buns 294
- Cookies 336
- Croquettes 501
- Meringue 207
- Rolls 196, 357, 546
- - Chocolate 357
- - France 357
- - Germany 357
- - Great Britain 357
- - Miniature.............. 357
- - Various 357
- Tart Filling 221
- Tartlets................. 835
- Wine Cream Torte 595
Sylvana Cakes 401
- Fancies 461
Sylvia Gâteau 574
Syrups 655
- Apple 655
- Blackberry 655
- Blackcurrant 655
- Cherry 655
- Coffee 655
- Gum Arabic 656
- Lemon 656
- Maidenhair 656
- Orange 656
- Orgeat 656
- Pomegranate 656
- Quince 656
- Raspberry 656
- Red Currant 656
- Rhubarb 656
- Savarins and Babas 665
- Stock................... 758

T

Taillaules 294
Tantallon 501
Tarragona Biscuits 501
Tarts, Dessert 734
- Amarena 735
- Apple 735
- - Alsatian 735
- - American 694
- - Condé 735
- - Curd 694
- - Dutch 735
- - English 735
- - Meringue 736
- - Streusel 735
- - Swabian 736
- - Trellised 736
- Apricot 736
- - Streusel 737
- Bilberry 737, 738
- Cherry 737
- - covered 737
- Christmas Pie 694
- Coconut Custard 738
- - Meringue 738
- Damson 739

- Dilston 695
- Florida 738
- Fruit 738
- Golden 695
- Gooseberry 738
- Greengage 738
- Lemon 739
- - Chiffon 739
- - Meringue 739
- Meringue 739
- Orange 739
- - Chiffon 740
- Orleans Custard 695
- Peach 739
- Pear 740
- Pineapple 740
- Plum 739, 740
- Prune 740
- Raisin 740
- Rhubarb 741
- Strawberry 741
- - Modern Style 741
- Yorkshire Curd 695
Tartlets, Alexandra Cream .. 321
- Almond Cream 321
- - Holland 321
- - Honey 208
- - Switzerland 321
- Apple Dutch 322, 336
- - Frangipane 321
- - Italy 410
- - Oxford 323
- - Switzerland 410
- Apricot 316, 336
- Bakewell 411
- Berkley 834
- Bettina 743
- Calcutta 834
- Cherry 417
- Chocolate Cup 321
- Christmas 321
- Cinnamon 419
- Coconut 419
- Custard 321
- Devilled Wensleydale 834
- Dutch Apple 322, 336
- Fondant Marshmallow..... 322
- Frangipane (Walnut) 324
- Fruit 433
- Ginger 322
- Golden 322
- Gooseberry 322
- Grape 322
- Greengage Marshmallow... 322
- Guayaquil 324
- Hollandaise 322
- Iced 434
- Jam 322
- Lemon 435
- - Marshmallow 322
- - Meringue 323
- Linz 436
- Maids of Honour 336
- Maraschino 323
- Marion Delorme 834
- Neapolitan Peach 439
- Nougatine 323
- Nut 323
- Orange 337, 441
- Oxford Apple 323
- - Filling 222
- Peach 323, 441
- Pineapple 323
- - Cup 323
- Praline 324
- Punch 324

- Rajah 834
- Raspberry 444, 496
- Rice 324
- Roumanian 835
- Strawberry 448
- Swiss 835
- Victoria Basket 324
- - Cream 325
- - Crown 325
- Viennese................. 451
- - Sand 451
- Walnut 324
- - Marshmallow........... 324
- - Raisin 325
- Wensleydale, devilled ... 834
Teacakes, London........... 295
- Yorkshire 296
- - fruited............... 296
- - Wheatmeal 297
- - - fruited............. 297
Tebaldi Mignons 526
Tempering Couverture 246
Thalhof Torte 567
Thin Biscuits 501
- Wine Biscuits 502
Tiered Cake 601
Tijger Broodjes 295
Tirrenia Gâteau 590
Toasts (see under savoury toasts) 836
Tobacco Rolls 303
Toffees 628
Tommies 449
Tongues, Berlin 304
- Dragons 459
- Schaffhauser 461
Toppings, Cake 226
- Coconut 226
- Danish Pastry 226
- Easter Bread 226
- Honey................... 227
- Rum Apricot 226
- Streusel
- - baked 226
- - Butter 226
- - Chocolate 249
- Viennese................ 226
Toppings, Savoury 816
- Fish 816
- Meats 816
- Mousses 816
- Purées 816
- Various Other 816
Torino Gâteau 590
Torrone 643
Torta d'Arancio 401
- Maddelena 401
- Mandorlata 401
- Margherita 402
- Yolanda 402
Torten (see under Gâteaux
and Torten)............. 545
Tottenham Cake 449
Tourtes (see under Gâteaux
and Torten)............. 545
Treacle Scones 312
Tree Shortbreads 326
Triestines 295
Trouville Biscuits.......... 502
Truffle Macaroons 539
- Rolls 360
- Slices................. 350
- Tourte 594
Truffles, light............. 621
Tuiles 502, 518
- pearled 516
Turban Cakes 402

Turin Gâteau	575	
– Genoese	202	
Turkish Delight	641	
– Savoury Biscuits	833	
Turnover Scones	312	
Turnovers	337	
Tuscanians	519	
Tutti-frutti	449	
– Squares	449	
Two Piece Puff Tarts	337	

U

Utrechters	449

V

Vacherin	458
Valencia Gâteau	575
Vanilla Almond Crescents	539
– – Croquettes	449
– Biscuits	502
– Custard	241
– Gâteau	587
– Marzipan Biscuits	502
– Patience Biscuits	502
– Pretzels	442
– Sticks	503
Various Cold Desserts	743
– Bettina Tartlets	743
– Cannoli Siciliani	743
– Champagne Flip	743
– Cherry Slices	744
– Chipolata Pudding	744
– Curdled Milk Rolls	744
– Delice Williamine	745
– Lemon Cream Madame Lacroix	745
– Mont-Blanc of Chestnuts	745
– Profiteroles with Chocolate	745
– Victoria Rings	746
Various Hot Desserts	695
– Buchteln	695
– Cannoli, Ticino Style	696
– Clafoutis limousin	696
– Emperor's Schmarren	696
– Fisherman's Flan	742
– Fried Custard	696
– Fruits	647
– Jam Puffs	696
– Kesari Bhata	697
– Prague Cakes	697
– Rice Condé	697
– Savarin rubané	697
– – Taiwan	698
– Semolina Subrics	698
– Timbale Bourdaloue	698
– Tutti-frutti Rissoles	698
Veal and Ham Pie	842
– Filling	818
Vendée Biscuits	503
Venetian Chocolate Tartlets	325
– Shutters	330
– Squares	449

Victoria Basket Tartlets	324
– Cheese Cakes	315
– – Filling	222
– Cream Tartlets	325
– Crown Tartlets	324
– Fancies	451
– Scones	312
– Slices	451
– Sponge	360
– Torte	594
Victorias	331
Vienna Fruit Pastries	449
Viennese Bases	197
– Biscuits	503
– Custard Rings	458
– Desserts	450
– Fancies	450, 457
– Fingers	450
– Fritters	303
– Horseshoe Biscuits	503
– Macaroons	450, 539
– Petits Fours	519
– Petits Fours glacés	524
– Rosettes	450
– Sand Tartlets	451
– Shells	451
– Squares	451
– Tartlet Filling	220
– Tarts	451
– Topping	226
– Tourte	576
Visitants	451
Visiting Cards	316
Vlechtbrood	289
Vosge Slices	452

W

Wafers, Almond	307
– Butter	307
– Marzipan	307
– Parisian	307, 308
Waffle Dressings	307
Waffles, Brussels	305
– Cinnamon	306
– Dairy cream	306
– Lille	306
– Recipes	305
– Basic Batter	305
– Sultan	306
– Vanilla	306
Walnut Cakes	402
– Cubes	524
– Custard	241
– Desserts	452
– Domes	452
– Duchesses	452
– Ganache Slices	452
– Gâteau	576
– Genoese	202
– Marshmallow Tartlets	324
– Raisin Tartlets	325
– Shortbreads	326

– Tartlets	324
– Tongues	539
– Torte	595
Walnuts	524
– Sablés	524
– Zurich	519
Water Icing	243
– Glaze	246
Wedding Cakes	403
Weesp Cookies	503
Weggen	295
Welsh Cakes	314, 452
– Pastries	823
– Rarebit	836
Wensleydale Tartlets	834
Wheatmeal Bread	296
– Farmhouse cake	403
– Rolls	296
– Scones	312
Whipped Cream Slices	335
White Chocolate Paste (modelling)	253
Wholemeal Bread	296
– Cheese Bread	296
– – Scones	312
Wiltshire Lardy Cake	284
Windmills	331
Windsor Cakes	403
– Rolls	360
Wine Biscuits	452, 504
– Cream	233
– – Lemon	233
– – Merlot	233
– – Tourte	595
– Custard	241
– Jelly	255
Witch's Cottage	611
Wrexham Ginger bread	373

Y

Yeasted Doughs	173
– for frying	303
– Goods	257
Yoghourt Desserts	746
– Cassis Shake	746
– Lemon Shake	746
Yorkshire Curd Tarts	321
– Filling	219
– Teacakes	296

Z

Zabaglione Cream	236
– Chocolate	236
– Coffee	236
– whipped	236
Zigomar Gâteau	595
Zuger Kirschtorte	595
Züngli Mixture	209
Zurich, Leckerli	539
– Marzipan Leckerli	539
– Nuts	504
– Walnuts	519